The Developing Person

Through Childhood and Adolescence

Christian Pierre. *Reading to Me* (front cover), *Festival Bandita* (back cover).
The luminous colors and figures in *Reading to Me* and *Festival Bandita* reflect the hope
and discovery apparent in all Pierre's paintings—of adults, animals, plants, landscapes,
and children. Pierre has lived in several cultures, under many life circumstances, but she
says she could never make herself paint anything depressing. Instead, by combining
colors, shapes, and composition in ways that reflect fantasy and reality, she allows us to
recognize human development. Note that the mother in *Reading to Me* focuses on the
big book, while her child snuggles against her cheek and looks outward with a wide-
eyed, happy expression. This is a metaphor for this textbook: The grownups read it
carefully to help the next generation of children develop an eager and secure outlook on
the world.

Sixth Edition

The Developing Person
Through Childhood and Adolescence

KATHLEEN STASSEN BERGER

Bronx Community College
City University of New York

WORTH PUBLISHERS

The Developing Person Through Childhood and Adolescence

Sixth Edition

Printed in the United States of America

ISBN: 0-7167-5257-3 (EAN: 9780716752578)

Fifth printing

Publisher: Catherine Woods

Senior Sponsoring Editor: Jessica Bayne

Developmental Editor: Cecilia Gardner

Production Editors: Vivien Weiss, Tracey Kuehn

Executive Marketing Manager: Renée Altier

Associate Managing Editor: Tracey Kuehn

Production Manager: Barbara Anne Seixas

Art Director, Interior and Cover Designer: Barbara Reingold

Layout Designer: Paul Lacy

Photo Editor: Meg Kuhta

Photo Researcher: Inge King

Senior Illustration Coordinator: Bill Page

Illustrations: Todd Buck Illustration and TSI Graphics, Inc.

Composition: TSI Graphics, Inc.

Printing and Binding: R. R. Donnelley & Sons Company

Cover Art: Christian Pierre, *Reading to Me* (front) and *Festival Bandita* (back)

Library of Congress Control Number: 2002110768

Worth Publishers

41 Madison Avenue

New York, NY 10010

www.worthpublishers.com

About the Author

Kathleen Stassen Berger received her undergraduate education at Stanford University and Radcliffe College, earned an M.A.T. from Harvard University and an M.S. and Ph.D from Yeshiva University. Her broad experience as an educator includes directing a preschool, teaching philosophy and humanities at the United Nations International School, teaching child and adolescent development to graduate students at Fordham University, and teaching social psychology to inmates earning a paralegal degree at Sing Sing Prison.

For the past 30 years Berger has taught at Bronx Community College of the City University of New York, recently as the elected chair of the Social Science Department. She has taught introduction to psychology, child and adolescent development, adulthood and aging, social psychology, abnormal psychology, and human motivation. Her students—who come from many ethnic, economic, and educational backgrounds and who have a wide range of interests—consistently honor her with the highest teaching evaluations. Her own four children attended New York City public schools, one reason that she was elected as president of the Community School Board in District Two.

Berger is also the author of *The Developing Person Through the Life Span* and *The Developing Person Through Childhood*. Her three developmental texts are currently being used at nearly 700 colleges and universities worldwide. Her research interests include adolescent identity, sibling relationships, and bullying, and she has contributed articles on developmental topics to the *Wiley Encyclopedia of Psychology*. Berger's inte[...] in college education is manifest in articles publ[...] 2002 by the American Association for Hig[...] Education and the National Education[...] Higher Education. She continues[...] with every semester and every ed[...]

Brief Contents

Contents

Part I

The Beginnings

Part II

The First 2 Years: Infants and Toddlers

Part III

The Play Years

Part IV
The School Years

Part V
Adolescence

Preface

Like so many people, I was profoundly affected by the events of September 11, 2001. From my home in New York City, I could smell the smoke from the World Trade Center site until almost Thanksgiving. Beyond deep gratitude that my family and students were unharmed, I felt renewed commitment to what we all do—teach the future professionals and parents who will raise the next cohort of children, or learn as much as we can to become a person who really helps children. As you know, education occurs not just in one memorable moment but cumulatively, in every day and every hour, and I was very grateful that I saw my students many times after that September morning. I realized again why I love teaching and why I put so much time and effort into revising every paragraph of this book.

In my own classroom, I start with high standards and clear expectations. But I'm aware that learning does not occur throughout the term unless I follow through with enthusiasm, humor, and intellectual honesty. I try to apply this insight to textbook writing as well.

The best developmental textbooks integrate theory and practice with such powerful clarity that students think deeply about the long-term implications of what they are learning. There should be no gap between theory and practice; the two inform each other. If my personal standards and experiences are evident in this text, I thank my heroes and mentors: not only my own gifted professors who studied directly with Erikson, Piaget, and Skinner, and not only the researchers whom I admire from the cool distance of the printed page—Ainsworth, Baltes, Bem, the Coles, Dweck, Garbarino, Gardner, the Gibsons, Lightfoot, Olweus, Plomin, Rogoff, Rutter, Schaie, Vygotsky, Whitborne, Zigler, and many more (which explains why the bibliography is longer than any comparable book's)—but also the thousands of peers and students who continue to teach me.

New Features

A number of aspects of this edition may be singled out for special mention:

- **Even stronger integration of theory and practice**   The five theories introduced in Chapter 2—psychoanalytic, behavioral, cognitive, sociocultural, and epigenetic—are applied repeatedly and in new ways, from explanations of how babies learn language to how children develop sexual identity. I want students to become accustomed to thinking from alternate perspectives. Nothing is quite so practical as a good theory, and nothing about child development is a mere abstraction. In this new edition, more than ever, theoretical insights are connected to practical issues. This linkage occurs in many ways, including the "Especially For . . ." questions in the margins as well as through a new series of features called "A Case to Study" that helps readers see how the experience of one developing person can illustrate a universal truth.
- **Up-to-date research citations**   Every year brings new concepts and research about human development. The best of these are integrated into the

text, including hundreds of new references on many topics—challenges to Piaget's theories, infant language, emotional regulation, theory of mind, psychoactive drugs, and social conflicts in childhood among them.

■ **New material on schooling** Education is a crucial foundation of childhood, and many who study this book will be educators. Accordingly, this edition highlights up-to-date, international research on education-related issues: the effects of infant day care, phonics versus whole language, standardized testing, multiple intelligences, special education, bilingual instruction, group problem solving, teacher–student ratios, and many more. The goal is twofold: to provide information (through new material on such topics as special-education laws and categories, family income and day care) and to encourage student readers to think critically, scientifically, and analytically about those issues.

■ **New learning features** With every edition, changes in the narrative are made to enhance readers' understanding of what scientists who study children actually do. Readers are offered many opportunities to test their observational and analytical skills by applying what they have learned to actual children. A series of new features, called "Thinking Like a Scientist," illuminates the thinking and research process. I have also increased the number of observational quizzes for photographs and have added some for graphs and tables so that quantitative data will be examined more carefully and will be better understood.

Ongoing Features

Many characteristics of this text have been acclaimed since the first edition and have been retained in this revision:

■ **Language that communicates the excitement and challenge of the field** An overview of the science of child development should be lively, just as children are. Consequently, I have added more summarizing and transitional statements to clarify the logical connection between one idea and the next. Sentences are shorter and less daunting, although I still choose some challenging vocabulary to deepen comprehension.

■ **Coverage of diversity** Cross-cultural, international, multi-ethnic, rich and poor—all these words and ideas are vital to appreciating how all our children develop. Studies of various groups make it clear that we all are the same and that each of us is unique. Chapter 1 includes a multifaceted discussion (class-tested with my own students) of where children sleep in various cultures. Similarly, every subsequent chapter refers to differences and similarities, from the many variations of immigrant development to the epigenetic ways in which nature and nurture interact. New research on Romanian adoptees, appreciation of Brazilian street children, cultural variations in childbirth practices, and advantages and disadvantages of various approaches to second-language learning are among the many diversity-related topics discussed throughout the book.

■ **Up-to-date coverage** My students and my four children help me keep current through their questions and concerns, not only in research but also in practice. My academic mentors nurtured my curiosity as well as a rational suspicion that makes me eager to read and analyze hundreds of journal articles and books on everything from anorexia to zygosity. The recent explosion of research in neuroscience and genetics has challenged me to explain many complex findings and speculative leaps.

■ **Topical organization within a chronological framework** The book's basic organization remains unchanged. Four chapters begin the book with coverage of definitions, theories, genetics, and prenatal development, used not only as a developmental foundation but also as the structure for explaining the life-span perspective, plasticity, nature and nurture, multicultural understanding, risk analysis, the damage–repair cycle, family bonding, and many other concepts that yield insights for all of human development. The ensuing parts of the book correspond to the major periods of growth. Each part contains three chapters, one for each of the three domains of development: biosocial, cognitive, and psychosocial. The topical organization within the chronological framework is a useful scaffold for student understanding of the interplay between age and domain as children actually experience it. The chapters are color-coded with tabs in the margins: The pages of the biosocial chapters have pale green tabs; the cognitive chapters have lilac tabs; and the psychosocial chapters have peach tabs.

■ **Relevant features** In some books, boxes are tacked on to make the text seem more current or multicultural than it really is. In this edition, four series of deeper discussions appear as integral parts of the text, and only where they are relevant. These features include two series that readers have particularly liked in earlier editions (called "Changing Policy" and "In Person") and two series that are new to this edition (called "A Case to Study" and "Thinking Like a Scientist"). You will see that these are not spin-offs or add-ons; they are extensions of ideas explored in the text, and thus provide material for critical thinking.

■ **Pedagogical aids** Each chapter ends with a summary, a list of key terms (with page numbers indicating where the word is introduced and defined), and key questions for reviewing important concepts. Terms are defined in the margins where they are introduced (in boldface) in the text and again in a glossary at the back of the book. The outline on the first page of each chapter and the system of major and minor subheads facilitate the widely used survey–question–review method of study. Observational quizzes inspire readers to look more closely at data and photographs, and the "Especially for . . ." questions in the margins apply concepts to real life (examples of these features are shown in the margin).

Examples of an "Especially for . . . " question, an Observational Quiz for a graph, and an Observational Quiz for a photograph are presented below and on the next page.

?Especially for Educators: An infant day-care center has a new child whose parents speak a language other than the one the teachers speak. Should the teachers learn basic words in the new language, or should they expect the baby to learn the majority language? (See answer, page 190.)

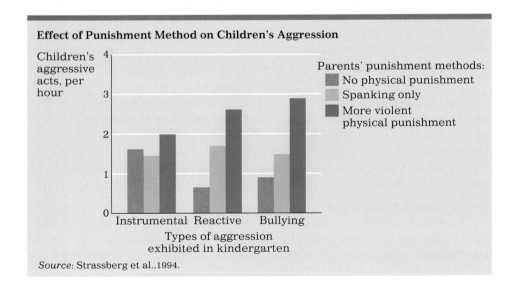

Effect of Punishment Method on Children's Aggression

Children's aggressive acts, per hour

Parents' punishment methods:
■ No physical punishment
■ Spanking only
■ More violent physical punishment

Instrumental   Reactive   Bullying
Types of aggression exhibited in kindergarten

Source: Strassberg et al.,1994.

FIGURE 10.1 Punishment and Aggression All the children, regardless of how their parents punished them, were about equally likely to exhibit instrumental aggression. The typical child did so once or twice an hour. By contrast, children who were severely punished by their parents were most often the bullies. The most interesting result involves reactive aggression. Children who were spanked interpreted such actions as hostile, and thus as requiring an aggressive response, twice as often as children who had not been physically punished.

?Observational Quiz (see answer, page 316): Could young children become bullies if their parents never spanked them?

■ **Photographs, tables, and graphs that are integral to the text**   Students learn a great deal by studying this book's illustrations, because Worth Publishers encourages authors to choose photos, tables, and graphs, to write captions, and to alter designs to better fit the words—not vice versa. As one result, photos and captions are instructional, supplementing and extending the text. Appendix A furthers this process by presenting at least one chart or table per chapter, containing detailed data for further study.

Learning Is Fun The original purpose of the Head Start program was to boost disadvantaged children's academic skills. The most enduring benefits, however, turned out to be improved self-esteem and social skills, as is evident in these happy Head Start participants, all crowded together.

?Observational Quiz (see answer, page 291): How many of these children are in close physical contact without discomfort or disagreement?

Content Changes for the Sixth Edition

Human development, like all sciences, builds on past learning. Many facts and concepts must be restated in every edition of a textbook—stages and ages, norms and variations, dangers and diversities, classic theories and fascinating applications. However, the study of development is continually changed by discoveries and innovations, so no paragraph in this sixth edition is exactly what it was in the fifth edition, much less the first. Extensive updating has been done, particularly in the coverage of multiculturalism and diversity—including such subject areas as gender, disabilities, ethnicity, and poverty. This updating is evident on virtually every page. Entire sections that have considerable emphasis on diversity are indicated here by blue bullets.

Chapter 1: Introduction
● ■ "Butterflies and Warfare" section (various trajectories of change)
● ■ Emphasis on the cultural contexts of development
● ■ "Who Sleeps with Whom?" section (cultural values)
● ■ A Case to Study: "This Sense of Liberation" (growing up on a Georgia farm)
● ■ Thinking Like a Scientist: Race and Biology (archaic and current concepts)

Chapter 2: Theories of Development
■ Increased coverage of behaviorism, including social learning
■ Updated and expanded coverage of epigenetic systems theory
● ■ Greater emphasis on sociocultural theory, including Vygotsky's work

- • ■ Application of theory: continuity–discontinuity, difference–deficit, nature–nurture
  - ■ Thinking Like a Scientist: What Is a Mother For? (Harlow's surrogate mothers)
  - ■ In Person: My Beautiful, Hairless Babies (why I adore my children)

Chapter 3: Heredity and Environment
  - ■ The practices and controversies surrounding genetic testing (especially in the context of the Human Genome Project)
- • ■ A Case to Study: What Do People Live to Do? (a young couple's quandary over their Down syndrome fetus)
- • ■ Changing Policy: Too Many Boys? (sex selection before birth)
- • ■ In Person: Whose Baby Is It? (alternate reproduction techniques)
- • ■ Changing Policy: Genetic Counseling: Decisions and Values

Chapter 4: Prenatal Development and Birth
- • ■ Prenatal testing to prevent transmission of HIV
  - ■ Recent discoveries about fetal learning and sensation (especially hearing)
  - ■ Changing Policy: Preventing Drug Damage (extensively updated)

Chapter 5: The First 2 Years: Biosocial Development
  - ■ New research on sleep at various ages
  - ■ Expanded discussion of brain growth, including expansion, pruning, sculpting
- • ■ New information on nutrition, malnutrition, and undernutrition
  - ■ A Case to Study: Toni's Well-Child Visit (identifying the signs of early deprivation)
- • ■ Thinking Like a Scientist: Plasticity and Young Orphans (Romanian adoptees)
- • ■ Changing Policy: SIDS Among Asian Infants (cohort and cultural insights)

Chapter 6: The First 2 Years: Cognitive Development
  - ■ Research-based challenges to Piaget's theories of early cognition
  - ■ Changing Policy: Policy Implications of Some Modern Research Methods
  - ■ Expanded coverage of information processing
- • ■ The effects of culture on language acquisition
  - ■ Three views of how infants learn language

Chapter 7: The First 2 Years: Psychosocial Development
  - ■ Expanded coverage of temperament, including exuberance, fearfulness
  - ■ More on emotions and social context (synchrony, social referencing)
- • ■ Expanded coverage of attachment (not only types A, B, and C but also type D)
  - ■ Expanded discussion of infant day care and father care, including a table on characteristics of high-quality care
  - ■ A Case to Study: Jacob's Parents on Autopilot (a boy's need to develop social connections)

Chapter 8: The Play Years: Biosocial Development
  - ■ Significance of brain development, especially the prefrontal cortex (with implications for education)
- • ■ Gender, cultural, and age variations in development of motor skills
- • ■ Updated coverage of injury control and of primary, secondary, and tertiary prevention of injury
- • ■ Updated discussion of incidence and prevention of child maltreatment, including failure to thrive, shaken-baby syndrome, and post-traumatic stress disorder
  - ■ A Case to Study: The Neglect of Neglect: A 2-Year-Old Boy (early recognition of warning signs)

Chapter 9: The Play Years: Cognitive Development

- Expanded coverage of Vygotsky's theory
- Thinking Like a Scientist: What Did Cinderella Do with the Pumpkin? (comparing theories)
- More explanations and data on theory of mind, including theory-theory
- Expanded coverage of children's information-processing abilities (simple arithmetic, memory, and theory of mind)
- New insights into language development, including the role of cognition
- The pros and cons of early schooling (including the qualities of good pre-K programs)

Chapter 10: The Play Years: Psychosocial Development

- Importance of emotional regulation and emotional intelligence
- Updated, multicultural research on prosocial and antisocial behavior
- Section on the influence of television and video games (reviews harm and benefits)
- Changing Policy: Turning Off the TV (who decides—parents or society?)
- New cross-cultural comparisons of parenting practices

Chapter 11: The School Years: Biosocial Development

- In Person: Two Mexican-American Children in California
- Relationship between brain development and motor control
- Updated coverage of autism, Asperger's, AD/HD, and ADD
- New data and tables on special education in the United States
- A Case to Study: Billy: Dynamo or Dynamite? (parents, teachers, and AD/HD)
- Changing Policy: Changing Tests (multiple intelligences)

Chapter 12: The School Years: Cognitive Development

- International data on children's understanding of logic
- Information processing in the school years (emphasizing brain development)
- Applications of moral education: Kohlberg, Gilligan, Rest
- Various approaches to teaching reading, math, and languages
- New discussion of educational standards and class size

Chapter 13: The School Years: Psychosocial Development

- Updated research on ways to treat and discourage bullying
- New section on prosocial behavior, including gender differences
- Updated coverage of family functions and structures (including adoptive and foster families)
- Rethinking relationship between stress and poverty, particularly family function
- Changing Policy: More Divorce, More Trouble?

Chapter 14: Adolescence: Biosocial Development

- New research on timing of puberty—genes, stress, evolution
- Updated material on risks of teenage sex
- Expanded discussion of origins of eating disorders
- New coverage of cultural context and drug use, especially gateway drugs
- A Case to Study: Julia, the Conscientious Student and Julia: Too Thin, As If That's Possible
- Changing Policy: Postponing Teenage Drug Experimentation (ads, education)

Chapter 15: Adolescence: Cognitive Development

- Formal operational thought and egocentricism as alternate modes
- Intuitive/analytic theories of cognition, with examples
- Discussion of school problems: dropouts, boredom, high-stakes testing
- Revised discussion of adolescent risk taking regarding jobs and sex
- Changing Policy: High Schools: Where and When (20th-century changes)

Chapter 16: Adolescence: Psychosocial Development
- ●■ Identity formation among various ethnic groups and nations
- ●■ New discussion regarding culture and gender in adolescent moods and social development
- ■ Restructured discussion of adolescent romance and sex
- ■ In Person: Talk to the Children; Be Careful What You Say (sex education and the Berger daughters)

Appendix A: Supplemental Charts, Graphs, and Tables
- ■ Quantitative data (in chart, graph, or table form) or further exploration, keyed to each chapter

Appendix B: More About Research Methods
- ■ Discussion of library research, observation, and the case study
- ■ Section on how research validity can be enhanced (through representative sampling, use of a comparison group)
- ■ Listing of key books and journals
- ■ Hints about using the Internet for research

Appendix C: Three Research Assignments

Supplements

As an instructor myself, I know how important good supplements are. I have been known to reject a textbook adoption if the publisher produced inferior and inaccurate ancillaries. Fortunately, Worth Publishers has a well-deserved reputation for the high quality of the supplementary materials it produces for both professors and students, and Worth's sales representatives are the most knowledgeable and helpful in the business. Accompanying this edition you will find the following:

Exploring Child Development: A Media Tool Kit for Understanding Development

This CD series (also available for instructors on VHS and DVD) was prepared by a talented team of instructors, including Lisa Huffman (Ball State University), Tom Ludwig (Hope College), Tanya Renner (Kapiolani Community College), Stavros Valenti (Hofstra University), Catherine Robertson (Grossmont College), and Connie Varnhagen (University of Alberta). Combining video, animations, self-tests, and interactive exercises, the *Media Tool Kit* offers students hands-on, interactive learning. These activities range from investigations of classic experiments (e.g., the visual cliff and the Strange Situation) to observations on children's play. The student tool kit includes more than 40 interactive video-based activities, quizzes, and flashcards tied to every chapter of the book. The instructor tool kit includes more than 200 video clips and animations, along with teaching tips and discussion starters.

Journey Through Childhood Observational Video

Bringing observational learning to the classroom, this new two-video set allows students to watch and listen to real children as a way of amplifying their reading of the text. The video enables students to observe children from birth through adolescence, in settings from day-care centers to schools, homes, and doctors' offices, and from a multitude of cultures and communities across the globe (Africa, Europe, Latin America, and Asia). Noted experts in child development—

among them Patricia Greenfield, Charles Nelson, Barbara Rogoff, and Carolyn Rovee-Collier—talk about their work in areas ranging from the biology of early brain development to prosocial behavior in middle childhood. This video set contains more than four hours of footage, including one hour of unnarrated observational clips. An observation workbook for the instructor provides teaching and activity tips. A student workbook helps students sharpen their observational skills and relate text material to real-life settings.

The *Scientific American Frontiers* Videos for Developmental Psychology

This remarkable resource provides instructors with 17 video segments of approximately 15 minutes each, on topics ranging from language development to nature–nurture issues. The videos can be used to launch classroom lectures or to emphasize and clarify course material. The *Faculty Guide* by Richard O. Straub (University of Michigan) describes each segment and relates it to specific topics in the text.

Child Development Telecourse

This new Child Development TeleWeb Course, developed by Coast Learning Systems and Worth Publishers, teaches the fundamentals of child development. The course also explores the variety of individual and developmental contexts that influence development, such as socioeconomic status, culture, genetics, family, school, and society. Each video lesson includes real-life examples interwoven with commentary by experts. In addition, video lessons describe the whole child, while others focus on topics such as fathers, maltreatment, and school. The course includes 26 half-hour video lessons, a *Telecourse Study Guide,* and a *Faculty Manual* with test bank.

Instructor's Resources

This collection of resources, compiled by Richard O. Straub, has been hailed as the richest in developmental psychology. This manual features chapter-by-chapter previews and lecture guides, learning objectives, springboard topics for discussion and debate, handouts for student projects, and supplementary readings from journal articles. Course planning suggestions, ideas for term projects, and a guide to audiovisual and software materials are also included. New to this edition are additional media teaching suggestions.

Study Guide

The *Study Guide,* by Richard O. Straub, helps students evaluate their understanding and retain their learning longer. Each chapter includes key concepts, guided study questions, and reviews that encourage students' active participation in the learning process; two practice tests and a challenge test help them assess their mastery of the material. New to this edition are additional application and observation activities for each chapter of the book.

PowerPoint Slides

A number of presentation slides are available on the Web site or on a CD-ROM. There are two prebuilt PowerPoint slide sets for each text chapter—one featuring chapter outlines, the other featuring all chapter illustrations. These slides can be used as is or customized to fit individual needs. Catherine Robertson has also produced a set of lecture slides featuring tables, graphs, and charts from the book.

The Worth Image and Lecture Gallery

Using Worth's Image and Lecture Gallery, located at www.worthpublishers.com/ilg, instructors can browse, search, and download illustrations from every Worth title and prebuilt PowerPoint presentation files for specific chapters, containing all chapter art or all chapter section headings in text form. Users can also create personal folders on a personalized home page for easy organization of the materials.

Overhead Transparencies

This set of 75 full-color transparencies consists of key diagrams, charts, graphs, and tables from the textbook.

Test Bank and Computerized Test Bank

The test bank, by the author and Clark Alexander, includes at least 80 multiple-choice and 50 fill-in, true-false, and essay questions for each chapter. Each question is keyed to the textbook by topic, page number, and level of difficulty. The Diploma computerized test bank, available for Windows and Macintosh, guides instructors step-by-step through the process of creating a test. It allows instructors to add an unlimited number of questions, edit questions, format a test, scramble questions, and include pictures, equations, and multimedia links. Online testing is also available.

Companion Web Site

The book's companion Web site (www.worthpublishers.com/berger) is an online educational setting for students and instructors. The companion Web site is free and does not require any special codes or passwords. Student resources include: chapter outlines, annotated Web links, online quizzes with immediate feedback and instructor notification, interactive flashcards and frequently asked questions about developmental psychology. For instructors, the Web site includes a full array of teaching tools, such as PowerPoint Slides, syllabus posting, an online gradebook, and links to various resources, including WebCT, Blackboard, and the Worth Image and Lecture Gallery.

Thanks

I'd like to thank those academic reviewers who have read this book in every edition and who have provided suggestions, criticisms, references, and encouragement. They have all made this a better book. I want to mention especially those who have reviewed and commented on this edition:

Mary Beth Ahlum *Nebraska Wesleyan University*
Joseph Allen *University of Virginia*
Leonard Austin *Black Hills State University*
Janette B. Benson *University of Denver*
Chris Boyazis *Bucknell University*

Priscilla Coleman *University of the South*
Tim Croy *Eastern Illinois University*
Peggy DeCooke *State University of New York, Purchase*
Ruth Doyle *Casper College*
Rosanne Dlugosz *Scottsdale Community College*

M. J. Eliason *University of Iowa*

Eugene Geist *Ohio University*

Tracey R. Gleason *Wellesley College*

Michelle de Haan *University College, London*

Robin Harwood *University of Connecticut*

Rebecca Hendrix *Northwest Missouri State University*

Christie Honeycutt *Stanly Community College*

Doug Hughey *Mount San Antonio College*

Andrew Johnson *Park University*

Mary Kay Jordan-Fleming *College of Mount St. Joseph*

Ken Kallio *State University of New York, Geneseo*

Laurie Katz *Middle Tennessee State University*

Kathleen Kleissler *Kutztown University*

Ada Lie *Milwaukee Area Technical College*

Harriett Light *North Dakota State University*

Martha G. Maddox *Houston Baptist University*

Angela Provitera McGlynn *Mercer County Community College*

Julie Ann McIntyre *Russell Sage College*

Joyce Munsch *Texas Tech University*

Barbara J. Myers *Virginia Commonwealth University*

David A. Nelson *Brigham Young University*

Larry J. Nelson *Brigham Young University*

Gail Overby *Southeast Missouri State University*

Susan Rogala *University of Michigan*

Pamela Schulze *University of Akron*

Fred Smiley *Cameron University*

Ken Springer *Southern Methodist University*

Siu-Lan Esther Tan *Kalamazoo College*

Grace van Thillo *Mount San Jacinto College*

Luis G. Valerio *University of Southern Colorado*

Dedication

Whenever I tell my story of how a junior assistant professor became an author writing the sixth edition of a textbook, I am struck by my good fortune. An eager, innocent novice found the best textbook publisher in the industry. Bob Worth himself promised that if I signed with Worth Publishers, I would have to work much harder than with any other company, but the final product would be better. Peter Deane, the book's first developmental editor, proved him right. Throughout the years, many editors, artists, designers, sales representatives, marketing managers, and CEOs have guided my work from its beginning as streams of words and ideas to its current position as a leading textbook sold in twelve nations, four languages, and every state of the United States. The process continues; my latest team of helpers includes Jessica Bayne, Cele Gardner, Tracey Kuehn, Renée Altier, and Catherine Woods—each of whom has taken a personal interest in my work, far beyond professional requirements. I thank them all, and dedicate this edition to them.

Kathleen Stassen Berger

July 2002

The Developing Person
Through Childhood and Adolescence

Introduction

scientific study of human development The science that seeks to understand the ways in which people change and remain the same as they grow older.

You are about to begin a fascinating journey, following human development from the moment of conception until about age 20. This chapter guides that journey. It outlines your direction, helping you anticipate the signposts, prepare for the climate, interpret the map, and read the compass. The directions, signposts, climate, map, and compass can be considered, respectively, the definitions, domains, contexts, methods, and ethics that guide our study.

Definitions: Change over Time

The **scientific study of human development** seeks to understand how and why people—all kinds of people—change and how they stay the same as they grow older. This definition has several key aspects. One is that developmental study is a *science,* using data, analysis, and methods similar to those used in all the other sciences. Another key phrase is *all kinds of people*—which includes people of many cultures, income levels, and backgrounds. Later in this chapter we describe scientific methods and human diversity in some detail.

Now we focus on the pivotal aspect of this definition: *change over time.* Each millisecond of life can be studied intensely, and developmental scientists sometimes do precisely that, examining one moment very carefully. For example, the split-second timing of the early interaction between a caregiver and newborn—the sequence of widening eyes, bobbing heads, relaxing lips, averted glances, tensed fingers, grunts, squeaks, coos, and so on indicate the relationship between the two. Such moments are significant in themselves but even more fascinating is how they reflect past experiences (such as in the birth process) and predict future ones—later that day, that week, that year, that life. Researchers look for "patterns of sound and silence" that become the rhythm of life (Jaffe et al., 2001, p. 5). Disrupted interactions, as would happen with neglect by a parent or lack of response by an infant, warn of abuse or brain damage—a warning that, properly heeded, can avert serious harm.

Each moment is understood to be only one small step in a very long journey, a journey that begins long before birth and continues through childhood, adulthood, and the next generation. As you can see from the parent–infant example above, developmentalists describe the moments of life, but they also do much more: They seek to understand how those moments are strung together and what could happen if different events had occurred in one moment, leading to an entirely different outcome. In seeking this understanding, developmentalists examine *every kind of change*—simple growth, radical transformation, improvement, and decline—and *every kind of continuity,* from day to day, year to year,

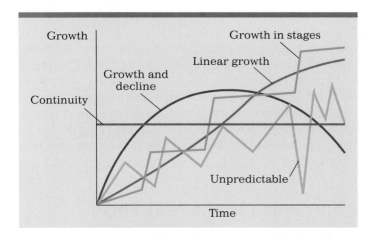

FIGURE 1.1 Patterns of Developmental Growth Many patterns of developmental growth have been discovered by careful research. Although linear (or near-linear) progress seems most common, scientists now find that almost no aspect of human change follows the linear pattern exactly.

linear change A process in which change occurs in a gradual, regular, predictable sequence.

dynamic systems A process of continual change within a person or group, in which each change is connected systematically to every other development in each individual and every society.

butterfly effect The idea that a small action or event (such as the breeze created by the flap of a butterfly's wings) may set off a series of changes that culminate in a major event (such as a hurricane).

and generation to generation. The elaborate genetic codes that lay the foundation for human growth; the countless particular experiences that shape and refine development; the impact of prenatal development; the multiple influences of family, school, friends, culture, and community—all are examined in the light of ever-changing social and cultural contexts.

Figure 1.1 illustrates some of these many kinds of change. Although **linear change** (like the blue line, gradually increasing day by day) is easiest to envision, it is least likely to occur. Only clock time ticks on, hour by hour, in a linear fashion, and clock time is a mechanical product of human creation. Development speeds up, slows down, and follows various trajectories; the specifics depend on which aspect of development, in whom, at what age is being described. For example, body weight increases very quickly in the early prenatal days, reverses in the first days after birth, then speeds up, slows down, and slows down even more until puberty, when it increases rapidly and then stops—unless the person overeats, diets, or gets sick. The path is not linear at all. Discovering and describing all the varied paths of change is one of the reasons the study of human development is so intriguing: We can always be surprised by what changes occur when, especially in our own lives or bodies.

Butterflies and Warfare

Beyond variability, developmentalists have made three important discoveries about change. First, life involves the continuous interplay of change and continuity, with each moment and each aspect potentially affecting all the others. To capture this idea, development is described as the product of **dynamic systems** (Lerner, 1998; Yoshikawa & Hsueh, 2001). "Dynamic" refers to the continual change within each person and in every social group, and "systems" highlights the fact that each change is connected systematically to every other development in each individual and every society. For instance, fluctuations in body weight are affected by genes, appetite, nutrition, caregiving, exercise, culture, food supply, and time of year. Weight is part of a system, interacting with other parts of the system.

One leader in the systems approach, Urie Bronfenbrenner, notes that even seemingly distant forces of international politics and traditional heritage have an impact on each developing person (Bronfenbrenner, 1979; Bronfenbrenner & Morris, 1998). To describe the various immediate and distant forces that affect a child, Bronfenbrenner has distinguished five systems: intimate, interfacing, community, cultural, and time (which he called, respectively, microsystems, mesosystems, exosystems, macrosystems, and chronosystems). He contends that all research should consider the reciprocal and dynamic relationships among all these five systems, using what he calls an *ecological approach* to studying human development (see Figure 1.2). Bronfenbrenner is particularly interested in the contexts of development, the importance of which is now recognized by all developmental scientists, as explained later in this chapter.

The second discovery is that a small change can have a very large effect on a dynamic system. This is called the **butterfly effect**, after a 1972 speech by weather expert Edward N. Lorenz entitled "Predictability: Does the Flap of a Butterfly's Wings in Brazil Set Off a Tornado in Texas?" The possibility that small input may result in large output applies to human thought and actions as well as to the natural sciences. A tiny change, a small gesture, a single spoken word may have a profound effect (Masterpasqua & Perna, 1997).

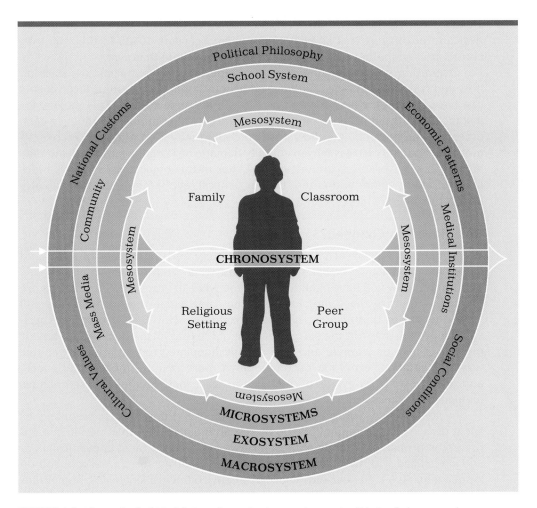

FIGURE 1.2 The Ecological Model According to developmental researcher Urie Bronfenbrenner, each person is significantly affected by interactions among a number of overlapping systems. *Microsystems* intimately and immediately shape human development. The primary microsystems for children include the family, peer group, classroom, neighborhood, and sometimes a church, temple, or mosque. *Mesosystems* refer to interactions among the microsystems, as when parents coordinate their efforts with teachers to educate the child. Surrounding and supporting the microsystems are the *exosystems,* which include all the external networks, such as community structures and local educational, medical, employment, and communications systems, that influence the microsystems. Influencing all three of these systems is the *macrosystem,* which includes cultural values, political philosophies, economic patterns, and social conditions. Bronfenbrenner has recently added a fifth system, the *chronosystem,* to emphasize the importance of historical time. Together, these systems provide the context of human development.

The third, seemingly opposite, discovery is that a large change may have no perceptible effect. For example, a group of 87 young refugees from war-torn Bosnia, aged 4 to 6 years (all of whom had fled their homes and most of whom had been shot at, lost family members, seen dead bodies, and been very hungry), were surprisingly "high on positive characteristics and low on psychological symptoms and problems" (Dybdahl, 2001, p. 1225). The ordeal had much more impact on their mothers, but the aid workers observing the children reported that "the majority managed to cope and function in everyday life" (p. 1226). How and why they emerged relatively unscathed is a topic for research, but it does seem that young children can cope with quite difficult experiences as long as they are with their parents, and that having a close bond to a protective,

Three Insights

1. Interacting systems: A change in one thing affects many other things.
2. The butterfly effect: A small change can become huge.
3. Power of continuity: A large change can be inconsequential.

steady caregiver helps children endure adversity of many kinds, including illness and poverty as well as war (Burlingham & Freud, 1942). In this example, continuity (the mother–child bond) was more powerful than war.

Overall, in seeking to understand change, developmentalists are learning how and why small changes can have enormous impact, while some large events can have no effect. Never forget that life is a dynamic system. This means, for instance, that the Bosnian mothers and children will continue to influence each other as time goes on. A child's positive coping may help a mother recover; a mother's ongoing distress may eventually damage her child; a father's death may limit both survivors. Research described later in this book reveals who is more likely to affect whom and when, but, in general, every family member always affects the others.

How Have You Changed?

The dynamic interplay of change and continuity and the impact of small and large changes become easier to understand when you look at your own life. Think about how you have changed since you were 10 years old. Some things are the same: You are the same sex, have the same family background, are still "you"—whatever that means. All that is continuity. However, everyone experiences a growth spurt in the second decade of life that turns them from a boy or girl into a man or woman, and that change happened to you in unforgettable ways. In addition, everyone becomes much more mature, more experienced, and, ideally, wiser as events and education teach new lessons. These changes happened to you as well.

In adolescence, you may have tried addictive drugs, gotten pregnant, or spent time in jail (although, if we go by research data rather than public perceptions, you probably did none of these). However, even the most uneventful teenage life is filled with thoughts and experiences that transform a person: You no longer think like a 10-year-old. Your social environment has altered, sometimes radically. Although some college students still live with their parents, socialize with old friends, and hang out in the same places that they did when they were children, most have shifted their social context. Indeed, some have experienced monumental transformations—perhaps divorce, marriage, death or birth of significant family members, a move to a new town or even a different nation.

Interestingly, such major changes may be forgotten or inaccurately remembered by the people who experience them. According to a 1997 survey of about 5,000 ninth-grade boys throughout the United States, 14 percent had had inter-

How Have You Changed Since Childhood? Many colleges have a spring festival, when students can act like kids again—as these sophomores at LeMoyne College in Syracuse, New York, are doing. Although blowing bubbles may seem to be child's play, the two have obviously changed since childhood. Change is evident not only in their physical size and shape but also in their willingness to be friends with someone of the other sex.

? *Observational Quiz* (see answer, page 6): One type of change is historical. Can you see three signs that this photo was taken in 2000, not twenty years before?

STEVE RUARK / SYRACUSE NEWSPAPERS / THE IMAGE WORKS

course before age 13. Two years later, another survey asked the same questions of most of the same boys, now in the eleventh grade; this time, only 8 percent reported having had sex before age 13 (Centers for Disease Control, August 14, 1998; CDC, June 9, 2000). Bravado? Bragging? Embarrassment? See page 25 for more on this.

To summarize, both the passage of time and changes over time sometimes seem obvious, as does continuity; but to know why and how they occur requires looking both forward and backward. Developmentalists examine the present moment, but they also look at what happened before and what happens after, always seeking the links that make a life, remembering that causes and consequences may not be what they seem. Change in one area of life dynamically alters the other areas, but minor changes can have a powerful effect and major events are not always traumatic.

A Life-Span Perspective

To understand all the dynamic systems over time, scientists look beyond childhood, not only because adults help guide the next generation and because every adult is a grown-up child but also because a firm understanding of what the future may hold is needed to help each child now. The scientific study of child development has benefited enormously from the scientific study of the entire life span (Dixon & Lerner, 1999; Smith & Baltes, 1999). In the "reciprocal connection" between the study of childhood and adulthood (Baltes et al., 1998), the **life-span perspective** helps us see sources of *continuity* from the beginning of life to the end (such as with biological sex, family of origin, and perhaps personality) and *discontinuity* (such as with language skills in infancy and with health habits in adulthood).

The life-span perspective actually envisions five distinct characteristics of development, each of which is illustrated throughout this text (Baltes et al., 1998; Smith & Baltes, 1999). Development is all of the following:

- **Multidirectional:** Change is not always linear, as we have just seen. Gains and losses, compensations and deficits, predictable growth and unexpected transformations are all part of the human experience.
- **Multicontextual:** Each human life must be understood as embedded in many contexts, as further described in this chapter.
- **Multicultural:** Many cultural settings—each with a distinct set of values, traditions, and tools for living—must be understood and appreciated, as is also illustrated in this chapter.
- **Multidisciplinary:** Many academic fields—especially psychology, biology, education, and sociology, but also neuroscience, economics, medicine, anthropology, history, and more—contribute data and insight to the science of development, as is apparent throughout this book.
- **Plastic:** Every individual, and every trait within each individual, can be altered at any point in the life span, as we will now explain.

This last characteristic, *plasticity,* or the capability of change, is probably the most encouraging tenet of the life-span perspective. The term *plasticity* denotes two complementary aspects of development: Human characteristics can be molded into different forms and shapes (as plastic can be), yet people maintain a certain durability (again, like plastic). Plasticity provides both hope and motivation—hope because change is possible, and motivation because what occurs at any moment helps lay the foundation for what follows. At the same time, plasticity emphasizes a sobering truth: People cannot become what they are not. We each have unique genes, families, and experiences, and those provide the raw material from which we mold and shape our lives.

life-span perspective A view of human development that takes into account all phases of life, not just childhood or adulthood.

multidirectional A characteristic of development, referring to its nonlinear progression—gains and losses, compensations and deficits, predictable and unexpected changes.

multicontextual A characteristic of development, referring to the fact that each human life takes place within a number of contexts—historical, cultural, and socioeconomic.

multicultural A characteristic of development, which takes place within many cultural settings worldwide and thus reflects a multitude of values, traditions, and tools for living.

multidisciplinary A characteristic of development encompassing the idea that dozens of academic disciplines contribute data and insight to the science of development.

plastic A characteristic of development that indicates that individuals—including their personalities as well as their bodies and minds—change throughout the life span.

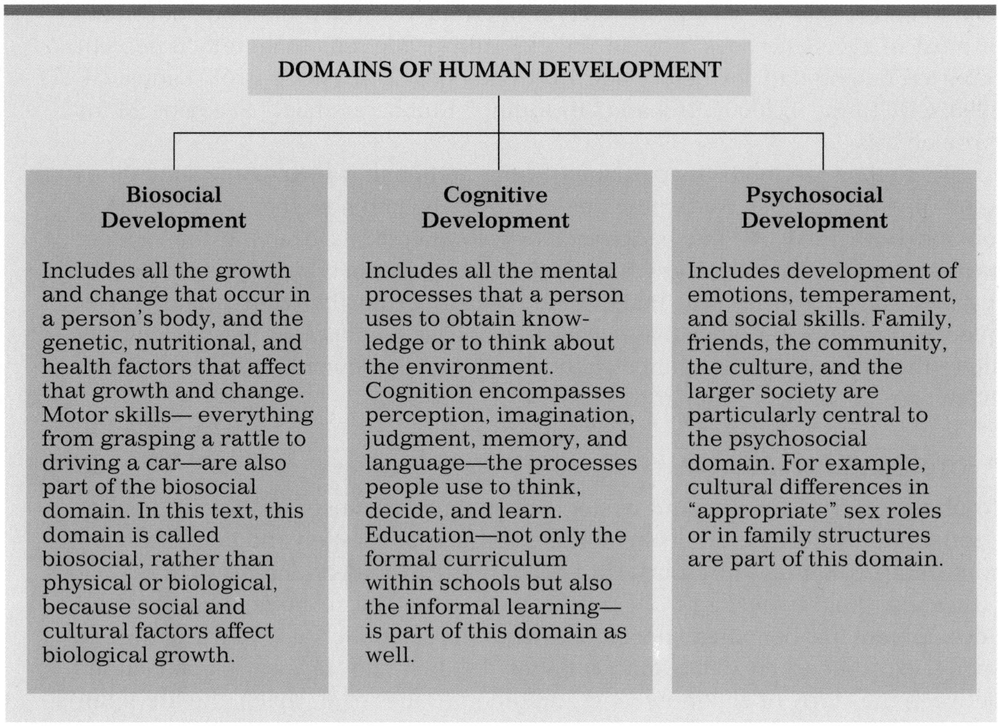

DOMAINS OF HUMAN DEVELOPMENT

Biosocial Development	Cognitive Development	Psychosocial Development
Includes all the growth and change that occur in a person's body, and the genetic, nutritional, and health factors that affect that growth and change. Motor skills— everything from grasping a rattle to driving a car—are also part of the biosocial domain. In this text, this domain is called biosocial, rather than physical or biological, because social and cultural factors affect biological growth.	Includes all the mental processes that a person uses to obtain know-ledge or to think about the environment. Cognition encompasses perception, imagination, judgment, memory, and language—the processes people use to think, decide, and learn. Education—not only the formal curriculum within schools but also the informal learning— is part of this domain as well.	Includes development of emotions, temperament, and social skills. Family, friends, the community, the culture, and the larger society are particularly central to the psychosocial domain. For example, cultural differences in "appropriate" sex roles or in family structures are part of this domain.

FIGURE 1.3 **The Three Domains** The division of human development into three domains makes it easier to study, but remember that very few factors belong exclusively to one domain or another. Development is not piecemeal but holistic: Each aspect of development is related to all three domains.

Three Domains of Development

To organize this multifaceted study, we can divide development into three major domains (see Figure 1.3): body, mind, and spirit, or the biosocial, cognitive, and psychosocial domains:

- The **biosocial domain** includes the brain and body, as well as changes in our biological selves and in the social influences that direct our physical growth.
- The **cognitive domain** includes thought processes, perceptual abilities, and language mastery, as well as the educational institutions that encourage our intellectual growth.
- The **psychosocial domain** includes emotions, personality, and interpersonal relationships with our family, friends, and the wider community.

All three domains are important at every age. For instance, understanding an infant involves studying his or her health (biosocial), curiosity (cognitive), and temperament (psychosocial), as well as dozens of other aspects of development from all three domains. Similarly, understanding adolescents requires studying the physical changes that turn a child's body into an adult one, the intellectual development that allows logical thinking about sexual passion and future goals, and the new patterns of friendship and courtship that lead to the intimate relationships of adulthood.

In practical terms, given a particular developmental change, it is not always obvious which domain it belongs to. Where would you place infertility, or learn-

biosocial domain The realm of the brain and body, as well as changes in our biological selves and in the social influences that direct our physical growth.

cognitive domain Our thought processes, perceptual abilities, and language mastery, as well as the educational institutions that encourage our intellectual growth.

psychosocial domain Our emotions, personality, and interpersonal relationships with family, friends, and the wider community.

!Answer to Observational Quiz (from page 4): Loose, printed t-shirts, backward baseball caps, and plastic lidded spout cups were rare before 1980.

ing a second language, or being a classroom bully? If you guessed biosocial, cognitive, and psychosocial, respectively, you are in accord with the placement of these topics in this text. But you also probably realized that there is overlap. For instance, a child is a bully for biological and cognitive reasons as well as social ones. Each person grows as an integrated whole.

All Kinds of People

Development is not only about many types of changes, reciprocal systems, and three major domains; it is also about *all kinds of people*. Remarkable similarities as well as dramatic differences are apparent among the 6 billion humans now alive and the billions more who once lived. Some aspects of development are universal for almost everyone: learning to walk and talk, developing relationships with family and friends, seeking love and learning. Many other aspects of life vary, depending on place, time, and circumstance. To highlight both the universal and the unique, this book includes many examples, quotations, anecdotes, and descriptions of many individuals.

A Case to Study

"This Sense of Liberation"

As you read the following passage, notice not only the impact of all three domains but also similarities and differences between this person and the children you know. Which aspect of this boy's life are true for everyone, which ones are true for most people but not all, and which ones seem unique?

My most persistent memory as a farm boy was of the earth. There was a closeness, almost an immersion, in the sand, loam, and red clay that seemed natural, and constant. The soil caressed my bare feet, and the dust was always boiling up from the dirt road that passed fifty feet from our front door, so that inside our clapboard house the red clay particles, ranging in size from face powder to grits, were ever present, particularly in the summertime, when the wood doors were kept open and the screen just stopped the trash and some of the less adventurous flies. . . .

There is little doubt that I now recall those days with more fondness than they deserve. . . . From as early in March until as late in October as weather and my parents permitted, I never wore shoes. The first warm days of the year brought not only a season of freshness and rebirth, but also a time of renewed freedom for me, when running, sliding, walking through mud puddles, and sinking up to my ankles in the plowed fields gave life a new dimension. I enjoyed this sense of liberation. . . .

There were some disadvantages to bare feet. There was always the possibility of stepping on old barbed wire or a rusty nail, with the danger of tetanus. Another problem was

at school. The pine floors were not sanded and polished but rough, the dust kept down by regular applications of used motor oil. We soon learned to pick up our feet with each step, because splinters were prevalent and a threat to bare feet that slid for even an inch across the surface.

Our most common ailments were the endemic ground itch, ringworm, boils and carbuncles, and sties on our eyes, plus the self-inflicted splinters, cuts, abrasions, bruises, wasp or bee stings. . . . On different occasions, I had both arms and three ribs broken, but my most memorable injury was just a small splinter in my wrist. . . . My arm was swollen only slightly, but I couldn't bend my wrist or move my fingers without intense pain, so I stayed at home instead of going to the field. One day, after our noon meal, as Daddy was leaving to go to work, he said, "The rest of us will be working while Jimmy lies here in the house and reads a book." I was stricken by his remark, knowing that he was disgusted with me when he called me "Jimmy" instead of "Hot." . . . My good reputation as a worker was important to me, and my father's approval was even more precious.

Not knowing what to do, I went out into the pasture near our home, ashamed of my laziness while my Daddy had to work even harder than usual. Desperate for a cure, I finally put my hand against a fencepost with my fingers upward, wrapped my belt tightly around it, and then slowly raised my arm to force my wrist to bend. All of a sudden, to my delight, there was a big eruption of pus, in the midst of which was a half-inch piece of blackened wood. I ran back to the house, got on my bicycle, pedaled it as fast as possible to the cotton field, and reported to Daddy for work. When I showed him the splinter, he smiled and said, "It's good to have you back with us, Hot."

[Carter, 2001, pp. 15, 29, 78–82]

It is easy to see the interplay of the three domains in this excerpt. Jimmy's desire for his father's approval (psychosocial) gave him the idea (cognitive) of strapping his hand to a fence to self-treat the infection in his arm (biosocial).

Both the universal and the unique are evident as well. Jimmy's attitudes and emotions are common among all children, including not only his wish for respect from adults but also his acceptance of conditions (dust, heat, bare feet) that those growing up in other places might think intolerable. By contrast, some specific conditions are very unusual: Perhaps you guessed from the red clay, dirt road, and clapboard house that Jimmy lived in rural Georgia, not far from Alabama, at a place and time that most people alive today would find strange.

It is also apparent that development is dynamic, ever-changing: Childhood for this happily barefoot lad is unlike that of any young child today, many of whom "need" several costly pairs of name-brand shoes. These differences highlight the crucial importance of the historical, cultural, and economic contexts of development.

A Clapboard Home Long grass now covers the loam and red clay that eighty years ago felt liberating to the boy named Jimmy. He sometimes slept with the farm family who lived here, although his own home was larger, with more windows, a stone's throw away.

PHYLLIS PICARDI / STOCK SOUTH / PICTUREQUEST

The Contexts of Development

As you might imagine, neither in a single book nor in everyday life can anyone simultaneously consider all the contextual factors that bear on any aspect of development. Throughout this text, we will examine a great many such factors, including families, schools, and nations, exploring how they push development in one direction or another. They are all interactive and reciprocal, with a small change sometimes becoming the butterfly whose wingbeat produces a major shift and a massive disaster sometimes not being strong enough to alter an individual's life course.

At the outset, however, we need to describe and define three contexts that can affect virtually every phase of development: the historical context, the cultural context, and the socioeconomic context. As Figure 1.4 suggests, these three contexts do not act in isolation.

The Historical Context

cohort A group of people whose shared birth year, or decade, means that they travel through life together experiencing the same major historical changes.

All persons born within a few years of one another are said to be a **cohort,** a group of people whose shared age means that they travel through life together (although they don't necessarily know one another). The idea is that all the people in a particular cohort are subject to the same history—the same prevailing assumptions, important public events, technologies, and popular trends. How

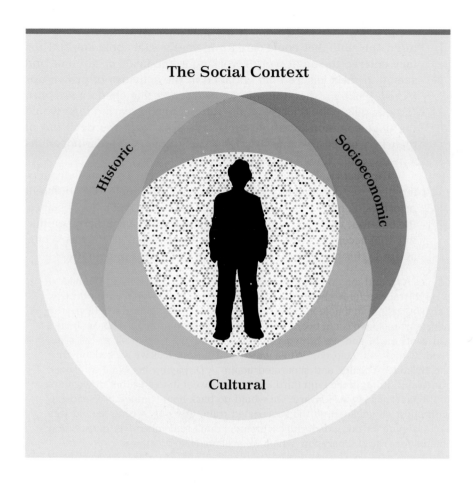

The Social Context

Historic

Socioeconomic

Cultural

FIGURE 1.4 Contexts Within Contexts Three broad contexts within the social context—history, socioeconomic status, and culture—affect human development in many ways—sometimes distantly, sometimes directly, sometimes individually, sometimes in combination. Because these three contexts overlap, it is often impossible to determine whether a particular effect comes from cohort, social class, or ethnic heritage.

❓Observational Quiz (see answer, page 10) Can you guess the significance of the multicolored dots?

history affects the lives and thoughts of a specific person depends partly on how old the person was when a given historical experience occurred. People in a specific cohort tend to be affected in the same way; those in different cohorts are generally affected differently. You can confirm this by asking members of other generations of your family about the war in Vietnam, Princess Diana's death, smoking marijuana, or even the appropriate use of a cell phone.

As profound economic, political, and technological changes occur over the years, basic concepts about how things "should be" are influenced by how things *were* before such changes took place. Scholars have discovered that our most cherished assumptions about how things should be are not always generally accepted. Instead, such an assumption is likely to be a **social construction,** an idea built more on shared perceptions of social order than on objective reality. As social shifts occur, social constructions also change.

Right now, for example, perceptions about the role of computers in society are shifting, cohort by cohort. The oldest cohorts tend to fear computers and are quick to see the Internet as a source of problems—pornography, social isolation, obesity, crime. The middle cohorts see computers as powerful tools to be mastered. The youngest cohorts see them as appliances, no more remarkable than toothbrushes or bicycles; they want fast, colorful, and audible ones in their bedrooms. Each cohort is partly correct; each has its own social construction. In fact, new inventions, from the radio to the automobile, and probably even the first campfire or plowed field, have always been judged by the older generations who grew up without them as corrupting the youth, who no longer do things the traditional way (Wartella & Jennings, 2000).

Even the most basic ideas about human development can change. For example, our very concept of childhood, as a precious and extended stage of life, is a

social construction An idea that is built more on shared perceptions of social order than on objective reality.

"You'd better ask your grandparents about that, son—my generation is very uncomfortable talking about abstinence."

Changing Values To some extent, the experiences and values of late adolescence influence each cohort for a lifetime. Maturity does not usually change those values, but at least it can make each generation realize the limitations of its historical context.

culture The specific manifestations of a social group's design for living, developed over the years to provide a social structure for the group members' life together.

! *Answer to Observational Quiz* (from page 9): Note that the dots are the same colors as the contexts and the overlap between the contexts. That means the dots signify that every context is apparent in some way in every immediate circumstance.

social construction. In many historical contexts, children were nurtured only until they could care for themselves (at about age 7). Then they entered the adult world, working in the fields or at home and spending their leisure time engaged in the activities of grown-ups (Ariès, 1962). Further, the social construction that children are born "little angels" would lead to quite different child rearing than would the once-common idea that adults have to "beat the devil out of them" in order to turn children into proper, God-fearing adults (Hwang et al., 1996; Straus, 1994).

The historical context of development is thus continually changing because "differences in year of birth expose people to . . . different priorities, constraints, and options" (Elder et al., 1995). For instance, the barefoot farm boy in A Case to Study lived in a southern community that accepted racial segregation without question. He was White, and A.D., his best friend, was Black. He writes that sometimes

Daddy let A.D. and me go to Americus to see a movie by ourselves. We had to walk up the railroad to Archery, find the little red leather flag left for the purpose, and stick it upright in a hole in the end of a crosstie. The engineer would see the signal and stop so we could board in front of the section foreman's house. It cost fifteen cents each, and we parted company during the ride to sit in the seats marked "white" and "colored." When we arrived in Americus we walked together to the Rylander Theater and separated again, A.D. paying his dime at a back entrance and sitting in the high third level while I went in to sit either downstairs or in the first balcony. Afterward, we would go back home, united in friendship though physically divided on the segregated train. Our only strong feeling was one of gratitude for our wonderful excursion; I don't remember ever questioning the mandatory racial separation, which we accepted like breathing.

[Carter, 2001, pp. 95–96]

When they got older, both Jimmy and A.D. fought against racial segregation, which they came to believe was very wrong. But their childhood historical and cultural context had created a racist social construction that was "accepted like breathing."

The Cultural Context

Culture is the second pervasive context of development. When social scientists use the term **culture**, they include hundreds of specific manifestations of a social group's *design for living,* developed over the years to provide a social structure for the group members' life together (Kluckhohn, 1949). Culture includes values, assumptions, and customs, not only physical objects (clothing, dwellings, cuisine, technologies, works of art, and so on). The term *culture* is sometimes used rather loosely, as in "the culture of poverty," "the culture of children," or "the culture of America." However, whenever culture is considered as part of the social context, the emphasis is more on values, behaviors, and attitudes than on the specific foods, clothes, and objects of daily life.

Survival Within the Cultural Context

Culture guides human development in a multitude of interrelated ways, helping families thrive within their communities. Here is one example: In many marginal agricultural communities, children are an economic asset because they work on the family's farm. Later, they perpetuate the family unit by remaining on the land, raising their own children, and caring for their aged parents. Thus, every newborn benefits the entire family group. If that family is also poor and dependent on subsistence farming, then nutrition and medical care are inadequate. As a

JOAN LEBOLD COHEN / PHOTO RESEARCHERS, INC.

Cherish the Child Cultures vary tremendously in how much they value children. China's "one-child" policy urges every family to limit reproduction, which could be taken as a sign either that children are not as valuable as older people or that each child is destined to be precious.

?Observational Quiz (see answer, page 14): What three signs suggest that this community enjoys this boy?

result, infant mortality is high—a serious loss to the family unit, which needs a new generation to work the land. Therefore, infant care is designed to maximize survival and emphasize cooperation. Typical cultural practices for babies in poor rural communities include the following:

- Breast-feeding on demand
- Immediate response to crying
- Close body contact, frequent touching, and caressing
- Keeping the baby beside the mother at night
- Constant care by siblings and other relatives

All these measures protect the fragile infant from an early death while establishing the value of interdependence among family members (LeVine et al., 1994).

In contrast, middle-class parents in postindustrial nations need not fear that their infant will die, but they have other concerns. They buy cribs, strollers, disposable diapers, high chairs, car seats, and educational toys—all quite expensive items that rural families never purchase. Even food, child care, and shelter are far more costly in an urban than a rural community, which is one reason most women in developed nations want only one or two children and most women in developing countries want three to five (Tsui et al., 1997) (see Appendix A, Chapter 1). The payoff for urban parents comes not when the child begins herding the sheep but when the young adult graduates from college and lands a prestigious job.

Therefore, hoping to ensure their children's future success in a technological and urbanized society, middle-class parents focus their child-rearing efforts on intellectual growth and emotional independence. They typically provide intense cognitive stimulation, talking to their babies more than touching them, putting them to sleep by themselves in their own cribs in their own rooms, and ignoring their young children's whining, crying, fussing, and clinging so as not to "spoil" them.

Who Sleeps with Whom?

As noted above, a specific cultural difference appears when parents decide where their children will sleep. Suppose you are asked to arrange the sleeping places for a family of six moving into a new apartment. The family consists of a

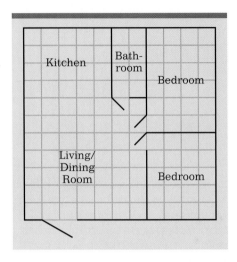

Who Sleeps Where? A six-person family needs to sleep in the apartment shown above. Can you figure out where? We have a mother, father, two daughters ages 2 and 15, and two sons ages 6 and 9.

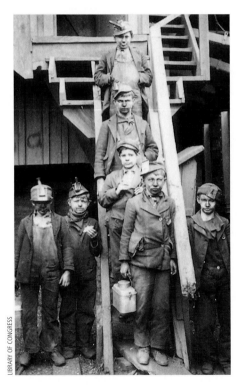

Why Not Put the Children to Work? The current view of childhood as a special period given over to formal education and play is a fairly recent one. As late as 1900, one out of every five children between the ages of 10 and 16 in the United States worked, often at dirty and dangerous jobs in factories, mills, and mines. These "breaker" boys, who usually started their work at age 10, had the task of picking out slate and rubble from crushed coal as it came down shutes from giant processors. Their hours were long; their environment was choked with coal dust; and their pay was less than a dollar a day.

husband and wife, two daughters aged 15 and 2, and two sons aged 6 and 9; the apartment has a living–dining room, a kitchen, one bathroom, and two bedrooms. Think a moment and see the figure at left before reading on. Have you figured it out? If you are from a non-Western culture, you see two easy solutions: Either the males sleep in one room and the females in another, or everyone sleeps in one room, perhaps on mats on the floor, with the second bedroom as the reading, studying, and computer room. What might seem like crowding may be preferred by people from the many cultures whose members always seek the company of others, awake or asleep (Schweder et al., 1998).

If you are from a Western culture, however, you believe in

> the ritualized isolation of children during the night, the institution of "bedtime," and the protection of the privacy of the "sacred couple" upheld by a cultural norm mandating the exclusive co-sleeping of the husband and wife.
>
> *[Schweder et al., 1998, p. 873]*

Your Western culture has taught you that husband and wife must sleep together, without the children. You have been warned that it is important for even young infants to sleep in separate cribs (Nakamura et al., 1999). You also believe that the 15-year-old is not a child, but a young woman who needs some privacy. This family has a problem without a solution, except the one my students suggested: "They must move."

Sleeping places are only one of hundreds of cultural variations. Each culture endorses certain parental strategies—not just for sleeping but also for talking, feeding, disciplining, encouraging, playing, and so on—that guide children to develop abilities, values, and expectations that are well suited for that place and time. Everyone grows up to "promote, promulgate, and share their understandings and practice with their children" (Schweder et al., 1998, p. 866). How does this relate to sleeping arrangements? Children who sleep with their parents are taught to depend on their parents for warmth and protection; children who sleep alone are taught to be independent of their families, becoming bold and independent as adults. Both practices seem to result in reasonably healthy adults, albeit with contrasting attitudes about their relationships with their parents, with Western young adults eager to get their own place, and non-Westerners often continuing to live with their parents even after marriage.

The Children's House For about 20 years, a third practice was common in hundreds of *kibbutzim* (the plural of *kibbutz,* a kind of farming commune developed in Israel, whose members share work, meals, income, and child care). In every kibbutz, the children once spent several hours each day with their parents, but slept in the same room with other children in a "Children's House," without adults. (The adults took weekly turns monitoring the children by intercom, in case an emergency arose during the night.) This custom changed, first in a few kibbutzim, then in others.

These changing patterns offered an opportunity for scientists to compare sleeping practices, as one researcher did. Three groups of 16- to 18-year-olds who had been raised in more than a dozen kibbutzim were studied; 33 had spent all their nights away from their parents; 34 had begun life sleeping in Children's Houses but switched before age 6 to sleeping near their parents; and 33 had always slept near their parents. This study also included a fourth group of 31 adolescents who had never lived on a kibbutz but had been raised in the city in their parents' homes. When the researcher evaluated these four groups of adolescents, particularly their emotions regarding their parents, the last three groups were quite normal (see Figure 1.5). However, many who had always slept apart from their parents, especially the boys, had difficulty talking about and relating to their family members (Scharf, 2001), a result similar to that of other research on kibbutz-raised children (Aviezer et al., 1994). Virtually all Israeli kibbutzim now

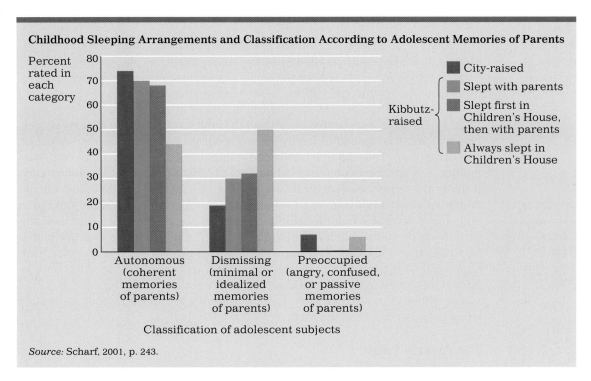

Childhood Sleeping Arrangements and Classification According to Adolescent Memories of Parents

Source: Scharf, 2001, p. 243.

FIGURE 1.5 **The Cost of Early and Continuing Nighttime Separation from Parents** The adolescent subjects' tape-recorded reminiscences about their parents were rated by trained researchers who did not know which of the four sleeping arrangements the subjects had experienced in childhood. The subjects were rated as autonomous, dismissing, or preoccupied, according to the criteria established for the Adult Attachment Interview. The subjects who, as children living on a kibbutz, had slept in a Children's House rather than near their parents were least likely to be rated as autonomous. Overall, the three groups of kibbutz-raised subjects were more likely to be rated as dismissing, with distorted memories of their parents, than were the city-raised subjects.

encourage parents to have their infants and children sleep near them; the Children's Houses are empty at night (Oppenheim, 1998).

The Need for Parents Extensive research led to the contemporary idea that children develop best if their parents are nearby (Bowlby, 1969, 1973, 1988). Today children who are hospitalized usually have their parents beside them (40 years ago the parents were kept away, to minimize infections). Families in the midst of war (such as the Bosnian mothers) stay together. Before the research, during World War II, thousands of English children were sent away from the cities (which were targets for German bombing) to stay with foster families in the countryside; they survived, but many developed psychological problems as debilitating as physical injury might have been (Burlingham & Freud, 1942).

Looking at cultural contexts makes it apparent that there are numerous wonderful and diverse ways to raise children, and each society and each set of parents make choices that could have been quite different. However, comparing cultures also makes it clear that some human needs are universal. For example, although most cultural variations in child rearing make sense within a given cultural context, raising children without a dedicated caregiver (though not necessarily a biological parent) is never satisfactory. Studies of orphans adopted from Romania as well as abused foster children from the United States suggest that children can recover from early separations if the caregivers are loving and patient, but it is much better to avoid the need for such recovery in the first place (Bowlby, 1988; Chisholm, 1998; Dozier et al., 2001).

Especially for Social Scientists: Can you think of any cultural assumptions that might have led to the now-universal practice in Israel of having kibbutz children sleep near their parents?

Especially for Parents: If you think one-year-olds should not sleep in their parents' room, why do you think that?

socioeconomic status (SES) An indicator of a person's social and economic standing, measured through a combination of family income, educational level, place of residence, occupation, and other variables.

*!**Answer to Observational Quiz** (from page 11): At least four adults are smiling at him; he is eating an apple that was brought to the market for sale; he is allowed to sit on the table with the food. If you noticed another sign—his new green sandals—give yourself bonus credit.

poverty line The minimum annual income a family needs to pay for basic necessities, as determined by the federal government. A family whose income falls below that amount is considered poor.

Response for Social Scientists (from page 13): Researchers as well as leaders in Israel assume that children should have strong relationships with their parents. Could this assumption itself be a social construction?

Response for Parents (from page 13): If you think the child should be in a separate room because the parents need privacy, you should know that children always sleep near their parents in India—and yet that country has an overpopulation problem. People obviously can have sex in many places and times other than in their shared bedroom at night. If your reason has to do with teaching the child, at a young age, to be independent, you are correct: The child is likely to learn not to depend on the parents for warmth and comfort while sleeping.

The Socioeconomic Context

The third major contextual influence on development is **socioeconomic status**, abbreviated **SES** and sometimes called "social class" (as in "middle class" or "working class"). SES is part of the social context because it influences many of the social interactions and opportunities a person might have.

Socioeconomic status is *not* simply a matter of how rich or poor a person is. Rather, SES is most accurately measured through a combination of several overlapping variables, including family income, educational level, place of residence, and occupation. The SES of a family consisting of, say, an infant, a nonemployed mother, and an employed father who earns $12,000 a year would be lower-class if the wage earner happens to be an illiterate dishwasher employed full time at minimum wage and living in an urban slum. But the same family configuration and annual income would be middle-class if the wage earner is a graduate student living on campus and teaching part time. The point of this example is that SES reflects not just financial status: It entails *all* the advantages and disadvantages, and *all* the opportunities and limitations, that may be associated with an individual's social status. Social class is as much a product of the mind as of the wallet, although obviously some mental attitudes are more difficult to sustain when basic needs cannot be met.

The Poverty Line

In official government statistics, SES is usually measured solely by family income (adjusted for inflation and family size), perhaps because the effects of education and occupation are difficult to quantify. In 2002 in the contiguous United States, a family of four with an annual income below $18,100 was considered to be at the bottom of the SES scale (U.S. Department of Health and Human Services, 2002). Their $18,100 was a dollar amount called the **poverty line**, which is calculated as the minimum amount needed to pay for basic necessities. (In Alaska and Hawaii, the poverty line is set somewhat higher.)

Looking only at family income is simplistic yet sometimes useful, especially when income falls below the poverty line. The reason is that inadequate family income both signals and creates a social context of limited opportunities and heightened pressures. These, in turn, make life much more difficult to manage than it is for families higher up on the socioeconomic ladder. For example, throughout the world infant mortality, child neglect, inadequate schools, and adolescent violence are all much more common among the poor than among the affluent (McLoyd, 1998). Of particular concern in the United States is that the poorest age group is also the youngest, in part because most publicly subsidized benefits (health care, food, housing, Social Security) that are age-related begin after age 65 (see Figure 1.6 and a state-by-state breakdown in Appendix A, Chapter 10).

Families and Neighborhoods

Although low income is a rough but useful indicator of poverty, and although poverty is a rough but useful signal for severe problems, we cannot simply say that lack of money creates overwhelming developmental difficulties. A better and more precise indicator is needed to differentiate between those low-SES individuals, families, and neighborhoods that are overcome by poverty and those that seem relatively protected.

Supportive relationships within the family are one crucial variable. For example, studies of children living in poverty find that some are "resilient: bouncing back from adversity, they become well-adjusted and successful, while others become angry, lonely, law-breaking, and failures" (Werner & Smith, 1992; see also Rutter et al., 1998). One difference is nurturant, involved parents. Even if adults

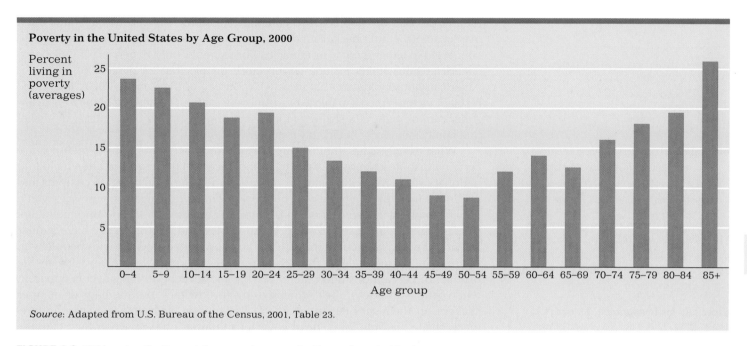

Poverty in the United States by Age Group, 2000

Source: Adapted from U.S. Bureau of the Census, 2001, Table 23.

FIGURE 1.6 Children Are the Poorest Someone who goes to bed hungry, in a crumbling house or apartment, in a crime-ridden community is more likely to be a child than an adult. To those who study child development, this seems unfair—especially because some older adults who are not actually poor "spend down" their assets in order to qualify for government subsidies. Who should support the poor of other generations—the society as a whole or the family members of those who are poor?

are poor, unmarried, and victims of childhood neglect and abuse, they can become good parents, and the quality of parenting is the single most sensitive predictor of a resilient child (Duncan & Brooks-Gunn, 2000; Wyman et al., 1999).

Neighborhoods are another crucial variable, as you might guess from the emphasis on the mesosystem. If people show concern for each other and for their immediate surroundings—getting rid of trash on the street, repairing broken windows, and so on—the children will be healthier and more successful than children of equally poor families who live in neighborhoods where the adults care only about themselves. The importance of "collective efficacy," which is the ability of the neighbors to create a functioning community, has been shown in detailed, block-by-block analyses in Chicago and New Orleans (Cohen et al., 2000; Sampson et al., 1997) and probably is true overall. Finally, again as our understanding of development would predict, a change in income level is more influential than the absolute level. For example, one study of impoverished families whose income improved over three years—even though it was still below average—found that the children did as well as middle-class children (Dearing et al., 2001).

Economics and Ethnic Groups

To say, as we did earlier, that "social class is as much a product of the mind as of the wallet" is not to say that money does not matter. It *does* matter, but it is only one of several factors that constitute social class, and social class is only one of the factors

Don't Go There Not just poverty but neglect and crime are evident in this scene on Chicago's South Side. In communities where incomes are low but the residents care about the neighborhood, abandoned cars are towed away, not stripped, and empty buildings are rebuilt, demolished, or at least boarded up, not left with broken windows for rats and drug addicts to enter.

that affect child development. To complicate matters, socioeconomic status often overlaps with ethnic background, so a particular pattern of development can be connected to either income or ethnicity. For example, only 10 percent of European-American households include six or more people, but 25 percent of Hispanic-American households are that large (U.S. Bureau of the Census, 2000). Is that the result of income (the Hispanic average income is about 60 percent of the European-American) or culture (a strong emphasis among Hispanics on familism, the belief that family members should stay together)?

ethnic group A collection of people who share certain attributes, almost always including ancestral heritage and often including national origin, religion, customs, and language.

What exactly is an ethnic group? Briefly, members of an **ethnic group** share certain attributes, almost always including ancestral heritage and often including national origin, religion, customs, and language. (*Heritage* refers to customs and traditions from past generations; *national origin* merely means birthplace, which may or may not signify customs.) Because of this shared background, members of an ethnic group recognize and identify with one another. They have similar attitudes and daily encounters with the social world, especially with people who realize they are members of that ethnic group. Accordingly, ethnicity is partly the product of perceptions and reactions. This social recognition aspect is apparent when people broadcast their ethnicity—by, for instance, putting flags or bumper stickers on their cars ("Honk if you're Italian") or wearing distinctive apparel (neck chains, jackets, pins, head coverings, and so on)—or when they take the opposite approach, working to rid themselves of an accent or mannerism that reveals their ethnic roots.

Especially for Immigrants: Why might it be unwise for you to abandon the customs of your native culture?

One of the many complications of ethnicity (and one of the reasons people are not always happy when others recognize their ethnic heritage) is that, in every nation of the world, economic opportunities, occupational choices, and residential patterns are linked to ethnic identity. Any research that finds differences between people based on ethnicity or race may actually be uncovering differences in SES, or vice versa (Bradley et al., 2001). Becoming aware of this problem is an essential step for students and researchers, but it is often impossible to disentangle SES, culture, ethnicity, and race (Smith, 2000), as the Thinking Like a Scientist feature explains.

race A social construction by which biological traits (such as hair or skin color, facial features, and body type) are used to differentiate people whose ancestors came from various regions of the world.

Thinking Like a Scientist

Race and Biology

Sometimes *race* is considered an element of ethnicity. Indeed, outsiders mistakenly assume that people of the same racial background are also from the same ethnic background, and statisticians often categorize people by race rather than by ethnicity. However, as social scientists emphatically point out, **race**—defined as the biological traits (such as hair or skin color, facial features, and body type) that people use to distinguish one group from another—is much less influential on development than ethnic background (Goodman, 2000). The Human Genome Project (discussed in Chapter 3) has found that genetic distinctions *between* racial groups are few and insignificant compared with genetic distinctions between members of one family or another *within* any racial group.

For this reason, social scientists prefer to discuss ethnicity, not race, although sometimes data are reported only by race. In that case, race is used as the only available marker for ethnicity.

Ethnic identity, however, is not primarily genetic; it is a product of the social environment and the individual's consciousness. Two people may look like close relatives but may have quite different upbringings, heritages, and community settings and therefore quite different ethnic identities. Or two people may be very different in appearance but still share an ethnic identity. This is readily apparent in many Latin American ethnic groups. These groups include people of African, European, and Indian descent who are united in a single ethnicity by their common language and original homeland. Similarly, people of African descent who lived for many generations in the Caribbean do not generally consider themselves black, at least as people born in the United States define "black" (Waters, 2000). In fact, immigrant children from many nations resent being categorized racially (Suarez-Orozco & Suarez-Orozco, 2001). They recognize that racial designations can be used artificially to set them apart and exclude them; people from the Middle East, for instance, are categorized as white in the United States but as non-white in England.

The realizations that ethnic categories are not genetic and that racial categories are misleading are changing the way scientists report research. For example, the 1970 U.S. census used only three racial categories—white, Negro, and other. Millions of Spanish-speaking citizens insisted that they did not belong in these categories, and millions of Asian-Americans and Native Americans resented being dismissed as "other." Three new categories were added in 1980: "Asian and Pacific Islander," "American Indian, Eskimo, Aleut," and "Hispanic, may be of any race" (although those who checked off "Hispanic" were also asked to designate "white" or "black"). Allowing Hispanics to be tallied separately has been particularly useful for those who care about the well-being of children; the census has revealed that the proportion of children under age 18 who are of Spanish heritage has doubled since 1980, from 9 to 18 percent; this increase lends urgency to the need to improve bilingual education as well as many other social services for children.

For the 2000 census, some scientists advocated getting rid of all racial categories, but this idea was rejected. Instead, a sixth category was created, separating "Asian" from "Native Hawaiian, and Pacific Islander." Respondents were also allowed to check several new racial categories, including "More than one race."

Social scientists increasingly recognize that all racial categories are imprecise, because each contains at least a dozen quite distinct ethnic groups. More and more studies try to specify the ethnic background of the subjects. At this point in the historical context, ethnic and racial categories remain socially and economically powerful, affecting how children develop, and therefore they are often reported in research. Data collected prior to 2000 are often reported using the old racial categories. By the 2010 census, these classifications may change again.

The Person Within Systems and Contexts

Awareness of the overlaps among culture, SES, and ethnicity leads to another, even more important, realization: Although each context always affects how an individual develops, a person within a context or system is never like a part in a complex machine, responsive only to the mechanical pushes and pulls of that context. No one is exactly like the statistically "average" person of his or her cohort, socioeconomic status, or culture. Not only is each person guided in divergent directions by many contextual influences, whose power varies from individual to individual, age to age, situation to situation, and family to family, but also each person has unique genes and experiences.

Consequently, each of us differs in unexpected ways from any stereotypes or generalities that might seem pertinent, and our individual differences demand as much scientific respect and scrutiny as any of the commonalities that link us to a particular group. In

Not the Usual Path If we were to consider only this woman's past history or the cultural values that her dyed hair and polished fingernails suggest, we would say that she belongs at home with her grandchildren and old-age pension. However, individual uniqueness can override contextual limitations—which explains why she is about to walk the Appalachian Trail from Maine to Georgia. If we use a life-span perspective, this is not a surprise, because she always enjoyed exercise and the outdoors, and covering the trail's entire 2,160-mile length was her lifelong ambition.

VINCE DE WITT / STOCK, BOSTON

CRISTOBAL HERRERA / AP PHOTO

Jimmy Carter in Havana, Cuba, in 2001.

fact, each of us is an active participant in every context that includes us. We contribute to the history of our cohort, we help form our economic circumstances, and we construct our own personal meanings from our cultural background (Rogoff, 1997; Valsiner, 1997). This power of the developing individual is demonstrated by every person who is the focus of the features in this book called "A Case to Study." Remember that barefoot farm boy from southwest Georgia? Given his historical, cultural, and economic contexts, he was destined to become a farmer like his father. But he did not. He went to the U.S. Naval Academy (the first in his family to attend college), became an engineer, and at the age of 52 was elected the 39th president of the United States. Today Jimmy Carter is a renowned humanitarian on the world stage. To reinforce the same point—that domains interact and that contexts are powerful—the In Person feature presents a personal story, that of my brother's son David.

In Person

My Nephew David

In the spring of 1967, in rural Kentucky, an epidemic of rubella (German measles) struck two particular victims— David's mother, who had a rash and a sore throat for a couple of days, and her 4-week-old embryo, who was damaged for life. David was born in November, with a life-threatening heart defect and thick cataracts covering both eyes. Other damage included minor malformations of the thumbs, feet, jaw, and teeth, as well as of the brain.

The historical context was crucial. Had David been conceived a decade later, widespread use of the rubella vaccine would have protected him from damage. Had he been born a few years earlier, he would have died. Indeed, some doctors expected David to live briefly as a severely retarded child requiring custodial care. But in 1967 the new miracle of microsurgery saved his tiny heart and his life.

My brother is a professor and his wife is a nurse; their cultural and socioeconomic contexts encouraged them to seek outside help rather than accept their fate. They asked advice from a teacher at the Kentucky School for the Blind, who told them to stop blaming themselves and stop overprotecting David. If their son was going to learn about his world, he had to explore it. For example, rather than confining David to a crib or playpen, they were to provide him with a large rug for a play area. Whenever he crawled off the rug, they were to say "No" and place him back in the middle of it. He would learn to use his sense of touch to decide where he could explore safely without bumping into walls or furniture. They followed this advice.

Nonetheless, progress was slow. Rubella had damaged much more than David's eyes and heart. At age 3, he could not yet talk, chew solid food, use the toilet, coordinate his fingers, or even walk normally. An IQ test showed him to be severely mentally retarded. Fortunately, although most children with rubella syndrome have hearing defects, David's hearing was normal.

David's fifth birthday occurred in 1972. By then, the social construction that children with severe disabilities are unteachable was being seriously challenged. David's parents found four schools that would accept a child with multiple handicaps. In accordance with the family's emphasis on education, they enrolled him in all four. He attended two schools for children with cerebral palsy: One had morning classes, and the other—40 miles away—afternoon classes. (David ate lunch in the car with his mother on the daily trip.) On Fridays these schools were closed, so he attended a school for the mentally retarded. On Sundays he spent two hours in church school, which was his first experience with "mainstreaming"—the then-new idea that children with special needs should be educated with normal children. Particularly in the church community, the cultural-ethnic context of northern Kentucky benefited David, for accepting the disabled and helping neighbors are basic Appalachian values.

At age 7, David entered a public school, one of the first severely disabled children to be mainstreamed. Rubella continued to hinder his biosocial, cognitive, and psychosocial development. His motor skills were poor (among other things, he had difficulty controlling a pencil); his efforts to read were limited by the fact that he was legally blind; and his social skills were seriously impaired (he pinched people he didn't like, hugged girls too tightly, cried and laughed at inappropriate times).

During the next several years, development in the cognitive domain proceeded rapidly. By age 10, David had skipped a year of school and was a fifth-grader. He could read—with a magnifying glass—at the eleventh-grade level and was labeled "intellectually gifted" according to tests of verbal and math skills. Outside of school he began to learn a second language, play the violin, and sing in the choir.

David now calls his college experience an "adversity," and certainly many of his peers and professors were unprepared for a student like him. He sometimes seemed to learn too well, asking precise questions and remembering numbers and words that most students would forget. He sometimes took offense at inadvertent slights. But he finally graduated, a double major in Russian and German. He studied in Germany to refine his translating skills and now earns his living as a translator (an interesting choice for someone who cannot see social nuances of facial expressions and therefore learned to listen carefully). His latest report is that he is

> generally quite happy, but secretly a little happier lately, especially since November, because I have been consistently getting a pretty good vibrato when I am singing, not only by myself but in congregational hymns in church. [He explained vibrato:] when a note bounces up and down within a quarter tone either way of concert pitch, optimally between 5.5 and 8.2 times per second.
>
> *[David, 2002]*

Amazing. David is both knowledgeable and happy, and he continues to develop his skills. He also has a wry sense of humor. When I told him that I wasn't progressing as fast as I wanted to in revising this text, even though I was working very hard every day, he replied, "That sounds just like a certain father I know." As his aunt, I have watched David defy many pessimistic predictions. The rubella damage will always be with him, limiting his development. But David proves again that no human is entirely or inevitably restricted by any of life's domains, systems, or contexts.

Three Brothers Studying the development of other people is fascinating in many ways, not the least of which is that no human is untouched by understanding the personal story of another. I have learned many things from David, shown in this recent family photo with his two older brothers, Bill (left) and Michael (right). One is the role of siblings: Bill and Michael protected their younger brother, but David also taught them, making them more nurturant than most young men in their community. I know this firsthand—these boys were the closest thing my daughters had to big brothers, and they tolerated teasing that some older cousins would have put a stop to.

KATHLEEN BERGER

Developmental Study as a Science

Because the study of human development is a science, it follows objective rules of evidence. Because it concerns human life and growth, it is also laden with personal implications and applications. This interplay of the objective and the subjective, of the individual and the universal, of young and old, of past, present, and future makes developmental science a dynamic, interactive, and even transformative study. Of all the sciences, the study of human development is the least static, least predictable, and least narrow. It also may have the most noble goal: "explaining, assessing, and promoting change and development" (Renninger & Amsel, 1997, p. xi). In other words, developmental scientists seek not only to understand and measure human change but also to use their knowledge to help all people develop their full human potential.

This lofty goal is of vital importance. Everyone has heartfelt opinions about how children should grow and why they turn out the way they do. By definition, opinions are subjective and tend to be biased, or influenced by our particular

Response for Immigrants (from page 16): Since cultures develop for reasons, a custom that seems superficial and old-fashioned in your new country may be part of an interdependent design for living; changing one custom may affect many other aspects of your life. This does not mean that change is bad; it simply means that aspects of both the old culture and the new culture should be examined before being adopted or discarded.

backgrounds and experiences. To move beyond opinions and controversy, developmentalists use the scientific method to seek evidence—not biased or wishful thinking—to gain the knowledge we need to use (Shonkoff, 2000; Thompson & Nelson, 2001). In fact, one of the goals of all science is to question assumptions, to disprove what "everyone knows," and even to reexamine the results of other scientific research (Feynman, 1985; Popper, 1965).

The Scientific Method

scientific method An approach to the systematic pursuit of knowledge that, when applied to the study of development, involves five basic steps: Formulate a research question, develop a hypothesis, test the hypothesis, draw conclusions, and make the findings available.

hypothesis A specific prediction that is stated in such a way that it can be tested and either confirmed or refuted.

replication The repetition of a scientific study, using the same procedures on another group of subjects, to verify or refute the original study's conclusions.

The **scientific method,** as it applies to developmental study, involves four basic steps and sometimes a fifth:

1. *Formulate a research question.* On the basis of previous research or a particular theory or personal observation, pose a question about development.
2. *Develop a hypothesis.* Reformulate the question into a **hypothesis,** which is a specific prediction that can be tested.
3. *Test the hypothesis.* Design and conduct a research project that will provide evidence—in the form of data—about the hypothesis.
4. *Draw conclusions.* Use the evidence to support or refute the hypothesis. Describe any limitations of the research and any alternative explanations for the results.
5. *Make the findings available.* Publishing the research is often the fifth step in the scientific method. It involves describing the procedure and results in sufficient detail that other scientists can evaluate the conclusions or replicate the research. **Replication** is the repetition of a scientific study, using the same procedures on another group of subjects, to verify or refute the original study's conclusions.

Some Complications

In actual practice, scientific investigation is less straightforward than these five steps would suggest. The linkages among question, hypothesis, test, and conclusion are sometimes indirect, and the design and execution of research are influenced by (fallible) human judgment (Bauer, 1992; Howard, 1996). Human biases tend to guide the choice of which topics to examine, which methods to use, and how to interpret the results.

Sometimes major industries that have an economic stake in the results of scientific studies either sponsor or subsidize research and distort the conclusions. It has been proven in court that the tobacco industry has done this regarding the harm done by nicotine and other toxins in cigarettes for years, and they continue to hamper scientific studies of the effects of advertising, international marketing, and secondhand smoke (Ong & Glantz, 2001). Most other social practices have economic implications, such as creating more public day-care centers, reducing the amount of lead in old houses, providing vouchers for private schools, funding contraception or abortion, using drugs to quiet disruptive children—although in all these cases the evidence is less clear-cut than it was for tobacco. Minimizing the effects of cultural values, political pressures, personal wishes, and financial support is a challenge. It is also one goal of the methods and procedures of science—and not an easy goal to reach (Hunt, 1999; Shonkoff, 2000).

variables The qualities that may differ, or vary, during a scientific investigation.

Further, there is always a question of whether researchers are aware of all the relevant **variables**—qualities that may differ, or vary, during an investigation. People vary in sex, age, education, ethnicity, economic status, nationality, values, jobs, family background, personality—the list could go on and on. Moreover, developmental researchers must deal with both *intrapersonal variation,* which is variation within one person from day to day, and *interpersonal variation,* which is variation between people or between groups of people. The two kinds of variation are not always easily distinguished.

Partly because of this complexity, certain controversies echo throughout the study of development, each time with different issues and questions—and often with different responses:

- *Nature–nurture.* How much and which aspects of development are affected by genes and how much and which aspects by environment?
- *Continuity–discontinuity.* How much of human growth builds smoothly and gradually on previous development, and how much transformation occurs suddenly?
- *Difference–deficit.* When a person develops differently from most other people, when is that difference considered diversity to be celebrated and when is it considered a problem to be corrected?

Each of these controversies is further explained and explored throughout this text, especially in Chapter 2, on theories of development.

Two other issues seem contentious to those unfamiliar with developmental study, though they are not issues for developmentalists:

- *Religion–science.* Do the tenets of religious faith and the methods of science necessarily conflict?
- *Individual–society:* Can we study the individual person without studying the family, the community, and the culture?

To both of these questions, the answer from scientists who study development is "no." Religion and science are complementary, not conflicting (Gould, 1999), and individuals are inextricably involved with their social group (Cole, 1996). Some of the most emotional questions about human life—who should have sex with whom, who should hurt whom, who should be rich or poor, and when and how all these things might happen—benefit from the scientific method and the perspective of other cultures and cohorts. Prepare for some new ideas.

Research Methods

Between the questions developmental scientists ask and the answers they find lies their methodology—not only the steps of the scientific method but also the specific strategies used to gather and analyze data. These strategies are critical because "the ways that you attempt to clarify phenomena in large measure determine the worth of the solution" (Cairns & Cairns, 1994). In other words, *how* research is designed affects the *validity* (does it measure what it purports to measure?), *accuracy* (are the measurements correct?), *generalizability* (does it apply to other populations and situations?), and *usefulness* (can it solve real-life problems?) of the conclusions.

Some general strategies to make research valid, accurate, and useful are described in Appendix B. Now we turn to specific methods of testing hypotheses: observations, experiments, surveys, and case studies. Remember, the overall goal is to find evidence that answers questions and minimizes human biases.

Observation

An excellent method to test hypotheses regarding human development is **scientific observation**—that is, observing and recording, in a systematic and objective manner, what people do. Observations often occur in a naturalistic setting, such as at home, in a workplace, or on a public street. Typically, the observing scientist tries to be as unobtrusive as possible, so that the people being studied (the research subjects) act as they normally do.

scientific observation A method of testing hypotheses by unobtrusively watching and recording subjects' behavior either in a laboratory or in a natural setting.

Do Not Disturb: Science in Progress Does any 6-month-old understand that cups go on saucers, that circles are not squares, and that mothers know the answers when a child does not? In this laboratory observation, one scientist elicits the answers while another videotapes the results for later analysis.

Observation can also occur in a laboratory. In this setting, the scientists sometimes are not visibly present at all; they may sit behind one-way windows that allow them to peer, unnoticed, into the experimental room, or they may record data with a video camera placed on the wall. In the laboratory, scientists study many aspects of behavior, such as the rate and duration of eye contact between infant and caregiver, the patterns of dominance and submission that emerge as an entire family discusses its vacation plans, the heart rate and brain activity of a child watching a frightening movie, and many more.

Already mentioned at the beginning of this chapter is observational research on the moment-by-moment interaction between a parent and an infant. This is sometimes done with great precision, using two video cameras and analyzing the tapes frame by frame on a computer to see whether a new baby really can observe a parent's rapidly changing facial expression or vocalization and respond to it. The answer is "yes," a finding that could not have been made without very careful and objective observations (Rochat, 2001).

Observation has one major limitation. It does not indicate what causes the behavior we observe. If we notice that one mother spanks her children and another does not, or that one 11-year-old sneaks a beer and another abstains, *why* do such differences appear? Naturalistic observation can note many characteristics of these two 11-year-olds, but it cannot explain why one variable occurs with another. For instance, in the United States, young adolescents who abuse alcohol are more likely to be male than female and more likely to be non-Hispanic white (European-American) than black (African-American) (Johnston et al., 2001). But why?

correlation A number indicating the degree of relationship between two variables, expressed in terms of the likelihood that one variable will occur when the other variable does. A correlation is not an indication that one variable *causes* the other.

Naturalistic observation provides no definitive answers about causes. The data can prove that certain variables correlate with other variables, not that one causes another. A **correlation** exists between two variables if one variable is more (or less) likely to occur when the other occurs. For example, a correlation exists between being a male European-American teenager and drinking beer. Are hormones, upbringing, advertising, or peer pressure the reason? Correlation indicates a connection, but it does not specify the reason for that connection. Are African-American adolescents better protected from alcohol abuse by religion, income, or family influences than European-Americans? Correlation cannot provide the answer.

Even when two variables are strongly (or highly) correlated, we should not, even must not, say that one variable causes the other. Table 1.1 illustrates the three types of correlational connections, using the correlation between wealth and education as an example.

TABLE 1.1 There Is a Strong Positive Correlation Between Wealth and Education

Possible explanation:	Income → education (Wealthy families pay for good schools and colleges.)
Possible explanation:	Education → income (Well-educated people earn more.)
Possible explanation:	Family values → income → education (Hard work and no drugs produce higher levels of both income and education.)
Conclusion:	Education and income are somehow connected.

Whenever there is a strong correlation between two variables, either of the variables could be the cause or both could be caused by a third variable. Correlation is not causation.

A correlation is *positive* if the occurrence of one variable makes it *more* likely that the other will occur. A correlation is *negative* if the occurrence of one variable makes it *less* likely that the other will occur. Because of the way correlation is calculated, the highest positive correlation is expressed as +1.0 and the greatest negative correlation as −1.0. Most actual correlations are neither so high nor so low: A correlation of 0.5 is impressive. Two variables that are not related at all have a correlation of zero, or 0 (exactly halfway between +1.0 and −1.0). We mentioned earlier that observation has confirmed that some parents spank their children more often than others. Correlation suggests reasons for this variation. As you can see from Table 1.2, the reason does not seem to be the child's sex, at least for 4- to 5-year-olds. This study found a positive correlation between spanking and behavior problems, and a negative one between spanking and the warmth of the parent's feelings toward the child. This link is intriguing—but once again, other research needs to reveal what causes what. The best way to do this is to conduct an experiment.

The Experiment

An **experiment** is an investigation designed to untangle cause from effect. In the social sciences, experimenters typically expose a group of people to a particular treatment or condition to see if their behavior changes as a result. In technical terms, experimenters manipulate an **independent variable** (the imposed treatment or special condition). They then note how that change affects the specific behavior they are studying, which is called the **dependent variable.** Thus, the independent variable is the new, special treatment; the dependent variable is the response (which may or may not be affected by the independent variable). Finding out which independent variables affect which dependent variables, and how great that effect may be, is the purpose of an experiment.

By comparing changes in a dependent variable that occur after an independent (experimental) variable has been imposed, researchers are often able to uncover the link between cause and effect. This is the reason experiments are performed: No other research method can so accurately pinpoint what leads to what.

In a typical experiment (diagrammed in Figure 1.7), two groups of subjects are studied: an **experimental group,** which is given a particular treatment (the independent variable), and a **comparison group** (also called a *control group*), which does not get the special treatment but is similar to the experimental group in other ways (such as age, ethnicity, SES). In the study of the Bosnian refugees mentioned at the beginning of this chapter, data were collected on a dozen variables for all the mothers and children. Half of the mothers were then given special counseling (the independent variable) to help them cope with their children's reactions to their wartime experiences. These women's children constituted the experimental group. The other mothers received no counseling; their children were the comparison group.

After five months, all the children were examined again. Few significant differences were found between the experimental and comparison groups of children. (*Significant* and *insignificant* are statistical terms that indicate the likelihood that the results did or did not occur by chance. In this study, improvements in the experimental group were so slight, and the total number of children involved was so small, that most changes were insignificant—that is, they could have happened by chance.) The one significant change was biological: The experimental children gained more weight over the five-month period than the other children (Dybdahl, 2001). In trying to understand why the counseling sessions were not more effective, the author speculates that the treated mothers shared what they learned with the comparison-group mothers, so that all benefited from an

TABLE 1.2 Correlations Between Spanking of 4- to 5-year-olds and Other Variables

Child is female	−0.06
Parent is warm toward child	−0.23
Child has behavior problems	+0.46

Source: McLoyd & Smith, 2002.

experiment A research method in which the researcher tries to determine the cause-and-effect relationship between two variables by manipulating one variable (called the *independent variable*) and then observing and recording the resulting changes in the other variable (called the *dependent variable*).

independent variable In an experiment, the variable that is introduced or changed to see what effect it has on the dependent variable.

dependent variable In an experiment, the variable that may change as a result of the introduction of or changes made in the independent variable.

experimental group In an experiment, the subjects who are given a particular treatment.

comparison group In an experiment, the subjects who are not given special treatment but who are similar to the experimental group in other relevant ways. (Also called the *control group*.)

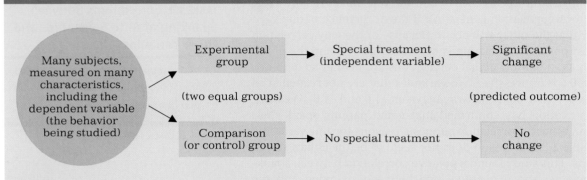

Procedure:

1. Divide subjects into two groups that are matched on important characteristics, especially the behavior that is the dependent variable on which this study is focused.

2. Give special treatment, or intervention (the independent variable), to one group (the experimental group).

3. Compare the groups on the dependent variable. If they now differ, the cause of the difference was probably the independent variable.

4. Publish the results.

FIGURE 1.7 How to Conduct an Experiment

?*Observational Quiz* (see answer, page 26):
Does the experimental group always change?

intervention that was intended for only half of them. It is also possible that counseling did not produce changes that helped the children emotionally (remember, they were all surprisingly unscathed by the civil war) but did help the mothers focus on nutrition—an important factor, since all these children had been underfed.

With all experiments, other questions remain. First, to what degree do the findings from an artificial experimental situation apply in the real world? A major problem with many experiments is that the controlled situation, with the scientist manipulating the independent variable, is different in important ways from normal, everyday life.

In addition, in most experiments (except those with very young children) the participants know they are research subjects. Subjects, especially adults, may attempt to produce the results they believe the experimenter is looking for, or, especially if they are adolescents, they may try to undermine the study. Even if the subjects do not react in either of these ways, almost all experimental subjects are more nervous than they otherwise would be. This reaction leads to the third problem: Is it ethical to make people nervous in such a way? Perhaps, but not always, as is discussed at the end of this chapter. Certainly it is not ethical to harm subjects in any way. It would be highly unethical (as well as artificial) to try to learn more about spanking, for instance, by asking some parents to spank their children more often.

Ideally, an experiment avoids these pitfalls by relying on natural conditions, which become the independent variable. Natural conditions can create an experimental and a comparison group. In the study of the kibbutz children, the independent variable was children's sleeping conditions (either near or apart from their parents), and the dependent variable was the adolescents' emotional relationships to family members. This study was a *natural experiment,* recommended as the most accurate and ethical way to conduct developmental research on children (Bronfenbrenner, 1979).

The Survey

In the research method called the **survey**, information is collected from a large number of people by personal interview, by written questionnaire, or by some other means. This is an easy, quick, and direct way to obtain data. Surveys are especially useful when scientists want to learn about children, since an obvious way of doing so is to ask parents or teachers.

Unfortunately, getting valid data through an interview or questionnaire is more difficult than it seems, because these methods are vulnerable to bias from both the researcher and the respondents. In addition, many people who are interviewed give answers that they think the researchers want, or that express opinion rather than fact, or that they think will make them seem wise or good.

For example, remember the survey that asked 5,000 boys if they had had sex before age 13? In ninth grade, 14 percent said "yes," but in the eleventh grade only 8 percent of the same boys said "yes." This was a paper-and-pencil survey conducted in classrooms, and researchers had no way to question the boys more closely. It could be that boys are likely to boast in ninth grade (is it "cool" to say "yes" to sex at that age?) or that they were more ashamed by eleventh grade (is it "good" to postpone sex at that age?). Or maybe the phrase *sexual intercourse* means something different at ages 14 and 16, or perhaps some of the early-experienced boys had left school or were out sick or refused to answer the questions in eleventh grade—or perhaps they really did forget. Since, for ethical reasons, the survey was confidential and anonymous, the researcher did not know which of the boys gave conflicting answers on the two surveys, much less why they did so. As you can see, surveys are useful for collecting a great deal of data, but accuracy and interpretations are problematic.

The Case Study

A **case study** is an intensive study of one individual. Typically, the case study is based on interviews with the subject regarding his or her background, current thinking, and actions; it may also utilize interviews of people who know the individual. Additional case-study material may be obtained through observation, experiments, and standardized tests, such as personality inventories and intelligence tests. A true case study is much more detailed than the excerpts presented in the feature called "A Case to Study" in this book.

Case studies can provide a wealth of detail, which makes them rich in possible insights. Many developmentalists prefer case studies precisely for that reason: The complexity of a human life is easier to comprehend through the rich *qualitative,* or descriptive, information of a case study than through a *quantitative* study involving sheer numbers.

However, the collection and interpretations of case-study information reflect the biases as well as the wisdom of the researcher. Even when a case study is carefully collected and interpreted, the conclusions apply with certainty to only one person. The case study has two important uses:

- To understand a particular individual very well
- To provide a provocative starting point for other research

However, no confident conclusions about people in general can be drawn from a sample size of 1, or even 10 or 20, no matter how deep and detailed the study is.

Clearly, there are many ways to gather developmental data, and each method compensates for the weaknesses of the others. Researchers can observe people in naturalistic or laboratory settings, or they can experimentally elicit reactions under controlled conditions or take advantage of unusual natural experiments. They can survey hundreds or even thousands of people, or interview a smaller

survey A research method in which information is collected from a large number of people by personal interview, by written questionnaire, or by some other means.

case study A research method in which one individual is studied intensively.

! *Answer to Observational Quiz* (from page 24): No. Note the word *predicted*. The hypothesis is that change will occur for the experimental group and not the control group, but the reason for doing the experiment is to discover whether that prediction does indeed come true.

number of people in great depth, or study one life in detail. Because each method has weaknesses, none of them provide data with ample scope and precision to merit broad conclusions. But each brings researchers closer to the issues and answers. Together they can either support or refute theories and hypotheses.

Studying Changes over Time

Remember the definition on page 1: The scientific study of human development seeks to understand how and why people—all kinds of people—change, and how and why they remain the same, as they grow older. Accordingly, for research to be truly developmental, it must be able to deal with things that change and continue *over time*. Developmental scientists need to design their research so that it includes time, or age, as a factor. Usually they accomplish this with one of three basic research designs: cross-sectional, longitudinal, or cross-sequential (as illustrated in Figure 1.8).

Cross-Sectional Research

cross-sectional research A research method in which groups of people who differ in age but share other important characteristics are compared.

The most convenient, and thus more common, way to include age in a developmental study is by designing **cross-sectional research.** In a cross-sectional study, groups of people who differ in age but share other important characteristics (such as level of education, socioeconomic status, and ethnic background) are compared.

Cross-sectional design seems simple enough, but it is very difficult to ensure that the various groups being compared are similar in every important background variable except age. Let's look at a simple, hypothetical example of cross-sectional research.

Suppose a group of 10-year-olds are found to be taller by about 12 inches (30 centimeters) than a comparable group of 6-year-olds. It seems reasonable to conclude that during the four years between ages 6 and 10, children gain a foot in height. However, even such an obvious conclusion might be wrong. In fact, other research shows that most children grow less than that—about 10 inches (25 centimeters)—between those ages. It could be that the particular 10-year-olds in the study were better nourished throughout their lives than the particular 6-year-olds or that they had some other relevant characteristic that was not accounted for. Certainly, if the 10-year-old group included more boys than girls or more Africans than Asians than the 6-year-old group, the height difference would reflect sex or ethnicity as well as age.

Compare These with Those The apparent similarity of these two groups in gender and ethnic composition makes them candidates for cross-sectional research. Before we could be sure that any difference between the two groups is the result of age, we would have to be sure the groups are alike in other ways, such as socioeconomic status and religious affiliation. These two groups are not exactly the same, but we cannot tell whether the cross-sectional differences are significant or not.

VIC BIDER / INDEX STOCK IMAGERY

SW PRODUCTION / INDEX STOCK IMAGERY

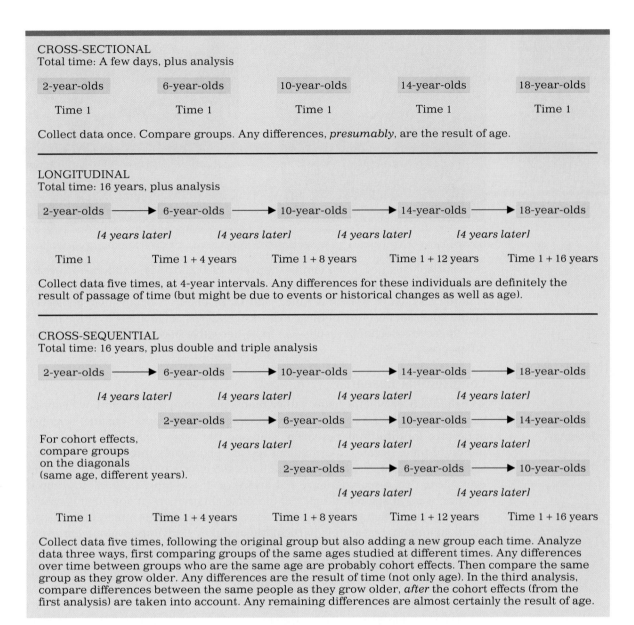

CROSS-SECTIONAL
Total time: A few days, plus analysis

| 2-year-olds | 6-year-olds | 10-year-olds | 14-year-olds | 18-year-olds |
| Time 1 | Time 1 | Time 1 | Time 1 | Time 1 |

Collect data once. Compare groups. Any differences, *presumably*, are the result of age.

LONGITUDINAL
Total time: 16 years, plus analysis

2-year-olds ⟶ 6-year-olds ⟶ 10-year-olds ⟶ 14-year-olds ⟶ 18-year-olds

[4 years later] *[4 years later]* *[4 years later]* *[4 years later]*

Time 1   Time 1 + 4 years   Time 1 + 8 years   Time 1 + 12 years   Time 1 + 16 years

Collect data five times, at 4-year intervals. Any differences for these individuals are definitely the result of passage of time (but might be due to events or historical changes as well as age).

CROSS-SEQUENTIAL
Total time: 16 years, plus double and triple analysis

2-year-olds ⟶ 6-year-olds ⟶ 10-year-olds ⟶ 14-year-olds ⟶ 18-year-olds

[4 years later] *[4 years later]* *[4 years later]* *[4 years later]*

2-year-olds ⟶ 6-year-olds ⟶ 10-year-olds ⟶ 14-year-olds

For cohort effects, compare groups on the diagonals (same age, different years).

[4 years later] *[4 years later]* *[4 years later]*

2-year-olds ⟶ 6-year-olds ⟶ 10-year-olds

[4 years later] *[4 years later]*

Time 1   Time 1 + 4 years   Time 1 + 8 years   Time 1 + 12 years   Time 1 + 16 years

Collect data five times, following the original group but also adding a new group each time. Analyze data three ways, first comparing groups of the same ages studied at different times. Any differences over time between groups who are the same age are probably cohort effects. Then compare the same group as they grow older. Any differences are the result of time (not only age). In the third analysis, compare differences between the same people as they grow older, *after* the cohort effects (from the first analysis) are taken into account. Any remaining differences are almost certainly the result of age.

FIGURE 1.8 Which Is Best? Cross-sequential research is the most time-consuming and most complex approach, but it also yields the best information about development. This is one reason why hundreds of scientists conduct research on the same topics, replicating one another's work—to gain some of the advantages of cross-sequential research without having to wait all those years.

Of course, good scientists try to make cross-sectional groups similar in every major background variable. Nevertheless, even if two cross-sectional groups were identical except for age, they would still reflect cohort differences because each age group was born in a different historical period. In this example, even four years could make a difference in the typical diet, as some additives are banned and as new snacks are introduced each year.

More broadly, factors in any domain could change over four years. Biological: A particular childhood disease might have been controlled and then eliminated (as polio was) or nutrition could have dramatically decreased over a four-year period (if, for instance, a nation were torn by civil war). Cognitive: Popular opinion about ideal weight could make children so weight-conscious that many of them undereat. Psychosocial: How children spend their time within

ALL PHOTOS: © GEORGE GOODWIN

each society changes. For example, between 1950 and 1954, children's television watching increased from zero to an average of almost three hours a day, making children less active and thus fatter, and fatter children begin their adolescent height spurt sooner. Any of these historical patterns could affect average height, and thus cross-sectional results would be deceptive because they ignore cohort differences.

Longitudinal Research

longitudinal research A research method in which the same individuals are studied over a long period of time.

To help discover whether age, rather than some other background or historical variable, is really the reason for an apparent developmental change, scientists undertake **longitudinal research,** studying the *same individuals* over a long period of time. Because longitudinal research compares information about the same people at different ages, it eliminates the effects of background variables, even those that researchers are not aware of. If we know how tall a group of children were at age 6 and how tall the same children are at age 10, it is easy to figure out how much they grew, on average, during the four intervening years.

Longitudinal research is particularly useful in studying development over a long age span (Elder, 1998). It has yielded valuable and sometimes surprise findings on many topics, including the following:

- *Children's adjustment to divorce.* The negative effects linger, but not for every child (Hetherington & Kelly, 2002).
- *The role of fathers in child development.* Even 50 years ago, fathers were far more influential regarding their children's future happiness than the stereotype of the distant dad implies (Snarey, 1993).
- *The consequences of an early delay in motor or language abilities.* Motor delays often disappear; language delays usually persist (Silva, 1996).
- *Prevention of teenage delinquency.* One factor is patient parenting at age 5, using conversation rather than physical punishment to correct the child's behavior (Pettit et al., 2001).

Repeated longitudinal research can uncover not only change but also the process of change. Do children learn to read suddenly, by "breaking the code," or gradually? The answer could not be found by simply comparing preliterate 4-year-olds and fluently reading 8-year-olds. However, following children month by month reveals the answer: Reading is usually a gradual process, although certain aspects can be grasped quite suddenly (Adams et al., 1998).

You will learn the results of many longitudinal studies throughout this book. Nevertheless, this design has some serious drawbacks. Over time, some subjects may withdraw, move far away, or die. These changes can skew the ultimate results if those who disappear differ from those who stay in the study (more rebel-

A Longitudinal Look at Kirsten Longitudinal research is ideal for discovering, as the definition of developmental study on page 2 states, "how and why people change, and how and why they remain the same, as they grow older." These photographs of Kirsten at 5 months, 18 months, 5 years, 8 years, and 12 years illustrate this well. In some ways, change is obvious—from baldness to chest-length hair, for instance. Similar changes can be seen for almost all children, although Kirsten's pattern was somewhat unusual since she didn't really start to grow a full head of hair until she was almost 3 years old. In other ways, continuity is clear: She is emotionally engaging at every age. This is most obvious when, as a toddler, she hid something forbidden from her parents, but it is apparent in the other snapshots as well.

Now, at age 13, it is not surprising that she is distinctive in predictable ways, such as her ballet, writing, social sensitivity, and cheerleading. She is also typical of her cohort in other ways—she likes boys, computers, and television—as cross-sectional research would show as well. Longitudinal research (and, in this case, even longitudinal photos) also helps spot the impact of unusual events, which are not typical of either that child or children in general.

? *Observational Quiz* (see answer, page 31): Kirsten's parents got divorced. Can you spot when?

lious? of lower SES?). In addition, the research itself may affect those who remain (who might "improve" over a series of tests, for example, only because they become increasingly familiar with the questions). This makes the results of longitudinal research less applicable to the average developing person, who is not in such a study.

Perhaps the biggest problem of all is that a longitudinal investigation is very time-consuming and expensive. It involves far more commitment from scientists and funding agencies than does cross-sectional research.

Cross-Sequential Research

As you can see, both cross-sectional research and longitudinal research allow scientists to look at development over time, but each design has flaws. Because these two methods tend to make up for each other's disadvantages, scientists have devised various ways to use the two together (Hartman & George, 1999). The simplest is **cross-sequential research** (also referred to as *cohort-sequential* or *time-sequential* research) (Schaie, 1996). With this design, researchers first study several groups of people of different ages (a cross-sectional approach) and then follow those groups over the years (a longitudinal approach).

Using cross-sequential design, we can compare findings for a group of, say, 50-year-olds with findings for the same individuals at age 30, as well as with findings for groups who were 50 a decade or two earlier and groups who are 30 years old now. Cross-sequential research thus allows scientists to disentangle differences related to chronological age from those related to historical period. Scientists using this method are like prospectors for gold, sifting through other elements to find genuine nuggets of age-related development. In fact, every method is useful, and none are perfect, as Figure 1.8 illustrates. A better metaphor might be trying to assemble a jigsaw puzzle, with each study contributing a piece but none of them making a complete picture in themselves.

cross-sequential research A hybrid research method in which researchers first study several groups of people of different ages (a cross-sectional approach) and then follow those groups over the years (a longitudinal approach). (Also called *cohort-sequential* or *time-sequential research*.)

Ethics and Science

Every scientist must be concerned with the ethics of conducting and reporting research. At the most basic level, researchers who study humans must ensure that their subjects are not harmed and that subjects' participation is voluntary and confidential. Each academic discipline and professional society involved in the study of human development has a **code of ethics**, or set of moral principles. In developmental studies, the need to protect the participants is especially acute when they are children.

code of ethics A set of moral principles that is formally adopted by a group or organization.

Ethics for Child Development Researchers

The Society for Research in Child Development (SRCD, 1996) includes the following precautions in its code of ethics:

- The investigator should use no research operation that may harm the child either physically or psychologically.
- Before seeking consent or assent from the child, the investigator should inform the child of all features of the research that may affect his or her willingness to participate and should answer the child's questions in terms appropriate to the child's comprehension. [The child is free to] discontinue participation at any time.
- Investigators working with infants should take special effort to explain the research procedures to the parents and be especially sensitive to any indicators of discomfort in the infant.
- The investigators should keep in confidence all information obtained about research participants.
- In reporting results, . . . the investigator should be mindful of the social, political, and human implications.

Such ethical guidelines—developed and enforced partly as a result of past abuses—deal with only part of the problem. For contemporary researchers, the thorniest issues arise not during but before and after the research. Every proposed study must be analyzed ahead of time to see if its benefits will outweigh its costs in time, money, and even momentary distress.

In human development, the possibility of distress varies with the subject's age and condition (Thompson, 1992). A young child may become upset by a few minutes of separation from a caregiver; older children are more susceptible to loss of self-esteem and privacy; parents of adolescents may not want anyone to ask their offspring anything about sex, drugs, or discipline. Often, the studies with the greatest potential benefit involve the most vulnerable groups, such as infants who have been maltreated or children who are suspended from school. Ironically, some groups (women, children, drug addicts) were excluded as subjects of research into drug treatments for AIDS because experimental drugs might have done them unexpected harm; as a result, the first AIDS treatments proven effective had never been tested on the people who might need them most (Kahn et al., 1998).

Especially for Future Researchers: What question in child development do you think needs to be further investigated? What do you think the problems with such research might be?

The Implications of Research

Once an investigation has been completed, additional ethical issues arise concerning the reporting of research findings. An obvious breach of scientific ethics is to "cook" the data, arranging the numbers so that a particular conclusion seems the only logical one. Sometimes this can be done unintentionally, which is one reason replication is so important. Deliberate deception regarding the data is cause for ostracism from the scientific community, dismissal from a teaching or research position, and, in some cases, criminal prosecution. Further, *"in reporting results, . . . the investigator should be mindful of the social, political, and human implications of his [or her] research"* (SRCD, 1996).

What does "mindful" of implications mean? An example makes it clear. A storm of controversy was evoked by a study of college students who had become sexually involved with adults before reaching the legal age of consent (Rind et al., 1998). The research correctly reported that the consequences depended on many factors. The actual article was a *meta-analysis,* which is a compilation of data from many other sources, so no research subjects were directly involved.

However, talk-show hosts and political candidates condemned the study—not because of its results, but because of their own misinterpretation of it. Such misinterpretation occurred for many reasons, but one reason was that the authors and editors were not sufficiently mindful of the inferences that other people might draw. The basic problem is that:

> Scientists are committed to verifying their claims in terms of the logic-based system of thinking. . . . Scientists sometimes forget that media personalities, elected politicians, and many others operate under very different rules from psychologists and other scientists. . . . Like it or not, scientists operate not only within a scientific context but also a societal one.
>
> [Sternberg, 2002, pp. 193, 194]

In another research project, a group of college students who listened to Mozart before taking a cognitive test scored higher than another group who heard no music (Rauscher et al., 1993; Rausher & Shaw, 1998). This "Mozart effect" was also misinterpreted; the governor of Georgia ordered that all newborns receive a free Mozart CD in order to improve their intelligence, and Florida passed a law requiring every state-funded infant day-care center to play classical music. The actual initial study was irrelevant to infants, and the results for college students could not be replicated (Nantais & Schellenberg, 1999; Steele et al., 1999).

As these examples demonstrate, even when the scientific method is carefully used and proper safeguards for the subjects are in place, ethics requires a concern for the implications of the results. Conclusions must be honestly and carefully reported; hasty generalizations are often false. Scientific methodology and integrity are the bases of our study of human development, and that is all the more reason to make sure the implications are carefully interpreted.

What Should We Study?

Finally, every reader of this book should consider the most important ethical issue of all: Are scientists studying the issues that are crucial to human development?

- Do we know enough about infant growth to ensure that every baby reaches full potential?
- Do we know enough about human sexual urges and actions to prevent sexually transmitted diseases, stop unwanted pregnancy, halt sexual abuse, and cure infertility?
- Do we know enough about stress, poverty, and prejudice to enable humans to be happier and healthier?
- Do we know enough about angry children to prevent a child from becoming a bully, a delinquent, and then a violent criminal?

The answer to all these questions is a loud *NO!* Sometimes the particulars of informed consent and confidentiality distract us from the larger ethical concerns, such as answering the questions just posed.

Ethics means far more than taking care of the subjects and reporting research carefully and honestly. It also means choosing to investigate issues that should be explored and then reporting results conscientiously and accurately. This chapter has noted many social problems that have been relieved by developmental research, including racial segregation, premature death of disabled children, and distorted parent–child interactions. Many more examples in which scientific findings have enhanced child development are cited throughout this book. Other issues still need research. Children still suffer because many questions have not been answered, or even asked. The next cohort of developmental scientists will continue this work, building on what is known. Read on.

!Answer to Observational Quiz (from page 29): Kirsten's parents ended their marriage about when Kirsten was 8 (fourth picture). Signs of this disruption are that she is thoughtful, unsmiling, with arms held close.

Response for Future Researchers (from page 30): Almost any issue that you care about is a valid subject for research, partly because scientists work best if they truly want to learn the answers. Beyond the problems of time, money, and protection of subjects, the crucial question is whether you are prepared to obtain results that contradict your own social constructions. Some of the best and bravest scientists surprise themselves as well as their culture.

SUMMARY

Definitions: Change over Time

1. Human development is a science that seeks to understand how people change over time. Sometimes these changes are linear—gradual, steady, and predictable—and sometimes not.

2. Development is the product of dynamic systems. Any one change affects an interconnected system, and any one person affects all the other people in a family or social group.

3. Change may be small or large, caused by something seemingly insignificant, like the flap of a butterfly's wings, or something large and pervasive, like a civil war. Development can seem to be continuous, or unchanging, for a period of time, and then a massive transformation can suddenly occur.

4. The life-span perspective reminds us that development is multidirectional, multicontextual, multicultural, multidisciplinary, and plastic. *Plasticity* means that change is always possible but never unrestricted: Childhood becomes the foundation for later growth.

5. Development can be divided into three broad aspects, called domains. The biosocial domain includes physical growth, the cognitive domain includes intellectual growth, and the psychosocial domain includes emotions and the social context. All three are important for every person at every point of development.

The Contexts of Development

6. Each individual develops within three contexts: historical, cultural, and socioeconomic. Since each person has unique genes and experiences, contexts do not determine an individual's development, but they always influence it.

7. The historical context is crucial, with all people in each cohort affected by the events and the social beliefs that prevailed when they were young. Such beliefs are often social constructions, or values that shift as the historical context changes.

8. Communities raise children in diverse ways, with each culture encouraging habits and personality traits that will help people function well in that culture.

9. Family income and residence, as well as the education level of the parents, determine a child's socioeconomic status. Particularly if family income falls below the poverty line, children are handicapped by their SES in crucial ways, including health, education, and even survival.

10. It is not easy to disentangle the effects of income and ethnicity. Although it is sometimes used in popular speech, scientists now find "race" a confusing and misleading category. Scientists prefer to group people by ethnicity, SES, age, or culture.

Developmental Study as a Science

11. The scientific method leads researchers to question assumptions and gather data to test conclusions. Although far from infallible, scientific methods help researchers avoid biases and guide them in asking questions that might not otherwise be asked.

12. Among the research methods used by scientists are observation, experiments, surveys, and case studies. Each method has strengths and weaknesses.

13. The most robust (solid) conclusions can be drawn when similar results are found in replications using various methods with many subjects in diverse cultures. Well-designed experiments are useful but difficult to conduct in human development, unless natural circumstances happen to create an experimental group.

14. Many statistical methods further scientific research. One is correlation, the calculation of a number that indicates how two variables are connected, though it does not prove that one variable causes the other. Another statistic is significance, which indicates the degree of possibility that a particular result occurred by chance.

15. To study growth over time, scientists use three strategies: cross-sectional research (comparing people of different ages), longitudinal research (studying the same people over time), and cross-sequential research (combining the first two methods).

Ethics and Science

16. Ethics is crucial in all sciences, perhaps especially in developmental research when children are involved. Not only must subjects be protected, but results must be clearly reported and understood.

17. Appropriate application of insights from scientific research depends partly on the integrity of the scientific methods used but even more on careful explanation and interpretation of the conclusions. The most important ethical issues of all are: Are the critical questions being asked, and is needed research being conducted?

KEY TERMS

scientific study of human
  development (p. 1)
linear change (p. 2)
dynamic systems (p. 2)
butterfly effect (p. 2)
life-span perspective (p. 5)
multidirectional (p. 5)
multicontextual (p. 5)
multicultural (p. 5)
multidisciplinary (p. 5)

plastic (p. 5)
biosocial domain (p. 6)
cognitive domain (p. 6)
psychosocial domain (p. 6)
cohort (p. 8)
social construction (p. 9)
culture (p. 10)
socioeconomic status (SES)
  (p. 14)
poverty line (p. 14)

ethnic group (p. 16)
race (p. 16)
scientific method (p. 20)
hypothesis (p. 20)
replication (p. 20)
variables (p. 20)
scientific observation (p. 21)
correlation (p. 22)
experiment (p. 23)
independent variable (p. 23)

dependent variable (p. 23)
experimental group (p. 23)
comparison group (p. 23)
survey (p. 25)
case study (p. 25)
cross-sectional research (p. 26)
longitudinal research (p. 28)
cross-sequential research
  (p. 29)
code of ethics (p. 29)

KEY QUESTIONS

1. Give an example of each of several kinds of change in human development.

2. What are some of the contexts and systems that would be particularly relevant in shaping your personal development? Explain your choices.

3. What are some of the reasons that a major social change might *not* affect a child's development very much?

4. How do researchers in child development benefit from the life-span perspective?

5. Give an example (not from the book) of development that is affected by all three domains.

6. How might the historical context differ for someone born in 1950 and someone born in 2000?

7. How might a young child's sleeping situation affect his or her adult values and personality?

8. Why is income not identical with socioeconomic status?

9. How does the condition of a child's neighborhood moderate or magnify the effects of poverty?

10. Why do people sometimes confuse SES, ethnicity, and race?

11. Pick two of the four methods of research, and show how the advantages of one compensate for the disadvantages of the other.

12. Why is cross-sectional research the easiest way to study development?

13. What are the advantages of cross-sequential research?

14. In what ways does the scientific method reduce human biases?

15. What are the most difficult ethical issues in the study of human development?

Chapter Two

Theories of Development

A s we saw in Chapter 1, the scientific effort to understand human development usually begins with questions. One of the most basic is: How do people develop into the persons they ultimately become?

- Do early experiences—of breast-feeding or bonding or abuse—linger into adulthood, even if they seem to be forgotten?
- How important are specific school experiences in human intelligence?
- Can a person develop moral values without being taught them?
- Do a person's chances of becoming a violent adult depend on whether he or she grows up in, say, Chile or Cambodia or Canada?
- If your parents or grandparents suffer from depression, schizophrenia, or alcoholism, will you develop the same condition?

For every answer, more questions arise: Why or why not? When and how? And, perhaps more important of all, so what?

What Theories Do

Each of the five questions listed above is answered by one of the five major theories described in this chapter. To frame various questions, and to begin to answer them, we need some way to determine which facts about development are relevant. Then we need to organize those facts to lead us to deeper understanding. In short, we need a theory.

A **developmental theory** is a systematic statement of principles and generalizations that provides a coherent framework for studying and explaining development. Developmental theorists "try to make sense out of observations . . . [and] construct a story of the human journey from infancy through childhood or adulthood" (Miller, 2002, p. 2). Such a story, or theory, is more than a set of assumptions and facts; it connects facts and observations, putting the details of life into a meaningful whole. Theories are also quite practical, in three ways:

- Theories offer insight and guidance for everyday concerns by providing a broad and coherent view of human development.
- Theories form the basis for hypotheses that can be tested by research studies. Thus, theories "provide a point of departure," " a conceptual context" for individual scientists who study according to their own particular research interests (Renninger & Amsel, 1997, p. ix).

developmental theory A systematic statement of principles and generalizations that provides a coherent framework for studying and explaining development.

■ Theories generate discoveries: "New facts change the theory, and changes in the theory generate new experiments and thus new facts" (Miller, 2002, p. 4).

Not just five, but hundreds of theories are relevant to the study of development. Some originated with extraordinary intellectual leaders, who fashioned what are called **grand theories,** "because each offered a powerful framework for interpreting and understanding change and development [and was] meant to apply to the change and development of all individuals, in all contexts, across all contents" (Renninger & Amsel, 1997, p. ix). Some are called **minitheories,** because they are intended to explain only a part of development or to relate to only a particular group of people, rather than to explain everything, everywhere, for everyone (Parke et al., 1994). And some are called **emergent theories,** because they arise from several accumulated minitheories and may become the new systematic and comprehensive theories of the future.

In this chapter we will focus on three grand theories—psychoanalytic theory, behaviorism, and cognitive theory—and two emergent theories—sociocultural theory and epigenetic systems theory. These five theories, and several others, will be further described and applied in relevant discussions later in this book.

grand theories Comprehensive theories that have traditionally inspired and directed thinking about development. Psychoanalytic theory, behaviorism, and cognitive theory are all grand theories.

minitheories Theories that focus on some specific area of development but are less general and comprehensive than the grand theories.

emergent theories Recently formulated theories that bring together information from many minitheories but that have not yet cohered into theories that are comprehensive and systematic.

Grand Theories

In the first half of the twentieth century, two opposing theories—psychoanalytic theory and behaviorism (also called learning theory)—began as theories of psychology and later were applied to human development more broadly. By mid-century, cognitive theory had overtaken these first two, becoming the dominant seedbed of research hypotheses. In regard to some ideas, proponents of each of these grand theories often scorned the other two; yet all of them agreed on many basic principles. Before we examine the points of disagreement and agreement, we will briefly describe each theory.

psychoanalytic theory A grand theory of human development that holds that irrational, unconscious drives and motives, many of which originate in childhood, underlie human behavior.

Psychoanalytic Theory

Psychoanalytic theory interprets human development in terms of intrinsic drives and motives, many of which are irrational and unconscious, hidden from awareness. These basic underlying forces are viewed as influencing every aspect of a person's thinking and behavior, from the smallest details of daily life to the crucial choices of a lifetime. Psychoanalytic theory also sees these drives and motives as providing the foundation for the universal stages of development that every human experiences. For everyone, each stage entails specific developmental tasks, from the formation of human attachments in infancy to the quest for emotional and sexual fulfillment in adulthood.

Freud at Work In addition to being the world's first psychoanalyst, Sigmund Freud was a prolific writer. His many papers and case histories, primarily descriptions of his patients' bizarre symptoms and unconscious sexual urges, helped make the psycho-analytic perspective a dominant force for much of the twentieth century.

Freud's Ideas

Psychoanalytic theory originated with Sigmund Freud (1856–1939), an Austrian physician who developed this theory based on his clinical work with patients suffering from mental illness. He listened to their accounts of dreams and fantasies, as well as to their "uncensored" streams of thought, and constructed an elaborate, multifaceted theory. According to this theory, development in the first six years occurs in three stages, each characterized by sexual interest and pleasure centered on a particular part of the body. In

AKG / PHOTO RESEARCHERS, INC.

Childhood Sexuality? The girl's interest in the statue's anatomy may reflect simple curiosity, but Freudian theory would maintain that it is a clear manifestation of the phallic stage of psychosexual development, when girls are said to feel deprived because they lack a penis.

infancy, that body part is the mouth (the *oral stage*); in early childhood, it is the anus (the *anal stage*); in the preschool years, it is the penis (the *phallic stage*). (See Table 2.1 for descriptions of the stages in Freud's theory.)

Freud maintained that at each of these stages, sensual satisfaction from stimulation of the mouth, anus, or penis is linked to the major developmental needs and challenges that are associated with that stage. During the oral stage, for example, the baby not only gains nourishment through sucking but also experiences sensual pleasure and becomes emotionally attached to the mother, who provides this oral gratification. During the anal stage, pleasures related to control and self-control—initially with defecation and toilet training—are paramount.

One of Freud's most influential ideas was that each stage includes its own potential conflicts between child and parent, as, for instance, when an adult tries to wean a baby from the beloved bottle. According to Freud, how the child experiences and resolves these conflicts—especially those related to weaning, toilet training, and childhood sexual curiosity—determines the person's lifelong personality and patterns of behavior. An adult may not know it, but the fact that he or she smokes cigarettes (oral), or keeps careful track of money (anal), or is romantically attracted to a much older partner (phallic) signifies unconscious problems rooted in a childhood stage.

Another developmental aspect of Freud's theory is its conception of the personality as consisting of three distinct systems: id, ego, and superego. The *id* represents the unconscious psychic energy that we devote to satisfying our basic urges toward survival, aggression, and reproduction. The *superego* is a strict moral judge, especially of impulses that the parents or culture would condemn. The *ego* tries to make rational choices and to cope with the reality of daily life, partly by keeping the id's unconscious lust and the superego's guilt under control. Infants are governed primarily by the id: They want their own needs to be met immediately, including their psychosexual need for oral pleasure. As children grow older, their egos develop; they continue to assert themselves but also begin to accommodate the external world's demands. Especially in early childhood, at about the phallic stage, parents and the society teach the child which impulses need to be controlled and thus foster development of the superego. The emotionally healthy person develops a strong ego, able to cope with the urges of both the id and the superego.

CORBIS

What's in a Name?—Erik Erikson As a young man, this neo-Freudian changed his last name to the one we know him by. What do you think his choice means? (See caption to photo below.)

Erikson's Ideas

Freud had many followers who became famous psychoanalytic theorists in their own right. Although they all acknowledged the importance of unconscious, irrational forces and of early childhood, each expanded and modified Freud's ideas. The most notable of these neo-Freudians was Erik Erikson (1902–1994), who formulated his own version of psychoanalytic theory.

Erikson spent his childhood in Germany, his adolescence wandering through Italy, and his young adulthood in Austria. Just before World War II, he arrived in the United States, where he studied Harvard students, children at play, and Native American cultures. Erikson proposed eight developmental stages covering the entire life span, each of which is characterized by a particular challenge, or *developmental crisis,* which is central to that stage of life.

As you can see from Table 2.1, Erikson's first five stages are closely related to Freud's stages. Erikson, like Freud, believed that problems of adult life echo unresolved conflicts of childhood. For example, an adult who has difficulty establishing a secure, mutual relationship with a life partner may never have resolved the crisis of early infancy, *trust versus mistrust.* However, Erikson's stages differ significantly from Freud's in their emphasis of the person's relationship to the family and culture, not just to his or her own sexual urges.

In Erikson's theory, the resolution of each developmental crisis depends on the interaction between the individual's characteristics and whatever support is provided by the social environment. In the stage of *initiative versus guilt,* for example, children between ages 3 and 6 often want to undertake activities that exceed their abilities or the limits set by their parents. Their efforts to act independently leave them open to pride or failure, depending partly on how they go about seeking independence, partly on the reactions of their parents, and partly on their culture's expectations. As an example of the last influence, some cultures *encourage* assertive 5-year-olds as being creative spirits who know their own minds; other cultures *discourage* them as being rude or fresh children. The children internalize, or accept, these reactions, and later, as adults, some are much bolder and others are more self-critical than their peers in other cultures.

Developmentalists owe a debt of gratitude to Freud and to the neo-Freudians who extended and refined his concepts. Many psychoanalytic ideas are widely accepted today—for example, that unconscious motives affect our behavior and that the early years are a formative period of personality development.

SYLVAIN GRANDADAM / PHOTO RESEARCHERS, INC.

Who Are We? The most famous of Erikson's eight crises is the identity crisis, during adolescence, when young people find their own answer to the question "Who am I?" Erikson did this for himself by choosing a last name that, with his first name, implies "son of myself" (Erik, Erik's son). Although the identity crisis is universal, particulars vary from place to place and time to time—with each cohort distinguishing itself from the slightly older cohort in some way.

? *Observational Quiz* (see answer, page 40): Where and when do you think this photograph was taken?

TABLE 2.1 Comparison of Freud's Psychosexual and Erikson's Psychosocial Stages

Approximate Age	Freud (Psychosexual)	Erikson* (Psychosocial)
Birth to 1 year	*Oral Stage* The mouth, tongue, and gums are the focus of pleasurable sensations in the baby's body, and sucking and feeding are the most stimulating activities.	*Trust vs. Mistrust* Babies learn either to trust that others will care for their basic needs, including nourishment, warmth, cleanliness, and physical contact, or to lack confidence in the care of others.
1–3 years	*Anal Stage* The anus is the focus of pleasurable sensations in the baby's body, and toilet training is the most important activity.	*Autonomy vs. Shame and Doubt* Children learn either to be self-sufficient in many activities, including toileting, feeding, walking, exploring, and talking, or to doubt their own abilities.
3–6 years	*Phallic Stage* The phallus, or penis, is the most important body part, and pleasure is derived from genital stimulation. Boys are proud of their penises, and girls wonder why they don't have one.	*Initiative vs. Guilt* Children want to undertake many adultlike activities, sometimes overstepping the limits set by parents and feeling guilty.
7–11 years	*Latency* This is not a stage but an interlude, during which sexual needs are quiet and children put psychic energy into conventional activities like schoolwork and sports.	*Industry vs. Inferiority* Children busily learn to be competent and productive in mastering new skills or feel inferior and unable to do anything well.
Adolescence	*Genital Stage* The genitals are the focus of pleasurable sensations, and the young person seeks sexual stimulation and sexual satisfaction in heterosexual relationships.	*Identity vs. Role Diffusion* Adolescents try to figure out "Who am I?" They establish sexual, political, and career identities or are confused about what roles to play.
Adulthood	Freud believed that the genital stage lasts throughout adulthood. He also said that the goal of a healthy life is "to love and to work."	*Intimacy vs. Isolation* Young adults seek companionship and love with another person or become isolated from others because they fear rejection and disappointment. *Generativity vs. Stagnation* Middle-aged adults contribute to the next generation through meaningful work, creative activities, and/or raising a family, or they stagnate. *Integrity vs. Despair* Older adults try to make sense out of their lives, either seeing life as a meaningful whole or despairing at goals never reached.

*Although Erikson described two extreme resolutions to each crisis, he recognized that there is a wide range of outcomes between these extremes. For most people, the best resolution of a crisis is not either extreme but, rather, a middle course.

Behaviorism

The second grand theory arose in direct opposition to psychoanalytic theory. Early in the twentieth century, John B. Watson (1878–1958) argued that if psychology was to be a true science, psychologists should study only what they could see and measure: human behavior, not human thoughts and hidden urges. In Watson's words:

> Why don't we make what we can *observe* the real field of psychology? Let us limit ourselves to things that can be observed, and formulate laws concerned only with those things. . . . We can observe behavior—what the organism does or says.
>
> [Watson, 1924/1998, p. 6]

According to Watson, anything can be learned. He said:

> Give me a dozen healthy infants, well-formed, and my own specified world to bring them up in and I'll guarantee to take any one at random and train him to become any type of specialist I might select—doctor, lawyer, artist, merchant

! *Answer to Observational Quiz* (from page 38): The signs suggest Asia, and the fact that overt rebellion is difficult in a small Asian town suggests a large city. If you guessed Tokyo, score one correct. A sharp eye on the T-shirt and an accurate memory of when Mohawk hairstyles were in fashion would give you another correct answer—probably 1992.

behaviorism A grand theory of human development that focuses on the sequences and processes by which behavior is learned. (Also called *learning theory*.)

conditioning According to behaviorism, any process in which a behavior is learned. See *classical conditioning* and *operant conditioning*.

classical conditioning The process by which a neutral stimulus becomes associated with a meaningful stimulus so that the organism responds to the former stimulus as if it were the latter. (Also called *respondent conditioning*.)

chief, and yes, even beggar-man and thief, regardless of his talents, penchants, tendencies, abilities, vocations, and race of his ancestors.

[Watson, 1924/1998, p. 82]

Other psychologists agreed, partly because they found it difficult to study the unconscious motives and drives identified in psychoanalytic theory. Actual behavior, by contrast, could be studied far more objectively and scientifically. Thus was developed the theory called **behaviorism.** It is also called *learning theory* because the focus is on the ways we learn specific behaviors—ways that can be described, analyzed, and predicted with far more scientific accuracy than the unconscious drives proposed by psychoanalysts (Horowitz, 1994; Uttal, 2000).

Laws of Behavior

Laws of behavior are said to apply to every individual at every age, from newborn to octogenarian. These laws provide insights into how mature competencies are fashioned from simple actions and how environmental influences shape individual development. In the view of behaviorists, all development involves a process of learning and, therefore, does not occur in specific stages that depend on age or maturation (Bijou & Baer, 1978).

Learning occurs through **conditioning,** as a particular response comes to be triggered by a particular stimulus (see Figure 2.1). There are two types of conditioning: classical and operant.

Classical Conditioning A century ago, Russian scientist Ivan Pavlov (1849–1936) began to study the link between stimulus and response. While doing research on salivation in dogs, Pavlov noted that his experimental dogs began to drool not only at the sight of food but also, eventually, at the sound of the approaching attendants who brought the food. This observation led him to perform his famous experiment in which he taught a dog to salivate at the sound of a bell. Pavlov began by ringing the bell just before presenting food to the dog. After a number of repetitions of this bell-then-food sequence, the dog began salivating at the bell's sound even when there was no food nearby.

This simple experiment was one of the first scientific demonstrations of **classical conditioning** (also called *respondent conditioning*). In classical conditioning, an organism (any type of living creature) comes to associate a neutral stimulus with a meaningful one and then responds to the former stimulus as if it were the latter. In Pavlov's original experiment, the dog associated the sound of

The Founder of Behaviorism John Watson was an early proponent of learning theory whose ideas are still influential today.

A Contemporary of Freud Ivan Pavlov was a physiologist who received the Nobel Prize in 1904 for his research on digestive processes. It was this line of study that led to his discovery of classical conditioning.

ARCHIVES OF THE HISTORY OF AMERICAN PSYCHOLOGY, THE UNIVERSITY OF AKRON

SOVFOTO

> **Learning occurs through:**
>
> ■ **Classical conditioning**   Through association, neutral stimulus becomes conditioned stimulus.
> ■ **Operant conditioning**   Through reinforcement, weak or rare response becomes strong, frequent response.
> ■ **Social learning**   Through modeling, observed behaviors become copied behaviors.

FIGURE 2.1 Three Types of Learning
Behaviorism is also called learning theory, because it emphasizes the learning process, as shown here.

the bell (the neutral stimulus) with food (the meaningful stimulus) and responded to the sound as though it were the food itself. That response was a conditioned response, which meant learning had occurred.

Operant Conditioning The most influential North American proponent of behaviorism was B. F. Skinner (1904–1990), who agreed with Watson that psychology should focus on the scientific study of behavior. Skinner also agreed with Pavlov that classical conditioning explains some types of behavior. However, Skinner believed that another type of conditioning—**operant conditioning** (also called *instrumental conditioning*)—plays a much greater role in human behavior, especially in more complex learning. In operant conditioning, the organism learns that a particular behavior produces a particular consequence. If the consequence is useful or pleasurable, the organism will tend to repeat the behavior to achieve that response again. If the response is unpleasant, the organism will tend not to repeat the behavior.

Once a behavior has been conditioned (learned), animals (including humans) continue to perform it even if pleasurable consequences occur only occasionally. Almost all of a person's daily behavior, from socializing with others to earning a paycheck, can be understood as a result of operant conditioning. For instance, when a baby first gives a half smile in response to a full stomach, a mother might smile back. Soon the baby is conditioned by the mother's responsive smile to give a bigger smile, and the mother picks the baby up to reinforce the smile. As time goes on, the baby becomes a smiling toddler, a cheerful child, an outgoing adolescent, and a friendly adult—all because of early operant conditioning and periodic reinforcing.

In operant conditioning, the process of repeating a consequence to make it more likely that the behavior in question will recur is called **reinforcement** (Skinner, 1953). A consequence that increases the likelihood that a behavior will be repeated is therefore called a *reinforcer.* The mother's early reinforcement produces a socially responsive, smiling adult.

The study of human development has benefited from behaviorism. That theory's emphasis on the causes and consequences of observed behavior has led researchers to see that many behavior patterns that seem to be inborn, or to result from deeply rooted emotional problems, are actually learned. If something is learned, it can be unlearned, which is a very hopeful message. Although it is not easy to break old habits and patterns, we are never stuck in our past. This realization has encouraged scientists to find ways to eliminate particular problem behaviors—among them temper tantrums, phobias, and addictions—by analyzing all the reinforcements and past conditioning and then breaking the stimulus–response chains that sustained the unwanted behaviors.

Like any good theory, behaviorism has also been a source of hypotheses for scientific experiments, such as those described in Thinking Like a Scientist.

operant conditioning The process by which a response is gradually learned via reinforcement or punishment. (Also called *instrumental conditioning.*)

reinforcement The process by which a behavior is followed by results that make it more likely that the behavior will be repeated. This occurs in operant conditioning.

Rats, Pigeons, and People B. F. Skinner is best known for his experiments with rats and pigeons, but he also applied his knowledge to human problems. For his daughter, he designed a glass-enclosed crib in which temperature, humidity, and perceptual stimulation could be controlled to make her time in the crib enjoyable and educational. He wrote about an ideal society based on principles of operant conditioning, where, for example, workers in less desirable jobs would earn greater rewards.

Thinking Like a Scientist

What Is a Mother For?

Because theories help organize perceptions, they make it easier for scientists to interpret their observations. True scientists welcome not only findings that confirm a theory but also data that don't fit their expectations. For example, Harry Harlow's experiments confirmed some conventional wisdom about mother–infant attachment and disproved other aspects.

Both behaviorism and psychoanalytic theory originally assumed that the reason children love their mothers is that the mothers satisfy basic hunger and sucking needs. In other words, they held that "the infant's attachment to the mother stemmed from internal drives which triggered activities connected with the libations of the mother's breast. This belief was the only one these two theoretical groups ever had in common" (Harlow, 1986).

Harlow, a psychologist who studied learning in infant monkeys, observed something that made him question the centrality of food:

> We had separated more than 60 of these animals from their mothers 6 to 12 hours after birth and suckled them on tiny bottles. The infant mortality rate was a fraction of what would have obtained had we let the monkey mothers raise their infants. Our bottle-fed babies were healthier and heavier than monkey-mother-reared infants. . . . During the course of our studies we noticed that the laboratory-raised babies showed strong attachment to the folded gauze diapers which were used to cover the . . . floors of their cages.

> *[Harlow, 1986, p. 103]*

In fact, the infant monkeys seemed more emotionally attached to the cloth diapers than to their bottles. This was contrary to the two prevailing theories. Psychoanalytic theory would say that the infant would love whatever satisfied its oral needs (the nipple), and behaviorism would predict that the infant would become attached to whatever provided reinforcing food (the bottle). Accordingly, Harlow set out to make a "direct experimental analysis" of human attachment via his monkeys.

Using monkeys to study emotional processes in humans may seem a stretch to some people, but not to Harlow, who had been trained as an experimental psychologist. He knew that it would be unethical to separate human infants from their mothers, but he believed that "the basic processes relating to affection, including nursing, contact, clinging, and

Clinging to "Mother" Even though it gave no milk, this "mother" was soft and warm enough that infant monkeys spent almost all their time holding on to it. Many infants, some children, and even some adults cling to a familiar stuffed animal when life becomes frightening. According to Harlow, the reasons are the same: All primates are comforted by something soft, warm, and familiar to touch.

HARLOW PRIMATE LABORATORY, UNIVERSITY OF WISCONSIN

even visual and auditory exploration, exhibit no fundamental differences in the two species" (Harlow, 1958).

Harlow provided infant monkeys with two "surrogate" (artificial) mothers, both the right size, with a face that included obvious eyes. One surrogate was made of bare wire, and the other was made of wire covered by soft terrycloth. He divided his monkeys into two groups. One was fed by a bottle periodically put through the chest of the cloth "mother"; the other was fed by a bottle put through the chest of the wire "mother." The hypothesis to be tested was that the cloth surrogate might be reinforcing, even for the monkeys that were fed by the wire mother.

To collect his data, Harlow measured how much time each baby spent holding on to one or the other of the two surrogates. The monkeys who had a cloth mother that provided milk clung to it and ignored the bare-wire, nonfeeding mother. However, beyond the few minutes needed to suck the milk, even the babies that fed from the wire mother had no interest in holding on to it, going to it only when hunger drove them to do so. No attachment to, or love for, the nourishing wire mother could be observed, but the cloth mothers seemed to win the infants' affection (see Figure 2.2).

This reaction was so strong that Harlow then wondered whether the cloth surrogate mothers might also reassure infant monkeys when frightening events occurred, just as a real mother does when a scared youngster runs to her. He set up another experiment, putting an unfamiliar mechanical toy into a cloth-reared infant monkey's cage. The monkeys immediately sought comfort from its cloth mother, scrambling to cling to it with one hand and then timidly exploring the new object with the other.

Wire mothers provided no such reassurance. Monkeys who were exposed to the same stress without the cloth mother's presence showed obvious signs of fright—freezing, screaming, shivering, hiding, urinating. It seems, then, that mothering is not primarily about feeding, but about touching, comforting, and holding, which Harlow called "contact comfort" or "love" (Harlow, 1958).

Harlow's research is a classic example of the use of theories. Although his study disproved an aspect of both behaviorism and psychoanalytic theory, that is not the most significant point. Remember, theories are meant to be useful, not necessarily true. (If they were known to be true in every aspect, they would be scientific laws, not theories.)

In this example, because he knew what the psychoanalytic and behavioral theories said about love and comfort, the baby monkeys' interactions with the gauze diapers caught Harlow's attention. That led to closer observation, a hypothesis, a clever series of experiments, and some amazing results. For decades, perhaps centuries, no one had questioned the idea that feeding creates loyalty—until actual observations conflicted with both grand theories. This conflict prompted an alert scientist to ask new questions.

Both psychoanalytic theory and behaviorism were revised and expanded in response to Harlow's experiments and to other evidence. Advice to caregivers changed as well: Crying infants should be picked up and cuddled, even if they are not hungry. The result has been much more cradling and less crying—all because a scientist compared a theoretical prediction with his own observations and performed ingenious experiments to test his hypothesis.

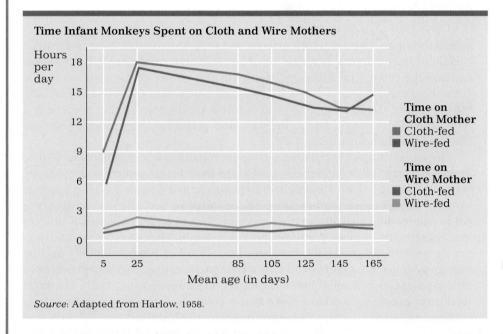

Time Infant Monkeys Spent on Cloth and Wire Mothers

Source: Adapted from Harlow, 1958.

FIGURE 2.2 Softer Is Better During the first three weeks of Harlow's experiment, the infant monkeys developed a strong preference for the cloth-covered "mothers." That preference lasted throughout the experiment, even among the monkeys who were fed by a wire-covered mother.

? Observational Quiz (see answer, page 46): At five days, how much time did the wire-fed monkeys spend on the cloth mothers compared with the cloth-fed monkeys?

Social Learning

Originally, behaviorists sought to explain all behavior as arising directly from a chain of learned responses, the result of classical and operant conditioning. However, one characteristic of every grand theory is that it is sufficiently comprehensive and thought-provoking that later scientists revise and extend it. One revision of behaviorism, based on thousands of studies, began with the realization that all creatures appreciate the touch, warmth, reassurance, and example of other similar beings. This extension is called **social learning theory.** Humans, even more than other animals, learn many behaviors by observing the behavior of others, without personally experiencing any reinforcement. Humans also strive for the feelings of pride and acceptance that other people can give.

An integral part of social learning is **modeling,** when people observe behavior and then copy it. For children, parents are the first models. Modeling is not simply imitation, because people model only some actions, of some individuals, in some contexts. For example, you undoubtedly know some adults who

social learning theory An application of behaviorism that emphasizes that many human behaviors are learned through observation and imitation of other people.

modeling In social learning theory, the process in which people observe and then copy the behavior of others.

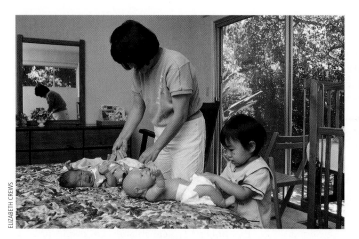

Social Learning in Action Social learning validates the old maxim "Actions speak louder than words." If the moments here are typical for each child, the girl in the left photo is likely to grow up with a ready sense of the importance of this particular chore of infant care. Unfortunately, the boy on the right may become a cigarette smoker like his father—even if his father warns him of the dangers of this habit.

? *Observational Quiz* (see answer, page 46): Beyond what they are doing, what else shows that these children imitate their parents?

self-efficacy In social learning theory, the belief that one is effective; self-efficacy motivates people to change themselves and their contexts.

cognitive theory A grand theory of human development that focuses on the structure and development of thinking, which shapes people's attitudes, beliefs, and behaviors.

Would You Talk to This Man? Children loved talking to Jean Piaget, and he learned by listening carefully—especially to their incorrect explanations, which no one had paid much attention to before. All his life, Piaget was absorbed with studying the way children think. He called himself a "genetic epistemologist"—one who studies how children gain knowledge about the world as they grow up.

repeat their parents' behavior patterns, but others who work hard never to copy certain of their parents' actions. From a behaviorist perspective, both reactions confirm the theory, because they testify to the power of the original example. Generally, modeling is most likely to occur when the observer is uncertain or inexperienced (which explains the readiness of children to use modeling) and when the model is someone admirable and powerful, nurturing, or similar to the observer (Bandura, 1986, 1997).

Social learning is related to self-understanding, social reflection, and feelings of efficacy. Self-confidence—developed from looking at the examples set by others as well as more directly from reinforcement by parents and teachers—leads to **self-efficacy**, the belief that one is effective. Self-efficacy motivates people to change themselves and their environment. In an individual, self-efficacy is associated with high aspirations and achievement (Bandura et al., 2001). In a group, self-efficacy becomes *collective efficacy* when effective family and community systems join, as they did in the crime-preventing neighborhoods of New Orleans and Chicago mentioned in Chapter 1 (Sampson et al., 1997). Overall, behaviorism encourages action, since better conditioning with precise reinforcers is likely to change a child, a family, or a culture.

Cognitive Theory

The third grand theory is **cognitive theory,** which focuses on the structure and development of thought processes and understanding. Cognitive researchers try

to determine how a person's thinking, and the expectations that result from a particular understanding, affect the development of attitudes, beliefs, and behaviors. In other words, to understand people, don't delve into what they have forgotten from childhood (as in psychoanalytic theory) or what has happened to them (as in behaviorism), but instead find out what they think.

Jean Piaget (1896–1980) was the major pioneer of cognitive theory. Although originally trained in the natural sciences, Piaget became interested in human thought processes when he was hired to field-test questions for a standard intelligence test for children. Piaget

TABLE 2.2 Piaget's Periods of Cognitive Development

Approximate Age Range	Name of Period	Characteristics of the Period	Major Gains During the Period
Birth to 2 years	Sensorimotor	Infant uses senses and motor abilities to understand the world. There is no conceptual or reflective thought; an object is "known" in terms of what an infant can *do* to it.	The infant learns that an object still exists when it is out of sight (*object permanence*) and begins to think through mental actions as well as physical actions.
2–6 years	Preoperational	The child uses *symbolic thinking,* including language, to understand the world. Sometimes the child's thinking is *egocentric,* causing the child to understand the world from only one perspective, his or her own.	The imagination flourishes, and language becomes a significant means of self-expression and of influence from others. Children gradually begin to *decenter,* that is, become less egocentric, and to understand and coordinate multiple points of view.
7–11 years	Concrete operational	The child understands and applies logical operations, or principles, to help interpret experiences objectively and rationally rather than intuitively.	By applying logical abilities, children learn to understand the basic concepts of conservation, number, classification, and many other scientific ideas.
12 years through adulthood	Formal operational	The adolescent or adult is able to think about abstractions and hypothetical concepts and to reason analytically, not just emotionally.	Ethics, politics, and social and moral issues become more interesting and involving as the adolescent becomes able to take a broader and more theoretical approach to experience.

was supposed to find the age at which most children could answer each question correctly, but he found the children's wrong answers much more intriguing.

How children think is much more important and more revealing of mental ability, Piaget concluded, than *what* they know. Moreover, understanding how people think reveals how they interpret their experiences and thus explains how they construct their values and assumptions.

Piaget maintained that there are four major periods, or stages, of cognitive development: the *sensorimotor* period, the *preoperational* period, the *concrete operational* period, and the *formal operational* period (see Table 2.2). These are age-related, and, as you will see in later chapters, each has features that permit certain types of knowing and understanding (Piaget, 1952b, 1970a,b).

Movement from one period to another is propelled by the human need for **cognitive equilibrium**—that is, a state of mental balance. What Piaget meant is that each person attempts to make sense of new experiences by reconciling them with his or her existing understanding. Cognitive equilibrium occurs when one's present understanding "fits" new experiences, whether this fitting involves a baby's discovery that new objects can be grasped in the same way as familiar objects or an adult's explanation of shifting world events as consonant with his or her political philosophy.

Figure 2.3 diagrams how the need for cognitive equilibrium is fulfilled. When a new experience does not seem to fit existing understanding, the individual falls into a state of *cognitive disequilibrium,* an imbalance that initially produces confusion. Disequilibrium then leads to cognitive growth when the person modifies old concepts and constructs better ones to fit the new experience if

cognitive equilibrium In cognitive theory, the state of mental balance that enables a person to reconcile new experiences with existing understanding. People strive to attain cognitive equilibrium.

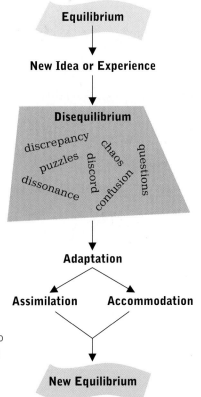

FIGURE 2.3 **Challenge Me** Most of us, most of the time, prefer the comfort of our conventional conclusions. According to Piaget, however, when new ideas disturb our thinking, we have an opportunity to expand our cognition with a broader and deeper understanding.

!*Answer to Observational Quiz* (from page 43): Three hours, or one-third less time. Note that later on, the wire-fed monkeys spent equal, or even more, time on the cloth mothers compared with the cloth-fed monkeys.

Response for Older Brothers and Sisters (from page 43): An older sibling is an ideal role model because he or she has survived or—better yet—succeeded within the same family and community context in which the younger child lives but has human weaknesses that are also apparent. By contrast, distant role models are portrayed as unusually skilled or fortunate, with no weaknesses—unless a particular foible reaches the headlines and causes children to lose faith in the former hero.

!*Answer to Observational Quiz* (from page 44): Their clothes and hair.

necessary, thus moving to a higher stage. In Piaget's terminology, cognitive adaptation occurs in two ways:

■ Reinterpreting new experiences so that they fit into, or *assimilate* with, the old ideas
■ Revamping old ideas so that they can *accommodate* the new

Assimilation is easier, since it does not require much adjustment. But accommodation is sometimes necessary, and it produces significant intellectual growth— a new form of thinking that is more inclusive than before.

You may experience cognitive disequilibrium, for example, when a friend's argument reveals logical inconsistencies in your views, when your favorite chess strategy fails against a skilled opponent, or when your mother does or says something you never expected her to. In the last example, you might assimilate your mother's unusual statement by deciding that it was just something she heard and didn't really mean. Growth occurs if, instead, you adjust your previous conception of your mother to accommodate a new, expanded, and more comprehensive view of who she is.

(a)   (b)

(c)   (d)

How to Think About Flowers A person's stage of cognitive growth influences how he or she thinks about everything, including flowers. (a) To a baby, in the sensorimotor stage, flowers are "known" through pulling, smelling, and perhaps tasting. (b) A slightly older child might be egocentric, wanting to pick and eat the vegetables now. (c,d) At the adult's formal operational stage, flowers can be part of a larger, logical scheme—either to earn money or to cultivate beauty. Note, however, that thinking is an active process throughout the life span.

According to cognitive theory, babies poke, pull, and taste everything they get their hands on; preschool children ask thousands of questions; school-age children become avid readers and information collectors; adolescents try out a wide variety of roles and experiences; and adults continually increase their knowledge and expertise in areas that interest them—all because people at every age seek cognitive challenges.

Recognition of this active searching is the very essence of Piaget's theory of human cognitive development. Unlike psychoanalytic and learning theories, which depict children as buffeted and shaped by influences beyond their control, cognitive theory portrays a much more active person, one who seeks ways to comprehend the world.

Not What He Expected Water spraying out of a pipe that he can hold in his hand—a surprising event that is likely to trigger first cognitive disequilibrium and then cognitive growth.

?Observational Quiz (see answer, page 48): This boy is 14 months old, in the sensorimotor period, and at an age when he loves to experiment. What is he likely to do next?

Limitations of the Grand Theories

All three of the theories we have just described deserve to be called "grand." They are insightful and provocative, stimulating not only for researchers in human development but also for historians, educators, novelists, and, particularly, psychotherapists. Thousands of clinical professionals still use techniques originated by Freud, Skinner, or Piaget. Further, each of these three theories has made significant contributions to developmental science, as already shown.

However, the grand theories, as they attempted to explain the development of all humans everywhere, were probably too wide-ranging. The central idea that every person, in every culture, in every nation, passes through certain fixed stages (Freud, Erikson, Piaget) or can be conditioned according to the same laws of reinforcement (Watson, Pavlov, Skinner) does not seem applicable to the actual diversity of human beings worldwide. Careful observation of any living, breathing, growing person evokes surprise and puzzlement, no matter what grand theory or basic assumption the observer might hold. This is already evident from the surprising examples in Chapter 1: the butterfly effect, the Bosnian 5-year-olds unscathed by war, and the eleventh-graders who seemed to forget that they had had sex before age 13.

In other words, all three grand theories seem much less comprehensive and inclusive now than they once did. This is apparent in the central controversies of development (continuity/discontinuity, difference/deficit, nature/nurture), discussed at the end of this chapter. It also becomes apparent when the theories of physics and biology are compared with the theories about human development in terms of their scientific rigor. As one critic writes:

> No field of biology can match the precision and power of physics, because unlike electrons or neutrons, all organisms are unique. But the differences between, say, two *Escherichia coli* bacteria or two leafcutter ants are trivial compared to the differences between any two humans, even those who are genetically identical. Each individual mind may also change dramatically when its owner is spanked, learns the alphabet, reads *Thus Spoke Zarathustra*, takes LSD, falls in love, gets divorced,

No Theories Allowed These three elderly women are in a nursing home where research in human development has not yet been applied. Being confined to wheelchairs, unable to see or hear each other, means that they are cut off from the comforts of human contact (psychoanalytic), of homemade food (behaviorism), and of intellectual stimulation (cognitive theory). Although none of the grand theories are considered comprehensive in the twenty-first century, any one of them could suggest improvements in the situation depicted here.

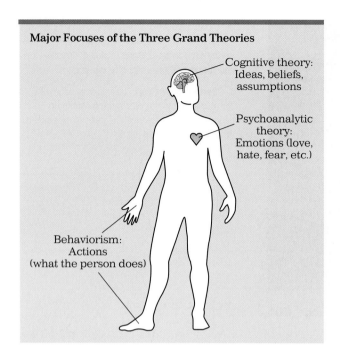

Major Focuses of the Three Grand Theories

Cognitive theory: Ideas, beliefs, assumptions

Psychoanalytic theory: Emotions (love, hate, fear, etc.)

Behaviorism: Actions (what the person does)

FIGURE 2.4 **Major Focuses of the Three Grand Theories**

sociocultural theory An emergent theory that holds that human development results from the dynamic interaction between each person and the surrounding culture, including all the social forces, near and distant, that affect that person.

!Answer to Observational Quiz (from page 47): He will want to use all his senses and motor skills, so he might put the pipe to his mouth to taste it, rub it on his belly to feel the cold, shake it up and down to see and hear what happens, and—watch out—aim it at you to see your reaction.

undergoes Jungian dream therapy, suffers a stroke. The variability and malleability of minds enormously complicate the search for general principles of human nature.

[Horgan, 1999, p. 6]

Each grand theory begins with a different focus: human emotions (psychoanalytic theory), actions (behaviorism), and thoughts (cognitive theory) (see Figure 2.4). The main conflict among the three theories involves what should be studied and how. As you might imagine, psychoanalytic theorists typically rely on case studies, behaviorists do experiments, and cognitive theorists observe and ask questions. However, all three grand theories seem to ignore major cultural differences and to underestimate the power of genes. New theories are needed to fill the gap, and at least two are emerging (Greene, 1997; Overton, 1998).

Emergent Theories

The three grand theories originated almost a century ago as theories of psychology. By contrast, the two emergent theories are recent and multidisciplinary. They include observations, mini-theories, and hypotheses from all the many sciences—in addition to psychology—that currently study human development. *Sociocultural theory* draws on research in education, sociology, and history; *epigenetic systems theory* is based on research from biology, genetics, ethology, and neuroscience. In part because of their scope and in part because of their recency, neither theory has become a comprehensive, coherent whole. However, as you will now see, both provide significant frameworks for the study of human development.

Sociocultural Theory

Although "sociocultural theory is still emerging and is not a single consolidated view," it stresses a new appreciation of the social context that developmentalists now recognize (Rogoff, 1998, p. 687). **Sociocultural theory** seeks to explain the growth of individual knowledge, development, and competencies in terms of the guidance, support, and structure provided by the society. Social change over time results from individual choices. Note the bidirectional influence of culture and person: People are affected by society, but people also change society.

The central thesis of sociocultural theory is that human development is the result of dynamic interaction between developing persons and their surrounding culture. According to this theory, culture is not simply an external variable that impinges on the developing person; it is integral to development (Cole, 1996).

The power of culture cannot be understood simply by comparing one particular practice in one place or ethnic group with another, as "cross-cultural" research did in the past. Instead, each culture is seen as a unique "design for living," and children learn that design from objects and people—from their parents, teachers, and peers, in their homes, schools, and neighborhoods. Consider a very simple example: What do you do if a 6-month-old baby starts to fuss? You could find a pacifier, turn on a musical mobile, change the diaper, give a bottle, pick up the baby and walk around, sing a lullaby, offer a breast, shake a rattle, or close the door so the noise won't bother anyone. Each of these is "the right thing to do" according to parents in some cultures but not in others. Few of these parents are aware that their culture has so shaped their attitudes that they respond to a baby's cry in a particular way, yet this is precisely what happens, according to sociocultural theory.

Guided Participation

A major pioneer of the sociocultural perspective was Lev Vygotsky (1896–1934), a psychologist from the former Soviet Union. Vygotsky was particularly interested in the cognitive competencies that developed among the culturally diverse people of his huge country, including such skills as the proper use of tools in an agricultural community and the appropriate use of abstract words among people who had never been to school. In the sociocultural view, these competencies develop from interactions between novices and more skilled members of the society, who act as tutors or mentors in a process called an **apprenticeship in thinking** (Rogoff, 1990, 1998).

COURTESY OF DR. MICHAEL COLE, LABORATORY OF COMPARATIVE HUMAN COGNITION, UC, SAN DIEGO

The Founder of Sociocultural Theory Lev Vygotsky, now recognized as a seminal thinker whose ideas on the role of culture and history are revolutionizing education and the study of development, was a contemporary of Freud, Skinner, Pavlov, and Piaget. Vygotsky did not attain their eminence in his lifetime, partly because his work, conducted in Stalinist Russia, was largely inaccessible to the Western world and partly because he died young, at age 38.

The implicit goal of this apprenticeship is to provide the instruction and support that novices need in order to acquire the knowledge and capabilities that are valued by their culture. The best way to accomplish this goal is through **guided participation:** The tutor engages the learner in joint activities, offering not only instruction but also direct involvement in the learning process.

Note that this apprenticeship depends on social interaction, not on a student's own discovery or on a teacher's lecture. Neither student nor teacher is ever passive; one person learns from another, through the words and activities that they engage in *together* (Karpov & Haywood, 1998). This is one crucial difference between sociocultural theory and the grand theories of the past: "Cognitive development occurs in and emerges from social situations" (Gauvain, 1998, p. 191). Adults learn from children as well as vice versa, and both adults and children learn as much from their peers as from older or younger individuals.

The concept that a culture's patterns and beliefs are social constructions (as explained in Chapter 1) is easy for sociocultural theorists to understand. However, the fact that something is socially constructed does not reduce its power or importance; quite the opposite. Values are among the most potent forces, shaping the development of every member of the culture. This point was stressed by Vygotsky, who himself was a teacher and argued that mentally and physically disabled children can learn (Vygotsky, 1925/1994). If people believe that "every child can learn," they are likely to find a way to teach every child.

The Zone of Proximal Development

According to sociocultural theory, *what* people need to learn depends on their cultures, but *how* they learn is always the same, whether they are learning a manual skill, a social custom, or a language. Cultural context, social customs, and guided participation are always part of the process.

apprenticeship in thinking In sociocultural theory, the process by which novices develop cognitive competencies through interaction with more skilled members of the society, often parents or teachers, who act as tutors or mentors.

guided participation In sociocultural theory, the process by which a skilled person helps a novice learn by providing not only instruction but also a direct, shared involvement in the learning process.

Especially for Teachers: Following Vygotsky's precepts, how might you teach reading to an entire class of first-graders at various skill levels?

R. ROWAN / PHOTO RESEARCHERS, INC.

A Temporary Support Structure Scaffolds support workers as they construct a new building or repair an existing one, such as the California state capitol in Sacramento, shown here. Similarly, expert teachers erect educational scaffolds, using hints, ideas, examples, and questions to support the novice learner until a solid cognitive structure is formed.

zone of proximal development In sociocultural theory, the range of skills that a learner can exercise and master with assistance but cannot yet perform independently. According to Vygotsky, learning can occur within this zone.

Response for Teachers (from page 49): First of all, you wouldn't teach them "to read"; you would find out where each child was and what he or she was capable of learning next, so that instruction would be tailored to each child's zone of proximal development. For some this might be letter recognition; for others, comprehension of paragraphs they read to themselves. Second, you wouldn't teach the whole class. You would figure out a way to individualize instruction, maybe by forming pairs, with one child teaching the other, by setting up appropriate computer instruction, or by having parents or ancillary teachers work with small groups of three or four children.

For learning to occur, a teacher (who can be a parent or peer as well as a professional) draws the learner into his or her **zone of proximal development,** which is the range of skills that the learner can exercise and master with assistance but cannot yet perform independently. Through sensitive assessment of the learner's ability and capacity for growth, the teacher engages his or her participation, guiding the transition from assisted performance to independent achievement. The teacher must avoid two ever-present dangers, boredom and failure, both of which are outside that ideal zone. Some frustration is permitted, but the learner must be actively engaged, never passive or overwhelmed (see Figure 2.5).

To make this rather abstract-seeming process more concrete, let's take a simple example—a father teaching his 5-year-old daughter to ride a bicycle. He probably begins by slowly rolling her along, supporting her weight while telling her to keep her hands on the bars and her feet on the pedals, to push the right and left pedals in rhythm, and to look straight ahead. As she becomes more comfortable and confident, he begins to roll her along more quickly, noting out loud that she is now able to keep her legs pumping in a steady rhythm. Within another lesson or two he is jogging beside her, holding on to just the handlebar. When he senses that, with a little more momentum, she could maintain her balance by herself, he urges her to pedal faster and slowly loosens his grip until, perhaps without her even realizing it, she is riding on her own.

Note that this is not instruction by rote. First, some children need more assurance than others; from the start the instruction process is modified for the particular learner. Second, even knowing the child, a parent needs to listen and

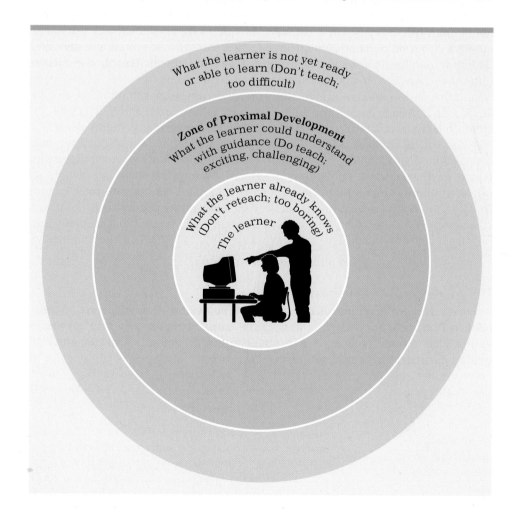

FIGURE 2.5 The Magic Middle Somewhere between the boring and the impossible is the zone of proximal development, where interaction between teacher and learner results in knowledge never before grasped or skills not already mastered. The intellectual excitement of that zone is the origin of the joy that both instruction and study can bring.

sense exactly whether more support or more freedom is needed at each moment, so the process is constantly modified. And third, such skills are almost impossible to transmit unless the teacher has mastered them: If a father intellectually understands the general principles but does not know how to ride, he is best advised to let his bike-riding wife do the instructing.

Such excursions into and through the zone of proximal development are commonplace, not only in childhood but throughout life. Ideally, the learning process follows the same general pattern in all instances: The mentor, sensitively attuned to the learner's ever-shifting abilities and motivation, continually urges the learner on to new levels of competence, while the learner asks questions and shows signs of progress that guide and inspire the mentor. The particular skills and processes vary enormously from culture to culture, but the overall social engagement is the same.

Sociocultural theorists have been criticized for overlooking developmental processes that are not primarily social. Vygotsky's theory, in particular, has been viewed as neglecting the role of genes in guiding development, especially with regard to neurological maturation in mental processes (Wertsch, 1985; Wertsch & Tulviste, 1992). The other emerging theory, which we will now discuss, begins with genetics.

MARK ANTMAN / THE IMAGE WORKS

Learning to Ride Although they are usually not aware of it, children learn most of their skills because adults guide them carefully. What would happen if this father let go?

Epigenetic Systems Theory

Epigenetic systems theory emphasizes the interaction of genes and the environment, an interaction that is seen as dynamic and reciprocal (Dent-Read & Zukow-Goldring, 1997; Goldsmith et al., 1997). This is the newest developmental theory, but it builds on several established bodies of research. Many disciplines of the natural sciences, including evolution, genetics, and ethology, provided a foundation for this theory. Further, both Erikson and Piaget described aspects of their theories as "epigenetic."

epigenetic systems theory An emergent theory of development that emphasizes the interaction of genes and the environment—that is, both the genetic origins of behavior (within each person and within each species) and the direct, systematic influence that environmental forces have, over time, on genes.

Before and After the Genes

To understand what is involved in this theory, let us begin by examining the root word *genetic* and the prefix *epi*. The word *genetic* refers both to the genes that make each person (except monozygotic twins) unique and to the genes that each human has shared with all other humans for hundreds of thousands of years. Many of our basic "human" genes, about 98 percent of them, are also shared with other primates (Gibbons, 1998).

In emphasizing this genetic foundation, epigenetic systems theory stresses that we have powerful instincts and abilities that arise from our biological heritage. Even the timing and pace of certain developmental changes are genetically guided.

The fact that genes substantially affect every aspect of human behavior was at first unknown and then disputed for most of the twentieth century. (That explains why the earlier grand theories did not give heredity a substantial role in explaining human development.) Now research has shown that every psychological as well as every physical trait, from blood type to bashfulness, from metabolic rate to moodiness, from voice tone to vocational aptitude, is influenced by genes. Molecular genetics is beginning to explain exactly which genes interact with which factors to produce which traits (McGuffin et al., 2001).

No longer ignored, the power of genes is now sometimes exaggerated. That is an error that epigenetic systems theory seeks to avoid—as is evident in the prefix *epi*, which means (among other things) "before," "after," "on," and "near." Thus, *epigenetic* refers to all the factors that affect the expression of the genetic instructions. Some are stress factors, such as injury, temperature, and crowding.

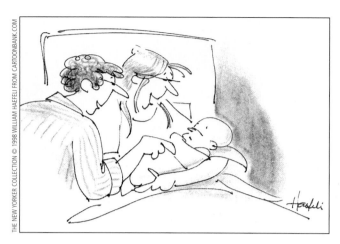

"Isn't she marvelous? Our own little bundle of untapped potential."

The Epigenetic Systems Perspective
Although these parents may not realize it, their words echo the essence of epigenetic systems thought—that each human is born with genetic possibilities that must be nurtured in order to grow.

Some are facilitating factors, such as nourishing food, loving care, and freedom to play. These and other epigenetic factors are part of, or arise from, the environment in which the organism develops, from the first cell to the complete organism, from the moment after conception to the moment before death.

Obvious and direct epigenetic effects are easier, and more ethical, to find in lower animals than in people. For example, some species of animals develop abnormal facial features or change the color of their fur (all genetic traits) depending on environmental conditions. One amazing example occurred when experimenters incubated a clutch of alligator eggs at various temperatures. All those which developed at about 32° Centigrade became male; all that developed below that temperature became female (Ferguson & Joanen, 1982).

Many other epigenetic factors have been shown to affect human body and brain development, especially in the early months (Dawson et al., 2000). One expert explains, "Brain development is not just a genetic process but an epigenetic one." Even identical twins, who have identical genes, are born with different brain structures, because of the *"epi"* aspects of genetics (Johnson, 1999).

As development progresses, most people move along the course set by earlier genetic–environmental interactions. However, a suddenly different context may totally change the epigenetic patterns that are already in place (Tarter et al., 1999). For example, it is well known that a person's propensity to become addicted to drugs is affected by genes. That genetic potential is further developed through exposure to an addictive drug. However, as one team of researchers explains:

> Within the epigenetic model, each intermediary phenotype [genetic manifestation] is an outcome as well as a precursor to a subsequent outcome contingent on the quality of person–environment interactions. . . . Indeed, sudden shifts . . . can occur. In this regard, it is noteworthy that 86 percent of regular heroin users among soldiers in Vietnam abruptly terminated consumption upon return to the United States (Robins, Helzer, & Davis, 1975). In effect, a substantial change in the environment produced a major phenotype change.
>
> *[Tarter et al., 1999, p. 672]*

Adaptation of the Genes

selective adaptation The idea that humans and other animals gradually adjust to their environment; specifically, the process by which the frequency of particular genetic traits in a population increases and others decrease over generations, depending on whether a given trait contributes to the survival of the species.

So far we have focused on epigenetic factors within individuals. However, some epigenetic factors relate to the evolutionary adaptation of the entire human species. Over the generations, the frequency of some genetic traits in a population increases and others become rarer. This process is called **selective adaptation.**

As a result of selective adaptation over centuries, species have developed certain specific traits—such as plumage or rituals or songs—that have a decidedly genetic origin and that enhance the ability to mate and reproduce. Experimental research has shown, for example, that deafening a baby bird temporarily so that it cannot learn the melody of local birdsong results in an impaired ability to mate later on. This finding demonstrates that both the genetic and the epigenetic are crucial. Indeed, an estimated 90 percent of all species that have existed at one time or another have become extinct because their genes did not adapt adequately to environmental change and their reproduction fell below the replacement rate (Buss et al., 1998).

Humans have adapted well thus far, so their numbers keep rising. In fact, some think, our epigenetic adaptability is the most crucial human quality distinguishing us from other animal species. Specific epigenetic factors within humans are hard to pin down by experiments, partly because both human genes and the human context are more diverse than those of nonhuman animals and partly because ethical research on human epigenetic factors is difficult to perform (Gottlieb et al., 1998).

There is no doubt, however, that humans vary in the pathways they follow from their genetic base, depending on the conditions in which they live. Some genes are never expressed; others are made more potent in response to the environment. Many psychological disorders, including schizophrenia, autism, antisocial personality disorder, and depression, have a genetic component, but none of them are purely genetic; they are all epigenetic (Reiss & Neiderhiser, 2000; Rutter & Sroufe, 2000; Sanchez et al., 2001). As an example, the rate of schizophrenia among people of West Indian descent living in England is significantly higher than the rate among native-born people in England or among West Indians living out their lives in the West Indies (Jamaica, Trinidad, the Bahamas). The probable cause is psychosocial stresses that are greater for West Indians in England than for other groups (McKenzie & Murray, 1999).

A more familiar example is height. Each person is genetically programmed to grow to a certain height. That person can overeat and stretch every day but will not grow taller. However, a child who is not adequately nourished will be several inches shorter than the genetic potential would have allowed. Thus, on an individual level, the genes for height combine with influences from the early environment to yield an individual's eventual height. On a species level, we humans are taller than our genetic cousins the chimpanzees because greater height was adaptive for humans.

Systems That Support Development

Finally, this theory also emphasizes *systems*. The critical aspect of a system, as scientists use the term, is that change in one part of the system causes corresponding adjustments and changes in every other part (an idea so basic to our current understanding of development that it was introduced at the beginning of Chapter 1). This is true for the biological systems that foster the development of an individual (e.g., the cardiovascular system), the systems that support an entire species (in an ecosystem), and the systems that govern all nature (Magnusson, 1996, 2000; Masterpasqua, 1997; Lewis & Granic, 2000).

One example of how the environment causes a systemic change is the effect of human handling on rat pups. It has long been realized that rats become smarter if they are frequently held when they are young. Some scientists thought that the rats learned from their early human involvement. Not so. More recent research shows exactly how handling produces systemic change: Handling increases the mother's licking and grooming of her pup, which leads to decreased release of stress hormones, which leads to increased tolerance of potentially stressful conditions, which, in adulthood, leads to less brain degeneration than in unhandled rats (Sapolsky, 1997). Obviously, none of these changes could occur as a direct result of genes, but all of them are part of an elaborate, systemic interaction between nature and nurture.

This example raises important questions for humans, which the researcher wryly addressed:

> It is a rare parent of a newborn who does not feel panic built around the consequences that her or his actions now have. Developmental studies have indicated that the quality, quantity, and timing of infant stimulation can have long-lasting effects—and soon the anxious parent is convinced that one lullaby sung off-key ensures that a child will not only one day be a sociopath, but will also never use dental floss. If mothers of newborn rats harbor similar anxieties, a report by Liu and colleagues affirms their worries: The authors show that subtle stimulation in a rat's infancy has marked consequences that are probably life-long.
>
> *[Sapolosky, 1997, p. 1620]*

We will soon discuss the implications of such research for humans. We already know, however, that each individual is (among other things) an epigenetic system, continually adjusting to a never-ending flux of proteins, hormones, and electrical charges that occur in response to biochemical and physical forces inside and outside the body. Genes form the foundation of that system, but they never act alone (Goldsmith et al., 1997).

Each body cell is a system in itself, with numerous proteins and genetic instructions; all the cells and genes within one person are also a system; and the collections of all the people in a family, in a culture, and in the world are systems as well. The conclusion that "individual development is most appropriately viewed as a hierarchically organized system" represents "the triumph of epigenesis" over the archaic idea that everything is determined by the genes (Gottlieb et al., 1998).

As you remember from the dynamic systems approach described in Chapter 1, each society and each species is also a system, gradually shaping its common genetic heritage in such a way as to adapt to the changing world. Humans depend on each other, not only economically and politically but also for survival. Survival, apparently, is why I adore my children.

ethology The study of patterns of animal behavior, particularly as that behavior relates to evolutionary origins and species survival.

In Person

My Beautiful, Hairless Babies

The epigenetic systems approach focuses on both the "micro" interactions of genes at the individual level and the "macro" genetic systems that have developed within the species over time. In the latter respect, epigenetic theory builds on a well-established theory called *ethology* (Hinde, 1983). **Ethology** is the study of patterns of animal behavior, particularly as that behavior relates to evolutionary origins and species survival.

The ethological perspective has particular relevance for infancy, not just that of rat pups, as discussed in the text, but that of human babies as well. Many of the instinctive behaviors of young infants and their caregivers tend to promote survival (Marvin, 1997).

Infant Instincts

Infants come into the world already equipped with social predispositions and social skills that help ensure their nurturance and development. For example, they can distinguish the sounds and rhythms of speech, recognize the facial expressions of fear and pleasure, and distinguish one person from another by smell, by touch, and by sound. Despite being so obviously immobile and helpless, human infants are genetically programmed to display reflexes, including the grasping, clinging, crying, and grunting that summon adults or keep them nearby. In the beginning, infants accept help from anyone—a good survival strategy in the centuries when women regularly died in childbirth. By the time they are able to crawl, however, infants have become emotionally attached to their specific caregivers, as well as fearful of unfamiliar situations.

Over the course of human history, infants who stayed near nurturing and protecting adults were more likely to survive. Hence, selective adaptation produced this genetic makeup to keep infants safe from harm.

Adult Impulses

Correspondingly, caregiving adults are genetically equipped to nurture babies. Logically, no reasonable adult would ever put up with being a parent. It is irrational to endure the sleepless nights, dirty diapers, and frequent cries of a baby, or the rebellion of a teenager, or all the tribulations of the years in between. Fortunately, however, genetic impulses are not logical. Humans are programmed to cherish and protect children. As the mother of four, I have been surprised by the power of this programming many times. With my first-born, I asked my pediatrician if she wasn't one of the most beautiful, perfect babies he had ever seen.

"Yes," he said, with a twinkle in his eyes, "and my patients are better looking than the patients of any other pediatrician in the city."

With my second newborn, the hospital offered to sell me a photo of her—hairless, chinless, and with swollen eyelids—at 1 day old; I glanced at it and said "no." The photo didn't look at all like her—she looked almost ugly. I was similarly enamored of my third and fourth. For the fourth, however, a new thought came to me: I am not only a woman who loves her children; I am a woman who loves her sleep, a genetic trait I have shown all my life; my mother called me "a good napper." In the predawn hours, as I roused myself yet again to feed my fourth baby, I asked myself how selective forgetting had allowed me, once again, to choose a disruptive addition to my life that was guaranteed to deprive me of my precious slumber. The answer, of course, is that some instincts are even stronger than the instinct for self-preservation.

Open Wide Caregivers and babies elicit responses from each other that ensure survival of the next generation. The caregiver's role in this vital interaction is obvious, but ethology has shown that infants starve if they do not chirp, meow, whine, bleat, squeal, cry, or otherwise signal hunger, and then open their mouths wide when food arrives. Both the baby birds and 5-month-old Jonah obviously know what to do.

Comparisons and Controversies

Each of the theories presented in this chapter has contributed a great deal to the study of human development (see Table 2.3).

- *Psychoanalytic theory* has made us aware of the importance of early childhood experiences and of the impact of the "hidden dramas" that influence daily life.
- *Behaviorism* has shown us the effect that the immediate environment can have on behavior.
- *Cognitive theory* has brought us to a greater understanding of how intellectual processes and thinking affect actions.
- *Sociocultural theory* has reminded us that development is embedded in a rich and multifaceted cultural context.
- *Epigenetic systems theory* emphasizes the inherited forces that affect each person—and all humankind—within particular contexts.

In order, these five theories present us with: the unconscious processes; the environment; the intellect; the culture; and the genes. No comprehensive view of development can ignore any one of these factors.

TABLE 2.3 Five Perspectives on Human Development

Theory	Basic Focus	Fundamental Depiction of What People Do	Emphasis on Early Years?	Relative Emphasis on Nature or Nurture?
Psychoanalytic	Psychosexual (Freud) or psychosocial (Erikson) stages	Battle unconscious impulses and overcome major crises	Yes (especially in Freudian theory)	More nature (biological, sexual impulses are very important, as are parent–child bonds and memories)
Behaviorism	Conditioning through stimulus and response	Respond to stimuli, reinforcement, and models in the environment	No (conditioning and reconditioning are lifelong)	More nurture (direct environmental influences produce various behaviors)
Cognitive	Thinking, remembering, analyzing	Seek to understand experiences while forming concepts and cognitive strategies	No (new concepts and control processes are developed throughout life)	More nature (person's own mental activity and motivation are key)
Sociocultural	Social context, expressed through people, language, customs	Learn the tools, skills, and values of society through apprenticeships	Yes (family and school acculturation are critical)	More nurture (interaction of mentor and learner, within cultural context, is pivotal)
Epigenetic systems	Genes and their expression, in individuals and species	Express impulses, interests, and patterns inherited from ancestors and developed from childhood	Yes (early biochemical forces alter the manifestation of genes)	Nature begins the process; nurture affects it via hormones, enzymes, toxins, and selective adaptation

Each theory has had its critics. Psychoanalytic theory has been faulted for being too subjective; behaviorism, for being too mechanistic; cognitive theory, for undervaluing genetic differences; sociocultural theory, for neglecting individuals; and epigenetic systems theory, for neglecting society.

At the beginning of this chapter we noted that theories are not meant to be correct in every detail but are intended to be useful, to provide a perspective that might not otherwise come to mind. Let us now apply these five theories to the three controversies mentioned in Chapter 1 (page 21), to see how useful they really are.

Continuity Versus Discontinuity

The first major controversy is whether development is *continuous,* with children growing a little day by day, or *discontinuous,* with growth occurring in spurts or stages. Each of the five theories answers this question in a distinct way.

Freud and Erikson described distinct stages, and Piaget was also a stage theorist. Piaget said that the transitions between his four stages occurred at about ages 2, 6, and 11—about the same ages at which Freud and Erikson also said new stages began. However, Freud and Erikson added a stage in toddlerhood, and Erikson added three more in adulthood. Moreover, although they were all stage theorists, who saw biology as a potent force, they each focused on different things—Freud on body parts and sex, Erikson on the relationship between personality and social context, and Piaget on thought processes. These differences pale when compared with the third grand theory, behaviorism, which has no stages at all, but instead insists that the same principles of learning apply to every human and other animal, of every age, and that any variations occur because of the environment, not the person.

The two emergent theories also differ. According to sociocultural theory, each culture constructs its own stages, setting an ideal time for weaning from the breast, for school, for having a first baby, for resuming sex after a baby is born. These social clocks vary depending on the place and time: A first pregnancy, for instance, was once expected at about age 18, but now most cultures expect first pregnancies several years later. Thus, stages exist, but they are set by a social clock, not by the maturation of the individual.

According to epigenetic systems theory, growth begins internally, with genetic forces, not society. The first days, months, and years of life, when the most plasticity is present, is the time when cognitive enrichment, emotional security, and adequate nutrition are especially important, because many epigenetic effects occur between conception and age 2. Similarly, at puberty, genes for sexual arousal mature. Parents must teach teens about contraception, become vigilant chaperones, or expect a grandchild, because the emerging genetic forces unleash a new set of compulsions that cannot be ignored. Thus, the epigenetic systems perspective includes intervals that resemble stages—called sensitive phases, time windows, or critical periods—but these are unlike the stages described by any other theory.

The basic issue—whether development occurs gradually or in stages—is not just theoretical. If there are stages, then parents must adjust to whatever stage their children are in at any given time. The toddler's temper, the school-age child's collection of beach rocks, the teenager's rebellion are all "just a stage," something that will be outgrown. If there are no stages, then societies and parents need to be continuously active in guiding a child; every day, every year, is equally crucial.

Normal Difference or Harmful Deficit?

The second major controversy is whether differences between children are normal variations or problematic deficits. This controversy arises from a painful history known to every developmentalist. Until the last decade or so, "deficit-oriented models and comparative studies have dominated research" (Fisher et al., 1998). Most research focused on white, middle-class, native-born children in wealthy nations; children who were from other cultures or who were poorer were found to be deficient because they deviated from the norms set for middle-class, majority children. For instance, "culturally deprived" children were slower to develop language, more likely to be physically punished, less likely to do well in school.

These differences once seemed to be deficits—and well-intentioned developmentalists hoped to help all children develop language more quickly, to encourage all parents to replace physical punishment with reasoning, to help everyone learn more in school. As we now see it, that attitude was arrogant and experts were too hasty, culturally insensitive, and prejudiced when they decided that differences were deficits. We now know that some cultures communicate more by touch than by talk, that some children develop better with stricter parenting than the middle-class ideal, that the reason for a child's failure may lie with the teacher or the curriculum, not the child.

However, it is an easy escape from a hard problem to say that all children and families are fine and that every difference is equally beneficial. Remember Chapter 1's discussion of research on where children sleep? There are many differences that do not seem to be deficits: Children may safely sleep beside their parents or in another room. But there are also differences that are more constructive than others: Children seem to develop best if a caregiver is within earshot at night, available to comfort the child. The more we learn, the more we realize that children grow in many wondrous and diverse ways, but also the more we realize that some things—low birthweight, child neglect, and social isolation among them—are not harmless differences but damaging deficits. The challenge is identifying what is really harmful and what is not. Two difficult questions, related to our understanding of cultural diversity, remain:

■ At what point does a difference become a deficit? Must the difference be quite large and obvious, and must the behavior be a pivotal one, or is any small deviation enough to be a deficit? The answer is not clear, even with physical characteristics: When is a child too short, too fat, too thin? Published norms, as in the height/weight tables that most pediatricians use, were based on thousands of middle-class European-Americans. If an African-American child is taller than normal at age 11 (and many are), is that a deficit? If a Pakistani child is shorter at age 6 (and most are), is that a deficit—even if it is normal for Pakistani children?

■ This raises a second question: Can something be a deficit even if it is not a major deviation? In 1950, "only children" were unusual and were assumed to be spoiled or emotionally distressed. Today, single-child families are typical in many nations, including Italy, Germany, and China, and such children are found to be smarter, more confident, and more likely to graduate from college than their peers. Have historical circumstances changed, making "only" children no longer a deficit, or have research assumptions changed? A more problematic example is unmarried motherhood, which was once considered a serious deficit for the mother as well as the child but which is now widely accepted and quite common in some countries (see Figure 2.6).

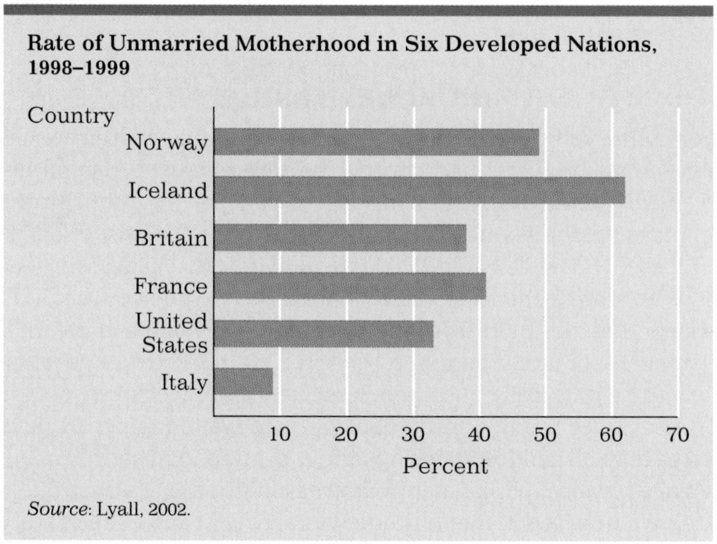

FIGURE 2.6 Increasing Deficit or Merely Cohort Change? These are the percentages of all births, not just first births. In all these nations, the percentage of couples who live together without being married has increased dramatically in the past three decades, with many educated and financially stable couples choosing not to marry. No longer are births to unmarried mothers considered a sign of poverty and ignorance. Even the Crown Prince of Norway lived with his future wife and had a baby before they married.

? Observational Quiz (see answer, page 60): Does the United States have more unwed mothers than any other developed nation?

Rate of Unmarried Motherhood in Six Developed Nations, 1998–1999

Source: Lyall, 2002.

How do theories help us deal with such complex questions? All viable developmental theories are quite broad and flexible; none of them suggest that there is only one, narrow, right way to raise a child. Thus, they provide a guide to normal variations. Most differences are acceptable, and only a few are really harmful. The complication is that each theory has a different view of what constitutes a deficit.

■ *Psychoanalytic theory*. Intimate maternal care is crucial for the first five years of a child's life. A *deficit* appears when a mother does not spend enough time with her child, or is not sufficiently responsive, for the pair to develop a close bond. Ideally, she breast-feeds until the baby is at least 1 year old, toilet trains relatively late, and tolerates the child's sexual curiosity. As Erikson stressed, there are limits to permissiveness, but guidance is preferred over punishment as the parental response.

■ *Behaviorism.* Many people (fathers, siblings, babysitters) can take care of the baby as well as the mother can. Feeding may occur in various schedules and modes, toilet training may be early or late, masturbation may be forbidden or encouraged. What is crucial is that the parents decide exactly what they want the child to learn and then use patience, modeling, and reinforcement to teach it step by step. For example, too much aggression in school is a *deficit*; as an example of a behaviorist remedy, the Oregon Social Learning Center retrains parents and teachers of such children, with specific behaviorist techniques that reinforce nonaggression (Reid et al., 2002).

■ *Cognitive theory.* Children advance cognitively if they are encouraged to explore and discover. A *deficit* is evident if children are slow to develop or are so "good" that they are always quiet, never curious and talkative. Parents should listen, talk to, play with, and encourage their children; teachers should let children follow their own interests.

■ *Sociocultural theory.* Each culture has its own approved system for raising children. Thus, any deficits identified under the first three theories—children who are afraid of their own sexual drives, or who are too aggressive, or who are too quiet—might be considered normal in some cultures. A *deficit* occurs when a child who has been raised by the standards of one culture does not function well in another. Immigrants who do not prepare their children for a new way of functioning may be creating a deficit, although at least some of the deficit may be blamed on the new culture (Suarez-Orozco & Suarez-Orozco, 2001). Docility, shyness, and "proper" manners may be a deficit in a brash, individualized culture.

■ *Epigenetic systems theory.* Genes vary from person to person, so diversity is to be expected. But genetic expression is also influenced by the environment, especially early in life. Thus, a *deficit* would be any environmental condition that does not provide proper nurturance for the developing child: the mother's drug abuse during pregnancy, lack of sensory stimulation in early infancy, too much fear and stress in toddlerhood, a depressed mother in early childhood. To keep these environmental deficits from impairing genetic expression, children in such homes should be cared for by someone else (perhaps a foster mother) or enrolled in early extensive day care.

As you can see, the solution to a deficit offered by epigenetic theory is the opposite of the solution offered by psychoanalytic theory. Similarly, a curious and talkative child who is doing well according to cognitive theory might not be doing well according to sociocultural theory, and so on. No wonder the difference/deficit issue is controversial: Each theory, and indeed each observer, sees different deficits. In practical terms, every parent has experienced the disapproval of a relative or friend, or even a stranger, for something their child did that seemed perfectly acceptable to them. (An excerpt from an article, supposedly by a meddlesome stranger, is reprinted here from the satirical newspaper *The Onion*.)

Nature or Nurture?

The very practical implications of the developmental theories we have been discussing are highlighted by the central controversy of human development: the debate over the relative influence of heredity and environment in shaping personal traits and characteristics. This debate is often called the *nature–nurture controversy* (Dixon & Lerner, 1999).

Now, There's a Stranger Who Could Use Some of My Child-Rearing Advice . . . Take, for example, the mother I recently saw giving her child a Hi-C drink box. Concerned that she mistakenly thought Hi-C was made with real fruit juice, I told her that it's largely artificial. Sadly, she felt threatened by my superior parenting skills and told me to "get lost." I assured her that it was an understandable mistake for her to think Hi-C was real fruit juice. The product's box, after all, deceptively features a bevy of oranges, apples, and grapes. I told her not to feel bad or embarrassed and then gently advised her to read labels more carefully in the future. "Anything called a 'fruit drink' or 'juice cocktail' is probably only 5 or 10 percent juice, at most," I told her. "So you should really try to avoid those."

Instead of thanking me for the free advice, this woman showered me with invective and urged me to "get my own damn kids."

—*from* The Onion, *March 28, 2002, p. 9*

nature A general term for the traits, capacities, and limitations that each individual inherits genetically from his or her parents at the moment of conception. Nature refers only to genes, not to other biological forces.

nurture A general term for all the environmental influences that affect development after an individual is conceived. Nurture includes the prenatal environment, as well as all the ecosystems described in Chapter 1.

Nature refers to the traits, capacities, and limitations that each person inherits genetically from his or her parents at the moment of conception. Body type, sex, and genetic diseases are obvious examples. Nature also includes a host of intellectual and personality characteristics that are powerfully influenced by genes (such as facility with numbers, attraction to novelty, sociability, and tendency to depression).

Nurture refers to all the environmental influences that come into play after conception, beginning with the mother's health during pregnancy and including all the individual's experiences in the outside world—in the family, the school, the community, and the culture at large.

The nature–nurture controversy has taken on many names, among them *heredity versus environment* and *maturation versus learning*. Under whatever name, the basic question remains: How much of any given characteristic, behavior, or pattern of development is the result of genes and how much is the result of experiences? Note that the question asks "How much?" not "Whether" or "Which ones?" All developmentalists agree that both nature and nurture interact to produce every specific trait; no characteristic develops as an exclusive response to either nature or nurture. Development is epigenetic, not merely genetic. Yet the specifics are hotly debated.

An Example: The Origins of Sexual Orientation

Let us look at the nature–nurture debate as illustrated by the question of how sexual orientation is determined. Most psychiatrists and psychologists once assumed that adult homosexuality resulted from unusual patterns in the mother–father–child relationship, a belief strongly endorsed by psychoanalytic theory. Other psychologists asserted that a person learned to be homosexual through reinforcement and modeling. The cognitive perspective held that a person's concept of appropriate sexual interaction influenced his or her orientation—that the idea itself led to the action.

All these explanations from the three grand theories clearly emphasized nurture over nature. However, new research suggests that homosexuality is at least partly genetic (Bailey et al., 2000). For example, a man is more likely to be gay if his mother's brother or his own brother—especially his identical twin—is homosexual (Hamer et al., 1993; Pool, 1993; Whitam et al., 1993). Further evidence that nature has a strong impact on sexual orientation comes from studies of children raised by lesbian mothers. Most of these children are heterosexual, in similar proportions to children raised by heterosexual parents (Golombok & Tasker, 1996). This finding supports an epigenetic perspective, in that any genetic factors that affect sexual orientation are not changed by the child's family or cultural environment.

The sociocultural view would regard nurture as very important—not the immediate mother–father–child nurture, but the cultural context. Each society has its own standards and expectations for sexual behavior. Looking at various cultures, one can find places where every boy is expected to be homosexual during adolescence and other places where homosexuality is considered perverse (Schlegel & Barry, 1991). Both the epigenetic systems and the sociocultural theories raise the difficult question of whether sexual orientation is an inborn biological fact or a behavior of sexual expression. Is it possible for someone to be homosexual but not know it? Is our sexuality something we learn, something we are born with, or something that develops in the interaction between nature and nurture?

All five perspectives guide our thinking to some extent, making us wary of choosing a simple answer from only one theory. Indeed, virtually no social scientist today believes that a warped mother–son relationship causes homosexuality (as psychoanalytic theory might hold) or that homosexuality is encouraged by the

! Answer to Observational Quiz (from page 58): As the chart shows, at least four countries have a higher *percentage* of unmarried mothers than does the United States. In fact, dozens of other countries do. However, this may be a trick question: Since the United States is one of the world's most populous *developed* nations, it does have a larger *number* of unwed mothers than most other countries.

environment (behaviorism) or that homo-sexuality is logically chosen after intellec-tual reflection (cognitive theory). Thus, all three grand theories, at least in their sim-plest, all-inclusive versions, are inadequate for explaining sexual orientation.

Yet the evidence for a genetic influence on homosexuality is far from conclusive (Hamer, 1999; Rice et al., 1999). Culture may also play a role, as is evidenced by varying rates of homosexuality from nation to na-tion and from cohort to cohort (Bailey et al., 1993; Maddox, 1993).

The human implications of the question are profound, which illustrates again why the nature–nurture debate is often contro-versial. If homosexuality is primarily the result of culture, those who are concerned about the future sexual orientation of the young should look to the influence of school curriculum, television programming, and laws about marriage, because these all reflect culture. In contrast, if the primary influences on a person's sexual orientation are genetic, different issues should be debated—and perhaps the debate itself is unnecessary.

Both of these positions may be too extreme for those who take "a develop-mental perspective." According to two psychologists:

Building for the Future The proud parents beam as their 19-month-old son uses blocks to make a tall building. Erik Erikson and other psychoanalytic theorists would be happy, too: Erikson observed that boys build towers and girls create circular enclosures. Psychoanalytic theorists might not be so happy, how-ever, with these parents' sexual orientation.

> Those who dichotomize sexual orientation into pure biological or social causation fall into a dangerous quagmire. To deny any role for biology affirms an untenable scientific view of human development. Equally harsh and deterministic would be to deny the significance of the environment.
>
> [Savin-Williams & Diamond, 1997, p. 235]

Policy and Practice

Theories about nature and nurture are implicit in many public policies. They are interwoven into many controversies, not only the one concerning sexual orienta-tion but also those concerning alcohol exposure before birth, class size and school learning, causes and consequences of teenage pregnancy, laws governing divorce, and attitudes regarding "welfare" or "social assistance." Political philos-ophy affects a person's preference for nature or nurture, difference or deficit, continuity or discontinuity. Using another example, one developmentalist explains, "Individual differences in aggression can be accounted for by genetic or social-ization differences, with politically conservative scientists tending to believe the former and more liberal scientists the latter" (Lewis, 1997, p. 102).

On a more personal level, all prospective parents wonder just what influence their nurturing might have: Are they as significant as psychoanalytic and learn-ing theories contend, or is the child's own thinking the determining factor, as cognitive theory might claim? Perhaps the emerging sociocultural or epigenetic systems theories can provide insight, attributing much of a child's behavior to either culture or genes. Indeed, for all three controversies, one can see that the theories aid us in contemplating ideas that our political, religious, or personality preferences might have ignored. In this way, at least, all five theories are useful for offering us new ideas to consider, even if we ultimately reject them. Develop-mental theories provide some perspective and values as a starting point. Scien-tific methods, as you learned in Chapter 1, guard against the undue influence of personal beliefs, and theories are one more tool toward the same goal.

Especially for Students Age 20 or So: The text cites teenage pregnancy as a controversial issue in which both nature and nurture are relevant. It is obvious how teenage pregnancy is partly nurture (influences of culture and family), but, from your experience, how could nature be involved?

Eclecticism and You

eclectic perspective The approach taken by most developmentalists, in which they apply aspects of each of the various theories of development rather than adhering exclusively to one theory.

Until a new grand theory is tested and established, most developmentalists will continue to take an **eclectic perspective.** That is, rather than adopt any one of these theories exclusively, they make selective use of many or all of them. When 45 leaders in the field were asked to identify their approach to developmental studies, "clear theoretical labels were hard to come by," with many describing themselves through some combination of terms, such as "cognitive social learning," "social interactive behaviorist," and even "social evolutionary cognitive behaviorism" (Horowitz, 1994, p. 243). The state of research in human development has been accurately characterized as "theoretical pluralism" because no single theory fully explains the behavior of humans as they go through life (Dixon & Lerner, 1999).

In later chapters, as you encounter elaborations and echoes of the five major theories and various minitheories, you will no doubt form your own opinion of the validity and usefulness of each. Probably you will also take an eclectic view— one that chooses the best from each theory to guide your exploration of development. You may even begin to devise a coherent, comprehensive, systematic approach of your own.

Response for Students Age 20 or So
(from page 61): The age at puberty, the strength of the sex drive, and the tendency to seek (or avoid) spontaneous adventure are all genetic. A particular person might reach puberty early, at about age 11, and have a powerful drive for sexual satisfaction and a zest for risky adventure, all because of genes. A person with those genetic impulses would be much more likely to become pregnant before age 20 than a person who experienced puberty late, has a relatively weak sexual drive, and is temperamentally cautious.

SUMMARY

What Theories Do

1. A theory provides a framework of general principles that can be used to guide research and explain observations. Each developmental theory interprets human development from a somewhat different perspective, but all developmental theories attempt to provide a context for understanding how individual experiences and behavior change over time. Theories are practical in that they aid inquiry, interpretation, and research.

Grand Theories

2. Psychoanalytic theory emphasizes that human actions and thoughts originate from powerful impulses and conflicts that often are not part of our conscious awareness. Freud, the founder of psychoanalytic theory, explained how sexual urges arise during childhood. Parents' reactions to conflicts associated with these urges have a lasting impact on personality.

3. Erikson's version of psychoanalytic theory emphasizes psychosocial contexts, with individuals shaped by the interaction of personal characteristics and social forces. Erikson described eight successive stages of psychosocial development, each of which involves a developmental crisis.

4. Behaviorists, or learning theorists, believe that the focus of psychologists' study should be behavior, which can be observed and measured. This theory seeks to discover the laws that govern the relationship between events and the reactions they produce.

5. Behaviorism emphasizes various forms of conditioning—a learning process. In classical conditioning, a neutral stimulus becomes associated with a meaningful stimulus, and eventually the neutral stimulus alone produces the response first associated with the meaningful stimulus. In operant conditioning, certain responses, called reinforcers, are used to make it more likely that certain behaviors will be repeated.

6. Social learning theory recognizes that much of human behavior is learned by observing the behavior of others. The basic process is modeling, in which we first observe a behavior and then repeat it. Generally, the person being observed is admirable in some way, or the behavior is one that the observer is motivated to repeat.

7. All theories lead to research that tests various hypotheses. Harlow's studies of mother love among baby monkeys revealed that comforting contact was more important than food in establishing the mother–infant bond.

8. Cognitive theorists believe that a person's thought processes have an important effect on his or her understanding of the world, and thus on the person's development. Piaget proposed that an individual's thinking develops through four age-related periods.

9. Piaget believed that cognitive development is an active and universal process. Curiosity is guided by the search for cognitive equilibrium, which is a person's ability to explain a new situation with existing understanding. When disequilibrium occurs, people develop cognitively by modifying their understanding to cover the new situation.

Emergent Theories

10. Sociocultural theory explains human development in terms of the guidance, support, and structure provided by culture. For Vygotsky, learning occurs through the social interactions learners share with more knowledgeable members of the society. They guide learners through the zone of proximal development.

11. Epigenetic systems theory begins by noting that genes are powerful and omnipresent, potentially affecting every aspect of development. This theory also stresses an ongoing interaction between the genes and environmental forces, which can range from prenatal toxins to lifelong stresses. This interaction can halt, modify, or strengthen the effects of the genes, both within the person and, over time, within the species.

12. Epigenetic systems theory also focuses on the systems, within the individual as well as the species, that support development. In one such system, infants are born with various drives and reflexes

that help ensure their survival, while adults are normally also equipped with innate predispositions to nurture babies, no matter what sacrifices might be required.

Comparisons and Controversies

13. Psychoanalytic, learning, cognitive, sociocultural, and epigenetic systems theories have each contributed to the understanding of human development, yet no one theory is broad enough to describe the full complexity and diversity of human experience.

14. Each of the five major theories reviewed here has a somewhat different position on the issues of development. The continuity–discontinuity controversy concerns the question of whether development occurs smoothly or in stages. The difference–deficit controversy asks when something that is unusual (a difference) becomes harmful (a deficit).

15. The nature–nurture controversy centers on how much influence heredity has on development, as compared to how much influence the environment has. Every researcher agrees, however, that both factors influence human development.

16. Each theory provides a useful perspective; none is complete in itself. Most developmentalists are eclectic, adopting aspects of various theories rather than following any single theory.

KEY TERMS

developmental theory (p. 35)
grand theories (p. 36)
minitheories (p. 36)
emergent theories (p. 36)
psychoanalytic theory (p. 36)
behaviorism (p. 40)
conditioning (p. 40)

classical conditioning (p. 40)
operant conditioning (p. 41)
reinforcement (p. 41)
social learning theory (p. 43)
modeling (p. 43)
self-efficacy (p. 44)
cognitive theory (p. 44)

cognitive equilibrium (p. 45)
sociocultural theory (p. 48)
apprenticeship in thinking
 (p. 49)
guided participation (p. 49)
zone of proximal development
 (p. 50)

epigenetic systems theory
 (p. 51)
selective adaptation (p. 52)
ethology (p. 54)
nature (p. 60)
nurture (p. 60)
eclectic perspective (p. 62)

KEY QUESTIONS

1. What functions does a good theory perform?

2. What is the major assumption of psychoanalytic theory?

3. What are the key differences between Freud's and Erikson's ideas concerning development?

4. What is the major focus of behaviorism?

5. What are the differences between classical conditioning and operant conditioning?

6. According to Piaget, how do periods of disequilibrium lead to mental growth?

7. What are the main differences among the grand theories?

8. According to sociocultural theory, how does development occur?

9. Give an example of guided participation that is not in the text.

10. According to epigenetic systems theorists, how can genetic instructions change?

11. What are the main differences between the two emergent theories?

12. What are the three main ongoing controversies in development?

13. Pick one controversy, and explain the different perspectives taken by the five theories.

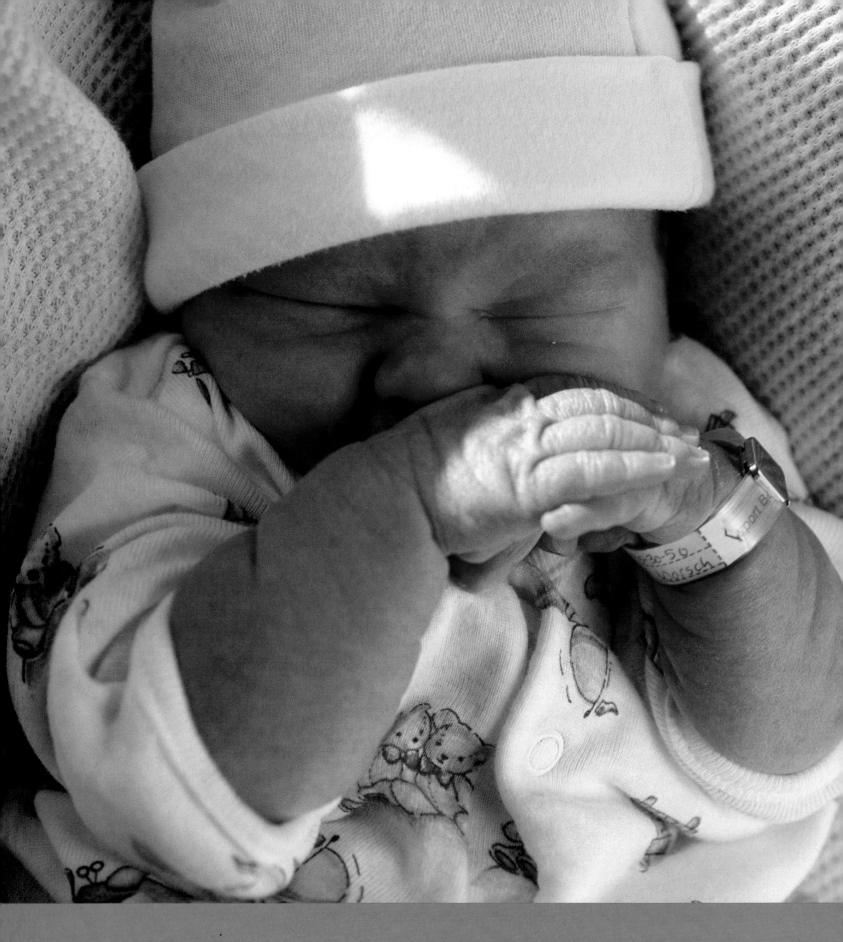

Part I

When considering the human life span, most people ignore or take for granted the time from conception through birth. Indeed, among all the nations of the world, China seems to have been the only one to include the prenatal period when reckoning age. Yet these 266 or so days could not be more crucial. On the very first day, for instance, our entire genetic heritage is set, affecting not only what we see when we look in the mirror but also many of the abilities, talents, and disabilities that characterize each of us. Survival is much more doubtful and growth much more rapid during the prenatal period than at any other time in our lives. At the end of prenatal development, birth usually provides more anticipation, worry, excitement, and joy on the part of parents than any other day of childhood. Indeed, the impact of the physiological and emotional events of that day can be felt for weeks, months, even years.

These early days, usually uncounted and underemphasized, are the focus of the next two chapters.

The Beginnings

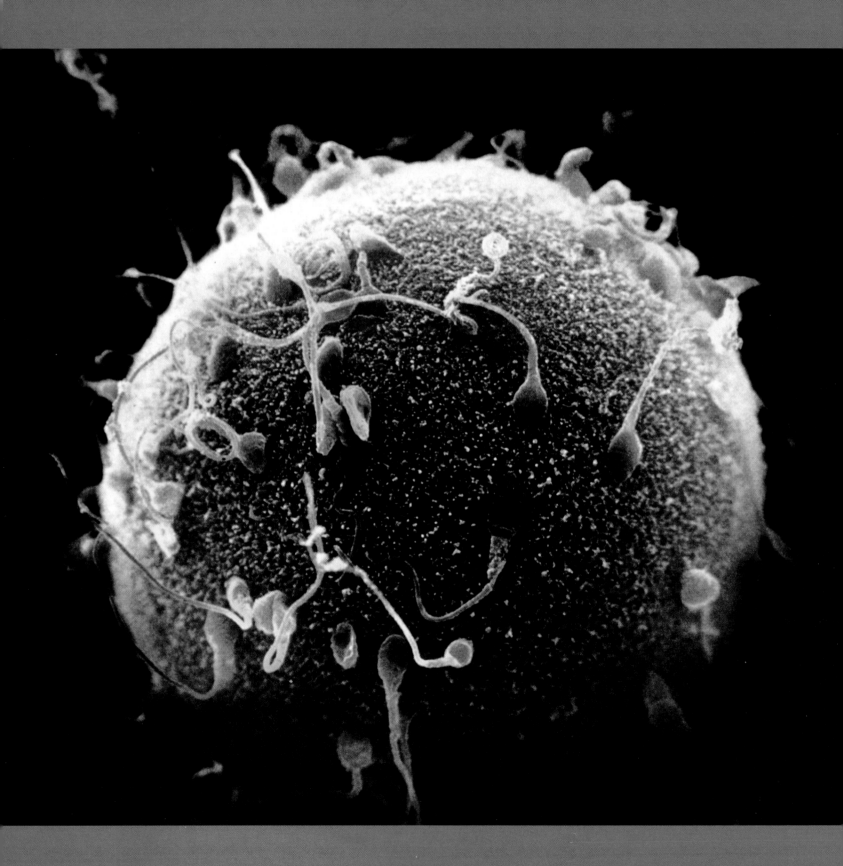

Heredity and Environment

Genetics has taken a lead role in the drama of human development. Prospective parents seek to predict which physical and psychological traits their children will inherit; the Human Genome Project promises to decipher the invisible genetic code that directs human growth; everyone consulting a doctor about any pain or peculiarity is questioned about ancestral and familial conditions; and anyone who studies child development realizes that genes are the foundation of all the growth we seek to understand.

Yet in many ways genetics remains a mystery, a plot difficult to follow, with strange twists and turns. This chapter goes behind the scenes to explain not only what genes are but how they work. Genes are pervasive and powerful, and you will learn more about the many ways in which their influence becomes apparent in each developing person.

Remember from Chapter 2, however, that genetic influence is actually *epigenetic*. Genes are influenced by their ongoing interaction with the *environment*, which includes everything nongenetic, from the nourishment of the fetus to the macrosystem of the growing child. The interaction between heredity and the environment, or between nature and nurture, is dynamic, complex, and varied. Indeed, "it may well be that outcome variability is built into individual development as a fact of nature" (Wachs, 2000). Rather than determining the course of our lives, genes are a major cause of the variability, diversity, and surprises that make human development the fascinating subject that it is. Understanding the basic facts about genes—what they are, where they are located, how they work together, and when they interact with the environment—is the topic of this chapter, one that you are likely to find surprising and fascinating.

Genetics: Foundations in Biology and Ethics

As you know from Chapter 1, a central tenet of human growth is *plasticity:* People are molded by their life experiences. Yet plasticity requires some raw material to be shaped, some basic substance to start the developmental process. Genes provide that raw material. Understanding them aids in understanding all past, present, and future generations and individuals, including me and you. How do your genes distinguish you from everyone else? How do they restrict, guide, and motivate you—in ways that your parents never wished or you yourself never imagined?

The general facts about child development and the specific questions about each of us lead directly to practical applications and ethical quandaries surrounding genetics—human cloning, selective abortion, surrogate parenthood, eugenics, disability accommodation, genetic testing, sex selection, donor gametes, infertility treatment, international adoption, to name just a few. We cannot duck these topics, because "once we take development seriously, we must also take genetics seriously" (Pennington, 2001). The question "What can humans become?" raises another question: "What *should* people become?"

Accepting people as they are, yet using genetic knowledge for the good of all humanity, has both ethical and logical pitfalls. To introduce this urgent topic, we look in on a couple who are arguing about the baby they are expecting.

A Case to Study

What Do People Live to Do?

John and Martha are in their 20s, both graduate students at Harvard, expecting their second child in five months. Martha's initial prenatal screening revealed abnormally low levels of alpha-fetoprotein (AFP). A low AFP level could indicate that her fetus has Down syndrome, in which each cell of the body has 47 chromosomes (instead of the usual 46) and which produces distinctive facial characteristics, serious health problems, and mental retardation. To recheck the AFP results (Down syndrome is rare when the parents are under 35) and to allow time for a more definitive test called amniocentesis, another blood test was immediately scheduled.

John met Martha at a café after a nurse drew the second blood sample, before the laboratory reported the new levels. Later, Martha wrote about their conversation.

"Did they tell you anything about the test?" John said. "What exactly is the problem?" . . .

"We've got a one in eight hundred and ninety-five shot at a retarded baby."

John smiled, "I can live with those odds."

I tried to smile back, but I couldn't. . . . I wanted to tell John about the worry in my gut. I wanted to tell him that it was more than worry—that it was a certainty. Then I realized all over again how preposterous that was. "I'm still a little scared."

He reached across the table for my hand. "Sure," he said, "That's understandable. But even if there is a problem, we've caught it in time. . . . The worst case scenario is that you might have to have an abortion, and that's a long shot. Everything's going to be fine."

. . . "I might *have to have* an abortion?" The chill inside me was gone. Instead I could feel my face flushing hot with anger. "Since when do you decide what I *have to* do with my body?"

John looked surprised. "I never said I was going to decide anything," he protested. "It's just that if the tests show something wrong with the baby, of course we'll abort. We've talked about this."

"What we've talked about," I told John in a low, danger-ous voice, "is that I am pro-choice. That means I decide

whether or not I'd abort a baby with a birth defect. . . . I'm not so sure of this."

"You used to be," said John.

"I know I used to be." I rubbed my eyes. I felt terribly con-fused. "But now . . . look, John, it's not as though we're decid-ing whether or not to have a baby. We're deciding what *kind* of baby we're willing to accept. If it's perfect in every way, we keep it. If it doesn't fit the right specifications, whoosh! Out it goes." . . .

John was looking more and more confused. "Martha, why are you on this soapbox? What's your point?"

"My point is," I said, "that I'm trying to get you to tell me what you think constitutes a 'defective' baby. What about . . . oh, I don't know, a hyperactive baby? Or an ugly one?"

"They can't test for those things and—"

"Well, what if they could?" I said. "Medicine can do all kinds of magical tricks these days. Pretty soon we're going to be aborting babies because they have the gene for alco-holism, or homosexuality, or manic depression. . . . Did you know that in China they abort a lot of fetuses just because they're female?" I growled. "Is being a girl 'defective' enough for you?"

"Look," he said, "I know I can't always see things from your perspective. And I'm sorry about that. But the way I see it, if a baby is going to be deformed or something, abortion is a way to keep everyone from suffering—*especially* the baby. It's like shooting a horse that's broken its leg. . . . A lame horse dies slowly, you know? . . . It dies in terrible pain. And it can't run anymore. So it can't enjoy life even if it doesn't die. Horses live to run; that's what they do. If a baby is born not being able to do what other people do, I think it's better not to prolong its suffering."

". . . And what is it," I said softly, more to myself than to John, "what is it that people do? What do we live to do, the way a horse lives to run?"

[Beck, 1999, pp. 132–133, 135]

The second AFP test came back low but in the normal range, "meaning there was no reason to fear that Adam had Down syndrome" (p. 137).

This episode reminds us of the subjective values and opinions that surround the objective facts about genetic differences. We will return to John and Martha, and to other values and opinions, later. First, however, let us outline those "objective facts about genetic differences."

From One Cell to Trillions

Human development begins very simply, when a male reproductive cell, or *sperm* (plural: *sperm*), penetrates the membrane of a female reproductive cell, or *ovum* (plural: *ova*). Each human **gamete** (the name for any reproductive cell, whether it comes from a male or female) contains more than a billion genetic instructions in the form of chemical codes.

At conception, when the sperm and ovum combine, the two gametes form a complete set of instructions for creating a person. Those instructions are not always followed to the letter. They must be read and interpreted, and the necessary components must be found. Genetic instructions begin by directing growth and become more complex as life unfolds (Johnston & Edwards, 2002).

Growth Begins

For the first hour or so after a sperm enters an ovum, the two cells maintain their separate identities, side by side, enclosed within the ovum's membrane. Suddenly they fuse, and a living cell called a **zygote** is formed: Two reproductive cells have literally become one, and the genetic material from one parent matches up with the genetic material from the other.

Within hours, the zygote begins the first stages of growth through a process of *duplication* and *division*. First, the combined genetic material from both gametes duplicates itself, forming two complete sets of the genetic code for that person. Then these two sets move toward opposite sides of the zygote, and the zygote divides neatly down the middle. Thus, the one-celled zygote has become two cells, each containing a complete set of the original genetic code. These two cells duplicate and divide to become four; these four, in turn, duplicate and divide to become eight; and so on.

At about the eight-cell stage, a third process, *differentiation*, is added to duplication and division. Cells begin to specialize, taking different forms and reproducing at various rates, depending on where in the growing mass they are. Before differentiation, any one of the cells could become a whole person; after differentiation, this is no longer true. The next nine months of development from a mass of cells to a newborn baby are described in Chapter 4. But now you need to know about genes and cells.

When you (or I, or any other person) were newborn, your body had about 10 trillion cells, almost half of them in your immature brain. By adulthood, your cells have increased to more than 100 trillion. But no matter how many cells you have, and no matter how much division, duplication, differentiation, and specialization has occurred, each body cell carries a copy of the complete genetic instructions inherited by the one-celled zygote. This explains why DNA testing of any body cell can identify "the real father" or "the guilty criminal" or "the long-lost twin" when the traditional methods of identification fail.

The Genetic Code

The basic unit of genetic instruction is the **gene.** A gene is a discrete segment of a **chromosome,** which is a molecule of *DNA* (*deoxyribonucleic acid*). Except for sperm and ova, every normal human cell has 23 pairs of chromosomes (46 chromosomes in all), which collectively carry between 30,000 and 40,000 distinct

gamete A reproductive cell; that is, a cell that can reproduce a new individual if it combines with a gamete from the other sex.

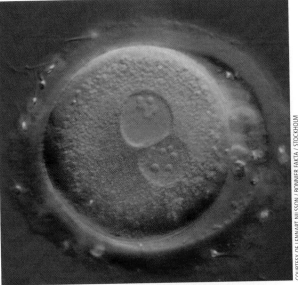

The Moment of Conception The ovum shown here is about to become a zygote. It has been penetrated by a single sperm, whose nucleus now lies next to the nucleus of the ovum. Shortly, the two nuclei will fuse, bringing together about 40,000 genes that will guide future development.

zygote The single cell formed from the fusing of a sperm and an ovum.

gene The basic unit for the transmission of heredity instructions.

chromosome A carrier of genes; one of the 46 molecules of DNA (in 23 pairs) that each cell of the body contains and that, together, contain all human genes.

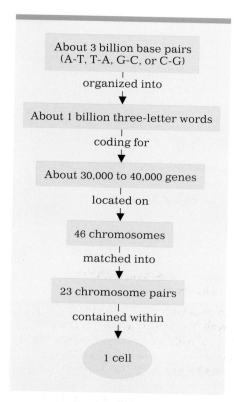

About 3 billion base pairs
(A-T, T-A, G-C, or C-G)

|
organized into
↓

About 1 billion three-letter words

|
coding for
↓

About 30,000 to 40,000 genes

|
located on
↓

46 chromosomes

|
matched into
↓

23 chromosome pairs

|
contained within
↓

1 cell

FIGURE 3.1 **What Every Human Cell Contains**

genetic code The sequence in which pairs of chemical bases appear along each segment of the DNA molecule.

Human Genome Project An international effort to map the complete human genetic code.

genes (see Figure 3.1). Each cell has the same DNA message. In fact, with rare exceptions, even when a human has an abnormal number of chromosomes (as in the 47 chromosomes of Down syndrome), every body cell still has those same chromosomes with those same genes.

The instructions from each gene are "written" in a chemical code made up of pairs of only four chemical *bases*—adenine, guanine, cytosine, and thymine, abbreviated A, G, C, and T, respectively. These chemical bases normally combine in only four pairings, A-T, T-A, G-C, and C-G, a fact that might seem to provide a very limited genetic vocabulary. In fact, there are approximately 3 billion base pairs in the DNA of every human and thousands of base pairs in every gene, which means that many, many sequences are possible.

On each gene the code letters are written in a particular sequence of three-letter words that direct the formation and combination of twenty amino acids. These amino acids, in turn, direct the synthesis of hundreds of different kinds of proteins, including enzymes that serve as the body's building blocks and regulators. Following genetic instructions, certain cells become neurons (brain cells), others become the lens of the eye, others become the valves of the heart, and so on throughout the body.

The influence of genes doesn't stop there. Through some sort of on–off switching mechanism, genes control life itself, instructing cells to grow, to repair damage, to take in nourishment, to multiply, to atrophy, to die. Even certain kinds of cognitive development involve genes that switch on at particular ages, propelling maturation in specific areas of the brain (Plomin et al., 2001).

The Human Genome Project

The precise nature of a gene's instructions is determined by the **genetic code**—that is, the sequence in which the pairs of chemical bases appear along each segment of the DNA molecule. The **Human Genome Project** is an international effort to map the complete genetic code. (A *genome* is all the genetic information, or hereditary material, that an organism possesses.) Originally scheduled to be completed by 2005, the Human Genome Project progressed so rapidly that two rough drafts were ready in 2000. The two drafts are similar overall, but different in details; both are still missing several segments, and both have already been enormously useful in locating genetic disabilities and developing treatments.

We now know that about 99 percent of all the genes are basically the same for all humans worldwide. Moreover, we share this genetic base with many other species of animals. This makes it easy to learn more about people by studying mice, monkeys, and even flies and worms.

For example, every mammal embryo is genetically commanded to make seven neck bones. Because of the influence of other genes, those seven bones in a whale's neck become flat, thin disks; those in a giraffe's neck become elongated; and those in a human's neck are in between—probably more than we would need if our bodies were perfectly designed to avoid neck injuries, but adequate as a template to accommodate mammalian diversity (Barnett, 1998). Thus, to learn about human neck injuries, we can study the neck of any mammal.

Reading the Code A small segment of a DNA molecule is sequenced into bands, with one color for each of the base pairs. These pairs direct the synthesis of enzymes and proteins that, in turn, direct the formation of a living creature. One small change in a gene might result in a physical anomaly or a mental quirk. A few hundred different genes might result in a giraffe instead of a whale.

Similarly, the gene that produces the legs of a butterfly is exactly the same gene that shapes the four legs of a cat, the many legs of a centipede, and the two legs of a person. The differences between your legs and those of other creatures are governed by a regulator gene that advises the leg gene as to the particular shape and number of legs to make (Pennisi & Roush, 1997).

The regulator genes, which guide growth and development throughout the body, make up much of the 1 percent of genetic differentiation between humans and other animals, and between one human and another. One percent may not seem like a lot, but it means that "about 3 million of our 3 billion base pairs differ among people" (Plomin et al., 2001, p. 51). A minor difference can have a major impact, as seen with genes that vary by just a letter or two.

"Reading" the Genome

Matt Ridley, who has written extensively on genetics, has provided a useful analogy between the human genome and a book.

> Imagine that the genome is a book.
>
> There are twenty-three chapters, called CHROMOSOMES.
> Each chapter contains several thousand stories, called GENES.
> Each story is made up of paragraphs, called EXONS, which are interrupted by advertisements called INTRONS.
>
> Each paragraph is made up words, called CODONS.
> Each word is written in letters called BASES.
>
> There are one billion words in the book, which makes it . . . as long as 800 Bibles. If I read the genome out to you at the rate of one word per second for eight hours a day, it would take me a century. If I wrote out the human genome, one letter per millimetre, my text would be as long as the River Danube. This is a gigantic document, an immense book, a recipe of extravagant length, and it all fits inside the microscopic nucleus of a tiny cell that fits easily upon the head of a pin.
>
> - [Ridley, 1999, p. 7]

A normal alteration is called an **allele,** one of several possible letter sequences that some genes have. Note that everyone has one allele or another of those variable genes; it is not that there is a standard, normal version and a mutant form. An allele makes it less likely that you will be a flaming redhead, a fluent reader, or senile when you are very old. Other alleles make it more likely that those things will happen. An allele even makes you more or less fearful (Hariri et al., 2002)

allele One of the normal versions of a gene that has several possible sequences of base pairs.

Continuity and Diversity

Paradoxically, the common and universal characteristics of human development are contrasted with unique and distinctive ones. Both are always apparent and both are crucial. Interpretation of developmental events is continually switching from universal to unique, from half-full to half-empty, depending on whether one prefers to emphasize that humans are all one species or that each human is an individual.

Now we consider some aspects of this paradox, as manifested in chromosomes, in sex determination, in species-specific characteristics, and in genetic diversity (as it relates to twins and as it is achieved through alternate means of conception).

Chromosomes: Same Cells, Different People

As we have noted, each human usually has 46 chromosomes, which are duplicated in every body cell except gametes. The chromosomes are arranged in 23 distinct pairs. One member of each pair is inherited from the mother, and the

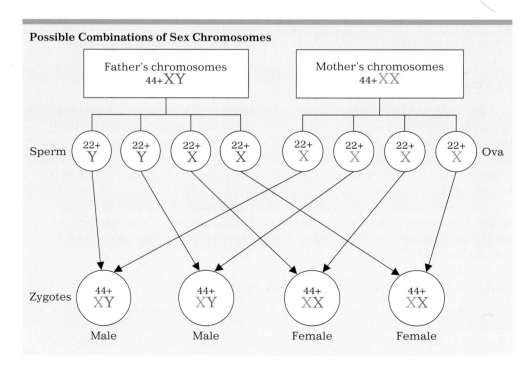

Mapping the Karyotype A *karyotype* portrays a person's chromosomes. To create a karyotype, a cell is grown in a laboratory, magnified, and then usually photographed. The photo is cut into pieces and rearranged, matching the pairs of chromosomes, from pair 1, the largest pair (*top left*) to pair 23, here the XY of a normal male (*bottom right*).

? *Observational Quiz* (see answer, page 74): Is this the karyotype of a normal human?

twenty-third pair The chromosome pair that, in humans, determines the zygote's (and hence the person's) sex, among other things.

XX A twenty-third pair that consists of two X-shaped chromosomes, one from the mother and one from the father.

XY A twenty-third pair that consists of one X-shaped chromosome from the mother and one Y-shaped chromosome from the father.

other one is inherited from the father. When the chromosomes pair off, the genes pair off, too, again with one from each parent (although, since many genes can have several alleles, a specific gene from one parent may not exactly match its mate from the other parent).

This very specific genetic and chromosomal pairing is encoded for life in every cell—with one important exception. When the human body makes sperm or ova, cell division occurs in such a way that each gamete receives only one member of each chromosome pair. This is why sperm and ova each have only 23 chromosomes: to ensure that when they combine, the new organism will have a total of 46 chromosomes. In other words, genetically, we are whatever we are: Every cell of your body, from the soles of your feet to the lining of your gut to the dancing neurons of your brain, contains the distinct code that makes you you, and every cell of my body contains the unique code that makes me me. And half of every cell's code is from your mother and half from your father.

The one exception becomes relevant if you and I reproduce. My gametes each contain only half of my genes; your gametes each contain only half of your genes. This means that our children would be neither yours nor mine but ours—half you, half me. It also guarantees genetic diversity in each child, male or female.

Sex Determination

Of the 23 pairs of human chromosomes, 22 are closely matched pairs called auto-somes, with the two chromosomes of each pair containing similar genes in al-most identical positions and sequence. The **twenty-third pair,** which is the pair that determines the individual's sex (among other things), is a different case. In the female, the twenty-third pair is composed of two large X-shaped chromo-somes. Accordingly, it is designated **XX**. In the male, the twenty-third pair is composed of one large X-shaped chromosome and one much smaller Y-shaped chromosome. It is designated **XY**.

Obviously, because a female's twenty-third chromosome pair is XX, every ovum that her body creates will contain either one X or the other—but always an X. And because a male's twenty-third pair is XY, half of his sperm will contain an X chromosome and half will contain a Y. That Y chromosome (but not the X) contains a gene (called SRY) that directs a developing fetus to make male organs.

FIGURE 3.2 Determining a Zygote's Sex Any given couple can produce four possible combinations of sex chromosomes; two lead to female children, and two to male. In terms of the future person's sex, it does not matter which of the mother's Xs the zygote inherited. All that matters is whether the father's Y sperm or X sperm fertilized the ovum. However, for X-linked conditions it matters a great deal, since typically one, but not both, of the mother's Xs carries the trait.

Possible Combinations of Sex Chromosomes

Father's chromosomes
44+XY

Mother's chromosomes
44+XX

Sperm

22+Y   22+Y   22+X   22+X   22+X   22+X   22+X   22+X   Ova

Zygotes

44+XY   44+XY   44+XX   44+XX

Male   Male   Female   Female

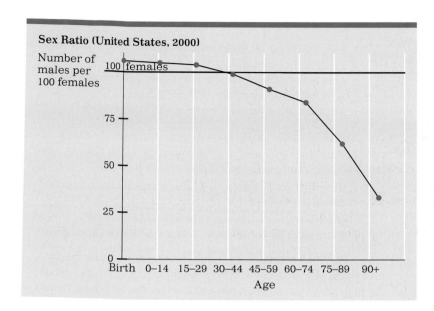

Sex Ratio (United States, 2000)

Number of males per 100 females

FIGURE 3.3 **Too Many Baby Boys?** Worldwide, slightly more males than females are born each year. Given the slightly higher rate of death among males in childhood (and assuming no unequal, major killer, such as war), the result is a roughly equal number of men and women of reproductive age. In the past, many women died in childbirth, whereas today heart attacks kill many more men than women—which is the main reason why the sex ratio now favors women after age 45. (Men are also somewhat more likely than women to die from other causes.) What would be the effect on marriage and divorce rates, on health costs, on crime statistics, and on population growth if couples had far more boys than girls, or vice versa?

Thus, the critical factor in the determination of a zygote's sex is which sperm reaches the ovum first—a Y sperm, creating a male (XY), or an X sperm, creating a female (XX) (see Figure 3.2).

Every now and then, a gene carried by a man renders either his X sperm or his Y sperm immobile, so that he can father only sons or only daughters. Other factors can also affect the survival of male or female embryos. However, the overall sex ratio (the proportion of males to females in a given population) at birth has always been roughly equal, and females increasingly outlive males with advancing age (see Figure 3.3). Now our expanding knowledge of genetics allows humans to alter the sex ratio dramatically. Whether or not to use that knowledge is an ethical issue, as the following Changing Policy feature explains.

Changing Policy

Too Many Boys?

Unless wars, epidemics, or other catastrophes occur, about an equal number of men and women reach young adulthood, the prime reproductive age. Should nations, or individuals, be allowed to change the natural sex ratio?

Some have tried. Numerous societies have allowed female infanticide (a practice so common that it had to be explicitly forbidden in the Koran) or have allowed husbands to divorce or even kill wives who produced only daughters (as did England's Henry VIII). For centuries, pregnant women were advised to eat certain foods, sleep on one side, or pray to the moon to make sure their baby was a boy or girl.

Today we know better:

- Sperm, not ova, determine a baby's sex.
- Each zygote is already XX or XY; no prenatal action can change that.

Moreover, we now have the potentially dangerous ability to discover, via prenatal testing, whether an embryo is destined to be male or female. This knowledge has been put to use in China, where, each year between 1990 and 1993, more than a million couples aborted female fetuses because sons are favored and couples are forbidden to have more than one child. In reaction, the Chinese government has outlawed abortion for the purpose of sex selection; as a result, virtually all the Chinese infants available for international adoption are girls. The same problem emerged in India, where laws against sex selection exist but are not enforced. In the state of Punjab, only 79 females are born for every 100 males (Duggar, 2001).

Couples in the United States who do not wish to abort have another alternative. For decades, cattle breeders have successfully used sperm sorting and artificial insemination to produce only male or only female calves, depending on whether beef or milk is the desired product. A similar sperm-sorting technique is available experimentally for humans and is said to have a 95 percent success rate (Grifo et al., 1994).

Do we need a social policy to regulate this new technology? Before answering, consider the social consequences if only half as many girls were born as are born today:

In family life

- Fewer single mothers, fewer widows, more never-married men
- Weaker family ties between siblings, parents and children, grandparents and grandchildren (because women maintain the family network)
- More children per woman, fewer children per man
- More children with learning disabilities, hyperactivity, conduct disorders; fewer adolescents with depression, eating disorders

In economic life

- More engineers, architects, billionaires; fewer nurses, teachers, secretaries
- Greater demand for fast food, fast cars, guns, prostitutes
- Less demand for fashionable clothes, household furnishings, kitchen equipment
- More violent crimes of all kinds, and thus a greater need for police, judges, prisons

In health care

- Lower average life span, more accidental deaths, more suicides, more homicides
- Less ongoing medical care; fewer specialists in gynecology, arthritis, gerontology; fewer nursing homes
- More people suffering from drug and alcohol abuse

In community life

- Increased attendance at professional sports events; decreased attendance at libraries
- Increased participation in sports teams; decreased participation in churches
- More wars; fewer day-care centers
- More votes for conservative policies; fewer for liberal ones

Do you disagree, insisting that cultural practices, not biological sex, determine who participates in athletics or religion or politics? Your protest is valid for all fifteen items. Neither genes nor chromosomes determine behavior, although sex-linked hormones do make one sex more likely to act in certain ways than the other (Ridley, 1999).

If you had only one child, would you prefer a son or a daughter? The Ethics Committee of the American Society for Reproductive Health (2001) reported that sperm sorting is still experimental and should not have "widespread use" but may be permitted in some cases. What do you think?

The Human Species

The vast majority of each person's genes are identical to those of every other human being, male or female, related or not (Plomin et al., 2001). As a result of the instructions carried by genes, each new member of the human race shares certain characteristics with everyone else, alive or dead or not yet born:

- Common physical structures (such as the pelvic alignment that allows humans to walk upright)
- Common behavioral tendencies (such as the urge to communicate through language)
- Common reproductive potential (allowing any male and female human to produce a new member of the species)

These species-specific characteristics, and thousands of others, have been fashioned throughout a long evolutionary history, promoting survival by enabling humans to live successfully on Earth (Ridley, 1999).

The remainder of each person's genes differ in various ways from those of other individuals. Such a difference usually takes the form of an allele that has only one or two changes in the thousands of letter combinations. The diversity that these small variations in the genetic code provide, over generations, is essential for human adaptation to new environments and needs. Thus, the fact that each human differs genetically from others means that our species is able to survive as conditions and circumstances change. For example, some genetic variants confer special resistance to malaria, cholera, tuberculosis, or alcoholism (Ridley, 1999).

Answer to Observational Quiz (from page 72): No, there are 24 pairs here. This photo shows the two different possibilities for the twenty-third pair. (The normal female XX is just to the left of the normal male XY.)

Our diversity also benefits the entire community through specialization and cooperation. Because each of us inherits specific talents and abilities, each of us is better at some tasks or activities than at others. By specializing in those particular tasks, performing them for others as well as for ourselves, together we achieve more than if we all had to be our own priest, artist, carpenter, farmer, cook, doctor, teacher, and so on. We gain intellectually as well, by exchanging and combining ideas and perspectives. Both our commonalties and our diversities allow the survival of the human species.

The Mechanisms of Diversity

Given that each sperm or ovum from a particular parent contains only 23 chromosomes, how can every conception be genetically unique? The answer is that when the chromosome pairs divide during the formation of gametes, chance alone determines which one of each pair will wind up in one gamete and which in the other. A vast number of chromosome combinations are possible. According to the laws of probability, there are, in fact, 2^{23}—that is, about 8 million—possible combinations. In other words, approximately 8 million chromosomally different ova or sperm can be produced by a single individual.

In addition, just before a chromosome pair in a man's or woman's body divides to form sperm or ova, corresponding segments of the pair are sometimes broken off and exchanged, altering the genetic composition of both pair members. Through the new combinations it produces, this *crossing-over* of genes adds greatly to genetic diversity. In addition, gene strands can replicate, repeat, mutate, duplicate, and even turn themselves upside down—often creating a nonviable zygote in the process, but sometimes creating a somewhat unusual child (Miller & Therman, 2001).

All things considered, a given mother and father can form more than 64 trillion genetically distinct offspring, all full brothers and sisters but each quite different from the others. Outsiders might see strong family resemblances in siblings (once a neighbor said my four children were "like four peas in a pod"). But every parent knows that each child is unlike the others. It is no exaggeration to say that every zygote is unique. No wonder it is sometimes said that the parents of one child believe in nurture but the parents of two or more children believe in nature (Wright, 1998). Siblings do not react the same way to the same parental behavior, because each child has his or her own genetic instructions.

Twins Although every zygote is genetically unique, not every newborn is. In some pregnancies, the growing cluster of cells splits apart in the early stages of duplication and division, creating two or four or even eight identical, independent clusters. These cell clusters become **monozygotic twins** (identical twins) or monozygotic quadruplets or monozygotic octuplets, so named because they originated from one (*mono*) zygote.

Because they originated from the same zygote, monozygotic multiple births share identical genetic instructions for physical appearance, psychological traits, vulnerability to diseases, and everything else. Every letter of their genetic code is the same, including alleles and mutations. They are natural, original clones. If conception occurs in a laboratory instead of inside a woman's body, it is technically possible to split a human organism at the two- or four- or eight-cell stage. These monozygotic multiples could be implanted in the uterus. At the moment, such cloning is considered unethical and illegal, and the natural incidence of monozygotic twins (about 1 in every 270 births) is holding steady for every ethnic group, in every nation, in mothers of every age.

It is even possible to take a cell from a living adult animal, place it in a medium to grow, and then implant it to develop and be born—a clone of the original, as has occurred in sheep, mice, and cats. Human cloning is illegal for

Any Monozygotic Twins Here? Sometimes twins are obviously dizygotic, as when they are of different sexes or, like the girls on the bottom, differ notably in coloring, size, and perhaps visual acuity. However, sometimes dizygotic twins can look a lot alike, just as two siblings born a year or two apart can share many physical characteristics.

? *Observational Quiz* (see answer, page 76): What do the similarities and differences of the boys in the top photo suggest about their zygosity?

monozygotic twins Twins who have identical genes because they were formed from one zygote that split into two identical organisms very early in development.

dizygotic twins Twins who were formed when two separate ova were fertilized by two separate sperm at roughly the same time. Such twins share about half their genes, like any other siblings.

!Answer to Observational Quiz (from page 75): They are almost monozygotic. Their similarities include every obvious genetic trait—coloring, timing of tooth loss, thickness of lips, and shape of the ears and chin. Their differences include exactly the kinds that might be imposed by parents who have trouble distinguishing one child from the other—the color of their eyeglass frames and the length of their hair.

infertile Referring to a couple who are unable to produce a baby after at least a year of trying.

assisted reproductive technology (ART) A general term for the various techniques designed to help couples conceive.

in vitro fertilization (IVF) A technique for helping couples conceive in which ova are surgically removed from a woman, mixed with sperm, and inserted into the woman's uterus once viable zygotes have formed.

ethical reasons, among them that many deaths occur before one clone survives (IFFS Surveillance, 2001), and animal clones are not normally healthy.

Few twins are monozygotic. **Dizygotic twins** (fraternal twins) begin life as two separate zygotes created by the fertilization of two ova at roughly the same time. Dizygotic conceptions may occur as frequently as one in every six pregnancies, but usually only one twin develops past the embryo stage. Dizygotic births occur naturally about once in every 60 births, with considerable variation among ethnic groups. (Women from Nigeria, for example, spontaneously produce dizygotic newborns about once in every 25 births; women from England, once in 100; and women from Japan, once in 700 [Gall, 1996]). Age is also a factor: Women in their late 30s are three times as likely to have dizygotic twins as women in their early 20s (Mange & Mange, 1999). Dizygotic twins share no more genes than do any other offspring of the same parents; that is, they share about 50 percent of the genes governing individual differences. They may not be of the same sex or look like each other, or they may look a great deal alike, just as non-twin brothers and sisters sometimes do.

Other multiple births, such as triplets and quadruplets, may likewise be monozygotic, dizygotic, trizygotic, quadrazygotic, and so on (or even some combinations of these). Over the past decade, the incidence of multiple births from separate zygotes has doubled in most medically advanced nations because of the increased use of fertility drugs and other methods of helping infertile couples have children. Indeed, the rate of triplet births has increased by 500 percent since 1980 in the United States (Jones & Schnorr, 2001).

Generally, the more embryos that develop together in one uterus, the smaller, less mature, and more vulnerable each one is. This means that the increase in multiple births, which has produced many happy couples, has increased medical costs, infant mortality, and the incidence of children with special needs. For this reason, Finland limits to two the number of zygotes that can be implanted at one time. The limit is three in Norway and four in several other nations. The United States has no legal limit, and that raises more ethical questions (IFFS Surveillance, 2001).

Alternate Means of Conception Between 2 and 30 percent of all couples are **infertile,** defined as unable to produce a baby after at least a year of trying. (As a result of cultural practices and inadequate medical care, "infertility varies from country to country and from cohort to cohort" [Bentley & Mascie-Taylor, 2000, p. 1]). In developed nations, many such couples turn to **assisted reproductive technology (ART),** which employs dozens of techniques to help couples conceive. One is **in vitro fertilization (IVF):** Ova are surgically removed from a woman and mixed with sperm; if viable zygotes begin to duplicate and divide, some are inserted into the uterus and the pregnancy proceeds normally. IVF is now "routine" (Fishel et al., 2000) and results in delivery of at least one newborn about 30 percent of the time (American Society for Reproductive Medicine, 2002), for a total of almost a million children in at least 40 nations since the first "test-tube" baby was born in 1978. If IVF produces several healthy embryos, all of them could be inserted, some could be frozen for later use, some could be used for research, or some could be destroyed; various nations, clinics, and couples make the full range of choices (IFFS Surveillance, 2001).

A related, newer (1992) procedure is already almost routine: injecting one viable sperm into an ovum in vitro as a way of overcoming male infertility (Bentley & Mascie-Taylor, 2000). (Males are the primary cause of about 40 percent of cases of infertility, females account for another 40 percent, and the remaining 20 percent are mutual or undetermined [Diamond et al., 1999]).

Other types of ART include separating biological parenthood from child rearing. It is possible for a woman to donate an ovum and a man to donate sperm, for the resulting embryos to be inserted into the uterus of another woman, who relinquishes the newborn to be raised by yet another mother and/or father, who may or may not be married. At birth, the child has three mothers and two fathers; later marriages and divorces could mean even more parents. The following explores the complications that infertility and ART may produce.

In Person

Whose Baby Is It?

Many questions are raised by assisted reproductive technology. At the broadest level are questions regarding rights and obligations:

- Should third-party donors, whether of sperm, ova, or wombs, have any parental rights?
- Should ART be available to everyone, no matter what their marital status, sexual orientation, lifestyle, age, or motives?
- Does an embryo conceived in vitro have a right to be implanted rather than frozen and destroyed after five years (as law in England requires)?
- If a woman, through ART, conceives so many embryos that they probably cannot survive, is she obligated or forbidden to abort some of them to save the others?
- Do children have the right to know if the parents who raise them are not their biological parents?
- Does society, through laws, religious prohibitions, or medical ethics, have the right to allow or forbid any form of ART?

Compassionate, thoughtful people—including developmentalists—differ widely in their responses to these legal and ethical issues. A survey of 39 developed nations found that some outlaw practices that others encourage (IFFS Surveillance, 2001). However, all agree that the answer to the question "Whose baby is it?" involves not just the mother or father but also the society that developed the laws and procedures that allowed the birth through ART.

ART also gives rise to economic questions. Even though infertility is more common among poorer adults, fertility options become more readily available as income rises. In the United States, the average cost of having a baby through IVF is about $32,000 if the woman is under age 35 and $90,000 if she is older (Hughes & Giacomi, 2001), which puts it beyond the reach of many couples. In other countries, national medical care covers some of the costs, which means doctors decide who qualifies for the procedure.

Similar economic issues involve selling gametes, "renting" a womb, and international adoption. It is usually low-income, unmarried women who carry a fetus for someone else, in exchange for expenses and a fee. And when adoption takes place across national borders, children from poor, politically unstable regions are transferred to families in wealthier, more powerful communities. International adoptions cost between $15,000 and $50,000, with almost all of that money going to lawyers, adoption agencies, temporary guardians, government officials, airfare, and other expenses, and almost none to birth parents (M. S. Rosenthal, 1996).

One final question: Should laws, medical ethics, and contemporary culture encourage infertile individuals to willingly, even obsessively, incur great financial cost (as well as psychic stress and, sometimes, physical pain) in attempting to have their own biological children?

The following quotes attest to the devastating effect that infertility can have on the individual:

Infertility takes the whole person. I used to feel attractive; I used to feel like I had a wonderful personality; I used to feel like I was smart; I used to feel like I could have a child if I wanted a child. And now all those things are shattered.

[quoted in Sandelowski, 1993]

I just cannot imagine ever feeling good about anything again. I do not even know if my husband will stay with me when he realizes that children are not an option for us. My guess is he will find someone else who will be able to give him a baby. Since I cannot do that, I cannot imagine that he would be happy with me. I am not happy with me.

[quoted in Deveraux & Hammerman, 1998]

Do not be too quick to criticize those who pursue the unconventional, irrational, and perhaps selfish quest for parenthood. In addition to the sociocultural assumptions and cognitive processes that encourage contemporary couples to seek alternative means of conception, the human species has a powerful biological impulse to pass genes on to the next generation. As one infertile woman explained:

When you take away being able to have a child biologically, it is like having to face death—almost like having half of you die. Having kids is the main way that people deal with the fact that they are mortal.

[quoted in Hodder, 1997]

There is a genetic imperative to procreate, an urge that is crucial to the survival of the species (Barkow et al., 1992; Buss, 1994). As epigenetic systems theory (discussed in

Chapter 2) would explain, not everyone feels this biological need, nor should everyone have children. But those who are fertile, or who are happily child-free, may be too judgmental about other people's reactions to "one of nature's cruelest tricks, infertility" (Cooper-Hilbert, 1998).

The rates of infertility vary dramatically by nation, with a rate of 30 percent in some African nations too poor to pro-vide routine gynecological care to their citizens (Caldwell & Caldwell, 2000). Worldwide, most infertile couples can be helped by ART if they get assistance while they are under age 35, but few can afford it (Fishel et al., 2000; Hughes & Giacomi, 2001). Is this fair? And is it fair that some children are neglected and unloved while some adults go through extreme difficulty and major expense to conceive their own?

From Genotype to Phenotype

As we have seen, conception brings together, from both parents, genetic instructions concerning every human characteristic. Exactly how do these instructions influence the specific traits that a given offspring inherits? The answer is usually quite complex, because most traits are both **polygenic**—that is, affected by many genes—and **multifactorial**—that is, influenced by many factors, including factors in the environment. This is particularly true for the genes that affect our most important organ, the brain (Pennington, 2001).

To grasp the complexity of genetic influences, we must first distinguish between a person's genetic inheritance—his or her genetic *potential*—and the actual *expression* of that inheritance in the person's physiology, physical appearance, and behavioral tendencies. The sum total of all the genes a person inherits is the **genotype** (the genetic potential). The genotype is present in each zygote and on every nonreproductive cell of a person's body. Many genes on the genotype never affect the actual person, however.

The sum total of all the actual, expressed traits that result from the genes—including physical traits such as bushy eyebrows and nonphysical traits such as a hunger for excitement—is the person's **phenotype** (the genetic expression). The phenotype is what can be observed by looking at a person, by analyzing the person's body chemistry, or by noting the person's behavior. Thus, everything from memory to madness is part of the phenotype.

Clearly, we all have many genes in our genotypes that are not apparent in our phenotypes. In genetic terms, we are **carriers** of these unexpressed genes; that is, we "carry" them in our DNA and can pass them on to our sperm or ova and thus to our offspring. When a zygote inherits a gene that was only carried (not expressed) by one parent, the zygote will have that gene in the genotype. That gene may then be expressed in the phenotype or may simply be carried again, with a chance of affecting the next generation, if other genes and the environment make expression in the phenotype possible.

Gene–Gene Interaction

Whether or not a genetic trait becomes expressed in the phenotype is determined by two levels of interaction:

■ Interaction among the proteins synthesized from the specific amino acids coded by the genes that affect the trait
■ Ongoing interaction between the genotype and the environment

We will look first at interactions among the genes themselves.

polygenic Referring to inherited traits that are influenced by many genes, rather than by a single gene.

multifactorial Referring to inherited traits that are influenced by many factors, including factors in the environment, rather than by genetic influences alone.

genotype A person's entire genetic inheritance, including genes that are not expressed in the person.

phenotype All the genetic traits, including physical characteristics and behavioral tendencies, that are expressed in a person.

carrier A person who has a gene in his or her genotype that is not evident as part of the phenotype but that can be passed on to the person's offspring.

Additive Genes

One common pattern of interaction among genes begins with an **additive gene.** When genes interact additively, the phenotype reflects the contributions of all the genes that are involved. The many genes that affect height, hair curliness, and skin color, for instance, usually interact in an additive fashion.

Consider an unlikely scenario: A tall man whose parents and grandparents were all very tall marries a short woman whose parents and grandparents were all very short. Assume that every one of his height genes is for tallness and that hers are all for shortness. The couple's children will inherit tall genes via the father's sperm and short genes via the mother's ova. Because the genes affecting height interact additively, the children will be of middling height (assuming that their nutrition and physical health are adequate). None of them will be as tall as their father or as short as their mother, because each will have at least one gene for tallness and one gene for shortness, somehow "averaged" together.

In actuality, most people have both kinds of ancestors—relatively tall ones and relatively short ones—so children are often taller or shorter than both their parents. My daughter Rachel is of average height, which is shorter than my husband or me, but taller than either grandmother. Rachel must have inherited a grandmother's shortness genes from our genotypes, even though it is not apparent in our phenotypes. How any additive trait turns out depends on all the contributions of whichever genes (half from each parent's varied genotype) a child happens to inherit. Every additive gene that is on a person's genotype has some impact on the phenotype. I myself am tall because my father was very tall; I would have been even taller if my mother had not been so short.

Dominant and Recessive Genes

Less common are *nonadditive patterns,* in which the phenotype shows the influence of one gene much more than that of others. One kind of nonadditive pattern is the *dominant–recessive pattern.* When a gene pair interacts according to this pattern, the phenotype reveals the influence of the more powerful gene, called the **dominant gene.** The other, weaker gene, the **recessive gene,** is not expressed in any obvious way.

Sometimes the dominant gene completely controls the characteristic and the recessive gene is merely carried, with its influence not evident at all in the phenotype. In other instances, the outcome reflects *incomplete dominance,* with the phenotype influenced primarily, but not exclusively, by the dominant gene.

Hundreds of physical characteristics are determined according to the dominant–recessive pattern (with some epigenetic modification due to environmental factors and the influence of other genes). Blood types A and B are both dominant and O is recessive, leading to a complex relationship of genotype and phenotype in blood inheritance. (See Appendix A.) Brown eyes are also said to be dominant over blue eyes, and many genetic diseases are recessive. However, with eye color and many diseases, additive interactions are also apparent.

X-Linked Genes

Some genes are called **X-linked** because they are located only on the X chromosome. If an X-linked gene is recessive—as are the genes for most forms of color blindness, many allergies, several diseases, and some learning disabilities—the fact that it is on the X chromosome is critical. Recall that males have only one X chromosome. Thus, whatever recessive genes a male happens to inherit on his X chromosome cannot be counterbalanced or dominated by genes on his second X chromosome—he has no second X. Any recessive genes on his X chromosome will be expressed in his phenotype. This explains why traits

additive gene A gene that, through interaction with other genes, affects a specific trait (such as skin color or height).

THOMAS DiGORY / STOCKPHOTOS / THE IMAGE BANK

Skin Color Is Inherited But . . . Using "black," "white," "red," and "yellow" to denote human skin color is misleading, because humans actually have thousands of skin tones, each resulting from the combination of many genes, and none of them is one of these four colors. Depending on which half of each parent's skin-color genes children happen to inherit, each child can be paler, ruddier, lighter, darker, more sallow, more olive, or more freckled than either parent. This is particularly apparent in many African-American families, like this one, whose ancestors came from at least three continents.

dominant gene The stronger of an interacting pair of genes.

recessive gene The weaker of an interacting pair of genes.

X-linked Referring to a gene that is on the X chromosome.

Especially for History Students: Some genetic diseases may have changed the course of history. For instance, the last czar of Russia had four healthy daughters and one son with hemophilia. Once called the royal disease, hemophilia is X-linked. How could this rare condition affect the monarchies of Russia, England, Austria, Germany, and Spain?

Inheritance of an X-Linked Recessive Trait
The phenotypes on lines 1 and 2 are normal because their genes are normal. Those on lines 3 and 4 are normal because the abnormal X-linked gene is recessive and the normal gene is dominant. Those on lines 5 and 6 are color-blind because they have no dominant, normal X.

TABLE 3.1 **The 23rd Pair and X-Linked Color Blindness**

X indicates an X chromosome with the X-linked gene for color blindness

23rd Pair	Phenotype	Genotype	Next Generation
1. XX	Normal woman	Not a carrier	No color blindness from mother.
2. XY	Normal man	Normal X from mother	No color blindness from father.
3. XX	Normal woman	Carrier from father	Half her children will inherit her X. The girls with her X will be carriers, the boys with her X will be color-blind.
4. XX	Normal woman	Carrier from mother	Half her children will inherit her X. The girls with her X will be carriers, the boys with her X will be color-blind.
5. XY	Color-blind man	Inherited from mother	All his daughters will have his X. None of his sons will have his X. All his children will have normal vision, unless their mother also had an X for color blindness.
6. XX	Color-blind woman (rare)	Inherited from both parents	Every child will have one X from her. Therefore, every son will be color-blind. Daughters will be only carriers, unless they also inherit an X from the father, as their mother did.

carried on the X chromosome can be passed from mother to son but not from father to son (since the Y does not carry the trait). (See Table 3.1.)

More Complications

As complex as the preceding descriptions of gene interaction patterns may seem, they make gene–gene interaction appear much simpler than it actually is. That is because, to be able to discuss interaction at all, we are forced to treat genes as though they were separately functioning "control devices." But, as we have noted, genes merely direct the creation of 20 amino acids, the combination of which directs the synthesis of thousands of kinds of proteins and enzymes, which then form the body's structures and direct its biochemical functions. The proteins of each body cell are continually affected by other proteins, enzymes, nutrients, and toxins that direct the cell's functioning (Masoro, 1999).

The genes themselves do not always function as the textbooks say they do. For example, a dominant gene might not actually "penetrate" the phenotype completely. Such incomplete penetrance may be caused by temperature, stress, or many other factors. Sometimes the split of a chromosome pair at or before conception is not precise, resulting in a person who is a *mosaic,* that is, who has a mixture of cells, some with a dominant gene, some without. A person could have one blue eye and one brown, or many other mosaicisms. And in the additive pattern, some genes contribute substantially more than others, either because they are naturally partially dominant or because their influence is amplified by the presence of certain other genes.

Moreover, certain genes behave differently depending on whether they are inherited from the mother or from the father. The full scope of, and the reason for, this parental **genetic imprinting,** or tagging, of certain genes has yet to be determined. We know that imprinting involves hundreds of genes but does not

genetic imprinting The tendency of certain genes to be expressed differently when they are inherited from one parent rather than the other.

occur on every chromosome (Hurst, 1997). Some of the genes that influence height, insulin production, and several forms of mental retardation affect a child in different ways—even in opposite ways—depending on which parent they came from.

Further, some genes mutate in the process of duplication, and some twenty-third chromosome pairs do not split precisely. In addition, the letter-code sequence on some genes may be repeated too many times—an error that becomes more serious with each generation. Usually such mistakes lead to the death of the embryo or serious problems in the infant, but sometimes they work to the advantage of the child or even the society. With thousands of genes and billions of letters, the interaction of normal and abnormal is always complex—and occasionally beneficial.

Such polygenic complexity is particularly apparent in **behavioral genetics,** which is the study of the genetic origins of psychological characteristics (Plomin et al., 2001). These include personality traits such as sociability, assertiveness, moodiness, and fearfulness; psychological disorders such as schizophrenia, depression, and attention-deficit/hyperactivity disorder; and cognitive traits such as memory for numbers, spatial perception, and fluency of expression. Mental retardation, for example, has been studied in great depth and detail. Virtually every type of inheritance pattern, including additive, dominant–recessive, X-linked, polygenic, multifactorial, and imprinting, is evident in at least one of the major forms of mental retardation. The complications that can affect genetic expression, causing mental retardation and other disorders, are listed in Table 3.2.

The same is probably true for all aspects of personality and intellect, including high intelligence. Every behavioral tendency is affected by many pairs of genes, some interacting in the dominant–recessive mode, some additive, and some creating new combinations of epigenetic functioning that are not yet catalogued or understood. And almost every behavior pattern can be caused by several different sets of genes (Rutter & Sroufe, 2000). One list of the "epigenetic rules" of behavioral genetics is particularly pertinent to the study of development:

1. Large numbers of genes interact to produce a trait.
2. Environmental factors are important, affecting whether or not a trait is expressed and what form that expression takes.
3. Environmental influences change during the life span. A trait that was quite plastic early in life can become difficult to alter once it is formed.
4. Despite rule 3, even adults retain developmental flexibility.
5. Despite all the rules above, the "butterfly effect" operates for behavioral genetics. For instance, a seemingly small factor such as birth order can affect genetic expression.

[Tobin, 1999]

behavioral genetics The study of the genetic origins of psychological characteristics, such as personality patterns, psychological disorders, and intellectual abilities.

Response for History Students (from page 79): Hemophilia is a painful, episodic disease that once (before blood transfusions became feasible) killed a boy before adulthood. Though rare, it ran in European royal families, whose members often intermarried, which meant that many queens (including Queen Victoria) were carriers of hemophilia and thus were destined to watch half their sons die of it. All families, even rulers of nations, are distracted from their work when they have a child with a mysterious and lethal illness. Some historians believe that hemophilia among European royalty was an underlying cause of the Russian Revolution of 1917 as well as the spread of democracy in the nineteenth and twentieth centuries.

TABLE 3.2 Complications at Conception That Affect Genetic Expression

Genes amplified or nullified by other genes

Genes affected by nutrients and toxins in the mother's body

Incomplete penetrance of dominant genes

Mosaic, caused by variable split of chromosomes

Extra or missing genes, caused by uneven split of chromosomes

Imprinting, affected by whether the gene came from the mother or father

Mutations caused by minor transcription errors as gametes are formed

Extra repetitions of a three-letter "word" (some variation is normal; too much may cause serious diseases)

"I don't know anything about
the bell curve, but I say
heredity is everything."

The Inheritance of the Throne Some people
have much more to gain than others from the notion
that genes are more influential than environment.

Nature and Nurture

In order to examine the complex interplay of heredity and the environment, researchers would like to distinguish the impacts of each of these two forces. This
is difficult because, within any given trait, nature and nurture are intertwined at
every moment. When the trait in question is an obvious physical one, the impact
of genes on the phenotype seems fairly obvious. Family resemblances in facial
features, coloring, or body shape can make it easy to say, "He has his mother's
nose," meaning "That's hereditary."

But when a trait is a psychological one, especially one that changes over
time, the fact that it runs in families could be explained by nurture just as easily
as by nature. If children of highly intelligent parents excel in school, their school
performance could be attributed entirely to genetics, entirely to the family environment (which is likely to encourage reading, intellectual curiosity, and high academic standards), or to a combination of nature and nurture in any proportion.
How, then, do scientists distinguish genetic from environmental influences on
psychological characteristics?

Comparing Twins

One approach to solving this puzzle has been to study twins, who are a natural
experiment. As we have seen, monozygotic twins have all the same genes,
whereas dizygotic twins, like any other two siblings from the same parents,
share only half their genes. Thus, if monozygotic twins are much more similar to
each other on a particular trait than dizygotic twins are, genes probably play a
significant role in the development of that trait. Conversely, if both kinds of twins
are equally likely to have a characteristic, environment is probably the reason.

Such twin comparisons have revealed that virtually all psychological traits
are strongly influenced by genetics. There is, however, one major problem with
this approach: It assumes that twins growing up in a particular family share the
same environment. In fact, twins in the same family sometimes have quite separate experiences—both in obvious ways, such as when one twin but not the other
suffers a serious illness or learns from an extraordinary teacher, and in more
subtle ways, such as when parents punish one twin more harshly or when one
twin defers to the other (Reiss, 1997). This means that twins may diverge on a
particular trait not because they have different genes, but because they had different childhood experiences, even though both grew up in the same family.

In fact, monozygotic twins actually share both more differences *and* more
similarities than a mathematical model would predict. For example, compared to
dizygotic twins, monozygotic twins are more likely to be markedly different in
birth weight, with the heavier baby born first, a fact that means the lighter twin
may have been oxygen deprived for a moment. As they are growing up, relatives
and friends may treat monozygotic twins more similarly than they treat dizygotic
twins, partly because whatever traits they share (a particular way of laughing,
a particular anxiety) make people react in the same way to both of them. This
similarity may make the twins themselves try to be distinct—by pursuing different careers, for instance. This means that the notion that both kinds of twins
raised in the same family always have the same environment is mistaken (Plomin
et al., 2001). Indeed, they may experience environmental similarities or differences because they are twins, not because of their genes. To confirm the finding
of omnipresent genetic effects, another approach is needed.

Comparing Adoptees

Studying adopted children is another natural way to distinguish the impact of
genes from that of upbringing. Traits that show a strong correlation between

adoptees and their biological parents seem to have a genetic basis; traits that show a strong correlation between children and their adoptive parents suggest environmental influence. Blended stepfamilies, with children of various biological connections to one another (as full, half-, or nonsiblings) and to their parents, also reveal differences between nature and nurture (Reiss & Neiderhiser, 2000). Best of all, researchers can study identical twins who were separated at birth and adopted by different families.

The results from all these studies confirm that virtually every psychological characteristic and personal trait is genetically influenced. At the same time, these studies reinforce another, equally important conclusion: Virtually every psychological characteristic and personal trait is also affected by the person's environment (Bouchard, 1994, 1997). Nature always interacts with nurture, and vice versa. As four leading researchers explain:

> The first message is that genes play a surprisingly important role throughout psychology. The second message is just as important: Individual differences in complex psychological traits are due at least as much to environmental influences as they are to genetic influences.
>
> *[Plomin et al., 2001, p. 323]*

More Precision: Molecular Genetics

Neither twins nor adoptees nor step-siblings can tell us exactly how genetic and environmental influences combine. Behavioral traits are particularly likely to be polygenic and multifactorial, with each impinging factor having a small and variable influence that is hard to detect. In fact, "genes that influence the susceptibility of complex traits . . . do not act on their own, but interact with one or many genes and environmental factors. On their own, they explain only a small portion of the variance of the complex phenotype" (Sherman & Waldman, 1999, p. 55).

How can "a small portion" be detected? Detailed analytic and statistical techniques developed in conjunction with the mapping of the genetic code in the Human Genome Project have been very helpful. This area of research involves **molecular genetics,** which includes the study of the chemical codes that constitute a particular molecule of DNA. Particularly promising is a locating technique called *quantitative trait loci (QTL)* (Plomin et al., 2001; Rowe & Jacobson, 1999). Instead of simply using the family connection (such as mother–child or brother–brother) as a measure of genetic closeness, researchers can now look directly at a pattern of genes that two individuals share on a particular chromosome. If two people with the same genetic locus (location for a particular gene pattern) and code are also similar in some aspect of their phenotypes, researchers can conclude that the particular gene contributes something to that trait.

QTL has already found a gene that contributes to reading disability (Cardon et al., 1994), one that contributes to high intelligence (Chorney et al., 1998), one that influences attention-deficit disorder (Thapar et al., 1999), and another for language fluency (Fisher et al., 1999). Note that these genes "contribute"; they do not cause. Many genes and many aspects of the environment create and sustain each human trait.

As we learn more about various alleles of genes, it becomes increasingly important to realize that when we say something is "genetic," we do not mean that its genetic origins are substantial, fixed, or unalterable. We mean that it is part of a person's basic foundation, affecting many aspects of life while determining none (Johnston & Edwards, 2002). As one expert put it, "A gene is a framed canvas upon which the psychological environment paints the person" (Brown, 1999). Every trait, action, and attitude of every living organism has a genetic component—

molecular genetics The study of genetics at the molecular level, including the study of the chemical codes that constitute a particular molecule of DNA.

without genes, no behavior could exist. Yet when one asks whether there can be purely genetic explanations for behavior,

> The simple answer to this question is "no." . . . Even when characterized in detail at the DNA level, genes do not, all by themselves, explain much. The genes have to be translated into phenotypes, and typically have to function in a specified environment. Furthermore, genes do not act in a solitary manner—they act in concert with other genes, often with many genes.
>
> *[Schaffner, 1999]*

Environmental Influences on Emotional Conditions

Environment affects every human characteristic. Consider our emotions—love and hate, joy and fear, admiration and envy. Every emotion is partly genetic, and the genes that affect the power and expression of our emotions help to make each personality unique. But emotional expression is also influenced by the individual's environment: One of the first lessons that parents teach their infants is how and when to express their feelings. The instructions vary, as does the receptivity of the infants.

Let us examine the influence of the environment on traits that are sometimes said to be "genetic": painful shyness, schizophrenia, and alcoholism. You will see that many influences after birth affect how the genes for those traits are expressed.

Painful Shyness

Being fearful of talking in public, of making new friends, of expressing emotions—being shy—is a personality trait that psychologists refer to as *inhibition,* which can become a characteristic called *social phobia* (Beidel & Turner, 1998). Many studies have found that levels of inhibition are more similar in monozygotic twins than in dizygotic twins—an indication that genes affect this trait and its opposite, called extroversion (see Figure 3.4). Further evidence comes from linkages between inhibition and other genetic traits. Compared to other infants, babies who will later be shy show quicker *startle reactions* (when they are surprised by a sudden loud noise, for instance), reacting with more motor activity and frightened crying. Then, as toddlers, they are less active overall but more fearful (as you would expect

an inhibited child to be) (Calkins et al., 1996; Kagen, 1994). As preschoolers, inhibition is still present in these children.

However, inhibition is also affected by the social atmosphere. If parents are able to encourage their shy children without shaming or embarrassing them, the children may learn to relax in social settings and may become less observably shy. For example, a longitudinal study of infants from 4 months to 4 years of age found that behavior over these years correlated with brain activity; the correlation was found not only for inhibition but also for exuberance and anger (Fox et al., 2001). Because brain activity in the first few months of life is the direct outgrowth of genetic instructions, the emotions in these very young infants were probably genetic.

Shyness Is Universal Inhibition is more common at some ages (late infancy and early adolescence) and in some gene pools (natives of northern Europe and East Asia) than others. But every community includes some individuals who are unmistakably shy, such as this toddler in Woleai, more than 3,000 miles west of Hawaii.

THE PURCELL TEAM / CORBIS

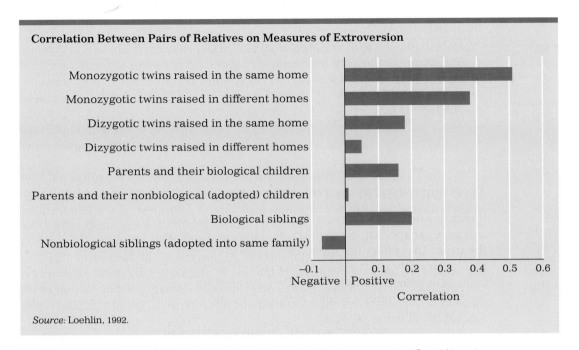

Correlation Between Pairs of Relatives on Measures of Extroversion

Source: Loehlin, 1992.

FIGURE 3.4 Both Nature and Nurture These correlations suggest that genes are quite influential in how shy or outgoing people feel. Note especially the much higher correlations between monozygotic than dizygotic twins.

? *Observational Quiz* (see answer, page 86): Can you see three indications from these correlations that the environment also affects this trait?

The study also showed that emotional expression and brain patterns in some infants changed between the ages of 4 months and 4 years. Inhibition was particularly likely to decrease if the child was placed in a good day-care center before age 2 (Fox et al., 2001). Apparently, the day-care experience, which includes regular interaction with other infants, encouraged the shy children to be more outgoing, and that was enough to shift the genetic pattern.

Alternatively, if a shy child's parents are themselves very shy and avoid contact with strangers, but nonetheless blame their child for being fearful, the child might grow up much more socially timid than if the parents were outgoing—and might be dramatically more inhibited than most other children.

The point here is not that genetically based tendencies disappear as life experiences accumulate. Shy people probably always feel a twinge of inhibition when entering a new school, for instance, or arriving at a party full of strangers—and these tendencies affect their life course. But life experiences and cultural context do make a difference. A longitudinal study in the United States found that shyness slowed down young men's career advancement, but this was not found to be the case in similar longitudinal research in Sweden. The researchers speculated on one reason for the difference:

> Swedish culture values shy, reserved behavior . . . and support systems of various
> sorts made it possible for Swedish boys to enter universities and careers without
> being assertive.
>
> *[Kerr et al., 1996]*

The same conclusion applies to other psychological traits that have strong genetic influences, including intelligence, activity level, aggression, and even religiosity. In each case, various dimensions of environment can enhance, inhibit, or alter the phenotypic expression of a person's heredity (Wachs, 2000).

!Answer to Observational Quiz (from page 85): First, all the correlations are far lower than 1.0, which would be a 100 percent correlation. From this you can see that even monozygotic twins, who are genetically identical, have some aspects of their lives that they do not share and that make them differ on the trait of extroversion.

Second, twins raised in the same family have higher correlations than do twins raised in different families, which shows that shared environment has an influence.

Third, although there is the same genetic similarity (50 percent shared genes) between biological parent–child and biological sibling–sibling pairs, the correlation is higher for siblings. Because the environments shared by siblings are more similar than are the environments of parents and children, it again seems likely that inhibition and extroversion are affected by the environment.

There is also a fourth indication, but it is speculative. What do you make of the slight negative correlation between two unrelated children adopted into the same family? Do such adoptees try to be somewhat different from each other? If they do, then environment is again the reason.

Especially for College Students Who Enjoy a Party: You wonder if one of your male friends is an alcoholic, because he sometimes drinks too much. He may be okay, though, because he can still talk clearly after drinking twice as much as you do. What should you ask him?

Schizophrenia

Psychopathologies such as depression, antisocial behavior, phobias, and compulsions, as well as virtually every other neurotic or psychotic disorder, are also genetically based traits that are subject to strong environmental influence. For example, relatives of people with schizophrenia have a higher-than-normal risk of developing the illness themselves, with about 75 percent of the variation in schizophrenia traceable to genes (Rutter, 2002). Most striking is the fact that if one monozygotic twin develops schizophrenia, about two-thirds of the time the other twin does, too.

Viewed another way, however, the same statistic reveals the importance of the environment: One-third of monozygotic twins whose twin has schizophrenia are not themselves afflicted (Cannon et al., 1999). Moreover, many people diagnosed with schizophrenia have no close relatives with the illness, and most close relatives of schizophrenics do not themselves develop the disorder. Even if that relative was their mother or father, about 88 percent of the biological offspring are *not* diagnosed as schizophrenic (Plomin et al., 2001). Obviously, schizophrenia is multifactorial, with environmental elements—possibly a slow-acting virus, head injury, inadequate oxygen at birth, or other physical insult—playing a pivotal role (Cannon et al., 1999).

Using genetic and epidemiological techniques, scientists are advancing in the treatment and prevention of schizophrenia. It is now known that one gene that predisposes for schizophrenia is on chromosome 6 (Sherman & Waldman, 1999). This gene does not act alone: Some people with the gene do not develop schizophrenia; some people without it, do. One predisposing factor is birth during late winter, probably because some virus more prevalent in late fall or early winter can affect a vulnerable fetus (Mortensen et al., 1999).

A similar scenario is apparent for Alzheimer's disease. Early-onset Alzheimer's is genetically dominant; if a person inherits the gene, he or she develops the disease before age 50. But late-onset Alzheimer's is multifactorial. A gene on chromosome 19 comes in several alleles. People with ApoE4 are more likely to develop the disease, and those with another allele (ApoE2) almost never do. A double dose of the ApoE4 allele (one from each parent) almost always leads to Alzheimer's if the person lives long enough. Nevertheless, a few people with two copies of this destructive allele never develop the disease, because they benefit from other, protective genes and a favorable environment (Vickers et al., 2000).

Alcoholism

At various times, drug addiction, including alcoholism, has been considered a moral weakness, a personality flaw, and a sign of psychopathology (Leonard & Blane, 2000). Alcoholics were once locked up in jails or in mental institutions. When that didn't stop the problem, entire nations banned alcohol, as the United States did during Prohibition, from 1919 to 1933. People who are not alcoholics have long wondered why some people just can't stop drinking to excess, and alcoholics have kept trying and failing to stop after one or two drinks.

Now we know that some people's inherited biochemistry makes them highly susceptible to alcohol addiction. Anyone can abuse alcohol, but each person's genetic makeup creates an addictive pull that can be overpowering, extremely weak, or something in between.

Evidence for "alcoholism genes" is found in the fact that some ethnic groups (such as those from the British Isles and from northern Russia) have a much higher proportion of alcoholics than others. Biochemistry allows some people to "hold their liquor," drinking so much that they become alcoholics, and causes others, notably many East Asians, to sweat and become red-faced after just a few sips of alcohol. This embarrassing response, particularly for women, is an incentive to avoid alcohol (McGue, 1995). Some people become sleepy, others nauseated, others aggressive, and others euphoric when alcohol hits their brains, and each person's reaction increases or decreases the eagerness to have another drink.

Alcoholism is not simply a biochemical reaction; it is psychological as well as physical. Not surprisingly, genes predispose a person to have certain personality traits that correlate with abusive addictions: a quick temper, a readiness to take risks, and a high level of anxiety. Thus, alcoholism is polygenic, with almost every alcoholic inheriting a particular combination of biochemistry-affecting and temperament-affecting genes that push him or her toward abusive drinking. Originally this was more true for men than women, because women were typically discouraged by their cultures from drinking to excess. Now that women in many cultures are free to follow their genetic impulses, the heritability of alcoholism in females is more than 50 percent (Heath et al., 1997).

Alcoholism Genes and Cultural Pressures

Although no ethnic group or gender is immune to alcoholism, the disease is much more prevalent in some ethnic groups (such as the British) than others (such as the Japanese) and, until recently, was much more common in men than women. There are three reasons behind these trends: selective adaptation, religious prohibition, and public policy.

For centuries in the British Isles, beer and wine were actually healthier for people than water, because the fermentation process killed many of the harmful bacteria that thrived in drinking water. Thus, being able to drink alcohol in quantity was adaptive in most of Europe. East Asians had a different solution to the problem of bacteria: They boiled their water and drank it as tea. This explains why about half of all Asians lack the gene for an enzyme necessary to fully metabolize alcohol: Their ancestors didn't need it.

Culture counts. If a person with a strong genetic tendency toward alcoholism spends a lifetime in an environment where alcohol is unavailable (in a devout Islamic family in Saudi Arabia, for example), the genotype will never be expressed in the phenotype. Similarly, if the person lives in a nation where alcohol is readily available (such as the United States or Japan) but belongs to a religion that forbids it (Mormon or Adventist, for instance) or a gender that never gets drunk (Japanese women), they are likely to escape their genetic destiny.

In contrast, if the same person is allowed to drink frequently at an early age, the potential of the genes will be released, as is true in Russia and Australia, among other places. Further, if a culture promotes alcohol consumption, with peer pressures that lead to alcohol abuse, genetically susceptible people become active alcoholics. Even for them, personal choices dramatically alter the outcome. Some alcoholics die of the disease before they are 30; others spend decades alternating among abuse, controlled drinking, and abstinence; still others recognize the problem, get help, and are sober and productive throughout a long life.

Developmental issues also have an impact. A person is most likely to become an active alcoholic between ages 15 and 25, even though the genotype has been present since conception. Another vulnerable period is old age: When the metabolism shifts, older people are more likely to become abusive drinkers. Among some ethnic groups, alcohol is taboo for women, which is one reason Mexican-American babies almost never have fetal alcohol syndrome unless the mother was raised in the United States and became acculturated. Among some American Indian tribes on reservations, alcohol is forbidden; among other tribes, it is readily available, with disastrous results for all who are affected—especially newborns, teenagers, and the elderly.

FABIAN FALCON / STOCK, BOSTON

All Alcoholics? Probably not. These farm workers in Provence, France, pause for a meal—complete with bread, wine, glasses, and a tablecloth. Drinking alcohol with friends and food is not a sign of alcoholism; habitually drinking alone is. Of course, cultural pressure to drink creates problems, which is one reason France has a high rate of cirrhosis, but this might not be a pressure group: One of the two bottles is water.

Can public policy have any effect here? Apparently yes. In the United States between 1980 and 1990, alcohol consumption per capita was reduced by 10 percent. Moreover, between 1980 and 1999, stricter enforcement of drunk-driving laws reduced the number of fatal accidents involving drunk drivers—from 26 percent to 17 percent overall and from 24 percent to 14 percent among 16- to 20-year-olds (U.S. Bureau of the Census, 2001). Workplace employee-assistance programs and insurance policies that consider alcoholism as a treatable disease have also had an effect, but this seems to have diminished recently. Drinking and alcohol-related problems were at the same level or worse at the end of the 1990s as at the beginning (Greenfield et al., 2000; Midanik & Greenfield, 2000).

These examples—painful shyness, schizophrenia, and alcoholism—make it quite clear that genes, the prenatal and postnatal biochemical environment, and the more distant social environment are all powerful influences on human development. Their complex interaction is involved in every aspect of development at every age and in every era. And in each person's life, the results of earlier genetic–environmental interactions guide further development. That said, we must also stress that the outcome is never predetermined, even at age 70 or 80. As one biologist explains:

> At every stage of development, from moment to moment, the growing organism is interacting with a varying environment; and the form of each interaction depends on the outcome of earlier interactions. This process is indescribably complicated—which is why it is never described and rarely even acknowledged. The extreme of intricacy is reached in human development, for the conditions which we and our children experience are often the products of deliberate, sometimes intelligent, choice.
>
> *[Barnett, 1998]*

Response for College Students Who Enjoy a Party (from page 86): Your friend's ability to "hold his liquor" is an ominous sign; his body probably metabolizes alcohol differently from the way most other people's do. Alcoholics are often deceptive about their own drinking habits, so you might ask him about the drinking habits of his relatives. If he has either alcoholics or abstainers in the family, you should be concerned, since both are signs of a genetic problem with alcohol. Ask him whether he can have only one drink a day for a month. Alcoholics find such restricted drinking virtually impossible.

On a practical level, this means we must not ignore the genetic component in any given trait—whether it be something wonderful, such as a wacky sense of humor; something fearful, such as a violent temper; or something quite ordinary, such as the tendency to get bored with our routine. However, we must not forget that the environment affects every trait, in ways that change as maturational, cultural, and historical processes unfold, with an impact that can be chosen or changed, depending on the people and society. Genes are always part of the tale, influential on every page, but they never determine the plot or the final paragraph.

Inherited Abnormalities

We now give particular attention to genetic and chromosomal abnormalities, for three reasons:

- Disruptions of normal development provide insight into the complexities of genetic interactions.
- Knowledge of the origins of genetic and chromosomal abnormalities suggests how to reduce or limit their harmful consequences.
- Misinformation and prejudice compound the problems of those who are affected by chromosomal and genetic abnormalities.

Chromosomal Miscounts

Sometimes when gametes are formed, the 46 chromosomes divide unevenly, producing a sperm or an ovum that does not have the normal complement of exactly 23 chromosomes. If such a gamete fuses with a normal gamete, the result is a zygote with more or fewer than 46 chromosomes. This is not unusual. An estimated half of all zygotes have an odd number of chromosomes. One count found 9,080 different chromosomal abnormalities in which part of or a whole chromosome was missing or misplaced (Borgaonkar, 1997). Most such zygotes do not even begin to develop, and most of the rest never come to term—usually because a **spontaneous abortion,** or *miscarriage,* occurs. About 5 percent of stillborn (dead-at-birth) babies also have more than 46 chromosomes (Miller & Therman, 2001).

> **spontaneous abortion** The naturally occurring termination of a pregnancy before the fetus is fully developed. (Also called *miscarriage.*)

Once in about every 200 births, a baby survives with 45, 47, or, rarely, 48 or 49 chromosomes. In every case, the chromosomal abnormality leads to a recognizable *syndrome,* a cluster of distinct characteristics that tend to occur together. In many cases—for instance, trisomy-18 (Edwards') and trisomy-13 (Patau) syndromes—the newborn lives for only a short time.

Prenatal Detection

Over the past 30 years, researchers have refined prenatal tests that are used selectively to detect whether chromosomal abnormalities are indeed present (Goetzel & D'Alton, 2001).

Alpha-Fetoprotein Assay A sample of the mother's blood can be tested for the level of alpha-fetoprotein (AFP), an indicator of neural-tube defects, multiple embryos, or, as Martha and John feared in this chapter's Case to Study, Down syndrome. About 10 percent of all pregnant women exhibit high or low AFP, but most of these are false alarms, caused by miscalculation of the age of the fetus or some other normal variation. The test itself is not risky, but unexpected AFP levels indicate that additional testing is needed, as Martha and John learned.

Ultrasound A sonogram, or ultrasound image, uses high-frequency sound waves to produce a "picture" of the fetus. If done early in pregnancy, sonograms can reveal problems such as an abnormally small head or other body malformations, excess spinal fluid accumulating on the brain, and several diseases (for instance, of the kidney). In addition, sonograms are used to diagnose twins, to estimate fetal age, to determine the position of the placenta, and to reveal the rate of fetal growth. No known risks to mother or fetus result from sonograms, unlike the X-ray that it replaced. Sonograms are routine in England and Canada, but in the United States they are used only about half the time. The reasons for the differences are cultural and political, in that England and Canada, but not the United States, provide free prenatal care to everyone (Heyman & Henriksen, 2001).

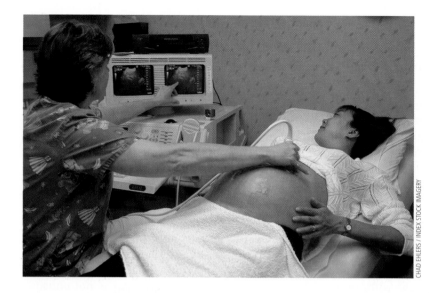

There's Your Baby For many parents, their first glimpse of their future child is an ultrasound image. The outline of the fetus's head and body are visible once an expert points them out. Measuring the width of the head is the best way to estimate fetal age, and the presence of more than one heartbeat is the first signal that a multiple birth is expected.

Amniocentesis In amniocentesis, about half an ounce of the fluid inside the placenta is withdrawn through the mother's abdominal wall. The fluid contains sloughed-off fetal cells that can be cultured and analyzed to detect chromosomal abnormalities as well as many other genetic and prenatal problems. The amniotic fluid also reveals the sex of the fetus (useful knowledge if an X-linked disorder is likely). Amniocentesis cannot be safely performed until midpregnancy (at least 14 weeks), and many detected abnormalities have uncertain consequences. Both these facts make the woman's decision about continuing the pregnancy very difficult. About once in 200 pregnancies, amniocentesis causes a spontaneous abortion.

Chorionic Villi Sampling In chorionic villi sampling (CVS), a sample of the placental tissue that surrounds the fetus is obtained and analyzed. This test provides the same information as amniocentesis, but CVS is usually performed earlier, at about the 10th week of pregnancy (Goetzel & D'Alton, 2001). This benefit comes at a price, however: Compared to amniocentesis, CVS is slightly less accurate and three times as likely to cause a spontaneous abortion.

Pre-Implantation Testing New techniques allow genetic testing to occur even earlier than CVS. If conception occurs in vitro ("in glass," or in a laboratory dish, with sperm being added to ova that have been surgically removed from the mother), one cell can be removed from each zygote at the four- or eight-cell stage and analyzed genetically. If a possible genetic defect is *not* found, the remaining developing cells can be inserted into the uterus. About 25 percent of the time, the cell mass implants, grows, and becomes a newborn without the chromosomal or genetic abnormality that the couple sought to avoid.

Pre-implantation testing is controversial and unusual, available only in specialized centers that screen for about 20 of the most commonly inherited conditions (Simpson et al., 1999). But some couples would not risk reproduction without the assurance of pre-implantation analysis. Experimenting on lower animals, researchers have added a gene or chromosome at the pre-implantation stage to replace a defective one—a measure not yet performed on human embryos.

Risks and Benefits of Testing The ideal (not always attained) is to reserve testing for suspected cases of serious, well-understood conditions, for which diagnosis is quite accurate and treatment or prevention is available (Wingerson, 1998). Unfortunately, uncertain diagnosis, especially of unusual chromosomal abnormalities, means that many pregnant couples are faced with puzzling results (either positive or negative) or ambiguous findings. Doctors usually decide which tests should be done and when, and prospective parents are often unprepared to interpret the data. As a consequence, nations differ in when and to whom prenatal tests are offered, and couples with identical results sometimes make opposite decisions.

In fact, doctors vary widely in the way they present prenatal tests to prospective parents. For instance, in one British hospital that required doctors to offer genetic tests to all pregnant patients, one doctor spoke to a patient of the "tremendous amount of heartache if we get a false positive" (quoted in Heyman & Henriksen, 2001, p. 100). Another told a patient to ask herself, "How do I feel about having a Down syndrome baby?" (p. 145) and then work back from there to decide about getting tested. Not surprisingly, the patient of the first doctor decided to have no genetic tests, and the second doctor's patient had amniocentesis. In this hospital, women over age 35 were warned about their increased risk of having a baby with Down syndrome but were not told about other relatively common syndromes or serious complications. Concern focuses on the problem that is lifelong and more readily dealt with by abortion, not on those whose victims die in early infancy or those that are apparent after birth.

As for Martha and John, even though their second AFP test indicated that their fetus was unlikely to have Down syndrome, Martha still had a gut feeling that something was wrong. She volunteered for amniocentesis and got bad news: Her fetus had the extra chromosome of Down syndrome after all. She decided not to abort and gave birth to Adam. Years later, when Martha was talking to a group about her decision to continue her pregnancy, a woman in the audience said that she had been in the same situation but had made the "wrong" decision. Martha replied that there was no right or wrong decision; every decision about prenatal testing is difficult, and each choice has costs (Beck, 1999). (We return to John and Martha in Chapter 4.) Let's look at Down syndrome in more detail.

Down Syndrome

Down syndrome is the most common extra-chromosome condition: There is a third chromosome at the twenty-first pair, which is why the syndrome is also called trisomy-21. Most embryos and newborns with trisomy-21 die. A few decades ago, almost all such children died in early childhood, but advances in treatment mean that now most survive well into adulthood (though seldom into old age).

Some 300 distinct characteristics can result from the presence of that extra chromosome, but no individual with Down syndrome is quite like another, either in symptoms or in their severity. Despite this variability, almost all people with trisomy-21 have certain specific facial characteristics—a thick tongue, round face, slanted eyes—as well as distinctive hands, feet, and fingerprints. Many also have hearing problems, heart abnormalities, muscle weakness, and short stature.

In terms of neurological development, almost all individuals with Down syndrome experience mental slowness. Their eventual intellectual attainment

Earning His Daily Bread This man with Down syndrome works in a cafeteria, and, by all reports, is a steady, conscientious employee.

? *Observational Quiz* (see answer, page 93): Visible are four signs of Down syndrome; not visible (and perhaps not present) are at least four other signs. Name all eight.

varies: Some are severely retarded; others are average or even above average. Usually—but not always—those who are raised at home and given appropriate cognitive stimulation progress to the point of being able to read and write and care for themselves (and often much more), while those who are institutionalized tend to be, and to remain, much more retarded (Carr, 1995).

Many young children with trisomy-21 are unusually sweet-tempered; they are less likely to cry or complain than most other children. Temperament may be a liability, however. If a Down syndrome child is more passive and less motivated to learn than others, that characteristic produces a slower learning rate and a lower IQ as time goes on (Wishart, 1999).

People with Down syndrome age faster than other adults. For them, the ailments of old age begin in middle adulthood (Hassold & Patterson, 1999). By that time, they "almost invariably" develop Alzheimer's disease, which severely impairs their limited communication skills and makes them much less compliant (Czech et al., 2000). They are also prone to a host of other problems more commonly found in older persons, including cataracts and certain forms of cancer. Consequently, their mortality rate begins to rise at about age 35, and their life expectancy is lower than that of other mentally retarded adults and much lower than that of average people (Strauss & Eyman, 1996).

This generally pessimistic description, however, does not reflect the actual experience of many individuals with Down syndrome. It is true that all have language difficulties, and many have other serious medical problems. But they may still become happy, proud, and successful young adults. One gave the following advice to others:

> You may have to work hard, but don't ever give up. Always remember that you are important. You are special in your own unique way. And one of the best ways to feel good about yourself is to share yourself with someone else.

> [Christi Todd, quoted in Hassold & Patterson, 1999]

Abnormalities of the Twenty-Third Pair

Every newborn infant has at least one X chromosome in the twenty-third pair; an embryo cannot develop without an X. However, about 1 in every 500 infants either is missing a sex chromosome (thus the X stands alone) or has two or more other sex chromosomes in addition to the first X. These abnormalities usually impair cognitive and psychosocial development as well as sexual maturation. In many cases, treatment with hormone supplements can alleviate some of the physical problems, and special education may remedy some of the deficits related to psychological functioning.

The specific features of any syndrome vary considerably from one individual to another. In fact, in many cases, the presence of abnormal sex chromosomes goes undetected until a seemingly normal childhood is followed by an abnormally delayed puberty. This is particularly likely for a boy who has *Klinefelter syndrome, XXY.* Such a boy will be a little slow in elementary school, but it is usually not until puberty—when his penis does not grow and fat begins to accumulate around his breasts—that his parents wonder if something is seriously wrong.

The Fragile X One of the most common syndromes associated with the sex chromosomes is **fragile-X syndrome,** which is genetic in origin. In some individuals, part of the X chromosome is attached to the rest of it by such a thin string of molecules that it seems about to break off (hence the name of the syndrome). This abnormality in the chromosome is caused by the mutation of a single gene, which has more than 200 repetitions of the "word" CGG (Plomin et al., 2001). The mutation involved in the fragile X intensifies as it is passed from one generation to the next, with more repetitions.

fragile-X syndrome A genetic disorder in which part of the X chromosome is attached to the rest of it by a very thin string of molecules; often produces mental deficiency in males who inherit it.

Of the females who carry it, most are normal (perhaps because they also carry one normal X chromosome), but one-third show some mental deficiency. Among the males who inherit a fragile-X chromosome, about 20 percent are apparently completely normal, about 33 percent are somewhat retarded, and the rest are severely retarded. The last group is relatively large: The cognitive deficits caused by fragile-X syndrome represent the most common form of inherited mental retardation. In addition to cognitive problems, the fragile X is often associated with inadequate social skills and extreme shyness (Dykens et al., 1994; Hagerman, 1996).

The wide range of effects produced by this disorder is somewhat unusual. However, the more we learn about other abnormal genes, chromosomes, and syndromes, the more diversity we find in their effects. For example, schizophrenia, as you already learned, is genetic, but the specific form (e.g., hebephrenic, paranoid) is not (Plomin et al., 2001).

Causes of Chromosomal Abnormalities

Chromosomal abnormalities are caused by many factors, some genetic and some environmental (such as the parents' exposure to excessive radiation). However, the variable that most often correlates with chromosomal abnormalities is maternal age. According to one detailed estimate, a 20-year-old woman has about 1 chance in 800 of carrying a fetus with Down syndrome; a 39-year-old woman has 1 chance in 67; and a 44-year-old woman has 1 chance in 16 (see Appendix A for the month-by-month, age-specific incidence).

Other chromosomal abnormalities are less common, but virtually all follow an age-related pattern (Snijders & Nicolaides, 1996). Because about half of all fetuses with these abnormalities are aborted spontaneously and some others are aborted by choice, the actual birth rate of infants with chromosomal abnormalities is lower than these statistics would suggest. Many doctors recommend prenatal testing for chromosomal abnormalities whenever a pregnant woman is 35 or older, although this step is controversial.

Harmful Genes

While relatively few people are born with abnormal chromosomes, everyone has at least 20 genes (usually additive or recessive) that could produce serious diseases or handicaps in the next generation (see Table 3.3.). Most of the 7,000 *known* genetic disorders are dominant, since whenever a dominant gene is inherited, it is apparent in the person's phenotype. With a few exceptions, dominant disorders are not seriously disabling because people with disabling dominant disorders are unlikely to have children and thus are unlikely to pass their genes on. One exception is *Huntington's chorea,* a central nervous system disease caused by a genetic mutation (again, too many triplets, this time more than 35 CAGs) that remains inactive until adulthood, by which time a person could have had many children (as the original Mr. Huntington did).

Another dominant disorder that can be severe is *Tourette syndrome,* which is quite common but variable. About 30 percent of those who inherit the gene exhibit recurrent uncontrollable tics and explosive outbursts of verbal obscenities. The remaining 70 percent experience milder symptoms, such as an occasional twitch that is barely noticeable and a postponable impulse to speak inappropriately.

Recessive and multifactorial disorders are less likely to be recognized but actually claim many more victims, largely because such disorders can pass unchecked (and unnoticed) from carrier to carrier for generations. As a result, carrier status can easily become widespread in a population. Among the more commonly known recessive disorders are cystic fibrosis, thalassemia, and sickle-cell anemia, with as

! *Answer to Observational Quiz* (from page 91): Four visible signs: round head, short stature, large hands, slanted eye sockets. Not visible: mental retardation, heart abnormalities, muscle weakness, thick tongue.

TABLE 3.3 Common Genetic Diseases and Conditions

Name	Description	Prognosis	Probable Inheritance	Incidence*	Carrier Detection†	Prenatal Detection?
Albinism	No melanin; person is very blond and pale.	Normal, but must avoid sun damage.	Recessive.	Rare overall; 1 in 8 Hopi Indians is a carrier.	No	No
Alzheimer's disease	Loss of memory and increasing mental impairment.	Eventual death, often after years of dependency.	Early onset—dominant; after age 60—multifactorial.	Fewer than 1 in 100 middle-aged adults; 20 percent of all adults over age 80.	Yes, for some genes; ApoE4 allele increases incidence	No
Breast cancer	Tumors in breast that can spread.	With early treatment, most are cured; without it, death within 3 years.	BRCA1 and BRCA2 genes seem dominant; other cases, multifactorial.	1 woman in 8 (only 20 percent of breast cancer patients have BRCA1 or 2).	Yes, for BRCA1 and BRCA2	No
Cleft palate, cleft lip	The two sides of the upper lip or palate are not joined.	Correctable by surgery.	Multifactorial.	1 in every 700 births; more common in Asian-Americans and American Indians.	No	Yes
Club foot	The foot and ankle are twisted.	Correctable by surgery.	Multifactorial.	1 in every 200 births; more common in boys.	No	Yes
Cystic fibrosis	Mucous obstructions, especially in lungs and digestive organs.	Most live to middle adulthood.	Recessive gene; also spontaneous mutations.	1 in 2,500; 1 in 20 European-Americans is a carrier.	Sometimes	Yes, in most cases
Diabetes	Abnormal sugar metabolism because of insufficient insulin.	Early onset (Type I) fatal without insulin; for adult onset (Type II), variable risks.	Multifactorial; for adult onset, environment is crucial.	Type I: 1 in 500 births; more common in American Indians and African-Americans. Type II: 1 adult in 10.	No	No
Deafness (congenital)	Inability to hear from birth on.	Deaf children can learn sign language and live normally.	Multifactorial; some forms are recessive.	1 in 1,000 births; more common in people from Middle East.	No	No
Hemophilia	Absence of clotting factor in blood.	Death from internal bleeding; blood transfusions prevent damage.	X-linked recessive; also spontaneous mutations.	1 in 10,000 males; royal families of England, Russia, and Germany had it.	Yes	Yes
Hydro-cephalus	Obstruction causes excess water in the brain.	Brain damage and death; surgery can make normal life possible.	Multifactorial.	1 in every 100 births.	No	Yes

*Incidence statistics vary from country to country; those given here are for the United States. All these diseases can occur in any ethnic group. When certain groups have a high or low incidence, it is noted here.
†Studying the family tree can help geneticists spot a possible carrier of many genetic diseases or, in some cases, a definite carrier. However, here "Yes" means that a carrier can be detected even without knowledge of family history.

Name	Description	Prognosis	Probable Inheritance	Incidence*	Carrier Detection†	Prenatal Detection?
Muscular dystrophy (13 diseases)	Weakening of muscles.	Inability to walk, move; wasting away and sometimes death.	Duchenne's is X-linked; other forms are recessive or multifactorial.	1 in every 3,500 males develops Duchenne's.	Yes, for some forms	Yes, for some forms
Neural-tube defects (open spine)	Anencephaly (parts of the brain missing) or spina bifida (lower spine not closed).	Anencephalic—severe retardation; spina bifida—poor lower body control.	Multifactorial; defect occurs in first weeks of pregnancy.	Anencephaly—1 in 1,000 births; spina bifida—3 in 1,000. More common in Welsh and Scots.	No	Yes
Phenylketo–nuria (PKU)	Abnormal digestion of protein.	Mental retardation, hyperactivity; preventable by diet.	Recessive.	1 in 10,000 births; 1 in 100 European-Americans is a carrier; especially Norwegians and Irish.	Yes	Yes
Pyloric stenosis	Overgrowth of muscle in intestine.	Vomiting, loss of weight, eventual death; correctable by surgery.	Multifactorial.	1 male in 200, 1 female in 1,000; less common in African-Americans.	No	No
Schizo-phrenia	Severely distorted thought processes.	No cure; drugs hospitalization, psychotherapy, relieve symptoms.	Multifactorial.	1 in 100 people develop it by early adulthood.	No	No
Sickle-cell anemia	Abnormal blood cells.	Possible painful "crisis"; heart and kidney failure; treatable with drugs.	Recessive.	1 in 500 African-Americans; 1 in 10 African-Americans and 1 in 20 Latinos is a carrier.	Yes	Yes
Tay-Sachs disease	Enzyme disease.	Apparently healthy infant becomes weaker, usually dying by age 5.	Recessive.	1 in 4,000 births; 1 in 30 American Jews and 1 in 20 French-Canadians are carriers.	Yes	Yes
Thalassemia	Abnormal blood cells.	Paleness and listlessness, low resistance to infections.	Recessive.	1 in 10 Greek-, Italian-, Thai-, and Indian-Americans is a carrier.	Yes	Yes
Tourette syndrome	Uncontrollable tics, body jerking, verbal obscenities.	Often imperceptible in children; worsens with age.	Dominant, but variable penetrance.	1 in 250 births.	Sometimes	No

Sources: Briley & Sulser, 2001; Klug & Cummings, 2000; Mange & Mange, 1999; McKusick, 1994; National Academy of Sciences, 1994; Shahin et al., 2002.

genetic counseling A process of consultation and testing that enables individuals to learn about their genetic heritage, including conditions that might harm any children they may have.

many as 1 in 12 North Americans being a carrier for one or another of the three. Most genetic research has been done in Europe and North America; undoubtedly, many other dominant and recessive conditions are prevalent in Asia, Africa, and South America that have not yet been named and described (Wright, 1998).

Genetic counseling, which is the process of testing a person to discover what genetic conditions are present on the genotype and then advising that person how likely the condition is to occur in his or her offspring's phenotype, is widely available in developed nations. Often, but not always, a couple can learn what their chances are of bearing a child with a specific genetic disease and can seek advice about how to prevent such an outcome. In the United States, genetic counselors try to follow two ethical guidelines.

■ The results are kept confidential, beyond the reach of insurance companies and out of public records.
■ The final decision is made by the clients, not by the counselor, whose job is to provide facts and options, not to impose values and conclusions.

A problem arises in interpreting these guidelines, however. Should test results be kept confidential, even from other family members who are directly affected? And should a client be allowed to make a decision that the counselor believes is unethical? Most counselors answer "yes" to both questions, but many members of the public answer "no." The disagreement is explained in the following Changing Policy feature.

Changing Policy

Genetic Counseling: Decisions and Values

Until recently, after the birth of a child with a serious or even fatal genetic or chromosomal disorder, couples thought fate rather than genetics was to blame. They often went on to have more children, who were likely to have the same problem or be carriers of it.

Today, many couples worry about their genes even before they marry. Almost every adult has a relative with a serious disease that may well be genetic. Genetic counseling can help relieve such worries, although it also requires careful decision making by the prospective parents.

In general, prenatal, preconceptual, or even prenuptial genetic counseling and testing are recommended for:

■ Individuals who have a parent, sibling, or child with a serious genetic condition
■ Couples who have a history of early spontaneous abortions, stillbirths, or infertility
■ Couples who are from the same ethnic group or subgroup—especially if the group is a small one and most particularly if the couple are close relatives
■ Women age 35 or older

When a couple begins genetic counseling, the counselor constructs a family history, charting patterns of health and

sickness over the generations, particularly with regard to early deaths and unexplained symptoms. The counselor then explains specific conditions based on age, ethnicity, and genetic history and discusses what the options will be if testing reveals high risk of serious conditions. This last step is crucial; as options increase, so do choices. The couple then decides whether to proceed with genetic testing.

There is an interesting paradox here. Genetic counselors, scientists, and the general public usually believe it best to proceed with testing because some information is better than none. However, high-risk individuals (who are most likely to hear bad news) do not necessarily agree, especially if the truth might jeopardize the marriage, health insurance coverage, or the chances of parenthood (Duster, 1999). If the genetic tests would reveal only the risk to the adult, not to a prospective child, most high-risk adults say they would rather not know about their own fate.

As a result of testing, couples can know the approximate odds that their prospective child will have a serious genetic problem. Of course, odds are risk assessments, not guarantees. If both partners have the recessive gene for sickle-cell anemia, for instance, and the couple plans to have several children, then all of them, some of them, or none of them

Genetic Counseling in Action Early in genetic counseling the prospective parents typically view a chart, such as the one held by the female counselor, that helps them understand inheritance patterns and risks. The counselors also look for signs that the two individuals will be able to understand and mutually decide on their next steps.

WILL AND DENI MCINTYRE / PHOTO RESEARCHERS, INC.

? *Observational Quiz* (see answer, page 99): At least one sign is evident that these two prospective parents will face their dilemma together. What is it?

could have the disease. Probability laws tell us that one child in four will be afflicted, two in four will be carriers, and one in four will not even be a carrier; but each new pregnancy is a new risk.

There are no guarantees. Even when a couple is at low risk, a spontaneous mutation or an inaccurate test may result in a child with a genetic disease. Two additional complications are that most diseases vary in severity and knowledge sometimes brings shame instead of power. A mother of a child with a recessive disorder explains:

> I feel responsible and his dad feels the same way. It's like we have done something. We have shamed ourselves real bad, but you just have to deal with it. Society puts people down about a whole lot of things. . . . You know, they don't take kindly when you do something to a child.

> *[quoted in Duster, 1999]*

Thus, testing itself is far less neutral and objective than it may appear to be. Indeed, most genetic counselors believe that being value-neutral is neither necessary nor desirable (Mahowald et al., 1998). Nonetheless, patient autonomy is a high priority in genetic counseling, and this can create thorny dilemmas. For example, what would you advise in the following four cases if you were the genetic counselor?

1. A pregnant couple are both achondroplastic dwarfs, a genetic condition that affects appearance but not intellect. They want genetic analysis of their fetus, which they intend to abort if it would become a child of normal stature.

2. A 40-year-old woman chooses to be tested and hears bad news: She has the BRCA1 gene, which gives her about an 80 percent chance of developing breast cancer before age 70, and perhaps ovarian or colon cancer as well. She refuses to believe the evidence and insists that no one tell her family, including her mother, her four sisters, and her three daughters. Several of them probably have the gene and may be in the early stages of cancer without knowing it.

3. A 30-year-old mother of two daughters (no sons) learns that she is a carrier for hemophilia. She requests pre-implantation analysis, demanding that only male embryos without her hemophilia-carrying X chromosome be implanted. This means that female zygotes, only half of which would even be carriers, would be given no chance to develop.

4. A couple has a child with cystic fibrosis. They want to know whether they both have the recessive gene or whether their child's condition was a spontaneous mutation (as is often the case). If the latter is true, they could have another child with very little risk of cystic fibrosis. During testing, the counselor learns that the wife has the gene but the husband does not—and also realizes that the husband is not the biological father of the child.

[adapted from Science News, 1994]

Many college students are tempted to break confidentiality for dilemmas 2 and 4 and to refuse to test the clients in dilemmas 1 and 3. What would you do?

Choosing to Have a Child

As the Changing Policy feature makes clear, genetic testing is a tool, not an answer. Novices need guidance to make effective use of this tool. Some genetic counselors are better guides than others. More and more genetic counselors are going to be needed, and you might consider this profession; imagine yourself as the counselor in the following episode.

After having a newborn die with a trisomy, a pregnant couple disagreed about amniocentesis. The woman wanted it, but the man didn't. The husband asked the counselor, "Well, what are we to do?"

The counselor answered, "It's not my problem. I am not you. You'll have to come to some resolution with your conscience and work it out with your wife."

An alternative approach was suggested by an expert on genetic counseling: "When you ask me 'What are we to do?' what do you see as the problem?" (Kessler, 2000, pp. 154, 156). This challenge causes the couple to think about many aspects of their situation: their religious beliefs, their relationship, what it would be like to experience the death of another newborn, which risks they were willing to accept, their feelings of shame and guilt, how they felt about raising a child with medical or psychological problems. Any one of these might be the core issue; a good counselor helps the couple explore any issues that are important to them.

Fortunately, the results of genetic testing do not usually end a marriage or a couple's hopes of becoming parents. Some couples may learn that only one partner carries a harmful recessive trait and therefore none of their children will have the disease. Others may learn that their risk of bearing a child with a serious illness is not much higher than that of any other couple.

Even if both partners are carriers of a serious condition or are at high risk in other ways, they still have many alternatives, as Figure 3.5 indicates. Some may avoid pregnancy and, perhaps, plan to adopt. Some might choose a reproductive alternative such as artificial insemination with donor sperm, in vitro fertilization with a donor ovum, or in vitro fertilization using the parents' own gametes followed by genetic testing of the cell mass before it is inserted into the uterus. If testing during pregnancy reveals serious problems, a couple can consider abortion or begin gathering information that will help them deal with the child-care problems that may lie ahead.

Some may decide to postpone pregnancy until promising treatments—either prenatal or postnatal—are further developed. Genetic engineering (altering of an organism's genetic instructions through the insertion of additional genes) is the most innovative of these, but it has not yet proved feasible on a large scale. Many other, more conventional, treatments have already made a dramatic difference for those with sickle-cell anemia, cystic fibrosis, and various other conditions.

Obviously, decisions about conception are not based simply on genetic analysis. Two couples with identical odds of conceiving zygotes with the same condition might make quite different choices—depending on their age,

Especially for a Friend: A female friend asks you to go with her to the hospital, where she is planning to be surgically sterilized. She says she doesn't want children, especially since her younger brother recently died of sickle-cell anemia, a recessive disease. What, if anything, should you do?

Not Too Old to Have a Healthy Baby The only age group to have an increase in birth rate over the past decade is women over 39. While older couples have a higher risk of conceiving an embryo with chromosomal abnormalities, modern medical care and prenatal monitoring can help the parents produce a healthy baby.

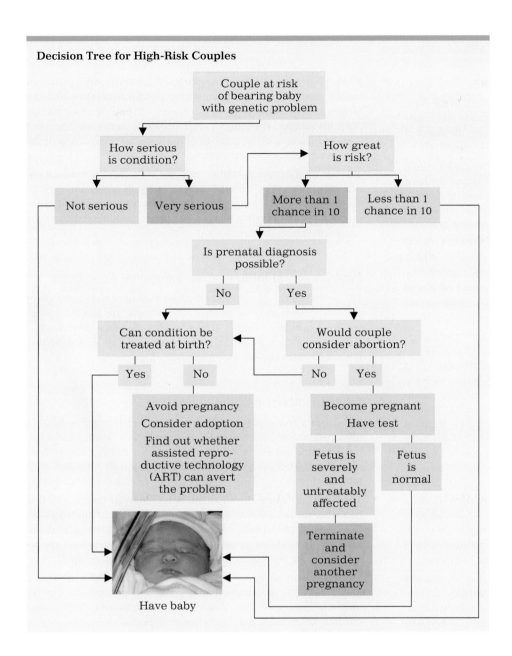

Decision Tree for High-Risk Couples

Couple at risk
of bearing baby
with genetic problem

How serious
is condition?

How great
is risk?

Not serious | Very serious

More than 1
chance in 10 | Less than 1
chance in 10

Is prenatal diagnosis
possible?

No | Yes

Can condition be
treated at birth?

Would couple
consider abortion?

Yes | No

No | Yes

Avoid pregnancy

Consider adoption

Find out whether
assisted repro-
ductive technology
(ART) can avert
the problem

Become pregnant

Have test

Fetus is
severely
and
untreatably
affected | Fetus
is
normal

Terminate
and
consider
another
pregnancy

Have baby

FIGURE 3.5 **At-Risk Decision Making** With the help of a genetic counselor, even couples who know they run a risk of having a baby with a genetic defect might decide to have a child. Although the process of making that decision is more complicated for them than it is for couples with no family genetic illness and no positive tests for harmful recessive genes, the outcome is usually a healthy baby. Genetic counselors provide facts and alternatives; couples make decisions.

ethnicity, religion, finances, ethics, personal relationship, and the number and health status of any other children they may have. Counseling begins with objective facts but ends with a very personal decision.

A child with special needs is ultimately the primary responsibility of the parents. Doctors, neighbors, teachers, and political leaders may all have opinions, and certainly can offer help, but the mother and father are the ones who must pound on a child's chest to loosen mucus (cystic fibrosis), hold the body still for the injection (diabetes, hemophilia), and ignore the stares or comments of strangers (almost all disabilities). They are also the ones who kiss their children good-night and watch them dream. Finally, they are the ones who hope that each newborn will become a toddler, a preschooler, a school-age child, a teenager, and, ultimately, a happy and healthy adult. The rest of this book describes that ongoing process, filled with problems and promise for every child—none of whom are "perfect." In the process, we will try to answer Martha's question: What do people live to do, the way a horse lives to run?

! *Answer to Observational Quiz* (from page 97): They are holding hands.

Response for a Friend (from page 98): Ask her to go with you to a genetic counselor for testing instead. She may not even be a carrier of the sickle-cell trait (you know she doesn't have the disease, so she has one chance in three of not being a carrier). Even if she is a carrier, she can have a child with the disease only if she marries a man who is also a carrier. Further, many women decide in their 30s that they want to have a child after all; urge your friend not to do anything irreversible.

SUMMARY

Genetics: Foundations in Biology and Ethics

1. Genes provide the foundation for all development, in the form of instructions for the formation of a functioning body and brain. Genes never act alone; all development is epigenetic, the result of interaction between heredity and the environment.

2. Conception occurs when two gametes (a sperm and an ovum) combine, creating a single cell called a zygote. The zygote contains all the genetic material—half from each of the two gametes—needed to create a unique developing person. That cell duplicates the entire set of instructions many times to form each new cell, so that every cell in the body contains the individual's complete DNA code.

3. About 30,000 to 40,000 genes, each with precise, chemically coded instructions, direct the creation of a sequence of amino acids, which trigger specialization and interaction between genes and cells to form a human being. Genes are arranged in precise locations on chromosomes. Humans usually have 23 pairs of chromosomes (46 in all).

4. The Human Genome Project is a massive, international effort to map every letter of the genetic code for the human species. This project has identified many detailed letter-by-letter transcriptions, which have led to detection and treatment of disabilities and diseases. Most (99 percent) of the genetic code is identical for every human being. However, some genes come in alternate versions, called alleles, and each human's code is unique in some details.

5. The twenty-third pair of chromosomes determines the individual's sex. Zygotes with an XX pair at the twenty-third location become female and those with an XY become male, with an X or Y sperm being the deciding factor. Recent understanding of genetics and chromosomes has made it possible to determine a fetus's sex and then decide whether to continue the pregnancy.

6. Genes provide genetic continuity, ensuring that all humans share common physical structure, behavioral tendencies, and reproductive potential. Genes also ensure genetic diversity, which allows humans to continue to evolve through adaptation and natural selection.

7. Every person has a unique combination of genes, with one important exception. Sometimes a zygote separates completely into two or more genetically identical cells, creating monozygotic twins, triplets, and so on, each with exactly the same genes as the others.

From Genotype to Phenotype

8. The sum total of all the genes a person inherits is the person's genotype. The expression of those genes, in combination with many influences of the environment, is the person's phenotype, or observable traits. Genes in the genotype interact in many ways to influence the phenotype, usually in an additive fashion but sometimes in a dominant–recessive pattern.

9. Some genes are located only on the X chromosome. Traits controlled by such genes are passed from mother to son but not from father to son, because a male inherits his only X chromosome from his mother. Thus, males are more likely to express recessive X-linked traits, such as color blindness, since no matching dominant gene appears on the other sex chromosome.

10. Genes affect every human trait, not only physical characteristics but also intellect, emotions, attitudes, preferences, and personality. However, from the moment of conception and continuing throughout life, humans are plastic; genes are affected by many factors in the environment.

Environmental Influences on Emotional Conditions

11. To distinguish genetic and chromosomal influences, researchers study twins and adopted children, and analyze the particular letter codes on genetic molecules at specific locations on a chromosome. Gene–environment interactions are complex, as illustrated by shyness, schizophrenia, and alcoholism.

Inherited Abnormalities

12. Chromosomal abnormalities occur when the zygote has too few or too many chromosomes, or when a chromosome has missing or extra genetic material. Most such embryos are spontaneously aborted early in pregnancy. Of the rest, most die soon after birth.

13. When an extra chromosome is attached to the twenty-first pair, this causes trisomy-21, or Down syndrome. A person with Down syndrome usually survives until middle adulthood, with numerous physical and intellectual problems. Chromosomal abnormalities in the fetus become more common as women age.

14. Extra or missing sex chromosomes—such as XXY, XYY, or a lone X—are the most common chromosomal abnormality that allows a person to survive. Another common abnormality of the sex chromosomes is fragile-X syndrome, which is caused by a gene that undercuts some of the genetic material in the X. Fragile X is particularly serious in males because they have only one X.

15. Every individual carries some genes for genetic handicaps and diseases. Most dominant disorders are not seriously disabling; they would not be passed on to the next generation if they were. Recessive disorders claim more victims and can be very serious, but they remain common because carriers are healthy and can pass on a destructive gene to their children.

16. Genetic testing and evaluation of family background can estimate a couple's risk of conceiving an embryo with a genetic problem. If the risk is high, the couple can adopt, remain childless, or obtain fetal testing on which to base their additional decisions. Each option is difficult, but genetic counselors can help clients understand the facts.

KEY TERMS

gamete (p. 69)
zygote (p. 69)
gene (p. 69)
chromosome (p. 69)
genetic code (p. 70)
Human Genome Project (p. 70)
allele (p. 71)
twenty-third pair (p. 72)
XX (p. 72)

XY (p. 72)
monozygotic twins (p. 75)
dizygotic twins (p. 76)
infertile (p. 76)
assisted reproductive
  technology (ART) (p. 76)
in vitro fertilization (IVF)
  (p. 76)

polygenic (p. 78)
multifactorial (p. 78)
genotype (p. 78)
phenotype (p. 78)
carrier (p. 78)
additive gene (p. 79)
dominant gene (p. 79)
recessive gene (p. 79)

X-linked (p. 79)
genetic imprinting (p. 80)
behavioral genetics (p. 81)
molecular genetics (p. 83)
spontaneous abortion (p. 89)
fragile-X syndrome (p. 92)
genetic counseling (p. 96)

KEY QUESTIONS

1. How many zygotes, genes, and chromosomes make one person?

2. How can detectives use genetic information to prove a person guilty or innocent of a crime?

3. How is genetic diversity among people ensured, and why is diversity important for the human species?

4. How do alleles affect human development?

5. What is the difference between genotype and phenotype?

6. What are the differences and similarities between the two types of twins?

7. Why does a person's sex affect the expression of a recessive X-linked gene?

8. What research strategies are used to distinguish genetic from environmental influences?

9. How can environment influence physical traits, such as height and weight, that are strongly genetic?

10. Why is alcoholism more common in some nations than in others?

11. Compare the severity and frequency of human dominant and recessive disorders.

12. What factors affect a child's odds of being born with genetic abnormalities?

13. Why might one couple with a Down Syndrome fetus get an abortion and another continue with the pregnancy?

14. Why are privacy and confidentiality important values for genetic counselors?

Chapter Four

Prenatal Development and Birth

germinal period The first two weeks of development after conception; characterized by rapid cell division and the beginning of cell differentiation.

embryonic period Approximately the third through the eighth week after conception, the period during which the rudimentary forms of all anatomical structures develop.

fetal period The ninth week after conception until birth, the period during which the organs grow in size and complexity.

Our primary focus in this chapter is on the astounding biological transformation from a single-cell zygote to a fully formed baby. As you will see, this is a social, not just biological, event. The mother-to-be's health habits and activities, the community's laws and practices, and the culture's customs regarding birth are just some of the myriad contextual factors that make some newborns—those fortunate enough to be born to certain mothers in certain communities and cultures—much better prepared for a long and happy life than others. Fathers also can make a difference, and so can the fetus itself—especially if the mother is particularly concerned about its well-being.

From Zygote to Newborn

The most dramatic and extensive transformation of life occurs from the beginning to the end of the prenatal period. The entire process is awesome, but to make it easier to study, human growth before birth is often divided into three main periods. The first 2 weeks of development are called the **germinal period**; the third through the eighth week is the **embryonic period**; and the ninth week until birth is the **fetal period**. (Alternative terms for these and other milestones of pregnancy are discussed in Table 4.1 on page 104.)

Germinal: The First 14 Days

You learned in Chapter 3 that, within hours after conception, the one-cell zygote, traveling slowly down the fallopian tube toward the uterus, begins the process of cell division and growth (see Figure 4.1 on page 104). At about the eight-cell stage the process of differentiation begins. The cells take on distinct characteristics and gravitate toward particular locations that foreshadow the types of cells they will become. One unmistakable sign of differentiation occurs about a week after conception, when the multiplying cells (now numbering more than 100) separate into two distinct masses. The outer cells form a protective circle that will become the *placenta* (the organ that surrounds and protects the developing creature), and the inner cells form a nucleus that will become the embryo.

TABLE 4.1 Timing and Terminology

Popular and professional books use various confusing phrases to segment pregnancy. This may help.

■ *Beginning of pregnancy:* In this text, pregnancy begins at conception, which is also the starting point of *gestational age.* However, the organism does not become an *embryo* until about two weeks later, and pregnancy does not affect the woman (and cannot be confirmed by blood or urine testing) until implantation. Paradoxically, many obstetricians date the onset of pregnancy from the date on which the woman's last menstrual period (LMP) began, about 14 days *before* conception.

■ *Length of pregnancy:* Full-term pregnancies last 266 days, or 38 weeks, or 9 months. If the LMP is used as the start, pregnancy lasts 40 weeks, sometimes expressed as 10 lunar months.

■ *Trimesters:* Instead of *germinal period, embryonic period,* and *fetal period,* some writers divide pregnancy into three-month periods called *trimesters.* Months 1, 2, and 3 are called the *first trimester;* months 4, 5, and 6, the *second trimester;* and months 7, 8, and 9 the *third trimester.*

■ *Due date:* Although doctors assign a specific due date (based on the woman's LMP), only 5 percent of babies are born on their exact date. Babies born between three weeks before and up to two weeks after are considered "on time." Babies born earlier are called *preterm;* babies born later are called *post-term.*

implantation Beginning about a week after conception, the burrowing of the organism into the lining of the uterus, where it can be nourished and protected during growth.

The first task of the outer cells is to achieve **implantation**, that is, to embed themselves in the nurturant environment of the uterus. The cells nestle into the uterine lining, rupturing tiny blood vessels in order to obtain nourishment and to build a connective web of membranes and blood vessels linking the mother and the developing organism. This connective web allows the organism to grow over the next nine months or so.

Implantation is far from automatic, however. At least 60 percent of all natural conceptions and 70 percent of all in vitro conceptions that are inserted into the uterus fail to properly implant (see Table 4.2; Bentley & Mascie-Taylor, 2000). Most new life ends even before the embryo begins to form or the woman suspects she is pregnant.

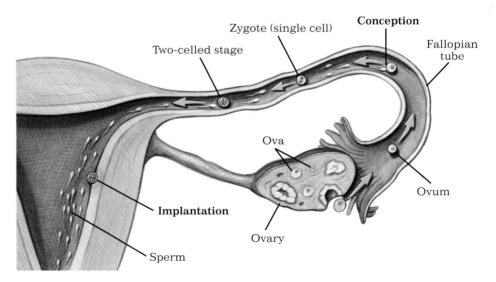

FIGURE 4.1 The Most Dangerous Journey In the first 10 days after conception, the organism does not increase in size because it is not yet nourished by the mother. However, the number of cells increases rapidly as the organism prepares for implantation.

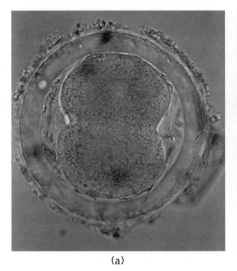
(a)

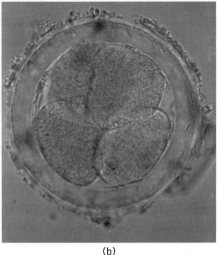
(b)

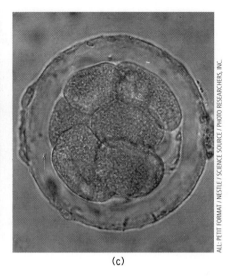
(c)

First Stages of the Germinal Period
The original zygote as it divides into (a) two cells, (b) four cells, and (c) eight cells. Occasionally at this early stage, the cells separate completely, forming the beginning of monozygotic twins, quadruplets, or octuplets.

TABLE 4.2 **Vulnerability During Prenatal Development**

The Germinal Period
At least 60 percent of all developing organisms fail to grow or implant properly, and thus do not survive the germinal period. Most of these organisms are grossly abnormal.

The Embryonic Period
About 20 percent of all embryos are aborted spontaneously, most often because of chromosomal abnormalities.

The Fetal Period
About 5 percent of all fetuses are aborted spontaneously before viability at 22 weeks or are stillborn, defined as born dead after 22 weeks.

Birth
About 31 percent of all zygotes grow and survive to become living newborn babies.

Sources: Bentley & Mascie-Taylor, 2000; Moore & Persaud, 1998.

Embryo: From the Third Through the Eighth Week

The start of the third week after conception initiates the *embryonic period,* during which the formless mass of cells becomes a distinct being—not yet recognizably human but worthy of a new name, *embryo.* First the developing organism begins differentiating into three layers, which eventually form key body systems. Then a perceptible sign of body formation appears, a fold in the outer layer of cells. At 22 days after conception this fold becomes the **neural tube,** which will later develop into the central nervous system, including the brain and spinal column (Larsen, 1998).

The head starts to take shape in the fourth week after conception. It begins as a featureless protrusion. Eyes, ears, nose, and mouth start to form within days. Also in the fourth week, a blood vessel that will become the heart begins to pulsate, making the cardiovascular system the first to show any activity. By the fifth week, buds that will become arms and legs appear, and a tail-like appendage extends from the spine. The upper arms and then forearms, palms, and webbed

neural tube A fold of outer embryonic cells that appears about three weeks after conception and later develops into the central nervous system.

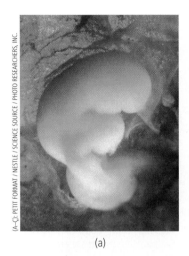

(a)

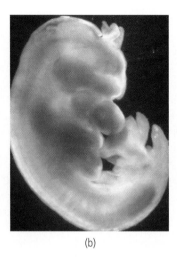

(b)

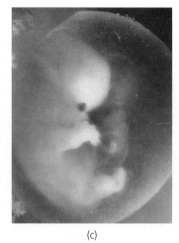

(c)

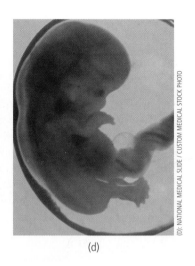

(d)

The Embryonic Period (a) At 4 weeks past conception, the embryo is only about ⅛ inch (3 millimeters) long, but already the head (top right) has taken shape. (b) At 5 weeks past conception, the embryo has grown to twice the size it was at 4 weeks. Its primitive heart, which has been pulsing for a week now, is visible, as is what appears to be a primitive tail, which will soon be enclosed by skin and protective tissue at the tip of the backbone (the coccyx). (c) By 7 weeks, the organism is somewhat less than an inch (2½ centimeters) long. Eyes, nose, the digestive system, and even the first stage of toe formation can be seen. (d) At 8 weeks, the 1-inch-long organism is clearly recognizable as a human fetus.

fingers appear about 5 weeks after conception. Legs, feet, and webbed toes, in that order, emerge a few days later, each having the beginning of a skeletal structure (Larsen, 1998).

At 8 weeks after conception, the embryo weighs about 1/30 ounce (1 gram) and is about 1 inch (2½ centimeters) long. The head has become more rounded, and the features of the face have formed. The embryo has all the basic organs and body parts (except sex organs) of a human being, including elbows and knees. The fingers and toes separate (at 52 and 54 days after conception, respectively), and the "tail" is no longer visible, having been incorporated into the lower spine at about 55 days.

Fetus: From the Ninth Week Until Birth

The organism is called a *fetus* from the ninth week after conception until it is born. That one name covers tremendous change, from a tiny, sexless creature smaller than the final joint of your thumb to a boy or girl who could nestle comfortably in your arms. We will now describe some of the details of this transformation.

The Third Month

Although the zygote already has a pair of chromosomes that determines sex, it seems as if sex organs are an afterthought in biological development. Not until the third month do the sex organs take discernible shape. Earlier, at the sixth week, the *indifferent gonad* appears, a cluster of cells that can develop into male or female sex organs. Through the seventh week, males and females are virtually identical (Larsen, 1998). Then, if the embryo is male (XY), the SRY gene on the Y chromosome sends a biochemical signal that initiates the development of male sexual organs. If the embryo is female (XX), no such signal is sent and the indifferent gonad develops female sex organs—first the vagina and uterus and then the external structures (Koopman et al., 1991).

Sex organs take several more weeks to develop, but by the twelfth week after conception the external genital organs are fully formed. Another sex-related development is that the newly formed organs begin to send hormones to the developing brain, directing small variations, depending on the sex of the developing person. Most functions of the brain are gender-neutral, and all sex-related functions are epigenetic, depending on internal and external factors that continue throughout life. However, the sex differences in brain organization occur, for the most part, in mid-gestation (Cameron, 2001).

At the end of the third month, the fetus has all its body parts, weighs approximately 3 ounces (87 grams), and is about 3 inches (7.5 centimeters) long. You should be aware, though, that early prenatal growth is very rapid and that there is considerable variation from fetus to fetus, especially in body weight. The numbers given above—3 months, 3 ounces, 3 inches—have been rounded off for easy recollection. (For those on the metric system, "100 days, 100 millimeters, 100 grams" is similarly useful.) Actually, at 12 weeks after conception, the average well-nourished fetus weighs about 1½ ounces (45 grams), while at 14 weeks the average weight is about 4 ounces (110 grams) (Moore & Persaud, 1998). So you can see that the 3-month, 3-ounce point is just a moment in a period of rapid change, a norm that is easy to remember but rarely precisely followed.

By the end of the third month, the fetus can and does move almost every part of its body—kicking its legs, sucking its thumb, even squinting and frowning. It changes position easily within the **placenta,** which is now fully formed. The placenta is composed of membranes and interwoven blood vessels connected to the umbilical cord, which brings nourishment to the fetus.

The Middle Three Months: Preparing to Survive

In the fourth, fifth, and sixth months, the heartbeat becomes stronger and the digestive and excretory systems develop more fully. Fingernails, toenails, and buds for teeth form, and hair (including eyelashes) grows. Amazing as all that is, the most impressive growth is in the brain, which increases about six times in size and begins to react to stimuli. The brain develops many new neurons (in a process called *neurogenesis*) and synapses, or connections between neurons (*synaptogenesis*), in the middle trimester. This process continues for years, as you will see in later chapters (Bourgeois, 2001; Takahashi et al., 2001), but the entire central nervous system first becomes responsive and sentient during mid-pregnancy. Some of the stages of prenatal brain growth and development are shown in Figure 4.2 on page 108.

Advances in fetal brain functioning may be the critical factor in the attainment of the **age of viability** (the age at which a preterm newborn can survive), because it is the brain that regulates basic body functions, such as breathing and sucking. Viability now begins at about 22 weeks after conception (Moore & Persaud, 1998). Babies born before 22 weeks' gestational age rarely survive more than a few days, because even the most sophisticated respirators and heart regulators cannot maintain life in a fetus whose brain has not yet begun to function. If such babies survive, they are nearly always severely brain-damaged. At 25 weeks, the brain shows signs of awareness of stimulation, and the heart rate increases, with the heartbeat now making a loud noise (Joseph, 2000). At 26 weeks, the survival rate improves to about 50 percent, with 14 percent of the survivors being severely mentally retarded and 12 percent having cerebral palsy (Lorenz et al., 1998).

At about 28 weeks after conception, brain maturation takes a "striking" leap forward (Carlson, 1994). At that time the brain-wave pattern shifts from a flat pattern to one with occasional bursts of activity, resembling the sleep–wake cycles of a newborn. Similarly, because of ongoing brain maturation, the heart rate becomes regulated by body movement (speeding up during activity, slowing during rest) between 28 and 32 weeks after conception (DiPietro et al., 1996). Movement patterns also become responsive, with regular cycles of rest and activity beginning at about 25 to 28 weeks, as the brain matures (Joseph, 2000). Largely because of this neurological awakening, the odds of survival are much better for a preterm infant who is at least 28 weeks old.

Weight is also crucial to viability. By 28 weeks, the typical fetus weighs about 3 pounds (1,300 grams), and its chances of survival have increased to 95 percent. The smallest newborn ever to survive was born in Florence, Italy, in February

placenta The disk-shaped temporary organ that connects the wall of the uterus and the umbilical cord. The placenta allows oxygen and nourishment to flow to the fetus and permits carbon dioxide and wastes to flow away but maintains the separation of the mother's and fetus's circulatory systems.

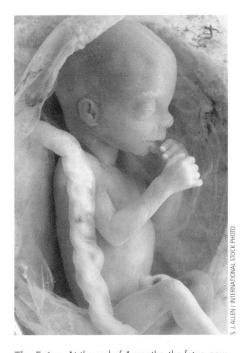

S.J. ALLEN / INTERNATIONAL STOCK PHOTO

The Fetus At the end of 4 months, the fetus, now 6 inches long, looks fully formed but out of proportion—the distance from the top of the skull to the neck is almost as large as that from the neck to the rump. For many more weeks, the fetus must depend on the translucent membranes of the placenta and umbilical cord (the long white object in the foreground) for survival.

?*Observational Quiz* (see answer, page 108): Can you see eyebrows, fingernails, and genitals?

age of viability The age (about 22 weeks after conception) at which a fetus can survive outside the mother's uterus if specialized medical care is available.

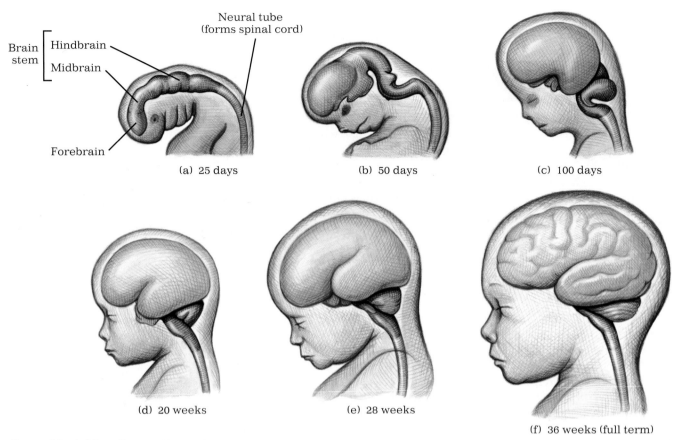

(a) 25 days   (b) 50 days   (c) 100 days

(d) 20 weeks   (e) 28 weeks

(f) 36 weeks (full term)

Source: Adapted from Cowan, 1997, p. 116

FIGURE 4.2 Prenatal Growth of the Brain
Just 25 days after conception (a), the central nervous system is already evident. The brain looks distinctly human by day 100 (c). By the 28th week of gestation (e), the various sections of the brain are recognizable, at the very time brain activity begins. When the fetus is full-term (f), all the parts of the brain, including the cortex (the outer layer), are formed, folding over one another and becoming more convoluted, or wrinkled, as the number of brain cells increases.

! Answer to Observational Quiz (from page 107): Yes, yes, and no. Genitals are formed, but they are not visible in this photo. That object growing from the lower belly is the umbilical cord.

2002. The tiny baby girl weighed just 10 ounces. Fetuses that small are usually less than 20 weeks old and are stillborn. But little Pearl had four advantages: her sex (girls have better survival odds), her birth process (elective cesarean, which puts no stress on the fetus), her birthplace (an advanced medical center), and her fetal age (27 weeks). The obstetrician was "completely taken aback" by her weight, but her maturity helped her survive (D'Emilio, 2002).

The Final Three Months: From Viability to Full Term

Attaining the age of viability simply means that life outside the womb is possible. Each day of the final three months of prenatal growth improves the odds, not only of survival but also of a healthy and happy first few months for baby and parents. A viable preterm infant born in the seventh month is a tiny creature requiring intensive hospital care, dependent on life-support systems for each gram of nourishment and for every shallow breath. By contrast, after nine months or so, the typical full-term infant is a vigorous person, ready to thrive at home on mother's milk—no expert help, oxygenated air, special food, or technical assistance required.

The critical difference between the fragile preterm baby and the robust full-term newborn is maturation of the respiratory and cardiovascular systems. This occurs in the last three months of prenatal life. During that period, the lungs begin to expand and contract, exercising the muscles that are involved in breathing by using the amniotic fluid surrounding the fetus as a substitute for air. The fetus takes in fluid through mouth and nose and then exhales it, much as a fish would. At the same time, the valves of the heart go through a final maturation that, at birth, enables the circulatory system to function independently.

In addition, the fetus usually gains a critical 4.5 pounds (2,000 grams) or more of body weight in the last 10 weeks, increasing to about 7½ pounds (3,400 grams)

TABLE 4.3 Average Prenatal Weights*

Period of Development	Weeks After Conception	Weight (Nonmetric)	Weight (Metric)	Notes
End of embryonic period	8	1/30 oz	1 g	A birthweight below 2 lb (1,000 g) is considered extremely low birthweight (**ELBW**).
End of first trimester	13	3 oz	100 g	
At viability (50–50 chance of survival)	24	22 oz	600 g	
End of second trimester	26–28	2–3 lb	1,000–1,300 g	Below 3½ lb (1,500 g) is very low birthweight (**VLBW**).
End of preterm period	35	5½ lb	2,500 g	Below 5½ lb (2,500 g) is low birthweight (**LBW**).
Full term	38	7½ lb	3,400 g	Between 5½ and 9 lb (2,500–4,500 g) is considered normal weight.

*To make them easier to remember, the weights are rounded off (which accounts for the inexact correspondence between metric and nonmetric measures). Actual weights vary. For instance, a normal full-term infant can weigh between 5½ and 9 pounds (2.5 and 4 kilograms); a viable infant, especially one of several born at 26 or more weeks, can weigh less than shown here.

at birth (see Table 4.3). This weight gain is primarily fat, which will insulate the newborn and provide calories that will be burned while the mother's breast milk is being fully established. The weight gain also ensures that the developing brain is well nourished; severe malnutrition in the second or third trimester reduces the child's ability to learn (Georgieff & Rao, 2001).

In many ways, the relationship between mother and child begins during the final three months, for during this time the size and movements of the fetus make her very aware of it, and her sounds, smells, and behavior become part of fetal consciousness.

Especially for Fathers-to-Be: When does a man's nongenetic influence on his children begin?

In Person

The Listening Fetus

The fetus is no passive passenger in the womb, nor is the pregnant woman simply "carrying" the fetus. Development is interactive, even before birth (Kisilevsky & Low, 1998). Toward the end of prenatal development, fetal sensory systems begin to function. Interaction between fetus and mother-to-be is apparent. For example, how much amniotic fluid the fetus swallows depends partly on the taste of that fluid: Fetuses swallow sweetened fluid more rapidly than noxious fluid, and thus their lungs, digestion, and nutrition are intimately related to the particulars of their mother's diet (Carlson, 1994). Immediately after birth, the smell of amniotic fluid is more soothing than other smells or than no smell at all, again indicating sensory adaptation before birth (Varendi et al., 1998). Further, at about the twenty-seventh week, the eyelids open, and the fetus perceives the reddish glow of sunlight or other bright illumination that diffuses through the woman's belly (Kitzinger, 1989).

The most remarkable fetal learning involves hearing, with the first fetal responses to noise evident at the twenty-eighth week of gestation (Aslin & Hunt, 2001). This comes as no surprise to most mothers-to-be, who have felt the developing person quiet down for a lullaby or startle with a kick when a door slams. But many people do not realize that newborns remember certain sounds heard before birth. The most obvious example is that infants typically stop crying when they are held with an ear close to the mother's heart, comforted by the familiar rhythm they have heard for months. Few mothers know this explicitly, but most instinctively cradle their infants on their left side, close to their heart.

Newborns also remember voices heard in the womb (Fifer & Moon, 1995). In a series of experiments, pregnant women read the same children's book aloud daily during the ninth month. Three days after birth, their infants listened to recordings of the same story, read either by the infant's own mother or by another baby's mother. Laboratory monitoring indicated that the newborns paid greater attention to the recordings of their own mother's voice. What's more, the newborns responded less when their mothers read an unfamiliar story than when they read the familiar one.

In other words, the newborns remembered both who talked to them before birth and what was said—or, to be accurate, they recognized the vocal rhythms and the speech patterns (Nazzi et al., 1998). Not surprisingly, then, infants born to monolingual English or Spanish mothers, when listening to the taped speech of a stranger speaking English or Spanish, preferred to listen to their native language (Moon et al., 1993).

Such results suggest that fetuses prepare more than just their reflexes and organ systems for physiological functioning after birth; they also begin to accustom themselves to the particulars of the social world that they soon will join. Meanwhile, mothers begin to identify features of their future offspring: Almost all pregnant women, by the last three months, are talking to, patting, and dreaming about their long-awaited child. Most women share this joy with the baby's father; the mother may urge him to put his hand on the rippling bulge on her belly where the fetus is kicking, engage him in detailed discussions about names and various child-raising issues, and review their plan for getting to the hospital. All this anticipation is much more likely if both parents wanted and planned the pregnancy—but, in fact, almost half the babies born in the United States are conceived unintentionally (CDC, April 26, 2002). Ideally, however, bonding begins at conception, as both parents begin eating healthier foods, eliminate contact with toxins (including pesticides, cleaning fluids, and secondhand smoke), and decrease stress.

Of course, pregnancy itself is stressful, especially if the baby might not be healthy. Remember John and Martha, the young couple you met in Chapter 3, whose amniocentesis revealed trisomy-21? One night at 3:00 A.M., after about seven months of pregnancy, Martha was crying uncontrollably. She told John she was scared.

"Scared of what?" he said, "Of a little baby who's not as perfect as you think he ought to be?" . . .

"I didn't say I wanted him to be perfect," I said. "I just want him to be normal. That's all I want. Just normal."

"That is total bullshit. . . . You don't want this baby to be normal. You'd throw him in a dumpster if he just turned out to be normal. What you really want is for him to be superhuman."

"For your information," I said in my most acid tone, "I was the one who decided to keep this baby, even though he's got Down's. You were the one who wanted to throw him in a dumpster."

"How would you know?" John's voice was still gaining volume. "You never asked me what I wanted, did you? No. You never even asked me. . . ."

[Beck, 1999, p. 255]

This episode ended well, with a long, warm, and honest conversation between the two prospective parents, the first one they had had since Martha had gotten pregnant. Both parents now understood better what their Down syndrome fetus meant to them. Adam, their future son, became an important part of their relationship. Such honest discussions between parents are crucial throughout pregnancy to form a "parental alliance," a shared commitment to cooperate in raising the child.

Although there are good reasons to talk to the fetus as well as to talk about it, prospective parents are not always rational. My husband and I became so impatient for the birth of our first child that we bought a puppy one month before the due date. Despite all the time and stress the dog entailed, we enjoyed caring for this small creature. A day after Bethany was finally born, I telephoned from the hospital to ask how the puppy was.

"Fine," my husband said. "She wagged her tail when I told her she had a little sister."

Now Hear This Big sister talks to her future sibling—and there is evidence that the fetus can hear and, to some extent, understand.

JON FEINGERSH / CORBISSTOCKMARKET.COM

Risk Reduction

Now we will describe some of the many toxins, illnesses, and experiences that can harm a developing person in the months before birth. Do not let this topic alarm you. As you will see, knowledge is protective, and most fetuses are born completely unaffected by the potential hazards we discuss here. Keep two facts in mind:

■ Despite the complexity of prenatal development and the many dangers to the developing organism, the large majority of babies are born healthy and capable.
■ Most hazards can be avoided, or their effects reduced, through care taken by an expectant woman, her family, and the community.

Thus, prenatal development should be thought of not as a dangerous period to be feared, but as a natural process to be protected. The goal of *teratology,* the study of birth defects, is to increase the odds that every newborn will have a healthy start in life.

Scientists now understand a great deal about **teratogens,** the broad range of substances (such as drugs and pollutants) and conditions (such as severe malnutrition and extreme stress) that increase the risk of prenatal abnormalities. These abnormalities include physical problems that are obvious at birth and more subtle impairments, such as learning disabilities, that first appear in elementary school. A specific teratogen may damage the body structures, the growth rate, the neurological networks, or all three.

Teratogens that can harm the brain, and therefore make a child hyperactive, antisocial, retarded, and so on, are called **behavioral teratogens.** Although they do not cause problems as readily apparent as missing limbs or sightless eyes, behavioral teratogens can be far more damaging over the life of the person than physical defects. About 3 percent of all fetuses are born with major structural anomalies, another 2 percent with minor problems (Green, 2001), and between 10 and 20 percent with behavioral difficulties that could be related to prenatal damage.

Determining Risk

Teratology is a science of **risk analysis,** of weighing the factors that affect the likelihood that a particular teratogen will cause harm. Although all teratogens increase the *risk* of harm, none *always* cause damage. The ultimate impact depends on the complex interplay of many factors, both destructive and protective. Exposure to a particular teratogen might be of low risk for one embryo, probably causing no harm at all, and of high risk for another, almost certainly causing damage. Obviously, a goal of risk analysis is to pinpoint exactly what separates these two outcomes in order to improve the odds for all babies.

For developmentalists, another goal is that couples, as soon as a pregnancy is confirmed, begin to prepare for the commitment required to care for another person. This care cannot always be perfect, and its object is a small being who is not perfect. Some contend that the very word *risk* "smuggles in an unexamined negative value about the adversity of the condition [of pregnancy]" (Heyman & Henriksen, 2000, p. 7). It is impossible to be dispassionate and neutral about human development at any stage, or to guarantee ideal growth. Knowing that life can never be risk-free, we use the word *risk* as shorthand in discussing probability.

Response for Fathers-to-Be (from page 109): Before conception, through his influence on the mother's attitudes and health.

teratogens Agents and conditions, including viruses, drugs, chemicals, stressors, and malnutrition, that can impair prenatal development and lead to birth defects or even death.

behavioral teratogens Teratogens that tend to harm the prenatal brain, affecting the future child's intellectual and emotional functioning.

risk analysis The process of weighing the potential outcomes of a particular event, substance, or experience to determine the likelihood of harm. In teratology, risk analysis involves an attempt to evaluate all the factors that increase or decrease the likelihood that a particular teratogen will cause harm.

A Week for Fingers The impact of a potential teratogen partially depends on when the developing organism is exposed to it. This is because there is a critical period in the formation of every body part during which the part is especially vulnerable. Shown here are three stages in finger development that define the critical period: (a) notches appear in the hand at day 44; (b) fingers are separated and lengthened by day 50; (c) fingers are completely formed by day 55, and the critical period for hand development is over. Other parts of the body, including the eyes, heart, and central nervous system, take much longer to complete development, so the critical period during which they are vulnerable to teratogens lasts for months rather than days.

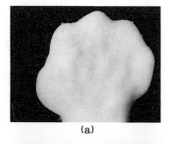
(a)

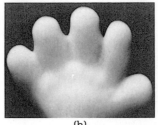
(b)

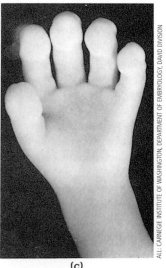
(c)

ALL: CARNEGIE INSTITUTE OF WASHINGTON, DEPARTMENT OF EMBRYOLOGY, DAVID DIVISION

Timing of Exposure

One crucial factor in teratology is timing—the age of the developing organism. Some teratogens cause damage only during specific days early in pregnancy, when a particular part of the body is forming. Others can be harmful at any time, but the severity of the damage depends on when exposure occurred.

The time of greatest susceptibility is called the **critical period.** As you can see in Figure 4.3, each body structure has its own critical period: It begins for the ears, limbs, and eyes at about four weeks after conception, for the lips at about five weeks, and for the teeth and palate at about seven weeks. The entire embryonic stage can be called a critical period for physical structure and form, with the specifics varying somewhat week by week (Moore & Persaud, 1998). Because those first two months are critical, most obstetricians today recommend that all couples who are considering pregnancy get counseling, start taking multivitamins, stop taking psychoactive drugs, and update their immunizations (Kuller et al., 2001).

For conditions (such as severe malnutrition) and substances (such as heroin) that disrupt and destabilize the overall functioning of the woman's body, there

critical period In prenatal development, the time when a particular organ or other body part is most susceptible to teratogenic damage.

FIGURE 4.3 Critical Periods in Human Development The most serious damage from teratogens is likely to occur in the first 8 weeks after conception (light shading). However, significant damage to many vital parts of the body, including the brain, eyes, and genitals, can occur during the last months of pregnancy as well (dark shading).

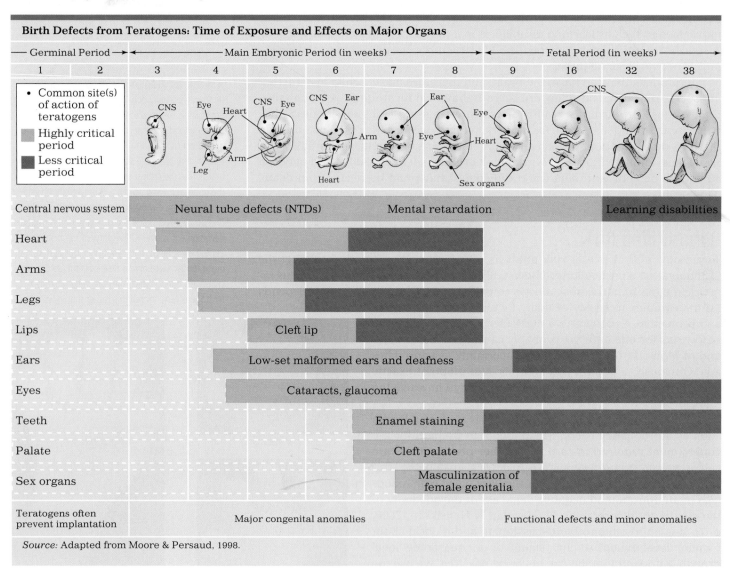

Source: Adapted from Moore & Persaud, 1998.

are two critical periods. The first is at the very beginning of pregnancy, when stress during the germinal period can impede implantation. The second critical period is toward the end of pregnancy, when the fetus most needs to gain weight and when the cortex of the brain is developing. At this time the fetus is particularly vulnerable to damage that can cause learning disabilities. Further, near the end of pregnancy, instability of the mother's body systems (for instance, if she has chills or the shakes) can loosen the placenta or cause hormonal changes, both of which can precipitate birth.

Note that for behavioral teratogens there is no safe period. The brain and nervous system can be harmed throughout prenatal development and infancy.

Amount of Exposure

A second important factor is the dose and/or frequency of exposure. Some teratogens have a **threshold effect;** that is, they are virtually harmless until exposure reaches a certain level, at which point they "cross the threshold" from being innocuous to being damaging. Indeed, a few substances, such as vitamin A, are actually beneficial in small amounts but fiercely teratogenic in large quantities (Kraft & Willhite, 1997). Vitamin A is an essential part of a good prenatal diet, so vitamin A is a component of most multivitamins for pregnant women; but more than 10,000 units per day may be too much.

For most teratogens, experts are reluctant to specify a threshold below which the substance is safe. One reason is that many teratogens have an **interaction effect;** that is, one poison intensifies the effects of another. Alcohol, tobacco, and marijuana are among the substances that interact, together doing more harm than any one of them would do alone.

Genetic Vulnerability

A third factor that determines whether a specific teratogen will be harmful, and to what extent, is the developing organism's genes. When a woman carrying dizygotic twins drinks alcohol, for example, the twins' blood alcohol levels are exactly equal; yet one may be more severely affected than the other (Maier et al., 1996). This difference probably involves a gene affecting a specific enzyme (alcohol dehydrogenase) that is crucial to the breakdown of alcohol. Similar genetic susceptibilities are suspected in other birth disorders, including cleft palate and club foot (Hartl & Jones, 1999). Because of epigenetic variability, even monozygotic twins may be affected differently. For example, all four of the monozygotic Genain quadruplets (born in 1930) developed schizophrenia, but the severity and type of each woman's condition varied (Plomin et al., 2001).

Genes are also implicated in the teratogenic effect of a deficiency of folic acid (a B-complex vitamin) in the mother-to-be's diet. Researchers have known for several years that folic-acid deficiency can produce *neural-tube defects*—either *spina bifida,* in which the spine does not close properly, or *anencephaly,* in which part of the brain does not form. Neural-tube defects occur more commonly in certain families and ethnic groups (specifically, Irish, English, and Egyptian) and not often in others (most Asian and African groups). That fact led to research that found the source: A defective gene produces an enzyme that prevents the normal utilization of folic acid (Mills et al., 1995).

In some cases, genetic vulnerability is related to the sex of the developing organism. Generally, male (XY) embryos and fetuses are at greater risk than female (XX). This is one explanation for a known fact: Male fetuses are more often aborted spontaneously. In addition, newborn boys have more birth defects, and older boys have more learning disabilities and other problems caused by behavioral teratogens. Autism, for instance, is largely genetic, but about four times as many boys as girls are autistic.

Especially for the Friend of a Pregnant Woman: Suppose that your friend is frightened of having an abnormal child. She refuses to read about prenatal development because she is afraid to learn about what could go wrong. What could you tell her?

threshold effect The phenomenon in which a particular teratogen is relatively harmless in small doses but becomes harmful once exposure reaches a certain level (the threshold).

interaction effect The phenomenon in which a teratogen's potential for causing harm increases when it is combined with another teratogen or another risk factor.

Response for the Friend of a Pregnant Woman (from page 113): Reassure her that almost all pregnancies turn out fine, partly because most defective fetuses are spontaneously aborted and partly because protective factors are active throughout pregnancy. Equally important, the more she learns about teratogens, the more she will learn about protecting her fetus. Many birth defects and complications can be prevented with good prenatal care.

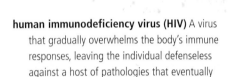

human immunodeficiency virus (HIV) A virus that gradually overwhelms the body's immune responses, leaving the individual defenseless against a host of pathologies that eventually manifest themselves as AIDS.

Hope for the Future Marilis and Anol, of the Dominican Republic, are especially delighted with their 18-month-old daughter, Yolanda, because their first child died of AIDS at age 2. Both parents are HIV-positive, but Yolanda is not. To avoid transmitting the virus to her baby, Marilis took the anti-AIDS drug AZT during her pregnancy, delivered Yolanda by cesarean section, and gives the baby formula rather than breast-feeding her. Yolanda, too, received AZT for the first 6 weeks of her life. Marilis and Anol hope that their story will inspire other people to do all they can to reduce the transmission of HIV.

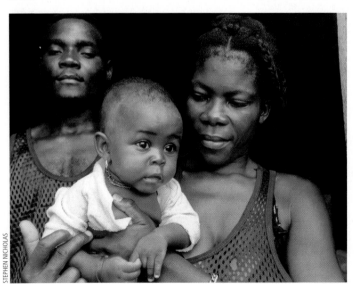

STEPHEN NICHOLAS

Specific Teratogens

Because of the many variables involved, risk analysis cannot precisely predict the results of teratogenic exposure in individual cases (Jacobson & Jacobson, 1996). However, decades of research have revealed the possible effects of some of the most common and damaging teratogens. More important, much has been learned about how individuals and society can reduce the risks.

Diseases

Many diseases, including most viruses and virtually all sexually transmitted diseases, can harm a fetus. Here we will focus on only two conditions, rubella and HIV, that also illustrate the potential for public health measures to prevent birth defects.

Rubella One of the first teratogens to be recognized was *rubella* (sometimes called *German measles*). Rubella was long considered a harmless childhood disease. But 50 years ago doctors discovered that if a woman contracts rubella early in pregnancy, her embryo might suffer blindness, deafness, heart abnormalities, and brain damage. (Some of these problems and their effects were apparent in my nephew David's story in Chapter 1.)

The seriousness of this teratogen became all too evident in a worldwide rubella epidemic in the mid-1960s. In the United States alone, 20,000 infants had obvious rubella-caused impairments, including hundreds who were born both deaf and blind (Franklin, 1984). Thousands more showed no immediate effects because damage was done only to the brain, but behavioral or learning problems appeared later in childhood (Enkin et al., 1989).

Since that epidemic, widespread immunization—either of preschool children (as in the United States) or of all adolescent girls who are not already immune (as in England)—has reduced the rubella threat. Consequently, only two rubella-syndrome infants were born in the United States in 2001 (CDC, January 4, 2002). Other teratogenic diseases (for example, chicken pox) likewise have been controlled by immunization and now rarely damage fetuses.

Pediatric AIDS No immunization is yet available for the most devastating viral teratogen of all: the **human immunodeficiency virus (HIV).** HIV gradually overwhelms the body's natural immune response, becoming *AIDS (acquired immune deficiency syndrome)* when the person's immune system can no longer fight off any of dozens of debilitating and deadly infectious diseases.

Pregnant women with HIV transmit the virus, prenatally or during birth, to about 25 percent of their infants. HIV overwhelms a very young body faster than a fully grown one. Consequently, worldwide, most of the 570 million HIV-positive infants born in 2000 will die before age 5 (Parker, 2002). In medically advanced nations, hundreds of HIV-positive children survive to adolescence, attending school, making friends, and understanding their illnesses (Brown et al., 2000). Like other children with innate vulnerability (to conditions such as juvenile diabetes, sickle-cell anemia, and asthma), HIV-positive children enjoy their lives; but their survival makes the need for prevention more obvious, because parents, doctors, and the children themselves suffer year after year.

Prevention of pediatric AIDS may now be possible. If a pregnant HIV-positive woman takes antiretroviral drugs (such as ZDV and AZT) starting 14 weeks after conception and gives birth by cesarean section and if the newborn is given antiretroviral drugs and is not breast-fed, then mother-to-child transmission of HIV is reduced from about 25 percent to 8 percent. Indeed, comprehensive counseling and free treatment for all pregnant women in the state of Michigan reduced the known rate of transmission from 19 percent to 3 percent in just seven years (1993–2000) (CDC, February 8, 2002). Most of the mothers who actually transmitted the virus during these seven years did not start taking antiretroviral drugs by mid-pregnancy. Michigan's success makes it clear why half a million children still develop AIDS each year. For successful prevention, the medical infrastructure must provide early counseling, adequate prenatal care, and free antiretroviral drugs. None of these steps are taken in the nations of sub-Saharan Africa, where 20 million adults carry the virus, or in many other countries (Jha et al., 2001).

In addition, women must go to a doctor early in pregnancy, learn their HIV status, and take the drugs. Each step of this process demands some courage. One woman from central Africa said, "I am going to die anyway. My baby might live but what is the point, as there will be no mother to raise my baby" (quoted in Bassett, 2002). (She has a point; even HIV-negative African babies are likely to die if their mother dies of AIDS.) Even in most of the United States, some pregnant women choose not to know their HIV status, and some obstetricians do not routinely test for HIV. In contrast, Michigan law requires confidential counseling and testing to be offered to all pregnant women, "regardless of their race, age, or marital or socioeconomic status" (CDC, February 8, 2002).

In short, early and diligent prenatal care can reduce the dangers posed to the fetus by infectious diseases, but such care is often lacking. Even in the United States, the wealthiest nation of the world, 240 newborns had congenital syphilis in 2001 (CDC, January 4, 2002); the severe damage that this disease causes to the fetal brain and body can easily be prevented if the mother is diagnosed, treated, and cured early in pregnancy. Overall, about 25 percent of pregnant women in the United States who choose to give birth also choose not to obtain prenatal care until after the critical first trimester (CDC, April 26, 2002).

Medicines and Drugs

The vital importance of prenatal counseling and care is underscored by the evidence on the many medicines that can damage a fetus. The list of proven teratogenic medicines includes tetracycline, anticoagulants, bromides, anticonvulsants, phenobarbital, retinoic acid (a common treatment for acne, as in Accutane), and most hormones. Other prescription drugs and nonprescription drugs (such as aspirin, antacids, and diet pills) may be teratogenic. Obviously, then, women who might become pregnant, or who are pregnant, should avoid taking any medication unless it is recommended by a doctor who is both well versed in teratology *and* aware of the possible pregnancy.

Prenatal damage is also caused by *psychoactive drugs*—that is, drugs that affect the psyche (see Table 4.4). Beer and wine, liquor, cigarettes and smokeless tobacco, heroin and methadone, LSD, marijuana, cocaine in any form, inhalants, and antidepressant pills are the most common preventable teratogens. All psychoactive drugs slow down fetal growth and increase the risk of premature labor. All can affect the developing brain, producing both short-term and long-term deficits. For days or weeks after birth, infants who were prenatally addicted to any of these drugs sleep fitfully, startle easily, cry unhappily, suck voraciously, eat erratically, and show other signs of drug withdrawal.

As they develop, such children may exhibit learning difficulties, impaired self-control, poor concentration, and overall irritability. Beyond these general effects, each drug varies in its specific effects. Thus, tobacco causes low birthweight, while alcohol causes **fetal alcohol syndrome (FAS),** the leading teratogenic cause of mental retardation. Definitive longitudinal data on both FAS and the less severe

Especially for Social Workers: When is it most important to convince women to be tested for HIV—a month before pregnancy, a month after conception, or immediately after birth?

BOB DAEMMRICH / THE IMAGE WORKS

Drug Abuse Smoking and drinking are an essential part of daily life for millions of young women, many of whom find these habits impossible to give up when they become pregnant. If you met this woman at a party and you thought complete abstinence was too much to ask, temperance might be a reasonable suggestion. Taking a few puffs and a few sips, or using just one drug and not the other, might prevent damage to the fetus's developing body and brain.

fetal alcohol syndrome (FAS) A cluster of birth defects, including abnormal facial characteristics, slow physical growth, and retarded mental development, that is caused by the mother's drinking excessive quantities of alcohol when pregnant.

TABLE 4.4 Effects of Psychoactive Drugs on Prenatal Development

Drug	Usage	Effects
Alcohol	3 or more drinks daily, or binge drinking of 5 or more drinks on one occasion early in pregnancy	Causes *fetal alcohol syndrome (FAS)*. Symptoms include a small head, abnormal facial characteristics (wide spacing between the eyes, a flattened nose and a narrow upper lip, unusual eyelids, and missing skin indentation between nose and upper lip), overall growth retardation, learning disabilities, and behavior problems (including poor concentration and impaired social skills).
	More than ½ oz. of absolute alcohol a day	Causes *fetal alcohol effects (FAE)*. FAE does not observably affect facial appearance or physical growth, but it affects brain functioning. The first sign is noisy, higher-frequency cries at birth. Later signs, on cognitive tests, include lower IQ (by about 5 points).
	Moderate drinking: less than 1 or 2 servings of beer or wine or 1 mixed drink a few days per week	Probably has no negative effects on prenatal development, although this is controversial.
Tobacco	Maternal smoking early in pregnancy	Increases risk of certain rare abnormalities, including malformation of the limbs and the urinary tract.
	Maternal smoking late in pregnancy	Reduces birthweight and size. Babies born to habitual smokers weigh, on average, about 9 oz. (250 g) less, and they are shorter, both at birth and in the years to come. They may have asthma.
	Paternal smoking	Reduces birthweight by about 2 oz. (45 g) on average.
Marijuana	Heavy use	Affects the central nervous system, as evidenced by the tendency of affected newborns to emit a high-pitched cry that denotes brain damage.
	Light use	Has no proven long-term effects.
Heroin	Any use	Because of the physiological "highs" and "crashes" of the addiction (such as the reduction of oxygen, irregular heartbeat, and sweating and chills that occur during withdrawal), heroin causes slower fetal growth and premature labor. (See also *methadone,* below.)
Methadone	Later in pregnancy	Moderates the effects of heroin withdrawal during pregnancy but is as addictive as heroin. Heavily addicted newborns require regulated drug doses in the first days of life to prevent the pain and convulsions of sudden opiate withdrawal.
Cocaine	Any use	Causes overall growth retardation, problems with the placenta, and specific learning problems in the first months of life. Research on long-lasting effects is confounded by the effects of poverty and the ongoing addiction of the mother. The major concern is in language development.
Solvents	Especially early in pregnancy	Causes smaller heads, crossed eyes, and other abnormalities.

Overall sources: Larsen, 1998; Lyons & Rittner, 1998.

condition called FAE (fetal alcohol effects) are now available. The data leave no doubt that alcohol is a behavioral teratogen. It increases hyperactivity, reduces concentration, and causes specific learning deficits, particularly in spatial reasoning and arithmetic (Streissguth & Connor, 2001).

Such definitive longitudinal research on the effects of specific illegal drugs is not available, because it is virtually impossible to locate a sizable representative sample of newly pregnant women who use one, and only one, illicit drug at a steady and measurable dose. Illicit drug users almost always use several legal as well as illegal drugs—not just their drug of choice—so interactive effects are common.

Furthermore, when a mother-to-be is *addicted* to an illicit drug, the fetal hazards are compounded by her erratic sleeping and eating habits; her bouts of anxiety, stress, and depression; and her increased risk of accidents, violence, and sexual abuse. One study of more than 3,000 women found that most of those who used psychoactive drugs quit during pregnancy. The unfortunate exceptions were the 100 or so who were physically abused by their partners; they were more likely to continue drug abuse (Martin et al., 1996). Finally, severely addicted women are

Response for Social Workers (from page 115): Voluntary testing and then treatment can be useful at any time, since women who learn that they are HIV-positive are more likely to get treatment, in order to reduce the likelihood of transmission, and to avoid pregnancy. If pregnancy does occur, diagnosis early in pregnancy is best, since abortion is one option and taking antiretroviral drugs such as AZT is another—one that prevents many cases of pediatric AIDS.

BOTH: GEORGE STEINMETZ

Differences and Similarities The differences between these two children are obvious at a glance: One is an African American teenager, the other a Swedish toddler. One similarity is obvious, too: Both are girls. However, the most important similarity—fetal alcohol syndrome—is apparent only on closer observation.

? *Observational Quiz* (see answer, page 119): How many of the five visible facial characteristics of fetal alcohol syndrome can you see in both girls?

often malnourished and sick, unsupported by concerned family members, and without medical care. After a baby is born, all these problems typically surround the child for years, along with possible additional stresses from an absent or abusive father and a poor and dangerous neighborhood. So targeting prenatal use of a particular illegal drug as *the* cause of the child's learning problems is obviously unscientific. Targeting it as a signal that a woman is in serious trouble, and that she and her fetus need ongoing, intensive help, makes sense.

Changing Policy

Preventing Drug Damage

Despite the ambiguity of much of the longitudinal research on drug use, the evidence leads to a strong recommendation: Pregnant women should avoid drugs entirely, because nothing is risk-free, even an occasional indulgence.

Nevertheless, many women in their prime reproductive years drink alcohol, smoke cigarettes, or use illicit drugs. Most continue their drug use in the first weeks before they realize that they are pregnant. It is already late, after the early formation of the embryo. To make matters worse, those who are addicts, alcoholics, or heavy users of multiple drugs are least likely to stop on their own, least likely to recognize their condition in the first few weeks and obtain early medical care, and often excluded from residential drug treatment programs.

General education is not enough. For example, the danger of tobacco and alcohol use during pregnancy is well known, and warning signs are displayed on cigarette packs and in liquor stores and bars. Yet about one in six pregnant women in the United States smoked during the final three months of pregnancy, with those under age 25 twice as likely to smoke as those over age 35 (CDC, September 24, 1999). Similarly, in a 1999 U.S. survey, 13 percent of pregnant women admitted drinking, at least a little, and 3.3 percent said that they had drunk a lot within the previous month—at least one

drink per day or five or more drinks on one occasion, a level that is definitely risky (see Figure 4.4 on page 118). This rate has not declined substantially in the past decade (CDC, April 5, 2002). Worse, the actual amount and prevalence of drinking are undoubtedly higher, because many alcoholics hide the extent of their drinking. A careful assessment in Seattle, Washington, of babies born in 1981 found that 3 in 1,000 had fetal alcohol syndrome and another 6 in 1,000 had less obvious brain damage (Sampson et al., 1997). The overall rate, about 1 in 100, shows that while not every pregnant drinker harms her fetus, far too many do. In fact, alcohol remains the leading teratogenic cause of mental retardation (Jacobs et al., 2000).

What can be done, beyond general education? The research suggests five protective steps:

1. *Abstinence from all drugs even before pregnancy.* The best course is to avoid drugs altogether. This can make a dramatic difference, as is shown by data on babies born to women who have recently emigrated to North America. For many reasons, including poverty and lack of medical care, immigrants are at high risk for prenatal and birth complications of every kind. However, their newborns weigh more, are born with fewer defects, and show less evidence of behavioral teratogens than do native-born children of the same

ethnicity (Beiser et al., 2002; Hernandez & Charney, 1998). One reason is that immigrants are more often drug-free, not only because of cultural patterns but also because their husbands and parents discourage any substance use in pregnancy.

2. *Abstinence from all drugs after the first month.* The teratogenic effects of psychoactive drugs accumulate throughout pregnancy. Thus, early prenatal care, with routine testing for drug use and effective treatment toward abstinence, would reduce fetal brain damage substantially. In fact, because the last three months of pregnancy are critical for brain development, a drug-free second half of pregnancy *may* be enough to prevent brain damage if drug use during the first half was moderate (Maier et al., 1996). Since alcohol and tobacco are at least as teratogenic as illegal drugs, they need to be tested for and targeted just as much as cocaine, heroin, marijuana, and the like.

3. *Moderation throughout pregnancy* (if abstinence from all drugs is impossible). The prenatal effects of psychoactive drugs are dose-related, interactive, and cumulative. Therefore, each dose that is reduced, each drug that is eliminated, and each day that is drug-free represents less damage that can be caused.

4. *Social support.* Maternal stress, psychological problems, loneliness, and poor housing correlate with prenatal complications as well as with drug use (Kramer et al., 2001). In fact, the correlation between psychoactive drugs and prenatal problems may be due, in part, to a hidden factor—psychological difficulties (Robert, 1996). If this is true, then befriending, encouraging, and assisting pregnant drug users may not only reduce their use of teratogens but also aid fetal development, even without directly affecting drug use. (Of course, the assistance should not include any help in obtaining or using drugs.)

5. *Postnatal care.* Babies born with alcohol, cocaine, or even heroin in their systems sometimes become quite normal, intelligent children if they receive optimal care (Koren et al.,

1998; Richardson, 1998). Thus, another way to protect children is to ensure sensitive nurturance after birth (through parenting education, preventive medicine, home visits, early day care, and, if necessary, adoption). Social prejudices work against these children. For instance, the assumption that "crack babies" are destined to have serious learning problems might reduce educational outreach. Social intervention to repair the damage from maternal alcohol abuse is minimal: 80 percent of such children are cared for by someone other than their mothers but very few receive any special services (Streissguth & Connor, 2001). One study found that cocaine-exposed infants whose mothers received help were significantly better off, physically and cognitively, by age 3 than a comparison group from similar low-SES families who neither were exposed to cocaine before birth nor received special services afterward (Kilbride et al., 2000).

One preventive measure that does *not* seem to help is prosecuting pregnant women who use drugs. Jailing such women enforces drug abstinence, and, ironically, imprisoned pregnant women have healthier babies than their peers outside the walls (Martin et al., 1997). However, the threat of prosecution and imprisonment keeps thousands of pregnant women away from prenatal care. This increases fetal damage that might have been prevented (Lyons & Rittner, 1998). When it comes to imprisoning drug addicts, the math is simple. If preventing drug abuse in one pregnant woman by keeping her in jail results in ongoing drug abuse in 99 other women who avoid all prenatal care, the harm far exceeds the benefit. If there were some way to get all 99 to reduce their drug use, however, the benefits might be substantial.

How much harm is prevented by any measure short of total abstinence before pregnancy starts? No one knows for certain. We cannot know until all newborns who were exposed to drugs before birth are assured of excellent care after birth—a distant goal (Byrd et al., 1999).

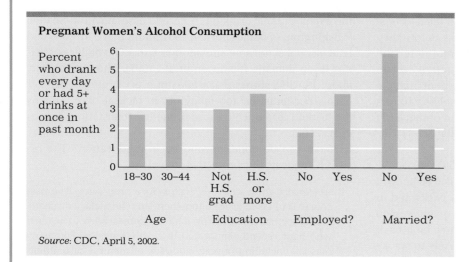

Pregnant Women's Alcohol Consumption

Percent who drank every day or had 5+ drinks at once in past month

Source: CDC, April 5, 2002.

FIGURE 4.4 Wisdom Doesn't Cut It Logically, one might think that older women and women with job experience and education would never drink to the point of endangering their fetus, but this isn't so. The only factor that seemed to make a powerful difference was marriage.

Low Birthweight

Another signal that something may be amiss is a newborn who weighs less than expected. Underweight is not always a handicap, but it is an obvious sign of vulnerability and thus has been studied intensively. We begin with definitions. **Low birthweight (LBW)** is defined by the World Health Organization as a weight of less than 5½ pounds (2,500 grams) at birth. LBW babies are further grouped into *very-low-birthweight (VLBW)* babies, weighing less than 3 pounds (1,500 grams), and *extremely-low-birthweight (ELBW)* babies, weighing less than about 2 pounds (1,000 grams). The rate of LBW varies enormously from nation to nation (see Figure 4.5); the U.S. rate of 7.6 percent in 2000 was twice that of some other developed nations, and it is not improving (see Figure 4.6 on page 120).

Many factors can cause low birthweight, including malnutrition and poverty. As you will see, the worst problems occur when several factors combine. Technically and traditionally, LBW is not a teratogen, but it is caused by

low birthweight (LBW) A birthweight of less than 5½ pounds (2,500 grams).

!Answer to Observational Quiz (from page 117): All five: wide-set eyes, large and unusual eyelids, flat nose bridge, narrow upper lip, missing indentation in the skin between the nose and the upper lip.

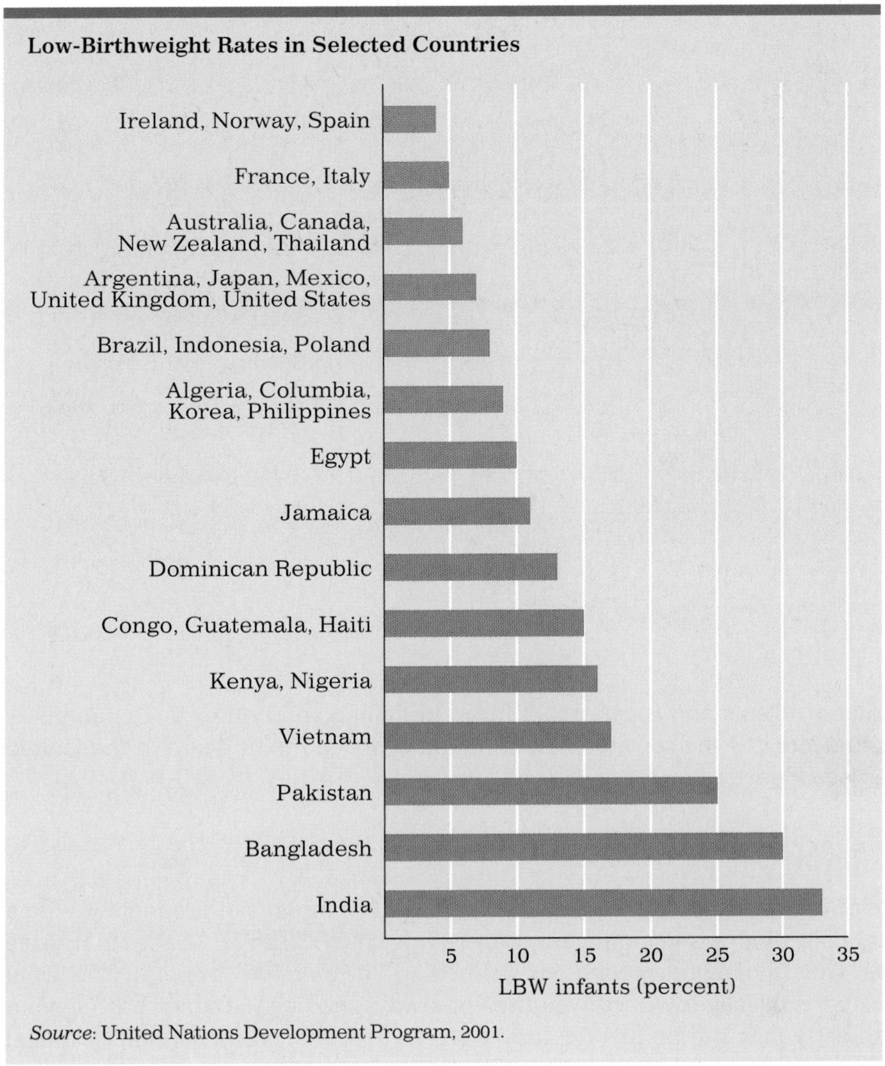

Low-Birthweight Rates in Selected Countries

Source: United Nations Development Program, 2001.

FIGURE 4.5 Low Birthweight Around the World The LBW rate is often considered a reflection of a country's commitment to its children, but a society's wealth also affects the resources it can devote to caring for pregnant women and their babies. Even so, some of the world's richest nations have surprisingly high LBW rates.

FIGURE 4.6 Not Improving
The LBW rate is often taken to be a measure of a nation's overall health. In the United States, the rise and fall of this rate are related to many factors, among them prenatal care, maternal use of drugs, overall nutrition, and number of multiple births.

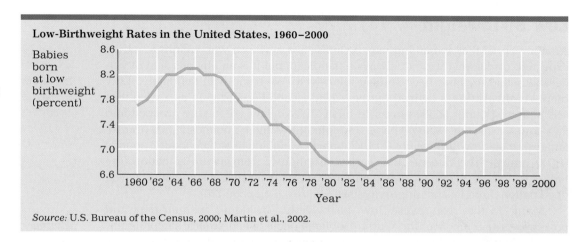

Low-Birthweight Rates in the United States, 1960–2000

Source: U.S. Bureau of the Census, 2000; Martin et al., 2002.

FIGURE 4.7 Why Babies Die Three causes of infant mortality have taken a marked downturn over the past 15 years. In two of them (congenital abnormalities and respiratory distress), intense research and medical technology have made a difference, with advanced genetic testing and counseling, neonatal intensive care, and new drugs given to newborns. Deaths caused by low birthweight are increasing, however.

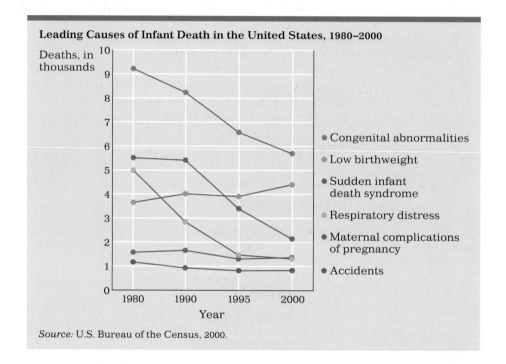

Leading Causes of Infant Death in the United States, 1980–2000

- Congenital abnormalities
- Low birthweight
- Sudden infant death syndrome
- Respiratory distress
- Maternal complications of pregnancy
- Accidents

Source: U.S. Bureau of the Census, 2000.

prenatal problems and it can result in brain damage and other birth complications. Indeed, it is the second most common cause of infant death in the United States (see Figure 4.7).

Too Soon

Remember that fetal body weight doubles in the last months of pregnancy, with a typical gain of almost 2 pounds (about 900 grams) occurring in the final three weeks. Thus, a baby born **preterm,** defined as 3 or more weeks before the usual 38 weeks, is usually low birthweight. Not always, however. Babies born even a month early may not be LBW if they were well nourished throughout prenatal development. They may weigh 6½ pounds (more than 3,000 grams), well above the 5½-pound (2,500-gram) cutoff. Most preterm infants, however, are too small as well as too early.

There are many causes of preterm births. A placenta may become detached from the uterine wall, or a uterus may be unable to accommodate further fetal growth. This last factor helps explain why small women and women bearing mul-

preterm birth Birth that occurs three weeks or more before the full term of pregnancy has elapsed, that is, at 35 or fewer weeks past conception rather than at the full term of about 38 weeks.

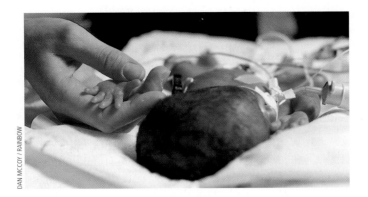

A Hand or a Handout? A number of factors—including maternal malnutrition and infection—are potential contributors to low birthweight, and often they occur in combination. Frequently these factors are related to poverty. Preventing them by giving a supportive hand during pregnancy, not a handout after the fact, would reduce the rate of LBW considerably.

tiple fetuses often go into labor weeks before the due date. Conditions that disrupt the physiological equilibrium of the mother (such as a high dose of psychoactive drugs, extreme stress, or chronic exhaustion) can also precipitate preterm birth. A previous preterm birth is a risk factor for having another. Women with an unusually short *cervix* (the passageway from the uterus to the vagina) are more likely than other women to begin labor early (Goldenberg et al., 1998).

Another key factor is infection, which stimulates chemicals that interfere with fetal development and trigger uterine contractions. A minor vaginal infection linked to early birth is *bacterial vaginosis,* which is easily cured with standard antibiotics if detected early. In the United States, this infection alone is responsible for an estimated 8 percent of all preterm births (Meis et al., 1995). Even a pregnant woman's untreated gum disease leads to a sevenfold increase in the rate of low birthweight (Offenbacher et al., 1996).

Too Small

Not all low-birthweight babies are preterm. Some fetuses simply gain less weight than they should. They are called *small-for-dates* or **small for gestational age (SGA).**

Remember Pearl, the newborn who weighed only 10 ounces? She was so small because her mother had an illness that affected blood circulation throughout her body, especially to her fetus. That was the reason she had an elective cesarean section at 27 weeks: Continuing the pregnancy would have put her life in danger.

Maternal behavior is a far more common cause of SGA than is illness. Taking any psychoactive drug slows fetal growth, but tobacco is the worst, as well as the most prevalent, culprit. Cigarette smoking is implicated in 25 percent of all low-birthweight births in the United States (Chomitz et al., 1995). Evidence for a connection between smoking and low birthweight comes from Sweden, where good nutrition and medical care make LBW less than half as common as in the United States. Between the mid-1980s and the mid-1990s, smoking in Sweden declined 24 percent (from 29 to 22 percent of the population), and correspondingly the total rate of SGA births declined 18 percent (from 3.4 to 2.8 percent of all births) (Cnattingius & Haglund, 1997).

Nutrition and Poverty

Another common reason for slow fetal growth—and hence for low birthweight—is maternal malnutrition, whether before or during pregnancy, long term or temporary. Women who begin pregnancy underweight, eat poorly during pregnancy, and consequently do not gain at least 3 pounds (1½ kilograms) per month in the last six months of pregnancy run a much higher risk than others of having a low-birthweight infant. Indeed, women who gain less than 15 pounds (7 kilograms),

Especially for Women of Childbearing Age: If you have decided to become pregnant soon, you obviously cannot change your genes, your age, or your economic status. But you can do three things in the next month or two that can markedly reduce the chance of having a low-birthweight baby a year from now. What are they?

small for gestational age (SGA) A term applied to newborns who weigh substantially less than they should, given how much time has passed since conception. (Also called *small-for-dates.*)

Would a Glass of Milk Be Better? A balanced diet is important throughout pregnancy and especially toward the end, when, among other special requirements, calcium is needed to build bones and teeth. For the many women of African or Asian descent who are lactose-intolerant and cannot digest much milk, yogurt is a good substitute.

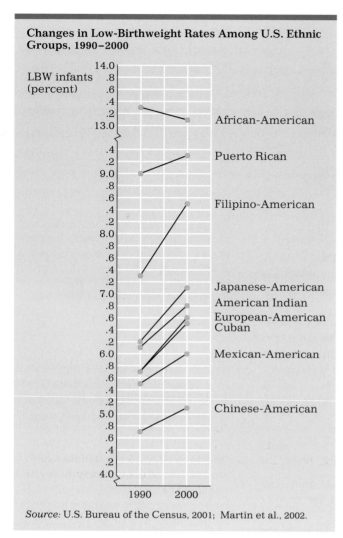

Changes in Low-Birthweight Rates Among U.S. Ethnic Groups, 1990–2000

LBW infants (percent)

1990   2000

Source: U.S. Bureau of the Census, 2001; Martin et al., 2002.

FIGURE 4.8 Poverty Plus The rate of low birthweight is rising in the United States, but poverty is not the only reason.

Response for Women of Childbearing Age (from page 121): Avoid all drugs, check your weight (gain some if you are under the norm), and receive diagnosis and treatment for any infections—not just sexual ones but infections anywhere in your body, including your teeth and gums.

even if they are nonsmokers who begin pregnancy overweight, still have a higher risk of preterm and SGA babies (Hellerstedt et al., 1997).

Obese women should gain 15 to 25 pounds (7 to 11½ kilograms) during pregnancy; normal-weight women, 25 to 35 pounds (11½ to 16 kilograms); and underweight women, 28 to 40 pounds (Kuller et al., 2001). Unfortunately, three risk factors—being underweight, undereating, and smoking—tend to occur together. Malnutrition (not age) is the primary reason young teenagers tend to have small babies: They tend to eat sporadically and poorly, and their diet is inadequate to support the growth of their own bodies, much less that of another developing person (Buschman et al., 2001).

Virtually all the risk factors for low birthweight correlate with poverty (Hughes & Simpson, 1995). Compared with women of higher socioeconomic status, pregnant women at the bottom of the economic ladder are more likely to be ill, malnourished, teenaged, and stressed. If they are employed, their jobs often require long hours of physically stressful work, exactly the kind of work that correlates with preterm and SGA birth (Ceron-Mireles et al., 1996). They often receive late or inadequate prenatal care, breathe polluted air, live in overcrowded conditions, move from place to place, and ingest unhealthy substances, from psychoactive drugs to spoiled foods—all of which can have deleterious effects on the developing fetus (Shiono et al., 1997).

Poverty is part of the explanation for differences between nations and, within the United States, for ethnic and historical differences (see Figure 4.8). Of the 21 million low-birthweight infants born each year, 20 million *are* in developing nations, with 7 million in India alone (Costello & Manandhar, 2000). Within the broad racial categories used by the U.S. Bureau of the Census, the poorer subgroups (for example, Appalachian whites, Filipino Asians, inner-city native-born blacks, and Puerto Rican Hispanics) have underweight newborns more often than the wealthier subgroups.

Socioeconomic status is only a rough gauge, and other factors sometimes have more effect. This is apparent with another Hispanic group—Americans of Mexican descent. Their LBW rate is only 6 percent, much lower than for other groups with similar income and education. Cultural values and paternal support are among the probable reasons for this relatively low rate (Aguirre-Molina et al., 2001).

The Normal Birth

Finally, the birth day arrives. For a full-term fetus and a healthy mother, birth can be simple and quick. At some time during the last month of pregnancy, most fetuses change position for the final time, turning upside down so that the head is low in the mother's pelvic cavity. They are now in position to be born in the usual way, head first. (About 1 in 20 does not turn and is born "breech," that is, buttocks first.)

At about the 266th day after conception, the fetal brain signals the release of certain hormones that pass into the mother's bloodstream. These hormones trigger her uterine muscles to contract and relax, starting the process that becomes active labor. In fact, the "triggering process" is not yet fully understood. It is "an extremely complex system involving various hormones and tissues," and irregu-

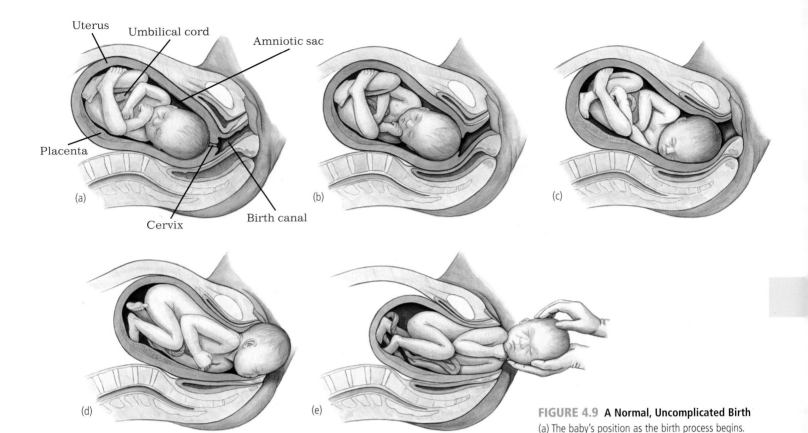

Uterus Umbilical cord Amniotic sac

Placenta

(a)

Cervix Birth canal

(b)

(c)

(d)

(e)

FIGURE 4.9 **A Normal, Uncomplicated Birth**
(a) The baby's position as the birth process begins.
(b) The first stage of labor: The cervix dilates to
allow passage of the baby's head. (c) Transition: The
baby's head moves into the "birth canal," the
vagina. (d) The second stage of labor: The baby's
head moves through the opening of the vagina
("crowns") and (e) emerges completely. The head is
turned, and the rest of the body emerges.

lar contractions typically occur hours, days, or even weeks before active labor begins (Chow & Yancey, 2001). Nonetheless, contractions eventually become strong and regular, less than 10 minutes apart. The baby is born, on average, after eight hours of active labor for first births and three hours for subsequent births (Chow & Yancey, 2001). The sequence of a normal birth is shown in Figure 4.9.

The Newborn's First Minutes

People who have never witnessed a birth might picture the newborn being held upside down and spanked by the attending doctor or midwife to make the baby start crying and therefore breathing. Actually, newborns usually breathe and cry on their own as soon as they are born. In fact, they sometimes cry as their heads emerge from the birth canal, even before their shoulders—one by one—appear.

As the first spontaneous cries occur, the newborn's circulatory system begins to function; soon the infant's color changes from a bluish tinge to pink, because oxygen circulates throughout the system. The eyes open wide; the tiny fingers grab anything they can; the even tinier toes stretch and retract. The newborn is instantly, zestfully, ready for life.

Checking for Problems

Nevertheless, there is much for those attending the birth to do. Any mucus that might be in the baby's throat is removed, especially if the first breaths seem shallow or strained. The umbilical cord is cut to detach the placenta, leaving the "belly button." The infant is wiped dry of fluid and blood, weighed, and wrapped to preserve body heat. If the birth is assisted by a trained health worker—as are 99 percent of the births in industrialized nations and about half of all births worldwide (Rutstein, 2000)—the newborn is immediately checked for body functioning.

One common means of assessing the newborn's condition is a measure called the **Apgar scale** (see Table 4.5). From a brief examination, the examiner assigns a score of 0, 1, or 2 to the heart rate, breathing, muscle tone, color, and

Apgar scale A means of quickly assessing a newborn's body functioning. The baby's color, heart rate, reflexes, muscle tone, and respiratory effort are scored (from 0 to 2) one minute and five minutes after birth and compared with a standard for healthy babies (a perfect 10).

TABLE 4.5 **Criteria and Scoring of the Apgar Scale**

Score	Color	Heartbeat	Reflex Irritability	Muscle Tone	Respiratory Effort
0	Blue, pale	Absent	No response	Flaccid, limp	Absent
1	Body pink, extremities blue	Slow (below 100)	Grimace	Weak, inactive	Irregular, slow
2	Entirely pink	Rapid (over 100)	Coughing, sneezing, crying	Strong, active	Good; baby is crying

Source: Apgar, 1953.

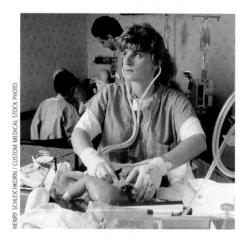

100 or More Heartbeats per Minute A minute after birth, this newborn is undergoing his first exam, the Apgar. From the newborn's ruddy color and obvious muscle tone, it looks as if he will do very well, with a score of 7 or higher.

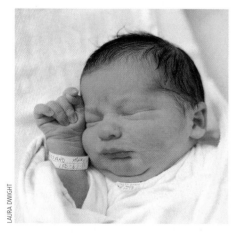

Picture Perfect One-day-old James looks bruised, scraped, and squashed—a perfectly normal, beautiful newborn.

reflexes at one minute after birth and again at five minutes (Moster et al., 2001). A low score at one minute is a warning, but usually newborns improve quickly. If the five-minute total score is 7 or better, there is no danger. If the five-minute total score is below 7, the infant needs help establishing normal breathing. If the score is below 4, the baby is in critical condition and needs immediate medical attention to prevent respiratory distress and death. Few newborns score a perfect 10, but most readily adjust to life outside the womb.

The Parents' Reaction

Immediately after birth, some doctors give the newborn first to the father, perhaps also allowing him to cut the umbilical cord to separate the baby from the placenta (which has not yet been expelled by the mother). Fathers are now welcome in delivery rooms, since they are much more likely to contribute psychological support than to cause medical complications. The mother gets her turn, often cradling the newborn against her skin and perhaps offering the breast for the first time. Some infants are too dazed or drugged (from birth anesthesia) to react, but most begin sucking vigorously. They have flat noses and virtually no chins, so it is easy to latch on to the nipple.

Here is a warning for those who have never seen a newborn until their own is handed to them: Newborns look strange. Especially if they are born a bit early, their skin may be covered with a waxy white substance called *vernix*; if they are a bit late, their skin is often red and wrinkled. Whatever color their complexion will eventually take on, at birth their skin is usually lighter, is often uneven in color (with whitish, bluish, or reddish patches), and sometimes shows visible bruises and birthmarks. The body looks strange, too. Not only is the baby chinless and the hair merely fuzz, but the skull is sometimes misshapen as a result of the bones' pushing together to squeeze through the birth canal. A pulse is visible in the top of the head, where the skull has not yet fused. And the tiny legs and arms flail out, or tuck in, instead of extending quietly and straight.

All these characteristics are temporary. The Apgar score and the birthweight are the critical measures of early health—not the newborn's appearance (Moster et al., 2001). With every day that passes, the newborn looks more normal (advertisements involving "newborns" typically feature babies several weeks old) and behaves more predictably. (The particulars of their early physical development and reflexes are described in Chapter 5.)

Medical Attention

How closely any given birth approaches the foregoing description depends on many factors. Among them are the mother's preparation for birth (gained through prenatal classes, books, conversations with women friends and relatives, or personal experience), the physical and emotional support provided by birth attendants (both professional and familial), the position and size of the fetus, and the cultural context (Creasy, 1997).

Almost every birth in every developed nation now occurs amid some medical activity, typically including drugs to dull pain or speed contractions; sterile procedures that involve special gowns, gloves, and washing; and electronic monitoring of both the mother and the fetus. Often surgery is performed. The most common is an *episiotomy* (a minor incision of the tissue at the opening of the vagina to speed the last moments before birth). An episiotomy is performed in about 80 percent of births but is actually needed less than 30 percent of the time (Chow & Yancey, 2001). The other common operation is major surgery: In about 22 percent of births in the United States, a **cesarean section** is performed to remove the fetus through incisions in the mother's abdomen and uterus (Martin et al., 2002).

Worldwide, the actions of doctors, midwives, and nurses save millions of lives each year—the lives of mothers as well as of infants. Indeed, a lack of medical attention during childbirth is a major reason why motherhood is still hazardous in the least developed nations; about one of every twelve African women dies of complications of pregnancy and childbirth (Tsui et al., 1997).

Medical attention makes delivery faster, easier, and safer. In many nations (including some of the most advanced), increasing numbers of trained midwives fill the gap between the busy, highly trained obstetrician, who specializes in serious complications, and the neighborhood "granny nurse," whose help is most welcome in uncomplicated births but whose expertise is limited. In developed countries, licensed midwives not only deal with medical aspects but also understand the psychic impact of birth on the new mother. As one midwife stresses, "Let's not leave any woman holding her baby without having conveyed to her our complete respect and belief in her ability to think clearly, to make decisions, and to be a good parent" (quoted in Walton & Hamilton, 1998).

Many North American mothers today use a professional birth coach, called a *doula*, to ease labor, reduce medical intervention, and facilitate breast-feeding (Douglas, 2002).

From several perspectives, there seems little to fault in a medicalized, technological approach to birth. Most women prefer to give birth in a hospital rather than at home, want pain relief instead of a drug-free birth, and prefer medical attention to being left alone. In some nations, such as England, about half of all births occurred at home in 1970; now almost all women choose to give birth in a hospital. Indeed, the Netherlands is unique among developed nations in its high rate of home births: about 35 percent (Ferguson, 1997).

At the same time, many aspects of hospital births, including the routine use of medication, intravenous fluids, electronic monitoring, and episiotomy, have been criticized as being rooted more in medical tradition than in medical necessity (Ferguson, 1997). Even worse, financial considerations or fear of lawsuits may affect medical decisions. For example, one careful study in the Midwest found that the rate of cesarean deliveries was 17 percent among women with private insurance, 14 percent for those with government insurance (i.e., Medicaid), and only 10 percent for those who had no insurance (Aron et al., 2000).

As a result of these criticisms, by the early 1990s only 41 percent of all U.S. hospital births occurred in delivery rooms with high-tech equipment, whereas 53 percent occurred in the *labor room*—typically a smaller, more homelike room where a woman stays, with her husband or other familiar person, from the time she enters the hospital until she and her baby have recovered from the birth (Nichols & Zwelling, 1997). In this setting, doctors and nurses intervene when

cesarean section A means of childbirth in which the fetus is taken from the mother surgically, through an incision that extends from the mother's abdomen through the uterus.

Same Event, Thousands of Miles Apart Both these midwives—one in New York City and the other in Rajasthan, India—are assessing the size, position, and heartbeat of a developing fetus. Which pregnancy is more likely to result in a healthy baby? If the birth is of high risk, high-tech medical equipment might be critical. However, if the pregnancy is a normal one, as most pregnancies are, the experience and empathy of the trained attendant are more important than the diagnostic tools used.

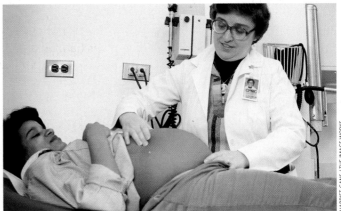

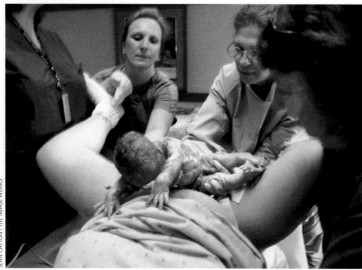

No Doctor Needed In this Colorado Springs birthing center, most babies are delivered with the help of nurse-midwives. This newborn's bloody appearance and bluish fingers are completely normal; an Apgar test at 5 minutes revealed that the baby's heart was beating steadily and that the body was "entirely pink."

needed, but the woman has much more control. The facts that it is *her* room and that she is with *her* husband make it *her* birth—and that itself reduces anxiety, pain, and complications. Even if there are complications, they seem to cause less stress.

Another 5 percent of U.S. births occur in freestanding *birthing centers,* which are even more family-centered. As one woman recounts:

> When we arrived at the Birthing Center to have the baby, we were told to go right to the room we had chosen ahead of time. There weren't any strong hospital odors, no people rushing around, no papers for Gary to fill out while I was wheeled off down a long hall without him. We just walked together to our room.
>
> There is always some amount of anxiety in starting labor; but the atmosphere at the Birthing Center was so relaxing that it had a calming effect on me. The thing that meant the most to my husband was his feeling that he belonged there. No one made him feel that he was in the way. (The comfortable recliner in our room helped, too.)
>
> I can remember how great it felt to be able to get up and shower to relieve my back labor and to take a walk out in the hall when I felt the need to walk. I wasn't confined to bed; I was in control.
>
> Several hours later, our third daughter was born. She never left us to go to the nursery with harsh lights and lots of other crying babies. She remained in our quiet room with us. We could hold her when she wanted to be held and feed her when she wanted to be fed. Gary and I both were there when the pediatrician checked her.
>
> Even though it was my most difficult labor and delivery, it was our happiest.
>
> *[quoted in La Leche, 1997]*

Only 1 percent of U.S. births take place at home—about half of these by choice and attended by a midwife, and half due to unexpectedly rapid birth (Nichols & Zwelling, 1997). Such births are usually quite normal and healthy, but any complications that arise can become serious problems.

Birth Complications

If a fetus is already at risk because of low birthweight, preterm birth, genetic abnormality, or teratogenic exposure, or because the mother is unusually young, old, small, or ill, birth complications may occur. The crucial concept to emphasize is that birth risks and complications are part of a continuum, beginning long before the first contractions and continuing in the months and years thereafter.

As an example, **cerebral palsy** (difficulties with movement control resulting from brain damage) was once thought to be caused solely by birth procedures such as excessive pain medication, slow breech birth, or misapplied forceps. (Forceps are sometimes used to pull the fetal head through the birth canal.) However, cerebral palsy often results from genetic vulnerability; worsened by teratogens and a birthing process that includes **anoxia**—a temporary lack of oxygen that can cause brain damage. Anoxia is always risky—that's why nurses listen closely to the fetal heart rate during birth and why the newborn's color is one of the five criteria on the Apgar scale. How long a baby can experience anoxia without brain damage depends on genes, weight, drugs in the bloodstream, and a host of other factors.

Similarly, low-birthweight infants are at risk for many problems before, during, and immediately after birth, especially when they are very early or very

cerebral palsy A disorder that results from damage to the brain's motor centers, usually as a result of events during or before birth. People with cerebral palsy have difficulty with muscle control, which can affect speech or other body movements.

anoxia A lack of oxygen that, if prolonged, can cause brain damage or death.

small. These problems sometimes affect them throughout life, but here, too, the impact depends on many influences. As we have already seen, such problems begin even before conception, if a woman is underweight, smokes cigarettes, or takes other drugs. Taking an ongoing developmental perspective, we look at the sequence of these influences after birth.

First, Intensive Care . . .

Vulnerable infants are typically placed in intensive-care nurseries where they are confined to enclosed *isolettes* (so that their environment can be monitored and controlled). They are hooked up to one or another machine, and surrounded by bright lights and noise. Although these measures are often medically warranted, they also deprive neonates of certain stimulation, such as the gentle rocking they would have experienced if they still were in the womb or the regular handling involved in feeding and bathing if they were at low risk. To overcome this deprivation, many hospitals provide high-risk infants with regular massage and soothing stimulation, which aid weight gain and increase overall alertness (Als, 1995).

Ideally, parents share in this early caregiving, in recognition of the fact that they, too, are deprived and stressed (Goldberg & Divitto, 1995). Not only must they cope with uncertainty about their baby's future, but they must also struggle with feelings of inadequacy and perhaps with sorrow, guilt, and anger. Such emotions are relieved somewhat if they can cradle and care for their vulnerable newborn. Anything that strengthens the family may forestall difficulties later on.

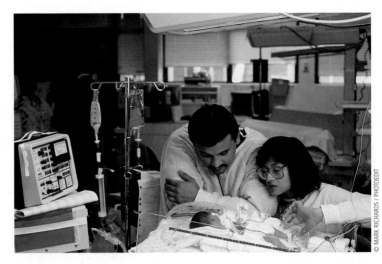

Getting to Know You If these new parents were kept at a distance, they might be troubled by the intravenous drips, the beeping monitor, and the protective plastic of the intensive-care nursery. Through the intimacy of closeness and touch, the LBW patient becomes, to the parents, simply "our baby."

. . . Then Home

For high-risk infants who survive, complications await, including minor medical crises and slow development. Preterm infants are often late to smile, to hold a bottle, and to communicate. As the months go by, short- and long-term cognitive difficulties may emerge. Cerebral palsy, first evident weeks after birth, affects 20 percent of those who weighed less than 35 ounces (1,000 grams) at birth and 7 percent of those who weighed between 3½ and 5½ pounds (1,500 and 2,500 grams) (Hack et al., 1995). High-risk infants who escape such obvious impairments are nevertheless more distractible, less obedient, and slower to talk (Girouard et al., 1998; Taylor et al., 2000).

Fortunately, long-term handicaps are not inevitable. Some newborns who had heart defects or other serious abnormalities, or were very small, can and do develop quite normally (Cherkes-Julkowski, 1998; Miller et al., 2001). Thus, parents of high-risk infants should not assume either that birth was the child's last major challenge or, conversely, that severe intellectual and medical problems will soon emerge.

Risks increase when the infant is very, very tiny—less than 3½ pounds (1,500 grams)—or when medical complications affect brain development for days or weeks, or when the infant is raised in a home already burdened by low socioeconomic status (Taylor et al., 1998). Preterm babies are always "more work and less fun," and their mothers rate them as more difficult and less adaptable (Langkamp et al., 1998). But even when mothers are young and poor, intervention—including parent-support programs and intensive high-quality day care beginning at age 1—can result in substantial intellectual gains for the child and notable benefits for the family (Holloman & Scott, 1998; Ramey et al., 1992).

"I suppose this puts my new bike on the back burner?"

Bike Versus Baby? Often neglected in the medicalization of birth are older siblings. Few are as sophisticated as this boy, making the connection between the additional expense that the new baby represents and his own material condition, but most miss their mother. If the mother is gone for several days because she is recovering from surgery or other complications, and if she comes home tired, depressed, distracted, or in pain, siblings may resent the innocent cause of it all.

Bonding After Birth

parent–newborn bond The strong feelings of attachment that arise between parents and their newborn infants.

postpartum depression The profound feeling of sadness and inadequacy that is experienced by some new mothers, leading to an inability to eat, sleep, or care normally for their newborns.

Now we discuss one final topic that is important for all families of newborns, no matter what their risk. Popular attention has been captured by the concept of the **parent–newborn bond,** an almost instant connection between parents and newborns as they touch each other in the first hours after birth. Newspaper and magazine articles have rhapsodized over the joy and the necessity of forming this special bond. Many people have come to believe that bonding is a critically important "magical social glue." As one mother who was deprived of early contact said, "It made me feel like a rotten mother when I didn't get to bond with my first two children. Made me feel they were going to go out and rob a bank" (quoted in Eyer, 1992).

However, the popular concept that early touch leads to a close mother–newborn bond that lasts a lifetime is false—not supported by the evidence and actually contrary to the research. That contradiction itself makes scientists ask, "Why was the notion of essential bonding so quickly accepted, when the research evidence was so sparse?" This issue is discussed in detail in the following Thinking Like a Scientist feature.

Thinking Like a Scientist

Bonding in Goats, Rats, and Humans

Recognizing the close genetic similarity—more than 98 percent—between humans and other mammals arouses researchers' renewed interest in parent–infant interactions among other animals as a way of understanding human behavior better (Corter & Fleming, 1995; Fleming & Corter, 1995). Comparative research on bonding led first to an appreciation of the importance of the first hours after birth and then to a rejection of a simplistic, dogmatic interpretation of the evidence.

Many female animals nourish and nurture their own young and ignore, reject, or mistreat the young of others, guided by hormones that make them act maternally and by a sense of smell that helps them recognize their own offspring. And many male animals kill newborns that seem abnormal or that do not seem to be theirs.

In some species, contact must occur within a critical period in order for bonding to take place. For example, if a baby goat is removed from its mother immediately after birth and returned a few hours later, the mother sometimes rejects it, kicking and butting it away no matter how pitifully it bleats or how persistently it tries to nurse. However, if a newborn goat remains with a mother who nuzzles and suckles it for the critical first five minutes and then is separated from her, the mother goat welcomes its return (Klopfer, 1971). Sheep and cows react in like fashion. Other species display a pronounced form of bonding, with touching in the "sensitive" period soon after birth helpful but not essential (Rosenblith, 1992).

Newborn animals are also primed to seek out their mothers. Even baby rats have multiple pathways for bonding, including acute senses of smell and taste that enable them to identify their particular mother before birth and thus lead blind newborns to nuzzle up to her (Hofer & Sullivan, 2001). Newborn rats signal severe distress with a high-pitched cry, inaudible to humans but piercing to mother rats, who respond with licking and nuzzling. This mutual mother–newborn bond is crucial for metabolism, temperature regulation, heart rate, and cognition and hence allows the newborn rats to thrive (Hofer, 1995).

Does a corresponding sensitive time period exist for bonding in humans? Some early research (with a few dozen women) suggested that it did. In those studies, the benefits of immediate contact after birth and extended contact during the first days of life were apparent over the entire first year. This was especially true for first-time mothers who were very young, poor, or otherwise stressed or whose preterm infants might have been deemed too frail to be touched. The mothers who had held their fragile infants soon after birth were more attentive and attached to them a year later than were the mothers who had barely seen their infants in the early days (Grossman et al., 1981; Klaus & Kennell, 1976; Leifer et al., 1972).

This research is credited with ending several hospital routines, including preventing mothers from holding their newborns for the first 24 hours and barring parents from intensive-care units. All these practices were originally thought to protect mother and child; all are now seen as unnecessary, even cruel.

Today almost no one questions the wisdom of early contact between mother and child. It can provide a wondrous beginning to the parent–child relationship, as suggested by this mother's account:

> The second he came out, they put him on my skin and I reached down and I felt him and it was something about having that sticky stuff on my fingers . . . it was really important to feel that waxy stuff [vernix] and he was crying and I made soothing sounds to him. . . . And he started calming down and somehow that makes you feel—like he already knows you, he knows who you are—like animals or something, perhaps the smell of each other . . . it was marvelous to hold him and I just touched him for a really long time and then they took him over but something had already happened. Just instant love.
>
> *[quoted in Davis-Floyd, 1992]*

But is this early contact essential for formation of the mother–child bond, as has been claimed? Absolutely not. Scientists always look for evidence to refute as well as to confirm their hypotheses. Researchers have discovered that many animals, including horses and dogs, do not automatically reject their newborns, as goats do, if they do not nuzzle them at birth. In addition, substantial research on primates (which are genetically closest to humans) begins with *cross-fostering,* a strategy in which newborns are removed from their mothers and given to another female, or even a male, to be raised. In monkeys, a parent–child relationship sometimes develops that is strong enough to overcome an infant monkey's genetic tendency to be excessively fearful. Cross-fostering is actually beneficial in many cases (Suomi, 2002).

Such research on animals led to larger, longitudinal studies of human newborns. The overall conclusion: Immediate or extended early skin-to-skin togetherness makes no measurable long-term differences in the mother–child relationship (Lamb, 1982; Myers, 1987). In retrospect, this makes sense. All mammals are similar, but each species is designed for nurturing the next generation of that species. All humans need extensive parental nurturance, through the infant's nighttime feeding, the toddler's temper, the preschooler's incessant questioning, the schoolchild's self-absorption, and the adolescent's rebellion—punctuated by illness, disappointment, and other unhappy events. Surely, the relationship between human parent and child could not hinge on bonding at birth. Nature is not so foolhardy as to create one, and only one, pathway for survival.

Diane Eyer, a social scientist, has concluded that instant bonding is a *social construction* (see Chapter 1), an idea formed as a rallying cry against the medicalization, depersonalization, and patriarchy of the traditional hospital birth. Eyer argues that women and developmental experts were ready to believe that newborns and mothers need to be together from the start, so it took only a tiny nudge from scientific research for the mystique of early bonding to become generally accepted. She fears that this zealous acceptance came at a high price: the setting of a standard of instant affection and "active love right after birth . . . that many women find impossible to meet" (Eyer, 1992).

Especially for Social Scientists: When is animal research used too quickly to support conclusions about people?

Depression and Love

Indeed, rigidly believing in bonding may be worse than not promoting it at all. If a medicated mother, exhausted from the birth process, is handed her infant for 10 minutes while the episiotomy is stitched, and then the baby is whisked away because "bonding" has supposedly occurred, she may feel guilty for not experiencing a surge of love. Or if an inexperienced mother does not hold her infant in the minutes after birth, all her doubts about her ability to be a good mother may overwhelm her.

One possible consequence is **postpartum depression**, the feeling of inadequacy and sadness that between 10 and 20 percent of women feel in the days and weeks after birth (called *baby blues* in the mild version and *postpartum psychosis* in the most severe form). Postpartum depression lasting more than a few weeks has a long-term impact on the child, so it should be diagnosed and alleviated as soon as possible (Goodman & Gotlib, 2002; Hay et al., 2001). There are many possible reasons for postpartum depression. A developmental perspective notes that some causes predate the pregnancy (such as earlier bouts of major depression, financial stress, marital problems) and others are specific to the particular infant (health, feeding, or sleeping problems) (Ashman & Dawson, 2002). The father can be crucial in caring for the newborn and for the mother.

Expressions of Love Smell and touch are essential components for mother–infant bonding for many animals, including the nuzzling lions seen here. Fortunately, bonding between humans can occur in varied ways, with early contact not at all essential—although physical intimacy, from breast-feeding at infancy to hugs at adolescence, sustains close attachment between parent and child.

One cause is directly related to the first hours after birth: the mother's perception that she is incompetent (O'Hara, 1997). For mothers who are vulnerable to depression, or for first-time low-income mothers, individual observation and discussion with a nurse or doctor of their own newborn's reflexes and motor skills improve their mothering skills and attentiveness to their babies in the next weeks (Brazelton & Cramer, 1991; Hart et al., 1999; Wendland-Carro et al., 1999). They benefit from seeing their newborn grasp a finger so tightly that the baby's body weight can be supported, or stare directly at a person's eyes, or suck and swallow in rhythm.

Fortunately, immediate contact is neither necessary nor sufficient for bonding. Millions of loving and dedicated biological, adoptive, or foster mothers and fathers never touched their children when they were newborns.

Does this mean that hospital routines can go back to the old ways, separating mother and newborn? Never. As one leading developmentalist states:

> I hope that the weakness of the findings for bonding will not be used as an excuse to keep mothers and their infants separated in the hospital. Although such separation may do no permanent harm for most mother–infant pairs, providing contact in a way that is acceptable to the mother surely does no harm and gives much pleasure to many. It is my belief that anything that may make the postpartum period more pleasurable surely is worthwhile.
>
> [Rosenblith, 1992]

In general, the mother's hormonal and physiological condition during the hours and days right after birth "is clearly a state of intense affect" (Corter & Fleming, 1995). In this emotional period, everything possible should be done to help the mother cherish her infant's touch, smell, and appearance. But the mother should never be overwhelmed with a cultural ideal she cannot reach—lest the "bonding experience" between a crying, scrawny newborn and an exhausted mother lead to anger, rejection, and depression. Love between a parent and a child is affected by interactions throughout pregnancy, birth, infancy, childhood, and beyond. As the chapters that follow reveal, the parent–infant relationship is critical for healthy development; the specifics of its formation are not.

Response for Social Scientists (from page 129): When it supports a point of view that is popular but not yet substantiated by research data, as in the social construction about mother–infant bonding.

SUMMARY

From Zygote to Newborn

1. The first two weeks of prenatal growth are called the germinal period. During this period, the single-cell zygote develops into an organism of more than 100 cells, travels down the fallopian tube, and implants itself in the uterine lining. Most zygotes do not develop, and never implant.

2. The period from the third through the eighth week after conception is called the embryonic period. The heart begins to beat and the eyes, ears, nose, and mouth begin to form. By 8 weeks, the embryo has the basic organs and features of a human, with the exception of the sex organs.

3. The fetal period extends from the ninth week until birth. By the twelfth week all the organs and body structures have formed. The fetus attains viability when the brain is sufficiently mature to regulate basic body functions, around the twenty-second week after conception.

4. The average fetus weighs approximately 3 pounds at the beginning of the last three months of pregnancy and 7½ pounds at birth. Maturation of brain, lungs, and heart ensures survival for more than 99 percent of all full-term babies. Toward the end of prenatal development, the fetus can hear and respond to movement, and the parents can prepare for birth and beyond.

Risk Reduction

5. Diseases, drugs, and pollutants can all cause birth defects. Some teratogens cause explicit physical impairment. Others, called behavioral teratogens, harm the brain and therefore impair intellect and actions during childhood.

6. Whether a particular teratogen will harm a particular embryo or fetus depends on the timing and amount of exposure and on the developing organism's genetic vulnerability. To protect against prenatal complications, a woman can avoid or limit her exposure to teratogens, maintain good nutrition, and seek early and competent prenatal care.

7. Particularly when psychoactive drugs, the most common teratogens in developed nations, are at issue, social support from the

woman's family and community is important. Immigrant women tend to be drug-free because their families and communities discourage drug use during pregnancy.

8. Epidemic in Africa, and ongoing in developed nations, is the HIV virus. If women know their HIV status before they become pregnant and take AZT during pregnancy, most pediatric AIDS can be prevented. In fact, most teratogens can be prevented with good public and personal health.

Low Birthweight

9. Low birthweight (under 2,500 grams, or 5½ pounds) arises from a combination of the mother's poor health or nutrition, smoking, drinking, drug use, and age, as well as the fetus's genes, and whether twins or other multiples are developing.

10. Preterm or small-for-gestational-age babies are more likely than full-term babies to suffer from stress during birth and to experience medical difficulties, especially breathing problems and brain damage. Long-term cognitive difficulties may occur, depending on whether the newborn was of very low birthweight, had serious medical problems, or is being raised in an impoverished home.

The Normal Birth

11. Birth typically begins with contractions that push the fetus, head first, out from the uterus and then through the vagina. The Apgar scale, which rates the neonate's vital signs at one minute after birth and again at five minutes after birth, provides a quick evaluation of the infant's health.

12. Medical intervention in the birth process can speed contractions, dull pain, and save lives. However, many aspects of the medicalized birth have been faulted. Contemporary birthing practices are aimed at finding a balance, protecting the baby but also allowing the mother and father more involvement and control.

Birth Complications

13. Birth complications, such as unusually long and stressful labor that includes anoxia (a lack of oxygen to the fetus), have many causes. Vulnerable newborns are placed in an intensive-care unit for monitoring and treatment. Long-term handicaps are not inevitable for such children, but careful nurturing is required once they are taken home. Anoxia and very low birthweight increase the risk.

14. Many women feel unhappy, incompetent, or uninterested in the days immediately after giving birth. In its mild form, called "baby blues," this postpartum depression lifts if the father and others are supportive. More serious is postpartum psychosis, which requires professional treatment.

Bonding After Birth

15. Ideally, both parents spend time with their baby in the hours and days after birth. However, early, skin-to-skin contact between mother and child is much less important for humans than for some animals. The human parent–infant bond develops continuously over a long period of time.

KEY TERMS

germinal period (p. 103)	behavioral teratogens (p. 111)	fetal alcohol syndrome (FAS) (p. 115)	Apgar scale (p. 123)
embryonic period (p. 103)	risk analysis (p. 111)	low birthweight (LBW) (p. 119)	cesarean section (p. 125)
fetal period (p. 103)	critical period (p. 112)	preterm birth (p. 120)	cerebral palsy (p. 126)
implantation (p. 104)	threshold effect (p. 113)	small for gestational age (SGA) (p. 121)	anoxia (p. 126)
neural tube (p. 105)	interaction effect (p. 113)		parent–newborn bond (p. 128)
placenta (p. 107)	human immunodeficiency virus (HIV) (p. 114)		postpartum depression (p. 129)
age of viability (p. 107)			
teratogens (p. 111)			

KEY QUESTIONS

1. What occurs during the germinal period?

2. What occurs during the embryonic period?

3. What major developments occur during the fetal period?

4. What makes a fetus more likely to survive if born at 38 weeks rather than at 24?

5. What increases or decreases the harm of teratogens?

6. What public health measures can prevent rubella and pediatric AIDS?

7. What are some effects of drug abuse on the fetus?

8. What can be done to reduce the damage done by a pregnant woman's use of psychoactive drugs?

9. What are the causes and consequences of low birthweight?

10. What is the relationship among the newborn's appearance, the Apgar scale, and health?

11. What are the advantages and disadvantages of the intensive-care nursery?

12. How is the formation of the parent–infant bond different in animals and in humans?

Part II

Adults usually don't change much in a year or two. Sometimes their hair gets longer or grows thinner, or they gain or lose a few pounds, or they become a little wiser. But if you were to be reunited with friends you haven't seen for several years, you would recognize them immediately.

If, in contrast, you were to care for a newborn twenty-four hours a day for the first month, and then did not see the baby until a year later, you probably would not recognize him or her. After all, would you recognize a best friend who had quadrupled in weight, grown 14 inches, and sprouted a new head of hair? Nor would you find the toddler's behavior familiar. A hungry newborn just cries; a hungry toddler says "more food" or climbs up on the kitchen counter to reach the bananas.

A year or two is not much time compared to the almost eighty years of the average life span. However, children in their first two years reach half their adult height, develop cognitive abilities that have often surprised researchers, and learn to express almost every emotion—not just joy and fear but also many others, including jealousy and shame. And two of the most important human abilities, talking and loving, are already apparent.

The next three chapters describe these radical and wonderful changes.

The First 2 Years: Infants and Toddlers

Chapter Five

The First 2 Years: Biosocial Development

norm A standard, or average, that is derived or developed for a specific group or population.

In the first 2 years of life, rapid growth is obvious in all three domains. Picture biosocial development, from birth to age 2: Roll over . . . sit . . . stand . . . walk . . . run! Reach . . . touch . . . grab . . . throw! Listen . . . taste . . . stare . . . see! Each object, each person, each place becomes something to explore with every sense, every limb, every organ, while clothes are outgrown before they become too stained or torn to wear.

To scientists studying infants, invisible developments are even more striking. Small infant brains become larger, with neurons connecting to one another at a dizzying, yet programmed, pace. Tiny stomachs digest food and more food, dispatching nourishment for brain and body activity as well as for phenomenally rapid growth.

Parents and cultures are essential to this process, which is bio*social*—not merely biological—development. Adults provide the nurture that enables infant growth, with specifics that must change daily because infants change daily. As one expert explains, "Parenting an infant is akin to trying to hit a moving target" (Bornstein, 1995a, p. 13).

In this chapter we will describe that target as it moves, presenting the norms of physical development, including the average weight, height, and motor skills at key ages. (A **norm** is a standard, or average, that is derived or developed for a specific group or population.) Throughout, we emphasize the brain growth that provides the foundation for all other growth. We will also explain what parents and cultures must provide—the stimulation, encouragement, vaccinations, nutrition, and many other things needed to make sure development proceeds on schedule. As you will learn, there is much normal variation here—fussing babies do not always need to be fed (although some families always feed them), tiny infants can eat rice flour or lemon juice or mashed banana (although some families would never give them that) (DeLoache & Gottlieb, 2000) and still grow. However, ignorance and indifference contribute to the neglect and even to the death of an estimated 10 million of the world's infants each year (Rice, Sacco, Hyder, & Black, 2000). The knowledge about both norms and variations that you will gain from this chapter will help the infants you know and some whom you will never meet make it safely to age 2 and beyond.

Body Changes

Monitoring and protecting health are critical throughout life. During most of childhood in developing nations, that monitoring includes visiting the doctor for preventive "well-child" care once a year, which is often enough. In infancy, however, growth is so fast and the consequences of neglect so severe that medical checkups, including measurement of height, weight, and head circumference, should occur every few weeks or months—not only to spot signs of trouble but also to guide parents, who are the first, and the best, defense against illness and injury.

Body Size

Every medical checkup for children under age 2 begins with weighing and measuring, for good reason. Except for prenatal development, the most dramatic changes in size and proportion occur in infancy. Any slowdown is a cause for immediate concern.

Exactly how rapidly does normal growth occur? At birth the average North American weighs a little more than 7 pounds (3.2 kilograms) and measures about 20 inches (51 centimeters). This means that the typical newborn weighs less than a gallon of milk and is about as long as the distance from a man's elbow to the tips of his fingers.

Newborns get smaller before they get bigger. In the first days of life, most lose between 5 and 10 percent of their birthweight because they eliminate more as body wastes than they take in as nourishment. Then they recover that loss and begin to gain, doubling their birthweight by the fourth month and tripling it by the end of the first year. Much of the weight increase in the early months is fat, to provide insulation for warmth and a store of nourishment. This stored nutrition is essential to keep the brain growing if teething or the sniffles temporarily interfere with eating, which often happens for a day or two. Fortunately, if nutrition is not quite adequate, the body stops growing but not the brain, a phenomenon called **head-sparing** (Georgieff & Rao, 2001).

Infants grow longer as well as heavier. In each of the first 6 months they add more than an inch (2.5 centimeters), making them half a foot longer by half a year. Then they slow down, but not by much. At their first birthday, typical babies stand 30 inches (75 centimeters) tall and weigh almost 22 pounds (10 kilograms).

Physical growth is less in the second year, but it is still rapid. By 24 months most children weigh almost 30 pounds (13 kilograms) and measure between 32 and 36 inches (81–91 centimeters), with boys typically slightly taller and heavier than girls. This means that typical 2-year-olds are already astonishingly tall, in that they have achieved half of their adult height. They are also about 15 to 20 percent of their adult weight. (See Appendix A for age norms of height and weight on pages A-6 and A-7.)

The numbers here and in the preceding paragraphs are *norms,* and they need to be carefully interpreted. An average child is at the 50th **percentile**, a number that would represent the midpoint if all the values were ranked from 1 to 99, with the lowest one-hundredth at the zero percentile and the highest one-hundredth at the 99th percentile. Thus, the 50th percentile is midway, with 49 percent of the children above it and 49 percent below it. A child can be said to be normal if he or she is between the 25th and 75th percentiles, as half of all children are. This isn't necessarily good or bad, merely typical. For example, a child could be genetically small, consistently below the 25th percentile, but quite healthy, especially if both parents were well nourished as children but are short adults. Other children might be genetically large, but not obese, if they are tall as well as heavy for their age, perhaps as high as the 90th percentile for both height and weight.

This means that children need to be compared not only to the norms of other children who are the same age, but also to their parents, their siblings, and their own growth patterns. Indeed, although pediatricians and nurses pay special heed to the 10 percent of children who are in the bottom five or top five percentiles, the critical factor is not the absolute number but the gain: A drop in per-

head-sparing A phenomenon by which the brain continues to grow even though the body stops growing as a result of malnutrition.

percentile Any point on a ranking scale of 1 to 99. For example, the 50th percentile is at the midpoint of such a scale, with half the subjects ranking higher and half ranking lower on a given value, such as height or weight.

centile rank alerts parents and professionals that something might be wrong. With this information as background, consider the following report on a baby named Toni.

A Case to Study

Toni's Well-Child Visit

Which Baby Is Older? Every child grows at his or her own rate. A wise pediatrician always keeps this fact in mind. These infants, visiting the doctor for a well-baby checkup, are twins, so they are exactly the same age; but one is significantly smaller (and has much less hair) than the other. If the smaller twin's curiosity and finger dexterity are any indications, however, he is developing completely normally.

Toni is a 17-month-old girl who has been brought to the doctor for a well-child visit. She was last seen at the age of 11 months and is behind in immunizations. Toni was born at term to an 18-year-old mother and weighed 3,850 grams (75th percentile) and measured 50 centimeters in length (50th percentile). Prenatal history was negative for problems, and her health has been good, according to her mother. At Toni's last visit, her height and weight were at the 50th percentile.

Today Toni weighs 9,400 grams (20th percentile) and is 79 centimeters tall (40th percentile). Development, according to her mother, is normal, although her language skills are delayed—she has only a five-word vocabulary. Toni's mother describes Toni as busy, always on the go. The family history for medical problems is negative. Toni's mother is 5 feet 5 inches tall and weighs 130 pounds. Her father is reported to be about 6 feet tall. He is not in the household.

There have been no significant illnesses since the 11-month visit. The physical exam, as well as screening laboratory tests, are essentially negative except for mild anemia.

Toni's mother has recently (within the past 4 months) returned to work as a waitress. She has pieced together a patch-work of child care. The child is cared for by a variety of family members. She [the mother] has indicated that she is afraid of using strangers. She has a difficult time giving a feeding history because multiple providers feed Toni, who apparently do not communicate with each other about her intake. Mealtimes vary from household to household as do other routines, such as naps and bedtime. Toni's mother's meals are also erratic, and the two rarely eat a meal together. Toni falls asleep in front of the television every night and generally awakens too late for breakfast at home, prior to rushing out in order to accommodate her mother's work schedule.

[Yoos et al., 1999, pp. 380, 381, 383]

Toni's case will be used throughout this book's three chapters on infancy. For easy reference, the facts of the case are listed in Table 5.1 (on the next page) with spaces for you to indicate which aspects of Toni's development you think are strengths, which are normal, and which are worrisome.

From Chapter 4, you can already recognize several strengths. A full-term, 8½-pound infant, born to an 18-year-old mother, is beginning life very well. (A birth-weight below 5½ pounds or a mother younger than 16 would be a risk.)

The first two items are positive signs as well, although this might not be as obvious. True, 6 months elapsed between Toni's checkups, 3 months more than recommended for toddlers. But this interval is shorter than many: In the United States, 13 percent of children had no doctor or clinic visits in a year, a percentage that jumped to 36 percent for children in poor and uninsured families (National Center for Health Statistics, 2000). Further, many teenage parents use various health care providers, which makes accurate records regarding immunizations, birth complications, and weight gain unavailable. Thus, that Toni's mother brought her for a well-child checkup only a few months late and that Toni's medical history is available are both positive signs.

Records are particularly useful in this case. Toni's 17-month measurements, by themselves, are not worrisome, especially since her father's height might mean she is genetically destined to be tall and thin. However, longitudinal data show that her weight has dropped from the 75th to the 50th to the 20th percentile. In addition, Toni is mildly anemic, her mother had difficulty giving a feeding history, caregivers do not communicate about Toni's eating, household routines vary, Toni's height as well as weight percentiles are decreasing, and Toni doesn't eat breakfast. Although no single one of these facts in itself means that Toni is malnourished, the combination of items 9, 10, 11, 22, 29, 30, 31, and 33 is ominous.

Be assured that because of "head-sparing," Toni's malnutrition had not yet damaged her brain. Acute malnutrition results in **wasting** when body weight is at the bottom 3 percent of the norms, and chronic malnutrition results in **stunting,** when height is at the bottom 3 percent of the norms. Typically, reduced weight is the first sign of malnutrition, stunted height is the next, and finally comes slow head growth (Rao & Georgieff, 2000). There is no indication that Toni's head circumference was too small, weight and height are still in the normal range, and this case was published partly to show when intervention would be needed. Further discussion and follow-up recommendations for Toni are presented in Chapter 7.

TABLE 5.1 Aspects of Toni's Development: A Checklist

Fact	Strength	Normal Development	Danger Sign
1. Toni—brought by mother for well-child visit	_____	_____	_____
2. Doctor or clinic—has Toni's past history, uses it as reference	_____	_____	_____
3. Toni—behind on immunizations	_____	_____	_____
4. Toni—born at term	_____	_____	_____
5. Mother—18 years old when Toni was born	_____	_____	_____
6. Toni—birthweight 3,850 grams (about 8½ pounds) = 75th percentile	_____	_____	_____
7. Toni—birth length 50 centimeters (about 20 inches) = 50th percentile	_____	_____	_____
8. Mother and Toni—good health, no serious prenatal problems	_____	_____	_____
9. Toni—11 months, weight and height at 50th percentile	_____	_____	_____
10. Toni—17 months, weight 9,400 grams (about 21 pounds) = 20th percentile	_____	_____	_____
11. Toni—17 months, height 79 centimeters (about 31 inches) = 40th percentile	_____	_____	_____
12. Toni—normal development, according to mother	_____	_____	_____
13. Toni—five-word vocabulary	_____	_____	_____
14. Toni—busy, always on the go, according to mother	_____	_____	_____
15. Family—no serious medical problems	_____	_____	_____
16. Mother—5 feet, 5 inches; 130 pounds (1.65 meters; 59 kilograms)	_____	_____	_____
17. Father—about 6 feet (1.83 meters)	_____	_____	_____
18. Father—not in household	_____	_____	_____
19. Toni—no significant illness over past 6 months	_____	_____	_____
20. Toni—physical exam normal	_____	_____	_____
21. Toni—most laboratory tests normal	_____	_____	_____
22. Toni—mild anemia	_____	_____	_____
23. Mother—exclusive caregiver for the first year	_____	_____	_____
24. Mother—recently went back to work	_____	_____	_____
25. Mother—works as waitress	_____	_____	_____
26. Child care—many family members each do a few hours	_____	_____	_____
27. Child care—mother afraid of using strangers	_____	_____	_____
28. Mother—difficulty giving feeding history (a list of what has been consumed over a few days)	_____	_____	_____
29. Caregivers—do not communicate with each other about Toni's eating	_____	_____	_____
30. Routines and rules—vary from household to household	_____	_____	_____
31. Mother and Toni—rarely eat together	_____	_____	_____
32. Toni—falls asleep in front of TV at night	_____	_____	_____
33. Toni—awakens too late to eat breakfast	_____	_____	_____

Sleep

Young infants spend most of their time sleeping and eating. It is obvious why they eat so much: You would, too, if you had to double your weight in 4 months. However, it is not obvious why they sleep so much or even why they sleep at all. What *is* known is that throughout childhood, regular and ample sleep correlates with brain maturation, learning, emotional regulation, and psychological adjustment in school and within the family (Bates et al., 2002; Sadah et al., 2000). In addition, more growth hormones are excreted from the brain during sleep than during wakefulness, another possible reason that infants sleep as much as they do and that older adults sleep less (see Figure 5.1).

Many new parents are troubled not by how much infants sleep but by when they do it. Parents want infants to sleep soundly through the night, but infants are too immature—in their brain, digestion, and circadian rhythm—to comply. To some extent, this mismatch is created by the time and schedule urgency of modern civilization. In most developing nations, by contrast, babies are always near their mothers and family harmony is not disturbed if an infant or child wakes several times each night.

Between birth and age 1, the infant's *total* daily sleep is reduced by only 3 hours or so—from about 16 hours a day for the newborn to 13 hours for the 1-year-old. However, although older infants still sleep a lot, the length and timing of their sleep gradually become more closely matched to the day–night activities of the family. No newborns but about one-third of all North American 3-month-olds and 80 percent of all 1-year-olds "sleep through the night" (defined as sleeping for at least 6 straight hours beginning some time in the evening). However, a third of all 1- to 3-year-olds still waken and demand attention during the night (C. M. Johnson, 1991). In fact, waking up several times during the night is still common among preschool and school-age children (Weissbluth, 1999).

Over the first months, changes in the stages of sleep are more notable than the relatively small reduction in number of hours slept. **REM sleep** (rapid eye movement sleep, also characterized by dreaming and rapid brain waves) declines, as does "transitional sleep," the dozing stage when a person is half awake. At about 3 or 4 months, quiet sleep (also called slow-wave sleep) increases markedly (Salzarulo & Fagioli, 1999).

Infants who are preterm or who have immature central nervous systems spend more time in REM sleep than do normal infants (Cornwell et al., 1998; Ingersoll & Thoman, 1999). The fact that REM sleep decreases as a person ages is puzzling, because REM sleep in adults correlates with vivid dreams, and newborns probably have little to dream about. One explanation is that REM sleep

REM sleep Rapid eye movement sleep, a stage of sleep characterized by flickering eyes behind closed lids, dreaming, and rapid brain waves.

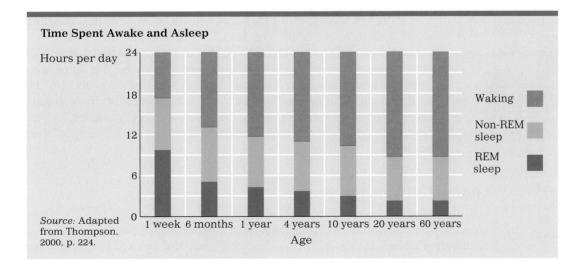

FIGURE 5.1 Sweet Dreams
On average, the older we are, the less sleep we get, probably because older people dream less. At age 60, we spend only about one hour per night dreaming. The mystery is, What can newborns be dreaming about for nine hours every day?

allows reorganization and interpretation of daily events. For adults, this often means dreaming to sort out the emotions, but for young infants, more basic mental processing of all the stimuli that have reached the brain is needed.

As we have just seen with Toni, a theme throughout this chapter is that both nature and nurture are influential in every aspect of physiological development. This is certainly true of sleep. Infants by nature sleep a great deal and wake up often. However, infants' sleep cycles are influenced by their parents' caregiving practices as well as by brain maturation. Thus, even older infants whose parents respond to their predawn cries with food and playtime are likely to wake up night after night. For the same reason, firstborns often exhibit more sleep problems, as in this report from one mother:

> I have strong opinions, having raised my first taking him wherever I went, whenever I went, confident he would adapt. While he was always happy, he was never a good sleeper and his first 4 years were very hard on me (I claim he didn't sleep through the night until he was 4, but I could be wrong, I was so sleep-deprived).
>
> The second came along 15 months after Sam and, forced to do less, he had more of a schedule and was a better sleeper.
>
> Bryn came along 18 months ago: 8 years after Sam. I was determined to give her a schedule. . . . I did and little interferes with it. I don't want it to. She is a good sleeper . . . no, she is a GREAT sleeper, happy to go to bed. I am convinced, anecdotally, that schedules are the most important part of this. When I talk to new mothers, I give them this advice: Let the baby determine the schedule, then let nothing interfere with it. (Freda, personal communication, 1997)

That is good advice. Developmentalists agree that insisting that an infant conform to the parents' busy schedule, rather than vice versa, can be frustrating to the parents and, in some cases, harmful to the infant.

Early Brain Development

The brain grows faster than the rest of the body, and head circumference is included in early checkups, for good reason: Brain size precedes brain functioning, and brain functioning makes all other development possible. Remember from Chapter 4 that the age of viability does not depend on body structures (all are present 10 weeks before viability) or body size (under 2 pounds, or 1,100 grams, is sometimes viable), but instead on brain maturation. After a full-term birth, sheer survival no longer depends on ongoing brain maturation, but neurological growth remains essential for the development of the senses, motor skills, and intellectual accomplishments that we will soon describe.

Therefore, no aspect of biosocial growth is more critical than the rapid growth of the brain, "by far the most complex structure in the known universe" (Thompson, 2000, p. 1). Recall that the newborn's skull is disproportionately large. That's because it must be big enough to hold the brain, which at birth has already attained 25 percent of its adult weight. (The neonate's body weight, by comparison, is typically only 5 percent of the adult weight.) By age 2, the brain is about 75 percent of its adult weight, while the body is only about 20 percent of its adult weight (see Figure 5.2).

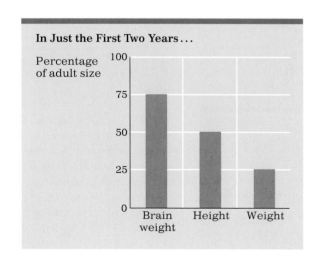

In Just the First Two Years...

FIGURE 5.2 **Growing Up** Two-year-olds are barely talking and are totally dependent on adults, but they have already reached half their adult height and three-fourths of their adult brain size. This is dramatic evidence that biosocial growth is the foundation for cognition and social maturity.

Connections in the Brain

Like brain weight, head circumference provides a rough idea of how much growth goes on within the skull. The head typically increases from 34 to 46 centimeters (about 35 percent) within the first year. Not as easy to measure for individual babies, but much more significant as a developmental process, are

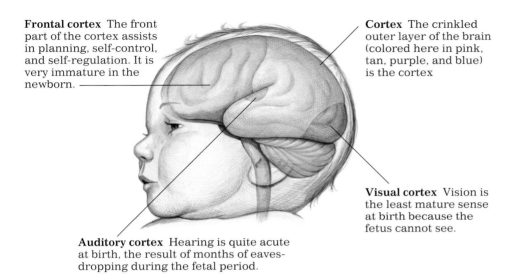

Frontal cortex The front part of the cortex assists in planning, self-control, and self-regulation. It is very immature in the newborn.

Cortex The crinkled outer layer of the brain (colored here in pink, tan, purple, and blue) is the cortex

Visual cortex Vision is the least mature sense at birth because the fetus cannot see.

Auditory cortex Hearing is quite acute at birth, the result of months of eavesdropping during the fetal period.

FIGURE 5.3 **The Developing Cortex** The cortex consists of six thin layers of tissue that cover the brain. It contains virtually all the neurons that make conscious thought possible. Some areas of the cortex, such as those devoted to the basic senses, mature relatively early. Others, such as the frontal cortex, mature quite late.

changes in the brain's communication systems. Recent research has revealed a great deal about early brain growth, with many implications for early child rearing. To understand this connection requires some familiarity with the structure and functioning of the brain (see Figure 5.3).

Basic Brain Structures

The brain's basic communication system begins with nerve cells, called **neurons.** Most neurons are created before birth, at a peak production rate of 250,000 new brain cells per minute at mid-pregnancy (Bloom et al., 2001). In infancy, the human brain has billions of neurons, about 70 percent of which are in the **cortex,** the brain's outer layer (also called the neocortex and sometimes called "the gray matter"). Only mammals (not birds or insects) have a cortex, which is the location of most thinking, feeling, and sensing. (Other parts of the brain participate in these functions, but the cortex is the crucial, and conscious, part.)

Various areas of the cortex specialize in particular kinds of thoughts. For instance, there is a visual cortex, an auditory cortex, and an area dedicated to the sense of touch for each body part, even for each finger or, in rats, for each whisker (Bloom et al., 2001). Definitive research linking particular brain areas to particular brain functions is easier to conduct with lower animals than with humans, and easier for studying motor skills than for studying how the brain thinks and analyzes ideas. As a result, scientists are not certain which human brain areas specialize in which kinds of memory, which parts of speech, which aspects of creative consciousness, and so on. However, it seems likely that areas of the human cortex specialize in those functions as well. At the same time every important concept seems to arise from several brain areas, involving many neurons. One science reporter explains:

> It's a complicated world out there, visually, full of things that look a lot alike. Yet people rarely identify a TV remote control as a cell phone or confuse a pencil with a swizzle stick. . . . In the past few years, brain imaging studies have identified one region [of the area of the brain called the ventral temporal cortex] that specializes in recognizing faces and another that processes places. More recently, researchers have found that even mundane objects such as shoes, chairs, and plastic bottles also light up distinct areas in part of the brain.
>
> *[Helmuth, 2001, pp. 196, 198]*

Neurons are connected to other neurons by intricate networks of nerve fibers called **axons** and **dendrites** (see Figure 5.4). Each neuron has a single axon and numerous dendrites, with the latter spreading out like the branches of

neuron A nerve cell of the central nervous system. Most neurons are in the brain.

cortex The outer layer of the brain in humans and other mammals; it is the location of most thinking, feeling, and sensing.

axon A nerve fiber that extends from a neuron and transmits electrical impulses from that neuron to the dendrites of other neurons.

dendrite A nerve fiber that extends from a neuron and receives electrical impulses transmitted from other neurons via their axons.

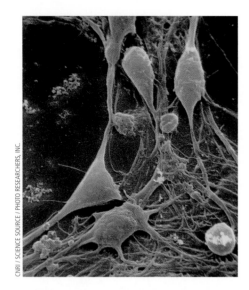

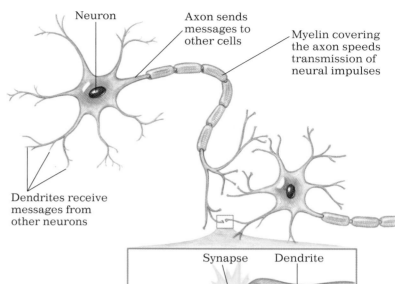

Neuron

Axon sends messages to other cells

Myelin covering the axon speeds transmission of neural impulses

Dendrites receive messages from other neurons

Synapse   Dendrite

Axon

Neurotransmitters

In the synapse, or intersection between an axon and dendrite, neurotransmitters carry information from one neuron to another.

FIGURE 5.4 How Two Neurons Communicate The link between one neuron and another is shown in this simplified diagram. The infant brain actually contains billions of neurons, each with one axon and many dendrites. Every electrochemical message to or from the brain causes thousands of neurons to fire simultaneously, each transmitting the message across the synapse to neighboring neurons. The electron micrograph above shows several neurons, greatly magnified, with their tangled but highly organized and well-coordinated sets of dendrites and axons.

synapse The intersection between the axon of one neuron and the dendrites of other neurons.

transient exuberance The great increase in the number of neurons, dendrites, and synapses that occurs in an infant's brain over the first 2 years of life.

Electric Excitement This infant's delight at his mother's facial expressions is visible, not just in his eyes and mouth but also in the neurons of the outer layer of his cortex. Electrodes map his brain activation region by region and moment by moment. Every month of life up to age 2 shows increased electrical excitement.

a tree. The axon of one neuron meets the dendrites of other neurons at intersections called **synapses,** which are critical communication links within the brain. To be more specific, a neuron communicates by sending an electrical impulse through its axon to the synapse, where it is picked up by the dendrites of other neurons. The dendrites bring the message to the cell bodies of those neurons, which, in turn, convey the message to still other neurons. Axons and dendrites do not touch at synapses. Instead, the electrical impulse excites brain chemicals, called *neurotransmitters,* which carry information from the axon of the sending neuron, across the *synaptic gap,* to the dendrites of the receiving neuron.

Exuberance and Speed

At birth, the brain contains more than 100 billion neurons, far more than any person will ever need, with comparatively few dendrites and synapses (although toward the end of prenatal development, synapses are already forming) (Bourgeois, 2001). During the first months and years, major spurts of growth and refinement in axons, dendrites, and synapses are particularly notable in the cortex. This is probably the major reason that brain weight triples in the 2 years after birth.

Indeed, an estimated fivefold increase in the density of dendrites in the cortex occurs from birth to about age 2, in a process called **transient exuberance.** As a result, in some cases as many as 15,000 new connections may be established *per neuron;* the total number of connections has been estimated at a quadrillion—that is, a million billion (Thompson, 2000). This exuberant proliferation enables neurons to become connected to, and communicate with, a greatly expanding number of other neurons within the brain. Synapses and dendrites continue to form throughout life, though much less rapidly (Huttenlocher & Dabholkar, 1997).

Experience Enhances the Brain

Experts agree that the specifics of brain structure and growth depend partly on the infant's experience. The most dramatic example arises from the pruning process that closely follows the growth process (see Figure 5.5). This pruning comes as no surprise when you remember that the exuberance of early dendrite growth is called *transient*. Exuberance is a transitional stage between the immaturity of the newborn brain and the maturity of the older child or adult. Soon after the exuberant expansion, some neurons wither because their synapses do not connect.

Why? Some neurons establish fewer dendrites, or their dendrites do not find any useful synapses, because experience does not activate that part of the brain. Underused neurons are inactivated (Bloom et al., 2001). This process is called *pruning* because it resembles the way a gardener prunes a rose bush by cutting away some stems to enable more, or more beautiful, roses to bloom. It has also been called "sculpting" because it is like the way a sculptor takes a block of stone or wood and chisels it into a work of art, discarding the useless chips. The point of both these analogies is that this cell death benefits the developing person's thinking ability. Indeed, one form of mental retardation (fragile-X syndrome) occurs when too many neurons survive (Comery et al., 1997).

Another example of the importance of experience comes from reactions to stress. The production of stress hormones by the brain is lifelong, but the amount produced relates partly to early experiences (Gunnar & Vasquez, 2001). If too many stress hormones are required early on (for instance, if an infant is terrified or anticipates pain much of the time), then the developing brain loses the capacity to react normally to stress, and later the child will be hypervigilant (always on the alert) or seemingly indifferent (not happy, sad, or angry) instead of having normal reactions. If a kindergarten teacher complains that a certain child is always angry or afraid, or that another child is never affected by anything, the cause could be the excessive production of stress hormones in infancy. If an adult loves or hates too quickly, extremely, and irrationally, again the cause could be abnormal brain growth in infancy resulting from early abuse (Teicher, 2002).

Note that this is what "could be." Scientists are certain that early experiences are crucial for normal brain development and that bombarding infants with too many experiences might be counterproductive. However, they are not sure how much experience, or what kind, is needed. Guidance in answering these questions comes from a useful distinction between typical and atypical experiences drawn by William Greenough, a scientist who bridges the divide between neuroscientific research and human experience.

Greenough has identified two experience-related aspects of brain development. **Experience-expectant** brain functions require basic common experiences in order to develop, and **experience-dependent** functions depend on particular, and variable, events (Greenough et al., 1987). Expected experiences *must* happen for normal brain maturation to occur, and they almost always do happen: The brain is designed to expect them and use them for growth. By contrast, dependent experiences *might* happen, and if they do, one brain will differ from another; but such variations do not make one mind better or worse than the other.

Human brains are designed for the *expected* experiences that virtually all normal infants have, no matter where they are raised. In deserts and the Arctic, on isolated farms and in crowded cities, we expect that all babies will have things to see and hear, have people to feed and carry them; as a result, their brains will develop normally as a member of the human species. Some particular experi-

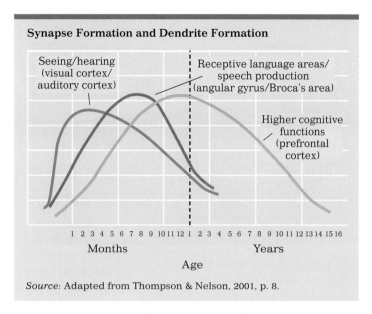

Synapse Formation and Dendrite Formation

Seeing/hearing (visual cortex/auditory cortex)

Receptive language areas/speech production (angular gyrus/Broca's area)

Higher cognitive functions (prefrontal cortex)

1 2 3 4 5 6 7 8 9 10 11 12 | 1 2 3 4 5 6 7 8 9 10 11 12 13 14 15 16
Months — Years
Age

Source: Adapted from Thompson & Nelson, 2001, p. 8.

FIGURE 5.5 **Brain Growth in Response to Experience** These curves show the rapid rate of experience-dependent synapse formation for three functions of the brain (senses, language, and analysis). After the initial increase, the underused neurons are gradually pruned, or inactivated, as no functioning dendrites are formed from them.

? *Observational Quiz* (see answer, page 146): Why do both "12 months" and "1 year" appear on the "Age" line?

experience-expectant Refers to brain functions that require basic common experiences (which the infant can be expected to have) in order to grow.

experience-dependent Refers to brain functions that depend on particular, and variable, experiences in order to grow.

Let's Talk Infants evoke facial expressions and baby talk, no matter where they are or which adults they are with. Communication is thus experience-expectant: Young human brains expect it and need it.

? *Observational Quiz* (see answer, page 146): Are these two father and daughter? Where are they?

ences, such as which language the baby hears or how the mother reacts to frustration, vary. *Depending* on those various experiences, infant brains will be structured one way or another. As a result, each person is a product of a particular family and culture as well as another member of the human race.

For example, human brains "expect" some sort of verbal communication and are primed to listen for and understand it; consequently, children learn to communicate at a far more advanced level than the most carefully taught chimpanzee or poodle. Only extreme deprivation—say, if a baby is profoundly deaf or if no one ever speaks to him or her—will prevent a human from learning to communicate with spoken words. Language learning is so innate that deaf children readily learn to communicate with gestures if anyone uses sign language with them. If no one does (as happened with a group studied in Nicaragua), when deaf children find each other, they will develop their own sign language, particularly if they are under age 10 when they meet (Senghas & Coppola, 2001).

How does experience-dependent language differ from universal brain expectancy? Your brain expects you to listen and talk, but its fine-tuning depends on the specific language you learned as an infant. Your neurons now show greater electrical excitement to words of your own language than to words of a language you never heard—even if you pretend not to understand the first language and fake comprehension of the second. You may fool others with your facial expressions and fibs, but you cannot fool your brain. Moreover, the way your adult brain is structured makes it very hard for you to learn an idiom or a pronunciation that is unlike any in your mother tongue.

The idea that some aspects of brain development are experience-expectant helps us know what kinds of stimulation infants need at what ages. Proliferation and pruning occur first in those parts of the cortex that are connected to the eyes and ears, at about 4 months in humans. Consequently, diagnosis of blind or deaf newborns and treatment with surgery or visual or auditory aids should occur in the first weeks of life, to prevent premature atrophy of neurons. If early visual or auditory neuronal connections are not made, those areas of the brain sometimes become dedicated to other senses, such as touch. Braille, for that reason, is easier for a blind person to learn to read than it is for a person who can see, because blind people have more brain power dedicated to the sense of touch.

Thinking Like a Scientist

Plasticity and Young Orphans

Neuroscientists once thought that brains were formed by genes and prenatal influences and that experience had nothing to do with neurological structures, unless it took the form of massive prenatal poisoning, as with fetal alcohol syndrome. By contrast, many social scientists once thought that the environment over the years of childhood was crucial, that cultures (according to anthropologists) or society (according to sociologists) or parents (according to psychologists) could be blamed for or credited with how children turned out. Now most scientists, especially developmental-

ists, are multidisciplinary, believing in *plasticity* (first described on page 5)—that is, the concept that personality, intellect, habits, and emotions change throughout life for a combination of reasons, not just one (Wachs, 2000). Brain structure and experience influence each other. Intriguing evidence along these lines comes from studies of musicians who play stringed instruments. The areas of their brains dedicated to finger sensitivity are more developed than are those of nonmusicians, especially if they began practicing daily as children (Elbert et al., 1995).

However, the concept of plasticity implies, just as the neuroscientists of old emphasized, that these are certain brain-based limits on how and when experience affects brain structure. Developmentalists now recognize, as do all scientists, that certain early physiological and experiential constraints guide human development (although they do not determine it) and that experiences have an impact (although not always a major one). In other words, as scientists recognize the influence of both nature and nurture on plasticity, they share the same dilemma: Too much emphasis on genetics is too rigid, but too much emphasis on experience is naive. How much, and when, does experience affect the brain? Two research projects—with caged rats and with adopted babies—provide some answers as well as further questions.

William Greenough and his colleagues raised some rats together in stimulating, toy-filled, large cages and others alone in small, barren cages, without toys or other stimulation. On autopsy, the brains of the rats in the first group were far better developed, with more dendrite branching, than the brains of the rats in the second group (Greenough & Volkmar, 1973). The same effect may apply to humans. As you already read, musicians' brains change in specific ways (such as increased finger sensitivity), especially if they began playing their instruments before age 10 (Elbert et al., 1995). Intense, early education for children of mentally retarded, socially deprived mothers improves the children's thinking and self-concept (Ramey & Ramey, 1998). This does not mean that extraordinary stimulation is needed for normal development. In fact, some contend that rats in the wild have a natural enrichment, where they encounter varied vegetation, rocks and hiding places, insects, birds, and fellow rats of many ages and temperaments. It does, however, demonstrate that experience affects brain structures.

How does this research on rats apply to humans? A chilling natural experiment is providing new urgency, and new data, on this question. It began with the Romanian dictator Nicolae Ceausescu. In the 1980s, his government forbade all birth control and paid parents a bonus for every baby born—but did not provide the economic infrastructure that made childrearing financially reasonable. More than 100,000 children were abandoned to the streets or to crowded, understaffed, state-run orphanages (D. E. Johnson, 2000). These children were malnourished, neglected, and deprived of normal social stimulation. They were overburdened with stress without any social reassurance and love to buffer it. In 1989, after Ceausescu was ousted and killed, thousands of these children were adopted by North American or Western European families who believed that "lots of love and good food would change the skinny, floppy waif they found in the orphanage into the child of their dreams" (D. E. Johnson, 2000, p. 154).

All the children were wasted and stunted, with head circumferences far below normal, but they all improved quickly (O'Connor et al., 2000). However, during early childhood many still showed signs of emotional damage: They were too friendly to strangers or too angry without reason or too frightened of normal events (Chisolm, 1998). If scientists expected dire consequences, the news is good: "The human infant has built-in 'buffers' against early adversity" (O'Connor et al., 2000). If they expected complete recovery, the news is bad: The identification of "persistent deficits in post-institutionalized children is repeated in all longitudinal studies of Romanian orphans" (D. E. Johnson, 2000, p. 152). Most (91 percent) of the adoptive parents were more positive than negative about their adoption experience (Groze & Ileana, 1996).

In the years to come, more research on these children will reveal how much recovery, under what circumstances, is possible for children who are severely deprived in infancy. We already know that the particulars of the early years have a greater effect than those of the adoptive homes, almost all of which are highly nurturing. The Romanian adoptees who have recovered are those who were adopted very young, at least before age 2, and were cared for by their birth parents for a while before being turned over to the orphanage.

Is damage that still exists at age 4 or 6 permanent? Scientists would like to answer that question, but they must withhold final judgment until further research on these children, now approaching adolescence, is conducted. "Subsequent transition, such as school entry, may bring about opportunities for developmental progress or, alternatively, maladjustment" (O'Connor et al., 2000, p. 388). Thinking like a scientist, in this case, means condemning every government, culture, or family that allows young children to be raised without the experiences they need, but it also means humbly admitting that there is much about early brain development and later experiences that we do not yet know.

For those who care about child development, the crucial question is whether early deprivation will cause a child to become mentally retarded or emotionally stunted—perhaps never able to appreciate poetry or sustain a loving relationship. Prolonged stress, severe malnutrition, extremely preterm birth, repeated abuse—all can seriously damage the brain as well as the body (Gunnar, 2000; D. E. Johnson, 2000; National Research Council & Institute of Medicine, 2000;

Especially for Social Workers An infertile couple in their late 30s asks for your help in adopting a child from Eastern Europe. They particularly want an older child. How do you respond?

! *Answer to Observational Quiz* (from page
144): The man's straight black hair, high cheek-
bones, and weather-beaten face indicate that he
could be an Indian from North or South America.
Other clues pinpoint the location more closely.
Note his lined, hooded jacket and the low, heat-
conserving ceiling of the house—he is an Inuit in
northern Canada. A father's attention makes a baby
laugh and vocalize, not look away, so this man is
not the 6-month-old baby's father. She is being held
by a family friend whom she is visiting with her
parents.

! *Answer to Observational Quiz* (from page
143): "One year" signifies the entire year, from day
365 to day 729, and that is indicated by its location
between "12 months" and "2 years."

sensation The response of a sensory system when
it detects a stimulus.

perception The mental processing of sensory
information.

Rose & Feldman, 2000). The evidence from studies of the Romanian adoptees is
that such deprivation sometimes results in severe damage but that a family can
help a child reduce that damage.

Our understanding of the brain now leads developmentalists to hope that
caressing a newborn, talking to a preverbal infant, and showing affection toward
a small person may be essential first steps toward developing that person's full
human potential. If such experiences are missing from the early weeks and
months, that is tragic. But human brains are designed to be adaptable, and some
plasticity is retained throughout life. New connections and pathways can develop, as long as new experiences continue (Greenough, 1993). It is never too
late, but earlier is much better.

The Senses and Motor Skills

You learned in Chapter 2 that Piaget called the first period of intelligence the *sensorimotor* stage, thus emphasizing that cognition depends on the senses and
motor skills. The same concept—that infant brain development depends partly
on the sensory experiences and early movements of the baby—underlies the
pages you have just read. Now we will look explicitly at those early sensory and
motor skills, especially at norms for their development. One reason for emphasizing norms is that infants who are slow to develop their senses and motor skills
may also be slow to develop their minds. Indeed, severe mental retardation is
sometimes signaled by a 6-month-old who, say, stares blankly or does not sit up.
However, you will also learn that variations from these norms can be quite normal, as my own daughters illustrate.

Sensation and Perception

The senses all function at birth. Babies are born with eyes open, with ears sensitive to noise, and with smell, taste, and touch responsive to the world around
them. Throughout their first year, infants rely heavily on their senses as an aid to
cognition, using them to sort and classify their many experiences. Indeed, "infants spend the better part of their first year merely looking around" (Rovee-
Collier, 2001 p. 35).

You may wonder why, if newborn senses are so capable, it takes months before they seem to perceive much of anything. To understand the reason, you
need to understand a logical distinction between sensation and perception.
Sensation occurs when a sensory system detects a stimulus, as when the inner
ear reverberates with sound or the pupil and retina of the eye intercept light.
Thus, sensations begin where an outer organ (eye, ear, skin, tongue, or nose)
meets anything in the external world that can be seen, heard, touched, tasted, or
smelled. That happens as soon as the newborn is held close to the mother's body,
for human bodies offer a feast for all the senses. The sensory systems begin to
develop before birth and become particularly acute in infancy. For instance, a
1-year-old can hear many very quiet sounds that most adults can no longer
sense, although the ability to hear does not guarantee that the brain is able to
perceive. An adult might not hear a whisper as well as an infant does but will
perceive and understand it much better once it is sensed.

Perception occurs when the brain becomes activated by a sensation and
attempts to notice and process it. Perception occurs in the cortex, usually as the
result of a message sent from one of the sensing organs. Perception depends on
experience: A person has to have some notion of the significance of the sensation. The connection between sensation and perception is particularly close in
early infancy, as the sense organs are all functioning and the baby is trying to

understand and interpret all those sensations. Of course, some sensations are beyond understanding at first: A newborn has no way to know that the letters on a page might have significance, or even that the smell of roses and the smell of garlic might need to be differentiated. In adulthood, the connection between sensation and perception is likely to break down for the opposite reason: The mind already has many thoughts and experiences, which might lead someone to ignore various sensations ("Sorry, I wasn't listening") or to perceive things that are not sensed ("I thought I saw her, but I was mistaken").

Cognition is one step beyond perception, when a person actually thinks about what he or she has perceived. Indeed, cognition can occur without either sensation or perception; a person can imagine something. Babies, however, are not yet able to imagine, because they have not yet sensed and perceived very much. Thus, there is a sequence, from sensation to perception to cognition. A baby's sense organs must function if this chain of comprehension is to begin. No wonder that the parts of the cortex dedicated to the senses develop rapidly; this is needed so that all the other developments can occur.

Listening

Hearing is already quite acute at birth. Certain sounds seem to trigger reflexes, even without conscious perception, probably because fetuses heard those sounds during the last trimester in the womb. Sudden noises startle newborns, making them cry; rhythmic sounds, such as a lullaby or a heartbeat, soothe them and put them to sleep. Even in the first days of life, infants turn their heads toward the source of a sound, and they soon begin to adapt that response to connect sight and sound, with increasing accuracy (Morrongiello et al., 1998).

Young infants are particularly attentive to the human voice, a striking example of genetic programming for social interaction. One overview of hearing in childhood explains:

> Infants are exposed to a variety of different sounds in their native environments. Some of these are produced with great frequency by other active, non-human creatures, such as family pets, and others by electromechanical devices, such as alarm clocks. Yet, the sounds that infants choose to imitate, the ones which seem to attract their attention most, are the ones produced by other human beings.
>
> [Aslin et al., 1998, p. 158]

Not only sensation but also perception of sounds is apparent from birth. Newborns distinguish voices, rhythms, and language, preferring the voice, rhythm, and mother tongue they have heard in the womb. The sensitivity of newborns to human speech is also shown by their ability to differentiate one consonant from another, one vowel from another, and even words with meaning (such as *taste, snow, mommy*) from words that are merely grammatical (such as *the, on, your*) (Shi et al., 1999).

As time goes on, the infant's sensitive hearing combines with the developing brain to distinguish patterns of sounds and syllables. For example, if infants hear repetitions of a particular nonsense sound—in one experiment, *pabiku*—they quickly become accustomed to it and are more surprised at hearing another three-syllable word than the old, familiar *pabiku* (Saffran et al., 1996). They also become accustomed to the rules of language, such as which syllable is usually stressed (various English dialects have different rules), whether changing voice tone is significant (as it is in Chinese), whether certain sound combinations are often or never repeated, and so on. All this is based on very careful listening to human speech, even speech not directed to them and, obviously, in a language they do not understand (Jusczyk, 1997; Marcus, 2000).

Response for Social Workers (from page 145): You would advise them that such a child requires more time and commitment than most children do, and you would assess their readiness to cope with that. You might ask if both of them are prepared to cut down on their working hours in order to have time to meet with other parents of international adoptees, to schedule weekly professional help (for speech, nutrition, physical development, and/or family therapy), and so on. In addition, you would explain that adoptees who adjust well are typically under age 2 and that older adoptees need as much attention as babies. You might encourage them instead to adopt a special-needs child from their own area, to become foster parents, or to volunteer at least 10 hours a week at a day-care center. One reason for making this recommendation is to assess their willingness to help a real—not imagined—child. If they are willing to do all this, and understand why it may be necessary, you might help them adopt the child they want.

Before Leaving the Hospital Even as he sleeps, this newborn has his hearing tested via vibrations of the inner ear in response to various tones. The computer interprets the data and signals any need for more tests—as is the case for about one baby in 100. Normal newborns hear quite well.

binocular vision The ability to focus the two eyes in a coordinated manner in order to see one image.

Is This Really Edible? Newborns can taste sweet, and—as this young lady demonstrates—toddlers can taste bitter. At her age, she is able to react, possibly by spitting out the bitter arugula but perhaps by swallowing it and taking another bite. One-year-olds, being curious, sometimes overcome their distaste in order to experiment.

Looking

Vision is the least mature of the senses at birth, partly because the fetus can see very little and thus the connection between the eyes and the visual cortex cannot form until the baby enters the world of lights, colors, and shadows. Newborns focus on objects between 4 and 30 inches (10 and 75 centimeters) away and merely stare at whatever they see (most often the faces of their caregivers) as if trying to figure out who or what they might be. Their distance vision is about 20/400, which means that they perceive objects that are 20 feet (6.1 meters) away no better than adults with 20/20 vision see the same objects at 400 feet (122 meters).

Within a few weeks, increasing experience with all the objects within view and maturation of the visual cortex combine to improve visual ability. For example, 1-month-olds' gazes often wander or seem to get stuck on an insignificant part of an object: Their ability to focus and *scan* (that is, move the eyes systematically to view an entire object from side to side and top to bottom) is quite imperfect. When looking at a face, for example, they might stare at a peripheral feature, such as the hairline, and then glance off into space. By 6 weeks, they look more intently, finally recognizing their caregivers and smiling—somewhat tentatively and fleetingly, but smiling nonetheless. Over time, scanning is more organized, more efficient, and centered on important aspects of a visual stimulus. Thus, 3-month-olds look more closely at the eyes and mouth, which contain the most information. Those infants who become most adept at scanning, focusing attention, and then momentarily looking away (rather than just staring at one spot) also become the most cognitively skilled on other measures of intellectual growth (Choudhury & Gorman, 2000; Rose et al., 2001a). This finding confirms the link between the early development of the senses and the increasing number of dendrites and synapses in the brain.

One of the best examples of early learning is the development of **binocular vision,** the ability to focus the two eyes in a coordinated manner in order to see one image. Because using both eyes together is not possible until the baby is outside the womb, many newborns seem to use one eye or the other to focus, or momentarily to use the two eyes independently, seeming temporarily wall-eyed or cross-eyed. At about 14 weeks, binocular vision appears quite suddenly (Held, 1995).

Touching, Tasting, Smelling

As with vision and hearing, taste, smell, and touch function at birth and rapidly adapt to the social world. For example, one study found that a taste of sugar calmed 2-week-olds but had no effect on 4-week-olds—unless accompanied by a human face looking reassuringly at the baby (Zeifman et al., 1996). Similar adaptation occurs for the senses of smell and touch. As babies learn to recognize their own caregiver's smell and handling, they respond by relaxing, even when their eyes are closed, when cradled by the one who usually holds and feeds them. The ability to be comforted by the human touch is one of the important "skills" tested in the Brazelton Neonatal Behavioral Assessment Scale (26 items of newborn behavior, as well as several reflexes, used to measure normal newborn functions). Response to cuddling is one measure of social adaptability that almost all newborns demonstrate.

In addition, in the early months—long before their limited eye control permits careful visual inspection and long before their fine motor skills can grab and finger an object—babies like to mouth things, exploring them with their tongues, gums, and lips, which are sensitive to touch, smell, and taste. In fact, research shows that they begin to recognize objects by mouth at 1 month of age (Gibson & Walker, 1984). This could help explain why infants a few months old might start to suck an unfamiliar brand of pacifier, recognize by taste and feel that something is amiss, and then spit it out, rather than immediately realizing on inspection that it is not the familiar one, as an older infant does.

The entire package of early sensation seems organized for two goals: social interaction (to become familiar with and connect with caregivers) and comfort (to be soothed amid the disturbances of daily newborn life). Even the sense of pain and the sense of motion, not among the five basic senses because no body part is dedicated to them, are attuned in infants to aid both socialization and comfort. Early breast milk, for instance, seems to have a mild anesthetic quality, so the newborn literally feels happier at the mother's breast, connecting taste, touch, and smell with that experience, and sight as well (a breast-feeding woman's face is exactly within the limited focusing range of a newborn's eyes). Similarly, crying infants often appreciate the sense of motion as well as touch, so many a new parent finds that rocking, carrying, or even putting the baby in the car and driving through the neighborhood will make the baby calm down and sleep—thus again connecting infant comfort with social interaction. In sum, the infant seems genetically programmed with the early senses that are primed to help him or her join the human family and be happy to do so.

Motor Skills

We now come to the most visible and dramatic body changes of infancy, those that ultimately allow the child to "stand tall and walk proud." Thanks to their on-going changes in size and proportion and their increasing brain maturation, infants markedly improve their motor skills, which are their abilities to move and control their bodies.

Because of the growing independence they afford the child, motor skills open new possibilities for discovery of the world. As one review of motor skills puts it:

> Gaining control over the arms and hands is one of the major achievements of the infant. . . . Once infants can reach for and grasp objects, they no longer have to wait for the world to come to them; their hands now bring objects close enough for tactile, auditory, visual, and buccal [mouth] exploration.
>
> *[Bertenthal & Clifton, 1998, p. 67]*

Walking and climbing are even more revolutionary. New vistas are seen, new dangers are within reach, and, fortunately for safety's sake, new fears develop. The development of motor skills—including the usual sequence and timing of their emergence—and the various factors that might cause one child to develop certain skills "behind" or "ahead of" schedule provide insight into how the infant is developing overall.

Reflexes

Strictly speaking, the infant's first motor skills are not skills at all but reflexes, or involuntary responses to particular stimuli. Three sets of reflexes are critical for survival and become stronger as the baby matures:

■ *Reflexes that maintain oxygen supply.* The **breathing reflex** begins in normal newborns even before the umbilical cord, with its supply of oxygen, is cut. Additional reflexes that maintain oxygen are reflexive *hiccups* and *sneezes,* as well as *thrashing* (moving the arms and legs about) to escape something that covers the face.

■ *Reflexes that maintain constant body temperature.* When infants are cold, they *cry, shiver,* and *tuck in their legs* close to their bodies, thereby helping to keep themselves warm. When they are hot, they try to *push away* blankets and then stay still.

Response for Grandparents (from page 148): No. Experience-expectant brain development is programmed to occur for all infants, requiring only the stimulation that virtually all families provide—warmth, reassuring touch, overheard conversation, facial expressions, movement. Extras such as baby talk, music, exercise, mobiles, and massage may be beneficial, but they are not needed for normal development.

breathing reflex An involuntary physical response, involving inhaling and exhaling, that ensures an adequate supply of oxygen and the discharge of carbon dioxide.

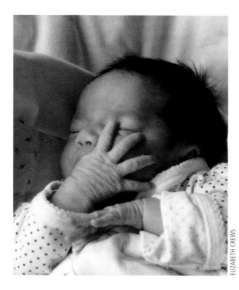

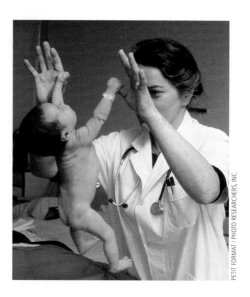

Never Underestimate the Power of a Reflex For developmentalists, newborn reflexes are mechanisms for survival, indicators of brain maturation, and vestiges of evolutionary history. For parents, they are mostly delightful and sometimes amazing. This is demonstrated by three star performers: a 2½-week-old infant stepping eagerly forward on legs too tiny to support her body; a 3-day-old infant, still wrinkled from being immersed in amniotic fluid, contentedly sucking his thumb; and a newborn grasping so tightly that his legs dangle in space.

sucking reflex An involuntary physical response in which newborns suck anything that touches their lips.

rooting reflex An involuntary physical response in which babies seek a nipple by turning their heads toward anything that brushes against their cheeks and trying to suck on it.

gross motor skills Physical abilities involving large body movements, such as waving the arms, walking, and jumping.

fine motor skills Physical abilities involving small body movements, especially of the hands and fingers, such as drawing and picking up a coin.

■ *Reflexes that manage feeding.* The **sucking reflex,** which is crucial to their taking in nourishment, causes newborns to suck anything that touches their lips—fingers, toes, blankets, and rattles, as well as natural and artificial nipples of various textures and shapes. The **rooting reflex** causes babies to turn their mouths toward anything that brushes against their cheeks—a reflexive search for a nipple—and start to suck. Even if a mother does nothing but put a newborn within striking distance of the nipple, the neonate instinctively grasps and sucks with sufficient skill to feed (Koepke & Bigelow, 1997). *Swallowing* is another important reflex that aids feeding, as are *crying* when the stomach is empty and *spitting up* when too much has been swallowed too quickly.

Gross Motor Skills

Gross motor skills, which involve large body movements, emerge directly from reflexes. Newborns placed on their stomachs reflexively move their arms and legs as if they were swimming and attempt to lift their heads to look around. As they gain muscle strength, they start to wiggle, attempting to move forward by pushing their arms, shoulders, and upper bodies against the surface they are lying on. Although these initial efforts usually get them nowhere (or even move them backward), infants persist in these motions whenever they have the opportunity. Usually by the age of 5 months or so, they become able to use their arms, and then legs, to inch forward on their bellies.

By the age of 7 months, most infants have succeeded at this belly-crawl. A few months later, usually between 8 and 10 months after birth, most infants can lift their midsections and crawl (or *creep*) on "all fours," coordinating the movements of their hands and knees in a smooth, balanced manner (Adolph et al., 1998). Within the next couple of months, most infants also learn to climb up onto couches and chairs—as well as up onto ledges and windowsills, and down into other dangerous places, including pools and lakes.

Walking shows a similar progression: from reflexive, hesitant, adult-supported stepping to a smooth, speedy, coordinated gait (Bertenthal & Clifton, 1998). On average, a child can walk while holding a hand at 9 months, can stand alone momentarily at 10 months, and can walk well, unassisted, at 12 months.

Interestingly, once an infant can take steps, walking becomes the preferred mode of movement—except when speed is an issue; then many new walkers quickly drop to their hands and knees to crawl. Two-year-olds are proficient walkers and almost never crawl except when, with a mocking grin, they pretend to be babies. Within 6 months, mastery of walking leads to mastery of running (Bertenthal & Clifton, 1998). Each of these motor skills may seem to appear suddenly, but actually each day of active practice at walking brings speedy running closer.

Fine Motor Skills

Fine motor skills are those that involve small body movements, usually of the fingers. Infants are born with a reflexive grasp, but they seem to have no control over it. During their first 2 months, babies excitedly stare and wave their arms at an object dangling within reach; by 3 months of age they can usually touch it. But they cannot yet grab and hold on unless the object is placed in their hands, partly because their eye–hand coordination is too limited.

By 4 months of age they sometimes grab, but their timing is off: They close their hands too early or too late, and their grasp tends to be of short duration. Finally, by 6 months of age, with a concentrated stare and deliberation, most babies can reach for, grab at, and hold onto almost any object that is of the right size. They can hold a bottle, shake a rattle, and yank a sister's braids. Moreover, they no longer need to see their hands in order to grab; they can grasp a moving object that is illuminated in an otherwise dark room (Robin et al., 1996), although when the lights are on, they use vision to help them carefully reach for objects (McCarty & Ashmead, 1999).

By the time they are 6 months of age, most infants can transfer objects from one hand to the other. By 8 or 9 months, they can adjust their reach in an effort to catch objects that are tossed toward them. And by 11 or 12 months, they can coordinate both hands to enclose an object that is too big for one hand alone (de Róiste & Bushnell, 1996). They can also point at objects and figure out what someone else is pointing at. Before 1 year, those who will speak sign language are already forming appropriate gestures—although still in a baby-talk version, without all the grammatical nuances that adult sign language includes.

The Whole Body

The distinction between gross motor skills and fine motor skills is important to educators, who are interested in the relationship between large body movements and the critical fine motor skill of writing letters with a pencil. However, for the developing child, all these skills build on one another, with gross motor skills enhancing fine motor skills and vice versa. Once able to sit steadily, a child becomes much better at reaching for and manipulating objects. Once able to grab, a child can hold onto chair legs, tabletops, and crib rails. This, in turn, makes standing, walking, and climbing possible, strengthening the leg muscles in the process.

At this point, toddlers can poke, pick, pinch, pull, squeeze, and throw hundreds of objects that were previously beyond reach. They can even hide or run away if they choose. Skilled fine motor movements, such as taking the top off a bottle of bleach, pushing a marker along a living room wall, or unlocking a cabinet door, do not mature until a few months later. However, careful attention to "babyproofing" the home is needed, especially with regard to poisons and breakables, long before the infant demonstrates such dexterity.

KENNETH MURRAY / PHOTO RESEARCHERS, INC.

Mind in the Making Pull, grab, look, and listen. Using every sense at once is a toddler's favorite way to experience life, generating brain connections as well as commotion.

Now a Toddler As this very young lady begins to walk, she demonstrates why such children are called toddlers: They move unsteadily from side to side as well as forward.

? *Observational Quiz* (see answer, page 153): What emotions and fine motor skills usually accompany early walking, as shown here?

BRADY

Variations and Ethnic Differences

Although all healthy infants develop the same motor skills in the same sequence, the age at which these skills are acquired varies greatly from infant to infant. Table 5.2 shows the age at which half of all infants in the United States master each major motor skill and the age at which 90 percent master each skill.

These averages, or norms, are based on a large representative sample of infants from a wide range of ethnic groups. Representative sampling is necessary because norms vary from group to group and place to place. For example, throughout infancy, African-Americans are more advanced in motor skills than Americans of European ancestry (Rosser & Randolph, 1989). Internationally, the earliest walkers in the world seem to be in Uganda, where, if well nourished and healthy, the typical baby walks at 10 months. Some of the latest walkers are in France, where taking one's first unaided steps at 15 months is not unusual.

What factors account for this variation? Of primary importance are inherited factors, such as how active, how physically mature, and how fat a particular child might be. The power of genes is suggested by the fact that identical twins are far more likely to sit up, and to walk, on the same day than are fraternal twins. Striking individual differences in the strategies, effort, and concentration that infants apply to the mastering of motor actions affect the timing of motor-skill achievements (Thelen et al., 1993). These differences may be genetic as well.

Patterns of infant care are also influential. For example, in many African cultures, infants are held next to an adult's body, usually in the upright position, virtually all day long; they are cradled and rocked as the adult works. Continually feeling the rhythm and changes of an adult's gait tends to stimulate the infant to

Safe and Secure Many Navajo infants still spend hours each day on a cradle board, to the distress of some nonnative adults, until they see that most Navajo babies are quite happy that way. The discovery in the 1950s that Navajo children walked at about the same age as European-American children suggested that maturation, not practice, led to motor skills. Later research found that most Navajo infants also received special exercise sessions each day, implying that practice plays a larger role than most psychologists once thought.

?Observational Quiz (see answer, page 154): Is a 6-month-old developing normally if he or she can sit propped up but cannot stand up, even while holding on?

TABLE 5.2 Age Norms (in Months) for Gross Motor Skills*

Skill	When 50% of All Babies Master the Skill	When 90% of All Babies Master the Skill
Lifts head 90° when lying on stomach	2.2 months	3.2 months
Rolls over	2.8	4.7
Sits propped up (head steady)	2.9	4.2
Sits without support	5.5	7.8
Stands holding on	5.8	10.0
Walks holding on	9.2	12.7
Stands momentarily	9.8	13.0
Stands alone well	11.5	13.9
Walks well	12.1	14.3
Walks backward	14.3	21.5
Walks up steps (with help)	17.0	22.0
Kicks ball forward	20.0	24.0

Source: The Denver Developmental Screening Test (Frankenburg et al., 1981).

Note: These norms came from a large cross-section of infants in 1960 in the western half of the United States. Accordingly, infants born more recently or babies from other nations may have different norms.

practice movement. This may well give African babies an advantage in gross motor skills over infants who spend much of each day in a crib or playpen.

Although some North American parents believe crawling helps later cognitive development by patterning the brain, and most delight in their baby's first steps, many other cultures discourage or even prevent infants from developing their motor skills. The people of Bali, Indonesia, never let their infants crawl, for babies are considered divine and crawling is for animals (Diener, 2000). By contrast, the Beng people in the Ivory Coast are proud when their babies start to crawl but do not let them walk until 1 year. In fact, as a grandmother was said to warn, "Your husband may have to spank the baby for trying to walk too early" (Gottlieb, 2000, p. 83). Although the Beng do not recognize the connection, one reason for this prohibition may be birth control, because in this culture, walking signifies that the mother is ready to resume sexual relations. According to tradition, a baby will die if the parents have sex before the baby walks.

❗️*Answer to Observational Quiz* (from page 151): Walking is thrilling to most toddlers, a source of pride and joy (see infant's face)—and perhaps disobedience, if the seated woman is unwilling to follow along and so asks her to stop. Finger skills take a leap forward, too: Notice the dirt in the baby's right hand and the extended finger pointing on the left.

In Person

The Normal Berger Daughters

Cultural beliefs affect American parents and babies as much as they do other peoples around the world, as I learned from personal experience. When I had my first baby, Bethany, I was a graduate student, so I had already memorized such norms as "sitting by 6 months, walking by 12." During her first year, Bethany reached all the developmental milestones pretty much on time. However, at 14 months, she was still not walking. I became a little anxious. I then began to read about developmental norms with a sharper eye and learned three comforting facts. First, variation in timing is normal. Second, when late walking is a sign of a problem, it is accompanied by other signs, and Bethany showed no other signs of delayed development: She was growing normally, using two hands to grab, and beginning to talk. Third, norms for motor-skill development vary among cultures. Remembering that my grandmother was Alsatian, I decided that Bethany's later walking was an expression of her French genes.

Two months later, Bethany was walking and my second child, Rachel, was born. Motivated by my experience with Bethany's late walking, I began marshaling evidence that motor skills follow a genetic timetable, taught that truth to my students, and received from them additional testimony as to the power of genes. Among my students who were immigrants, those from Jamaica, Cuba, and Barbados expected babies to walk earlier than did students who had emigrated from Russia, China, and Korea. Among my students who were born in North America, both expectations as to walking norms and personal experience followed racial lines. Many of my African-American students proudly cited their sons, daughters, or younger siblings who walked at 10

months, or even 8 months, to the chagrin of their European-American classmates.

Believing now in a genetic timetable for walking, I was not surprised when Rachel took her first steps at 15 months—over Christmas vacation at Grandma's house. Our third child, Elissa, also walked "late"—though on schedule for a Berger child with some French ancestry. By then I was not worried at all about her late motor-skill development, partly because her older sister Bethany had become the fastest runner in her class. I taught all my students about genetic variation in developmental norms and told them they could start worrying when a child didn't sit up by 8 months or walk by 16 months, but not before that.

By the time our fourth child, Sarah, was born, I was an established professor and author, able to afford a full-time caregiver, Mrs. Todd, who was from Jamaica. Mrs. Todd thought Sarah was the brightest, most advanced baby she had ever seen, except, perhaps, her own daughter Gillian. I agreed, of course, but I cautioned Mrs. Todd that Berger children walk late.

"She'll be walking by a year," Mrs. Todd told me. "Maybe sooner. Gillian walked at 10 months."

"We'll see," I replied, confident in my genetic interpretation.

However, I had not anticipated Mrs. Todd's dedication to seeing her prediction come true. She bounced baby Sarah on her lap, day after day. Sarah loved it. By the time Sarah was 8 months old, Mrs. Todd was already spending a good deal of time bent over, holding Sarah by both hands and practicing walking—to Sarah's great delight. Lo and behold, with Mrs. Todd's urging and guidance, Sarah took her first step at exactly 1 year—late for a Todd baby, but amazingly early for a Berger.

As a scientist, I know that a single case proves nothing. It could be that the genetic influences on Sarah's walking were different from those on her sisters. She is only one-eighth French, after all, a fraction I had ignored when I was explaining Bethany's late walking to myself. But in my heart I think it much more likely that practice, fostered by a caregiver with a cultural tradition different from mine, made the difference. From that day forward, as I teach, I always emphasize both nature and nurture in describing motor skills. I am also more appreciative

when my students tell me of variations and discrepancies from the "norms" of development.

My Youngest at 8 Months When I look at this photo of Sarah, I see evidence of Mrs. Todd's devotion. Sarah's hair is washed and carefully brushed, her dress and blouse are cleaned and pressed, and the carpet and footstool are perfect equipment for standing practice. Sarah's legs—chubby and far apart—indicate that she is not about to walk early, but given all these signs of Mrs. Todd's attention to caregiving, it is not surprising, in hindsight, that my fourth daughter was my earliest walker.

HAZEL HANKIN

Although variation in the timing of the development of motor skills is normal, an infant who shows a pattern of slow development—that is, development several months behind the norms for babies of the same culture and ethnicity—should be checked to ensure that no problem is impeding the child's progress. Slow infants may be mentally retarded, physically ill, seriously neglected—or perfectly fine.

Preventive Medicine

In the long history of humankind, there have been many instances when the body growth, brain connections, and sensorimotor skills just described did not occur. As you will now see, the story of preventive medicine is one of the most encouraging tales of the past 50 years.

!*Answer to Observational Quiz* (from page 152): Yes. By age 6 months, the average baby can stand up while holding on, but 40 percent master this skill later, between 6 and 10 months.

Precise worldwide statistics were not collected half a century ago, but it is safe to say that at least 6 billion children were born between 1950 and 2000. At least 1 billion of them survived childhood only because of advances in newborn care, childhood immunization, oral rehydration therapy (giving restorative liquids to children with diarrhea, thus saving 3 million young children *per year*), nutrition, and other public health measures (Rutstein, 2000; Victora et al., 2000).

According to reliable current statistics, in the healthiest nations (such as Japan, the Netherlands, and France), fewer than 1 in 200 children who survive birth die before age 5. Even in the nations with the most childhood deaths (Malawi, Niger, and Ethiopia), fewer than 20 percent of newborn survivors die before age 5 (McDevitt, 1998). In 1900, by contrast, no matter where they were born, about 1 in 3 children died before age 5 (Bogin, 1996). More young lives can be saved in the next decade or two if public health improvements continue.

Immunization

Most of the children who died 50 years ago were sick with measles, whooping cough, pneumonia, or some other obvious illness. Even in the twenty-first century, these diseases kill thousands of malnourished children each year, but today the diseases themselves are much less common (Rutstein, 2000). The reason is **immunization** (which primes the infant's innate immune system to defend against a specific contagious disease), a scientific development said to have had "a greater impact on human mortality reduction and population growth than any other public health intervention besides clean water" (Baker, 2000). There is no evidence that immunization causes autism or any other problem—quite the opposite, in fact.

A person can be immunized against a contagious disease in many ways— through injection, ingestion, inhalation, or naturally (by catching the disease and surviving). Usually the best method is a vaccine, which involves giving the person a small dose of inactive disease (often via a "shot" in the arm) that prepares the immune system to resist the actual disease if it is encountered. The best timing, vaccination method, and dose for each illness are topics of ongoing research. Particularly urgent are the development, testing, and approval of vaccinations against AIDS, malaria, cholera, typhoid, and shigellosis, which together kill more than a million children each year in developing nations (Russell, 2002). (Current childhood immunization schedules for the United States are given in Appendix B.) Although much remains to be done, especially in poor nations, stunning successes in applying past research include the following:

■ Smallpox, the most lethal disease for all children in past centuries, has been eradicated worldwide. Since 1971, routine vaccination against smallpox has not been recommended, because it is no longer necessary. In fact, stockpiles of the virus and the vaccine are kept only as a precaution against bioterrorism, not because any new natural outbreak is expected.

■ Polio, a crippling and sometimes fatal disease, is almost extinct, thanks to widespread vaccination begun in 1955. No new cases of polio have occurred in the United States or several other nations for more than a decade.

■ Measles (rubeola), which can be fatal in the first months of life because it can cause dehydration, is disappearing from the world, thanks to a vaccine developed in 1963. In all of the Americas, only about 1,000 cases of measles occurred in 2000, down from 53,683 just three years earlier (CDC, November 3, 2000). In the United States, fewer than 100 cases were reported in 2000, a marked contrast to the peak of 777,000 in 1958. That impressive progress is outdistanced by 32 smaller American nations, which reported no cases at all in 2000. In contrast, many nations of Africa and Asia still

immunization A process that stimulates the body's immune system to defend against attack by a particular contagious disease.

STEVE RUBIN / THE IMAGE WORKS

Look Away! The benefits of immunization justify the baby's brief discomfort, but many parents still do not appreciate the importance of following the recommended schedule of immunizations for their children.

have thousands of cases each year, down from hundreds of thousands a decade ago.

■ In the United States, the "highest level ever reported" of immunization was attained in 1998, when 79 percent of the nation's children were fully protected (with a total of 15 doses, including booster shots) against polio, measles, diphtheria, tetanus, mumps, pertussis, hepatitis, and influenza (CDC, September 22, 2000).

Immunization protects children not only against the mild versions of childhood diseases but also against serious complications, among them deafness, blindness, sterility, meningitis, and even death. Less obviously, immunization of each child protects many other people: Infants too young for their first vaccinations may die if they catch a disease from an older child who has not been immunized; a fetus whose mother contracts rubella may be born blind, deaf, and brain-damaged; healthy adults with mumps or measles suffer much more than a child; and vulnerable adults (the elderly, those who are HIV-positive, or chemotherapy patients whose immune systems are impaired) can be killed by any number of "childhood" diseases. Chicken pox, for instance, can be fatal, but less than half of all U.S. children are fully immunized against it (*MMWR*, June 22, 2000). Although the vaccine has been available and recommended since 1995, a 23-year-old mother in Pennsylvania caught it from her two preschool children and died in 1997. If 90 percent of all preschool children are successfully immunized, a disease is unlikely to spread. This woman would not have died if she had not caught chicken pox from her children, but they would not have caught it if all their friends had been immunized, and so on. Thus, every unimmunized child is a potential carrier of death to a family member or a neighbor.

Sudden Infant Death Syndrome

Infant mortality worldwide has plummeted in recent years, for three main reasons (see Figure 5.6). Two of the reasons have already been mentioned: the advances in newborn care described in Chapter 4 and the widespread immunization just mentioned. The third reason is the drop in the number of sudden deaths of seemingly healthy babies each year.

In **sudden infant death syndrome (SIDS)**, infants who are at least 2 months old and appear to be completely healthy—already gaining weight, learning to shake a rattle, starting to roll over, and smiling at their caregivers—

Especially for Nurses and Pediatricians
A mother refuses to have her baby immunized because she says she wants to prevent side effects. She wants your signature to apply for a religious exemption. What should you do?

sudden infant death syndrome (SIDS) A set of circumstances in which a seemingly healthy infant, at least 2 months of age, dies unexpectedly in his or her sleep.

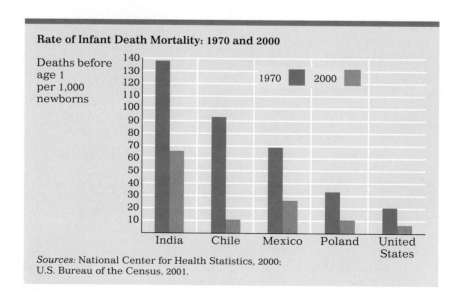

FIGURE 5.6 **More Babies Are Surviving**
Improvements in public health—better nutrition, cleaner water, more widespread immunization—over the past three decades have meant millions of survivors.

? *Critical Thinking Question* (see answer, page 158): The United States seems to be doing very well on reducing infant deaths. Can you suggest another way to present the U.S. data that would lead to another impression?

die unexpectedly in their sleep. In 1990 in the United States, 5,000 babies died of SIDS, with similar rates in Canada, England, Australia, and virtually every other European and American nation. That rate has been cut in half, primarily because infants are now less likely to sleep on their stomachs.

The diagnosis of SIDS is assigned at autopsy when other causes have been ruled out, but because there was no apparent sickness, superstitions and suspicions may run rampant—a cat sucked out the baby's breath, or a witch put a curse on the family, or a jealous older child suffocated the baby, or a parent murdered the infant. If the parents slept with the baby, "overlaying" was once suspected, but we now know that a parent rarely rolls over onto a baby accidentally (about 20 cases per year in the United States) and is usually drunk or drugged when it does happen (Nakamura et al., 1999). Conversely, because child abuse has sometimes been misdiagnosed as SIDS, immediate and expert investigation is always necessary.

Especially for Police Officers and Social Workers If an infant dies suddenly, what would you look for to distinguish SIDS from homicide?

Changing Policy

SIDS Among Asian Infants

A key risk factor in SIDS is ethnic background. Generally, within ethnically diverse nations such as the United States, Canada, Great Britain, Australia, and New Zealand, babies of African descent are more likely, and babies of Asian descent less likely, to succumb to SIDS than are babies of European descent. For decades, pediatricians thought the reasons for this difference were either genetic (racial) or related to ethnicity (such as the rate of teenage pregnancy).

Fortunately, new attention to culture, not race, led to a closer look at specific infant-care routines that may be widespread in one ethnic group and rare in others. For example, Bangladeshi infants in England tend to be low in both birthweight and socioeconomic status, yet they have *lower* rates of SIDS than white British infants, who are more often of normal birthweight and middle-class. If not genes, then what?

Bangladeshi infants, even when they sleep, are usually surrounded by many family members in a rich sensory environment, continually hearing noises and feeling the gentle touch of their caregivers. Therefore, they do not sleep deeply for very long. By contrast, their white British age-mates tend to sleep in their own private spaces in an environment of enforced quiet, and these "long peri-

JEFF GREENBERG / MRP / PHOTO RESEARCHERS, INC.

ods of lone sleep may contribute to the higher rates of SIDS among white infants" (Gantley et al., 1993).

Similarly, Chinese infants, born either in China or elsewhere, have a low rate of SIDS (Beal & Porter, 1991). Why? First, Chinese parents tend to their babies periodically as they sleep, caressing a cheek or repositioning a limb; second, most Chinese infants are breast-fed, which makes them sleep less soundly (cow's milk is harder to digest, so it causes a deeper sleep). Therefore, Chinese infants are unlikely to fall into a deep, nonbreathing sleep.

As pediatricians, nurses, and anthropologists compared the specifics of infant care among Asians and Europeans, they noticed one other critical factor: sleeping position. In all the ethnic groups with a low incidence of SIDS, babies were put to

Practices Among the Maya Every culture has some traditional practices that are protective of infants and some that are dangerous.

? *Observational Quiz* (see answer, page 158): Can you spot at least one protective and one dangerous practice here?

sleep on their backs; in all those with high rates, babies slept on their stomachs. The expressed reasons varied. For example, until recently, Benjamin Spock's (1976) book of advice for parents, which has sold more than 30 million copies, recommended stomach sleeping:

> A majority of babies seem, from the beginning, to be a little more comfortable going to sleep on their stomachs. . . . There are two disadvantages to babies sleeping on their back. If they vomit, they're more likely to choke. Also, they tend to keep the head turned toward the same side, usually toward the center of the room. This may flatten that side of the head. It won't hurt the brain, and the head will gradually straighten out, but it may take a couple of years.
>
> *[Spock, 1976, p. 199]*

In Turkey, meanwhile, mothers were advised to swaddle their newborns

> for several months until the baby seems strong and healthy . . . [and] never put a swaddled baby to sleep on its stomach, for it would not be able to breathe. Instead, put the baby down to sleep on its back.
>
> *[Delaney, 2000, p. 131]*

Both these experts were mistaken: Babies sleeping on their stomachs can breathe, and babies sleeping on their backs do not choke. Neither "expert" realized the connection between SIDS and sleeping position. In fact, Spock wrote:

> Every once in a while, a baby between the ages of 3 weeks and 7 months is found dead in bed. There is never an adequate explanation, even when a postmortem examination is done. . . . Though crib death has been studied extensively, there is no satisfactory, scientific explanation.
>
> *[Spock, 1976, pp. 576–577]*

Finally, in about 1990, researchers began to pay attention to cultural variations in sleeping positions and advised a group of non-Asian mothers to put their infants to sleep on their backs. Other mothers with similar backgrounds were given no special advice; most put their babies to sleep on their stomachs, as their mothers and Dr. Spock had recommended. The results were dramatic: Far fewer infants died when they slept on their backs. For example, one comparison study found that the risk of SIDS was only one-fourth as high when infants slept supine (on their backs) instead of prone (Ponsoby et al., 1993).

It is now accepted that "back to sleep" (as the public-awareness slogan puts it) is safest, and policy as well as practice has changed. Most caregivers heed this advice, although some still lay babies on their sides—better than on their stomachs, but not as safe as on their backs. In the United States, in the 4 years between 1992 and 1996, the stomach-sleeping rate decreased from 70 to 24 percent, and the SIDS rate dropped from 1.2 to 0.7 per 1,000, a "remarkable success" (Pollack & Frohna, 2001). Note that changing sleeping position is not a magic cure: Reducing cigarette smoking, preventing low birthweight, and encouraging breast-feeding are among the other protective practices.

!*Answer to Observational Quiz* (from page 157): The infant sleeps on her back, near her mother, and thus her risk of SIDS is lower than it would be if she slept on her stomach. However, the spaces within the crib walls appear large and flexible enough for a small head or limb to get stuck. After some tragic deaths, the United States regulates the distance between the slats of a crib—no more than 3 inches.

Nutrition

We have described the growth of infants' body and brain, motor skills, and sensory abilities; we have also cited current practices that almost guarantee the survival of a healthy, well-loved newborn. Nutrition has been mentioned throughout this chapter because it is connected to everything else. You have learned that pediatricians closely monitor early weight gain, that head-sparing will probably protect Toni from her temporary undernourishment, and that oral rehydration therapy prevents malnutrition from being fatal to a child with measles. Finally, we focus directly on nutrition.

!*Answer to Critical Thinking Question* (from page 156): The same data could be presented in terms of rate of reduction in infant mortality. Chile's rate in 2000 was only 10 percent of what it had been in 1970—much better than the U.S. rate, which in 2000 was 35 percent of what it had been in 1970. At the same time, India's reduction is even less impressive: only about 50 percent. (Other data show that about 25 developed nations have lower infant mortality rates than the United States.)

Breast Is Best

For most newborns, good nutrition starts with mother's milk, beginning with *colostrum,* the thick, high-calorie nourishment in the woman's breasts at the birth of her child. Within a few days, the breasts begin making less concentrated milk, which is the ideal infant food, not only because its consistency provides a good balance of liquid and calories but also because it helps prevent almost every infant illness, allergy, ache, and pain (Isolauri et al., 1998). Breast milk is always sterile and at body temperature; it contains more iron, vitamins C and A, and many other nourishing substances than cow's or goat's milk; it provides antibodies to protect against any disease that the mother is immunized against. The specific fats and sugars in breast milk make it more digestible, and probably better for the infant brain, than any prepared formula (Talukder, 2000).

The only situations in which formula may be better than breast milk are when the mother is HIV-positive, is using toxic drugs (such as heroin), or has some other condition that makes her milk decidedly unhealthy. Even mothers who are undernourished would benefit from using the money now spent on formula to purchase a better diet for themselves and then to breast-feed their infants. The World Health Organization (WHO) recommends that infants be fed exclusively with breast milk for the first 4 to 6 months. At that point, other foods can be added—especially cereals and fruits, which are relatively easy to digest and provide the vitamins and minerals an older infant needs. Breast-feeding should continue until the infant is 2 years old or so (WHO, 1990).

Given that "breast is best" and that all babies must nurse to survive, why do infant feeding practices vary from one culture to another? For example, some cultures advocate putting the newborn on a 4-hour schedule of formula, switching to a 6-hour schedule as soon as possible, and abandoning the night feeding (at about 2 A.M.) when the infant is 2 to 3 months old. Others recommend breast-feeding at the first whimper, which can be every half hour or so, until the infant is at least 1 year old.

Preferred feeding schedules also vary from generation to generation. One developmental researcher writes:

> It is easy to forget how rapidly ideas about parenting have changed. I was brought up as a Truby King baby. Influenced by this New Zealand pediatrician, my father, also a physician, believed that babies should be fed on a strict 6-hour schedule. Whenever we visited my father after our first child was born, at 6 p.m. he would start to fidget in his chair and say, "Isn't it time he was nursed?"
>
> *[Hinde, 1995 p. xi]*

This researcher was influenced by the attitudes of his own era, not his father's era, so his son was fed whenever the son cried, rarely at precisely 6 o'clock because, usually, he had been fed an hour or two before and hunger had not yet reappeared.

Remember that every aspect of child care is connected to the surrounding culture. In cultures in which babies were quickly put on rigid schedules, adults were scheduled, too, working from 9 to 5, graduating from high school by age 18, retiring at age 65. In the twenty-first century, that has changed for almost everyone, and feeding schedules have changed as well. Most contemporary experts recommend feeding infants "on demand," whenever they seem hungry. Fortunately, human breasts increase milk production if they are emptied often. Because supply adjusts to demand, hungry babies can be satisfied as they grow. Indeed, mothers of twins and even triplets sometimes breast-feed them all.

The current cultural belief that "the child knows best" is tempered by the reality that some babies are too quiet to demand enough milk whereas others want to suck continuously, exhausting their mothers. Feeding on demand needs to be balanced with common sense and with attention to the height and weight standards discussed at the beginning of this chapter (Yoos et al., 1999). Remember, however, that more is not necessarily better. Formula-fed infants tend to weigh above the 50th percentile, which actually predicts overweight, not optimal health, later on.

Response for Nurses and Pediatricians (from page 156): It is very difficult to convince people that their traditional child-rearing methods are wrong, although, given what you know, it is your obligation to try. In this case, you might listen respectfully and then cite cases you know of when a child got seriously ill or an adult died from a childhood disease. Ask the mother to ask her parents and grandparents if they have known anyone who was seriously ill from polio, tuberculosis, or tetanus. If you cannot convince this mother, do not despair—vaccination of 95 percent of toddlers is usually sufficient to protect the 5 percent whose parents reject vaccination. If the mother is refusing vaccination for religious reasons, you could discuss the risks with her pastor and then sign the form, perhaps adding a warning letter. Keep the relationship open, as she may change her mind later.

Response for Police Officers and Social Workers (from page 157): An autopsy, or at least a speedy examination by a medical pathologist, is needed, because any suspicions of foul play need to be substantiated with evidence or firmly rejected so that the parents can grieve. However, your careful notes about the immediate circumstances—such as the position of the infant when he or she was discovered, the state of the mattress and nearby blankets, the warmth and humidity of the room, and the baby's health (any evidence of a cold)—can be informative. Further, while SIDS victims sometimes turn blue overall, and thus might seem bruised, they rarely display signs of specific injury or neglect, such as a broken limb, a scarred face, an angry rash, or a skinny body. Especially if maltreatment is evident and the dead baby is not between 2 and 4 months of age, something other than SIDS may have occurred.

Malnutrition

Malnutrition in infancy is complicated, widespread, harmful, and political. Severe malnutrition is easy to see when it has continued for several months, but undernutrition can be destructive as well. Not apparent at all, except by laboratory test, are specific vitamin or mineral deficiencies, but these, too, may harm brain development for many years. We will discuss each of these nutritional problems in turn, noting what can be done to prevent damage.

Severe Malnutrition

protein–calorie malnutrition A condition in which a child does not consume sufficient food of any kind to thrive.

In infancy, the most serious nourishment problem is **protein–calorie malnutrition,** which occurs when a child does not consume sufficient food of any kind to thrive. Roughly 8 percent of the world's children, most of them in developing nations, are severely malnourished during their early years because they simply are not getting enough calories and protein (Rutstein, 2000).

Severe malnutrition can be detected by comparing an infant's weight and height with the norms discussed at the beginning of this chapter or the more detailed measurements presented in Appendix B. As you no doubt remember, a child who is genetically small may not be malnourished, but weight loss during the first 2 years is a sign that the child is acutely malnourished or *wasted.* Other signs are that the child's birthweight has not tripled by age 1 or that the 1-year-old's legs and cheeks are not chubby with baby fat.

Even more ominous, over the long term, is the situation of *stunted* infants and children, who are far too short as well as too thin for their age. A third of the children in developing nations are stunted (de Onis et al., 2000) (see Figure 5.7). Chronically malnourished infants suffer in three ways:

1. Their brains may not have enough nutrition to develop normally. As you remember, the brain is the last organ to be affected, thanks to "brain saving"; but if malnutrition has continued long enough to affect the baby's height, it may also be affecting the brain.

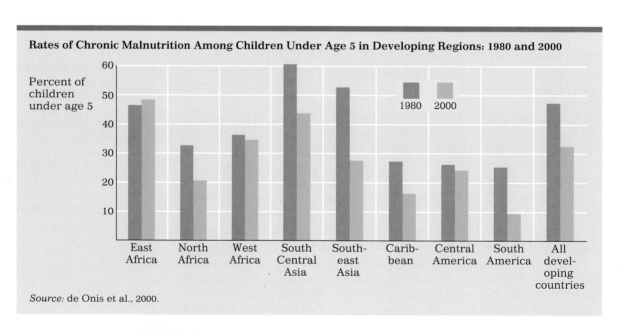

Rates of Chronic Malnutrition Among Children Under Age 5 in Developing Regions: 1980 and 2000

Source: de Onis et al., 2000.

FIGURE 5.7 Except in Southern Africa Children in every region of the world are being fed better than they were twenty years ago, although children in all the poorer nations far exceed the 3 percent expected from normal height variation. Among chronically malnourished children, the body uses calories not for growth but for basic survival. Civil war and AIDS have reduced child nourishment in one area of the world, sub-Saharan Africa.

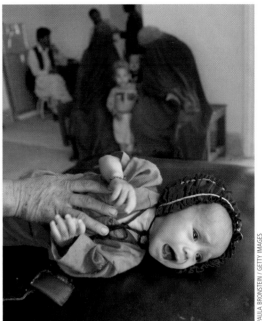

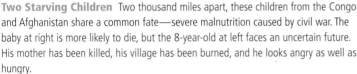

Two Starving Children Two thousand miles apart, these children from the Congo and Afghanistan share a common fate—severe malnutrition caused by civil war. The baby at right is more likely to die, but the 8-year-old at left faces an uncertain future. His mother has been killed, his village has been burned, and he looks angry as well as hungry.

2. Malnourished children have no body reserves to protect them if disease strikes. As you have read, about half of all infant deaths occur because malnutrition makes a childhood disease much more lethal than it normally would be (Rice et al., 2000). When civil war and poverty are widespread, almost every child is malnourished. In the 1990s, East Africa was the only area of the world where malnutrition and infant death increased—a tragedy rooted in political conflict.

3. Some diseases—notably, two serious conditions called marasmus and kwashiorkor—are the direct result of malnutrition.

In the first year of life, severe protein–calorie malnutrition causes **marasmus,** a disease in which growth stops, body tissues waste away, and the infant eventually dies. Prevention of marasmus begins prenatally and continues with breast-feeding beginning within an hour after birth, when the mother's breasts still secrete colostrum. Unfortunately, few cultures recognize that colostrum is highly nutritious and provides protective antibodies (Talukder, 2000).

As they get older, malnourished children may progress to **kwashiorkor,** a condition caused by a deficiency of protein in which the child's face, legs, and abdomen swell with water; this swelling sometimes makes the child appear well fed to anyone who doesn't know the real cause of the bloating. In children with kwashiorkor, the essential organs claim whatever nutrients are available, so other parts of the body become degraded. This includes the children's hair, which usually becomes thin, brittle, and colorless—a telltale sign of systemic malnutrition.

Kwashiorkor itself is usually not fatal, but it makes the child vulnerable to death from almost any other disease, including measles, diarrhea, and even the flu. Kwashiorkor may result when a woman has babies too close together, which prevents her from breast-feeding the older child for at least a full 2 years. One consequence of kwashiorkor is reduced organ size, which makes the person, even as an adult, have reduced caloric needs but also reduced energy (Henry, 1996).

marasmus A disease of severe protein–calorie malnutrition in which growth stops, body tissues waste away, and the infant eventually dies.

kwashiorkor A disease of chronic malnutrition in which a deficiency of protein causes the child's face, legs, and abdomen to bloat, or swell with water, and makes the child more vulnerable to other diseases, such as measles, diarrhea, and influenza.

undernutrition Inadequate nutrition that does not cause visible wasting or stunting but causes the person to be shorter than the norm for healthy, well-fed members of the same ethnic group.

Undernutrition

Much more common than severe malnutrition is **undernutrition**, which causes children to be smaller than their genes would otherwise dictate. Undernutrition is defined as inadequate nourishment, such that a person is not visibly wasted or stunted, but still is shorter than the norm for healthy, well-fed members of the same ethnic group. Undernutrition is primarily a problem in developing nations, but it is not unknown in developed ones. Some overweight adults may actually have been undernourished as children and therefore eaten more than they needed as adults to fill their childhood hunger gap. Toni might have become such an example if the health care provider had not alerted her mother to the problem. Undernutrition is caused by a complex interaction of political, economic, and familial problems that together mean less breast-feeding, less nourishment for mothers, and inadequate food intake for children (Pollitt et al., 1996; Wright & Talbot, 1996).

For example, many mothers switch from breast milk to formula too quickly. In developing nations, one reason for the widespread use of formula is that many hospitals have women (called "mothercraft" nurses) who are employed by manufacturers of formula to visit new mothers, give them a free sample of bottled formula, and explain how to use it. This practice is in violation of a United Nations code established in 1961 (Riordan & Auerbach, 1998). Both politics and economics come into play here (Baumslag & Michels, 1995). International food corporations conduct these campaigns because once a mother's breast milk has dried up (after a few days of not nursing), the infant is a "customer" for their formula for months. Political pressure favors formula as well, since mothercraft nurses are local women who are gainfully employed and who make the work of the hospital easier. Of course, the UN depends on local governments for enforcement, and local governments are hesitant to reduce the number of jobs. Cultural influences are mixed: Traditionally, all infants were breast-fed, but many women want to be more modern and independent. Only public health advocates, doctors, and developmentalists are wholeheartedly in favor of breast-feeding.

Parents want the best nutrition for their infants, but they do not always know what is best. In some communities, undernutrition is evident only in retrospect, as when families emigrate to well-nourished nations and teenagers grow to tower over their stunted grandparents. In Guatemala, civil war between 1979 and 1982 fostered a generation of undernourished children. Adults who left for Florida or California had children who grew significantly taller, heavier, and more muscular than their cousins whose parents stayed behind (Bogin, 1995). If you are significantly taller than your parents or grandparents, they may have been undernourished.

Undernutrition is certainly a way to cut down on population growth, but this viewpoint is short-sighted, since high rates of maternal and infant illness, death, and impaired intellectual development are bound to affect a nation adversely. Worldwide, better education for women, readily available family-planning services, and preventive health care for every infant would produce a much healthier and more intelligent population in another generation or two. Note, however, that these benefits are not immediate, which is why "nutritional intervention, without attention to psychosocial risk factors, may be ineffective" (Metallinos-Katsaras & Gorman, 1999).

Specific Deficiencies

Custom undermines good nutrition in every nation. Many developing countries have thousands of infants who appear well fed but do not get enough vitamin A or iodine and who risk blindness or mental retardation as a result. Usually good sources of missing vitamins are available, but the culture sees these foods as taboo.

Developed nations, too, have specific nutritional deficiencies. For example, about three out of every four 6-month-olds in the United States are exclusively formula-fed. The reasons are almost all cultural: fathers' jealousy, employers' restrictions, and mothers' wish for convenience (Riordan & Auerbach, 1998). Breast-feeding in public is much less common in the United States than in some other parts of the world, so breast-feeding women must choose among staying at home (restrictive), expressing milk from the breast to a bottle (inconvenient at best), and feeding the baby with strangers nearby (considered immodest and bizarre).

These cultural attitudes promote widespread formula feeding. Is there any harm in that, when sterile water is readily available and the cost of formula is not a burden? Some people assert that bottle feeding harms family bonding, child development, or social values, but such effects are difficult to trace scientifically. However, there are some immediate health consequences in specific vitamin and mineral deficiencies. Breast-fed babies are gradually weaned to a cup beginning at about 9 months, but bottle-fed babies are more difficult to wean. Iron deficiency among bottle-fed babies is one consequence, caused by *milk anemia,* which occurs when toddlers are given a bottle of milk (which has no iron) with every nap and every meal. One careful survey in Massachusetts found that 15 percent of all 6- to 12-month-olds were iron deficient, with the rate about 21 percent among Hispanics and 42 percent among those of Asian ancestry (Sargent et al., 1996). Iron deficiency can cause serious brain retardation, but usually there are no symptoms unless the child's teeth show early signs of decay—a result of the constant presence of sugar on the gums, called "milk mouth." The permanent teeth soon replace the rotted baby teeth, but the effect of an early nutritional deficiency can remain throughout life (Lozoff, et. al, 2000).

Also fairly common in the early years is a deficiency of zinc, a mineral found in seafood, beef, and poultry as well as in breast milk. Children become stunted in their first years as a result of this deficiency, but they can catch up if they get enough zinc-rich food (Golden, 1996). However, giving malnourished children vitamins and minerals does not necessarily make things right, because brain damage may already have occurred or too much of one nutrient might deplete another (Lozoff et al., 2000). Prevention is much better, but cultural practices tend to divorce infant care from mother care, and inadequate attention to the needs of mothers makes malnutrition in children more prevalent. In fact, the cultural pressure for young mothers to work is evident in recent laws restricting welfare eligibility, as well as in the experience of mothers like Toni's, our case study.

This chapter has described physical growth of all kinds from birth to age 2. An underlying theme is that healthy biological growth is the result not simply of genes and nutrition but also of a social environment that provides opportunities for growth, such as lullabies and mobiles for the infant's senses, encouragement for developing the first motor skills, protection against disease, and so on. Political leaders, parents, and even child development experts sometimes make mistakes, and, as you have read, some of the 150 million babies born into the world this year will suffer. Everyone—family, friends, communities, and cultures—needs to pay attention to the newest members of our species, providing all their needs for body and brain development.

Not So Natural Few middle-class American mothers learn how to breast-feed from their mothers, for whom formula feeding was considered "modern" 30 years ago. Consequently, support groups like this one provide instruction and encouragement.

SUMMARY

Body Changes

1. In the first 2 years of life, infants grow taller, gain weight, and increase in head circumference—all indicative of development. The norm at birth is slightly more than 7 pounds, 20 inches (about 3⅓ kilograms, 51 centimeters).

2. Infants typically double their birth weight by 4 months, triple it by 1 year, and more than quadruple it by 2 years, when they weigh about 30 pounds (14 kilograms). Norms for height and head circumference show steady, though less dramatic, increases.

3. Percentiles indicate how a child compares to others the same age, which makes them useful over time to see whether a child's growth is proceeding as it should. Some normal children are consistently smaller or larger than others. In malnourished children, first weight, then height, then head circumference slow down, and these declines are indicated by a drop in percentiles.

4. Sleep gradually decreases over the first 2 years (from about 17 hours a day to 13), with less REM sleep, less night waking, and more slow-wave sleep over time. As with all areas of development, variations in sleep patterns are normal, caused by both nature and nurture.

Early Brain Development

5. The brain increases dramatically in size, from 25 percent to 75 percent of its adult weight in the first 2 years. Complexity increases as well, and transient exuberance of cell growth, dendrite development, and synapse connections occur.

6. Experience is vital for brain formation, particularly for linkages between one neuron and another. In the first year, parts of the cortex dedicated to the senses and motor skills mature. If neurons are unused, they atrophy, and the brain regions are rededicated to other sensations. Normal stimulation allows experience-expectant maturation.

7. Most experience-dependent brain growth reflects the varied, culture-specific experiences of the infant. Therefore, one person's brain differs from another's, but all normal infants are equally capable in the basic ways—emotional, linguistic, and sensual—that all humans share.

8. The precise harm to brain development caused by early deprivation is not yet known. However, research on lower animals and maltreated humans emphasizes that the early years may be critical for later brain functioning.

Senses and Motor Skills

9. All the senses operate at birth, with hearing the most mature and vision the least mature. Vision improves quickly; binocular vision emerges at about 14 weeks. Infants use all their senses to strengthen their early social interactions.

10. The only motor skills apparent at birth are reflexes, including the survival reflexes of sucking and breathing. Reflexes indicate brain maturation and provide a foundation for later skills.

11. Gross motor skills involve movement of the entire body, from rolling over to sitting up (at about 6 months), from standing to walking (at about 1 year), from climbing to running (before age 2). Variations in these norms depend on both genes and culture.

12. Fine motor skills are more difficult for infants, but they gradually develop the hand and finger control needed to grab, aim, and manipulate almost anything within reach.

Preventive Medicine

13. About a billion infant deaths have been prevented in the past half-century because of improved medical care and public health measures. One major innovation is immunization, which has eradicated smallpox and virtually eliminated polio and measles. However, new vaccines and increased levels of immunization are necessary.

14. Sudden infant death syndrome (SIDS) once killed about 5,000 infants per year in the United States, but this number has been reduced by half since 1993. The major reason is that researchers looked closely at cultural habits regarding infant care and discovered that putting infants to sleep on their backs makes SIDS less likely.

Nutrition

15. Breast-feeding is best for infants, partly because breast milk reduces disease and promotes growth of every kind. However, feeding practices are heavily influenced by culture and politics. Many families use formula in bottles instead of breast milk.

16. Severe malnutrition stunts growth and even causes death, typically through marasmus, kwashiorkor, or severe dehydration resulting from a "minor" illness. In addition, many of the world's infants are wasted and stunted, growing less than they should.

17. Undernutrition and specific vitamin and mineral deficiencies are more common than severe malnutrition. They can reduce intellectual capacity and physical growth. The solution to malnutrition is complex, requiring a reassessment of cultural priorities.

KEY TERMS

norm (p. 135)
head-sparing (p. 136)
percentile (p. 136)
wasting (p. 138)
stunting (p. 138)
REM sleep (p. 139)
neuron (p. 141)
cortex (p. 141)

axon (p. 141)
dendrite (p. 141)
synapse (p. 142)
transient exuberance (p. 142)
experience-expectant (p. 143)
experience-dependent (p. 143)
sensation (p. 146)
perception (p. 146)

binocular vision (p. 148)
breathing reflex (p. 149)
sucking reflex (p. 150)
rooting reflex (p. 150)
gross motor skills (p. 150)
fine motor skills (p. 151)
immunization (p. 155)

sudden infant death syndrome
 (SIDS) (p. 156)
protein–calorie malnutrition
 (p. 160)
marasmus (p. 161)
kwashiorkor (p. 161)
undernutrition (p. 162)

KEY QUESTIONS

1. What do measurements at a well-baby checkup reveal about brain development?

2. How does culture affect an infant's sleep patterns?

3. In what ways can 1-year-olds be said to have more brain power than adults?

4. What could explain the belief that deaf people read facial expressions very well?

5. Can you give an example, from your own experience, of the difference between sensation and perception?

6. How are gross motor skills related to early reflexes?

7. What fine motor skills are required for reading and writing?

8. What evidence indicates that norms of motor skills are partly genetic?

9. Why are infants at least four times more likely to survive today than a century ago?

10. Is it possible for babies sleeping on their backs to die of SIDS? Why or why not?

11. Why are so many of the world's children undernourished?

12. How do the advantages of breast milk compare to the advantages of formula?

Chapter Six

The First 2 Years: Cognitive Development

This chapter is about infant *cognition,* a word that means "thinking" in a very broad sense. Cognition involves intelligence and learning, memory and language, facts and concepts, beliefs and assumptions, teaching and education. You might wonder, "Intelligence in babies?" Yes, indeed.

Imagine, for a moment, that you are a newborn, just beginning to have thoughts. New and constantly changing images, sounds, smells, and body sensations bombard your limited consciousness. You try to make sense of them, connecting smells with visual images, tastes with feelings. You develop perceptions of objects, of people, even of parts of your own body; you figure out which relate to you, and how, and when. Then you put it all together: sensations, sequences, objects, people, events, permanent and transient features, causes and effects. And this is just the beginning of your cognition.

By the end of the first year—and often much sooner—you will have categories for organizing and thinking about the objects you experience, you will understand how your own actions can make things happen, you will have goals and know how to reach them, and you will begin to talk. By the end of the second year, you will speak in sentences, think before acting, and pretend to be someone or something (a mother, an airplane) that you know you are not.

No wonder, then, that infant intelligence is a major topic: There is much to describe.

We begin with the framework provided by Jean Piaget for observing the amazing intellectual progress from newborns who know nothing, on to toddlers who are able to make a wish and blow out their birthday candles. Then we consider more recent research on affordances, categories and concepts, and memory, that suggests that infant brain and perceptual development is faster and deeper than even Piaget realized. This all comes to fruition in child language—an intellectual accomplishment that actually begins before birth, even though the first words are not spoken until about age 1, followed by gradual acquisition of grammar. How all this happens is a topic of great interest and controversy, as you will learn.

Sensorimotor Intelligence

It is impossible to understand the first two years of cognitive development without referring to Piaget, a Swiss scientist born in 1896. By carefully observing his own three children, Piaget discovered that infants are active learners. From those detailed observations and from hundreds of studies of other children, Piaget concluded that humans of every age and circumstance actively seek to comprehend their world and that their understanding occurs in four specific, age-related

sensorimotor intelligence Piaget's term for the intelligence of infants during the first (sensorimotor) period of cognitive development, when babies think by using their senses and motor skills.

periods. Each of these periods is characterized by a particular kind of thinking, a way to understand the world.

The first of those periods begins at birth, then accelerates so rapidly that six distinct substages occur before age 2. Because infants learn through their senses and motor skills, Piaget called this first period **sensorimotor intelligence.** Piaget's works (including 26 major books) "continue to be an important source of inspiration for contemporary infant research" (Rochat, 2001, p. 7).

All developmentalists owe Piaget a great deal, especially regarding infancy. The following passage is one of thousands that exemplify his contributions. Piaget is observing his 3-month-old son, Laurent:

> I place the string which is attached to the rattle in his right hand, merely unrolling it a little so that he may grasp it better. For a moment nothing happens, but at the first shake due to chance movement of his hand, the reaction is immediate: Laurent starts when looking at the rattle and then violently strikes his right hand alone, as if he felt the resistance and the effect. The operation lasts a full quarter of an hour during which Laurent emits peals of laughter. The phenomenon is all the more clear because, the string being slack, the child must stretch his arm sufficiently and put the right amount of effort into it.

> *[Piaget, 1952b, p. 162]*

This passage illustrates three of Piaget's attributes: his keen powers of observation; his close attention to sequence, the essence of development; and his fascination with the details of infant discovery. In all these, Piaget has been a role model for generations of developmentalists, who not only use careful observation, paying particular attention to sequence, but also share Piaget's fascination with the details and the delights of infant behavior. You remember from Chapter 2 that some specific conclusions reached by Piaget are no longer considered valid. We will discuss these deficiencies further in this chapter. But to benefit from Piaget's insights, we present the six stages of sensorimotor intelligence (see Table 6.1).

Stages One and Two: Primary Circular Reactions

primary circular reactions The first of three types of feedback loops, this one involving the infant's own body, in which the infant takes in experiences and tries to make sense of them.

The first two stages of sensorimotor intelligence are examples of **primary circular reactions,** which are reactions that involve the infant's own body. Stage one, called the *stage of reflexes,* lasts only for a month. It includes reflexes (described on page 150), such as sucking and grasping, and also senses, which are so responsive at birth that they seem like reflexes. Simple inborn actions and reactions are all that newborns can use for sensorimotor intelligence, but these simple reflexes soon begin to help infants think as well as react. Sensation becomes perception, which becomes cognition; reflexes become deliberate.

At this point, the baby enters stage two, *first acquired adaptations* (also called the stage of first habits). This change from reflexes to deliberate action occurs because repeated use of reflexive responses provides information about what the body does and how that action feels. Infants adjust their body reactions in accord with this information from their body. This adjustment still involves their own body (making it a primary circular reaction), but it also ushers in **adaptation** of reflexes and senses to the specifics of the context. *Adaptation* is a key word in Piaget's understanding of cognition, meaning that taking in new information and responding to it become part of the thinking process.

adaptation The cognitive process by which new information is taken in and responded to.

Assimilation and Accommodation

assimilation The process of taking new information into the mind by incorporating it into previously developed mental categories, or schemas.

Adaptation occurs in two complementary ways: by assimilation and by accommodation (as you learned in Chapter 2). **Assimilation** means taking new information into the mind by incorporating it into previously developed mental categories, or

TABLE 6.1 The Six Stages of Sensorimotor Intelligence

For an overview of the stages of sensorimotor thought, it helps to group the six stages into pairs. The first two stages involve the infant's responses to its own body (sometimes called *primary circular reactions*):

Stage One (birth to 1 month)	*Reflexes*—sucking, grasping, staring, listening.
Stage Two (1–4 months)	*The first acquired adaptation* (assimilation and coordination of reflexes)—sucking a pacifier differently from a nipple; grabbing a bottle to suck it.

The next two stages involve the infant's responses to objects and people (sometimes called *secondary circular reactions*):

Stage Three (4–8 months)	*An awareness of things*—responding to people and objects.
Stage Four (8–12 months)	*New adaptation and anticipation*—becoming more deliberate and purposeful in responding to people and objects.

The last two stages are the most creative, first with action and then with ideas (sometimes called *tertiary circular reactions*):

Stage Five (12–18 months)	*New means through active experimentation*—experimentation and creativity in the actions of the "little scientist."
Stage Six (18–24 months)	*New means through mental combinations*—considering before doing provides the child with new ways of achieving a goal without resorting to trial-and-error experiments.

action patterns—in Piaget's terminology, "schemas." **Accommodation** means taking new information into the mind in such a way as to readjust, refine, or expand previous schemas.

Adaptive processes occur throughout life. Indeed, for Piaget, adaptation is the essence of intelligence. There are numerous definitions of *intelligence* (according to my Webster's dictionary, it includes the abilities to learn, to understand, to respond quickly, to remember), but for Piaget, an unintelligent person is rigid, stuck, unable or unwilling to adapt his or her cognitive processes to include new ideas, to find a new equilibrium.

In the first two stages of infancy, adaptation via both assimilation and accommodation is obvious: Babies eagerly and actively adapt their reflexes and senses to whatever experiences they have. The reflexive grasp, for instance, is automatic and tight whenever something is put in the newborn's hand; within a few months, however, the baby grasps only certain things, because accommodation has occurred. Similarly, the senses assimilate everything at first but then begin to accommodate the particular sights and sounds of the infant's immediate surroundings—focusing on faces, for instance, and ignoring the bright lights that first captured the attention. Sucking is another example of this assimilation/accommodation process, one that we will explain in detail.

Sucking as a Stage-Two Adaptation

Newborns suck anything that touches their lips; sucking is one of the strongest and most apparent reflexes. In fact, newborns turn their heads to try to suck anything that touches their cheeks. These reflexes of rooting and sucking confirm that for the newborn, everything is assimilated into the general schema "the world is for sucking"; no accommodation is needed.

accommodation The process of taking new information into the mind in such a way as to readjust, refine, or expand previous mental categories, or schemas.

Stage Two Sucking everything is a mere reflex in the first month of life, but by 3 months Katie has already learned that some objects afford better sucking than others. Many infants her age have learned not to suck on people's faces, but with this mother, that adaptation is not necessary.

ROBERT ULLMAN

However, at about the age of 1 month, infants start to adapt sucking. Some items, such as the nipple of a bottle (for a breast-fed infant), merely require assimilation: The same old sucking reflex brings nourishment. Others require more accommodation: Pacifiers need to be sucked without the tongue-pushing and swallowing reflexes, since they do not provide food. This adaptation is a sign that infants have begun to organize their perceptions; they are "thinking."

In other words, adaptation in the early weeks relies primarily on reflexive assimilation—everything suckable is assimilated as worthy of being sucked until accommodation occurs. After several months, new responses are established because adaptation has occurred, organizing the sucking reflex into nonreflexive actions: Suck some things to soothe hunger, suck others to bring comfort, and suck still others (fuzzy blankets, large balls) not at all. If the baby is hungry, only familiar nourishing nipples will do—all other objects are rejected. Similarly, when babies are not hungry but want the reassurance of rhythmic sucking, they will suck a pacifier. If no pacifier has been offered in the stage of reflexes, infants begin sucking their thumbs, fingers, or knuckles (a choice that depends on whatever the baby first assimilates). If infants a few months old are full and their stomachs hurt, sucking is probably not what they want: They push away a bottle stuck into their crying mouth and may resist a pacifier as well. They want pain relief, perhaps available only if someone carries them, putting pressure on their bellies.

Especially for Parents: When should parents decide whether to feed their baby only by breast, only by bottle, or using some combination, and when should they decide whether or not to offer a pacifier?

secondary circular reactions The second of three types of feedback loops, this one involving people and objects, in which the infant takes in experiences and tries to make sense of them.

Stages Three and Four: Secondary Circular Reactions

In stages three and four, development switches from primary circular reactions, involving the baby's own body (stages one and two), to **secondary circular reactions,** involving the baby with an object or with another person.

Stage Three: Making Interesting Sights Last

During stage three (age 4 to 8 months), infants interact diligently with people and objects to produce exciting experiences. Realizing that rattles make noise, for example, they shake their arms and laugh whenever someone puts a rattle in their hand. Even the sight of something that normally delights an infant— a favorite toy, a favorite food, a smiling parent—can trigger an active attempt at interaction.

Vocalization of all sorts increases a great deal at this time, and not just in a chorus (as with younger infants—when one newborn in the nursery cries, they all tend to cry). Now that babies realize that other people can and will respond, they love to make a noise, listen for a response, and answer back. Interestingly, by the age of 3 or 4 months, babies are already unlikely to make sounds at the same moment that someone is talking to them, causing a deceptive downward shift in the frequency of vocalization at about 4 months (Hsu et al., 2000). This is an example of a secondary circular reaction, because infants incorporate other people into their cognitive schema. The "interesting sights" are outside their own bodies.

Overall in this third stage, infants become more aware of objects and of other people; they recognize some of the specific characteristics of the things in their environment, and they develop ways to continue whatever sensation they seek. Sometimes they repeat a specific action that has just elicited a pleasing response from some person or thing.

Stage Four: New Adaptation and Anticipation

Stage four, which occurs from about 8 months to 1 year, is sometimes called "the means to the end," because babies now think about a goal and begin to understand how to reach it. This is a much more sophisticated kind of thinking than occurs in stage 3, when babies merely understand how to continue an experience once it is underway.

Stage Three This 7½-month-old knows that a squeal of delight is one way to make the interesting experience of a tickle from Daddy last.

In stage four, babies adapt in new, more deliberate ways. They anticipate events that will fulfill their needs and wishes, and they try to make such events occur. A 10-month-old girl who enjoys playing in the tub might see a bar of soap, crawl over to her mother with it as a signal to start her bath, and then remove all her clothes to make her wishes crystal clear—finally squealing with delight when she hears the bath water being turned on. Similarly, if a 10-month-old boy sees his mother putting on her coat to leave without him, he might begin tugging at it to stop her or he might drag over his jacket to signal that he is coming along.

Senses and motor skills (and probably brain maturation as well) advance to make such anticipation possible. Careful experimental studies have found that at 8½ months, but not before, infants search for a concealed object using "landmarks" (visible spatial clues) (Lew et al., 2000). At about the same age, but not before, they anticipate where an interesting sight will appear and they look in that direction (Reznick et al., 2000). Organizing spatial perceptions in the brain and remembering the location of past sights require some neurological associations between memory and place, which is probably impossible before certain dendrite networks form.

All our examples of anticipation also reveal **goal-directed behavior**—that is, purposeful action. The baby's obvious goal-directedness at this age stems from the development of an enhanced awareness of cause and effect as well as better memory for actions already completed (Willatts, 1999). That cognitive awareness coincides with the emergence of the motor skills infants need to achieve their goals.

Thus, a stage-four baby might see something from across the room, be attracted to it, and crawl toward it, ignoring many interesting distractions along the way. Or the baby might grab a forbidden object—a box of matches, a thumbtack, a cigarette—and cry with rage when it is taken away. Because the baby is now goal-directed, the wailing continues even if the infant is offered a substitute that he or she normally finds fascinating.

Piaget thought that the concept of **object permanence** begins to emerge during stage four. Object permanence refers to the awareness that objects or people continue to exist when they are no longer in sight. At this point—and usually not before—infants actively search for objects that are no longer in view. Researchers have since shown that the concept of object permanence actually begins to emerge much earlier. However, the *goal-directed* search for toys that have fallen from the baby's crib, rolled under a couch, or disappeared under a blanket does not begin to emerge until about 8 months, just as Piaget indicated.

Response for Parents (from page 170): Within the first month, the stage of reflexes. If parents wait until the infant is 4 months or older, they may discover that they are too late. It is difficult to introduce a bottle to a 4-month-old who has been exclusively breast-fed or a pacifier to a baby who has already adapted the sucking reflex to a thumb.

goal-directed behavior Purposeful action initiated by infants in anticipation of events that will fulfill their needs and wishes.

object permanence The realization that objects (including people) still exist even when they cannot be seen, touched, or heard.

Thinking Like a Scientist

Object Permanence Revisited

Peek-a-Boo The best hidden object is Mom under an easily moved blanket, as 7-month-old Elias has discovered. Peek-a-boo is the most fun from about 7 to 12 months. In another month, Elias will search for more conventionally hidden objects. In a year or two, his surprise and delight at finding Mom will disappear.

Although it no doubt seems obvious to you that an object, an animal, and your mother continue to exist when you cannot see them, Piaget discovered that it is not at all obvious to very young infants. If a 5-month-old sees a ring of keys, for instance, and reaches for it, simply moving it out of reach is likely to create a fuss and frustration, but "disappearing" it behind your back or even in your closed hand produces only a fleeting expression of disappointment. No further crying or reaching transpires.

Quite literally, out of sight is out of mind. When an infant does demonstrate object permanence (in this case by trying to pry open your hand to get the keys), that is considered a marker of intelligence. Consequently, object permanence has been the subject of intense developmental research. The design and implications of that research continue to be controversial (Baillargeon, 1999).

To understand that controversy, we begin with an appreciation of Piaget's discovery. Before Piaget, it was assumed that infants understood objects in the same way that adults do. Piaget developed a simple experiment that proved that assumption wrong. An adult shows an infant an interesting toy and then covers it up with an easy-to-remove blanket or cloth. If the infant then removes the cover to get the toy, that means that he or she realizes that the toy still exists, even though it was momentarily out of sight.

Various forms of this experiment have been replicated with thousands of infants in virtually every university, every city, and every nation of the world. The findings:

- Infants younger than 8 months do not search for hidden objects.
- At about 8 months, infants search if they can do so immediately but lose interest or forget if they have to wait a few seconds.
- By 2 years, the concept of object permanence is quite well understood. However, even 3-year-olds playing hide-and-seek may become fearful that someone has really disappeared, or they may hide themselves in obvious places (such as behind a coat rack with their feet still visible or as a big lump under a sheet on a bed).

Does failure to search mean the infant has no concept of object permanence? Could other weaknesses of the young brain or body—lack of motivation, imperfect motor skills, or fragile memory—mask an understanding that objects still exist when they are not seen? For almost 50 years, the scientific community accepted Piaget's conclusions. Then, beginning in the 1980s, some researchers raised questions and set about answering them (Spelke, 1993).

One clever experiment startled developmental researchers when it was first published (Baillargeon, 1987). Infants age 3 to 5 months sat directly in front of a screen attached on one side to a table. The screen was made to pivot upward, front to back, from flat to full height and then down to flat again (see Figure 6.1). This action took place immediately in front of the baby, and the screen was tall, so that at its full height everything behind it was hidden from view. The experimenter made the screen pivot many times, until the infants were no longer interested in watching it rise and fall. When babies seemed bored with the routine rise and fall, a large, solid box was placed on the far side of the table, positioned so that the screen would hit it as it pivoted backward.

Two experimental conditions followed. In one, called the *possible event,* the screen pivoted again, up and then back, until it hit the box and stopped, as one would expect. In the other, called the *impossible event,* the screen pivoted up and down as before, through the entire 180-degree arc, as if no box were in the way. (In fact, although the babies couldn't see it happen, the box dropped through a trap door before the screen reached it.)

(a) Habituation

(b) Placing the box

(c) Possible event

(d) Impossible event

FIGURE 6.1 The Old Screen-and-Box Game The basic steps of Renée Baillargeon's test of object permanence—a test that does not depend on the infant's searching abilities or motivation to search. (a) The infant is habituated to the movement of a hinged screen that rotates through a 180-degree arc toward and (as shown) away from the infant. (b) With the infant observing, a box is placed in the backward path of the screen. Then the infant witnesses two events: (c) the "possible" event in which the screen's movement through the arc is stopped by the box, and (d) the "impossible" event, in which the screen completes its movement through the arc as though the box did not exist. Infants as young as 4½ months stare longer at the "impossible" event, indicating their awareness that the box does exist even though they cannot see it behind the screen.

By 4½ months, infants stared longer at the "impossible" event than at the "possible" one, as recorded on videotape and counted in milliseconds. Their longer stares signified their expectations that the box continued to exist when it was hidden from view. This means that the 4½-month-old infants had some concept of object permanence and were surprised when an object seemed to disappear. Apparently Piaget was mistaken in concluding that infants younger than 8 months have no notion of object permanence. As one leading researcher summarizes:

> Until fairly recently, the study of children's cognitive development was dominated by the theory of Jean Piaget. Piaget's theory was detailed, elaborate, comprehensive, and, in many important respects, wrong.
>
> *[Tomasello, 2000, p. 37]*

Most developmentalists still respect Piaget's work and commend him for his two most basic ideas: (1) Infants do not understand everything that adults assume they understand and (2) young infants are smarter than many people realize. Piaget's error was in not realizing that infants are more intelligent, at younger ages, than even he knew.

Where's Rosa? At 18 months, Rosa knows all about object permanence and hiding. Her only problem here is distinguishing between "self" and "other."

Especially for Parents: One parent wants to put all the breakable or dangerous objects away because their toddler is now able to move around independently. The other parent says that the baby should learn not to touch certain things. Who is right?

BOB DAEMMRICH PHOTO, INC.

A boy with a purpose At ten months, this little boy is goal-oriented, stuffing the bread into his mouth with his left hand. In a few months, he will also experiment, probably by dropping crumbs on the floor, dipping the bread in gravy, or conducting many other creative experiments.

tertiary circular reactions The third of three types of feedback loops, this one involving active exploration and experimentation, in which the infant takes in experiences and tries to make sense of them.

"little scientist" Piaget's term for the stage-five toddler (age 12 to 18 months), who actively experiments with objects to learn about their properties.

mental combinations Sequences of actions that the toddler in Piaget's stage six of sensorimotor intelligence (age 18 to 24 months) develops intellectually before actually performing them.

deferred imitation A mental combination in which an infant perceives something that someone else does and then performs the same action a few hours or even days later.

Stages Five and Six: Tertiary Circular Reactions

In their second year, infants begin experimenting in thought and deed. Actually, they experiment first in deed and then in thought, because toddlers typically act first and think later. **Tertiary circular reactions** mean that, rather than simply responding to their own bodies (primary reactions) or to other people or objects (secondary reactions), 1-year-olds take independent and varied actions to actively discover the properties of people and objects. They not only take such action, they delight in their discoveries. Remember that Toni, in our case study in Chapter 5, was "always busy"? That is just as it should be. Indeed, discovery is so rewarding that a toddler might do something that is uncomfortable (taste detergent, squeeze under a bed) to learn more about the world.

Stage Five: New Means Through Active Experimentation

Stage five (age 12 to 18 months) builds directly on the accomplishments of stage four, as infants' goal-directed and purposeful activities become more expansive and creative after the first birthday. Toddlerhood is a time of active exploration and experimentation, a time when babies "get into everything," as though trying to discover all the possibilities their world has to offer.

Because of the experimentation that characterizes this stage, Piaget referred to the stage-five toddler as a **"little scientist"** who "experiments in order to see." Having discovered some action or set of actions that is possible with a given object, stage-five infants seem to ask, "What else can I do with this? What happens if I pour water on the cat?" Their scientific method is one of trial and error, but their devotion to discovery sounds familiar to every adult researcher—and to every parent.

Stage Six: New Means Through Mental Combinations

In the final stage of sensorimotor intelligence (age 18 to 24 months), toddlers begin to anticipate and solve simple problems by using **mental combinations,** a kind of intellectual experimentation that supersedes the active experimentation of stage five. They try out various actions mentally, before actually performing them, to think about the consequences their actions might bring. Thus stage-six children can invent new ways to achieve a goal without resorting to trial-and-error experiments. Consider how Piaget's daughter Jacqueline solved a problem she encountered at the age of 20 months:

> Jacqueline arrives at a closed door with a blade of grass in each hand. She stretches out her right hand toward the knob but sees that she cannot turn it without letting go of the grass. She puts the grass on the floor, opens the door, picks up the grass again and enters. But when she wants to leave the room, things become complicated. She puts the grass on the floor and grasps the doorknob. But then she perceives that in pulling the door toward her she will simultaneously chase away the grass which she placed between the door and the threshold. She therefore picks it up in order to put it outside the door's zone of movement.
>
> *[Piaget, 1952b, p. 162]*

Being able to use mental combinations also makes it possible for the child to pretend. A toddler might lie down on the floor, pretend to go to sleep, and then jump up laughing. Or a child might sing to a doll before tucking it into bed. This is in marked contrast to the behavior of the younger infant, who might treat a doll like any other toy, throwing it, biting it, or banging it on the floor.

As you can see, mental combinations include thinking about consequences before acting and pretending—both quite sophisticated intellectual accomplishments. One other significant intellectual accomplishment involving both thought and memory begins at stage six, according to Piaget. **Deferred imitation,** when an infant sees (or hears, or otherwise perceives) something that someone else does and then imitates that behavior, is another example of a mental combination (Piaget, 1962). He describes an incident involving Jacqueline, who at 16 months observed another child

> who got into a terrible temper. He screamed as he tried to get out of a playpen and pushed it backward, stamping his feet. Jacqueline stood watching him in amazement, never having witnessed such a scene before. The next day, she herself screamed in her playpen and tried to move it, stamping her foot lightly several times in succession.
>
> *[Piaget, 1962, p. 63]*

You may have noticed that Jacqueline was not yet 18 months old, the age at which stage 6 begins. Actually, Piaget was not rigidly age-bound. He cites several instances when his own children were slightly ahead of the norms. He was quite adamant about sequences, though: The behaviors of stage six follow, never precede, those of stage five. However, as with object permanence, later research has shown that he was mistaken: Deferred imitation can begin as early as 9 months. To understand how Piaget again underestimated children, it is useful to realize how scientific methods, and consequently public policies regarding infant development, changed in the course of the twentieth century.

Can You Hear Me Now? How does this baby know about using a cellular phone? Months of watching adults have led to this moment of deferred imitation.

Changing Policy

Policy Implications of Some Modern Research Methods

Scientific investigation has advanced since Piaget's day. A major innovation is the development of complex statistical methods, which can detect small differences (such as milliseconds of visual attention) and can compile data from hundreds of subjects to prevent overgeneralization from a small sample (as Piaget did with his own three children). A related insight is that background factors—not only age but also sex, family structure, socioeconomic status, culture, cohort, and so on—can make a major difference in how a child develops.

Two important research tools not available to Piaget are habituation studies and fMRI. **Habituation** (from the word *habit*) refers to the process of getting used to an object or event through repeated exposure to it, as when an infant hears the same sound or sees the same picture again and again until he or she seems to lose interest in it. One of the wonderful characteristics of very young infants is that they enjoy novel stimuli and soon become habituated to (or bored by) the same old experience. Habituation is thus a boon for researchers studying infant development.

If a baby becomes habituated to one stimulus and then is presented a new one, any of several indicators—a longer or more focused gaze; a faster or slower heart rate; more or less muscle tension around the lips; a change in the rate, rhythm, or pressure of suction on a nipple—reveal that the baby detects a difference between the two stimuli. If no change occurs, that means the baby cannot yet perceive the difference. By watching for signs of habituation, scientists have learned, for instance, that even 1-month-olds can detect the difference between a *pah* sound and a *bah* sound, between a circle with two dots inside it and a circle without any dots, between a smooth pacifier and a bumpy one.

fMRI (functional magnetic resonance imaging, a brain-imaging technique) reveals brain activity by showing increases in oxygen supply to various parts of the brain as a person tries to remember a word or watches an exciting movie (Casey et al., 2001). The fMRI depicts the brain areas where, for instance, the recognition of faces and the recognition of places occur. Probably the most important insight to date from fMRI and other brain scans is that various parts of the brain are specialized for various activities but that no one part functions alone (Casey et al., 2001). Connections between parts are thus crucial, and experience helps form those connections (as explained in Chapter 5). (The major new brain-scanning techniques are listed in Table 6.2.)

The main conclusion relevant to public policy is that the early years of life, once thought to be intellectually empty, are now known to be prime time for cognitive development. Indeed, developmentalists now worry about the opposite danger: Since we know that substantial cognitive development occurs in the first three years, some politicians and members of the media act as if those years are the only ones that provide a foundation for learning. Not so. As a report from 20 leading developmentalists summarizes:

> Early experiences clearly affect the development of the brain. Yet the recent focus on "zero to three" as a critical or particularly sensitive period is highly problematic, not because this isn't an important period for the developing brain, but simply because the disproportional attention to the period from birth to 3 years begins too late and ends too soon. (National Research Council and Institute of Medicine, 2000)

Experts concerned about the interface between developmental research and public policy worry that the colorful pictures of brain activity may inspire journalists and politicians to make unrealistic conjectures about the pace of cognitive development (Thompson & Nelson, 2001). Piaget himself was concerned about "the American question," which was always asked by audiences in the United States but not elsewhere: "How can we speed up cognitive development?" Piaget pointed out that maturation fosters cognition at the appropriate time, and he developed his theory to show that the intellect evolves over time in a series of stages.

It is possible that all the recent research, especially the sophisticated technology and analyses that are now available, has actually distracted scientists from the essential developmental perspective. As always, the interpretation of the data from scientific research is the crucial contribution from scientists who know the various questions and issues regarding that perspective. Perhaps the makers of public policy need to be reminded that the entire context of development is more important than any specific activity that might stimulate one part of the brain at one stage of development.

TABLE 6.2 Some Techniques Used by Neuroscientists to Understand Brain Function

Technique	Use
EEG (electroencephalogram)	Measures electrical activity in the top layers of the brain, where the cortex is.
ERP (event-related potential)	Notes the amplitude and frequency of electrical activity (as shown by brain waves) in specific parts of the cortex in reaction to various stimuli.
fMRI (functional magnetic resonance imaging)	Measures changes in activity anywhere in the brain (not just the outer layers).
PET (positron emission tomography)	Also (like fMRI) reveals activity in various parts of the brain. Locations can be pinpointed with precision, but PET requires injection of radioactive dye to light up the active parts of the brain.

Because of practical and ethical concerns, none of these techniques have been used with large, representative samples of normal infants.

habituation The process of getting used to an object or event through repeated exposure to it.

fMRI Functional magnetic resonance imaging, a technique in which the brain's magnetic properties are measured to detect changes in activity levels anywhere in the brain.

Information Processing

Piaget was a "grand" theorist of cognition throughout the life span, with an appreciation of shifts in the nature of cognition that occur at about ages 2, 6, and 12. His sweeping stage overview contrasts with another view of infant cognition, one that arises from **information-processing theory**, a perspective on human thinking processes modeled on computer analysis of data. No computer can match the mind's capacity for reflection, creativity, and intuition. However, information-processing theorists suggest that a step-by-step description of the mechanisms of human thought, by analogy to the steps by which computers process data, aids our understanding of the development of cognition at every age.

information-processing theory A perspective that compares human thinking processes, by analogy, to computer analysis of data, from sensory input through brain reactions, connections, and stored memories to output.

Information-processing researchers look not only at such specific fields of study as neuroscience and linguistics, but also at the comprehensive processing of information, from input through output. Information processing begins with input in the form of sensory messages picked up by the five senses; proceeds to brain reactions, connections, and stored memories; and concludes with some form of output. For infants, the output might consist of moving a hand to uncover a hidden object, or saying a word to signify recognition of a person, or focusing the eyes to demonstrate that a stimulus is noticed.

Although many researchers in infant cognition do not explicitly use the information-processing perspective in their work, this perspective helps tie together the various aspects of infant cognition that are the topic of extensive study and exciting discoveries. We will review three of these aspects now: affordances, categories, and memory. Each of these refers to a step in information processing: Affordances concern perception (or, by analogy, input); categories refer to the organization of concepts by the brain (or programming); and memory involves retrieval of ideas already learned or of past experiences (or output).

A Hole Is to Dig As for any scientist, discovery and application are the motivating forces for infant activity. Clamshells have many uses, one for clams, one for hungry people, and another—shown here—for toddlers on the beach.

Affordances

Perception, remember, is the mental processing of information that arrives at the brain from the sensory organs. It is the first step of information processing—the input to the brain. One of the puzzles of adult development is why two people can have radically different perceptions of the same situation. The same question applies to infants.

A lifetime of thought and research led Eleanor and James Gibson to conclude that perception is far from an automatic phenomenon that every baby, everywhere, experiences in the same way (E. Gibson, 1969; J. Gibson, 1979). For infants, as for the rest of us, perception is a cognitive accomplishment that requires selection from a vast array of possibilities: "Perceiving is active, a process of obtaining information about the world. . . . We don't simply see, we look" (E. Gibson, 1988, p. 5).

The Gibsons contend that the environment (people, places, and objects) *affords,* or offers, many opportunities to be perceived and to be used in a wide variety of ways (E. Gibson, 1997). Each of these opportunities for perception and interaction is called an **affordance.** Which particular affordances are perceived and acted on depends on four factors: sensory awareness, immediate motivation, current development, and past experience.

As a simple example, a lemon may be perceived as something that affords smelling, tasting, touching, viewing, throwing, squeezing, and biting (among other things). Which affordance a particular person perceives and acts on depends on the four factors just mentioned. Consequently, a lemon might elicit quite different perceptions from an artist about to paint a still life, a thirsty adult in need of a refreshing drink, and a teething baby wanting something to gnaw on. This example implies (correctly) that affordances require an ecological fit between the individual and his or her environment. Hence, affordances arise both from specific qualities of an object and from the way the individual subjectively perceives the object.

Affordances are not limited to objects; they are also perceived in the physical characteristics of a setting and the living creatures in it (Reed, 1993). A toddler's idea of what affords running might be any unobstructed surface—a meadow, a

affordance An opportunity for perception and interaction that is offered by people, places, and objects in the environment.

Response for Parents (from page 174): It is easier and safer to babyproof the house, because toddlers, being little scientists, want to explore. However, it is also important for both parents to encourage and guide the baby, so it might be better to leave out a few untouchable items for teaching purposes than to get a divorce.

It's OK to Grasp Daddy's Nose Infants quickly learn what objects are of the right size and proximity for grasping. If the adults in their life allow it, graspability also affords sociability, an impulse that requires one to distinguish appropriate objects from inappropriate ones.

graspability The perception of whether or not an object is of the proper shape, size, texture, and distance to afford grasping.

visual cliff An experimental apparatus designed to provide the illusion of a sudden dropoff between one horizontal surface and another.

long hallway in an apartment building, or an empty road. To an adult eye, the degree to which these places afford running may be restricted by such factors as a bull grazing in the meadow, neighbors in the hallway, or traffic on the road.

Graspable?

All the senses are active processors from the moment of birth. Infants learn what parts of the visual array best afford focusing, what sounds merit listening, and so on. In terms of actions controlled by the infant, the grasping and sucking reflexes are among the first to afford information.

Graspability—whether an object is the right size, shape, and texture for grasping and whether it is within reach—is an early affordance. This is vital information, since infants learn about their world by handling objects. Extensive research has shown that infants perceive graspability long before their manual dexterity enables them to actually grasp successfully. They look intently at objects that seem graspable and ignore ones that do not, even before they are able to aim and adjust their arms and hands to grab the possibly graspable thing (Wentworth et al., 2000). By 5 months, infants are able to grab objects successfully, usually taking longer to coordinate their hand movements than do older babies and adults. This shows that deliberate and thoughtful perception precedes an action that will soon become automatic (McCarty & Ashmead, 1999).

The fact that babies perceive graspability so early helps explain how they explore a face. Once they have some control over their arm and hand movements, they will grab at any face that comes within their reach. But their grabbing is far from haphazard: They do not grab at the eyes or mouth (although they might poke at them), because they already perceive that these objects are embedded and thus do not afford grasping. A tug at the nose or ears is more likely, because these features do afford grasping. Even better are eyeglasses, earrings, and long mustaches—all of which are quickly yanked by most babies, who perceive at a glance the graspability these objects afford.

Sudden Drops

The affordances that an infant perceives in common objects evolve as the infant gains experience with those objects. An example is provided by the **visual cliff**, an apparatus designed to provide the illusion of a sudden dropoff between one horizontal surface and another.

Depth Perception Like thousands of crawling babies before him, this infant refuses to crawl to his mother because the visual-cliff apparatus makes him think there is a dropoff between himself and her.

?Observational Quiz (see answer, page 180): What does he see when he looks down?

Researchers once thought that perception of a visual cliff was purely a matter of visual maturity: 8-month-olds could see the difference; younger babies, because of their inadequate depth perception, could not. "Proof" came when 6-month-olds could be enticed to wiggle forward over the supposed edge of the visual cliff, in contrast to 10-month-olds, who fearfully refused to budge, even when their mothers called them (E. Gibson & Walk, 1960).

Later research found, however, that this hypothesis was wrong. In fact, even 3-month-olds notice the difference between a solid surface and an apparent cliff, as evidenced by their slowed heart rate and wide-open eyes when they are placed over the "edge." But they do not realize that one affordance of the cliff is falling. That realization comes when they start crawling, and their memory of a caregiver's fear (or perhaps their own tumble off a bed) teaches them that the edge of a precipice (as in stairs that go down) affords danger and pain (Campos et al., 1978).

Movement and People

Despite all the variations from one infant to another in the particular affordances they perceive, two general principles of perception are shared by all infants. One is **dynamic perception,** which is perception primed to focus on movement and change. Infants love to attend to objects that move. As soon as they can, they move their own bodies—grabbing, scooting, crawling, walking—and, to their delight, these movements change what the world affords them. Likewise, other creatures that move, especially their own caregivers, are among the first and best sources of pleasure. That is one reason it's almost impossible to teach a baby not to chase and grab a dog, a cat, or even a cockroach.

dynamic perception Perception that is primed to focus on movement and change.

One Constant, Multisensual Perception
From the angle of her arm and the bend of her hand, it appears that this infant recognizes the constancy of the furry mass, perceiving it as a single entity whether it is standing still, rolling in the sand, or walking along the beach.

The second universal principle of infant perception is that they are fascinated by other people. This characteristic may have evolved over the many centuries when humans of all ages survived by learning to attend to, and rely on, each other. This fascination underlies another of the surprising competencies of young infants: coordinating vision and hearing by matching face with voice.

An experiment that demonstrates this begins with two side-by-side frames on a video screen, with two people facing the camera and talking. Only one voice is heard on the audiotape. By 6 months, infants match the speakers' voice to the face on the film, ignoring the face of the other person, whose mouth movements are not synchronized with the sounds (Kuhl & Meltzoff, 1988). With this task, as with all affordances, selectivity is apparent. Seven-month-olds connect speech and face when the person is happy, angry, or interested. However, they prefer not to look at a sad face, even when the voice matches it. They would much rather stare at the happy face even when it does not match the voice (Soken & Pick, 1999).

One team of researchers who study infant matching of face and voice refer directly to affordances:

> Given that infants are frequently exposed to their caregivers' emotional displays and further presented with opportunities to view the affordances (Gibson, 1959, 1979) of those emotional expressions, we propose that the expressions of familiar persons are meaningful to infants very early in life.
>
> [Kahana-Kalman & Walker-Andrews, 2001, p. 366]

As with the earlier research, these researchers presented infants with two moving images on a video screen. Both images were women visibly expressing joy or sorrow, accompanied by an audiotape of one woman's happy or sad talk. This study differed from earlier work in two ways. First, the infants were much younger, only 3½ months old. Not surprisingly, given their immaturity, when the infants did not know the woman, they failed to match the verbal emotion with the face. Like the 7-month-old infants in the study just mentioned, they looked slightly more at the happy face, but unlike them, they showed no sign of matching visual and auditory stimuli.

The second difference between this study and earlier research was that half the infants saw a video of a stranger, but the other half were presented with two images (happy and sad) of their own mothers, with an audio that was either their mother's happy words or her sad ones. In this case, the infants successfully matched visual and vocal emotions. They looked longest of all at their happy mothers, talking in a happy way, but they also looked at their sad mothers when the audio they heard was their mother's sad voice—an amazing display of the very young infant's ability to perceive and interpret speech.

These experimenters noticed something else that was not reported in the earlier research. When they saw and heard their happy mothers, as opposed to the happy strangers, infants smiled twice as quickly, seven times as long, and much more brightly (with cheeks raised as well as mouth upturned) (Kahana-Kalman & Walker-Andrews, 2001). Obviously, experience had taught these babies that a smiling mother affords joy, especially if you smile back. The affordances of a smiling stranger, however, even on a video, are more difficult to judge.

Categories and Concepts

Understanding objects or people one by one, moment by moment, is much easier than forming a general concept or perception, especially when that concept seems to include an entire category of experiences. Yet that is precisely what infants apparently do—they categorize affordances within the first year of life. As we just saw, very young infants quickly form at least two categories for adult women: their own mother in one category and smiling strangers in another. You will learn in Chapter 7 that infants form other social categories, responding quite differently to fathers than to mothers, to children than to adults, and to friends than to strangers. Even more impressive is that infants form categories using intellectual, not social, concepts.

Early Categories

Infants younger than 6 months can categorize objects on the basis of their shape, color, angularity, density, relative size, and, to the amazement of researchers, number (up to three objects) (Haith & Benson, 1998). Taken as a whole, the evidence suggests that young infants do not merely perceive the difference between shapes (such as circles versus squares) or relative sizes (such as larger and smaller); they also apply organizing principles that enable them to develop a concept of what is, or is not, relevant for inclusion in each category. Many researchers believe that a rudimentary understanding of such categories may be biologically based ("hard-wired" in the brain) but that experience with different objects and events is also essential for developing the innate ability to sort things into categories.

To use the term introduced in Chapter 5, basic categories are *experience-expectant*. For instance, the brain awaits visual stimuli of some curved things and some angular things; once these things are seen, the category is quick to emerge. Also important is basic number—at least the distinction between "one" and "more than one." Babies also understand simple spatial relationships. For example, infants as young as 3 months seem to understand "above" and "below." At least, after they see several depictions of a small diamond-shaped dot above a

Especially for Parents: This research on early affordances suggests a crucial lesson about how many babysitters an infant should have. What is it?

! Answer to Observational Quiz (from page 178): He sees a visual cliff. It has the same attractive pattern as the surface on which he rests, but he perceives a 1-meter drop (that's why he hesitates).

line, they stare longer when the diamond switches to being below the line. However, the above–below distinction escapes them if the target object varies from trial to trial—from the diamond to, say, a tiny arrow, the letter *E,* a plus sign, and then a triangle. By the age of 6 months, though, varying the object does not distract babies from paying attention to an object below a line after seeing various objects above it (Quinn et al., 1996).

The fact that babies can do this suggests that they are forming concepts, not just habits—again, well in advance of Piaget's stages. Repeated exposure to particular patterns is closely connected to the interpretation of information that is processed. For the preverbal infant, of course, categories do not have the verbal labels that older children learn to connect with them. In fact, categories are probably "not accessible to conscious awareness" (Ashby & Waldron, 2000, p. 12).

Once an object is categorized, however, that will aid the infant's understanding of what actions that object affords, and that knowledge, in turn, will facilitate assimilation of vocabulary once the brain is ready for language. Such labels eventually make reading possible. Recognizing letters requires noticing some categories ("rounded" and "angular" are important for *U* and *V,* "above" and "below" are important for *d* and *p*) and ignoring others (an *O* is still an *O,* whether it is printed in roman or italic type). Thus many educators believe that the academic achievement of the older child and adult begins in early infancy—a belief that is further explored in this chapter's later discussion of baby talk.

Given the importance of dynamic perception, it is not surprising that infants are particularly likely to categorize objects that move. Thus, categories of living things are developed early. By the end of the first year, babies can discriminate between photographs, all of the same size, of the following:

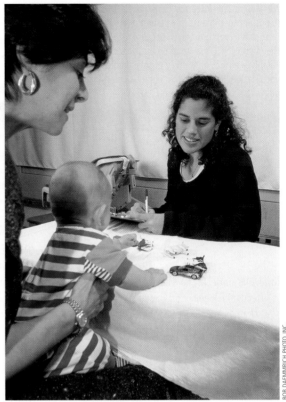

Research in Progress Even at 4 months, this infant has a sense of objects—which ones are graspable, suckable, throwable. The psychology student taking notes is observing in search of a theory to explain (among other things) why the baby is ignoring the red car.

- Birds and other animals, recognizing that parakeets and hawks are in the same category but that horses are different (Roberts, 1988)
- Men and women, children and adults, and beautiful people and less attractive ones (Rubenstein et al., 1999)
- Dogs and cats (Mandler & McDonough, 1998)

Are these merely categories, or are they concepts—ideas that require some organization of perception and selective cognition? The answer can be debated and depends partly on the definition of *concept.* However, there is no doubt that quite specific perceptual understanding is required for some of these categories. For example, can you identify the difference between a child and an adult when same-size photos of both are presented? (One key is the shape of the head and the proportion of the nose and jaw; 1-year-olds seem to know this.)

Are Categories Universal?

Is this tendency of young brains to categorize objects true for all children everywhere? In a series of experiments, Jonas Langer (2001) displayed objects of various shapes to toddlers and allowed them to play with the objects in any way they wished. At the outset, three rectangles were placed with one circle, and three circles with one rectangle. Some 21-month-olds spontaneously put all the rectangles in one pile and all the circles in another; before age 3, all the children, without prompting, piled all the objects in together according to shape categories. They did not yet verbalize the shape labels (although one girl rebuked the tester, saying, "No. Belongs this way"), because, according to Langer and to many others, cognitive categories precede the vocabulary for such clusters.

In replications of the rectangles-and-circles experiment, three very different groups of children—middle-class European-Americans, low-income toddlers

Response for Parents (from page 180): It is important that infants have time for repeated exposure to each caregiver, because infants adjust their behavior to maximize whatever each particular caregiver affords in the way of play, emotions, and vocalization. Parents should find one steady babysitter rather than several.

infantile amnesia The inability, hypothesized by Freud, to remember anything that happened before the age of 2 or anything except very important events before the age of 5.

reminder session A perceptual experience that makes a person recollect an idea or thing but that does not test one's actual memory for it.

exposed before birth to crack-cocaine, and extremely impoverished Indian children in Peru—sorted the shapes correctly at almost identical ages. At least on this measure, the minds of young children apparently develop according to the same timetable, no matter what their immediate educational context is. Langer also notes that, although the emotional maturity of these three groups of children reflected their varied circumstances, their conceptual development did not (Langer, 2001; Langer et al., 1998). This observation suggests that, for basic categories and concepts, brain maturation is the crucial factor, but for emotional interactions, experience-dependent factors dominate. In other words, all infants seem to have the brainpower and motivation to develop cognitive categories. Thus, using the information-processing metaphor, they have a default program that enables them to think.

Memory

Piaget, along with virtually every other psychologist of his day, underestimated infant memory. The most extreme view was presented by Sigmund Freud, who described **infantile amnesia**, a hypothesis he thought was a fact—that no one could remember anything that happened before age 2 or very much before age 5. Current research shows that they were wrong, or at least not completely right.

Very Early Memories

Scientists have confirmed that infants have great difficulty storing new memories in their first year and that older children are often unable to describe what happened when they were young. But developmentalists now agree that young infants can remember if certain conditions exist:

■ Experimental conditions are similar to real life.
■ Motivation is high.
■ Special measures aid memory retrieval.

The most dramatic evidence for infant memory comes from a series of innovative experiments in which 3-month-old infants were taught to make a mobile move by kicking their legs (Rovee-Collier, 1987, 1990). The infants lay on their backs, in their own cribs, connected to a brightly colored mobile by means of a ribbon tied to one foot. Virtually all the infants began making some occasional kicks (as well as random arm movements and noise) and realized after a while that kicking made the mobile move. They then kicked more vigorously and often, sometimes laughing at their accomplishment. So far, this is no surprise—we know that such control of movement is highly reinforcing to infants. In fact, 3-month-old Laurent Piaget demonstrated that 80 years ago, as you read at the beginning of this chapter. But could infants remember this experience?

When some infants had the mobile-and-ribbon apparatus reinstalled in their cribs *1 week later,* most started to kick immediately—indicating that they did remember. But when other infants were retested *2 weeks later,* they began with only random kicks. Apparently they had forgotten what they had learned.

However, the lead researcher, Carolyn Rovee-Collier, developed another experiment that demonstrated infants could remember after 2 weeks *if* they were given a brief reminder session prior to the retesting (Rovee-Collier & Hayne, 1987). A **reminder session** is any perceptual experience that might make a person recollect an idea or thing but that does not test the actual memory. In this particular reminder session, 2 weeks after the initial training the infants watched the mobile move but were *not* tied to the ribbon and were positioned so that they could *not* kick. The next day, when they were again connected to the mobile and positioned so that they could move their legs, they kicked as they had learned to do 2 weeks earlier. In effect, their faded memory had been reactivated by watching the mobile move on the previous day.

Further research shows that the specific conditions of the reminder session can make remembering either easier or harder (Adler et al., 2000). For example, a mobile in the same room is easier to remember than the identical mobile in a different room. It is even better if identical music is playing and identical smells are in the air (Rubin et al., 1998). A slight difference—for example, between a mobile with an obvious letter *Q* and one with an obvious letter *O*— can make remembering much less likely (Gerhardstein et al., 1998).

Rovee-Collier believes that natural reminder sessions are part of every infant's daily experience, because the same events and circumstances occur day after day. For example, parents regularly shake a rattle and then put it in the baby's hand. If one day they simply show the rattle, the infant might reach out to grab and shake it, remembering what the rattle does. Such events are common, and if adults are alert, they will notice that very young infants can remember. They will also notice that infants do not remember much. Under the age of 6 months, they recall only for a limited period of time, only under specific conditions, and probably only events that include their own activities.

Overall, however, early memories can be "highly enduring, and become even more so after repeated encounters with reminders" (Rovee-Collier & Gerhardstein, 1997). Repetition and reminders are key: Infants under 6 months do not remember meeting their grandparents when they see them again a year later, nor do they remember a sudden trauma, such as emergency surgery. Early in life, under the best conditions, long-term storage and retrieval of memories appear to be fragile and uncertain, facilitated by repetition, reminders, and active involvement of the infant.

He Remembers! In this demonstration of Rovee-Collier's experiment, a young infant immediately remembers how to make the familiar mobile move. (Unfamiliar mobiles do not provoke the same reaction.) He kicks his right leg and flails both arms, just as he learned to do several weeks ago.

A Little Older, a Little More Memory

After about six months, infants become capable of retaining information for longer periods of time, with less training or reminding. Toward the end of the first year, even deferred imitation is apparent. For example, suppose a 9-month-old watches someone playing with a toy the baby has never seen before. The next day, if given the toy, the 9-month-old is likely to play with it in the same way as the person he or she observed had played. (Younger infants do not usually do this.)

Over the next few months, deferred imitation becomes more elaborate; children are particularly likely to imitate other children (Heimann & Meltzoff, 1996; Oliver Ryalls et al., 2000). Infants retain more details, including the sequence of events, and they can duplicate those details days later, prompted by only minimal clues associated with the experience—such as a sound or a part of the setting (Bauer & Mandler, 1992). A 1-year-old, for instance, might stare intently as an adult opens the refrigerator, takes out an egg carton, and cracks a few eggs into a bowl. The next day (perhaps when the adult has left the refrigerator open while answering the phone), the child might take out the egg carton and crack all the remaining eggs—in a bowl, if it happens to be visible and within reach, or in the sink or the garbage pail or even on the floor, if not.

By the middle of the second year, toddlers are capable of remembering and reenacting even more complex sequences. They can also *generalize* their memories, moving from particular details to the general concept just as they did with affordances and categories several months earlier.

In one experiment, 16- and 20-month-olds first watched an experimenter perform various activities, such as putting a doll to bed, making a party hat, and cleaning a table (Bauer & Dow, 1994). For each activity, the experimenter used particular props and gave a brief "instruction" for performing each step. For instance, to clean the table, the experimenter wet it with water from a white spray bottle, saying "Put on the water"; wiped it with a paper towel, saying "Wipe it"; and placed the towel in a wooden trash basket saying "Toss it." A week later, most toddlers remembered how to carry out the sequence just from hearing "Put on the water. Wipe it. Toss it." They did this not only when given the same props the experimenter had used but also when given quite different props (for instance, a clear spray bottle, a sponge, and a plastic lidded garbage can).

Thus, they had formed and remembered a general scheme of the activity; they were not just reenacting a memorized sequence, triggered by visual props. To make sure the toddlers were remembering the sequence and not merely playing imaginatively, the experimenters presented the instructions and the props to toddlers who had *not* seen the demonstration. Those youngsters played with the objects but did not perform the specific actions in order (Bauer & Dow, 1994).

Implicit and Explicit Memories

To understand why psychologists have differed on the age at which infants remember, you need to understand another significant discovery relating to infant memory, this one from neuroscience. Memory is not one thing, "not a unitary or monolithic entity" (Schacter & Badgaiyan, 2001, p. 1). People are inaccurate when they say "I have a good memory" or "My memory is failing," because fMRI research finds many distinct brain regions devoted to distinct aspects of memory. Thus, we have a memory for words, for images, for actions, for smells, for experiences, for "memorized" facts, for "forgotten" faces, and so on. Each type of memory is encoded by neurons in a particular part of the cortex. At least for adult verbal memories, separate networks become dedicated to names of vegetables, of animals, of tools, of people, and so on (Gabrieli, 1998; Rolls, 2000). (For the basics about the brain's structure and function, see Chapter 5.)

Because there are many types of memory, it is not surprising that infants remember some things better than others: That's the way human brains are constructed. Thus, early memories are *both* fragile and enduring, depending on which type of memory is described. One crucial difference is the storage and retrieval process, with infants storing within their brains many memories of emotions and sensations that they cannot readily retrieve. To further understand what is and is not remembered, we differentiate between implicit and explicit memory (C. A. Nelson, 1997).

Implicit memory is memory of events, objects, and experiences that can be recognized but not necessarily recalled; that is, implicit memories are evoked when certain cues are present, but they cannot be brought to mind independently of reminders. As an adult, you become aware of implicit memory when an object unexpectedly and suddenly triggers a memory, or when you learn something so fast that you must have known some aspect of it earlier (as happens if you study a language you knew as a child but "forgot"), or when something seems vaguely, inexplicably familiar (a phenomenon called *déjà vu,* which is French for "already seen").

Explicit memory is available for instant recall; a person can demonstrate it on demand. Often, explicit memory involves material that was deliberately studied and memorized. Evidence of explicit memory might be performance on a straightforward test, such as a history quiz, or an informal measure, such as being asked "When is your mother's birthday?"

You probably have an explicit memory of the address of your childhood home, because your parents taught it to you in case you got lost. You may not realize, however, that you also implicitly remember the color and texture of your

implicit memory Memory of events, objects, and experiences that can be recognized when certain cues are present but cannot be recalled without reminders.

explicit memory Memory that is available for instant recall; often involves material that was deliberately studied and memorized.

first bedspread—until you see it again and a flood of memories return. Virtually all current researchers agree that different parts of the brain are involved in implicit and explicit memory and that implicit memories are stored and retrieved better in early childhood than explicit ones are. In fact, explicit memory is usually verbal, which is why it is impossible to store explicit memories before learning to talk.

Affordances, categories, and memory—all these elements of cognition make it clear that infants under age 2 are not only aware of their surroundings but are actively thinking and learning about them. They are processing the information they gather, interpreting and organizing it. It is crucial that the particular context allows the young mind to grow and that parents, educators, psychologists, and politicians pay much more attention to cognitive development in infancy than they did a decade or two ago. Even beyond the nonverbal accomplishments of the very young, thinking and remembering are the foundation for the most amazing accomplishment of all, learning language. As you read about early communication, look for links between cognition as already described and language as it develops.

Language: What Develops in Two Years?

Language, with thousands of basic vocabulary words, hundreds of idiomatic phrases, dozens of rules of grammar, and, for English at least, dozens of exceptions to those rules, is the most impressive intellectual achievement of the young child. In fact, language is the most impressive accomplishment of all humans—it differentiates our species from all others and is probably the reason human brains are more complex than those of any other animal. For instance, humans and gorillas are close relatives, with about 99 percent of their genes in common, and gorillas actually are bigger than people. But the adult gorilla's brain is only one-fourth as big as the human's, which also has far more dendrites, synapses, and so on (Thompson, 2000). This means that a 2-year-old human has three times as much brainpower as a fully grown gorilla. The size of the cortex is the key difference here. Other animals communicate, but none have anything approaching the neurons and networks that support one or more of the 6,000 human languages.

Children around the world follow the same sequence of early language development (see Table 6.3). The timing and depth of the linguistic ability vary; the most advanced 10 percent of 2-year-olds know more than 550 words, and the least advanced 10 percent speak fewer than 100 words—a fivefold difference (Merriman, 1998). (Some explanations are discussed at the end of this chapter.) But the sequence of language learning is the same for almost all, with every human surpassing even the smartest ape many times over. We now describe this sequence.

First Noises and Gestures

Infants are equipped to learn language even before birth, partly due to brain readiness and partly due to their auditory experiences during the final prenatal months (Aslin et al., 1998). As you have read, newborns prefer hearing speech over the sounds; they prefer listening to **baby talk**—high-pitched, simplified, and repetitive adult speech that is quite distinct from normal speech. As scientists use the term, *baby talk* is not the way babies talk but the way

baby talk The high-pitched, simplified, and repetitive way adults speak to infants; also called *child-directed speech, motherese.*

Too Young for Language? No. The early stages of language are communication through noise, gestures, and facial expressions, very evident here between this Kung grandmother and granddaughter.

ANTHONY BANNISTER / CORBIS

TABLE 6.3 The Development of Spoken Language: The First 2 Years

Age*	Means of Communication
Newborn	Reflexive communication—cries, movements, facial expressions.
2 months	A range of meaningful noises—cooing, fussing, crying, laughing.
3–6 months	New sounds, including squeals, growls, croons, trills, vowel sounds.
6–10 months	Babbling, including both consonant and vowel sounds repeated in syllables.
10–12 months	Comprehension of simple words; simple intonations; specific vocalizations that have meaning to those who know the infant well. Deaf babies express their first signs; hearing babies use specific gestures (e.g., pointing) to communicate.
12 months	First spoken words that are recognizably part of the native language.
13–18 months	Slow growth of vocabulary, up to about 50 words.
18 months	Vocabulary spurt—three or more words learned per day.
21 months	First two-word sentence.
24 months	Multiword sentences. Half the infant's utterances are two or more words long.

*The ages of accomplishment in this table reflect norms. Many healthy and intelligent children attain these steps in language development earlier or later than indicated here.
Sources: Bloom, 1993; Lenneberg, 1967.

adults talk to babies (sometimes called *child-directed speech* or *motherese*). Moreover, even 1-month-olds can distinguish among many different speech sounds, including those that adults no longer hear—and among sounds that they have heard only in a research laboratory (Kuhl, 1994). The sound of the human voice—whether it comes from mother or father, another child, a stranger, or even someone speaking a foreign language—is always fascinating to them.

Vocalization

Very young babies do much more than listen. They are noisy creatures—crying, cooing, and making a variety of other sounds even in the first weeks of life. These noises gradually become more varied until, by the age of 4 months, most babies have verbal repertoires that include squeals, growls, gurgles, grunts, croons, and yells, as well as some speechlike sounds (Hsu et al., 2000).

The first sounds are actually reflexes, uttered whether or not someone else is talking, but by 4 months they are more deliberate, uttered now as conversation, with the pauses that are proper to turn-taking. If caregivers have been attentive in the early weeks, a whimper now means "I'm awake and hungry," and the response "Oh, I'm coming" is usually sufficient. With the right response from an adult, the infant has no need to go to the next step of the communication process, a loud, demanding cry (perhaps meaning "Get me food now!").

Note the link here to cognition. The first noises follow Piaget's sequence from reflexes to adaptation and then to communication that will "make interesting sights last." Affordances are also notable in an infant's reaction to adults. For some babies, any adult is perceived as affording food, and a mere whimper is enough to make that affordance become actuality. For other babies, a loud cry is needed to access that affordance. For yet other babies, no noise makes any difference because adults are indifferent, not affording anything at all. Ideally, adults afford communication on many levels, and infants act on their perceptions, making noises that communicate in the first months of life.

Babbling

By 6 or 7 months, babies begin to repeat certain syllables (*ma-ma-ma, da-da-da, ba-ba-ba*), a phenomenon referred to as **babbling** because of the way it sounds. Babbling is experience-expectant learning; all babies do it if given half a chance. Moreover, the sounds they make are similar no matter what language their parents speak. However, over the next few months, babbling begins to vary and to incorporate more and more sounds from the native language, perhaps as infants imitate the sounds they hear (Boysson-Bardies et al., 1989; Masataka, 1992). Many cultures assign important meanings to some of these sounds, with *ma-ma-ma, da-da-da,* and *pa-pa-pa* usually taken to apply to significant people in the infant's life (Bloom, 1998). (See Appendix A, page A-4.)

Deaf babies begin to making babbling sounds several months later than hearing infants, and they make the sounds less frequently. However, deaf infants may actually begin babbling manually at about the same time hearing infants begin babbling orally (Petitto & Marentette, 1991). Analysis of videotapes of deaf children whose parents communicate via sign language reveals that before their tenth month, these infants use about a dozen distinct hand gestures—most of which resemble basic elements of the American Sign Language used by their parents—in a rhythmic, repetitive manner analogous to oral babbling.

Actually, by 10 months hearing as well as deaf babies communicate with gestures, such as pointing at objects and lifting their arms to be picked up. And both hearing and deaf babies do some spontaneous manual babbling as well as oral babbling. For obvious reasons, however, deaf infants reduce their oral babbling and increase their gesturing just when hearing babies do the opposite. (Petitto & Marentette, 1991).

babbling The extended repetition of certain syllables, such as *ba-ba-ba*, that begins at about 6 or 7 months of age.

First Words

Finally, at about 1 year of age, the average baby speaks a few words, not pronounced clearly or used precisely. Usually, caregivers hear and understand the first word before strangers do, which makes it hard for researchers to pinpoint exactly what a 12-month-old can say (Bloom, 1998). For example, at 13 months, Kyle knew standard words such as *mama,* but he also knew *da, ba, tam, opma,* and *daes,* which his parents knew to be, respectively, "downstairs," "bottle," "tummy," "oatmeal," and "starfish" (yes, that's what *daes* meant) (Lewis et al., 1999).

The Language Explosion

Once an infant's vocabulary reaches about 50 words, it suddenly begins to build rapidly, at a rate of 50 to 100 words or even more per month (Fenson et al., 1994). In fact, one scholar says the child becomes a "vacuum" for words, scooping them up at the rate of one word every 90 waking minutes (Pinker, 1994). This language spurt is sometimes called the **naming explosion**, because the first words include a disproportionate number of nouns, or naming words.

Every toddler seems to learn more nouns, especially those that refer to animate creatures (mostly humans), than verbs, adjectives, or other parts of speech (Gentner & Boroditsky, 2001). Almost universally, labels for each significant caregiver, sibling, and sometimes pet (often *dada, mama, nana, papa, baba, tata*) appear between 12 and 18 months. Other frequent words refer to the child's favorite foods and, if toilet training is an issue, elimination (*pee-pee, wee-wee, poo-poo, doo-doo*), used as labels first for the product, then for the process).

No doubt you have noticed that all these words have a similar structure: two identical syllables, each a consonant followed by a vowel. Variations follow that pattern: in addition to *baba,* many infants say *bobo, bebe, bibi,* or, more complicated, not just "mama" but also *ma-me, ama,* and the like. The reason is that

naming explosion A sudden increase in an infant's vocabulary, especially in the number of nouns, that begins at about 18 months of age.

short, two-syllable words with *m, n, t, d,* or *p* are easiest for the child to say because they follow directly from babbling. The spontaneous noises of the infant are interpreted and used by every culture to form words, not vice versa. This facilitates early communication for both parties.

The first words also reflect the cognitive characteristics of infancy, including the salience of things that afford action, social interaction, and dynamic perception—all key elements in information processing. The importance of building on the infant's own preferences and perceptions became obvious in an experiment in which 12-month-olds were presented with two unnamed objects, a brightly colored moving one and a stationary beige one (Hollich et al., 2000). An adult tried to teach the name of the beige one by looking at the object, touching it, repeating the name many times—but the infants showed no inclination to learn. They just were not interested, although they could have learned if they had wanted to. The experimenters knew this because they successfully and quickly taught 12-month-olds the names of other, more interesting objects.

The first words soon take on nuances of tone, loudness, and cadence that are precursors for the first grammar, in that a single word—called a **holophrase**—conveys a particular message in the way that it is spoken. You can imagine a meaningful sentence encapsulated in "Dada!" "Dada?" and "Dada." Each is a holophrase.

Although all new talkers say many names at first, soon cultural influences are apparent. For example, by 18 months, English-speaking infants learn more nouns than Chinese or Korean infants, who learn more verbs than children elsewhere. (The number of nouns is greater than the number of verbs in all three of these languages, but the proportions differ). One explanation is directly linguistic: Chinese and Korean are "verb-friendly" languages, in that adults use more verbs and place them at the beginnings or ends of sentences. In English, verbs take varied forms and positions, and they change in illogical ways (think of "go," "gone," "will go," "went"); they are thus harder for novice learners (Gentner & Boroditsky, 2001).

Another explanation considers the entire social context: Playing with toys and learning about objects are crucial in North American culture, whereas East Asian cultures emphasize human interactions. To figure out your own bias here, think about what you would do if a 1-year-old was fussing in her crib. Would you give her a toy, turn on a mobile, find a pacifier, offer a bottle, pick her up, rub her back, hum a lullaby, speak to her, or close the door? The first four are object-centered, the next four are interaction-centered, and the last one suggests that you are too tired to cope.

Within each culture, family and personality influences also affect the characteristic vocabulary of the infant. Some infants are called "referential," because they primarily learn words that refer to objects; others are "expressive," because they know more social words (such as *up, no, hi, please*) and use them to express their emotions and relationships. This distinction seems connected to the kinds of words the caregivers deem important (D'Odorico et al., 2001; K. Nelson, 1981).

Early Errors

When toddlers start learning language, they make certain mistakes (Clark, 2001). One common inaccuracy is **underextension**, applying a word too narrowly. For example, *cat* names only the family cat and no other feline. A toddler might learn one name and then resist learning any alternatives—insisting that the little fuzzy, yellow, winged thing is definitely not a "chick," as Grandpa keeps calling it, because it is a "bird" (Shatz, 1994). This is actually evidence of a general word-

Especially for Educators: An infant day-care center has a new child whose parents speak a language other than the one the teachers speak. Should the teachers learn basic words in the new language, or should they expect the baby to learn the majority language?

holophrase A single word that is used to express a complete, meaningful thought.

A Family in Nairobi This baby's intellectual development is well nourished.

? ***Observational Quiz*** (see answer, page 190): Can you spot four signs of this?

underextension The too-narrow application of a word, as when a toddler uses *cat* to refer only to the family cat and no other feline.

learning strategy that usually works quite well, called the *mutual exclusivity bias*. It means that each object has one, and only one, name (Merriman, 1998).

The opposite tendency also appears, with words being applied beyond their meaning. This **overextension** might lead a child to call two people *Mama*. It is easy to see why *Mama* would be overextended: Toddlers hear several people called *Mama*, hear their own mother called by another name, and know several people who act mother-ish. As another example, many toddlers can count—up to two or maybe three. Any quantity more than three is a big number and, in a wonderful overextension, is haphazardly called *four, forty,* or any other number word, all meaning "more than two" (Spelke & Tsivkin, 2001).

Difficulties are particularly likely to emerge if the concepts are cognitively unclear. For example, Korean has five single words for two English pairs: *put on* and *put in*. In both languages, young children sometimes overextend or underextend these words (Bowerman & Choi, 2001).

Early Grammar

Adults tend to notice misuses of vocabulary while failing to notice the toddler's linguistic progress. In fact, the dominant theme of language learning is not the mistakes of young learners but their overall speed and efficiency.

Toddlers seem to "experiment in order to see" with words, just as the little scientist that Piaget described (stages 5 and 6) experiments with objects. Little scientists become little linguists. It is not unusual for 18-month-olds to walk down the street pointing to every vehicle, asking "Car?" "Truck?" and even "Fire engine?" "Motorcycle?" Or, again and again, "Wha' dat?"—perhaps to confirm their hypothesis about which words go with which things, or perhaps simply because they enjoy conversation and "What's that?" keeps the talk coming.

Grammar includes all the methods that languages use to communicate meaning, apart from the words themselves. Word order, prefixes, suffixes, intonation, loudness, forms of verbs, pronouns and negations, prepositions and articles—all of these are aspects of grammar. Each language has its own rules, which is the reason it is difficult to learn a new language. Yet infants begin using grammar almost as soon as they begin to talk in holophrases.

Two-Word Sentences

Grammar is even more evident soon after the naming explosion, when toddlers start to put words together. As a general rule, the first two-word sentence occurs at about 21 months of age, with some normal infants achieving this milestone at 15 months and others not reaching it until 24 months.

Combining words demands considerable linguistic understanding because word order affects the meaning of a sentence. However, even in their first sentences, toddlers demonstrate that they have figured out the basics. They declare "Baby cry" or ask "More juice" rather than the reverse.

"Kitty Jumping Down"

Now that you know all the specific steps that lead up to the 2-year-olds' abilities, you can analyze the grammar in a personal account about my daughter Sarah, who, at 24 months, was determined to distract me from revising an earlier edition of this textbook. She said:

"Uh, oh. Kitty jumping down."
"What drawing? Numbers?" [said as her words were being transcribed]
"Want it, paper."
"Wipe it, pencil."
"What time it is?" [said about my watch]

overextension The application of a word beyond its true meaning, as when a child calls two or more people *Mama*.

grammar All the methods—word order, verb forms, and so on—that languages use to communicate meaning, apart from the words themselves.

Motherese Infants' verbal understanding advances well ahead of their abilities at verbal production. *Fishee* is probably one of dozens of words that this child readily recognizes even though he has yet to say them himself.

These sentences show that Sarah had a varied vocabulary and a basic understanding of word order. For example, Sarah said "Kitty jumping down" (noun, verb, adverb) rather than "Down jumping kitty" or any of the four other, less conventional possible combinations of these three words. Sarah's speech also shows that she had much to learn, for she incorrectly used the pronoun *it* and its referent together ("it, paper," "it, pencil"), omitted personal pronouns, and used declarative rather than inquisitive word order in asking a question ("What time it is?").

Beyond demonstrating specifics of English vocabulary and grammar, Sarah's words show something even more impressive. By the time she reached age 2, Sarah had learned the universal function of language—to express one's thoughts and wishes to another using accepted signals, codes, and cues. Despite my preoccupation and nonresponsiveness, Sarah produced seven successive sentences crafted to entice me into a dialogue. The final question—"What time it is?"—reveals considerable sophistication about the rules of polite conversation: Sarah must have noticed that I almost always answer that particular question, even when the person who asks it is a stranger on the street.

Theories of Language Learning

Worldwide, people who weigh less than 33 pounds (15 kilograms) and are not yet 2 years old can already speak one or sometimes two languages. They already recognize words and patterns by 8 months, and by age 2 they communicate quite well to their monolingual parents, who could not do nearly as well if they had to learn a completely new language in 2 years. If they are bilingual, they already show evidence of knowing which listeners understand which languages. The process of language learning continues throughout childhood, with some teenagers able to compose lyrics or deliver orations that move thousands of their co-linguists. How does this happen?

Answers to this question have come from three schools of thought, each with its own history, body of research, and committed scholars. One theory says that infants are directly taught; a second theory holds that infants naturally understand language; a third theory says that social impulses propel infants to communicate. Each of these theories has implications for caregivers and early childhood educators, all of whom want their young charges to speak fluently and well, but none of whom want to waste their time teaching something that a 1-year-old cannot learn or would learn just as well without any instruction. As you will see, the first of the three perspectives on early language mastery originated in behaviorism, the second is epigenetic, and the third relates to sociocultural theory.

Theory One: Infants Are Taught

The seeds of the first perspective were planted more than 50 years ago, when the dominant theory in North American psychology was behaviorism, or learning theory. The essential idea was that all learning is acquired, step by step, through associations and reinforcements. In language learning, B. F. Skinner (1957) noticed that spontaneous babbling at 6 to 8 months is usually reinforced. Typically, every time the baby says "ma-ma-ma-ma," a grinning mother appears, repeating the sound as well as showering the baby with attention, praise, and perhaps food. These affordances of mothers are exactly what the infant wants. Obviously, the baby will make those sounds again to get the same rewards.

An early criticism of this theory of early language reinforcement held that most parents are very poor teachers, and thus parents could not generate the amazing language learning that infants display. But later research found that this criticism underestimated parents. Most parents are excellent intuitive instructors. For instance, parents who talk to their young infants typically name each object: "Here is your *bottle,*" "There is your *foot,*" "You want your *juice*?" and so on, often touching and moving the named object at the same time as they speak the target word loudly, clearly, and slowly (Gogate et al., 2000). They also use baby talk, capturing the baby's interest with higher pitch, shorter sentences, elongated words, stressed nouns, and simpler grammar.

All these features help infants associate words with things. Just as Pavlov's dogs learned to associate the sound of a bell with the smell of the food (see Chapter 2), infants associate objects with names they have heard often, and that is how they learn their first words (L. Smith, 1995). The current applications of this theory are more nuanced than the original form, but the core ideas are the same: Parents are the first teachers, frequent repetition is instructive, and well-taught infants become well-spoken children, perpetuating the accents, gestures, and phrases (grammatically correct or not) of their first role models.

Research Support for Theory One

Support for the view that children must be taught language begins with an undeniable fact: Wide variations are apparent in language fluency, especially when children from various cultures are compared. Some 3-year-olds converse in elaborate sentences; others just barely put one simple word together with another. In all cultures, parents of the most verbal children teach language throughout infancy, singing, explaining, listening, and responding; parents of the least verbal children rarely talk to their babies and don't even realize that their children's language delays are connected to parental practices (Law, 2000).

The importance of parental input has been confirmed by thousands of studies. One recent one (Tamis-LeMonda et al., 2001) is notable for its longitudinal design and detailed charts, although its conclusions are not surprising. The subjects were 40 mother–infant pairs from intact, middle-class, English-speaking, European-American families. The mothers (and the fathers) had all attended some college; most had college degrees. This sample obviously excluded many families with different structures or backgrounds. However, the exclusion was deliberate in order to rule out factors such as poverty, single parenthood, low SES (see Chapter 1), and ethnicity as the cause of any differences.

Periodically the researchers checked each infant's language progress, noting particularly the age at which he or she reached each of five steps in language acquisition: imitation, first spoken word, first 50 words, first two-word sentence, and talking about the past (which requires use of basic grammar). When the infants were 9 months old, and again at 13 months, each mother–infant pair played for 10 minutes in a well-equipped playroom, where their every sound and movement was videotaped. Later, several researchers analyzed each tape, frame by frame. Among the specifics tallied were how often the mothers responded to their infants. The responses were sorted into six categories:

1. Affirmation (e.g., "Yes," "That's right," "Good job")
2. Imitation of vocalization (e.g., saying "ball" after the child says "ball")
3. Description (e.g., "That's a spoon you are holding.")
4. Question (e.g., "What is that?")
5. Play prompt (e.g., "Why don't you feed the doll?")
6. Exploration prompt (e.g., "What else can we do?")

Cultural Values If his infancy is like that of most babies raised in the relatively taciturn Ottavado culture of Ecuador, this 2-month-old will hear significantly less conversation than infants from most other regions of the world. According to many learning theorists, a lack of reinforcement will result in a child who is insufficiently verbal, and in most Western cultures that might be called educational neglect. However, each culture tends to encourage the qualities it most needs and values, and verbal fluency is not a priority in this community. In fact, people who talk too much are ostracized, and those who keep secrets are valued, so encouragement of language may itself be maltreatment here.

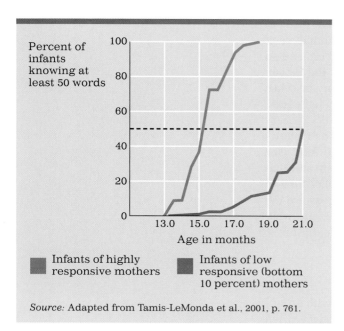

Percent of infants knowing at least 50 words

Age in months

■ Infants of highly responsive mothers

■ Infants of low responsive (bottom 10 percent) mothers

Source: Adapted from Tamis-LeMonda et al., 2001, p. 761.

FIGURE 6.2 Maternal Responsiveness and Infants' Language Acquisition Learning the first 50 words is a milestone in early language acquisition, as it predicts the arrival of the naming explosion and the multiword sentence a few weeks later. Researchers found that half the infants of highly responsive mothers (top 10 percent) reached this milestone as early as 15 months of age, and the other half reached it by 17 months. The infants of nonresponsive mothers (bottom 10 percent) lagged significantly behind.

language acquisition device (LAD) Chomsky's term for a hypothesized brain structure responsible for the innate human ability to learn language, including the basic aspects of grammar.

Although all the mothers had similar ethnic and economic backgrounds, their responses in all six categories varied tremendously. For example, one mother never responded by imitating her child's vocalization; another mother imitated 21 times in 10 minutes. Overall, mothers were more likely to respond with descriptions (category 3) than anything else, partly because most young infants said very few words. This meant that the mothers had few opportunities to react to what the infant said but many opportunities to talk about what the infant was doing. Again, the range was vast: One mother used description only 4 times in 10 minutes; another used it 33 times.

The frequency of maternal responsiveness predicted the rate of language acquisition many months later, as Figure 6.2 dramatically illustrates. All of the 13-month-old infants whose mothers were in the top 10 percent of responding reached the 50-word stage by 17 months. By contrast, at 21 months, only half of those infants whose mothers were in the lowest 10 percent had 50-word vocabularies.

An astute critic might notice that these tallies are *responses* and point out that in order for a mother to respond, her infant must act. The assumption is that the mothers' behavior caused the infants' language, not vice versa; but in order for a mother to respond, her baby must do something that can be responded to. Could it be that some babies did very little, thus causing both low maternal responses and their own delayed language learning? Remember that correlation does not prove causation: Perhaps, instead of unresponsive mothers, this research measured unresponsive 9-month-olds who were slow to learn language because of their nature, not their nurture. (If you asked this question, congratulations! This is exactly the kind of issue that astute developmentalists raise because they do not want to blame parents unfairly for patterns that are initiated and sustained by their children.)

To test this possibility, the researchers examined the longitudinal data carefully. They found that early maternal response was much more predictive of later language development than was infant action or inaction at 9 or 13 months. Even if their infants were relatively quiet, some mothers were quite verbal, suggesting play activities, describing things, and asking questions. Nonverbal infants with that kind of mother usually became talkative later on. According to this behaviorist viewpoint, adults teach language, and then infants learn it. This theory holds that the main linguistic difference between one child and another comes from their caregivers, not their genes. Before you conclude that parental teaching is key, however, consider the second viewpoint.

Theory Two: Infants Teach Themselves

The seeds of the second perspective were planted soon after Skinner first proposed his theory of verbal learning. Noam Chomsky (1968, 1980) and his followers believe that language is too complex to be mastered so early and so easily through step-by-step conditioning. Chomsky noted that all young children worldwide learn the rudiments of grammar and that they all do so at approximately the same age. This, he said, implies that the human brain is uniquely equipped with some sort of structure or organization that facilitates language development. This structure would have been produced by centuries of evolution that made it adaptive for humans to use words to communicate with each other.

Somewhat boldly, Chomsky labeled this theoretical facilitator the **language acquisition device,** or **LAD.** The LAD enables children to quickly and effectively derive the rules of grammar from the speech they hear every day, regardless of whether their native language is English, Thai, or Urdu. Other theorists have proposed the existence of other innate structures to facilitate other features of language learning (Pinker, 1994).

No reputable researcher argues that language emerges *automatically,* because they all know that development is epigenetic—that is, it depends on the interaction between genes and many other factors. A more thoughtful version of this idea is that infants are active and thinking beings (as we have seen time and time again), which makes them quite ready to use their minds to understand and speak whatever language is offered (Gopnik, 2001). Further, the various languages of the world, as different as they are, are all logical, coherent, and systematic. Infants, who are also logical, are primed to grasp the particular language they are exposed to, making language "not a 'trigger' but a 'nutrient'" (Slobin, 2001, p. 438).

Another way to express this idea is to say that language is *experience-expectant* (see Chapter 5). Words are "expected" by the developing brain, which quickly and efficiently connects neurons and synapses to support whichever of the thousands of possible languages the infant hears. The differences between one language and another seems enormous only because we tend to be oblivious to the similarities: All languages have names for people, objects, actions, and adjectives; all languages ask questions using the same basic scaffold; all languages use add-ons of some sort to indicate tense and other aspects of grammar. This is the *deep structure* of language, imbedded in LAD. The *surface structure,* consisting of pronunciation and vocabulary, are *experience-dependent;* but language itself is not.

Research Support for Theory Two

Research supports this perspective as well. In fact, think about everything you have learned so far in this chapter. Babies are eager learners—of categories and concepts, of motor skills and sensory affordances. Further, the infant brain is closely attuned to human speech. Long before infants start talking, their brains attend to speech sounds and their minds develop categories, to be expressed in words later, once the surface structure of their particular language is deciphered.

In the first weeks of life, long before they talk, infants already adapt their reflexes to respond differently to their own caregivers and to strangers. Remember that they laugh at their own mothers, but not at strangers; and they babble a *mama* sound (not yet referring to mother) at less than 6 months (Goldman, 2001). No wonder they say "mama" and "dada" as soon as their brains are sufficiently mature and their tongue and lips are under enough control to coordinate thought and speech. No reinforcement or teaching is needed; all they need is for dendrites to grow, mouth muscles to strengthen, and synapses to connect during the transient exuberance. Many researchers believe that genetic programming endows babies with intellectual strategies and linguistic constraints that make it easy for them to construct language when the time comes (Markman, 1989; Pinker, 1994).

As you have learned, early categorization seems to be part of the human experience, and the development of language follows those ideas. One researcher, Jonas Langer (2001), explains that, in infancy, "developing cognition provides the foundational grammatical abilities" (p. 38); in other words, thought leads to both grammar and vocabulary. Current evidence for this theory comes from a surprising source: children who cannot hear or see. As you remember, deaf infants babble and then learn sign language according to the same sequence and timing, with activation in the same part of the brain, as hearing children learn spoken language (Schirmer, 2000). Moreover, blind babies spontaneously use gestures, although they have never seen them used (Iverson et al., 2000). For these infants, at least, language comes from within, not from parental example and reinforcement.

In another study that suggests that infants teach themselves (Akhtar et al., 2001), toddlers age 23 to 27 months were brought into a playroom, where they first played with familiar toys. Then they saw four buckets, each containing an unseen, unfamiliar object (such as a wallpaper roller). There were two versions of this experiment. In both versions, three of the objects were unnamed ("I'm going to show you what's in here") and one object was called a *toma* ("I'm going to show you the toma"). The made-up word *toma* was chosen because the children had never heard it, but it was fairly easy for them to remember.

In the first version of the experiment, the experimenter brought each object out of a bucket, demonstrated it to the child, and allowed the child to play with it before replacing it in its bucket. In the second version, the child was asked to wait for a turn, and the experimenter showed the same four objects to another person, who was allowed to play with them before returning them to the bucket. During this version, the child sat off to one side, neither looked at nor spoken to by the experimenter, but merely overhearing what was said.

In the final step for both versions, the experimenter displayed all four novel objects in front of each child and asked, "Can you give me the toma?" Care was taken not to clue the child—the experimenter didn't look at the toma, or place it in a preferred position. Children generally selected the correct object. Indeed, every child who had been directly taught (version one) selected the "toma," showing that they all had learned its name in this brief process. More impressive was the finding that even when children merely overheard (version two)—never touching or playing with the "toma" or realizing that the word would later be important—75 percent successfully selected it. The experimenters also tested two groups of children 6 months older; all these 2½-year-olds successfully learned merely from overhearing. According to the experimenters:

> That children learn words through overhearing calls into question the view that language learning requires joint attention between child and adult. . . . Many parents reported that their children knew many more words than they had been explicitly taught (including some that parents would prefer their children had not learned!). We do not expect the findings of this study to come as a surprise to most parents of young children, nor is it expected these findings will surprise researchers studying cultural differences in language socialization.

> *[Akhtar et al., 2001, pp. 427, 428]*

The people who might be most surprised would be the strong advocates of the first perspective, which holds that babies must be taught directly. Advocates of the second perspective believe that infants learn well enough without such instruction. According to this perspective, communication, not verbosity, is the heart of human relationships, and that is what all humans share. To deny that is to ignore the unity of the human race.

Theory Three: Social Impulses Foster Infant Language

The third theory is called *social-pragmatic,* because it perceives the crucial starting point to be neither vocabulary nor the thought–language connection but the pragmatic (practical) reason for language: communication. According to this perspective, infants communicate in every way they can because humans are social beings, dependent on each other for survival and happiness.

Even when they cannot do anything but look and listen, newborns look searchingly at human faces and listen intently to human voices. Before 1 year, infants vocalize, babble, gesture, listen to vocalization, and point—with an outstretched little index finger that is soon accompanied by a very sophisticated glance to see if the other person is looking in the right spot. These and many other examples show how humans are compelled to be social from the very start.

That compulsion, not explicit teaching or brain maturation (the first two perspectives), makes infants learn language, "as part of the package of being a human social animal" (Hollich et al., 2000). They seek to understand what others want and intend, and therefore "children acquire linguistic symbols as a kind of by-product of social action with adults" (Tomasello, 2001).

Research Support for Theory Three

If a 1-year-old is focusing intently on playing with an unnamed new toy, and an adult utters a word that might be that toy's name, would the child learn that word as the name of the mystery toy? From a purely behaviorist, learning-by-association perspective, the answer might seem to be "yes," but the actual answer is "no." Toddlers in such a situation interrupt their activity, look up, analyze the direction of the adult's gaze, figure out what object the adult was looking at when the word was said, and then assign the new word to that object, not to the fascinating toy in front of them (Baldwin, 1993). This suggests that infants are socially focused more than self-focused and that they consider language a useful social tool more than an abstract system for labeling objects.

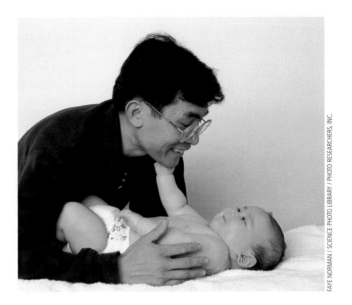

Not Talking? No words yet, but this infant communicates well with Dad, using eyes, mouth, and hands. What are they telling each other?

Indeed, the research studies cited to support the first and second perspectives can also be used to support this third, social-pragmatic, perspective. Perhaps the reason mothers had a powerful impact on language learning (Tamis-LeMonda et al., 2001) is not that mothers can be skilled teachers, but rather that their infants want to learn whatever they think their mothers want them to learn. Thus, if a mother repeats words and utters new ones, so will her toddler; if a mother says little, so will her toddler.

The impressive ability of toddlers to learn by overhearing, described above (Akhtar et al., 2001), may demonstrate the power of social interest, which motivated the toddler's attention whether or not the toddler personally handled the "toma." Remember that the experimenter showed the toy to another person while the toddler looked on; the social interaction may have captured the child's attention and thereby taught the word.

With the social-pragmatic perspective in mind, consider a dialogue between one toddler and his mother at bedtime:

> **Mother:** And when you get up in the morning, you'll go for a walk.
> **Nigel:** Tik.
> **Mother:** And you'll see some sticks, yes.
> **Nigel:** Hoo.
> **Mother:** And some holes, yes.
> **Nigel:** Da.
> **Mother:** Yes, now it's getting dark.
> **Nigel:** I wa. *(Repeats this 12 times.)*
> **Mother:** What?
> **Nigel:** I wa. *(Repeats this 6 times.)* Peaz.
> **Mother:** What do you want in bed? Jamie? (his doll)
> **Nigel:** No!
> **Mother:** You want your eiderdown? (his quilt)
> **Nigel:** *(Grins.)* Yeah!
> **Mother:** Why didn't you say so? Your eiderdown.
> **Nigel:** Ella. *(Repeats 2 times.)*
>
> *[Halliday, 1979]*

Note that Nigel repeated the phrase "I wa" an amazing 18 times, all in an attempt to get his message across. He believed that his mother would respond, so he did not quit until he communicated, even adding a social nicety ("peaz") in case politeness was required for this particular social interaction. The word *eiderdown* was not one he had been taught, nor did it fit into a concept or category. It was a social request, part of a longer conversation about a previous social interaction, and thus quite pragmatic. This dialogue may be more typical of early language learners than any of the laboratory experiments that underpin the other two theories.

A Hybrid Theory

Which of these three perspectives is correct? Social scientists, including developmental psychologists, linguists, and neuroscientists, are dedicated to scientific evidence, even if it contradicts their hypotheses. In fact, the original theories of both Skinner and Chomsky have been refuted and rejected by research, which is why the current versions as explained here are less rigid than their original versions (Markman, 1989; Plunkett, 1997). Research can be found to support each of these current perspectives, and research is open to interpretation, almost never directly proving anything. This does not make research useless; it is far better than the raw opinions that almost everyone holds based on their own memories or their own philosophy. But many studies must all lead in the same direction before firm conclusions can be drawn. We are not there yet with early language learning. However, many scientists seek to reconcile all the research, acknowledging the merit of each (e.g., Bowerman & Levinson, 2001; Boysson-Bardies, 1999; Gelman & Williams, 1998; K. Nelson, 1996).

One recent attempt at integration was published in a monograph written by three scholars, based on twelve experiments designed by eight researchers (Hollich et al., 2000). The authors developed a hybrid (which literally means a new creature, formed by combining two other living things) of previous theories. They called their model an *emergentist coalition,* since it combines valid aspects of several theories.

Given that children learn language to do numerous things—indicate intention, call objects by name, put words together, talk to their family, sing to themselves, express their wishes, remember the past, and much more—it seems to these researchers that some aspects of language are best learned in one way at one age, others in another way at another age. Further, just as neuroscientists have recently discovered that memories arise from many parts of the brain and that each memory is retrieved under different conditions, language may also be learned and expressed by many parts of the brain. In fact, fMRI research finds that the cortex contains not one language center, but many. Similarly, decades of cross-cultural studies have found that cultures vary tremendously in language acquisition practices. Obviously, not every community functions linguistically in the same way. Not every infant follows an identical pattern, nor does every parent teach the same way.

A broad developmental perspective suggests that language develops in many ways for many reasons. As with newborn bonding, with motor skills, with reflexes and senses, and with experience-expectant brain growth of all kinds, some aspects of human development are too vital to rely on only one pathway toward achievement. Since communication is crucial for humans, nature provides many paths toward that goal. Each path may be preferred, or may be more efficient, in some stages, cultures, and families, but every child (except those who are severely brain-damaged) must learn language. That is how humans are designed.

This returns the child, not the developmental theorist, to center stage. As one expert concludes:

Lots of Communication Mother–toddler conversations that are rich with facial expressions, gestures, and the dramatic intonation of an occasional word are universal, as is illustrated by this winning pair in a Mexican market.

HAZEL HANKIN / STOCK, BOSTON

Word learning theories will have to come to terms with the fact that children in the typical, everyday word learning scenario are more than perceivers, receivers, or possessors of external supports. Instead, the word learning child is a child with feelings and thoughts about other persons, a child engaged in dynamic real-life events, a child learning to think about a world of changing physical and psychological relationships—in short, a child poised to act, to influence, to gain control, a child reaching out to embrace the learning of language for the power of expression it provides.

[Bloom, 2000, p. 133]

A Note for Caregivers

What does this controversy about early language mean for caregivers? Ideally, all three paths just described converge, and all are used for each baby's onward progress. The infant is deliberately taught and encouraged, the brain and curiosity are nourished and supported, and the social drive of the young human is appreciated and even celebrated. It also means that, if a 1-year-old is not progressing in language, something may be seriously wrong.

Remember 17-month-old Toni, whom you met in Chapter 5? She had an expressive vocabulary of only 5 words, and she fell asleep in front of the TV each night (see Table 5.1 on page 138). Five words are about average at 13 months, but many infants Toni's age already speak 50 words. Further, the best language teacher is an adult who knows the child's imperfect noises well, interpreting and repeating the words responsively; this makes television a poor teacher, especially during infancy (Barr & Hayne, 1999).

As applied to Toni, the emergentist-coalition model would notice problems with Toni's situation from all three theoretical perspectives. Toni's delayed language may be caused by a combination of (1) inadequate teaching from her patchwork of caregivers (behaviorist); (2) problematic conceptual development, perhaps related to poor nutrition or disorganized, erratic experiences (epigenetic); and (3) social discouragement and perhaps depression caused by her mother's sudden return to work and inadequate substitute care (social-pragmatic). The medical practitioners who reported on Toni's situation were rightly concerned about her eating and daily routines, and they assigned a community health worker to help Toni's mother improve her overall care. Given what we know about early infant cognition and brain development, her delayed speech may be more worrisome than her percentile decline in weight.

Worrisome, yes; cause for panic, no. Remember that the sociocultural perspective suggests that no particular norm is universal; everything must be considered in context. The language delay indicates that it is time to check Toni's hearing and to pay attention to other aspects of communication. The written report does not mention whether she uses gestures or whether her mother provides encouraging touch and facial expressions. This information is crucial. If Toni and her mother communicate well and relate to each other with evident fondness, then Toni may be fine, on the verge of her language explosion. Given the adaptability and plasticity of humans, some normal children do not talk very much until age 2, and then they catch up with their peers.

All the research and norms presented in this chapter alert caregivers to the intellectual importance of these first 2 years. If the next generation is to become bright, verbal, high achievers in a society that values knowledge (where respect and wealth are accorded to the inventor of technology, the computer whiz, the rocket scientist, the brain surgeon), then providing infants with objects, words, and social play may be essential. Or maybe not. But given the joy that Laurent Piaget expressed as he pulled the string, and the persistence of Sarah in getting me to talk, and the pleasure that all infants display when their efforts lead to discovery, accomplishment, and social responses, there is surely no harm in providing opportunities for learning from the very start. The next chapter, on psychosocial development, continues our examination of the caregivers' role in infant development.

SUMMARY

Sensorimotor Intelligence

1. Through careful observation of his own three children, Piaget realized that very young infants are active learners, seeking to understand their complex observations and experiences. Infant cognition is characterized by sensorimotor intelligence, the first of Piaget's four stages of cognitive development.

2. At every stage of intelligence, people adapt their thoughts to the experiences they have. This continual process of assimilation and accommodation is evident even in the first acquired adaptations, from about 1 to 4 months, as the sucking reflexes accommodate the particular nipples and other objects that the baby learns to suck.

3. Sensorimotor intelligence develops in six stages, beginning with reflexes and ending with the toddler's active exploration of the world. A pair of stages occurs in each of three circular reactions, or feedback loops, in which the infant takes in experiences and tries to make sense of them. Primary circular reactions involve the infant's own body; secondary circular reactions involve other people and objects; and tertiary circular reactions involve active exploration and experimentation.

4. Object permanence is a key concept in sensorimotor intelligence. Infants gradually develop this concept over the first 2 years of life. In Piaget's classic experiment, infants begin to search for hidden objects at about 8 months, although they have some dawning realization of object permanence months before that.

Information Processing

5. Another approach to understanding infant cognition is information-processing theory, which looks at each step of the thinking process, from input to output. This method is useful because infants sometimes seem to understand more than they can demonstrate through their actions.

6. The perceptions of a young infant are attuned to the particular affordances or opportunities for action, that are present in the infant's world. For example, infants learn that some objects afford grasping and that some people (especially their mothers) afford happy interactions.

7. Objects that move are particularly interesting to infants, both as early affordances and as objects that can be understood when the baby develops general categories, such as "big" and "small," "above" and "below." The early development of concepts and cat-

egories in the infant's thinking, even before the first words are uttered, is an example of the impressive cognitive development of the young child.

8. Infant memory is fragile, but not completely absent, as Freud thought when he described infantile amnesia. Reminder sessions help trigger memories. Implicit, unspoken memories are easier to recall than explicit memories, which are typically connected to words and are remembered without reminders.

Language: What Develops in Two Years?

9. Communication is apparent throughout the first year. Even very young infants pay special attention to voices and facial expressions, and they use their own early noises to communicate. Caregivers who use baby talk facilitate this learning.

10. Infants babble at about 6 months and speak their first words at about 1 year. Vocabulary builds very slowly at first until about 18 months, when a naming explosion begins.

11. The first evidence of grammar is apparent in the holophrase, one word that expresses an entire thought. Toward the end of the first year, toddlers begin putting two words together, showing by their word order that they understand the rudiments of grammar.

12. Toddlers make interesting mistakes in their early language, including overextension and underextension, using words to mean more than, or less than, they actually mean in the particular language the toddler speaks. In all phases of language development, children reflect their culture and their caregivers' speech.

Theories of Language Learning

13. Many theories of language development attempt to explain how infants learn as much as they do. The three main theories emphasize difference aspects of early language learning: that infants must be taught, that their brains are genetically attuned to language, and that their social impulses foster language learning.

14. Each of these theories seems partly true. The challenge for developmental scientists is to formulate a hybrid theory that uses all the insights and research on early language learning. The challenge for caregivers is to respond appropriately to the infant's early attempts to communicate, providing a rich and comprehensible language experience at the proper level for learning.

KEY TERMS

sensorimotor intelligence (p. 168)

primary circular reactions (p. 168)

adaptation (p. 168)

assimilation (p. 168)

accommodation (p. 169)

secondary circular reactions (p. 170)

goal-directed behavior (p. 171)

object permanence (p. 171)

tertiary circular reactions (p. 174)

"little scientist" (p. 174)

mental combinations (p. 174)

deferred imitation (p. 174)

habituation (p. 175)

fMRI (p. 175)

information-processing theory (p. 176)

affordance (p. 177)

graspability (p. 178)

visual cliff (p. 178)

dynamic perception (p. 179)

infantile amnesia (p. 182)

reminder session (p. 182)

implicit memory (p. 184)

explicit memory (p. 184)

baby talk (p. 185)

babbling (p. 187)

naming explosion (p. 187)

holophrase (p. 188)

underextension (p. 188)

overextension (p. 189)

grammar (p. 189)

language acquisition device (LAD) (p. 192)

KEY QUESTIONS

1. Why did Piaget call the first period of intelligence "sensorimotor"?

2. How does the way a baby eats change as the baby moves through the first four stages of sensorimotor intelligence?

3. Can you think of an idea you used to believe that you have changed your opinion about because you have adapted to new experiences or information?

4. What are the affordances of most North American 6-month-olds?

5. In what ways was Piaget mistaken about infant development?

6. If there are certain early memories you want a baby to retain, what would you do?

7. What is the difference between a category and a concept? How are these ideas related?

8. Can you think of a concept you believe that you did not really understand well until you knew the word to describe it?

9. What evidence is there that toddlers use grammar?

10. Why might one 2-year-old's vocabulary be four times as large as another's?

11. What cultural differences are there in early language learning?

12. What would happen if parents never talked baby-talked to their baby?

Chapter Seven

The First 2 Years: Psychosocial Development

Psychosocial development, by definition, involves the combination of two elements: the *psyche* (from the Greek word meaning "soul, spirit, feelings") and the *social context* (family, community, culture). This chapter is about that combination: the interaction between an infant's emotions, temperament, and personality, on the one hand, and the entire social world, including mother, father, other caregivers, and society as a whole, on the other. There are many ways in which such an interaction can go well—a "goodness of fit" that allows the baby's temperament and the surrounding social world to come together to support ongoing development. With some adjustments by both partners, this fit usually occurs. We focus first on the infant's contribution to this partnership and then on the caregiving context. Throughout, we note the varieties of interaction, from the infant's secure attachment (whether to mother, father, day-care provider) to development that is detached, disorganized, disturbed, destructive. As we will see, theories lead to practice: What can be done to ensure that every infant achieves that goodness of fit.

Emotional Development in Infancy

In many ways, expressions of emotion become the vital code that enables one person to connect with another, the window that allows outsiders to look into a person's thoughts and allows the person inside to look outward. As the infant becomes older, both processes are at work: The infant's emotions become easier for others to read, just as the infant becomes better able to read the emotional expressions of others.

The diversity of family circumstances and of inborn traits means that some infants develop much more smoothly than others. Of necessity, this chapter describes the typical course of development, but we must not forget the many other psychosocial paths that infants and caregivers take. To help us keep this point in mind, we begin and end the chapter with two cases—Toni (whom we first met in Chapter 5) and Jacob.

A Case to Study

Jacob's Parents on Autopilot

Here is a father's description of his third child, Jacob:

> We were convinced that we were set. We had surpassed our quota of 2.6 children and were ready to engage parental auto-pilot. I had just begun a prestigious job and was working 10–11 hours a day. The children would be fine. We hired a nanny to watch Jacob during the day.
>
> As each of Jacob's early milestones passed we felt that we had taken another step toward our goal of having three normal children. We were on our way to the perfect American family. Yet, somewhere back in our minds we had some doubts. Jacob seemed different than the girls. He had some unusual attributes. There were times when we would be holding him and he would arch his back and scream so loud that it was painful for us.
>
> *[Jacob's father, 1997]*

Jacob was unable to relate to his parents (or to anyone else) for the first two years of his life, although his parents paid little attention to the problem. They already had two daughters; if they noticed that something was odd, they told themselves "boys are different" and blamed Jacob's inability to talk on a nanny who did not speak English well. His father continues:

> Jacob had become increasingly isolated [by age 2]. I'm not a psychologist, but I believe that he just stopped trying. It was too hard, perhaps too scary. He couldn't figure out what was expected of him. The world had become too confusing, and so he withdrew from it. He would seek out the comfort of quiet, dark places and sit by himself. He would lose himself in the bright, colorful images of cartoons and animated movies.

Jacob was finally diagnosed with a "pervasive development disorder" at age 3. This is a catchall diagnosis that can include autistic reactions (discussed in detail in Chapter 11). At the moment you need to know only that the psychosocial possibilities for Jacob and his parents were unappreciated at this point. First, his despairing parents were advised to consider residential placement, because he would never be normal and they, at least, would no longer be constantly reminded of their "failure." (This recommendation ignored the commitment that most parents feel toward their children.) Second, Jacob's father reports satisfaction that his son successfully passed the "milestones" described in earlier chapters—he gained weight, sat up, walked, played with objects, all on schedule. (Again, a crucial point is ignored: These milestones are connected to biosocial growth, not psychosocial development.) Thus, Jacob's early social problems were overlooked, even though some evidence—such as his reaction to being held and his failure to talk—should have raised the alarm. Other telltale data—smiling, social play, imitation—are not even reported, but should have been.

Toni's situation is another example of the inappropriate focus on biosocial rather than psychosocial difficulties. The case manager's report on Toni does mention some worrisome social factors—the mother went back to work when Toni was about 1 year old, Toni's father is "not in the household," many relatives provide "patchwork care," the mother does not trust strangers to care for Toni—but these are not properly evaluated. For example, if proper evaluation reports that the father is financially supportive and actively involved in her care, it does not matter where he lives; but all we are told is that he does not live in the household. In this chapter we focus on that missing piece: the elements that an infant's emotional and social world should contain for optimal development.

Age Norms

To some extent, early emotional development follows age-graded norms, which are related to physical and cognitive development. For instance, in the first year, before infants walk and talk, they have a smaller range of emotions than in the second year, when more mobility coincides with more emotion. Let us look at the usual sequence of emotional development (which is summarized in Table 7.1).

The First Year

Newborns seem to have only two identifiable emotions: distress and contentment. They cry when they are hungry or in pain, when they are tired or fright-

Stranger Wariness Becomes Santa Terror
For toddlers, even a friendly stranger is cause for alarm, especially if Mom's protective arms are withdrawn. Ironically, the most frightening strangers are men who are unusually dressed and who act as if they might take the child away. Santa Claus remains terrifying until children are about 3 years old.

ened (as of a loud noise or a sudden loss of support), and sometimes for no apparent reason. Reflexive fear appears when a newborn is startled, but this does not seem to be an emotional reaction, in that it is not a conscious response to a perception. They look happy and relaxed when they are recently fed and drifting off to sleep.

After the first few weeks, recognizable emotions become obvious. Curiosity, or at least interest, is shown when infants stare at something new, or hear an interesting voice, or watch a mobile. Interest in people becomes pleasure, evidenced first by the social smile at about 6 weeks and then, at 3 or 4 months, by laughter when a caregiver makes faces and noises that offer the right combination of familiarity and novelty. Full smiles, with open mouth and raised cheeks, are almost never seen at 2 months, but are easy for mothers to elicit at 5 months (Messinger et al., 1999). As we saw in Chapter 6, for 4-month-olds even a video of their happy mothers brings a wide grin (Kahana-Kalman & Walker-Andrews, 2001).

Anger emerges a little later, because anger is usually triggered by frustration, and frustration arises when someone or something prevents individuals from doing something they expect to do. Thus, a certain maturation of motor skills and conscious awareness is a prerequisite for anger. At about 4 months, infants show anger when their hands are held down and an interesting object is put in front of them—they want to reach for it but cannot. Anger becomes increasingly powerful and targeted once babies understand more about the who, what, and why of frustration. Thus the 8-month-old's anger when Daddy puts away the magazine with colorful photos that the infant tried to see is not nearly as strong as when an older sister dangles a favorite toy just out of reach.

Fully formed fear emerges at about 9 months. Then it builds rapidly, becoming more frequent as well as more apparent to an onlooker, and is most clearly expressed in two ways: stranger wariness and separation anxiety:

▪ **Stranger wariness** is evident when an infant no longer smiles at any friendly face and cries if an unfamiliar person moves too close, too quickly. This fear of strangers can be seen fleetingly at 6 months and is full-blown by 10 to 14 months.
▪ **Separation anxiety** is typically expressed in tears or anger when a beloved caregiver leaves, even for just a few minutes. The peak time for this fear of abandonment is 9 to 14 months.

The strength of many of these emotions depends on the social experiences of the infant, particularly on how responsive the parent is, as we will soon see in the

TABLE 7.1
Ages When Emotions Emerge

Age	Emotional Expression
Birth	Crying Contentment
6 weeks	Social smile
3 months	Laughter Curiosity
4 months	Full, responsive smiles Anger
9–14 months	Fear of social events (strangers, separation from caregiver)
18 months	Pride Shame Embarrassment

stranger wariness Fear of unfamiliar people, exhibited fleetingly at 6 months and at full force by 10 to 14 months.

separation anxiety Fear of abandonment, exhibited at the departure of a beloved caregiver; usually strongest at 9 to 14 months.

discussion of social referencing. Temperamental differences, discussed below, are also apparent. But by the end of the first year, every normal child expresses joy, distress, interest, fear, and anger.

The Second Year

Throughout the second year and beyond, anger and fear typically decrease and become more targeted toward things that are really infuriating or terrifying. Although decreasing frequency and more focused expression of fear and anger are the most common pattern from about 18 months on, for some toddlers these emotions spread and increase rather than decrease. Similarly, both laughing and crying tend to be more discriminating, so that the experiences that once reliably triggered shrieks of joy or pain no longer do so. For example, toddlers tumble often as they begin to run, but between falling down and reacting, 1-year-olds seem to pause to decide whether the fall was fun or hurtful. Then, and only then, do they burst into tears or laughter.

New emotions typically appear toward the end of the second year: pride, shame, embarrassment, and even guilt. Because these emotions require an awareness of what other people might be thinking, they emerge from the social context. In fact, throughout the first two years, the social context elicits, guides, and identifies the various emotions of the child, so that a 2-year-old not only experiences and expresses a wide range of emotions but also knows which emotions are welcomed and which ones are discouraged by the particular family and culture (Rothbart & Bates, 1998). For example, anger is almost never expressed in some families ("Don't you dare raise your voice to me"), but in other families anger is a common reaction, even to minor transgressions. All emotions, particularly pride and shame, show some cultural as well as familial variation (Eid & Diener, 2001).

Temperament

As you have just seen, the emotions of the first two years follow a timetable set by the maturation of genetic impulses; yet the social context also has an effect. The interaction between nature and nurture is evident in reactions that seem, at first, to be powerfully genetic: the aspects of personality called temperament.

Temperament is defined as "constitutionally based individual differences in emotional, motor, and attentional reactivity and self-regulation" (Rothbart & Bates, 1998, p. 109). Thus, temperament is primarily genetic and biological, and it emphasizes those behaviors that make each person somewhat different from all others. As an example of temperamental tendencies, we might note that one person is a *cautious* individual whereas another is a *risk taker*, or, in terms introduced in Chapter 3, one person is *inhibited* and the other is *uninhibited*.

Temperament is epigenetic, not merely genetic: It begins in the multitude of genetic instructions that guide the development of the brain and then is affected by the prenatal environment, especially the nutrition and health of the mother, and probably by postnatal experiences as well. As the person develops, the social context and the individual's experiences continue to influence the nature and expression of temperament. All these influences interact with the biological tendencies of the child (Dawson et al., 2000).

Current research confirms that infants are born with definite, distinct temperaments and that these are genetic in origin and affect later personality. However, researchers also stress that early temperamental traits can change; there is much more stability, from year to year, in temperament after age 2 than before it (Lemery et al., 1999). Further, in adulthood, almost any basic trait may take either a benign or a destructive turn. The cautious person may become either stable and trustworthy or fearful and stagnant; the risk taker may become either innovative and brave or erratic and foolhardy.

temperament According to Rothbart and Bates (1998), "constitutionally based individual differences in emotion, motor, and attentional reactivity and self-regulation."

Thinking Like a Scientist

Measuring Temperament

Although no one doubts that infants have inborn traits, measuring how those traits have shaped them has proven difficult. Many attempts to quantify temperamental differences begin with brain research: Scientists record brain activity, measure various parts of the cortex, assess various biochemical reactions to stress, and so on. This research is exciting but frustrating: The correlations found thus far between neurological measurements and childhood behavior are small and sometimes contradictory (Gunnar, 2000; National Research Council & Institute of Medicine, 2000; Thompson & Nelson, 2001). Intriguing findings are beginning to emerge, as you learned in the previous two chapters, but firm neurological evidence regarding infant brains and emotional expression is elusive.

Accordingly, most research on temperament still relies on many checklists and assessments reported by parents (Rothbart & Bates, 1998). One major advantage that these instruments have over neurological measures is that some of them have been used in many nations, over several decades, and thus have made possible a cross-cultural developmental perspective.

The most famous, comprehensive, and long-term study of children's temperament is the classic New York Longitudinal Study (NYLS), begun more than four decades ago (Thomas & Chess, 1977; Thomas et al., 1963). For this study, parents of very young infants were interviewed repeatedly and extensively. The researchers detailed the various aspects of the infants' behavior, and they described the approach they used to reduce the possibility of parental bias:

> For example, if a mother said that her child did not like his first solid food, we asked her to describe his actual behavior. We were satisfied only when she gave a description such as, "When I put the food into his mouth he cried loudly, twisted his head away, and let it drool out."
>
> *[Chess et al., 1965]*

According to the researchers' initial findings, in the first days and months of life babies differ in nine characteristics:

- *Activity level.* Some babies move around a great deal in their bassinets, and, as toddlers, they are nearly always running; others tend to stay in one place.
- *Rhythmicity.* Some babies eat, sleep, and defecate on schedule almost from birth; others are unpredictable.
- *Approach–withdrawal.* Some babies delight in everything new; others withdraw from every new situation.
- *Adaptability.* Some babies adjust quickly and happily to new experiences; others do not.
- *Intensity of reaction.* Some babies chortle when they laugh and howl when they cry; others merely smile or whimper.
- *Threshold of responsiveness.* Some babies sense every sight, sound, and touch and react to it, usually with distress; others seem oblivious.
- *Quality of mood.* Some babies seem constantly happy, smiling at almost everything; others are always irritable.
- *Distractibility.* Some babies can easily be distracted from a fascinating but dangerous object or a distressful experience; others cannot be sidetracked.
- *Attention span.* Some babies play happily with one toy for a long time; others flit from one thing to another.

The lead New York Longitudinal Study (NYLS) researchers, Alexander Thomas and Stella Chess (1977), believe that "temperamental individuality is well established by the time the infant is two to three months old." They found that about a third of all infants were hard to classfiy but that most infants can be clustered into one of three types:

- Easy (40 percent)
- Difficult (10 percent)
- Slow to warm up (15 percent)

Difficult babies are irregular, intense, disturbed by every noise, unhappy, and hard to distract for very long—quite a handful, even for an experienced parent. Easy babies are the opposite of difficult. Slow-to-warm-up babies are unwilling to approach or adapt to new experiences but they do adjust with time. This information is useful to parents of a "difficult" infant, who need not blame themselves but do need to work harder to guide and encourage their child. In fact, recent research has found that highly active, fearless boys tend to develop many types of psychological problems later on. This is less true for girls, perhaps because parents and the community work harder to rein in a young girl's "boisterous" behavior (Colder et al., 2002).

Another group of researchers began by studying adults and came up with a different list of basic traits, called the "Big Five":

- *Extroversion:* outgoing, assertive, and active behavior
- *Agreeableness:* kind, helpful, and easygoing feelings
- *Conscientiousness:* organized, deliberate, and conforming impulses
- *Neuroticism:* anxious, moody, and self-punishing thoughts
- *Openness:* imaginative, curious, and artistic attitude, welcoming new experiences

As you can see, these five tendencies are not identical to the nine characteristics of the NYLS, but there are many similarities. The **Big Five** are a central group of personality traits that seem to be evident in all humans, no matter what their cohort or culture. They are found in international studies of adult personality as well as in descriptions of children's traits by parents from many nations (Kohnstamm et al., 1996; McCrae et al., 1999). These findings confirm that temperament is probably innate and that patterns that distinguish one infant, child, or adult from another transcend culture or child-rearing specifics. Other research finds that temperament is linked to biological and neurological patterns (in heartbeat, crying, activity level, and such) that appear in the first months of life, so parents should not be blamed or credited for all their infants' actions (Huffman et al., 1998; Rothbart & Bates, 1998).

Temperament and Caregiving

approach–withdrawal The term used in the NLYS for a trait whose measurement helps classify children as fearful, outgoing, or low-reactive.

Big Five A central group of personality traits that seem to be evident in all humans: extroversion, agreeableness, conscientiousness, neuroticism, and openness.

goodness of fit A pattern of smooth interaction between the individual and the social milieu, including family, school, community.

Even though they do not determine temperament, culture and child-rearing practices have an effect on infant emotions. This is particularly apparent with the trait called **approach–withdrawal** in the New York Longitudinal Study (NYLS), which is closely related to the Big Five traits of openness and neuroticism. In one widely used laboratory measure of this trait, infants are confronted with toys or noises that might be frightening. For 4-month-olds, these are typically mobiles and recorded sounds; for older children, they might be a noisy, moving robot or a clown who tries to play with the child. Most infants show some interest as well as distress, perhaps at 4 months staring but then turning the head away. However, some infants express joy, smiling and reaching out to the toy; others are inhibited and quiet; still others are very upset, crying and kicking.

One longitudinal study found that children in each of these three distinctive groups—positive, inhibited, and negative—tended to show consistent patterns in their brain functioning as well as behavior from age 4 months to 4 years (Fox et al., 2001). That consistency, however, was not shown by every child. In fact, if predictions about the children's ongoing temperament were based solely on their reactions at 4 months, half of them would be wrong. The highly distressed children were most likely to change, especially if they were in a day-care setting where they could learn to control their fear. The exuberant children were least likely to change, either in their behavior or in their brain patterns (see Figure 7.1). This difference makes sense: An exuberant temperament already fits well with the expectations of most families and preschools, but a fearful one can (and should) be encouraged to shift over time.

In addition, the difference highlights a crucial finding from temperament research: **Goodness of fit** among caregiver, caregiving context, and infant allows development to proceed well, with a smooth interaction between family and

Twins They were born on the same day and now are experiencing a wading pool for the first time.

? *Observational Quiz* (see answer, page 208): Are these monozygotic or dizygotic twins?

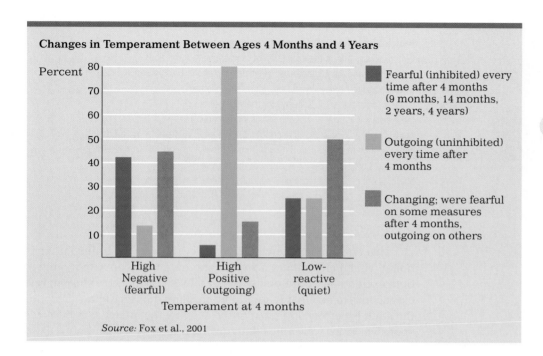

Changes in Temperament Between Ages 4 Months and 4 Years

Source: Fox et al., 2001

FIGURE 7.1 **Do Babies' Temperaments Change?** The temperamental patterns of the 4-month-olds in this study tended to continue, especially if they were already happy and outgoing.

? *Observational Quiz* (see answer, page 209): Which category of infant was most likely to keep changing after the assessment at 4 months?

baby being the critical factor, not the behavior of either in isolation. When there is goodness of fit, parents of slow-to-warm-up children give them time to adjust to new situations; parents of exuberant, happy, curious children make sure that they do not hurt themselves while exploring their surroundings; parents of difficult children patiently guide them and build a positive interaction with them.

Emotions in the Social Context

Regulation of emotions and cultural variations are mentioned in Chapter 5's discussion of early brain development. They are also major themes of Chapter 10, since emotional regulation is an important foundation for the school years. Now, however, we need to look at early emotional responses, especially at two specific psychosocial responses that directly affect infant emotions: social referencing and self-awareness.

Early Emotional Responses

It is difficult to be a responsive parent even to an "easy" newborn, much less a difficult one. Pain and pleasure seem to arise from the newborn's stomach, not the parents' devotion. Parents who anticipate joyous exchanges may be disappointed to discover that their very young infant spends most of the day sleeping, awakening mainly to cry and eat, rarely responding to a caregiver's shows of emotion. Parents sometimes try to elicit some response, with limited success. One developmentalist reports:

> A father in the swimming pool lowers his two-month-old daughter toward the water's surface. He holds her so that he can have a clear view of her face and so she can see his entire face. While staring at her intensely, the father gently lets one of her bare feet touch the water and briskly removes it while commenting with a loud, high-pitched voice "Oootch, it's cold!" and displaying a greatly exaggerated expression of pain. This routine is repeated many times in a row, each time after a pause during which the infant regains her calm.

[Rochat, 2001, p. 132]

Which Sister Has a Personality Problem? Culture always affects the expression of temperament. In Mongolia and many other Asian countries, females are expected to display shyness as a sign of respect to elders and strangers. Consequently, if the younger of these sisters is truly as shy as she seems, her parents are less likely to be distressed about her withdrawn behavior than the typical North American parent would be. Conversely, they may consider the relative boldness of her older sister to be a serious problem.

colic A condition in which indigestion causes an infant to engage in prolonged bouts of crying and to sleep less at night than other infants.

! *Answer to Observational Quiz* (from page 206): True tests of zygosity involve analysis of blood type, although physical appearance often provides some clues. Here such clues are minimal: We cannot see differences in sex, coloring, or hand formation—although the shapes of the skulls seem different. The best clue from this photo is personality. Confronting their first experience in a wading pool, these twins are showing such a difference on the approach–withdrawal dimension of temperament that one would have to guess they are dizygotic.

synchrony A coordinated interaction between caregiver and infant, who respond to each other's faces, sounds, and movements very rapidly and smoothly.

This episode is noteworthy in several ways. First, this father is doing what many fathers do, engaging his child in an activity that is both exciting and frightening, but carefully making sure she can reference him to see that it should be thrilling, not terrifying. Second, the adult is performing most of the activity; the infant is, at best, responsive. Third, given her immaturity, a return to calm and a fixed stare are typically the best response that he can elicit. Indeed, many new parents find that managing to get a crying infant to sleep is a major success.

Even this success eludes some parents. Infants with **colic**—(an imprecise term used by parents to refer to painful indigestion)—engage in prolonged bouts of crying (typically in the late afternoon and early evening), and they sleep much less at night than other infants (White et al., 2000). Such crying makes parents feel helpless and angry, worried that they are failures or that their baby already hates them. The high-pitched, persistent wailing of a "colicky" baby is very unpleasant and unsettling to listen to (Zeskind & Barr, 1997). Research confirms that infants under 3 months of age often become upset for reasons that have little to do with the quality of their care. Boys, for instance, are usually fussier than girls, even though parents tend to try harder to comfort them (Weinberg et al., 1999).

An infant's responses in the first three months are not predictive of later temperament or even emotional reactions to stress (White et al., 2000). A newborn's brain and stomach may take a few months to adjust to the world outside the womb, particularly to the sleep–wake cycle that the parents prefer. Eventually these early problems become a distant memory. The emotional responses of the parents are crucial, with many becoming needlessly upset at their newborn's behavior. In fact, parents in the early weeks are best advised to be patient rather than to feel responsible for early fussiness (van IJzendoorn & Hubbard, 2000).

Synchrony

Parents can and do rejoice when their 3-month-old begins to respond to them in special ways (Rochat, 2001). Although any face elicits a social smile at about 6 weeks, by the time an infant is 3 months old a sensitive and familiar caregiver is able to provoke wider grins, lilting noises, cooing, and other reactions that signify special status.

At this point, **synchrony** can begin. Synchrony is a coordinated interaction between caregiver and infant, who respond to each other with split-second timing. Synchrony has been variously described by researchers as the meshing of a finely tuned machine (Snow, 1984), an emotional "attunement" of an improvised musical duet (Stern, 1985), and a smoothly flowing "waltz" that is mutually adaptive (Barnard & Martell, 1995). The critical factor is the timing of the interaction, such that each partner responds to the other almost instantly, in a chain of mutual communication. Synchrony helps infants learn to read other people's emotions and to develop some of the basic skills of social interaction, such as taking turns and paying attention, that they will use throughout life.

Synchrony also helps infants learn to express their own feelings. A sensitive parent responds to every hint ("Ooh, are you hungry?" "Aahaaa, you're tired," "Uuumm, you see the rattle?") by mirroring (copying) each expression with exaggerated facial movements and a solicitous tone of voice as well as with actions, such as getting food, putting the head to the shoulder, handing over the rattle (Gergely & Watson, 1999).

Imitation is pivotal. Infants sometimes imitate caregivers: Even newborns can imitate mouth movements, and as their imitation improves over the first year, they begin to feel the emotions that go with the expressions their faces make (just as adults who laugh begin to feel better). But parents' imitation of infants, not infants' imitation of parents, is the force that drives the synchronous activity. If an emotion is visible from an infant's expression (and infants all over the world make the same facial expressions in response to the same stimuli) and the infant sees a familiar face mirroring that emotion, then the infant begins to connect his or her internal state with the external expression (Rochat, 2001).

Learning Through Play

Even though emotional communication is a serious and important job in the first months, synchrony is most evident not in serious dialogue, but in play. Playful interactions may occur in almost any context—during a feeding, a diaper change, or a bath, for example. After a while, they can be initiated by either the adult or the infant: The caregiver might notice the baby's expression or vocalization and echo it (by cooing when the baby coos), or the baby might notice the adult's wide-eyed beaming and break into a grin.

What really distinguishes episodes of synchrony from routine caregiving are the playful, moment-by-moment actions and reactions of both partners. To complement the infant's animated but quite limited repertoire, as well as to elicit new or increased reactions, caregivers perform dozens of actions that seem to be reserved exclusively for babies. Typically, they may open their eyes and mouths wide in exaggerated expressions of mock delight or surprise; make rapid clucking noises or repeat one-syllable sounds ("ba-ba-ba-ba," "di-di-di-di," "bo-bo-bo-bo"); raise and lower the pitch of their voices; change the pace of their movements (gradually speeding up or slowing down); bring their faces close to the baby's and then pull back; tickle, pat, poke, lift, rock, stroke, and do many other simple things. (You may well recognize some of these behaviors as your own spontaneous reaction to a baby—sometimes surprising yourself and amusing those around you!)

Infants' responses complement the actions of adults: They may stare at their partners or look away, vocalize, widen their eyes, move their heads forward or back, or turn aside. A skilled caregiver notices a signal, such as a glance away, that the infant does not want to play. However, some infants need to give very obvious signals—falling asleep, freezing expressionless, or, like Jacob, arching their backs and screaming. Such signals mean that something is wrong in the

Especially for College Men Who Are Not Yet Fathers Imagine you have a male friend who has an infant niece. He says he is afraid he might look silly if he tried to play with her. What do you tell him?

!Answer to Observational Quiz (from page 207): The quiet babies changed the most, perhaps because they were neither distinctly fearful nor distinctly outgoing at 4 months.

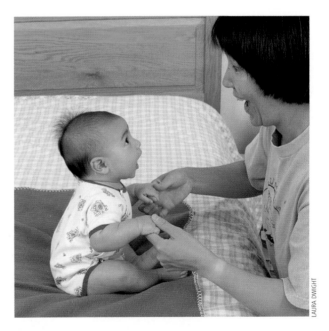

Emotion Shared Three-month-old Mathias and his mother experience synchrony, with eyes wide and staring, mouths open, and hands touching. What would you call the emotion they are sharing—excitement, pride, exhilaration? The experience may be too powerful for any ordinary word to describe.

social interaction: Either the caregiver is too intrusive, not letting the baby rest, or the baby is overwhelmed.

Crucial in all this is that the caregiver be responsive, realizing that babies sometimes just want to look around, to eat, or to sleep. At other times the infant wants interaction but signals that the caregiver's timing or intensity is out of sync. How to repair a failed interaction is as important for both parties to learn as how to sustain interest. Again, the main burden of synchrony falls on the adult: In frame-by-frame studies of videotaped interaction, the caregiver picks up on the baby's signals and elaborates on them more than vice versa (Feldman et al, 1999). Successful breast feeding requires such synchrony, which is one reason it is recommended even when nutrition is not an issue (see Appendix A, Chapter 7).

Reactions to a Still Face

Babies learn to expect certain reactions, as evidenced in a creative experiment using the **still face technique** (Tronick, 1989; Tronick et al., 1978). In the classic condition, a 3- to 4-month-old infant is placed facing the mother, who is first told to play with the baby. Typically, the mother begins the behavior of synchrony, with exaggerated tone, expressions, and so on, and the baby reciprocates with smiles and joy. Then the mother is told to erase all expression and to stare at the baby with a "still face" for a minute or two. Not usually at 2 months, but clearly by 6 months, babies get very upset at the still face: They frown, fuss, drool, look away, kick, or vocalize. Two video cameras record both partners, and then frame-by-frame comparisons reveal the sequence of reactions. The mutuality of the synchrony is apparent, as are the baby's surprise and distress when the mother does not respond. The same conditions and reactions apply with fathers or other significant people, but less so with strangers.

Interestingly, babies are much more upset by their still-faced parents than by their parents' departure for a minute or two (Field, 1994). From a developmentalist's perspective, this is very healthy, because it shows that the baby is used to interactive play. Even more impressive, by 5 months infants have adjusted their style to their social experiences. If a stranger, when placed in front of the infant, responds quickly, with lots of smiling, infants reciprocate *if* their mother acts the same way. However, if their mother is more low-key, infants may be quiet or even cry at an exuberant stranger; they respond better to a stranger whose behavior is similar to their mother's (Bigelow, 1999).

Although synchrony is evident early in life, it becomes more frequent and more elaborate as time goes on; thus, a 6-month-old is a much more active and responsive social partner than a 3-month-old. Parents and infants spend about an hour a day in face-to-face play, although wide variations are apparent from baby to baby, time to time, culture to culture (Baildam et al., 2000; Lee, 2000). Toward the end of the first year, face-to-face play almost disappears; once infants can move around and explore on their own, they are no longer content to stay in one spot and mirror an adult's facial expressions. Even when infants are on the move, however, they look to caregivers for emotional cues, as we will now see.

Social Referencing

The search for information about another person's feelings is called **social referencing.** A mother's glance of calm reassurance or words of caution, a father's expression of alarm, pleasure, or dismay—each can become a guide to action, telling an infant how to react to an unfamiliar or ambiguous event. (We saw this with the father who allowed his very young daughter's foot to touch the water

still face technique A method of studying synchrony by assessing the infant's reaction when the caregiver stops engaging in synchronous behavior and merely stares at the baby for a minute or two.

social referencing Seeking information about an unfamiliar or ambiguous object or event by observing someone else's expressions and reactions. That other person becomes a reference, consulted when the infant wants to know how to react.

in the swimming pool.) Social referencing becomes increasingly distinct and important after crawling (at about 9 months) and walking (at about 12 months) make infants independently mobile, when active exploration by Piaget's "little scientist" begins (Derochers et al., 1994). Toddlers search for emotional cues in gaze and facial expressions, pay close attention to outbursts of pleasure or disgust, and watch carefully to detect the intentions behind the actions of others (Baldwin, 2000).

Social referencing is particularly noticeable at mealtime, when infants look to caregivers for cues about new foods. This explains why caregivers the world over smack their lips, pretend to taste, and say "yum-yum" (or the equivalent) as they feed toddlers their first beets, liver, spinach, or whatever. They are trying to lead the infants to like whatever is offered. For their part, toddlers become quite astute at reading expressions, insisting on the foods that the adults *really* like.

Referencing Mom

An everyday example of social referencing is toddlers' willingness to respond to their mother's requests. As every parent knows, toddlers often refuse to do as they are told. In an experiment, only about one toddler in four obeyed their mother's request to pick up dozens of toys that they had not spilled (Kochanska et al., 2001). However, the same toddlers were much more likely to comply when their mothers told them not to touch some very attractive toys within easy reach. Social referencing entered the picture because mothers used tone and expression as well as words to make this prohibition clear and to point out the specifically forbidden toys.

To be specific, when the mothers made it clear to their 1-year-olds that they should not play with certain available toys, about half of the 14-month-olds and virtually all of the 22-month-olds obeyed their mother, even when she was out of sight. Indeed, 80 percent of the older toddlers not only acquiesced but seemed to accept the mother's judgment (which the researchers called *committed compliance*), one even saying "no-no touch" as a reminder (Kochanska et al., 2001). It is interesting to contrast these toddlers' wholesale acceptance of the message they received via social referencing with typical reactions at older ages: Preschoolers more often touch the forbidden toys when the mother is not present, and adolescents ask for reasons and argue back. Unlike these older children, toddlers rely on their parents as reliable social references and accept their judgments, typically looking repeatedly at the adult's facial expression.

Referencing Dad

Early research on the psychosocial context of development usually studied mother–infant relationships, partly for practical reasons and partly because in those days it was assumed that mothers were the main caregivers. Now it has become apparent that people other than mothers can and do provide important care for infants. Research has not caught up to the specific effects of siblings, grandparents, and others (although their influence can be substantial), but much is now known about fathers. Infants use Dad as a social reference as much as Mom, if both are present. In fact, fathers tend to be more encouraging than mothers, who are more protective. As a result, when toddlers are about to begin exploring, they often seek a man's approval as a spur for their curiosity (Parke, 1995).

As researchers looked closely at mothers, fathers, and infants, they discovered a curious difference: Although fathers provide less basic care, they play

MICHAEL S. YAMASHITA / CORBIS

Social Referencing Is it dangerous or joyous to ride in a bicycle basket through the streets of Osaka, Japan? Check with Mom to find out.

Response for College Men (from page 209): Go ahead and play. Infants need adults who are willing to look silly, because making odd noises and facial expressions is part of synchrony and play—both important for infant development. This is not only how infants learn; it is also what fathers throughout the world do, bringing great joy to their babies.

Especially for Grandmothers A grandmother of an infant boy is troubled that the baby's father stays with him whenever the mother is away. She says that men don't know how to care for infants, and she notes that he sometimes plays a game in which he tosses his son in the air and then catches him.

Up, Up, and Away! The vigorous play typical of fathers is likely to help in the infant's mastery of motor skills and the development of muscle control.

Goodness of Fit Attachment to the father can be very strong, especially for boys. If the mother is unavailable for any reason, a secure attachment to the father or another caregiver can make the difference in the child's emotional health.

more. In general, infants look to fathers for fun and to mothers for comfort (Lamb, 2000; Parke, 1996). Compared to mothers' play, fathers' play is more noisy, emotional, boisterous, physical, and idiosyncratic (as fathers tend to make up active and exciting games on the spur of the moment).

In the first year of a baby's life, fathers are more likely to move the baby's legs and arms in imitation of walking, kicking, or climbing; to zoom the baby through the air (playing "airplane"); or to tap and tickle the baby's stomach. Mothers tend to caress, murmur, or sing soothingly; to combine play with caretaking routines such as diapering and bathing; or to use standard sequences that involve only one part of the body, such as peek-a-boo and patty-cake. Not surprisingly, young infants typically laugh more, and cry more, when playing with Daddy.

In all probability, physically active play helps the children master motor skills and develop muscle control (Pellegrini & Smith, 1998). In addition, play with Daddy may contribute to the growth of social skills and emotional expression. In one study, one or the other parent sat passively nearby while their 18-month-olds met a stranger. The toddlers were more likely to smile and play with the new person when the father was present than when the mother was; the difference was especially apparent among the boys. The authors of the study speculated that previous boisterous, idiosyncratic interactions with Dad made his presence a signal to be bold and playful (Kromelow et al., 1990).

Similar speculations have been raised about fathers' teasing, which requires the baby's social response to an unpredictable game—and thereby may increase not only excitement but also emotional regulation and social understanding (Pecheux & Labrell, 1994). Another study, this one of very-low-birthweight infants in Japan, found that these high-risk infants were much more likely to develop normal social skills if their fathers were actively involved with them (Itoigawa et al., 1996). And in Israel, father–infant involvement led to an increase in exploratory play (Feldman et al., 1997).

The fact that fathers are good playmates in many cultures does not mean they are limited to that role. If they are called on and their culture allows it, fathers are quite capable of providing all necessary emotional and cognitive nurturing, speaking baby talk, and forming secure relationships as both secondary and primary caregivers (Geiger, 1996; Lamb, 1997).

Diversity is obvious, as each couple cooperates to raise their children. Every set of parents develop their own roles, which may or may not conform to cultural generalities but which work well for their family. In fact, diversity is more evident for fathers' involvement than mothers' (Marsiglio et al., 2000). Nevertheless, fathers' involvement generally benefits children's development, even if fathers forge their own way of caring for their offspring. Cultures or individual mothers who discourage fathers' participation may thus be impairing children's growth. One study found that adolescent boys who did not know their fathers were more likely to abuse drugs and be arrested, as well as to become fathers themselves before age 20 (Fagot et al., 1998). In general, the father's involvement in infant care benefits the mother's self-confidence, the child's later development, and the emotional strength of the father himself (Aldous et al., 1998; Eggebeen & Knoester, 2001; Vandell et al., 1997). Apparently, throughout today's changing world, mothers and fathers together are better able to meet all their infant's needs—biological, cognitive, and psychosocial—than is either parent alone (Cabrera et al., 2000).

Self-Awareness

Another foundation for emotional growth becomes evident in later infancy with the onset of **self-awareness**, which is a person's realization that he or she is a distinct individual whose body, mind, and actions are separate from those of other people. This emerging sense of "me" and "mine" fosters the growth of many self-conscious emotions, from pride and confidence to guilt, shame, and embarrassment. Notice, however, that we discuss self-awareness within our discussion of "emotions in the social context." That's because awareness of self arises from awareness of others, and, simultaneously, self-awareness leads to new consciousness of others. That consciousness fosters other-directed emotions, including defiance and jealousy as well as empathy and affection. As one developmentalist explains:

> With the emergence of consciousness in the second year of life, we see vast changes in both children's emotional life and the nature of their social relationships. . . . With consciousness the child can feel what I have called self-conscious emotions, like pride at a job well done or shame over a failure.
>
> *[Lewis, 1997, p. 132]*

The onset of self-awareness is strikingly evident when infants of various ages are compared. Very young infants have no sense of self. In fact, a prominent psychoanalyst, Margaret Mahler, theorized that for the first 4 months of life infants see themselves as part of their mothers. They "hatch" at about 5 months, and spend the next several months developing a sense of themselves as separate from their mothers (Mahler et al., 1975). Psychoanalytic theories have not been proved to be universally applicable, but there is no doubt that the infant emerges as a self-aware individual occurs gradually over the first year.

During the second year, the period from 15 to 18 months "is noteworthy for the emergence of the Me-self, the sense of self as the object of one's knowledge" (Harter, 1998). This can be seen in the following two examples, one about a series of experiments and the other about one normal toddler.

Rouge on the Forehead

The emerging sense of self was demonstrated in a classic experiment (Lewis & Brooks, 1978). Babies looked in a mirror after a dot of rouge had been surreptitiously put on their noses. If the babies reacted to the mirror image by touching their own noses, that meant they knew they were seeing their own faces. By trying this experiment with 96 babies between the ages of 9 and 24 months, the experimenters found a distinct, age-related developmental shift. None of the babies under 12 months reacted to the mark as if it were on their own faces (they sometimes smiled at and touched the dot on the baby in the mirror). However, most of those between ages 15 and 24 months did react with self-awareness, perhaps by touching their own faces with an expression of curiosity and puzzlement.

The link between self-awareness and self-conscious emotions was shown in a later extension of the rouge-and-mirror experiment (Lewis et al., 1989). In this study, 15- to 24-month-olds who showed self-recognition in the mirror also looked *embarrassed* when they were effusively praised by an adult; that is, they smiled and looked away, covered their faces with their hands, and so on. Infants without self-recognition—that is, those who had not recognized that the rouge was on their own noses—were not embarrassed.

self-awareness A person's realization that he or she is a distinct individual whose body, mind, and actions are separate from those of other people.

Response for Grandmothers (from page 211): Fathers can be great caregivers, and most mothers prefer that the father provide care. It's good for the baby and the marriage. Being tossed in the air is great fun (and no harm, as long as the father is a good catcher!). A generation ago, mothers didn't let fathers care for infants, so today's grandfathers may feel unable to do it. Fortunately, today's mothers less often act as gatekeepers, shutting the fathers out.

A Beautiful Bonnet At 18 months, Austin recognizes himself, obviously delighted by his colander hat. Once self-recognition begins at about this age, many children spend hours admiring themselves with various hats, makeup, and other accessories. Almost every view of themselves is a joy; children are not yet worried about looking stupid or ugly.

Self-awareness soon becomes linked with self-concept, as toddlers figure out the extent of their abilities. One of the interesting aspects is the importance of toddlers' self-evaluations. Toddlers who are told "You're very smart" probably appreciate the compliment, but usually they can already feel quite smart, pleased, and proud about what they have done. In fact, one study found that boys who receive *less* parental praise become *more* proud of themselves, perhaps because they are better able to form their own positive self-evaluations (Belsky et al., 1997). Another longitudinal study found that positive comments from a mother to a 2-year-old did not lead to more pride or less shame by age 3 (Kelley et al., 2000). However, certain negative comments ("You're doing it all wrong") diminished effort and increased shame. Neutral suggestions, in addition to guiding toddlers to complete activities on their own, fostered the willingness to try new challenges later on (Kelley et al., 2000). It seems that building self-esteem is more complicated than simply praising a toddler; it also entails enabling children to accomplish things that make them feel proud.

Juice on the Floor

How can a toddler's own pride be more compelling than parental approval? Look, for example, at Ricky, the grandson of a noted psychologist. Shortly before his second birthday, Ricky teased his mother by deliberately pouring a cup of juice onto a rug. Evidence that Ricky knew he was being naughty was his reaction to his mother's scolding: He was unsurprised and unfazed by her angry words and was quite willing to help her clean up the mess. Only when his mother sent him to his room did he protest angrily, apparently not having anticipated such punishment. Later that day he told his grandmother, "Juice on a floor." Her response was "Juice doesn't go on the floor," delivered somewhat sternly. "Yes, juice on a floor, juice on a floor," Ricky laughingly repeated several times, pretending to turn an imaginary cup upside down. As Ricky's grandmother comments:

> The boy's pleasure at watching the juice spill and anger at being sent to his room are emotions that are typical at all periods of infancy, but his obvious pride at his ability to act counter to convention or his mother's wishes is possible only when self-awareness is firmly established.

[Shatz, 1994]

Theories About Caregiving

Thus far we have focused on the infant half of the psychosocial partnership, including both the epigenetic, maturational aspects of emotion and the interface with the social context of development. Here we turn to the other half, the caregiver. We begin by reviewing what our five major theories (introduced in Chapter 2) have had to say about the importance of caregivers, particularly of mothers. As you will see, the theories that developed before the middle of the twentieth century placed mothers at the center of infant growth and development, while more recent theories do not.

Psychoanalytic Theory

By far the strongest emphasis on the early relationship between parent and child arises from psychoanalytic theory, which holds that the first two or three years of life are pivotal for later personality and psychological health. The mother–child relationship is considered particularly crucial. To be specific, there are lifelong consequences if a parent–child relationship goes wrong, these theorists assert, and usually the mother is to blame. Sigmund Freud, who established the frame-

"I get along fine with people my age and I get along fine with people your age—it's the ones in the middle who give me all kinds of problems."

Parents Are the Problem According to psychoanalytic theory, the inevitable conflicts between parents and young children create the need for personality quirks and defensive measures.

work for this view, believed that the experiences of the first four years "play a decisive part in determining whether and at what point the individual shall fail to master the real problems of life" (Freud, 1918/1963). He thought that the mother was "unique, without parallel, established unalterably for a whole lifetime as the first and strongest love-object and as the prototype of all later love relations" (Freud, 1940/1964).

Freud: Oral and Anal Stages

As we noted in Chapter 2, Freud viewed human development in terms of psychosexual stages that occur at specific ages. According to Freud (1935), psychological development begins in the first year of life with the **oral stage,** so named because the mouth is the young infant's prime source of gratification. In the second year, the infant's prime focus of gratification shifts to the anus—particularly the sensual pleasure of bowel movements and, eventually, the psychological pleasure of controlling them. Accordingly, Freud referred to this period as the **anal stage.**

According to Freud, both the oral and anal stages are fraught with potential conflicts that can have long-term consequences. If a mother frustrates her infant's urge to suck—by, say, weaning the infant from the nipple too early or preventing the child from sucking on fingers or toes—the child may become distressed and anxious and eventually become an adult with an *oral fixation.* Such a person is stuck (fixated) at the oral stage and therefore eats, drinks, chews, bites, or talks excessively, in quest of mouthy pleasures that were denied in infancy.

Similarly, if toilet training is overly strict or if it begins before the child is mature enough to participate (before 18 months), interaction between parents and child may become locked into a conflict over the toddler's refusal or inability to comply. This conflict, too, may have important consequences for the child's future personality. The child becomes fixated and develops an *anal personality;* as an adult, he or she may seek control of self and others and demonstrate an unusual need for regularity in all aspects of life.

Freud's ideas have been extremely influential. The importance of unconscious memories from early childhood and of the mother–infant relationship are still emphasized by many psychoanalytic theorists (Fonagy & Target, 2000). However, research has failed to link specific oral- and anal-stage conflicts with later personality traits. The overall pattern of parental warmth and sensitivity, or coldness and domination, affects the child's emotional development much more than the particulars of either feeding or toilet training. This broader perspective is reflected in the theory of Erik Erikson.

Erikson: Trust and Autonomy

As you remember from Chapter 2, Erikson believed that development proceeds through a series of developmental crises, or challenges, that occur over the life span. In the first crisis of infancy, which Erikson labeled **trust versus mistrust,** the infant learns whether the world is essentially a secure place where basic needs will be readily satisfied or an unpredictable arena where needs are met only after much crying—and sometimes not even then. Erikson (1963) contended that babies begin to develop a sense of security when their mothers provide food and comfort with "consistency, continuity, and sameness of experience." When interaction with the mother inspires trust and security, the child (and later the adult) experiences confidence in engaging with and exploring the world.

oral stage Freud's term for the first stage of psychosexual development, in which the infant obtains pleasure through sucking and biting.

anal stage Freud's term for the second stage of psychosexual development, in which the anus becomes the main source of gratification, particularly the sensual pleasure of bowel movements and, eventually, the psychological pleasure of controlling them.

KEN CAVANAUGH / PHOTO RESEARCHERS, INC

A Moment of Bliss Freud thought that oral gratification through breast feeding was an erotic experience as well as, in his day, a nutritional necessity. Modern psychologists question the power and even the existence of Freud's stages, but his emphasis on the universality of unconscious, primitive urges may not be as far-fetched as some believe.

trust versus mistrust Erikson's term for the first crisis of psychosocial development, in which the infant learns whether the world is essentially a secure place where basic needs are always met or an unpredictable arena where needs (for food, comfort, etc.) are sometimes unmet.

autonomy versus shame and doubt Erikson's term for the second crisis of psychosocial development, in which toddlers either succeed or fail in gaining a sense of self-rule over their own actions and bodies.

The next crisis, which occurs in toddlerhood, is **autonomy versus shame and doubt.** Toddlers want autonomy, or self-rule, over their own actions and bodies. If they fail in their effort to gain it, either because they are incapable or because their caregivers are too restrictive, they feel ashamed of their actions and doubtful of their abilities. According to Erikson, the key to meeting this crisis and gaining a sense of autonomy is parental guidance and protection:

Firmness must protect him [the toddler] against the potential anarchy of his as yet untrained sense of discrimination, his inability to hold on and let go with discretion. As his environment encourages him to "stand on his own feet," it must protect him against meaningless and arbitrary experiences of shame and of early doubt.

[Erikson, 1963]

If parents accomplish this, the child will become increasingly self-confident when new challenges arise.

Like Freud, Erikson believed that problems that begin in early infancy can last a lifetime. He maintained that the adult who is suspicious and pessimistic or who always seems burdened by shame may have been an infant who did not develop sufficient trust or a toddler who did not achieve sufficient autonomy.

Curiosity or Naughtiness? According to Erikson, how parents react to their children's efforts at autonomy can shape how young children resolve the psychosocial crisis of autonomy versus shame and doubt. If you were 21-month-old Shaquille's parent, how would you react to his destructive exploration of a cassette tape?

Behaviorism

From the perspective of behaviorism, or traditional learning theory (discussed in Chapter 2), an infant's emotions and personality are molded as parents reinforce or punish the child's spontaneous behaviors. If parents smile and pick up their baby at every glimmer of an infant grin, the baby will become a child—and later an adult—with a sunny disposition. Responses in early synchrony teach a child some very important lessons about communicating: Take turns, and repair a broken line of communication when necessary. Similarly, if parents continually tease their infant by, say, removing the nipple as the baby is contentedly sucking or by playfully pulling at a favorite toy that a toddler is clutching, that child will develop a suspicious, possessive nature and will not be securely attached to anyone.

The strongest statement of this early view came from John Watson, the leading behaviorist of the time, who cautioned:

Failure to bring up a happy child, a well-adjusted child—assuming bodily health—falls squarely upon the parents' shoulders. [By the time the child is 3] parents have already determined . . . whether . . . [the child] is to grow into a happy person, wholesome and good-natured, whether he is to be a whining, complaining neurotic, an anger-driven, vindictive, over-bearing slave driver, or one whose every move in life is definitely controlled by fear.

[Watson, 1928]

Later theorists in the behaviorist tradition incorporated social learning into their view of personality formation. They found that infants observe and then imitate personality traits of their parents, even if they are not directly reinforced for doing so. A child might develop a quick temper, for instance, if a parent regularly displays anger and in return gets respect—or at least obedience—from other family members.

Social referencing strengthens this learning by observation. Generally, if toddlers receive more signals of interest and encouragement than of fear and prohibition as they explore, they are likely to be more outgoing and less aggressive than they would have been if the opposite messages had been received (Calkins, 1994). If an infant or toddler sees few signals of any kind (as might happen if the primary caregiver is depressed, neglectful, or overtired), the child may become relatively emotionless and passive (Field, 1994).

Like psychoanalytic theorists, behaviorists usually emphasize the importance of the mother in a child's early years. For example, having a social initiative ignored by the mother is a powerful punishment for infants, who naturally strive to make social contact. A depressed mother does not respond to her infant's bids for synchrony, and once the infant is able to move around, her behavior becomes even less encouraging: "Depressed mothers are more likely to withdraw from their children and respond with little emotion or energy, or to become intrusive and hostile toward them" (National Research Council and Institute of Medicine, 2000).

Other Theories

The psychoanalytic and behaviorist theories developed in the early twentieth century and had become popular by mid-century. At that time, it was widely believed that good mothers did not work outside the home, at least until their youngest child entered kindergarten. Other, more recent theories are somewhat less focused on early maternal care.

Cognitive Theory

Cognitive theory holds that a person's thoughts and values determine his or her perspective on the world. Cognitive theorists believe that our early family experiences are important primarily because our thoughts, perceptions, and memories make them so, not because they are buried in our unconscious (as psychoanalytic theory maintains) or burned into our brain patterns (according to behaviorism). Regarding synchrony, cognitive theory suggests that newborns know nothing about whether relationships are supposed to be trusting, encouraging, liberating, or restrictive. What infants do is try to develop a general concept of what to expect from people, in much the same way that, as we saw in Chapter 6, they develop affordances of objects or events.

To be specific, infants use their early relationships to develop a **working model,** a useful set of assumptions that become a frame of reference that can be called upon later in life (Bretherton & Munholland, 1999). It is called a "model" because these early relationships are seen as a prototype or blueprint; it is called "working" because it is useful in practice but is just a guide, not a fixed and final creation.

For example, if a 1-year-old girl develops a working model, based on how her mother responds to her, that people are not to be trusted, then she will use that assumption whenever she meets a new person. All her childhood relationships will be insecure, and as an adult she will be suspicious of humanity, always on guard against further disappointment. To use Piaget's terminology, people develop a cognitive schema to organize their perceptions of all humans, just as babies develop a schema to organize their perception of objects—deciding, for instance, that small objects are graspable. It is the interpretation of early experiences that is crucial, not necessarily the experiences themselves (Schaffer, 2000). This is true for many infant cognitions, such as the concept of self and the role of

working model In cognitive theory, a set of assumptions that are used to organize perceptions and experiences.

temperament traits such as fear and curiosity. We all develop many working models, which are subject to change as the need for adaptation arises.

Sociocultural Theory

The sociocultural perspective emphasizes the many ways in which the entire social context can have a major impact on infant–caregiver relationships. For example, if the culture encourages mothers to nurse at the baby's first whimper and to soothe every distress, the infant will be likely to develop into a trusting, contented adult.

The sociocultural perspective also says that children can change after infancy if their social context changes. A dramatic recent example is the thousands of children in Romania who had been surrendered to orphanages and were adopted by couples from other countries in the early 1990s. None of these children had experienced synchrony or responsive caregiving of any kind in infancy; in fact, "without exception, children adopted from Romania experienced very gross global deprivation" (O'Connor et al., 2000, p. 379). However, some of them developed warm and supportive relationships with their new parents—evidence of sociocultural power.

In truth, many later adoptees who had had a severely deprived infancy did not adapt perfectly: By age 6 they still had not attained normal cognitive or social development. But the fact that some had done so suggests that change after the first year is possible and that even the worst social context in the early years can be replaced by a better social-cultural situation, to which the children will respond. Other research, with children whose infancy was less disturbed, also finds that personality and emotional traits are affected by current cultural conditions as much as or more than by early ones (O'Connor et al., 2000).

Epigenetic Systems Theory

Epigenetic systems theory holds that each infant is born with a genetic predisposition to develop certain traits that affect emotional development. Temperament is real. As we have seen in our discussion of temperament, the emotions of the infant are universal in their emergence but vary from child to child in the frequency and intensity of their expression. Change is possible, because genes permit selective adaptation to the environment. The central idea of epigenetic systems theory—that all human behavior is imbedded in a social and biological context that changes in mutually adaptive ways over time—seems as true in the first years of life as in the final days.

Each of our five major theories provides useful, and sometimes contrasting, perspectives on two of the most extensively studied aspects of infant psychosocial development: attachment and day care.

Attachment

The relationship between child and parent is lifelong. Even adult children and their aging parents have episodes of quick-response interaction, with mutual glances and laughter, that are similar to the exchanges they had when the child was a few months old and synchrony between parent and child first appeared. Love, affection, and closeness between parents and children are possible at any age. At each stage, however, the expression of that relationship changes, and the usual terminology changes as well.

The term *synchrony* is usually reserved for the first year, when preverbal play predominates. Another term, **attachment**, describes the relationship be-

attachment According to Ainsworth (1973), "an affectional tie that one person or animal forms between himself and another specific one—a tie that binds them together in space and endures over time."

tween slightly older infants and their caregivers. Attachment, according to Mary Ainsworth (1973), "may be defined as an affectional tie that one person or animal forms between himself and another specific one—a tie that binds them together in space and endures over time." In addition to being lifelong, attachment is a person-specific emotional bond. If someone loses an attachment figure, other people and other attachments can meet some of the same needs, but the original attachment figure cannot be replaced. For this reason, adults may always be affected by the death of a parent during their childhood.

When people are attached to each other, they try to be near each other and they interact in many ways. Infants show their attachment through **proximity-seeking behaviors,** such as approaching, following, and climbing onto the caregiver's lap, and through **contact-maintaining behaviors,** such as clinging, resisting being put down, and using social referencing once they are able to move around on their own. Caregivers show their attachment by keeping a watchful eye on the baby even when there is no danger and by responding affectionately and sensitively to the baby's vocalizations, expressions, and gestures. Many a mother or father, awakening at 3 A.M. to go to the bathroom, then tiptoes to the crib to gaze fondly at their sleeping infant. During the day, many like to smooth the toddler's hair or pat a hand or a cheek. These are just a few of many obvious examples of proximity-seeking and contact-maintaining behaviors. Attachment not only deepens the parent–child relationship but, over our long evolutionary history, may have contributed to human survival by keeping infants near their caregivers and keeping caregivers vigilant.

Secure and Insecure Attachment

The concept of attachment was originally developed by John Bowlby (1969, 1973, 1988), a British developmentalist who was inspired both by psychoanalytic theory and by ethology, particularly by observation of the interactions of monkeys. His ideas inspired a young American graduate student named Mary Ainsworth, who devoted her career to defining and measuring attachment.

Ainsworth realized, as many other scientists have, that universal human characteristics are most easily noticed in a place where one's usual cultural blindness is removed. She therefore went to Uganda, in central Africa, to observe mothers and infants. In Uganda, while the specifics of mother–infant interaction differed from those in England or the United States (for example, there was more physical contact but no kissing), the bonds of affection were still visible in various proximity-seeking and contact-maintaining behaviors (Ainsworth, 1967). Ainsworth discovered that virtually all normal infants develop special attachments to the people who care for them but that some infants are more secure in their attachments than others—a fact later confirmed by hundreds of other researchers (Cassidy & Shaver, 1999).

Secure attachment (called type B) provides comfort and confidence, as evidenced first by the infant's attempt to be close to the caregiver and then by the infant's readiness to explore. In such a relationship the caregiver acts as a **secure base for exploration** from which the child is willing to venture forth. The child might, for example, scramble down from the caregiver's lap to play with a toy but periodically look back and vocalize a few syllables or return for a hug.

By contrast, **insecure attachment** is characterized by an infant's fear, anxiety, anger, or seeming indifference toward a caregiver. The insecurely attached child has much less confidence, perhaps playing without trying to maintain contact with the caregiver or being unwilling to leave the caregiver's arms. Both these extremes are signs of insecure attachment; the first is called **insecure-avoidant** (type A) and the second **insecure-resistant/ambivalent** (type C) (see Table 7.2).

proximity-seeking behaviors Actions (such as approaching, following, and climbing into the lap) that are evidence of attachment—specifically, the desire to be physically close to someone to whom one is emotionally attached.

contact-maintaining behaviors Actions (such as clinging, resisting being put down, and using social referencing) that are evidence of attachment—specifically, the desire to remain physically close to the person to whom one is emotionally attached.

secure attachment A relationship of trust and confidence; during infancy, a relationship that provides enough comfort and reassurance to enable independent exploration of the environment.

secure base for exploration The caregiver's role in a relationship of secure attachment, in which the child freely ventures forth and returns.

insecure attachment A relationship that is unstable or unpredictable; in infancy such relationships are characterized by the child's fear, anxiety, anger, clinging, or seeming indifference toward the caregiver.

insecure-avoidant Referring to a pattern of attachment in which one person tries to avoid any connection with another, as an infant who is uninterested in the caregiver's presence or departure and ignores the caregiver on reunion.

insecure-resistant/ambivalent Referring to a pattern of attachment in which anxiety and uncertainty keeps one person clinging to another, as an infant who resists active exploration, is very upset at separation, and both resists and seeks contact on reunion.

TABLE 7.2 Patterns of Attachment in Infancy

Pattern of Attachment	Characteristics	Range of Occurrence*
Secure (type B)	Explores freely when the caregiver is present, using the caregiver as a "secure base." May be distressed at separation, always greets the caregiver on reunion. If distressed during separation, seeks contact and comfort during reunion, then settles down to continue play.	50–65%
Insecure-avoidant (type A)	Explores freely, seems uninterested in the caregiver's presence or departure. On reunion, ignores or actively avoids caregiver.	10–25%
Insecure-resistant/ambivalent (type C)	Resists active exploration. Preoccupied with caregiver. Upset at separation. On reunion, both resists and seeks contact, showing anger, passivity, or clinging. Does not easily return to play.	10–25%
Disorganized (type D)	Neither plays freely nor responds to the caregiver in any one coherent mode. May cry and then hit; may "freeze"; trance-like; may move in slow motion or other stereotyped manner; may show fear of parent.	5–20%
Not classified	Some children fit into none of the four categories.	Rare

* The percentages show a range because infant populations vary. This is particularly true internationally. Insecure German infants are more likely to be type A. Insecure Japanese infants are more likely to be type C. In the United States, abused, preterm, or brain-damaged infants are more likely to be type D.

Sources: Adapted from Braungart-Rieker et al., 2001; Goldberg et al., 1995; Vondra & Barnett, 1999.

Measuring Attachment

Ainsworth developed a now-classic laboratory procedure, called the **Strange Situation,** to measure an infant's attachment to a caregiver (usually the mother) by evoking the child's reactions to somewhat stressful conditions. In a well-equipped playroom, the subject infant is closely observed in eight three-minute-long episodes. In a given segment, the infant is with the caregiver, with a stranger, with both, or alone. The first episode has caregiver and child together, and then every three minutes the stranger or the caregiver leaves or enters the playroom, so the infant's reactions to these potentially stressful comings and goings can be observed.

The infant's reactions indicate motivation to be near the caregiver (proximity-seeking and contact-maintaining behaviors) and ability to use the caregiver's presence as a secure base (having confidence to venture forth). The key observational aspects of the Strange Situation are the following:

Strange Situation A laboratory procedure developed by Mary Ainsworth to measure attachment by evoking an infant's reactions to stress, specifically episodes of a caregiver's or stranger's arrival at and departure from a playroom where the infants can play with many toys.

- *Exploration of the toys.* A securely attached toddler plays happily when the caregiver is present.
- *Reaction to the caregiver's departure.* A securely attached toddler may or may not show some sign that the caregiver is missed—a loud cry, or perhaps only a pause and a woeful look.
- *Reaction to the caregiver's return.* A securely attached toddler exhibits a welcoming response when the caregiver returns to the room after leaving—especially when this occurs for a second time.

(a)

(b)

(c)

The Attachment Experiment In this episode of the Strange Situation, Brian shows every sign of secure attachment, (a) He explores the playroom happily when his mother is present; (b) he cries when she leaves; and (c) he is readily comforted when she returns.

Almost two-thirds of all normal infants tested in the Strange Situation demonstrate secure attachment (type B). The mother's presence in the playroom is enough to give them courage to explore the room and investigate the toys; as you read earlier, the father's presence makes some infants even more confident. The caregiver's departure may cause some distress (usually expressed through verbal protest and a pause in playing); and the caregiver's return is a signal to reestablish positive social contact (by smiling or climbing into his or her arms) and then resume playing. This balanced reaction—being concerned about the caregiver's departure but not overwhelmed by it—reflects secure attachment.

Most of the remaining infants show either insecure-avoidant (type A) or insecure-resistant/ambivalent (type C) attachment. Researchers using Ainsworth's A/B/C designations found some infants who fit into none of these categories; such infants are classified as **disorganized,** or type D. The percentages of children classified as A, B, C, and D vary, partly because groups of infants differ in their family and cultural experiences and therefore in their attachment patterns.

disorganized A category of attachment that is neither secure nor insecure but is marked by the child's and caregiver's inconsistent behavior toward each other.

Attachment and Social Context

Ainsworth's Strange Situation has been used in thousands of studies, and her seminal concepts regarding early relationships have inspired much additional research. Some researchers have developed a structured questionnaire to rate attachment in infants or older children; others have developed a set of conditions and criteria to measure preschoolers' attachment; still others have refined ways to quantify and categorize the attachments that adults had to their parents long ago. The concept of attachment has been extended to refer to teenagers and their friendships, to spouses and their marriages, and to people's reactions to death (Cassidy & Shaver, 1999; Noppe, 2000). Attachment has been measured in many cultures, internationally and within nations, and always about half or two-thirds of the infants are rated as securely attached, especially when cultural variations are taken into account (Posada et al., 1995; True et al., 2001; van IJzendoorn & Kroonenberg, 1988). No developmentalist doubts that attachment is vital to the human species and that infants are powerfully disposed to use familiar people as bases for emotional comfort and exploration.

Experts also agree that an infant's attachment is affected by many factors, including the personalities of both parent and child, the past quality of their relationship, and the conditions in the family and culture. A history of responsive, caring interaction is probably the most important factor in predicting secure attachment (Sroufe, 2002). A secure relationship is more likely if the caregiver has provided the following:

(a)

(b)

Personality of Caregiver Both nature and nurture may be in evidence here, in that the mother's personality obviously affects the quality of interaction with her offspring. Adults typically use special social behaviors (a) with their young infants—leaning in close, opening their eyes and mouths wide in exaggerated expressions of surprise or delight, maintaining eye contact—because those behaviors elicit the baby's attention and pleasure. But such behaviors are subdued or absent when the adult is depressed or stressed (b), and this makes social interaction much less enjoyable for each partner.

- Overall sensitivity to the infant's basic needs (e.g., for food, stimulation, soothing)
- Responsiveness to specific signals, such as vocalizations and facial expressions
- Play in which the caregiver actively encourages ongoing development

Not surprisingly, greater synchrony in early interactions between a mother and a young infant tends to produce more secure attachment to the mother by the time the child is a toddler (Isabella & Belsky, 1991; Thompson, 1998; Volker et al., 1999). Note that these conclusions follow quite logically from Erikson's emphasis on early trust and from the behaviorists' stress on early learning.

The infant's characteristics directly affect the likelihood of secure attachment; some infants, by temperament, have more difficulty forming attachments than others (Pipp-Siegel et al., 1999; Poehlmann & Fiese, 2001). Fathers, too, are influential, either indirectly, through their influence on the mother's ability to be a secure base, or directly, in that some infants are securely attached to their fathers but not to their mothers. In the latter case, the attachment to the father can protect the infant from the worst consequences of insecure attachment to the mother (Goodman & Gotlib, 1999). The nature of the parents' marriage, the birth of another baby, death or serious illness in the family—all affect attachment. Marital conflict and divorce are particularly likely to lead to insecure attachment, primarily because those situations directly affect the mother's responses to her child (Thompson, 2000).

As with all of development, no single factor determines attachment status. For example, a healthy, happy newborn raised in an economically comfortable family by a well-adjusted mother will almost always demonstrate secure attachment to her at age 1. In contrast, if an infant had a low birthweight (but is not handicapped) *and* if the mother has symptoms of depression (but is not clinically depressed), secure attachment is less likely, occurring in only 32 percent in one sample. The same study found that if the mother was quite happy, even if the infant was of low birthweight, 75 percent became securely attached (Poehlmann & Fiese, 2001). The interaction of various protective and debilitating factors is crucial, with normal infants being genetically predisposed to develop a secure attachment to someone.

The Importance of Attachment

Experts agree about the nature of attachment, but they disagree about its implications. Attachment at age 1 may be a powerful influence on the child's social and personality development in the years to come, or it may merely indicate one moment in a long developmental history. In both cases, the correlation may be positive, and positive correlations have been found in hundreds of longitudinal studies. Thus, children who continue to explore the environment and are not overly dependent on the mother or father are likely to interact with teachers in a friendly and appropriate way, to seek help when needed, to work independently when possible, and to display many social skills—making friends, deflecting conflicts, cooperating in play. By contrast, insecure infants tend to become more aggressive and less able to learn as they grow older. The correlation is definite, which means that every parent should strive for secure attachment and every psychological professional should be concerned about insecure attachments in babies at age 1.

Since correlation is not causation, it is not certain that attachment *causes* such later development. Some researchers are convinced that age 1 is a critical period, or at least a sensitive one, for emotional and social development. They believe that if secure attachment does not develop then, it is difficult to establish later. This is in line with psychoanalytic and behaviorist theories.

Cognitive and sociocultural theorists agree that secure attachment indicates a healthy social relationship, but they think that security merely signifies a supportive caregiver who will probably continue to be effective. As evidence for this view, siblings tend to have the same attachment status, even though siblings differ genetically and in other ways; this fact suggests that some mothers are culturally and cognitively more sensitive than others and that their sensitivity continues over the years (van IJzendoorn et al., 2000). Similarly, twins' attachment to their mother is usually the same, whether they are monozygotic (identical) or dizygotic (fraternal); again, this indicates that the mother's sensitivity is more influential than the child's temperament (O'Conner & Croft, 2001).

Insensitive care also usually continues, pushing the child toward being overly fearful (type A, insecure-avoidant, in Ainsworth's terms), overly distressed (type C, insecure-resistant/ambivalent), or overly angry and aggressive (type D, disorganized) over the years, not only because of early issues of trust or reinforcement but also because of current care (Kochanska, 2001).

The fact that a mother's personality and responsiveness are major influences on both infant attachment and later development suggests that attachment is an indicator, not a cause, of a child's future emotional growth. When the parents' responses to the child change, emotional relationships change as well. For example, early research among higher-income, intact families found very high stability of attachment (above 80 percent) from age 1 through the preschool years. However, recent research on economically diverse samples finds that stability occurs only about half the time, with the most stable being type B (secure) and type D (disorganized) (Thompson, 1998). Factors that disrupt a family, such as abuse or divorce, can shake loose a secure attachment, as had happened to most (61 percent) of a group of 18-year-olds who were secure at age 1 but experienced disruptive family events before age 12 (Beckwith et al., 1999).

Warning Signs of Insecure Attachment

The finding that attachment status may be an indicator, not a determinant, of future emotional development is particularly important when something seems to be amiss in the child's first emotional relationships. For example, it is estimated that 10 percent of mothers of young infants (20 percent of low-income mothers) are depressed; insecure attachment is much more common in such cases (Thompson, 1998). However, even in such cases, insecurity is not inevitable and need not be long-lasting. First, the mother's attitudes or even the degree of her depression is not the determining factor;

Nobody's Children These orphans in Kabul, Afghanistan, are living casualties of years of civil war. They appear well nourished, but, with their parents dead and with no adult to develop an attachment to, they are emotionally deprived. Also, this Spartan orphanage gives them physical shelter but inadequate mental stimulation. These conditions lessen their chances of developing normally.

JOHN MOORE / AP PHOTO

TABLE 7.3 How Disturbed Mothers Develop Type D Attachment in Their Infants

Mothers of type D infants are at least three times more likely than mothers of types A, B, and C infants to exhibit these behaviors:

Laugh when infant is crying	Pull infant by the wrist
Invite approach and then distance	Mock and tease the infant
Use friendly tone while maintaining threatening posture	Tell a crying infant to hush
Direct infant to do something and then say not to do it	Ignore an infant who falls down
Display a sudden change of mood, not elicited by the context	Use a loud or sharp voice
Handle the infant as though the infant were not alive	Remove a toy with which the infant is engaged
Display a frightened expression	Hold infant away from body with stiff arms
Withhold a toy from the infant	Speak in hushed, intimate, sexy tones to the infant
Neglect to soothe a distressed infant	Talk in "haunted" or frightened voice

Source: Adapted from Lyons-Ruth et al., 1999.

instead, her overt responses to the infant's attempts at synchrony or need for attachment create the relationship. Thus, simply knowing that a mother is distressed does not mean that valid conclusions about the mother–child relationship can be drawn; the actual interaction must be measured. Second, at least in the early years of life, children can recover from periods of maternal depression, and they respond more to their mother's current behavior than to her behavior months earlier (National Research Council & Institute for Medicine, 2000).

If a mother is too withdrawn, infants are likely to develop a type A (insecure-avoidant) attachment pattern. Essentially, type A infants ignore the person who is already ignoring them and explore the environment, often seeking another attachment figure. If they succeed in this search—that is, if a father, grandparent, or another caregiver provides secure attachment—these infants often develop normally (Goodman & Gotlib, 1999). Similarly, type C (insecure-resistant/ambivalent) infants sometimes manage to induce change in their caregivers that allows a more secure, less manipulative relationship to develop.

The most serious problems arise in type D (disorganized) infants, who often become hostile and aggressive in later childhood (Lyons-Ruth, 1996). They are disorganized because their mother's inconsistent behavior makes it impossible to devise an effective attachment strategy. Instead of responding appropriately, these mothers give conflicting messages—love/hate, sad/glad—that are beyond the ability of a 1-year-old to decipher and respond to coherently (see Table 7.3). Not surprisingly, if infants are unable to learn any effective strategy for dealing with other people, even an avoidant or resistant strategy, they lash out in pain and confusion, becoming hostile and aggressive for no apparent reason in preschool and later (Lyons-Ruth et al., 1999).

Infant Day Care

Almost all infants are cared for, part of the time, by people other than their mothers. In fact, more than half of all 1-year-olds in the United States were in "regularly scheduled" nonmaternal care in 1999, and the percentage rises every year (National Research Council & Institute of Medicine, 2000). Other nations have even higher rates.

The specifics vary from culture to culture. In many places, especially for a young infant, "nonmaternal care" means care by a relative, usually fathers or grandmothers. As a child's age and family income increase, nonmaternal care becomes more likely to take the form of an organized and structured program conducted outside the baby's home. Here we will use the term *day care* in the latter, more formal sense.

Research on Infant Day-Care Programs

Assumptions and theories about how day care affects infant psychosocial development vary widely. Observers influenced by psychoanalytic theory insist that continuous maternal care is better for young children than any alternative. Those influenced by sociocultural theory contend that alternative caregivers are as good as, and sometimes better than, mothers. Most employed mothers believe that care by a relative, especially the father, is preferable. In fact, however, most infants are cared for by nonrelatives outside the home (Riley & Glass, 2002).

In general, recent research finds that children are not harmed by, and sometimes benefit from, nonmaternal care (Lamb, 1998). In fact, the evidence is overwhelming that good preschool education (from age 3 to age 5) is beneficial, helping children learn more language, think with more perspective, develop better social skills, and achieve more in the long term, as Chapter 9 describes in detail. Here we look at nonmaternal care in the first two years, which is more controversial, especially with regard to attachment.

Support for the conclusion that day care is not harmful and is often beneficial is being provided by a massive (1,300 children), multistate (10 regions) longitudinal (from birth to age 3) study by the National Institute of Child Health and Development (NICHD Early Child Care Research Network, 1996, 1998, 1999, 2000, 2001, 2002).

According to this study and other current research, an infant who regularly attends a day-care center that has a low teacher–child ratio is likely to do well in almost every aspect of cognitive and social development (Melhuish, 2001). Infants in day care play with several peers and many safe, age-appropriate toys and learn to express thoughts verbally sooner than do children who stay at home. (Table 7.4 summarizes the characteristics of high-quality day care.) According to the Early Child Care Research Network, the *only* condition in which early day care seems detrimental is when the mother is already insensitive *and* when the infant spends many hours each week in a poor-quality program (too few caregivers, with too little training).

In some cases, out-of-home day care is better than in-home care (Ramey et al., 2002). For example, the longitudinal study of children's emotions from 4 months to 4 years, cited earlier, found that infants who were most fearful at 4 months were more likely to become outgoing over the next four years if they entered day care before age 2. To be specific, 75 percent of those fearful infants who experienced early nonparental care were sociable, not fearful, on at least one later assessment. By contrast, of those who stayed exclusively with their mothers, 70 percent remained consistently inhibited through age 4 (Fox et al., 2001). Among the possible explanations is that toddlers who do not always receive solicitous care from one person must figure things out on their own and

Especially for Day-Care Teachers A mother who brings her child to your care says that she knows she is harming her baby but must work out of economic necessity. What do you say?

TABLE 7.4 High-Quality Day Care

High-quality day care has four essential characteristics:

1. *Adequate attention to each infant.* This means a low caregiver-to-infant ratio and a small group of infants. The ideal situation might be two reliable caregivers for five infants. Infants need to be able to rely on one or two adults, so continuity of care from the same caregivers is very important.

2. *Encouragement of sensorimotor exploration and language development.* Infants should be provided with a variety of easily manipulated toys and should have a great deal of language exposure through games, songs, and conversations.

3. *Attention to health and safety.* Cleanliness routines (such as handwashing before meals), accident prevention (such as the absence of small objects that could be swallowed), and safe areas for exploration (such as a clean, padded area for crawling and climbing) are all good signs.

4. *Well-trained and professional caregivers.* Ideally, every caregiver should have a degree or certificate in early-childhood education and should have worked in this field for several years. Turnover should be low, morale high, and enthusiasm evident.

ELIZABETH CREWS

Infant Day Care Three adults and four babies in this Berkeley, California, day-care center—not a bad ratio. It is also safe (no sharp edges, for example), nurturing (note the hugs), and it encourages cognition (lots of books and toys).

hence "increase in independence and decrease in fearfulness" (Fox et al., 2001, p. 18). When the mother is severely depressed, the home is conflict-filled, or the family is neglectful, day care not only is a lifesaver for the infant but also may help repair a destructive family context (Lamb, 1998; NICHD, 2000).

Some research, however, finds that the benefits of day care disappear if the caregiver is harsh, insensitive, or overwhelmed. Other research finds that the quality of day care is not very significant, since even an infant who spends 40 hours a week in day care still spends 128 hours a week at home. The NICHD study of infant day care found that mediocre day care was generally harmless. Infants were likely to become insecurely attached or to show other signs of deprivation only if all of the following were true:

■ Their own mothers were insensitive.
■ Day-care quality was not just mediocre, but poor.
■ They spent more than 20 hours per week in day care.

Even under these circumstances, girls had fewer problems than boys, and steady care was better than care from an assortment of caregivers (as we saw in the case of Toni in Chapter 5) (NICHD, 1997).

Interpreting the Evidence

Even though most research finds that day care is generally beneficial, you may have read some alarming reports that early day care impairs infant development, particularly in such areas as attachment between mothers and infants and aggressiveness. Why do such contrary examples surface in the media? There are two reasons. The first is that many uninformed people seize on exceptions that confirm their prejudices, ignoring the more widespread examples that support the opposite view. Thus, headlines make it seem as if the most common sexual abusers of children are trusted nonrelatives (teacher, scout leader, coach, priest) whereas in reality, most abusers are the child's own parents.

The second reason some people jump to the wrong conclusions is that, among the dozens of factors studied, some are enhanced by infant day care and some are not. This is always the case when many variables are evaluated. It is a mistake to focus on any one correlation, especially when the effects are small (as they are when the impact of maternal and nonmaternal care in the first two years of life is studied). For almost every variable, the dominant effects arise from the nature of the home environment—whether or not an infant, toddler, or preschooler is also in day care.

Although almost all cognitive and biosocial development advances further in day care than at home, effects on psychosocial development are less clear-cut. For example, the NICHD study correlated fifteen aspects of children's interactions (six at 24 months and nine at 36 months) with nine aspects of caregiving, including the mother's education, mother's sensitivity, and the child's hours in day care from birth on. Maternal education was a significant correlate for six of the variables, and maternal sensitivity was a significant correlate for twelve of

Response for Day-Care Teachers (from page 225): Reassure her that you will keep her baby safe and you will develop the baby's mind and social skills through synchrony and attachment. More important, tell her that the quality of mother–infant interaction at home is more essential than anything else for psychosocial development; mothers who are employed full time usually have wonderful, secure relationships with their infant. If need be, you can teach her ways of being a responsive mother.

the variables, all in a favorable direction. (For example, children of more educated, sensitive mothers were rated as being more positive in sharing, taking turns, and other aspects of social play.) When these fifteen variables were compared to hours spent in early day care, ten showed no correlation, two were favorable, and three were unfavorable (NICHD, 2001). Thus, not every item measured favors day care. Some critics still contend that early, extensive nonmaternal care is sometimes harmful to mother–infant harmony (Belsky, 2001).

Conclusions in Theory and Practice

You have seen in this chapter that the first two years are filled with psychosocial developments, all of which result from genes, maturation, culture, and caregivers. Each of the five major theories seems plausible, yet they differ in assessing the significance of the particular experiences of the first two years of life. To evaluate these differences, first study Figure 7.2 and think about possible explanations for the findings charted there; then try thinking like a scientist.

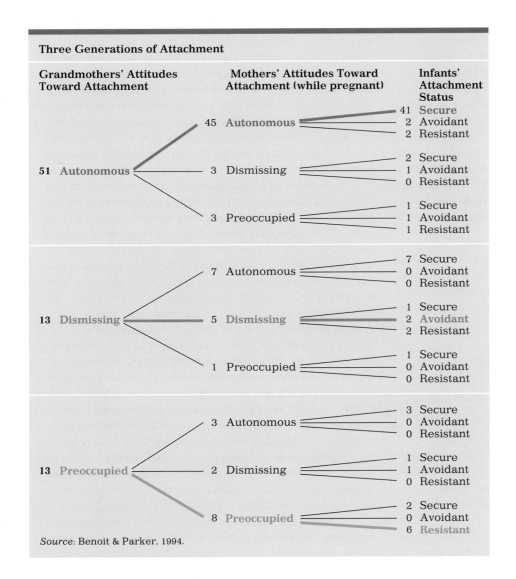

Three Generations of Attachment

Source: Benoit & Parker, 1994.

FIGURE 7.2 Adult Attachment and Attitudes Using the Adult Attachment Interview, researchers rated the attachment attitudes of 77 pregnant women and those of their mothers. The ratings comprised three categories: autonomous (valuing attachment objectively), dismissing (tending to devalue attachment), and preoccupied (emotional about attachment). (A fourth category, called unresolved, exists but was not significant in this study.) About a year after the women gave birth, "blind" observers (researchers who knew nothing of the subjects' previous ratings) rated the attachment quality of the women and their infants by using the Strange Situation. The results show that the attachment attitudes tend to be transmitted intergenerationally (e.g., of the 51 autonomous grandmothers, 45 had autonomous daughters). Further, the attitudes of the mothers seem to be reflected in the quality of their infants' attachment (e.g., of the 55 autonomous mothers, 51 had securely attached infants).

Thinking Like a Scientist

Explaining Continuity in Attachment Status from Childhood to Adulthood

To help you interpret the data in Figure 7.2, you should know that researchers administered an adult attachment interview (AAI) to 77 pregnant women and to their mothers. During the hour-long interview, the subjects were asked questions about childhood attachment experiences, perception of early trust and security, and current relationships with parents and adult partners (Main, 1995). About a year after the pregnant subjects gave birth, the researchers tested their infants in the Strange Situation (Benoit & Parker, 1994). As you can see from Figure 7.2, attachment patterns tended to be passed down, with 64 percent of the families having the same attachment status in all three generations. However, the mothers in the middle generation were all European-American, all married, and mostly middle-class. This is a segment of the population in which continuity is more common than in samples with more varied socio-economic status or ethnicity. To simplify analysis, Figure 7.2 reflects only three categories for toddlers (called secure, avoidant, and resistant) and adults; but actually, toddlers and adults can be classified into four categories. For adults, these four categories are the following:

- *Dismissing.* Dismissing adults devalue the importance and influence of their past attachment relationships. Sometimes they idealize their early relationships with their parents without being able to provide specific examples to support their view. (Similar to type A, insecure-avoidant attachment in children)

- *Autonomous.* Autonomous adults value close relationships and regard them as influential. They are not overwhelmed by emotions concerning their childhood attachments; they can discuss them objectively, including negative as well as positive aspects. (Similar to type B, secure attachment)

- *Preoccupied.* Preoccupied adults are very involved with their childhood experiences. They are unable to speak about early attachment relationships objectively, and they often show considerable emotion when asked about their relationships with their parents. (Similar to type C, insecure-resistant/ambivalent attachment)

- *Unresolved.* Unresolved adults have not yet reconciled their past attachments with their current ones. They are still trying to understand parental rejection, death, or other early experiences. (Similar to type D, disorganized attachment)

Now let's analyze the data. Did you notice in the graph that mother–infant attachment status was more often in agreement (81 percent) than grandmother–mother attachment status (75 percent)? Did you also see that secure attachments are the ones most likely to be transmitted? Almost 90 percent of the autonomous grandmothers had autonomous daughters, and more than 90 percent of the autonomous daughters had securely attached infants. By contrast, dismissing or preoccupied mothers were more likely to have offspring with a different attachment status. What do these findings mean? Certainly they suggest that a person's experiences in infancy are durable, lasting into adulthood and then being passed down from mother to child, especially if the pattern is a beneficial one. It is impossible to tell from these data which (if any) of the three grand theories—psychoanalytic, behaviorist, or cognitive—is correct. But one's early experiences and one's interpretation of those experiences clearly seem important.

Both the sociocultural and the epigenetic systems theories also offer explanations for the remarkable continuity in attachment patterns from generation to generation. Because all the subjects were middle-class North American women, they might be expected to share cultural values and socially accepted behaviors across the generations. Therefore, an alternative explanation is that the data reveal the impact of culture rather than of early experiences. Moreover, note that the number of secure attachments increased from one generation to the next: 51 of the grandmothers, 55 of the mothers, and 59 of the infants were securely attached. This generational drift may follow from the changes in cultural values that occurred over the course of the twentieth century. Secure attachment is the most desirable pattern today, but that may not have been the case 50 years ago. Also note that category A diminished most over three generations, decreasing from 13 to 10 to 7. To interpret this trend, a sociocultural perspective is again useful. Remember that avoidant infants play independently, a behavior that may have been encouraged by the mother who had more children and fewer household conveniences than her modern counterpart. For today's young mothers, as represented by this sample, that is less often true. In fact, half of these children were first-born, and the average age of the mothers was 30, so probably relatively few encouraged their infants to be very independent, ignoring their mothers as they explored a new playroom. Therefore, these mothers did not raise dismissing/insecure-avoidant toddlers, even if their own mothers had raised them to be more independent.

Temperament may also help explain the intergenerational continuity, which would favor an epigenetic systems view. Genes are obviously passed from one generation to the next, so the apparent continuity seen here could be epigenetic; that is, anxious parents might conceive anxious children who show type C (insecure-resistant/ambivalent) attachment in the Strange Situation.

Although continuity is apparent, so is discontinuity. Even within this restricted, middle-class group of families, 39 percent changed in attachment patterns from one generation to the next. Thus, the data can be interpreted in many ways.

What conclusions can be drawn from such research? Certainly there is some continuity in attachment across the generations, but no single theory stands out as the best interpretation of continuity or change. The first two years are important, but early emotional and social development can probably be altered by the mother's behavior, the father's support, the quality of day care, cultural patterns, and inborn traits. We do not know whether one influence, such as a good day-care center, can completely compensate for another, such as a depressed mother. Prevention, intervention, and compensation remain important for early psychosocial development, but we do not yet know exactly how and when.

"We do not yet know exactly how and when" is a scientifically accurate statement as regards almost every controversial assumption about child development. But this statement does not resolve many practical issues. On the basis of what you have learned, you could safely advise parents to play with their infants, respond to their physical and emotional needs, let them explore, maintain a relationship with them, pay attention to them, and expect them to be sometimes angry, sometimes proud, sometimes uncertain. These parental actions may or may not have a powerful impact on later development, but they certainly make infants happier than they would be if their parents were indifferent.

Such generalities are not good enough for our two toddlers, Toni and Jacob, or for all the other thousands, even millions, of infants who show signs of under-nutrition, delayed language development, poor social skills, abnormal emotional development, and other deficits. Here we must leave scientific uncertainty and skepticism, and be specific. Toni and Jacob cannot wait for definitive answers.

A Practical Approach for Toni

We can interpret Toni's experiences to highlight her emotional distress. Toni's social world was turned upside down when her mother went back to work. Having lived exclusively with her mother (with no father or siblings in the household), Toni suddenly finds herself being cared for, outside her home, by a variety of family members. The mother's reported mistrust of strangers is ominous, since social isolation and fear of outsiders may keep Toni and her mother from getting the support they need. No wonder Toni is losing weight and not talking much; she may be angry, depressed, or fearful.

Like all toddlers, Toni needs stability of care, but she has none. The ideal solution is a day-care center that is near her home and has all four characteristics of high-quality care described earlier in this chapter. However, such care is very expensive in the United States and is not always supported by public funds. Inadequate care, with frequently changing caregivers, may be all that is available for Toni. Could that be good enough? Perhaps, but the research suggests that it is risky. It would be much better if one person were the alternative caregiver—perhaps the father, perhaps a grandmother, perhaps a neighbor who stays home with a toddler of her own. The author of the case study recently reported that a social worker has been assigned to help Toni's mother coordinate her care and find a good day-care center in her neighborhood. We hope she found one.

A Practical Approach for Jacob

With Jacob, the withdrawn toddler whom we met at the beginning of this chapter, the need for immediate action is glaringly obvious. Jacob may be autistic or brain-damaged; he may be understimulated by the nanny who does not speak English; he may be suffering from a lack of parental attention, as is suggested by the father's admission that he and his wife were "ready to engage parental autopilot." All infants need one or two people who are emotionally invested in them from the first days of life, and it is not clear that Jacob had anyone.

In any case, something had to be done. Jacob had been evaluated at a major teaching hospital and had been seen by at least 10 experts, none of whom had anything encouraging to say. Fortunately, Jacob's parents consulted a psychologist who was skilled in helping infants with emotional problems. He said, "Now I am going to teach you how to play with your son," showing them a way to build a relationship with him. They learned about "floor time," four hours a day set aside for the parents to get on their son's level and interact with him: imitate him, act as if they were part of the game, put their faces and bodies in front of his, create synchrony even though Jacob did nothing to initiate it. The father reports:

> We rebuilt Jacob's connection to us and to the world—but on his terms. We were drilled to always follow his lead, to always build on his initiative. In a sense, we could only ask Jacob to join our world if we were willing to enter his. . . . He would drop rocks and we would catch them. He would want to put pennies in a bank and we would block the slot. He would want to run in a circle and we would get in his way. I remember a cold fall day when I was putting lime on our lawn. He dipped his hand in the powder and let it slip through his fingers. He loved the way it felt. I took the lawn spreader and ran to the other part of our yard. He ran after me. I let him have one dip and ran across the yard again. He dipped, I ran, he dipped, I ran. We did this until I could no longer move my arms.
>
> *[Jacob's father, 1997]*

Jacob's case is obviously extreme, but many infants and parents have difficulty establishing synchronistic interaction. From the perspective of early psychosocial development, nothing could be more important.

> In Jacob's case it worked. He said his first word at age 3, and by age 5, . . . he speaks for days at a time. He talks from the moment he wakes up to the moment he falls asleep, as if he is making up for lost time. He wants to know everything. "How does a live chicken become an eating chicken? Why are microbes so small? Why do policemen wear badges? Why are dinosaurs extinct? What is French? [A question I often ask myself.] Why do ghosts glow in the dark?" He is not satisfied with answers that do not ring true or that do not satisfy his standards of clarity. He will keep on asking until he gets it. Rebecca and I have become expert definition providers. Just last week, we were faced with the ultimate challenge: "Dad," he asked: "Is God real or not?" And then, just to make it a bit more challenging, he added: "How do miracles happen?"
>
> *[Jacob's father, 1997]*

Miracles do not always happen, although it is amazing that almost all infants, almost all the time, develop relationships with their close family members. The significance of early psychosocial development is now obvious to every developmentalist, and, it is hoped, to every reader of this text and parent or teacher of a young child. The first two years are the foundation for a long developmental history, with later opportunities to shift course. The first such opportunity arises during early childhood, which is the subject of the next three chapters.

SUMMARY

Emotional Development in Infancy

1. Two emotions, contentment and distress, appear as soon as an infant is born. They are soon joined by anger when efforts are frustrated at about 4 months of age. Although reflexive fear is apparent in very young infants, fear of something specific, including fear of strangers and fear of separation, does not appear until toward the end of the first year.

2. In the second year, increasing social awareness leads to more selective fear, anger, joy, and distress. At that point, toddlers begin to express new emotions that are social in nature, such as jealousy and shame.

3. Temperament includes basic personality traits that seem to be genetic. An infant may be easy, difficult, or slow to warm up, according to the New York Longitudinal Study, which measured nine basic traits that have stability over the years.

4. Another categorization of temperament, or personality, is the Big Five (extroversion, agreeableness, conscientiousness, neuroticism, and openness to experience. All these traits seem to be evident, and fairly stable, in people of all ages in many nations.

Emotions in the Social Context

5. Although temperament originates in the child, not in the family, parents can inhibit or guide a child's temperament. Fear, particularly, is moderated by parents and other caregivers.

6. By age 3 months, infants become more responsive and social, and synchrony begins. Synchrony involves moment-by-moment interaction between a baby and an adult. The caregiver needs to be responsive and sensitive, interpreting the infant's signals for play or rest.

7. By age 6 months, infants adjust to the particulars of their caregiver's responses and expect other adults to behave in similar ways. Infants look at other people's facial expressions to detect whether a particular object or experience is frightening or enjoyable, a process called social referencing.

8. Fathers are wonderful playmates for infants, who frequently consult them as social references. Each family is different, but generally mothers are more nurturing and fathers more exciting and more likely to encourage exploration.

9. The increasing self-awareness of toddlerhood allows further development of the more social emotions, such as pride and embarrassment.

Theories About Caregiving

10. According to all five major theories, caregiver behavior is especially influential in the first two years of life. Freud stressed the mother's impact on early oral and anal pleasure; Erikson expanded on Freud's ideas, emphasizing early trust and autonomy.

11. Behaviorists emphasize learning, with parents serving as their baby's first teachers about various emotions—when to be fearful or joyful, for instance. Learning occurs partly through reinforcement and partly through observation, as we saw with social referencing.

12. Cognitive theory holds that infants develop working models, or cognitive hypotheses, based on early experiences. Cultural influences and genetic tendencies are stressed by sociocultural theory and epigenetic systems theory.

13. Every theory recognizes the importance of the early relationship between the infant and caregiver. The two must form an attachment that allows the infant to rely on the caregiver for security and support; this bond gives the infant courage to explore the environment. Attachment to the mother at age 1 correlates with later relationships in school and beyond.

Attachment

14. Attachment is measured by the baby's reaction to the caregiver's presence in or departure from a strange playroom. Some infants seem indifferent (type A—avoidant) or overly dependent (type C—resistant/ambivalent), instead of secure (type B). The most worrisome form of attachment is disorganized (type D). Infants with disorganized attachment are likely to develop serious psychological problems later in life, perhaps becoming loners or criminals.

Infant Day Care

15. Day care for infants seem, on the whole, to be a positive experience, especially for cognitive development. Psychosocial characteristics, including secure attachment, are more influenced by the quality of home care than by the number of hours spent in nonmaternal care. Quality of care within an organized program—especially when it comes to staff training and experience—is also important for the infant's development.

Conclusions in Theory and Practice

16. Exactly how critical early psychosocial development might be is still debated by experts. However, for practitioners, it is obvious that all infants need caregivers who are committed to them, available for and responsive in play, and dedicated to encouraging each aspect of early development.

KEY TERMS

stranger wariness (p. 203)
separation anxiety (p. 203)
temperament (p. 204)
Big Five (p. 205)
approach–withdrawal (p. 206)
goodness of fit (p. 206)
colic (p. 208)
synchrony (p. 208)
still face technique (p. 210)

social referencing (p. 210)
self-awareness (p. 213)
oral stage (p. 215)
anal stage (p. 215)
trust versus mistrust (p. 215)
autonomy versus shame and
    doubt (p. 216)
working model (p. 217)
attachment (p. 218)

proximity-seeking behaviors
    (p. 219)
contact-maintaining behaviors
    (p. 219)
secure attachment (p. 219)
secure base for exploration
    (p. 219)
insecure attachment (p. 219)
insecure-avoidant (p. 219)

insecure-resistant/ambivalent
    (p. 219)
Strange Situation (p. 220)
disorganized (p. 221)

KEY QUESTIONS

1. What is the difference between emotions in the first year and in the second year?

2. What is the usual development of fear in infancy?

3. Provide a specific example of synchrony, describing a creative interaction—either real or hypothetical—at least four responses by each partner.

4. How did researchers develop the nine temperamental traits of the New York Longitudinal Study?

5. Name and define each of the Big Five characteristics.

6. What are the similarities in the explanations of infant personality offered by psychoanalytic theory and behaviorism?

7. Give an example of a working model you might have, and how it might change with experience.

8. What are the differences in the explanations of infant personality offered by epigenetic systems theory and sociocultural theory?

9. What might an observer look for to find out whether an infant was securely or insecurely attached?

10. Describe at least two alternative explanations for the correlation between early attachment and later development.

11. What are the characteristics of high-quality day care?

12. Why might the general public misinterpret research on infant day care?

BIOSOCIAL

Body, Brain, and Nervous System Over the first 2 years, the body quadruples in weight and the brain triples in weight. Connections between brain cells grow into increasingly dense and complex neural networks of dendrites and axons. As neurons become coated with an insulating layer of myelin, they send messages faster and more efficiently. The infant's experiences are essential in "fine-tuning" the brain's ability to respond to stimulation.

Motor Abilities Brain maturation allows the development of motor skills from reflexes to coordinated voluntary actions, including grasping and walking. At birth, the infant's senses of smell and hearing are quite acute; although vision at first is sharp only for objects that are about 10 inches away, visual acuity approaches 20/20 by age 1 year.

Health The health of the infant depends on nutrition (ideally, breast milk), immunization, and parental practices. Survival rates are much higher today than they were even a few decades ago.

COGNITIVE

Perceptual Skills The infant's senses are linked by both inter-modal and cross-modal perception, allowing information to be transferred among senses. The infant is most interested in affordances, that is, what various experiences and events offer to the infant. Movement and personal sensory experiences contribute to the perception of affordances.

Cognitive Skills The infant's active curiosity and inborn abilities interact with various experiences to develop early categories, such as object size, shape, texture, and even number, as well as an understanding of object permanence. Memory capacity, while fragile, grows during the first years. The infant progresses from knowing his or her world through immediate sensorimotor experiences to being able to "experiment" on that world through the use of mental images.

Language Babies' cries are their first communication; they then progress through cooing and babbling. Interaction with adults through "baby talk" teaches them the surface structure of language. By age 1, an infant can usually speak a word or two, and by age 2 is talking in short sentences.

PSYCHOSOCIAL

Emotions and Personality Development Emotions change from quite basic reactions to complex, self-conscious responses. Infants become increasingly independent, a transition explained by Freud in terms of the oral and anal stages, by Erikson in terms of the crises of trust versus mistrust and autonomy versus shame and doubt. While these theories emphasize the parents' role, research finds that much of basic temperament—and therefore personality—is inborn and apparent throughout life.

Parent–Infant Interaction Early on, parents and infants respond to each other by synchronizing their behavior in social play. Toward the end of the first year, secure attachment between child and parent sets the stage for the child's increasingly independent exploration of the world. The infant becomes an active participant in this social interaction, first in directly reacting to others and then in seeking out opinions through social referencing. By age 2, toddlers have definite personalities, the product of the interaction of nature and nurture.

Part III

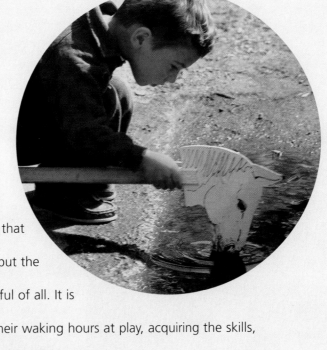

The period from ages 2 to 6 is usually called early childhood, or the preschool period. Here we shall call it the "play years" as well, to underscore the importance of play during that time. Play occurs at every age, of course, but the years of early childhood are the most playful of all. It is then that young children spend most of their waking hours at play, acquiring the skills, ideas, and values that are crucial for growing up. They chase each other and dare themselves to attempt new tasks, developing their bodies; they play with words and ideas, developing their minds; they invent games and dramatize fantasies, learning social skills and moral rules.

The playfulness of young children can cause them to be delightful or exasperating. To them growing up is a game, and their enthusiasm for it seems unlimited—whether they are quietly tracking a beetle through the grass or riotously turning their play area into a shambles. Their minds seem playful, too, for the immaturity of their thinking enables them to explain that "a bald man has a barefoot head" or that "the sun shines so children can go outside to play."

If you expect them to sit quietly, think logically, or act realistically, you are bound to be disappointed. But if you enjoy playfulness, you will enjoy caring for, listening to, and even reading about children between 2 and 6 years old.

Chapter Eight

The Play Years

The Play Years: Biosocial Development

Between ages 2 and 6, significant development occurs on several fronts. The most obvious changes are in size and shape, as chubby toddlers seem to stretch upward, becoming thinner as well as taller. Less obvious but more crucial changes occur in the brain. Maturation turns a clumsy, impulsive 2-year-old into a deft, deliberate, 6-year-old.

Rapid growth and active play make young children vulnerable to many biosocial hazards, including injury and abuse. That aspect of early childhood is covered in this chapter as well, to aid not only in the recognition of abuse but also in its prevention. There is much that can be done to ensure a happy, pain-free early childhood for every 2- to 6-year-old.

Size and Nourishment

As in infancy, the young child's body and brain develop according to powerful epigenetic forces—biologically driven and socially guided, both experience-expectant and experience-dependent (see Chapter 5). However, there are marked differences between infancy and early childhood in biological growth, from gaining weight to adding height, from getting upright to running around, from the emergence of motor skills and emotional expressions to the control of movement and affect.

Body Shape and Growth Rates

During the play years, children generally become slimmer as the lower body lengthens and some baby fat melts away. Gone are the protruding belly, round face, short limbs, and large head that characterize the toddler. By age 6, body proportions are similar to those of an adult, although muscles and stature are obviously quite different, and the kindergartner is more straight than curvaceous.

Steady increases in height and weight accompany these changes in proportions. Each year from ages 2 through 6, well-nourished children add almost 3 inches (about 7 centimeters) in height and gain about 4½ pounds (2 kilograms) in weight. By age 6, the average child in a developed nation weighs about 46 pounds (21 kilograms) and measures 46 inches (117 centimeters). As my nephew said at that point, "In numbers I am square now." These are averages; actual children vary a great deal, especially in weight, and, as noted in Chapter 5, percentiles are more useful than norms in monitoring the growth of a particular child (see Appendix A).

When many ethnic groups live together in one developed nation (such as England, France, Canada, Australia, or the United States), children of African descent tend to be tallest, followed by Europeans, then Asians, and then Latinos. These are very broad generalities; many of these broadly designated ethnic groups and many individual families exhibit quite different inherited height patterns (Eveleth & Tanner, 1990). Even in developed nations, height is particularly variable among children of African descent, because various groups living in Africa over many centuries developed more genetic diversity than did people on any other continent.

Cultural patterns also have an impact on growth rates. Traditionally on the Indian subcontinent and in many South Asian families today, males are better fed and cared for. Consequently, girls are not only much shorter and smaller than boys but also more likely to die (their death rate is almost twice as high) between ages 1 and 4 (Costello & Manandhar, 2000). By contrast, in many North American families with ample food, mealtimes are family rituals that require that children be polite and quiet to earn extra helpings of dessert. In those families, the boys may be the skinny ones.

Many factors influence growth, including birth order, sex, and geography; moreover, first-borns, males, and those living in cities at sea level tend to be taller than their opposites. The three most influential factors, each accounting for several inches of height by the end of childhood, are genes, health, and nutrition. The last factor—nutrition—is largely responsible for dramatic differences between children in developed and underdeveloped nations. In the Netherlands, average 4-year-olds are already taller than 6-year-olds in India, Nepal, or Bangladesh (Eveleth & Tanner, 1991; United Nations, 1994). Similar height disparities occur when children living in Africa or South America are compared to children of the same African or Latino descent who grow up in Europe or North America. Genetically, such children are quite similar, but marked differences in food supply cause dramatic contrasts in height. Improved nutrition is also the primary reason that the average height for 40-year-old men in the United States was 5 feet, 8 inches in 1960 and increased to 5 feet, 10 inches by 1990 (U.S. Bureau of the Census, 1986, 1999).

Genes, health, and malnutrition were covered in Chapter 5. Although undernutrition continues to be a concern in early childhood, we need not discuss inadequate protein or calories again here. However, new concerns arise regarding a balanced diet for young children in nations where food is abundant.

Eating Habits

Compared to infants, young children—especially modern children, who play outdoors less than their parents or grandparents did—need far fewer calories per pound of body weight. Appetites decrease between ages 2 and 6, which causes many parents to fret, threaten, and cajole ("Eat all your dinner, and you can have ice cream"). However, reduced appetite in early childhood is not a medical problem, unless a child is unusually thin or gains no weight at all.

Percentiles indicate whether children are losing or gaining weight compared to their peers; they are certainly a better guide to malnourishment or overnourishment than the leftovers on the dinner plate. Overweight, and worry about being too fat, can be a problem in early childhood (Ambrosi-Randic, 2000). Childhood obesity is discussed in detail in Chapter 11, because it is even more problematic during the school years.

The major nutritional problem in early childhood is an insufficient intake of iron, zinc, and calcium. Foods containing these crucial minerals get crowded out by other foods. Sweetened cereals and drinks, advertised as containing 100 percent of a day's vitamin requirements, are a poor substitute for a balanced diet, for two reasons. First, some essential nutrients have not yet been identified. Second, it is easy for a child to consume too much of one nutrient and not enough of another if fortified cereals rather than fresh fruits and vegetables are the mainstay of the diet. Indeed, high-calorie foods can cause vitamin or mineral deficiencies if they reduce an already small appetite.

Too much sugar is also the leading cause of early tooth decay, the most prevalent disease of young children in developed nations (Lewit & Kerrebrock, 1998). Many cultures promote children's eating of sweets, in the form of birthday cake, holiday candy, Halloween treats, and such. The details (e.g., chocolate Easter bunnies or Hanukkah gelt) depend on family ethnicity and religion, but the general trend is pervasive and hard to resist.

A related problem is that many children, like most adults, eat too few fruits and vegetables and consume too much fat. No more than 30 percent of daily calories should come from fat, but six out of seven young children in the United States exceed that limit. Interestingly, one North American study found that children whose family income is either below the poverty level or three times above it are more likely to exceed this 30 percent than are those whose family income is between the two extremes (Thompson & Dennison, 1994).

Adding to the complications of feeding young children is the fact that many are quite compulsive about daily routines, including meals. This phenomenon is called *just right,* in reference to the child's need for a particular experience to occur in a particular sequence and place and to have certain characteristics. For example:

> Whereas parents may insist that the child eat his vegetables at dinner, the child may insist that the potatoes be placed only in a certain part of the plate and must not touch any other food; should the potatoes land outside of this area, the child may seem to experience a sense of near-contamination, setting off a tirade of fussiness for which many 2- and 3-year-olds are notorious.
>
> *[Evans et al., 1997]*

Most food preferences and rituals are far from nutritionally ideal. (One 3-year-old I know wanted to eat only cream cheese sandwiches on white bread; one 4-year-old, only fast-food chicken nuggets.) The insistence on eating only certain foods, prepared and placed in a particular way, would be pathological in an adult but is normal for young children. About 1,500 parents answered questions about the desire of their 1- to 6-year-olds to have familiar routines and habits (Evans et al., 1997). They reported that more than 75 percent of the 2- to 4-year-olds displayed one or more of the following attitudes:

■ Preferred to have things done in a particular order or in a certain way
■ Had a strong preference for wearing (or not wearing) certain articles of clothing
■ Prepared for bedtime by engaging in a special activity, routine, or ritual
■ Had strong preferences for certain foods

By age 6, this rigidity begins to fade. The items measuring demand that things be "just right" (e.g., "liked to eat food in a particular way") showed a marked decline after age 3 (see Figure 8.1).

Each to His Own Lifelong food preferences are formed during early childhood, which may be one reason why the two children on the right seem dubious about the contents of the pink lunchbox, broccoli and all. Nevertheless, each of these children appears to be a model of healthful eating.

FIGURE 8.1 Young Children's Insistence on Routine This chart shows the average scores of children (who are rated by their parents) on a survey indicating the child's desire to have certain things—including food selection and preparation—done "just right." Such strong preferences for rigid routines tend to fade by age 6.

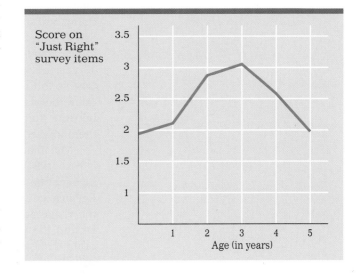

Given both the power and the transience of this behavior in normal children, parents should probably be tolerant. Insistence on a particular bedtime routine, a preferred pair of shoes, or favorite cup can usually be accommodated until the child no longer wants the item. Malnutrition is another story; the best tactic here is to offer ample healthy foods when the child is hungry and to cut down on high-calorie snacks. This approach, however, is rarely taken in the United States, where children typically consume several snacks each day. For example, the past 20 years have seen a decline in calcium consumption because the traditional snack of milk and cookies has been replaced with soda pop and a candy bar (Jahns et al., 2001).

Brain Growth and Development

Brain development begins very early in life, as we described in Chapters 4 and 5. Indeed, by age 2, most pruning, or sculpting, of dendrites has already occurred, as has major brain growth: The 2-year-old brain weighs 75 percent as much as the adult brain.

Since most of the brain is already functioning by age 2, what remains to develop? The most important parts! Brain weight continues to increase faster than the child's body weight, reaching 90 percent of adult weight by age 5 and almost 100 percent by age 7—when the rest of the child's body still has about 100 pounds (45 kilograms) to gain. More important, those functions of the brain that make us most human are the ones that develop after infancy, enabling quicker, more coordinated, and more reflective thought.

Speed of Thought

myelination The process by which axons become insulated with a coating of *myelin*, a fatty substance that speeds transmission of nerve impulses from neuron to neuron in the brain.

After infancy, continued proliferation of the communication pathways results in some brain growth, but the more life-changing transformations occur because of increased myelination. **Myelination** is the process by which neurons (nerves) become insulated with a coating of *myelin*, a fatty substance that speeds transmission of nerve impulses between neurons and from neurons to the brain. Myelination enables the child to think and react much quicker than the toddler can. This greater speed is apparent with single thoughts—as when children recognize familiar faces or hear their own names—but becomes pivotal when several thoughts must occur in rapid succession.

With increasing myelination, thoughts follow each other quickly enough that a child can perform one task and then immediately remember to do the next: hear and then speak, catch and then throw a ball, scan an entire scene to find one thing, and so on. Of course, parents of young children must still be patient when listening to them talk, helping them get dressed, or watching as they try to write their names—all these tasks are completed more slowly by 3-year-olds than by 13-year-olds. However, young children are certainly quicker than toddlers, who take so long with even the simplest task that they might forget what they were doing before they finish. Parents' patience eventually pays off, as children soon become quicker and more precise at exactly those tasks their parents guided them toward completing "all by themselves."

Myelination is not essential for basic communication between neurons, but it *is* essential for fast and complex communication. Experience affects the rate of myelination: Practice makes thoughts come more quickly (Merzenich, 2001). Because young infants spend almost all their waking hours looking and listening, the visual and auditory cortexes are among the earliest to become myelinated. During the play years, myelination proceeds most rapidly in the areas of the brain dedicated to memory and reflection. A 5-year-old, for example, can stop and think, can remember last year, and can act after some reflection—all of which are impossible for a 1-year-old, whose neurons are excited by a particular event and who acts on that impulse immediately. For 1-year-olds, inadequate myelination means that the message has not yet reached another part of the brain, making coordinated reflection impossible. Myelination continues through early adulthood (Sampaio & Truwit, 2001).

Connecting the Brain's Hemispheres

One particular part of the brain that grows and myelinates rapidly during the play years is the **corpus callosum**, a band of nerve fibers that connect the left and right sides of the brain (see Figure 8.2). The corpus callosum is "250–800 million fibers that do nothing other than keep the hemispheres coordinated in their processing" (Banich & Heller, 1998, p. 1). As a result, throughout childhood, communication between the two brain hemispheres becomes markedly more efficient, allowing children to coordinate functions that involve the entire brain or body (Banich, 1998).

Left Side, Right Side

Although it looks as if the two sides of the body and brain are identical, in many crucial ways they are not. **Lateralization** is specialization of the two sides of the body or brain, so that one side is dominant for a certain function. You already know about hand dominance, either because you are left-handed yourself or because you have noticed that some of your friends prefer using their left hand for certain tasks. But you may not realize that lateralization is also apparent in arms, legs, feet, eyes, and ears. For instance, if you pick up a telephone (usually with your dominant hand), you almost always put it to your dominant ear—the ear that is specialized for understanding speech. In most people, this is the right ear, because the right ear is connected to the left side of the brain (so are the right eye, the right arm, and so on), which is where speech is best processed. However, if you routinely had to listen to sentimental melodies with only one ear, the left ear would probably be your unconscious choice, because the right side of the brain is better at processing tunes and emotions (Ivry & Robertson, 1998).

Such specialization begins before birth, prompted by genes or prenatal hormones and, as epigenetic theory would predict, continues with early experience. Newborns, sleeping in their cribs, usually turn their heads rightward (or leftward, for those who will be left-handed), typically also bending their limbs toward one side rather than straight up and down. (Adults do this, too—think about how your head, arms, and legs are positioned when you sleep by yourself.) This is evidence for the prenatal origins of sidedness. As infants lie in their cribs, they face toward one hand, moving it as they watch, gaining dexterity, making that hand dominant. Thus early experience may influence hand preference. Later experience definitely makes a difference, as is evident in the millions of infants with a left-handed preference who were trained to be right-handed.

Why would anyone force a child to change hand preference? Unless you are left-handed yourself, you may not realize that all societies are organized to favor right-handed people. This bias is apparent in language (in Latin, *dexter* means "right" and *sinister* means "left"), customs, tools, and taboos. In many Asian and African nations today, the left hand's only function is wiping after defecation; it is a major insult to give someone anything or to perform any other observable action with that "dirty" hand. In Western cultures, using the right hand to shake hands is a

corpus callosum A long, narrow strip of nerve fibers that connects the left and right hemispheres of the brain.

lateralization Literally, "sidedness," here referring to the differentiation of the two sides of the body or brain so that one side specializes in a certain function. Brain lateralization allows the left side of the brain to control the right side of the body, and vice versa.

FIGURE 8.2 Connections Two views of the corpus callosum, a band of nerve fibers (axons) that convey information between the two hemispheres of the brain. When developed, this "connector" allows the person to coordinate functions that are performed mainly by one hemisphere or the other. (a) A view from between the hemispheres, looking toward the right side of the brain. (b) A view from above, with the gray matter not shown in order to expose the corpus callosum.

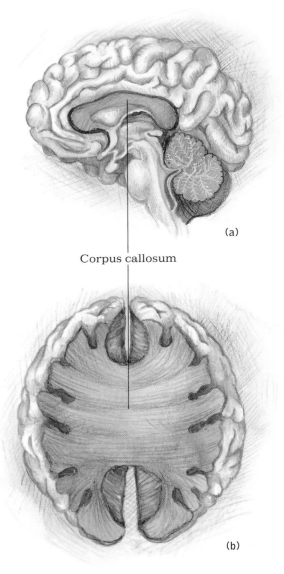

(a)

Corpus callosum

(b)

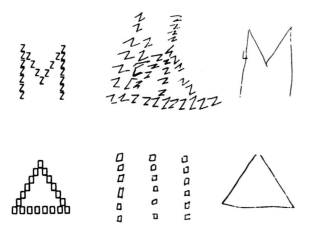

FIGURE 8.3 Copy What You See
Brain-damaged adults were asked to copy the figure at the left in each row. One person drew the middle set, another the set at the far right.

? *Observational Quiz* (see answer, page 244): Which set was drawn by someone with left-side damage, and which set by someone with right-side damage?

custom that has its origin in the intent to prove that the dominant hand is not holding a weapon. Many tools—scissors, steam irons, faucets, screws—are designed for right-handed people. Such circumstances may explain why many parents try to train their children to be right-handed and why the incidence of left-handedness decreases with age.

Not only in hands but also in the brain, plasticity favors youth (Merzenich, 2001). Damage to the left side of the brain, where most language functions are located, is more serious in adults than in young children. When the left side of the brain is entirely gone (as may happen when a major brain tumor is surgically removed), young children often switch language functions to the right side, learning to talk, listen, and read quite well. Interestingly, although such children test in the normal range on various tests of language abilities, some subtle deficiencies in fluency are evident, proof that the whole brain is needed for most complex tasks (Stiles, 1998). Adults suffer far more impairment if one side of their brain is damaged, as shown in Figure 8.3.

Through such findings, neurologists have determined that the brain's hemispheres specialize: The left half controls the right side of the body and contains the areas dedicated to logic, analysis, and language; the right half controls the left side of the body and generalized emotional and creative impulses. Some people assume that this means people are either left-brained or right-brained. Not true. In fact, every cognitive skill requires both sides of the brain, just as every important motor skill requires both sides of the body (Efron, 1990; Springer & Deutsch, 1998). Without a mature corpus callosum, "the hemispheres of young children are more functionally disconnected than those of adults" (Banich, 1998, p. 36) and some skills are clumsy, wobbly, and slow. As newly myelinated fibers carry faster signals between the two hemispheres, better thinking and faster movement are possible.

Gender- and Age-Related Variations

Although all adults (except those few whose brains are "split" surgically to relieve life-threatening epilepsy) have approximately 500 million fibers in their corpus callosum, some people, especially left-handed males, have more than others (Clarke et al., 1998). Presumably, young left-handed boys adjust to a world designed for right-handed people by developing stronger neural connections. Proportionally, the corpus callosum is usually thicker in female brains than in male ones. For this male–female variation, researchers have many hypotheses and presumptions, both genetic and cultural, but no consensus.

These gender variations related to handedness are small compared to the age-related growth in the size of the corpus callosum in young children. Six-year-olds coordinate their brains and bodies much better than younger children do. A simple example is hopping on one foot while using both arms for balance; few children under age 4 can do this. A more complicated example is skipping, which demands not only balance and coordination of both sides of the body but also quick switching between the two. Myelination and left–right equilibration allow mastery, progressing from step–slide–hop at age 4—too slow to be a real skip—to smooth skipping by age 8 or 10 (Loovis & Butterfield, 2000).

A less visible but more crucial application of left–right coordination is information processing (explained in Chapter 6), which connects and interweaves sensory perceptions, emotions, cognitions, and body movements. Reading, writing, and many other intellectual skills call for such multitasking. This requires not only the corpus callosum but also the ability to choose between various inputs, selecting some and inhibiting others, planning and analyzing. For this, the prefrontal cortex is essential.

Planning and Analyzing

The **prefrontal cortex** is the final part of the human brain to reach maturity. Sometimes called the *frontal cortex* or *frontal lobe,* it is an area in the very front part of the brain's outer layer (the cortex) that is least developed in nonhuman primates and absent in rats and other lower animals. Maturation of the prefrontal cortex is not completed until mid-adolescence (Bloom et al., 2001). One reason it develops so slowly is that it emerged relatively recently in the evolutionary sequence (Darling et al., 1998).

prefrontal cortex The area at the front of the cortex of the brain that specializes in the "executive function," planning, selecting, and coordinating thoughts. (Also called the *frontal lobe* or *frontal cortex*.)

The Prefrontal Cortex as Executive

The prefrontal cortex is also called the *executive* area of the brain, because it directs and controls the other parts (Umilta & Stablum, 1998). Its specific functions include planning, analyzing, selecting responses, and coordinating messages from many parts of both cerebral hemispheres. A crucial executive function is to inhibit, or halt, various impulses, stopping immediate reactions, especially emotional ones. Children's gradual development of emotional control reflects not only their increasing myelination but also the maturation of the prefrontal cortex; this is confirmed by many studies that reveal particular advances of the prefrontal cortex at about age 3 or 4 (Posner & Rothbart, 2000).

The prefrontal cortex assists in self-control and self-regulation. Neonates cannot muffle a cry of pain or stay awake when drowsiness hits. As the neurons of the frontal area become more interconnected and their axons more myelinated, infants gradually become better able to regulate their responses, sleep–wake patterns, and emotions. As you saw in Chapters 5 and 7, by age 1, sleep is already more regular and emotions are more nuanced and responsive to the external world (think of shrieks of joy at a father's tickling but cries of anger when a sibling does the same thing). This begins a long period of emotional regulation via the frontal lobe, which "shows the most prolonged period of postnatal development of any region of the human brain" (Johnson, 1998, p. 33), with dendrite density increasing throughout adolescence.

Some brain functions in the prefrontal cortex seem experience-expectant: Every normal human has the requisite experiences to regulate emotions by middle childhood. For that reason, something is seriously wrong in the brain or in the family if a 10-year-old has a kicking, screaming temper tantrum, although it is quite normal for a 2-year-old to have one. Other aspects of self-control are experience-dependent, influenced by the particular culture. For example, are all children taught to wait for dessert until after dinner, to answer strangers politely, to give up their naps, to repress tears or curses or laughter? No. Some kinds of emotional regulation are unique to particular cultures, and children in all cultures depend on quite specific instruction from adults and peers.

Impulsiveness and Perseveration

Understanding the functioning of the prefrontal cortex sheds light on the ongoing development of the child. Since they have little mental ability to plan and select, very young children are both impulsive and perseverative. Both impulsiveness and perseveration are signs of brain damage in older children or adults, but they are typical of normal children who are very young.

Impulsiveness is obvious; just imagine a 3-year-old who jumps from task to task, unable to sit down and be still for very long, even in church or other settings that require quiet. Impulsiveness is also obvious in a day-care center with many children and toys, where some younger children want to play immediately with whatever toy another child has but then, when they can have that toy because the other child has begun to play with something else, they no longer want it.

perseveration The tendency to persevere, or stick to, one thought or action even when it has become useless or inappropriate.

Perseveration is the tendency to persevere, or stick to, one thought or action long after it is time to move on. An adult may think a child should stop building a tower long before the child does. That is not really perseveration. True perseveration is more detrimental, such as putting the same simple puzzle together a dozen times or more, or cutting one's chicken into dozens of tiny pieces instead of taking one bite.

Now picture perseveration as it normally occurs in young children. Some 2-year-olds sing the same song again and again, or scribble the same drawing, or resist having their favorite TV show interrupted and "lose it," throwing a temper tantrum. That temper tantrum itself may perseverate, with the child's crying becoming uncontrollable, unstoppable, as if the child were stuck in that emotion until exhaustion sets in. This age is sometimes called the "terrible twos": These children's brain patterns lead them to deviate from adult standards of decorum, because emotions are not yet regulated.

Although impulsiveness and perseveration seem opposites, they actually are two manifestations of the same deficiency—a lack of self-control, of appropriate focus, of emotional balance. In other words, they are signs of an undeveloped prefrontal cortex, which characterizes all 2-year-olds and far fewer 5-year-olds. Gradually, children become less likely to bump into walls or each other as they learn to "look before they leap."

! Answer to Observational Quiz (from page 242): The middle set, with its careful details, reflects damage to the right half of the brain, where overall impressions are found. The person with left-brain damage produced the drawings that were just an M or a Δ, without the details of the tiny z's and squares. With a whole functioning brain, people can see both "the forest and the trees."

Educational Implications of Brain Development

Brain development is not smooth and linear; brain functions do not improve at exactly the same age for every child (Fisher, 1997; Haier, 2001). Even by age 6, some children have not yet acquired the neurological maturity expected after years of experience-expectant brain growth, particularly of the corpus callosum and prefrontal cortex. However, most 6-year-olds (and a few 4- and 5-year-olds) are ready to do the following:

- Sit in one place for an hour or so
- Scan a page of print, moving the eyes systematically from left to right (or, for some languages, from top to bottom or right to left), not allowing the eyes to dart around the page
- Balance the sides of the body, enabling skipping, galloping, and kicking or catching balls
- Draw and write with one hand, accurately copying shapes or letters
- Listen and think before talking
- Remember important facts and instructions for more than a few seconds
- Control emotions, with tears, temper, or laughter seldom erupting at the wrong time

As you can imagine, experience is crucial to all these abilities (Merzenich, 2001). Children whose family life is too stressful or whose emotions are too unchanneled are severely handicapped in their brains as well as their actions (De Bellis, 2001). First-grade teachers assume normal neurological maturity, which is why formal education typically begins at age 6, when appropriate instruction can guide a child to read, add, write, and so on. This is also why it is frustrating to both child and adult to try to teach a 4-year-old to read a page of print. Unless the script is large and simple (most 3-year-olds can "read" the M of a McDonald's sign from a hundred feet away), the child's brain is not ready.

During the school years, many deficiencies in cognition, peer relationships, emotional control, and classroom learning are directly tied to inadequate lateralization of the brain and to immaturity and asymmetry (an uneven balance) of the frontal cortex. The signs and consequences of these deficiencies are discussed in later chapters. The main point to remember here is that the brain provides the foundation, as was already explained in Chapter 5's discussion of senses and motor skills. Any impediment to normal growth of the brain puts all other accomplishments, including academic achievement, on shaky ground, because many parts of the cortex and many connections between neurons are involved in attaining them.

Mastering Motor Skills

As bodies grow slimmer, stronger, and less top-heavy, maturation of the prefrontal cortex permits greater impulse control, and the increased myelination of the corpus callosum permits coordination of the extremities. These developments permit children between 2 and 6 years to move with greater speed and grace. They become more capable of directing and refining their own activity.

Gross Motor Skills

Gross motor skills—which, as we saw in Chapter 5, involve large body movements such as running, climbing, jumping, and throwing—improve dramatically. If you watch a group of children at play, you will see that 2-year-olds are quite clumsy, falling down frequently and sometimes bumping into stationary objects. But by age 5, many children are both skilled and graceful. Most North American 5-year-olds can ride a tricycle, climb a ladder, pump a swing, and throw, catch, and kick a ball. Some of them can even ice-skate, ski, whiz along on in-line skates, and ride a bicycle, activities that demand balance as well as coordination. Skills vary by culture, of course; in certain nations, some 5-year-olds swim in ocean waves or climb cliffs that few adults in other nations would attempt. Underlying the development of such skills is a combination of brain maturation and guided practice.

Related to both brain maturation and practice is **activity level,** which is measured either by how much children move parts of their bodies while they remain in one place or by how much their whole bodies move from one spot to another. Some children sit quietly, not budging; other fidget, jiggle, tap, jump, walk, and run all the time. The main difference between these two extremes is age. From a peak at about age 2, activity level gradually declines throughout childhood (Eaton & Yu, 1989). Given what we now know about the prefrontal cortex, this makes sense: Children are better able to control their body movements once they can inhibit responses.

Another factor in activity level is gender: Boys are generally more active than girls. This is certainly cultural and hormonal, but it may be neurological as well, because young girls' brains seem to mature faster than those of young boys even before birth. Differences in activity level begin with biology, although these inborn distinctions are probably encouraged by the environment, so that preschoolers differ more by gender than infants do (Campbell & Eaton, 1999).

Experience also has an impact on gender differences as well as on control of the body while moving around. Many hours and months of climbing, for instance, enable refinement of brain patterns, allowing a child to climb up the ladder of a playground slide and descend with little risk of falling off. (Until then, it's best for a parent to stand near the slide, ready to catch an uncoordinated adventurer.)

Generally, children learn basic motor skills by teaching themselves and learning from other children, rather than through adult instruction. According to sociocultural theory, learning from peers is probably the ideal way for children to master skills needed for the future. As long as a child has the opportunity to play in an adequate space and has suitable playmates and play structures,

More Curiosity Than Caution As they master their gross motor skills, children of every social group seem to obey a universal command: "If it can be climbed, climb it." That command is usually heard louder than any words of caution—one reason direct supervision is needed during the play years.

activity level A measure of how active children are, taking into account both body movements while in one place and movement from one spot to another.

gross motor skills develop as rapidly as maturation, body size, and innate ability allow. Unfortunately, neither opportunity nor play space can be taken for granted, especially in large cities.

Several factors during the play years correlate with serious criminal behavior in adolescence and adulthood, including poor motor control, living in crowded urban areas, and difficulty making friends (Loeber & Farrington, 2000; Moffitt & Caspi, 2001). No single one of these problems predicts lawbreaking, but they can be closely interrelated. This pattern is one of many reasons for communities to build, and parents to use, safe playgrounds exclusively for children under age 6, where they can practice gross motor skills and learn how to make friends by playing with peers. These skills are also learned in good early day care as (described in Chapters 7 and 9), which has proven to be an antidote to juvenile delinquency as well (Zigler & Styfco, 2001).

Fine Motor Skills

Fine motor skills, which involve small body movements (especially those of the hands and fingers), are much harder to master than gross motor skills. Such actions as pouring juice from a pitcher into a glass, cutting food with a knife and fork, and achieving anything more artful than a scribble with a pencil are difficult for young children, even with great concentration and effort. They can spend hours trying to tie a bow with their shoelaces, producing knot upon knot instead.

Reasons for Difficulty

The chief reason many children experience difficulty with fine motor skills is simply that they have not yet developed the necessary muscular control, patience, and judgment—in part because their central nervous system is not yet sufficiently myelinated. Many fine motor skills involve two hands and thus two sides of the brain: The fork stabs the meat while the knife cuts it, one hand steadies the paper while the other writes, and it takes two hands to tie shoes, button shirts, pull on socks, and even zip zippers. If one hand does not know what the other hand is doing because the corpus callosum and the prefrontal cortex are still immature, shoelaces get knotted, paper gets ripped, zippers get stuck, and so on.

For many young children, neurological immaturity is compounded by short, stubby fingers. Unless caregivers keep these limitations in mind when selecting utensils, toys, and clothes, frustration and destruction can result: Preschool children may burst into tears when they cannot fasten their jackets, or they may mash a puzzle piece into place when they are unable to position it correctly, or they may tear up the paper when they cannot cut it with their blunt "safety" scissors. Fortunately, such frustrations usually fade as a child's persistence at and practice of fine motor skills gradually lead to mastery. Adults can help by offering tools, time, and encouragement, as well as noticing, for example, which hand is dominant so the left-handed child has a pair of left-handed scissors.

ROYCE BAIR

Especially for Immigrant Parents You and your family eat with chopsticks at home, but you want your children to feel comfortable in Western culture. Should you change your family eating customs?

What Is She Accomplishing? The papier-mâché animals produced by this girl and her preschool classmates are more likely to be mushy and misshapen than artistic. However, the real product is development of eye–hand coordination. With intensive, dedicated practice, fine motor skills are mastered by the school years, when children's artwork is sometimes truly remarkable.

Artistic Expression

During the play years, children are creative and not yet very self-critical. They love to move around and express themselves. This makes all forms of artistic expression a joy—dancing around the room, building an elaborate block construction, making music by pounding in rhythm, and putting marks on paper.

Creative endeavors are evidence that play can be important work. On the simplest level, "the child who first wields a marker is learning in many areas of his young life about tool use" (Gardner, 1980). Few children try to reproduce in their art exactly what they see. Instead, they realize the affordances provided by clay, paste, or paint and use them to express their symbolic understandings (Pufall, 1997). Even the first scribbles are patterned and meaningful to the young child (Kellogg, 1967).

The pictures children draw are often closely connected to their perception and cognition. For that reason, it is better to ask "What is it?" than to guess. For example, in one study young children were asked to draw a balloon and, later, a lollipop. Even though the actual drawings were indistinguishable, children were quite insistent as to which was which (Bloom, 2000) (see Figure 8.4).

Drawings of the human figure show developmental progress. Almost always, 2- to 3-year-olds draw a "tadpole"—a circle for a head with eyes and sometimes a smiling mouth, and then a line or two beneath to indicate the rest of the body. Tadpoles are drawn universally, in all cultures, and hence are called "strikingly characteristic" of children's art (Cox, 1993). With time, the dangling lines become legs, and sometimes a circle is placed between them to indicate a stomach. By age 5, a torso is added and, after 5, arms and hands (Cox, 1997).

Drawing seems to require that the artist think about what to draw; manipulate the pencil, crayon, or brush to execute the thought; and then view, refine, and perhaps explain the product. A developmental study of children's painting found that 3-year-olds did none of this. Usually they just plunked the brush into a color, pulled it out dripping wet, and then pushed it across the paper without much forethought or skill. However, by age 5 most children took care to get just enough of the chosen hue on the brush, planned where to put each stroke, and stood back from their work to examine the result (Allison, 1985). In doing so, 5-year-olds experience a sequence that not only provides practice with fine motor skills but also involves coordination of action and thought and, in the end, enhances artistic accomplishment. It is easy to see the gradual maturation of the prefrontal cortex in this process: Self-judgment is beyond the youngest children and quite typical of the oldest ones.

By age 5 many children are eager to practice their skills, drawing essentially the same picture again and again, with the later versions more detailed and better proportioned. In this case, perseveration aids mastery. Drawing is also a way in which children communicate and hence may provide useful insight to psychologists and social workers who know how to interpret their pictures (Silver, 2001). However, many quite normal and intelligent young children do not display their intellect or emotions in their art. A child who is able to see and reproduce such details as fingers, ears, jewelry, and shoes at age 5 is certainly observant, thoughtful, and skilled—and thus probably pretty intelligent. However, a 5-year-old whose drawings are still quite primitive is not necessarily less intelligent. Thus, meaningful analysis of a young child's art before age 8 is problematic.

A lollipop

A balloon

The experimenter

The child

FIGURE 8.4 Which Is Which? The child who made these drawings insisted that the one at top left was a lollipop and the one at top right was a balloon (not vice versa), and that the drawing at bottom left was the experimenter and the one at bottom right was the child (not vice versa).

(a)

(b)

(c)

ALL: LAURA DWIGHT

No Ears? Strategically connected circles, lines, and dots are the mainstays of 1- to 6-year-olds' drawings of human figures. However, continuous development of fine motor skills is apparent as time goes on. (a) Like 2-year-old Peter, most very young children connect legs to the head, making a "tadpole person." (b) The family members that 4-year-old Elizabeth draws are hairless, armless, and unisex—but they all have belly buttons, feet, noses, and big smiles that reach their foreheads. (c) By age 5, this boy draws his mother with eyelashes, arms, and fingers.

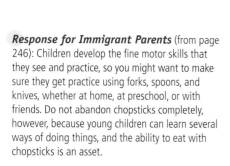

Response for Immigrant Parents (from page 246): Children develop the fine motor skills that they see and practice, so you might want to make sure they get practice using forks, spoons, and knives, whether at home, at preschool, or with friends. Do not abandon chopsticks completely, however, because young children can learn several ways of doing things, and the ability to eat with chopsticks is an asset.

Nevertheless, just as every neighborhood should have protected space for running and safe equipment for climbing, so should every child have blank paper and paint for developing fine motor skills. A sketch pad and a box of markers are no less educational toys than traditional alphabet blocks or counting games.

Injuries and Death

In all but the most disease-ridden or war-torn countries of the world, accidents are by far the most common causes of childhood death. In the United States, a newborn has about 1 chance in 650 of dying from an unintended injury before age 15—four times the risk that he or she will die of cancer, the leading lethal childhood disease (National Center for Health Statistics, 2000). The rate for boys is almost twice that for girls: A boy's odds of dying accidentally before age 15 are about 1 in 500 and a girl's about 1 in 800, with increased death rates in both genders as income falls.

Looking at the entire world, unintended injuries cause millions of premature deaths each year: Not until age 40 does any disease overtake accidents as a cause of mortality. Accidents occur at every age, but 1- to 4-year-olds have even higher rates of serious injuries than do slightly older children, aged 5 to 15. (Late adolescents and the elderly also have higher-than-average rates.)

Age-related trends are also apparent in which situations are most dangerous. Car crashes are by far the leading killer of teenagers and young adults, but not of young children. The direct cause of death is more often a deadly poison that is gulped down, a fire that burns more than 80 percent of a small body, a fall that shatters a skull, a small object or large amount of water that stops all breath. Drowning, in fact, is the leading cause of death for young children in the dozen or so American states where home swimming pools are common.

Why such high death rates for such small children? As you read earlier in this chapter, neurological immaturity makes young children particularly unable to think things through, so they impulsively plunge into dangerous places and activities. They need protection, but society often does not provide it. As one team of experts explains, "Injuries are not unpredictable, unavoidable events. To a large extent, society chooses the injury rates it has" (Christoffel & Gallagher,

1999, p. 10). Other statistics make the need for reducing the injury rate even more apparent: For small children, the rate of nonlethal injuries reported by hospitals and doctors is about 400 times the rate of injury-caused deaths.

How could a society *choose* injury, pain, and lifelong damage for any of its children? The central idea is that prevention is a choice made not only by parents but also by manufacturers, legislators, and the individuals who might drive a car after drinking, smoke in bed, and so on. To understand this, consider the implications of the vocabulary that is commonly used. The word *accident* implies that an injury is a random, unpredictable event, an "act of God" or—if anyone is to be blamed—of a careless parent and an accident-prone child. Using the word *accident* thus allows the general public to feel blameless. Yet, as you just read, "society chooses the injury rate it has." Experts now refer to **injury control** or **harm reduction**, not "accident prevention." *Injury control* implies that, although complete prevention is not always possible, harm can be minimized if appropriate social controls are in place. Death and serious injury can be controlled and usually prevented; minor "accidents" may be inevitable, but the harm can be reduced. Putting controls in place and reducing harm are choices that society makes.

Three Levels of Prevention

Prevention and control begin long before any particular child or parent does something foolish or careless. A wise society starts with **primary prevention**, changing the overall background conditions to make injuries less likely. Primary prevention does not require any forethought by individuals at the time; instead, it fosters conditions that reduce everyone's chance of injury. Then comes **secondary prevention**, steps that avert harm in the minutes before it would occur. **Tertiary prevention** occurs after the fact, reducing damage from any particular trauma and thus saving lives as well as preventing permanent disabilities. Let us look at an example incorporating all three levels of prevention.

An Example: Pedestrian Deaths

More than 100,000 pedestrians were killed by motor vehicles in the United States between 1980 and 2000, most of them under age 15 or over age 65. *Primary prevention* could reduce pedestrian deaths by means of better sidewalks, fewer cars, slower speeds, pedestrian bridges, wider roads, longer traffic signals, brighter street lights, perception tests before driver's license renewal, rigorous annual auto inspections, strengthened law enforcement, or all ten of these and more—anything that makes traffic conditions safer overall.

Secondary prevention occurs right before a crash. Requiring flashing lights on stopped school buses, employing school-crossing guards, refusing alcohol to teenagers, improving car brakes, enforcing drunk-driving laws, providing better visibility on curving roads, insisting that children walk with adults—all these are secondary prevention measures because they decrease the chance that a particular child will be killed by a particular driver at a particular spot. Whenever a pedestrian is hit, analysis of secondary prevention looks at why it happened at this stretch of road and not 500 feet away, why this particular driver now and not another who just drove by or this driver on another day, why this person and not the dozens of other pedestrians, and so on. Answers to these questions reveal that secondary prevention is always possible: No particular injury is random, even though it is unexpected.

Finally, *tertiary prevention* reduces damage after impact. Protective helmets, laws against hit-and-run driving, speedy and well-trained ambulance drivers, emergency room procedures that reduce brain swelling, effective rehabilitation techniques—all these reduce the harmful results. There is a "golden hour" after a crash: If an injured person gets to an emergency room within that time, the

injury control/harm reduction The idea that accidents are not random but can be made less harmful with proper control. In practice, this means anticipating, controlling, and preventing dangerous activities.

primary prevention Actions that change overall background conditions to prevent some unwanted event or circumstance, such as injury, disease, or abuse.

secondary prevention Actions that avert harm in the immediate situation, such as stopping a car before it hits a pedestrian.

tertiary prevention Actions that are taken after an adverse event occurs, aimed at reducing the harm or preventing disability. Immediate and effective medical treatment of illness or injury is tertiary prevention.

Especially for Urban Planners Describe a neighborhood park that would benefit the community.

(a)

(c)

(b)

Protective Settings In order for parents to safeguard their children from injury, they first need to be aware of safety hazards and then need to take whatever action is necessary to prevent accidents. In two of these photos, the parents are to be commended: The parents of the child in (b) not only put a helmet on their skater but protected his knees, wrists, elbows, and hands as well. The mother in (c) probably has been securing her child in a safety seat from infancy. However, the boy in (a) may be in trouble. What is immediately below him? We hope it is a "safety surface" designed to prevent serious injury or an adult ready to catch him. Such forethought is essential for injury control.

chances of recovery are much better. Yet too often shock, guilt, and inefficiency use up that hour (Christoffel & Gallagher, 1999).

Many of these three levels of prevention have been instituted in the United States in the past 20 years, with very good results. The annual pedestrian death rate decreased from more than 8,000 in 1980 to about 5,000 in 2000 (U.S. Bureau of the Census, 2001), with similar trends worldwide. This downward trend may change: Injury-control advocates are dismayed that the U.S. Congress has repealed the 55-mile-per-hour speed limit on highways, a law that was enacted in the mid-1970s to save fuel but that also substantially reduced motor vehicle deaths.

Parents, Education, and Protection

To further stress the need for prevention, consider the relationship between income and injury. Socioeconomic differences are apparent among and within nations, with the poorest nations having the most childhood deaths not only from disease and malnutrition but also from other causes (Mohan, 2000). Within the United States, a fatal home fire is six times more likely to occur in low-income neighborhoods than in high-income communities (Christoffel & Gallagher, 1999). In Montreal, Canada, socioeconomic status is the most powerful predictor of young pedestrians being hit by a car, with the poorest children six times more likely to be injured than the richest (Macpherson et al., 1998).

Injury control requires parents to institute safety measures *in advance* to reduce the need for vigilant supervision. There is a distinction here between prevention, which is the task of everyone in every society, and protection, which is the immediate job of the parents. Ideally, an overall climate of prevention makes it easier for parents to protect their children. For instance, compared to adults, children are more likely to drown, choke on a nonfood object, tumble from a bicycle, suffocate in a fire, or fall out of a window. Precautions that parents can take—such as teaching children to swim, removing swallowable objects from reach, requiring a helmet for bicycling, and installing smoke alarms and window guards—would prevent many deaths. The goal is not to change the nature of the child but to change the nature of the child's situation, as with laws that prevent

Response for Urban Planners (from page 249): The adult idea of a park—a large, grassy open place—is not best for young children, and they are the ones who need parks most. For them, you would design an enclosed area, small enough and with adequate seating to allow caregivers to socialize while watching their children. The playground surface would need to be protective (since young children are clumsy), and equipment that encourages both gross motor skills (such as climbing) and fine motor skills (such as a large sandbox) would be useful. Swings are not very beneficial, because they do not develop many motor skills. Teenagers and dogs should be accommodated elsewhere.

active, curious children from swallowing a lethal dose of baby aspirin by forbidding manufacturers to put that many pills into a single bottle.

Educational campaigns are often launched to promote safety; their effects are mixed. General, broad-based television announcements and poster campaigns do not have a direct impact on children's risk taking. The best results from educational broadsides may be to increase public support for laws and other safety programs. Similarly, educational programs in schools can teach children to verbalize safety rules, but classroom education appears to have little effect on children's actual behavior (Rivara, 1994). Parental behavior is also difficult to change through education, especially if older children in the family have already survived childhood without sitting in a car seat, strapping on a wrist guard, or sleeping in flame-retardant pajamas.

Both prevention and protection are needed, but neither occurs through education alone. Public health advocates believe that laws that apply to everyone are more effective than educational efforts that assume that people are ready to learn and willing to change. "Too often, we design our physical environment for smart people who are highly motivated" (Baker, 2000), whereas in real life, everyone has moments of foolish indifference. At those moments, automatic safety measures save lives.

Changing Policy

Fences All Around the Pool

Only half as many 1- to 5-year-olds in the United States were fatally injured in 1999 compared to 20 years earlier, thanks to laws about poisons, fires, and cars. However, safety laws are difficult to write, pass, and enforce. For example, one Australian city, Brisbane, had no law requiring private swimming pools to be fenced in but had nine times as many child drownings as another, Canberra, that did have such a law. The need for legislation seemed obvious (Baker, 2000). A law was written in 1978, requiring that every Brisbane swimming pool be surrounded on all four sides by a high fence whose gate had a self-locking latch. Objections involving fencing costs, private property, parental responsibility, and community aesthetics stalled the bill until 1990 and led to poor enforcement. Then a 3-year-old drowned in a motel pool that had no self-locking gate. That death finally brought enforcement (Nixon, 2000).

Beyond unanticipated objections and lax enforcement, loopholes based on faulty assumptions can thwart prevention. In southern California, a pool-fencing ordinance passed with one small modification: The fourth side of the pool enclosure could be the wall of a house, with a door that could lock. Child drownings did not decline, partly because children could get to their families' swimming pools through that door (Morgenstern et al., 2000). Parents and legislators somehow imagined that only trespassing children would drown; they did not realize the family's own children were

vulnerable. Policy and practice must reflect the reality that no parent is always wise and careful, and no child is always safe and secure.

Safe and Happy? The type of pool fence shown here—with a locked gate and bars that are too high for a young child to climb and too closely spaced to be squeezed through—should be legally required everywhere to prevent accidental drownings.

? *Observational Quiz* (see answer, page 253): Can you identify at least three potential dangers that lurk in this apparently safe situation?

Child Maltreatment

Throughout this chapter and elsewhere in this text, we have assumed that parents naturally want to foster their children's development and protect them from every danger. Yet daily, it seems, reporters describe shocking incidents of parents who harm their offspring. However, sensational cases represent only a small portion of all maltreatment cases. And, as experts in child maltreatment point out, "Journalism is an impatient enterprise and the tragic, bungled case will always be more newsworthy . . . than the small successes of family reunification or the incremental process of reform" (Larner et al., 1998).

Not only do sensational cases distract attention from other, far more typical incidents, but the emotional reaction to the extremes obscures the lessons we need to learn. Such lessons begin with an understanding of what abuse is, then lead to knowledge of its "causes and consequences," and finally teach us how to treat and, even better, prevent maltreatment of every sort. Among the research findings: Reporting suspicions is likely to be helpful to the child, but parental practices need to be considered in context, not in cultural isolation.

Changing Definitions of Maltreatment

Until about 1960, child maltreatment was thought of as obvious physical assault and was assumed to result from the rare outburst of a mentally disturbed person, typically someone the family did not know or trust. However, we now recognize that maltreatment is neither rare nor sudden, that almost 90 percent of the perpetrators are the child's own parents, and that most of the rest are close relatives or family friends (U.S. Department of Health and Human Services, 2001). This reality began to dawn on professionals when emergency personnel in a large Boston hospital noticed patterns of injuries—such as bones broken in a certain way; burns on specific body parts; X-rays that showed old, untreated fractures—that never showed up when children accidentally fell or otherwise injured themselves. Once *battered child syndrome* was discovered, described, and labeled, effective efforts to prevent maltreatment could begin (Kempe et al., 1962).

With this recognition came a broader definition: **Child maltreatment** includes all intentional harm to, or avoidable endangerment of, anyone under 18 years of age. Thus, child maltreatment includes both **child abuse**—deliberate action that is harmful to the child's physical, emotional, or sexual well-being—and **child neglect**—failure to appropriately meet a child's basic physical or emotional needs. Note that abuse is deliberate, inflicted with the intention of doing harm, which is one reason it is so hurtful. The child understands that he or she is not protected and loved by the parent who engages in extreme punishment. (Sexual abuse is discussed in Chapter 14.)

Compared to physical abuse, neglect is twice as common and can be even more damaging (Garbarino & Collins, 1999). Consequently, signs of neglect are important to recognize, and they might be missed if someone looks only for broken bones or cigarette burns. One sign of neglect is called **failure to thrive;** it becomes apparent when an otherwise healthy infant or young child gains no weight. Typically, the mother explains that the child refuses to eat, but if hospitalization produces rapid weight gain, nonorganic failure to thrive is confirmed. Often the hospital discharges the child, who returns to the neglectful home. A trained home visitor may help to prevent further neglect (Grantham-McGregor et al., 1994).

child maltreatment All intentional harm to, or avoidable endangerment of, anyone under 18 years of age.

child abuse Deliberate action that is harmful to a child's physical, emotional, or sexual well-being.

child neglect Failure to meet a child's basic physical, educational, or emotional needs.

failure to thrive A situation in which an infant or young child gains little or no weight, despite apparent, normal health.

reported maltreatment Maltreatment about which the police, child welfare agency, or other authorities have been officially notified.

substantiated maltreatment Maltreatment that has been reported, investigated, and verified.

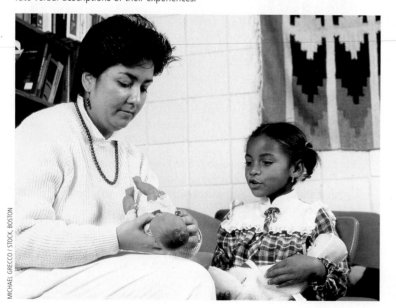

Show Me What Happened Professionals like this social worker sometimes use dolls to elicit information about possible maltreatment or other events from children who are too young to provide accurate verbal descriptions of their experiences.

MICHAEL GRECCO / STOCK, BOSTON

Another sign of maltreatment, more often found after infancy, is *hypervigilance,* or excessive watchfulness: The child seems unable to concentrate on anything because he or she is always nervously looking around. Hypervigilance can signify abuse if children are routinely hit for no reason, but it is also a sign of neglect if children often witness frightening events (Dutton, 2000; Kerig et al., 2002). The event most often witnessed by neglected children in developed nations is their father beating up their mother; in developing nations it is gunfire and torture in civil war. Children can also suffer from *medical neglect,* when a life-threatening illness is not treated (Dubowitz, 1999), or from *educational neglect,* when an older child receives no schooling (Gelles, 1999).

Reported and Substantiated Maltreatment

Reported maltreatment cases are those about which the authorities have been informed, and **substantiated maltreatment** cases are those that have been investigated and verified (see Figures 8.5 and 8.6). Since 1993, the number of *reported* cases of maltreatment in the United States has been about 3 million a year, and the number of *substantiated* cases has been not quite 1 million, an annual rate of 1 child in every 70. This 3-to-1 ratio between reported and substantiated cases is attributable to three factors:

- A particular case may be reported many times but will be tallied as only one substantiated case because it involves just one child, who is repeatedly abused.
- Before a case is substantiated, investigators must find some proof—usually visible, unmistakable injuries or malnutrition or credible witnesses (such as the other parent and the maltreated child).
- The report may be mistaken or even deliberately misleading (especially when the child's feuding parents or other relatives are fighting over custody).

In many countries around the world, laws now require that any teacher, health professional, police officer, or social worker who becomes aware of possible maltreatment must report it. These laws have made a difference. Reporting has increased, and in the United States more than half of all reports of maltreatment come from such professionals. With better awareness, many public and private organizations now tally reports of abuse and neglect, monitor treatment, and fund research into prevention.

Intergenerational Bonding Devoted grandfathers, such as this one in Su Zhou, China, prevent the social isolation that is a prerequisite for serious abuse. Can you imagine this man's response if he thought his granddaughter was underfed, overdisciplined, or unloved?

!*Answer to Observational Quiz* (from page 251): (1) The fence may not surround all four sides of the pool area. (2) The child's sunglasses may not be shatterproof. (3) The sunglasses may not provide effective protection from the sun's ultraviolet rays. (4) The toy car tempts the young driver to venture onto the street.

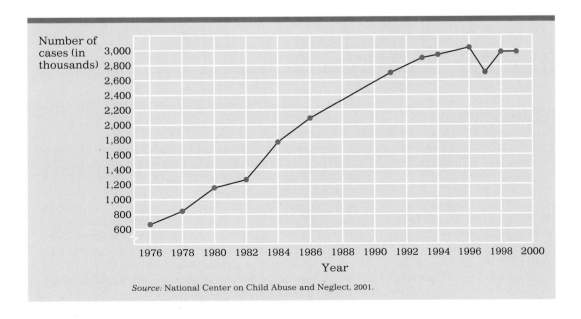

Source: National Center on Child Abuse and Neglect, 2001.

FIGURE 8.5 Reported Cases of Child Maltreatment, United States, 1976–1999 After doubling in the 1970s and doubling again in the 1980s, the number of children reported as maltreated has leveled off. What explanations are possible for this pattern?

FIGURE 8.6 Substantiated Cases of Child Maltreatment, United States, 1990–1999
The number of substantiated cases of child maltreatment in the United States is too high, but there is some good news: The number of cases has declined by almost 20 percent from the peak in 1994.

? *Observational Quiz* (see answer, page 255): The dot for 1999 is close to the bottom of the graph. Does that mean it is close to zero?

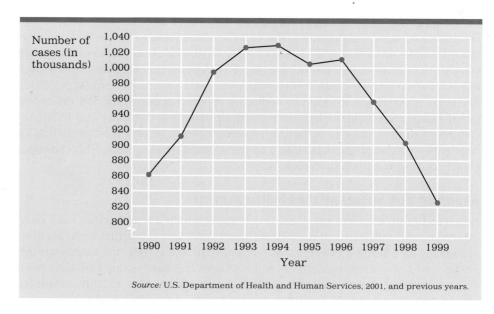

Source: U.S. Department of Health and Human Services, 2001, and previous years.

differential response A way of reacting to child-maltreatment reports that distinguishes between those that require immediate investigation (possibly leading to foster care and legal prosecution) and those that are less serious (possibly leading to supportive measures to encourage better care).

Further, child protection agencies are developing procedures to act more swiftly (most cases are now investigated within 48 hours), more decisively, and more differentially. This last factor, **differential response**, means that high-risk cases can be treated one way, with immediate investigation and removal of the child, and low-risk cases another, with an offer of help (such as placement in a free preschool program, income supplementation, or health benefits) (Waldfogel, 1998). A policy of differential response reduces paperwork and relieves the emotional burnout that can occur when one social worker tries to give equal attention to every report. Instead, social workers have both the mandate and the time to proceed full force in high-risk cases, and they can link low-risk families to various benefits to prevent matters from worsening.

It is just as important for those who care about children to spot and report the signs of neglect as it is to spot evidence of physical abuse. Most children who experience one form of maltreatment suffer others as well, over a long period of time; noticing and halting one episode will stop many more, not only for that child but probably for brothers and sisters as well. Many hospital workers and police officers are now trained to distinguish forms of maltreatment and to respond appropriately.

A Case to Study

The Neglect of Neglect: A 2-Year-Old Boy

Three million reported cases of maltreatment per year are a lot, but even more cases, especially of neglect, are not reported. Consider the following.

B. V., a 2-year-old male, was found lying face down in the bathtub by an 8-year-old sent to check on him. He had been placed in the bathtub by his mother, who then went to the kitchen and was absent for approximately 10 minutes. B. V. was transported by ambulance to a local hospital. He was unresponsive and had a rectal temperature of 90 degrees Fahrenheit.

After medical treatment, the child's breathing resumed, and he was transported to a tertiary care hospital. B. V. remained in the pediatric intensive care unit for 9 days with minimal brain function and no response to any stimuli. He was then transferred to a standard hospital room where he died 2 days later. The mother refused to have an autopsy performed. Subsequently, the death certificate was signed by an attending physician, and cause of death was pneumonia with anoxic brain injury as a result of near-drowning.

The CPS [Child Protection Service] worker advised B. V.'s mother that 10 minutes was too long to leave a 2-year-old in the bathtub unsupervised. B. V.'s mother replied that she had done it many times before and that nothing had happened.

Further examination of the medical chart revealed that prior to B. V.'s death, he had a sibling who had experienced an apparent life-threatening event (previously termed a "near miss" sudden infant death syndrome). The sibling was placed on cardiac and apnea (breathing) monitors for 7 to 8 months. In addition B. V. had been to the children's hospital approximately 2 weeks prior for a major injury to his big toe. B. V.'s toe had been severed and required numerous stitches. The mother stated that this incident was a result of the 4-year-old brother slamming the door on B. V.'s foot. Furthermore, B. V. had been seen in a different local hospital for a finger fracture the month before his death. None of the available reports indicate the mother's history of how the finger fracture occurred.

[Bonner et al., 1999, pp. 165–166]

No charges were filed in the death of B. V. The team who reported this case explain:

This case illustrates chronic supervisory neglect but also shows that a child's death can occur in a short period of time. The mother's self-reported practice of leaving the child in the bathtub unsupervised is an example of a pattern of chronic failure to supervise in a manner appropriate for the age and development of the child. Also note that the series of suspicious events that preceded the death did not result in protective or preventive services for the family.

[Bonner et al., 1999, p. 166]

This case is chilling for many reasons. Many signs that something was amiss in this family—the near-miss SIDS, the broken finger, the severed toe—were ignored. Even B. V.'s death did not result in charges against the mother or in the mother herself admitting that she had been neglectful.

Who Is to Blame? This note was left at a makeshift memorial outside the Texas home where Andrea Yates drowned her five children. It attests to the possibility that some parents, overwhelmed by their children's needs and demands, will become negligent or abusive; sometimes the child's death is the outcome. In the Yates case, the pressures of caring for five young children were increased by the mother's longstanding mental illness. Greater vigilance by and support from family, friends, and the community at large (members of the clergy, health-care providers, and others) might help to prevent some of these tragedies.

At this point nothing was written about the possible emotional trauma suffered by the 8-year-old who found his dying brother and by the 4-year-old who reportedly severed the toddler's toe, yet both of them are likely to be traumatized. These children are also at high risk of maltreatment. Indeed, the most serious injury to a child's mental health is caused not by abuse itself but by the chronic trauma of feeling helpless and endangered (De Bellis, 2001).

The Cultural and Community Context

Cultural diversity makes the problem of substantiating reports of child maltreatment even more complex. Before a particular practice can be considered abusive, customs and community standards must be taken into account (Hansen, 1998). Examples include the numerous customs that give children pain: pierced ears, circumcision, castor oil, forced feeding of hated foods, ceremonial facial scars, permed or tightly braided hair, encouragement of sports that bring exhaustion and bruises, forced sleeping alone despite tears of protest, and harsh words designed to shame a child into proper behavior. Such practices are considered commonplace in some cultures and abusive in others (Freeman, 2000).

In some neighborhoods, not letting children play freely outside is considered maltreatment; in others, letting a child play outside unsupervised for even 10 minutes is considered neglectful. One contrast is between Japan and the United States, both rich and highly educated nations. The Japanese say, "Before seven, among the gods" to advise parents that young children are pure and not to be punished; but Westerners hold the "view that Japanese adults are indulgent with

Answer to Observational Quiz (from page 254): No. The number is actually 826. Note the little squiggle on the graph's vertical axis below the number 800. This means that many numbers between zero and 800 are not shown.

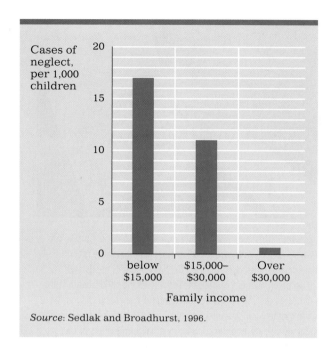

Cases of neglect, per 1,000 children

Source: Sedlak and Broadhurst, 1996.

FIGURE 8.7 What Correlates with Maltreatment—Income, Sex, Age, Race? Rates of neglect skyrocket as family income falls, with the highest rates of neglect found among single mothers who have either four or more children or only one child. Abuse also correlates with income. Fathers are more likely than mothers to be perpetrators of abuse (as opposed to neglect). Interestingly, neither age nor race correlates with maltreatment.

their children . . . not playing their roles as socializing agents properly" (Chen, 1996). Despite such variation, two aspects of the overall context seem universally conducive to maltreatment: poverty and social isolation.

Poverty

No matter how maltreatment is defined or counted, it occurs more frequently and more severely as family income falls (see Figure 8.7) (Drake & Zuravin, 1998). This is particularly true for physical abuse and all forms of neglect, which fall most heavily on children under age 6 who have:

■ Three or more siblings
■ An unemployed father
■ A mother who did not complete high school
■ Homes in a poor, high-crime neighborhood

All these factors signify poverty and lead to greater poverty. Living in a poor neighborhood makes maltreatment worse because the child has few avenues of escape or neighbors willing to intervene (Lynch & Cicchetti, 1998). For example, B. V.'s medical care is typical of low-income children, who are taken to various hospital emergency rooms and treated by overworked staff who do not know the family history. If B. V. had had a private pediatrician, the maltreatment would probably have been noticed and addressed.

Social Isolation

A related risk factor is social isolation. Every society has certain "family values" to guide parents in caring for their children. One of these values, the belief that each family should decide how to live within its own home, is an especially useful principle in nations with diverse ethnic and religious groups, such as the United States and Canada. However, this value can boomerang when children need intervention, because it encourages privacy and social isolation. Signs of maltreatment become "not my business," and abuse continues and worsens.

The combination of an overstressed parent, low income, unwanted children, and social isolation—rather than any one factor alone—provides fertile ground for maltreatment. Low-income neighborhoods with less social isolation also have markedly less child abuse (Korbin et al., 1998). Poverty adds to a family's stress, but it does not *cause* maltreatment. Most low-income parents provide adequate and loving care for their children, especially if they have nearby friends and relatives who are supportive (Crittenden, 1999).

Consequences of Maltreatment

Cultural values do not cause abuse—every society values its young—but some cultural practices can be misused. Thus, maltreatment comes in many forms, usually occurs in families with many children, and often is ignored until serious harm has been done. What are the results if maltreatment is not spotted and stopped? Maltreatment impairs every aspect of child development, especially education and social skills.

Maltreated children have difficulty learning, not only because they are less likely to be taught, guided, encouraged, or even talked to but also because they may develop brain patterns that make learning difficult. The most serious pattern is **shaken baby syndrome,** which results when infants are held by the shoulders and shaken back and forth, sharply and quickly, to stop their crying. Sometimes

shaken baby syndrome A serious condition caused by maltreatment involving shaking a crying infant back and forth, sharply and quickly. Severe brain damage results from internal hemorrhaging and broken neural connections.

the neck breaks, but even if not, ruptured blood vessels in the brain and broken neural connections lead to severe damage.

Another form of brain damage can occur in a child who is often terrorized or despondent. Such extreme stress can halt normal brain development, flooding the mind with irrational fantasies and uncontrollable flashbacks. As one team of authors explains:

> Exceptionally large quantities of stress hormones and neurotransmitters may be released during the trauma which lead to high levels of activation of the sympathetic nervous system. This may cause the brain to enter a very different biochemical state than is usually the case when ordinary experiences are encoded into memory.
>
> *[Macfie et al., 2001]*

As a result, memory may be impaired and logical thinking delayed until long past 6 years, the age at which the prefrontal cortex should mature. Damage to the corpus callosum sometimes results from too many stress hormones in infancy (Teicher, 2002).

Many maltreated children are hyperactive and hypervigilant, startled at any noise, quick to counterattack for an imagined insult, confused between fantasy and reality. These are all symptoms of **post-traumatic stress disorder (PTSD)**, a syndrome that was first described in combat veterans but is also apparent in some abused children (De Bellis, 2001; Dutton, 2000). Another brain disorder can occur in children whose mothers are clinically depressed, unable to provide the encouragement and emotional guidance that young children need. Such children can develop an asymmetry of the prefrontal cortex in which the right side develops more than the left, a pattern that makes negative emotions (fear, sadness, anxiety) dominant and depression more likely (Dawson & Ashman, 2000). Depressed children, like stressed children, have difficulty learning.

Even without damage to blood vessels or nerve connections in the brain, abuse disrupts learning in many other ways. At the simplest level is nourishment: As you remember from Chapter 5, long-term malnutrition impedes brain growth. Many neglected infants are underfed; many neglected preschoolers eat few healthy foods (Wachs, 2000). Another very basic problem occurs when a child is injured: Pain and absence from school or preschool impair learning. Less dramatic, but just as disruptive, is the mental state of children who are worried about their own safety or that of their family members; these children have trouble concentrating. Some have disruptive fantasies, distorted self-concepts, and disturbing thoughts that interfere with normal childhood learning. Finally, active intelligence requires curiosity, yet many mistreated children are punished for exploration, for asking questions, even for moving around. Bluntly put, they are punished for trying to learn, so they stop trying.

Beyond the intellectual and academic handicaps, deficits are even more apparent in social skills. Maltreated children tend to regard other people as hostile and exploitative, and hence they are less friendly, more aggressive, and more isolated than other children. The longer their abuse continues and the earlier it started, the worse are their relationships with peers (Bolger et al., 1998). A maltreated child is likely to be a difficult member of any group, often a bully or a victim or both. As adolescents and adults, people who were severely maltreated in childhood (either physically or emotionally) often use drugs or alcohol to numb their emotions, choose unsupportive relationships, become victims or aggressors, sabotage their own careers, eat too much or too little, and generally engage in self-destructive behavior (Crittenden et al., 1994; Wolfe et al., 1998).

post-traumatic stress disorder (PTSD) A syndrome in which a victim or witness of a trauma or shock has lingering symptoms, which may include hyperactivity and hypervigilance, displaced anger, sleeplessness, sudden terror or anxiety, and confusion between fantasy and reality.

What Happens Next? The child may be spanked, hit, or just yelled at, but fear will certainly be involved. This fear causes the release of stress hormones that will halt learning and make normal exploration less likely in the future. In addition to considering this psychic damage, the father might think about the true cause of the damage to the lamp: Could the child have broken it if the parents had not left it within reach?

FELICIA MARTINEZ / PHOTOEDIT

permanency planning The search for a long-term solution to a problem. In the case of an abused child, such a plan may involve return to parents who have changed, long-term foster care, or adoption.

How to Prevent Further Maltreatment

When a case of maltreatment has been substantiated, the first priority is to protect the child. This often means removing the child from the parents. Removal should not be done haphazardly and temporarily. Instead **permanency planning,** which is planning for the long-term care of the child, should begin immediately. Sometimes permanency planning means setting goals that the parents must meet if they want their child returned (such as parental education and drug rehabilitation, with several months of "clean and sober" time and a series of supervised child visits). Permanency planning may also mean finding a foster or adoptive home that can keep the child until adulthood.

Foster Care

foster care A legally sanctioned, publicly supported plan that transfers care of maltreated children from parents to someone else.

kinship care A form of foster care in which a relative of the maltreated child becomes the approved caregiver.

Over the years, many children have been raised by "foster parents"—usually relatives or neighbors—because their biological parents died or were too poor or too ill to care for them. Even today, such informal foster care is common. However, in contemporary society, **foster care** generally means a legally sanctioned, publicly supported arrangement in which children are officially removed from their parents' custody and entrusted to another adult or family who is paid to nurture them.

Even though maltreated children often bring behavioral problems, learning disabilities, or traumatic memories into foster care, their foster families usually treat them well. Foster parents are responsible for only 1 in 200 cases of substantiated abuse. A positive outcome is especially likely when the foster parents are committed to the child and when they have the resources to address whatever emotional, physical, and social problems the child might have (Curtis et al., 1999).

Often a good parent–child relationship is created, and the child in long-term foster care eventually becomes a loving and successful adult. The notion of *intergenerational transmission*—that children who are abused will inevitably abuse their own children—is false. Only about a third do so (though, of course, any rate of maltreatment is too high).

About 600,000 children in the United States are in foster care, a number that has risen over the past decade (U.S. Department of Health and Human Services, 2001; see Appendix B). About half the children in foster care in the United States are from minority groups, almost all of them are from low-income families, and many of them have multiple physical, intellectual, and emotional problems—partly as a result of intervention that came too late. The average length of stay in foster care has decreased (to two years), the number of children needing foster care has risen (to about 200,000 additional children per year), and the number of adults willing to foster children has declined. Finding hundreds of thousands of new placements each year that match the needs of the children is a daunting task (Curtis et al., 1999).

The Chosen Family Two of these three children are adopted, and adoption is probably the best solution for children whose birth parents are unable to care for them. The third child, the 6-week-old girl, is a foster child who could be returned to her mother—which might protect the legal rights of the original family but likely not the emotional needs of the child.

STEPHANE MAZE / CORBIS

Kinship Care

Fortunately, the use of another form of foster care, called **kinship care,** has increased. In kinship care, a relative of the maltreated child becomes the approved caregiver. About one-fourth of all foster children in the United States are staying with relatives, who receive some financial support for doing what, traditionally, they might have done on their own (U.S. Department of Health and Human Services, 2001).

Many experts have raised concerns about the quality of kinship care. The available kin are usually the grandparents who raised the abusive parents in the first place and who are older, poorer, less healthy, and less educated than traditional foster parents. Indeed, some states and cities have policies that make it very diffi-cult for any kin to be officially sanctioned and reimbursed to care for their mis-treated relatives. Other communities find that subsidizing kinship care seems the best plan—especially since kin are more likely to allow the biological parents to see their children, thus making family reunification more likely. This goal itself is controversial, with some agencies believing that biological bonds need strength-ening so more families can eventually care for their own children, and others be-lieving that parents who abuse their children should not be given a chance to terrorize them again (Gelles, 2000).

That there are diverse opinions about kinship care is indicated by comparing Baltimore, where 2 of every 3 foster-care children are with kin, to Norfolk, Virginia, 100 miles away, where only 2 of every 100 foster children are in kinship care (Curtis et al., 1995). Generally, children fare as well in kinship homes as in the homes of strangers if the kin receive the same screening, supervision, and support as other foster parents (Berrick, 1998).

Adoption and Other Outcomes

Adoption is the final option. It is the preferred choice when parents are incompe-tent and children are young. **Adoption** legally separates the children from their biological parents and commits them to lifelong care from their adoptive par-ents. Thus, this solution is a permanent commitment and is better for the child. Judges and biological parents must release children for adoption, and often they are reluctant to do so. (Adoptive families are further discussed in Chapter 13.)

Older children who have witnessed and endured years of maltreatment in their biological family are least likely to be available for adoption, least likely to be adopted if they are available, and most likely to hate themselves, distrust oth-ers, and feel so angry at life that they suffer no matter where they are raised. Permanency planning for them is difficult. Such children are often sent to group homes—which may be better than living on the street but sometimes create new problems faster than they solve old ones. As one child says:

> My parents didn't want me. I lived in three foster homes. My foster parents didn't want me. Now, I live in a group home, and I'm a loner. Probably for what's hap-pened to me in my life, I'll never fit in.
>
> *[quoted in Kools, 1997]*

Three Levels of Prevention, Again

It is now apparent that, just as with injury control, there are three levels of prevention of child maltreatment. The ultimate goal of child-care policy is to keep all maltreat-ment from ever beginning. This is called *primary preven-tion* because it must occur before the problem starts. Stable neighborhoods, family cohesion, income equality, and measures that decrease financial instability, family isolation, and teenage parenthood are all examples of pri-mary prevention; their nature and impact are described in every chapter of this book.

Secondary prevention involves spotting warning signs and intervening to keep a problem situation from getting worse. For example, insecure attachment, especially of the disorganized type, is a sign of a disrupted parent–child relationship. Slow weight gain, late language development, poor emotional regulation, and unusual play patterns are some other troubling signs. Secondary prevention includes

Especially for the General Public You are asked to give a donation to support a billboard campaign against child abuse. You plan to make $100 in charitable contributions this year. How much of this total should you contribute to the billboard campaign?

adoption The process whereby legally designated, nonbiological parents are given custody and care of a child.

Cultural Differences This baby waits outside alone while his mother eats sweets in the café.

? *Observational Quiz* (see answer, page 260): What signs indicate that this is maltreatment?

Response for the General Public (from page 257): Maybe nothing. Educational campaigns rarely change people's habits and thoughts, unless they have never thought about an issue at all. If you want to help prevent child abuse and neglect, you might offer free babysitting to parents you know who seem overwhelmed by their child-care responsibilities but who have little money for babysitters.

! Answer to Observational Quiz (from page 259): None! The baby is obviously well-cared-for, with a hat to protect him from the sun, warm and colorful socks, and a chance to experience the fresh air and the view. If you thought this was neglect, you need to note from the sign that this café is in Germany, where toddlers are often parked in carriages or strollers outside restaurants without injury, kidnapping, or any other distress. (A Danish mother did the same thing in New York City in 1997. She was arrested and jailed, and her baby was put in temporary foster care. Which incident was maltreatment?)

measures such as home visits by a social worker, high-quality day care, and preventive medical treatment—all designed to help high-risk families.

Obviously, secondary prevention is tricky. Efforts to identify families that might be incubating problems can make a problem worse. A systems approach (first described in Chapter 1) is needed to bring about any social change, because "many of the most effective solutions to social problems are not readily apparent and may even be counterintuitive. . . . Any single action may reverberate and produce . . . unintended consequences" (Garbarino & Collins, 1999, p. 4). Reformers must consider the overall context and specific conditions, and then must use scientific methods to evaluate the results of any program (Thompson & Nelson, 2001). For instance, one program providing social support to depressed mothers was found to be worse than no intervention at all, perhaps because intervention made the mothers feel even more inadequate (National Research Council & Institute of Medicine, 2000). It is clear that secondary prevention must *not* do any of the following:

- Stigmatize certain families as inadequate
- Undermine atypical family or cultural patterns that actually nurture children
- Create a sense of helplessness in the family, leading them to rely on outsiders rather than strengthening their confidence, skills, and resources.

Tertiary prevention—intervention to reduce the harm done by actual abuse—sometimes comes too late. We have already detailed many of the lifelong intellectual and social costs of child maltreatment that is not halted before it is obvious, repeated, and substantiated.

Theory and research in human development suggest that prevention programs should be broad enough to involve the entire social context. We know that poverty, youth, drug abuse, isolation, and ignorance tend to correlate with unwanted births, inadequate parenting, and then injured and mistreated children. Measures to raise the lowest family incomes, discourage teenage pregnancies, treat addicts, encourage community involvement, and increase parental education may be the most cost-effective approach to prevention after all.

SUMMARY

Size and Nourishment

1. Children continue to gain weight and height during early childhood. Generally, they become thinner and more active.

2. Height and weight variations are caused primarily by genes in developed nations and by nutrition when children from various parts of the world are compared. Percentiles are better indicators of normal growth than number of pounds.

3. Many young children have unbalanced diets during these years, eating more fat and sugar and less iron and calcium than they need. Such poor eating habits are exacerbated by the child's insistence on having everything "just right" and by a cultural emphasis on eating snacks that are nutritionally poor.

Brain Growth and Development

4. The brain reaches adult size by age 7. More important than size, myelination of axons and dendrites speeds messages from one part of the brain to another. This enables more reflective, coordinated thought and memory, as well as quicker responses.

5. With better myelination, various parts of the brain can specialize. Some functions occur more on the left side of the brain, and the right hemisphere specializes in other functions. The corpus callosum connects the two sides of the brain; about 500 million nerve fibers carry messages back and forth.

6. The thickness of the corpus callosum varies. Left-handed people and females tend to have slightly more connecting fibers than

their right-handed or male counterparts. For everyone, however, the corpus callosum increases markedly during the play years.

7. Maturation of the prefrontal cortex, the executive area of the brain, is the final neurological development during these years. It makes formal education possible and enables children to achieve better impulse control.

Mastering Motor Skills

8. Gross motor skills continue to develop, so that many clumsy 2-year-olds become 5-year-olds able to move their bodies in whatever ways their culture values and they themselves have practiced.

9. Muscular control, practice, and brain maturation are also involved in the development of fine motor skills. One developmental progression of fine motor skills is seen in drawings of the human figure, which typically begins by looking like a tadpole with arms but, in the play years, comes to resemble a real person, with facial features, fingers, and clothes that reflect personality.

Injuries and Death

10. Accidents are by far the leading cause of death for children and young adults, with 1- to 4-year-olds, boys, and low-income children more likely to suffer a serious injury or premature death. Culture, community conditions, and biology combine to make such children more vulnerable.

11. Prevention and injury control must occur on many levels, including long before and immediately after each harmful incident. Parents must protect their children, but they cannot do it alone. Laws seem more effective than educational campaigns.

Child Maltreatment

12. Child maltreatment occurs far too often, usually as ongoing abuse and neglect by a child's own parents. Physical abuse is the most obvious form of maltreatment, but neglect is more common and perhaps more harmful in the long term.

13. Witnessing violence can be very destructive. Adult protection and concern are a vital buffer for the child, which is one reason parental maltreatment is especially harmful.

14. About 3 million cases of child maltreatment are reported in the United States each year, about 1 million of which are substantiated. Differential response, in which serious and emergency cases are separated from less troubling ones, is crucial in saving the children from further abuse and getting help to families who can be helped.

15. Foster care, adoption, and kinship care are all necessary and beneficial in some cases of child maltreatment. It is important to support these alternatives to parental care when permanency planning indicates, but it is also important to identify parents who are temporarily overwhelmed by the needs of their children and provide support services for them.

KEY TERMS

myelination (p. 240)	primary prevention (p. 249)	substantiated maltreatment (p. 253)	kinship care (p. 258)
corpus callosum (p. 241)	secondary prevention (p. 249)	differential response (p. 254)	adoption (p. 259)
lateralization (p. 241)	tertiary prevention (p. 249)	shaken baby syndrome (p. 256)	
prefrontal cortex (p. 243)	child maltreatment (p. 252)	post-traumatic stress disorder (PTSD) (p. 257)	
perseveration (p. 244)	child abuse (p. 252)	permanency planning (p. 258)	
activity level (p. 245)	child neglect (p. 252)	foster care (p. 258)	
injury control/harm reduction (p. 249)	failure to thrive (p. 252)		
	reported maltreatment (p. 253)		

KEY QUESTIONS

1. What could our society do to improve the nutrition of young children?

2. In what ways is faster thinking also better thinking?

3. How and why do the left and right sides of the brain function differently?

4. In terms of brain maturation, why do children rarely begin formal education before age 5 or 6?

5. What is the usual progression of children's drawing of the human figure?

6. Which is more effective in preventing injury: public service advertisements or public laws?

7. What is the difference between the terms *harm reduction* and *accident prevention?*

8. Give an example of each of the three levels of prevention?

9. What are the various types of child maltreatment?

10. What kinds of maltreatment are most common and most harmful?

11. Why are many more cases of maltreatment reported than substantiated?

12. What are the advantages and disadvantages of kinship care?

Chapter Nine

The Play Years: Cognitive Development

One of the delights of observing young children is listening to their fanciful and subjective understanding. They beguile us with imaginative, even magical, thinking when they chatter away with an invisible playmate, or wonder where the sun sleeps, or confidently claim that they themselves sleep with their eyes open. At the same time, they startle us when they are confused by metaphors (as in "Mommy is tied up at the office" or "The car's engine just died") and when they are illogical about common occurrences, such as believing that the moon follows them when they walk at night or that buttons are alive because they hold up pants (Carey, 1999). At 3 years of age, they believe that wishes usually come true and that adults, children, and probably cats and dogs (but not babies) can make such wishes (Woolley et al., 1999). Clearly, their thinking is often dictated by their own subjective views, but it also reflects guidance and explicit instruction. This chapter describes both—the magic of what is, and the education that can be.

Research on intellectual development before age 7 has inspired a completely new understanding of early schooling, which was once thought of as merely "day care" but is now considered an important learning experience. One developmental psychologist explains:

> People often call this the "preschool period," but that's not only a mundane name for a magic time, it's also a misnomer. These three-ish and five-ish years are not a waiting time before school or even a time of preparation for school, but an age stage properly called "early childhood" that has a developmental agenda of its own.
>
> *[Leach, 1997, p. 431]*

The goal of this chapter is to understand that "developmental agenda," from the theories to the facts about cognitive development, from the language explosion to early education.

How Children Think: Piaget and Vygotsky

For many years, the magical and self-absorbed nature of young children's thinking dominated developmentalists' descriptions. In this we were guided by Jean Piaget, the Swiss developmentalist whose theories were discussed in Chapter 2 and who called such thinking *egocentric* (literally, "self-centered"). Piaget thought young children were severely and inevitably limited by their own perspective. The label "egocentric" stuck, not only to the children but also to our thoughts about them.

However, more recent research has highlighted another side of early childhood cognition. This side was suggested first by scientists who skillfully used naturalistic observation to chronicle exactly what children said and did. Analyze the following interaction between a 2-year-old child and his mother, who had been trying to hold his sweet tooth in check:

> *(Child sees chocolate cake on table.)*
> **Child:** Bibby on.
> **Mother:** You don't want your bibby on. You're not eating.
> **Child:** Chocolate cake. Chocolate cake.
> **Mother:** You're not having any more chocolate cake, either.
> **Child:** Why?
> **Mother:** *(No answer)*
> **Child:** *(Whines)* Tired.
> **Mother:** You tired? Ooh! *(Sympathetically)*
> **Child:** Chocolate cake.
> **Mother:** No chance.
>
> [adapted from Dunn et al., 1987, p. 136]

Is this 2-year-old illogical, unaware of his social context? Not at all. He is showing strategic skill in pursuing his goal—from asking for his bib (which, unlike cake, is a noncontroversial request) to eliciting his mother's sympathy by feigning fatigue. He is, as Lev Vygotsky would recognize, thinking beyond the bounds of egocentrism. To develop an understanding of both the egocentrism and the social awareness of early cognition, we consider both Piaget and Vygotsky.

Piaget: Preoperational Thought

Piaget's term for cognitive development between the ages of about 2 and 6 is **preoperational thought**. Because he assumed that the ultimate goal of cognition is the ability to reason logically, Piaget emphasized what children cannot do rather than what they can do. Until about age 6 or 7, according to Piaget, children cannot yet think *operationally;* that is, they cannot develop a thought or an idea according to a set of logical principles and then change their conclusions about a given problem when the logical rules change. For instance, they know that Mother is Mother, but they cannot grasp that Mother was once Grandma's baby girl.

Obstacles to Logical Operations

Young children may not yet be capable of logical thought, but that does not mean that they are stupid. Rather, it means that their thinking reflects four prelogical characteristics. The first is **centration**, a tendency to focus thought on one aspect of a situation to the exclusion of all others. We already saw centration in Chapter 6, with the underextension of first words. This continues with later words and concepts. Young children may, for example, insist that lions and tigers are not cats because they center on the house-pet aspect of the cats they know. Or they may insist that Father is a *daddy,* not a brother, because they center on the role each family member fills for them.

A particular type of centration is ego-centration, better known as **egocentrism.** The egocentric child contemplates the world exclusively from his or her personal perspective. In the daddy example above, the fact that the child centers on the man's relationship to the child is an example of egocentrism. As Piaget described it, young children are not necessarily selfish; they would, for example, rush to comfort a tearful parent. But the comfort would come in a decidedly egocentric form, such as a teddy bear or a lollipop.

A second characteristic of preoperational thought is its **focus on appearance** to the exclusion of other attributes. A girl given a short haircut might worry that she has turned into a boy; a boy might refuse to wear a pink shirt because he is

---

Four Aspects of Preoperational Thought

1. Centration
2. Focus on appearance
3. Static reasoning
4. Irreversibility

preoperational thought Piaget's term for cognitive development between the ages of about 2 and 6; characterized by centration (including egocentrism), focus on appearance, static reasoning, and irreversibility.

centration A characteristic of preoperational thought in which the young child focuses on one aspect of a situation to the exclusion of all others.

egocentrism A type of centration in which the young child contemplates the world exclusively from his or her personal perspective.

focus on appearance A characteristic of preoperational thought in which the young child ignores all attributes except appearance.

not a girl. Or upon meeting, say, a tall 4-year-old and a shorter 5-year-old, a child might mistakenly insist that "bigger is older."

Third, preoperational children use **static reasoning,** assuming that the world is unchanging, always in the state in which they currently encounter it. If anything does change, it changes totally and suddenly. When she awakened on her fifth birthday, my daughter Rachel asked, "Am I 5 yet?" Told "yes," she grinned, stretched out her arms, and said, "Look at my 5-year-old hands."

Finally, **irreversibility** means that preoperational thinkers fail to recognize that reversing a process can restore whatever existed before the transformation occurred. A 3-year-old who cries because his mother put lettuce on his hamburger might not think to suggest removing the lettuce. Indeed, he might refuse to eat the hamburger even after the lettuce is removed, because he believes that what is done cannot be undone. If his mother takes the contaminated hamburger away, secretly removes the lettuce, and then brings the "new" hamburger, the child might happily eat.

Conservation and Logic

Piaget devised many experiments to test and illustrate the ways in which these four preoperational characteristics—centration, focus on appearance, static reasoning, and irreversibility—limit young children's ability to reason logically. In several experiments, he studied children's understanding of **conservation,** the principle that the amount of a substance is unaffected by changes in its appearance. Piaget found that conservation, which is taken for granted by older children and adults, is not at all obvious to young children. Rather, young children tend to focus exclusively on one facet of shape or placement.

As an example, suppose two identical glasses contain the same amount of liquid. Then the liquid from one of the glasses is poured into a taller, narrower glass. If young children are asked whether one glass contains more liquid than the other, they will insist that the narrower glass, with the higher liquid level, contains more. They make that mistake because they center on the liquid's height, noticing only the static appearance and ignoring the fact that they could reverse the process and re-create the liquid level they had seen a moment earlier.

Similarly, if an experimenter lines up seven pairs of checkers in two rows of equal length and asks a 4-year-old whether both rows have the same number of checkers, the child will usually say "yes." But suppose that, as the child watches, the experimenter elongates one of the rows by spacing its checkers farther apart. If the experimenter asks again whether the rows have the same number

static reasoning A characteristic of preoperational thought in which the young child assumes that the world is unchanging.

irreversibility A characteristic of preoperational thought in which the young child fails to recognize that reversing a process can restore whatever existed before the transformation occurred.

conservation The principle that the amount of a substance is unaffected by changes in its appearance.

Demonstration of Conservation Professor Berger's daughter Sarah, here at 5 ¾, demonstrates Piaget's conservation-of-liquids experiment. First, she examines both short glasses to be sure they contain the same amount of milk. Then, after the contents of one are poured into the tall glass and she is asked "Which has more?" she points to the tall glass, just as Piaget would have expected. Later she added, "It looks like it has more because it's taller," indicating that some direct instruction might change her mind.

HAZEL HANKIN

Tests of Various Types of Conservation

Type of Conservation	Initial Presentation	Transformation	Question	Preoperational Child's Answer
Liquid	Two equal glasses of liquid.	Pour one into a taller, narrower glass.	Which glass contains more?	The taller one.
Number	Two equal lines of checkers.	Increase spacing of checkers in one line.	Which line has more checkers?	The longer one.
Matter	Two equal balls of clay.	Squeeze one ball into a long, thin shape.	Which piece has more clay?	The long one.
Length	Two sticks of equal length.	Move one stick.	Which stick is longer?	The one that is farther to the right.

FIGURE 9.1 Conservation, Please According to Piaget, until children grasp the concept of conservation at (he believed) about age 6 or 7, they cannot understand that the transformations shown here do not change the total amount of liquid, checkers, clay, and wood.

of checkers, most children will reply "no." Other conservation tasks, shown in Figure 9.1, produce similar results. Children are not logical, at least about conservation, until about age 7.

Piaget believed that preoperational children focus on appearances, ignoring or discounting transformations, because they are not yet logical. However, notice that Piaget's operational tests of cognition depend on the child's words, not actions. Other research finds that even 3-year-olds can distinguish appearance from reality if the test is nonverbal (Sapp et al., 2000). Also, children can remember and report transformations in a gamelike setting, such as when a toy puppet, rather than the adult experimenter, does the rearranging. Contemporary researchers now believe that Piaget underestimated conceptual ability during early childhood, just as he did during infancy. He designed his experiments to reveal what young children seemed *not* to understand, rather than to identify what they *could* understand. According to Vygotsky (1978), such underestimation is an error that many adults make: They notice what children cannot do rather than helping them learn what they can.

Vygotsky: Children as Apprentices

Like Vygotsky and Piaget, every developmentalist, every preschool teacher, and every parent knows that young children strive to understand the world that fascinates and sometimes confuses them. One researcher even coined the term **theory-theory** to highlight the idea that children attempt to construct a theory to explain everything they see and hear:

> More than any animal, we search for causal regularities in the world around us. We are perpetually driven to look for deeper explanations of our experience, and broader and more reliable predictions about it. . . . Children seem, quite literally, to be born with . . . the desire to understand the world and the desire to discover how to behave in it.
>
> [Gopnik, 2001, p. 66]

theory-theory Gopnik's term for the idea that children attempt to construct a theory to explain everything they see and hear.

Thus, according to theory-theory, the best conceptualization of, and explanation for, mental processes is that humans always seek reasons, causes, and underlying principles. Although theory-theory is not universally accepted, no one doubts that children are active thinkers, not passive ones; agents, not recipients (Bloom & Tinker, 2001; Brandtstädter, 1998).

Vygotsky also emphasized another point: Children do not strive alone; their efforts are embedded in a social context. They ask questions—how machines work, why weather changes, where the sky ends—assuming that others know the answers.

Meanwhile, parents, as well as older children, early-childhood educators, and many others, do more than just answer. They try to guide a young child's cognitive growth in numerous ways:

- Presenting challenges for new learning
- Offering assistance with tasks that may be too difficult
- Providing instruction
- Encouraging the child's interest and motivation

In many ways, then, a young child is an **apprentice in thinking** whose intellectual growth is stimulated and directed by older and more skilled members of society. With the help of these mentors, children learn to think by means of their **guided participation** in social experiences and in explorations of their universe.

Vygotsky made yet a third important point: The fact that children want to learn, and then do so, is evidence of their cognitive ability. In fact, "What children can do with the assistance of others might be in some sense even more indicative of their mental development than what they can do alone" (Vygotsky, 1978, p. 85).

If this social-apprenticeship aspect of cognitive development seems familiar, that's because it is given particular emphasis in the sociocultural perspective discussed in Chapter 2. Vygotsky's ideas are one basis for extensive research that emphasizes the cultural foundations of growth and development. In contrast to many developmentalists (including Piaget) who regard cognitive growth as a product of individual discovery propelled by personal experience and biological maturation, Vygotsky believed that cognitive growth is driven by culture. More specifically, Vygotsky saw cognition not as a process of private discovery but as a social activity, with parents and other teachers motivating, channeling, and constructing children's learning.

How to Solve a Puzzle

To see how Vygotsky's approach works in practical terms, let's look at an example. Suppose a child tries to assemble a jigsaw puzzle, fails, and stops trying. Does that mean the task is beyond the child's ability? Not necessarily. The child may do better if given guidance that:

- Structures the task to make its solution more attainable
- Focuses attention on the important steps
- Provides motivation

An adult or older child might begin by praising the child for choosing a hard puzzle and then by encouraging the child to look for a missing puzzle piece for a particular section ("Does it need to be a big piece or a little piece?" "Do you see any blue pieces with a line of red?"). Suppose the child finds some pieces of the right size, and then some blue pieces with a red line, but again seems stymied. The tutor might become more directive, selecting a piece to be tried next, or rotating a piece so that its proper location is more obvious, or actually putting a

Guided Participation Through shared social activity, adults in every culture guide the development of their children's cognition, values, and skills. Typically, the child's curiosity and interests, rather than the adult's planning for some sort of future need, motivate the process. That seems to be the case as this Guatemalan girl eagerly tries to learn her mother's sewing skills.

apprentice in thinking Vygotsky's term for the young child whose intellectual growth is stimulated and directed by older and more skilled members of society.

guided participation The process by which young children, with the help of mentors, learn to think by having social experiences and by exploring their universe.

piece in place with a smile of satisfaction. Throughout, the tutor would praise momentary successes, maintain enthusiasm, and help the child recognize that together they are progressing toward the goal of finishing the puzzle.

The critical element in guided participation is that the partners interact to accomplish the task, with the tutor sensitive and responsive to the precise needs of the child. Eventually, as a result of such mutuality, the child will be able to succeed independently—the ultimate goal of Vygotsky's "apprenticeship in thinking."

Such interactive apprenticeships are commonplace and continual. Everywhere in the world, adults provide guidance and assistance to teach various skills that are valued in the culture—perhaps putting together a puzzle, skinning a small snake, or forming a tortilla. Soon, children who are given such guided practice learn to perform the tasks on their own. Eventually, *they* become the tutors, guiding younger children to master skills that other children, who are the same age but live in a distant country, might never dream of trying.

Scaffolding

Key to the success of apprenticeship is the tutor's sensitivity to the child's abilities and readiness to learn new skills. According to Vygotsky (1934/1986),

> The only good kind of instruction is that which marches ahead of development and leads it. It must be aimed not so much at the ripe as at the ripening functions. It remains necessary to determine the lowest threshold at which instructions may begin, since a certain ripeness of functions is required. But we must consider the upper threshold as well: instruction must be oriented toward the future, not the past.

As you saw in Chapter 2, Vygotsky believed that for each developing individual at each skill level, there is a **zone of proximal development (ZPD),** that is, a range of skills that the person can exercise with assistance but is not quite able to perform independently. How and when children master potential skills depends, in part, on the willingness of others to **scaffold,** or sensitively structure, participation in learning encounters. Most caregivers do this, at least to some extent (Conner et al., 1997; Rogoff, 1998). For example, a study of adults reading to 3-year-olds found very sensitive scaffolding—explaining, pointing, listening—toward the zone of proximal development in response to the child's needs at the moment (Danis et al., 2000).

Vygotsky believed that words can be part of a scaffold and that verbal interaction is a cognitive tool, essential to intellectual growth in two ways. First, internal dialogue, or **private speech,** occurs when people talk to themselves, and this helps them develop new ideas (Vygotsky, 1987).

zone of proximal development (ZPD)
Vygotsky's term for a range of skills that a person can exercise with assistance but is not quite able to perform independently.

scaffold A sensitive structuring of the young child's participation in learning encounters.

private speech Vygotsky's term for the internal dialogue which occurs when people talk to themselves and through which new ideas are developed and reinforced.

Language as Mediation One of the problems with cultural transmission of knowledge is that children are ready to learn whatever they are told—as myths about storks or cabbage patches, bogeymen or witches attest.

Calvin and Hobbes by Bill Watterson

Researchers have found that preschoolers use private speech to review what they know, decide what to do, and explain events to themselves and, incidentally, to anyone else within earshot. Older preschoolers use private speech more selectively and effectively than younger ones (Winsler et al., 2000).

The second way in which language advances thinking, according to Vygotsky, is as the *mediator of the social interaction* that is vital to learning. Whether this **social mediation** function of speech occurs during explicit instruction or only during casual conversation, whether it is intellectual interpretation or simply enthusiastic comment, language as a tool of verbal interaction refines and extends a person's skills. Language allows a person to enter and traverse the zone of proximal development, because words provide a bridge from the child's current understanding to what is almost understood.

social mediation A function of speech by which a person's cognitive skills are refined and extended.

Comparing Piaget and Vygotsky

The theories of Piaget and Vygotsky are "compatible in many ways" (Rogoff, 1998, p. 681). However, each perspective suggests limitations of the other, as a comparison of the two theorists reveals (see Table 9.1).

Thinking Like a Scientist

What Did Cinderella Do with the Pumpkin?

How would scientists figure out whether Piaget or Vygotsky was correct—that is, how egocentric or socially oriented young children actually are? Can you imagine an experiment that would elicit the child's ability to take the perspective of someone other than themselves? In one experiment designed to measure perspective, or egocentrism, in children aged 3 to 5, young children heard two familiar fairy tales, one with the verb *came* or *went,* the other with the verb *take* or *bring*. The first fairy tale included either this passage:

Little Red Riding Hood was sitting in her bedroom when her mother went (or *came*) and asked her to go to her grandmother's house.

or this one:

Cinderella was looking and looking in the kitchen for a pumpkin so that she could bring (or *take*) it to her fairy godmother.

[Rall & Harris, 2000, p. 208]

The children were then asked questions, such as "Little Red Riding Hood was in her bedroom and what happened next?" The researchers wanted to know whether the children would repeat the verb they had heard or change it. When the verb was consistent with the main character's location (as are *came* and *take* above), most children repeated it exactly, but when it was inconsistent (as are *went* and *bring*), they changed it three times more often than they

repeated it verbatim. For example, although they were told that the mother *went* in, they said the mother *came* in; although they heard that Cinderella wanted to *bring* the pumpkin to her fairy godmother, they said she wanted to *take* it to her.

The authors of this study assert that it shows that Piaget was in error. Specifically:

The findings of the present study indicate that such perspective-taking is not just an occasional capacity that is sometimes deployed to override a predominantly egocentric stance. The systematic tendency to misrecall inconsistent verbs indicates, rather, that children spontaneously and tenaciously maintain an alternative perspective.

[Rall & Harris, 2000, p. 206]

Yet this experiment seems to indicate that neither Piaget nor Vygotsky was completely right. Do children strive on their own to reflect the appropriate perspective? Many contemporary theorists believe that they do—that children are less egocentric than Piaget believed and less dependent on parental guidance than Vygotsky believed. A third perspective is that motivation, self-organization, and social orientation are among the innate characteristics of children. If all three explanations are partly correct, then adults, ideally, should provide: time and opportunity (according to Piaget); guidance and scaffolding (according to Vygotsky); respect and freedom (for the children themselves).

Comparing Two Theories Both theories emphasize that learning is not passive but is affected by the learners. The two theories share concepts and sometimes terminology; the differences are in emphasis.

TABLE 9.1 Concepts from the Theories of Piaget and Vygotsky

Piaget	Vygotsky
Active Learning The child's own search for understanding, motivated by the child's inborn curiosity.	**Guided Participation** The adult or other mentor's aid in guiding the next step of learning, motivated by the learner's need for social interaction.
Egocentrism The preschooler's tendency to perceive everything from his or her own perspective and to be limited by that viewpoint.	**Apprenticeship in Thinking** The preschooler's tendency to look to others for insight and guidance, particularly in the cognitive realm.
Structure The mental assumptions and modalities (schema) the child creates to help him or her organize an understanding of the world. Structures are torn down and rebuilt when disequilibrium makes new structures necessary.	**Scaffold** The building blocks for learning put in place by a "teacher" (a more knowledgeable child or adult) or a culture. Learners use scaffolds and then discard them when they are no longer needed.

Information Processing

As you have just read, developmentalists debate the origins of the cognitive accomplishments that occur during early childhood. However, no one doubts that young children demonstrate amazing competence in many areas. Social competencies are further discussed in Chapter 10; grammar and vocabulary are described at the end of this chapter; the curiosity and creativity of the young child are evident throughout the three chapters on the play years. Now we look closely at mathematics, memory, and theory of mind—all of which are aspects of the particular way that young children process information.

After Ten Comes Eleven The day, the date, the season, and the weather are all concepts that are part of the curriculum of a good preschool. Young children's ability to grasp these concepts—as well as to develop an understanding of number—is a good deal stronger than researchers or educators once imagined.

JOHN LEI / STOCK, BOSTON

Simple Arithmetic

Even infants have some perceptual awareness of quantity, noticing, for example, the difference between two and three objects (although you may remember that researchers do not all agree about the meaning of this perception) (Chiang & Wynn, 2000). The connection between numbers and objects continues to be quite shaky in early childhood. When asked to count a group of objects, younger preschoolers are likely to delete numbers from the number sequence (counting "one, two, four, seven, . . ."), to count the same item more than once, or to omit some items. It takes time to master basic counting principles, which include the following:

■ *Stable order.* In counting, numbers must be said in a fixed order: 1, 2, 3 is not the same as 3, 2, 1.
■ *One-to-one correspondence.* Each item being counted gets one number, and only one.

■ *The cardinal principle.* The last number in a count represents the total of the items being counted.

The fact that counting ability improves progressively was illustrated by a study in which 2½- and 4-year-olds were presented with two displays of dots, one of five dots and the other of thirteen, and were asked to "count the dots and touch each dot as you count it" (see Figure 9.2). The younger children seemed to understand what they had been asked to do, but their performance was poor. Typically, they failed to touch at least two dots of the five-dot display and an average of eight dots in the thirteen-dot display. They also miscounted, some saying only "one, two, three" for both displays, ignoring the one-to-one principle.

By contrast, most of the 4-year-olds performed perfectly on the five-dot display and averaged only two counting mistakes and two pointing errors on the thirteen-dot display. Indeed, many 4-year-olds did the thirteen-dot task with no errors (Saxe et al., 1987). Presumably, in 18 months these children had learned the three principles, just mentioned, that are necessary for accurate counting.

How Number Skills Develop

What contributes to the child's developing understanding of number? One factor is simple maturation, of three different kinds:

■ Brain development that continues throughout childhood
■ Maturation of language, enabling the young child to conceptualize and express number
■ Maturation in the sense emphasized by Piaget—that is, the flowering of the child's innate curiosity and exploration of the world of objects

In some cultures, another factor that promotes number competence is the particular language children speak. One hypothesis about the general math superiority of East Asian children over European and American youngsters is that the languages they speak—Japanese, Korean, and Chinese—are much more logical in their labeling of numbers. For instance "eleven, twelve, thirteen," and so on, are called "ten-one, ten-two, ten-three," and so on, in the Asian languages (Fuson & Kwon, 1992). This linguistic ordering advances young Asian children's intuitive grasp of the number system as soon as they begin to talk.

Another way in which the Chinese language, in particular, fosters number learning is that its names for the numbers are short, one-syllable words. Because all children's brains have limited storage and processing capacity, a child's brain can process more one-syllable Chinese numbers than one- and two-syllable English ones (such as "seven, twenty, sixty")—and, for that matter, more English numbers than Welsh ones, which often have three syllables. The more numbers the memory can contain, the easier it is to count, add, and perform other arithmetic operations (Schneider & Pressley, 1997).

A final factor in building number competence is the structure and scaffolding support provided by parents, other adults, and older children. "Structure" and "scaffolding" do not mean a formal curriculum, but just natural interaction, as Vygotsky would emphasize. In many families, parents and offspring frequently use numbers together—counting small quantities, playing number games ("one, two, button my shoe . . ."), pushing television-channel buttons, sorting coins, and measuring (as in putting the allotted spoonfuls of cocoa mix into a glass of milk). Through such shared activities, number concepts come within the children's capabilities, because apprenticeship has naturally put counting into their zone of proximal development.

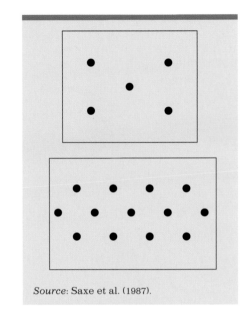

Source: Saxe et al. (1987).

FIGURE 9.2 Up for the Count In the experimental game of "count the dots," 2½- and 4-year-olds were asked to count and touch each dot in these two different displays. Most 2½-year-olds made several errors, even on the five-dot display. But some 4-year-olds did both tasks perfectly. They had already learned the most basic of counting rules: Count each object once, and only once.

Especially for Early-Childhood Educators
What does young children's understanding of number imply for preschool education?

Memory

Preschoolers are notoriously poor in memory, even when compared with children only a few years older. Ask a school-age child "What did you do today?" and you may get a detailed accounting. Ask that older child what happened in a television sitcom, and again you might hear more specifics than you ever wanted to know. Ask a preschooler the same questions, however, and you are likely to hear "I don't remember" or "I liked it" or a string of seemingly irrelevant details.

Even with skilled help from a patient mother who knows her child and understands the basics of early memory, at age 2 memory is far from fluent. This example is typical:

> **Mother:** Did you like the apartment at the beach?
> **Rachel:** Yeah, and I have fun in the, in the, water.
> **Mother:** You had fun in the water?
> **Rachel:** Yeah, I come to the ocean.
> **Mother:** You went to the ocean?
> **Rachel:** Yeah.
> **Mother:** Did you play in the ocean?
> **Rachel:** And my sandals off.
> **Mother:** You took your sandals off?
> **Rachel:** And my jamas off.
> **Mother:** And your jamas off. And what did you wear to the beach?
> **Rachel:** I wear hot cocoa shirt.
> **Mother:** Oh, your cocoa shirt, yeah. And your bathing suit.
> **Rachel:** Yeah, and my cocoa shirt.
> **Mother:** And did you go in the water?
> **Rachel:** *(No response)*
> **Mother:** Who went in the water with you?
> **Rachel:** Daddy and Mommy.
> **Mother:** Right. Did the big waves splash you?
> **Rachel:** Yeah.
>
> *[Hudson, 1990, pp. 180–181]*

The difficulty is not primarily deficient memory circuits in the brain. Basic information processing is quite possible. Sometimes young children remember particular events or details very well, as Rachel remembered the "hot cocoa shirt." From Chapter 6 you know that memory is encoded in several parts of the brain, both explicitly and implicitly, and that for adults a memory of one type (perhaps an overheard tune) often evokes another memory (perhaps the person with you when you first heard that song). Young children have great difficulty with such connections, partly because the corpus callosum between the brain's hemispheres is not well myelinated but also because the prefrontal cortex is underdeveloped. Consequently, children have not yet had much practice acquiring strategies for deliberately storing memories of past events or for retrieving them from memory on demand. Retrieval is particularly troublesome for young children (Rovee-Collier et al., 2001).

Another very practical problem is that young children do not yet know what should be encoded into memory for later retrieval and what is irrelevant. Rachel seemed to forget that she wore a bathing suit and played in the waves, surely the most important parts of a trip to the beach, although probably not the topic of extended explanation at the time. Some types of memories are obviously easier to form, to store, or to retrieve than others, with memories for emotional experiences being among the strongest (Lagattuta & Wellman, 2001).

Source Memory

source memory The ability to recall the person who said or did something or the place where something occurred.

For people of all ages, the most difficult part of memory is called **source memory**, recollection of the person who said or did something or the place where something occurred—specifically, remembering who, when, where, and how we

ANNIE GRIFFITHS BELT / CORBIS

Remember That Picnic? The children at this Sephardic Jewish family's picnic in Israel will, typically, have a faulty source memory, incorrectly remembering some of the participants and some of the things that happened. They may have a very accurate memory of other particular aspects of the occasion, however, such as a bee sting, an unusual food, or a sudden downpour.

learned certain facts (Roberts, 2000). People sometimes believe that they read a statement in a textbook when they actually overheard it on the street or that their mother gave them the new sweater that they actually bought themselves. Source confusion makes people think something has been verified by expert research when actually it is just someone's offhand opinion—a particular problem for teachers of the social sciences!

Source memory is especially difficult for children. They may insist that a certain person did something when that person was nowhere nearby, or they may think that they always knew a fact that they actually just learned (Esbensen et al., 1997). When positive behavior is described, young children are likely to claim that they did more than they actually did; when negative behavior is described, they take less blame and may not acknowledge their responsibility, not to avoid punishment but because they have genuinely forgotten (Ratner et al., 2000). Thus, young children may not be deliberately lying but merely demonstrating their inadequate source memory.

A surprising disconnect between fact and knowledge was found when children were guided to use one of their five senses to detect a certain property of various substances, such as smelling bubble bath to see if it was strawberry or lemon, or touching water to see if it was warm or cold (O'Neill & Chong, 2001). An experimenter demonstrated what to do (noisily sniffing the bubble bath, for instance); then children did the same thing, using the appropriate sense to answer each of the five questions. When they were then asked a specific question, they could easily give accurate answers (for instance, "The water was cold"). Next they were asked, "How do you know?" Most 3-year-olds (57 percent) and many 4-year-olds (37 percent) did not correctly identify the source of their knowledge, often coming up with inaccurate responses even though they had just used smell, touch, taste, and so on, and had just correctly said what they had discovered. The researchers write:

> The presentation of our findings in this format—a written journal article—makes it hard to convey the difficulty 3-year-olds had in answering questions about the source of their knowledge of the properties in question. Nor is it easy to convey here how odd children's responses often appeared. . . . Many 3-year-olds seem

Response for Early-Childhood Educators (from page 271): Since arithmetic concepts depend on both maturation and experience, counting games, songs, and questions ("How many children are here?" "What is the date?" "How many crackers should we count out?") should be part of every day's curriculum, with children actively participating. Playing store, play money, games with dice or numbers, adding, and subtracting will help move children to the next level. Learning the differences among written numbers (1-2-3, etc.) is as important as learning *A-B-C.*

entirely unaware of how their own sensory actions were related to the property knowledge they had gained only seconds earlier . . . To watch a child sniff a swimming pool and tell you that that is how they found out it contained cold water is quite striking.

[O'Neill & Chong, 2001, pp. 812, 813]

Following the Script Preschoolers remember what routinely happens in their lives by following a script in their play. This young lady has learned something about tea parties, and she has a dog who follows her script. Other preschoolers act out scripts one wishes they had never experienced.

script A mental road map of a familiar sequence of events.

Script Creation

In other ways, however, young children are remarkably capable of storing useful representations of past events. One way they do this is by forming scripts of recurring experiences. A **script** is a mental road map of a familiar sequence of events, useful at any stage of life to aid memory and comprehension.

Each script acts as a kind of self-made scaffold, or skeletal outline. By age 3, for example, children can tell you what happens in a restaurant (you order food, eat it, and then pay for it), at a birthday party (you arrive, give presents, play games, have cake and ice cream, sing "Happy Birthday"), and at bedtime (first a bath, then a story, then perhaps a prayer, and then lights out) as well as during other everyday events. As we saw in Chapter 8's discussion of eating routines, any change—such as a birthday pie replacing a birthday cake—is objectionable precisely because it does not fit the script.

Memories of Special Experiences

Under certain circumstances, children show excellent long-term memory not only for experiences that have happened so many times that a script is formed but also for unique experiences—including disasters, celebrations, and family births or deaths—especially if they had been the topic of conversation (Howe, 1997). One study began with 2½-year-olds and their mothers in a make-believe camping and fishing experience with 30 distinctive toy objects provided by the experimenters (Haden et al., 2001). At ages 3 and 3½, the same children were engaged in two other make-believe events; bird-watching and opening an ice-cream store. A day after each event, the children were asked which of the toy objects they remembered. There were age-related trends: The children remembered, on average, 50 percent of the objects at age 2½ and 70 percent at age 3½. The researchers noted that older children made more comments about their experiences: The 3½-year-olds made almost four times as many such remarks as they had made one year earlier (Haden et al., 2001). One factor that affected memory was whether or not the mother and child had talked together about the object—naming the map, grill, sleeping bag, and so on (Haden et al., 2001).

Considerable other research (Ratner et al., 2000; Schneider & Bjorklund, 1998) likewise indicates that, particularly in young children, four factors are likely to aid memory:

■ Social interaction
■ Personal participation
■ Conversation that names the objects and experiences
■ Specific questions asked by a friendly, knowledgeable person

All four of these factors point to the importance of language as a social mediator between memory and the mind, just as Vygotsky claimed. This is true at age 2 and older, but not for 1-year-olds, because they cannot yet easily use words to solidify memories (Herbert & Hayne, 2000).

In one study, children who had had a medical emergency (a broken bone, swallowed poison) at age 1 or 2 were interviewed long after the event. Those who were not yet talking at the time of the trauma remembered very little, but those who were at least 2 years old had vivid and accurate memories, even if the interview took place at age 4. Source memory, as might be expected, was imperfect, but other aspects of memory were solid. Specifically, most children were quite correct about what happened and what the treatment was, but less accurate about who did what to them and why (Peterson & Rideout, 1998).

Conversation during early childhood may be pivotal in explaining children's recall because "marked individual differences that are observed among mothers in memory conversations with their young children have a long-term impact on the development of children's skills for retrieving and reporting" (Haden et al., 2001). One practical implication of this research is that parents can help their children remember better by eliciting memories and adding details in conversations with the children, as Rachel's mother did. Longitudinal research confirms that 3-year-olds with such parental guidance develop better memory skills by age 6 (Reese et al., 1993).

As such studies show, young children can remember accurately, but they also sometimes become confused about what happened. In another series of experiments, an interview after a medical checkup included misleading questions (Goodman et al., 1990). Questions such as "[The nurse] touched your bottom, didn't she?" and "How many times did she kiss you?" were asked, either in a friendly, encouraging manner or in an intimidating, stern one. Older children, age 5 to 7, were rarely misled: Less than 9 percent did they falsely affirm something that had not happened, whether the questioning was friendly or stern. In contrast, 10 percent of the 3- and 4-year-olds responded untruthfully to the friendly questions, and 23 percent of them were misled by the stern questions.

Would you believe her? As the only eyewitness to the slaying of a playmate, 4-year-old Jennifer Royal was allowed to testify in open court. Her forthright answers, and the fact that she herself had been wounded, helped convict the accused gunman. While most developmentalists agree that, when questioned properly, children can provide reliable testimony about events they have experienced or witnessed, many advocate arranging a more sheltered way for children to give testimony.

One example of a child's erroneous agreement with stern questions in real life occurred in a notorious day-care abuse case, during which the following exchange took place:

> **Prosecutor:** Did she touch you with a spoon?
>   **Child:** No.
> **Prosecutor:** No? Okay. Did you like it when she touched you with the spoon?
>   **Child:** No.
> **Prosecutor:** No? Why not?
>   **Child:** I don't know.
> **Prosecutor:** You don't know?
>   **Child:** No.
> **Prosecutor:** What did you say to Kelly when she touched you?
>   **Child:** I don't like that.
>
> *[quoted in Ceci & Bruck, 1998, p. 741]*

From research involving questioning of children after a stressful encounter, three useful guidelines have emerged (Cassel et al., 1996; Lamb et al., 2000; Pipe et al., 1999; Schneider & Pressly, 1997):

- Children should be presented with a structured sequence of questions.
- Children should be interviewed by a neutral professional.
- Children should be interviewed only once (and videotaped for later trial use).

Adults also misremember important details, especially after a long delay or if source memory is needed. Nobody always tells the truth. Indeed,

> The safest conclusion that can be reached at this point in time is that subjects of all ages will lie when the motives are right. Children may be no different from adults in this regard. Thus the argument that children are incapable of "lying"

should be discounted, as should the insinuation that they are hopeless liars. . . . Children have tremendous strengths in recollecting their pasts, provided that the adults do not do anything to usurp their memories.

[Ceci & Bruck, 1998, pp. 765, 766]

In fact, this statement could serve as a summary of all that we know about memory during young childhood. It can be surprisingly good and surprisingly poor, as with source memory. Throughout early childhood, impressive competencies and amazing lapses coexist in the same child at the same moment.

Theory of Mind

Human mental processes—thoughts, emotions, motives, beliefs, and intentions—are among the most complicated and thought-provoking phenomena in a young person's world. Whether trying to understand a playmate's unexpected anger, determine when a sibling will be generous, or avoid an aunt's too-wet kiss, children want to understand and predict what goes on in another person's mind. To do so, they develop a kind of "folk psychology," an understanding of human mental processes called **theory of mind.** This is a third area (along with numbers and memory) in which young children's ability has often been underestimated.

Emergence by Age 4

Social referencing by toddlers (discussed in Chapter 6) indicates that they realize their caregiver might be expressing fear or joy. But a 1-year-old's social referencing is linked to facial expressions and particular words, not to imagined concepts of what a person might be thinking. Indeed, the fact that people are thinking, even when they are not expressing those thoughts, seems unknown to children under age 3. Actually interpreting, predicting, and remembering someone else's thoughts is even more difficult, and doing so typically begins around age 4 (Wellman et al., 2001). (See Table 9.2.)

In truth, it takes a lifelong effort to understand how the mind works, including all the varieties of thought processes that occur in many contexts (Kuhn, 2000). Every student of human development strives to understand cognition; no one succeeds completely. However, in "an important intellectual change at about 4 years" (Perner, 2000. p. 396), young children suddenly grasp something about theory of mind that they did not know before.

What is it that children understand? Between the ages of 3 and 6, children come to realize that mental phenomena may not reflect reality. This idea leads to the theory-of-mind concept that individuals can believe various things and, therefore, that people can be deliberately deceived or fooled—an idea beyond most younger children, even when they have themselves been deceived. Consider an experiment in which an adult shows a 3-year-old a candy box and asks, "What is inside?" The child says, naturally, "Candy." But, in fact, the child has been tricked:

> **Adult:** Let's open it and look inside.
> **Child:** Oh . . . holy moly . . . pencils!
> **Adult:** Now I'm going to put them back and close it up again. *(Does so)* Now . . . when you first saw the box, before we opened it, what did you think was inside it?
> **Child:** Pencils.
> **Adult:** Nicky *(friend of the child)* hasn't seen inside this box. When Nicky comes in and sees it . . . when Nicky sees the box, what will he think is inside it?
> **Child:** Pencils.
>
> *[adapted from Astington & Gopnik, 1988, p. 195]*

This experiment has become a classic, performed with thousands of children from many cultures. When it is replicated exactly, 3-year-olds almost always make

---

theory of mind An understanding of human mental processes.

TABLE 9.2 Age at Which Theory of Mind Emerges

Age (years)	Place
3	None
3½	Baka (Cameroon)
	Canada
4	Australia
	Korea
	United States
4½	Austria
	United Kingdom
5	Japan
6	None
7	Quechua (Peru)

Source: Adapted from Wellman et al., 2001.

Understanding How Others Think This table shows the average age at which theory of mind appears in children of various cultures. A child was said to have developed theory of mind when he or she correctly answered half the theory-of-mind questions asked. These findings are based on a detailed meta-analysis of 143 studies. Children from every society studied (except those in rural Peru) showed rapid growth in theory of mind from age 4 to age 5½.

Especially for Social Scientists Can you think of any connection between Piaget's theory of preoperational thought and 3-year-olds' errors in this theory-of-mind task?

the same mistake. They seem to confuse belief and reality, and this "realist bias" makes it difficult for them to remember ever having believed something that contradicts what they now see (Mitchell & Kikuno, 2000).

Until age 4, children are notoriously bad at fooling other people. They play hide-and-seek by hiding in the same place time after time or somehow signify the truth when they try to tell a lie. Their understanding of what other people are likely to think or believe is very limited, although some research finds that they can figure out strategies to trick someone else by age 3, a year younger than they can realize that they themselves have been tricked (Hala & Chandler, 1996).

Contextual Influences on Theory of Mind

Recently, developmentalists have asked what, precisely, strengthens theory of mind at about age 4. Is it nature or nurture, brain maturation or experience? Consider one study, in which 68 children aged 2½ to 5½ were presented with four standard theory-of-mind situations, including a Band-Aid box that really contained pencils (similar to the candy-box experiment described above) (Jenkins & Astington, 1996). More than one-third of the children succeeded at all four tasks (for example, they understood that someone else might initially believe, as they had, that the Band-Aid box would contain Band-Aids); more than one-third failed on three or four tasks; and the remaining 26 percent were in between, succeeding at two or three tasks. Not surprisingly, age had a powerful effect: The 5-year-olds were most likely to succeed on all four tasks and the 3-year-olds most likely to fail every time. This result suggests that maturation of the executive function of the brain (the prefrontal cortex), which usually reaches a new level of growth at about age 4, may be the underlying factor here (Moses, 2001).

Interestingly, however, as a predictive variable, general language ability was as significant as maturation: The greater a child's verbal proficiency (at any age), the better he or she did (Jenkins & Astington, 1996). Other research also finds that language ability, particularly the ability to use the words *think, believe,* and *know,* precedes theory-of-mind development (de Villiers & de Villiers, 2000). Of course,

Brotherly Love In addition to their shared joy, these brothers, aged 5 years and 11 months, are both learning the intricacies of social interaction. Such sharing is one reason that children with siblings usually develop a theory of mind more quickly than "only children" do.

ERIKA STONE / PHOTO RESEARCHERS, INC.

MICHAEL NEWMAN / PHOTOEDIT

Friendly Lion Halloween is fun for the children in this Santa Monica, California, elementary-school classroom, because they are past the preoperational stage in which a frightening appearance might mean a frightening reality. (Inside the lion costume is Richard Riordan, the mayor of Los Angeles at the time the photo was taken.)

ELIZABETH CREWS / THE IMAGE WORKS

Now the Green One This 14-month-old is, for the moment, following his 4-year-old sister's instructions to stack the plastic rings the "right" way, something no toddler normally does. Both are content now, but what if he wanted to put the blue one next? Both siblings would advance in theory of mind.

Theory of Mind Is Advanced by . . .

1. Maturation of prefrontal cortex
2. Language: *believe, think*
3. An older sibling
4. A culture that anticipates the future

---

imaginary companion A make-believe person or other creature that a young child talks to and plays with.

language ability may be partly the result of brain maturation, but specific language interaction also plays a pivotal role.

In the Jenkins and Astington (1996) study, when the effects of both age and language ability were accounted for, a third important factor emerged: having at least one older brother or sister. Siblings particularly aided younger children whose language ability was not quite up to par for their age. Another researcher estimates that, in theory-of-mind development, "Two older siblings are worth about a year of chronological age" (Perner, 2000, p. 383).

Before concluding that maturation, with a little help from language and siblings, produces theory of mind at age 4, consider one more study (Vinden, 1996). All the 4- to 8-year-olds in a village in Peru were tested on a culturally appropriate version of the candy-box situation, in this case a sugar bowl that contained tiny potatoes. Of course, the children at first thought the bowl contained sugar, as anyone from that village would. But surprisingly, even up to age 8, many of these children answered theory-of-mind questions incorrectly: They could not explain why someone would initially expect sugar to be in a sugar bowl and then be surprised to discover potatoes.

Culture is probably the key difference between the Peruvian and the North American children. In the Peruvians' mountainous, isolated village, "there is no reason or time for elaborate deception . . . where subsistence farmers, working from dawn to dusk just to survive, . . . live mostly on the landscape of action, and not on the landscape of consciousness" (Vinden, 1996. p. 1715). Neither their language nor their culture describes false belief or "how people's thoughts might affect their actions." Thus, culture is a fourth crucial factor in the development of theory of mind (Lillard, 1998; Vinden, 1996).

Imagination Throughout Life

The development of the understanding of human mental processes—particularly knowing how someone could think something that is not true—is an important topic for all social scientists. Variations of the original theory-of-mind experiment, and interpretation of the surprising ignorance at age 3 and insight at age 4, continue to intrigue researchers (Carruthers & Smith, 1996; Mitchell & Riggs, 2000; Wellman et al., 2001). From a developmental perspective, however, the sudden onset of theory of mind at about age 4 should not lead us to think that younger children are clueless or adults always wise. According to the explanation of theory of mind offered by *theory-theory*, people of all ages have theories about their experiences and observations. Thus, people naturally develop theories of mind, beginning with quite primitive and incorrect theories and progressing toward more accurate ones as development continues. Certainly our entire understanding of human development includes conflicting theories, as Chapter 2 demonstrates.

Particularly during the play years, imagination and creative theorizing are apparent. By age 2, children are already able to pretend, and they understand that pretending means acting as if something were true even though it isn't. Pretending becomes much more elaborate, interactive, and detailed as time goes on. Even before they could pass the standard tests of theory of mind, many young children create vivid **imaginary companions**, make-believe people or other creatures that they talk to and play with. Such children are quite normal in many ways, but their theories of mind are often more advanced than those of their less imaginative age-mates. At age 4, although they usually believe, quite firmly, that their imaginary creatures are real, they also know, quite logically, the difference between imagined thinking and acknowledged reality (Taylor, 1999).

TABLE 9.3 Summary of Children's Thinking from Ages 2 to 6

Memory for emotional events—good, even at age 2

Memory for details—good, but more fragile than it is for older children

Source memory—poor, even worse than for older children

Knowing the names of numbers—good by age 2 or 3

Counting in sequence—gradual mastery during early childhood

Using numbers correctly to count—poor until about age 4

Awareness of emotions, in self and others—good (based on appearance, not theory of mind)

Theory of mind—poor until about age 4

Imaginary companions—common from ages 4 to 6; does not impede theory of mind

It is evident that children during the play years make significant cognitive strides. (Their achievements are summarized in Table 9.3.) It is also evident that their remaining errors are not very different in kind (although they are less sophisticated) than the errors made by older children and adults.

Language

As we noted in Chapter 6, humans normally begin talking at about 1 year, with new vocabulary and phrases added slowly at first. Toward the end of toddlerhood, when the naming explosion occurs, the pace and scope of language learning increase dramatically, ushering in early childhood, when rapid linguistic advances occur. Over the past thirty years, developmentalists have wondered if early childhood is a *sensitive* or *critical* period for language development. A **sensitive period** is a time when a certain type of development occurs most rapidly; a **critical period** is a time when a certain type of development must occur or it will never happen. Some scientists once called early childhood a critical period for language learning, because they believed that if language structure and pronunciation were not learned in early childhood, then the necessary brain neurons and synapses would no longer be available and language would never be mastered (Lenneberg, 1967; Scovel, 1988). This turns out to be an exaggeration: Humans can and do master their native language after early childhood and can learn second languages even after puberty (Bialystok, 2001).

Although not a critical period, early childhood does seem to be a *sensitive period* for language learning—a time when vocabulary, grammar, and pronunciation can be rapidly and easily learned, not only because of neurological characteristics of the developing brain but also because most young children have a powerful social motivation and an absence of self-criticism. Thus, language can be learned any time during the life span, but it is best learned during early childhood; the words and grammar learned then will last a lifetime. To realize how impressive this early linguistic mastery is, consider the details of acquiring vocabulary, grammar, and a second language.

Vocabulary

In early childhood, vocabulary increases exponentially, from about 500 words at age 2 to more than 10,000 at age 6. One scholar says that 2- to 6-year-olds learn 10 words a day (Clark, 1995); another estimates 1 new word every two waking hours from about ages 2 to 20 (Pinker, 1994). Although these estimates vary, partly because children and contexts themselves vary, all agree that the most rapid vocabulary expansion usually occurs before age 7.

Response for Social Scientists (from page 276): Children who focus on appearance and on static conditions, who cannot mentally reverse a process, and who egocentrically believe that everyone else thinks as they do would naturally believe that they had always known that the candy box held pencils and that their friend would know that, too.

sensitive period A time when a certain type of development occurs most rapidly.

critical period A time when a certain type of development must occur or it will never happen.

Universal Language All 1-year-olds point and smile, indicating their readiness to communicate. Starting at this moment and for the next four years, parents can readily teach their child one language or two.

? *Observational Quiz* (see answer, page 282): Look closely at the baby's face and sweater. Can you guess which two languages he is learning?

ALEXANDER FARNSWORTH / THE IMAGE WORKS

fast mapping The speedy and not very precise process of acquiring vocabulary by mentally "charting" new words.

How does this happen? As you remember from Chapter 6, one explanation is that, after a year or so of painstakingly learning one word at a time, the human mind has developed an interconnected set of categories for vocabulary, a kind of grid or mental map on which to chart the meanings of various words. This speedy and not very precise process of acquiring vocabulary by "charting" new words is called **fast mapping** (Woodward & Markman, 1998). Children quickly learn new animal names, for instance, because they can be mapped in the brain close to old animal names. *Tiger* is easy if you already know *lion, zebra* is easy if you already know *horse,* and so on. Similarly, children learn new color names by connecting them with those they already know.

The process is called fast mapping because, rather than stopping to figure out an exact definition and waiting until a word has been understood in several contexts, the child simply hears a word once or twice and sticks it on a mental language map. [Something similar occurs when someone is asked, for instance, where Nepal is. Most people can locate it approximately ("near India") in their mental map of the world, but few can locate it precisely, citing each border.]

Closely related to fast mapping is logical extension: After learning a word, children apply it to other, unnamed objects in the same category. It is as if children use their available vocabulary to cover all the territory within their range (Behrend et al., 2001).

Young children's fast mapping is aided by the way adults label new things for them. A helpful parent might point at an animal the child is watching at the zoo and say, "See the *lion* resting by the water. It's a *lion!* A very big cat." In less than a minute, *lion* enters the child's vocabulary. Zoos, museums, and children's first picture books do the same thing: organize animals and objects into categories.

In general, children use some basic principles to help them learn language (Woodward & Markman, 1998). One set of assumptions is that syntax is an important clue (Jaswal & Markman, 2001). When English-speaking children are told, for instance, that something is *a dax, dax, daxing,* or *daxy,* they decide that *dax* means a common noun, a proper noun, a verb, or an adjective, respectively. Another set of assumptions is that words refer to whole objects rather than to their parts, that each object has only one label (an example of underextension), and that adults who are talking authoritatively are probably using words correctly (Sabbagh & Baldwin, 2001). Of course, children must be in a social context where they hear people conversing in order for this type of fast mapping to occur. For this reason, children who have older siblings map out the differences among *I, you, he,* and *she* more quickly than first-borns do. Fast mapping and the presence of siblings do not always combine well, however, as I learned from my daughters.

In Person

Fast Mapping: Mommy the Brat

Fast mapping has an obvious advantage, in that it fosters quick vocabulary acquisition. However, it also means that children *seem* to know words because they use them, but actually their understanding is quite limited. One very simple common example is the word *big,* a word even 2-year-olds use and apparently understand. In fact, however, young children often use *big* when they mean *tall* or *old* or *great* ("My love is so big!") and only gradually come to use *big* correctly (Sena & Smith, 1990).

A more amusing example involves a 3-year-old who told her father that her preschool group had visited a farm, where she saw some Dalmatian cows. Luckily her father (my student) remembered that, a week before, the girl had met her uncle's Dalmatian dog, so he understood his daughter's fast-mapping mistake and reported it to the class.

When adults realize that children often do not fully comprehend the meanings of words they use, it becomes easier to understand—and forgive—the mistakes children make. I still vividly recall an incident that stemmed from fast mapping when my youngest daughter, then 4, was furious at me.

Sarah had apparently fast-mapped several insulting words into her vocabulary. However, her fast mapping did not provide precise definitions or reflect nuances. In her anger, she called me first a "mean witch" and then a "brat." I smiled at her innocent imprecision, knowing the first was fast-mapped from fairy tales and the second from comments she got from her older sisters. Neither label bothered me, as I don't believe in witches and my brother is the only person who can appropriately call me a brat.

But then Sarah let loose an X-rated epithet that sent me reeling. Struggling to contain my anger, I tried to convince myself that fast mapping had probably left her with no real idea of what she had just said. "That word is never to be used in this family!" I sputtered. My appreciation of the speed of fast mapping was deepened by her response: "Then how come Rachel [her older sister] called me that this morning?"

The vocabulary-building process occurs so quickly that, by age 5, some children seem to understand and use almost any term they hear. In fact, 5-year-olds can learn any word or phrase, if it is explained to them with specific examples and used in context, or if they themselves can figure out what the word means. A teacher who was my student asked her preschoolers what they had done over the weekend. Among standard answers—watch television, go to church, buy groceries—one child answered:

"I went to a protest."
"What is a protest?" another child asked.
"A lot of people get together, walk around, and yell," the first child replied.
The second child nodded, mapping that word into her vocabulary.

Young children cannot comprehend *every* word they hear. Abstract nouns and metaphors are difficult because there is no referent in their experience and because the fast-mapping process is quite literal, allowing only one meaning per word. A mother, exasperated by her son's frequent inability to find his belongings, told him that someday he would lose his head. He calmly replied, "I'll never lose my head. If I feel it coming off, I'll find it and pick it up." Another mother warned her child who was jumping on the bed:

Mother: Stop. You'll hurt yourself.
   Child: No I won't. *(Still jumping)*
Mother: You'll break the bed.
   Child: No I won't. *(Still jumping)*
Mother: OK. You'll just have to live with the consequences.
   Child: *(Stops jumping)* I'm not going to live with the consequences. I don't even know them.

[*adapted from* The New York Times, *November 2, 1998*]

Hi, Grandma This boy has been having telephone conversations with his grandmother since he was 1 year old. At first, he mostly listened and then cried when the phone was taken away. Now, almost 3 years old, he chatters away unstoppably, revealing an extensive grasp of vocabulary and grammar. However, he still doesn't necessarily provide all the details that would let his grandmother follow the conversation; he may sometimes refer to events she has no knowledge of and people she does not know or tell the ending of a story without a beginning.

overregularization The young child's tendency to apply the rules of grammar even when doing so is not necessary or appropriate.

❗**Answer to Observational Quiz** (from page 280): A good guess would be Swedish and English. The photograph was taken in Stockholm, Sweden. Many Swedish babies, including this one, have blue eyes and fair skin, and the baby's sweater has an American flag on the front.

Young children also have difficulty with words expressing comparisons—such as *tall* and *short, near* and *far, high* and *low, deep* and *shallow*—because they do not understand the *relative* nature of these words (Oliver Ryalls, 2000). Once young children know which end of the swimming pool is the deep end, for instance, its depth becomes their definition of *deep*. They might obey parental instructions to stay out of deep puddles by splashing through every puddle they see, insisting that none of those is *deep*.

Words expressing relationships of place and time—such as *here, there, yesterday*, and *tomorrow*—are difficult as well. More than one pajama-clad child has awakened on Christmas morning and asked, "Is it tomorrow yet?" As with toddlers, however, it is easy to focus on children's vocabulary mistakes, forgetting the language explosion from ages 2 to 6, which adds thousands of new words each year. The play years could appropriately be called the language years, except that so much else develops as well.

Grammar

The *grammar* of a language includes the structures, techniques, and rules that are used to communicate meaning. Word order and word repetition, prefixes and suffixes, intonation and pronunciation—all are part of this element of language.

By the time children are 3 years old, their grammar is quite impressive: English-speaking children not only place the subject before the verb but also put the verb before the object and the adjective before the noun. They say "I eat red apple," not any of the 23 other possible combinations of those four words. They can form the plurals of nouns; the past, present, and future tenses of verbs; and the subjective, objective, and possessive forms of pronouns. They can rearrange word order to create questions and can use auxiliary verbs ("I *can* do that"). They are well on their way to mastering the negative, having progressed past the simple "no" of the 2-year-old ("No sleepy" or "I no want it") to more complicated forms ("I am not sleepy" or "I don't want any more"). By age 6, most can also understand "tag" questions ("This is mine, *isn't it*?").

Parental input and encouragement lead directly to faster and more correct language use (Barrett, 1999). In a study of twins (who are often delayed in language development), researchers found that the speed and depth of language learning depended more on how much the parents spoke to each twin than on genetics (Rutter et al., 2000).

Following the Rules

Young children learn their grammar lessons so well that they often tend to apply the rules of grammar even when they should not. This tendency, called **overregularization**, creates trouble when a child's language includes many exceptions to the rules. As an example, one of the first rules that English-speaking children apply is to add -*s* to form the plural. Overregularization leads many young children to talk about foots, tooths, sheeps, and mouses. They may even put the -*s* on adjectives when the adjectives are acting as nouns, as in this dinner-table exchange between my 3-year-old and her father:

> **Sarah:** I want somes.
> **Father:** You want some what?
> **Sarah:** I want some mores.
> **Father:** Some more what?
> **Sarah:** I want some more chickens.

Although technically wrong, overregularization is actually a sign of verbal sophistication; it shows that children are applying the rules. Indeed, as young children become more conscious of grammatical usages, they exhibit increasingly sophisticated misapplications of them. A child who at age 2 correctly says she "broke" a glass may at age 4 say she "braked" one and then at age 5 say she "did broked" another.

Children comprehend more complex grammar, and more difficult vocabulary, than they produce. Thus, although it is a mistake to expect proper grammar, it is also an error to always "talk down" to the level of a young child. Some grammatical forms (the future subjunctive, the distinction between *whoever* and *whomever*) are beyond many young children, but most other forms are potentially within their comprehension. Vygotsky's zone of proximal development suggests that a zone of potential improvement lies between the simple grammatical forms that are well understood and those that are as yet incomprehensible. In that zone, social mediation by adults and older children facilitates a child's language learning.

Learning Two Languages

In today's world, bilingualism is an asset. But should infants and young children be addressed in two distinct languages? Some argue that the primary task of young children is to become proficient in one and only one language. In fact, some contend that English-language deficiencies are the underlying reason that many Spanish-speaking children in the United States underperform their classmates, repeat a grade, and then drop out before high school graduation. (Chapters 12 and 15 discuss education for older children.) Others argue that everyone should learn to speak at least two languages and that the language-sensitive years of early childhood are the best time to do it.

Learning a second language is more difficult than it may seem, because it depends not only on exposure and motivation but also on the language's similarity to the language that the child already uses. Thus it is more difficult for an English-speaking child to learn Chinese (which is very different from English) than Italian (which uses the same alphabet as English and is easy to pronounce). Remarkably, very young children learning two languages master the distinct grammars quite well, using not only the proper word order but even the characteristic pauses and gestures soon after the vocabulary explosion (Bates et al., 2001; Mayberry & Nicoladis, 2000). These are the best years to learn native pronunciation, another argument in favor of early childhood as a sensitive period for language learning. Most 6-year-olds still have difficulty with pronunciation, but by then their neurons and dendrites have at least adjusted to the languages they hear.

The cross-linguistic errors in vocabulary, grammar, and pronunciation of bilingual children mirror those of monolingual children, with one exception: When they are stumped, they sometimes borrow a grammatical form or word from the other language, if it is easier than the one in the language they are speaking. That kind of language mixing is sensible, but generally children use each language, or both languages, only to the people who understand and expect it. Apparently, children can separate one language from another, not becoming confused (Bialystok, 2001).

For a comprehensive grasp of this issue, we must acknowledge that culture, not just language, is at issue. One group of researchers explains:

> A question of concern to many is whether early schooling in English for language minority children harms the development and/or maintenance of their mother tongue and possibly children's language competence in general. . . . Such debate quickly and unfortunately becomes highly politicized, and productive scholarly discussion of the issues is hampered by extreme and emotional political positions.
>
> [Winsler et al., 1999, p. 350]

No, Timmy, not "I sawed the chair." It's "I saw the chair" or "I have seen the chair."

Correct Grammar
This mother has obviously become too accustomed to her son's overregularization.

SUSAN KUKLIN / PHOTO RESEARCHERS, INC.

One Family's Multiculturalism One of the first cultural preferences to travel successfully is food, and Italian cuisine is one of the world's most popular. This family lives in New York, the parents were born in Taiwan, their children are learning to speak both Chinese and English—and they all love pepperoni pizza.

Evidence exists that *both* monolingualism and bilingualism advance cognitive development. Supporters of bilingualism point out, correctly, that children who speak two languages by age 5 are less egocentric in their understanding of language and more advanced in their theories of mind. On the other side, advocates of monolingualism point out, also correctly, that bilingual proficiency comes at the expense of vocabulary development in the dominant language, slowing down literacy (Bialystok, 2001). In fact, many Asian-Americans make a *language shift,* becoming more fluent in English than in their native language, to the sorrow of their parents and grandparents (Min, 2000; Wong & Lopez, 2000).

Parents are reluctant to choose between one language and another if they believe one choice deprives children of their roots, heritage, and identity and the other deprives them of success in a new country, where achievement depends on reading, writing, and communicating in another tongue (Suarez-Orozco & Suarez-Orozco, 2001). The best solution seems to be to avoid that split by allowing children to become "balanced bilinguals," fluent in two languages.

Is that possible? Yes. Developmental research confirms that, in these sensitive play years, children *can* become equally fluent in two or more languages, but they seldom do so (Romaine, 1999). Usually bilingual children are less fluent in either language than monolingual children of the same socioeconomic status are in one (Bialystok, 2001). Often, children learn one language for family and emotional talk and one for school and logical talk, and they have difficulty finding the appropriate words and tone when using the home language at school, or vice versa.

How can a young child master two languages equally? Ideally, bilingual couples expose their children to twice as much language as a typical monolingual family would, with each parent using one language and explaining vocabulary, correcting grammar, reading books, singing songs, and so on. The same principles of language learning—the language explosion, fast mapping, overregularization, parental encouragement—apply to two languages as well as to one.

Another possibility is to send the child to a preschool where the second language is taught. This strategy can work well not only in Canada, Switzerland, the Netherlands, and other countries where everyone is expected to become bilingual but even in the United States. One cluster of bilingual preschools in California not only taught proficiency in English but also advanced the children's knowledge of Spanish, their native tongue. In fact, their mastery of Spanish exceeded that of children in the same community who did not attend preschool (Winsler et al., 1999). Preschool education itself seems to advance children in many other aspects of cognition as well, as we will now examine.

Early-Childhood Education

By now, it is no doubt evident to you that young children are learning every day. But 30 years ago, as mothers of young children entered the workforce in increasing numbers, the question of whether early education was beneficial for young children became urgent. Some parents and political leaders assumed that it was harmful for mothers to work outside the home. Others believed it was not. No

one knew for sure. Developmentalists did extensive research, using various methodologies and samples, and found that preschool education is usually helpful, not harmful. Even education before age 2 can be helpful for cognitive development, as we saw in Chapter 7. Developmentalists are now interested in which one of all the forms of preschool education seems most beneficial, for which children, where, and when.

Happy Kindergartners These photos show happy kindergartners in teacher-directed exercise in two settings, the United States and Japan.

? *Observational Quiz* (see answer, page 287): If you were a stranger to both cultures, with no data other than what you see in the photos, what would you conclude about the values, habits, and attitudes adults hope to foster in these two groups of children?

Where: Cultural Differences

Early childhood programs vary a great deal from one nation to another. Many explicitly foster national and ethnic pride, as children sing patriotic songs, memorize prayers, learn to respect their elders, listen to inspiring stories, and so on. By contrast, other programs encourage individualism, with various corners and tables set up for the children, alone or in groups, to choose among—to dress up, paint a picture, work a puzzle, build a block tower, and so on. Some schools require young children to wear uniforms; others want children to wear comfortable clothes that they can get dirty. Some separate boys and girls; others encourage the sexes to participate in all activities together. Some emphasize reading and math; others stress social and emotional development.

Why do programs differ, even though young brains and impulses are the same no matter where the children live? A sociocultural perspective reminds us that early education includes preparation not only for formal schooling but also for adult life and that every nation differs in values, customs, and priorities, which means that every nation establishes a distinct network of early childhood education (Wollons, 2000). As one example, adults in Japan place great emphasis on social consensus and conformity. Therefore, Japan's preschools provide training in the behaviors and attitudes appropriate for group activity: Children are encouraged to show concern for others and to contribute cooperatively to the group (Rohlen & LeTendre, 1996). At the same time, Japanese mother–child bonds are strong throughout childhood, so mothers have a specific role in preschool: to support their young child's learning. Japanese mothers and teachers discourage assertiveness, independence, and self-expression—precisely the qualities that many Western preschool teachers encourage (Rothbaum et al., 2000).

In the United States, preschools are often designed to foster self-confidence and self-reliance and to give children a good academic start through emphasis

Especially for Parents In finding a preschool program, what should a parent look for?

on language skills and letter recognition. Since most North American preschools are privately or parochially sponsored, they vary a great deal in rules, curricula, and values. Some stress personal development; others, academic skills (Reynolds, 2000). Certain preschools have distinct educational curricula, such as those inspired by Italian educator Maria Montessori, by Jean Piaget, or by learning theory. Most are more broadly "developmental," encouraging children to express themselves in imaginative play, to learn to get along with other children, and to master self-care behaviors such as putting on a coat, going to the bathroom, and eating lunch without adult help. As a rough guide to these variations, see Table 9.4.

TABLE 9.4 Types of Early-Education Programs

Over the past 20 years, the content and values of many early-education programs have changed as developmental research is published; therefore, a program's name may no longer reflect its curriculum. Nonetheless, this guide may serve as a starting point for distinguishing among various types of programs.

Differences in the Purpose of the Program

Day-care center. Originally designed to care for children while their parents worked, day-care centers were open all day, from about 8 A.M. to 6 P.M., and served children as young as 1 or 2. Day care originally literally provided care—meals, naps, outdoor play—but not formal education. Health habits and safety were stressed.

Preschool. Originally intended to prepare children for school, preschools usually focused on learning. They were primarily attended by older children, about age 4, for a few hours a day. Language learning was emphasized, often through book reading and vocabulary building. Development of fine motor skills, with all the children tracing letters or pasting colored paper, and gross motor skills, especially those requiring balance, was also considered important.

Nursery school. Similar to preschools in that they were often part-time programs, nursery schools usually accepted younger children, age 2½ to 3, and therefore were less structured.

Difference in Emphasis Placed on Academic Skills

Developmental or child-centered. These terms imply that the program stresses child development and growth, often using a Piaget-inspired model that allows children to discover ideas at their own pace. Therefore, materials and the physical space are organized in such a way that children are encouraged to play, with dress-up materials, an art corner, puzzles on accessible shelves, blocks of many sizes, and other toys that lend themselves to self-paced, social interaction.

Montessori or Reggio-Emilio. Maria Montessori opened nursery schools for poor children of Rome in the first half of the twentieth century. She believed that children need structured, individualized projects that will give them a sense of accomplishment, such as completing particular puzzles, using a sponge and water to clean a table (even if it is not dirty), and drawing shapes. Current Montessori schools still emphasize individual pride and accomplishment, although many tasks are different. A current Italian model, called Reggio-Emilio, builds on these concepts, with each child learning constantly.

Readiness curriculum. The basic idea is that children need to prepare for school, so they need to learn letters, numbers, shapes, and colors, as well as how to listen to the teacher, sit quietly, and work in groups. Praise and other reinforcement are given for good behavior, and time-outs (not being able to play with the other children) are used as punishment. Readiness programs are quite structured, more teacher-directed than child-centered, but they also take into account the abilities of the child. Musical appreciation, artistic expression, emotional regulation, and social skills are usually included among the goals.

Academic. Such programs explicitly teach basic school skills, including reading, writing, and arithmetic, typically using "direct instruction" by a teacher. For example, young children are given practice in forming letters, sounding out words, counting objects, and writing their names. Homework can be assigned to practice basic skills. Listening to the teacher is key. If a 4-year-old learns to read, that is a success, whereas in a developmental program, it would be cause for suspicion that the child was not being allowed to play creatively.

When: Historical Differences

One historical difference dwarfs these international variations. Not too long ago, the world's children stayed home until first grade—which is why it was called "first" and why young children were called "preschoolers." Now most mothers are in the labor force and need some kind of early childhood program for their young children. In addition, over recent decades, researchers have discovered not only that young children have amazing cognitive potential but also that this potential is best actualized by specific teaching and learning practices. Seventy years ago even kindergarten was optional and innovative, an export from Germany (hence the name, which is German for "children garden"). Now some form of kindergarten thrives everywhere (Wollons, 2000).

Statistics confirm these changes. For example, in the United States in 1970, only 30 percent of married mothers with children under age 6 were in the labor force, and only 20 percent of all 3- and 4-year-olds were in an organized program of any type (including nursery school, preschool, and day-care centers, which used to provide babysitting care, not education). As you can see from these percentages, back then even employed mothers usually found relatives to care for their children at home.

Between 1970 and 2000, the percentage of employed mothers doubled. The most dramatic increase occurred among mothers of infants and very young children (see Figure 9.3). Today, almost all 5-year-olds are in some sort of school, although 24 of the 50 states still do not require school attendance until age 7 (U.S. Department of Education, 2001). By age 4, most children are already attending an organized educational program (see Figure 9.4). In fact, recent research suggests that age 4 is already late; 2- and 3-year-olds learn language and many other skills from being in school (NICHD, 2000; National Research Council & Institute of Medicine, 2000).

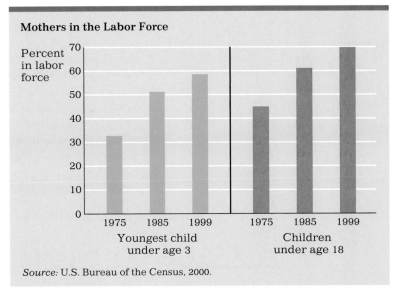

Mothers in the Labor Force

Source: U.S. Bureau of the Census, 2000.

FIGURE 9.3 **Most Mothers Now Work Outside the Home**

!Answer to Observational Quiz (from page 285): The most obvious difference is the greater emphasis on individualism in the United States—no uniforms, diverse ethnicity, smaller group size. Evaluation of this contrast depends on the values of the beholder. Three other differences might have caught your attention (you are an excellent observer if you spotted all three): The Japanese head teacher is male (virtually never the case in a U.S. early-childhood classroom); the Japanese children are segregated by gender (indicated by the hats as well as position), and none of the U.S. children have their arms in the correct position, while all the Japanese children do.

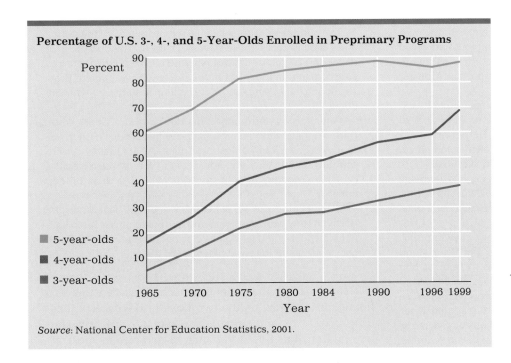

Percentage of U.S. 3-, 4-, and 5-Year-Olds Enrolled in Preprimary Programs

- 5-year-olds
- 4-year-olds
- 3-year-olds

Source: National Center for Education Statistics, 2001.

FIGURE 9.4 **Changing Times** As research increasingly finds that preschool education provides a foundation for later learning, more and more young children are in educational programs. Currently, almost half of all 3- and 4-year-olds are in school. That proportion is expected to increase even more in the twenty-first century.

Response for Parents (from page 286): There is much variation, and there is no right answer that fits every parent's values. However, children should be engaged in learning, not allowed to sit passively or to squabble with each other. Before deciding, parents should look at several programs, staying long enough to see the children in action.

Many of today's adults who grew up before the expansion of early-childhood education in the 1970s may still equate "school" (and hence "preschool") with sitting at desks in rows, memorizing times tables, and practicing penmanship—skills beyond the zone of proximal development for even the brightest 4-year-old. For them, a "preschool" child is literally what the word says, a child before school age. If such adults were asked whether massive amounts of public money should underwrite schools for young children, where one goal is to encourage children's play (Jones & Reynolds, 1992), they might ask, "Why pay for play?" Perhaps the account in A Case to Study would convince them. It surely would give them a better idea of what preschool is like. It also illustrates how a preschool setting offers varied experiences, facilitates social interaction, and expands language as few families do, or even can.

A Case to Study

Hold On with Both Hands

The children were settling in for a videotaped movie and a little boy offered Peter the empty chair beside his own. . . . Peter's thumb went into his mouth. . . . Miss Murray put a stuffed teddy bear in Peter's lap and whispered, "You need to hold onto Mr. Bear and don't let him get away until the story is over. Help him listen too, by holding him in your lap with both hands." Peter held Mr. Bear in a death grip with both arms. The little boy who had offered Peter the chair asked if he could have an animal and Miss Murray pulled one out of the basket on the shelf. The movie was *Jack and the Beanstalk*, a favorite of many of the children. The two boys held their stuffed animals and echoed the giant's "Fee, fie, foe, fum" in their best and deepest "giant" voices.

The last activity of the day was a watermelon party. The class went out on the grass near the classroom door to begin the festivities. The teacher placed the watermelon in the middle of the circle of children and they all admired it and talked about how it grew. The teacher encouraged the children to touch it and allowed them to try and pick up the "Monster Melon."

Peter was fascinated. "Boy, this is real, real, big!" he exclaimed, trying to lift up one end of the melon. "I bet my Dad could pick it up though. He's real strong." He ran his hands along the sides and ends of the melon and then commented, "It's like a ball . . . but not really . . . just sorta like a ball."

The teacher made the first cut, lengthwise, and then she and Miss Murray (another teacher) each took a group of children to cut the two halves into smaller pieces. One at a time, the children were allowed to help cut their own slice of watermelon. The children were soon busy biting, chewing, spitting seeds, and enjoying the sloppy affair. But Peter stood immobile. He was holding his watermelon in front of him with the pink juice running down his arms. He looked forlorn and helpless, seeming not to know what to do with the slice of watermelon. It then dawned on Miss Murray that Peter may have never experienced watermelon before or perhaps he couldn't relate this cold slab of wetness to the neat chunks he may have been given at home.

She took Peter's index finger and poked it into the pink part of the melon and then into the firmer rind. She explained that the soft part was for eating, but there were small, hard bits called "seeds" all mixed up in it. She helped Peter find a seed and feel how hard and slippery it was. She then encouraged him to take a bite and asked him if his teeth or tongue had found any seeds yet. Perplexed, he nodded his head "yes," but he didn't know how to spit them out. They just slid down his chin. Miss Murray coaxed Peter to blow the seeds out, but he was only minimally successful. Even so, he managed to get a few seeds into the air instead of on his chin. From the look on Peter's face, it was safe to say that he did not especially enjoy this new experience. This was confirmed when Peter announced sheepishly, "I like my mom's watermelon better—hers doesn't have seeds."

The buckets of water available for cleanup were the source of as much fun as the watermelon itself. The splashing of water and giggling that accompanied it were much more to Peter's liking. In the midst of the fun, a taller version of Peter strode into view and said, "Hey there, Buddy . . . whatcha doin'?"

Peter turned and hugged his dad's knees. "Guess what, Dad? We had watermelon today, and guess what? Their watermelon has a lot of seeds. And guess what? I know how to spit now! I can show you how to spit. Wanna see me spit? I can show Mommy how to spit too. What d'ya think of that, huh?"

Peter's father smiled, patted his son on the back, and said, "Okay, Buddy, we'll go home and show Mommy how to spit. Find my pocket and let's go." Peter put his fingers in his dad's back pocket and followed him toward the gate.

[Bishop, 1993]

The most obvious benefit of school as compared to home is friendship, as the two boys in the excerpt illustrate. Same-sex and same-age playmates are preferred by children, but this is difficult to arrange in most at-home settings. Likewise, the facilitated sharing (here, of the chair, the stuffed animal, and the giant voices) are common in preschool but virtually impossible at home. Wise and experienced teachers know how to encourage children to give up thumb-sucking, to use a knife, and to spit out seeds without making them feel singled out for their normal insecurities and lack of skill. Moreover, the distinction between imagination and reality is clarified even as both are being encouraged, as in the "Fee, fie, foe, fum" chant.

Varied experiences are also more likely to happen at preschool. Peter was probably not the only child who, for the first time that day, wielded a knife, spat out seeds, or tried to lift a "monster melon." Such new experiences teach words as well as motor skills—here, *spit, slippery, oval,* and *monster* became better understood.

Social skills also develop as children share—here, the carrying and cutting, eating and spitting, washing and drying. In this instance, the preschool children learned an additional lesson: that disabilities need not prevent a person from taking part in normal activities. Did you guess? Peter is blind.

Who: Individual Differences

Some children need an organized program of early education more than others, because during these years, if children simply learn on their own, some achieve far more than others. To be specific, the achievement gap between the most and least accomplished is narrow in infancy—almost all children begin to walk and talk at about 12 months—but it widens with every year of early childhood. As a result, kindergartners differ a great deal in their ability to learn, talk, or even listen (Morrison et al., 1997). Then this divergence in achievement stabilizes—maintaining a wide gap—throughout the school years.

This fact suggests a strategy: Shore up the academic skills of children at high risk before first grade. "Risk" is variously interpreted: In general, children who are from low-income, minority, immigrant families are more likely to fall behind in school than are other children. These are overly broad, catch-all categories, but initially they were used to define **high risk**, meaning—in education—that the chances of poor achievement were notably higher than average.

The first massive public effort to create quality preschools in the United States was Project Head Start, a federal program launched in 1965 and designed for low-income or minority children who, at least in theory, needed a "head start" on their education. Two thousand new programs were created and funded; after a year, or sometimes only a summer, Head Start 4-year-olds gained an average of 5 IQ points. This result led to rejoicing among developmentalists (Horowitz & Paden, 1973). In retrospect, that celebration was premature, because the gains seemed to fade as children moved through elementary school. Disappointment and defunding were narrowly averted (Zigler & Muenshow, 1992) as three important facts became evident:

- There is no quick fix for cognitive deficits.
- The quality of Head Start programs varied, from excellent to awful.
- When careful scientific studies of early education were done, extensive and long-lasting benefits became evident.

Three research projects have used scientific research to follow up on preschool children: one in Michigan, called Perry or High/Scope (Schweinhart & Weikart, 1997); one in North Carolina, called Abecedarian (Campbell et al., 2001); and one in Chicago, called Child–Parent Centers (Reynolds, 2000). All three programs enrolled children for several years before kindergarten, all compared groups of experimental children with matched groups of control children, and all reached the same conclusions: Early education has substantial long-term benefits, which become apparent when the children are in the third grade or later. To be specific, children in these three programs scored higher on math and reading

high risk Term used by educators to refer to a child whose chances of poor achievement are notably higher than average. More generally, high risk refers to someone with an increased likelihood of some negative experience, such as catching a disease or dropping out of school.

Learning Is Fun The original purpose of the Head Start program was to boost disadvantaged children's academic skills. The most enduring benefits, however, turned out to be improved self-esteem and social skills, as is evident in these happy Head Start participants, all crowded together.

? Observational Quiz (see answer, page 291): How many of these children are in close physical contact without discomfort or disagreement?

achievement tests than other children from the same backgrounds, schools, and neighborhoods. They were significantly less likely to be placed in special classes for slow or disruptive children or to repeat a year of school. In adolescence, they had higher aspirations and a greater sense of achievement. And the young adults who had participated in the High/Scope program were found to be more likely to attend college and less likely to go to jail (Haskins, 1989; Zigler, 1998) (longitudinal data on the other programs have not yet been reported).

All three research projects found that direct cognitive training of the children was useful. Although the programs cost several thousand dollars per child per year (perhaps as much as $10,000 annually per child in 2001 dollars), in the long run significant savings were made, largely because later special education was less likely (Karoly et al., 1998). Full-day care in an accredited program (not a special program) costs about $8,000 per year in 2001 dollars; Head Start is cheaper, about $5,000 per child per year, primarily because it usually provides only half-day care for only 34 weeks (National Research Council and Institute of Medicine, 2000). Other research finds that much cheaper projects, with short-term intervention of questionable quality, may not help at all (Cowan & Cowan, 2001; St. Pierre et al., 1997; Van Tuijl et al., 2001; Zigler & Styfco, 1993). Explicit and direct education of children over the years is a better investment than general instruction or emotional support for parents. Developmentalists believe that good early education is, eventually, a money saver.

What about children who are not at high risk? Preprimary education does not help every child equally. The children most likely to benefit are those who are neediest: low-income, from high-crime neighborhoods, with mothers who are poorly educated. Most longitudinal research on more advantaged children in the United States and elsewhere finds that every child *could* benefit from a quality preschool setting. However, children who stay at home, with ample opportunity to play, also fare well (Erel et al., 2000; Warash & Markstrom-Adams, 1995). For example, one carefully controlled study of very-low-birthweight infants (another group sometimes considered at high risk) found that most of them later benefited from intensive early education—except for a small group whose mothers were college graduates. This last group did no better, and no worse, than children of equally low birthweight who had stay-at-home mothers who were also college graduates (Brooks-Gunn et al., 1993; Ramey & Ramey, 2000). A key finding is that quality matters. As a review by 22 experts concludes:

In sum, the positive relation between child care quality and virtually every facet of children's development that has been studied is one of the most consistent findings in developmental science. While child care of poor quality is associated with poorer developmental outcomes, high-quality care is associated with outcomes that all parents want to see in their children, ranging from cooperation with adults to the ability to initiate and sustain positive exchanges with peers, to early competence in math and reading.

[National Research Council and Institute of Medicine, 2000]

What constitutes high-quality education? Some basics seem obvious and have been described in Chapter 6: safety, adequate space and equipment, a low adult–child ratio, positive social interactions among children and teachers, and trained staff who are unlikely to leave their jobs. (One of the best questions parents can ask is "How long has each staff member worked at that center?") Beyond that, curriculum may be important, especially during the play years. Worst seem to be programs that have no philosophy or direction. Best may be programs with an emphasis on learning, reflected in a curriculum that includes extensive practice in language, fine and gross motor skills, and early number skills. Such a curriculum has proven cognitive benefits for high-risk children (Reynolds, 2000).

A curriculum of this sort is more likely to be offered in an organized program than informally at home. In the United States, for this reason, three-fourths of high-income families (income above $75,000) choose center-based care (see Appendix A, Chapter 9). Apparently, those who can afford it prefer an organized licensed program to at-home care by a relative, a nanny, or a neighbor.

The factor that determines whether a child develops better at home or in a center is whether the mother is not only able and willing to stay at home but also able to provide excellent care—finding regular playmates, offering art projects, organizing field trips, singing, reading, playing games, and so on. Low-risk children seem to be better off at home with such a mother than attending a crowded, unsafe center, where discipline is considered more important than cognition; high-risk children are usually better off in a center, although here, too, quality counts.

Of course, the need to make that comparison shows how much the times have changed. Until a few decades ago, it was widely assumed that young children were *always* better off with their mothers at home. Then research proved the benefits of organized group care. Now developmentalists point out that children are not *always* better off in day care. The crucial factor is quality of care and the specifics of learning opportunities, not where that early education takes place (Melhuish, 2001).

Conclusions

Considering all the research about cognitive development between the ages of 2 and 6, the benefits of a high-quality educational program for young children come as no surprise. In the ongoing debate over how children think, described earlier in this chapter, most developmentalists are now tilting toward Vygotsky. The influence of culture, the power of scaffolding on various cognitive abilities, and the discovery of the benefits of high-quality education all support sociocultural theory. Few developmentalists or educators are content to follow Piaget, especially if his ideas are interpreted to mean waiting until the child discovers learning, letting time lead to cognitive growth.

Past history, however, teaches that new research will find additional abilities in the brains of 2- to 6-year-olds and additional strategies to develop that potential. Evaluation studies, longitudinal comparisons of similar groups of children with varied experiences, are still too rare. Some readers of this book will be among those who undertake the research, parent the children, and staff the schools that will again revise our view of the thoughts of the very young.

❗ Answer to Observational Quiz (from page 290): All five—not four (look again at the right-hand side of the photograph)!

SUMMARY

How Children Think: Piaget and Vygotsky

1. Piaget stressed the egocentric and illogical aspects of thought during the play years. He called this stage preoperational thought because young children cannot yet use logical operations to think about their observations and experiences.

2. Piaget noted many characteristics of preoperational thinking. Young children's thinking is largely prelogical. They sometimes focus on only one thing (centration) and use only their own viewpoint (egocentrism), remaining stuck on appearances and on current reality. They cannot understand that things change, actions can be reversed, and other people have other perspectives.

3. Vygotsky stressed the social aspects of childhood cognition, noting that children learn by participating in various experiences, guided by more knowledgeable adults or peers. That guidance assists learning within the zone of proximal development, which includes the knowledge and skills that the child has the potential to learn.

4. According to Vygotsky, the best mentors use various clues, guidelines, and other tools to provide a scaffold for new learning. He believed that learning occurs in social interaction, not in isolation. Language is a bridge of social mediation between the knowledge that the child already has and the learning that the society hopes to impart. For Vygotsky, words are a tool for learning that both mentor and child use.

Information Processing

5. Young children have some concept of quantity, but they do not yet understand several key counting principles. Experience as well as maturation gives the 5-year-old a better understanding of the number system.

6. Memory is apparent in young children, although they do not necessarily focus on what adults want them to remember. The most important aid to memory seems to be conversation about the past that promotes verbal scaffolding.

7. Retrieval becomes more accurate when questions are explicit and nonthreatening. Source memory is particularly fragile and open to distortion. If a sequence of events becomes familiar, a script forms, which both reflects and aids memory.

8. Memories at every age are often distorted and fragile. This is even more true in early childhood, which means that adults who want young children to tell the truth must ask specific questions, neither leading nor threatening the child, soon after the experience.

9. Children develop a theory of mind, understanding what others might think, throughout early childhood. Notable advances in theory of mind occur at around age 4. At that point, children become less egocentric and better able to understand the differences among perception, emotion, and fact.

Language

10. Language develops rapidly during early childhood, which is probably a sensitive period, but not a critical period, for language learning. Vocabulary increases dramatically, with thousands of words added between ages 2 and 6. In addition, basic grammar is mastered, and many children speak more than one language.

11. Bilingualism is controversial, largely because language use is intimately connected to culture and heritage. Ideally, children become balanced bilinguals, equally proficient in two languages, by age 6. This ideal is not easily attained.

Early-Childhood Education

12. Organized educational programs during early childhood advance cognitive and social skills. This is particularly true for high-risk children, whose homes may not provide them with the intellectual stimulation and instruction they need. It may also be true for low-risk children.

13. Quality matters: Education works best if there is a clear curriculum and if the adult–child ratio is low. The training and continuity of early-childhood teachers are also important.

14. According to longitudinal research on comprehensive childhood education programs, especially those that begin with very young children and involve their mothers, early intervention works. Graduates of these programs are less likely to need special education or to repeat a grade and more likely to become employed, law-abiding, happy adults.

KEY TERMS

preoperational thought (p. 264)
centration (p. 264)
egocentrism (p. 264)
focus on appearance (p. 264)
static reasoning (p. 265)
irreversibility (p. 265)

conservation (p. 265)
theory-theory (p. 266)
apprentice in thinking (p. 267)
guided participation (p. 267)
zone of proximal development
    (ZPD) (p. 268)

scaffold (p. 268)
private speech (p. 268)
social mediation (p. 269)
source memory (p. 272)
script (p. 274)
theory of mind (p. 276)

imaginary companion (p. 278)
sensitive period (p. 279)
critical period (p. 279)
fast mapping (p. 280)
overregularization (p. 282)
high risk (p. 289)

KEY QUESTIONS

1. How did Piaget and Vygotsky differ in their understanding of the causes of development?

2. Describe how a parent might scaffold a learning skill, such as reading a book.

3. Which counting principles do 3-year-olds understand, and which ones do they not understand?

4. How do contextual and cultural differences affect how easy it is for children to learn to count?

5. What would be easy and what would be difficult for a 3-year-old to remember?

6. How do scientists find out if a child has a theory of mind?

7. How does an imaginary companion help and hinder a child's thought processes?

8. Why is the question whether children should learn a second language so controversial?

9. What is the difference between a child-centered and an academic preprimary school?

10. What are the reasons for and against sending a 3-year-old to early education?

Chapter Ten

The Play Years: Psychosocial Development

Picture a typical 2-year-old and a typical 6-year-old, and consider how emotionally and socially different they are. Chances are the 2-year-old still has many moments of clinging, of tantrums, and of stubbornness, vacillating between dependence and self-assertion. Further, the 2-year-old cannot be left alone, even for a few moments, wherever curiosity might lead to danger or destruction. If a parent takes a 2-year-old and a 6-year-old to the playground, and then gets absorbed in reading the newspaper, after five minutes the 6-year-old will be playing safely nearby with friends, but the 2-year-old may be at the top of a very high slide or tasting a pretend cake in the sandbox or completely out of sight.

In general, by age 6, children have both the confidence and the competence to be quite independent and yet know their limits. A typical 6-year-old does many things alone and is proud of that—perhaps fixing breakfast before school and even helping to feed and dress a younger sibling. This child shows affection toward family members without obvious clinging, exasperating demands, or exaggerated self-will. The 6-year-old might say good-bye to Mom or Dad at the door of the first-grade classroom and then take care of business: following classroom routines, befriending certain classmates and ignoring others, respecting and learning from teachers.

This chapter details how that 2-to-6 transformation occurs and why some 6-year-olds have not yet achieved the emotional control just described. As you will see, parents and peers are pivotal socializing agents in this process, but the child's own maturation and motivation are important, too. This is apparent in all of psychosocial development, but is especially clear in the area of sex and gender.

Emotional Development

As you remember from the chapters on infancy, 2-year-old children have a sense of themselves and their goals, and they are beginning to develop a range of emotions. During the play years all three of these—self, goals, and emotions—come together.

Emotional Regulation

The pivotal accomplishment between ages 2 and 6 is the "ability to inhibit, enhance, maintain, and modulate emotional arousal to accomplish one's goals" (Eisenberg et al., 1997). Pride is tempered by guilt (and vice versa); joy, by sadness; anger, by fear; fear, by rituals. All are regulated and controlled by the 3- or 4-year-old in ways unknown to the exuberant, expressive, and often overwhelmed toddler.

Close Connection Unfamiliar events often bring temperamental patterns to the surface, as with the curious boy and his worried brother, who are attending Colorado's Pikes Peak or Bust Rodeo breakfast. Their attentive mother keeps the livelier boy calm and reassures the shy one.

?Observational Quiz (see answer, page 298): Mother is obviously a secure base for both boys, who share the same family and half the same genes, but are different ages: One is two and the other is four. Can you tell which boy is younger?

SEAN CAYTON / THE IMAGE WORKS

emotional regulation The ability, beginning in early childhood, to direct or modify one's feelings, particularly feelings of fear, frustration, and anger.

externalizing problems Difficulties that arise from a child's tendency to externalize emotions, or experience emotions outside the self, lashing out in impulsive anger and attacking other people or things.

internalizing problems Difficulties that arise from a child's tendency to internalize emotions, or inhibit their expression, being fearful and withdrawn.

This ability, called **emotional regulation**, is developed in response to society's expectations that children "manage frustration" and "modulate emotional expression" (Sroufe, 1996). Most children accomplish this difficult task quite successfully: They are friendly to new acquaintances but not too friendly; angry but not explosive; frightened by a clown but not terrified.

Emotional regulation begins with impulse control. Some children have **externalizing problems:** Their emotions are external or outside them, as they lash out in impulsive anger and attack other people or things. They are "undercontrolled" and need to learn to regulate their anger. Other children have **internalizing problems:** They are fearful and withdrawn. Their inhibition may be an automatic reaction or a fearful strategy, but in any case, "internalizing children appear to lack the spontaneity and flexibility of control that may be needed for positive adjustment" (Eisenberg et al., 2001). Both externalizing and internalizing children must master the art of emotional regulation, first recognizing and accepting their emotions and then regulating expression, exercising some control but not too much.

Maturation and Learning

Part of emotional regulation is neurological, a matter of brain functioning, and part of it is learned, a matter of social awareness. As we saw in Chapter 8, the ability to regulate one's emotions, to think before acting, to decide whether and in what way to display joy or anger or fear, is directly related to the maturation of the prefrontal cortex. Normally, advances occur at about age 4 or 5, as the child becomes less likely to throw a temper tantrum, provoke a physical attack, or burst into uncontrollable giggles. Normally, social experiences reinforce this maturation, as families and communities encourage children to control their emotions.

Not every child develops the ability to regulate emotions at the same age, for four sets of reasons: genes, early stresses on the brain, early care, and current social influences.

Genetic Variations First, genetic influences come into play: Some people are naturally emotionally expressive and others more inhibited, a range found in infants as well as adults. In the study of brain patterns and behavior in 153 children aged 4 months to 4 years described in Chapter 7, considerable stability was found not only in emotional reactions (laughing or crying when a strange clown appeared, for instance) but also in electrical activity in the prefrontal cortex. Just as with adults, young children who were more fearful had greater activity in their right prefrontal cortex, while those who were more exuberant showed more activity in their left prefrontal cortex (Fox et al., 2001). This indicates that some of the variation in emotional expression is genetic. Consequently, some children need to work to regulate their exuberance, others must try to overcome their anxiety, and still others have neither problem, controlling their emotions more easily.

Early Stress The second set of brain-related differences in emotional regulation is the result of damage during brain development, either prenatally (if the pregnant woman was stressed, ill, or a heavy drug user) or postnatally (if the infant was chronically malnourished, injured, or frightened). Repeated exposure to extreme stress kills some of the neurons of the brain and stops others from developing properly (Sanchez et al., 2001), possibly making some young children physiologically unable to regulate their emotions by thinking and remembering. Instead, even an ordinary stressor—such as an unexpected loud noise or a critical remark—could release a flood of stress hormones, particularly a hormone called cortisol. A 4- or 5-year-old might overreact, experiencing terror or fury at something that another child would consider only mildly upsetting (De Bellis, 2001).

To complicate our understanding of the impact of early stress on later brain maturation, some research finds lower, not higher, levels of cortisol in children who had experienced abuse (Gunnar & Vasquez, 2001). Their blunted stress response may be an early sign of depression if it indicates that their emotions are already dampened and distorted instead of regulated. In either case, early stresses can change the electrical activity, dendrite growth, and production of various hormones in the brain.

Care History We already know, from previous chapters, a third set of influences on emotional regulation: the child's early care experiences. These may either soothe or aggravate the child's reaction to the stresses of infancy. We cannot experiment directly on human infants, but one study of rat pups exposed to stresses that usually cause brain abnormalities found that the effects of that stress disappeared if the rats were raised by nurturing, stress-combating mothers. Such mothers licked, nuzzled, groomed, and fed the rat pups even more than an average rat mother would (Kaufman & Charney, 2001). In humans, one particular influence, as you might imagine after reading Chapter 7, is the quality of the child's attachment to the caregiver. Secure children are best able to control their emotional outbursts (Kochanska, 2001; Laible & Thompson, 1998).

The effects of a child's past care are revealed in many ways, including reactions to another child's cry of pain. Children who have been well nurtured and have formed secure attachments regulate their own emotions and express empathy, comforting the hurting child, reassuring the frightened child, or getting help if need be. By contrast, children with insecure attachments respond abnormally to other children's distress. Some do whatever

> . . . would precisely further distress the child (e.g., scaring a child with the very mask that had been frightening, taunting a crying child and calling him or her a "cry baby," or punching a child with a stomach ache in the stomach). . . . [Others] would often become upset themselves when another was distressed (e.g., holding their own lip and seeking a teacher's lap when another child had fallen).
>
> *[Sroufe, 1996]*

Current Experiences Finally, one key difference between humans and most other animals is that human children depend on their parents for years, not merely for

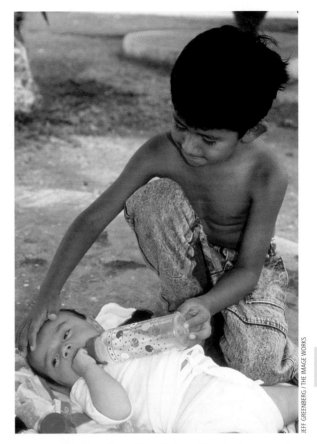

Emotional Regulation Older brothers are not famous for being loving caregivers. However, within the Mayan culture, older children learn to regulate their jealousy and provide major care for younger siblings while their parents work.

*?**Observational Quiz*** (see answer, page 299): What do you see that suggests that this boy is paying careful attention to his brother?

!*Answer to Observational Quiz* (from page 296): Size is not much help, since children grow slowly during these years and the heads of these two boys appear about the same size. However, emotional development is apparent. Most two-year-olds, like the one at right, still cling to their mothers; most four-year-olds are sufficiently mature, secure, and curious to watch the excitement as they drink their juice.

a few months. Accordingly, it is theoretically possible that parenting practices *after* infancy could be significant in a child's development. Parenting in childhood might have a major impact on emotional regulation, no matter what the child's earliest experiences in infancy had been. Some evidence points in that direction: a mother's current state of depression, current levels of stress hormones, and current patterns of protection seem quite influential in the child's ability to cope with stress and to regulate emotions, sometimes for the better (if a mother who was depressed has recovered) and sometimes for the worse (if a mother becomes depressed) (Susman et al., 2001).

The best research on the relative impact of caregiving in infancy and in early childhood focuses on children who were seriously deprived early in life but then were well nurtured. Such was the experience of the adopted Romanian children mentioned in Chapter 7. Most children adopted before 8 months of age, and some adopted after 8 months, showed normal levels of stress hormones by age 4 or so (Chisholm, 1998; Gunnar et al., 2001). Thus, good caretaking seems able to compensate for high stress and poor caretaking experienced in the early months of life, even repairing the brain damage that may have occurred.

For other adopted children, especially those adopted in toddlerhood, good later caregiving did not prevent emotional difficulties (externalizing or internalizing) or marked delays in emotional regulation. Many were overly friendly, too irritable, or overly distractable. For unknown reasons, some, but not all, children seem to bounce back after early deprivation; resilience probably depends on a combination of genes and experiences (Luthar et al., 2000).

A leading team of developmental researchers summarized:

> In sum, then, there are multiple converging pathways—including not only the neural circuits that are activated by physical, psychological, and immunological stressors, but also the influence of genetics, early experience, and ongoing life events that determine the neural response to different stressors.
>
> [Cicchetti & Walker, 2001]

Fear: An Example

Given that some, but not all, caregiving protects against brain abnormalities and that multiple pathways converge, we need to know exactly what parents can do to encourage emotional regulation. One emotion that often seems mishandled by parents in early childhood is fear.

Every normal young child is somewhat fearful. Refusal to go to sleep alone, vivid nightmares, and sudden terror at seeing a masked person are common. However, some parents teach their infants to keep fear at bay by repeatedly responding to the infant's anxiety with reassurance, modulating early fear even at age 1. Comforting touch and tone soothe anxiety at every stage of life. Then, in the "terrible twos," parents teach their children to moderate all the negative emotions, including anger and fear (Kochanska et al., 1997).

The best teacher is example, so ideally parents never express fear when a dog approaches, thunder roars, or a mouse scampers across the floor. The circuits of the child's developing brain respond to such experiences. Gradually, innate emotional triggers are connected to intellectual responses via the corpus callosum, the band of tissue between the brain's hemispheres described in Chapter 8. This connection allows the 4-year-old girl to stand her ground when a circus clown approaches or the 4-year-old boy to restrain himself when another child bumps into him, with neither bursting into tears or launching a self-protective attack.

Learning can also work in the opposite direction. Some young children develop a **phobia**: an irrational and exaggerated fear that terrifies the person. Phobias probably have their roots in genetic protection of the entire human race:

phobia An irrational fear that is strong enough to make a person avoid the feared object or experience.

Our ancestors had good reason to fear spiders, snakes, and heights, which is why many twenty-first-century humans instinctively fear such things more than modern killers such as cigarettes and cars.

Phobias are particularly likely if a child's parents are also somewhat phobic, not only for genetic reasons but also because children become quite astute at sensing their parents' feelings. When a worried parent says "Let's pet the nice doggie," children will notice the hesitant hand, the fast breathing, or the sudden startle if the dog moves. In this case, learning is added to a genetic tendency, and the child becomes afraid.

Thus, emotional regulation is a normal, expected outcome of early childhood, but all four factors—a child's genetics, early physiological stress, early care, and current social context—can delay or distort emotional regulation.

Who's Chicken? Genes and good parenting have made this boy neither too fearful nor too bold. Appropriate caution is probably the best approach to meeting a chicken.

Self-Expression

As you remember, in toddlerhood children gradually realize that they exist as independent people, distinct from others. This awareness becomes, during early childhood, the **self-concept**, which is people's understanding of who they are. By age 2 or 3, a child's self-concept includes such notions as that he or she is a boy or a girl; a brother, sister, or only child; and, of a certain age, religion, and ability. From the self-concept flow many other emotions. In fact, self-concept has been called "the cornerstone of both social and emotional development" (Kagan et al., 1995). Typically, self-concept turns from factual to evaluative, becoming **self-esteem,** or pride in oneself (Davis-Kean & Sandler, 2001). Children with relatively high self-esteem at age 5 tend to be more accepted over the years by other children (Verschueren et al., 2001). Self-esteem that is too high, however, tends to create other problems. A positive, but balanced, self-concept is probably best.

A noteworthy aspect of self-concept and self-esteem is that children in the play years feel older, stronger, and more skilled than younger children or than they themselves once were. One of the worst insults to call a 3-year-old is "baby," and one of the most positive comments is "big boy" or "big girl." The significance of this feeling, as well as young children's skill in negotiation, is shown in this episode involving three 4-year-old girls:

> **Beth:** How about this. Pretend he married two of us and you were the sister. OK? You were the sister of us—OK? Of both of us, cause you were the littler one.
> **Celia:** No, I don't want to be a little one.
> **Beth:** No, you're both, you're big. Um, let's pretend.
> **Annie:** But we were a little bigger.
> **Beth:** You're 20.
> **Celia:** Yeah.
> **Beth:** And both of us are 21.
> **Celia:** OK, so that means . . .
> **Annie:** So, we're one month older than you.
>
> [Furth, 1996]

The young ladies' chronological understanding clearly is immature, but their social skills are not. All three want to maintain their self-esteem as big girls without giving up their social interaction, and they combine assertion and compromise to achieve that end.

For children of all ages, psychologists emphasize the importance of developing a positive self-concept. (In fact, too much self-criticism is one sign of psychosocial problems in a young child.) Normally, young children have no such

self-concept People's understanding of who they are.

self-esteem People's pride in themselves.

❗Answer to Observational Quiz (from page 297): Look at his hands, legs, and face. He is holding the bottle and touching the baby's forehead with delicacy and care; he is positioning his legs in a way that is uncomfortable but suited to the task; and his eyes and mouth suggest he is giving the baby his full concentration.

ONE BIG HAPPY   **By RICK DETORIE**

Know-It-Alls Have Something to Learn
Like many preschoolers, Ruthie thinks her art is worth money and she would love to be the rescuer of another child, an animal, or even a bird. In the real world, however, that self-concept will need some modification.

problem; typical 2- to 6-year-olds form quite favorable impressions of themselves. They regularly overestimate their own abilities, believing that they can win any race, skip perfectly, count accurately, and compose beautiful songs. They enjoy undertaking various tasks, and they expect all others—grandparents, playmates, stuffed animals—to be a patient, admiring audience for their showing off. The next day, they might gather the identical audience for a repeat performance. Self-confidence is tied to competence, and competence demands repeated demonstrations of mastery.

Such typically high self-esteem was demonstrated in a laboratory test in which 4- to 6-year-olds were given two minutes to solve an impossible puzzle. When they failed, they were asked to guess how many of two additional puzzles they could solve if they tried. Almost all the children, despite having just failed, answered "both." When the same children were asked to indicate how smart they were by awarding themselves one, two, three, four, or five stars (representing the range from "not smart at all" to "very smart"), more than 90 percent confidently chose five stars (Stipek et al., 1995).

Theories of Emotions

Normal emotional regulation during early childhood has been described by every theorist who has studied this stage. Freud observed a burst of self-importance, anger, and fear during these years; these emotions are submerged by parental actions, so that the next stage, called *latency* (which means quietness and inactivity), can begin. More specifics about many theories, including Freud's, are discussed later in this chapter. Here, however, we need to mention two theorists who have specifically considered the emotions of young children: Erik Erikson and Daniel Goleman.

Initiative Versus Guilt

One crucial aspect of emotional development during early childhood was described by Erik Erikson almost half a century ago. Positive enthusiasm, effort, and self-evaluation characterize ages 3 to 6, according to Erikson's psychosocial theory (first discussed in Chapter 2). During the developmental stage that Erikson calls **initiative versus guilt,** self-esteem is largely defined by the skills and competencies that demonstrate independence and initiative. Most young children leap at almost any opportunity to show that "I can do it!" Spontaneous play becomes goal-directed.

Children do *not* want to do just *anything,* as infants do in Piaget's sensorimotor period and as toddlers do in Erikson's autonomy stage. Now, in the initiative stage, they want to *begin and complete something* and take pride in their accomplishment. Accordingly, attention span becomes much longer. Many 3- or 4-year-olds can spend up to an hour in one episode of pretend play or in practicing a new motor skill or in creating a work of art—something no normal toddler does.

Erikson also believed that, as the larger society motivates them to take on new activities, children develop their sense of themselves and others, feeling guilt when their efforts result in failure or criticism. Guilt is a more mature emotion than is shame. Guilt comes from within the child who is unhappy at having done a bad thing; shame comes from knowing that someone else might see what the child has done and be critical (Tangney, 2001). Both shame and guilt originate from social standards, but guilt indicates that the child has taken on these standards as his or her own.

Erikson's historic overview still applies. Over the last decade of the twentieth century, developmentalists intensely studied the psychosocial development of young children (Eisenberg, 2000). As you remember, all the basic human emotions are already evident by the end of infancy: from early joy and fear to more complex anger and sadness, and, by age 2, self-aware emotions such as jealousy and embarrassment. These emotions continue to be evident during the years from 2 to 6, but now children have an additional developmental task: to express and modulate emotions in ways sanctioned by their social context. As Erikson recognized, when autonomy has become initiative and shame has become guilt, then children have internalized the social standards of their culture and emotions are properly regulated.

Emotional Intelligence

Daniel Goleman (1998) is another theorist who stresses the importance of emotional regulation. He contends that the ability to modulate and direct emotions is crucial to **emotional intelligence,** an understanding of how to interpret and express emotions. Emotional intelligence develops throughout life, but particularly during early childhood. It is during these formative years that the reflective and intellectual areas of the cortex, especially the prefrontal cortex, gradually come to govern the rush of fear, anger, and other passion from the *amygdala,* an emotional hotspot deep within the brain. According to Goleman, when caregivers use children's natural attachment to teach them how and when to express feelings, the children will become balanced and empathetic human beings, neither overwhelmed by nor unresponsive to their own emotions. This is so crucial for any adequate functioning that it is more important than conventional intelligence, according to Goleman.

In Chapter 11 we will discuss various concepts of intelligence, including the conventional definitions that stress verbal and logical abilities. You will also see that a leading alternative view, proposed by Howard Gardner, again stresses emotions—specifically, the ability to understand one's own and other people's

initiative versus guilt The third of Erikson's eight stages of psychosocial development, in which the young child eagerly begins new projects and activities and feels guilt when his or her efforts result in failure or criticism.

emotional intelligence Goleman's term for the understanding of how to interpret and express emotions.

emotions. Similar ideas are expressed in a report from 22 leading researchers on early childhood, who emphasize again and again the importance of learning to regulate emotions (National Research Council and Institute of Medicine, 2000). They write:

> The developmental tasks of this period range from the mastery of essential building blocks for learning and the motivation to succeed in school, to the ability to get along with other children, to make friends, and become engaged in a social group, as well as the capacity to manage powerful emotions.
>
> *[p. 386]*

As you see, in listing six tasks of early childhood, they begin with one cognitive task, then cite four emotional tasks, and conclude with emotional regulation.

Although we have detailed the impact that brain maturation and stress have on emotional growth (including theory of mind in Chapter 9), it is also apparent that human relationships provide essential guidance in emotional expression and regulation. These experts explain:

> Regulation in early development is deeply embedded in the child's relations with others. Providing the experiences, supports, and encouragement that enable children to take over and self-regulate in one area of function after another is one of the most critical elements of good caregiving.
>
> *[National Research Council and Institute of Medicine, 2000, p. 122]*

The rest of this chapter is about those social "experiences, supports, and encouragement" that young children receive from their parents, their peers, and their culture.

Prosocial and Antisocial Behavior

Ultimately, emotions are expressed in relation to the social world, particularly behavior related to **peers,** who are other people of about the same age and status as the child. For young children, peers are other children in the neighborhood, play group, and preschool who become friends, acquaintances, or enemies. Many psychologists believe that children learn about their own and other people's emotions through playing with peers. Even the best parent is less desirable than a peer when it comes to the give-and-take of play.

Few children are neutral in their relationships with peers. Typically they are either **prosocial,** behaving in ways that help another person without obvious benefit to themselves, or **antisocial,** behaving in ways that are deliberately hurtful or destructive (Caprara et al., 2001). In both types of behavior, intent is crucial: Actions that are intended to be hurtful are antisocial, even if they do not actually affect the target. Accordingly, children must be old enough to be able to regulate their emotions before they can justifiably be called either prosocial or antisocial, because they must be able to form the intention to help or harm.

How old is old enough? That is an open question: Some cultures and researchers credit or blame children for their behavior at much younger ages than others. However, most agree that newborns who reflexively cry when another one cries are not yet prosocial and that 1-year-olds who refuse to share are not yet antisocial. By age 4 or 5, though, children should have developed a theory of mind and thus should be able to act in a deliberately prosocial or antisocial manner (Eisenberg, 2000).

Empathy and Sharing

Expressing sympathy, offering to share, and including a shy child in a game or conversation are all examples of prosocial behavior. Such behavior, which is

peers People who are about the same age and status as oneself.

prosocial Behaving in ways that help other people without obvious benefit to oneself.

antisocial Behaving in ways that are deliberately hurtful or destructive.

indicative of social competence, appears during the later play years, continues to develop during the school years, and is correlated with emotional regulation (Eisenberg et al., 1997).

Prosocial attitudes also correlate with the making of new friends. Throughout the period from age 2 to 5, violent temper tantrums, uncontrollable crying, and terrifying phobias diminish, and the capacity for self-control—such as not opening a wrapped present immediately if asked to wait—becomes more evident (Kochanska et al., 2001). By school age, children tend to like other children best if they are neither overcontrolled nor undercontrolled in their emotions.

Empathy involves much more than simply following a parent's or teacher's moral prescription to share a toy or comfort another child; it is a prosocial emotion from the heart. **Empathy** is a person's true understanding of the emotions of another, including the ability to figure out what would make that person feel better. It is not egocentric. It is also more complex than mere sympathy, which means feeling sorry *for* someone, not *with* someone.

Because empathy indicates a certain level of understanding of the self and theory of mind, it is not usually evident until about age 4. It is not surprising that prosocial behaviors of all kinds correlate with popularity and friendship during childhood (Ladd, 1999)—and it is empathy that is the source of these helpful impulses. A young child who is lonely and unliked by peers may need special help in developing social skills. Such help can be, and often is, provided by trained teachers in a high-quality preschool—an addition to the list of reasons, given in Chapter 9, that a child's participation in Head Start sometimes affects his or her self-esteem and social relationships in adulthood. Young adults who were well educated in their early years were found, as adults, to be more likely to be married and less likely to be in prison. This amazing longitudinal connection may link empathy, social skills, and one's life situation as an adult.

What Will She Do? By age three or four, children can respond with empathy to another child's distress, as the girl on the left is doing. Such emotions usually lead to prosocial actions: She is likely to ask the distressed boy at right to play with her at the sand table.

empathy A person's true understanding of the emotions of another, including the ability to figure out what would make that person feel better.

Aggression

Both prosocial and antisocial behavior take many forms. However, **aggression** is a form of antisocial behavior that is of particular concern; it begins with inadequate emotional regulation during early childhood, and it can become a serious social problem as time goes by (Coie & Dodge, 1998). As one group of researchers reports:

> Children with [emotional] control problems observed by home visitors at ages 3 and 4 years were seen by teachers as more hostile and hyperactive in the classroom at age 5 years. . . . Early onset aggression, in particular, is likely to become entrenched and linked to multiple problems late in development.
>
> [Zahn-Waxler et al., 1996]

In other words, although almost all 2-year-olds are aggressive, a child who is more angry and hurtful at age 3 and 4 than other children is headed for trouble at age 5, 10, or even 15 or 25 (Loeber & Farrington, 2000). Here we will look at the forms, causes, and consequences of aggression that are specific to children aged 2 to 6.

Remember that emotions need to be regulated, not repressed, and that some assertion and self-protection are universal, and probably beneficial, aspects of early development. Accordingly, the consequences of aggressive actions taken by a young child are not always dire: Every normal child sometimes hurts another

aggression Hostile attitudes and hurtful or destructive actions that stem from anger or frustration.

child or adult by deliberately hitting, kicking, biting, pinching, hair-pulling, name-calling, arm-twisting, or the like. Parents are often shocked when this first happens, especially since they are likely to be the first victims when the angelic infant in their arms suddenly looks at them and then inflicts pain. Typically, parents teach emotional restraint—for instance, by saying "No" and then putting the baby down so that the hurtful action is not repeated. (The parent should never laugh or retaliate; both responses teach the wrong lessons.)

Although parents are no longer likely to be victims by the time the child is 3, other children sometimes are. Aggressive behavior normally increases between ages 1 and 4 because, as children become aware of themselves and their needs and begin to play more with peers, they become more likely to defend their interests. In fact, a 4-year-old who never lashes out is likely to become overwhelmed by anxiety or depression later on, perhaps victimized by bullies or by his or her own fears. But even though 4-year-olds are more aggressive than 2-year-olds, they are usually much more controlled: They do not hurt everyone in their path, but instead choose their issues and targets.

Researchers recognize four forms of aggression:

- **Instrumental aggression** is used to obtain or retain something, such as a toy or other object.
- **Reactive aggression** involves angry retaliation for an intentional or accidental act.
- **Relational aggression** is designed to inflict psychic, not physical, pain.
- **Bullying aggression** consists of an unprovoked attack.

Instrumental aggression is common in the play years and is the form of aggression that is most likely to increase from age 2 to 6. Although it should be discouraged as a strategy, instrumental aggression involves objects more than people, is quite normal, and therefore is not of serious concern.

Reactive aggression is more worrisome, because it can indicate a lack of emotional regulation. A 2-year-old might be expected to react to any hurt with aggression, but a 5-year-old should be able to stop and think, figuring out not only whether the hurt was intentional but also whether reciprocal aggression is likely to make the situation better or worse.

Relational aggression, as when a child teases or taunts another, can be even more hurtful than physical aggression (Miller & Olson, 2000). Victims and perpetrators of relational aggression are more likely to be lonely and unwilling to share with others than are victims and perpetrators of instrumental aggression. A 3-year-old who has a toy snatched by another child is likely to cry and try to get it back; but if another child calls him or her dirty, dumb, or bad, the remedy is less obvious. Friendships are severed by relational aggression but not usually by instrumental aggression (Crick et al., 1999).

Bullying aggression is the most troublesome of all. It is not only the most hurtful form of aggression toward other children but also indicates that the bully has a troubled family situation and will probably be involved in worse aggression later. Bullies and victims are discussed in detail in Chapter 13, because the most serious harm occurs during the school years. One aspect, however, is directly relevant to early childhood: Both bullies and victims are characterized by inadequate and immature emotional regulation. This is another reason adults should guide children to understand and control their emotions before the first grade (Mahady et al., 2000).

instrumental aggression Aggressive behavior that is aimed at getting or keeping an object desired by another.

reactive aggression Aggressive behavior that is an angry retaliation for some intentional or accidental act by another person.

relational aggression Aggressive behavior that takes the form of insults or social rejection.

bullying aggression Aggressive behavior that takes the form of an unprovoked physical or verbal attack on another person.

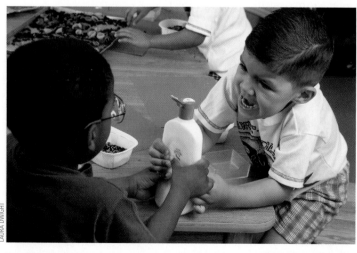

LAURA DWIGHT

Me First! An increase in aggression by about age 4 is typically accompanied by an increase in self-control. This struggle will not escalate to instrumental aggression if both children have learned some emotional regulation and if neither has been misguided by racism or by a false image of maleness.

Adult guidance is only one of many influences on prosocial and antisocial behavior. To some extent, developmental processes are also at work. It is typical for children to become more prosocial and less aggressive between ages 3 and 6. However, with some children, antisocial behavior does not decrease (Campbell, 1995). The reasons range from genetic and prenatal influences to the impact of school and society. Now we look at an influence that is particularly powerful during early childhood: playing with peers.

Learning Social Skills Through Play

During childhood, play is the most productive and adaptive activity that children can undertake. Indeed, the fact that play is both universal and variable, related to the culture and the gender as well as the age of the playmates, makes it an ideal forum for learning specific social skills (Sutton-Smith, 1997). Although children play when they are alone or with adults, they are much more likely to play with other children.

Compare the peer interactions of a 2-year-old and a 5-year-old. The younger child's social play consists mainly of simple games (such as bouncing and trying to catch a ball and becoming angry or upset if the other child does not cooperate). By contrast, the more sophisticated 5-year-old has learned how to gain entry to a play group, to manage conflict through the use of humor, and to select and keep friends and playmates.

More than 70 years ago, a researcher named Mildred Parten (1932) outlined five types of childhood play, from the least social to the most social:

■ *Solitary play*. A child plays alone, seemingly unaware of any other children playing nearby.
■ *Onlooker play*. A child watches other children play.
■ *Parallel play*. Children play with similar toys in similar ways, but they do not interact.
■ *Associative play*. Children interact, sharing materials and emotions, but they don't seem to be playing the same game or to be concerned that the other is not cooperating.
■ *Cooperative play*. Children play together, either jointly creating an elaborate game or structure or taking turns.

As you can see, one indicator of social skill development is how children play with peers, because only with age-mates do children themselves assume responsibility for initiating and maintaining harmonious social interaction. Whether learning how to share crayons or sand toys, or how to include everybody in the construction of a spaceship, or how to respond to a friend's accusatory "That's not fair," children must deal with playmates who are not always understanding and self-sacrificing (as a mother might be). Specifically, how does this social play occur? It takes many forms, but two are especially prominent in early childhood; rough-and-tumble play and sociodramatic play.

Rough-and-Tumble Play

One beneficial form of social play is called **rough-and-tumble play,** because it looks quite rough and the children seem to tumble over each other as they play. In fact, the term first came from scientists who studied baby monkeys in East Africa (Jones, 1976). They noticed that the monkeys seemed to chase, attack, roll over in the dirt, and wrestle, quite roughly, but without really hurting each other. If another monkey wanted to play, all it had to do was to come close, catch the eye of a peer, and then run away as if being chased. This was an invitation, which the other monkey almost always accepted. Since the monkeys did not hurt each

rough-and-tumble play Play that mimics aggression through wrestling, chasing, or hitting but that actually occurs purely in fun, with no intent to harm.

LAURA DWIGHT

Male Bonding Sometimes the only way to distinguish aggression from rough-and-tumble play is to look at the faces. The hitter is not scowling, the hittee is laughing, and the hugger is just joining in the fun. Another clue that this is rough-and-tumble play comes from gender and context. These boys are in a Head Start program, where they are learning social skills, such as how to avoid fighting.

other, ethologists called this play, to distinguish it from rough fighting. They noted that the young monkeys who were most likely to fight were least likely to engage in rough-and-tumble play, which led them to conclude that rough-and-tumble play helped monkeys learn to avoid aggression.

When the scientists left the jungle and returned to their families, they were surprised to realize that their own children did the same things as the baby monkeys—that human youngsters also engage in rough-and-tumble-play! It became very obvious that, although a distinguishing characteristic of such play is its mimicry of aggression, rough-and-tumble play is clearly prosocial, not antisocial. Unlike aggression, rough-and-tumble play is both fun and constructive; it teaches children how to enter a relationship, assert themselves, and respond to the actions of someone else while exercising gross motor skills, all without hurting the other person (Pellegrini & Smith, 1998). Adults who are unsure whether they are observing a fight that should be broken up or a social activity that should continue should look for a "play face." Children almost always smile, and often laugh, in rough-and-tumble play, whereas they frown and scowl in real fighting.

Rough-and-tumble play is universal. It has been observed in Japan, Kenya, and Mexico as well as in every income and ethnic group in North America, Europe, and Australia (Boulton & Smith, 1989). There are some cultural and situational differences, however. One of the most important is space and supervision: Children are much more likely to instigate rough-and-tumble play when they have room to run and chase and when adults are not directly nearby. This is one reason the ideal physical environment for children includes ample safe space for gross motor activities, with adults within earshot but not underfoot (Bradley, 1995).

In addition, rough-and-tumble play usually occurs among children who have had considerable social experience, often with each other. Not surprisingly, then, older children are more likely to engage in rough-and-tumble play than younger ones. In fact, the incidence of rough-and-tumble play increases with age, peaking at about age 8 to 10 and then decreasing (Pellegrini & Smith, 1998). Finally, boys are much more likely to engage in rough-and-tumble play than are girls. Indeed, girls typically withdraw from boys' rough-and-tumble play (Fabes, 1994). The reason may be hormonal or cultural or both. (Sex differences are discussed at the end of this chapter.)

Sociodramatic Play

sociodramatic play Pretend play in which children act out various roles and themes in stories that they create themselves.

In the type of social play called **sociodramatic play,** children act out various roles and themes in stories they themselves have created, taking on "any identity, role, or activity that they choose. They can be mothers, babies, Cinderella, or Captain Hook. They can make tea or fly to the moon. Or they can fight, hurt others, or kill or imprison someone" (Dunn & Hughes, 2001). From simple plots at age 2 (a mother–baby script that consists mainly of eating, sleeping, and waking) to elaborate ones by age 5 (such as a trip through the jungle confronting various challenging animals, people, and geological barriers), sociodramatic play provides a way for children to do the following:

■ Explore and rehearse the social roles they see being enacted around them
■ Test their own ability to explain and convince others of their ideas
■ Regulate their emotions through imagination
■ Examine personal concerns in a nonthreatening manner

The beginnings of sociodramatic play can be seen in solitary or parallel play, when a toddler "feeds" or "cuddles" or "punishes" a doll or stuffed animal. Sociodramatic play greatly increases in frequency and complexity between the ages of 2 and 6. As young children develop their theory of mind and their emotional regulation, they seek other children to practice what they have learned.

The social experiences that young children have as they negotiate, cooperate, and persuade in let's-pretend play are crucial opportunities (as we saw earlier with the three girls negotiating to be "sisters") (Hobson, 2000). Children can, for instance, use sociodramatic play to try out various means of managing their emotions, as in dealing with a scary situation in the dark (in a tent made of blankets, quickly opened if the darkness becomes overwhelming) or providing nurturance to an injured playmate (who falls down dead and needs to be miraculously revived) or exhibiting courage when the bad guys attack (with machine guns, bombs, or swords). In this sense, then, sociodramatic play is a testing ground for early psychological knowledge, always protecting the self-esteem of the players and teaching them cooperation.

Sociodramatic play can also reveal anger and aggression. In one study comparing hard-to-manage 4-year-olds and their friends, the former were likely to turn sociodramatic play episodes toward violence and death, which are not the usual themes of such play (Dunn & Hughes, 2001). For these children, doctor play became pain and surgery; fantasy play involved killing ("You must go and find your fortune" "Why?" "Because your mother is going to be killed in a minute"); and play fighting became frightening (a hard-to-manage child brandishes a sword saying, "Kill. Kill. Kill me"—to which his friend responds "No" and drops his weapon). This study found that the children whose pretend play was most violent at age 4 became 6-year-olds who were least likely to understand prosocial behavior.

Although both sexes engage in sociodramatic play, girls are more likely to do so, and they are less likely than boys to use violent themes. For their part, boys are more likely to engage in rough-and-tumble play, which seems designed to teach the participants to express their power and strength without actually hurting their playmates. Both sexes apparently learn important prosocial skills as they play. The best setting for children to practice these social skills with peers is a high-quality educational program where children have many friends and where teachers help them master fear and anger and learn to modify their emotional expressions in response to the reaction of their playmates.

In a good early-childhood program, children can develop a wide range of social skills as they interact with peers (National Research Council and Institute of Medicine, 2000). They can also make many friends. Indeed, friendships are remarkably consistent during the play years. Young children choose regular playmates, usually of the same age and sex, and then their ongoing rough-and-tumble play or sociodramatic play together becomes complex, involving more self-disclosure, intimacy, and reciprocity than does their play with casual acquaintances. In fact, two close friends sometimes develop ongoing plots, roles, routines, and scripts, quickly returning to another episode of the same story each time they play together.

Sociodramatic Play Just like the boys in the previous photograph, these girls are developing their social skills—in this case, as store owner and grocery shopper.

?Observational Quiz (see answer, page 308): Which specifics of the girls' fantasy play are similar to the real thing, and which are not?

The Influence of Television and Video Games

Young children spend almost 20 hours per week watching television (Nielsen Media Research, 2000), and North American households have more television sets and personal computers than bathrooms—which used to be counted as the indicator of modernity. Other research confirms that 2- to 4-year-olds spend about 3 hours per day watching television and that 5- to 6-year-olds spend about 2 hours, only about 15 minutes of which is educational (Huston et al., 1999).

! *Answer to Observational Quiz* (from page 307): The particular hats, necklaces, and shoes are all quite different from those their mothers would likely wear to the store, and the stock, the money holder, and the grocery bag are quite different. However, the essence of shopping is here: Money is exchanged for goods, and both participants politely play their roles.

It is easy to understand why this is so. Parents quickly learn that the "idiot box" is a good babysitter: It keeps children relatively quiet and in one room for hours at a time. Advertisers know that young children are gullible and demanding, so that a program that keeps their uncritical attention creates a strong market and large profits for junk foods and expensive toys.

Some critics suggest that any time spent watching television is destructive, becausee it keeps children from physical activity, imaginative play, reading, and family interaction. Although this point may be valid, there is no proof that merely viewing TV, hour after hour, is destructive. There is evidence, however, that the messages conveyed on the screen are influential, as confirmed by a longitudinal study that surveyed children at about age 5 and again at about age 16. Those who had watched educational television as young children (mostly *Sesame Street* and *Mr. Rogers' Neighborhood*) became teenagers who earned higher grades and did more reading than other high-school students, especially if they were boys. By contrast, those who watched violent TV programs had lower grades, especially if they were girls (Anderson et al., 2001). Using a variety of statistical safeguards, the researchers found causation, not merely correlation. In other words, those parents who encouraged their children to watch *Mr. Rogers* might also be parents who encouraged their children to get good grades, but this research found that educational television in and of itself had a positive impact.

The fact that content is crucial is one reason video games are of great concern to many developmental researchers. Remember that good science is accumulated slowly and deliberately, with various methods and diverse populations and samples, over a period of years. Developmentalists are reluctant to state flatly that violent video games are worse than violent TV programs, that they lead directly to death and injury. However, it is certain that both are destructive, pushing children to be more violent than they would otherwise be (Bushman & Anderson, 2001). One developmentalist explains, "It seems likely that the impact of watching characters being killed on television will be exceeded for a child playing a computer game who is doing the virtual killing" (Larson, 2001).

Changing Policy

Turning Off the TV

Most policy makers seem resigned to the impact of TV and video games on young children. Instead, they save their criticism for the parents who let infants watch television (an increasing number of programs, such as *Barney* and *Teletubbies*, target youngsters under age 2), or who let their teenagers play violent video games.

Film and TV executives say the media are merely reflecting reality, but critic Michael Medved (1995) asks, if TV violence is part of everyday life,

> . . . then why do so few people witness murders in real life but everybody sees them on TV and in the movies? The most violent ghetto isn't in South Central L.A. or Southeast Washington, D.C.; it's on television. About 350 characters appear each night on prime-time TV, but studies show an average of seven of these people are murdered every night. If this rate applied in reality, then in just 50 days everyone in the United States would be killed and the last one left could turn off the TV.

[pp. 156–157]

Watching television may be particularly harmful in early childhood, not only because of all the hours that are spent in front of the screen but also because young children are just beginning to learn about society, culture, and emotions. Television teaches many potentially destructive lessons. Developmentalists focus on several aspects:

- Advertisements with faulty messages about nutrition, promoting foods high in fat, sugar, and salt
- Perpetuation of sexist, ageist, and racist stereotypes
- Depiction of violent solutions for every problem with no expression of empathy

At 10 A.M. on Saturday mornings, more than half of all North American children are watching TV (Comstock & Scharrer, 1999). What do they see and learn? The "good guys," whether in cartoons or police dramas, do as much hitting, shooting, and kicking as the bad guys, yet the consequences of their violence are sanitized, justified, or made comic. They are never portrayed as bloodthirsty or evil. In cartoons, a person or object blown to smithereens is funny and a person who stops to think about consequences dies. All the good guys are male, even on educational television (Big Bird, Barney, even Bugs Bunny). Virtually no hero, in cartoon or human form, is nonwhite, although villains often are. Women are portrayed as victims or adoring girlfriends of the heroes, almost never as leaders—except in a very few sex-stereotyped programs that few boys watch.

Video games are worse in every respect—more violent, more sexist, more racist. Almost all the characters in 33 popular Nintendo and Sega Genesis video games are male and Anglo, and 80 percent of the games include violence or aggression as an essential strategy the child must use to score points (Dietz, 1998).

Children who watch violent television are likely to be more aggressive than children who do not, and children who are already inclined to be aggressive are likely to watch the most violent programs. In fact, "well over 1,000 studies . . . point overwhelmingly to a causal connection between media violence and aggressive behavior in some children" (U.S. Congress, 2000). Six major organizations concerned with the psychological and physical well-being of children (the American Psychological Association, the American Academy of Pediatrics, the American Medical Association, the American Academy of Child and Adolescent Psychiatry, the American Academy of Family Physicians, and the American Psychiatry Association) suggest that parents turn off the TV.

Obviously, not every child who watches televised violence or plays violent video games becomes a bully or a victim, a racist or a sexist. The impact of video violence has been compared to that of cigarette smoking: Not every smoker is guaranteed to die of lung cancer, but many will (Bushman & Anderson, 2001). To take this comparison a step further: No responsible parent would give a child a cigarette, or even deliberately blow smoke in a child's direction. Why, then, do parents turn on the TV for their children to watch?

The current public policy debate revolves around the question of whether an emphasis on parental responsibility is adequate or whether the judgment and power of parents are overwhelmed by the commercialization of children's television, which requires programs to be as eye-catching as possible in order to draw a wide audience for the unhealthy snacks and the expensive toys of the sponsors. The division of responsibility for such decisions between individual parents and governmental policy is a matter of societal debate. This is an ongoing public policy issue that the next generation may decide.

Wrong Lessons Learned Preschoolers are eager for knowledge, and these boys are learning to shoot the bad guys whenever they appear. The most frightening aspect of television watching at this age is that children absorb it totally, without a firm understanding of the difference between real and pretend.

Parenting Patterns

We have seen that many things—including genes, peers, gender, and culture—affect children's behavior. Parenting patterns are also very influential (Maccoby, 2000; Patterson, 1998). However, it is important to neither exaggerate nor understate the role of parents—mistakes often made in the media or by social scientists of earlier periods.

Contemporary students of socialization largely agree that early researchers often overstated conclusions from correlational findings; relied excessively on singular, deterministic views of parental influence; and failed to attend to the ■ potentially confounding effects of heredity. Contemporary researchers have taken steps to remedy many of these shortcomings. Unfortunately, the weaknesses of old studies still permeate presentations of socialization research in introductory textbooks and the mass media, partly because they appeal to preferences for simple generalizations.

[Collins et al., 2000]

In other words, the general public would like to believe that parents alone determine a child's personality, an error made by theorists as dissimilar as Sigmund Freud and John B. Watson 80 years ago (see Chapter 7). Current research places much less emphasis on parents, but the way mothers and fathers relate to their children is still important (Maccoby, 2000).

Baumrind's Three Styles of Parenting

The contemporary study of parenting patterns has been greatly influenced by the early work of Diana Baumrind (1967, 1971), who began with 100 preschool children, all from California and almost all European-American and middle-class. As a careful researcher, Baumrind used many measures of behavior, several of them involving naturalistic observation. First, she observed the children's activities in preschool and, on the basis of their actions, rated their self-control, independence, self-confidence, and other attributes. She then interviewed both parents of each child and observed parent–child interaction in two settings, at home and in the laboratory, in search of possible relationships between the parents' behavior at home and the child's behavior at preschool.

Baumrind found that parents differed on four important dimensions:

- Expressions of *warmth*, or nurturance, which ranged from very affectionate to quite cold
- Strategies for *discipline*, which might involve explanation, criticism, persuasion, and/or physical punishment
- The quality of *communication*, which ranged from extensive listening to demands for silence
- Expectations for *maturity*, evident in how much responsibility and self-control was demanded

On the basis of these four dimensions, Baumrind identified three basic styles of parenting:

1. **Authoritarian parenting.** The parents' word is law, not to be questioned. Misconduct brings strict punishment, usually physical, although authoritarian parents do not cross the line into physical abuse. Demands for maturity are high, and parent–child communication, especially about emotions, is low. Although they love and care about their children, authoritarian parents seem aloof, showing little affection or nurturance.
2. **Permissive parenting.** The parents make few demands on their children, hiding any impatience they feel. Discipline is lax because demands for maturity are low. Permissive parents are nurturant and accepting, and they communicate well with their offspring. They view themselves as available to help their children but not as responsible for shaping how their children turn out.
3. **Authoritative parenting.** Authoritative parents are similar in some ways to authoritarian parents, in that they set limits and enforce rules. However, they also listen to their children's requests and questions and discuss feelings and problems. Family rule is more democratic than dictatorial. The parents demand maturity of their offspring, but they are also nurturant and understanding, forgiving (rather than punishing) a child when demands for maturity are not met.

The characteristics of these three styles are summarized in Table 10.1.

authoritarian parenting Baumrind's term for a style of child rearing in which standards for proper behavior are high, misconduct is strictly punished, and parent–child communication is low.

permissive parenting Baumrind's term for a style of child rearing in which the parents seldom punish, guide, or control the child but are nurturant and communicate well with the child.

authoritative parenting Baumrind's term for a style of child rearing in which the parents set limits and provide guidance for their child but are willing to listen to the child's ideas and to make compromises.

TABLE 10.1 Characteristics of Baumrind's Parenting Styles

		Characteristics			
			Communication		
Style	Warmth	Discipline	Parent to Child	Child to Parent	Expectations of Maturity
Authoritarian	Low	Strict, often physical	High	Low	High
Permissive	High	Rare	Low	High	Low
Authoritative	High	Moderate, with much discussion	High	High	Moderate

All three styles of parenting reflect underlying love and concern. The authoritarian parent thinks it is important for the child to learn to behave properly; the permissive parent believes that learning happens best through conversation. In contrast, two other styles of parenting have been identified: **neglectful parenting,** in which the parents do not seem to care at all, and **indulgent parenting,** in which the parents accommodate the child's every whim. These two types are abusive and thus clearly harmful, unlike the three parenting styles that Baumrind described.

Baumrind and others have continued to study parenting styles, following the original 100 children as they grew and studying thousands of other children of various backgrounds and ages. Based on this research they have come to some basic conclusions:

- *Authoritarian* parents raise children who are likely to be conscientious, obedient, and quiet; however, the children are not especially happy. They are more likely to feel guilty or depressed.
- *Permissive* parents raise children who are even less happy and who lack self-control, especially within the give-and-take of peer friendships.
- *Authoritative* parents raise children who are more likely to be successful, articulate, intelligent, happy with themselves, and generous with others.

Follow-up research has also found that, at least for middle-class families of European ancestry, the initial advantages of the authoritative approach are likely to grow even stronger over time, helping children to achieve in school, adolescents to avoid drug abuse, and young adults to have high self-esteem. Specifically in early childhood, researchers still find that authoritative strategies foster self-control and emotional regulation (Mauro & Harris, 2000). Other research finds that the best way to promote prosocial behavior and to limit aggression is to induce children to think through and verbalize the human consequences of their actions (Hoffman, 2001). This process is central to authoritative parenting.

Many studies have found the link between any one of the three basic parenting styles and the child's behavior to be less direct and inevitable than it appeared in Baumrind's original research. First, the child's temperament needs to be considered. A fearful child needs gentle parenting, and a bolder child needs more restrictive (but still warm) parenting (Bates et al., 1998; Kochanska et al., 1997). Second, community and cultural differences sometimes undercut, sometimes emphasize, and almost always influence the child's perception of the quality of parenting. Effective Asian- and African-American parents are often stricter than effective European-American parents (Darling & Steinberg, 1997; Wachs, 1999).

This last finding surprised developmentalists, who then hypothesized that, to some extent, more authoritarian parenting is required when families live in stressful, violent neighborhoods: Children need more guidelines in such places. However, non-European parents who are middle-class also tend to impose strict guidelines and occasional physical punishment, and they have more child-rearing success than do European-American parents who use the same strategies.

neglectful parenting An abusive style of child rearing in which the parents do not seem to care about their child at all.

indulgent parenting An abusive style of child rearing in which the parents accommodate the child's every whim.

Baumrind named two of her three parenting styles with almost the same word; only the last syllables differ. How will you remember them? One student said "authoritarian" *Is Awfully Negative* (*-ian*), but "authoritative" *Is Very Excellent* (*-ive*). Maybe this memory trick will work for you, too.

GEORGE GERSTER / PHOTO RESEARCHERS, INC.

What Kind of Parenting? The relationship between these two Botswana bushmen suggests authoritative, not authoritarian, parenting and serves as a reminder that parenting practices follow cultural and ethnic lines, not racial ones. In the largely democratic communities in the open areas of the Kalahari Desert, unlike urban neighborhoods, parents do not have to be strict.

The crucial factors seem to be parental warmth, support, and concern for the child, which are expressed in ways that vary with the family's cultural background and current circumstances.

Parents who seem authoritarian or permissive may raise well-adjusted children, depending on the child's personality and the circumstances. However, there is *no* evidence that abusive, indifferent, or neglectful parents are effective (Maccoby, 2000; McGroder, 2000).

Many parents today are raising young children while coping with extraordinary stresses of their own. Single parenthood, marital conflict, social prejudice, civil war, inadequate income—all of these can reduce a parent's patience, time, and warmth toward young children (McLoyd, 1998b). These factors are discussed in some detail in Chapter 13. One general point should be made here: No single one of these stresses always harms children. Some parents cope very well, and some children are quite resilient (Luthar et al., 2000). Low-income minority parents who are consistent and nurturant raise young children who can regulate their emotions and are ready for success in school and later life, just as can middle-income majority parents who are equally consistent and nurturant (Garner & Spears, 2000). One factor that contributes to nurturance is community support for parenting, evidence for which can be partly determined by looking at the percentage of children living in poverty (see Appendix A, Chapter 10)

Among the indicators of parental warmth are caressing or hugging the child, answering the child's questions, and asking the child to participate in a conversation between adults. Such warmth buffers the potentially harmful effects of strict standards of behavior (McLloyd & Smith, 2002).

Punishment

How a parent disciplines a child is an integral part of parenting style. No developmentalist would suggest that young children should do whatever they please; but, given what researchers have learned about cognition, it is apparent that proactive and preventive discipline is preferable to punishment after the misdeed. Four specific recommendations are listed in Table 10.2.

TABLE 10.2 Relating Discipline to Developmental Characteristics During Early Childhood

Remember theory of mind. Young children gradually understand things from other viewpoints. Hence involving empathy ("How would *you* feel if . . .?") will increase prosocial and decrease antisocial behavior.

Remember emerging self-concept. Young children are developing a sense of who they are and what they want, sometimes egocentrically. Adults should protect that emerging self: They should not force 3-year-olds to share their favorite toys, nor should they tell them, "Words will never hurt me." Relational aggression is painful, as young children know.

Remember the language explosion and fast mapping. Young children are eager to talk and think, but they are not always accurate in their verbal understanding. Hence a child who doesn't "listen" should not necessarily be punished, because a command might be misunderstood. However, conversation before and after an event helps the child learn.

Remember that young children are not yet logical. The connection between the misdeed and the punishment needs to be immediate and transparent. A child might learn nothing from waiting several hours to be spanked for deliberately breaking a dish but might learn a lot from having to pick up the pieces, mop the floor, and perhaps contribute some saved pennies toward a replacement.

Techniques of Disciplines

However, no disciplinary technique works quickly and automatically. Instead, over the years from 2 to 6, children gradually learn to reflect on the consequences of their actions, and their actions become more in line with expectations. Culture is a strong influence on disciplinary techniques. Japanese mothers, for example, use reasoning, empathy, and expressions of disappointment to control their children's social behavior more than North American mothers do. These techniques work quite well, partly because of the mother–child relationship referred to as *amae* (a very close interpersonal relationship, especially dependency on the mother), which is much stronger in Japan than in North America (Rothbaum et al., 2000). Parents in the United States are more likely than Japanese parents to allow and even encourage emotional expressions of all sorts, including anger. Perhaps as a result, in a series of experimental situations designed to elicit distress and conflict, American 4- to 5-year-olds were more aggressive than their Japanese counterparts (Zahn-Waxler et al., 1996).

One disciplinary technique often used in North America is the **time-out,** which involves requiring the child to stop all activity and sit in a corner or stay indoors for a few minutes. Other punishment practices are withdrawal of a privilege, such as television watching, and withdrawal of affection, as when the parent expresses disappointment or gives the child a stern "look." Each of these techniques may have unintended consequences. Developmentalists stress the need for parents to prevent misdeeds whenever possible and to choose punishments carefully, noting the effect on the child.

time-out A disciplinary technique in which the child is required to stop all activity and sit in a corner or stay indoors for a few minutes.

What About Spanking?

Many developmentalists wonder whether punishment in any form has a boomerang effect—whether children who are criticized develop low self-esteem, whether those who are shamed feel that they are not loved, whether those who are physically punished learn to be more aggressive. This question raises many cultural issues. In Sweden, for instance, physical punishment of children is against the law for parents as well as for teachers. By contrast, in some Caribbean nations, all parents are expected to physically punish their children and to be very sparing of praise (Durbrow, 1999). In the United States, physical punishment is more commonly accepted in the South than in the North.

More than 90 percent of today's adults in the United States were spanked when they were young, and most consider themselves none the worse for it. Indeed, most parents not only in North America but also throughout Asia, Africa, and South America believe that spanking is acceptable, legitimate, and necessary at times (Durrant, 1996; Levinson, 1989). They are especially likely to spank their children at ages 2 to 6, when the children are considered "old enough to know better" but "not old enough to listen to reason." Spanking is so common that parents of all types resort to it: permissive types in exasperation, authoritative types as a last resort after a series of warnings, and authoritarian types as a legitimate consequence of breaking a rule.

Angela at Play Research suggests that being spanked is a salient and memorable experience for young children, not because of the pain but because of the emotions. Children seek to do what they have learned; they know not only how to place their hands but also that an angry person is able to do the hitting. The only part of the lesson they usually forget is what particular misdeed precipitated the punishment. Asked why she is spanking her doll, Angela will likely explain "She was bad."

However, many developmentalists are particularly concerned about spanking. Do children who are physically punished learn to be more aggressive? The answer is probably "yes." Domestic violence of any type—from spanking a child to letting siblings "fight it out" to exposing children to mutual insults or hitting between the parents—may make children aggressive with peers and, later on, with their own families (Straus, 1994).

Not every child in every family will learn to be aggressive from being spanked. Spanking poses that risk, but it is not a determining factor. It is to be avoided if possible, but it is not always destructive (McLloyd & Smith, 2002). For example, one research team (Strassberg et al., 1994) set out to study the relationship between punishment at home and aggression at school. They tracked 273 children aged 4 to 6 and their parents from many socioeconomic and cultural backgrounds. Roughly one-third were single parents; about three-fourths were European-Americans.

Before their children entered kindergarten, the parents were asked how frequently they had spanked, hit, or beaten their children over the past year. If the parents asked the difference between spanking and hitting, *spanking* was defined as "an open hand or an object on the child's buttocks in a controlled manner," whereas *hitting* was "the impulsive or spontaneous use of a fist or closed hand (or object) to strike the child more strongly than one would while spanking." (*Beating,* apparently, did not need to be defined.) Of the 408 parents surveyed, 9 percent never used physical punishment, 72 percent spanked but did not use more violent punishment, and 19 percent hit and/or beat, as well as spanked, their preschool children.

Six months later, observers, blind to the children's punishment history, recorded their behavior in kindergarten, taking particular note of acts of aggression. For an accurate snapshot of behavior, the observation phase was divided into 12 five-minute segments per child, occurring over several days. Within each segment, the observers recorded how many times each child engaged in instrumental, reactive, or bullying aggression.

Bullying aggression, as expected, was clearly associated with being violently punished (see Figure 10.1), particularly among "a few extremely aggressive children," mostly boys who were frequently hit or beaten as well as spanked by both of their parents. No surprise there.

The incidence of *instrumental aggression* was not surprising, either, since it is quite normal for young children to fight to get or keep hold of something, such as a toy. This type of aggression showed no correlation with the kind of

FIGURE 10.1 Punishment and Aggression All the children, regardless of how their parents punished them, were about equally likely to exhibit instrumental aggression. The typical child did so once or twice an hour. By contrast, children who were severely punished by their parents were most often the bullies. The most interesting result involves reactive aggression. Children who were spanked interpreted such actions as hostile, and thus as requiring an aggressive response, twice as often as children who had not been physically punished.

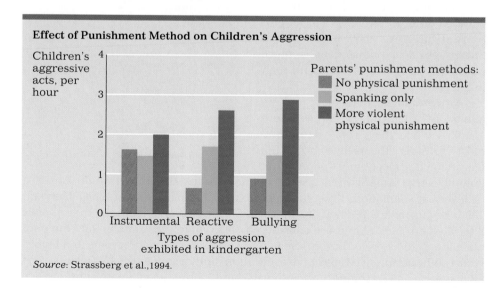

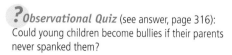 *Observational Quiz* (see answer, page 316): Could young children become bullies if their parents never spanked them?

punishment the children experienced at home. Children fought over posses-
sions and privileges whether they had been spanked, beaten, or not physically
punished at all.

However, *reactive aggression*—retaliation against another child for a real or
imagined wrong—was surprisingly common among children who were spanked.
Compared to children who were never spanked, those who were spanked retali-
ated more than twice as much. They angrily shoved, punched, or kicked at any
provocation, rather than asking the other child for an explanation, complaining
to the teacher, assuming it was an accident, or compromising their own actions.

The researchers point out that while violent punishment (hitting or beating)
seems to lead a child to be aggressive under all circumstances (to be a bully),
spanking does not. Rather, it seems to create a specific emotional-response
pattern—a quick physical reaction to a perceived attack—probably because
the child connects spanking to anger, a powerful emotion for a 4-year-old
(Strassberg et al., 1994). Generally, the gender of the child or the spanking parent or the frequency of spanking did not matter. Even a few spankings a year
by only one of the parents was still likely to make the child higher in reactive
aggression. There was one gender-related exception: Boys who were spanked
by their fathers reacted as if they had been hit as well as spanked; that is, they
tended to become bullies.

Although no single study proves a general point, the conclusions of this
study have been refined, not contradicted, by other research. For example, one
prospective, longitudinal study of adolescent mothers found that those who
controlled their children by yelling, grabbing, and spanking had children whose
aggressive and disruptive behavior increased between the ages of 3 and 6. The
correlation was more powerful for European-American than African-American
mothers, perhaps because the latter scored high on measures of warmth and affection as well as control (Spieker et al., 1999). As already pointed out, the overall
context of family support may be more powerful than any particular parental behavior. The general conclusion seems to be that although physical punishment
may be quick and effective at age 2 or 3, it may have negative repercussions later,
especially if the child experiences it as emotional rejection.

Further research clarifies the differences between families. Harsh discipline
was much more harmful to young children's development if it was accompanied
by parental anger and distress, especially if the parent's distress was related to
the child's negative emotions (such as the child's being upset at being teased or
scared of the doctor or nervous about going to a new school) (Fabes et al., 2001).
Children probably should be allowed to express anger, fear, or sorrow without
the parents themselves becoming upset. The physical impact of punishment is
only one part of a triad: The child's cognitive and emotional reactions are as important as the child's physical sensations.

Especially for Parents Suppose you agree that spanking is destructive, but you sometimes get so angry at your child's behavior that you hit him or her.

Boy or Girl: So What?

Male or female identity is an important feature of self-understanding during the
play years, as well as a particular concern of many parents. Social scientists distinguish between **sex differences,** which are the biological differences between
males and females, and **gender differences,** which are culturally imposed differences in the roles and behaviors of the two sexes. Curiously, although true *sex*
differences are far less apparent in childhood (when boys and girls are about the
same size and shape) than in adulthood (when physical differences become more
visible and anatomy becomes critical in sexual intercourse, pregnancy, and
birth), *gender* differentiation seems more significant to children than to adults.

sex differences Biological differences between males and females.

gender differences Culturally imposed differences in the roles and behavior of males and females.

(a)

(b)

Two Sets of Cousins Same day, same trampoline, and similar genes and culture, because these eight children are cousins. But sex or gender differences are quite apparent in the later preschool years. Of course, no one should read too much into a photograph. Nonetheless, this group, like any group of preschoolers, offers suggestive evidence of boy–girl differences, here including one specific aspect of their wearing apparel.

? Observational Quiz (see answer, page 320): What sex or gender differences can you see?

! Answer to Observational Quiz (from page 314): Yes, although bullies were three times as likely to be the product of a home in which physical punishment more violent than spanking was used.

Developmental Progression of Gender Awareness

Even at age 2, gender-related preferences and play patterns are apparent. Children already know whether they are boys or girls, can identify adult strangers as mommies or daddies, and apply gender labels (Mrs., Mr., lady, man) consistently. That simple cognitive awareness becomes, by age 3, a rudimentary understanding that male and female distinctions are lifelong (although some pretend, hope, or imagine otherwise). By age 4, children are convinced that certain toys (such as dolls and trucks) and certain roles (such as nurse and soldier) are appropriate for one gender but not the other (Bauer et al., 1998; Ruble & Martin, 1998). When given a choice, children play with children of their own gender, a tendency that is apparent at age 2 and is clear-cut by age 4, with children becoming more selective and exclusive as they mature (Martin & Fabes, 2001). Partly because of their largely gender-segregated play patterns, victims of physical aggression in preschool are more often boys, while most victims of relational aggression are girls (Crick et al., 1999).

A child who follows same-sex play patterns does not necessarily understand biological sex differences. A leading researcher of gender identity, Sandra Bem, described the day her young son Jeremy

> naively decided to wear barrettes to nursery school. Several times that day, another little boy insisted that Jeremy must be a girl because "only girls wear barrettes." After repeatedly asserting that "wearing barrettes doesn't matter; being a boy means having a penis and testicles," Jeremy finally pulled down his pants as a way of making his point more convincingly. The boy was not impressed. He simply said, "Everybody has a penis; only girls wear barrettes."
>
> *[Bem, 1989]*

As in this example, even though children confuse gender and sex throughout the play years, a child's awareness of differences is soon associated with what is good, bad, or simply wrong (Fagot & Leinbach, 1993). By age 6, children have well-formed ideas (and prejudices) and also know which sex is better (their own) and which sex is stupid (the other one) (Ruble & Martin, 1998).

Young children also insist on dressing in stereotypic ways: Shoes for preschoolers are often designed with such decorations as pink ribbons or blue footballs, and no child would dare wear the shoes meant for the other gender. Such dress codes become rigidly enforced by first grade, with some of the cruelest barbs of relational aggression used against children who dress oddly.

When they reach school age, a few children still may have a good friend of the other sex, but they rarely play with that friend when other children are around (Kovacs et al., 1996). Awareness that a person's sex is a biological characteristic that is not changed by clothing or activities develops gradually, not becoming solid until age 8 or so (Szkrybalo & Ruble, 1999).

Many young children also learn that sexual stereotyping is morally wrong, at least when other people do it. This was demonstrated in a study of 4-year-olds who were told several stories of sexual exclusion; for example: "A group of boys are playing with a truck. Sally comes over and asks if she can play. Two of the boys say that Sally cannot play because she is a girl. Is it all right or not all right for the boys to tell Sally she can't play?" Most of the girls (72 percent) and about half the boys (52 percent) said it was "not all right." Other types of examples elicited other responses, but noteworthy is that many children put aside their personal preferences (very few girls would actually try to join a group of boys in school) when moral judgments about sex discrimination must be made (Theimer et al., 2001).

Theories of Gender Differences

Experts disagree about what proportion of observed gender differences is biological—perhaps a matter of hormones, of brain structure, or of body size and musculature—and what proportion is environmental—perhaps embedded in centuries of cultural history or in the immediate, explicit home training each child receives (Beal, 1994). One reason for their disagreement is that the topic is so vast, individual experiences so varied, and the research so various that firm conclusions are difficult to reach. To develop a framework for analyzing the conflicting evidence, we need a theory. Fortunately, we have five theories, first described in Chapter 2.

Psychoanalytic Theory

Freud (1938) called the period from about age 3 to 6 the **phallic stage,** because he believed its central focus is the *phallus,* or penis. At about 3 or 4 years of age, said Freud, the process of maturation makes a boy aware of his male sexual organ. He begins to masturbate, to fear castration, and to develop sexual feelings toward his mother. These feelings make him jealous of his father—so jealous, according to Freud, that every son secretly wants to replace his dad. Freud called this the **Oedipus complex,** after Oedipus, son of a king in Greek mythology. Abandoned as an infant and raised in a distant kingdom, Oedipus later returned to his birthplace and, not realizing who they were, killed his own father and married his mother. When he discovered what he had done (after disaster struck the entire kingdom), he blinded himself in a spasm of guilt.

Freud believed that this ancient story still echoes through history because every man feels horribly guilty for the incestuous and murderous impulses that were buried in his youthful unconscious mind. Boys fear that their fathers will inflict terrible punishment if this evil secret is ever discovered, and therefore they hide their feelings, even from themselves. Specifically, boys cope with their guilt and fear through **identification,** a defense mechanism that allows a person to ally him- or herself with another person by symbolically taking on that person's behavior and attitudes. Since they cannot replace their fathers, young boys strive to become them, copying their fathers' masculine mannerisms, opinions, and actions.

Boys also develop, again in self-defense, a powerful conscience, called the **superego,** that is quick to judge and punish "the bad guys." According to Freud's

Response for Parents (from page 315): The worst time to spank a child is when you are angry, because you might seriously hurt the child and because the child will associate anger with violence and may follow your example. Better to learn to control your anger and develop other strategies for disciplining your child or preventing him or her from misbehaving in the first place.

phallic stage Freud's term for the third stage of psychosexual development, which occurs in early childhood and in which the penis becomes the focus of psychological concern as well as physiological pleasure.

Oedipus complex In the phallic stage of psychosexual development, the sexual desire that boys have for their mothers and the related hostility that they have toward their fathers.

identification A defense mechanism that lets a person symbolically take on the behaviors and attitudes of someone more powerful than him- or herself.

superego In psychoanalytic theory, the part of the personality that is self-critical and judgmental and that internalizes the moral standards set by parents and society.

theory, a young boy's fascination with superheroes, guns, kung fu, and the like comes directly from his unconscious urges to kill his father. An adult man's obsession with crime and punishment might be a product of an imperfectly resolved phallic stage. In this perspective, homosexuality, either overt or latent, is also evidence of a poorly managed phallic stage, as is homophobia.

Freud offered two overlapping descriptions of the phallic stage in girls. One form, the **Electra complex** (also named after a figure in classical mythology), is similar to the Oedipus complex: The little girl wants to eliminate her mother and become intimate with her father. In the other version, the little girl becomes jealous of boys because they have penises, an emotion Freud called *penis envy*. The girl blames her mother for this "incompleteness" and decides that the next best thing to having a penis is to become sexually attractive so that someone who does have a penis—preferably her father—will love her (Freud, 1933/1965). Her *identification* is with women her father finds attractive; her superego strives to avoid his disapproval.

Thus, the origins and consequences of the phallic stage are basically the same for girls as for boys. Biological impulses within a family context first produce lust and anger and then give rise to guilt and fear. By the end of the play years, these emotions have caused the development of a strict superego that mandates gender-appropriate behavior and harsh punishment for those who do not abide by the code. No wonder, then, that 5-year-olds seem obsessed by gender appropriateness; this is their best defense against unconscious urges.

Other psychoanalytic theorists agree that male–female distinctions are important to the young child's psychic development, although many disagree about the specifics.

Electra complex In the phallic stage of psychosexual development, the female version of the Oedipus complex: Girls have sexual feelings for their fathers and accompanying hostility toward their mothers.

In Person

Berger and Freud

As a woman, and as the mother of four daughters, I have always regarded Freud's theory of sexual development as ridiculous, not to mention antifemale. I am not alone. Psychologists generally agree that Freud's explanation of sexual and moral development is one of the weaker parts of his theory, reflecting the values of middle-class Victorian society at the end of the nineteenth century more than any universal developmental pattern. Many female psychoanalysts (e.g., Horney, 1967; Klein, 1957; Lerner, 1978) have been particularly critical of Freud's idea of penis envy. They believe that girls envy not the male sex organ but the higher status males are generally accorded. They also suggest that boys may experience "womb envy," wishing that they could have babies and suckle them. Virtually no contemporary psychologist or psychiatrist believes that homosexual urges are caused by problems during the phallic stage.

However, my own view of Freud's theory as utter nonsense has been modified somewhat by my four daughters. Our first "Electra episode" occurred in a conversation with my eldest, Bethany, when she was about 4 years old:

Bethany: When I grow up, I'm going to marry Daddy.
Mother: But Daddy's married to me.
Bethany: That's all right. When I grow up, you'll probably be dead.
Mother: *(Determined to stick up for myself)* Daddy's older than me, so when I'm dead, he'll probably be dead, too.
Bethany: That's OK. I'll marry him when he gets born again.

At this point, I couldn't think of a good reply, especially since I had no idea where she had gotten the concept of reincarnation. Bethany saw my face fall, and she took pity on me:

Bethany: Don't worry, Mommy. After you get born again, you can be our baby.

Our second episode was also in conversation, this time with my daughter Rachel, when she was about 5:

Rachel: When I get married, I'm going to marry Daddy.
Mother: Daddy's already married to me.
Rachel: *(With the joy of having discovered a wonderful solution)* Then we can have a double wedding!

The third episode was considerably more graphic. It took the form of a "valentine" left on my husband's pillow by my daughter Elissa, who was about 8 years old at the time. It is reproduced here.

Finally, when Sarah turned 5, she also expressed the desire to marry my husband. When I told her she couldn't, because he was married to me, her response revealed one more reason why TV can be pernicious: "Oh yes, a man can have two wives. I saw it on television."

I am not the only feminist developmentalist to be taken aback by her own children's words. Nancy Datan (1986) wrote about the Oedipal conflict: "I have a son who was once five years old. From that day to this, I have never thought Freud mistaken." Obviously, these bits of "evidence" do not prove that Freud was correct. I still think he was wrong on many counts. But Freud's description of the phallic stage now seems less bizarre than it once did.

Pillow Talk Elissa placed this artwork on my husband's pillow. My pillow, beside it, had a less colorful, less elaborate note—an afterthought. It read "Dear Mom, I love you too."

Behaviorism

In contrast with psychoanalytic theorists, behaviorists believe that virtually all roles are learned and hence are the result of nurture, not nature. Therefore, to behaviorists, the gender distinctions that are so obvious by age 5 are evidence of years of ongoing reinforcement and punishment, rather than the product of any specific stage.

What evidence supports this theory? Parents, peers, and teachers all reward "gender-appropriate" more than "gender-inappropriate" behavior (Etaugh & Liss, 1992; Fagot, 1995; Ruble & Martin, 1998). Parents praise their sons for not crying when hurt, for example, but caution their daughters about the hazards of rough play. This male–female distinction seems to be more important to young boys than to older boys or to girls of any age (Banergee & Lintern, 2000). For example, in the study cited above about which sex should be allowed to play with trucks or dolls, boys were more likely to endorse exclusion than girls were (Bauer et al., 1998). Similarly, boys are criticized for being "sissies" more than girls are criticized for being "tomboys," and fathers, more than mothers, expect their daughters to be feminine and their sons to be tough. The same reinforcements and punishments occur in adulthood: A man who goes out in public wearing a skirt and lipstick is likely to be ostracized or even beaten up, particularly by other men; a woman who

Modeling Much gender-role learning happens without adult realization or intention. This father did not ask his son to pretend to fix his toy lawnmower, just as no mother asks her daughter to pretend to iron the clothes, set the table, or wear high heels. The impulse to copy obviously comes from the children—which is one of the reasons the lessons are learned so well, even when we would rather teach something else.

goes out wearing pants and no makeup is unlikely to be criticized at all and may instead be admired, particularly by other women.

Behaviorists stress that children learn about proper behavior not only through direct reinforcement (such as a gift or a word of praise) but also by observation. They model their behavior particularly after those people they perceive to be nurturing, powerful, and yet similar to themselves. For young children, those people are usually their parents. Ironically, parents of young children follow sex-stereotyped roles more than do men or women of any other life stage. This means that if boys and girls model their behavior after that of their fathers and mothers, they will act in relatively stereotypical ways. In addition, young children of either sex who have older brothers become more masculine and those who have older sisters become more feminine, just as behaviorism would predict (Rust et al., 2000).

Thus, conformity to gender expectations is still rewarded, punished, and modeled, especially for young children and especially for boys. This may explain why girls and women can aspire to male occupations but boys cannot aspire to female roles without experiencing massive disapproval, especially from other males. Note again that this gender prejudice is strongest during the play years. If a college man aspires to be a nurse or a preschool teacher, most of his classmates will respect his choice. If a 4-year-old boy wants the same thing, his peers will probably soon set him straight. As one professor reports:

> My son came home after 2 days of preschool to announce that he could not grow up to teach seminars (previously his lifelong ambition, because he knew from personal observation that everyone at seminars got to eat cookies) because only women could be teachers.
>
> *[Fagot, 1995]*

Cognitive Theory

In explaining gender identity and gender differences, cognitive theorists focus on children's understanding—on the way a child intellectually grasps a specific matter at hand. Young children, they point out, have many gender-related experiences but not much cognitive complexity. They tend to see the world in intellectually simple terms. They see male and female as complete opposites, on the basis of appearances at the moment, even when past evidence (such as the father whom they saw cleaning the living room) contradicts such a sexist assumption.

Remember that the basic tenet of cognitive theory is that a person's thinking determines how the world is perceived and how that perception is acted on. Young children's thinking about gender follows their cognitive patterns, which are static and egocentric. When personal experience is ambiguous or contradictory, young children search for the "script" they have formed describing appropriate gender behavior. For example, when researchers gave children unfamiliar, gender-neutral toys, the children first tried to figure out if the toys were for boys or for girls and then decided whether or not they personally would like to play with them (Martin et al., 1995).

Sociocultural Theory

Proponents of the sociocultural perspective note that many traditional cultures emphasize gender distinctions, and these quickly become the model for the gender patterns adopted by children. In societies where adult behavior is strictly separated by gender, girls and boys attend sex-segregated schools beginning in kindergarten, and they virtually never play together (Beal, 1994). They are also taught different skills. For instance, in rural communities throughout the world, girls tend the chickens and the younger children, while boys tend the larger animals, such as sheep, pigs, and cattle (Whiting & Edwards, 1988). As a result,

! Answer to Observational Quiz (from page 316): The most obvious ones are in appearance. The girls have longer hair, and the colors and styles of their clothes are different. Did you notice the wearing-apparel difference—that the soles of all four boys' shoes are black, whereas the girls' are white or pink? Now let's get more speculative. The girl on the left, who may need to establish her alliance with the group since she is the only one in colors a boy might wear, is looking at and talking with her cousins—a very female thing to do. In addition, the girls' facial and body expressions suggest they are much more comfortable with this close contact. In fact, the two boys on the left seem about to relieve their tension with a bout of rough-and-tumble play.

gender distinctions are clear and inflexible in the mind and behavior of both children and adults.

Sociocultural theorists point out that the particulars of gender education—such as which activities are promoted for which sex—vary by region, socio-economic status, and historical period. Nevertheless, every society has powerful values and attitudes regarding preferred behavior for men and women, and every culture teaches these to the young. After 30 years of feminism and campaigns for gender equity in North America, one might naively imagine that any remaining sex differences would be biological, not cultural. This is not true: Gender stereo-types are still omnipresent for young children. Consider Halloween dress-up, a peculiarly North American custom. Only 10 percent of children's costumes in a recent study of 469 different costumes were gender-neutral, with most of those neutral ones designed for babies. Girls were pumpkin princesses, blushing brides, and beauty queens; boys were warriors and villains of all sorts, including Hercules, Dracula, and Jack the Ripper, the serial killer. Even animal costumes were sex-specific, with girls as black cats and pink dragons, boys as lions and T-Rex dinosaurs (Nelson, 2000).

To break through the restrictiveness of cultural gender expectations and to encourage individuals to define themselves primarily as a human being, rather than as a male or female, many parents and teachers embrace the idea of an-drogyny. As a biological term, *androgyny* is defined as the presence of both male and female sexual characteristics in one person or other living thing. As developmentalists use the term, **androgyny** means a balance, within a person, of traditionally male and female psychological characteristics. To achieve an-drogyny, boys should be encouraged to be nurturant and girls to be assertive, so that with maturity and patience they will develop less restrictive and gender-bound behavior patterns.

Sociocultural theory stresses, however, that androgyny (or any other gender concept) cannot be taught to children simply through cognition or parental rein-forcement. The only way children will be truly androgynous is if their entire culture promotes such ideas and practices—something no culture has yet done. Why not? The reasons may lie buried far deeper in human nature than the politi-cal forces or social values of the moment, as epigenetic systems theory suggests.

Epigenetic Systems Theory

We saw in Chapter 2 that epigenetic systems theory contends that every aspect of human behavior, including gender attitudes and roles, is the re-sult of interaction between genes and early experience—not just for the individual but also for the species. The idea that many gender differences are genetically based is supported by recent research in neurobiology, which finds biological differences between male and female brains.

These brain differences are probably not the result of any single sex-linked gene. More likely, they appear because sex hormones pro-duced by XX (female) or XY (male) chromosomes begin to circulate in the fetal stage, affecting the development of the brain. Those hormones continue to influence brain development throughout childhood (Gaulin, 1993; Hines, 1993). The social context may then enter the picture by af-fecting the brain in ways that program proper male and female behavior.

This programming is not inevitable. Remember: Although epige-netic systems theory stresses the biological and genetic origins of behav-ior, it also stresses that the manifestations of those origins are shaped, enhanced, or halted by environmental factors. Here is one example: Infant girls seem to be genetically inclined to talk earlier than boys. However, the language areas of an infant's brain do not develop fully

Especially for Gender Idealists Suppose you want to raise an androgynous child. What would happen if you told no one your newborn's sex, dressed it in yellow and white, not pink or blue, and gave it a gender-neutral name, such as Chris or Lee?

androgyny A balance, within a person, of tradi-tionally male and female psychological characteristics.

Nature or Nurture? At first glance, the boy–girl differences seen here seem entirely cultural. The boy must have seen a fireman, and the girl a fancy lady, if not in person then on television. However, epi-genetic theory urges us to go deeper, to see if something innate is also portrayed in this photo.

SYBIL SHACKMAN

unless someone talks to the infant. Suppose a boy is an only child, raised in a household with several adult women. He may be talked to, sung to, and read to by all his devoted caregivers. He will probably develop superior verbal ability in his brain, because of the interaction between his genetic potential (which might be slightly less than that of the typical girl) and his social environment (which is much richer than that of most children of either sex). Environmental factors will have enhanced his genetic capabilities greatly.

This is not the usual scenario. In a family that includes one man, one woman, and two or more children of both sexes, language stimulation differs by sex. Since girls are more responsive to language and since mothers are usually more verbal than fathers, mother–daughter pairs typically talk most and father–son pairs, least. This will likely turn the females' slight linguistic advantage in their brain circuitry into a notably higher level of language proficiency (Leaper et al., 1998).

Conclusion: Gender and Destiny

The first and last of our five theories—psychoanalytic theory and epigenetic systems theory—emphasize the power of biology as regards gender development. A reader who is quick to form opinions might decide that the gender-based behaviors and stereotypes exhibited by young children are unchangeable. This conclusion might be reinforced by the fact that gender awareness emerges very early, by age 2, or that the play patterns and social interactions of young boys and girls differ. But the other three theories—behaviorism, cognitive theory, and sociocultural theory—all present persuasive evidence for the influence of family and culture in guiding and shaping the powerful gender patterns we see by age 5. Actually, even psychoanalytic theory and epigenetic systems theory acknowledge that some learning occurs in gender development as well. Boy–girl differences are partly innate, a matter of sex; but much is taught, a matter of gender.

Thus, our five theories, collectively, have led to at least two conclusions and one critical question.

■ Gender differences are biological, not merely cultural: The biological foundation for gender differences includes hormonal influences on the brain as well as on bodily organs.
■ Biology is not destiny: Children are shaped by their experiences.

This raises the question: What gender patterns should children learn, ideally? Answers vary. In those cultures and families that encourage each child to develop his or her own inclinations, many children grow up to choose gender-based behaviors, express emotions, and develop talents that would be taboo—or even punished—in cultures that adhere to strict gender guidelines. Strict societies and families encourage gender separation, widening whatever innate sex distinctions there may be. In those societies, adults fall naturally into two worlds, one designed for men and one for women.

To what extent do you want children to meet gender expectations, and to what extent do you want them to be androgynous? Is harm done to individuals' development by requiring them to adhere to social guidelines and thereby to change their natural orientation, so that they become either more or less gender-bound than they might naturally be?

If you agree that the theories we have examined have at least some merit, you must conclude that both nature and nurture influence gender behaviors. But theories don't answer questions about moral and social values. Perhaps that is why various cultures and individuals—and the theories themselves—come to such different conclusions about gender.

Response for Gender Idealists (from page 321): Since babies are raised by a society and community as well as by the parents, and since at least some gender differences are biological, this attempt at androgyny would not succeed. First, other interested parties would decide for themselves that the child was male or female. Second, the child would sooner or later develop gender-specific play patterns, guided by the other boys or girls.

SUMMARY

Of course, the same can be said about the proper expression of aggression, or the preferred parenting style, or the degree of emotional regulation that should be evident in a person. The research describes what is, and what can develop, during early childhood. Each reader, each family, each culture decides what should be.

Emotional Development

1. Regulation of emotions is crucial during the play years when children learn emotional control. Both externalizing and internalizing problems can be seen as indications of inadequate self-control and self-expression, because poorly regulated emotions can make a child explosively angry or painfully withdrawn.

2. Emotional regulation is made possible by brain maturation, particularly of the prefrontal cortex. Too many stressful experiences in infancy affect the production of stress hormones, impeding normal development. A final biological influence is genetic, with emotional regulation possibly impeded by inherited exuberance or inhibition.

3. A child's experiences with caregivers also affect the development of emotional control. If infants are emotionally deprived, particularly if they are not comforted and cuddled, they may have difficulty regulating their emotions later on. Further, children's current experiences—especially if their primary caregiver is depressed—affect their current emotional development.

4. Many children during the play years are fearful. They learn from their parents and peers to control their fears. Extreme, irrational fears are phobias, which result from both genetic influence and parental example.

Theories of Emotions

5. The play years include the crisis of initiative versus guilt, Erikson's name for the psychosocial crisis that results from the impulse to begin and complete various projects. Children normally develop pride and self-esteem; if this stage of development does not go well and the child does not have normal feelings of pride, the child internalizes feelings of guilt.

6. Emotional intelligence is the ability to understand one's own feelings and goals, as well as the ability to interpret and adjust to the emotions of others. Early childhood is a crucial period for the development of this kind of intelligence.

Prosocial and Antisocial Behavior

7. Children develop patterns of interaction with peers. Children are generally prosocial, in that they often share with and care for others. Some children are antisocial, deliberately hurting others. Aggression is the most common childhood expression of antisocial behavior, which can become criminal behavior later on if it is not regulated.

8. Aggression takes many forms in early childhood. Instrumental aggression is the most common, as children fight over toys and privileges. Reactive aggression is also common. More worrisome are relational and bullying aggression, which can become very hurtful to both aggressor and victim if the pattern persists.

9. Children learn to control their emotions, particularly their antisocial ones, through play with peers. Cooperation gradually develops through rough-and-tumble and sociodramatic play, both of which require adjustment to the needs and imaginations of one's playmates.

10. Television promotes aggression and takes time from play with peers. The themes and characters of television programs tend to reflect sexism, racism, and ageism. Video games are probably even worse, although longitudinal, controlled research is not complete. The long-term consequences of watching TV seem to depend more on the content of the programs than on the mere fact of watching.

Parenting Patterns

11. Parents are very influential in the development of young children's behavior. Three classic styles of parenting have been identified: authoritarian, permissive, and authoritative. Generally, regardless of parenting styles, parents who express warmth and who set guidelines raise children who become better achievers, with more self-control.

12. Punishment should fit not only the age and temperament of the child but also the culture. Generally, developmentalists are concerned that any physical punishment risks increasing reactive and bully aggression in the child. Parental conversations with the child about misbehavior tend to promote prosocial behavior.

Boy or Girl: So What?

13. Even 2-year-olds correctly use sex-specific labels, such as boy and girl, mommy and daddy. During early childhood, children become more aware of gender differences in clothes, toys, future careers, and playmates, becoming quite stereotyped by age 6. Although sex differences are minimal in the play years, gender distinctions are of major importance to the children themselves.

14. Each major theory has a perspective on these expressed gender distinctions. Freud emphasized that children are attracted to the opposite-sex parent and eventually seek to align themselves with the same-sex parent.

7

15. Behaviorists hold that gender-related behaviors are learned through reinforcement and punishment (especially for males) and social modeling. A young child learns these primarily from his or her parents. Cognitive theorists note that simplistic preoperational thinking leads to gender stereotypes, and sociocultural theorists point to the many male–female distinctions apparent in every society.

16. Gender differences are partly the result of hormones affecting brain formation in the months before and after birth. This epigenetic systems explanation makes it clear that gender differences are not determined by either biology or culture, but are affected by both.

17. Gender and sex are both cultural and biological in origin and function. Individuals and societies must decide whether these distinctions are harmful and restrictive or natural and necessary.

KEY TERMS

emotional regulation (p. 296)
externalizing problems (p. 296)
internalizing problems (p. 296)
phobia (p. 298)
self-concept (p. 299)
self-esteem (p. 299)
initiative versus guilt (p. 301)
emotional intelligence (p. 301)
peers (p. 302)

prosocial (p. 302)
antisocial (p. 302)
empathy (p. 303)
aggression (p. 303)
instrumental aggression (p. 304)
reactive aggression (p. 304)
relational aggression (p. 304)
bullying aggression (p. 304)

rough-and-tumble play (p. 305)
sociodramatic play (p. 306)
authoritarian parenting (p. 310)
permissive parenting (p. 310)
authoritative parenting (p. 310)
neglectful parenting (p. 311)
indulgent parenting (p. 311)
time-out (p. 313)

sex differences (p. 315)
gender differences (p. 315)
phallic stage (p. 317)
Oedipus complex (p. 317)
identification (p. 317)
superego (p. 317)
Electra complex (p. 318)
androgyny (p. 321)

KEY QUESTIONS

1. Why is it important for children to learn to regulate their emotions?

2. How do biological factors influence children's emotional regulation?

3. How might a child develop pride and initiative?

4. What does research on adopted children suggest about the role of parents in emotional regulation?

5. How does a child's expression of aggression typically change with age?

6. What is the difference between instrumental aggression and relational aggression?

7. How do other children help a child learn to regulate emotions?

8. How can an adult distinguish rough-and-tumble play from fighting?

9. What relationship is there between Parten's five types of social play and sociodramatic play?

10. How does parent–child communication differ in Baumrind's three styles of parenting?

11. What styles of parenting are always destructive of child development?

12. What do developmentalists believe about the long-term impact of spanking?

13. What are the sex and gender differences among young children?

14. According to Freud, how does the development of boys and girls differ?

15. What are the similarities between behaviorism and the sociocultural perspective on early gender differences?

16. In what ways does the epigenetic systems perspective differ from the other four theories?

17. Is true androgyny possible? Why or why not?

BIOSOCIAL

Brain and Nervous System The brain continues to develop, attaining 90 percent of its adult weight by the time the child is 5 years old. Both the proliferation of neural pathways and myelination continue. Coordination between the two halves and the various areas of the brain increases, allowing the child to settle down and concentrate when necessary, and to use various parts of the body in harmony. Gross motor skills, such as running and jumping, improve dramatically. Fine motor skills, such as writing and drawing, develop more slowly.

Maltreatment Child abuse and neglect, potential problems at every age, are particularly likely in homes with many children and few personal or community resources. Recognition of the problem has improved, but treatment is still uneven. Distinguishing the ongoing problems of a family that needs support, and the immediate danger for a child who needs to be removed and placed in foster care, is critical for long-term development. Planning a permanent solution for a maltreated child is much better than repeatedly moving the child from one house to another.

COGNITIVE

Cognitive Skills Children think in magical ways, self-centered yet aware of others. Many cognitive abilities, including some related to number and memory, become more mature, if the social context is supportive. Children begin to develop a theory of mind, in which they take into account the ideas and emotions of others. Social interaction, particularly in the form of guided participation, is of help in this cognitive advancement. At the same time, however, children's thinking can be quite illogical and egocentric.

Language Language abilities develop rapidly; by the age of 6, the average child knows 10,000 words and demonstrates extensive grammatical knowledge. Children also learn to adjust their communication to their audience, and use language to help themselves learn. Preschool education helps children develop language and express themselves, as well as prepares them for later education and adult life. Long-term benefits are apparent, especially for children with stressful home lives.

PSYCHOSOCIAL

Emotions and Personality Development Self-concept emerges, as does the ability to regulate emotions. Children boldly initiate new activities, especially if they are praised for their endeavors.

Play Children engage in play that helps them master physical and intellectual skills and that teaches or enhances social roles. As their social and cognitive skills develop, children engage in ever more complex and imaginative types of play, sometimes by themselves and, increasingly, with others.

Parent–Child Interaction Some parenting styles are more effective than others in encouraging the child to develop autonomy and self-control. Those that are most responsive to the child, with much communication, seem to do best, although guidance is needed and too much permissiveness is destructive. Parenting styles are influenced by cultural and community standards, and the authoritative style is usually—but not always—best.

Gender Roles Increasingly, children develop stereotypic concepts of sex differences in appearance and gender differences in behavior. The precise roles of nature and nurture in this process are unclear, but both of these forces are obviously involved.

SHARON SCHOOL DISTRICT

Part IV

f someone asked you to pick the best years of the entire life span, you might choose the years from about 6 to 11 and defend your choice persuasively. Physical development is usually almost problem-free, making it easy to master dozens of new skills. With regard to cognitive development, most children are able to learn quickly and think logically, provided the topic is not too abstract. Moreover, they are usually eager to learn, mastering new concepts, new vocabulary, and new skills with a combination of enthusiasm, perseverance, and curiosity that makes them a joy to teach. Indeed, we call these the "school years" because every culture worldwide takes advantage of the fact that children in these years are especially ready and eager to learn.

Finally, the social world of middle childhood seems perfect: Most school-age children think their parents are helpful, their teachers fair, and their friends loyal. The child's moral reasoning and behavior have reached that state where right seems clearly distinguished from wrong, without the ambiguities and conflicts that complicate morality during adolescence. As you will see, however, not every child escapes middle childhood unscathed.

The next three chapters celebrate the joys, and commemorate the occasional tragedies, of middle childhood.

The School Years

Chapter Eleven

The School Years:
Biosocial Development

Context changes. The most important aspect of development during the school years is that the social context changes and expands as children enter wider educational and cultural communities. No longer do children depend on their families to provide all forms of physical maintenance—that is, to clothe, feed, and clean them—or to send or not send them to a preschool. By age 6 or 7, self-care (dressing, eating, bathing) is taken for granted, and school attendance is mandated, with a state-approved curriculum and many schoolmates.

Of course, children still depend on their families in many other ways, especially emotionally, as detailed in Chapter 13. Further, the family influences the school-age child's every biosocial attribute, as this chapter explains. But a new measure of independence allows the child to look beyond the family and to rely on teachers and peers as sources of pride, achievement, and, above all, comparison. Perhaps because their context expands or because their maturing prefrontal cortex makes analysis and comparison possible, school-age children become keenly aware of differences among themselves. Almost every child sometimes feels odd, lonely, isolated, inadequate, or, to use Erikson's word, inferior.

Adults also notice differences, clustering children of a certain type together—by age, ethnicity, intelligence, or disability. Some schools even "track" children, so that, for example, a given fourth grade class is made up entirely of children of a certain maturity and reading level. This chapter describes biosocial development, including similarities among all school-age children but also significant differences—in size, in health, in psychopathology. As you learn more about differences, be careful: Children who are designated "special" are not so different from those designated "normal," or average in every aspect of growth—and no child is completely normal. Once we look closely at real children, it becomes obvious that every child has unique strengths and liabilities. Diversity splinters into further diversities; multiculturalism becomes multi-multi-multi-cultural. To highlight this point, we begin with two children who seem at first to belong in the same category, Mexican-Americans living in Southern California. Both are now adolescents, old enough to have some perspective on their elementary school years.

In Person

Two Children of Mexican Heritage in California

In the following accounts, Yolanda Piedra and Paul Chavez reflect on their first years in the United States.

Yolanda:

When I got here [from Mexico at age 7], I didn't want to stay here, 'cause I didn't like the school. And after a little while, in third grade, I started getting the hint of it and everything and I tried real hard in it. I really got along with the teachers . . . they would start talking to me, or they kinda like pulled me up some grades, or moved me to other classes, or took me somewhere. And they were always congratulating me.

Actually, there's one friend of mine . . . she's been with me since first grade until eighth grade, right now. And she's always been with me, in bad or good things, all the time. She's always telling me, "Keep on going and your dreams are gonna come true."

[Interviewer: What do you remember about Cinco de Mayo?]

That's my favorite month, 'cause I like dancing. And in elementary school they had these kinds of dances, and I was always in it . . .

Sometimes you get all tangled up with the grades or school or the teachers, 'cause you don't understand them. But you have to get along with them and you have to work for it. So actually, I feel good about it because I like working, making my mind work.

[Interviewer: Is your mother involved in school?]

No, first of all, 'cause she understands English, but she's just embarrassed, shy to talk. . . . And 'cause she's always busy. . . . My mom says that they want me to go to school. That way, I won't be stuck with a job like them. They want me to go on, try my best to get something I want. . . .

I see some other kids that they say, like they'd say they're Colombian or something. They try to make themselves look cool in front of everybody. I just say what I am and I feel proud of myself . . . it's okay for me being born over there 'cause I feel proud of myself. I feel proud of my culture.

[quoted in Nieto, 2000]

Paul:

I grew up . . . ditching school, just getting in trouble, trying to make a dollar, that's it, you know? Just go to school, steal from the store, and go sell candies at school. And that's what I was doing in the third or fourth grade. . . . I was always getting in the principal's office, suspended, kicked out, everything starting from the third grade.

My fifth grade teacher, Ms. Nelson . . . she put me in a play and that like tripped me out. Like why do you want me in a play? Me, I'm just a mess-up. Still, you know, she put me in a play. And in the fifth grade, I think that was the best year out of the whole six years. I learned a lot about the Revolutionary War. . . . Had good friends. . . . We had a project we were involved in. Ms. Nelson . . . just involved everyone. We made books, this and that. And I used to write, and wrote two, three books. Was in a book fair. . . . She got real deep into

you. Just, you know, "Come on now, you can do it." That was a good year for me, fifth grade.

You need to educate your mind . . . somebody gets born and throw 'em into the world, you know, they're not gonna make it. You get someone, you born 'em, you raise 'em and encourage 'em, then they're gonna make it.

. . . My mom, I wouldn't change nothing, nothing. My dad, I would . . . just have him be there for me when I was younger. I could have turned out different if he was there.

[Interviewer: Is your mother involved in school?]

My mom, she's not really. . . . She's too busy doing her own thing. She gets out of school, makes dinner, cleans the house, goes to church, comes home, irons for my two sisters. . . .

I think right now about going Christian, right? Just going Christian, trying to do good, you know? Stay away from drugs, everything. And every time it seems like I think about that, I think about the homeboys. And it's a trip because a lot of the homeboys are my family too, you know? . . .

Let's say I'm Chicano and dress like a gang member. They're gonna look at you like one of these crazy kids, you know, Mexican kid . . . I don't really know if it's 'cause I'm Brown or it's 'cause of my gang tattoo, so I can't really pinpoint. But for me, as far as me being a Chicano, it's prideful, it's pride of your race, of what you are.

[quoted in Nieto, 2000]

Surely you have noticed differences between these two children. In the third grade Paul considered himself "just a mess-up," whereas Yolanda was beginning to get "the hint of it." Yolanda's friend encouraged her to "keep on going," whereas Paul's friends kept him from "going Christian." When we look at them as individuals, their differences seem to override their shared heritage.

Despite the many differences between Yolanda and Paul, and the differences among all the 15 million other children under age 20 of Hispanic heritage living in the United States, and the differences among the 600 million school-age children in the world (U.S. Bureau of the Census, 2001), development between the ages of 7 and 11 follows universal patterns. All these children grow in weight and height, and they become more independent and competent. As the author who gathered these interviews points out, most school-age children are proud of their ethnic backgrounds (as both Yolanda and Paul are), most remember at least one teacher fondly, most are encouraged by their parents to get an education, and all consider friends important (Nieto, 2000). Many also feel their parents do not really understand school ("too busy"). Physical discipline and mastery (in sports of many kinds and, for Yolanda and Paul, dancing and acting) contribute to self-image and cognition as well as to growth.

A paradox is obvious here: Each child is unique and all children are similar. Now we begin to examine some of the particulars of biosocial development during the school years.

A Healthy Time

In general, genetic and developmental factors are protective, making children age 7 to 11 the healthiest group of humans. They are least likely to die or become seriously ill or injured (see Figure 11.1). Even unintended injuries and serious abuse, which are the leading causes of morbidity and mortality during childhood, occur less often from 7 to 11 than before or after those years. (These topics were first discussed in Chapter 8.)

Therefore, during this period, called **middle childhood** because it is after early childhood and before early adolescence, most parents can relax a little. School-age children not only stay healthy and avoid dangers but they are also capable of self-care: getting dressed, walking to school, brushing their teeth, washing up, and amusing themselves without parental assistance or supervision. In fact, most prefer playing apart from adults, especially when they are with their friends. (No adult ever noticed that Paul sold stolen candy.) Middle childhood is usually a happy, easy time.

middle childhood The period from age 7 to 11.

Typical Size and Shape

Children grow more slowly from age 7 to 11 than they did a few years earlier or than they will a few years later. "More slowly" refers to the *rate of increase,* because children actually gain at least as much weight each school year as they did at age 3 or 4. The proportional gain is less, however, and that makes all the difference; for example, a typical 8-year-old already weighs 55 pounds (25 kilograms), so a gain of 5 pounds is taken in stride.

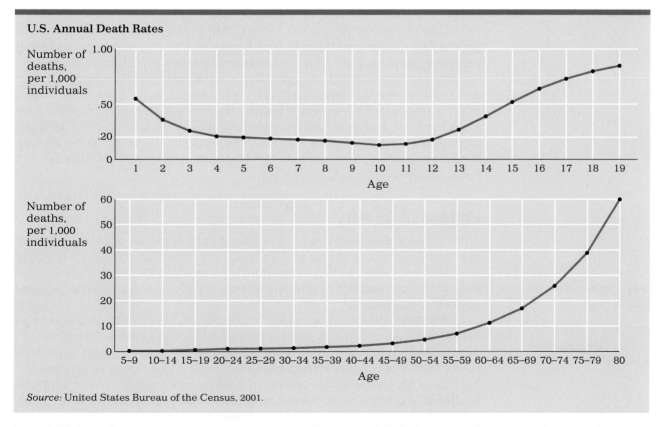

Source: United States Bureau of the Census, 2001.

FIGURE 11.1 **Death at an Early Age? Almost Never!** Schoolchildren are remarkably hardy, as measured in many ways. These charts show that death rates for 7- to 11-year-olds are lower than those for children under 7 or over 11, 15 times lower than their parents' rates, and 1,000 times lower than their grandparents' rates.

All The Same These boys are all friends in the third grade, clowning in response to the camera—as school-age boys like to do. Outsiders might notice the varied growth rates and genetic differences, but the boys themselves are more aware of what they have in common.

Growth varies, depending on genes, gender, and nutrition. Generally, each year from age 7 to 11, well-nourished children gain 5 to 7 pounds (about 3 kilograms) and at least 2 inches (almost 6 centimeters); by age 10, they weigh about 70 pounds (32 kilograms) and are 4½ feet (1.37 meters) tall. (See Appendix A, pages A–6 and A–7, for specifics.) Obviously, children who are malnourished or undernourished gain less weight, as we saw in Chapter 8. Bear in mind that undernutrition does not disappear with age or occur only in poor countries. For instance, one study of low-income schoolchildren in Philadelphia and Baltimore found that 8 percent were often hungry, which correlated not only with less growth and poorer health but also with poor functioning in school—including excessive absences, inattention, and emotional outbursts (Murphy et al., 2001).

Typically, however, school-age children eat enough food, becoming stronger and healthier. They get fewer high fevers, persistent colds, or bumps and bruises than they did earlier. They seem to become slimmer as their height increases, their limbs lengthen, and their body proportions change. Muscles become stronger as well. Thus, the average 10-year-old throws a ball twice as far as the average 6-year-old. Lung capacity expands, so with each passing year children can run faster and exercise longer.

Childhood Obesity

There is one major exception to this generally placid picture of children's gradual growth: obesity or excess body fat sufficient to put the individual's health at risk. More precisely, to be **overweight** is to be up to 20 percent above ideal weight for one's age and height, and **obesity** involves being 20 percent or more above this benchmark.

Childhood obesity is increasing in the United States (U.S. Department of Health and Human Services, 2000). Experts believe that between 20 and 30 percent of North American children are obese, a rate that has doubled since 1980 (Dietz, 1999). For children, obesity reduces exercise and increases blood pressure; both these developments are associated with serious health problems in middle adulthood, including heart disease, stroke, and diabetes (Freedman et al., 1999). Although the causes of obesity predate these years and the consequences extend throughout life, obesity is discussed here primarily because anything that makes a child look different (from freckles to feet, from eyeglasses to larger body size) takes a particularly heavy social and emotional toll during the school years.

overweight A body weight that is up to 20 percent above the weight that is considered ideal for the person's age and height.

obesity A body weight that is 20 percent or more above the weight that is considered ideal for the person's age and height.

The significance of being overweight or obese has changed over time. For most of history, starvation was a common threat to survival. A layer of body fat to protect against famine signified health, wealth, and high status. Good fathers were "breadwinners" who "brought home the bacon"; good mothers prepared abundant "home cooking" for the family; and good children were fat and happy, rewarded for cleaning their plates, punished by not getting dessert or being sent to bed without any supper.

It is not surprising, then, that people from nations where starvation was prevalent continue customs that once protected against early death. For example, in the United States, the most recent immigrants from Mexico, as a group, have the highest rate of obesity; Hispanic children are twice as likely as non-Hispanic white children to be overweight. In many other ways, immigrant children born in Mexico are healthier than their U.S.-born peers; but in childhood diet, they are worse off (Flores & Zambrana, 2001). The United Nations now considers obesity a public health problem of "epidemic" proportions in many regions, including North America (World Health Organization, 1998).

There are many reasons why one child might be heavier than another. Genetic differences are part of the explanation, including differences in genes that affect activity level, taste preferences, body type, and metabolism. Adopted children whose biological parents were obese are more often overweight (no matter what the weight of their adoptive parents) than other adoptees (Grilo & Pogue-Geile, 1991).

However, genes never act in isolation, and genes change very little from one generation to the next. Environmental factors, including the following, are the major reasons for the recent increase in childhood obesity (Robinson & Killen, 2001):

Family Favorites School-age children are primed to learn whatever their parents value, whether it be playing sports, arguing, reading, cooking, or eating. Rosa's mother is teaching her how to follow a recipe—a very useful skill. She may be teaching some other, less beneficial behaviors as well.

- *Lack of exercise.* The body is a machine that uses energy every moment, and the balance between the calories spent in activity and the calories consumed determines weight gain or loss. In childhood, *nature* predisposes most children to be very active but contemporary *nurture* urges them to "sit down and be quiet." City and suburban children get few chances to run around outdoors in unrestricted exploration, and in school, physical education has often been reduced to waiting your turn in the gym.
- *Poor-quality food.* The foods advertised on children's television, sold in school vending machines, and bought by children at fast-food restaurants are high in fat and sugar and low in nutrition. Such products are profitable because humans have evolved a preference for high-calorie foods that prevent starvation. But in the twenty-first century, children who eat whatever they want, whenever they want, are almost always unhealthy.
- *Television watching.* How much children watch television correlates with how much they weigh (Anderson et al., 2001). Children move less and snack more when they watch TV. Even worse, one study found that small children go into a kind of trance when they watch television: Metabolism (basically, the rate at which the body burns calories) drops by 12 percent in most children and by 16 percent in obese children (Klesges, 1993).
- *Cultural values.* Every holiday is celebrated with unhealthy food, from Christmas candy to Hanukkah gelt, from birthday cakes to Thanksgiving pies.

Crash diets are not the answer, for several reasons. One is that rapid weight loss at any age triggers physiological changes that evolved to prevent starvation: With dieting, appetite increases and metabolism decreases until the previous weight is reached. Further, severe diets impede growth and harm health during childhood.

Bribes and ultimatums are no good, either. Comments like "You can't have dessert until you eat your broccoli" and "Aren't you ashamed of how fat you are?" reinforce the child's dislike of healthy foods, enhance the attractiveness of

Especially for Teachers: A child in your class is overweight, but you are hesitant to say anything to the parents, who are also overweight, because you do not want to insult them. What should you do?

Will She Drink Her Milk? The first word many American children read is "McDonald's," and they all recognize the golden arches. Fast food is part of every family's diet, and that is one reason the rate of obesity has doubled in every age group in the United States since 1980. Even if the girl at left stops playing with her straw and drinks the milk, she is learning that soda and French fries are desirable food choices.

Response for Teachers (from page 333): Speak to the parents, not accusingly (because you know that genes and culture have a major influence on body weight), but helpfully, to alert them to a potential social and health problem. Most parents are very concerned about their child's well-being and will be glad to work with you to improve the child's snacks and exercise. If they are overweight themselves, they will probably appreciate your concern about their child.

sweets, and push the child toward overeating for emotional comfort. Even worse, children who become obsessed with body size become adolescents with eating disorders, including bulimia and anorexia nervosa, as will be discussed in Chapter 14 (Fisher & Birch, 2001).

The best way to get obese children to slim down is to increase their physical activity (Dietz, 1995). However, since overweight children tend to move more slowly and awkwardly than other children, they are not often selected for teams, invited to join backyard games, or inclined to exercise on their own. Adults need to encourage overweight children by exercising with them, especially in activities that can be done at any size, such as walking, bicycling, and swimming.

Proper health habits can counter even the genetic tendency toward obesity. As Figure 11.2 indicates, by age 10, the child's own weight is much more critical than his or her genes in determining whether that child will become an overweight adult (Whitaker et al., 1997).

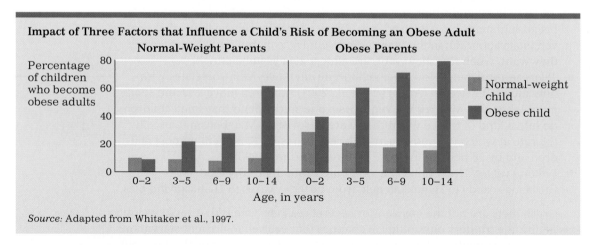

Source: Adapted from Whitaker et al., 1997.

FIGURE 11.2 Predicting Obesity This graph compares three risk factors for adult obesity: the child's age, the child's weight, and the parents' weight. For young children, the parents' weight—normal or obese—is the biggest risk factor; for older children, a child's own weight is the strongest predictor.

? *Observational Quiz* (see answer, page 336): Is it possible for a 6- to 9-year-old whose parents are of normal weight to be obese in adulthood?

Chronic Illness

We noted earlier that middle childhood is generally a healthy time. In fact, it is healthier now in every nation of the world than it was just 30 years ago. Chronic sore throats are uncommon, one reason that tonsillectomy—a type of surgery "practically every child" experienced as recently as 1980 (Larson, 1990)—is relatively rare today. Hearing impairments and anemia are only half as common as they were, and fewer than 200 children in the United States were diagnosed with AIDS in 2001, down from 1,000 in 1992. Even in Africa, where inadequate medical care and scarce drugs still mean that almost a million HIV-positive infants are born each year, most die before age 5. Starvation and infectious diseases and even war also target the youngest children. Thus, worldwide, the period from 7 to 11 is the healthiest time of life.

However, in middle childhood children are more aware of one another's, and their own, minor physical imperfections. This means that even wearing glasses, walking with a limp, or blowing one's nose too often makes children very self-conscious. In addition, some conditions are more likely to emerge during the school years than earlier, including Tourette's syndrome (uncontrollable noises or movements), stuttering, and some allergies. Worst of all is anything that prevents normal play or school attendance. In fact, school absence and lateness are among the strongest correlates of all the problems of childhood, from low achievement to sexual abuse, from being left back to breaking the law. The most common medical problem that causes absences from school is childhood asthma.

Already Too Late A nurse uses an inhaler to open a young asthma patient's airways. Such hospital care is tertiary prevention, which will avoid even more serious consequences; but it represents a failure of primary and secondary prevention.

Asthma on the Rise

Asthma is a chronic inflammatory disorder of the airways that affects between 10 and 20 percent of school-age children in North America. It is three times as common as it was only 20 years ago, and its incidence is expected to double again by the year 2020 (Pew Environmental Health Commission, 2000). For almost half of them, severe symptoms disappear by late adolescence (Clark & Rees, 1996).

asthma A chronic inflammatory disorder of the airways.

Many researchers are studying the causes of asthma. Among these are the following:

- Genes on chromosomes 2, 11, 12, 13, and 21.
- Infections that once protected against asthma but now rarely occur. (Children who never experience viral infections are more likely to develop asthma.)
- Exposure to allergens such as pet hair, dust mites, cockroaches, and air pollution.

Actually, allergens are triggers, not causes. Indeed, Eastern European nations have very heavy pollution but much less asthma, and 100 years ago most families had pets but asthma was rare (Cookson & Moffat, 1997). However, for those who are vulnerable, several aspects of modern life—carpeted floors, more bedding, dogs and cats living inside the house, airtight windows, less outdoor play, and urbanization (which crowds people together in buildings where cockroaches multiply)—increase the risk (Carpenter, 1999).

Prevention of Chronic Illness

Let us apply to chronic illness our understanding of the three levels of prevention that we discussed in Chapter 8. Tertiary prevention, which is the prevention of serious consequences once an ailment is recognized, occurs every day in physicians' offices and hospital emergency rooms. For asthma, prompt use of injections, inhalers, and pills that are prescribed and monitored by specialists markedly reduces the rate of acute wheezing and overnight hospitalizations. A clinical pathways approach (following a standard procedure for testing and treating in the hospital) reduces hospital stays for acute asthma attacks (Glauber et al., 2001). Unfortunately, less than half the asthmatic children in the United States receive adequate tertiary prevention; those from Spanish-speaking homes are particularly likely to get inadequate care (Halterman et al., 2000). Indeed, for every chronic illness, good medical care is not always available to school-age children in the United States. Overall, one-third have no private health insurance; the proportion rises to more than half for African-American and Hispanic 6- to 11-year-olds (U.S. Department of Health and Human Services, 2000).

Secondary prevention begins earlier. If there is a genetic history of allergies, ridding the house of allergens *before* the disease appears and breast-feeding newborns cut the rate of asthma in half (Gdalevich et al., 2001). Breast-feeding and immunizations also reduce the risk of many other diseases.

Primary prevention is the best approach of all to asthma and every other childhood disease. Proper ventilation of schools and homes, decreased pollution, eradication of cockroaches, and safe outdoor play spaces would make life and health better for school-age children, especially those who might become asthmatic.

The benefit of primary prevention was demonstrated by a natural experiment during the Summer Olympics in Atlanta, Georgia. The city imposed traffic restrictions, encouraged carpooling, and offered free mass transit for 17 days in order to ease the movement of athletes and spectators. An unexpected consequence was a sudden dip in the incidence of acute asthma. Compared to four weeks earlier and four weeks later, Medicare asthma treatments decreased by 42 percent and HMO asthma claims were down 44 percent (Friedman et al., 2001). Visits to hospital emergency rooms for asthma treatment also declined, even though hospitals and insurance agencies reported no change in the frequency of other acute-care incidents involving children (injuries, heart ailments, accidental poisoning, etc.).

Development of Motor Skills

Partly because children grow more slowly during middle childhood, many become quite skilled at controlling their own bodies. School-age children can master almost any basic skill, sometimes with impressive grace and precision, as long as it doesn't require too much strength or split-second judgment of speed and distance.

Every motor skill involves several abilities, some requiring a certain body size and level of brain maturation. From a developmental perspective, age is crucial. For instance, **reaction time** (the length of time it takes a person to respond to a particular stimulus) is a consequence of brain maturation, especially ongoing myelination. Because of neurological development, hand–eye coordination, balance, and judgment of movement (including time, distance, and trajectory) continue to develop during the school years, and thus 12-year-olds are better in all of these abilities than 9-year-olds, who in turn are better than 6-year-olds. Reaction time shortens with each year until about age 16; then it stabilizes and, beginning at about age 20, slows down again, so that older adults (aged 60–81) are about as quick as 8-year-olds (Williams et al., 1999). Before describing in more detail the brain maturation that underlies motor skills, we examine variations in gender, culture, and genes.

! Answer to Observational Quiz (from page 334): Yes, but the odds of being an obese adult increase if the 6- to 9-year-old is already obese. In adulthood, 28 percent of children in this age group are obese, compared to only 8 percent of the ones whose weight was normal at ages 6 to 9. The other side of the coin is that most 6- to 9-year-olds grow up to be normal-weight adults. Specifically, as the graph shows, if they have normal-weight parents, 72 percent of the obese children in this age group become normal-weight adults, as do 92 percent of the normal-weight children.

reaction time The length of time it takes a person to respond to a particular stimulus.

The Influence of Gender and Culture

Boys and girls are just about equal in their overall physical abilities, although boys tend to have greater upper-arm strength and girls to have greater flexibility. Consequently, although some sports, such as soccer, are gender-neutral, boys have the advantage in baseball and girls have the edge in gymnastics. However, even for these physical activities during middle childhood, biological differences between the sexes are minimal: Boys can do cartwheels, and girls can hit home runs. The fact that they usually don't is not because they are unable to learn but because the social setting discourages them.

Expertise in many areas, athletic prowess among them, depends on cultural influences that are rarely the same for both sexes. That is why certain activities (gross motor ones, as well as fine motor ones) are favored by girls (jump rope, knitting, penmanship) and others (football, video games, hammering) are favored by boys, even though both sexes are equally endowed. Beginning at about age 4, and increasingly until about age 12, gender differences in play patterns are dramatic. Boys tend to choose to play with other boys in relatively large groups (five or more) in organized games that encourage conflict, rivalry, and gross motor skills. Girls form smaller, more intimate groups, where competition is discouraged and fine motor skills are practiced (Maccoby, 2002).

National policies also affect children's motor-skill development. For example, the average schoolchild in France or Switzerland gets three hours a week of physical education, compared to one and a half hours in the United States and only one hour in England and Ireland. During such classes and during recess, boys tend to be much more active than girls (Armstrong & Welsman, 1997). By eighth grade, more than half of girls and one-third of boys in the United States no longer exercise regularly (U.S. Department of Health and Human Services, 2000). Japan requires daily physical activity for all schoolchildren; most Japanese schools are equipped with gyms and athletic fields, and 75 percent also have swimming pools.

Unfortunately, many sports that adults value (and often push children into) demand precisely those skills that are most difficult for children and put greater emphasis on winning than children want. Softball and baseball, for example, demand throwing, catching, and batting, all of which involve more distance judgment, better hand–eye coordination, and quicker reaction times than many elementary school children possess. Younger children are therefore likely to drop the ball even if it lands in their mitts, since they are slow to enclose the ball. They are similarly likely to strike out, because they swing too late to hit a pitched ball. For all but the most talented or determined, continual disappointment and embarrassment can lead to refusal to play.

A Fair Contest? Three against two might seem unfair, unless you look at the boys' body positions. Although the sexes do not differ much in physical strength at this age, gender differences are already having powerful effects. The boys won.

Genetic Variations

Hereditary differences also affect the development of motor skills. Some children, no matter how hard they try, can never throw or kick a ball with as much strength and accuracy as others. The same is true for fine motor skills. Some children naturally write more neatly than others, and those children are more likely to practice their penmanship, refining the curve of the *s* and the slant of the *t*, for instance. Adults need to provide extra motivation and time for the children who have less natural skill. About 6 percent of all children are considered to have a motor coordination disability sufficiently serious that it interferes with school achievement (American Psychiatric Association, 2000). These children need concentrated help. Practice and patience are particularly important during the brain development that is the foundation for all the skills of middle childhood.

Brain Support for Motor Development

Remember that the brain, proportionally large at birth, continues to grow more quickly than the rest of the child's body, reaching adult size at about age 7. By then, not only the basic areas of the sensory and motor cortexes are functioning; so, too, are more complex language, logic, memory, and spatial areas, each with many dendrites reaching out to other neurons as experiences accumulate.

Also recall that, in early childhood, emotional regulation, theory of mind, and left–right coordination begin to emerge as the maturing corpus callosum connects the two hemispheres of the brain and as the prefrontal cortex plans, monitors, and evaluates all the impulses from the various sectors of the brain. Hemispheric specialization makes the brain more efficient overall.

Now, in middle childhood, ongoing maturation of those parts of the brain as well as of the cerebellum becomes apparent in both motor and cognitive development, which are neurologically connected to each other (Diamond, 2000). For example, several behaviors common in early childhood—emotional outbursts, perseverance, inattention, the insistence on routines—can now be controlled. Now the executive brain functions well, allowing the child to analyze consequences before lashing out in anger or dissolving in tears, for example, or to knowing when a curse word seems advisable (on the playground to a bully, perhaps) and when it doesn't (during math class or in church).

Two other advances in brain function become increasingly evident in middle childhood. The first is the ability to attend to information from many areas of the brain at once. In the classroom, children must listen to the teacher, write down what is important, and ignore another child's whispering; in the cafeteria, children must understand another child's gestures and facial expressions and respond quickly and appropriately; on the ball field, children must not only calculate the trajectory of a batted ball but also start running in the right direction while noting where other teammates are positioned and whether anyone besides the batter is trying to reach base.

These multiple demands for action and inaction from various parts of the brain are beyond the thinking capacity of 3-year-olds, who zero in on only one aspect of a situation. The thoughtful and competent older child must select and coordinate the simultaneous impulses from all parts of the brain, developing "large-scale cortical networks" that link the various parts together so that the person thinks in a coordinated manner and is not confused by myriad signals from the millions of scattered neurons in various areas (Bressler, 2002). This coordination requires extensive myelination and increased production of neurotransmitters.

The second advance that becomes apparent in middle childhood is in **automatization,** a process by which thoughts and actions are repeated in sequence

automatization A process by which thoughts and actions are repeated in sequence so often that they become automatic, or routine, and no longer require much conscious thought.

so often that they become automatic, or routine, and no longer require much conscious thought. Almost all behaviors that originate in the cortex require careful, slow, and focused concentration the first few times they are performed. After many repetitions, with a particular sequence of neurons firing together, behavior becomes more automatic, more patterned, and requires less neuronal effort because firing one neuron leads to a chain reaction that fires an entire sequence.

Automatization becomes easier and quicker as brain maturation speeds the signals between one part of the brain and another. You can readily see this in reading, which begins with the child using the eyes (sometimes aided by a finger and the lips) to sound out letters and guess at words; this series of fine motor skills leads to interpretation in the brain. Then reading gradually becomes so automatic that a person can glance at billboards or cereal boxes and read, even when not intending to do so.

Automatization can also be seen in the development of gross motor skills. It is the brain more than the muscles that throws the ball toward the catcher's mitt instead of into the dugout. If a particular communication network is flawed, as seems to be the case in some forms of childhood psychopathology, then the person will be unable to produce the coordinated responses that the activity requires. The problem may not be in a specific part of the brain but rather in "inattention to the whole" (Fisher, 1998), as we will describe later in this chapter.

A child's motor habits, especially in coordinating both sides of the body and performing complex tasks, benefit from connections formed in the brain, as the corpus callosum between the brain's hemispheres continues to mature. Further, neurons that fire together are strengthened together, so practicing any particular skill—from moving a pencil on paper to kicking a ball toward a goal post—gradually makes processing in the brain faster and more efficient (Merzenich, 2001). Hours of practicing penmanship or throwing a softball, or cutting one's meat with knife and fork smooth out brain pathways and make the typical 10-year-old much more adept than the typical 5-year-old, as well as far more adept than a 10-year-old who has not practiced these skills.

According to research on lower animals, brain development is advanced through play, especially the active, erratic, rough-and-tumble frolicking that many children love (see Chapter 10). Indeed, one expert believes that such play particularly helps boys overcome their genetic tendency toward hyperactivity and learning disabilities, because rough-and-tumble play helps regulate the frontal lobes of the brain (Panksepp, 1998). Whether or not this is true, it is apparent that children's impulses toward active play may need to be guided but should not be repressed. When not restricted, rough-and-tumble play increases for boys from early to middle childhood, aiding not only motor skills but probably emotional regulation and interpretation as well (Pellegrini & Smith, 2001).

Brain Music If this boy is to become a competent violinist, the brain must coordinate arms, hands, fingers, ears, and memory. All this is possible only after practice has made some of it automatic. Automatization frees the brain's cortex for more emotional and coordinated expression in response to the conductor.

Children with Special Needs

All parents watch with pride and satisfaction as their offspring become smarter, taller, and more skilled. For many parents, however, these feelings mingle with worry and uncertainty when their children unexpectedly encounter difficulties in one area of development or another. Often delay, overactivity, or clumsiness in motor skills is the first problem to be noticed; other problems become apparent once formal education begins (Lerner, 2000). Although developmental problems usually originate in the brain, the observable symptoms and the many factors that inhibit or amplify those genetic tendencies are social and cognitive (Rutter & Sroufe, 2000). That is, the symptoms of disability become more apparent on the playground or in the classroom (when a child's ability is compared to that of others the same age) than at home or in the pediatrician's office. Consider Billy, a third-grader with a problem at school.

You will soon read more about Billy's diagnosis and treatment. The psychiatrist found him to be a **child with special needs**, one who requires extra help in order to learn. The specific diagnosis that gives rise to "special needs" might be

child with special needs A child who, because of a physical or mental disability, requires extra help in order to learn.

A Case to Study

Billy: Dynamo or Dynamite?

Billy was a typical 8-year-old in many ways. He was born full term after an uncomplicated pregnancy; he sat up, walked, and talked at the expected ages. His parents were proud of their first-born child and only son's energy and curiosity: "Little Dynamo," they called him affectionately. They did not consider him handicapped—he walked, talked, and even began to read on schedule, and he looked quite normal. True, he sometimes needed to be reminded to wash his hands before dinner and sometimes upset his little sister. Doesn't every boy do that? But Billy's third-grade teacher, Mrs. Pease, insisted that he see a psychiatrist because his behavior in class was "intolerably disruptive" (Gorenstein & Comer, 2002, p. 250), as the following episode illustrated:

Mrs. Pease had called the class to attention to begin an oral exercise: reciting a multiplication table on the blackboard. The first child had just begun her recitation when, suddenly, Billy exclaimed, "Look!" The class turned to see Billy running to the window.

"Look," he exclaimed again, "an airplane!"

A couple of children ran to the window with Billy to see the airplane, but Mrs. Pease called them back, and they returned to their seats. Billy, however, remained at the window, pointing at the sky. Mrs. Pease called him back, too.

"Billy, please return to your desk," Mrs. Pease said firmly. But Billy acted as though he didn't even hear her.

"Look, Mrs. Pease," he exclaimed, "the airplane is blowing smoke!" A couple of other children started from their desks.

"Billy," Mrs. Pease tried once more, "if you don't return to your desk this instant, I'm going to send you to Miss Warren's office." Billy, seemingly oblivious to her threats, remained at the window, staring excitedly up at the sky.

Mrs. Pease, her patience wearing thin, addressed Billy through gritted teeth, "Billy, come with me back to your seat!" she said. . . . By now she was almost 10 minutes into the lesson period and still had not finished a single multiplication table.

Mrs. Pease tried to resume the lesson. "Who can tell me 3 times 6?" she asked.

Fifteen children raised their hands, but before she could call on anyone, Billy blurted out the correct answer. "Thank you, Billy," she said, barely able to contain her exasperation, "but please raise your hand like the others."

Mrs. Pease tried again. "Who knows 3 times 7?" This time Billy raised his hand, but he still couldn't resist creating a disruption.

"I know, I know," Billy pleaded, jumping up and down in his seat with his hand raised high.

"That will do, Billy," Mrs. Pease admonished him. She deliberately called on another child. The child responded with the correct answer.

"*I* knew that!" Billy exclaimed.

"Billy," Mrs. Pease told him, "I don't want you to say one more word this class period."

Billy looked down at his desk, sulkily, ignoring the rest of the lesson. He began to fiddle with a couple of rubber bands, trying to see how far they would stretch before they broke. He looped the rubber bands around his index fingers and pulled his hands farther and farther apart. This kept him quiet for a while; by this point, Mrs. Pease didn't care what he did, as long as he was quiet. She continued conducting the multiplication lesson while Billy stretched the rubber bands until finally they snapped, flying off and hitting two children, on each side of him. Billy let out a yelp of surprise, and the class turned to him.

"That's it, Billy," Mrs. Pease told him, "You're going to sit outside the classroom until the period is over."

"No!" Billy protested. "I'm not going. I didn't do anything!"

"You shot those rubber bands at Bonnie and Julian," Mrs. Pease said.

"But it was an accident."

"I don't care. Out you go!"

Billy stalked out of the classroom to sit on a chair in the hall. Before exiting, however, he turned to Mrs. Pease. "I'll sue you for this," he yelled, not really knowing what it meant.

[Gorenstein & Comer, 2002, pp. 250–251]

any of dozens of conditions, including aggression, anxiety, Asperger syndrome, attachment disorder, attention-deficit disorder, autism, bipolar disorder, conduct disorder, depression, developmental delay, Down syndrome, and dozens more. All of these begin with a biological anomaly, which might be the extra chromosome of Down syndrome or simply an inherited tendency toward a particular emotion. A special need may also result directly from an obvious physical handicap, such as blindness, deafness, or paralysis, but less than 10 percent of the children with special needs have visible physical disabilities that affect learning.

In 1999 about 13 percent of all schoolchildren in the United States received special educational services, up from 8 percent in 1977 (National Center for Education Statistics, 2001) (see Table 11.1). Special-needs children who have not been identified as such probably amount to another 13 percent, which means that about one out of every four 7- to 11-year-olds is a special-needs child. Of those who have been identified, usually the teacher (not the parent or pediatrician) begins the process of formal identification by making a *referral,* writing a

TABLE 11.1 Prevalence of Some Categories of Childhood Psychopathology: United States

Categories	DSM-IV-R 2000	Students Receiving Special Education (as percent of all students)	
	2000	1975	1999
Mental Retardation (MR)*	1%	2%	1%
Significantly delayed adaptation to life, often measured by a score of less than 70 on an IQ test			
Specific Learning Disorder or Disability (LD)	6%	2%	6%
Academic achievement substantially below expected in a basic academic skill			
Communicative Disorders	11%	3%	2%
DSM-IV-R includes several types, including:			
Expressive—Understanding but poor expression (5% at school age; 12% under age 3)			
Receptive-expressive—Deficits in understanding and expression (3% of school-age children)			
Phonological—Child's speech cannot be understood (2%)			
Stuttering—Severe disturbance in fluency (1%) (rare before age 5)			
Pervasive Developmental Disorder (PDD)	0.01	0.01†	0.14
(Includes autism and Asperger syndrome)			
Attention deficit/hyperactivity disorder (AD/HD, ADD)	5%	**	**
Inattentiveness, impulsivity, and/or overactivity (see text for clarification of definitions and symptoms)			
Conduct Disorder (CD)	5%	**	**
Bullying, threatening, cruelty to people or animals, lying			
Oppositional Defiant Disorder (ODD)	8%	**	**
Negativity, disobedience, hostility toward authorities			
Serious Emotional Disturbance (ED)	††	0.6%	1%
Totals: §	25%	8%	13%

*Specialists often refer to categories using only abbreviations. To help with interpretation, the common abbreviations are given in parentheses.

†Autism data compare 1990 and 1999, since autism was not a recognized category in 1975.

**These categories are not qualified for special education, according to U.S. law.

††This is not a category in DSM-IV-R, which uses more specific categories for serious emotional problems.

§Totals include additional children not listed in specific categories. For DSM-IV-R, these include uncommon psychological disturbances, such as feeding disorders, tic disorders, and attachment disorders. For special education, these include severe physical problems, such as blindness and deafness. Some children have *comorbid* disabilities, so the DSM total of 25 percent is less than the sum of all categories. The current educational total does not include all children who might benefit from special services, because only those referred, diagnosed, and accepted for special education are tallied. Disorders of speech are not often diagnosed, and three common problems— attention-deficit disorder, conduct disorders, and oppositional behavior—are not recognized as educational categories. A few children with those problems receive special services because they are learning-disabled or emotionally disturbed, but most simply go without any special help.

Sources: American Psychiatric Association, 2000; National Center for Education Statistics, 2001.

TABLE 11.2 Laws Regarding Special Education in the United States*

PL (Public Law) 91-230:   Children with Specific Learning Disabilities Act, 1969

Recognized learning disabilities as a category within special education. Before 1969, learning-disabled children received no special education or services.

PL 94-142:   Education of All Handicapped Children Act, 1975

Mandated education of all school-age children, no matter what disability they might have, in the *least restrictive environment (LRE)*—which meant with other children in a regular classroom, if possible. Fewer children were placed in special, self-contained classes, and even fewer in special schools. This law required an *individual educational plan (IEP)* for each child, specifying exactly what educational goals are next to be reached, and periodic reassessment to evaluate progress.

PL 105-17: Individuals with Disabilities Education Act [IDEA], 1990; updated 1997

Refers to "individuals," not children (to include education of infants, toddlers, adults), and to "disabilities," not handicaps. Emphasizes parents' rights to be consulted and to agree to, or refuse, referral, testing, placement, and IEP. Parents may invite interpreters and advocates, and may appeal any decision.

*Other nations have quite different laws and practices, and states and school districts within the United States interpret these laws in various ways. Parents and teachers should consult local support groups and authorities, including legal experts, if necessary.

individual education plan (IEP) A legally required required document specifying a series of educational goals for each child with special needs

special request for evaluation based on specific behaviors. According to law, other professionals are required to observe and test the child and then to conclude whether or not the child has special needs. The parents then meet with the professionals to hear about the problem, the test, and the diagnosis, and are asked to agree on an **individual education plan (IEP)** (see Table 11.2).

Some teachers (such as Mrs. Pease) are much more likely than others to refer children for evaluation, and some states recognize more special-needs children than others do. Rhode Island is highest at 18 percent; Arizona is lowest at 10 percent. This gap is influenced more by state policy than by the nature of the children (U.S. Department of Education, 2001). Many children are not referred or properly diagnosed if their problems are not obvious to the teacher, and many parents do not recognize their children's problems or agree with the experts' solutions. Other nations have different laws and procedures for referral, evaluation, and planning.

Developmental Psychopathology

developmental psychopathology A field in which knowledge about normal development is applied to the study and treatment of various disorders, and vice versa.

Psychologists and psychiatrists who study childhood disorders have joined with those who study normal development to create the field of **developmental psychopathology.** In developmental psychopathology, knowledge about normal development is applied to the study and treatment of various disorders, and vice versa. As for all development, the emphasis is on "biological, psychological, social and cultural processes" that produce "multiple risks and protective factors" (Cicchetti & Sroufe, 2000, p. 256). The reality that any child, whether with special needs or not, is continually changing as time goes on is recognized by developmental psychopathologists. The "core identity" of developmental psychopathology involves "discovering processes of development, with the goal of comprehending the emergence, progressive unfolding, and transformation of patterns of adaptation and maladaptation over time" (Cicchetti & Sroufe, 2000, pp. 258–259).

Given this emphasis, it is not surprising that research in developmental psychopathology has provided four lessons that apply to all children:

1. *Abnormality is normal.* Most children sometimes act in ways that are decidedly unusual, and most children with serious disorders are, in many respects, quite normal. If we ignore this complexity, we may "seriously distort the variability of development" for all children (Fischer et al., 1997). Children

with psychological disorders should be viewed primarily as children—with the many developmental needs that all children share—and only secondarily as children with special challenges.

2. *Disability changes over time.* The behaviors associated with almost any special problem change as the person grows older. A child who seems severely handicapped at one stage of development may seem quite capable at the next stage, or vice versa. In fact, "discontinuity in disorders from childhood to adulthood" is typical (Silk et al., 2000). Such changes are not simply due to the passage of time; they result from the interplay of maturation, treatment, and contextual change.

3. *Adolescence and adulthood may be better or worse.* Many children with seemingly serious disabilities, even blindness or mental retardation, become happy and productive adults once they find a vocational setting in which they can perform well. Conversely, any disability that makes a child unusually aggressive and socially inept becomes more serious during adolescence and adulthood, when physical maturity and social demands make self-control and social interaction particularly important (Davidson et al., 1994; Lahey & Loeber, 1994).

4. *Diagnosis depends on the social context.* The official fourth edition (revised) of the diagnostic guide of the American Psychiatric Association, the ***Diagnostic and Statistical Manual of Mental Disorders,*** or **DSM-IV-R,** recognizes that the "nuances of an individual's cultural frame of reference" need to be understood before any disorder can be diagnosed (American Psychiatric Association, 2000, p. xxxiv). Nonetheless, many researchers believe that DSM-IV-R does not go far enough in this direction, because disorders may not reside "inside the skin of an individual" but "between the individual and the environment" (Jensen & Hoagwood, 1997).

> ***Diagnostic and Statistical Manual of Mental Disorders* (DSM-IV-R)** The American Psychiatric Association's official guide to the diagnosis of mental disorders. The fifth edition will soon be published.

We have space to focus on only three of the many categories of disorders that developmental psychopathologists study: autism, learning disabilities, and attention-deficit disorders. Each originates in the biosocial domain, and each is a typical example of many disorders. Knowledge of these three will help us understand the development of all children, no matter what special needs they might have.

Autism

Autism is one of several types of **pervasive developmental disorders,** which are severe problems that affect many aspects of psychological growth of a child under age 3. According to physician Leo Kanner (1943), a child with **autism** has an "inability to relate in an ordinary way to people . . . an extreme aloneness that, whenever possible, disregards, ignores, shuts out anything that comes to the child from the outside." This severe form of the disorder is quite rare; it occurs in about 1 of every 2,000 children, according to DSM-IV-R (American Psychiatric Association, 2000).

> **pervasive developmental disorders** Severe problems, such as autism, that affect many aspects of psychological growth of a child under age 3.

> **autism** A pervasive developmental disorder marked by an inability to relate to other people in an ordinary way, by extreme self-absorption, and by an inability to learn normal speech.

The first of the four lessons from developmental psychopathology—"abnormality is normal"—makes us seek similarities between people diagnosed as "abnormal" (in this case, as autistic) and people considered "normal." First, many children and adults have less severe symptoms that seem autistic, with fairly normal speech and intelligence but severely impaired social interaction. They are sometimes diagnosed as *high-functioning autistic,* or as having **Asperger syndrome;** they are also self-absorbed but may be quite intelligent and verbally adept (Barnhill et al., 2000; Green et al., 2000). Second, some completely normal people are much better than others in social interaction.

> **Asperger syndrome** A set of less severe symptoms of autism, in which the individual has fairly normal speech and intelligence but severely impaired social interaction.

When the entire spectrum of autistic-like disorders is taken into account, about 1 child in 300 shows autistic traits—and four times as many boys as girls

(Szatmari, 2001). Particular genes probably make some embryos more vulnerable than others, and teratogens that harm the embryonic brain stem about three weeks after conception probably exacerbate the genetic weakness (Rodier, 2000). (Recall from Chapter 4 that a *teratogen* is a substance or condition that can impair prenatal development and cause birth defects.) The number of such children has increased, particularly in California, where five times more children were diagnosed as autistic in 1994 than in 1990. A theory that autism is caused by childhood immunizations has been disproved, although it is easy to understand why parents might believe it, since the symptoms of poor social interaction and deficient language are not obvious at birth but coincide with the MMP injections given in the first year (Dales et al., 2001). Other theories, such as increased diagnosis in children who previously would have been diagnosed as mentally retarded or some new teratogen, are still under investigation.

The Early Path of Autism

Autism is truly a *developmental* disorder (as is emphasized by lesson 2 in our list above: "Disability changes over time"). As babies, many autistic children seem quite normal and sometimes unusually "good" (that is, undemanding), although they are often hypersensitive to noise or other stimulation, and the way they roll over, sit up, crawl, and walk may be less coordinated than the norm (Teitelbaum et al., 1998). However, severe deficiencies appear in three areas:

■ Ability to communicate
■ Social skills
■ Imaginative play

At age 1 or 2, autistic children lack spoken language or normal responses to others, have "difficulties in understanding the signs and signals" of human communication, and thus lose out on many opportunities to learn (Leekam et al., 2000). During the play years, many autistic children continue to be mute, not talking at all, while others engage exclusively in a type of speech called *echolalia*, in which they repeat, word for word, television jingles or questions that are put to them ("Good morning, John" is echoed with "Good morning, John"). They avoid spontaneous interaction with peers, such as the rough-and-tumble play and sociodramatic play described in Chapter 10. Instead, they engage in repetitive movements (such as spinning a top over and over) or compulsive play (assembling a puzzle in a particular order time after time).

Hope for Autism The prime prerequisite in breaking through the language barrier in a nonverbal autistic child, such as this 4-year-old, is to get the child to pay attention to another person's speech. Note that this teacher is sitting in a low chair to facilitate eye contact and is getting the child to focus on her mouth movements—a matter of little interest to most children but intriguing to many autistic ones. Sadly, even such efforts were not enough: At age 13 this child was still mute.

Autism in Later Childhood and Beyond

Lesson 3—"adolescence and adulthood may be better or worse"—is also apparent. In adolescence and adulthood the lack of social understanding often proves to be the most distinctive and devastating characteristic of autism (Gillham et al., 2000). Human relationships are the usual path toward learning and self-concept, yet autistic individuals appear to lack an awareness of the thoughts, feelings, and intentions of other people (Ziatas et al., 1998). Their theory of mind and emotional regulation are woefully inadequate. Many seem cold, aloof, and uninvolved until something triggers an outburst of laughter or fury. This pattern is frustrating for other people, who are bewildered by the unexpected explosions. Teachers and parents are best advised to ignore such emotional extremes and to use behavioral techniques to teach language and social skills, ideally beginning before age 5.

As children with autism grow older, their symptoms vary widely. Most score in the mentally retarded range on intelligence tests, but a closer look at their intellectual performance shows isolated areas of remarkable skill (such as memory for numbers or ability to put puzzles together). In general, their strongest cognitive skills are in abstract reasoning; their weakest, in social cognition (Scott & Baron-Cohen, 1996; Scheuffgen et al., 2000). For example, on a trip to the grocery store, an autistic child might quickly calculate that each apple in a bag of a dozen costs exactly 10½ cents and then blurt out to strangers that they must buy apples at this bargain price. Some autistic children never speak or have only minimal verbal ability, but many who are diagnosed as autistic in infancy learn to express themselves in language by age 6, becoming quite fluent by adulthood if given intensive behavioral training (Shrebman, 2000).

Given our understanding of the importance of social context (lesson 4, "diagnosis depends on the social context"),

> people with Asperger syndrome or high-functioning autism might not necessarily be disabled in an environment in which an exact mind, attracted to detecting small details, is an advantage. In the social world there is no great benefit to such a precise eye for detail, but in the world of math, computing, cataloging, music, linguistics, craft, engineering, or science, such an eye for detail can lead to success rather than disability. In the world of business, for example, a mathematical bent for estimating risk and profit, together with a relative lack of awareness of the emotional states of one's employees or rivals, can mean unbounded opportunities.
>
> *[Baron-Cohen, 2000, pp. 497–498]*

One autistic adult, Temple Grandin, remembers the unusual repetitive play of her childhood:

> When left alone, I would often space out and become hypnotized. I could sit for hours on the beach watching sand dribbling through my fingers. I'd study each individual grain of sand as it flowed between my fingers. Each grain was different, and I was like a scientist studying the grains under a microscope. As I scrutinized their shapes and contours, I went into a trance which cut me off from the sights and sounds around me.
>
> *[Grandin, 1996]*

Grandin developed verbal skills beyond those of most autistic children, in part because of unusual support from her parents and teachers and, later, medication and therapy. She became an engineer and an international expert in the design of humane slaughtering facilities for animals. However, even as a successful professional, she was still puzzled by the normal give-and-take of human emotions, describing herself as being like an "anthropologist on Mars," bewildered by the customs she observed (Sacks, 1995).

ROSALIE WINARD

Temple Grandin and Friends Temple Grandin understands cattle so well that she feels more comfortable with them than with most humans. Although this trait is partly the result of her autism, she has turned it into a strength. She is famous for designing slaughtering sheds in which the animals are killed quickly, without feeling panic or fear.

mentally retarded Having severe delays in all areas of mental development.

learning-disabled Having a marked delay in a particular area of learning that is not associated with any obvious physical handicap, overall mental retardation, or unusually stressful home environment.

aptitude The potential to learn, or master, a particular skill or body of knowledge.

IQ tests Aptitude tests designed to measure a person's intellectual aptitude, or ability to learn in school. This aptitude was originally defined as mental age divided by chronological age, times 100—hence, intelligence quotient, or IQ. An example:

Actual age of three children: 12, 12, 12
Mental ages of the three: 15, 12, 8
IQ of each of these three:
15/12 = 1.25 × 100 = 125 (superior)
12/12 = 1 × 100 = 100 (average)
8/12 = 0.75 × 100 = 75 (slow learner)

achievement tests Measures of reading ability, math knowledge, science facts, writing skills, or any other subject matter that has actually been mastered.

norm-referenced Of achievement-test scores, based on a certain level of achievement that is usual, or normal (such as a certain grade level).

criterion-referenced Of achievement-test scores, based on a certain standard of performance.

Learning Disabilities

The second type of psychopathology we will describe, learning disability, is much more common than autism. Indeed, almost half of the special-needs children in the United States are diagnosed as learning-disabled (U.S. Department of Education, 2001). Children vary in how quickly and how well they learn to read, write, and do arithmetic; **mentally retarded** children are severely delayed overall in mental development, with no particular achievement area that lags notably behind the rest. By contrast, **learning-disabled** children fall markedly behind in a particular aspect of learning but have no obvious physical handicap, no overall mental retardation, and no unusually stressful home environment that would explain their learning difficulty. Thus, the crucial factor in the diagnosis of learning disability is a *measured discrepancy* between expected learning and actual accomplishment in a particular academic area. To understand this difference between aptitude and achievement, you need to know more about the tests that measure these constructs.

Aptitude and Achievement

In theory, **aptitude** is the potential to learn, or master, a particular skill or body of knowledge. Aptitude is different from achievement, which is what a person has already accomplished. A person could have the aptitude for reading but never learn to read, or a person could have the aptitude to repair computers but never be taught to do so. The most important aptitude for school-age children is intellectual aptitude, or the ability to learn in school. This aptitude is measured by **IQ tests.** "IQ" is an abbreviation for "intelligence quotient." Originally, an IQ score was actually a quotient (the answer to a division problem), found by dividing the child's mental age (as measured by performance on an intelligence test) by his or her chronological age and then multiplying the result by 100. A score between 85 and 115 is considered average. Today, IQ tests use a slightly more complicated formula to make sure the overall distribution of scores follows the normal curve (see Figure 11.3), but the underlying concept is the same.

Achievement tests measure reading ability, math knowledge, science facts, writing skills, and whatever else has actually been mastered. Achievement tests are usually either **norm-referenced,** which means they are based on a certain level that is usual, or normal (such as a certain grade level), or **criterion-referenced,** which means they are based on a certain standard of performance. A child who scores at the fourth-grade level in achievement either reads as well as a typical fourth-grader (norm-referenced) or reads as well as expected after four years of schooling (criterion-referenced).

FIGURE 11.3 In Theory, Most People Are Average Almost 70 percent of IQ scores fall within the normal range. Note, however, that this is a norm-referenced test. In fact, actual IQ scores have risen in many nations; 100 is no longer exactly the midpoint. Further, in practice, scores below 50 are slightly more frequent than indicated by the normal curve shown here, because severe retardation is the result, not of the normal distribution, but of genetic and prenatal causes.

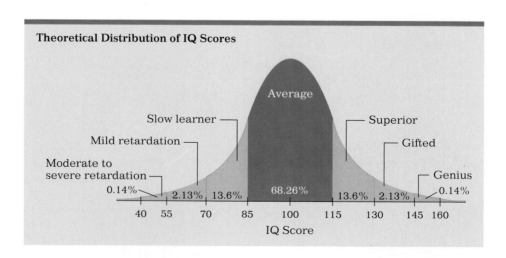

Setting both norms and standards gets more complicated as the school-age population becomes more diverse. Especially with bilingual children, educators and psychologists are increasingly cautious in using standardized tests to assess aptitude, achievement, or special needs, since test scores are often misleading (Lerner, 2000). For example, the two children you met at the start of this chapter, Yolanda and Paul, were below the norms and standards by the third grade, but neither of them was designated as needing special education. In fact, Yolanda's teachers pulled her "up some grades," recognizing that her ability was higher than her test scores indicated.

IQ Tests

Two highly regarded IQ tests are the *Stanford-Binet* and the *Wechsler* intelligence tests. The **Wechsler Intelligence Scale for Children (WISC)** is designed for school-age children. Both the Stanford-Binet and the WISC are given by a trained examiner to one child at a time; on both, the test items are varied to hold the child's interest as well as to assess many abilities, including vocabulary, general knowledge, memory, and spatial comprehension. The examiner reads the questions to the child to avoid measuring reading achievement. Some items are timed, but the child is not rushed; even finishing a particular puzzle after time is up is praised (although no points are given) (Kaufman & Lichtenberger, 2000).

IQ tests are quite reliable in predicting school achievement and somewhat reliable in predicting adult career attainment. In other words, children of above-average IQ earn above-average grades in school, are quite likely to attain above-average amounts of higher education, and are somewhat likely as adults to earn above-average income, to have a professional or managerial job, and even to be married and homeowners, at least in the United States (Sternberg et al., 2001).

IQ tests are *not* designed to identify particular learning or behavioral problems because they are supposed to be measures of general aptitude, not specific achievements or disabilities. Many learning-disabled children score normally on intelligence tests, although sometimes the scores on particular subtests are scattered around the norm—some unusually high and others unusually low (Kaplan et al., 2000). A mismatch between IQ score and achievement is a clue that something is amiss in the child, the home, or the school. Indeed, according to the guidelines in many states, a discrepancy between aptitude and achievement scores indicates a learning disability. The specifics vary, with a one-year discrepancy usually considered sufficient to signal disability at age 7 and a two-year discrepancy at age 11 (Lerner, 2000). Such a discrepancy indicates that more tests are needed.

Wechsler Intelligence Scale for Children (WISC) An IQ test designed for school-age children; it is administered by a trained examiner to one child at a time, and the questions are varied to hold the child's interest and to assess many abilities, including vocabulary, general knowledge, memory, and spatial comprehension.

Performance IQ This puzzle, part of a performance subtest on the Wechsler IQ test, seems simple until you try to do it. Actually the limbs are difficult to align correctly and time is of the essence, with a bonus for speed and failure after a minute and a half. However, this boy has at least one advantage over most African-American boys who are tested. Especially during middle childhood, boys tend to do better when their examiner is of the same sex and race.

Changing Policy

One Intelligence Score or Many?

Using a single test score to designate intelligence runs counter to the fact that children develop at different rates, depending on their genes, family, school, and culture (Sternberg et al., 2001). Only in theory, not in fact, can any test measure potential without also measuring achievement, or do so without reflecting the culture. Actually, IQ tests reflect knowledge of vocabulary, understanding of basic math, and familiarity with cultural ideas and artifacts—all of which are learned, not innate. Performance on an IQ test also reflects the ability to pay attention and concentrate, to express thoughts verbally, and to ask questions of a stranger if instructions are unclear.

When the children who will be taking the test have significantly different cultural backgrounds, the possibility of bias adds emotion and clouds interpretation. Caution is needed in interpreting any test scores, especially when doing so may lead to either good or bad consequences, such as more individualized teaching or repetition of a grade.

Another criticism of IQ tests applies to every child, in every culture and family. Humans may have many intelligences, not just one, which would mean that the very idea of using one test to measure intelligence is based on a false and narrow assumption. Indeed, researchers are finding that, just as there are many discrete functions within the brain, there are many kinds of abilities and many ways to demonstrate potential and then express achievement. Robert Sternberg (1996), for example, describes three distinct types of intelligence:

- *Academic* (measured by IQ and achievement tests)
- *Creative* (evidenced by imaginative endeavors)
- *Practical* (seen in everyday interactions)

In the usual academic test setting, according to Sternberg, the highly creative or practical child might become stressed and distracted. Such a child might become quite successful in adulthood, however, when many styles of learning and expressions of achievement are valued (Ferrari & Sternberg, 1998).

Similarly, Howard Gardner (1983) described seven distinct intelligences: linguistic, logical-mathematical, musical, spatial, bodily-kinesthetic, interpersonal (social understanding), and intrapersonal (self-understanding). Gardner believes that every normal person has all these intelligences. Our neurological variations give each of us particular strengths and weaknesses. For example, a man may be an able writer because of strong linguistic intelligence but may get lost easily when driving a car because spatial intelligence is weak. A woman may paint extraordinary portraits because her spatial, bodily-kinesthetic, and social understanding intelligences are strong, but linguistic weakness may make her unable to describe her work.

Recently, Gardner added an eighth intelligence—*naturalistic,* the ability to understand life in the natural world (as in biology, zoology, or even farming) (Torff & Gardner, 1999). Naturalistic intelligence was added because some people have a gift for it and some cultures (more often in Africa than in North America) seem to encourage it.

Standard IQ tests measure only linguistic and logical-mathematical ability, not all that brains contain. The fact that most schools emphasize language and math explains why

OWEN FRANKEN / STOCK, BOSTON

Gardner's Intelligences

- Linguistic
- Logical-mathematical
- Musical
- Spatial
- Bodily-kinesthetic
- Interpersonal (social understanding)
- Intrapersonal (self-understanding)
- Naturalistic

Demonstration of High IQ? If North American intelligence tests truly reflected all the aspects of the mind, children would be considered mentally slow if they could not replicate the proper hand, arm, torso, and facial positions of a traditional dance, as this young Indonesian girl does brilliantly. She is obviously adept in kinesthetic and interpersonal intelligence. Given her culture, it would not be surprising if she were deficient in the logical-mathematical intelligence required to use the Internet effectively or to surpass an American peer on a video game.

traditional IQ tests predict school success. However, if intelligence is the multifaceted jewel that Gardner (1993) believes it to be, schools will need to develop a broader curriculum so that every child can shine. Moreover, if IQ tests, as currently used, predict college and occupational success, then not only elementary schools but also colleges and career standards may need to change to reflect a broader understanding of human potential. The gifted musician or artist may need to be valued and paid as much as the gifted financier.

Some advocates for the learning-disabled insist that the current criterion-based achievement tests used for school promotion should be abandoned. However, as the director of the California Department of Education's Division of Standards says, "When special ed kids get out of school, they don't go to special ed town, they go out and compete with all the rest of us" (Spears, quoted in Lewin, 2002). Tests are a policy issue, and values differ; the director is one of many educators who insist that traditional tests, based on aptitude and achievement in reading, writing, and math, should be maintained. In truth, some testing can be very helpful. If experts can develop "new theories of intelligence . . . , researchers can begin to acquire deeper insight into how and why some children develop to the best of their potential, while, sadly, others do not" (Ferrari & Sternberg, 1998, p. 935).

Specific Learning Disabilities

No matter how achievement is measured, some children seem unable to learn as well as other children in one subject area or another. Abnormal processes in one particular region of the brain, rather than physical or environmental handicaps, are presumed to be the cause of learning disabilities (Hallahan & Keogh, 2001). Inherited abnormalities in brain structure are often identified as the underlying deficiency (Alarcon et al., 2000).

The most common learning disability is **dyslexia,** which is unusual difficulty with reading. Most dyslexic children seem bright and happy in the early years of school, volunteering answers to difficult questions, diligently completing their worksheets, sitting quietly and looking at their books in class. However, as time goes on, it becomes clear that they are reading only with great difficulty or not at all. They guess at simple words (occasionally making surprising mistakes) and explain what they have just "read" by talking about the pictures. In fact, if a child is advanced in comprehension through the use of contextual clues but is behind in ability to match letters to sounds, that is a sign of dyslexia (Nation & Snowling, 1998) (see Figure 11.4).

Another fairly common learning disability is **dyscalculia,** or difficulty with math. This disability usually becomes apparent at about age 8, when even simple number facts, such as 3 + 3 = 6, are memorized one day and forgotten the next. It soon becomes clear—especially with word problems—that the child is guessing whether numbers should be added, subtracted, multiplied, or ignored. Almost

dyslexia Unusual difficulty with reading.

dyscalculia Unusual difficulty with mathematics.

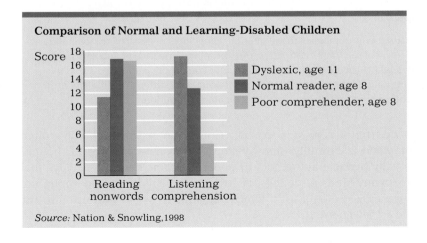

Comparison of Normal and Learning-Disabled Children

Legend:
- Dyslexic, age 11
- Normal reader, age 8
- Poor comprehender, age 8

Source: Nation & Snowling, 1998

FIGURE 11.4 Reading and Comprehension In this study, three groups of children were compared, all reading at the third-grade level. The children in one group were dyslexic, and they were age 11, on average. The children in the other two groups were 8 years old, but half of them were normal readers and the other half had problems with reading comprehension. As you can see, the groups differed markedly in their ability to read and pronounce a nonword (letters combined to make a possible word that does not mean anything, such as *wug* or *tedork*) or to comprehend a passage read to them. Each group would require a different pattern of reading instruction.

The Joy of Books These third-graders are fortunate: They all seem to know how to read, and their classroom includes many books and this wonderful reading tent, where they can take off their shoes and relax with a book of their choice. A teacher who provides such individualized opportunities for readers is probably also sensitive to the special needs of the dyslexic for intense, one-on-one training in specific skills.

everything the child knows about arithmetic is a matter of rote memory rather than understanding.

Other specific academic subjects that may reveal a learning disability are spelling and handwriting. A child might read at the fifth-grade level but repeatedly make simple spelling mistakes ("kum accros the rode"), or a child might take three times as long as any other child to copy something from the chalkboard, and then produce only a large, illegible scrawl. Children also can be disabled primarily in speech, motor coordination, or social skills. Although these disabilities are less likely to be referred for expert diagnosis, they often signal other problems, as we will now see.

Early Diagnosis: A Dilemma

Many educators believe that the key to treating learning disabilities is to identify them early, before the child starts to fall behind in school (Molfese & Martin, 2002). Early diagnosis is difficult, however, if it depends on a discrepancy between actual and expected school achievement; but some children do fall behind in speech, motor skills, or social skills by age 4, and such a lag may signal a learning disability. Our understanding of neuroscience is very helpful here. If learning disabilities originate in the brain, and if brain pathways are formed through the practice of various activities, then children can be taught new ways of thinking in time to avoid failing in school. As an expert on attention-deficit disorders explains:

> Executive functions comprise those mental capacities necessary to formulate goals, and to achieve them, and carry out the plans effectively, and are at the heart of all socially useful, personally enhancing, constructive and creative activities. With executive functioning intact an individual can suffer . . . impairment in any of the other areas of the brain and still be able to function.
>
> *[Fisher, 1997, p. 77]*

In short, the prefrontal cortex is crucial. Childhood psychopathology often improves if the child is carefully, step-by-step, taught new patterns of thought that can eventually become automatic. In general, brains develop in ways that compensate for many kinds of deficits, as long as the child is young enough to learn to plan general strategies and alternate sequences that end up with the same academic achievement.

Older children and adults can also be trained to use their brains differently; such training can change the connections between neurons. However, the training must be very precise. For example, a person with dyslexia should receive specific discrimination training between rapid, similar sounds (Bedi, 2001).

About half of children with learning disabilities also have poor social skills. When a person has more than one disorder, that is called **comorbidity**; it is very common for all types of psychopathology. It may well be that the learning disability leads to the social disability, or at least makes it worse—another point in favor of early diagnosis. It may also be that several problems stem from one brain abnormality, one teratogen, or one childhood context. In any case, however, comorbidity adds to the burden, and treating one problem is likely to help the others.

Attention-Deficit Disorders

One of the most puzzling and exasperating of childhood problems is **AD/HD (attention-deficit/hyperactivity disorder)**, in which the child has great difficulty concentrating for more than a few moments at a time. Actually, AD/HD children have three possible problems: They can be inattentive, impulsive, and overactive. After sitting down to do homework, for instance, an AD/HD child might repeatedly look up, ask irrelevant questions, think about playing outside, get up to get a drink of water, sit down, fidget, squirm, tap the table, jiggle his or her legs, and then get up again to get a snack or go to the bathroom. Often this need for distraction and diversion is accompanied by excitability and impulsivity.

The origin of attention-deficit/hyperactivity disorder seems to be neurological (Aman et al., 1998; Casey, 2001): a brain deficit that results in great difficulty in "paying attention" and in *not* reacting to irrelevant stimuli. The underlying problem may sometimes be an abnormality in some part of the brain, but more often it is that the neurotransmitters (particularly dopamine and norepinephrine) do not transmit signals quickly enough to enable the child to avoid distraction (Fisher, 1997). AD/HD may also result from genetic vulnerability, prenatal teratogens, or postnatal damage such as lead poisoning (Oosterlaan et al., 1998). Billy, the 8-year-old in the A Case to Study feature, was diagnosed with AD/HD, with his attention problems evident in that he looked at the airplane when he was supposed to stay in his chair, and he could not wait to say his math answer. Billy's response—"I'll sue you"—reveals his inattention to the social context.

Teachers notice such disruptive children, but a formal diagnosis may never be made. A checklist of the DSM-IV-R criteria for AD/HD was given to all teachers in every elementary school in one Tennessee county. Although fewer than 5 percent (the typical proportion) of the children had already been diagnosed as having AD/HD, actually 16 percent of the children met the criteria for the disorder (Wolraich et al., 1998). In this study, as happens generally, about four boys were diagnosed with AD/HD for every girl.

Problems Related to AD/HD

Attention-deficit disorder (ADD) may occur without the impulsivity and overactivity of the hyperactive child. Children with this form of the problem appear to be prone to anxiety and depression; they sometimes seem lost in thought, spaced out, distracted. Children with ADD or AD/HD are at increased risk of developing *oppositional defiant disorder* or *conduct disorder*; about 70 percent also have learning disabilities, more often in social skills and reading than in math (Fisher, 1998; Mayes et al., 2000; Pisecco et al., 2001).

Problems with attention, impulses, activity, opposition, and aggression may occur in a developmental sequence (Stormshak et al., 1998). The origins of such

comorbidity The presence of more than one disorder in one person at the same time.

AD/HD (attention-deficit/hyperactivity disorder) A condition in which a child has great difficulty concentrating for more than a few moments at a time and, as a result, is inattentive, impulsive, and overactive.

attention-deficit disorder (ADD) A condition in which a child has great difficulty concentrating (but, unlike a hyperactive child, is not impulsive and overactive); the child may be prone to anxiety and depression and may seem lost in thought, spaced out, or distracted.

Normal or Not? It's impossible to judge just from this photo. In some children, an action like this may be an isolated instance of showing off or of outrageous mischief. In children with AD/HD, these actions are commonplace. When such behavior is accompanied by aggression, the child may be at risk of developing a conduct disorder—possibly becoming the kind of stubborn, disobedient daredevil who is constantly in trouble at home, at school, and in the neighborhood.

problems are probably innate, perhaps genetic or prenatal. Then early caregiving may include either secure attachment, which alleviates the problem, or insecure attachment, which makes it worse. Toddlers who cannot pay attention may be especially unresponsive to parents' demands that they be quiet and stay put. Perhaps the attention-deficit child soon learns that he or she can concentrate better by moving around. Thus the child may begin with ADD but develop AD/HD by age 4 or 5. If the parents are too permissive, then the child never learns emotional regulation. If the parents are too strict, demanding quiet or concentration from a child who is unable to comply, the child may develop oppositional–defiant disorder, utterly refusing to comply with any authority. If that opposition ("I won't do it") is repeatedly met with aggression ("Do it or I'll spank you"), the child may become aggressive and disruptive.

In the classroom, aggression is especially likely to develop if the teacher insists that every child concentrate quietly at his or her desk, an impossible demand for a child with an attention-deficit problem. Learning to read, add, write, and so on would then become difficult, which explains why many AD/HD children seem both intelligent and learning-disabled. With time, social problems with peers also develop, as was beginning to happen with Billy when his rubber bands hit Bonnie and Julian.

Such a developmental sequence, as well as contextual considerations, would explain why these conceptually distinct disorders often occur in the same child (Stormshak et al., 1998). They also help explain cultural differences in the frequency of these disorders. Children in Britain, for instance, are rarely diagnosed as having AD/HD, but they are more likely to be diagnosed with conduct disorders than are children in the United States (Soussignan & Tremblay, 1996).

Help for Children with AD/HD

Not surprisingly, children with AD/HD are usually troublesome to adults and rejected by their peers. Medication, psychotherapy, and changes in the family and school environments can help some children, especially when all three approaches are combined. In general, the family and the school need to be very precise in determining the consequences of behaviors, making sure the child is rewarded for the correct, appropriate actions. Mrs. Pease should have said at the outset that children should raise their hands, and she should not have said, "Thank you, Billy" when he blurted out the answer. With special coaching, parents and teachers can learn to guide children with AD/HD (Scott et al., 2001).

For reasons not yet determined, certain drugs that stimulate adults have the reverse effect on many—but not all—children with attention-deficit problems. Among these psychoactive drugs are amphetamines (e.g., Adderall) and methylphenidate, known as *Ritalin,* widely prescribed for adults as a stimulant. For many children, the results of these drugs are remarkable: They can sit still and concentrate for the first time. Ritalin was prescribed for Billy, and his parents and teacher were taught how to help him. He "improved considerably" within two months, not only staying in his seat and concentrating on his school work, but also making some friends (Gorenstein & Comer, 2002). In fact, success with therapy and medication in cases such as Billy's has led to the use of drugs for children with other special needs, including those who are depressed or anxious (Aman & Langworthy, 2000; Del Mundo et al., 1999).

A reported 11 million prescriptions were written for Ritalin in 1999 (Shute et al., 2000). At least 20 other psychoactive drugs, including Prozac, Zoloft, and Paxil, are now prescribed for children, some of them as young as age 2 (Fisher, 1998). The dilemma with such drugs is that testing even Ritalin by giving it to children under age 6 has not been approved by the Food and Drug Administration, yet pediatricians will continue to prescribe psychoactive drugs to children as long as they seem to help. Moreover, some AD/HD children are not helped by medication, perhaps for genetic reasons (Bower, 1999). The most serious concern is that some children may be simply quieted. They remain educationally and socially needy, yet their teachers and parents never learn how to help them because the children are no longer disruptive. Ongoing changes at home and at school are essential. Drugs can, at best, control behavior; they cannot remedy learning problems. Moreover, drugs are often underprescribed or overprescribed (Angold et al., 2000).

Especially for Health Workers: Parents ask that some medication be prescribed for their kindergarten child, who is much too active for them to handle. How do you respond?

Issues in Educating Children with Special Needs

Once a child is referred for evaluation and testing and parents and professionals agree that the child has special needs, where should that child be educated? In many cases before 1960, the child was not educated at all: Public policy did not sanction allocation of public money to educate such children, and specialized private schools focused on children with obvious physical handicaps such as blindness. If retarded, disturbed, or otherwise disabled students were educated in schools, they were often placed in a separate classroom segregated from regular students, such as a small self-contained classroom on the top floor or at the end of a long hall. Besides making the children feel isolated and odd, this approach lumped all sorts of disabled children together—including those with overall retardation and delay—with no recognition of their individual strengths and abilities. Further, segregated classrooms impaired the development of normal social skills and slowed advancement in areas in which a child was not disabled.

The Least Restrictive Environment

In response, **mainstreaming** emerged about 35 years ago. The Education of All Handicapped Children Act of 1975 mandated that children with special needs be taught in the **least restrictive environment (LRE)** available. In practice, that often meant they should be taught with children in the general (main) classroom. The regular teacher was asked to be particularly sensitive to the special-needs children, perhaps using alternative methods to teach them or allowing them extra time to complete assignments and tests. The presumption was that they belonged *with* their peers, not apart from them.

mainstreaming A policy (mandated by the Education of All Handicapped Children Act in 1975) under which children with special needs must be taught in "the least restrictive environment" available, which usually means that they are taught with other children in the general classroom.

least restrictive environment (LRE) A legally required school setting that offers children with special needs as much freedom as possible to benefit from the instruction available to other children; often, in practice, the general classroom.

What Are These Children Learning? This deaf boy is fortunate—he is with his hearing peers and his teacher knows how to sign to him. Are the other children doing their work? One hopes, over the course of the year, they will learn more from the inclusion of the special child than they miss from the teacher's targeted attention.

ROBIN L. SACHS / PHOTOEDIT

Mainstreaming tended to become a "sink-or-swim" situation. Many teachers were untrained, unwilling, or simply unable to cope with the special needs of unusual children, especially in a classroom of 30 or so students. As one teacher complained:

> I do not have the training that you people [speech-language pathologists] have. However, I've been in the business for a long time, and I think I know when I see a child with a language problem. So I make all the referrals. Now I don't know what happens in the 1:1 session, or what kinds of tests you give the kids, but my speech person keeps sending these children back to me saying they don't have a language problem. Finally I just said to her, "Then you get in the classroom and see what is wrong."

> *[quoted in Constable, 1987]*

As with this teacher, not only did the children fail but the teachers did, too, when they used the same methods and goals with special-needs children that they used with the other children in the class. In our Case to Study, Mrs. Pease did not know what to do when Billy blurted out the correct answer, so she mishandled him, leading to further frustration.

Some schools set aside a **resource room**, where special-needs children would spend part of each day with a teacher who was trained and equipped to work with their disabilities. But pulling the child out of regular class undermined classroom social relationships and left the regular teacher unaccountable for the progress of the child. Further, scheduling resource-room time meant the child missed out on vital parts of the regular school day, either play periods or practice in academic skills.

The Most Effective Education

The most recent approach to placement is called **inclusion:** Children with learning disabilities are "included" in the regular class, as in mainstreaming. However, a specially trained teacher or paraprofessional assists with the special-needs children, for all or part of the day. This solution is expensive, and it requires adjustment on the part of both teachers, who are not used to working side by side. Nonetheless, children who need both social interaction with their schoolmates and special treatment for their learning difficulties may learn more than if they were to be pulled out of the regular class to learn in a resource room (Swenson, 2000; Waldron & McLeskey, 1998).

To take the idea of inclusion one logical step further, many teachers and parents now emphasize *integration,* the idea that each child within the classroom, learning-disabled or not, is a vital part of that social and educational group. Some experts suggest that almost every school-age child has some sort of special need and that therefore schools should develop an individualized education plan (IEP) for every student (Branson, 1998). This may be the ideal, but many parents are more interested in the practical implications of inclusion for their own children, whether normal or learning-disabled, and in the costs involved. If a school district is trying to save money by assigning special-needs children to a regular classroom of 30 children with only a part-time special educator, then the children would be better off with a resource room or self-contained classroom (Swanson, 1999).

resource room A room set aside in some schools for special-needs children to spend part of each day with a teacher who is trained and equipped to work with their disabilities.

inclusion A policy under which learning-disabled children are included in the regular class, as in mainstreaming, but are supervised by a specially trained teacher or paraprofessional for all or part of the day.

Every Child Is Special One reason for a school policy of inclusion is to teach children to accept and appreciate children who have special needs. The girl with Down Syndrome (in yellow) benefits from learning alongside her classmates, as they learn from her. An effective teacher treats every child as a special individual.

Unfortunately for children with special needs, no approach always solves their academic and social problems (Siperstein et al., 1997). From a developmental perspective, this is not surprising: All manner of disabilities, from severe physical impairment to subtle learning disabilities, are real, and long-standing. They may be improved by the proper educational context, but they are unlikely to disappear completely, as a study of inclusion in eight nations made clear (Booth & Ainscow, 1998).

Once parents, teachers, and the child understand that a learning disability does not stem from laziness, stupidity, or stubbornness, but from a brain pattern that needs to be restructured, then advances in the child's development can occur. This happened with the late Ennis Cosby, son of comedian Bill Cosby: "The happiest day of my life occurred when I found out I was dyslexic. I believe that life is finding solutions, and the worst feeling to me is confusion."

Conclusion

Specific suggestions for teachers and parents of children with special needs can be gleaned from the next two chapters, for everything that helps the cognitive development (Chapter 12) and psychosocial development (Chapter 13) of children in general will also help the development of special-needs children. A few particular suggestions arise from the research. Simply telling parents to be patient or responsive or strict does *not* work, but teaching them specific ways to encourage appropriate behavior in their child does (Scott et al., 2001). As far as teachers are concerned, direct instruction in teaching children skills (e.g., steps in problem solving, how to sound out a word) and in helping children use learning strategies is more effective than simply providing general instruction (Swanson, 1999).

What happens if a developmental problem is not recognized, diagnosed, or treated? This was the case for three-fourths of the AD/HD children in the Tennessee study mentioned earlier, more than half of the high-functioning autistic children, and probably most of the children with other disorders. Similarly, physical conditions like obesity, asthma, and even high blood pressure and heart disease have roots in childhood but are not usually diagnosed soon enough for effective early intervention.

Life-span developmental research finds that childhood problems rarely disappear but that the severity of their lifelong impact depends on the specifics of the home and school contexts. These contexts affect a person's fortune or misfortune in finding a vocation, a partner, and a community that will provide social support. Ideally, children with special needs are spotted by age 5 and their teachers and parents provide the necessary educational and emotional support. If not, many older children may still find ways to compensate for, overcome, or limit their difficulties in the larger social context (Rutter & Sroufe, 2000). Development during the school years is a multifaceted combination of risks and assets, with the particular educational and familial contexts usually able to prevent serious problems from growing worse as the child's development continues.

We continue this theme in the next two chapters, which focus specifically on what school-age children usually learn (a prodigious amount) and how they cope with their problems (quite well, for the most part) as well as on what schools and families can do to bring ongoing pride and success to every child. As we stressed at the beginning of this chapter with Yolanda and Paul, and you can now see with Billy as well, each child is unique, but all have common needs and concerns. Parents, teachers, and peers can help all of them in many ways.

Response for Health Workers (from page 353): On this topic, ideology far outdistances information. Medication helps some hyperactive children, but not all; it might be useful at age 4, but other forms of intervention should probably be tried first. Therefore, you should compliment the parents on their concern about their child but refer them to an expert in early childhood. The expert can evaluate the child and the family and then make recommendations, which may include medication but definitely will include behavior-management techniques geared to the particular situation.

SUMMARY

A Healthy Time

1. Middle childhood is generally a healthy time of steady growth and few serious illnesses. Because of their increasing independence and ability to care for themselves, school-age children join the wider social world, comparing themselves with others the same age.

2. Children perceive almost any physical difference between one child and another as a deficit, a reason to feel ashamed and lonely. The most common of these observable differences is childhood obesity, an increasing epidemic in developing nations.

3. The causes of childhood obesity are far deeper than the home environment: genes, culture, and national customs are at the root of the problem. However, parents and schools can add regular exercise and subtract high-fat snacks, making every child healthier.

4. Asthma is an increasingly common ailment among school-age children in developed nations. Although the origins are genetic and the triggers are specific allergens, primary prevention includes longer breast-feeding, more outdoor play, and reduced air pollution, which would benefit all children.

Development of Motor Skills

5. Both gross and fine motor skills continue to develop during middle childhood. However, many children do not have adequate practice and guidance, because schools and playgroups encourage the more able children, especially if they are boys, and allow the less skilled to become discouraged. Gender patterns of motor-skill development originate in children's preferences as well as in the culture.

6. Brain development continues during middle childhood, enhancing every other aspect of development. Particularly important are increased myelination and greater production of neurotransmitters, which speed communication between neurons. In addition, the prefrontal cortex and the corpus callosum continue to mature, allowing not only analysis and planning but also automatization and simultaneous use of the entire cortex.

Children with Special Needs

7. The field of developmental psychopathology uses an understanding of normal development to inform the study of unusual development. Four general lessons have emerged from the field: Abnormality is normal; disability changes over time; adolescence and adulthood may be better or worse; and diagnosis depends on the social context.

8. Some children with obvious educational or psychological disabilities are recognized, referred, evaluated, diagnosed, and treated in early childhood. For the most part, however, behavioral or learning problems are not spotted until the children enter elementary school and are compared with other children in a setting that demands maturity and learning.

9. About 13 percent of all school-age children in the United States receive special-educational services. These services begin with an IEP (individual educational plan) and assignment to the least restrictive environment—all with the parents' approval.

10. One of the most severe disabilities of childhood is autism, which is characterized by three main symptoms: odd and delayed language; lack of social awareness, with impaired interpersonal skills; and play that is repetitive and unimaginative.

11. Treatment for autism usually involves one-on-one teaching of language and social skills. If such special education is early and intense, some autistic children become successful adults. Children whose main problem is with social interaction, but who think and speak well, may be diagnosed as having Asperger syndrome.

12. Learning disabilities, especially in reading and math, are the most common reason for special education in the United States. Even though the number of special-education programs has doubled in the past two decades, experts estimate that about half of children with special needs are not in special education.

13. A learning disability is a discrepancy between actual and expected achievement, typically measured by an IQ test that quantifies intellectual aptitude. Such tests assess language and logical ability and predict school achievement. Intelligence is actually manifested in multiple ways, which conventional IQ tests are too limited to measure.

14. Decisions about the educational placement of special-needs children are complicated by conflicts between ideological concerns and practical needs, and sometimes between educational professionals and parents. The inclusion approach is controversial, although it is generally considered better than mainstreaming. Advocates of inclusion agree that resource rooms and special classes for learning-disabled children are still sometimes needed.

15. Children with attention-deficit/hyperactivity disorder (AD/HD) have potential problems in three areas: inattention, impulsiveness, and overactivity. Children who are not especially overactive but who have trouble concentrating and who seem anxious, depressed, and distracted may be diagnosed with attention-deficit disorder (ADD).

16. Most AD/HD children are learning-disabled as well. Long-term prognoses for AD/HD children improve if they master basic academic skills, achieve normal social interaction, and do not become oppositional and aggressive.

17. The best treatment for attention deficits is probably a combination of medication, home management, and education. Stimulant medication often helps AD/HD children focus, but it requires targeted teaching and careful home management.

18. All the potential problems of middle childhood benefit from prevention, early recognition, and targeted treatment. Each child has unique strengths and coping abilities, but all children need support and guidance both at home and at school.

KEY TERMS

middle childhood (p. 331)
overweight (p. 332)
obesity (p. 332)
asthma (p. 335)
reaction time (p. 336)
automatization (p. 338)
child with special needs (p. 340)
individual education plan
 (IEP) (p. 342)
developmental
 psychopathology (p. 342)

Diagnostic and Statistical
 Manual of Mental Disorders
 (DSM-IV-R) (p. 343)
pervasive developmental
 disorders (p. 343)
autism (p. 343)
Asperger syndrome (p. 343)
mentally retarded (p. 346)
learning-disabled (p. 346)
aptitude (p. 346)
IQ tests (p. 346)

achievement tests (p. 346)
norm-referenced (p. 346)
criterion-referenced (p. 346)
Wechsler Intelligence Scale
 for Children (WISC) (p. 347)
dyslexia (p. 349)
dyscalculia (p. 349
comorbidity (p. 351)
AD/HD (attention-deficit/
 hyperactivity disorder)
 (p. 351)

attention-deficit disorder
 (ADD) (p. 351)
mainstreaming (p. 353)
least restrictive environment
 (LRE) (p. 353)
resource room (p. 354)
inclusion (p. 354)

KEY QUESTIONS

1. How do nutrition and heredity affect stature and physique in middle childhood?

2. What are the causes of obesity?

3. How is asthma sometimes caused by modern life?

4. What factors affect which specific motor skills a child masters during the school years?

5. What gender differences and similarities are apparent in motor skills between ages 7 and 11?

6. What are the four lessons, applicable to all children, that research in developmental psychopathology has provided?

7. What are the three major characteristics of autism?

8. What are the signs of at least two specific learning disabilities?

9. How might the symptoms of AD/HD in a specific child change with age?

10. What are the arguments for and against the use of psychoactive drugs to control AD/HD?

11. What are the advantages and disadvantages of inclusion for students with learning disabilities?

Chapter Twelve

The School Years: Cognitive Development

concrete operational thought Piaget's term for the ability to reason logically about the things and events that one perceives.

School-age children are primed to learn, and they can learn almost anything that is not too abstract. They can learn how to multiply and divide fractions, how to prepare a balanced and delicious meal, how to surf the Web to find an obscure fact. These skills take time to master—each day from age 7 to 11 is an occasion for small advances in knowledge—and reflect both the child's motivation and the culture's priorities. But all children can learn, each in a way that is unique, partly because of subtle differences in the intricate connections of their brains and partly because their experiences vary with family, culture, and historical context.

If the story ended with that, then adults might simply offer basic learning and let children choose. However, not only are children at this age primed to learn, but the specifics of *what* they learn are each culture's bridge to the future. Thus, adults decide exactly what children should learn and how best to teach them. Should every child learn calculus and chemistry, or is it enough that they know how to count and categorize? Should children be taught to be quiet and respectful of authority or to be creative and rebellious, questioning every rule? Should children learn to suspect any stranger or to accept everyone? What religion, what language, what principles must be passed on, and what standards, groupings, and measurements should schools use?

We begin this chapter by considering the universals of thinking, especially as described by Jean Piaget, Lev Vygotsky, and information-processing theorists. We then turn to some controversial topics: moral development, code-switching, bilingual education, educational standards, reading techniques, and national differences. Developmentalists know that all children must learn and that each child is different; getting from one of these certainties to the other is complicated.

Building on Piaget and Vygotsky

Both Piaget and Vygotsky, as you remember from Chapter 9, emphasize the structures or scaffolding that children develop in preparation for learning during middle childhood (Rogoff, 1998). Piaget, with his four major stages of development, explicitly differentiates the school-age child from the younger version. In Piaget's view, the most important cognitive achievement of middle childhood is the attainment of **concrete operational thought**, whereby children can reason logically about the things and events they perceive. Beginning at about age 7, children understand logical principles, and they apply them in *concrete* situations, that is, situations that deal with visible, tangible, real things—things that are solid, just like the concrete poured to become a sidewalk or the foundation of a building. Children thereby become more systematic, objective, scientific—and educable—thinkers.

Vygotsky (1934/1994) believed that Piaget's attention to the actual thinking of the child was a marked improvement over the dull "meaningless acquisition" approach favored by the schools of his time. Such schools rendered the child "helpless in the face of any sensible attempt to apply any of this acquired knowledge" (pp. 356–357). However, Vygotsky was very critical of Piaget's view of the child as a socially isolated learner. To Vygotsky, instruction by others is crucial, with schools, peers, and teachers providing the bridge that is needed to connect the child's innate developmental potential with the skills and knowledge that formal education should provide.

Especially for Teachers: How might Piaget and Vygotsky help in teaching geography to a class of third-graders?

Logical Principles

To understand the place of logic in the development of concrete operational thought during middle childhood, consider three of the logical structures that Piaget describes: classification, identity, and reversibility. These ideas are difficult for younger children but are more easily grasped by school-age children.

Classifying Objects, Ideas, and People

classification The process of organizing things into groups (or categories or classes) according to some property they have in common.

Classification is the process of organizing things into groups (or *categories* or *classes*) according to some property they have in common. For example, a child's parents and siblings belong to the class called "family." Other categories include "toys," "animals," "people," and "food."

Classification leads to the related but more complicated concept of *class inclusion,* the idea that a particular object or person may belong to more than one class. For example, a baseball may be included in the classes of round objects, of sports equipment, and of small things, as well as in many other classes. Until school age, few children really understand class inclusion. As you remember, young children usually assume that each object has one and only one name and belongs to one and only one category (Inhelder & Piaget, 1958, 1964).

Consider the following experiment, similar to experiments conducted by Piaget. An examiner shows a child nine plastic dogs. Five of the dogs are collies; the others are a poodle, a Labrador retriever, and two German shepherds. First, the examiner makes sure that the child knows that all the plastic toys are types of dogs and that the child can name each breed. Then comes the crucial question: "Are there more collies or more dogs?" Until classification and class inclusion are firmly established (at about age 7), most children say "More collies." They do not understand that "dog" is the general category here and "collie" the subcategory, and that the general category includes (and so is greater than) the subcategory. So when they hear "collies" and realize that there are more collies than all the other breeds put together, they jump to the conclusion that there are more collies than dogs.

Once children do understand the relation between a category and its subcategories, they can understand the wide variety of relationships among people, objects, and events—all of which can, and usually do, belong to more than one class. They understand that categories or subcategories can be any of the following:

Learning by Doing This science teacher and student are demonstrating the effects of static electricity. Such demonstrations bring out the logical abilities of concrete operational children much better than do abstract descriptions in textbooks.

- *Hierarchical.* A child is simultaneously a human, primate, mammal, animal, and living creature, with each category belonging to the higher categories, and each higher category including more members than the lower categories do. For example, all humans are primates, but not all primates are human.
- *Overlapping.* A child, within a family, can be an offspring, a sibling, one of the girls, and one of those with curly hair; other family members are likewise in some of those categories but not all of them.
- *Separate.* A child may be a member of the Lee family and simultaneously a member of Mr. Smith's fourth-grade class, but the other members of Mr. Smith's class are not members of the Lee family.

Obviously, a child who can consistently and thoughtfully apply logical principles is better equipped to analyze problems, derive correct solutions, and ask follow-up questions than an intuitive, haphazard thinker would be. The ability to think logically also makes older children more objective, enabling them to think analytically, not just to react emotionally.

Identity and Reversibility

Identity is the idea that certain characteristics of an object remain the same even if other characteristics change. Children who understand identity realize that superficial changes in an object's appearance do not alter that object's underlying substance or quantity. In conservation tests (see page 265), for example, identity tells us that pouring a liquid from one container into a different container does not change the amount of liquid present. "It's still the same milk," a 9-year-old might say. "You haven't changed that."

School-age children also come to understand **reversibility**, the idea that sometimes a thing that has been changed can be returned to its original state by reversing the process by which it was changed. A school-age child might prove that the amount of liquid has not changed by pouring it back into the first container, thus reversing the process.

Identity and reversibility are both relevant to mathematical understanding. Children need a firm grasp of identity to realize, for example, that the number 24 is always 24, whether it is obtained by adding 14 + 10, or adding 23 + 1, or adding 6 + 6 + 6 + 6. This logical principle of identity also enhances scientific understanding, whether that means grasping the underlying oneness of the tadpole and the frog or seeing that frozen water is still H_2O. Similarly, reversibility is essential to a school-age child's understanding of math and science. For example, subtraction is the reverse of addition (if 5 + 9 = 14, then 14 – 9 = the original 5).

Logical principles also apply to everyday social encounters. Identity enables a school-age child to understand—as most preschoolers cannot—that his mother was once a child and that her baby picture is, in fact, a picture of his mother. School-age children are even able to imagine their parents growing old—and to promise, as one child did, always to be around to push their wheelchairs. Similarly, a school-age child might say, "Let's start over and be friends again, OK?" (reversibility). Later, when we discuss moral development, we will note that school-age children understand the categories of sex and race well enough to know when relying on such categories amounts to prejudice.

identity The idea that certain characteristics of an object remain the same even if other characteristics change.

reversibility The idea that sometimes a thing that has been changed can be returned to its original state by reversing the process by which it was changed.

LAURA DWIGHT

Measuring Soil Absorbency This science lesson in the fourth grade of a public school in New York City seems well designed for concrete operational thinking. The children analyze, investigate, and classify samples of soil by putting them in water, not by reading a textbook. Note also that each does his or her own work within a social setting—another sign of effective elementary education.

Logic and Culture

Piaget's basic idea about concrete operational thought—that children during middle childhood gradually come to comprehend and apply logical ideas that they did not understand before—remains valid. In math, in physics, and in explaining how people can or cannot catch physical or mental illnesses from someone else, children become more logical and less egocentric as they mature (Howe, 1998; Keil & Lockhart, 1999; Siegler & Jenkins, 1989). Indeed, in all these domains, the same research finds that sometimes older children make mistakes that younger children do not, again showing that school-age children apply their new logic even when it leads them astray.

Vygotsky's emphasis on the influence of the sociocultural context of learning adds to Piaget's ideas, illuminating why children learn and think as they do. According to Vygotsky, children are powerfully influenced by the people around them, who guide them in one direction or another, and by the cultural context. In physics, for instance, whether or not school-age children grasp certain concepts depends a great deal on the particulars of instruction and on the influence of their peers, as they learn within "a framework that was laid down by Piaget and embellished by Vygotsky" (Howe, 1998, p. 207).

Most of the research on children's cognition has been done in North America and England, but the same principles are apparent worldwide. In Zimbabwe, for example, children's understanding of the logical concept of classification was found to be influenced not only by their age but also by the particulars of their schooling and their family's socioeconomic status (Mpofu & van de Vijver, 2000). Japanese 4- to 11-year-olds' understanding of time, speed, and distance, as Piaget would predict, improved with age: Although younger children sometimes grasped the relationship between two of these three, they could not put all three together, as some of the oldest children could. However, comprehension of the reciprocity of time, speed, and distance varied much more than a straightforward stage theory would predict, suggesting that sociocultural factors were influential as well (Matsuda, 2001). Another study of Japanese children found that some mathematical skills closely followed Piaget (despite the mathematical advantages that some believe are conferred by Japanese families and language), but that other arithmetic strategies were definitely the result of specific school instruction (Naito & Miura, 2001).

The most detailed international example of the importance of culture and context comes from 6- to 15-year-old street children in Brazil, many of whom sell fruit, candy, and other products to earn their living. They have never attended school, but most become quite adept at pricing their wares, making change, and giving discounts for large quantities—a set of practices that must be recalibrated almost every day as inflation, wholesale prices, and demand change. These children calculate "complex markup computations and adjust for inflation in these computations by using procedures that were widespread in their practice but not known to children in school" (Saxe, 1999, p. 255). Thus, the demands of the situation, the social learning attained from other sellers, and their daily experience advance these children's cognitive performance in ways that neither maturation nor education could do alone. In short, learning is both developmental and sociocultural; both Piagetian and Vygotskyan.

Further research on Brazilian 4- to 14-year-olds confirms the special relationship of thinking and experience. The cognitive advantage of actually having dealt with money was greatest for children age 6 to 11, in middle childhood. Younger children were less able to understand the arithmetic problems as presented to them, even with experience,

Who Is the Smart One Here? Research on child street vendors in Brazil, such as this boy in São Paulo, reveals that few have attended school but that most have quite advanced arithmetic skills, allowing them to divide per-item cost, subtract to determine change, and even convert currency of another nation into the Brazilian equivalent—adjusted for inflation. Other research confirms that school-age children use their cognitive capacities to master whatever their culture values or requires, including the social skills needed—in this case, to convince tourists to buy lemons.

GEORGE ANCONA / INTERNATIONAL STOCK

and older ones could do just as well whether or not they had personal experience (Guberman, 1996).

Overall, Piaget constructed a valid sketch of cognitive development, but he underestimated the influence of context, instruction, and culture, and this, in turn, made him underestimate the variability from one child to another. Research inspired by Vygotsky and the sociocultural perspective fills in Piaget's outline with details of the actual learning situation.

Information Processing

A third approach to understanding cognition arises from *information-processing theory*. Like computers, people take in and store large amounts of information, then apply their mental processes to perform three functions: to search for specific items of information when they are needed, to analyze situations using the particular problem-solving strategies that are likely to yield correct solutions, and to express the best solution in a format that another person (or a networked computer) can understand.

Information-processing theory is useful precisely because people "can learn anything, sense or nonsense" (Simon, 2001, p. 205). Many 7- to 11-year-olds not only learn rapidly in school but also outscore their elders on computer games, repeat the rapid-fire lyrics of their favorite rap songs, and recognize out-of-towners by the clothes they wear. Some children, by age 11, beat their fathers at chess, play a musical instrument so well that adults pay to hear them, or write poems that get published. Other children that age run away from abusive homes and live by their wits on the street, and still others become soldiers in a civil war—having learned lessons that few adults want to know.

This enormous and impressive range of knowledge makes it clear that older school-age children are very different kinds of learners from, say, 4- or 5-year-olds. Not only do they know more, they also use their minds much more effectively, whether they must solve a problem or remember a piece of information to be retrieved easily when needed. As with a computer, greater efficiency means not simply having more information stored somewhere, but having better access strategies. This is the main reason 11-year-olds are better thinkers than 7-year-olds.

Memory

The **sensory register** is the first component of the information-processing system. It stores incoming stimulus information for a split second after it is received, to allow it to be processed. To use terms first explained in Chapter 5, *sensations* are retained for a moment while the person selects some sensations to become *perceptions*. This first step of information processing is quite good in early childhood and continues to improve slightly until about age 10. (For most people, hearing and vision are as sharp at age 10 as they will ever be, gradually declining from adolescence on.) Most sensations that come into the sensory register are lost or discarded, but meaningful information is transferred to working memory for further analysis.

It is in **working memory** (sometimes called *short-term memory*) that current, conscious mental activity occurs. Your working memory includes, at this moment, your understanding of this paragraph, any previous knowledge you recall that is related to it, and also, perhaps, distracting thoughts about weekend plans or the interesting person who sat next to you in class today. Working memory is constantly replenished with new information, so thoughts and memories are usually not retained for very long. Most are discarded, while a few are transferred to long-term memory, to be recalled later (as weekend plans were in this

Response for Teachers (from page 360): Here are two of the most obvious ways. First, use logic. Once children can grasp classification and class inclusion, they can understand cities within states, states within nations, and nations within continents. Organize your instruction to make logical categorization easier. Second, make use of children's need for concrete and personal involvement: You might have children learn first about their own location, then about the places where friends and family live, and finally about places beyond their personal experience via books, photos, guest speakers, and films.

sensory register The component of the information-processing system in which incoming stimulus information is stored for a split second to allow it to be processed.

working memory The component of the information-processing system in which current conscious mental activity occurs. Also called *short-term memory.*

long-term memory The component of the information-processing system in which virtually limitless amounts of information can be stored indefinitely.

Especially for Teachers: How might your understanding of memory help you teach 2,000 new words to a class of fourth-graders?

KAZ MORI / THE IMAGE BANK

Eye on the Ball This boy's concentration while heading the ball and simultaneously preparing to fall is a sign that he has practiced this maneuver enough times that he can perform it automatically. Not having to think about what to do on the way down, he can think about what to do when he gets up, such as pursuing the ball or getting back to cover his position.

knowledge base A broad body of knowledge in a particular subject area that makes it easier to master new learning in that area.

example). Working memory is one of the components that clearly improves in childhood (Meadows, 1993).

Finally, **long-term memory** stores information for minutes, hours, days, months, or years. The capacity of long-term memory—how much information can be crammed into one brain—is virtually limitless by the end of middle childhood. Together with the sensory register and working memory, long-term memory assists in organizing reactions to stimuli. Crucial here is not merely *storage* (how much material has been deposited in long-term memory) but also *retrieval* (how readily the material can be brought to the conscious mind to be used). Certain information is more readily retrievable (you remember your birth date more easily than your phone number), but all the information in long-term memory is stored somehow, unless something (such as a stroke) destroys it.

Speed of Processing

Older children are much quicker thinkers than younger children, and this greater speed benefits memory and a host of other cognitive skills (Williams et al., 1999). Speed directly increases mental capacity, because faster thinking makes it possible to hold and process more thoughts in one's conscious mind (working memory) at once. A sixth-grader can listen to the dinner-table conversation of her parents, respond to the interruptions of her younger siblings, think about her best friend, and still remember to ask for her allowance. In school, increased processing capacity means that she can answer a teacher's question with several relevant ideas rather than just one and, at the same time, monitor her words for accuracy and note her classmates' reactions to her answer.

Speed of thinking continues to increase throughout adolescence. In adulthood, it gradually slows down. Why does thinking speed increase even though adult brain size is reached by age 7? Neurological maturation, especially the ongoing myelination of neural axons and the development of the frontal cortex, partly accounts for these changes (Benes, 2001). But the advances seem more directly a matter of learning from experience than of simple maturation. Indeed, there is no evidence that the critical parts of the brain literally grow bigger during middle childhood. Instead, speed and capacity increase because as children learn to use their brains more efficiently, myelination increases and dendrites become more dense (Schneider & Pressley, 1997). As this happens, repetition makes many neurons fire in a coordinated and seemingly instantaneous way (Merzenich, 2001).

We saw in Chapter 11 that *automatization* is the process in which familiar, well-practiced mental activities become routine and automatic. As people use their intellectual skills, many processes that at first required hard mental labor now become automatic. This increases processing speed, frees up capacity, allows more to be remembered, and thus advances thinking in every way (Schneider & Pressley, 1997).

Progress from initial effort to automatization often takes years. Many children lose cognitive skills over the summer because the halt in daily schooling erases earlier learning (Huttenlocher et al., 1998). Not until something is overlearned does it become automatic.

Knowledge Base

Another aspect of thinking that takes years to develop is knowledge. Children know much more in the school years than in the play years. The more they know and remember, the more they can learn. That is, having an extensive **knowledge base,** a broad body of knowledge in a particular subject area, makes it easier to master new learning in that area. This fact is apparent not only in college classes but also in elementary school subjects, such as math and reading, and in psychological research. For example, one study compared fourth-graders of varied intelligence—some of whom were expert soccer players and others of whom were novices—on their ability to understand and remember a written passage about soccer (see Table 12.1). As expected, high-IQ children did somewhat better than low-IQ children—but this was true only for children who were at the same level of soccer expertise. When an expert soccer player with low intelligence was compared to a highly intelligent novice, the expert did better. In this experiment a larger knowledge base was sufficient to overcome slower thinking overall (Schneider et al., 1996).

Further research emphasizes that the connections between bits of information improve as the knowledge base expands. When people learn more about a particular topic, they remember how the new knowledge relates to the previous knowledge. This explains why learning by rote is fragile, while learning by comprehension of ideas endures.

Control Processes

The mechanisms that put memory, processing speed, and knowledge together are the **control processes,** which regulate the analysis and flow of information within the system. Control processes include selective attention, emotional regulation, and metacognition. When someone wants to concentrate on only one part of all the material in the sensory register, or summon a rule of thumb from long-term memory to working memory in order to solve a problem, control processes assume an executive role in the information-processing system.

If this sounds familiar, it is because you read in Chapter 8 about the maturation of the prefrontal cortex, where the brain regulates and coordinates emotions and thoughts. This part of the brain (actually several parts, including the medial prefrontal cortex, the orbital prefrontal cortex, the anterior cingulate, and the hypothalamus) is sometimes called the *executive function* precisely because it controls the other parts. The underlying problem of children with AD/HD (as we saw in Chapter 11) may well be that an underdeveloped prefrontal cortex reduces their ability to control their impulses; without control processes, a child blurts out words and is easily distracted (Karatekin, 2001).

Selective Attention

One of the most important control processes is the ability to focus one's thoughts on what is important. If you were to observe children learning in a kindergarten classroom and a fifth-grade classroom, you would see many differences in attention. Kindergartners are easily distracted, whether they are listening to a story or printing letters of the alphabet. While they are working, they chatter to each other, look around, fidget, call out to the teacher, and sometimes get up to visit friends or just wander around. Their curriculum is designed to be highly varied, with plenty of changes of activity, because the teachers know the nature of their 5-year-old charges.

By contrast, fifth-graders might work independently at desks or in groups around a table, managing to read, write, discuss, and seek assistance without distracting, or being distracted by, other students. Or they might all quietly follow a demonstration at the chalkboard, raising their hands to be called on rather than shouting out. Remember Billy, the boy with AD/HD, from Chapter 11, as he sat in class? The problem was not that he didn't know the right answer; in fact, he got angry precisely because he was right. The problem was that he could not wait quietly, with his hand raised, to be called on. As this example demonstrates,

TABLE 12.1 Who Remembers Most After Reading a Passage About Soccer?

	Intelligence	
	High IQ	**Low IQ**
Expert soccer players	Most	Second most
Novice soccer players	Third most	Least

Experts Versus Novices That intelligent children who are experienced soccer players remember the most, or that their opposites remember the least, about a written passage concerning soccer is not surprising. What is surprising is the group that came in second: those children who were not very intelligent overall but who happened to know a lot about soccer. Given a passage they had never seen before, both their comprehension and their memory were better than those of smarter children with less knowledge about the subject.

control processes The mechanism—selective attention, emotional regulation, and strategic thinking—that put memory, processing speed, and knowledge together in order to regulate the analysis and flow of information within the information-processing system.

selective attention The ability to screen out distractions and to focus on the details that will help in later recall of information.

metacognition "Thinking about thinking," or the ability to evaluate a cognitive task to determine how best to accomplish it, and then to monitor and adjust one's performance on that task.

They've Read the Book Acting in a play based on *The Lion, the Witch, and the Wardrobe* suggests that these children have metacognitive abilities beyond almost any preschooler. Indeed, the book itself requires a grasp of the boundary between reality (the wardrobe) and fantasy (the witch). "Thinking about thinking" is needed in order to appreciate the allegory.

?*Observational Quiz* (see answer, page 368): Beyond the book, what are three examples of metacognition implied here? Specifically, how does the ability to memorize lines, play a part, and focus on the play illustrate metacognition?

BACHMANN / PHOTO RESEARCHERS, INC.

toward the end of middle childhood, academic tasks are more difficult and take longer to complete, but teachers expect students to persist in the face of challenge, waiting and thinking.

Selective attention, the ability to screen out distractions and concentrate on relevant information, is the critical difference between the kindergartners and fifth-graders. Selective attention improves throughout middle childhood and beyond (Goldberg et al., 2001). Memory and thought depend on the improved ability to ignore most of the information that bombards the senses and to focus on details that will help in later recall—perhaps using an already-memorized address to remember a historical date. Focusing on what should be remembered and ignoring what should be forgotten are equally important components of selective attention (Cowan, 1997).

Improved Control

The ability to control one's mental processes begins during the preschool years, as children show signs of *emotional regulation*—holding their anger instead of hitting their friends, distracting themselves instead of crying at the dentist, and so on. This works in the opposite direction, too: Overly inhibited children become less shy and fearful. As you saw in Chapter 10, these processes are powerfully influenced by the responses within the family and by the values of the child's culture.

Metacognition

During the school years, control processes become markedly better, especially in regard to intellectual, not just emotional, efforts, which are reinforced by the school. Children develop **metacognition**, which means "thinking about thinking," the ability to evaluate a cognitive task to determine how best to accomplish it, and then to monitor and adjust one's performance on that task. For example, experimenters first tested 6- to 10-year-old children's knowledge base about animals, including their knowledge that woolly animals live in cold places. The experimenters then gave the children examples from a mythical planet that contradicted their previous knowledge. The older children were better able to alter their prior knowledge to accommodate the new information, even though they had a firmer knowledge base and hence required more adjustment than the younger children (Carmichael & Hayes, 2001). Thus, as middle childhood proceeds, children become better able to control their knowledge, changing their assumptions if necessary.

Much other research provides evidence for the marked advances in control processes and metacognition that take place over the school years (Case, 1998; Ferrari & Sternberg, 1998). For example, preschool children find it difficult to judge whether a problem is easy or difficult, or whether or not they remember a particular fact. Thus, when they try to study something, they cannot monitor or judge what they need to know, so they wastefully devote equal effort to the easy and the hard, to what is already known and what is not yet known. Children at the start of middle childhood still make this mistake; consequently, "young grade school children have enormous problems responding appropriately to monitoring activities" (Schneider, 1998).

By around age 8 or 9, children realize that they must identify challenging tasks. They become much more accurate about what they already know and thus more efficient when they study. They can evaluate their learning progress, judging whether they have learned a set of spelling words or science principles, rather than simply asserting (as many younger children do) that they know it all (Harter, 1999). In short, older children approach cognitive tasks in a more strategic and analytical manner. Storage and retrieval strategies improve as they learn how to pluck something from memory, when to use mnemonic devices (memory aids, such as "*i* before *e* except after *c*"), and when something is not worth learning. All this is part of metacognition, including both control processes and memory strategies (Meadows, 1993).

Language

To understand the thinking of the school-age child, it is vital to examine language, which is a cause, a consequence, and the best evidence, of cognitive development from ages 7 to 11. For example, younger children tend to use intuition and subjective impressions to interpret the results of a classroom science experiment ("Maybe the caterpillar just felt like becoming a butterfly"); in contrast, school-age children seek verbal explanations that are rational, consistent, and generalizable ("Does the caterpillar use the air temperature to know when it's time to start spinning a cocoon?"). Preoperational thinkers ask "Why?" but reject answers that are not to their liking; concrete operational thinkers ask "Why?" and then want to know more facts.

Similarly, 5-year-olds on the playground may argue over the rules of a game by using increasingly loud and assertive protests ("Is!" "Is not!" "Is!" "Is not!"), whereas 10-year-olds temper their arguments with reason and justification ("That can't be right, because if it was, we'd have to score points differently"). In both academic and nonacademic contexts, school-age children's logical thinking and precise use of language are crucial to their understanding, knowledge, and communication. How, and how much, language is learned often differentiates the cognitive achievements of school-age children.

Learning Vocabulary

Both Piaget and Vygotsky stress that the school years are the ideal time for teaching language. By some estimates, school-age children's rate of vocabulary growth exceeds that of younger children. Some children learn as many as 20 words a day during elementary school, reaching a vocabulary of nearly 40,000 words by the fifth grade. However, variation is enormous: 6-year-olds' vocabulary ranges between 5,000 and 20,000 words—a 400 percent difference (Moats, 2001). Children from low-income families are usually at the low end of this range, not only in vocabulary but also in syntax and sentence length (Hart & Risley, 1995). This means that, even if vocabulary doubles in size between ages 5 and 11, disadvantaged children know an average of only 10,000 words, compared to 40,000 words for more advantaged children.

The size of the child's vocabulary at the start of middle childhood depends on how much he or she has been exposed to

Response for Teachers (from page 364): Children can be taught strategies for remembering at this age, making links between working memory and long-term memory. Accordingly, you might break down the vocabulary list into word clusters, looking for root words, connections to the children's existing knowledge, applications, or (as a last resort) by first letters or rhymes. Active, social learning is useful; perhaps in groups the students could write a story each day that incorporates 15 new words. Each group could read its story aloud to the class. Four days a week, 15 new words a day, would be appropriate for this activity.

Connections Basic vocabulary is learned by age 4 or so, but the school years are best for acquiring expanded, derivative, and specialized vocabulary, especially if the child is actively connecting one word with another. With his father's encouragement, this boy in San Jose, California, will remember *Jupiter, Mars,* and the names of the other planets and maybe even *orbit, light years,* and *solar system.*

RACHEL EPSTEIN / THE IMAGE WORKS

Answer to Observational Quiz (from page 366): (1) Memorizing extensive passages requires an understanding of advanced memory strategies that combine meaning with form. (2) Understanding how to play a part so that other actors and the audience respond well requires a sophisticated theory of mind. (3) Staying focused on the moment in the play despite distractions from the audience requires selective attention.

new words that label experiences, which is not necessarily correlated with socioeconomic status (SES). For example, in one study researchers recorded 44 hours of conversations between 53 low-income mothers and their 5-year-olds during mealtime, playtime, and reading time. Despite their similar SES, these mothers varied widely in the amount of linguistic encouragement they gave their children. Some mothers simply told their children "eat"; other mothers used mealtime as an occasion for informal language instruction. For example:

Child: [makes gulping noise in throat]
Mother: Please stop.
Child: Okay.
Mother: Were you planning to eat more?
Child: No.
Mother: We kinda wasted some of that first piece of chicken there. Don't you think?
Child: No. [makes noise again]
Mother: Stop it now.
Child: Okay.
Mother: Now you're gonna have to roll up your sleeves and wash your hands and your face. Try not to get your pajama top wet. See how you do. You can wash your face with the face cloth.
Child: Okay.
Mother: Don't you make that gulping noise.
Child: [laughs for a while]

[adapted from Weizman & Snow, 2001, p. 269]

This child said only "okay" and "no," but the mother employed a fairly extensive vocabulary, including "planning," "wasted," "gulping," "roll up," and "face cloth," using each term in the immediate context so that it had concrete meaning for the child. Poverty put all the children in this study "at risk," but those 5-year-olds with mothers like this one became school-age children with large vocabularies, as measured on standardized tests (see Table 12.2). These findings "demonstrate that there is a powerful linkage between early exposure to sophisticated vocabulary—even if it constitutes as little as 1% of total maternal input—during

TABLE 12.2 Variability in Maternal Talking

During All Five Interactions	Average	Least	Most
Time spent by mother in interaction with child	50 minutes	28 minutes	90 minutes
Number of different words used by mother	1,073 words	381 words	1,636 words
Percentage of words not in child's basic vocabulary	1.8%	Less than 0.3%	More than 4.0%
During Mealtime Interactions Only			
Time spent by mother in interaction with child	20 minutes	1 minute	47 minutes
Number of different words used by mother	259 words	3 words	595 words
Percentage of words not in child's basic vocabulary	3.5%	None	More than 8%

Source: Weizman & Snow, 2001.

Talk to Me! In a detailed study of low-income mothers in the Boston area and their 5-year-old children, five interactions were recorded for each pair: two reading, two playing, and one mealtime. Despite their similar economic and geographic status, the mothers varied enormously in how much time they spent interacting with their child (by a factor of 3), how much they said (by a factor of 5), and, especially, how many words they used that were not part of a child's expected basic vocabulary (by a factor of 12). Note that the percentage of new words used by the mothers at mealtime—the only one of these five interactions that is always part of each child's day—was greater than the average (mean) percentage for all five interactions. By the time they reached second grade, the children who had heard the most varied maternal ■ talk were ahead of their peers in vocabulary acquisition.

mealtime and playtime conversation and later vocabulary performance in school" (Weizman & Snow, 2001, p. 276).

This conclusion has been supported by other research. Parents who read to, talk to, and instruct their preschool children and kindergartners foster the children's vocabulary and reading achievement in their later school career (Sénéchal & LeFevre, 2002; Sonnenschein et al., 1996).

Teaching New Words and Ideas

Vocabulary learning from ages 7 to 11 does not qualify as an "explosion," a sudden burst of new words that seems spontaneous, as in early childhood. Instead, given school-age children's logical minds and passion for new information,

> cognitive psychologists tell us that this requires a very systematic, analytical, and explicit approach. . . . Break down each domain to be learned into manageable elements that can be mastered. Then systematically build on that knowledge with new knowledge. This is the most efficient mode of learning for everybody, but it is the *essential* mode if the aim is to make up for lost time in knowledge and vocabulary.
>
> *[Hirsch, 2001, p. 7]*

This systematic building on prior knowledge is well suited to the intellect of school-age children. They increasingly link the content of the words with the overall context, realizing that the same statements can mean various things.

In one experiment, 4- to 10-year-old children heard a tape of a person saying 10 sentences with happy content in a sad voice ("My mommy gave me a treat") and 10 sentences with sad content but in a happy voice ("I lost my sticker collection") (Morton & Trehub, 2001). They were asked whether the person was actually happy or sad, a task that required them to interpret both the words they heard and the tone of the statement. Most younger children guessed wrong, judging on the basis of content alone: Sentences describing something good were judged as happy. With each year of age, the number who judged correctly on the basis of tone grew, from 5 percent to 55 percent. When asked if there was anything silly or tricky about the way the speaker talked, none of the 4-year-olds but all of the 9- and 10-year-olds explained that the speaker's emotions were sometimes different from the content (see Figure 12.1). These results show the development of linguistic sophistication over the years of middle childhood, as children come to understand the importance of the nuances of language, with tone, word choice, and context sometimes overriding the surface content of speech. Puns, sarcasm, and even irony are gradually understood, an achievement beyond the preschool child.

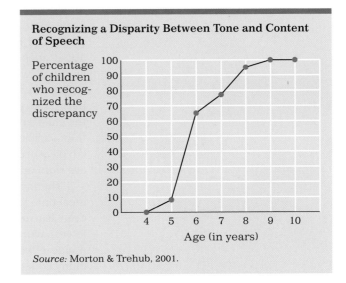

Recognizing a Disparity Between Tone and Content of Speech

Source: Morton & Trehub, 2001.

FIGURE 12.1 Do You Mean What You Say? A sudden leap of understanding occurs at the beginning of concrete operational thinking, when children can realize that a speaker is using a sad tone to describe a happy event, or vice versa. By age 9 or 10, all children are aware of this phenomenon.

An Application: Learning Apple Words

Consider what the combined insights of Piaget and Vygotsky might mean in vocabulary learning. Suppose a teacher asks a child to say the first thing that comes to mind on hearing, say, the word *apple*. A preschooler is likely to respond by referring to perceptions, appearance, or egocentric actions: *red, round,* or *to eat.* To expand this young child's knowledge, personal experience is required; apple-picking, apple-eating, and apple-juice-drinking are in the curriculum of good preschools, accompanied by lots of repetitive talk. In contrast, an older child, who could understand classification, might respond to *apple* by referring to an appropriate category ("fruit," "snack"). Suppose the teacher asks the older child to deduce the meaning of words that have *apple* as their root: *apple butter, apple cart, applesauce, apple cider, applewood.* School-age children, applying concrete logic, can do this without difficulty, adding several words to their vocabulary in a minute or two.

Piaget's scheme, which describes children as developing from preoperational (ages 2–6) to concrete operational (ages 7–11) to formal operational (age 12 on), also describes what school-age children find difficult: They are not yet at the stage of formal operations, which means that abstractions, analogies, or even metaphors may be problematic. Thus, some *apple* expressions—*apple polisher, the Big Apple, one rotten apple spoils the barrel*—are difficult to comprehend because the school-age child takes them literally, missing the connection between, say, a person and a rotten apple. Knowing what school-age children can learn easily, and what they have difficulty learning, helps adults as they try to guide each child into the *zone of proximal development,* as Vygotsky would call it, toward those words and ideas they can learn with a little assistance (see Chapter 2).

Expanding the Vocabulary

School-age children really enjoy words, as demonstrated in the poems they write, the secret languages they create, and the jokes they tell. Joke telling actually demands several skills not usually apparent in younger children: the ability to listen carefully; the ability to know what someone else will think is funny; and, hardest of all, the ability to remember the right words and sequence for telling the joke. Vocabulary is often key, with puns a mainstay of school-age humor. The intellectual flexibility required to understand a pun is the consequence of normal brain maturation that is typical by age 6 or 7. For example, "What's black and white and red all over?" with the classic answer "a newspaper" is funny from about ages 6 to 12 (but not earlier or later) because most children understand language well enough to know that *red* and *read* are pronounced the same. Once children understand and remember that riddle, the alternative answers (an embarrassed skunk, a sunburned zebra) become funny because their violation of the child's developing knowledge of logic becomes laughable. The other satisfaction is tricking someone who thought they knew the answer, which is a particular pleasure for the concrete operational child who believes that some answers are right and others are wrong.

The fact that children love words as well as learning makes these years the ideal time for teaching new vocabulary. One study found that in grades 3–5, children learned an average of three words per day; the children who knew the fewest words at the beginning learned more at school. In order to teach language effectively, adults should appreciate that children at this age can learn many codes and languages, as we will now see.

Code-Switching

In elementary school, children become sensitive to variations in the speech and tone of others, a process called *code recognition.* They realize, for example, that a father's increasingly terse and clipped speech is an indication of growing anger. They also understand that the entire set of linguistic conventions may be changed to suit particular audiences. The latter concept is apparent in this example:

> A brand-new black teacher is delivering her first reading lesson to a group of first-grade students in inner-city Philadelphia. She has almost memorized the entire basal-provided lesson dialogue [the introduction provided in the teacher's edition of the textbook] while practicing in front of a mirror the night before.
>
> *"Good morning, boys and girls. Today we're going to read a story about where we live, in the city."*

A small brown hand rises.

"Yes, Marti."

Marti and this teacher are special friends, for she was a kindergartner in the classroom where her new teacher student-taught.

"Teacher, how come you talkin' like a white person? You talkin' just like my momma talk when she get on the phone."

I was that first-year teacher many years ago, and Marti was among the first to teach me the role of language diversity in the classroom. Marti let me know that children, even young children, are often aware of the different codes we all use in our everyday lives. They may not yet have learned how to produce those codes or what social purposes they serve, but children often have a remarkable ability to discern and identify different codes in different settings.

[Delpit, 1995]

In addition to recognizing codes, children can change their own speech and tone from one form to another, a process called **code-switching.** Children in middle childhood censor profanity when they talk to adults, but use picturesque slang, curses, and drama on the playground. Bilingual children sometimes switch back and forth from one language to another within a single sentence when they are talking with other children who know both codes (Bialystok, 2001). These changes in code are a sign of linguistic sophistication. The bilingual code-switcher, for example, does not change at random but uses the words and phrases that are most likely to convey exactly what is meant. In all cases, the child code-switches in response to the context: The school-age child does not make the mistakes that younger children do, such as cursing in front of grandma or speaking French to a stranger in Japan.

code-switching The ability to change one's speech and tone from one form to another.

Formal and Informal Codes

In a universal example of code-switching, almost every school-age child shifts from formal communication in the classroom to informal communication with friends outside the school. In general, the **formal code,** sometimes called *elaborated code,* is characterized by extensive vocabulary, complex syntax, and lengthy

formal code Speech that is characterized by extensive vocabulary, complex syntax, and lengthy sentences. Also called *elaborated code.*

RICHARD HUTCHINGS / PHOTO RESEARCHERS, INC.

Recitation Classroom talk is distinct from street talk not only in vocabulary but also in grammar, sentence length, logic, intonation, and gesture. One way to stick to the formal code and avoid hand gestures is to read your report, as this 10-year-old is doing. In the classroom, unlike the playground, the listeners are supposed to be quiet, immobile, and attentive—a lesson these children have learned.

? *Observational Quiz* (see answer, page 372): How does the writing on the blackboard reflect concrete operational thought?

informal code Speech that is characterized by the use of relatively few words and simpler syntax and by reliance on gestures and intonation to convey meaning. Also called *restricted code*.

sentences. By comparison, the **informal code,** sometimes called *restricted code,* uses fewer words, employs simpler syntax, and relies more on gestures and intonation to convey meaning.

The formal code is relatively *context-free;* that is, the meaning is clear regardless of the immediate context. The informal code tends to be *context-bound;* that is, the meaning relies on shared understandings and experiences between speaker and listener, as well as on the immediate situation and subject at hand. A dispirited student might tell a teacher, in formal code, "I'm depressed today because [a detailed excuse that the teacher is likely to accept], and I would rather not read out loud or write my book report," and later confide to a friend informally, "I'm down; school ____s." The particular words chosen informally depend on the specific local code, but the tone and emphasis are universal in friend-to-friend communication.

Children of all backgrounds code-switch, changing pronunciation, grammar, and vocabulary depending on the context. Southern dialect, Ebonics, patois, Valley talk, Cockney, mountain speech, Newyorican, pidgin, street language, broken English, and slang all refer to informal codes. They are used not only by children but also by adults (especially when speaking with other adults who had similar childhood origins). Even children who do not use a designated, regionalized informal code (such as the ones just mentioned) tend to speak to their friends informally, with less crisp enunciation and nontextbook grammar.

!*Answer to Observational Quiz* (from page 371): If you can read it, you can see that the topic is German shepherds—what they "are," "have," and "do." Even if you can see only the diagram, you can tell that this lesson takes advantage of classification skills, with a connecting line linking each subcategory to the larger category.

Formal language is sometimes called *correct, proper, high,* or *standard* (as in *Standard English* or *High German/Hoch Deutsch*). Such adjectives imply that the formal code is preferable, but actually both codes are appropriate in their place. It is sometimes vital to speak in formal terms, partly because standard language is considered educated speech and its vocabulary is more precise. Indeed, the two pivotal academic skills learned during middle childhood—reading and writing—depend on understanding and employing formal language without the benefit of informal gestures, intonations, and immediate context.

At the same time, peer communication via informal code is also vital—not only for social acceptance but also for more direct, emotional dialogue. While many adults rightly insist that their children master proper language ("Say precisely what you mean in complete sentences, and don't use any slang"), the code that is used with peers is also evidence of the child's ability (Goodwin, 1990).

This same distinction can be made between children who speak the dominant language of a nation and those who have another mother tongue. Both languages are important, for different reasons, and educators need to find a way to foster fluent bilingualism—no easy task, as we will see later in this chapter.

Don't Tell the Teacher The best example of the informal code is the whispered secret—a few hurried words, not for public consumption, that convey shared emotional understanding.

Whether or not this task is attempted is a matter of national education policy (Alexander, 2000). The best approach for teaching children a second language is also a hotly contested issue. Accordingly, the specifics of the second-language debate are discussed on pages 383–385, in the section on education-related controversies. First we discuss one other kind of learning for which 7- to 11-year-olds are at the ideal age: moral education.

Moral Development

Beginning at about age 4, the various parts of the brain involved in emotions and intellect become better connected, as we have seen in previous chapters; this has implications for morality as well as for academic skills. School-age children can evaluate their own instincts, set moral values and then act on them, or remember moral prohibitions and refrain from actions that they decide are wrong. Moral development is not only a cognitive process; it is a cultural and social one as well. However, our major discussion of developing morality appears in this chapter on cognition because moral decisions stem from thought and logic, influenced by family and society (as are other cognitive accomplishments) (Colby, 2000; Walker et al., 2000). As a psychiatrist who studied children's morality writes:

> It's a real passion for them. . . . In elementary school, maybe as never before or afterward, given favorable family and neighborhood circumstances, the child becomes an intensely moral creature, quite interested in figuring out the reasons of this world: how and why things work, but also how and why he or she should behave in various situations.
>
> *[Coles, 1997]*

Kohlberg's Stages of Moral Development

Building on Piaget's theories and research, Lawrence Kohlberg (1963, 1981a,b) studied moral reasoning by presenting subjects with a set of ethical dilemmas. Responses to several scenarios allowed Kohlberg to describe how people reasoned about situations that demanded moral judgments. The most famous story involves the conflict between private property and human life as experienced by Heinz, a poor man whose wife is dying of cancer. A local pharmacist has developed the only cure, a drug sold for thousands of dollars—far more than Heinz can pay and 10 times what the drug costs to make.

> Heinz went to everyone he knew to borrow the money, but he could only get together about half of what it cost. He told the druggist that his wife was dying and asked him to sell it cheaper or let him pay later. But the druggist said "no." The husband got desperate and broke into the man's store to steal the drug for his wife. Should the husband have done that? Why?
>
> *[Kohlberg, 1963]*

Lawrence Kohlberg Kohlberg was a scholar, researcher, and philosopher who described the logical structures that underlie specific moral decisions.

In people's responses to such dilemmas, Kohlberg found three levels of moral reasoning—**preconventional, conventional,** and **postconventional**—with two stages at each level (see Table 12.3).

According to Kohlberg, *how* people reason, rather than what specific moral conclusions they reach, determines their stage of moral development. For example, reasoning that seeks social approval (stage 3) might produce opposite conclusions: Either Heinz should steal the drug (because people will blame him for not saving his wife) or he should not steal it (because people would call him a thief if he stole). But in both cases, the underlying moral precept is the same—that people should behave in ways that earn the praise of others, a stage-three way of thinking.

In every stage, what counts for Kohlberg are thought processes as verbalized by the person, not the final decision one way or the other. Children, adolescents, and adults gradually move up the hierarchy, reasoning at a more advanced stage as time goes on. A close examination of this process reveals that generally, during middle childhood, children's answers are at the first two levels—primarily

preconventional moral reasoning Kohlberg's first level of moral reasoning, in which emphasis is placed on getting rewards and avoiding punishments.

conventional moral reasoning Kohlberg's second level of moral reasoning, in which emphasis is placed on social rules.

postconventional moral reasoning Kohlberg's third level of moral reasoning, in which emphasis is placed on moral principles.

TABLE 12.3 Kohlberg's Three Levels and Six Stages of Moral Reasoning

Level I: Preconventional Moral Reasoning

Emphasis is placed on getting rewards and avoiding punishments; this is a self-centered level.

- *Stage One: Might makes right* (a punishment and obedience orientation). The most important value is obedience to authority, so as to avoid punishment while still advancing self-interest.

- *Stage Two: Look out for number one* (an instrumental and relativist orientation). Each person tries to take care of his or her own needs. The reason to be nice to other people is so that they will be nice to you.

Level II: Conventional Moral Reasoning

Emphasis is placed on social rules; this is a community-centered level.

- *Stage Three: "Good girl" and "nice boy."* Proper behavior is now behavior that pleases other people. Social approval is more important than any specific reward.

- *Stage Four: "Law and order."* Proper behavior means being a dutiful citizen and obeying the laws set down by society.

Level III: Postconventional Moral Reasoning

Emphasis is now on moral principles; this level is centered on ideals.

- *Stage Five: Social contract.* One should obey the rules of society because they exist for the benefit of all and are established by mutual agreement. If the rules become destructive, however, or if one party doesn't live up to the agreement, the contract is no longer binding.

- *Stage Six: Universal ethical principles.* General universal principles, not individual situations or community practices, determine right and wrong. Ethical values (such as "life is sacred") are established by individual reflection and may contradict the egocentric or legal values of earlier stages.

preconventional for 7- and 8-year-olds and conventional for 9- to 11-year-olds—although much depends on the specific context and on the child's opportunity to discuss moral issues. Almost no one, child or adult, reaches the highest level of all, universal ethical principles.

Kohlberg's Critics

Kohlberg's basic ideas—that cognitive maturation affects reasoning about moral dilemmas and that moral thinking advances in stages—are now confirmed (Boom et al., 2001; Gibbs et al., 1992; Rest et al., 1999b; Walker et al., 2001). Morality is not simply swallowed whole by children as they learn their culture. Moral development depends on the interplay of thought and experience, and both of those are intertwined with a child's cognitive maturation. All these factors are apparent in how self-absorbed (preconventional), culturally influenced (conventional), or principled (postconventional) people are in their responses to moral issues. Kohlberg's stress on childhood and adolescence is also widely accepted; although moral values develop throughout life, the decade from 6 to 16 is a crucial time when moral values are taught, ethical principles are tested, and religious beliefs are laid down.

Yet there are three major criticisms of Kohlberg and his stages: that his methods are flawed, that his hierarchy is biased in favor of Western elites, and that he ignores the moral development of women. The first criticism has to do with methodology. In assessing the three levels (and six stages) of moral thinking, examiners interview each individual, one by one, and score their oral responses.

This research method is cumbersome, time-consuming, and susceptible to scoring bias. The focus on logical, expressed explanations favors articulate respondents over those who may be equally moral but less verbal.

To avoid this methodological problem, James Rest, another prominent researcher, developed an alternate measure of moral thinking that asks people to read various dilemmas and then to rank 12 statements as possible resolutions for each situation. This questionnaire, called the **Defining Issues Test (DIT)**, has been used widely, comparing people of various ages and backgrounds (Rest et al., 1999a). Answers are easier to collect, tabulate, and compare than with Kohlberg's original method. Results from the DIT show that Kohlberg's three levels (self-centered, community-centered, and principle-centered) are valid. They also show that cultural differences affect moral judgments—a finding that leads to the second criticism.

Defining Issues Test (DIT) A questionnaire devised by James Rest that measures moral thinking by asking people to read various dilemmas and then to rank 12 statements as possible resolutions for each situation.

Cultural Differences

It is now well established that every culture has distinctive values and morals, which are sometimes connected to a particular religion, sometimes not. For example, children may hold the belief that eating beef (or pork, whale, or dog) is immoral; such a value is not universal but very culture-specific. Kohlberg was from a Western intellectual background. Did this influence his hierarchy?

To be specific, some critics of Kohlberg believe that his level III (stages 5 and 6) reflects only liberal, Western intellectual values. In many non-Western nations and among many non-Western ethnic groups within Western cultures, the good of the family, the well-being of the community, or adherence to religious tradition takes moral precedence over all other considerations (Wainryb & Turiel, 1995). This makes it harder for non-Westerners to score at Kohlberg's postconventional level or even to move up the hierarchy as fast as others. For example, in a study of teenagers in the Netherlands, Moroccan and Turkish students were significantly behind Dutch and Surinamese adolescents in Kohlberg's hierarchy (De May et al., 1999). The Moroccan and Turkish emphasis on family and community, taken as a handicap in Kohlberg's scheme, can be considered a higher form of moral thinking than the individualism and rationality enshrined by Kohlberg. It may be that Kohlberg's "philosophical emphasis on justice and psychological emphasis on reasoning" are too narrow and restrictive (Walker et al., 1995).

In contrast, Kohlberg's hierarchy may underestimate the reasoning capacity of some school-age children in some cultures. Canadian 6- to 10-year-olds, who were presumably too young to think past level I or II, were able to judge whether laws were just and to condone disobedience when a law was unjust—a stage-five reaction. These issues are not discussed in elementary school, presumably because they are thought to be beyond young children (Helwig & Jasiobedzka, 2001).

Morality and Gender

Carol Gilligan (1982) raised the third criticism, that Kohlberg overlooked significant gender differences, in part because his original research used only boys as subjects. Gilligan explains that females develop a **morality of care** more than a **morality of justice.** The morality of care makes girls and women reluctant to judge right and wrong in absolute terms (justice) because they are socialized to be nurturant, compassionate, and nonjudgmental (caring).

As an example, Gilligan cited the responses of two bright 11-year-olds, Jake and Amy, to the Heinz story. Jake considered the dilemma "sort of like a math

morality of care In Gilligan's view, the tendency of females to be reluctant to judge right and wrong in absolute terms because they are socialized to be nurturant, compassionate, and nonjudgmental.

morality of justice In Gilligan's view, the tendency of males to emphasize justice over compassion, judging right and wrong in absolute terms.

Carol Gilligan Gilligan is best known for comparing moral logic to real-life dilemmas. She pointed out that because females are often inclined to consider human relationships, they are less abstract and less dogmatic than men—and less advanced in Kohlberg's hierarchy of moral development.

problem with humans," and he set up an equation that showed that life is more important than property. Amy, in contrast, seemed to sidestep the issue, arguing that Heinz "really shouldn't steal the drug—but his wife shouldn't die either." She tried to find an alternative solution (a bank loan, perhaps) and then explained that stealing wouldn't be right because Heinz "might have to go to jail, and then his wife might get sicker again, and he couldn't get more of the drug."

Amy's response may seem just as ethical as Jake's, but Kohlberg would score it lower. Gilligan argues that this is unfair, because what appears to be females' moral weakness—their hesitancy to take a definitive position based on abstract moral premises—is, in fact,

> inseparable from women's moral strength, an overriding concern with relationships and responsibilities. The reluctance to judge may itself be indicative of the care and concern that infuse the psychology of women's development.
>
> *[Gilligan, 1982]*

Many researchers have tested Gilligan's ideas with children, by looking for a morality of care or a morality of justice. In one study, the moral dilemma presented was not Kohlberg's but a fable about a family of moles who invite a lonely and cold porcupine to share their underground home for the winter. He accepts, but then the moles realize that the porcupine's size and sharp quills make them very uncomfortable. They politely ask him to leave, but he refuses. What to do? One 8-year-old was very caring:

> They should all go on an expedition for marshmallows and stick the marshmallows on the porcupine's quills and then the moles will really, really, really not get pricked. Then the porcupine would be happy because he could live in the moles' house that suited him just fine and the moles could have tasty tidbits as well as a warm home because of the porcupine's body heat . . . and all would be happy.
>
> *[Garrod, 1993]*

This version of "the morality of care" found a way for everyone to be happy. By contrast, law and order were evident in another child's response, which is a good example of "the morality of justice":

> The central problem, as I see it, is that the moles want the porcupine to leave and he's refusing. I think that they should kick him out. They were nice to let him in in the first place. And it's not their fault that he has quills. They have a right to be comfortable in their own home . . . they can do what they want in their cave. It's like if a homeless man moved into my home while my family was vacationing in Florida. We'd definitely call the police.
>
> *[Garrod, 1993]*

Both these respondents were boys. Thus, in this research (and in other research involving the actual responses and actions of school-age children) there is no clear gender distinction regarding the morality of justice or the morality of care. Gilligan may have articulated an important difference in the way males and females are encouraged to respond in ethical situations, but the evidence from hypothetical dilemmas does not support a gender divide between a morality of care and a morality of justice (Walker, 1988). From all the cross-cultural research on moral development, however, researchers find that moral dilemmas are provocative issues for school-age children—who have opinions and like to express them.

Another conclusion about morality is also widely held: Abstract reasoning about the justice of hypothetical situations is not the only, or necessarily the best, way to measure moral judgment (Emler, 1998). What children actually do when they personally care about an issue is more reflective of morality than what they might say about Heinz, or porcupines, or any other hypothetical situation.

Prosocial Behavior: Two versions School-age children, such as these Habitat for Humanity builders and this Girl Scout, are able to perform many useful prosocial tasks. Although prosocial acts are performed without expectation of rewards, they can result in a very important benefit: a sense of connection. The adults' role is to find suitable prosocial activities for school-age children—not always an easy task because children don't always feel comfortable "helping." These boys, for instance, might not enjoy wearing a uniform and chatting with the elderly, but they certainly take pride in pounding nails with their friends.

Children's Actual Moral Behavior

As we have seen, during middle childhood children are passionately concerned with issues of right and wrong. Overall, these are the

> years of eager, lively searching on the part of children, whose parents and teach-
> ers are often hard put to keep up with them as they try to understand things, to
> figure them out, but also to weigh the rights and wrongs of this life. This is the
> time for growth of the moral imagination, fueled constantly by the willingness,
> the eagerness of children to put themselves in the shoes of others.
>
> *[Coles, 1997]*

The specifics depend heavily on the values of the child's parents and society. If a family and culture are conscientious about providing children with guided participation in their set of values, with both adult and child undertaking moral actions, school-age children learn and, eventually, behave accordingly (Goodnow, 1997). As you saw in Chapter 10, prosocial behavior—acts of sharing, helping, and caring—is learned in much the same way that antisocial behavior is—from parents, schools, and peers (Eisenberg et al., 1996).

Few children *always* follow their parents' moral standards, their culture's conventions, or their own best moral thinking; yet moral thought has a decided influence on children's actions (Eisenberg, 1986; Rest, 1983). Increasingly, as they grow older, children try to figure out their own standards of what the "right" thing to do is, and they feel guilty and ashamed when they do "wrong," even if no one else knows (Harter, 1996). For example, when children were asked whether they would break a law to help their siblings or peers, the answer was almost always "yes." In general, school-age children considered loyalty to siblings or peers—especially to a close friend—a compelling reason to ignore community standards of proper action. Many children said they would cheat, lie, or steal to help a needy friend (Smetana et al., 1991; Turiel et al., 1991). Further, authority figures—parents, teachers, police officers, store owners—are not necessarily seen as right, as the In Person feature illustrates.

Especially for Parents: Suppose you and your school-age children move to a new community that is 50 miles from the nearest location that offers instruction in your religious faith or secular value system. Your neighbor says, "Don't worry, they don't have to make any moral decisions until they are teenagers." What do you do?

In Person

Challenging the Adults

As a mother of four, teaching moral thinking and behavior is very important to me. I have often said that I would rather have my children become loving and caring adults than become successful and rich—although I take great pride in their successes. It is not surprising, then, that they also care about moral issues, sometimes taking actions that are not the ones I would choose.

For example, my daughter Sarah regularly gives her pocket money to homeless people and is quick to criticize me for rudely (her word) passing them by. The strength of her conviction was illustrated years ago when her fourth-grade class visited the local police precinct in New York City to hear an officer instruct them on street safety. Most of his talk was accepted without protest, until:

> **Officer:** Never take money out of your pocket while you are on the street—

> *(At this point, according to the mother who helped chaperone the school trip, Sarah raised her hand insistently, "the way children do who have to go to the bathroom right away.")*

> **Officer:** *(Interrupting his speech.)* Yes?

> **Sarah:** But what if a homeless man wants money?
> **Officer:** Your parents give you money for lunch, not to give away.
> **Sarah:** But what if you decide you don't need lunch?
> **Officer:** You should not give money to beggars; you don't know how they will spend it.
> **Sarah:** But what if you decide he really really needs it?
> **Officer:** Don't give it. Adults are taking care of the homeless people who really need help.
> **Sarah:** *(Shaking her head.)* Well, you aren't doing a very good job.

That incident made me proud, as the mother who telephoned me to report it knew it would.

Although I still disagree with Sarah about the most moral response to street beggars, I appreciate at least one aspect of this incident. Sarah's active sense of morality bodes well. Children who engage in moral discussion and feel personally responsible for their ethical behavior tend to be more accomplished than others, socially as well as academically (Bandura et al., 1996). Active reflection is much more likely to lead to moral action than is merely accepting social conventions and laws.

Because cultural and religious values shape moral perception, what is merely conventional in one culture may take on moral significance in another. Children behave in accord with their moral beliefs, nurtured by family, school, and, especially, the peer group. As they grow older, their actions become more ethical and less self-interested, because they have the social experiences, the cultural awareness, and the cognitive capacity to generate more persuasive arguments—both in convincing themselves to do the right thing and in justifying their actions to others (Emler, 1998). They maintain these patterns and values when they are fully grown, becoming better at recognizing true moral dilemmas.

One team of researchers asked third-graders, seventh-graders, and college students "whether it is all right" for other people to hold beliefs that they themselves did not hold (Wainryb et al., 2001). The beliefs tested were of four kinds: moral, conventional, psychological, and metaphysical. (In pretesting, the examiners determined that these subjects did not hold these particular beliefs.) Here are examples of the four kinds of beliefs tested:

- *Moral.* "It is all right to hurt children just because one wants to hurt them."
- *Conventional.* "The way to get a waiter's attention is to put one's fork in a glass."
- *Psychological.* "The way to be really good friends with someone is never to tell them how you feel about anything."
- *Metaphysical.* "Only people who die on Tuesday become angels."

GARY LANGLEY

Give Peace a Chance The setting is Israel; the sheep washers include Jews and Muslims. In all probability, these boys are aware that their cooperative efforts are in accord with moral values but are contrary to the social customs prevailing around them. The school years are a good time to teach children about other races and cultures, a lesson best learned through personal experience.

Not surprisingly, subjects were likely to judge moral beliefs that were divergent from their own to be "not all right" and divergent *metaphysical* beliefs to be "all right." Third graders were already quite similar to adolescents and adults in their moral judgments, particularly about what is tolerable (although odd) and what is beyond acceptance.

In two important ways, however, the third-graders differed from the older subjects. First, they more strongly believed that disagreements with conventional beliefs (putting a fork in a glass) were "not all right," especially when the person not only held the unconventional idea but also acted on it, even if that person's culture approved of such behavior. Second, they were more likely to judge someone who held any of these four types of divergent beliefs "insane" compared to the seventh-graders and college students, who more often thought such a person was merely "immature" or "uninformed." In other words, compared to adolescents and adults, school-age children were more critical and dismissive of people who thought differently from themselves. Likewise, another study found that, compared to college students, school-age children judged liars more harshly, especially liars who personally benefited from their lies (Barnett et al., 2000).

This tendency to be critical of other people who disagree is apparent in school-age children's everyday behavior: They increasingly want to dress, talk, and think like their peers, even if adults have other preferences. Does this conformity mean that children prefer other children who are just like them, including their own sex and ethnicity? Yes! However, when asked, they oppose exclusion based on race or sex. In one study, children in the first, third, and seventh grades were adamant that it was *not* all right to exclude a child just because he or she was different from other members of an after-school club. This moral judgment was made by 94 percent of the children when the difference was sex and 97 percent when the difference was race (Killen & Stangor, 2001). The third-graders were slightly more inclusive than the others. Other research suggests that school-age children come to their beliefs as a result of their thoughts and experiences, not just of an innate moral sensibility. In fact, by about age 11 almost all children have well-formed ideas of justice and fairness, and can think of instances when they themselves have been wronged (Evans et al., 2001). The advanced control processes that we have described mean that 11-year-olds are less likely to react to their feelings in a harmful way; nevertheless, they are well aware of immoral behavior in adults.

Response for Parents (from page 377): Your neighbor is mistaken: These are prime years for moral education. You might travel those 50 miles once or twice a week or recruit other parents to organize a local program. Whatever you do, don't skip moral instruction. Discuss and demonstrate your moral and religious values, and help your children meet other children who share those values.

Schools, Values, and Research

Worldwide, many ideological debates swirl around the content and the practice of elementary education. A review of educational practices in five cultures found that there is often a discrepancy between "expressed claim and observed reality," because "not uncommonly school structures are at variance with educational goals, frustrating or even contradicting them" (Alexander, 2000, p. 176). Virtually no nation has good information on the extent to which reforms and policies are actually implemented in the classroom. As a result, moving from what is known about the psychology and brain of the school-age child to what happens in the classroom is a hazardous journey.

Sometimes answers are not clearly established or well understood by scholars or the public. For that reason, developmentalists advocate large-scale outcome evaluations for every new or old educational practice, in which children from many cultures are compared. At other times the research leads in one direction but ideology seems disconnected from the research (Rayner et al., 2001). Developmental principles and research provide some guidance through the thicket of ideology, politics, and culture that surrounds educational controversies.

Deciding How Children Should Learn

Children can learn anything if it is "packaged" properly—but not everything all at once. Our understanding of cognition suggests that learning is easiest and most efficient if it is concrete, not abstract (Simon, 2001); builds on an established knowledge base; is connected to other material; and is taught directly and sequentially, with explicit goals and demands. What does this mean for school curricula?

Internationally and across the decades, adults have agreed that schools should teach reading, writing, and arithmetic. The school years are the best time for that academic learning, although about a fifth of the world's people never learn the basics and remain illiterate (United Nations, 2001). Beyond these three subjects, curricula vary. For example, in Russia and France, oral expression and reasoned argument are central to the elementary school curriculum; this is not so in India and the United States (Alexander, 2000). Specific national history is sometimes emphasized, sometimes not. In the United States, some observers point out that children do not know American history (one report found that only 32 percent of fourth-graders could name even one of the 13 original colonies [Hitchens, 1998]); other observers note that knowledge of science lags behind that of children in other nations (see Appendix A); and others report that health, or sports, or second-language learning are not part of every child's school day.

The much-publicized achievement of Japanese, Chinese, and Korean children in math and science, which is far superior to the achievement of children in the United States and Canada, led to pressure to have North American children spend more time learning and less time playing. This shift has indeed happened since the early 1980s (see Appendix A).

The debate about what specific skills to stress in elementary education is ongoing. School-age children are able and eager to learn almost anything, but they cannot learn everything at once. Comparing nations, comparing schools, and comparing children can show which educational strategies and curricula succeed, as we have seen. However, another set of criteria is needed to measure what should be valued. For example, the need "to ensure a competitive workforce . . . to fill the jobs of the future and compete in a global economy" led the United States to set the goal of being first worldwide in math and science by the year 2000. At that point, most Americans probably agreed that this was a desirable aim (National Endowment Goals Panel, 1997). But if math and science become priorities, and scores continue to rise, what will happen in literacy and creativity, areas in which the United States has traditionally excelled? Music, art, and physical education programs have been cut back in almost every public school. Emotional regulation and community values may be even more important. As one teacher said, "My trouble is too many children are sad, or mad, or bad; not that they can't add" (quoted in Thompson, 2001).

The Reading Wars

Two distinct approaches to teaching reading are used in the United States and in many other nations: phonics and whole language (Rayner et al., 2001). Clashes over the two approaches have been called the Reading Wars; these battles have sometimes been waged without concern for scientific evidence, developmental changes, or children's needs (Adams et al., 1998).

Traditionally, the **phonics** approach (from the root word for "sound") meant requiring children to learn the sounds of each letter before they began to decipher simple words. This works well in learning to read languages such as Italian, where the sound–letter connections are clear, but not as well in English, where there are many exceptions. In the first half of the twentieth century, schools in the United States were characterized by:

> drill and more drill . . . instruction in letter–sound relationships and pro-nunciation rules. . . . Children had to learn so much abstract material by rote before doing any significant amount of reading.
>
> *[Diederich, 1973, p. 7]*

By contrast, the **whole-language** approach begins by recognizing that language is an entire set of skills—talking and listening, reading and writing—all with the goal of communication. Children are encouraged to write on their own, inventing the spelling according to how the words sound. For example, one 4-year-old boy tried to keep others out of his room with this sign on his door: GNYS AT WRK (Bissex, 1980); a school girl named Karla wrote a stern note to her mother (see Figure 12.2). These demonstrate the whole-language idea that children can communicate their emotions in writing long before they have mastered standard spelling.

Both these approaches have merit. First, both maintain that motivation matters: Children learn best when they understand why they are learning. Abstract, decontextualized memorization is difficult—no wonder traditional phonics did not always succeed. Second, unlike talking, which is experience-expectant, reading is experience-dependent. Most children will not be able to figure it out on their own without explicit instruction in the relationship among sounds, letters, and words. Beginning readers often need to be taught how to translate spoken words into printed ones. Instruction in phonics and then practice with standard spelling are needed for children to be able to break the code and decipher words. Until then, children will not practice reading on their own. Without practice, automatization in reading will not occur, because brain patterns are established only through extensive repetition (Rayner et al., 2001; Stanovich, 2000).

Third, research emphasizes that each step of development, each component of language learning, and each child's learning style and maturation level are unique in crucial ways. In practical terms, this means that phonics is particularly useful for children who are just beginning to read and for the many children who need help with learning to decipher new words. If children speak another language or do not already have strong listening and speaking skills, they also need explicit vocabulary-building and pronunciation practice. In fact, every teacher

From karla to my mom
its No fare
that you mad
me Lat my Lade
bug Go Wat
If I was your
mom and I mad
you tack yo ur
Lade bug tam
Shp you wud
be sad like me
that lade bug
mat of bar a orfan
so you sod ov lat me
hav it ane wae

FIGURE 12.2 "You Wud Be Sad Like Me"
Although Karla, a first-grader, uses invented spelling, her arguments show that she is reasoning quite logically; her school-age mind is working quite well. (If you have trouble deciphering Karla's note, turn the book upside down for a translation.)
Source: Lerner, 2000, p. 462.

"From Karla to my mom. It's no fair that you made me let my lady bug go. What if I was your mom and I made you take your lady bug. I am sure you would be sad like me. That lady bug might have been an orphan. So you should have let me have it anyway.

phonics approach The teaching of reading by requiring children to learn the sounds of each letter before they begin to decipher simple words.

whole-language approach The teaching of reading by encouraging children to develop all their language skills—talking and listening, reading and writing—all with the goal of communication.

should use many methods and strategies, for there are "alternate pathways in learning to read" (Berninger et al., 2002, p. 295). Phonics should be part of instruction, but other aspects of literacy, taught in other ways, are important as well (Adams & Bruck, 1995; Rayner et al., 2001).

Teaching Math

In the United States, math was traditionally taught through rote learning; children memorized number facts, such as the multiplication tables, and filled page after page of worksheets. As a result, many children came to hate math and did poorly in it. In response, the U.S. government supported research devoted to improving the math curriculum, and experts, inspired by Vygotsky, found ways to make math a more active, engaging subject (Ginsburg et al., 1998).

One notable set of standards and practices came from the National Council of Teachers of Mathematics (1989), which developed a new curriculum emphasizing concepts and problem solving, estimating and probability. Recommended pedagogical techniques included social norms: "Students are obligated to explain and justify solutions, to attempt to make sense of solutions given by others . . . and to ask clarifying questions or challenge alternatives" (Cobb, 2000, pp. 464–465). The focus is on the process, not the product. One teacher asked the class how many runners were in a race that had two teams of six runners each. The children had already worked in pairs to come up with the process for answering, called the "answer solution."

> **Teacher:** Jack, what answer solution did you come up with?
> **Jack:** Fourteen.
> **Teacher:** Fourteen. How did you get that answer?
> **Jack:** Because 6 plus 6 is 12. Two runners on two teams . . .

> *(Jack stops talking, puts his hands to the side of his face and looks down at the floor. Then he looks at the teacher and at his partner, Ann. He turns and faces the front of the room with his back to the teacher and mumbles inaudibly.)*

> **Teacher:** Would you please say that again. I didn't quite get the whole thing. You had—say it again please.
> **Jack:** *(Softly, still facing the front of the room)* It's six runners on each team.
> **Teacher:** Right.
> **Jack:** *(Turns to look at the teacher)* I made a mistake. It's wrong. It should be twelve. *(He turns and faces the front of the room again.)*

> *(Jack's acute embarrassment . . . confounded the teacher's intention that the children should publicly express their thinking and, more generally, engage in mathematical practice characterized by conjecture, argument, and justification.)*

> **Teacher:** *(Softly)* Oh, okay. Is it okay to make a mistake?
> **Andrew:** Yes.
> **Teacher:** Is it okay to make a mistake, Jack?
> **Jack:** Yeah.
> **Teacher:** You bet it is. As long as you're in my class it is okay to make a mistake. Because I make them all the time, and we learn from our mistakes— a lot. Jack already figured out, "Ooops, I didn't have the right answer the first time" *(Jack turns and looks at the teacher and smiles),* but he kept working at it and he got it.
>
> [Cobb et al., 1993]

Nevertheless, changes in educational practice remain controversial: "Even mathematics—that cold, rational, neutral, nerdy subject matter—can become embroiled in political dispute, at least when hot issue of values are introduced" (Ginsburg et al., 1998, p. 437). The primary problem is that parents (and some teachers) disagree with the recommendation that children work in groups to find solutions to difficult problems on their own, without the textbooks, worksheets, or homework that parents understand.

Teacher practice seems more strongly influenced by culture than by research, as illustrated by an international study in which hundreds of math lessons were videotaped (Stigler & Hiebert, 1999). The researchers found that math instructors in Japan require children to collaborate on developing math solutions and proofs, after the teachers ensure step-by-step learning that makes such challenges surmountable. The same study found that, even though schools in the United States are diverse in population and structure, most math teachers stress basic procedures for solving simple problems, and these procedures are often presented in a scattered, repetitive way (Stigler & Hiebert, 1999). Math classes in the United States were found to be less difficult than those in the other parts of the world, but the children learned less. Children progress faster when they are taught strategies, not mere facts, and when they learn through teacher guidance and peer collaboration, not on their own. When the group problem solving that is the usual mode in Japan is tried in North America, it seems to work effectively (Johnson & Johnson, 1994).

Popular beliefs and actual learning are not necessarily connected. For example, children and parents in the United States are more satisfied with their math achievements, even though it is lower than are children and parents in Japan (Stigler & Hiebert, 1999). Similar discrepancies between cultural norms and real learning seem to exist in many nations, in math and in other subjects (Alexander, 2000).

> ❯ **Especially for Parents:** You are tired but are setting out to buy groceries. Your 7-year-old son wants to go with you. Should you explain that you are too tired to take him?

Learning a Second Language

Learning a second language is required in some nations (such as India and Canada) but not in others (such as the United States) (Alexander, 2000). As we saw in Chapter 9, learning two languages is easiest in early childhood. However, many children arrive in kindergarten speaking only one language, which makes schooling a crucial path toward bilingualism.

Almost every nation has a sizable minority whose members speak a non-majority language; for them, learning the majority language is a necessity. In fact, most of the estimated 6,000 languages of the world are never used in formal educational settings. Consequently, most of the world's children are educated in a language other than their mother tongue (Tucker, 1998).

While the best time to *learn* a second language by listening and talking is during early childhood, the best time to *teach* a second language seems to be during middle childhood. Because of their readiness to understand code-switching, their eagerness to communicate, their wish to be good students, their grasp of

Maintaining Tradition Some would say that these Vietnamese children in Texas are fortunate. They are instructed in two languages by a teacher who knows their culture, including the use of red pens for self-correction as well as teacher correction. Others would say that these children would be better off in an "English-only" classroom.

total immersion An approach to teaching a second language in which instruction occurs entirely in that language and the learner's native language is not used at all.

Response for Parents (from page 383): Your son would understand your explanation, but you should take him along. Any excursion is a learning opportunity. You wouldn't ignore his need for food or medicine; don't ignore his need for learning. While shopping, you can teach vocabulary (does he know *pimientos, pepperoni, polenta?*), categories ("root vegetables," "freshwater fish"), and math (which size is cheaper?). Explain in advance that you need him to help you find things and carry them, and that he can choose only one item that you wouldn't normally buy. Seven-year-olds can understand rules, and they enjoy being helpful.

logic, and their ear for nuances of pronunciation, children aged 7 to 11 are at their prime for being taught a second language.

No single approach to teaching a second language has yet been recognized as best for all children in all contexts (Bialystok, 2001). Strategies include both extremes—from **total immersion,** in which instruction occurs entirely in the second (majority) language, to *reverse immersion,* in which the child is taught in his or her first (native) language for several years, until the second language can be taught as a "foreign" language. Variations between these extremes include presenting some topics of instruction in one language and other topics in the other; presenting every topic in both languages; or conducting separate after-school classes in a "heritage language" to allow children to connect with their culture while learning all academic subjects in the dominant tongue. In the United States, three approaches attempt to avoid the shock of complete immersion in English for non-English-speakers (see Table 12.4).

Which teaching strategy is best? In Canada, immersion has succeeded with more than 300,000 English-speaking children who were initially placed in French-only classrooms. These children showed no decline in English skills (learned at home) or in other academic achievement (Edwards, 1994; Lambert et al., 1993). Indeed, even when Canadian children whose native language is English are immersed in two other languages—French and Hebrew—from the first to the sixth grade, they do well on achievement tests in all three languages (Genesee, 1998). Note, however, that this was a six-year program.

By contrast, reverse immersion works best in Guatemala, where children learn the second language (Spanish) only after they have already been well taught in their native Mayan language (Tucker, 1998). In Belgium, biculturalism

TABLE 12.4 **Three Strategies for Teaching English as a Second Language**

English as a Second Language (ESL)
Requires all non-English-speaking students to undergo an intensive instructional period together, with the goal of mastering the basics of English in six months or so. In classes using ESL, the teacher neither speaks in the child's native language nor allows the children to talk to each other in any language except English.

Bilingual Education
Requires that the teacher instruct the children in school subjects using their native language as well as English. In the early years, children are greeted, instructed, and (when necessary) disciplined in the two languages, in the hope that they will progress in both. Informal talk between one child and another is almost always in the native language, as is much of the teacher's informal conversation.

Bilingual–Bicultural Education
Recognizes that non-English-speaking children come to school with non-Anglo values, traditions, and perceptions that may need to be preserved. Implementation of the strategy may be as simple as celebrating special holidays (such as, for Mexican-American children, Three Kings Day, Cinco de Mayo, and the Day of the Dead), or it may be as complex as instituting new classroom strategies (such as cooperative learning or special discipline). Practically as well as politically, bilingual–bicultural education requires a large concentration of children whose parents value the native language. In the United States, bilingual–bicultural programs during school usually involve Hispanic children, and bilingual–bicultural after-school programs more commonly serve Asian children, if enough Koreans, Vietnamese, Hmong, or other groups live in the same area. In fact, one reason immigrants to the United States tend to settle near other people from the same area is to preserve the culture of the homeland for the children. Bicultural education thus happens naturally in the community, because parents fear that their children will become "Americanized" as well as English-speakers (Suarez-Orozco & Suarez-Orozco, 2001).

works with children of Italian ancestry, if Belgian-born and Italian-born teachers each teach the students for half a day (Byram, 1998). Thus, all three strategies can succeed—sometimes.

Immersion tends to fail if children are made to feel shy, stupid, or socially isolated because of their language difference. In such cases, this educational approach might more aptly be called *submersion,* because children are more likely to sink than swim (Edwards, 1994). Immersion that occurs after puberty, even if the children already have some knowledge of the second language, also impedes education (Marsh et al., 2000).

In the United States, many school systems use none of the three approaches outlined in Table 12.4. For most of the twentieth century, Native American children were sent to boarding schools to learn white ways. Many of them became sick, ran away, or became alienated from their families, victims of an attempt at cultural obliteration that has only recently been recognized (Coontz, 1998). Even today, many Spanish-speaking children who are instructed only in English become slow learners who repeat a grade or two until they are old enough to drop out of school. Unfortunately, the main alternative—bilingual education—does not necessarily produce children who are sufficiently fluent in English to perform well in an English-only high school. In both cases, their poor performance is blamed on their deficiency in English rather than on the teachers and educational programs that failed to take into account the special needs of such children (Romo & Falbo, 1996).

Success or failure in second-language learning seems to lie in the attitudes of the parents, the teachers, and the larger community. If both languages are valued as well as used extensively, then *additive bilingualism* occurs, with fluency in the second language added to fluency in the first. Sometimes, however, neither language is learned well, and the child is *semilingual,* not even monolingual— literally possessing only part of one language (Swain & Johnson, 1997). As one review regarding the need for well-trained language teachers explained, "Whether policies are overtly articulated, covertly implied, or invisibly in the making, the central concern in multilingual education appears to be how much status and recognition within the educational system should be given to the languages of the minority group" (Nunan & Lam, 1998). This is a political question more than a developmental one.

Teaching Moral and Civic Values

Some parents criticize or praise "godless schools," but actually all schools teach moral and civic values. The true controversy is over whose moral code and which values should be taught. In some schools, memorized prayers and recited commandments are part of each school day. For example, in many Islamic countries a major reason for schooling is to learn the Koran; in the United States, the Constitution prohibits the teaching of any particular religion in public schools, which 90 percent of young children attend. Religious tolerance is itself a national value in the United States (Marshall, 2001).

Developmental research indicates that middle childhood is a prime time for incorporating values as well as for memorizing texts—if not the Ten Commandments or a particular prayer, then the Pledge of Allegiance, the Bill of Rights, or a Shakespeare monologue. Language—the words in which a particular code is expressed—is a joy to school-age children. In middle childhood, moral and behaviorial rules are understood and often rigidly interpreted, whether they are the rules of the school administration (requiring school uniforms, for example), of the political culture (as in elections for student council representatives), or of the children themselves (forbidding them to rat on their friends). Adults should ensure that whatever values and principles their children learn are the ones they

Friendly Immersion The poster is in English, because this Toronto teacher is explaining a sign in the city, but all the instruction occurs in French, even though none of these children are native French speakers. Their parents chose it not only because French immersion works successfully in Canada but also because such programs have a reputation for academic rigor, including high standards for conduct and achievement. Attitudes, not just instruction, facilitate learning a second language.

themselves believe in. Given the concrete nature of school-age children's minds and their concern about fairness, adults need to teach morality not only by words but also by example.

Educational Structures and Policies

The importance of explicit practices is reflected in the need for instructional practices and school organization to reflect the goals of the educators or of the broader community. In addition to its academic curriculum, each school has a **hidden curriculum,** which is not published in any curriculum guide or even articulated by the staff but which influences every aspect of school learning. The hidden curriculum affects school structures and teacher actions. It is manifest in discipline tactics, in grades and teacher comments on report cards, in salaries, in school schedules, in the assignment of children to particular classes, and so on. Every culture creates its own hidden curriculum, usually without being aware of it until a change is suggested (Alexander, 2000). We will look now at two aspects of the hidden curriculum—class size and testing—that illustrate its complex relationship to our understanding of development.

hidden curriculum The unofficial, unstated, or implicit rules and priorities that influence the academic curriculum and every other aspect of school learning.

Class Size

It seems obvious to every parent and teacher, and to many politicians, that children learn better when there are fewer children in each class. Smaller class size is one reason some parents send their children to private schools, some politicians advocate charter schools or vouchers, and some teachers go on strike.

Surprisingly, the research supporting this popular assumption is weak. In fact, some data suggest that class size makes no difference in children's performance (Betts, 1995; Hanushek, 1999). The pupil/teacher ratio is far lower in the United States than in almost any other nation, having declined from 25 to 18 between 1969 and 1997 (Alexander, 2000), with no comparable advance in learning. Schools in the United States have more low-income and immigrant children and fewer qualified teachers than they had in the 1960s, so educational gains caused by reduced class size may be offset by losses resulting from other factors (Ehrenberg et al., 2001).

Advocates have looked for experimental (not correlational, as in the example above) evidence that smaller class size results in better learning. A massive experiment in Tennessee, involving 12,000 children in 70 schools, began in 1985 and continued for four years. Kindergarten children and teachers were randomly assigned to one of three classroom conditions: regular (22–26 children); regular with aid (22–26 children with a full-time teacher's assistant), or small (13–17 children). Children (especially nonwhite children) in the small classes learned more, and those in the regular classes with an aide did no better than those in regular classes without an aide. Follow-up research shows that even after the children had been in regular classes for years, those who once had small classes still outperform their peers (Finn et al., 2001).

Although smaller class size made some difference, there is disagreement about how substantial the benefits were, why they occurred, and whether the gains were worth the expense (Rayner et al., 2001). California, inspired by Tennessee, reduced class sizes in the early grades—but, unlike Tennessee, California had neither enough qualified teachers nor suitable classrooms for this expansion, and the average class-size reduction was only from 30 to 20, not 24 to 15. The California results were "disappointing"—statistically significant, but very small (Stecher & Bohrnstedt, 2000). During the same years California public schools reinstated the teaching of phonics and basic math and reduced bilingual education, so solid conclusions from California are elusive.

A review of all the research leaves many questions unanswered. The early grades may be crucial, but another year may be equally important—perhaps sixth grade, when puberty hits, or twelfth grade, when high school graduation should occur. Other reforms in the hidden curriculum—raising teacher salaries, improving professional education, extending school hours until 6 P.M., expanding the school year to 11 months a year, or including more sports, music, more reading—might have a great impact, or might be neutral, or might be destructive.

These questions are not yet answered because the connection between developmental research and practical policy is problematic (Thompson & Nelson, 2001). As one review explains:

> . . . reductions in class size are but one of the policy options that can be pursued to improve student learning. Careful evaluations of the impacts of other options, preferably through the use of more true experiments, along with an analysis of the costs of each option, need to be undertaken. However, to date there are relatively few studies that even compute the true costs of large class-size reduction programs, let alone ask whether the benefits . . . merit incurring the costs.
>
> *[Ehrenberg et al., 2001]*

Merely raising the question alerts us to the hidden assumption about class size. If Piaget is correct and learning happens individually, then smaller class sizes would be beneficial because the teacher could give each child more personal attention. However, if Vygotsky is right and learning is a social process that may include learning from peers, then reducing class size would be counterproductive.

Educational Standards and Testing

National and statewide standardized tests of children's academic achievement are popular in the United States; 98 percent of children are tested in both math and English at least once in elementary, middle, and high school. Many states require more frequent tests (usually beginning in third grade), and most states test achievement in science and social studies as well.

Learning to Learn These two classes, in Somalia *(left)* and Japan *(right),* are different from each other in many ways. However, they both share several characteristics that are rare in most nations where this textbook is used.

Experts disagree about what educational standards should be and how they should be measured. Flawed standards—too high, too low, too vague—undermine learning and increase stress. Even worse are standards that differ from what the tests assess, because then no one knows if the children are reaching the standards or not.

Few developmentalists oppose periodic assessment of educational achievement, since accurate longitudinal data are essential for science. However, many criticize specific testing practices, since tests are not necessarily accurate, valid, or aligned to standards, curricula, or learning. Too-difficult tests may lead to failure, with many children repeating grades and then dropping out; too-easy tests are useless; irrelevant or rigid tests crowd out creative and individualized learning and teaching. Teachers may begin "teaching to the test" in an effort to raise their students' scores so they will be rated as good teachers and perhaps earn merit pay. If the goal of a test is not to measure past teaching accomplishments but to reveal what children need to learn, then the testing process should occur within a zone of proximal development, with children offered assistance by friends and teachers as needed (Meijer & Elshout, 2001). This approach is taken in some European nations and in some informal assessments in the United States, but the usual practice is for children to take tests in a large group, sometimes without their own teachers present. The tests are scored elsewhere, so that teachers are unable to use the results to improve their instruction of each child. Most developmentalists would probably agree that "standards and assessment, though necessary, are not enough. . . . Standards set the course, and assessments provide the benchmarks, but it is teaching that must be improved to push us along the path to success" (Stigler & Hiebert, 1999, p. 2).

Testing and standards can alert us to hidden assumptions about how children learn. Frequent testing, high and measurable standards that must be met before promotion or graduation, and an overall emphasis on individual academic accomplishments seem to undermine an appreciation of every child's learning strength and style, of every teacher's professional judgment, and of cooperative learning. These two versions of how teaching and learning should be done reflect two hidden curricula whose supporters sometimes clash openly, as in British Columbia, Canada, when some parents wanted the school board to create a traditional school that would presumably have higher academic and behavioral standards than a more progressive school. Here are excerpts from three letters to the editor of the local newspaper (quoted in Mitchell, 2001, pp. 64–65). One mother wrote in favor of a traditional school:

> Our children's performances are much lower both in academic and moral areas. I noticed the children have learnt very little academically. They learned to have self-confidence instead of being self-disciplined; learned to speak up instead of being humbled; learned to be creative instead of self-motivated; and learned to simplify things instead of organizing. All of these characteristics were not balanced, and will be the source of disadvantage and difficulties in children in this competitive society.

Two other parents disagreed:

> These characteristics she disapproves of are the very characteristics I encourage in my children, as do their teachers and the public schools. Self-confidence, creativity, and individuality are wonderful qualities, which in no way detract from a child being respectful and pleasant, and achieving academic success.

> She wants her children to be self-disciplined, humble, self-motivated and organized, instead of being self-confident, assertive, creative and analytic. . . . These repressive, authoritarian, "traditional" parents who hanker for the days of yore, when fresh-faced school kids arrived all neatly decked out in drab-grey uniforms and shiny lace-up leather shoes, are a menace to society. They desire their kids to sit quietly in tidy serried ranks . . . should they err in any way, a thousand lines or a good beating will learn 'em real good.

Conclusion

This chapter has demonstrated the remarkable ability of children aged 7 to 11 to learn, not only grasping logic and accumulating facts but adding tens of thousands of words to their vocabulary, using dozens of strategies for learning, incorporating moral values that last a lifetime, generalizing concepts, and refining habits of thought and action.

We will close this chapter by reminding you of an example that stresses the strong intellectual capacity of the school-age child, if experience and motivation are in place. The young Brazilian street vendors whom we mentioned earlier in this chapter—all in middle childhood, with little formal education—do very poorly when given standard problems presented the way achievement tests usually present them (such as 420 + 80). However, when given oral problems involving fruit purchases and making change for a customer ("I'll take three coconuts. Here's a 10-real [the basic Brazilian unit of money] bill. How much do I get back?"), they solve the problems far more quickly and successfully, often using unconventional but effective math strategies (Carraher et al., 1985, 1988). In other words, although they seem to lack the cognitive strategies necessary to solve arithmetic problems, these children have developed sophisticated math abilities. In fact, the prices of the fruit they sell must be recalculated often, as wholesale prices vary with supply and as inflation changes the value of the currency. These unschooled children have mastered that math very well; their survival depends on it (Saxe, 1999).

To repeat the theme of this chapter: Children in the school years can and do learn whatever their culture and context teach. Parents, peers, and community leaders must decide what that should be.

SUMMARY

Building on Piaget and Vygotsky

1. According to Piaget, children enter the stage of concrete operational thought at about age 6 or 7. Egocentrism diminishes and logical ideas, including identity and irreversibility, are applied to every aspect of experience.

2. Their new logical abilities enable school-age children to understand classification, conservation, and many other concepts. This concrete operational understanding advances all forms of academic thinking, particularly in math, as well as social relationships.

3. Vygotsky stressed the social context of learning, including the role of teachers and peers in guiding each child's education. International research finds that maturation is one factor in the cognitive development of school-age children (as Piaget predicted) and that cultural and economic forces are also influential (as Vygotsky predicted).

Information Processing

4. An information-processing approach examines each step of the thinking process, from input to output, using the computer as a model. Humans are more creative than computers, but this approach is a useful guide to memory, perception, and expression.

5. Memory begins with the sensory register, which briefly stores information that reaches the brain from the sense organs. The information proceeds to working memory, where perceptions are processed for a short time in active consciousness. Some images and ideas are stored indefinitely in long-term memory.

6. Advances in memory during middle childhood occur primarily because of improvement in working memory, aided by selective attention and logical retrieval. Long-term memory increases as well, as more material in the knowledge base makes more learning possible.

7. Speed of thought accelerates with continued brain myelination. Faster processing advances every aspect of cognition, including working memory. Repeated practice makes thought patterns and skill sets almost automatic, requiring little time or conscious effort.

8. Children become better at controlling and directing their thinking as the prefrontal cortex matures. Consequently, metacognition advances and children learn better, particularly in school.

Language

9. Language becomes more logical and extensive as children move through middle childhood. Children who are exposed to a rich vocabulary at home and in school are likely to become very adept at articulating their thoughts and ideas.

10. By the end of middle childhood, children can interpret vocal tones and can comprehend nuances of meaning that they could not grasp earlier. Children also recognize that certain forms of speech are more appropriate in one context or another. Recognition of the difference between informal and formal speech codes leads to code-switching, which means that children speak informally with friends and formally at school.

Moral Development

11. School-age children are passionately concerned about moral questions. Kohlberg described three levels of moral reasoning, from preconventional (self-concerned) to conventional (community-centered) to postconventional (centered on moral principles). Individual responses to Kohlberg's moral dilemmas are sometimes difficult to score; another measure, the Defining Issues Test, uses a questionnaire to indicate moral development.

12. Kohlberg's stages have been criticized for being too abstractly rational, downgrading the morals of people from traditional, non-Western communities. In addition, he ranked the "morality of justice" higher than the "morality of care," although the latter may be preferred by those who are more concerned with human relationships than with absolute rules. Although some claim the "morality of care" to be more representative of females, research evidence does not support this assertion.

13. During the school years, children tend to value loyalty to their friends over adult standards. They can be quite rigid in their judgments of right and wrong, with a strong personal belief in justice and fairness.

Schools, Values, and Research

14. Many issues regarding education are hotly debated. Developmental research provides some answers, but most of the core issues require social choice, not just better research. Concern about education in the United States has led to more time spent in educating school-age children.

15. Internationally, all agree that children should learn to read and compute, but experts and nations disagree as to how that learning should occur and what else should be taught in schools. The arguments of both sides in the "Reading Wars" and math debates have merit. Nevertheless, some phonics instruction in reading and some group learning in math seem advisable.

16. During the school years, children are particularly open to learning a second language and absorbing moral and civic values. The specifics of second-language instruction and moral education remain controversial, with marked variations from nation to nation.

17. Smaller class size does not necessarily advance achievement, although a massive experiment in Tennessee that reduced class size to about 15 in kindergarten through the third grade resulted in higher achievement. It is not clear whether the Tennessee experiment is generalizable and cost-effective.

18. Over the past decade or so, the United States has moved toward higher standards of academic achievement and more frequent testing. Most scholars agree with the basic philosophy behind these trends, but many criticize the specifics.

19. Every decision about school-age children's cognition raises deep moral, political, and sociocultural issues. These children can and do learn a great deal; their families and communities must choose what to teach them.

KEY TERMS

concrete operational thought (p. 359)
classification (p. 360)
identity (p. 361)
reversibility (p. 361)
sensory register (p. 363)
working memory (p. 363)
long-term memory (p. 364)

knowledge base (p. 364)
control processes (p. 365)
selective attention (p. 366)
metacognition (p. 366)
code-switching (p. 371)
formal code (p. 371)
informal code (p. 372)

preconventional moral reasoning (p. 373)
conventional moral reasoning (p. 373)
postconventional moral reasoning (p. 373)
Defining Issues Test (DIT) (p. 375)

morality of care (p. 375)
morality of justice (p. 375)
phonics approach (p. 381)
whole-language approach (p. 381)
total immersion (p. 384)
hidden curriculum (p. 386)

KEY QUESTIONS

1. According to Piaget, what are the distinctive characteristics of cognition in middle childhood?

2. How might concrete operational thought aid in learning multiplication?

3. What does international research on school-age children find regarding Piaget's and Vygotsky's views?

4. Which step of memory improves most during middle childhood and why?

5. How are selective attention and speed of processing related?

6. How does an expanded knowledge base improve learning?

7. What would signify better control processing during middle childhood?

8. Why do children need both formal and informal speech codes?

9. How do jokes reflect children's understanding of language?

10. What are the three major criticisms of Kohlberg's stages of moral development?

11. What differences would you expect between 8-year-olds' moral values and adult moral actions?

12. What are the arguments for and against the phonics approach to teaching reading?

13. Which method of teaching a second language seems most effective?

14. What does research reveal about reductions in class size?

Chapter Thirteen

The School Years: Psychosocial Development

latency Freud's term for middle childhood, during which children's emotional drives are quieter, their psychosexual needs are repressed, and their unconscious conflicts are submerged.

industry versus inferiority The fourth of Erikson's eight crises of psychosexual development, in which school-age children attempt to master many skills and develop a sense of themselves as either industrious and competent or incompetent and inferior.

In middle childhood, children break free from the closely supervised and limited arena of the younger child. Usually with their parents' blessing but sometimes breaking the rules, school-age children explore the wider world of neighborhood, community, and school. They experience new vulnerability, increasing competence, ongoing friendships, troubling rivalries, and deeper social understanding. Although often beyond direct adult supervision, their lives are still shaped by family structures and community values.

Our goal in this chapter is to examine the interplay between expanding freedom and guiding forces. We will look first at emotional growth, then at peer and family influences that direct and propel that growth, and, finally, at strategies and strengths that enable most children to move forward, ready for adolescence. In tackling this topic, there is a danger of overloading the discussion by including every perspective and opinion from every pupil, teacher, or political leader—all of whom care about children. Indeed, adults from many professions—educators, sociologists, anthropologists, politicians, economists, and others—are concerned about how children develop during these years. To anchor our analysis, we begin with the perspectives on development in middle childhood that have been offered by the five major theories that were introduced in Chapter 2.

Theories of School-Age Development

Throughout the world, school-age children are noticeably more independent, more responsible, and more capable than younger children. This increased competence is recognized by parents and schools, in research results, and in every developmental theory.

Sigmund Freud described middle childhood as the period of **latency**, during which children's emotional drives are quieter, their psychosexual needs are repressed, and their unconscious conflicts are submerged. This makes latency "a time for acquiring cognitive skills and assimilating cultural values as children expand their world to include teachers, neighbors, peers, club leaders, and coaches. Sexual energy continues to flow, but it is channeled into social concerns" (Miller, 2002, p. 131).

Erik Erikson (1963) agreed with Freud that middle childhood is a quiet period emotionally, a period in which the child "becomes ready to apply himself to given skills and tasks." During Erikson's crisis of **industry versus inferiority**, children busily try to master whatever abilities their culture values. On the basis of their degree of success, they judge themselves as either *industrious* or *inferior*—that is, competent or incompetent, productive or failing, winners or losers.

Industry on Display One characteristic of school-age children is their obsession with collecting, whether their interest is stamps or insects, Harry Potter paraphernalia or, as shown here, Yu-Gi-Oh cards, which are the latest collecting fad in Japan. Children are much more industrious than adult collectors, busily counting, organizing, and trading their treasures.

social cognitive theory A perspective that highlights how the school-age child advances in learning, cognition, and culture, building on maturation and experience to become more articulate, insightful, and competent.

Developmentalists influenced by two other grand theories—behaviorism and cognitive theory—are concerned with the acquisition of new skills and self-understanding, respectively. The overview from these two theories is quite similar to that of psychoanalytic theory: School-age children meet the challenges of the outside world with an openness, insight, and confidence that few young children possess.

One offshoot of the grand theories, **social cognitive theory,** is particularly relevant to middle childhood because it highlights how the school-age child advances in learning, cognition, and culture (Bandura, 2001). Social cognitive theory stresses the combination of maturation and experience that allows school-age children to become much more articulate, reflective, and active, able to understand themselves and to be effective and competent. They think logically, as we saw in Chapter 12, and they apply their new learning ability to their expanding social world. In practical terms, 10-year-olds can explain their emotions to their parents, or decide to wake up early to study for a test, or choose which friend to phone for the homework assignment. All these actions make the older child more active than passive in the social world, displaying what Albert Bandura (1997) calls "social efficacy" and what the proud smile of any 10-year-old who has just won a race, earned a perfect grade, or finished a work of art conveys.

The two emergent theories, sociocultural and epigenetic systems, also acknowledge the new independence of school-age children but go further: Considering both current context and genetic factors, sociocultural theory looks not only at children from widely separated parts of the world—for instance, rural China versus urban Canada—but also at various subcultures within one nation or even on one city block. Yolanda and Paul, the children whom you met at the beginning of Chapter 11, were from the same nation (United States), state (California), region (Los Angeles area), and heritage (Mexican-American), yet their differences are apparent. Consider their opinions about education:

> *Yolanda:* I feel proud of myself when I see a [good] grade. And like I see a C, I'm going to have to pull this grade up. . . . I like learning. I like really getting my mind working. . . . [Education] is good for you. . . . It's like when you eat. It's like if you don't eat for the whole day, you feel weird.

> *Paul:* I try not to get influenced too much, pulled into what I don't want to be into. But mostly, it's hard. You don't want people to be saying you're stupid. "Why do you want to go to school and get a job? . . . Drop out." . . . They try to pull you down and then you just got to be strong enough to try to pull away.

> [quoted in Nieto, 2000, pp. 220, 221, 252]

Both these children have been affected by family and cultural influences that were radically different during middle childhood. Consequently, they are different from each other, as sociocultural theory would anticipate.

Finally, epigenetic systems theory considers how inherited impulses that mature during middle childhood have enabled families over the centuries to raise their children. Thus, genes within each human lead to maturation—not only biological but also social. For instance, during these middle-childhood years, to ensure survival of the next generation, children need to reach out to peers and adults, developing a social network that will guide them toward adulthood.

The human species still responds to the ancient genetic mechanisms: The 7- to 11-year-old develops a body and a brain that allow greater intellectual focus (selective attention), rationality (concrete operational thought), and physical hardiness (slowed growth and increased control). In prior centuries, these protected the child when parents typically had younger children who needed close attention. Indeed, among all primate species, it seems that normal maturation pulls developing children to become more independent of their mothers and more dependent on their peers in middle childhood (Suomi, 2002). At the same time, genetic impulses are shaped by the social environment, which is why epigenetic systems theorists study "the role of the environment in bringing about species-typical behavior" (Dent-Read & Zukow-Goldring, 1997, p. 11).

Notice that all five major theories describe the child from ages 7 to 11 in similar ways, as competent, eager, and manageable outside the home. Worldwide, cultures recognize the wonderful characteristics of this stage by selecting these years as the time to give the child more independence and responsibility, from attending first grade to making one's First Communion, from doing significant chores at home to facing major challenges at school. In the twenty-first century, even in the poorest nations, most school-age children are, in fact, in school (Alexander, 2000).

Celebrating Spring No matter where they live, 7- to 11-year-olds seek to understand and develop whatever skills are valued by their culture. They do so in active, industrious ways, as described in behaviorism as well as cognitive, sociocultural, psychoanalytic, and epigenetic systems theories. This universal truth is illustrated here, as four friends in Assam, northeastern India, usher in spring with a Bihu celebration. Soon they will be given sweets and tea, which is the sociocultural validation of their energy, independence, and skill.

Understanding Self and Others

Social scientists once categorized cultures, societies, and even individuals into two opposite groups: individualistic/collective, independent/dependent, self-oriented/other-oriented, introverted/extroverted (Triandis, 1989). This distinction was applied to entire regions of the world; for example, North America and Western Europe would be categorized as individualistic and Asia, Africa, and South America as collective. Today, such broad distinctions may still be made, but most scholars agree that every successful person and culture must find a balance, an interdependence, and that both autonomous and social forces are at work in every society (Harter, 1999; Oyserman et al., 2002).

Similarly, human development from birth to age 20 can be depicted as a progression from total dependence in infancy to self-determination in adolescence. Middle childhood is the time when children learn whatever skills they will need as adults, concretely (Piaget's word) or industriously (Erikson's word) going their own, self-centered way and shedding their dependence on parents during latency (Freud's word). However, research finds that self-development occurs in harmony with connection to parents and peers, no less in middle childhood than earlier. The following self-description could have been written by many 10-year-olds:

> I'm in the fourth grade this year, and I'm pretty popular, at least with the girls. That's because I'm nice to people and can keep secrets. Mostly I am nice to my friends, although if I get in a bad mood I sometimes say something that can be a little mean. I try to control my temper, but when I don't, I'm ashamed of myself. I'm usually happy when I'm with my friends, but I get sad if there is no one to do things with. At school, I'm feeling pretty smart in certain subjects like Language Arts and Social Studies. I got A's in these subjects on my last report card and was really proud of myself. But I'm feeling pretty dumb in Math and Science, especially when I see how well a lot of the other kids are doing. Even though I'm not doing well in those subjects, I still like myself as a person, because Math and Science just aren't that important to me. How I look and how popular I am are more important. I also like myself because I know my parents like me and so do other kids. That helps you like yourself.
>
> *[Harter, 1999, p. 48]*

It is evident that both children and their social contexts develop during the school years.

Read Their Expressions This girl seems hesitant to proceed, perhaps in anticipation of getting a cold shock. However, because of the expanded emotional understanding that is typical of school-age children, she probably realizes that if she stalls much longer, she is bound to get teased. This greater emotional understanding may also help her to control her anxiety long enough to take the plunge.

?*Observational Quiz* (see answer, page 398): What gender differences do you see?

social cognition A person's awareness and understanding of human personality, motives, emotions, intentions, and actions.

Social Understanding

The development of school-age children depends on advances in **social cognition,** that is, in understanding the social world. At younger ages, in their simple theory of mind, children began to realize that other people are motivated by thoughts and emotions that differ from their own. But preschoolers' early theorizing is prone to error, because their grasp of other viewpoints is quite limited and fragile.

During the school years, theory of mind evolves into a complex, multifaceted perspective. Cognitive advances allow children to understand that human behavior is not simply a response to specific thoughts or desires. Instead, they see behavior as actions that are influenced—simultaneously—by a variety of needs, emotions, relationships, and motives. The ability to regulate their own emotions improves (Eisenberg, 2000). For example, a preschooler who was told to stop getting into fights with his friends said he couldn't help it because sometimes the fight "just crawled out of me." By contrast, school-age children know what leads to the fights—and what might follow if they choose to fight back. They usually judge where, when, why, and with whom to fight according to this new, deeper understanding (but not always; see the discussion of bullying, page 402).

The development of social understanding was demonstrated in a simple study in which 4- to 10-year-olds were shown pictures and asked how the mother might respond and why (Goldberg-Reitman, 1992). In one picture, a child curses while playing with blocks. As you can see in the following typical responses, the 4-year-olds focused only on the immediate behavior, whereas the older children recognized the implications and possible consequences:

> *4-year-old:* "The mother spanks her because she said a naughty word."
> *6-year-old:* "The mother says 'Don't say that again' because it's not nice to say a bad word."
> *10-year-old:* "The mother maybe hits her or something because she's trying to teach her . . . because if she grew up like that she'd get into a lot of trouble . . . she might get a bad reputation."
>
> *[Goldberg-Reitman, 1992]*

Similar research and everyday experience tell us that younger children are likely to focus solely on observable behavior—not on motives, feelings, or social consequences. They know when an adult might protect, nurture, scold, or teach a child, but not why. Older children add three more elements:

■ They understand the motivation and origin of various behaviors.
■ They can analyze the future impact of whatever action a person might take.
■ They recognize personality traits and use them to predict a person's future reactions.

Developmental progression builds on these elements as children mature, a maturation evident in research on children's psychosocial understanding. For example, younger children recognize basic personality traits; they can say whether it is good or bad to have a particular characteristic. However, they are much less able than slightly older children to predict how having a particular personality trait might affect future actions (Alvarez et al., 2001). Overall, from ages 5 to 11, a "developmental sequence reflects children's growing understanding of the multiple or changing representations of emotional situations" (Terwogt & Stegge, 1998).

As a result of their new social cognition, children manage their own emotions better. They can mentally distract themselves to avoid becoming fidgety during a boring concert, for example, or can look attentive in class even when they are not paying attention. They can even mask or alter inborn tendencies. When a group of 7-year-olds looked at videotapes of themselves being shy at age 2, most were distressed to see how timid they had once been, but only a few still acted shy. Many said they had learned to understand themselves and adjust their timidity. As one explained, "I was a total idiot then [but] I learned a lot of new stuff, so now I'm not as scared as I was when I was a baby . . . I've gotten older and I don't want to be embarrassed" (quoted in Fox et al., 1996). This new self-understanding leads directly to better social skills, with children less fearful, less likely to start fights, and better able to concentrate as they mature (Brendgen et al., 2001; Nagin & Tremblay, 1999). Another consequence of maturing social cognition is more nuanced self-evaluation.

Self-Understanding

School-age children begin to make measurements of themselves, comparing quite specific abilities to those of their peers—as did the fourth-grader quoted on page 395. Nonacademic skills are also compared. A boy might, for example, realize that he is weak at playing the piano, OK at basketball, and a whiz at Nintendo.

Increased self-understanding comes at a price. Self-criticism rises and self-esteem dips, especially when children are asked general questions, such as "Are you smart?" and "Are you good?" Instead of simply answering "yes," as a younger child might, older children accept and use the specific standards set by their parents, teachers, and peers. This also means that they use **social comparison**, the ability to compare themselves with other people even when no one else explicitly makes the comparison. Then children examine their own actual behavior, abandoning the imaginary, rosy self-evaluation of preschoolers (Grolnick et al., 1997).

Older children feel personally at fault for their shortcomings and are less likely to blame luck or someone else. Further, as they compare themselves to others, "children become increasingly concerned about self-presentation" (Merrell & Gimpel, 1998). Other children are more important as both critics and commentators than they once were, and the opinions of parents or teachers (who are likely to say, in ignorance, "You are fine, stop worrying") are now discounted.

The Peer Group

In general, the most influential system for developing the self-concept is the **peer group,** a group of individuals of roughly the same age and social status who play, work, or learn together. It is almost impossible to overstate the importance of peers. As one group of researchers who did an extensive study of children during the school years reported, "Friends and being part of a peer group were central to living a full life and feeling good" (Borland et al., 1998, p. 28).

Most developmentalists consider getting along with peers to be crucial during middle childhood (although parents and teachers do not always agree) (Merrell & Gimpel, 1998). Indeed, some psychologists think peers are the deciding influence during the school years, far more important in determining personality and self-concept than parents (Harris, 1998). That position is extreme, but "ample evidence exists that difficulties with peers place a child at risk for developing subsequent problems of a psychological nature" (K.H. Rubin et al., 1998, p. 674). Being rejected by peers is a precursor to serious developmental

social comparison The tendency to assess one's abilities, achievements, social status, and other attributes by measuring them against those of other people, especially one's peers.

peer group An aggregate of individuals of roughly the same age and social status who play, work, or learn together.

! *Answer to Observational Quiz* (from page 396): All the girls look distressed, but the boys do not. The girls also seem more likely to cover their bodies, a recognition of their problems with social comparison, self-esteem, and gender norms that often accompany middle childhood. The boys may be unaffected by such problems or may have already learned to appear tough.

society of children The social culture of children, consisting of the games, vocabulary, dress codes, and rules of behavior that characterize their interactions.

The Rules of the Game These young monks in Burma are playing a board game that adults also play, but they have some of their own refinements of the general rules. The society of children often modifies the dominant culture, as is evident in everything from superstitions to stickball.

KYUYA KAMAZAWA / HAGA / THE IMAGE WORKS

problems later on, including juvenile delinquency, depression, and drug abuse (Laird et al., 2001). Conversely, even children who were harshly treated by their parents, and thus more likely to be victimized by their peers, are protected from victimization if they have a friend (Schwartz et al., 2001).

There is an important developmental progression here. Preschool children have friends and learn from playmates, of course, but they are more egocentric and therefore less needy of friends. In middle childhood, however, children tend to be concerned with the opinions and judgment of the entire group of classmates. They become more dependent on each other, not only for companionship but also for self-validation and advice. One reason for this dependence is that peer relationships, unlike adult–child relationships, involve partners who must learn to negotiate, compromise, share, and defend themselves as equals (Hartup, 1996). Children learn lessons from each other that adults cannot teach.

Because peers are so important to children, developmentalists are troubled if children have no free time to spend with each other. Many protective parents insist that their children come home immediately after school. In school, the push for higher standards and international competitiveness has reduced the time set aside for recess, for lunch, and, as we saw in Chapter 12, for playing outdoors, which often meant playing with neighborhood children. In addition, most parents are now employed outside the home, so after-school supervision sometimes means enrolling the children in organized programs. Children themselves, however, generally prefer the freedom to choose their own activities with their own friends (Belle, 1999).

This is not the only example of parents misperceiving what their children need. A study comparing parents' and children's perceptions of middle childhood found that parents worried most about predatory strangers and illicit drug use. The children were much more concerned about peer relationships, family conflicts, and parental use of alcohol or cigarettes (Borland et al., 1998). Thus, the peer group, which is often feared by the parents, can be very helpful to the children. The family's influence also remains strong, for good or ill. Fortunately, parents' influence is positive, for the most part, in preparing children to have close friends (Parke & Buriel, 1998; Updegraff et al., 2002).

The Society of Children

When school-age children play together, they develop patterns of interaction that are distinct from those of adult society and culture. Accordingly, some social scientists call the peer group the **society of children**, highlighting the fact that children create their own subculture, which is firmly in place by age 10 or so.

The society of children typically has special norms, vocabulary, rituals, and rules of behavior that flourish without the approval, or even the knowledge, of adults. Its slang words and nicknames are often ones adults would frown on (if they understood them), and its activities—such as (in the United States) hanging out at the mall, playing games at the playground, and having long, meandering phone conversations—do not invite adult participation (Opie, 1993; Zarbatany et al., 1990). Its dress codes become known to parents only when they try to get their son or daughter to wear something that violates those codes—as when a perfectly fine pair of hand-me-down jeans is something the child "would not be caught dead in" because, by the norms of the society of children, they are an unfashionable color, have the wrong label, are too loose or too tight. In some nations, including Brazil, Romania, and India, the society of children functions as the only socializing influence on homeless children whose parents or circumstances have forced them to live on their own.

Throughout the world, many of the norms and rules of the peer group implicitly encourage independence from adults, and some go even further, demanding distance from adult society. By age 10, if not before, the peer group pities children (especially boys) whose parents kiss them in public ("momma's boy"), teases children whose teachers favor them ("teacher's pet"), and despises those who betray other children to adults ("tattletale," "snitch," "rat"), especially adults in authority such as teachers or the police.

Close friends and the society of children are always powerful but not always positive (Hartup & Stevens, 1999). Children tend to take on the characteristics and values of those in their group. This makes the society of children one of the best sources of language learning—which is essential if a child needs to learn a second language, but less benign if the new code includes a marked regional accent and unacceptable slang and cursing, or if the values of the group include petty delinquency and antagonism to school. By age 9, Paul, the California boy you met in Chapter 11, believed that "I got in just to be in a gang, be somewhere, be known from somewhere." In elementary school he was already breaking rules, fighting, and getting suspended; by junior high he had a tattoo and a gang identity, which led him to drugs and crime by the end of adolescence.

By age 10 or 11, a circle of deviant, antisocial friends may make a child deviant and antisocial, ready to gang up on an outsider or to scorn one of the group. In sum, whether or not friends and the society of children are beneficial depends partly on who those children are.

Friendship

While acceptance by the entire peer group is valued, personal friendship is even more important (Erwin, 1998). Indeed, if they had to choose between being popular but friendless and having close friends but being unpopular, most children would take the friends. Such a choice is consistent with developmentalists' view of the close relationship between friendship and psychosocial development (Hartup & Stevens, 1999; Ladd, 1999). For example, one study found that children from violent and nonviolent homes said they had similar numbers of acquaintances, but the children from conflicted homes were less likely to have close friends and more likely to be lonely. The authors explained, "Skill at recruiting surface acquaintances or playmates is different, therefore, from the skill required to sustain close relationships," and the latter is needed if the child is to avoid loneliness, isolation, and rejection (McCloskey & Stuewig, 2001, p. 93).

Friends and Culture Like children everywhere, these children—two 7-year-olds and one 10-year-old—of the Surma people in southern Ethiopia model their appearance after slightly older children, in this case adolescents who apply elaborate body paint for courtship and stick-fighting rituals.

? *Observational Quiz* (see answer, page 400): Are these boys or girls, and which two are best friends?

As friendships become intense and more intimate, older children demand more of their friends, change friends less often, find it harder to make new friends, and are more upset when a friendship breaks up (Erwin, 1998). They are also pickier: They tend to choose best friends whose interests, values, and backgrounds are similar to their own. In fact, from ages 3 to 13, close friendships increasingly involve children of the same sex, age, ethnicity, and socioeconomic status (Aboud & Mendelson, 1996). When friendships across age, sex, ethnic, or SES lines flourish, they are based on a common need, interest, or personality trait (Hartup, 1996). Generally, however, having a best friend who is not the same age or sex correlates with being rejected or ignored by one's classmates and being unhappy (Kovacs et al., 1996). Having no friend at all is even worse.

Whereas most 4-year-olds say they have many friends (perhaps everyone in their nursery school class, with one or two exceptions), most 8-year-olds have a

! *Answer to Observational Quiz* (from page 399): They are girls. The short hair and necklaces give conflicting signals, from a Western perspective, but the unmistakable sign is that two of them have outlined their future breasts, in imitation of their older sisters. They are all friends, but the two younger girls are especially close: The photographer reports that they decorated their bodies in similar ways to show their affection for each other.

aggressive-rejected Referring to children who are actively rejected by their peer group because of their aggressive, confrontational behavior.

withdrawn-rejected Referring to children who are actively rejected by their peer group because of their withdrawn, anxious behavior.

small circle of friends. And by age 10, children often have one "best" friend to whom they are quite loyal. This trend toward fewer but closer friends is followed by both sexes, but it is more apparent among girls. Boys tend to emphasize group identity and loyalty, "using the group in their quest for recognition and self-esteem while they jockey for position within the group." By contrast, girls form smaller, more intimate networks and then are more concerned about being excluded from the small circle (Borland et al., 1998; Buhrmester, 1996; Erwin, 1998). By the end of middle childhood, many girls have one, and only one, best friend on whom they depend.

Rejected Children

All children occasionally feel left out or unwelcome by their peers, but only a small minority are spurned most of the time. For instance, in one study, for six consecutive years (from the first through the sixth grade), researchers asked 299 children which classmates they particularly wanted or did not want as playmates. Each year, the rankings were tabulated and clustered into three groups: popular, or often chosen (36 percent of the children fell into this category); average, or sometimes chosen (47 percent); and unpopular, or often rejected (17 percent). Almost all of the children (89 percent) changed from one category to another over the six years. Only 2 percent of the children were consistently unpopular (Brendgen et al., 2001).

Three distinct categories of unpopular children can be identified. One group consists of neglected, not really rejected, children. No classmate picks them as friends, but nobody avoids them, either. This lack of friends is far from ideal, but it may not be harmful to long-term psychosocial development. Two buffers that sometimes protect the self-esteem of neglected children are good family relationships and outstanding talents (such as the ability to play a musical instrument very well).

The other two types of unpopular children are not just neglected; they are actively rejected. They may be either **aggressive-rejected**—that is, disliked because of their antagonistic, confrontational behavior—or **withdrawn-rejected**—disliked because of their timid, anxious behavior. These seemingly opposite types of rejected children are similar in many ways: Both have problems regulating their emotions, and both are likely to come from homes where they have been mistreated in some way (Pollak et al., 2000).

In contrast, well-liked children are typically helpful and willing to assume the best about other children (Ladd, 1999). This is particularly true as regards

Following Social Rules This argument in a schoolyard is not just a fight between two boys but a sociocultural event.

? *Observational Quiz* (see answer, page 402): What can you see in the behavior of these four boys that suggests that they are aware of the rules of such confrontations?

BOB DAEMMRICH / THE IMAGE WORKS

TABLE 13.1 Examples of the Perceptions and Reactions of Popular and Unpopular Children

Situation	Child B's Type	Typical Interpretation	Typical Response
Child A spills a glass of milk on child B during lunch.	Aggressive-rejected	It was on purpose.	Pour milk on child A, or say something mean.
	Withdrawn-rejected	It was on purpose, or it was accidental.	Ignore it, or leave the table.
	Well-liked	It was accidental.	Get a towel, or ask how it happened.

emotional interpretations. Well-liked children assume that social slights, from a push to an unkind remark, are accidental and not intended to harm, and therefore they do not react with fear (as withdrawn children do) or anger (as aggressive children do) (see Table 13.1). In ambiguous situations, well-liked children try to solve the problem, perhaps by first asking the other child for an explanation (Erdley & Asher, 1996). Given a direct conflict between themselves and another, they seek not revenge, but rather a compromise that maintains the friendship (Rose & Asher, 1999).

These prosocial skills—benign social perceptions, insight into human relationships, and the tendency to help rather than to attack others—are rare in rejected children of either type (Ladd, 1999). Both aggressive-rejected and withdrawn-rejected children misinterpret other people's words and behavior, are poor listeners, and avoid social situations. They tend to be clumsy, awkward, and inept around other children.

Can I Play? If she dares to ask, she is likely to be rejected, because the rules of bonding at this age tend to exclude as well as include. The ability to deal with such situations is one of the most difficult skills taught by the society of children.

Teaching Social Skills

Since the school years are prime time for education, and since rejected children have apparently not learned how to get along with other children, it seems logical simply to teach them how to do so. However, efforts to teach social skills to rejected children have met with mixed success (Merrell & Gimpel, 1998; Sridher & Vaughn, 2001), as have all attempts to intervene by somehow "fixing" the child. As one review candidly reports, "Although intervention has been praised extensively by the teachers and parents involved and it is in great demand, it has been hard to show that . . . changes in aggressive behavior followed from the intervention" (Huesmann & Reynolds, 2001, p. 265).

There are three reasons why aggressive and withdrawn children do not learn better social skills:

- Defensive and destructive social responses are usually learned from the parents during early childhood; such lessons from home are hard to unlearn.
- Peer attitudes and actions resist change. For instance, even if rejected children learn how to start a friendly conversation, their efforts may fail because the other children fear that befriending an unpopular child will jeopardize their own social standing.
- Children sometimes say one thing and do another. A rejected child might verbalize what he or she should do in a given social situation but not actually do it when the time comes; emotions take over, and fear or aggression replaces logic.

In trying to remedy the rejection of withdrawn children, one must acknowledge the power of parents and peers by teaching the parents and training popular peers. Intervention before the third grade (when patterns are set and problems

! Answer to Observational Quiz (from page 400): The boy on the left, by his facial expression, knows he must stand his ground or risk losing status among his peers. The boy in the middle, angry as he is, keeps his hands down because to start hitting would be unacceptable. And the two boys at the right watch intently as judge, jury, and police, standing close enough to hold back or egg on the antagonist if the argument escalates and they decide intervention is appropriate. If the disagreement does escalate into a physical fight, other children will join the onlookers, not only to observe but also to monitor and moderate—making sure that neither boy unfairly pummels the other.

bullying A child's repeated, systematic efforts to inflict harm on another, particular child through physical, verbal, or social attacks.

typically emerge) and helping all the children to accept themselves and appreciate others are more effective than targeting the older rejected child for special assistance. Sometimes the best intervention is academic: Contrary to the popular misconception, school-age children who are accomplished students are less, not more, likely to be rejected by peers (Stipek, 2001).

It is even harder to turn around the rejection of aggressive children, partly because most 7- to 11-year-old aggressive-rejected children have a few awed and cowed friends (Brendgen et al., 2001; Ladd, 1999). As a result, they overestimate their acceptance and are oblivious of their unpopularity. When another child rejects them, they blame that child rather than themselves. Accordingly, they have no motivation to learn new social skills.

Ironically, these aggressive children often display a "veneer of self-satisfaction and invulnerability [that] may further decrease the likelihood that others will offer encouragement, warmth, and support" (Hughes et al., 1997). If an aggressive child makes an awkward attempt to do a good deed, other children will be wary; the aggressive child will be pushed back toward the familiar, hostile ways. The best solution for both types of rejected children is to change the entire social context.

Bullies and Their Victims

Any discussion of aggressive and withdrawn children is likely to bring to mind bullies and their victims. The behavior of bullies and victims occurs when these children are in a social context that allows active expression of aggressive and withdrawn temperaments.

Researchers define **bullying** as repeated, systematic efforts to inflict harm through physical attack (such as hitting, pinching, or kicking), verbal attack (such as teasing, taunting, or name-calling), or social attack (such as deliberate shunning or public mocking). Bullies are actively aggressive, and victims of bullying are "cautious, sensitive, quiet, . . . lonely and abandoned at school. As a rule, they do not have a single good friend in their class" (Olweus, 1999, p. 15). Victims are no more likely to be fat or homely or to speak with an accent than nonvictims are. However, victims are usually withdrawn-rejected children—anxious and insecure, unable or unwilling to defend themselves—and bullies are described as mean by other children (Boulton, 1999; Poulin & Boivin, 2000). Such characterizations are probably universal. For example, Chinese and Japanese children who are victims of bullying show the same characteristics as their Western counterparts (Rios-Ellis et al., 2000; Schwartz et al., 2001).

Bullying was once thought to be a normal part of children's play—not to be encouraged, of course, but of little consequence in the long run. However, developmental researchers who have looked closely at the society of children now realize that bullying is a serious problem, harming both the victim and the aggressor (Bukowski & Sippola, 2001; Garrity & Baris, 1996).

The leading researcher in this area is Dan Olweus, who has studied bullying for 30 years. The cruelty, pain, and suffering that he has documented are typified by the details of two cases (Olweus, 1993a):

Linda was systematically isolated by a small group of girls, who pressured the rest of the class, including Linda's only friend, to shun her. Then the ringleader of the group persuaded Linda to give a party and invite everyone. She did. Everyone accepted, but, following the ringleader's instructions, no one came. Linda was devastated, her self-confidence "completely destroyed."

Henry's experience was worse. Daily, his classmates called him "Worm," broke his pencils, spilled his books on the floor, and mocked him whenever he answered a teacher's questions. Finally, a few boys took him to the bathroom and made him lie, face down, in the urinal drain. After school that day he tried to kill himself. His parents found him unconscious, and only then learned about his torment.

Boys versus Girls

Children of both sexes can be bullies or victims, although gender differences exist. Boys who are bullies are often above average in size, whereas girls who are bullies are often above average in verbal assertiveness. Bullies' victims tend to be less assertive; boy victims are often physically weaker, whereas girl victims are more shy.

These gender differences are reflected in bullying tactics: Boys typically use force or the threat of force; girls often mock or ridicule their victims, making fun of their clothes, behavior, or appearance, revealing their most embarrassing secrets, or spreading destructive rumors about them. This gender-related difference in tactics reflects the difference between *physical* aggression and *relational* aggression. Physical aggression, as you remember from Chapter 10, involves punching, kicking, and causing the victim other physical pain; relational aggression involves undercutting the victim's friendships and self-esteem.

To some extent, gender norms condone bullying. As we have already noted, children are shunned by their peers if they complain to adults, so most children suffer bullying in silence. These norms allow bullies of both sexes to believe they are doing nothing wrong when the boys act tough or the girls gossip maliciously. They also mean that boys, in particular, become bullies because they consider it a sign of strength—a belief shared by many peers and even by some adults. Fewer girls become bullies, except in Japan, where social cooperation is so crucial that exclusion and the spreading of false rumors (two forms of relational aggression) are especially potent bullying weapons for girls (Morita et al., 1999).

Especially for Former Victims of Bullying: How can you overcome the psychic scars of having been a victim?

Bullying Around the World

Following the suicides of three victims, the Norwegian government asked Dan Olweus to determine the extent and severity of bullying. After concluding a confidential survey of nearly all of Norway's 90,000 school-age children, Olweus reported that bullying was widespread and serious (see Figure 13.1 on page 404); that teachers and parents were "relatively unaware" of specific incidents; and that even when adults noticed, they rarely intervened. Of all the children Olweus surveyed, 9 percent said they were bullied "now and then"; 3 percent were victims once a week or more; and 7 percent admitted that they themselves sometimes deliberately hurt other children, verbally or physically (Olweus, 1993b).

These numbers are equaled or exceeded in many other countries (Smith et al., 1999). For instance, confidential surveys found that 10 percent of British children bullied another child at least once a week (Smith et al., 1999), as did 18 percent of Italian and Australian children and 13 percent of Japanese children (Fonzi et al., 1999; Morita et al., 1999; Rigby & Slee, 1999). A study of a multiethnic, multi-income group of children in Los Angeles found that 10 percent (three-quarters of them boys) were teased and picked on and another 17 percent (most of them girls) were socially rejected (Graham & Juvonene, 1998).

Research in many nations finds wide variation among schools within the same community and much higher rates in locations where many adults are engaged in violence, such as the Palestinian territory, Ethiopia, and South Africa (Ohsako, 1999). Bullying is never completely absent, however. It occurs in every nation, in small rural schools and large urban ones, among well-to-do majority children and poor immigrant ones, among children of every race and religion (Smith et al., 1999).

A child's social status and behavior often change from year to year. For example, in the United States, when children from kindergarten through third grade were asked every year whether they had been the target of physical or relational aggression, only 4 percent said "yes" for all four years, but 60 percent said "yes" for at least one year (Kochenderfer-Ladd & Wardrop, 2001). The first years of elementary school are the time of greatest change, as some children learn to act in

FIGURE 13.1 Every Country Has Bullies
The rates of being bullied in the various grades as reported by Norwegian schoolchildren are typical of the rates in many other countries. This chart shows physical bullying only; relational bullying may increase with age. Although physical bullying is less common among older children, relational bullying becomes more devastating, because older children depend much more on peers for self-esteem.

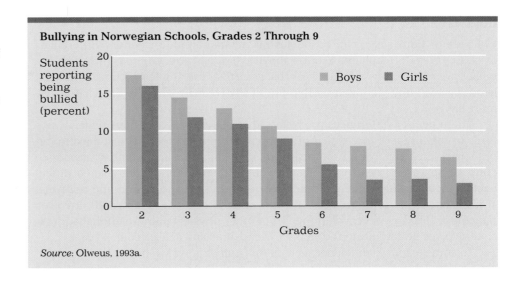

Bullying in Norwegian Schools, Grades 2 Through 9

Source: Olweus, 1993a.

Response for Former Victims of Bullying
(from page 403): Realize that it was not your fault; the bully was in the wrong and should have been stopped by adults at home and at school. Make sure your self-esteem is not still damaged. Write about the situation, see a psychotherapist, or talk it over with a supportive friend.

prosocial rather than antisocial ways and thus achieve more social acceptance (Haselager et al., 2002). To assess the cumulative frequency of bullying, other researchers asked older children if they *ever* were bullies or victims. Among U.S. middle-school students, 80 percent said they had engaged in bullying (Bosworth et al., 1999) and 77 percent said they had been victims (Hoover et al., 1992).

The Consequences of Bullying

A key word in the definition of bullying is *repeated*. Most children experience isolated attacks or social slights from other children and come through unscathed; and when the social play described in Chapter 10 turns hurtful, both the aggressor and the injured usually learn how to stop and repair the friendship. But when a child endures shameful experiences again and again—being forced to hand over lunch money, or to drink milk mixed with detergent, or to lick someone's boots, or to be the butt of insults and practical jokes, with everyone watching and no one defending—the effects can be deep and long-lasting. Bullied children are anxious, depressed, and underachieving during the months and years of their torment. To make matters worse, longitudinal studies show that a drop in self-esteem and an increase in loneliness follow the bullying experiences; even if the child is no longer bullied, negative effects linger (Kochenderfer-Ladd & Wardrop, 2001).

The picture is also ominous for bullies. As we have noted, in middle childhood bullies usually have friends who abet, fear, and admire them. They are brashly unapologetic about the pain they have inflicted "all in fun." Their parents do not stop them but instead are part of the problem, treating their children with a combination of neglect and hostility and using physical punishment, verbal criticism, and dominance to control and demean them (Olweus, 1993a).

However, bullies' popularity and school success fade over the years, as their peers become increasingly critical of their behavior. In reaction, bullies become more hostile, getting into trouble not only with peers and teachers but also with the police. In one longitudinal study, by age 24 two-thirds of boys who were bullies in the second grade had been convicted of at least one felony, and one-third of those who were bullies in the sixth through ninth grades had been convicted of three or more crimes, usually violent ones, and had already done prison time (Olweus, 1993b). This particular study came from Norway, but international research confirms that children who regularly victimize other children and challenge authority often become violent criminals (Moffitt et al., 2002).

Bullying is difficult to change. The origins of all kinds of antisocial behavior, including bullying, predate middle childhood and may lie in brain abnormalities

Especially for the Parents of a Bully:
Another parent has told you that your child is bullying his or her child, but your child denies it and explains that the other child doesn't mind being teased.

that are present at birth and that are then strengthened by insecure attachment, poor emotional regulation, and other deficits (Cairns & Cairns, 2001; Holden, 2000). In fact, aggression may be natural to all children. As one researcher quipped, "Babies do not kill each other because we do not give them access to guns" (Tremblay, 2000, p. 581).

Fortunately, there are two hopeful notes. First, children *do* change if family, school, and the society of children encourage them to. A longitudinal study found that about one-fourth of a group of 51 high-risk children who were unusually aggressive and uncontrolled in the first grade improved as time went on. By adolescence they were not delinquents, not bullies, and not particularly stressed, even though they still lived in low-income, violence-prone neighborhoods. The other three-fourths remained antisocial, with numerous signs that they had criminal futures (Aguilar et al., 2000). The researchers suspect that psychosocial influences, such as those provided by families and schools, are more powerful than biological ones, such as genetic inheritance and brain damage, which are difficult to change.

A second reason for hope is that careful research has shown how bullying can be reduced, as discussed in the Thinking Like a Scientist feature.

Jimmy, Sixth-Generation Pain in the Ass

© THE NEW YORKER COLLECTION 1997. JACK ZIEGLER FROM CARTOONBANK.COM

Like Father, Like Son If parents and grandparents use their greater physical power to punish and criticize their offspring, the children (especially the boys) are often hostile to everyone they know.

Thinking Like a Scientist

Don't Suffer Bullying in Silence

Bullies and victims share one firm cognitive assumption: Adults will not intervene. Robert Coles (1997) describes a 9-year-old boy who reported that one of his classmates, a girl, was cheating. The boy was then victimized, not only by the girl and her friends but more subtly by the teacher and the principal, who made excuses for the girl (her grandfather had died several months earlier). Coles believes the overall moral climate teaches many children to ignore the actions of bullies and the feelings and needs of victims of bullying.

A recent study in Ontario, Canada, that unobtrusively recorded playground bullying (verbal and physical) found that girls were as involved as boys, teachers intervened in only 4 percent of the situations, other children stopped 12 percent of the incidents, and the principal of the school with the most bullying denied that his school had any bullying at all (Pepler et al., 1999). Most children are sympathetic to victims, are afraid of bullies, and believe that teachers could stop the bullies but are "too soft. . . . The most she'll do is, like, go 'Don't do it again'" (quoted in Borland et al., 1998).

One 8-year-old explained how a bully in his class operated:

He sits across the aisle from me, and he doesn't give me any trouble, because I'm able to defend myself, and he knows it, but he's a bully, that's what he is, a real meanie. He tries to

get his way by picking on kids who he's decided are weaker than him. They help him with his homework—they give him answers. They give him candy from their lunches. They take orders from him. He cheats—I see him. I think the teacher knows, but the kid's father is a lawyer, and my dad says the teacher is probably afraid—she's got to be careful, or he'll sue her.

[quoted in Coles, 1997]

The children who made these observations may be right about the influence of teachers, and they are certainly right about the perception of children. This also can change. In England, when a pamphlet entitled "Don't Suffer in Silence" was distributed to all schoolchildren and teachers were trained in ways of responding to bullying incidents, bullying in primary schools was reduced by almost 50 percent (Smith et al., 1999).

Researchers now realize that intervention must change the social climate so that bully–victim cycles no longer spiral out of control. A "whole-school" approach is needed, as was first demonstrated in Norway. Dan Olweus had been studying bullying for many years when the Norwegian government asked him to design an intervention effort. Olweus first collected data from all the children and then, using an ecological approach, began to change the school culture. All

parents received pamphlets that described signs of victimization (such as a child's having bad dreams, no real friends, damaged clothes, torn books, or unexplained bruises). All students saw videotapes intended to evoke sympathy for victims. All teachers were given special training in intervention.

The second phase was more direct. In every classroom, students discussed reasons to stop bullying, ways to mediate peer conflicts, and how to befriend lonely children. The last action is particularly crucial: Having at least one protective peer "watching your back" not only prevents the escalation of bullying but reduces its emotional sting (Hodges et al.,

Shake Hands or Yell "Uncle" Many schools, such as this one in Alaska, have trained peer mediators who intervene in disputes, hear both sides, take notes, and seek a resolution. Without such efforts, antagonists usually fight until one gives up, giving bullies free rein. Despite Alaska's higher rate of alcohol abuse, the state's adolescent homicide rate is lower than the national average.

? *Observational Quiz* (see answer, page 408): Could this be one reason?

1999). Therefore, teachers organized cooperative learning groups within classes so that no child could be isolated and then bullied, and teachers halted each incident of name-calling or minor assault, recognizing the undercurrent beneath the bully's excuses and the terror behind the victim's silence or nervous laughter. Principals learned that adult supervision in the lunchroom, bathroom, and playground was pivotal, and they redeployed staff to keep watch and intervene.

If bullying occurred despite these preventive steps, counselors used very direct measures: conducting intensive family therapy with the bully and parents; removing the bully to a different class, grade, or even school; and helping the victim strengthen social and academic skills. (Note that bullies and their families bore the major burden. If the victim were to change school and the bully were to stay, the wrong child would be punished.)

Twenty months after this campaign began, Olweus resurveyed the children. Bullying had been reduced overall by more than 50 percent, with dramatic improvement for both boys and girls at every grade level (Olweus, 1992). These results are thrilling to developmentalists because they show that research can lead to an inexpensive, widespread intervention that effectively reduces a serious problem. Especially noteworthy is that the intervention did not attempt to change the children's nature—no drugs, no suspensions, no expulsions—but used children's normal desires to be friends and to do well in school. Adult guidance made prosocial behavior the norm, changing the school climate—which, again, is much easier at the beginning of middle childhood than at the end of adolescence. Olweus (1993a) concludes:

> It is no longer possible to avoid taking action about bullying problems at school using lack of awareness as an excuse . . . it all boils down to a matter of will and involvement on the part of adults.

Unfortunately, many school systems throughout the world have not yet even acknowledged the harm caused by bullying. A research team from Finland complains:

> It is somewhat strange that society provides education in a large variety of subjects of a scholarly nature, but when it comes to human relations, which is the source of both the greatest misery and the greatest joy in life, we do not consider it worth covering in our educational system.
>
> [Bjorkqvist & Osterman, 1999]

Many educators in many nations are beginning to address bullying, although some efforts are scattershot, some ineffective, and some (particularly in high school) self-defeating (Olewus, 2001; Smith et al., 1999). A whole-school approach, with involvement by all concerned over a period of years, can be very successful in middle childhood, if the "will and involvement" are present.

Family Influences

A debate rages between those who believe that parenting styles and processes are very influential and those who believe that a child's genes and peers are much more powerful than anything the parents might do (Maccoby, 2000). Putting it strongly, those who advocate the supremacy of parenting say:

> The vulnerabilities of older children may differ substantially in kind from those of young ones, but the potential consequences of risks remain equally great throughout the developmental period. The extent to which parents provide healthy and supportive environments for their developing children is a critical component in their lifelong well-being.
>
> *[Ramey, 2002, p. 48]*

And those who assert that heredity predominates contend:

> Children somewhat resemble their biological parents and siblings in personality, but the genes they have in common can account for almost all of the resemblance. These results indicate that being reared by conscientious parents does not, on average, make children more (or less) conscientious, that being reared by social parents does not, on average, make children more (or less) sociable, and that being reared by open-minded parents does not, on average, make children more (or less) open-minded.
>
> *[Harris, 2002, p. 5]*

All researchers agree that both nature and nurture are important. All agree that the interaction between the two is crucial and that nurture—the environment—involves not simply parenting practices but also other influences, such as school and friendships. These aspects of the environment are called "nonshared" because children in the same family do not share them. When researchers calculate the correlation between various genetic traits among parents and siblings (including twins, adoptees, and stepchildren), they find that roughly half of the traits seem genetic and half seem environmental, with most environmental effects "nonshared"—a blow to parents who thought they could mold their children's personalities (Plomin et al., 2001). But, as you remember from Chapters 1–3, exactly how scientists should quantify and interpret variables can be disputed. Moreover, developmentalists disagree about the meaning of nonshared influences. Do they mean that school and friends combined with genes determine a child's personality?

Most developmentalists answer "no", for two reasons. First, differences between siblings from the same family are much less than differences between children from extremely diverse families, such as between a well-educated, well-to-do suburban couple and an impoverished, illiterate single parent. Studies of adopted children, who share no genes with their adoptive parents, reveal that nonfamilial contextual factors are as powerful as genetic influences. Because parents choose neighborhoods and schools, they determine contexts. Thus, indirectly, they have a powerful effect. Second, virtually all the research is correlational and therefore static, from one moment in time, even though parent–child interaction is a dynamic, ever-changing system.

> As every parent knows, parents continually try to make up for their past errors with their children, and they are generally fairly successful at mid-life correction. They are constantly responsive to their past actions and to their child's current level of adaptation. A child who is getting into trouble will be met with a parent who intensifies her monitoring and restriction of the child, whereas a child's demonstration of responsibility will be met with a parent who grants greater freedom. Because of this responsivity, simple-minded correlational studies will misrepresent the relation between parenting behavior and child behavior. . . . The point is that the parent will titrate her actions in an exquisite manner when the child's behavior begins to deviate. So, too, the child's behavior is just as exquisitely responsive to changes in parenting.
>
> *[Dodge, 2002, p. 218]*

Response for the Parents of a Bully (from page 404): The future is ominous if the charges are true, and your child's denial is a symptom of a problem. (If your child were not a bully, he or she would be worried about the other child's misperception instead of categorically denying that any problem exists.) You might ask the teacher and guidance counselor what they are doing about bullying in the school. Since bullies often learn behavior at home, perhaps family counseling would help you to become less punitive and your child to become less aggressive. Because bullies often have a few friends who encourage them, you may need to monitor your child's friendships and perhaps even befriend the victim. Talk matters over with your child, as often as necessary. Ignoring the situation may lead to heartache later on.

!Answer to Observational Quiz (from page 406): Yes. Children learn their conflict-resolution patterns in elementary school and then tend to use them in adolescence

You may find one or another of the three quotations above more persuasive than the others, but the controversy is not yet settled. All developmentalists agree that genes, peers, and families are influential in middle childhood, and that dynamic, longitudinal, experimental studies are too scarce to be definitive (Demo & Cox, 2000). Keep this in mind as you read about family functions and structures. Decide for yourself the impact of parents during the school years.

Family Function

family function The ways in which a family operates to nurture the development of its children's potential: meeting their physical needs for food, clothing, and shelter; encouraging them to learn; developing their self-esteem; nurturing their friendships with peers; and providing harmony and stability at home.

Families may be classified in two ways; by function and by structure. **Family function** refers to how a family works to meet the needs of its members; **family structure** refers to how a family is legally constructed and how its members are genetically connected. Some family structures tend to function better than others, as we will see.

Although the details vary, families serve five essential functions for school-age children:

family structure The legal and genetic relationships among the members of a particular family.

1. *Meet physical needs by providing food, clothes, and shelter.* In middle childhood, children are old enough to dress, wash, and put themselves to bed, but they cannot yet obtain the basic necessities of life without their families' help.
2. *Encourage learning.* A critical task during middle childhood is to master academic skills. Families must get their children to school and then guide and motivate their education.
3. *Develop self-esteem.* As they become more cognitively aware, children become more self-critical. Families need to make their children feel competent, loved, and appreciated.
4. *Nurture peer friendship.* Families can provide the time, space, opportunity, and skills needed to develop peer relationships.
5. *Provide harmony and stability.* Children need to feel safe and secure, confident that family routines are protective and predictable.

Thus, a family that functions well provides material and cognitive resources as well as emotional security, so that the children grow in body and mind. No family functions perfectly for every child. Recurrent unresolved conflict between the adults is common but harmful, whether or not the child is directly involved in it and whether or not it leads to divorce (Cox & Brooks-Gunn, 1999; Cummings et al., 2002).

Mom Urges Fit Over Fashion The basic function of families is to provide children with basic necessities, such as clothing. When middle-class school-age children are involved, this is more difficult than it seems. The society of children is often quite specific about the most desirable brand, color, and design of every item of clothing, especially shoes.

JOHN BOYKIN / PHOTOEDIT

Styles of Parenting

You read in Chapter 10 about Diana Baumrind's (1967, 1971) classification of parenting styles: authoritarian, authoritative, and permissive. Think about how each of these three parenting styles relates to the five family functions just listed. If parents with a permissive style simply accept whatever their child does, they fail at all but the first function. The child needs both warmth and discipline, both encouragement and direction, as typified by the authoritative style. Research suggests that parents who actively promote education, self-esteem, and social skills have children who are more likely to achieve in school and to have solid friendships. Organization of family life is key; chaos is destructive (Maccoby, 2000).

Although authoritative families (warm, communicative, and demanding) generally raise more successful and self-confident children, a diversity of family styles can function well for children (Dishion & Bullock, 2002). For example, it is important that

parents be aware of what their children are doing, where, and with whom—a style that is more authoritarian (Dishion & McMahon, 1998; Pettit et al., 2001). Many immigrant families have an authoritarian style, which they may be wise to maintain even if it is atypical in the new culture, because immigrant children fare better if the family keeps its cultural identity and values (Suarez-Orozco & Suarez-Orozco, 2001).

Stress and Poverty

In the twenty-first century, almost every family tries to meet basic needs and encourage learning in its school-age children (functions 1 and 2 on our list), and most families realize that the child's self-esteem and friendship are important (functions 3 and 4). Providing harmony and stability (function 5) is another matter. Many children grow up in conflict-filled homes, violent neighborhoods, or unstable conditions, moving from place to place or having adults join or leave the household. All this impedes development in middle childhood.

Each year, about 20 percent of all children move from one residence to another, a rate three times that of adults over age 50 (U.S. Bureau of the Census, 2000). Even if the move is to a better place, school-age children are particularly disrupted because they have stronger neighborhood networks than younger or older people do. Unfortunately, the frequency of moves increases as income falls, with the poorest children moving, on average, 2 to 3 times *a year* before becoming homeless and moving into a shelter (Buckner et al., 1999).

Poverty interferes with a family's ability to serve all five basic functions for the school-age child. Yet although poverty increases the risk, it does not always interfere with effective family functioning (McLoyd, 1998a; White & Rogers, 2000). Even the poorest families usually manage to provide food, clothing, and shelter (function 1), but only some low-income families give their children what they need to learn well, make friends, and develop self-esteem (functions 2, 3, and 4).

Poverty puts adults under stress, and stress sometimes makes an adult a less effective parent—distracted, inconsistent, harsh, neglectful (Dodge et al., 1994; Pinderhughes et al., 2001). Perhaps function 5, harmony and stability, is most difficult to perform, since poor families are likely to be unemployed, undereducated, and unstable, with other adults joining or leaving the household and the home address changing as well.

Especially for Readers Who Are Not Yet Parents: Should children call their parents by their first names, participate freely in the adults' discussions, and wear whatever clothes, hairstyles, and accessories they choose? Or should children be expected to be seen and not heard, to do their household chores regularly and well, and to excel in school?

KATHERINE MCGLYNN / THE IMAGE WORKS

Fighting Homelessness Despite the anxiety evident in these children, this is a hopeful scene. The woman on the left, formerly homeless, is now living with her children in a stable community residence and is also studying for her high school degree, with the help of a college student. With secure housing and education or job training, many homeless families can become functional again.

Finally, poor children are exposed to much more violence than parents realize. According to one survey of 1,000 children on Chicago's South Side, 39 percent had witnessed a shooting (Bell & Jenkins, 1993). A similar study of 9- to 11-year-olds in Detroit found that two-thirds had seen someone beaten up or mugged; one-third had seen someone stabbed; one-fourth had seen someone shot; and one-sixth had seen someone killed. The children's mothers usually did not know that their children had witnessed such violence (Ceballo et al., 2001).

Family Structures

All five of the nurturing functions can be provided by any form of family, of any income. Structure does not determine function. A family's ability to function well is not determined by, but is affected by, its structure. As we have seen, structure refers to the legal bonds that hold the members together, as well as to their location—family members usually live together. The seven most common family structures are the following:

- The **nuclear family** consists of a father, a mother, and their biological children.
- The **extended family** consists of three or more generations of biologically related individuals.
- The **single-parent family** consists of one parent with his or her biological children.
- The **blended family** consists of two adults, the biological children from a previous earlier union of one or both adults, and any children the adults have together. Thus, stepparents, stepchildren, and stepsiblings may be part of the family.
- The **grandparent family** consists of children living with their grandparents instead of with their parents.
- The **adoptive family** consists of one or more nonbiological children whom adults have voluntarily, legally, and permanently taken to raise as their own.
- The **foster family** consists of one or more orphaned, neglected, abused, or delinquent children who are temporarily cared for by an adult individual or couple to whom they are not biologically related.

Is any family structure always best? No. Children can thrive in almost any family structure, especially if income is adequate and family interaction is supportive (Carlson & Corcoran, 2001; Lansford et al., 2001).

Children want and need some sort of family. A study of 1,000 8- to 12-year-olds included many children of various races, of single mothers, of low-income families, of stepparents, and of foster families (Brannen et al., 2000). Regardless of their circumstances, "children considered parents to be very important to them and their expectations of them were high." Their definition of parents—"people who never ever don't care about you" (p. 93)—emphasized caregiving, not legalities. More broadly,

> Children's criteria for family life included: the presence of children; living with at least one parent; a sense of security and a place to belong, and, most important of all, . . . unconditional love and care.
>
> [Brannen et al., 2000, p. 205]

In each generation and each society, tax policies, housing design, divorce laws, religious rituals, and mortality rates make some family structures more widely preferred and therefore more common. The family structure that is most common in the society usually works best for children.

Before 1900, many family forms were apparent in the United States and elsewhere, partly because more parents died young or went off in search of a better life, leaving their children to live in single-parent or blended families or to

nuclear family A family that consists of a father, a mother, and the biological children they have together.

extended family A family that consists of three or more generations of biologically related individuals.

single-parent family A family that consists of one parent and his or her biological children.

blended family A family that consists of two adults, the biological children from a previous union of one or both adults, and any children the adults have together.

grandparent family A family that consists of children living with their grandparents instead of with their parents.

adoptive family A family that consists of one or more nonbiological children whom an adult individual or couple have voluntarily, legally, and permanently taken to raise as their own.

foster family A family in which one or more orphaned, neglected, abused, or delinquent children are temporarily cared for by an adult individual or couple to whom they are not biologically related.

be informally fostered by relatives or neighbors. If parents divorced or separated, fathers were given custody, and they usually remarried or found a live-in housekeeper, because men were not considered capable of child care.

By the middle of the twentieth century in North America, a family of two parents living with their two or three biological offspring had become the norm. The nuclear family was glorified on early television programs (such as *Ozzie and Harriet*) and is still idealized by many Americans (Coontz, 1992).

If current trends continue, a minority—about 37 percent—of children born in the twenty-first century will live with both biological parents from birth to age 18. In the United States in 1998, 33 percent of all infants were born to mothers who were not married (U.S. Bureau of the Census, 2000). Another one-third are likely to live in a single-parent household before age 18 because of divorce or, less often, parental death. Many of these children will experience several changes in household composition—spending part of their childhood living with a grandparent, a stepparent, or a parent's live-in lover—and will witness several marital transitions, from marriage to divorce to remarriage to divorce again.

Given all these possible transitions and historical changes, defining a family structure merely by who lives in the household at a given time is misleading (Bengtson, 2001). Most American children today are being raised by multiple generations of adults in extended families. One reason for this is that adults are living longer: In 1900, only 21 percent of all 30-year-olds in the United States had living grandparents; now, 76 percent of 30-year-olds have at least one living grandparent. In fact, today's 20-year-olds are more likely to have a living *grandmother* (91 percent) than 20-year-olds a century ago were to have a living *mother* (83 percent) (Uhlenberg, 1996). Despite all the variations in family structure, most children grow up fairly well: They are equally close to their parents (see Figure 13.2) and are healthier and better educated (at least less likely to die young or drop out of school) than children in earlier years. Each family type has advantages and disadvantages.

> **Response for Readers Who Are Not Yet Parents** (from page 409): Each set of practices is typical in some families, and both sets can result in happy, successful children. If you judged one style or the other to be categorically wrong, think again.

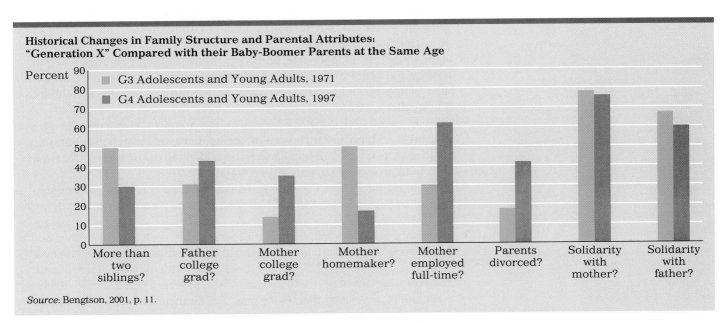

Historical Changes in Family Structure and Parental Attributes: "Generation X" Compared with their Baby-Boomer Parents at the Same Age

- G3 Adolescents and Young Adults, 1971
- G4 Adolescents and Young Adults, 1997

Source: Bengtson, 2001, p. 11.

FIGURE 13.2 Parent–Child Bonds Stay Strong This chart depicts generational changes within families. In 1971, generation one (G1) consisted of the elderly, G2 was their middle-aged children, and G3 was their adolescent and young-adult grandchildren—the "Baby Boomers." By 1997, G4, the great-grandchildren of G1, were approaching adulthood. Because this was a longitudinal study, all generations have the same gene pool and family heritage. This means that the dramatic changes—parental divorce and maternal employment, for instance—are real, historical shifts. It is comforting to see that solidarity with parents does not seem to be much affected by the various cohort changes.

Benefits of the Nuclear Family The nuclear family—two parents and their biological children, with no other relatives in the home—is considered ideal, but families with this structure make up less than half of all American households.

?*Observational Quiz* (see answer, page 414): This particular family illustrates three of the advantages that nuclear families are more likely to have. What are they?

The Nuclear Family

Although we have stressed that children can thrive in many family structures, children raised in nuclear families experience fewer health, academic, and emotional problems; and, as adults, they are more likely to have successful careers, satisfying family lives, and good mental health. Four reasons for these favorable trends have been identified:

■ *Parental alliance.* Two adults, both of whom have known and loved a child since birth, tend to provide more complete caregiving and an extra measure of warmth, discipline, and attention. When a "parental alliance" forms, both allies cooperate, compensate, and compromise to attain their mutual goal: healthy and successful children. Fathers, particularly, spend more time with their biological children in their own homes, and this benefits the children (Furstenberg, 1998).

■ *Genetic investment.* All mammals, including humans, have a genetic impulse to protect and nurture their own offspring, perhaps for genetic continuity. Child maltreatment and homicide are less likely to occur when children live with both biological parents (Davis & Daly, 1997).

■ *Parental mental health.* Parents who sustain a close marriage relationship tend to be psychologically healthier than parents who never marry or who get divorced.

■ *Financial advantage.* Married couples tend to be wealthier than other adults, for reasons that predate the child's birth and continue as long as the marriage does (see Figure 13.3). To be specific, individuals with more income and education are more desirable marriage partners and are more likely to meet and marry each other. Once married, financial security makes them more likely to have children and less likely to divorce.

Notice that the last two advantages actually predate parenthood. People who marry and stay married are generally richer, healthier, better educated, and less likely to be abusive or addicted. All these traits describe a good parent and a good spouse, but they are the cause of the good relationship, not the result. Moreover, because the children of two such people are more likely, because of genes and early nurturing, to be relatively easy to raise, the parents willingly invest time and money in parenting. No wonder, then, that children in nuclear families are more successful at school and as adults than children without the two-parent advantage.

Not all nuclear families confer well-being on their members. Some biological parents are unfit, and some marriages are destructive. Some spouses are so disturbed, addicted, or self-absorbed that they mistreat their children and interfere with their partner's child-rearing efforts. It is not necessarily wise for such couples to "stay together for the sake of the children." One review of cross-sectional and longitudinal research concluded that, although all children are "harmed by intense conflict, whether or not their parents live together, . . . children who live in intact families with persistently high levels of conflict are the most distressed of all" (Furstenberg & Cherlin, 1991).

The Single-Parent Family

The number of single-parent households has increased markedly over the past two decades, as births to unmarried parents and divorces of married ones have more than doubled in virtually every major industrialized nation. In the United States, most single mothers are in the labor force, including a large majority (83 percent) of those with children age 6 to 17, as well as most (68 percent) of those with children under age 6 (U.S. Bureau of the Census, 2000). The number of single fathers has increased by 500 percent over the past 30 years, to more than 1.7 million in 1999, and 88 percent of them are employed (U.S. Bureau of the Census, 2000) (see Appendix A).

No matter what their sex, nationality, ethnicity, or level of education, single parents are likely to work hard to fill the dual role of major provider and major caregiver—usually giving up personal recreation, social life, and sleep to do so. Single parents are also more likely to have experienced adverse life circumstances and to have inadequate income (Davies et al., 1997; Simons, 1996).

One important factor in the ability to be a patient and responsive parent is maturity, which tends to increase with age; yet single parents tend to be younger than married parents. In 1999, of all the U.S. households headed by someone under age 25, 55 percent were headed by a single parent. In fact, of all births to unmarried women in that year, about a third were to women under age 20, another third were to women aged 20 to 24, and the final third were to women aged 25 to 50. Thus, a disproportionate number of single parents are young, often lacking the emotional maturity and the financial resources to meet a child's needs. Having a baby during adolescence makes it worse: Teenage parenthood slows down maturation and earning power.

We must be careful not to blame the baby for problems that predate the pregnancy. Teenagers with less education, less money, and more personal problems are more likely to have sex with immature partners at an early age, without contraception—and thus are more likely to become single parents. A careful study found that about half the problems of children of teenage mothers were direct results, not of their mother's immaturity, but of her enduring characteristics (such as poverty) before and after she got pregnant (Jaffee et al., 2001). No wonder the offspring of teenage parents are more likely to have problems in school as they grow up—but neither their parents' age nor marital status is the primary reason.

Obviously, being raised by a single parent does not always hurt a child's development. The actual outcome is affected by all the factors listed in Table 13.2. A family's poverty has a greater impact on a child than

Average Income of U.S. Families, 1998

Source: U.S. Bureau of the Census, 2000.

FIGURE 13.3 No Father, No Money
Although some single mothers are quite wealthy (3 percent of families headed by a single woman have an income of more than $75,000 a year), most are poor. This may affect children as much as or more than the father's absence does.

The Single-Parent Family Single parents are of two distinct types: never married and formerly married. This divorcee is a pediatrician, so she and her daughter have a higher income than many single-parent families. To combat the other hazards faced by single parents—including loneliness, low self-esteem, and ongoing disputes with the former spouse—she has established a divorce resource center in her hometown in Michigan.

TABLE 13.2 The Impact of Single Parenthood on Child Development

Likely to Be Harmful If	Likely to Be Beneficial If
Low-income home	Middle-income home
Conflict-filled home	Peaceful home
Parent under age 25	Parent over 30
Parent is not high school graduate	Parent has college education
More than two siblings	Only child, or one sibling
Several changes (e.g., divorce, remarriage, divorce)	Stable family structure (no change ever or none within past five years)
No help from relatives	Grandparents actively helpful
Conflict with other parent	Cordial relations with other parent
Parent has live-in lovers	Parent not romantically involved
Parent socially isolated	Parent active with friends, church, etc.
Community hostile to single parents	Community supportive of single parents
If child is under age 5	
More than four caregivers	Two or three caregivers
No steady day care	High-quality preschool
Parent employed 60+ hours a week	Parent has part-time job
If child is over age 5	
Frequent change of school	Child stays in one school
Frequent change of neighborhood	Child stays in one neighborhood
Parent unemployed	Parent employed, flexible hours
Child hostile or friendless	Child has several friends

Source: Compiled from several sources, among them Angel & Angel, 1994; McLanahan & Sandefur, 1994.

⁝ Answer to Observational Quiz (from page 412): Shared concern for the children's well-being (note the helmets), shared activities (family vacations, dinners, or, as shown here, recreation), and higher income (bikes for everyone). Of course, some nuclear families have none of these, and some nontraditional families have them all.

whether or not the parents are married, were never married, or were married and divorced (Miller & Davis, 1997). Indeed, as we have seen, the correlation between single parenthood and children's problems often is actually a correlation among poverty, mental health, and childhood stress (Carlson & Corcoran, 2001).

One issue for single parents is whether they were never married or married and then divorced. In terms of a child's development, parental divorce seems particularly negative, although the specific effects are still under dispute, as the Changing Policy feature explains.

Changing Policy

More Divorce, More Trouble?

Developmentalists are engaged in an "ongoing, contentious debate over the consequences of marital disruption for adults and children" (Amato, 2000, p. 1270). The longitudinal evidence suggests that a certain coldness between husband and wife—short of open warfare—may be better for the children than separation and divorce. One longitudinal study of children of divorce began long before the parents thought of separation. In high-conflict marriages that ended in divorce, the children actually benefited from the breakup. However, most divorces occurred in low-conflict marriages, and here the children suffered as a result (Booth & Amato, 2001).

The disruption and discord of divorce almost always adversely affect the children for at least a year or two (Hetherington & Kelly, 2002). Immediately before and after a divorce, the children show signs of emotional pain, such as depression or rebellion, and symptoms of stress, such as lower school achievement, poorer health, and fewer friends. Whether this distress is relatively mild and short-lived or serious and long-lasting depends primarily on the stability of the child's life and the adequacy of caregiving (Amato, 1993). Recovery in the area of emotional health is typical after three years or so, but recovery in academic achievement is more problematic (Sun & Li, 2001).

Harmony and stability, so crucial to a well-functioning family, are jeopardized by divorce. For instance, the feeling of being abandoned by a trusted adult (parent, grandparent, babysitter)—even if that is not actually the case—is devastating to a child. Moving to a less desirable neighborhood and attending a different school can be particularly disruptive for children who are old enough to have best friends. Divorce also reduces the attention that parents give their children, partly because financial needs require that they work more hours or take a second job and partly because emotional needs make them resume their own social lives, dating and socializing with other adults. Divorce that occurs before or during middle childhood is likely to have longer-lasting effects than divorce that occurs when the child is older (Furstenberg & Kiernan, 2001).

Divorce does not have to be disastrous. An extensive study found that most parents of every family structure, including divorced families, were adequate and, consequently, that most children seemed to develop well enough. However, if a mother who was the primary caregiver was financially stressed, emotionally depressed, or inadequate as a parent (all at least twice as common among divorced as among married mothers), then the children were likely to suffer (Simons, 1996).

The parental alliance is likely to be undercut during divorce, with legalities, emotions, and sheer physical separation making cooperation difficult (Hetherington & Kelly, 2002). Divorce usually means an economic setback for the children, because even if the noncustodial spouse pays the full amount of child support mandated by the court, the custodial household's income is likely to be less than it was before the divorce. The economic loss is worse if child support is not paid in full or is withheld completely (Manning & Smock, 2000).

Theoretically, parents should share legal custody and finances and work out an equitable division of physical custody, deciding the child's physical whereabouts. Joint custody is not easy to carry out in practice, however, especially when the parents are fighting. Thus, the custody solution that at first appears fair may actually harm the children.

Indeed, no particular custody arrangement is always benign, because the ages, personalities, needs, wishes, and cir-

cumstances of the mother, father, and child all change over time (Galatzer-Levy & Kraus, 1999; Hetherington & Stanley-Hagan, 1999). Custodial fathers can do as well as mothers, partly because they usually choose to maintain active parenthood, and adults generally perform better when they have chosen a role rather than having it forced upon them. Typically, custodial fathers have more income than their ex-wives, more authority over their sons, and greater willingness to accept caregiving help from relatives of the other sex, including the children's mother. The last point is particularly important in enabling the child to maintain close ties to both parents. Children whose fathers have custody have close relationships with their mothers more often than vice versa (Hetherington et al., 1998).

The bottom line is that divorce is almost never good for children. Ironically, few marrying couples think they will ever divorce, but many couples avoid marriage, because they fear divorce. In Europe, a growing number have children outside of marriage, planning to stay together for decades without a marriage license. This is one way to avoid divorce, but—like other family forms—it may or may not function well for children.

"Wait a minute! When we decided to separate, I thought I was leaving home"

The Joy of Single Parenthood More and more men are becoming custodial fathers, not always out of choice.

Who Belongs to Whom? Only two members of this newly formed blended family chose each other. The success of their relationship, like that of all parents in blended families, will largely depend on how well the other family members work out their relationships with stepparents, stepsiblings, and other "acquired" relatives. Generally, the younger the children, and the more years that pass, the more likely it is that stepparents and even half-siblings will be accepted as one's own.

MICHAEL NEWMAN / PHOTOEDIT

The Blended Family

Most divorced parents remarry within a few years, and many unmarried parents marry eventually. When such a marriage ends loneliness, improves finances, reduces conflict with a former spouse, and creates a more stable household organization, it may benefit the children. There is, however, a complication. Most new partners are initially happy, but that is almost never the case for the children, who are likely to show stress due to the marriage or remarriage (Cherlin, 1992; Mott et al., 1997). They must suddenly negotiate a new set of family relationships, sharing the parent not only with a stepparent but often with half-siblings, stepgrandparents, and others, most of whom they would not select as relatives if they had a choice (Ganong & Coleman, 1994).

The same functions that are important to children in all other families—meeting basic needs, encouraging learning, enhancing self-esteem, fostering friendship, and providing harmony and stability—also are important to children in stepfamilies (Arendell, 1997). Even in the best circumstances, however, adequate family functioning in these five areas takes time to achieve.

Second marriages are more likely to end in divorce than first marriages, and the presence of children aged 9 to 15 increases the risk. The main reason is that children during these years want a stable family structure as they undergo their own emotional and sexual transitions. They add stress to a new marriage, particularly if a new stepparent changes the relationship they had with their parents or attempts to enforce different rules and routines (Hetherington et al., 1998).

LAURA DWIGHT

Blending In As indicated by her smile and her embrace of her 2-year-old half-brother, 7-year-old Alina seems happy in her blended family, with her biological mother, her stepfather, and their son. What do you make of her other hand, touching her mother's hand?

The Grandparent Family

Grandparents are increasingly responsible for child rearing (Bengtson, 2001). Some share responsibilities with one or both parents: About 4 percent of children in the United States live with one or both parents in their grandparents' household (U.S. Bureau of the Census, 2001).

(This figure does not include households of adult children whose parents have moved in with them.) Another 2 percent of children in the United States live with grandparents without any parent present, usually because the parents are dead, addicted, imprisoned, or mentally ill.

Children in grandparent families are more likely to benefit than to be harmed (Thomas et al., 2000). If the grandparent family is relatively free of conflict, providing stability as well as ongoing love and guidance, children are likely to thrive. When parents are involved in divorce, a new romance, or remarriage, grandparents can be a crucial source of continuity for the children (Ganong & Coleman, 1999). However, when grandparents feel stressed by the obligation to care for grandchildren, the result is added emotional and health problems for both generations (Shore & Hayslip, 1994). As one 53-year-old great-grandmother laments:

Grandmother Knows Best About 20,000 grandmothers in Connecticut are caregivers for their grandchildren. This 15-year-old boy and his 17-year-old sister came to live with their grandmother in New Haven after their mother died several years ago. This type of family works best when the grandmother is relatively young and has her own house, as is the case here.

> I have been taking care of all these kids for a mighty long time. Sandy [her daughter] needs so much help with her children. LaShawn [her granddaughter] I raised from a baby. Now she got two kids and I'm doing it again. I bathe, feed them, and everything. Three generations I raised. Lord Almighty! I'm tired, tired, tired. Sick too.
>
> *[quoted in Burton, 1995]*

One vulnerability affects only grandparent families: intergenerational conflict when parents and grandparents have different notions of how children should be raised. If grandparents are major caregivers, they often feel their rules and guidelines should prevail over those of the parents. As one young mother complains:

> It was a constant pull and a constant draining. . . . I didn't feel like she was my child at all. I really didn't have any say-so over anything.
>
> *[quoted in McDonald & Armstrong, 2001, p. 217]*

The Adoptive Family

We noted back in Chapter 3 that about one couple in six is infertile—that is, unable to conceive a child after at least a year of trying. Many of these couples wish to adopt a child. Adoption is much more difficult than it was 50 years ago, because birth control has become more widespread and fewer birth mothers are giving up their babies for adoption (Babb, 1999).

As a result, couples who want to adopt today are more determined and more carefully screened than in earlier times. They are also more willing to adopt older children, children with disabilities, and children from other nations (Romania, Russia, and China are the most popular sources of children among U.S. couples seeking to adopt). Another significant change is that many adoptions today are "open"; Adopted children, whose origins were once kept strictly confidential, now may know their birth mother's identity and whereabouts, and may even visit with her from time to time.

On the whole, being adopted does not produce either advantages or disadvantages in the children involved (Roehlkepartain et al., 1994). Most adopted children develop well; among those who do not, the reasons for their difficulties are the same as for their nonadopted peers—lack of family communication and warmth, poverty, lack of education, and early biological deficits (Miller et al., 2000). The Romanian and Russian children who were adopted by U.S. families in the 1990s had been housed in orphanages and severely deprived before they were adopted. They experienced marked improvement over their first few years with their new families, but, by middle childhood, their situations varied widely: Some had evident emotional problems and others were developing quite normally (O'Connor et al., 2000).

Unless they were adopted internationally, by a family of another race, or after infancy, adoptees' reaction to open adoption does not seem to be influenced in any particular direction: Some become very concerned about their adoptive status, while others seldom think about it (Kohler et al., 2002). In adulthood, although longitudinal research finds a somewhat higher risk of emotional problems, most adoptees are healthy and normal in their everyday functioning (Borders et al., 2000; Grotevant & Kohler, 1999).

In the development of adoptees, their overall personal history and social context work to both their advantage and disadvantage. The legal process of adoption can be long and difficult, so couples who do adopt tend to be particularly concerned about and involved with their children. This care and concern are pluses for the children, many of whom are deprived or disabled and benefit greatly from being adopted away from an inadequate birth family or impersonal institution. In fact, the less time a child spends in an institution, the better his or her eventual future will be. Furthermore, most genetic risks are moderated by supportive families. These are strong arguments in favor of speedy adoption (Borders et al., 2000; Glidden, 2000).

Cultural attitudes may work against a sound adoptive relationship. Informal adoption and foster care were common in the nineteenth century and are still readily accepted in many nations and among ethnic-minority groups in the United States (Terrell & Modell, 1994). However, some middle-class European-Americans are less tolerant; they "still consider adoption as a 'second-best' and suspect family form" (Wegar, 2000, p. 363). A change in this negative attitude would benefit adoptive families.

The Foster Family

Foster children have a far higher than average rate of learning and behavior problems when compared to biological children raised by families of the same economic level and relationship structure. Most of these difficulties begin before the child joins the new family (Fergusson et al., 1995). As mentioned in Chapter 8, continuity of care is crucial to the child's development, and thus permanent placement works to decrease the child's problems, especially if it occurs in the first year of life. But early, permanent placement is rare for foster children. Foster children typically have a long history of deprivation and several changes in caregivers before a permanent placement is made.

From a developmental perspective, foster parenthood should be encouraged when children cannot or should not be raised by their biological parents. Kinship care and stranger care are both good options, with the best option dependent on quality of care more than on genetic links. But responsive parenting, never easy, is particularly challenging if the child has been severely deprived. Although most foster families seem adequate, the challenges posed by foster children require unusually skilled care, and foster families (especially kinship families) tend not to be exceptionally warm or nurturant but, rather, the opposite (Orme & Buehler, 2001).

Especially for Readers Whose Parents Are Middle-Aged: Suppose your mother tells you she misses taking care of young children and she wants to become a foster parent. How do you advise her?

Many foster children have special emotional and academic needs, which are usually apparent by age 6. At the beginning of middle childhood, excellent homes and schools can usually forestall or prevent serious consequences, but neither the resources nor the expertise are available for the half a million foster families in the United States, or for millions more elsewhere (Altshuler & Gleeson, 1999; Lindsey, 2001). Many academic and psychosocial patterns become more pervasive and habitual by adolescence, so ignoring foster children under age 10 is a serious mistake when all of child development is kept in mind.

Context and Ethnicity

As developmentalists study children in various family structures, it becomes more and more clear that family functioning is crucial and that a wide range of family styles and structures can function well for children (Carlson & Corcorran, 2001; Patterson, 1995). This observation applies not only to all the forms discussed above but also to gay and lesbian families, families that use assisted reproduction to conceive, families of immigrants, multiracial families, families in which an older sibling raises a child, and so on (Bernardes, 1996; Golombok et al., 2001; Oswald, 2002; Patterson & Redding, 1996).

If a particular family type is accepted and supported by ethnic, cultural, or community values, the caregivers will probably be able to nurture the children entrusted to them. The reverse is also true: Adults who feel isolated, stressed, and unsupported usually do not function well for children, and rejecting parents raise maladjusted children—in Asia, Africa, and Europe as well as in the Americas (Khaleque & Rohner, 2002). Over the past 30 years, as social acceptance of nontraditional families has been increasing, the negative effects of non-nuclear families on children have been decreasing. The focus now is on how families function, not on how they are structured.

In the United States, Latino and Asian-American children are more likely to live in extended families, with married parents and grandparents in the same household (Glick & Van Hook, 2002). Especially if they are immigrants, children seem to do better in such families than in traditional nuclear families (Rumbert & Portes, 2001). Again, some generalities hold true:

> Family cohesion and the maintenance of a well-functioning system of supervision, authority and mutuality are perhaps the most powerful factors in shaping the well-being and future outcomes of all children, immigrant and non-immigrant alike.
>
> *[Suarez-Orozco & Suarez-Orozco, 2001, p. 82]*

However, immigrant children are particularly likely to experience a change in family structure, shifting every few years from a grandparent household, to a single-parent household, to an extended family, to a nuclear family. In one multi-ethnic study of children emigrating to the United States, only 20 percent arrived with their entire family; 62 percent remained in the original country while at least one, and sometimes both, parents left to find work, a home, and some stability (Suarez-Orozco & Suarez-Orozco, 2001).

These children immigrated not only to a new nation and to a changed family structure but also to marked cultural differences, most of them for the worse: restricted play space, a foreign tongue, no friends. Given what we know about the importance of school achievement, friendship networks, self-esteem, and stability during the school years, it is not surprising that many school-age children and adolescents who immigrate find adjustment difficult (Rumbert & Portes, 2001).

This wide range of outcomes is possible for all children. Although middle childhood can pose potential problems, many children do find ways to cope.

Coping with Problems

As you have seen in these three chapters on middle childhood, the expansion of a child's social world sometimes brings new and disturbing problems. The beginning of formal education forces learning disabilities to the surface, making them an obvious handicap. Speaking another language in school may hinder learning and provoke prejudice. The peer group may bring rejection and attack. Living in a family that is angry, impoverished, or unstable is destructive.

These problems of middle childhood are often exacerbated by long-standing problems that harm children of every age, such as having a parent who is

TABLE 13.3 Dominant Ideas About Challenges and Coping in Children, 1965–Present

1965	All children are the same, with the same needs for healthy development.
1970	Some conditions or circumstances—such as "absent father," "teenage mother," "working mom," and "day care"—inevitably harm any child.
1975	All children are *not* the same. Some children are resilient, coping easily with stressors that cause harm in other children.
1980	Nothing inevitably causes harm. Indeed, some nonnuclear families function very well, and both maternal employment and preschool education usually benefit children.
1985	Factors beyond the family, both in the child (low birthweight, prenatal alcohol exposure, aggressive temperament) and in the community (poverty, violence), are discovered to be very risky for the child.
1990	Risk–benefit analysis finds that some children seem to be "invulnerable" to, or even to benefit from, circumstances that destroy others. (Some do well in school despite extreme poverty, for example.)
1995	No child is invincibly resilient. Risk factors always harm children—if not academically, then psychosocially.
Today	Risk–benefit analysis involves the interplay among all three domains (biosocial, cognitive, and psychosocial), in many systems, and it includes factors within the child (genes, intelligence, temperament), the family (function as well as structure), and the community (including neighborhood, school, church, and culture).

Sources: Luthar et al., 2000; Walsh, 2002; Werner 1994.

This table simplifies the progression of the dominant ideas about the challenges that children face and about their ability to cope. Certainly the 1960s idea that all children are the same still seems true to some extent, and today's idea that risk–benefit analysis involves many factors is not a brand-new discovery. Nonetheless, the emphasis within the research has shifted over the past 40 years, as discovery, oversimplification, and criticism have yielded greater understanding of the complexity of the concept of resilience.

emotionally disturbed, drug-addicted, or imprisoned, or growing up in a community that is crumbling, violent, and crime-filled. Because of a combination of problems, some children fail at school, fight with their friends, fear the future, or cry themselves to sleep. Indeed, every academic and psychiatric difficulty that school-age children suffer can be traced, at least in part, to psychosocial stresses.

The stresses and hassles of middle childhood are so common that almost every child experiences some of them. Fortunately, the coping measures that school-age children develop are common as well. As a result, between ages 7 and 11, the overall frequency of psychological problems decreases as the number of evident competencies—at school, at home, and on the playground—increases (Achenbach et al., 1991; Smith et al., 2001). Many factors described in this chapter, among them the development of social cognition and an expanding social world, combine to protect school-age children against many of the stresses they encounter (Ackerman et al., 1999). According to some observers, some school-age children seem "stress-resistant," "resilient," or even "invincible" (Garmezy, 1985; Werner & Smith, 1992). That is an exaggeration. All children are affected by adversity, and some cope with it better than others do. Exactly what that means has changed over the past 40 years, as research has helped us understand the challenges and coping mechanisms of middle childhood (see Table 13.3).

Resilience and the Assessment of Stress

Resilience is now defined as "a dynamic process encompassing positive adaptation within the context of significant adversity" (Luthar et al., 2000). There are three important parts to this definition:

- Resilience is a *dynamic process,* not a stable trait. Thus a given child is not resilient in all situations. A particular child may become a good reader in a crowded classroom with an ineffective teacher, but that same child's self-esteem may suffer if he or she is rejected by peers. Another child may be resilient socially but not academically.
- Resilience is not the absence of pathology, but a *positive adaptation* to stress, resulting in some new strength or insight.
- The adversity must be *significant.* Research informs us which problems are not actually adverse (maternal employment, single parenthood) and which ones are (victimization by peers, neglect by parents).

To understand whether a particular stress is significant for a particular child, three questions must be answered: (1) How many other stresses is the child experiencing? (2) How does the stress affect the child's daily life? (3) How does the child interpret the stress?

In general, a single stressor does not cause obvious harm. However, if that vulnerability is added to other burdens—even mild ones that might be called "daily hassles" rather than "stressful events"—the child can suffer evident damage (Durlak, 1998; Shaw et al., 1994).

Daily routines are crucial. For example, having an emotionally dysfunctional parent may affect a child very little if the other parent compensates for, and protects the child from, the dysfunctional parent's irrationality. However, the situation may become overwhelming if the child of a schizophrenic or depressed mother must do any of the following:

- Manage his or her own daily care and school attendance
- Contend directly with the mother's confused, depressed, or irrational thinking
- Supervise and discipline younger siblings
- Keep friends away from the house

Such a situation is especially likely to cause harm if the child must also deal with poverty and high-risk living conditions, including an unsafe or unstable home and an unreliable supply of food and clothes. For a school-age child, poverty can become shameful, not simply a burden, and school a place of failure. That child may develop a lifelong tendency to feel inferior rather than industrious, as Erikson would put it.

The crucial strain of multiple stressors is seen in research on adopted and foster children. For example, being a foster child is stressful, but most children cope well enough. However, if adolescence finds them living in group homes, they display three times as many problems (such as getting drunk, skipping school, and being sick) as other stressed children who are still living with a biological parent (Miller et al., 2000).

A longitudinal study of babies in Hawaii born at high risk—in poverty, with birth complications, to parents who were alcoholic or mentally ill—found that two-thirds were unable to cope (they had internalizing or externalizing problems), but the other one-third did well if they avoided further stresses by achieving in school and having good friends and adult mentors who helped them (Werner & Smith, 1992). As adults, it was essential for them to escape their childhood stressors by leaving their family problems behind (Werner, 1994).

Community influences can counteract the effects of poverty, family stress, and even abuse (Garbarino et al., 1997). The community not only relieves the stress directly but also helps the child interpret it so that it does not cause guilt or shame. For example, poverty is much more stressful if the child's family is the only poor one in a neighborhood; then the child feels ashamed.

The child's own attitude is crucial. An intriguing study measured conflict between the parents of 8- to 11-year-olds, problems in these children, and the children's feelings of self-blame and threat. By far the most important correlate with the children's problems was whether the children blamed themselves for, or felt threatened by, their parents' marital discord: "Children who do not perceive that marital conflict is threatening to them and do not blame themselves for the conflict may be better able to [reduce] the negative impact of the stressor" (El-Sheikh & Harger, 2001, p. 883). This study found that cognitive appraisal was crucial in many ways, one of which is shown in Figure 13.4.

Another study of school-age children led to similar conclusions (Jackson & Warren, 2000). In this one, the children themselves evaluated events as positive or negative. As you might imagine, some items, such as the death of a family member, were always negative; other items, such as making the honor roll, were almost always positive. Remarkably, many items were rated as positive by some children but as negative by others, such as moving to a new home (45 positive, 16 negative), gaining a new stepparent (14 positive, 5 negative), and even the increased absence of a parent from the home (14 positive, 50 negative). The number of psychological symptoms shown by the children

Response for Readers Whose Parents Are Middle-Aged (from page 418): Foster parenthood is probably the most difficult type of parenthood, yet it can be very rewarding if all needed support is available and a permanent arrangement is likely. Advise your mother to make sure that doctors and psychotherapists are available, that the biological parents are unlikely to reclaim the child, and that the placement agency truly cares about children's well-being.

FIGURE 13.4 When Parents Fight and Children Blame Themselves Husbands and wives who almost never disagree are below the first standard deviation (−1 SD) in verbal marital conflict. By contrast, couples who frequently have loud, screaming, cursing arguments are in the highest 15 percent (+1 SD). In such high-conflict households, children are not much affected—*if* they do not blame themselves for the situation. However, if children do blame themselves, they are likely to have internalizing problems, such as nightmares, stomach aches, panic attacks, and feelings of loneliness.

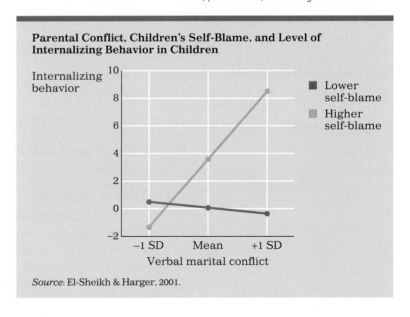

Parental Conflict, Children's Self-Blame, and Level of Internalizing Behavior in Children

Source: El-Sheikh & Harger, 2001.

depended more on their appraisal of the events than on the events themselves. Indeed, the crucial aspect was children's interpretations, which "lead some children to adapt well after an event seen as only mildly aversive or positive and other children to develop serious psychopathology after exposure to the same event perceived as intensely negative" (Jackson & Warren, 2000, p. 1452).

Focus on Competence

Research on resilience helps shift the focus from problems to strengths. This is particularly useful for all who are concerned about child development. Adults cannot remove all stressors—such as divorce, poverty, and immigration—but they can help children develop coping measures. That might make all the difference, as it did for the children in the Hawaii study and as it continues to do for the millions of 7- to 11-year-olds who must deal with difficult circumstances.

If a child has certain strengths (see Table 13.4), he or she can "sustain reasonably good development" even in the face of serious problems (Masten & Coatsworth, 1998). Particularly important are various personal competencies—especially social, academic, and creative skills—that can help the child deflect or avoid many of the problems he or she may encounter at home or in the community (Conrad & Hammen, 1993; Werner, 1994).

Competence can make up for disabling factors in several ways. One is through self-esteem. If children feel confident in at least one area of their lives, they become able to see the rest of their lives in perspective. They can believe, for example, that despite how others might reject or belittle them, they are not failures.

More practically, children with better-developed cognitive and social skills are better able to employ coping strategies against their problems—perhaps by changing the conditions that brought about a problem in the first place or by restructuring their own reaction to the problem (Masten & Coatsworth, 1998). You learned in Chapter 12 that, during middle childhood, children develop metacognition and become more logical, an advance that allows them to think rationally about thinking. They can use this ability to convince themselves that "it's not my fault" or "when I am older, I will escape this situation."

Because their cognitive abilities and, hence, their coping repertoires "increase and become more differentiated in middle childhood," older children may deal with the stresses of life better than children who are just beginning middle childhood (Aldwin, 1994). Thus, when a peer is suddenly antagonistic, a 6-year-old is likely to dissolve into tears or to launch a clumsy counterattack that merely brings further rejection. Older children are more adept at finding ways to disguise their hurt, keep a bully at bay, repair a broken friendship, or even make new friends to replace old ones.

TABLE 13.4 Strengths and Relationships That Help Children Cope with Stress

Source	Strength
Individual child	Good intellectual functioning
	Appealing, sociable, easygoing disposition
	Self-efficacy, self-confidence, high self-esteem
	Talents (artistic, athletic, academic)
	Religious faith
Child's family	Close relationship to a caring parent figure
	Authoritative parenting: warmth, structure, high expectations
	Socioeconomic advantages
	Connections to extended supportive family networks
Other	Bonds to prosocial adults outside the family
	Connections to prosocial organizations (e.g., a church, temple, mosque, or settlement house)
	Attendance at an effective school with understanding teachers
	Stable and cohesive neighborhood
	Supportive friendships

Social Support

Another important element that helps children deal with problems—one we have already touched on—is the social support they receive (Garmezy, 1993). Ideally, a strong bond with a loving and firm parent can see a child through many difficulties. Even in war-torn or deeply impoverished neighborhoods, when a child is strongly attached to a parent who has been present consistently since the child's infancy, the child tends to be resilient (Masten & Coatsworth, 1998). Immigrant

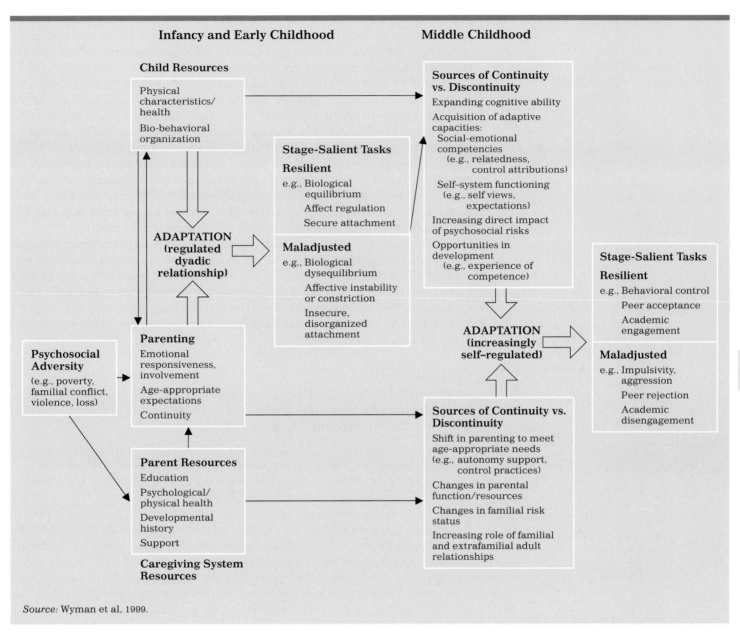

Infancy and Early Childhood

Middle Childhood

Child Resources

Physical characteristics/ health

Bio-behavioral organization

ADAPTATION (regulated dyadic relationship)

Stage-Salient Tasks

Resilient

e.g., Biological equilibrium

Affect regulation

Secure attachment

Maladjusted

e.g., Biological dysequilibrium

Affective instability or constriction

Insecure, disorganized attachment

Sources of Continuity vs. Discontinuity

Expanding cognitive ability

Acquisition of adaptive capacities:
Social-emotional competencies (e.g., relatedness, control attributions)

Self–system functioning (e.g., self views, expectations)

Increasing direct impact of psychosocial risks

Opportunities in development (e.g., experience of competence)

Psychosocial Adversity

(e.g., poverty, familial conflict, violence, loss)

Parenting

Emotional responsiveness, involvement

Age-appropriate expectations

Continuity

Parent Resources

Education

Psychological/ physical health

Developmental history

Support

Caregiving System Resources

ADAPTATION (increasingly self-regulated)

Sources of Continuity vs. Discontinuity

Shift in parenting to meet age-appropriate needs (e.g., autonomy support, control practices)

Changes in parental function/resources

Changes in familial risk status

Increasing role of familial and extrafamilial adult relationships

Stage-Salient Tasks

Resilient

e.g., Behavioral control

Peer acceptance

Academic engagement

Maladjusted

e.g., Impulsivity, aggression

Peer rejection

Academic disengagement

Source: Wyman et al, 1999.

FIGURE 13.5 An Organizational–Developmental Model of Resilience Note that, in comparing infancy and middle childhood, parenting is more crucial early on. By middle childhood, the child's own competence and relationships with people other than parents become crucial.

children tend to do surprisingly well, academically and emotionally, despite all their stresses, if their families and schools are supportive (Fuligni, 2001). An analysis of impoverished children living in very stressful conditions also found that parenting practices can be a buffer against adversity (Wyman et al., 1999).

As you can see from Figure 13.5, adaptation in middle childhood is increasingly a matter of the child's own ability to reach out for support. This is exactly what they try to do: Every school-age child tries to make friends, respect parents and other adults, and master the various skills that each culture values. And most succeed, not only surviving childhood but entering adolescence well prepared for the risks and rewards that lie ahead (Hawkins et al., 1999; Masten, 2001).

Continuity

Developmental research has repeatedly revealed that continuity is apparent from early childhood on: A child who was at risk at age 3 because of poor parenting, difficult temperament, poverty, and so on is probably still at risk at age 8 or 18. However, such risks remain potential, not actual, until or unless they erupt in violence, drug abuse, school failure, early sexual activity, or other destructive behavior. Although developmental research traces risk from age to age and generation to generation, a recent summary found that, overall, "discontinuities outweigh continuities" in risk and resilience (Rutter, 1998).

One of the benefits of the expanding social world of middle childhood is additional sources of social support, people who stick by the child despite adversity. Having a network of supportive family and friends is a much better buffer than having only one close person (Jackson & Warren, 2000). For example, a child whose parents are fighting bitterly on their way to divorce may spend hours on the phone with a friend whose parents have successfully separated; may often be invited to dinner at a neighbor's house where family harmony still prevails; or may devote himself or herself to helping a teacher or a coach or to working with a community group. Grandparents, peers, and even pets are often very helpful to children in middle childhood (Borland et al., 1998).

Community members can also help. One example comes from Jonathan Kozol's (1991) study of children in the South Bronx. A young fatherless boy, whose mother had AIDS, found himself intrigued by a neighborhood man who was a poet. The boy often heard quotations from great literature; learned to read, especially admiring Edgar Allan Poe ("Did you know he grew up in the Bronx?"); and aspired to become a writer himself. Such hope for the future can sustain many a deprived young person.

Religious Faith

An often powerful source of support is religion (Johnson et al., 2000). Especially for children in difficult circumstances, religious faith itself can be psychologically protective. The South Bronx boy wrote to Kozol:

> No violence will there be in heaven. There will be no guns or drugs or IRS. You won't have to pay taxes. You'll recognize all the children who have died when they were little. Jesus will be good to them and play with them. At night he'll come and visit at your house. God will be fond of you.
>
> *[quoted in Kozol, 1991]*

School-age children, almost universally, develop their own theology, influenced by whatever formal religious education they receive but by no means identical to it. This personal education helps them structure life and deal with worldly problems (Coles, 1990; Hyde, 1990). An 8-year-old African-American girl who, in the 1960s, was one of the first to enter a previously all-white school, remembers walking past a gauntlet of adults yelling insults:

> I was alone, and those people were screaming, and suddenly I saw God smiling, and I smiled. A woman was standing there, and she shouted at me, "Hey you little nigger, what are you smiling at?" I looked right up at her face, and I said "At God." Then she looked up at the sky, and then she looked at me, and she didn't call me any more names.
>
> *[quoted in Coles, 1990]*

In a way, this example illustrates many aspects of children's coping abilities, for it was not only faith but also a measure of self-confidence, social understanding, and skill at deflecting her own emotional reactions that enabled this child to deal with a very real threat.

Conclusion

We wish that all children could have an idyllic childhood, but that is never the case. Nor is a stress-free childhood necessary to a happy life. Research on coping in middle childhood clearly suggests that as they grow older, most children develop ways to deal with all varieties of stress, from minor hassles to major traumatic events.

This realization can guide adults who seek to be of help. If the home situation is difficult, for instance, any adult, from a caring teacher to a loving grandparent, can step in and make a critical difference. If parents decide to divorce, they should first figure out how to ensure that their children will receive the necessary material and emotional resources. Grandparents can take over, quite successfully, if a parent is incapable. Or if a child has a severe reading difficulty, helping the child develop talents in some other area—math or baseball or music—may be as important to the child's overall well-being as tutoring to overcome the learning disability.

Within neighborhoods, the attitude that everyone is responsible for all the children's behavior can also improve life for individuals (Sampson et al., 1997). More broadly, measures designed to enhance the social context, perhaps by making violent neighborhoods safer or improving job opportunities in impoverished communities, can benefit school-age children substantially.

> Successful children remind us that children grow up in multiple contexts—in families, schools, peer groups, baseball teams, religious organizations, and many other groups—and each context is a potential source of protective factors as well as risks. These children demonstrate that children are protected not only by the self-righting nature of development, but also by the actions of adults, by their own actions, by the nurturing of their assets, by opportunities to succeed, and by the experience of success. The behavior of adults often plays a critical role in children's risks, resources, opportunities, and resilience. Development is biased toward competence, but there is no such thing as an invulnerable child. If we allow the prevalence of known risk factors for development to rise while resources for children fall, we can expect the competent individual children and the human capital of the nation to suffer.
>
> *[Masten & Coatsworth, 1998]*

As you will see in the next three chapters, adolescence is a continuation of middle childhood as well as a radical departure from it. Stresses and strains continue to accumulate, and "known risk factors," including drug availability and sexual urges, become more prevalent. Fortunately, for many young people protective resources and constructive coping also increase. Personal competencies, family support, and close friends get most children through childhood and adolescence undamaged. Indeed, the same factors help each of us throughout our development, as we overcome the problems, and build on the strengths, that characterized the first years of our lives.

SUMMARY

Theories of School-Age Development

1. All three grand theories acknowledge that school-age children become more independent and capable in many ways. In psychoanalytic theory, Freud described latency, when sexual needs are quiet; Erikson emphasized industry, when children are busy mastering various tasks. Behaviorism and cognitive theory stress the new skills that maturation and wider social opportunities afford.

2. Social cognitive theory combines these grand theories to describe how children begin to think more deeply about their social context and to act effectively within it. The sociocultural and epigenetic systems theories also describe an increase in independence in middle childhood.

Understanding Self and Others

3. Research confirms these theories. The interplay of self-understanding and social perception is increasingly evident during the school years. Children figure out who they are partly by comparing themselves to others.

The Peer Group

4. Peers are crucial. Rejection by peers is devastating; intimacy with at least one good friend makes school and other challenges surmountable. Children typically group themselves together, forming their own subculture, with slang, rituals, and taboos that change from one community or nation to another.

5. Friendships become increasingly close and influential. Usually friends provide needed companionship and allow development of social skills, but sometimes they encourage deviant, antisocial behavior.

6. Rejected children may be neglected, withdrawn, or aggressive. All three types have difficulty interpreting the normal give-and-take of childhood. Usually rejection is temporary, but it is difficult to teach a rejected child to become more popular without also teaching parents and peers, because social skills are not learned in isolation.

7. Aggressive children can become bullies, who do obvious damage over the years to themselves and to their victims. Unless they change, many bullies become delinquent and then criminal, and many victims develop persistent feelings of mistrust and anxiety.

8. In most nations, boys are often bullies and tend to use physical attacks. Girls are more likely to use relational aggression, involving social exclusion and rumor spreading, which can be very destructive.

9. Adults can prevent most bullying. Because of various policies and attitudes, some schools have four times more bullying than others. There are international variations as well, but bullying is common worldwide—usually more than 10 percent of school-age children do it.

Family Influences

10. Families influence children in many ways, as do genes and peers. The five functions of a supportive family are to help the child meet physical needs; learn; develop friends; protect self-esteem; and live in a safe, stable, and harmonious home. This last function is crucial, but many families find it difficult, because adults fight, neighborhoods change, and violence is prevalent.

11. Generally, authoritative families balance support and discipline effectively. However, there are many variations: No one parenting style always functions best. Impoverished families find all five functions difficult to fulfill; poor children are at greater risk for emotional and behavioral problems.

12. Family structures that are common today include nuclear, extended, blended, grandparent, adoptive, and foster families. Less than half of all children born in the United States today will live in a nuclear family from birth to age 18. No one of these structures guarantees good—or bad—child development.

13. Nuclear families have natural advantages, including more stability and higher income. Divorce impedes child development, at least for a few years, particularly reducing school achievement.

14. The most difficult family structure may be foster families. Children enter such families with many problems, and foster parents are not guaranteed a permanent connection to their foster children. This is a particular problem in middle childhood, when stability and continuity are crucial.

Coping with Problems

15. School-age children tend to be resilient. Many cope well with major problems—learning disabilities, immigration, social rejection, families that are not supportive, poverty, violence.

16. In general, children benefit from social support (perhaps a best friend or a grandparent), natural assets (intelligence, a winning personality, a special skill), personal strengths (religious faith, a stable early childhood), and few stresses. The innate drive toward competence and independence keeps most school-age children from being overwhelmed by problems.

KEY TERMS

latency (p. 393)	social comparison (p. 397)	bullying (p. 402)	single-parent family (p. 410)
industry versus inferiority (p. 393)	peer group (p. 397)	family function (p. 408)	blended family (p. 410)
	society of children (p. 398)	family structure (p. 408)	grandparent family (p. 410)
social cognitive theory (p. 394)	aggressive-rejected (p. 400)	nuclear family (p. 410)	adoptive family (p. 410)
social cognition (p. 396)	withdrawn-rejected (p. 400)	extended family (p. 410)	foster family (p. 410)

KEY QUESTIONS

1. How do the five major theories differ in describing middle childhood?

2. How does a school-age child develop a sense of self?

3. The society of children strongly disapproves of tattletales. How does this affect child development?

4. Why is social rejection particularly devastating during middle childhood?

5. Describe the personal characteristics of a bully and a victim.

6. How do schools, families, and cultures contribute to the incidence of bullying?

7. What is the difference between family function and family structure?

8. Why is a safe, harmonious home particularly important during middle childhood?

9. What are the special advantages and disadvantages of adoption?

10. Compare the child-rearing advantages of never-married parents with those of divorced parents.

11. Why is coping with family problems easier during middle childhood than earlier?

Part IV

The Developing Person So Far:
The School Years, Ages 6 Through 11

BIOSOCIAL

Growth and Skills During middle childhood, children grow more slowly than they did during infancy and toddlerhood or than they will during adolescence. Increased strength and lung capacity give children the endurance to improve their performance in skills such as swimming and running. Slower growth contributes to children's increasing bodily control, and children enjoying exercising their developing skills of coordination and balance. Which specific skills they master depends largely on culture, gender, and inherited ability.

Special Needs Many children have special learning needs that may originate in brain patterns but that express themselves in educational problems. Early recognition, targeted education, and psychological support help all children, from those with autism to the much milder instance of a specific learning disability or ADHD.

COGNITIVE

Thinking During middle childhood, children become better able to understand and learn, in part because of growth in their processing capacity, knowledge base, and memory capacity. At the same time, metacognition techniques enable children to organize their learning. Beginning at about age 7 or 8, children also develop the ability to understand logical principles, including the concepts of identity, reciprocity, and reversibility.

Language Children's increasing ability to understand the structures and possibilities of language enables them to extend the range of their cognitive powers and to become more analytical in their use of vocabulary. Most children develop proficiency in several language codes, and some become bilingual.

Education Formal schooling begins worldwide, with the specifics of the curriculum depending on economic and societal factors. An individual child's learning success depends on the time allotted to each task, specific guided instruction from teachers and parents, and the overall values of the culture. Curricula and goals vary, and some variations are more crucial than others.

PSYCHOSOCIAL

Emotions and Personality Development School-age children come to understand themselves, as well as what is right in their relations with others. The peer group becomes increasingly important as children become less dependent on their parents and more dependent on friends for help, loyalty, and sharing of mutual interests. Rejection and bullying become serious problems.

Parents Parents continue to influence children, especially as they exacerbate or buffer problems in school and the community. During these years, families need to meet basic needs, encourage learning, develop self-esteem, nurture friendship, and—most important—provide harmony and stability. Parents in the midst of divorce may be deficient in all of these. Most single-parent, foster, or grandparent families are better than families in open conflict, but a family with two biological parents, both of whom are cooperative with each other and loving to the child, is generally best. Fortunately, school-age children often develop competencies and attitudes to defend against the stress that most experience. Friends, family, school, and community can all be helpful.

Part V

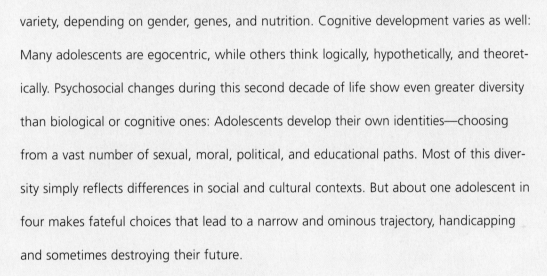

Adolescence is the period of transition from childhood to adulthood. It is probably the most challenging and complicated period of life to describe, to study, or to experience. The biological changes that begin adolescence are universal, but their expression and timing show enormous variety, depending on gender, genes, and nutrition. Cognitive development varies as well: Many adolescents are egocentric, while others think logically, hypothetically, and theoretically. Psychosocial changes during this second decade of life show even greater diversity than biological or cognitive ones: Adolescents develop their own identities—choosing from a vast number of sexual, moral, political, and educational paths. Most of this diversity simply reflects differences in social and cultural contexts. But about one adolescent in four makes fateful choices that lead to a narrow and ominous trajectory, handicapping and sometimes destroying their future.

Despite all the variations, there is also a commonality to the adolescent experience. All adolescents confront the same developmental tasks: They must adjust to their changing body size and shape, to their awakening sexuality, and to new ways of thinking. They all strive for the emotional maturity and economic independence that characterize adulthood. As we will see in the next three chapters, the adolescent's efforts to come to grips with these tasks are often touched with confusion and poignancy—and, eventually, success.

Adolescence

Adolescence: Biosocial Development

adolescence The period of biological, cognitive, and psychosocial transition from childhood to adulthood, usually lasting a decade or so.

During **adolescence**, humans everywhere cross a great divide between childhood and adulthood—biosocially, cognitively, and socioculturally. No one would call this process easy. The biological aspect is uneven but occurs fairly quickly, mostly before age 15; the cognitive and psychosocial aspects typically take longer, lasting at least until age 18 and often until age 22, 25, or even 30. Adjusting to all the changes of adolescence can be difficult and stressful.

Adolescence is *not* defined by its problems, but all adolescents experience moments of awkwardness, confusion, anger, and depression. Many make serious missteps on the path toward maturity. Some encounter obstacles that halt their progress completely. This chapter and the two that follow examine some of these problems, putting them in the perspective of the three domains of development (see Table 14.1).

The same developmental changes that cause difficulty also create excitement, challenge, and growth: "Adolescence in all industrial societies, and at all times during this century, constitutes a period of life that is full of [both] opportunity and risk" (Leffert & Petersen, 1995). The risk is real, but most adolescents seize the opportunity instead. The "adult public has come to view youth as a liability" (Gilliam & Bales, 2001, p. 11) and to believe "a rising cascade of bad news about teenagers" (Males, 1999, p. 13), but the public is mistaken. Compared to teenagers of the 1980s or to contemporary young adults, teenagers today less often break the law, have a baby, take drugs (legal or illegal), die of AIDS, kill themselves, or kill someone else.

Seriously troubled adolescents are in the minority; many "problems" are actually more problematic for the adults than the teenagers. For instance, the same music that disturbs adults makes young people jump with joy; the marathon phone calls that exasperate parents are a social lifeline; the Internet that adults consider dangerous is a window on an expanding world; the sexual awakening can begin a thrilling intimacy. Generalizations about adolescence, especially about its turbulence, must be made with care.

In this chapter, we outline the normative biological changes of adolescence—the rise in hormone levels, the new body shapes and sizes, the sexual maturation, and the reasons one teenager starts puberty earlier than another. We then discuss reactions to all these biological changes; and here variation, not generalization, is apparent. One adolescent is thrilled by the appearance of facial hair, another is horrified; one adolescent wolfs down a whole pizza, another slowly swallows half a cracker; some adolescents become unwilling victims of sexual abuse and others voluntarily abuse drugs of all sorts. These emotional responses to puberty, and the causes and consequences of such variations, are the heart of this chapter. Some common health hazards, including

TABLE 14.1 Overview of Issues in Adolescent Development

Topic	Description	Major Discussion
Decision making	Adolescent decides either to take risks or to be cautious.	Chapter 15 (Cognitive)
Delinquency	Adolescent breaks the law and risks getting arrested, convicted, and incarcerated.	Chapter 16 (Psychosocial)
Depression and suicide	Adolescent thinks about, attempts, and/or commits suicide.	Chapter 16 (Psychosocial)
Drug use and abuse	Includes legal and illegal drugs that jeopardize physical or mental health.	Chapter 14 (Biosocial)
Eating disorders	Adolescent becomes obese or develops anorexia or bulimia.	Chapter 14 (Biosocial)
Education about sex	Adolescent learns about sexuality, abstinence, safe sex, contraception.	Chapter 15 (Cognitive)
Homicide	Adolescent is a murderer or victim.	Chapter 16 (Psychosocial)
Peer pressure	Adolescent follows peer advice and copies peer behavior.	Chapter 16 (Psychosocial)
Sexual abuse	Young person is used for the sexual pleasure of an older or more powerful person.	Chapter 14 (Biosocial)
Sexual activity	Adolescent becomes sexually active, risking pregnancy.	Chapter 14 (Biosocial)
School dropouts	Reasons and remedies for school failure.	Chapter 15 (Cognitive)

Overlapping Problems, Overlapping Domains Every problem of adolescence originates in, and is affected by, all three domains of development. They are all health hazards (biosocial), worsened by immature reasoning (cognitive), influenced by parents, peers, and culture (psychosocial). In this text, each problem is discussed in detail in only one chapter, as indexed in this table.

poor nutrition, inadequate medical care, and foolish risk taking, are discussed here and in later chapters. We start at the beginning, when the body shifts away from childhood.

Puberty Begins

Puberty is the period of rapid physical growth and sexual maturation that ends childhood and begins adolescence, producing a person of adult size, shape, and sexual potential. The forces of puberty are unleashed by a cascade of hormones that bring on the numerous visible changes. Typically, growth and maturation are complete three or four years after puberty begins, although some individuals (more often late developers) gain an additional inch or two of height, and most (especially early developers) gain additional fat and muscle over the next decade. Why and when does puberty start?

Hormones

Hormones—dozens of them—affect every aspect of growth and development. The levels of certain hormones rise naturally at puberty, causing increased sexual interest and quicker mood shifts. The production of many hormones within the body begins deep in the base of the brain, in an area called the **hypothalamus**. A biochemical signal from the hypothalamus is sent to the **pituitary gland**, located next to the hypothalamus. The pituitary produces hormones that stimulate the **adrenal glands** (two small glands located above the kidneys at

puberty A period of rapid growth and sexual change that occurs in early adolescence and produces a person of adult size, shape, and sexual potential.

hypothalamus An area at the base of the brain that, in addition to regulating several maintenance activities (eating, drinking, and body temperature), directs the production of hormones via the pituitary gland.

pituitary gland A gland that, in response to a biochemical signal from the hypothalamus, produces hormones that regulate growth and control other glands, including the adrenal glands.

adrenal glands A pair of glands located above the kidneys that secrete the hormones epinephrine (adrenaline) and norepinephrine (noradrenaline), which help to arouse the body in time of stress.

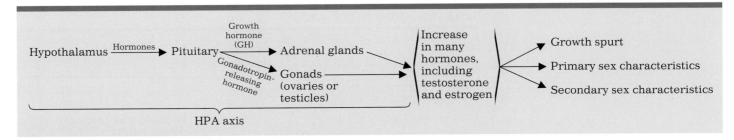

FIGURE 14.1 Biological Sequence of Puberty Puberty begins with a hormonal signal from the hypothalamus to the pituitary gland. The pituitary, in turn, signals the adrenal glands and the ovaries or testes to produce more of their hormones.

either side of the torso). This route, which is called the **HPA axis** (hypothalamus/pituitary/adrenal axis), is followed by many kinds of hormones to regulate stress, growth, sleep, appetite, sexual excitement, and various other changes in the body. The HPA axis also triggers the changes of puberty, not only the growth spurt but also the development of primary and secondary sexual characteristics, as will soon be described.

At puberty, the pituitary also activates the **gonads,** or sex glands (the ovaries in females and the testes, or testicles, in males). These are the first parts of the body to enlarge at puberty. In girls, the changes in the ovaries are invisible; in boys, the scrotum, which encases the testicles, increases in size and changes in color from red to pink.

One hormone in particular, GnRH (*gonadotropin-releasing hormone*), causes the gonads to dramatically increase their production of sex hormones, chiefly **estrogen** in girls and **testosterone** in boys. This increase, in turn, loops back to the hypothalamus and pituitary gland, causing them to produce more GH (growth hormone) as well as more GnRH, which causes the adrenal glands and gonads to produce even more sex hormones (see Figure 14.1).

Although testosterone is considered the male hormone and estrogen the female hormone, both boys and girls experience increased levels of estrogen and testosterone at puberty. However, the rate of increase is sex-specific: Testosterone production skyrockets in boys, up to 18 times the level in childhood, but increases much less in girls. Estrogen production increases up to 8 times in girls but not nearly as much in boys (Malina & Bouchard, 1991). Changes in facial hair, voice quality, and breast size also occur in both sexes—and again, the difference is in degree. Later we will discuss the psychological effects of these changes.

When Do Changes Begin?

You just read that the visible changes of puberty are themselves triggered by an invisible sequence of hormone production, which typically begins a year or more before the first pubic hair appears. But what starts the hormones? We know that the age of puberty is highly variable: Normal children begin to notice body changes some time between ages of 8 and 14. This considerable age range is one of the reasons puberty is often difficult for adolescents and their parents: It is hard to prepare for if you have only a vague notion of what might occur and when. Accordingly, it is useful to know that the changes of puberty, not only the sequence but also the timing, can be predicted by looking for a combination of four factors: sex, genes, body size, and stress.

Sex Differences in Timing

Boy–girl differences in onset of puberty are easiest to notice. Girls tend to begin puberty ahead of boys; many seventh-grade girls are several inches taller than

HPA axis The hypothalamus/pituitary/adrenal axis, a route followed by many kinds of hormones to trigger the changes of puberty and to regulate stress, growth, sleep, appetite, sexual excitement, and various other bodily changes.

gonads The pair of sex glands in humans. In females, they are called the ovaries; in males, they are called testes or testicles.

estrogen A sex hormone, secreted in greater amounts by females than by males.

testosterone A sex hormone, secreted in greater amounts by males than by females.

Male Pride Teenage boys typically feel serious pride when they first need to shave. Although facial hair is taken as a sign of masculinity, a person's hairiness is actually genetic as well as hormonal. Further evidence that the Western world's traditional racial categories have no genetic basis comes from East Asia: Many Chinese men cannot grow beards or mustaches, but most Japanese men can.

TABLE 14.2 Sequence of Puberty

Girls	Approximate Average Age*	Boys
Ovaries increase production of estrogen and progesterone[†]	9	
Uterus and vagina begin to grow larger	9½	Testes increase production of testosterone[†]
Breast "bud" stage	10	Testes and scrotum grow larger
Pubic hair begins to appear; weight spurt begins	11	
Peak height spurt	11½	Pubic hair begins to appear
Peak muscle and organ growth (also, hips become noticeably wider)	12	Penis growth begins
Menarche (first menstrual period)	12½	Spermarche (first ejaculation); weight spurt begins
First ovulation	13	Peak height spurt
	13½	
Voice lowers	14	Peak muscle and organ growth (also, shoulders become noticeably broader)
Final pubic-hair pattern	15	Voice lowers; visible facial hair
Full breast growth	16	
	18	Final pubic-hair pattern

*Average ages are rough approximations, with many perfectly normal, healthy adolescents as much as 3 years ahead of or behind these ages.

[†]Estrogen, progesterone, and testosterone are hormones that influence sexual characteristics, including reproductive function. All three are also provided, in small amounts, by the adrenal glands in both sexes. Major production, however, occurs in the gonads, with marked male–female differences.

their male classmates. Already by age 10, one or two girls in a class have developed visible breasts and begun to grow to woman-height; not until about age 17 has the last boy in the class sprouted facial hair and attained man-height. These are the extremes, but even the average girl seems to be about two years ahead of the average boy.

However, look closely at Table 14.2. Sex differences in age of puberty are not as great as they might seem. For example, the maximum height spurt occurs about midway in a girl's pubescence but is one of the later events for boys, which means that just looking at height is a misleading way to gauge progress (Reiter & Lee, 2001). The shortest boy in the class may already have massive amounts of testosterone circulating in his bloodstream, and his penis may be almost man-size. Note also that breast development is publicly visible on a girl's chest, but the first sign of gender differentiation in boys, enlargement of the testicles, is not publicly visible at all. Further, in recent years the age of puberty has been edging downward, more for boys than for girls (Reiter & Lee, 2001). One third of all boys in the United States show some genital changes at age 9 (Herman-Giddens et al., 2001).

Genes and Ethnicity

Genetic influences are more apparent in girls than in boys, primarily because **menarche**, the first menstrual period, is easier to date than **spermarche**, when a boy first produces live sperm. Menarche normally occurs between ages 9 to 15, with age 12 the average (Biro et al., 2001). Genes are the most powerful reason for that variation. For example, dizygotic twins (who share half their genes and presumably an almost identical family environment) reach menarche, on average, only 12 months apart; monozygotic twins typically differ by a mere 2.8 months if raised together and 9 months if raised apart (Farber, 1981). A daughter's age of menarche is also related to her mother's age of menarche, which occurred under

menarche A female's first menstrual period.

spermarche A male's first ejaculation of live sperm, whether through masturbation, a dream, or sexual contact with another person.

quite different historical and familial circumstances (Golub, 1992). Other pubertal changes, for boys as well as for girls, also follow familial patterns (Brooks-Gunn, 1991).

Perhaps for genetic reasons, the average age of puberty varies from nation to nation and from ethnic group to ethnic group. In Europe, for example, the onset of puberty tends to be relatively late for Belgians and relatively early for Poles (Malina et al., 1988). In the United States, African-Americans often begin puberty earlier (by almost a year, on average) and Asian-Americans later (again, by almost a year) than Americans of Hispanic or other European origin. Such categories are imprecise; the Human Genome Project has shown that variations within ethnic groups are much greater than differences among them. Genes are predictive of pubertal changes, but the pubescence of a child's biological parents is a more accurate guide than is the average for others of the same ethnicity.

An Awkward Age The normal variation in age of puberty is readily apparent in this junior high gym class in Texas.

?Observational Quiz (see answer, page 436): What three signs can you see that the boy in the foreground wants to be taller and the girl beside him wishes she were less conspicuous?

Body Fat

Another influence on the age of puberty is body fat. In general, stocky individuals experience puberty earlier than do those with taller, thinner builds. The onset of puberty correlates with accumulation of body fat in both sexes, although it is more obvious in girls (Vizmanos & Marti-Henneberg, 2000). Menarche does not usually occur until a girl weighs about 100 pounds (45–48 kilograms) (Berkley et al., 2000). Females who have little body fat (either because they are severely malnourished or because they are serious athletes) menstruate later and less regularly than the average girl.

For both sexes, chronic malnutrition reduces body fat and therefore delays puberty by several years. This is probably the primary reason puberty occurred as late as age 17 in Europe from about the sixteenth to the eighteenth century—with marked cohort and regional variations (Tanner, 1978). For the past two decades, the most malnourished regions of the world have been in east and south Africa, especially the rural areas (Rutstein, 2000); puberty occurs two to three years later in rural Kenya than in Nairobi, the capital city (Bledsoe & Cohen, 1993).

Stress in Families

The most recently recognized influence on the age of puberty is stress. For some years biochemists have noticed that stress levels affect hormone production throughout life (Sanchez et al., 2001). For example, abused children have either abnormally high or abnormally low levels of a key stress hormone, cortisol (Gunnar & Vazquez, 2001); those under extreme stress grow more slowly, a condition called *deprivation dwarfism*. One likely explanation for such dwarfism is that GH, growth hormone, is released during sleep, and troubled or insufficient sleep would impede the nightly surge of GH.

Stress is particularly likely to affect the sexual/reproductive systems by causing irregular menstruation in some young women when they go away to college or travel to distant lands; production of fewer viable sperm or mature ova in stressed adults; and spontaneous abortions or premature births in pregnant women under stress (Veldhuis et al., 1997).

Ironically, until recently, when scientists noted a correlation between puberty and family conflict, they assumed that "raging hormones" caused the stress. Now evidence is accumulating that the reverse may be true: Stress may cause production of the hormones that cause puberty (Belsky et al., 1991; Ellis & Garber, 2000; Kim & Smith, 1998; Wierson et al., 1993). For example, girls in New Zealand whose parents are divorced experience earlier puberty than do girls of married parents (Moffitt et al., 1992); girls from India who were raised by adoptive families in Sweden typically reach menarche a year or two earlier than girls in India or than Swedish girls raised by their biological parents (Proos et al., 1991), Polish teenagers of both sexes who live in cities mature earlier than their rural contemporaries (Hulanicka, 1999). Many boys in the United States today begin puberty about a year earlier than boys did in the 1960s (Herman-Giddens et al., 2001). Stress could be the explanation for all these differences.

The stress hypothesis gathered further support from a study that, controlling for nutrition, ethnicity, and genes, found two factors that influenced early puberty (Ellis & Garber, 2000): conflicted relationships within the family and an unrelated man (stepfather or mother's boyfriend) living in the home. The longer a woman had lived with a man who was not her daughter's father, the earlier the girl's puberty tended to be. Research on lower animals points toward the same conclusions. Earlier puberty, pregnancy, and death occur for stressed rats, mice, and opossums compared to their genetic relatives who are less stressed (Warshofsky, 1999), and infant female mice reach puberty earlier if they are exposed to unrelated adult male mice (Caretta et al., 1995).

Why would such factors trigger the hormones that start puberty? "Over the course of our natural selective history, ancestral females growing up in adverse family environments may have reliably increased their reproductive success by accelerating physical maturation and beginning sexual activity and reproduction at a relatively early age" (Ellis & Garber, 2000, p. 486). Remember that human genes are adaptive, responding to the social context. In trouble-free circumstances, children can mature slowly; they will have many years of adulthood during which they can replace themselves by having one or two children. But under stressful circumstances, when death might occur, early reproduction is needed for the species' survival. (Controlled comparisons of stress-hormone levels in a cross section of children before puberty, with longitudinal follow-up, have not been reported. Alternate explanations for the link between stress and puberty have been offered.)

The Biological Changes

Although puberty begins at various ages, the sequence is almost always the same. For girls, the visible changes include, in sequence, the onset of breast growth, initial pubic hair, peak growth spurt, widening of the hips, the first menstrual period (menarche), completion of pubic-hair growth, and final breast development. For boys, the visible physical changes of puberty include, in approximate order, initial pubic hair, growth of the testes, growth of the penis, the first ejaculation of seminal fluid (spermarche), peak growth spurt, voice deepening, beard development, and completion of pubic-hair growth (Biro et al., 2001; Herman-Giddens et al., 2001; Malina, 1990).

Adults might wish that puberty began in midadolescence and proceeded slowly, as it used to. However, once pubic hair appears, the child will become a man or woman—biologically, if not emotionally—in three to four years. As we now describe in detail, the changes puberty brings are not only rapid but pervasive.

Growth Spurt

growth spurt The period of relatively sudden and rapid physical growth of every part of the body that occurs during puberty.

A major **growth spurt** occurs in late childhood and early adolescence. This is just what the term suggests—a sudden, uneven, and somewhat unpredictable jump in the size of almost every part of the body. Growth proceeds from the extremities to the core (the opposite of the prenatal and infant growth spurts): The fingers and toes lengthen before the hands and feet; the hands and feet lengthen before the arms and legs; and the arms and legs lengthen before the torso.

Because the torso is the last part of the body to grow, many pubescent children are temporarily big-footed, long-legged, and short-waisted, appearing to be "all legs and arms" (Hofman, 1997).

He's Outgrown His Shoes The typical body proportions of the young adolescent are particularly noticeable in this runner: long legs, long feet, and a relatively short torso.

Wider, Taller, Then Stronger

While the bones lengthen, the child eats more and gains more weight than before, to provide energy for the many changes taking place. As a result, fat accumulates. In fact, parents typically notice that their children are cleaning their plates, emptying the refrigerator, and straining the seams of their clothes even before they notice that their children are growing taller.

By the end of middle childhood, usually between the ages of 10 and 12, all children become noticeably heavier, although exactly when, where, and how much fat accumulates depends partly on heredity, partly on diet and exercise, and partly on sex. Females gain more fat overall, so that eventually about a fourth of their body weight is fat, almost double the average for males (Daniluk, 1998). Sex differences in body fat are especially notable on the legs and hips, because evolution favored young adult females who had extra body fat to sustain pregnancy and lactation and favored young adult males who moved swiftly in the hunt.

A height spurt follows soon after the start of the weight increase, burning up some of the stored fat and redistributing some of the rest. About a year or two after that, a period of muscle increase occurs (Hofman, 1997). As a consequence, the pudginess and clumsiness typical of early puberty generally disappear a few years later. Overall, boys increase in muscle strength by at least 150 percent (Armstrong & Welsman, 1997). This is particularly noticeable in their upper bodies. Between ages 13 and 18 years, male arm strength more than doubles (Beunen et al., 1988).

The typical girl gains about 38 pounds (17 kilograms) and 9⅝ inches (24 centimeters) between the ages of 10 and 14; the typical boy gains about 42 pounds (19 kilograms) and about 10 inches (25 centimeters) between 12 and 16. Girls typically gain the most weight in their thirteenth year, and boys in their fourteenth year (Malina & Bouchard, 1991). (See Appendix A, page A-7.)

Note, however, that no child is typical. These data are the average of many individual growth spurts. At any age between 11 and 15, some individuals grow very little because their major growth spurt has not begun, some grow very little because their spurt is already over, and some are growing very rapidly. Thus, individual growth spurts are much more rapid than the overall average: During the 12-month period of their greatest growth, many girls gain as much as 20 pounds (9 kilograms) and 3½ inches (9 centimeters), and many boys gain up to 26 pounds (12 kilograms) and 4 inches (10 centimeters) (Tanner, 1991a).

Does He Like What He Sees? During adolescence, all the facial features do not develop at the same rate, and the hair often becomes less manageable. If B. T. here is typical, he is not pleased with the appearance of his nose, lips, ears, or hair.

Proper Proportions

One of the last parts of the body to take final form is the head, which reaches adult size and shape several years after final adult shoe size is attained. To the embarrassment of many teenagers, their facial features, especially the ears, lips, and nose (which are markedly larger in adults than in children), grow before the skull itself takes on the larger, more oval shape typical of adults. Next time you see a 14-year-old covering his ears with a hat, or her nose and mouth with a hand, remember that shame may be part of the reason.

At least as disturbing to some young people is the fact that the two halves of the body do not always mature at the same rate; one foot, breast, testicle, or ear may be notably larger than the other. Fortunately, none of these anomalies persist very long. Once the growth process starts, every part of the anatomy reaches close to adult size, shape, and proportion in three or four years. (For an adolescent, a year or two of waiting for normal body proportions can seem like an eternity.)

Organ Growth

While the torso grows, internal organs also grow. Over the course of adolescence, the lungs increase in size and capacity, actually tripling in weight. Consequently, the adolescent breathes more deeply and slowly than a child (a 10-year-old breathes about 22 times a minute, while an 18-year-old breathes about 18 times). The heart doubles in size and the heart rate decreases, slowing from an average of 92 beats per minute at age 10 to 82 at age 18. In addition, the total volume of blood increases (Malina & Bouchard, 1991).

These changes increase physical endurance, making it possible for many teenagers to run for miles or dance for hours without stopping to rest. Note, however, that the more visible spurts of weight and height occur before the less visible spurts of muscles and internal organs. This means that athletic training and weight lifting for an adolescent should be designed to match the young person's size of a year or so earlier. Exhaustion and injury may occur when demands on a young person's body do not take the lag in muscle and organ growth into account (Murphy, 1999). Sports injuries are the most common school accidents, as a result of poor judgment on the part of coaches and parents and of the aspirations and actions of the young people themselves (Patel & Luckstead, 2000). Almost half of all adolescent boys hope to become professional athletes—but fewer than 1 in 10,000 actually do so (Stiles et al., 1999).

These organic changes increase the child's need to sleep, and they change the diurnal (daily) cycles whereby the body responds to day and night. Because of hormonal shifts and increases (especially in the growth hormones), many teenagers crave sleep in the mornings and are wide awake at night, when their parents are conveniently asleep (Greydanus, 1997b; Wolfson & Carskadon, 1998). Ironically, school schedules are holdovers from earlier times, when many children lived on farms and had to help get the cows home before dark every day and harvest the crops every summer. As a result, millions of North American teenagers today are challenged by calculus and chemistry at 8:00 A.M. instead of at 11:30 A.M. to 3:00 P.M., when they are most alert, and they are bored by three months of summer vacation (Barber et al., 1998). If schedules were designed to accommodate bodily rhythms, school would begin at 10:00 and end at 5:00, difficult classes would be held in the early afternoon, and families would eat dinner at 7:00 in the evening or later (Larsen, 1998).

One organ system, the *lymphoid system,* which includes the tonsils and adenoids, actually decreases in size at adolescence. Having smaller tonsils and adenoids makes teenagers less susceptible to respiratory ailments. Mild asthma, for example, often switches off at puberty (Clark & Rees, 1996).

Finally, the hormones of puberty cause many relatively minor physical changes that are insignificant in the grand scheme but have substantial psychic impact. For instance, the oil, sweat, and odor glands of the skin become much more active. One result is acne, which occurs to some degree in about 90 percent of all boys and 80 percent of all girls (Greydanus, 1997a). Another result is oilier hair and smellier bodies, which is one reason adolescents spend more money on shampoo and deodorants than does any other age group. The eyes also undergo a change. The eyeballs elongate, making many teenagers sufficiently nearsighted to require corrective lenses. All told, no part of the older adolescent's body functions or appears quite the same as it once did.

Sexual Characteristics

Even more revolutionary than the growth spurt is a set of changes that transform boys into men and girls into women.

Reproductive Possibilities

The **primary sex characteristics** are those parts of the body that are directly involved in reproduction. During puberty, every primary sex organ becomes much larger. In girls, the ovaries and the uterus begin to grow and the vaginal lining thickens even before any outward signs of puberty appear. In boys, the testes begin to grow and, about a year later, the penis lengthens and the scrotum enlarges and becomes pendulous.

Menarche is usually taken to indicate sexual maturity and fertility in girls, although the first ovulation usually does not occur until several months later. For boys, the comparable indicator is spermarche, which may occur during sleep in a nocturnal emission (a "wet dream"), through self-stimulation with masturbation, or through sexual touch by another person, with or without intercourse. Today, masturbation is the most frequent precipitator of the first ejaculation; a few generations ago masturbation was considered so depraved that the dire warnings against it meant most young boys first ejaculated when they were asleep and dreaming.

Since menarche and spermarche now occur at younger ages than they once did, many parents, especially from low-income and immigrant families, do not prepare their children properly, according to several studies (e.g., Martin, 1996). Even when parents do discuss sexual maturation with their children, they may describe the biosocial significance of puberty not in terms of joy and excitement but in terms of unwanted sex, pregnancy, and disease (all of which are discussed later in this chapter). Even so, most young people today seem to face spermarche and menarche without the fearful anxiety, embarrassment, or guilt that their parents had. This fact is illustrated by a 13-year-old who, being away from home at menarche, called her mother in tears to announce the event. Her mother, remembering her own experience and mindful of the shame and misunderstanding that generations of women have experienced regarding menstruation, immediately reassured her about the glory of womanhood, the joy of fertility, the renewal of the monthly cycle, the evidence of health (since menstruation prevents disease and prepares the uterus for pregnancy), and so on. "I know all that," her daughter protested impatiently. "I'm glad I got my period. I'm crying because this means I won't grow much more, and I want to be tall!"

primary sex characteristics The sex organs— those parts of the body that are directly involved in reproduction, including the vagina, uterus, ovaries, testicles, and penis.

A Rite of Passage Cultures and families teach their youths whether puberty is shameful, prideful, or neither. Traditional religious celebrations to mark the passage from childhood to adulthood are now rare in mainstream culture, although the Sweet Sixteen, the gang initiation, and even the high school graduation have elements of it. However, many traditional groups still follow practices, such as that shown here among the Apache people, to guide the young person into the new status, with expectations for spiritual, intellectual, and social maturity.

Sexual Appearance

Along with maturation of the reproductive organs (primary sex characteristics) come changes in **secondary sex characteristics,** which are bodily characteristics that signify sexual development, although they do not directly affect reproductive ability. One obvious example is body shape, which is virtually unisex in childhood but differentiates at puberty. Males grow taller than females (by 5 inches, on average) and become wider at the shoulders (because historically they needed to do the heavy lifting and throwing). Females put on more fat all

secondary sex characteristics Body characteristics that are not directly involved in reproduction but that indicate sexual maturity, such as a man's beard or a woman's breasts.

That's What Friends Are For Jennifer's preparations for her prom include pedicure and hairstyle courtesy of her good friends Khushbu and Meredith. In every generation and society the world over, teenagers help their same-sex friends prepare for the display rituals involved in coming of age, but a senior prom in Florida in 2002 would have been unimaginable to the grandmothers of these three girls.

over and become wider at the hips (in preparation for childbearing) and gain more fat all over.

Breasts For most girls, the first sign of puberty is the "bud" stage of breast growth, when a small accumulation of fat causes a slight rise around the nipples. From then on, breasts develop gradually, with full breast growth reached when almost all the other changes of puberty are completed (Malina, 1990). Because our culture misguidedly takes breast development to be symbolic of womanhood, small-breasted girls often feel "cheated," even disfigured; large-breasted girls attract unwanted stares and embarrassing remarks. No wonder some bras are padded to enlarge, others are advertised as "minimizers," and the most common major cosmetic surgeries are the ones that increase or decrease breast size.

In boys, as well as girls, the diameter of the areola (the dark area around the nipple) increases during puberty. To their consternation, about 65 percent of all adolescent boys experience some breast enlargement (typically in mid-puberty) (Behrman, 1992). However, their worry is usually short-lived, since this enlargement normally disappears by age 16.

Breasts are so closely connected in our minds with sex and reproduction that they are mistakenly considered part of reproductive ability. That is false: Breasts are secondary sexual characteristics; they can be absent completely with no effect on conception, pregnancy, or birth.

Voice and Hair Another secondary sex characteristic is the voice, which becomes lower as the larynx grows. This change is most noticeable in boys. (Even more noticeable, to the chagrin of the young adolescent male, is an occasional loss of voice control that throws his newly acquired baritone into a high squeak.) The "Adam's apple," the visible lump in the throat, also becomes prominent in boys but not girls, which is why it is named for Adam, not Eve. Girls also develop somewhat lower voices, the underlying reason people think a low, throaty female voice is "sexy."

During puberty, existing hair on the head, arms, and legs becomes coarser and darker, and new hair grows under the arms, on the face, and in the groin area. Visible facial hair and body hair are generally considered distinct signs of manliness in American society. This notion is mistaken, because hairiness is inherited. How often a man needs to shave, or how hairy his chest is, is determined primarily by his genes, not his virility. Further, during puberty all girls develop some light facial hair, as well as more noticeable hair on their arms and legs, with the specifics of color and density more genetic than hormonal. Eyebrows grow bushier and eyebrow ridges become more prominent in males.

Attempted Mustache To teenagers, the appearance of a secondary sexual characteristic such as facial hair, though it may be barely visible, is a sign of increasing maturity.

Emotional Responses to Physical Growth

As you have already noticed, it is difficult to describe puberty without alluding to the emotional significance of the growth spurt and of sexual maturation. Now we explicitly describe emotional and social reactions to puberty, including their causes and consequences. Puberty gives rise to emotions of all sorts, from bliss to terror, from seeming unawareness to irrational obsession, in all observers—not only the adolescents who watch their bodies change in fascination and fear but also the parents, teachers, and strangers who view the developing person with a new perspective. To begin this topic, read one teenager's report and see if you can identify her emotions and those of her parents.

A Case to Study

Julia, the Conscientious Student

Julia is the elder daughter of married parents, part of a nuclear family living in the same suburban home until Julia went to college on a full academic/athletic scholarship. She is not a low-income, inner-city child of single parents, with many siblings, moving frequently, so she is not classified as "at risk" for drug abuse, delinquency, or unintended pregnancy. Julia's adolescence should be easy. At age 17, in the spring of her freshman year, Julia explains:

> In high school, I took advanced-level classes and earned good grades. I also got along quite well with my teachers, and ended up graduating in the top 10% of my class. I know this made my mother really proud, especially since she works at the school. She would get worried that I might not be doing my best and "working to my full potential." All through high school, she tried to keep on top of my homework assignments and test schedules. She liked to look over my work before I turned it in, and would make sure that I left myself plenty of time to study for tests.
>
> In addition to schoolwork, the track and cross-country teams were a big part of high school for me. I started running in junior high school because my parents wanted me to do something athletic and I was never coordinated enough to be good at sports like soccer. I was always a little bit chubby when I was a kid. I don't know if I was exactly overweight, but everyone used to tease me about my baby fat. Running seemed like a good way to lose that extra weight. . . .
>
> My parents didn't like me hanging out with boys unless it was in a group. Besides, the boys I had crushes on were never the ones who asked me out. So any free time was mostly spent with my close girlfriends. We would go shopping or to the movies and we frequently spent the night at each other's houses. I was annoyed that although I never did anything wrong, I had the earliest curfew of my friends. Also I was the only one whose parents would page me throughout the night just to check in. . . . I guess they were just worried and wanted to be sure that I was safe.

[quoted in Gorenstein & Comer, 2002, pp. 274–275]

At first, everything seems fine with Julia. She was a hardworking high school student, with parents who care about her and girlfriends to talk to. She was active on two sports teams, and athletic participation is usually good for health, self-confidence, and social skills (Murphy, 1999).

A more careful reading is less upbeat. Julia's outlook on her adolescence is amazingly unemotional, even though she describes several things her parents did that would make many teenagers angry—checking her homework, repeatedly phoning her when she was out with her friends, insisting on an early curfew. Julia says she *never* did anything wrong, and that itself is unusual. Why didn't she rebel? Perhaps her low body fat and avoidance of boys suppressed the hormone production, mood swings, and the bodily urges of normal development. Her parents may have been too closely involved, too fearful of adolescence. You will learn more about Julia, but first think about the relationship between hormones and moods.

Storm and Stress

Adolescents are expected to be moody, emotional, angry, and turbulent. A century ago the founder of American research on adolescence, G. Stanley Hall, described the normal, inevitable "storm and stress" of puberty in great detail (Hall, 1904). Yet, as we have noted, adolescence is not necessarily a time of violent emotional shifts, of ongoing war between teenagers and authorities, or even of overpowering sexual drives. What is the proper balance between these two opposite perspectives?

Raging Hormones

On the one hand, considerable evidence confirms that conflict, moodiness, and sexual urges usually rise during adolescence (Arnett, 1999a). Hormones are part of the explanation (Susman, 1997; Weisfeld, 1999). To be specific:

- Rapidly increasing hormone levels, especially of testosterone, cause more rapid arousal of emotions.

■ Hormones cause quick shifts in emotional extremes—from feeling great to feeling awful.

■ For boys, hormonal increases lead to more thoughts about sex, as well as more masturbation. (Girls have such thoughts, too, but they do not seem to be tied to hormone levels in the same way as they do for adolescent boys.)

■ For girls, the ebb and flow of hormones during the menstrual cycle produce mood changes, from happy at midcycle to sadness or anger a day or two before the period starts.

Especially for Parents of Teenagers: Why would parents blame adolescent moods on hormones?

All these hormonal effects are lifelong, but they are more erratic and powerful, and less familiar and controllable, in the years right after puberty begins (Susman, 1997).

Social Context

On the other hand, detailed studies suggest that hormone levels make a relatively small *direct* contribution to the daily emotional outbursts of puberty—that is, to the conflicts, moods, and sexual urges. A more potent hormonal influence on the overall emotional tone of adolescence, both positive and negative, is *indirect,* via the psychological impact of the visible changes. This impact is not caused by the hormonal rush itself, because "by the time physical characteristics indicate the beginning of this transitional period, puberty, as assessed by hormonal measurements . . . is well under way" (Reiter & Lee, 2001).

In other words, it *is* true that hormones *directly* cause moods and emotions to change more quickly than in childhood or adulthood, which makes some adults conclude that pubescent children are unpredictable. Hormones also make adolescents more intent on sexual activity, and therefore more emotional, aroused, and frustrated. However, hormones have their greatest impact *indirectly,* by producing visible signs of sexual maturation such as breasts and beards, and the adult shape and size, that make society expect new maturity. Adults and other teenagers react to these biological signs. These social responses, not primarily hormones, trigger adolescent moods and reactions.

Evidence for this view came from a study of adolescents in whom puberty was delayed, with no signs of pubescence for two years after the usual age of onset (Schwab et al., 2001). Doctors prescribed a two-year treatment, alternating three-month doses of testosterone or estrogen with three-month doses of placebo (a look-alike pill that was chemically inert). Researchers found few psychological effects that could be attributed to the relatively high levels, or low levels, of hormones in the bloodstream—although the overall effects of the increased physical development pleased the adolescents.

The researchers measured nine kinds of self-competence (including self-worth, academic competence, conduct, social acceptance), and most were the same whether they were measured after doses of placebo or after high or low doses of hormones. Only one hormonal effect was significant for both sexes: Teenagers with higher hormone levels were likely to agree that they "had enough skills to do a job well" (Schwab et al., 2001). In addition, boys (but not girls) increased in feelings of athletic competence with high hormone levels, and girls (but not boys) increased in self-perceived romantic appeal.

The role of hormones is crucial to understand because the social context affects pubescence dramatically. Even the one change that is most directly linked to hormones—thinking about sex—is powerfully affected by culture, which shapes sexual thoughts into enjoyable fantasies, shameful preoccupations, frightening impulses, or an impetus to action. In the United States and probably in many other nations, the reaction to sexual urges is markedly different for boys and girls, but at least one qualitative study concludes that this difference is primarily cultural, not biological, in origin (Martin, 1996). Quantitative studies of teenage sexual activity also find that, among contemporary adolescents, sexual activity levels are quite similar for boys and girls at various ages, with about a fourth of both sexes having had intercourse by about age 14, half by age 17, and 90 percent by age 21 (Hogan et al., 2000; Santelli et al., 2000).

Current teenage sexual activity is quite different from that of 40 years ago, when the "double standard" meant boys were sexually active at younger ages than girls. The most plausible explanation for the new standards is not hormone levels (which differ for the two sexes but have not changed much for decades) but contextual. In today's social context—rooted in the sexual revolution of the 1960s, which coincided with the availability of effective contraception—teenage girls are less likely to be censured by their families and peer groups for sexual activity.

Body Image

The relationship between puberty and emotions is evident in **body image**—that is, a person's concept of, and attitude toward, his or her physical appearance. According to many psychologists, developing a healthy body image is an integral part of becoming an adult (Erikson, 1968; Simmons & Blyth, 1987). Indeed, one researcher states that "body image lies at the heart of adolescence" (Ferron, 1997). Few adolescents are satisfied with their physiques; most imagine their bodies to be far less attractive than they actually are. Keep in mind that body image entails attitude and perception, not necessarily reality. This explains why teenagers can think they are fat and ugly when their parents insist they are handsome or beautiful. For body image, the opinions of self and peers are more significant than those of parents. An offhand criticism of one wayward feature outweighs a dozen compliments (Rosenblum & Lewis, 1999).

Negative self-appraisal has a major impact on self-esteem. Although self-concept is obviously influenced by success in athletics, academics, friendship, and other areas, a teenager's assessment of personal appearance is the most important determinant of self-esteem. Consequently, adolescents are "morbidly preoccupied with how they appear in the eyes of others" (Harter, 1998, p. 573). They may spend hours examining themselves in a mirror—worrying about their complexions, about whether their clothes make them look alluring and cool, not fat or geeky. If they can afford it, many search the stores relentlessly to buy the perfect shirt or pair of jeans. Some teenagers exercise or diet with obsessive intensity (perhaps lifting weights to build specific muscles or measuring food to the gram to calculate calories).

body image A person's concept of how his or her body appears. This self-evaluation may be quite different from the opinions of others or from any objective measures.

MICHAEL NEWMAN / PHOTOEDIT

Sexual Messages This teen couple is aware that everyone who lifts weights should have a spotter, to prevent accidents. However, note that they seem to be using the occasion to exchange messages through their eye contact, facial expressions, and clothing.

Sex Differences in Body Image

Concern with body image is especially likely to reach extremes for girls, because norms of attractiveness are "particularly punishing and very narrow for women" (Harter, 1998, p. 592).

The contrast in how boys and girls think about their bodies is shown in their reactions to menarche or spermarche. Each person's reaction is influenced by many factors, but girls are more likely to be upset and boys more often thrilled when these signs of reproductive possibility appear (Downs & Fuller, 1991).

Audrey, looking back from age 16, talks about getting her first period:

> I was really upset. I was crying. I remember it was on my birthday and I was like "God hates me." Just something about me I didn't want that stuff to start happening to me. . . . Well, you want to know, it sounds really irrational, but I do remember one thought I had. I thought it meant that I had to start having sex, and I felt really weird, and I felt really rushed. I was in the seventh grade, I mean, I was a

really late bloomer, and I didn't even start talking to guys until eighth or ninth grade. I was really shy and remember I was like I can't really talk to any guys today 'cause they'll know, they'll know. And I remember being in homeroom and thinking "Oh no, I can't face anyone that day."

[quoted in Martin, 1996, pp. 28–29]

A teenage boy's one worry may be his impulse to masturbate, as Brent explains:

I pretty much knew everything. I was only worried about getting AIDS through like masturbating or something (laughs), but umm, I actually talked to my dad about that so, I wasn't really worried about anything after the sixth grade.

What did your dad say when you talked to him?

He said, he sort of laughed. He told me stories about how he used to do it too, and he said "No, you can't get AIDS from doing that." And so I was happy, and he was happy, and that sort of opened the door for whatever conversations.

[quoted in Martin, 1996]

Another example of male–female difference in body image is the reaction to the body hair that both sexes grow. Many boys are thrilled with their facial hair, shaving long before there is any real need to. If they can, they grow sideburns, beards, "soul patches," or mustaches, and display their hairy chests. Girls, in contrast, diligently attempt to rid themselves of barely visible hairs, using waxes, bleaches, tweezers, creams, or razors. For many young women, shaving, including inexpert nicks, is a chosen rite of passage, more likely to be learned from girlfriends and older sisters than from mothers (Martin, 1996).

Too Early or Too Late

Every adolescent wants to experience puberty "on time," not much earlier or later than their friends do. In reality, given the normal range of puberty's onset, few adolescents mature exactly when their peers do. This is a particular problem for early girls and late boys, who are off "schedule" compared to the other sex as well as their own (Downs, 1990; Graber et al., 1994).

Think about the situation of the early-maturing girl. If she has large, visible breasts in the fifth grade, she is probably teased by the boys in her classroom; they are awed by the sexual creature in their midst. She herself is embarrassed. While trying to fit her feet into shoes that are too tight and her womanly body into a school chair designed for younger children, she may try to disguise her breasts in blouses several sizes too large. Early-maturing girls tend to have lower self-esteem and poorer body image than other girls, as a recent study in Scotland has confirmed (Williams & Currie, 2000).

After a period of feeling awkward, many early-maturing girls turn to a remedy for their self-esteem that is likely to impede their intellectual growth: romantic involvement. Older boys and young men find their combination of innocence and physical development attractive. Girls in these relationships may drink alcohol, smoke cigarettes, use other drugs, and become sexually active before girls typically do (Brooks-Gunn, 1991). One study found that age of menarche was a stronger predictor of age of first intercourse than any background restraint, including religion, ethnicity, and socioeconomic status (Bingham et al., 1990).

As for late-maturing boys, the tenth-grader who is still short and skinny is likely to be shunned by the girls, who protect their self-image by never holding hands with boys who are smaller than they

Who Is the Oldest? Height is a very poor guide to age during adolescence (though not in childhood). Given the discrepancies in the timing of growth after puberty, the shortest one of these high school students may be the oldest, and the tallest may be the youngest.

MICHAEL NEWMAN / PHOTOEDIT

are. Longitudinal research has found that in high school late-maturing boys tend to be talkative and restless, while early-maturing boys are socially popular and sports heroes (Jones, 1957, 1965). If late-maturing boys are in a school and culture that value intellectual accomplishments, and they themselves are academically inclined, they may excel at schoolwork, go on to college, and eventually succeed at careers that suit their talents (Downs, 1990). Asian-Americans tend to mature relatively late, as well as to graduate from high school and attend college at higher rates than other young Americans. The usual reason given for Asians' success is that their families value education and push them to succeed, but part of the reason could be simply that late maturation gives them fewer other options than their high school classmates have.

Early longitudinal research found that the low self-esteem of off-time maturation lingers even when young adults are finally about as tall as everyone else. Early-maturing girls tend to become mothers earlier; late-maturing boys tend to marry later and are less likely to hold leadership positions at work or in their communities (Jones, 1965; Livson & Peskin, 1980). More recent research on the lingering psychological effects of off-time puberty has not been reported. However, data on drug use do not hint that puberty has become easier. For example, in 2001 about 7 percent of male 15-year-olds used steroids to build up their muscles, twice as many as 10 years earlier (Johnston et al., 2001). Steroids are particularly likely to be used by late-maturing boys who are desperate to get taller and stronger. Cigarette smoking has not declined, and girls smoke about as much as boys (see Appendix A, page A-15). Many girls smoke to keep their weight down, and body fat speeds up the age of puberty—so early-maturing girls who smoke tend to be larger as well as more addicted to cigarettes compared to late-maturing girls. Ironically, as adults, early-maturing girls still tend to be heavier than their peers—and about an inch shorter (Biro et al., 2001).

Reactions to Sexual Impulses

Beginning with Freud, almost all psychologists and other social scientists have agreed that sexual relations are an important aspect of life. Puberty adds genetic compulsion to the more emotional and intellectual reasons for having sex. Every physically mature creature has an urge to mate and reproduce, so it is not surprising that most adolescents seek sexual interactions before they reach age 20. In many nations, they marry and have babies.

Although the average age of first marriage in the United States is about 24, most (between 50 and 60 percent) boys and girls experience sexual intercourse before they graduate from high school; more than a fourth are sexually active by age 14 (Hogan et al., 2000; Santelli et al., 2000). The cognitive aspects of sexual choices are discussed in Chapter 15. Here we describe two physiological hazards of early sexual activity: sexually transmitted diseases and unwanted pregnancies.

Especially for Young Adults: Suppose your parents never talked to you about sex or puberty. Was that a mistake?

Sexually Transmitted Diseases

Sexually active teenagers have higher rates of *gonorrhea, genital herpes, syphilis,* and *chlamydia*—the most common **sexually transmitted diseases (STDs)**—than any other age group. This is true worldwide, although the absolute rates of STDs are actually higher among 20- to 24-year-olds because many teenagers are not sexually active and thus are unlikely to contract an STD (Panchaud et al., 2000). Few STDs are serious if promptly treated, but untreated STDs can cause lifelong sterility and life-threatening complications. Sexually active adolescents also risk exposure to the HIV virus, a risk that increases if a person:

sexually transmitted diseases (STDs) Disease spread by sexual contact. Such diseases include syphilis, gonorrhea, herpes, chlamydia, and AIDS.

- Is already infected with other STDs
- Has more than one partner within a year
- Does not use condoms during intercourse

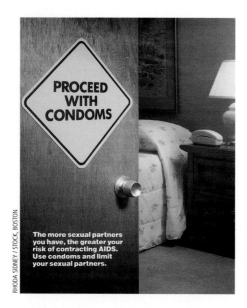

RHODA SIDNEY / STOCK, BOSTON

Better Protection For decades, sex educators have bemoaned the fact that teenage girls have been considered solely responsible for practicing birth control. However, as this poster suggests, the AIDS epidemic has changed advertising and individual practice, with clear results. Almost half of all sexually active boys use condoms regularly, and the rate of teen pregnancy has been decreasing since the late 1980s.

Response for Young Adults (from page 445): Yes, but maybe you should forgive them. Ideally, parents should talk to their children about sex, presenting honest information and listening to the child's concerns. However, many parents find this very difficult because they feel embarrassed and ignorant. Yes, their silence was a mistake—but no parent is perfect and sex is hard for many parents to talk about. Try asking them now.

All three of these conditions are common among teenagers and their sex partners (who are often unmarried young adults), making them the most likely to catch the virus. To be specific, recent data reveal that, by their senior year of high school, 22 percent of U.S. teenagers have already had four or more sexual partners and that only half (more younger than older teens) used a condom at last intercourse (CDC, June 28, 2002).

The younger people are when they contract an STD, the more reluctant they are to seek treatment and to alert their sexual partners. They may feel ashamed and afraid, and many young adolescents do not recognize the symptoms or know where inexpensive, confidential, and respectful medical treatment can be found. As a result, the reinfection rate is higher than that of older people.

For example, researchers in Washington State checked the legally mandated reports filed by every doctor or clinic treating cases of chlamydia. After a woman had one chlamydia infection, she was four times more likely to have a second one if she was under age 20 than if she was over 30 (Xu et al., 2000). The Washington teenagers were more likely than older women to see a different health care provider for each reinfection (Xu et al., 2000). Inadequately treated STDs not only reappear and spread, they may also cause PID (pelvic inflammatory disease), which blocks the fallopian tubes and thus makes pregnancy impossible. This means that early sexual activity coupled with erratic medical care can mean infertility later on.

Teenagers are *not* more sexually active than adults, but those who are active typically have more partners and poor or no medical care. These factors increase the risk and speed the transmission of sexually transmitted diseases in adolescents. Each infection with an STD makes the person more likely to catch another one. The possible consequences are not only infertility but also lifelong infection (with herpes, for instance) and even death (as with HIV/AIDS) (Valois et al., 1999).

Unwanted Pregnancies

The second developmental risk for sexually active adolescents is pregnancy. Unintentional pregnancy causes two distinct sets of problems, one for younger teens and the other for older ones.

Younger Adolescents If a girl becomes pregnant within a year or two of menarche, she is at increased risk of almost every complication—among them spontaneous abortion, eclampsia, stillbirth, cesarean section, a low-birthweight baby—all because her uterus and overall body functioning are not yet mature (Phipps & Sowers, 2002).

Moreover, in the first years after puberty, the body adjusts to new hormones, adds bone density, redistributes weight, and grows taller. Pregnancy slows down or stops all this, because the girl's body must respond to another set of hormones. Women who had their first child when they were under age 16 tend to be shorter and sicker later on, and to die at younger ages, than women who had their first baby at an older age. Part of the explanation is socioeconomic: Pregnancy occurs more often among poor teenagers, who tend to have health problems even if they do not become pregnant. The sheer biological burden of pregnancy, imposed on the body before it is ready, takes a heavier toll.

The induced abortion rate is highest among girls under age 15. In the United States in the 1990s, about half the pregnancies of girls aged 14 or under were terminated by abortion, compared to only one in six women aged 30 to 34 (U.S. Bureau of the Census, 2001). Abortion spares the young person the physical burden of pregnancy and birth and the psychological strains of motherhood, but abortion is particularly difficult, biologically and emotionally, for young teenagers.

Older Adolescents Because older teenagers are fully grown, pregnancy is no greater a physical problem for them than it is for women in their 20s. Serious birth complications are as rare from ages 16 to 19 as from age 20 up (Phipps & Sowers, 2002). However, problems abound once the baby is born. Eighty percent of teenage mothers in the United States are not married, primarily because very few of the fathers are ready to take on a lifetime commitment to the mother and the child. Although the father is typically several years older than the girl, he is unlikely to be a supportive father or even a helpful birth coach.

Teenage motherhood slows educational and vocational achievement and restricts social and personal growth. No matter what a teenager's level of family support, income, or intellectual capacity, becoming a mother reduces eventual academic achievement by three years on average (Klepinger et al., 1995). It also reduces her chance of employment and marriage, and, if she marries because she is pregnant, it increases her chances of being abused, abandoned, or divorced.

These conclusions are based on women in the United States, but a recent follow-up of the fertility and economic paths of all the women born in Sweden between 1941 and 1970 found the same long-term consequences, even though the political and social context was quite different. This study was sufficiently large (covering 140,000 adolescent births) that age and cohort effects were apparent. Although the averages for all teenage mothers were worse than for older mothers, the worst outcomes were found in the youngest mothers whose pregnancies occurred after 1960 (Olausson et al., 2001).

The likely consequences for the child are even more troublesome. Babies of young teenagers have a higher risk of prenatal and birth complications, including low birthweight and brain damage, than do infants from the same ethnic communities and educational backgrounds whose mothers are older. As they develop, children born to adolescents experience more mistreatment of all kinds and less educational success of any kind. In adolescence, they are more likely to become drug abusers, delinquents, dropouts, and—against their mothers' advice—parents themselves (Borkowski et al., 2002; Fergusson & Woodward, 1999; Jaffee et al., 2001).

It is important to realize that the problems of teenage pregnancy after age 15 are linked to culture and cohort. In previous decades, to be 17 years old, married, in love, and expecting a baby was ideal not only for the society but also for the young woman, whose husband usually was a few years older and employed. Even today in some nations—Burma, Bangladesh, and Yemen among them— only 5 percent of the older adolescents, virtually all of them male, are enrolled in higher education of any kind. The teen birth rate in those nations is more than four times that of Japan, Canada, or Western Europe, where young people are expected to stay in school until at least age 21 and where first-time parenthood at age 30 is not considered too late.

The rate of teen pregnancy is quite low in many industrialized nations. Even in the United States, where rates are far higher than in any European or East Asian nation, the annual teen birth rate is only half of what it was in 1970. In the United States in 2000, about 1 in 1,000 teenage girls under age 15 gave birth, as did fewer than 5 in 1,000 older teens (compared to 11 per 1,000 for women in their 20s) (Ventura et al., 2001).

From a developmental perspective, these rates are still too high. For the young girl's body, the older girl's future, and the baby's well-being, teenage pregnancy is to be avoided. The wiser choice, then, is to postpone sexual activity, thus avoiding the risk of disease, sterility, and pregnancy. If they do become sexually active, young people who use condoms every time they have sexual intercourse can avoid both disease and pregnancy.

sexual abuse The use of an unconsenting person for one's own sexual pleasure. Sexual activity is abusive whenever it is not mutual, whenever consent is not freely given, or whenever a person does not understand or feels obligated to agree to a sexual encounter.

child sexual abuse Any activity in which an adult uses a child for his or her own sexual stimulation or pleasure—even if the use does not involve physical contact. Child pornography, fondling, and lewd comments by strangers are all examples of child sexual abuse.

Sexual Abuse

Sexual abuse is defined as the use of an unconsenting person for one's own sexual pleasure. Accordingly, sexual activity is abusive whenever it is not mutual, whenever consent is not freely given, or whenever a person does not understand or feels obligated to agree to a sexual encounter.

Free consent is considered impossible for children or young adolescents to give. They have little understanding of the implications of sexual activity, and they are physically weaker than their elders and psychologically dependent on them. Accordingly, **child sexual abuse** is defined as any erotic activity that arouses an adult and excites, shames, or confuses a young person—whether or not the victim protests, whether or not genital contact is involved. Thus, sexual abuse may consist of sexualized teasing, taking erotic photographs, asking intrusive questions about the child's body, or invading the privacy of the child's bathing, dressing, or sleeping routines—especially once puberty begins.

As with other forms of maltreatment (see Chapter 8), the harm done by any act of sexual abuse increases if it is repeated, if it distorts the adult–child relationship, if it involves the child's sex organs, if it is coercive, or if it impairs the child's ability to develop normally with peers (Haugaard, 2000; Stevenson, 1999). In particular, ongoing sexual abuse by a parent damages a victim's ability as an adult to establish a trusting and intimate relationship with another adult. Typically fathers or stepfathers are the abusers, but mothers contribute by not recognizing the abuse and by not protecting the child (Sheinberg & Fraenkel, 2001).

Sexual victimization often begins in childhood, with parental fondling, explicit nudity, or suggestive comments—all of which confuse preschoolers or young children. Blatant sexual abuse typically begins at puberty (Stewart, 1997), particularly if the mother is away, the biological father is absent, and an unrelated male is in the household (Rowland et al., 2000). Prevalence studies of childhood sexual abuse range from more than 50 percent to less than 5 percent, depending on how abuse is defined (Haugaard, 2000). Broad definitions (such as "any sexual abuse") are preferred by developmentalists, who seek to prevent all possible harm; narrow definitions ("forced genital activity") are used by legal authorities, who prosecute offenders.

The age below which sexual activity is considered abuse also varies: In the United States in the nineteenth century, the "age of consent" was only 10. Some states permitted marriage as young as age 12. Currently in North America the age of consent is between 14 and 18, depending on local law (Donovan, 1997). (Some other nations still permit marriage at any age if the parents agree.)

For unmarried adolescents below the age of consent, even voluntary sexual intercourse is classified as "statutory rape"—that is, rape according to law or statute within a particular jurisdiction, although voluntary sexual intercourse between two teenagers is seldom prosecuted as rape. However, even without criminal charges, an interaction that begins voluntarily but progresses further than one party wants, or that involves a sexual interaction between a teenager and someone in authority (educator, clergy, relative), is sexual abuse. Sexual relations are least likely to be voluntary if the girl is under age 15 and her partner is age 18 or older (Elo et al., 1999).

Adolescent girls are prime targets for victimization by relatives, family friends, and especially young men they know. In a survey of young women of four ethnic groups in the United States, (African-, Native, Mexican-, and European-Americans), about one-third of each group reported sexual abuse; one-fifth of these respondents had been raped (Roosa et al., 1999). Young Canadian women report similarly high rates (DeKeseredy & Schwartz, 1998).

The *meaning* of being sexually victimized may be especially disturbing for older children and adolescents compared to younger children. At a time when they want to take pride in changes in their bodies, as they become increasingly self-aware and attracted to peers, sexual victimization can turn the world upside down. Indeed, adolescents often react to such maltreatment in ways that younger children rarely do—with self-destructive behavior (such as suicide, drug abuse, or running away) or with counterattack (such as vandalism or violence, aimed at society or directly at the perpetrator) (Ewing, 1990).

This is just as true for boys as for girls. In addition to bearing the stigma of unwelcome sexual activity, a molested boy is likely to feel shame at being weak and unable to defend himself and is also likely to worry that he is homosexual— all contrary to the macho image that many young adolescent boys strive to attain. The male perpetrator does not necessarily consider himself homosexual, nor is a boy's involvement a true indication of his sexual orientation. However, when the boy is, in fact, gay and is abused for it, the shame escalates. And when the sexual abuse of a boy occurs at home, typically by his father or stepfather, the problems of vulnerability and loss of self-esteem are multiplied (Finkelhor, 1994).

Although most sexual abusers are male, about 20 percent are female (Bagley & Thurston, 1996). Such abuse can be sexual teasing and fondling, which evokes confusion and shame, or more blatant abuse. Boys obviously are spared the problems of unwanted pregnancy that many sexually abused girls experience, but they often turn their anger outward. An estimated 30 to 50 percent of child molesters are adolescent boys who had been abused themselves (Jones et al., 1999).

The fact that an abuser had himself been abused is no excuse for victimizing a child or adolescent. However, every abuser is living testimony of past negligence, and victims suffer long after the act of incest or abuse, so ongoing treatment may be needed. Every problem of adolescence—unintended pregnancy, suicide, delinquency, eating disorders, and so on—is more common in victims of past sexual abuse than in other teenagers (Friedrich, 1998). For example, in a survey of more than 6,000 Minnesota high school students, boys who were sexually abused were 10 times more likely, and girls twice as likely, to have an eating disorder (Hernandez, 1995). Whenever an adolescent seems troubled, past sexual abuse is a possibility that should be explored in confidence, with effective help at the ready.

Health and Hazards

Adolescence is a healthy time. The minor illnesses of childhood (including flu, colds, earaches, and childhood diseases of all sorts) become much less common, because inoculations, bouts of illness, and years of exposure have increased immunity. The major diseases of adulthood are rare. The two main killers of adults, heart disease and cancer, almost never occur: A 15-year-old's chance of dying from them is only one-hundredth that of a 60-year-old (U.S. Bureau of the Census, 2001). Not only are teenagers innately quite healthy, but the health behaviors required of humans of all ages—eat right and exercise regularly—come naturally: Appetites increase (which is why they raid the kitchen at 2:00 A.M.), and the impulse to move is strong (as is evident in all-night dances, enthusiasm for sports, and difficulty just standing still).

Although diseases don't attack teenagers, their own actions do. The average annual death rate for teenagers aged 15 to 19 is five times that of children aged 5 to 9 (1:1,000 compared to 1:5,000). These rates are from the United States from 1970–2000, but other nations and cohorts have similar age gaps. In fact, in the

Twisted Memorial This wreck was once a Volvo, driven by a Colorado teenager who ignored an oncoming train's whistle at a rural crossing. The car was hurled 167 feet and burst into flames. The impact instantly killed the driver and five teenage passengers. They are among the statistics indicating that accidents (many of which result from unwise risk taking) kill ten times more adolescents than diseases do.

DOMINIC CHAVEZ / THE DENVER POST / AP PHOTO

United States the ratio is getting worse: Over the past 30 years, death rates declined about 65 percent for young children but only about 20 percent for older teens (U.S. Department of Health and Human Services, 2000). Accidental injury and death rates increase markedly, from about age 10 until a peak at age 25, and then they begin to decline. Two hazards, eating disorders and drug use, are discussed in detail below. (Other risks are discussed in Chapters 15 and 16.)

Nutrition

The rapid bodily changes of puberty requires fuel in the form of additional calories, as well as additional vitamins and minerals. In fact, the recommended daily intake of calories is higher for an active adolescent than for anyone else; the greatest calorie requirement occurs at about age 14 for girls and 17 for boys (Malina & Bouchard, 1991). During the growth spurt, the need for calcium, iron, and zinc (for both bone and muscle development) is about 50 percent greater than it was only two years earlier.

In developed nations, where sufficient high-quality food is readily available, most adolescents meet their basic caloric needs most of the time, typically consuming four or more meals a day even without breakfast. To assess whether a person is too thin or too fat, clinicians calculate **body mass index (BMI)**, dividing the person's weight in kilograms by height in meters squared. BMI in inches and pounds is shown in Table 14.3. Note that a healthy BMI for full-grown people (which includes almost all 18-year-olds) is between 19 and 24. Everyone has a

body mass index (BMI) A measure of obesity, determined by dividing a person's weight in kilograms by height in meters squared.

TABLE 14.3 Body Mass Index (BMI)

To calculate your BMI: Find your height, then look across that row. Your BMI is at the top of the column that contains your weight.

BMI	19	20	21	22	23	24	25	26	27	28	29	30	35	40
Height					Weight (pounds)									
4'10"	91	96	100	105	110	115	119	124	129	134	138	143	167	191
4'11"	94	99	104	109	114	119	124	128	133	138	143	148	173	198
5'0"	97	102	107	112	118	123	128	133	138	143	148	153	179	204
5'1"	100	106	111	116	122	127	132	137	143	148	153	158	185	211
5'2"	104	109	115	120	126	131	136	142	147	153	158	164	191	218
5'3"	107	113	118	124	130	135	141	146	152	158	163	169	197	225
5'4"	110	116	122	128	134	140	145	151	157	163	169	174	204	232
5'5"	114	120	126	132	138	144	150	156	162	168	174	180	210	240
5'6"	118	124	130	136	142	148	155	161	167	173	179	186	216	247
5'7"	121	127	134	140	146	153	159	166	172	178	185	191	223	255
5'8"	125	131	138	144	151	158	164	171	177	184	190	197	230	262
5'9"	128	135	142	149	155	162	169	176	182	189	196	203	236	270
5'10"	132	139	146	153	160	167	174	181	188	195	202	207	243	278
5'11"	136	143	150	157	165	172	179	186	193	200	208	215	250	286
6'0"	140	147	154	162	169	177	184	191	199	206	213	221	258	294
6'1"	144	151	159	166	174	182	189	197	204	212	219	227	265	302
6'2"	148	155	163	171	179	186	194	202	210	218	225	233	272	311
6'3"	152	160	168	176	184	192	200	208	216	224	232	240	279	319
6'4"	156	164	172	180	189	197	205	213	221	230	238	246	287	328
				Normal					*Overweight*				*Obese*	

Adult BMI Overall, the BMI for both men and women should be between 19 and 24, with more muscular people on the higher end of that range and less muscular people on the lower end (since muscle weighs more than fat). A BMI of 18 or below is considered anorexic; 30 or above is considered obese. The World Health Organization has set a BMI of 35 as severely obese. For more information on standards, exercises, and calculations, check the National Heart, Lung and Blood Institute's Web site at www.nhlbi.nih.gov.

natural weight, called either a set point or a "settling point," which is maintained as long as we eat only when we are hungry and avoid fried and high-calorie foods. Some genetic impulses can lead to overeating, but sociocultural restraints can counter them, permitting a normal BMI to be maintained (Pinel et al., 2000).

Fewer than one-fourth of high school seniors consume the recommended servings of fruits and vegetables a day (see Figure 14.2; CDC, June 9, 2000). This bodes ill for the future, since a diet with ample fruits and vegetables protects against the two leading killers of adults, heart disease and cancer. Even fewer high school seniors (9 percent of senior girls and 19 percent of senior boys) drink three glasses of milk a day. This is a dramatic decline from several decades ago, when most adolescents drank a quart or more of milk a day, and even a cutback from the ninth grade, when 13 percent of girls and 25 percent of boys drank at least three glasses of milk each day (CDC, June 28, 2002).

Inadequate milk consumption is particularly troubling because milk is a good source of calcium, a major contributor to bone growth. About half of adult bone mass is acquired during adolescence. Insufficient bone mass increases the risk of osteoporosis, a leading cause of disability, injury, and even death among older women. Today's teens prefer carbonated soft drinks over milk, thereby endangering their teeth, their bones, and the rest of their bodies (Harnack et al., 1999).

Part of the responsibility for poor eating habits lies with the adolescents themselves. (Teenagers rarely think rationally about the future, as explained in Chapter 15.) Schools, television, and the overall culture are also at fault. Families, too, share in the blame: It is rare for today's young people to sit down with their families to eat a meal of fresh foods that have been washed, cut, combined, seasoned, and cooked by a parent. According to a developmentalist whose special interest is adolescence, many European families still eat dinner together, although they do it later than North Americans traditionally did, at 7:00 or 8:00 P.M. rather than 6:00. If that custom were exported, North American teenagers might be healthier (Larsen, 1998). As it is, however, many of them are unaware of nutritional requirements. For example:

> Christina Green, a 17-year-old high school student in Delaware, Ohio, considers herself old-fashioned when she shops for groceries. Most of her friends buy meals to go, she said—"stuff they can eat right away or zap." She, on the other hand, picks up frozen pot pies and breaded chicken, fishsticks and pizza, boxed macaroni and cheese.
>   "I like a homemade meal," she said.
>   To many teen-agers, "homemade" has come to mean nothing more than "home heated."
>
> [O'Neill, 1998]

Most teenagers snack on their own or with peers and eat few meals at home. As a result, they are likely to get too much salt, sugar, fat, and preservatives in their diet, and not enough calcium or iron. Indeed, fewer than half consume the recommended daily dose of 15 milligrams of iron, a nutrient that is present mainly in green vegetables, eggs, and meat. Because each menstrual period depletes the body of some iron, females between the ages of 15 and 17 are more likely to suffer from iron-deficiency anemia (low blood hemoglobin) than any other subgroup of the population (Baynes & Bothwell, 1990). This means, for example, that if a teenage girl seems apathetic and lazy, she should have her hemoglobin checked before she is accused of a poor attitude or other psychological difficulties.

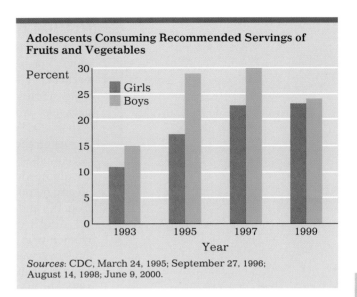

Adolescents Consuming Recommended Servings of Fruits and Vegetables

Sources: CDC, March 24, 1995; September 27, 1996; August 14, 1998; June 9, 2000.

FIGURE 14.2 Five or More a Day
Nutritionists recommend that everyone eat at least five portions of fruits and vegetables a day—and more would be better. Less than one third of high school seniors reach this minimum. Perhaps surprisingly, younger adolescents do better on this measure than seniors do.

A Thousand Hamburgers per Person per Year Some teenagers easily reach the thousand mark, wolfing down three burgers a day in after-school or midnight snacks, or even breakfast at noon. This Charlotte, North Carolina, basketball star knows that he should avoid high-fat foods and fill up on whole grains, fresh fruits, and various vegetables. However, for him and for most other teenagers, knowledge does not change habits.

Dieting As a Disease

Most teenagers eat too little or too much, or they eat wrong foods at the wrong times. For instance, vegetarianism suddenly becomes more popular at puberty, particularly among girls. This eating pattern can be healthy, but not the way many adolescents do it. They avoid not only meat and eggs but also milk products, just when their bodies need increased iron and calcium (Belamarich & Ayoob, 2001).

As already explained, body image is closely tied to self-concept. Girls are especially likely to worry that they are too fat, even when they are gaining the weight needed for their bodies to become womanly. It is normal to gain between 30 and 60 pounds—depending on height, muscle mass, and genetic body type—from the end of childhood to adulthood.

Adults do not set a very good example. Almost half of North American women who were dieting to lose weight had a BMI under 25—and thus were not at all overweight. Those who were young, well educated, and employed were the ones most likely to diet *and* the least likely to need to do so (Biener & Heaton, 1995). In the United States, the average 17- to 28-year-old woman would like to be 8 pounds lighter and the average man, 5 pounds heavier. Almost no young adults are satisfied with their present weight (Mintz & Kashubeck, 1999).

It is no surprise, then, that when body size changes dramatically at puberty, many young people want to stop the process. Almost every teenage girl (no matter what her weight) and many teenage boys diet for a few days or weeks—they become tired and short-tempered, they lose a few pounds and then gain a few, they ask for foods they never wanted before and refuse things they always liked—usually without serious consequences. About a fourth of all teenage girls in the United States have already tried diet pills, which are addictive (Johnston et al., 2001). Almost two-thirds of them had already stopped using these pills, usually because they had already learned on their own that the benefits (if any) do not outweigh the costs.

For about 1 teenager in 20, however, serious eating disorders become much more prevalent at the beginning of adolescence, at about age 12 or 13, and just after high school, at about age 18. A study of adolescents with abnormal eating patterns found that their mothers' direct suggestion that they diet was the most powerful influence (Vincent & McCabe, 2000). Let's look at two eating disorders that are becoming increasingly common: anorexia and bulimia nervosa.

Anorexia Nervosa

Anorexia nervosa is characterized by self-starvation; it occurs when individuals voluntarily eat so little and exercise so much that they risk death. In fact, between 5 and 20 percent of the victims of anorexia do die. One famous victim of anorexia was Karen Carpenter, a gifted singer who reached the top of the charts with "Rainy Days and Sundays" and other hits and who died at age 32.

According to DSM-IV-*R,* there are four symptoms of anorexia nervosa:

- Refusal to maintain body weight at least 85 percent of normal for age and height
- Intense fear of gaining weight
- Disturbed body perception and denial of the problem
- In adolescent and adult females, lack of menstruation

If someone's BMI is 18 or lower, or if she (or, less often, he) loses more than 10 percent of body weight within a month or two, anorexia is suspected (American Psychiatric Association, 2000).

From a developmental perspective, it is noteworthy that anorexia is a disease of the social context; in other words, the culture supports it. Anorexia was virtually unknown before 1950, and then it was first diagnosed in some high-

Especially for College Roommates: You and your roommate respect each other's privacy, but your roommate is jeopardizing his or her health by losing a lot of weight, or getting drunk every weekend, or practicing unsafe sex. What should you do?

anorexia nervosa A serious eating disorder in which a person restricts eating to the point of emaciation and possible starvation. Most victims are high-achieving females in early puberty or early adulthood.

Danger Signs Ashleigh, a California 13-year-old, may not have anorexia, but she looks very thin, especially in relation to her parents, standing behind her. If she weighs herself more often than once a week or so, she may be developing an obsession with thinness.

achieving, upper-class young women. Within a few decades, it became prevalent among adolescent girls in general in developed nations, and it is currently on the rise in developing nations, especially in urban areas (Gordon, 2000; Nasser, 1997). At one time African-Americans, citizens of any Asian or African nation, and Latinas in South or North America were immune to eating disorders. That is no longer true, and now "the unhealthy aspects of American culture are strong and far-reaching. Therefore it is critical that the possibility of eating and body image concerns are considered for all individuals, regardless of ethnic background" (Dounchis et al., 2001, p. 82). Overall, about 1 percent of women develop anorexia at some point in their lives, with rates much higher among athletes, particularly runners, gymnasts, dancers, and among men, wrestlers (Perriello, 2001; Thompson & Sherman, 1993).

A Case to Study

Julia Again: "Too Thin, As If That's Possible"

We return to Julia, who writes of her first year in college, at age 17.

> I have never before felt so much pressure. Because my scholarship depends both on my running and on my maintaining a 3.6 grade point average, I've been stressed out much of the time. Academic work was never a problem for me in the past, but there's just so much more expected of you in college.
>
> It was pressure from my coach, my teammates, and myself that first led me to dieting. . . . I know that my coach was really disappointed in me. He called me aside about a month into the season. He wanted to know what I was eating, and he told me the weight I had gained was undoubtedly hurting my performance. He said that I should cut out snacks and

> sweets of any kind, and stick to things like salad to help me lose the extra pounds, and get back into shape. He also recommended some additional workouts. I was all for a diet—I hated that my clothes were getting snug. . . . At that point, I was 5'6" and weighed 145 pounds. When I started college I had weighed 130 pounds. . . .
>
> Once I started dieting, the incentives to continue were everywhere. My race time improved, so my coach was pleased. I felt more a part of the team and less like an outsider. My clothes were no longer snug, and when they saw me at my meets my parents said I looked great. I even received an invitation to a party given by a fraternity that only invited the most attractive first-year women. After about a month, I was back to my normal weight of 130 pounds.

. . . I set a new weight goal of 115 pounds. I figured if I hit the gym more often and skipped breakfast altogether, it wouldn't be hard to reach that weight in another month or so. Of course, this made me even hungrier by lunchtime, but I didn't want to increase my lunch size. I found it easier to pace myself with something like crackers. I would break them into several pieces and only allow myself to eat one piece every 15 minutes. The few times I did this with friends in the dining hall I got weird looks and comments. I finally started eating lunch alone in my room. . . . I couldn't believe it when the scale said I was down to 115 pounds. I still felt that I had excess weight to lose. Some of my friends were beginning to mention that I was actually looking too thin, as if that's possible.

. . . All of which brings me to the present time. Even though I'm running great and I'm finally able to stick to a diet, everyone thinks I'm not taking good enough care of myself. . . . I'm doing my best to keep in control of my life, and I wish that I could be trusted to take care of myself.

Julia's roommate writes, in her spring semester:

There were no more parties or hanging out at meals for her. . . . We were all worried, but none of us knew what to do. . . . I looked in the back of Julia's closet. A few months ago I had asked to borrow a tampon. She opened a new box and gave me one. The same box was still there with only that one missing. For the first time, I realized how serious Julia's condition could be.

A few days later, Julia approached me. Apparently she just met with one of the deans, who told her that she'd need to undergo an evaluation at the health center before she could continue practicing with the team. She asked me point blank if I had been talking about her to anyone. I told her how her mother had asked me if I had noticed any changes in her over the past several months, and how I honestly told her yes. She stormed out of the room and I haven't seen her since. I know how important the team is to Julia, so I am assuming that she'll be going to the health center soon. I hope that they'll be able to convince her that she's taken things too far, and that they can help her to get better.

[quoted in Gorenstein & Comer, 2002, pp. 275–280]

Julia, with her rapid weight loss that she does not see as a problem, is a classic case of anorexia nervosa. She thinks she is finally able to stick to a diet and in control of her life, when in fact she is not at all in control but is addicted to exercise and weight loss. The vital organs, including the heart, need nourishment to function. Serious depression is also linked to anorexia, and suicide is a danger for Julia.

Undoubtedly you wonder why her coach, her parents, and her friends did not notice her problem sooner and insist that she get help. This time lag is common: "By the time the anorexic reaches the point at which the disorder is clinically identified, she has already become entrapped in a complex web of psychological attitudes" (Gordon, 2000). Before that point, many people encourage rapid weight loss instead of welcoming the normal gains of a healthy developing woman. Actually, just at the time that her coach suggested she diet, Julia's weight after a month of college (145 for an athlete who is 5'6") was within the normal BMI. She was not even marginally overweight, much less obese. Yet everyone seemed pleased when she lost 15 pounds in the next month. Although Julia was already anorexic by Thanksgiving, in evident danger, her parents and the fraternity boys continued to give her emotional incentives to continue dieting.

Bulimia Nervosa

bulimia nervosa An eating disorder in which the person, usually a female, engages repeatedly in episodes of binge eating followed by purging through induced vomiting or use of laxatives.

About three times as common as anorexia, especially among young female adults, is the other major eating disorder of our time, **bulimia nervosa.** This condition involves compulsive binge eating, in which thousands of calories worth of food may be consumed within an hour or two, followed by purging through either vomiting or inducing diarrhea by taking massive does of laxatives. Such behaviors are performed on occasion by many young adult women; some studies find that half of all college women have binged and purged at least once (Fairburn & Wilson, 1993), while other research finds bulimia present in virtually every city (but not every rural area) of the world (Nasser, 1997).

To warrant a clinical diagnosis of bulimia, bingeing and purging must occur at least once a week for three months, and the person must have uncontrollable urges to overeat and must show a distorted self-judgment based on misperceived body size. Between 1 and 3 percent of women in the United States are clinically bulimic during early adulthood (American Psychiatric Association, 2000). People who suffer from bulimia are usually close to normal in weight and therefore unlikely to starve to death. However, they can experience serious health problems, including severe damage to the gastrointestinal system and cardiac arrest from the strain of electrolyte imbalance (Gordon, 2000).

Theories of Eating Disorders

Although bulimia typically emerges in early adulthood, its origins lie in puberty or even earlier. According to longitudinal research, 12-year-olds who overeat to the point that they feel painfully stuffed are more likely to be bulimic by age 19 than are 12-year-olds who have never overeaten to that degree (Calam & Waller, 1998). Other research suggests that even in infancy and childhood,

> parental control in child feeding may have unintended effects on the development of eating patterns; emphasis on "external" cues in eating and decreased opportunities for the child to experience *self*-control in each . . . parental pressure to eat may result in food dislike and refusal, and restriction may enhance children's liking and consumption of restricted foods.
>
> *[Fisher & Birch, 2001, p. 35]*

Anorexia and bulimia are not the only serious eating disorders that become more common in adolescence. Some teenagers become obese, some binge without purging, some purge without bingeing. In all these disorders, eating is disconnected from the internal cue of hunger, instead serving some psychological or social need. The stresses, weight gain, and changing body shape of puberty, in a culture obsessed with thinness, make every contemporary teenage and young adult woman vulnerable (Gordon, 2000). Most do not develop a disorder, either for genetic reasons, because they have a habit of restraint, or because their mothers are not demanding and intrusive, like Julia's mother. But almost every female understands the wish to be a little thinner and thus ignores the early signs of disease.

From a developmental perspective, it is not surprising that the roots of eating disorders are in childhood and that genes, habits, and parental care contribute to the problem. But it is not obvious why females are so much more likely than males to be caught up in such destructive self-sabotage. Each theory of development offers an explanation:

- A *psychoanalytic* hypothesis is that women develop eating disorders because of a conflict with their mothers, who provided their first nourishment and from whom the daughters cannot psychically separate.

- *Behaviorism* notes that for some people with low self-esteem (more often women than men), fasting, bingeing, and purging "have powerful effects as immediate reinforcers—that is, [as means of] relieving states of emotional distress and tension" (Gordon, 1990), thus setting up a destructive stimulus–response chain.

- One *cognitive* explanation is that as women compete with men in business and industry, they want to project a strong, self-controlled, masculine image antithetical to the buxom, fleshy body of the ideal woman of the past.

- *Sociocultural* explanations include the contemporary cultural pressure to be "slim and trim" and model-like—a pressure that seems to be felt particularly by unmarried young women seeking autonomy from their parents, especially when the parents espouse traditional values (Nasser, 1997).

- The *epigenetic systems* perspective emphasizes the genetic roots of disorders and the impact they may have on the evolutionary mandate to reproduce. Since girls with eating disorders sometimes stop developing completely and do not ovulate at all, they avoid pregnancy. In addition, their bony appearance and their obsession prevent young men from becoming romantically interested in them. For girls who are frightened by the physical impulses of normal puberty, eating disorders can be a powerful defense.

No matter what the explanation, in many girls who should be proud of growing into independent young women, puberty triggers fear and a distorted body image.

Response for College Roommates (from page 452): How would you feel if your roommate died because you kept quiet? Discuss your concerns with your roommate, presenting facts as well as feelings. You cannot make anyone change, but you must raise the issue—and perhaps consult the college health service.

Drug Use and Abuse

The topic of drugs is a lightning rod for distorted statistics, latent prejudices, and murky thinking. Let's look for clarity, beginning with definitions. **Drug use** is simply the ingestion of a drug, regardless of the amount or effect. **Drug abuse** is the ingestion of a drug to the extent that it impairs the user's biological or psychological well-being. **Drug addiction** occurs when a person craves more of a drug in order to feel physically or psychologically at ease. Addiction is easiest to spot when absence of the drug arouses symptoms of withdrawal, such as restlessness, depression, or physical disturbance (dizziness, nausea, and the like).

Drug *abuse* is always harmful. Drug *use* may or may not be harmful, depending on the reasons for, and the effects of, the use. Whether or not drugs always have a harmful effect on adolescents is a matter of judgment. Some nations, including the United States, judge that almost any nonmedicinal drug use by persons under age 18 is harmful. Indeed, some jurisdictions within the United States forbid the sale of alcohol to anyone of any age or cigarette smoking except in a private home or out of doors. Some religions forbid any drug use, while others include drugs or alcohol as an essential part of religious ceremony.

The Gateway Drugs

Research on adolescent drug use has focused especially on the **gateway drugs:** alcohol, tobacco, and marijuana. These three are called gateway drugs because their use is often the initial step toward drug abuse and addiction, either to these drugs or to more obviously harmful substances. Not every teenager who tries gateway drugs goes on to harder drugs, but everyone who uses any, or many, harmful drugs began with gateway drugs (see Figure 14.3).

An additional danger is that adolescents who use gateway drugs tend to be more violent, a connection found in every ethnic group and income bracket and among drug users of both genders. For example, although girls are generally less violent than boys, they become increasingly destructive and hurtful when they use alcohol or marijuana (Dornbusch et al., 1999). The connection between gateway drugs and later polydrug use, violence, sexual activity, and school failure has been found again and again; drug use is both a cause and a symptom (Cairns & Cairns, 1994; Kandel & Davies, 1996; Raskin-White et al., 1999).

Most adolescents and many parents, relying on their personal experience, are unfazed by warnings that early drug experimentation will lead to dire consequences. On this topic, research is very helpful, because it shows that the gateway drugs have far more damaging effects on young adolescents than on adults.

Tobacco The use of tobacco decreases food consumption and interferes with the absorption of nutrients. As a result, a person's growth rate slows down. Young steady smokers are significantly shorter and smaller than they would have been if they had not started smoking until they were fully grown. In fact, cigarettes are the only forbidden drug that adolescent girls use as much as boys, partly because cigarettes reduce appetite, growth, and weight gain. This immediate benefit comes with a long-term cost: The girl who smokes becomes a less developed and shorter woman, often with an addiction that impairs lung capacity and increases cancer risk.

In both sexes, smoking markedly reduces fertility, an indication that the entire sexual/reproductive system is probably affected (Fiscella et al., 1998). Impairment is particularly likely when a young person's body is just beginning to adjust to the fluctuating hormones that characterize adulthood.

drug use The ingestion of a drug, regardless of the amount or effect.

drug abuse The ingestion of a drug to the extent that it impairs the user's biological or psychological well-being.

drug addiction A situation in which a person craves more of a drug in order to feel physically or psychologically at ease.

gateway drugs Drugs—usually tobacco, alcohol, and marijuana—whose use increases the risk that a person will later use harder drugs, such as cocaine and heroin.

FIGURE 14.3 Why Stop at the Gate? Adolescents sneer at scare tactics suggesting that use of gateway drugs will make them lifetime addicts or serious drug abusers. This happens only sometimes: It is not inevitable. However, there is truth in the second possibility: One way to avoid the use of hard drugs and their destructive consequences is to avoid any use at all of gateway drugs.

Gateway Drugs: Cause and Effect (Two Possibilities)

One

Use of → Sometimes but not usually leads to
Tobacco / Alcohol / Marijuana → Addiction / Use of harder drugs (cocaine, heroin, hallucinogens) / Unsafe sex, teen pregnancy / Violence, arrest

Two

Use of → Almost always begins with use of
Cocaine, crack / Heroin / Hallucinogens → Tobacco / Alcohol / Marijuana

Nicotine, a toxic chemical found in tobacco, is probably the most addictive drug of all. The great majority of adolescents who become steady smokers are quickly hooked. Yet, just as with other addictions (such as to weight loss or gambling), teenagers seem blithely unaware that they are at risk (Orford, 2001). For example, one study of teenage smokers found that only 5 percent thought they would still be smoking in five years, even though 75 percent of all adolescent smokers are still smoking in early adulthood. In this study, five out of six had tried to quit smoking, but only one in six had succeeded. The others had tried to stop and failed—but still believed that they would not be smoking as young adults (Siquera et al., 2001). This exaggerated sense of control is accompanied by another naive belief: Although research finds that the life span of the average adult smoker is reduced by 10 years because of cancer, stroke, and heart disease, 40 percent of eighth-graders believed there is "no great risk" in smoking half a pack of cigarettes a day (Johnston et al., 2001).

Looking Cool Their tight clothing, heavy makeup, multiple rings, and cigarettes are meant to convey to the world that Sheena, 15, and Jessica, 16, are mature, sophisticated women. Tobacco is the one gateway drug that girls use as much as boys, perhaps because boys have other ways of communicating their readiness to take on the world.

? *Observational Quiz* (see answer, page 458): Did these girls buy their own cigarettes?

Alcohol Drinking alcohol is more harmful in adolescence than in adulthood. One reason is that, even in small doses, alcohol loosens inhibitions and impairs judgment—dangerous in young persons who are already coping with major physical, sexual, and emotional changes. Another reason is that drinking in adolescence correlates with abnormal brain development; alcohol impairs memory and self-control by damaging the hippocampus and the prefrontal cortex (De Bellis et al., 2000; Brown et al., 2000).

Remembering that correlation is not causation, you may wonder whether these brain abnormalities predated the alcohol use, perhaps making these young people become drinkers because they could not think as clearly as normal adolescents. Neurologists tested this possibility by giving high doses of alcohol to lower animals, finding that alcohol does not merely correlate with the abnormalities, but causes them (White et al., 2000). Although some early drinkers already have emotional or attention difficulties, most early drinkers are well liked by their peers; they drink not because they are socially isolated but because they are part of a social group.

Especially for Older Brothers and Sisters: A friend said she saw your 13-year-old sister smoking. Should you tell your parents?

Marijuana The third gateway drug, marijuana, seriously slows down thinking processes, particularly those related to memory and abstract reasoning. Such impairment is especially problematic in early adolescence, when academic learning requires greater memory and a higher level of abstract thinking.

In addition, over time, repeated marijuana "mellowness" may turn into a general lack of motivation and indifference toward the future. The result is apathy at the very time when young people should be focusing their energy on meeting the challenges of growing up. This explains the results of a longitudinal study in which children who became marijuana users experienced a developmental slowdown in adulthood. They were later than their peers to graduate from college, to obtain steady employment, and to marry (Brook et al., 1999).

Celebrating Alcohol These young people in a Florida motel room, rejoicing in their beer, have temporarily—and artificially—overcome the awkwardness and unease that most teenagers feel with each other.

Patterns of Adolescent Drug Use

Almost every teenager tries one or more of the gateway drugs; by high school graduation, most have tried all three. This has been confirmed by numerous studies among many populations in various nations. One of the most notable and reliable of these is an annual, detailed, confidential survey of nearly 50,000 eighth-, tenth-, and twelfth-grade students from more than 400 high schools in the United States. Since its inception in 1975, this survey (called *Monitoring the Future*) has shown that more than 8 out

! *Answer to Observational Quiz* (from page 457): No, they bummed them from a stranger at this San Jose, California, shopping mall. If you answered no, you probably had in mind the fact that most states, including California, are strictly enforcing their laws against selling cigarettes to minors. You may also have noticed the awkward way the girls are holding their cigarettes and realized that they have not yet been smoking long enough to become addicted to nicotine, but are smoking to get attention.

generational forgetting The tendency of a particular cohort of young people to be ignorant of what the previous cohort learned about the consequences of the use of a drug because the younger group has not personally witnessed the effects of that drug.

of 10 high school seniors have drunk alcohol (more than a few sips), 2 out of 3 have smoked at least one cigarette, and about half have tried at least one illegal drug, usually marijuana (Johnston et al., 2002). The numbers vary somewhat from year to year, but the most recent survey still reports that 80 percent have tried alcohol and 54 percent have tried at least one illegal drug.

Experimentation and Regular Use In theory, one taste or puff is merely an experiment. However, these are called gateway drugs for a reason; Most one-time users become repeat users, and some become addicts or soon turn to other more harmful drugs. To discount the curious experimenter, a more valid measure of drug abuse may be drug use in the past 30 days. More than half of all high school seniors admit to using at least one drug in the past month, with alcohol the most common but cigarettes, marijuana, and other illegal drugs common as well (see Figure 14.4). Every use reported here is against the law, and actual use is higher than the percentage on the chart, not only because teenagers underreport their serious drug use, but also because high school absentees and dropouts do not receive this questionnaire.

The *Monitoring the Future* survey also finds that drug use, particularly daily use and abuse, increases throughout late adolescence among college and non-college youth (Johnston et al., 2002). Thus, although gateway drug use typically begins in adolescence, serious problems build from that point, usually reaching the level of abuse and addiction by the mid-20s. For example, in one recent year in Los Angeles, no teenager died of a drug overdose, but 562 adults did (Males, 1999). This does not mean that teen drug use is harmless, only that serious consequences are often not immediately evident. Members of each new generation begin this destructive journey, heedless of where it might lead.

Learning from Someone Else One problem is **generational forgetting**, the tendency of a particular cohort of young people to forget about the consequences of the use of a drug when they have not personally witnessed the effects of that drug. The use of certain drugs—crack, marijuana, and LSD among them— decreased in the 1980s as young potential users saw the effects on their older friends. Today, now that generational forgetting has taken place, the use of these drugs has risen again. For example, in 1979, 37 percent of high school seniors had smoked marijuana at least once, and daily in some cases, in the past 30 days. As young people began to see the long-term effects, the 30-day rate dropped to

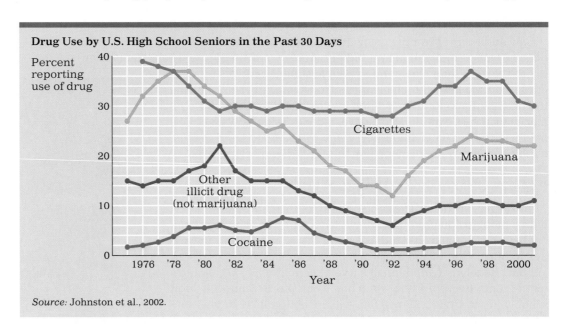

FIGURE 14.4 **Rise and Fall** By asking the same questions year after year, the Monitoring the Future study shows notable historical effects. It is encouraging that something in the society, not something in the adolescent, makes drug use increase and decrease. However, as Chapter 1 emphasized, survey research can not prove what causes change.

Drug Use by U.S. High School Seniors in the Past 30 Days

Percent reporting use of drug

Cigarettes

Marijuana

Other illicit drug (not marijuana)

Cocaine

Year

Source: Johnston et al., 2002.

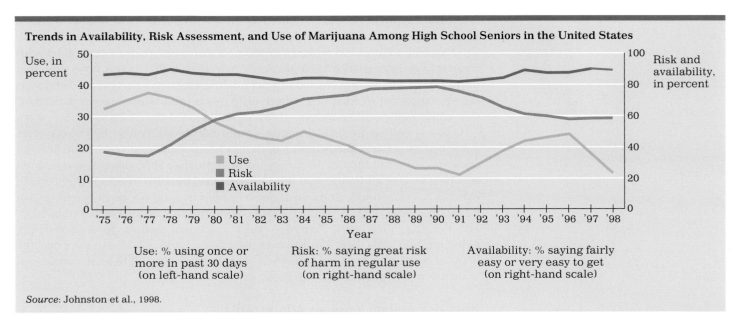

Trends in Availability, Risk Assessment, and Use of Marijuana Among High School Seniors in the United States

Use: % using once or more in past 30 days (on left-hand scale)

Risk: % saying great risk of harm in regular use (on right-hand scale)

Availability: % saying fairly easy or very easy to get (on right-hand scale)

Source: Johnston et al., 1998.

12 percent by the early 1990s. Because marijuana was then less popular, and that generation did not personally witness its consequences, 30-day use rose again, to 22 percent in 2001 (Johnston et al., 2002). Careful tracking of marijuana attitudes and use show that supply (always plentiful) and legality (never) do not affect use by adolescents nearly as much as attitudes do, with a lag of a year or two between attitudes and actions (see Figure 14.5).

Adolescents tend not to listen to warnings about drug use from older people. The evidence that might sway an adolescent is the testimony of a young addict who quit or the death of a well-known young hero. After basketball star Len Bias died suddenly of cocaine use in 1986, there was a dramatic decline (by a third) in past-month use of cocaine. As the memory lingered, cocaine use was low for eight years (the year before Bias died, the rate was 7 percent; seven years later, 1 percent). By 1993, those who were teenagers had never heard of Len Bias or other famous stars who had died of drugs; generational forgetting has led to a gradual increase in the use of cocaine and other drugs since 1993 (Johnston et al., 2001).

Cultural Differences

Researchers find that cohorts and cultures vary markedly in the psychological effects of adolescent drug use. There is some evidence that drug experimentation may have helped certain adolescent cohorts over rough spots in their lives. For example, a longitudinal study found that adolescents in California in the 1980s who never tried any drugs were more troubled psychologically, even as children, than those who experimented with at least one illegal drug and stopped (Shedler & Block, 1990). Similarly, an in-depth study on the East Coast of the United States found that drinking alcohol and smoking marijuana helped adolescents bond with their peers (Lightfoot, 1997).

Whether a particular teenager uses drugs, and what drugs he or she uses, depends largely on his or her peers as well as on the wider community. For instance, only 40 percent of ninth- to twelfth-graders in the heavily Mormon state of Utah had puffed on a cigarette even once, but 75 percent of ninth- to twelfth-graders in West Virginia had done so. Many of them were already daily smokers (CDC, June 9, 2000). For Mormon youth, smoking would not impress their friends or family, but West Virginia teens who smoked might be considered mature. Among many adolescents, aggression, drug experimentation,

FIGURE 14.5 Not Supply and Demand, but Attitude and Action Marijuana has been easily available to almost nine out of ten U.S. high school seniors over the past 25 years, but actual pot smoking is closely related to perception of risk, not to supply. These are patterns for high school seniors, a group most likely to be affected by their peers' attitudes. Adults and addicts are not as vulnerable to shifts in attitudes, except, perhaps, if those changing attitudes are their own.

Response for Older Brothers and Sisters (from page 457): Smoking is very addictive; you need to urge your sister to stop now. Most adolescents care more about immediate concerns than the distant possibility of cancer or heart disease, so tell her about a smoker you know whose teeth are yellow, who smells of smoke, and who is shorter than the rest of his or her family. Then tell your parents; they are your best allies in helping your sister have a healthy adolescence.

and misbehaving in class are admired as signs of maturity (Bukowski et al., 2000; Leaper & Anderson, 1997; Moffit, 1993a).

National culture also makes a difference. European nations have shown increases in drug use since 1980, particularly in heroin use, at the same time that overall drug use among North American adolescents has decreased. Variations are also apparent in Australia, where drug use is increasing in a particular pattern unlike that of either Europe or North America (Maxwell, 2000).

Closely related to such group-by-group norms are cohort-by-cohort averages. Just as music, clothes, and hairstyles change from one year to the next, so does drug use, not only in frequency (for lifetime use, 1978 saw an all-time high and 1992 saw an all-time low in the United States) but also in composition (marijuana is now stronger), in mode of delivery (heroin need not be injected), and in form (smokeless tobacco is much more common). New drugs come into fashion. For example, "ice" and "ecstasy" were unknown before 1990, and GBH, Ketamine, and bidis were almost never used before 1995, yet all five have become popular among high school seniors in recent years—and all five are considered quite harmful by medical researchers.

Drug Use Among Younger Adolescents

One other troubling problem is drug use among younger adolescents. The national survey of 400 high schools mentioned earlier also questioned eighth-graders (Johnston et al., 2002). In 2001 about 51 percent of all eighth-graders had already had at least one alcoholic drink and 37 percent had smoked at least one cigarette—numbers that, while high, are not significantly different from a decade ago. Other drugs that eighth-graders use include inhalants, which were tried by about 17 percent during the 1990s, even though single use can lead to brain damage and death.

However, use of some drugs is increasing among younger adolescents. In 2001, 20 percent of eighth-graders surveyed had tried marijuana (twice as many as in 1991) and 4 percent had tried cocaine, again twice as many as a decade before (Johnston et al., 2002). Another sample, smaller in size but focusing particularly on young adolescents, found that between seventh and ninth grades, cigarette smoking increased from 32 to 55 percent, alcohol drinking from 55 to 80 percent, and marijuana use from 4 to 23 percent (Griffin et al., 2000).

From these data, it seems that antidrug education, if it is intended to forestall the first use of various drugs, should occur at about age 12 or before. This is particularly important for parents to understand, because parents tend to condone occasional use of some substances by their children. One longitudinal New Zealand study found that half the parents allowed their very young children (age 9 or younger) to have an occasional sip of alcohol. A decade later, these same children were most likely to be alcoholics (Casswell, 1996) (see Figure 14.6). A study in Scotland found that parents of middle-school children were most worried about their children's use of illegal drugs, somewhat resigned about their early smoking and drinking, and oblivious to the dangers of solvent sniffing. In fact, the actual prevalence rates of these practices—rare, common, and

FIGURE 14.6 Almost Everybody Drinks This longitudinal study of New Zealanders found that 80 percent of all 18-year-olds had at least one alcohol-related problem in the past year. Problems ranged from the very serious (one in twenty had had a car crash) to the almost-normal (half had had hangovers). Perhaps most disturbing were signs of alcoholism: 44 percent had awakened unable to remember events of the night before, and 14 percent drank first thing in the morning. However, even in a teen culture where almost everyone drank, childhood drinking made a difference, as you can see. A child who had not tasted alcohol at age 9 was half as likely to have a problem related to alcohol at 18 as a child of 9 who had been given a drink (usually a beer). Most of those who were drinking by age 9 were in trouble by age 18, some of them with many more than three alcohol-related problems.

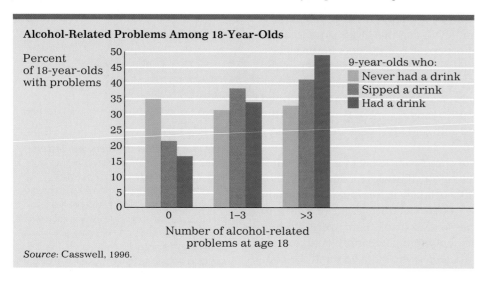

Alcohol-Related Problems Among 18-Year-Olds

Source: Casswell, 1996.

sometimes lethal, respectively—were the opposite of the parents' level of concern (Boyland et al., 1998). This raises a larger issue: What can be done to keep younger adolescents, in particular, away from gateway drugs?

Changing Policy

Postponing Teenage Drug Experimentation

If experimental use of gateway drugs cannot be completely prevented (and in some cohorts and cultures, this may be the case), it should at least be postponed until a young person is fully grown and mature enough to monitor the risks and recognize the early signs of possible addiction. How can this postponement be accomplished?

Some adults believe that any antidrug effort is a step in the right direction. This is not true; even well-intentioned efforts can boomerang. The best example is one of the most popular and costly drug education programs in the United States. In Project D.A.R.E. (Drug Abuse Resistance Education), police officers go into classrooms from kindergarten through high school to present a curriculum that emphasizes the harmfulness of drugs, including videos of the frightening consequences of illegal drug abuse. Parents, politicians, and police departments like the program, funding it generously and extensively; but longitudinal research has found that the only benefit is a short-term increase in knowledge about specific drugs.

Students who experience D.A.R.E. are no more likely to abstain from drugs over the high school years than those who do not (Clayton et al., 1996; Ennett et al., 1994; Wysong et al., 1994). Is there some long-term "sleeper" effect, protecting D.A.R.E. recipients in young adulthood? No. In fact, 10 years later, the only difference between one group of high school students who had experienced D.A.R.E. and another group who had not was that the D.A.R.E. group had lower self-esteem than the non-D.A.R.E. group (Lynam et al., 1999). Actual drug use by the two groups was similar, but the D.A.R.E group felt worse about themselves.

Another research project used group discussions among delinquent youth in an intense summer-camp experience as a way of guiding teenagers toward constructive behavior. Again, longitudinal research found that they fared worse: They were more likely to use drugs and to be arrested than those without such group training (Dishion et al., 1999). Finally, research evaluating antimarijuana advertisements found that some actually make smoking marijuana seem more attractive (Fishbein et al., 2002). Messages warning against other drugs can similarly backfire (Block et al., 2002).

Drug education programs must be carefully developed, with teen involvement, adult example, and accurate research findings and evaluation procedures. A recent decline in cigarette smoking among adolescents (see Figure 14.7) followed headline news about the addictiveness of nicotine, unethical business practices by tobacco companies, and the hazards of secondhand smoke, as well as higher taxes on cigarettes, and greater penalties for tobacco sales to minors. Advertisements aimed at young adolescents, such as those featuring the cartoon character Joe Camel, have been banned. Some states

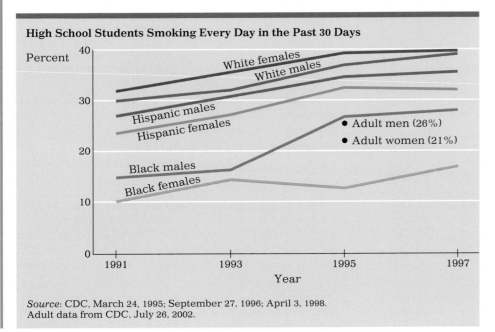

High School Students Smoking Every Day in the Past 30 Days

Source: CDC, March 24, 1995; September 27, 1996; April 3, 1998.
Adult data from CDC, July 26, 2002.

FIGURE 14.7 Current Cigarette Use Among Ninth- to Twelfth-Graders Cigarette use among U.S. high school students has begun to decline since 1997 (see Appendix A). However, the overall average of 35 percent for females and 38 percent for males is substantially above the average for adults.

have used the settlement money from successful lawsuits to fund youth antismoking campaigns. Florida was one. In that state from 1998 to 2000, smoking declined by 40 percent among middle school students (Bauer et al., 2000).

More generally, two grounds for hope have emerged from the research. One is that adolescent drug use is powerfully influenced by social conditions, cultural norms, and peer groups. Cigarette smoking among teenagers varies not only by generation but also by sex and ethnic group. In many nations, the rate of smoking among female adolescents is less than half that of males; the United States is the only nation where the smoking rate among girls sometimes exceeds the rate among boys. African-American teens have low rates of cigarette smoking as well as most other drug use. Thus, although the stresses of puberty sometimes seem to increase drug use (Wills et al., 1996), puberty does not make drug use inevitable or universal.

The second reason for hope is that researchers are finding factors that protect against drug use (Benson et al., 1998). One is an active, problem-solving style of coping (Wills et al., 2001); another is a sense of competence and well-being (Griffin et al., 2001); a third is cognitive maturity (Ammerman et al., 2001). A solid family and school background that enhances all these cognitive skills, while keeping drugs out of reach, may protect young people against addiction. Most addicts start their drug use in adolescence, even if they do not become addicts until later on.

Adolescent drug use and abuse are far from inevitable; advanced thinking and coping skills can postpone, moderate, or prevent drug use. Public policy that encourages parent–child conversations (not necessarily about drugs), that supports religious and community organizations, and that sponsors after-school sports, drama, music, and even midnight basketball may be a drug-prevention program in disguise.

Centuries ago puberty did not begin until age 16 or so, when the adolescent mind and social context may have been ready for the challenges of sexual awakening and the growth spurt. Today, however, when puberty begins at age 11 or 12, young people may not be cognitively or socially capable of the autonomy their bodies seek. Fortunately, the social context can make a difference in how teenagers respond to their biological growth. Education and social pressures still guide young people in positive and healthy directions. These issues are further explored in the next two chapters, on cognitive and psychosocial development.

SUMMARY

Puberty Begins

1. Puberty refers to the various changes that transform a child's body into an adult one. Biochemical signals from the hypothalamus to the pituitary gland to the adrenal glands and back again lead to increased levels of testosterone, estrogen, and various other hormones, causing the body to grow and change.

2. The visible changes of puberty normally occur any time from about ages 9 to 14; the child's sex, genetic background, body fat, and level of family stress all contribute to this variation. Girls generally begin and end the process before boys do, and contemporary young people in developed nations experience puberty earlier than young people growing up in earlier centuries or in impoverished areas of the modern world.

The Biological Changes

3. The growth spurt is an acceleration of growth in every part of the body. The peak weight increase usually comes before the peak height and then peak muscle increase. The lungs and the heart also increase in size and capacity. The entire process is usually completed about three to four years after it begins.

4. Sexual characteristics emerge at puberty. The maturation of primary sexual characteristics means that by age 13 or so, menarche and spermarche have occurred, and the young person is able to reproduce.

5. Secondary sexual characteristics are not directly involved in reproduction but signify whether the person is a man or a woman. Body shape, breasts, voice, body hair, and numerous other features differentiate males and females.

Emotional Responses to Physical Growth

6. Puberty is accompanied by many emotions. Some, such as quick mood shifts and thoughts about sex, are directly caused by hormones, but most are only indirectly hormonal. Instead they are caused by other people's reactions to the adolescent body changes; hence, they are more a matter of nurture than nature.

7. An adolescent's self-esteem often depends on body image. Girls are particularly troubled if their bodies do not seem to conform to their ideal. Boys who mature late and girls who mature early are stressed by the sociocultural consequences of not being "on time."

8. The biological impulse to become sexually active in adolescence is strong, for genetic reasons. Whether or not a teenager acts on that impulse depends largely on culture and context. Two common hazards are sexually transmitted diseases and unwanted pregnancies.

9. Childhood sexual abuse does not necessarily involve force or genital contact, but it is likely to make it difficult for the victim to establish normal, intimate relationships in adulthood. Puberty is often the most vulnerable time for sexual abuse, since older children are attractive to adults but are not yet able to protect themselves.

Health and Hazards

10. Adolescents tend to be healthy. Diseases are rare, both mild ones (such as colds and flu) and serious ones (such as cancer and heart disease). However, adolescents take risks that can lead to injury and accidental death at a rate five times that of younger children.

11. To sustain body growth, most adolescents consume large quantities of food, although they do not always make healthy choices. The most serious problems occur when eating disorders, such as anorexia and bulimia nervosa, take over. They can be lethal.

12. Adolescent eating disorders have roots in childhood, are partly genetic, and are influenced by culture. Early awareness and treatment of the problem are crucial, but cultural recognition of the dangers is not widespread.

13. Many adolescents use drugs, partly because they like to experiment, to rebel against adults, and to reduce the stresses of puberty. Drug abuse (including the gateway drugs—tobacco, alcohol, and marijuana) is even more harmful in adolescence than at later ages because of the physiological and psychological immaturity of the young person.

14. Each culture and cohort finds its own patterns of drug use and abuse during adolescence. Generational forgetting and some misguided adult attitudes make teen drug use an ongoing problem. Lessons learned from the research can somewhat modify and postpone drug use until the person is better able to make wise decisions.

KEY TERMS

adolescence (p. 431)
puberty (p. 432)
hypothalamus (p. 432)
pituitary gland (p. 432)
adrenal glands (p. 432)
HPA axis (p. 433)
gonads (p. 433)
estrogen (p. 433)

testosterone (p. 433)
menarche (p. 434)
spermarche (p. 434)
growth spurt (p. 436)
primary sex characteristics (p. 439)
secondary sex characteristics (p. 439)

body image (p. 443)
sexually transmitted diseases (STDs) (p. 445)
sexual abuse (p. 448)
child sexual abuse (p. 448)
body mass index (BMI) (p. 450)
anorexia nervosa (p. 452)

bulimia nervosa (p. 454)
drug use (p. 456)
drug abuse (p. 456)
drug addiction (p. 456)
gateway drugs (p. 456)
generational forgetting (p. 458)

KEY QUESTIONS

1. What problems are caused for adolescents by the sequence of the growth spurt?

2. Why would some adolescents begin puberty two years earlier than their peers?

3. What are the consequences of the variations among ethnic groups in average age of puberty?

4. Why are adolescents said to be moody during puberty?

5. What are the essential similarities in male and female growth during adolescence?

6. What are the crucial differences between male and female growth during adolescence?

7. Why would an adolescent be slow to obtain medical attention for sexual concerns? What are the consequences of this reluctance?

8. Compare the causes and consequences of anorexia and bulimia.

9. Why do adolescents try the gateway drugs, even though it is illegal for minors to purchase them?

10. Which approaches are effective in preventing adolescent drug use? Which are ineffective?

11. What is the relationship between a person's age and drug use, drug abuse, and drug addiction?

Chapter Fifteen

Adolescence: Cognitive Development

Talking with a 16-year-old about international politics, about hot new music, or about the meaning of life is obviously quite different from conversing on the same topics with an 8-year-old. Thanks to major advances in cognition, adolescents are increasingly aware of both world concerns and personal needs—other people's as well as their own—and they are more adult in their use of analysis, logic, and reason.

However, as thinking develops and knowledge increases, young people become more vulnerable to ideas, speculations, and insights that are troubling or even dangerous. They may appear tough-minded; at least, their frequent sarcasm, cynicism, and arrogance give this impression. But the opposite is more likely true. Adolescents can be naive, idealistic, troubled by their own introspections, and supersensitive to criticism, real or imagined.

In this chapter we will explore adolescent thought processes, including both their advanced logical powers (sometimes called analytic, or formal, thinking) and their greater emotional force (sometimes called intuitive, or egocentric, thinking). Then we will describe the mutual impact of adolescent minds and the schools where they study. Finally, we look at adolescent decision making, particularly regarding risk taking, vocations, and sex. Adolescents ask, "If we love each other, why shouldn't we show it by having sex?" and "Why should I study things I don't want to learn?" and even "What is the meaning of life?" and come up with answers that differ from those found by most adults. Teenagers are risk takers, but not without reason.

Intellectual Advances

Adolescent thinking advances in three ways: Basic cognitive skills continue to develop, logic emerges, and intuitive thinking becomes quicker and more compelling. Let's look at each of these three changes in turn.

More and Better Cognitive Skills

First, every basic skill of information processing, described in previous chapters, continues to progress during adolescence. Selective attention becomes more skillfully deployed, enabling students to do homework when they are surrounded by peers or blaring music (or both) *if* motivation is high. Expanded memory skills and a growing knowledge base allow adolescents to connect new ideas and concepts to old ones. Metamemory and metacognition help them become better students. This, in turn, deepens their understanding of calculus and chemistry, fads and friendship, and everything else they set their minds to.

Brain maturation also continues. Myelination is ongoing, making reaction time even shorter, not only on the athletic field but also in the classroom. Adolescents are able to grasp, connect, and refute ideas much faster than younger children can (Sampaio & Truwitt, 2001). The prefrontal cortex, in particular, becomes more densely packed and more efficient, enabling adolescents to plan their lives, to analyze possibilities, and to pursue goals much more effectively than children can. In fact, the executive functions of the brain, which originate primarily in the prefrontal cortex, improve markedly throughout adolescence but improve only slightly in young adulthood, when these functions slow down again (Cepeda et al., 2001). Memory increases as well, not only implicit but also explicit memory, so that the teenager can "cram" for a test all night, score well, and then forget most of the memorized facts a week later.

Language mastery improves. Vocabulary continues to build, adding technical as well as derivative words. The nuances of grammar are better understood; adolescents can figure out why certain rules are used and when exceptions should be made. This makes code-switching more sophisticated: Most adolescents have several speech codes, using different ones for parents and teachers, for same-sex and other-sex friends, and so on. Many adolescents develop a personal style in their writing and speech. Poets, diarists, and debaters emerge in every high school classroom.

hypothetical thought Thought that includes propositions and possibilities that may or may not reflect reality.

Hypothetical thought is thought that involves reasoning about propositions that may or may not reflect reality. For younger children, imagined possibilities (such as in pretend play) are always tied to the everyday world as they know or wish it to be. For adolescents, possibility takes on a life of its own. "Here and now" is only one of many alternatives that include not only "there and then" but also "long, long ago," "nowhere," "not yet," and "never."

The adolescent's ability to ignore the real and think about the possible is clear in this hypothetical example: If an impoverished college student were offered $100 to argue in favor of the view that government should *never* give or lend money to impoverished college students, he or she could probably earn the money by providing a convincing (if insincere) argument. This demonstrates that the college student has mastered the skill of hypothetical thought. By contrast, school-age children have great difficulty arguing against their personal beliefs, especially if those personal beliefs arise from their own situation. An 8-year-old would find it impossible to give three good reasons why parents should never give birthday presents to their children, even if the child knew this argument was "just pretend."

Abstraction Way Beyond Counting on Fingers and Toes This high school student explains a calculus problem, a behavior that requires a level of hypothetical and abstract thought beyond that of any concrete operational child—and of most adults. At the beginning of concrete operational thought, children need blocks, coins, and other tangible objects to help them understand math. By later adolescence, in the full flower of formal operational thought, such practical and concrete illustrations are irrelevant.

For almost any teenager, reflection about any serious issue becomes a complicated process. The complications were illustrated on a personal level by one high school student who wanted to keep her friend from making a life-threatening decision but did not want to judge her, because

> to . . . judge [someone] means that whatever you are saying is right and you know what's right. You know it's right for them and you know it's right in every situation. [But] you can't know if you are right. Maybe you are right. But then, right in what way?
>
> *[quoted in Gilligan et al., 1990]*

Although adolescents are not always sure what is "right in what way," they are quick to see what is "wrong." Unlike children, they do not accept current conditions because "that's how things are." Instead, they criticize what is, precisely because they can imagine how things could be, would be, should be in a world where justice was realized, people were always sincere, and the sanctity of human life was truly recognized. This is hypothetical thinking at its best.

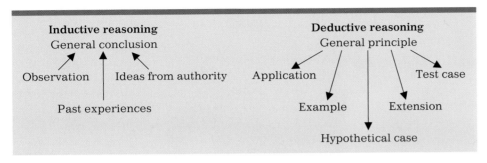

Inductive reasoning

General conclusion

Observation   Ideas from authority

Past experiences

Deductive reasoning

General principle

Application   Test case

Example   Extension

Hypothetical case

FIGURE 15.1 **Bottom Up or Top Down?** Children are more likely to draw conclusions on the basis of their own experiences and what they have been told, as you might expect from concrete operational thinkers. This is called inductive, or bottom-up, reasoning. Adolescents can think deductively, from the top down. One way to remember this distinction is that *in*ductive reasoning begins *in*side the problem; *de*ductive reasoning begins *de*tached from it. Since adolescents focus on the possible and the hypothetical, they are much more able to detach from reality.

As you saw in Chapter 12, during the school years, children increasingly use their accumulated knowledge of facts, as well as their personal experience, to reach conclusions. In essence, their reasoning goes like this: "If it waddles like a duck and quacks like a duck, then it must be a duck." Such reasoning from particulars ("waddles like" and "quacks like") to a general conclusion ("it's a duck") is called **inductive reasoning.**

During adolescence, as young people develop their capacity to think hypothetically, they soon become more capable of **deductive reasoning.** That is, they can begin with a general premise or theory, reason through one or more logical steps to draw a specific conclusion, and test the validity of that conclusion. Deduction is reasoning from the general to the specific: "If it's a duck, it will waddle and quack" (see Figure 15.1).

New Logical and Analytic Abilities

A second cognitive advance that occurs in adolescence is the development of deductive reasoning and hypothetical thought (Lutz & Sternberg, 1999; Moshman, 2000). Jean Piaget was the first to notice these new abilities, which he called

inductive reasoning Reasoning from one or more specific experiences or facts to a general conclusion.

deductive reasoning Reasoning from a general statement or principle, through logical steps, to a specific conclusion.

DOUG MARTIN / PHOTO RESEARCHERS, INC.

Deductive Reasoning High school chemistry classes first teach students the general principles and then ask them to test the principles with specific substances. There is no way a student could simply be given these materials and told to figure out some generalities, as a teacher of 8-year-olds, with much simpler and safer substances, might do. Younger children think inductively; these students think deductively as well.

Thinking Many Moves Ahead Unlike simple games of chance, which younger children enjoy, chess requires some deductive thinking, which involves general principles, such as protecting your king, focusing on the center, and changing strategies as the game progresses. These students are among 20 who played simultaneous chess games against an adult champion.

? *Observational Quiz* (see answer, page 471): Beyond the intellectual challenge of chess, what other type of problem do these adolescents seem to be solving?

formal operational thought In Piaget's theory, the fourth and final stage of cognitive development; arises from a combination of maturation and experience.

formal operational thought and identified as the fourth and final stage of his sequence of cognitive development. Formal operational thought arises from a combination of maturation and experience (Inhelder & Piaget, 1958).

Most developmentalists agree that adolescent thought is qualitatively different from children's thought (Fischer & Bidell, 1998; Flavell et al., 2001; Moshman, 1998). They disagree only about whether this change occurs quite suddenly as a new stage (Piaget) or gradually (information-processing theory), as the result of context (sociocultural theory) or biology (epigenetic systems theory).

Explanations differ as well. Information-processing theorists describe a new and higher level of cognition, the result of accumulated improvements in processing and memory. Sociocultural theorists point to intellectual advances that result when adolescents enter secondary school, where specialized teachers, changing classrooms, and long-term homework assignments constitute a new culture of learning. Epigenetic systems theory suggests that, just as genes trigger reproductive potential at puberty, genes permit intellectual deepening via new neural networks in the brain.

Hypothetical-Deductive Thought

The most prominent feature of the change in cognition that occurs at adolescence is the capacity to think of *possibility,* not just reality. Adolescents "start with possible solutions and progress to determine which is the real solution" (Lutz & Sternberg, 1999). This allows adolescents to think "outside the box" of tradition. They analyze probabilities, realizing with joy that some things are merely more possible than other, less probable, things; nothing is inevitable, and even the impossible can be considered (Falk & Wilkening, 1998). In Piaget's words:

> . . . there is a reversal of the direction of thinking between *reality* and *possibility* in the subject's method of approach. *Possibility* no longer appears merely as an extension of an empirical situation or of action actually performed. Instead, it is *reality* that is now secondary to *possibility.*
>
> [Inhelder & Piaget, 1958, p. 251; emphasis in the original]

This kind of possibility thinking is called *hypothetical-deductive thought*, because a hypothesis is something that is possible but not yet proven and because deductions are logical but not necessarily real.

An Example: Religious Freedom Versus Economic Justice The power of deductive thought is most evident when moral issues are involved, because then rationality is tested by competing principles. Adolescents can do more than reason from the general to the specific; they can even construct logical arguments and "deduce conclusions from premises explicitly known to be hypothetical or false" (Moshman, 1998, p. 957).

Consider an experiment that tested belief in freedom of religion (Helwig, 1995). When asked, three groups of adolescents—seventh-graders, eleventh-graders, and college students—in northern California all endorsed the abstract principle of free exercise of religion (in the U.S. Constitution's Bill of Rights). Then their easy endorsement was put to the test, with questions such as "What if a particular religion refused to allow low-income people to become priests?" This hypothetical *What-if* question would be rejected as impossible by most concrete operational thinkers, who have a very difficult time following any logical argument that begins with a false premise (Moshman, 2000). However, all three age groups of adolescents attempted to answer—and their answers varied by age. The youngest group switched quickly. Almost all of them (94 percent) abandoned freedom of religion if low-income priests were excluded. However, 81 percent of those in midadolescence (the eleventh-graders) stuck to their principles, using deductive reasoning to conclude that religious freedom held sway even when a particular religion seemed unfair.

If you are thinking that such cold logic is not always best, you may be reassured to learn that many psychologists hypothesize a fifth stage of reasoning that follows formal operational thought. This stage, sometimes called **postformal thought**, involves a struggle to reconcile logic and experience. In this experiment, the college students engaged in such a struggle: 38 percent decided that economic justice was a more important principle than religious freedom, while 62 percent felt that religious freedom was more important (see Figure 15.2).

When a person realizes that various moral values conflict, weighs the relative merits of each, and comes up with an overarching principle to guide behavior, that is logical deduction at its best. In Chapter 12's discussion of moral development, you learned that the last pair of Lawrence Kohlberg's stages, together called postconventional, require that the person understand conventional morality and then move beyond it. For instance, a person using postconventional reasoning would decide that Heinz should break the law and steal the expensive medicine because saving human life outweighs the need to respect property rights. Children virtually never reach postconventional moral reasoning; adolescents and adults sometimes do, if they can manage the intellectual challenge of coordinating various ethical perspectives (Carpendale, 2000). This is true not only for Kohlberg's stages but also for Carol Gilligan's "morality of care." In her description, struggling to balance the need for justice with the need to sustain human relationships is the most mature form of moral thought.

postformal thought A type of reasoning that, many psychologists believe, develops after formal operational thought. Postformal thought is well suited to solving real-world problems because it is less abstract and absolute than formal thought, more adaptable to life's inconsistencies, and more dialectical—capable of combining contradictory elements into a comprehensive whole.

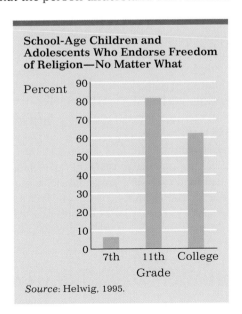

School-Age Children and Adolescents Who Endorse Freedom of Religion—No Matter What

Source: Helwig, 1995.

FIGURE 15.2 Adherence to Principle High school students are more capable of deductive reasoning than are middle schoolers, as shown by the fact that a much higher percentage of eleventh-graders were able to perceive religious freedom as a basic principle and to cling to it no matter what conflicting circumstances were proposed by the researcher. (College students were more aware that one of those conflicting circumstances might in itself represent a basic principle, so they were more likely than the eleventh-graders to temper their adherence to religious freedom.)

Thinking Like a Scientist

Piaget's Balance Experiment

Scientists not only develop theories but also develop experiments that refute or support their theories. To study the reasoning of children of various ages, Piaget and his colleagues devised a number of famous tasks designed to reveal the onset of hypothetical-deductive thought (Inhelder & Piaget, 1958). They sought to demonstrate that, "in contrast to concrete operational children, formal operational adolescents imagine all possible determinants, . . . systematically vary the factors one by one, observe the results correctly, keep track of the results, and draw the appropriate conclusions" (Miller, 2002).

In one experiment (diagrammed in Figure 15.3), children were asked to balance a scale with weights that could be hooked onto the scale's arms. To master this task, children must realize that the heaviness of the weights and their distance from the center interact reciprocally to affect balance, so that a heavier weight close to the middle can be counterbalanced with a lighter weight far from the center on the other side. This means that something half as far from the center must be twice as heavy (e.g., something weighing 6 grams and placed 4 centimeters to the left of the center will balance something weighing 12 grams and placed 2 centimeters to the right of the center).

This understanding, and a method to discover it, was completely beyond the ability of 3- to 5-year-olds. In Piaget's experiments, they randomly hung different weights on different hooks. By age 7, children realized that the scale could be balanced by putting the same amount of weight on both arms, but they didn't realize that the distance of the weights from the center of the scale is also important.

By age 10, near the end of the concrete operational stage, children often realized the importance of the weights' locations on the arms, but their efforts to coordinate weight and distance from the center to balance the scale involved trial-and-error experimentation, not logical deduction.

Finally, by about age 13 or 14, some children hypothesized that there is a relationship between a weight's distance from the center of the scale and the effect it has on a balance. By systematically testing this hypothesis, they correctly formulated the mathematical relation between weight and distance from the center and could solve the balance problem accurately and efficiently. Piaget attributed each of these advances to the children's attainment of the next-higher cognitive stage.

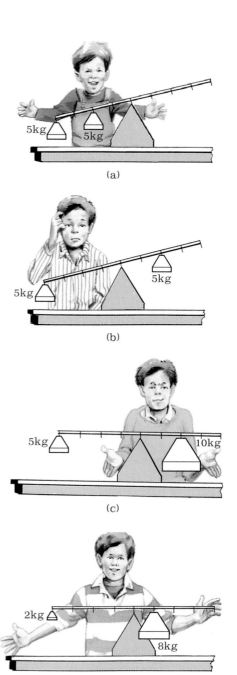

FIGURE 15.3 How to Balance a Beam Piaget's balance-scale test of formal reasoning, as it is attempted by (a) a 4-year-old, (b) a 7-year-old, (c) a 10-year-old, and (d) a 14-year-old. The key to balancing the scale is to make weight times distance from the center equal on both sides of the center; the realization of that principle requires formal operational thought.

Variations in Cognition

Hypothetical thought and deductive reasoning should make adolescents more flexible and resourceful thinkers. However, many adolescents (and adults) perform quite poorly on standard tests of deductive reasoning, such as the balance-scale task. Formal operational thought is not always demonstrated during adolescence, nor acquired by everyone. In fact, research with various populations in many nations over several decades finds that only about half of all adolescents and young adults perform at the formal operational level on Piaget's measures (Larivee et al., 2000).

Moreover, a teenager who can easily use deductive reasoning to figure out a mathematics problem may have great difficulty in deducing the solution to a problem in biology, or in assessing the ethics of various approaches to national health insurance, or in determining the most effective way to deal with a complex human dilemma. In other words, adolescents apply formal logic to some situations but not to others. It seems that each individual's intellect, experiences, talents, and interests affect his or her thinking at least as much as the ability to reason formally (Fischer & Bidell, 1998). Other researchers also stress the importance of human relationships and cultural contexts in advancing a particular adolescent toward formal operational thought (Case & Okamoto, 1996; Suizzo, 2000).

Educational and historical conditions have an effect as well. For example, one careful assessment of the reasoning processes of French 13- to 15-year-olds found about one-third at the concrete operational level, one-third at an intermediate level, and one-third at the formal operational level. Then, over a decade later, these assessments were repeated on another group of French students, similar in age and background to the first. They scored significantly higher. Despite variation from person to person and test to test, overall more than half scored at the formal level, most of the rest were in transition, and only a sixth were still at the concrete operational level (Flieller, 1999). This suggests that context (probably based on reforms of the French educational structure), not merely biology, affects attainment of hypothetical-deductive thought.

Piaget and his early followers realized that students vary, of course; no accurate observer would conclude that all adolescents think alike. However, they considered the differences insignificant, mere fluctuations. More recent scholars, however, believe that "variations in developmental level are routine and pervasive, and they need to be explained, not ignored" (Fischer & Rose, 1996, p. 209).

The strongest critics of Piaget are sociocultural theorists, who believe variations based on cultural or historical experiences prove the basic premise of their theory. This conclusion was reached by Vygotsky and Luria 80 years ago, when they found the peasants of eastern Russia stunningly illogical and simple-minded when asked questions that were routinely taught in secondary school (Luria, 1976).

More generally, because Piaget's tests of formal operational thought rely on examples (such as the scale-balancing problem) that might arise in high school science class, sociocultural theorists suggest that these tests of formal thought may be biased in favor of elite students who are exposed to a curriculum devised by Western educators. From the sociocultural perspective, it comes as no surprise that many adolescents and adults fail at such tests, even if they use hypothetical-deductive reasoning in other domains.

The sociocultural criticism of Piaget's stage theory may be too harsh, but research from all theoretical perspectives finds that adolescents are not always logical, even when they have earned high grades in their study of advanced science and math (Larivee et al., 2000). This fact has led to recognition of another form of thinking, which also becomes more prominent during adolescence, as you will now learn.

! Answer to Observational Quiz (from page 468): The photo shows partners who must collaborate in order to produce the desired outcome. How to work with another adolescent is the most urgent curriculum of all during the secondary school years, requiring speculation, strategy, and study of each individual case.

More Intuitive, Emotional Thought

The third change in adolescent cognition is the increasing importance of intuitive thinking. The fact that adolescents *can* use hypothetical-deductive reasoning does not necessarily mean that they *will* use it. Even college students, carefully taught statistical reasoning in lectures and laboratories, are amazingly varied in the extent to which they apply the concepts they have just learned (Lovett, 2001). Similarly, students in college as well as younger adolescents persistently cling to mistaken notions about perception (Winer et al., 2002).

Apparently, humans have "two parallel, interacting modes of information-processing" (Epstein, 1994, p. 709) and both modes advance during adolescence (Moshman, 2000):

■ The first kind is the formal, logical, hypothetical-deductive thinking described by Piaget. This is called *analytic* thought, because it involves rational analysis of many factors, calculating combinations and interactions, as in the problem of balancing the scale. Analytic thinking requires a certain level of intellectual maturity, brain capacity, motivation, and practice, which is why children cannot use it, but teenagers and adults who are schooled in scientific processes can.

■ The second type of information processing begins with a belief or an assumption and quickly and uncritically develops supporting ideas as if the original beliefs were facts. This is called *intuitive* (or *heuristic* or *experiential*) thought, in that ideas are discovered and applied, instead of hypothesized and analyzed. Intuitive cognition is quick and powerful; it feels "right," even when analysis might lead in a different direction. Brain maturation may aid this type as well, as puberty brings an emotional quickness to bear on every thought.

Adolescents sometimes prefer not to use analytic thought. Many avenues of research now reveal that the brain has at least two pathways, which are variously called conscious/unconscious, explicit/implicit, factual/creative, intellectual/emotional, and so on. No matter what they are called, these pathways develop independently, on parallel processing tracks, and do not always lead to the same conclusions (Epstein, 1994; Macrae & Bodenhausen, 2000; Stanovich, 1999). This two-track thinking is demonstrated by adolescents as they think about themselves and as they respond to logical problems.

Adolescent Egocentrism

Adolescents frequently think about themselves. When they do so, even those who reach formal thinking can lose their logical detachment. They worry about how others perceive them; they try to sort out their conflicting feelings about parents, school, and close friends; they think deeply (but not always realistically) about their future possibilities; they reflect, at length, on each day's experiences. Analyzing private thoughts and feelings, forecasting the future, and reflecting on experiences underlie the reflection and self-awareness—and enhanced capacity for self-centeredness—that distinguish adolescence.

New ventures in introspection are part of expanding self-awareness. However, they are often distorted by **adolescent egocentrism** (remember, from Chapter 9, that *egocentric* means "self at the center"), a self-view in which adolescents regard themselves as much more socially significant than they actually are (Elkind, 1967, 1984; Lapsley, 1993). Younger adolescents tend to hypothesize about what others might be thinking (especially about them) and then egocentrically take their hypotheses to be fact—a kind of deductive reasoning that can lead to very false conclusions.

Several false assumptions that characterize adolescent egocentrism have special names. One is the **invincibility fable,** the idea that they cannot be conquered

Especially for High School Guidance Counselors: Given what you know about adolescent thinking, should you spend more time helping students with college applications, with summer jobs, with family problems, or with high school course selection?

adolescent egocentrism A characteristic of adolescent thinking that sometimes leads young people to focus on themselves to the exclusion of others and to believe, for example, that their thoughts, feelings, and experiences are unique.

invincibility fable A teenager's false belief, stemming from adolescent egocentrism, that he or she cannot be conquered or even harmed by anything that might vanquish a normal mortal, such as unprotected sex, drug abuse, or high-speed driving.

or even harmed by anything that might vanquish a normal mortal. Because they falsely believe in their invincibility, some young people are convinced that they will never fall victim, as others do, to dangerous behavior. They deliberately take risks, believing they will survive unscathed. We saw in Chapter 14 that adolescent cigarette smokers believe that they will not become addicted, saying they will soon quit, even though almost every steady teenage smoker is still nicotine-addicted five years later. Drug abuse and addiction are never planned or anticipated, but they occur nevertheless. Similarly, high school students have academic knowledge of the risks of pregnancy and sexually transmitted diseases, yet few sexually active teenagers always use a condom; driver education is mandatory, but it does not prevent 15- to 24-year-olds from having the second-highest motor vehicle–injury rate of any age group (see Figure 15.4). In general, the invincibility fable leads to a dangerous sense of security that all too often has disastrous consequences.

A second logical lapse resulting from adolescent egocentrism is the **personal fable:** Adolescents imagine their own lives as unique, heroic, or even legendary. Justin, one of my teenage students, complained that it was patently unfair that millions mourned the Tejano singer Selena's tragic death. Using hypothetical thinking, he imagined that he might die but few would mourn or even care. I told him I would care; he dismissed that as unimportant. I also pointed out that Selena was extraordinarily talented and accomplished, that she brought joy to millions. He replied, "But I am very talented, too; if I died, millions would never experience the joy I would bring them." When I looked quizzical, he was annoyed at me: "How do you know I'm not just as talented as she was?" In the personal fable, the young person perceives him- or herself as exceptional, distinguished by unusual experiences, talents, perspectives, and values.

A third false conclusion stemming from egocentrism is called the **imaginary audience.** This arises from many adolescents' assumption that other people are as intently interested in them as they themselves are. As a result, they tend to

It's All About Me Personal perceptions cloud judgment at every age. However, egocentrism is particularly apparent in adolescence, when the discovery of self is not yet balanced by a deeper understanding of the breadth of human experience.

personal fable A teenager's false belief, stemming from adolescent egocentrism, that he or she is destined to have a unique, heroic, or even legendary life.

imaginary audience A teenager's false belief, stemming from adolescent egocentrism, that others are intensely interested in his or her appearance and behavior.

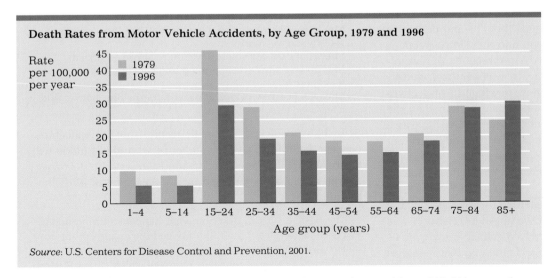

Death Rates from Motor Vehicle Accidents, by Age Group, 1979 and 1996

Source: U.S. Centers for Disease Control and Prevention, 2001.

FIGURE 15.4 Safer on the Road, but Not Safe Enough Adolescents and young adults aged 15–24 have seen the most improvement in motor vehicle safety. However, they still have the second-highest rate of death in motor vehicle accidents, just slightly below that of the oldest group, age 85 and older.

? *Observational Quiz* (see answer, page 476): The oldest groups are the only ones that have not experienced fewer motor vehicle deaths since 1979. Could this be because the population is aging, with far more people in the oldest age groups in 1996 than in 1979?

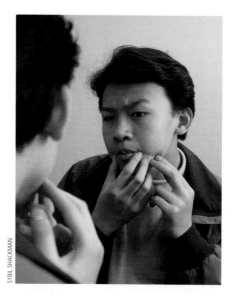

fantasize about how others react to their appearance and behavior. The imaginary audience can cause teenagers to enter a crowded room as if they believe themselves to be the most attractive human beings alive, or to avoid any attention because something as trivial as a slight facial blemish or a spot on a shirt becomes an unbearable embarrassment that everyone will notice.

As the acute self-consciousness resulting from the imaginary audience reveals, young people are not yet comfortable in the broader social world. This is one reason many seem obsessed with their hair, clothing, and so on, before going out in public. It also explains their need to fit in with their peer group, who presumably judge every visible nuance of their appearance and behavior. No wonder, then, that one adolescent remarked, "I would like to be able to fly if everyone else did; otherwise it would be rather conspicuous" (quoted in Steinberg, 1993).

Overall, adolescent egocentrism suggests that intense reflection about thoughts, feelings, and motives is a mixed blessing. The following personal accounts lend support to this observation.

Boys Do It, Too Although it is generally girls who are considered to be overly aware of minor flaws in their complexion or attire, the truth is that adolescent boys also pay exaggerated attention to their appearance. The cognitive capacity to think about oneself in egocentric terms makes many young people of both sexes spend hours combing their hair, adjusting their clothing, and searching for blemishes.

SYBIL SHACKMAN

In Person

Bethany and Jim

Teenagers' mastery of hypothetical thought and deductive reasoning is not always apparent, and their introspections can cause them to leap in the wrong direction. The unpredictability of adolescent thought was well demonstrated by my eldest daughter, Bethany, whose newfound perspectives on art and history made her absolutely certain that she wanted to visit the Metropolitan Museum of Art. It was a humid midsummer afternoon, and all her friends were out of town, so she prevailed on me to go with her. I was ready in five minutes but, because she was in her midteens, it took her much longer.

In fact, we left the house so late that I was concerned the museum would close soon after we got there. Hence, I was relieved that our subway train arrived quickly and moved us rapidly to our stop. But when we climbed up to street level from the station, we encountered a sudden downpour. Bethany became angry—at *me!*

She: You didn't bring an umbrella? You should have known.
Me: It's OK—we'll walk quickly. It's a warm rain.
She: But we'll get all wet.
Me: It's OK. We'll dry.
She: But people will see us with our hair all wet.

Me: Honey, no one cares what we look like. And we won't see anyone we know.
She: That's OK for you to say. You're already married.
Me: Do you think you are going to meet your future husband here?
She: No. People will look at me and think, "She'll never find a husband looking like that!"

Bethany's quickness to criticize me, and her egocentric concern with an imaginary audience who might judge her future possibilities, is echoed in almost every other teenager. Another example is reported by a father, himself a psychotherapist:

The best way I can describe what happens [during adolescence] is to relate how I first noticed the change in my son. He was about 13 years of age. One afternoon he and I were riding in a car on a four-lane highway which circles Boston, Massachusetts. I was driving 65 miles an hour in a 55-mile zone.

He suddenly turned toward me and shouted, "Dad!"

I was startled and responded by saying, "What is it, Jim!"

Then there was this pause as he folded his arms and turned slowly in my direction and said, "Dad, do you realize how fast you are driving this car?"

I was obviously embarrassed because after all, I did not want my son to notice that on occasion I break the law! I was able to put this over on him up to this age in his life. But more than that, I was taken aback by the new tone in his voice! I had not heard that before. It was a command, not a question!

Anyway, he was asking the question so I simply turned and said, "Oh, I'm doing 65 miles per hour!" (as if I didn't know it).

He then came right back at me and said, "*Dad!* Do you know what the speed limit is on this highway?"

Now my ego was hurt and I wanted to attack! This little voice in the back of my head was saying "Here comes early adolescent behavior, wipe it out now!"

Well, he was right, so I kept cool and responded by saying, "Yes, Jim, it's 55 miles an hour."

He then said, "*Dad!* Do you realize that you are traveling 10 miles over the speed limit!" I handled this one with calm because it at least indicated that he could add and subtract!

He continued, "*Dad!* Don't you care about my life at all! Do you have any idea of how many thousands of people lose their lives every year on our nation's highways who exceed the speed limit!"

Now I was beginning to get angry and I responded by saying, "Look, Jim, I have no idea how many people are killed every year, you were right I shouldn't have been speeding; I promise I won't ever do it again, so let us just forget it!"

Not being satisfied, he continued, "*Dad!* Any idea what would happen if the front wheel of this car came off doing 65 miles per hour, how many lives you might jeopardize!"

He kept on with this for another 10 minutes until I finally got him quiet for about 20 seconds! Then he came back at me and said, "Dad! I've been thinking about this."

Once he said that, I knew I was in deep trouble! You see, my son was so easy to deal with before he started to *think!* Who told him he had a right to start *thinking!* Before this all happened he would ask, *why,* and I would simply give him the answer and it was good enough!

[Garvin, 1994]

Note that both Bethany and Jim were focused on future possibilities, just as one might expect. And both followed an idea, albeit an egocentric one, to a logical conclusion.

The various forms that adolescent egocentrism can take are the most obvious forms of intuitive, emotional thought. At every age, humans have a "self-serving bias," which makes them take credit for good things that happen to them and avoid blaming themselves for bad things. It also makes them evaluate themselves more favorably than their friends, their friends more favorably than their other peers, and so on (e.g., Duval & Silvia, 2002; Suls et al., 2002). Adolescent egocentrism is a kind of thinking that everyone uses; it is just more obvious to adults when adolescents do it.

Notice also that adolescent egocentrism is not necessarily destructive, "not distorted, egocentric, and somewhat paranoid thinking" (Vartanian, 2001, p. 378) as it has sometimes been portrayed. Research does not support such a negative view, at least in regard to most adolescents. Instead, the imaginary audience and other aspects of personal, intuitive thinking "may signal growth toward cognitive maturity" and personal adaptation (Vartanian, 2001, p. 378).

Intuitive Conclusions

Intuitive thinking is also apparent when adolescents are not judging themselves, but are engaging in a task that is more abstract. The advantage of such thinking is that it is quick and emotional; the disadvantage is that it is often wrong (Moshman, 2000). For example, consider the following statement, to be refuted or substantiated. You are told that every card in a pack has a letter on one side and a number on the other. (Accept this as true; it is not a trick.) Then you are given a proposition to prove or disprove. The proposition is: *If a card has a vowel on one side, then it has an even number on the other side.* Confirm or disconfirm that proposition regarding the following four cards:

E   7   K   4

The challenge is to turn over the cards, *and only those cards,* that will confirm or disconfirm the statement. Which cards must be turned over?

While you are pondering (the answer will be presented soon), consider the research of Paul Klaczynski on the thought processes of hundreds of adolescents,

Response for High School Guidance Counselors (from page 472): It depends on what your particular students need; schools vary a great deal. However, all students need to talk and think about their choices and options so that they will not act impulsively. Therefore, providing information and a listening ear might be the most important thing you can do. You will also want to keep every student in challenging and interesting classes until they graduate. Encouraging teachers and administrators to improve educational structures and to increase student motivation is a worthwhile endeavor.

half younger (average age 13) and half older (average age 16). In one study (Klaczynski, 2001), adolescents were challenged by diverse problems of logic. For example,

> Timothy is very good looking, strong, and does not smoke. He likes hanging around with his male friends, watching sports on TV, and driving his Ford Mustang convertible. He's very concerned with how he looks and with being in good shape. He is a high school senior now and is trying to get a college scholarship.

> *Based on this [description], rank each statement in terms of how likely it is to be true. . . . The most likely statement should get a 1. The least likely statement should get a 6.*
> _____ Timothy has a girlfriend.
> _____ Timothy is an athlete.
> _____ Timothy is popular and an athlete.
> _____ Timothy is a teacher's pet and has a girlfriend.
> _____ Timothy is a teacher's pet.
> _____ Timothy is popular.

In ranking these statements, 71 percent of the 16-year-olds made at least one analytic error. They ranked a double statement (e.g., athlete *and* popular) as more likely than either of the single statements that it comprised (athlete *or* popular). That cannot be, and therefore is illogical and wrong. This is an example of intuitive thought because the adolescent jumps ahead to the more inclusive statement rather than sticking to the narrow, logical task at hand.

The Timothy example was only 1 of 19 possible problems. Almost all adolescents (even the younger ones) were analytical and logical on some of the problems and swayed by quick, illogical thinking on others. Generally, logic improved with age, although not necessarily with intelligence. Age differences were not nearly as substantial as a maturation theory of adolescent cognitive development would predict; adults are illogical with the same kinds of problems. Klaczynski (2001) is convinced that most adolescents are sufficiently competent to solve logical problems, but "most adolescents do not demonstrate a level of performance commensurate with their abilities" (p. 854).

What would motivate adolescents to use—or fail to use—their newly acquired analytic mode of information processing? In another series of experiments, Klaczynski (2000) first assessed how strongly the subjects felt about their particular religion and then asked them to evaluate research (not actual scientific studies) that supposedly led to favorable, neutral, or unfavorable conclusions. For example, in one fictitious study read by the adolescents, "Jennie" was said to be interested in the relationship between religious background and parenting skills. She observed six parents playing with their children. Three of the parents were said to be Baptist (or whatever religion the adolescent belonged to) and three, Catholic (or some other religion to which the adolescent did not belong). Supposedly, the three parents from one group (or the other) interacted with their children intelligently and warmly, playing challenging and enjoyable games, and the other three parents did not. Jennie concluded that parents who did not play well with their children (either the Baptists or Catholics, in this example) "are more likely to neglect and abuse children."

The adolescents were asked to judge the strength and persuasiveness of the conclusion. When the conclusion was *unfavorable to their own religion,* adolescents usually noticed and articulated the logical fallacies. In the parenting example, some realized that too few people were studied to draw significant conclusions, that the measures of parenting competence were not objective, or that the conclusion about child abuse did not follow from the data about parent–child interaction. In Klaczynski's sample, some adolescents even rejected the premise as implausible; one said, "I don't see why they did this research, because my religion can't make me a bad parent." However, when the conclusion was *favorable to their own religion* (remember, parents of their religion supposedly played warmly), adolescents were less likely to find fault with either the logic or the plausibility of the research.

Intuitive Thinking As an Intellectual Tool

In the study just mentioned regarding flawed research, the older adolescents (age 16) were better able than the younger group to use analytic reasoning, seeing the obvious weaknesses even in the research that favored their own religious background. But they also were *more* biased in favor of their own religion. They saw more and greater weaknesses in the unfavorable research compared to the favorable or neutral studies, in addition to having a *greater* tendency to dismiss the unfavorable research as implausible, impossible, and flat-out wrong (Klaczynski, 2000).

Interestingly, after reading the bogus research examples, the adolescents of both age groups became more convinced of the value of their own faith than they were before. In other words, analyzing research did not detract from beliefs already held; just the opposite. It seems that maturation (or education) in the second decade of life makes people better thinkers but that the improvements occur in both kinds of thought—the ability to analyze in order to justify one's own perspective and the ability to use one's prior assumptions to reach conclusions that are more intuitive than logical. Klaczynski (2000) concluded:

> Analytic reasoning competence . . . has long been considered the pinnacle of adolescent cognitive development [but] . . . biased use of judgmental heuristics [rules of thumb] . . . increases with age in some social arenas. One possible explanation for this unexpected finding is that . . . older adolescents are more flexible and are more geared toward cognitive economy.
>
> *[pp. 1347, 1361]*

Cognitive economy is exactly what might be expected as the knowledge base increases, as thinking proceeds more quickly, and as both analysis and intuition are more readily and powerfully available. It is probably more efficient to use formal, analytic thinking in science class and emotional, experiential thinking (which is quicker and more satisfying) in one's personal life. As the brain functions more quickly and in a more coordinated fashion, a person is able to think more forcefully—but that force can be applied in many directions.

To advance cognition, we need to understand both analytic and intuitive thought, because

> the assumption that we think in two fundamentally different modes has implications for human survival. . . . How we do think, I believe, is with two minds, experiential and rational. Our hope lies in learning . . . how to use them in a harmonious manner.
>
> *[Epstein, 1994, p. 721]*

For adolescents, harmonious thinking is usually social thinking. The task in the E–7–K–4 example is "notoriously difficult": Almost everyone wants to turn over the E and the 4, and almost everyone is wrong (Moshman, 2000). However, when college students who individually guessed wrong are given a chance to discuss the problem as a group, 75 percent get it right, avoiding the 4 card (even if the 4 card has a consonant on the other side, that doesn't disprove the statement) and selecting the 7 card (if it had a vowel on the other side, the proposition would be false) (Moshman & Geil, 1998). This example demonstrates a very important idea: Quick, intuitive thinking can, with discussion and guidance, evolve to become more logical, and then adolescents can and do change their minds.

Although formal operational thought is not universally used, it may be universally possible after age 11. Adolescents do not necessarily think logically; in fact, the easy, spontaneous, intuitive mode of thinking is often their first reaction, especially for issues that involve them. However, when encouraged by adults or peers, they can analyze the various possibilities. Combining both forms of thinking in "a harmonious manner," using both formal and personal thought, is not only possible but desirable. Brain maturation allows adolescents the capacity to be great thinkers in all three ways—existing skills; new hypothetical-deductive reasoning; and quicker, stronger intuition.

Schools, Learning, and the Adolescent Mind

Some things are obvious: Schools are important institutions in the public life of every society; the purpose of school is to educate; and many teenagers use school as a base for their self-discovery and social interaction. For adolescents, this last point may be most important: Making friends is a "high priority . . . often even higher than the pursuit of academic goals" (Covington, 2000).

As we have seen, adolescents have a greater knowledge base, expanded language skills, and better memory strategies than younger children do. They think more abstractly, analytically, hypothetically, and logically—as well as more personally, emotionally, intuitively, and experientially—than they once did. Secondary schools build on adolescents' cognitive strengths in many ways: adding details to their basic history and science knowledge; requiring them to write longer essays and to use symbols to express concepts that cannot be expressed concretely (∞, H_2O, 5_5); giving them long-term, elaborate assignments; and so on.

Because of these intellectual advances, secondary teachers are specialists in particular academic fields (not generalists, as primary school teachers are), qualified to answer challenging questions about the intricacies of cell biology, calculus, or poetry. By midadolescence, students are intellectually capable of understanding almost anything, from theoretical physics to ancient history, and most schools try to provide specialized classes and teachers who can guide students in a wide variety of subjects (Bransford et al., 1999). One reason bigger, more "comprehensive" high schools have been created is to enable students with various interests and abilities to find teachers who can accommodate them.

Unfortunately, teachers and schools are not always adept at harmonizing the analytic and intuitive aspects of adolescent cognition. Some do succeed. For example, when a high school sociology teacher explained the "bystander effect" (the unwillingness of observers to intervene, even when they could be helpful and when something is clearly wrong), one student challenged his explanation, as adolescents are wont to do with any piece of received wisdom that contradicts their intuition. The teacher was sufficiently aware of adolescent cognitive processes to ask the student to develop an experiment (using experiential or intuitive understanding) and then to analyze the results (using formal operational thinking). The student asserted that surely church members would intervene if they saw something contrary to the proper functioning of their congregation.

> To prove this assertion, the student made confidential arrangements with the minister to steal the collection plate *during the Sunday service.* "Theft Sunday" found numerous student "worshippers," who wanted to see what would happen. . . . Only shocked glances and frightened worshippers were evident as the student left the church immediately following her row's donation.
>
> *[Poplau, 2002, p. 12]*

Thus, all aspects of adolescent cognition were fostered by this teacher.

However, the optimum **person–environment fit**—that is, the best setting for personal development (which depends not only on the individual's stage of development and cognition but also on social traditions and educational

person–environment fit The match between a person at a given stage of development and his or her setting, including society, family, and peer group.

objectives)—is not always realized in secondary schools. Many critics point to a **volatile mismatch** (Carnegie, 1989) between the current needs of adolescents and the traditional structures of their schools (Bruner, 1996). To understand how this imbalance came to be, we examine historical and cultural variations in secondary schools in the following feature.

volatile mismatch A lack of fit between a person and his or her environment, which can change rapidly as the person or the environment changes.

Changing Policy

High Schools: Where and When

First, let us clarify the terminology. Educational institutions are usually divided into three categories, depending on the level of education they offer.

Primary schools (elementary schools) are those in which younger children learn basic academic skills. In developed nations for a hundred years or more, every 6- to 11-year-old was expected to be in school until about the sixth grade, mastering reading, writing, and arithmetic. As the twenty-first century begins, every nation in the world believes that a literate citizenry is crucial, and some offer universal primary education. Worldwide the rate of literacy is now high; about 80 percent or more of the people of the world can read—although the literacy rate for an individual nation ranges from 50 percent to almost 100 percent (United Nations Development Program, 2001).

Secondary education follows primary education, usually beginning at or just after puberty. In the United States, secondary schools are called high schools and often divided into junior and senior high schools. (Middle schools are between primary and secondary schools.) Nations vary in the proportion of children attending secondary schools (see Figure 15.5); the poorer countries still focus on primary education. However, virtually every government recognizes that economic growth, national health, and citizens' employment prospects depend on high rates of secondary education. All adolescents in developed nations are expected to learn several sciences, advanced math, literature, national as well as world history, and, often, a second or third language.

Tertiary education (also called higher education) follows secondary, and includes colleges (which usually offer only associate's or bachelor's degrees) and universities (which also offer master's, doctoral, and other professional degrees). Nations vary widely in the proportion of young people who go to college, from less than 5 percent to more than half, and in the proportion of college students who study science, math, or engineering—just 14 percent in the United States, 32 percent in Australia, and 41 percent in Nigeria (United Nations Development Program, 2001). The relatively low percentage of U.S. college students in the sciences may be misleading, because the total number who go to college is so high: Since 1995, about two-thirds of U.S. high school

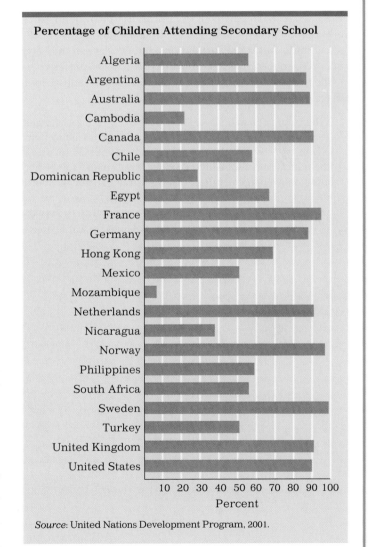

Percentage of Children Attending Secondary School

Source: United Nations Development Program, 2001.

FIGURE 15.5 Growing Recognition of Secondary Education's Importance These percentages were calculated by dividing the number of children in secondary school (grades 7–12) by the total number of children in the corresponding age group. Every nation has a certain proportion of children of the appropriate age who are not in school. Many countries (among them China, India, and Nigeria) emphasize elementary education; secondary school attendance data are not reported for those nations.

graduates have gone on to college, the highest rate of any major nation (U.S. Department of Education, 2001).

In every nation, high school graduates stay healthier, live longer, are richer, are more likely to marry, vote, and buy homes than their less educated contemporaries. U.S. statistics illustrate the point: Yearly income of heads of household (that is, the principal breadwinner, male or female) averages $16,154 for those who never attended high school, twice that ($34,373) for those with a high school diploma, and almost twice that again ($66,474) for those with at least a bachelor's degree (U.S. Bureau of the Census, 2000). High school attendance is one of the best deterrents against criminal behavior (Henry et al., 1999). High school graduates are more often employed, not only immediately but for the next 40 years; unemployment is twice as high among those who have not graduated (U.S. Department of Education, 2001). Other variables (family background, IQ, and income among them) affect all these statistical correlations, but even when they are equalized, education is a significant predictor of success.

The increased prevalence and importance of high school affects public policy in three ways:

1. When more of a nation's children attend high school, a larger percentage of the national income must go to education. About 5 percent of the gross domestic product is spent on the education in the United States and Canada; somewhat less (about 4 percent) in Japan and Australia; somewhat more (about 6 percent) in France, Sweden, and New Zealand (Organization for Economic Cooperation and Development, 2000). In every nation, education is now considered an essential government function, a legitimate competitor for national funds with other public expenses, from prisons to parks, from armies to ambulances.

2. Leaders question whether schools designed for one set of historical conditions meet the needs of another set. Many critics believe that high schools in the United States are still structured to educate the elite and discourage everyone else. In 1900, high school was a luxury; 92 percent of students left school before high school graduation. In 2000, only 21 percent dropped out (see Figure 15.6), but even that low rate is widely considered a serious problem because high school education has become a necessity.

3. As education becomes more pivotal and universal, the public and political leaders pay closer attention, regarding each high school dropout as a personal and national failure. As secondary education becomes more valued, issues related to it—vouchers, curriculum, promotion, funding, discipline, charter schools, school prayer, and so on—have increasingly become part of public debate. In the United States over the past 100 years, secondary schools—once only for the elite and supervised by an assortment of town boards, private boards, and churches—have come under increasing scrutiny. Education is now considered a major policy area by presidential candidates, Supreme Court judges, members of Congress, and the voting public.

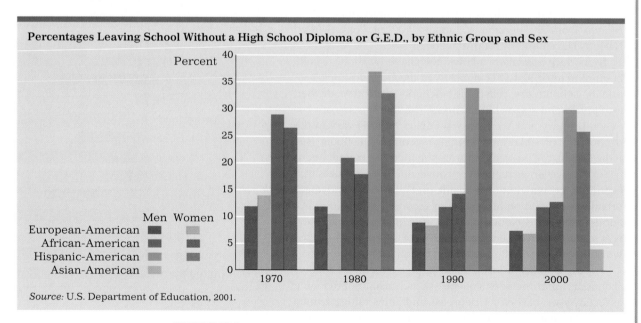

FIGURE 15.6 No Diploma Shown here are the percentages of adolescents and young adults, ages 16–24, who are not in high school and do not have either a high school diploma or a G.E.D. (General Educational Development) high school equivalency diploma. The percentage has decreased for some groups, but the dropout rate remains high among Hispanics.

? *Critical Thinking Question* (see answer, page 482): Why are no Hispanic rates shown for 1970?

School Structure

Secondary schools do not reflect the findings of current developmental research, as described earlier in this chapter. That research has demonstrated that supportive interaction among students and, especially, between teachers and students is crucial for helping adolescents find the harmonious balance between analytic and intuitive thought. However, compared to primary schools (which were designed for the cognitive abilities of younger children), most secondary schools still seem focused on the elite, in that they feature intensified competition, norm-referenced rather than criterion-referenced tests, rigid behavioral demands, and less individual attention.

Grades on report cards almost always decline as students move to secondary schools; the first year after primary school is usually a "low ebb" of learning (Covington & Dray, 2002, p. 48). Teacher–student conversations are almost impossible in large high schools, since the two groups have separate lunchrooms, bathrooms, and even parking lots. Hallways are designed to keep people moving, not to encourage the social interactions that teenagers need.

As mentioned in Chapter 14, even school schedules do not promote education. The first bell typically rings at 8:00 A.M., before adolescent minds are awake. The curriculum is divided into disciplines (originally delineated centuries ago, distinguishing biology from chemistry, history from language, psychology from ethics) and is often taught in 40-minute blocks by a variety of teachers, who instruct about 200 students in class each week and forget some students' names. Field trips are almost impossible to schedule. Schools let out for the summer, an echo of the days when most children had to help out on the family farm. Taken as a whole, all these factors hinder the expression of the wide-ranging curiosity and personal involvement that is central to adolescent cognitive development.

A related problem is school size. In large schools only a few of the more talented juniors and seniors can be involved in extracurricular activities, such as sports, theater, music, art, science fairs, and chess clubs. All these activities encourage student commitment to their schools and foster constructive relationships with teachers and with other students, thereby enhancing school attendance and academic performance (Eccles & Barber, 1999). Yet most (60 percent) students in the United States attend high schools with enrollments of more than 1,000 and few (3 percent) attend high schools, either public or private, with fewer than 200 students (U.S. Department of Education, 2001). Ironically, to save money, over the last decade schools have grown in size and cut back on extracurricular activities.

Lessons Their Ancestors Never Studied
Education today prepares students to think for themselves, not memorize facts. This photo shows a class in prehistory, in contrast to traditional history classes, which began with the first written texts. Note also the "hidden" curriculum—in the way learning occurs. The teacher is acting as a guide rather than as an authority figure. The students are encouraged to draw their own conclusions about the evidence before them. Moreover, this interracial school is in Johannesburg, South Africa. All these features impart lessons that, presumably, will serve these young people well in the twenty-first century.

!Answer to Critical Thinking Question
(from page 480): Before 1980, the U.S. government did not collect data on Hispanics. People with Latin American ancestors were categorized as either black or white.

Secondary schools vary a great deal not only in size but also in structure, curriculum, teacher preparation, goals, and values for reasons not directly related to human cognitive development. No one school design is best for all persons in all cultures. In the United States, local control of education means that communities, schools within communities, and even teachers within schools differ about curriculum and standards, as do groups of parents and students with each other. Internationally, education systems vary in expectations (virtually everyone graduates from high school in Japan and Norway, but only a third do in Brazil, Indonesia, and Mexico), in curriculum (language arts are stressed in France, math in China), in average class size (23 in Canadian high schools, 8 in Norwegian ones), in teacher training, in pedagogical methods, and in legal requirements (Alexander, 2000; U.S. Department of Education, 2001).

Worldwide, immigration has increased in recent years, and schools have not adjusted to the implications of this demographic shift. In the United States, an estimated 20 percent of schoolchildren have at least one parent who was born in another nation. Immigrants believe strongly in the power of education to give their children a brighter future, but immigrants' values and expectations often differ from those of the people who set educational policies and carry them out (Suarez-Orozco & Suarez-Orozco, 2001). Discrepancies in background between native-born parents and educators may also become volatile mismatches (Patrick & Pintrich, 2001). As one highly regarded analysis of learning suggests, "School failure may be partly explained by the mismatch between what students have learned in their home cultures and what is required of them in school" (Bransford et al., 1999).

Controversies in Education

The words *school failure* remind us that not every child succeeds according to whatever measure a family, a school, or a culture might use. Many education-related controversies (the Reading Wars, standards, group learning, bilingual education, and class size) were described in Chapter 12. Some of the issues on which developmentalists agree—the importance of social interaction, of teacher–student relationships, of extracurricular activities—have been mentioned in this chapter. Three additional issues—student motivation, high-stakes testing, and school violence—merit discussion here.

Student Motivation

Adolescents are often bored and unhappy in school ("Algebra sucks," "*The Odyssey* is boring"), especially when they are complaining to their friends (Larson, 2000). They seek to be "cool" and admired, which often means appearing detached from the excitement of learning. As students progress through high school, they become less attached to their school, a trend found particularly among boys (Wigfield et al., 1997).

Teachers are well aware of students' problems with motivation: 38 percent of public high school teachers consider student apathy their most serious problem, worse than drugs (14 percent), lack of challenge (10 percent), fighting (9 percent), and racial tension (7 percent). Teachers in private secondary schools agree: Although they mention fewer problems overall, they cite apathy as a serious problem four times as often as teachers in private primary schools do (U.S. Department of Education, 2001). As one review of secondary education explains, "The content and the way they are taught are sometimes unfit to capture the attention of the students" (Massimini & Delle Fave, 2000). Teachers, researchers, and developmentalists describe adolescents—honor students as well as delinquents—as having "high rates of boredom, alienation, and disconnection from meaningful challenge" (Larson, 2000).

To understand this problem, remember how adolescents think. They have the potential to learn, advancing in skills and developing analytic as well as intuitive thought. Adolescents are known for becoming excited and involved in intellectual efforts (Flavell et al., 2001). They will stay up all night to discuss things with their friends, create their own version of their life story (Habermas & Bluck, 2000), and find answers on the Internet to questions their parents never knew they had. Hypothetical and abstract thinking allow them to abandon simplistic, concrete thinking, focusing on possibility more than on reality. They construct more imaginative, comprehensive, and complex worldviews; they are no longer content with someone else's statements of facts, whether from a textbook or from a teacher. Adolescents are eager for lively intellectual interaction but

Reality and Fantasy Since teenagers can think analytically and hypothetically, they can use computers not only to obtain factual information and to keep in touch with friends but also to leave the reality of daily life and escape into the realm of imagination and fantasy. This temporary reprieve may be particularly important for adolescents like 17-year-old Julisa *(right)*. She is a student in a high school in Brownsville, Texas, that offers computer labs and other programs to help children of migrant laborers keep up with their peers.

highly vulnerable to self-doubt; they may be both extremely rational and extremely emotional. The brash young man who unhesitatingly challenges the ideas of long-ago thinkers may also avoid coming to class after his teacher makes a wisecrack at his expense.

All this suggests that adolescents need challenging intellectual activities that require social interaction within a supportive context; they want to express their hypothetical and nontraditional ideas without feeling alienated from school. Most would rather feign boredom, or stop trying, than risk being thought stupid (Dweck, 1999). In a longitudinal study of high school students of varied ability in eight communities, those who disengaged from class after a year (no longer doing the homework, never asking questions, and so on) were *not* those with low intellectual potential, but those who initially thought their achievement depended on others or on fate, not on their own efforts (Glasgow et al., 1997). Attitude, not aptitude, is crucial (Wigfield & Eccles, 2002).

In general, adolescents experience a dip in self-confidence in all academic subjects when they enter secondary school (Cole et al., 2001; Fredricks & Eccles, 2002; Jacobs et al., 2002). An adolescent's first reaction when grades decline is to study less—a **self-handicapping** technique that preserves their self-esteem but at obvious cost (Midgley & Urdan, 2001). They learn less, score lower, and perhaps join the million or so who drop out of school in the United States each year.

Low motivation is not inevitable (Wigfield et al., 1998). Extracurricular activities can sometimes pull adolescents back into the academic scene. The school play, the school band, the debating, chess, or math team, and various sports teams require—and get—from their members avid participation, extensive practice of various cognitive skills, and an intensity that contrasts dramatically with the apathy apparent in some classrooms (Larson, 2000). Many adolescents take a passionate interest in music, putting in hours of voluntary practice to learn to play an instrument, demonstrating that some activities are highly motivating for high school students (North et al., 2000). Adolescents who exercise more—whether in school or on their own—tend to have higher grade point averages as well as better relationships with their parents (Field et al., 2001).

Many parents and adolescents do not realize that too much passive leisure (e.g., watching a game, hanging out, and watching television) correlates with lower achievement and reduced self-esteem (McHale et al., 2001). One study found that ninth-graders who spent a lot of time hanging out with friends were likely to experience depression, low grades, and lack of ambition a few years later (Shanahan & Flaherty, 2001). By contrast, spending time in extracurricular

self-handicapping A person's deliberate selection of choices that will impede his or her success. Adolescents who do not study, who hand in homework late, who rush through tests, and who skip sleep are handicapping their academic success.

activities correlates with accomplishment (Broh, 2002; Shanahan & Flaherty, 2001). Various outlets, such as community organizations, church groups, Scouts, neighborhood activities, and volunteer work, provide the challenges adolescents seek, as long as adults organize them with "enough structure so that youth are challenged, but also enough flexibility" (Larson, 2000, p. 181).

Teachers play an important role in student motivation. A study of 300 tenth-grade students found that the best teachers "take pupils seriously," "have confidence in them," "push them to do well," and "make it easier for them to understand" (Tatar, 1998). Such learning enhances self-esteem. Students who believe that they can learn more if they put forth effort

> told us they felt smart, not only when they were striving to master new tasks, but also when they put their knowledge to work to help their peers learn. Thus within this framework, rather than being rivals for self-esteem, peers can gain self-esteem by cooperating and by facilitating each other's learning.
>
> *[Dweck, 1999]*

Another study that focused on early adolescents found that high teacher expectations tended to increase student interest and aspirations, and criticisms from teachers tended to decrease academic achievement (Wentzel, 2002). Contrary to what many teachers intuitively believe, motivation is not innate to the student but may be influenced by teachers and parents (Torff & Sternberg, 2001).

Note again that the school culture and climate, rather than the adolescent's innate ability, is the prime ingredient for success. Often, the family attitude is equally important.

All this suggests that the problem of poor motivation during secondary education can be overcome once families and schools understand what it involves and take the needed steps: "Motivation is not just a characteristic of the individual but also a result of the home and school environmental contexts" (Wigfield & Eccles, 2002, p. 5). As you will now learn, whether tests increase or decrease motivation is a controversial issue.

High-Stakes Tests

Some tests are called **high-stakes tests** because the consequences of a failing score are serious. In the United States, high-stakes tests have been used for decades to qualify people for professional licensing (lawyer, doctor, clinical psychologist, and so on) and for employment (Sackett et al., 2001). Although some Asian and European nations use high-stakes tests for entrance to, or graduation from, academic high schools, traditionally American secondary schools have relied instead on teacher grades and credits earned.

Since 1990, however, virtually every state legislature in the United States has mandated the use of standardized high-stakes tests to determine school promotion and/or high school graduation. This trend stems from the increasingly recognized need for accountability, achievement, and universal standards in secondary education, as the Changing Policy feature indicated (Elmore & Rothman, 1999). Many developmentalists wonder if high-stakes tests are antithetical to learning, since adolescent thinking thrives on questions more than answers, hypotheses more than facts, deduction rather than induction. Too much emphasis on right or wrong answers on a single test might narrow the curriculum (making it "a mile wide and an inch deep"), reward rote memorization, and discourage students (Kornhaber & Orfield, 2001; Phelps, 1998; Sacks, 1999). Ironically, many other nations (notably Japan and England) are now moving away from the use of a single test to determine a child's future.

The actual tests and the uses to which test scores are put vary from state to state; not all are developmentally destructive. However, one fear is that high-stakes tests increase ethnic, economic, and sexual inequality and decrease student effort and motivation (Maehr & Yamaguchi, 2001). Some research validates this

Especially for Junior High Teachers: You think your class is interesting and you know you care about your students, yet many of them cut class, come late, or seem to sleep through it. What do you do?

high-stakes tests Tests whose results have serious consequences for the people who take them—determining, for example, whether they will be promoted to the next grade or allowed to graduate from high school.

fear. For example, in the Boston suburbs (where most schools are considered quite good), scores on high-stakes tests were lower than teacher evaluations for girls in math and science and for African-American and Latino/a teenagers in every subject (Brennan et al., 2001). In general, student attitude, motivation, and persistence, as well as school structure and staff, are more influential than test scores in determining high school achievement as well as college-level skill mastery (Bruner, 1996; Cote & Levine, 2001; Dornbusch et al., 1996). Social scientists are eager for objective longitudinal data about tests and learning; at the moment, the political climate makes dispassionate analysis of high-stakes testing difficult.

Violence in Schools

Statistically, adolescents are safer in schools than in their neighborhoods and homes: Of all who are killed, 99 percent meet their fate somewhere other than in school. The injury rate is lower on school days from 8:00 A.M. to 3:00 P.M. than at other times. Although only 1 in 20 adolescents is afraid to go to school, and only 1 in 10 has *ever* brought a weapon to school, adolescents do sometimes harm other students and teachers (U.S. Department of Education, 2001).

AP / WIDE WORLD PHOTOS

Unsafe at School An agony of grief and fear is apparent in these girls' faces as they leave Columbine High School in Littleton, Colorado, on the day of the worst school shooting in American history. According to writings and tapes the gunmen left behind, the massacre was an extreme reaction to their feelings of being ostracized by the school's "jocks." The culture of a school can foster powerful feelings of rejection that some students may be unable to deal with appropriately.

School violence is not random. Students are more likely to be injured in the first years of middle or high school and at the beginning of a semester. Violence is likely to erupt when students feel most vulnerable and uncertain, which explains why pubescent boys in large schools, who feel shamed or disrespected by teachers or other students, are more likely to lash out with fists, knives, or guns (Aronson, 2000; Mulvey & Cauffman, 2001). Former bullies and victims are more violent than socially accepted students.

Because gunfire is so rare, it is impossible to anticipate which particular sixth- to twelfth-grade student out of the 24 million in the United States will use a weapon on any given day. Therefore, measures to reduce violence for everyone are more effective than targeting any particular student, who might become even more alienated upon being singled out (Mulvey & Cauffman, 2001). This indicates that effective antidotes to school violence should focus more on student motivation and social relationships than on metal detectors or isolated students. One psychologist described the dilemma this way:

> Some apparently sensible interventions could produce negative or even disastrous consequences, depending on what is actually going on in the school. . . . A few days after the Columbine tragedy, my 16-year-old grandson came home from high school and said, "Guess what? The principal sent around a notice asking us to report any kids who are dressing strangely, behaving weirdly, appear to be loners, or out of it."
>
> . . . The principal is shining his spotlight on the wrong part of the equation. Here's why: From my classroom research, I have found that the social atmosphere in most schools is competitive, cliquish, and exclusionary. The majority of teenagers I have interviewed agonize over the fact that there is a general atmosphere of taunting and rejection among their peers that makes the high school experience an unpleasant one. For many, it is worse than unpleasant—they describe it as a living hell, where they are in the out-group and feel insecure, unpopular, put-down, and picked on. By asking the "normal" students to point out the "strange" ones, my grandson's high school principal is unwittingly making a bad situation worse by implicitly sanctioning the rejection and exclusion of a sizable group of students whose only sin is unpopularity.

> *[Aronson, 2000]*

Fortunately, the same practices that foster education can also prevent violence. When students are engaged in learning, bonding with their teachers and fellow students, and involved in school activities outside the classroom as well as in it, they are unlikely to be destructive. Even more important, these practices

Response for Junior High Teachers (from page 484): Students need both challenge and involvement. Make sure your lessons are not too easy and that all students participate. For example, structure discussions by small groups that must report to the whole class, assign oral reports that must bring new information to the class, create debates and role-plays that require some rehearsing and practice, and so on. As a teacher, you probably value abstract ideas; remember that adolescents value each other's opinions and their own voices.

create a protective shield throughout the school, for "students are well aware of the problem children in their own classrooms . . . [but] for such information to flow from students to administrators requires an atmosphere where sharing in good faith is respected and honored" (Mulvey & Cauffman, 2001). (Our major discussion of adolescent violence and delinquency appears in Chapter 16.)

Conclusion: To Be or Not to Be

As the review of school violence suggests, a mismatch between the adolescent mind and the school setting can be dangerous. However, we should not conclude this section with the rare and dangerous event. Not only do most students learn, but every reader of this book probably had at least one teacher in secondary school who knew "how to get adolescent fires lit, how to have them develop the complex of dispositions and skills needed to take charge of their lives" (Larson, 2000, p. 170). Remember that adolescents combine the hypothetical and the experiential, the analytic and the intuitive, and that they can draw connections and ask questions on a much deeper level than when they were younger. In view of that, think about how Shakespeare's *Hamlet* can be taught in high school:

> Steven [the teacher] began his unit on *Hamlet* without even mentioning the name of the play. To help his students grasp the initial outline of the themes and issues of the play, he asked them to imagine that their parents had recently divorced and that their mothers had taken up with a new man. This new man had replaced their father at work, and "there's some talk that he had something to do with the ousting of your dad" (Grossman, 1990). Steven then asked students to think about the circumstances that might drive them so mad that they would contemplate murdering another human being. Only then, after students had contemplated these issues and done some writing on them, did Steven introduce the play they would be reading.
>
> [Bransford et al., 1999, p. 34]

Discussion led students to understand that the carnage in *Hamlet* is needless, useless, and pointless—the result of partial truths, imperfect analysis, and misinterpreted intuition—and to realize that, whatever their personal circumstances, they did not need to imitate Hamlet. In sum, good teaching not only makes learning exciting; it makes violence less appealing.

Adolescent Decision Making

An understanding that adolescent thinking is hypothetical and intuitive is important for another practical reason: to help students choose wisely. For the first time in their lives, teenagers make independent decisions that have far-reaching consequences. They decide what and how diligently to study, whether and where to go to college, whom to befriend, what courses to take, which career to pursue, which political organization to support, for whom to vote, how to express their religious beliefs, what to do about sex, which drugs and foods to consume (or abstain from), whether to get a job, how to spend their money.

However, because they think about possibilities, not practicalities, and because both egocentrism and intuitive thinking are easier than careful analysis, few adolescents actually decide such matters in a rational, explore-all-the-options manner. Adult guidance may help—or it may backfire.

Weighing Risks and Benefits

Adults are not necessarily wiser than teenagers in calculating the risks and benefits of various decisions (Gruber, 2001). Fears are not necessarily rational or proportional in adults of any age (Myers, 2001). Adolescents are *not* the most likely age group to drive drunk, or use heroin, or carry a gun—young adults are.

Suicide is at least three times more likely in the last decade of life than in the second. Many scholars who have studied adult decision making have found that it is often based on mistaken assumptions, damaging ignorance, and questionable priorities (Allwood & Selart, 2001; Byrnes, 1998; Ranyard et al., 1997). In fact, as you have discovered numerous times in this text, experts disagree about applications and implications of scientific research, which is one reason that careful methodology (described in Chapter 1) is so important.

Nevertheless, adults do their best to protect teenagers from poor judgment, for several reasons (O'Donoghue & Rabin, 2001):

■ The consequences of risk taking are more serious the younger a person is, not only if they become addicted, maimed, or killed, but also if they are expelled, arrested, or jailed.

■ Adolescent choices are long-lasting; "a significant determinant of the well-being of many older persons will be the risky decisions that they made in their youth," such as dropping out of school, having a baby, or joining a gang (Gruber, 2001, p. 25).

■ Adolescents typically overrate the joys of the moment and ignore future costs. Because they have not yet personally experienced the eventual consequences of their own actions, and because generational forgetting makes older peers poor teachers, adolescents are especially likely to disregard the risks of their immediate impulse to respond to a mind-altering drug, a sexually arousing situation, a disrespectful police officer, or a dangerous dare.

Every decision requires weighing risk against opportunity. Some people are "risk-averse"—they take great care to avoid doing anything that has a chance of ending in disaster. Others "throw caution to the winds"; they enjoy the thrill of spontaneity, of impulse, of being close to danger. Personality, culture, and life responsibility are all factors here (30-year-old parents are more cautious than 30-year-olds without families), as is mental set (adolescents with attention-deficit disorder are more vulnerable to all kinds of risks); but age is probably the strongest influence of all. The allure of risk increases from age 11 to age 18. Boys are somewhat more inclined than girls to seek thrills, such as parachuting or roller coasting, and to rebel against adult authority, as by engaging in secret drinking or sex (Gullone et al., 2000). Adolescent girls, while somewhat more cautious than boys (although less cautious than older or younger females), admire risk-taking boys, which encourages the boys to be even more daring. For many adolescents, behaviors that adults would consider foolhardy (skipping school, using drugs or alcohol, breaking the law, having unprotected sex, driving too fast, and so on) gain status and respect, strengthen friendship bonds, and loosen the inhibitions (Lightfoot, 1997). In adolescent culture, risk taking is viewed as brave, while caution is considered "goody-goody" or wimpish.

The rush of hormones, the new freedom, and the discovery that many adults are clueless or quiet about sex, drugs, and morality encourage teenagers to choose pleasure over caution. They discount consequences, miscalculate probabilities, and risk their futures (O'Donoghue & Rabin, 2001). Adults who want to guide them must first appreciate the attraction of social acceptance, of self-expression, and of rebellion. Good decision making requires, at a minimum, weighing alternatives, collecting information, taking action, and then reflecting on the results. And good decision making takes time to develop, as was shown by a study in which life dilemmas were posed to 204 subjects aged 14 to 37. During adolescence, each year brought wiser, more mature analysis. This gradual improvement suggests that "adolescents are acquiring reasoning capacities that

Which College, Where? As a 17-year-old basketball star, high school senior Niesha Butler had a critical decision to make—which of hundreds of colleges to choose. Her top list included Harvard, Virginia, Notre Dame, and Georgia Tech—although she thought of skipping college and turning pro because "if the money is there, why not?" That was a possibility her parents—who had banned television from their home years before—would not let her consider. She chose Georgia Tech, where she was awarded full scholarship and received living expenses.

MICHELLE AGINS / NYT PICTURES

may support both the acquisition and expression of wisdom-related knowledge and judgment" (Pasupathi et al., 2001, p. 358). Now let's explore adolescent decision making on two issues: employment and sex.

Making Decisions About Employment

Few adolescents can, or should, decide their future careers. When an adult asks a child "What do you want to do when you grow up?" the child is likely to answer that he or she wants to be a basketball star, president, pediatrician, or millionaire. In high school, such grandiose aspirations are still apparent. Among thousands of high school students of all backgrounds, unrealistic career expectations were found to be typical. For example, 37 percent expected (and 45 percent wanted) careers that only 1 percent of the employed population actually have. Most of the other 63 percent also had unrealistic goals; at least 95 percent of all teenagers will be disappointed in their vocational path unless some readjustment occurs (Csikszentmihalyi & Schneider, 2000). There are literally tens of thousands of occupations and jobs; no one can be expected to understand them all or to make a perfect match. Given the fluidity of the job market, it might be better to advise adolescents to learn as much as they can in every area and to stay flexible, since they will probably have more than one career and many jobs before they retire.

Adolescents would be well advised to consider this fact: Courses studied and leisure choices do make a difference. Taking challenging classes in high school is likely to lead to more success in college and then in the job market. In fact, one of the most effective ways in which students who were failing in the eighth grade improved their academic situation was to take challenging courses in high school (Cappella & Weinstein, 2001).

Jobs and School

One aspect of adolescent life that has surprised researchers is the extent of employment outside of school. In general, teenagers in the United States work more and learn less than teenagers elsewhere. The only part-time jobs they can usually get are boring, dead-end positions. Teenage workers take whatever job is available, seeking the best pay scale, the least effort, and the most social interaction. They do not learn how to do a methodical search of career possibilities, and family members rarely know of challenging jobs for teens that will teach values and skills. Instead of analysis and rational planning, adolescents use easier rule-of-thumb thinking ("jobs bring money"), and so do their parents ("work teaches responsibility"). Not coincidentally, one study found that seniors in high school who were employed, no matter how few hours per week they worked, had lower grades and poorer relationships with parents and friends. They also were more likely to smoke cigarettes—a gateway drug that indicates poor decision making in other areas as well (Largie et al., 2001).

Attitudes and practices regarding jobs and school vary a great deal from country to country (Hamilton & Wolfgang, 1996). In some nations, such as Japan, almost no adolescent is employed or even does significant chores at home, because the family and culture agree that the adolescent's job is to study. In other nations, including several in Europe, many older adolescents have jobs that are an integral part of their school curriculum. For example, in Germany most vocations require extensive apprenticeship; adolescents first choose a particular vocation and then are chosen by a particular employer, who trains them in conjunction with their schoolwork. In still other nations, including the United States, such school-to-work partnerships are relatively rare. When they are implemented by changing the structure of the school day and increasing the relevance of the school curriculum, they seem successful. Participants are more likely to graduate from high school and continue their education (Stern, 1997).

Even without formal school-to-work arrangements, almost all North American adolescents gain nonacademic experience in the job market—after school, on weekends, or during the summer—earning not only substantial spending money but also status in the eyes of their peers and respect from their parents (Mortimer et al., 1994). Indeed, their parents strongly approve of youth employment, citing increased responsibility, better money management, raised confidence, and work-related skills as benefits.

Sometimes such parents are correct if adolescents' job experience is relevant to adult employment and their earnings make a real family contribution. Under those circumstances the benefits of employment eventually outweigh the problems. This was apparent for almost every adolescent during the Great Depression of the 1930s, for most low-SES boys who found work in the military during World War II, and for rural youths in Iowa during the 1980s downturn in family farming. It is still true for adolescents living in the poorest enclaves of American cities (Elder, 1974; Shanahan et al., 1996).

Lessons Learned

As noted above, in today's job market meaningful jobs for teens are rare. Most research finds that, especially when adolescents are employed more than 20 hours a week, having a job means less time for study and lower grades. Adolescents conclude that work is routinely dull and that working hard is "a little bit crazy" (Greenberger & Steinberg, 1986). Moreover, the money earned usually goes to clothes, entertainment, cars, alcohol, and drugs—not to basic household necessities or savings accounts (Bachman & Schulenberg, 1993; Mortimer et al., 1996; Steinberg & Dornbusch, 1991). Provocative international data from European nations show a negative correlation between hours of after-school employment and learning in school (Kelly, 1998). Such correlations do not prove causation, but it is curious that U.S. fourth-graders, who obviously have no jobs, score much closer to their European peers on standardized tests than twelfth-graders do.

Even from one year to the next, having a job pulls down the grade point average (Steinberg, 1993). As adults, those who were employed extensively when teenagers are more likely to use drugs and less likely to feel connected to their families. There is one possible benefit: If someone had a stable work history (such as the same job and schedules for months or years) during adolescence, he or she is more likely to have a stable work history in adulthood (Mihalic & Elliott, 1997). In general, however, an adolescent's decision to work is made for the wrong reasons, sometimes with the unwitting encouragement of parents and teachers (Steinberg, 1996).

Making Decisions About Sex

Sometimes sex is presented as a biological drive rather than a cognitive choice. But the facts reveal that many decisions made by adolescents regarding sex are far from biologically inevitable. Among these facts are the following:

- International differences in teen birth rates are dramatic. Teenagers in the United States have far more babies than do their peers in any other developed nation, both because U.S. teens are more sexually active and because they use contraception less often and have fewer abortions (see Figure 15.7).
- Cultural differences in onset of sexual intercourse before age 18 are vast. In Mali, at that age, 72 percent of the girls but only 26 percent of the boys are sexually experienced. Brazil is almost the reverse: 29 percent of the girls and 63 percent of the boys. Other nations are sexually balanced, with either low rates, as in the Philippines (where only 6 percent of 17-year-old girls and 7 percent of the boys are sexually experienced) or high rates, as in Canada

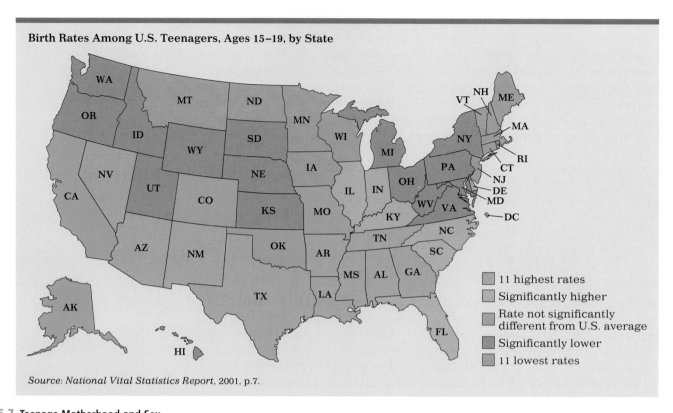

Birth Rates Among U.S. Teenagers, Ages 15–19, by State

- 11 highest rates
- Significantly higher
- Rate not significantly different from U.S. average
- Significantly lower
- 11 lowest rates

Source: National Vital Statistics Report, 2001, p.7.

FIGURE 15.7 **Teenage Motherhood and Sex Education** There are regional differences within the United States in birth rates among teenage girls. The reasons are not fully known, but the states with the highest birth rates tend to be the ones whose schools teach "abstinence only" in their sex-education classes. Is this a cause or a consequence of, or irrelevant to, the teen birth rate?

sexually active Traditionally, a euphemism for sexual intercourse; still in use, even though today many adolescents engage in many behaviors other than penile–vaginal penetration

(where about 50 percent of both sexes are sexually active by age 17 (Singh et al., 2000).

■ The teen birth rate worldwide has dropped significantly since 1990. In the United States, these decreases have occurred in every ethnic and age group, but most dramatically among African-Americans and among 15- to 17-year-olds (National Vital Statistics Report, 2001) (see Figure 15.8).

■ Use of contraception, particularly condom use among adolescent boys, has at least doubled in most nations since 1990 and has more than tripled in the United States.

Although neither biology nor dominant cultures changed much between 1990 and 2000, adolescents in almost every nation are making different decisions than adolescents did a mere 10 years ago. What changed their thinking? In the United States, detailed information from a representative sample of teenagers of every ethnic, regional, and economic group is scarce, because regulations imposed by the U.S. Congress forbid asking teenagers confidential questions unless their parents have given explicit, written permission. As a result, solid data are elusive. For example, one national survey found that, in 1995, among sexually active 15- to 17-year-old boys, 20 percent had had at least two partners in the past three months; another, similar survey found that almost twice as many, 38 percent, had (Santelli et al., 2000). (Although both surveys were done anonymously and privately, the first was conducted in the subjects' homes and the second at school. Did that make the difference?)

Researchers do not even know what **sexually active** means to teenagers. Ten years ago, adolescent couples who were sexually active did many things together, including masturbation, oral sex, shared bathing and sleeping, and penile-vaginal penetration, with the last on this list often the first intimate activity the couple performed. Consequently, almost all research on adolescent sex asks if the person has had intercourse. If the answer is "no," the person is assumed to be sexually inactive. However, adolescent sexual behavior is far more diverse than the "Did they or didn't they?" question about intercourse reveals (Whitaker et al., 2000). Some young people who have oral sex do consider themselves to be having sex (Horan et al., 1998; Remez, 2000; Sanders & Reinisch, 1999) and therefore do not think they need any guidance about intimate relationships, sexually transmitted diseases, or contraception—an uninformed and dangerously egocentric belief.

Sex Education in School

Almost all secondary schools provide sex education, often beginning at age 11 or so (Landry et al., 2000). In the United States, beyond providing the facts about sexually transmitted diseases, reproduction, and puberty, most high school programs teach how to tell a partner "no" about sex (CDC, August 18, 2000). From a developmental perspective, this is to be commended: Teenagers need not only experience with formal operational thinking (the facts of biological sex and reproduction) but also practice with emotional expression and social interaction.

According to recent data, 93 percent of schools in the United States teach about sex and health (a marked increase since 1980, and even since 1990), emphasizing how to avoid drugs, AIDS, and pregnancy. Most focus on the dangers of sex and the benefits of abstinence, sometimes exclusively. Only 43 percent teach the correct use of condoms, a decline over the past decade (CDC, August 18, 2000). Other research also finds that, compared to 1988, current teachers are less likely to explain methods of contraception (only 40 percent mention mifepristone, the drug that halts pregnancy in the first few weeks), less likely to provide referrals for medical treatment (now 35 percent, formerly 48 percent), less likely to discuss sexual orientation (51 percent, down from 68 percent), and more likely to claim that abstinence from intercourse is the only way to avoid pregnancy or disease (23 percent, up from 2 percent) (Darroch et al., 2000). About 35 percent of all school districts in the United States require that sexual abstinence be taught as the only acceptable alternative to marriage and forbid mention of contraception, but few classroom teachers are that dogmatic (Gold & Nash, 2001).

Some adults worry that if teenagers know too much about sex, they will be encouraged to try it. Given the nature of adolescent cognition, this worry seems needless. Adolescents are eager to learn what is possible, and they enjoy

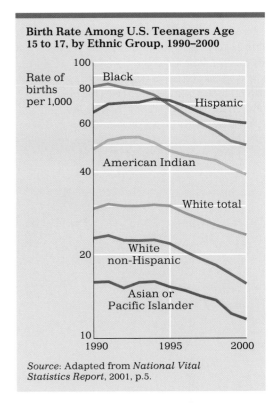

Birth Rate Among U.S. Teenagers Age 15 to 17, by Ethnic Group, 1990–2000

Source: Adapted from *National Vital Statistics Report*, 2001, p.5.

FIGURE 15.8 Fewer Children Having Children The recent across-the-board drop in the rate of births to adolescents aged 15 to 17 is especially remarkable for two reasons: The abortion rate among teenage girls has dropped slightly, and the rate of sexual activity among 15- to 17-year-old girls has not changed significantly.

A Public Kiss The specific ways in which physical affection is expressed depend on cohort and context, not just biological processes—as Mike knew when he presented Tiffany with a white carnation for Valentine's Day.

? *Observational Quiz* (see answer, page 492): In what year and in which country did this kiss occur?

! *Answer to Observational Quiz* (from page 491): The contemporary United States is one of the few countries where large, comprehensive high schools are common and rules against public displays of affection by students had been lifted by 1990. In fact, this high school is in Syracuse, New York, and the photograph was taken in 1999.

Especially for Religious Leaders: Suppose you believe very strongly in some tenet of your faith, but the youth group includes teenagers who act contrary to your belief. What do you do?

challenging conventional adult wisdom, but possibility does not necessarily become reality. A review of more than 100 sex-education programs by the Surgeon General of the United States found that teaching adolescents about contraception

> does not increase adolescent sexual activity, either by hastening the onset of sexual intercourse, increasing the frequency of sexual intercourse, or increasing the number of sexual partners. . . . Some evaluated programs increased condom use or contraception use more generally for adolescents who were sexually active.
>
> *[Satcher, 2001]*

From what we know about adolescent thinking—hypothetical, questioning, deductive—it makes sense that adolescents would want to learn all they could about sex and contraception, and that they would not necessarily act on this knowledge. Possibility does not mean actuality (see Appendix A). A Boston survey of high school students, both sexually active and not, found that they all agreed that schools should provide more factual information, not more moral instruction (Hacker et al., 2000). Many educators hope that morality will be taught at home, but adolescent–parent communication about sex is difficult, as we will see in the next chapter.

Cultures are dynamic, not static. They can work to decrease the birth rate as well as to foster it, and every nation has witnessed shifts (some increases, some decreases) in rates of adolescent sex, STDs, and pregnancy. One notable example comes from France, where nurses in all the public and church-sponsored schools were authorized, as of January 2000, to provide emergency contraception to any girl who requested it. They were also told to counsel girls who had impulsively had unprotected intercourse and to encourage them to talk to their parents. France's teen pregnancy rate is only a third as high as that of the United States, but the French want to reduce it further, and they believe that the best approach is to encourage adolescent contraception, not to try to stamp out adolescent sex. One government official explained:

> Young people, we assume, are going to be interested in sexual relationships. You can't forbid sex, but you can ask young people to be responsible. That's what this campaign is about—protecting young people.
>
> *[quoted in Boonstra, 2000]*

Risk Taking, Decision Making, and Cultures

Although culture and worldwide trends are influential, and obviously France and the United States have quite different contexts for adolescent decision making, no one is a helpless product of age, sex, culture, or cohort. The final decisions about sex, drugs, school, careers, and so on are made by individuals, perhaps in consultation with their peers and families. This point was forcefully made by researchers who analyzed the data from the Ad Health comprehensive, longitudinal study of U.S. teenagers (Blum et al., 2000). The results could be clustered: Each ethnic group had somewhat different patterns of teenager risks (see Table 15.1). Adolescents in all ethnic groups who lived with both their parents took fewer risks than did adolescents in single-parent homes; in general, adolescents from high-income families displayed more cautious behavior with sex and weapons, and more risky behavior with alcohol and cigarettes (as well as being more at risk for suicide). More significant, these researchers report that none of these factors explained much of the variance in risk taking from one adolescent to another:

Talking with Dad Teenagers who feel that their parents listen to them are more likely to postpone sexual intercourse, avoid using drugs, and go on to college. This father and daughter in an outdoor café in France are obviously communicating comfortably, and neither is shutting the other out.

MICHAEL KAGAN / STOCK, BOSTON

TABLE 15.1 Adolescent Risk Taking by U.S. Ethnic Group

Risky Behavior	Whites	Hispanics	Blacks
Smoking cigarettes: frequency and amount	Highest	Medium	Lowest
Drinking alcohol: frequency and amount	Highest	Medium	Lowest
Carrying a weapon or being involved in an incident where weapon was used: frequency scale	Lowest	Quite high	Highest
Sex: ever had intercourse	Lowest	Quite low	Highest
Suicidal thoughts, attempts: scale of seriousness	Highest	Quite high	Lowest

Source: Blum et al., 2000.

Risky Business This table, which uses the U.S. census ethnic categories for responses in the Ad Health study, shows the comparative risk taking of the three largest ethnic groups of adolescents. Not tallied are Asian-Americans, who are lowest on all five indicators, and Native Americans, who are relatively high. Knowing people's ethnicity, or even knowing their income or family structure, does not make it possible to predict how likely an individual is to take any particular risk. Much more relevant is knowing thought processes and immediate social context—family and peers.

> Knowing race/ethnicity, income, and family structure provides little predictive power at the individual level. . . . Rather we must look at neighborhood, family, school, peer and individual characteristics and how those characteristics interact within various demographic groups to truly understand the dynamics that contribute to specific risk behaviors.
>
> *[Blum et al., 2000]*

Even today, almost half of all U.S. high school seniors are virgins, and 96 percent of all teenage girls have never given birth. Why not? Most adolescents are in school, planning to go to college, expecting to become workers and taxpayers, husbands and wives, fathers and mothers. They take risks and follow their intuitions and emotions, but they also ask questions and analyze logical alternatives. The only way to know how adolescents make their choices—what facts, thoughts, and values they use—is to ask detailed questions of hundreds of them, from every region and group, and to listen to the answers carefully, without judging. Every reader of this book knows teenagers who could explain their sexual and other thoughts and practices. Embarrassing, perhaps—but think of the consequences of not asking.

Response for Religious Leaders (from page 492): This is not the time for dogma; teenagers intuitively rebel against authority. Nor is it the time to be quiet about your beliefs, because teenagers need some structures to help them think. Instead of going to either extreme, begin a dialogue. Listen respectfully to their concerns and emotions, and encourage them to think more deeply about the implications of their actions.

Not Me! A young woman jumps into the Pacific Ocean near Santa Cruz, California, while at a friend's birthday party. The jump is illegal, yet since 1975, 52 people have died on these cliffs. Hundreds of young people each year decide that the thrill is worth the risk, aided by the invincibility fable and by what they think are sensible precautions. (Note that she is wearing shoes. Also note that the dog has apparently decided against risking a jump.)

NORBERT SCHWERIN / THE IMAGE WORKS

SUMMARY

Intellectual Advances

1. All the aspects of information processing that have been developing since infancy continue to advance during adolescence. Selective attention becomes more focused, memory expands, control processes mature. Underlying all these advances is brain maturation. As myelination continues and coordination between various parts of the brain becomes more elaborate, adolescents become quicker and deeper thinkers.

2. Adolescents are no longer earthbound and concrete in their thinking; they prefer to imagine the possible, the probable, and even the impossible, instead of focusing on what is real. They develop hypotheses and explore, using deductive reasoning.

3. *Formal operational thought* is Piaget's term for adolescent and adult cognition, the fourth of his four periods of cognitive development. He tested and demonstrated formal operational thought with various problems that might be encountered by students in a high school science or math class, such as adjusting weights and their distance from the center to make a scale balance.

4. Not every adolescent or adult succeeds at Piaget's tests of formal thinking, perhaps because Piaget did not consider sociocultural variations and did not study variations of hypothetical-deductive thinking in every domain. However, many developmentalists believe that, with proper guidance and experience, all adolescents can sometimes reason logically and abstractly.

5. Intuitive thinking, also known as experiential or heuristic thinking, becomes more forceful during adolescence. One manifestation, called adolescent egocentrism, is highly self-centered and emotional, in contrast to the objective, abstract thinking of formal operational thought. Adolescent egocentrism gives rise to the invincibility fable, the personal fable, and the imaginary audience.

6. Adolescents sometimes use illogical, intuitive ways to solve problems, even though they are capable of logical thought. Ideally, both adolescents and adults combine analytic and intuitive thinking, using them harmoniously to find the best solutions.

Schools, Learning, and the Adolescent Mind

7. Secondary education has become more widespread over the past 100 years, as nations have come to realize that their citizens need more than literacy and other basic skills in order to function well in the future. High school graduation correlates with health, wealth, and employment, for individuals and nations.

8. The specifics of educating high school students are not straightforward. Various nations, cohorts, families, and communities differ in their goals and values, as well as in the traditions and structures of their schools. Internationally, nationally, and historically, schools vary widely in size, enrollment, requirements, and many other aspects.

9. For adolescent cognitive development, smaller schools with engaging instruction that invites logical as well as personal reflection seem best. Adolescents are more motivated when they discuss issues with each other and with adults, and when they are challenged within a supportive context. Motivation and attitude seem crucial for learning.

10. As students move from primary to secondary education, usually their grades fall and their engagement decreases. One reason is that secondary schools are more competitive than cooperative. Another reason is that teachers are knowledgeable in particular subjects rather than being involved with their students' learning overall.

11. Some students rebound in motivation and interest as they approach their senior year, especially if they participate in extracurricular activities. However, about a fifth of U.S. students drop out before earning their high school diploma.

12. High-stakes tests are controversial. They are intended to bring more accountability to high school curricula. Critics fear that they decrease motivation and discriminate, particularly against minority ethnic groups. Substantial, longitudinal evidence on this issue is not yet available.

13. School violence is less troublesome in the minds of students than it is for the adult public. Improving school relationships and increasing academic engagement, as some teachers do, may not only advance cognition but may also prevent violence.

Adolescent Decision Making

14. Adolescents have different priorities from adults, so they make choices adults do not condone. Some of these decisions involve taking risks, partly because emotional thinking and impulses are unchecked unless the adolescent takes time to discuss and reflect.

15. Given the complexity and discontinuity of career paths in today's world, the teen years are probably too early to settle on a career. Employment during high school is likely to undermine academic achievement instead of teaching useful adult skills.

16. Sex education is almost universal in U.S. schools, often starting at age 11 or even earlier. The specifics of contraception, sexual orientation, and medical services are not usually included. Worldwide, the teen birth rate is declining.

17. Although education, national policies, and cultural norms affect risk taking, much of the variation in personal risk taking depends on more immediate factors, such as personality, cognitive maturity, parental conversations, and peer groups.

KEY TERMS

hypothetical thought (p. 466)
inductive reasoning (p. 467)
deductive reasoning (p. 467)
formal operational thought
 (p. 468)

postformal thought (p. 469)
adolescent egocentrism
 (p. 472)
invincibility fable (p. 472)

personal fable (p. 473)
imaginary audience (p. 473)
person–environment fit (p. 478)
volatile mismatch (p. 479)

self-handicapping (p. 483)
high-stakes tests (p. 484)
sexually active (p. 490)

KEY QUESTIONS

1. What three kinds of advances typically occur in adolescent thought?

2. Give an example of your own use of deductive (not inductive) thinking.

3. What are the differences between analytic and intuitive thought?

4. How are the personal fable and the imaginary audience similar?

5. When would a person's reasoning processes be logical, and when would they be emotional?

6. Can you show how a harmonious combination of both analytic and intuitive thought could help in settling a controversy currently in the news?

7. Compared to 100 years ago, how does secondary education differ and how is it the same?

8. Why are young adolescents less motivated in school than children are?

9. What is the role of extracurricular activities in secondary schools?

10. Why should adults be concerned about the way adolescents make decisions?

11. What benefits might adolescents see in taking risks, such as skipping school with their friends?

12. How do students and politicians differ in their views about sex education in schools?

13. What are the positive and negative consequences of employment during high school?

14. How have adolescent sexual practices changed since 1990?

Chapter Sixteen

Adolescence: Psychosocial Development

identity A consistent definition of one's self as a unique individual, in terms of roles, attitudes, beliefs, and aspirations.

possible selves Various intellectual fantasies about what the future might bring if one or another course of action is chosen.

Adolescence starts when the physical changes of puberty transform a childish body into an adult one (see Chapter 14). Then the cognitive changes of adolescence enable the young person to move beyond concrete thought, to think hypothetically (see Chapter 15). However, the psychosocial changes—relating to parents with new independence, to friends with new intimacy, to society with new commitment, and to oneself with new understanding—are the critical ones that bring the young person to adulthood. Becoming an adult is not a matter of size or intellect; it requires social maturity (Grotevant, 1998).

The Self and Identity

Psychosocial development during adolescence is best understood as a quest for self-understanding, for answering the question "Who am I?" Momentous changes—growth spurt, sexual awakening, less personal schools, more intimate friendships, and risk taking—challenge each adolescent to find **identity,** a unique and consistent self-definition (Kroger, 2000; Larson & Ham, 1993).

The first step in the identity process is to establish the integrity of personality—that is, to align emotions, thinking, and behavior to be consistent no matter what the place, time, circumstances, or social relationship. "Two-faced," "wishy-washy," and "hypocritical" are among the worst accusations one adolescent can throw at another, in part because integrity is fervently sought but is frustratingly elusive.

Multiple Selves

In the process of trying to find their true selves, many adolescents experience **possible selves**—that is, diverse perceptions of who they really are, who they are in different groups or settings, who they might like to become, and who they fear becoming (Markus & Nurius, 1986; Markus et al., 1990). Many teenagers notice how much they are affected by changing settings and circumstances: Their behavior switches from reserved to rowdy, from cooperative to antagonistic, from loving to manipulative. Aware of the inconsistencies among these multiple selves, they ask which one, if any, is the "real me." One developmentalist noted, "The tortuous search for the self involves a concern with who or what I am, a task made more difficult given the multiple me's that crowd the landscape" (Harter, 1999, p. 68).

Ideally, when adolescents talk about their possible selves, they have specific plans for a particular course of education, career, and so forth. A teenager who combines fearfulness with high but nonspecific aspirations is a source of worry (Yowell, 2000).

false self A set of behaviors that is adopted by a person to combat rejection, to please others, or to try out as a possible self.

As they try to sort through their possible (and multiple) selves, adolescents frequently take on a **false self**, acting in ways that they know are contrary to their core being—even if they are not sure what that core being is. According to one group of researchers (Harter et al., 1996), adolescents display three distinct types of false selves:

■ *The acceptable false self.* This false self arises from the adolescent's perception that the real self is rejected by parents and peers—a perception often colored by the adolescent's own self-hate. Adolescents who adopt a false self in order to be accepted tend to feel worthless, depressed, and hopeless; they engage in self-betrayal to hide their true nature. They also report low levels of real self-understanding.

■ *The pleasing false self.* This second type of false self arises from a wish to impress or please others. It is quite common among adolescents. Those who adopt it appear to be less debilitated psychologically, and to have greater self-understanding, than those whose false selves arise from a sense of rejection.

■ *The experimental false self.* This type of false self is one that adolescents try out "just to see how it feels." Compared with adolescents who engage in the first two types of false behavior, these adolescents report the highest levels of self-esteem and self-knowledge, partly because although they acknowledge that their experimentation is not their usual, expected behavior, they do not feel it is fake.

This same group of researchers found a developmental progression: False and contradictory selves are most common in midadolescence and gradually become more coherent by late adolescence (Harter et al., 1997).

Identity Status

Younger children describe themselves primarily in terms of their skills in school, with friends, and perhaps on the athletic field. But adolescents distinguish their scholastic competence from other aspects of who they are, such as their job skills, romantic appeal, moral conduct, and peer acceptance (Harter, 1999). They also begin to ponder career options, political identification, religious commitment, and sexual ethics, questioning how these values fit together with expectations for the future and the beliefs acquired in the past. These are the four aspects—vocation, politics, religion, and sex—of identity first highlighted by Erik Erikson (1968).

As they deal with these increasingly diverse and complex aspects of selfhood, adolescents confront the psychosocial challenge referred to by Erikson as **identity versus role confusion.** For developmentalists like Erikson, the search for identity leads to the primary crisis of adolescence—a crisis in which the young person struggles to reconcile a quest for "a conscious sense of individual uniqueness" with "an unconscious striving for a continuity of experience . . . and a solidarity with a group's ideals" (Erikson, 1968).

The search for identity is ongoing throughout adolescence. Along the way an adolescent may experience more than one identity status or condition. The ultimate status, called **identity achievement,** is reached through "selective repudiation and mutual assimilation of childhood identifications" (Erikson, 1968). That is, adolescents ideally establish their own identities by reconsidering the goals and values set by their parents and culture, then accepting some and rejecting others. Adolescents who "achieve" identity know who they are; they remain connected to all the morals and attitudes they have learned earlier but are not inescapably bound to any of them.

identity versus role confusion Erikson's term for the fifth stage of development, in which the person tries to figure out "Who am I?" but is confused as to which of many roles to adopt.

identity achievement Erikson's term for the attainment of identity, or the point at which a person understands who he or she is as a unique individual, in accord with past experiences and future plans.

Some young people short-circuit this quest by never examining traditional values. The result is **foreclosure,** or closing out a process before it is complete. In foreclosure, an adolescent adopts parents' or society's roles and values whole-sale, rather than exploring alternatives and forging a personal identity. A typical example is the young man who has always wanted (or been pressured) to follow in his father's footsteps. If his father was a doctor, the adolescent might diligently study chemistry and biology in high school and take premed courses in college.

Other adolescents decide that the roles their parents and society expect them to fill are unattainable or unappealing, yet they cannot find alternatives that are truly their own. The reaction may be a **negative identity,** that is, an identity opposite whatever is expected. The teacher's child refuses to go to college, the religious leader's child becomes a prostitute—the crucial factor in negative identity is not the choice itself but the rebellious defiance that underlies it. One version of negative identity is *oppositional identity* (Ogbu, 1993), which occurs when the adolescent rejects the dominant culture by adopting and exaggerating a negative stereotype. For example, some gay young men proudly call themselves "queer," and some African-Americans take pride in being the "baddest."

Still other young people experience **identity diffusion,** typically having few commitments to goals or values—of parents, peers, or the larger society—and often being apathetic about taking on any role. These young people have difficulty meeting the usual demands of adolescence, such as completing school assignments, finding a job, and thinking about the future. Instead, they sleep too much, waste time watching television and hanging out, and claim not to care about anything because "nothing matters" or "whatever . . . ." If diffusion continues, an adolescent may move from one sexual or platonic relationship to another, never with passion and commitment. Almost every teenager experiences diffusion, at least for a short while, when the expectations from adult society become overwhelming.

Finally, in the process of finding a mature identity, many young people declare an **identity moratorium,** a kind of time-out during which they experiment with alternative identities without trying to settle on any one. In some cases, the culture provides formal moratoriums through various institutions. The most obvious example of an institutional moratorium in the United States is college, which usually requires that students sample a variety of academic areas before concentrating on any one. Being a full-time student also forestalls pressure from parents and peers to settle down, choose a career, and find a mate. Other institutions that permit a moratorium are the military, the Peace Corps, religious mission work, and various internships.

Dozens of studies have compared identity with cognitive or psychological development (Adams et al., 1992; Archer, 1994; Kroger, 2000). Table 16.1 shows some revealing combinations of statuses and traits. Note, for example, a strong ethnic identification among both achievers and foreclosers. These teens are proud to be Irish, Italian, Indonesian, or whatever they may be. However, those who have foreclosed are relatively high in prejudice, perhaps because they have simply seized on their own ethnicity without considering the merits of other backgrounds. By contrast, teens who have achieved identity are relatively low in prejudice, presumably because they are secure enough in their ethnic background that they do not need to put down others.

Extensive research, much of it longitudinal, confirms that many adolescents go through a period of foreclosure or diffusion, and then a moratorium, before they finally achieve

foreclosure Erikson's term for premature identity formation, which occurs when an adolescent adopts parents' or society's roles and values wholesale, without questioning and analysis.

negative identity An identity that is taken on with rebellious defiance, simply because it is the opposite of whatever parents or society expect.

identity diffusion A situation in which an adolescent does not seem to know or care what his or her identity is.

identity moratorium Erikson's term for a pause in identity formation that allows young people to explore alternatives without making final identity choices.

I'm a Big Girl Now Many adolescents worry that their true identity is hidden by various false selves. Young teenagers are likely to use their musical taste, their clothing and hairstyles, and sometimes their facial expression to make it very obvious to parents that they are no longer the obedient, predictable children they once were.

TONY FREEMAN / PHOTOEDIT

TABLE 16.1 Attitudes, Relationships, and Emotions Typical of the Major Identity Statuses

Characteristics	Identity Status			
	Foreclosed	**Diffused**	**Moratorium**	**Achieved**
Degree of anxiety	Tends to repress anxiety	Moderate	High	Moderate
Attitude toward parents	Loving and respectful	Withdrawn	Trying to distance self	Loving and caring
Degree of self-esteem	Low (easily affected by others)	Low ("empty")	High	High
Sense of ethnic identity	Strong	Neutral to ethnicity	Medium	Strong
Degree of prejudice	High	Neutral	Medium	Low
Kohlberg's moral stage	Preconventional or conventional	Preconventional or conventional	Postconventional	Postconventional
Dependence on others	Very dependent	Dependent	Self-directed	Self-directed
Cognitive processes	Simplifies complex issues; refers to others and to social norms for opinions and decisions	Complicates simple issues; defers to others in both personal and ideological choices	Thoughtful; procrastinates, especially in decisions; avoids referring to others' opinions or to norms	Thoughtful; makes decisions by both seeking new information and considering others' opinions
Attitude in college	Very satisfied as long as guidelines are clear	Variable, indifferent to most subjects unless motivated and "turned on"	Most dissatisfied (likely to change major)	Good; gets high grades
Relations with others	Stereotyped	Stereotyped or isolated	Intimate	Intimate

Source: Adapted from research reviewed by Archer, 1994; Kroger, 2000; Marcia et al., 1993; Moshman, 1999.

a mature identity. The process can take 10 years or more, with many college students still not clear about who they are or what they want to do (Grotevant, 1998; Marcia et al., 1993).

Is Achievement Always Best? Each of Erikson's four identity statuses is characterized by how much questioning and how much commitment the status includes. For Erikson and many other Western psychologists of his generation, the ideal was achievement, with the adolescent ranking high on both questioning and commitment; the least satisfactory was diffusion, with the young person seeming to have neither questions nor convictions. In today's society, might it be better to avoid commitment, staying in moratorium for years, or to choose foreclosure, avoiding the hard questions?

Status Versus Process

Erikson first described the identity crisis almost 50 years ago (Erikson, 1963, 1968). Although his clinical insights were not based on extensive longitudinal research, his formulation rang true; the identity crisis has become the best known of his eight stages. Shortly after that, James Marcia (1966) developed a series of questions to measure identity status, distinguishing foreclosure, diffusion, moratorium, and achievement based on commitments in the four core areas (vocation, religion, sex, and politics) that Erikson identified (see Table 16.2).

To illustrate status determination, consider religion. If a teenager self-identifies as a committed Christian, Jew, Muslim, Buddhist, or so on, specifies a subcategory such as Pentecostal or Orthodox, and worships and prays regularly, then that person has a religious identity. This identity is either foreclosed or achieved, depending on whether or not the person has asked the hard questions (e.g., why God allows suffering, why some people in that faith are immoral). Foreclosed members of a religious group have never really doubted; achieved members have questioned, struggled, and then developed their own satisfactory answers.

Those without a religious identity include both those in moratorium, who are questioning but who have not found

TABLE 16.2 Identity Status and Commitment

	No Commitment	**Commitment**
Not questioning	Diffusion	Foreclosure
Questioning	Moratorium	Achievement

Both theories emphasize that learning is not passive, but is affected by the learner. The two theories share concepts and sometimes terminology; the differences are in emphasis.

answers, and those in diffusion, who are indifferent and alienated—claiming, for instance, that "all religions are meaningless."

Developmentalists are more interested in ongoing processes than in status outcomes (Grotevant, 1998). This outlook has led to two additional questions:

1. Can a person achieve identity in one domain but still be searching in another? For example, could a person have foreclosed on religious identity, be diffused politically, in moratorium on vocational identity, and have achieved sexual identity? Yes. Indeed, in the twenty-first century, such a combination is not unusual. Vocational identity is particularly complex, since the choices are in the tens of thousands and since virtually no teens simply take up their parents' occupation, as many once did (Csikszentmihalyi & Schneider, 2000).

2. Is identity formed from within, when a person recognizes his or her true nature, or from without, after family and social forces push a teenager to adopt a particular identity? The answer is both: Identity is considered to be constructed, neither merely discovered nor blindly accepted (Muuss, 1996). In achieving a sexual identity (Moshman, 1999), for example, teenagers identify as homosexual or heterosexual, not entirely for biological or sociological reasons. People interweave nature and nurture to begin the complex process of developing their sexual orientation.

Gender Identity

Today, sexual identity is called **gender identity**, a term that refers to the person's self-identification as either male or female, with acceptance of all the roles and behaviors that society assigns to that sex. Originally, many experts in the psychoanalytic tradition, including Erikson, thought sexual identity meant realizing that one was either male or female, with the two sexes seen as opposites (Miller & Simon, 1980). Although gender identity could be confusing at puberty (partly because little information was supplied by embarrassed, secretive adults), and although some young adolescents experienced a brief period of homosexual experimentation, gender identity meant identifying oneself as a heterosexual male or female by adulthood (Erikson, 1968; Freud, 1958/2000).

Later research revealed that sexual orientation and gender identity are much more varied than a simple male–female division, perhaps because today's cohorts must answer more difficult questions. Each adolescent now makes a multitude of sexual decisions (as described in Chapter 15) and selects from various gender roles (first mentioned in Chapter 10). Some teenagers, for example, decide to have many heterosexual or homosexual or bisexual partners; some choose only one; some, none. They must also choose whether to date, whom to date, and what physical contact might be involved, since cultural rules are no longer dogmatically and universally enforced.

Even romance is optional, and if it is chosen, "falling in love" is done individually, with each person selecting (sometimes deliberately) a partner who may not match the expectations of parents or society. In India, Pakistan, and other nations, parents find husbands or wives for their children, a practice preferred by many adolescents from these cultures. Even in traditional Asian families, however, adolescents usually participate in the choice (Gibson-Cline 2000; O'Donnell & Sharpe, 2000).

gender identity A person's identification of the self as either male or female, with acceptance of all the roles and behaviors that society assigns to that sex.

Gay or Straight? These adolescents were among the 6,000 people who marched in the Gay/Straight Youth Pride parade in Boston in May 2001. This annual march is sponsored by the Massachusetts Governor's Safe Schools program with the goal of fostering self-esteem in teens, regardless of their sexual orientation.

MARILYN HUMPHRIES / THE IMAGE WORKS

Those who foreclose on being male or female can follow an easy set of rules, choosing an occupation, a course of study, a way of dressing, laughing, walking, and so on that signifies male or female, perhaps wearing see-through T-shirts or tight pants to make gender identity even more obvious. Some adolescents refuse to follow such patterns but instead may choose unisex hair and clothes, again making a statement. In gender identity, it is not easy to separate individual choice from social pressure, especially when we remember that resisting social pressure—as when a boy wears an earring—may be a negative identity that arises only in opposition to a social norm.

Some psychologists wondered if adolescent girls might avoid an identity crisis, because they would first seek intimacy (the next stage) and, once they found their sexual partner, develop their identity through him. Erikson (1968) wrote, "Something in the young woman's identity must keep itself open for the peculiarities of the man to be joined and of the children to be brought up" (p. 283). Perhaps "the construct of identity itself is biased toward the Western, masculine ideal of individual over relatedness" (S.J. Patterson et al., 1992, p. 14).

This hypothesis has not been verified: Contemporary young women are concerned with their own identity just as young men are. Females do seem slightly more concerned about family and interpersonal relationships, but all gender differences in identity formulation are a matter of frequency and degree, not of male–female opposites (Cross & Madson, 1997).

Today's adolescent girls plan careers and egalitarian marriages, and adults encourage them to achieve academically. Now more girls than boys graduate from high school and go on to college (in the United States, 55 percent of college students are female, compared to 40 percent in 1970). As one result, developmentalists are worried about boys who assert their male identity by rejecting "female" subjects such as literature (Rowan et al., 2002). Boys seek to validate their masculinity by being tough, in opposition to authority. Cursing in class, openly breaking the law, adopting an "attitude" of defiance—these are all admired by the other boys, who are loyal to their group. Consequently, "boys and men are in a state of identity confusion" because "modern society is littered with barriers and control on youthful assertiveness, particularly that of young men" (O'Donnell & Sharpe, 2000, pp. 113, 158).

Ethnic Identity

For members of minority ethnic groups in democratic societies, identity achievement entails additional stress. On the one hand, democratic ideology espouses a color-blind, open society in which background is irrelevant to achievement and in which all citizens develop their potential according to individual merits and personal goals. On the other hand, most minorities take pride in their ethnicity, expecting teenagers to honor their roots and cherish their heritage.

Hidden beneath both of these ideologies are instances of prejudice by the majority against the minority, attempts by minority members to mirror majority standards, and stereotypes from all sides. In adolescence, when appearance and mannerisms take on prime importance, coloring, cutting, straightening, or curling one's hair, wearing clothes and jewelry that are or aren't ethnic, and even talking "black" or "white," "Latino" or "Anglo," can become issues. Thus, identity formation requires finding the right balance between transcending one's background and immersing oneself in it. In Erikson's words, during adolescence "each new generation links the actuality of a living past with that of a promising future" (Erikson, 1968).

Linking past and future is particularly difficult when one's expectations of living by the democratic ideal are thwarted by social prejudice and institutionalized racism. As a result, "many ethnic minority youth . . . may have to deny large parts of themselves to survive, may internalize negative images of their group,

and [consequently] may fail to adopt an ethnic cultural identity" (Hill et al., 1994). In some cases, minority youths adopt a negative identity—rejecting wholesale the traditions of both their ethnic group and the majority culture.

Such resistance to external control may be seen in a decision one 15-year-old made in defiance of her childhood tradition:

> I wanted to feel free and independent. . . . I wanted a haircut. But I couldn't make myself do it. A haircut was a big decision. My hair was more than just a bunch of dead cells. It was a symbol of control. For my parents and relatives, long hair is considered an essential part of being a woman. Especially for "good Indian girls."
>
> [Chikkatur, 1997]

Torn by all these conflicts, one day this young woman decided and—before she told her family or changed her mind—had her hair cut. For the next month, as all her relatives criticized her, she alternated between thinking she had made a "huge mistake" and being "glad I cut my hair." She considered her haircut a symbol of her independence, not only from her family but also from the majority culture's expectations about beauty, marriage, and sexual orientation.

More often than choosing independence, as this young woman did, African-American, Native American, Mexican-American, and Asian-American adolescents choose foreclosed identity, and they do so more readily than European-Americans (Phinney, 1990; Rotheram-Borus & Wyche, 1994; Streitmatter, 1988). The searching process itself may be too difficult when criticism from one's own group or from the majority group is evoked (or assumed) by every action.

Peers, themselves torn by similar conflicts, can be very critical. Minority-group members may be branded "Oreos," "bananas," or "apples"—colorful on the outside but white inside. Whites who associate with blacks may be called "gray," or those who associate with Indians may be said to have "gone native." And these are the kinder comments.

In general, ethnic identity becomes more important when adolescents see their background as different from that of others, a perception based more on family history and other people's judgments than on their own conclusions. According to the 2000 United States census, 40 percent of all teenagers are not European-American. Consequently, the need for a distinct ethnic identity is becoming less pressing for young Americans of African or Latino or Asian descent, who will gradually come to see themselves not as descendants of a particular nation but, more generally, in broader ethnic categories. This "pan-ethnic" outlook distresses some parents, who remain loyal to their particular childhood home. Such ethnic identity issues are emotionally and politically complex (Falcon et al.,

The Same but Different Traditionally, minority identity in the United States focused on race, with young people of color needing to find their place in a white world. Currently, however, the issue has broadened to be seen as ethnic, not racial. These California high school students look physically similar but are from very different backgrounds: the one in the foreground of the left-hand photo is from Cambodia and the one in the right-hand photo is from Mexico. Each is finding her own bicultural identity. Their backgrounds differ, but the search is universal; many adolescents of European descent also struggle with issues of heritage and self.

2001). Young people become more connected to their peers in their new community, taking on their attitudes toward drugs, parents, or school (Hamm, 2000). For many young people, religion and SES affect attitudes more than ethnicity does (Montemayer, 2000).

Provocative research comes from a large longitudinal study of the relationships among academic grades, self-esteem, and identification with school. In the eighth grade, members of all ethnic groups showed some correlations among these three variables. As time went on, the correlations were maintained among the European-American children, weakened among the Latino-Americans, and disappeared among the African-Americans. In fact, by their senior year of high school, the black boys had high self-esteem, but their identity was not connected to their performance in school at all—which was fortunate for their self-confidence because their grades worsened with each year. A less optimistic possibility is that their achievement declined *because* they did not associate being a proud African-American man with being a good student.

Identity and Social Context

Cohort differences affect not only ethnic and gender identity but every other aspect of identity formation as well. We all develop within families and communities that are influenced by political and economic contexts. In fact, Erikson (1968) thought that the personal identity crisis and the surrounding historical circumstances "help to define each other and are truly relative to each other" (p. 23). Accordingly, each generation of developmentalists wonders how the overall social context helps or hinders identity achievement. Societies make identity easier to attain in two ways:

- By providing values that have stood the test of time and that continue to serve their function
- By providing social structures and customs that ease the transition from childhood to adulthood

Whether a given culture actually provides these values and social structures depends primarily on agreement among members of the culture and stable life circumstances from one generation to the next.

In a culture where virtually everyone holds the same moral, political, religious, and sexual values and where social change is slow, identity is easy to achieve. Most young people in such traditional societies simply accept the roles and values they grew up with—the only ones they have ever known. (An exception might be the occasional adolescent who possesses some special personality trait—quirky creativity, a rare passion, or an unusual talent—that is contrary to the traditional path within his or her culture. Such individuals become the prophets, the freaks, or the criminals, depending on the place and time.)

In modern industrial and postindustrial societies, by contrast, cultural consensus is rare and continuity is rarer still. Everything is open to question by almost everyone. Rapid social change, a broad diversity of values and goals, and an ever-expanding array of choices characterize such a society and make identity formation difficult. As one geneticist put it, "Pluralism in moral life and discourse masks a deep-seated conceptual confusion" (Carson, 1999, p. 191). When anything is possible, nothing is easy.

The Rite of Passage

Anthropologists note that the identity crisis was smoother and shorter in simple societies (Schlegel & Barry, 1991). Every young person knew what adulthood meant for him or her (because all the grownups followed similar, and quite visible, patterns), and cultures provided rites of passage. As you learned in Chapter 14, a **rite of passage** is a dramatic ceremony that marks the transition from childhood to adulthood. In traditional societies, the rite of passage meant group initiation of boys in their teens, who were ritually scarred on their faces and/or circumcised and then were taught the secrets of their ancestors while they recuperated. For girls, the rite of passage was more often individual, taking place after menarche, when a girl was presented to the community as eligible for marriage and motherhood.

Echoes of these ceremonies remain, even in industrialized, complex societies, in the form of the Sweet Sixteen, la Quinceañera, the debutantes' ball, the senior prom, the fraternity initiation, or even the wedding (the bachelor party, the bridal shower). Such ceremonies in developed nations are not as dramatic, painful, or universal as the traditional rites of passage. Developmentalists wonder whether the identity crisis itself is a social construction, the psychic price paid by teenagers who have no traditional mode of becoming adults (Elkind, 1981).

The Impact of Social Change

If social change produces the identity crisis, then teenagers would have a particularly difficult time in modern nations that are experiencing massive social change. Several teams of researchers looked specifically at teenagers in European countries where marked social change had occurred during the 1990s. They expected to find severe identity crises in nations such as the former East and West Germany (Silbereisen & von Eye, 1999), Armenia and Ukraine (Roberts et al., 2000), Hungary and Poland (van Hoorn et al., 2000), northern Finland and neighboring Russia (Puuronen et al., 2000).

In all these regions, nationalism, democracy, and capitalism had burst forth. Economic and political upheaval had disrupted the lives of adults, increasing unemployment, postponing marriage, decreasing births, shortening life. Adolescents should have been hard hit, experiencing massive identity crises and torn in many directions by such strong economic and political currents just when they were seeking to know themselves.

Researchers "expected more dramatic changes and bolder findings" (van Hoorn et al., 2000, p. 277) than they actually encountered. In every one of these national and international comparisons, most adolescents seemed oblivious to the wider political scene. For example, a 17-year-old boy in Pecs, Hungary, in 1994, who had just lived through massive social and political revolution and who could hear gunfire from the civil war in nearby Croatia almost daily, said

> I am interested in everything. I like new technology, computers, videos. I have a guitar that I play at home. I usually go to play basketball with my friends. . . . Briefly, I feel good, I am friendly and I have a sense of humor. . . . Love, friendship, honesty and self-assurance are the most important values in a person's life. There were no essential, important events in my life, only that I was born.
>
> *[quoted in van Hoorn et al., 2000, p. 22]*

The same sentiments could have been expressed by hundreds of thousands of teenagers in dozens of nations. These adolescents acknowledged the political changes when they were explicitly asked about them, but they were amazingly unaffected by them, even when economic disruption meant reduced income and increased job worries for them. Generally, they seemed not to notice that dramatic social upheaval had occurred. A 16-year-old, also from Hungary, said, "It's good that the Russian soldiers left but we don't really feel that they have" (p. 24).

Another team (Silbereisen & von Eye, 1999) studied possible differences among teenagers in Germany, all of whom had seen their nation transformed when the Berlin Wall came down and East and West Germany were reunited. Self-esteem was similar and quite high throughout Germany, on both sides of the former East-West divide. The variations that were found seemed related primarily to family, regional culture (e.g., south versus north), and school, with

LESTER SLOAN / WOODFIN CAMP & ASSOCIATES

The Rite of Passage These boys are participating in a puberty ritual in the Congo. The blue dye on their faces indicates that they are temporarily dead, to be reborn as men once the ritual is over. Such rites of passage, which are based on strong cultural cohesion regarding social roles and responsibility, make adolescence a quick and distinct transition for all concerned. In technologically sophisticated societies, rites of passage are less obvious, although the events surrounding high school graduation are similar in several ways.

rite of passage A dramatic ceremony that marks the transition from childhood to adulthood.

students in the college-bound high schools (*Gymnasium*) more confident than those in the least selective schools (*Hauptschule*), no matter whether they lived east or west of the old division.

International Identity Crisis In another series of studies, researchers surveyed adolescents worldwide (Gibson-Cline, 1996, 2000). In more than a dozen nations, 13- to 20-year-olds were asked, "Name one concern or problem that causes you to feel worried or pressured." Again, to their surprise, researchers found similarities that seemed to transcend national and economic divisions. Schooling problems predominated. Identity concerns were also apparent—no less so in China and India than in Canada or Japan (see Figure 16.1).

Not shown in the figure are other concerns that the researchers expected to find—about war, catastrophes, sexuality, poverty, and several other possible problems. None of these were mentioned by many teenagers. The researchers concluded, contrary to their expectations, that adolescents worry about personal, not political, issues. Even war did not concern many teenagers, except for about 8 percent in Israel, who mostly wondered if the required army service would disrupt their personal plans. AIDS and drug addiction were never mentioned.

A few gender, national, and economic differences emerged. For example, impoverished adolescents who were no longer in school were more concerned about material needs and finding a job. However, these differences were not found in every nation. When they were found, they were variations on a general theme: Even among the disadvantaged youth, identity concerns were more common than material concerns.

Losing the Farm A longitudinal, intense study of a very different group of teenagers—high school students in rural Iowa at a time of many farm foreclosures and few jobs—also found that family, school, and church influences were a successful buffer against the decline in material wealth or vocational promise (Elder & Conger, 2000).

Overall, in various kinds of studies in many cultures, family and peer relationships seem more important to current adolescents than the broader social context. Relations with parents and peers will be discussed in detail later. First, however, we will examine

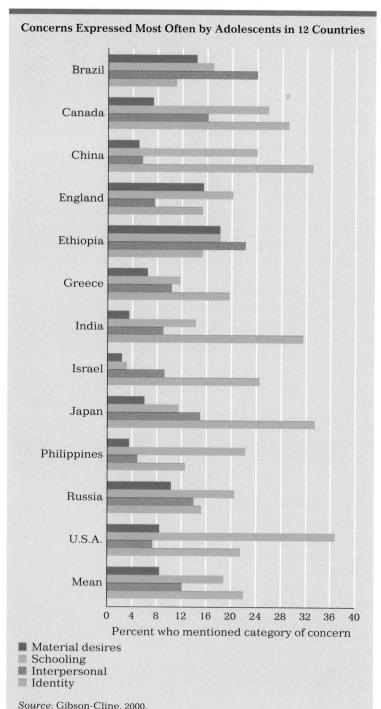

Concerns Expressed Most Often by Adolescents in 12 Countries

Percent who mentioned category of concern

- ■ Material desires
- ▨ Schooling
- ■ Interpersonal
- ▨ Identity

Source: Gibson-Cline, 2000.

FIGURE 16.1 Who Am I? In one of the most ambitious international studies of adolescents ever done, teams of researchers asked thousands of teenagers—male and female, older and younger, advantaged, disadvantaged, and poor—in four continents to "name one concern or problem that causes you to feel worried or pressured; please describe this concern in more detail." Of the fourteen possible categories, ten were rarely mentioned, including war, sexuality, and extreme poverty. The four categories most often mentioned were material desires (such as the need to earn money), schooling (such as worry about school failure), interpersonal (such as friendship), and identity (including self-concept). Answers varied by gender, age, SES, and nationality, but worldwide patterns were apparent. For example, identity was a concern among every group.

two potentially serious problems, depression and delinquency, both of which appear in almost every adolescent in the milder forms of lowered self-esteem and increased rebelliousness.

Depression and Self-Destruction

As you learned in Chapter 14, puberty brings intense and rapid changes of mood, from happy to sad (or even from ecstatic to despondent) and back again. Happier feelings lead to more activity and joy, and, as described in Chapter 15, perhaps to fantasies of invincibility and grandeur. Some adolescents, some of the time, feel on top of the world, destined for great accomplishments. This can be destructively unrealistic, but usually it simply reflects youthful energy and exuberance.

By contrast, adolescents can feel despondent and depressed, overwhelmed by the troubles of the world and their own inadequacies. Ironically, most of those who experience great happiness sometimes become depressed, crashing down after their joyful high. The reverse is not true: Those who are depressed do not necessarily feel unusually happy in the near future (American Psychiatric Association, 2000).

The Usual Dip

The general trend is more downward than upward. For example, a cross-sequential study showed that children from ages 6 to 18 feel less competent, on average, each year in most areas of their lives (see Figure 16.2). In the United States, young boys generally are most confident about themselves in athletics; thus, athletic self-concept is especially likely to dip during adolescence. Overall, this study found that feelings of competence become more similar in males and females as time goes on (Jacobs et al., 2002).

Many students in various places and nations drop in self-esteem at about age 12 (e.g., Eccles et al., 1998; Fredericks & Eccles, 2002; Harter, 1999; Marsh, 1989). Some show a more dramatic decline than the figures shown here and then a small rise—never as high as the childhood peak (e.g., Cole et al., 2001). The specifics depend on cohort, culture, and the particular ability being measured.

Is this decline troubling, or is it merely that teenagers lose some of the unrealistically high self-esteem that is common in younger children? Look closely at Figure 16.2. The halfway mark of 4 was exceeded in every year and in every area. At least according to this study (of middle-class, European-American youth), typical adolescents still think they are above average. Perhaps this is as it should be, given that a certain level of egocentrism is normal in adolescents. Self-esteem that is too high may lead to unrealistic expectations, and self-esteem that is too low may make a person stop trying.

Children who think that academic ability is innate, and that they themselves are naturally smart, may be rudely awakened at adolescence, when

FIGURE 16.2 All the Children Are Above Average U.S. children, both boys and girls, feel less competent in math, language arts, and sports as they move through grades 1–12. However, their scores on tests of feelings of competence indicate that, overall, teenagers still consider themselves above average in all three of these areas. Thus, while self-esteem declines in adolescence, it does not disappear; it just becomes more realistic.

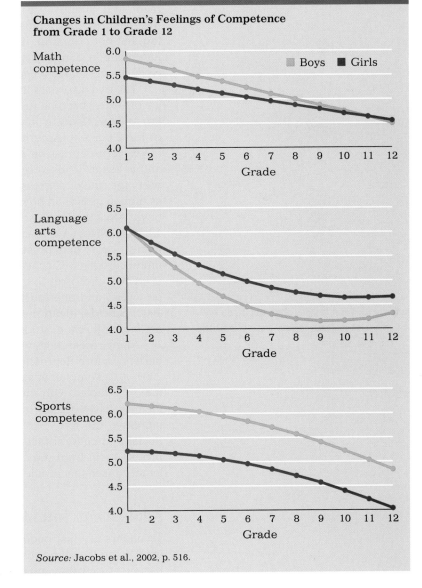

Changes in Children's Feelings of Competence from Grade 1 to Grade 12

Source: Jacobs et al., 2002, p. 516.

almost everyone's grades fall. Unless they understand the need for realistic goals, they may quit school or even quit life (Dweck, 1999). Extremes of self-doubt and self-confidence may have undesirable effects (Sniezek, 1999).

Does a drop in self-esteem prepare teenagers to compete realistically for jobs, colleges, and sexual partners, or does it make them vulnerable to self-destructive behavior such as drug use, sexual risk taking, and suicide? This question refers to the typical adolescent—when do high expectations provide motivation, and when do they lead to frustration? Some adolescents are more vulnerable to begin with because they lack support from family, friends, or school. A loss of self-esteem pushes them not toward realism but toward serious depression.

Mood Disorders in Adolescence

Not every moody adolescent suffers a disorder sufficiently serious that professional help is needed. To differentiate emotional variability from mood disorders, psychotherapists seek to understand whether the emotions affect a person's normal routines. If the person does not sleep, eat, talk, or move in a normal rhythm (either can't sleep or sleeps too much, under- or overeats, talks or moves far too quickly or far too slowly) and if that person has strong feelings of despair or elation that are not based on reality, these are warning signs. If the person's judgment and actions are not seriously affected, the condition is called either *dysthymia* (negative mood) or *hypomania* (mildly elevated mood)—both debilitating, but not crippling. If the symptoms are more extreme and distort a person's judgment in dangerous ways, a professional will diagnose major depression (very down), mania (very up), or bipolar disorder (alternately up and down).

The two disorders that include high energy and grandiosity, mania and bipolar disorder, become more common in adolescence and early adulthood. These are as likely to occur in males as females and have an overall lifetime prevalence of 1 to 2 percent (American Psychiatric Association, 2000).

Severe depression sometimes occurs in childhood, but it is relatively rare and is usually caused by parental abuse or neglect (Duggal et al., 2001). At puberty the rate of depression more than doubles, to about 15 percent, and is twice as high in girls as in boys, affecting about 1 in 5 teenage girls and 1 in 10 teenage boys. After the incidence of depression rises dramatically between ages 14 and 18, it stabilizes (A.C. Peterson et al., 1993). The primary cause in adolescence is a family history of depression, especially a depressed mother who was the primary infant caregiver (Cicchetti & Toth, 1998).

suicidal ideation Thinking about suicide, usually with some serious emotional and intellectual or cognitive overtones.

One-third of all U.S. adolescent girls say they have felt sad or hopeless in the past year, and one-fourth have seriously thought about suicide (CDC, June 28, 2002). **Suicidal ideation**—that is, thinking about committing suicide—is so common among high school students that it might be considered normal (Diekstra, 1995).

Many researchers wonder why adolescents, especially females, suddenly experience more depression than children (Ge et al., 2001; Hankin & Abramson, 2001; A.C. Peterson et al., 1993). The hormonal changes of puberty are one explanation, coupled with the psychic stresses of school, friends, sexual drives, and identity crises. Genes make a person vulnerable to mood disorders, and stress increases the risk, but social pressures throughout life also have an impact. Social and cultural factors can either push people over the edge of despair or protect them from the consequences of adolescent mood shifts—even the most lethal consequence, suicide.

Adolescent Suicide

Teenagers are just beginning to explore life's possibilities. Even if they experience some troubling event—failing a class, ending a romance, fighting with a parent—surely they must realize that better days lie ahead. Not always. This logi-

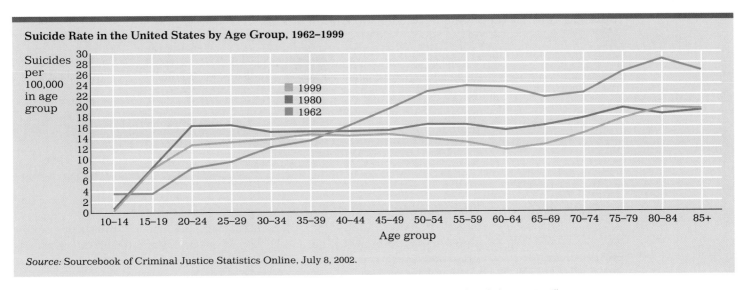

Suicide Rate in the United States by Age Group, 1962–1999

■ 1999
■ 1980
■ 1962

Source: Sourcebook of Criminal Justice Statistics Online, July 8, 2002.

FIGURE 16.3 So Much to Live For A historical look at U.S. suicide statistics reveals two trends. First, although their rate is still below that of adults, teenagers are twice as likely to take their own lives as they once were. Second, this increase in teen suicide is part of a life-span trend. Whereas rates used to rise in middle age, today young adults are more suicidal and older adults less so. Among the possible reasons are that drug abuse, increased parental divorce, and other factors have made adolescence more problematic and that better health care and pension plans have generally made the later years easier.

cal perspective is not shared by suicidal adolescents, who are so overwhelmed with pain or anger that, for a few perilous hours or days, death seems their only solution.

But before discussing this issue, we need to destroy a prejudice: Adolescents under age 20 are much less likely to kill themselves than adults are, now and in previous years, worldwide (see Figure 16.3). Why do many people still think suicide is an adolescent problem? Five reasons account for it:

- The rate, low as it is, is triple the rate in 1960.
- Statistics often lump adolescents and young adults together, and 20- to 24-year-olds typically have a much higher suicide rate.
- Every adolescent suicide, particularly that of younger adolescents (some 300 children age 10 to 14 kill themselves in the United States every year; see Figure 16.4), is shocking and grabs our attention.
- Social prejudice tends to consider teenagers as problems, hence distorting the evidence.
- Suicide attempts are more common in adolescence than later on.

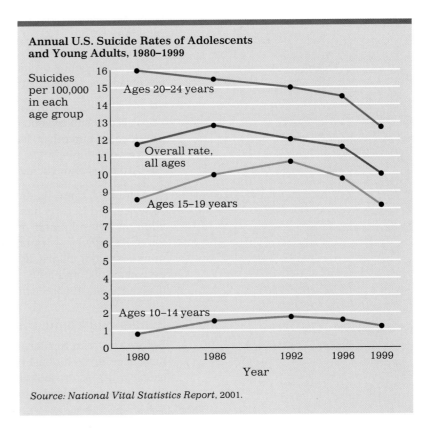

Annual U.S. Suicide Rates of Adolescents and Young Adults, 1980–1999

Ages 20–24 years

Overall rate, all ages

Ages 15–19 years

Ages 10–14 years

Source: National Vital Statistics Report, 2001.

FIGURE 16.4 Why? Suicide rates for adolescents have been rising over the past two decades, while rates for older individuals have been decreasing. Note, for example, that the rate for the youngest adolescents has doubled in that time, a cause for great concern.

TABLE 16.3 Suicidal Ideation and Parasuicide, United States, 1999

		Felt Sad or Hopeless	Seriously Considered Attempting Suicide	Planned Suicide	Parasuicide (Attempted Suicide)	Actual Suicide (Ages 14–18)
Overall		28%	19%	15%	8%	Less than 0.01% (about 7 per 100,000)
Girls:	9th grade	34	24	20	14	
	10th grade	38	30	23	15	About 2 per 100,000
	11th grade	35	23	16	8	
	12th grade	34	21	13	6	
Boys:	9th grade	21	12	9	6	
	10th grade	20	14	13	6	About 11 per 100,000
	11th grade	19	14	12	5	
	12th grade	25	16	10	5	

Sources: CDC, June 9, 2000, based on a survey of 1,600 students from 23 states. Actual suicide rates estimated from U.S. Bureau of the Census, 2000.

Parasuicide and Prevention

parasuicide A deliberate act of self-destruction that does not end in death. Parasuicide may be a fleeting gesture, such as a small knife mark on the wrist, or potentially lethal, as when a person swallows an entire bottle of sleeping pills.

Not only is suicidal ideation high in adolescence, but so is **parasuicide** (any deliberate act of self-destruction that does not result in death), with an international rate of between 6 and 20 percent. The results of one survey of suicidal ideation and parasuicide among adolescents are summarized in Table 16.3.

Experts prefer the word *parasuicide* over *attempted suicide* or *failed suicide* because this term does not judge severity or intention (Diekstra et al., 1995). Particularly in adolescence, most self-destructive acts are accompanied by extreme emotional agitation and confusion. Intent may not be clear, even to the self-destructive individuals themselves. Many who make a potentially lethal attempt soon feel relieved that they did not die and wonder what they could have been thinking.

Whether or not suicidal ideation eventually leads to a plan, a parasuicide, and death depends on factors that vary from community to community. In adolescence, five of the most influential are the following:

■ Availability of lethal means, especially guns
■ Parental supervision
■ Alcohol and other drugs
■ Gender
■ Attitudes about suicide in the culture

The first three factors make clear why the rate of youth suicide in North America and Europe has doubled since 1960: Adolescents have more guns, less adult supervision, and more alcohol and drugs because many parents are divorced, single, or working outside the home. In the United States, accessibility of guns is a major culprit; adolescent gunshot suicide increased by about 50 percent between 1980 and 1995. This accounts for virtually all of the recent increases (Kachur et al., 1995; Sickmund et al., 1997).

Gender and Ethnic Differences in Suicide

Before you read further, rank the suicide rates of the eight groups listed on the next page, from highest (1) to lowest (8). (Hispanics are not listed separately because the most recent data for 15- to 19-year-olds include them with either European- or African-Americans.) The actual rankings are given in Table 16.4.

_____ African-American females
_____ African-American males
_____ Asian-American females
_____ Asian-American males
_____ European-American females
_____ European-American males
_____ Native American females
_____ Native American males

Worldwide parasuicide is higher for females but completed suicide is higher for males. One reason is that when males attempt suicide, they use more lethal means—guns rather than pills—and hence it is harder to rescue them. Another reason is that boys are less likely to ask for help, and everyone contemplating suicide needs help to relieve the pain (Schneidman, 2001).

Cultural factors influence age differences. Japan's teen suicide rate is actually among the lowest (contrary to widespread belief), and Hungary's is among the highest. In Australia, aboriginal youth are particularly vulnerable, in part because of cultural romanticism regarding suicide (Tatz, 2001). Romanticism also underlies many **cluster suicides** among all groups of teenagers when a particular town or school sentimentalizes the "tragic end" of a teen suicide. Such publicity can trigger suicidal thoughts, talk, and attempts in other adolescents (Joiner, 1999). Cluster suicides are particularly common among Native Americans (Beauvais, 2000).

For youth in every nation, however, suicidal ideation and attempted suicide are "late clues," usually preceded by other signals that help is needed (Faberow, 1994). Reading these clues is everyone's "moral responsibility, something akin to omnipresent fire prevention" (Shneidman & Mandelkorn, 1994). Parents and teachers, as well as peers, can usually see the signs of teen suicide if they are alert to them. At every age, chronic depression, death of a close friend, drug abuse, loneliness, social rejection, and homosexuality correlate with suicide ideation and completion (Brent et al., 1999; Cochran & Mays, 2000; Prinstein et al., 2000).

cluster suicide A group of suicides that occur in the same community, school, or time period.

TABLE 16.4 Suicide Rates of 15- to 19-Year-Olds, by Ethnic Group

Rank	Ethnic Group	Suicides per 100,000
1	Native American males	36.5
2	European-American males	13.9
3	African-American males	10.0
4	Native American females	7.5
5	Asian-American males	6.5
6	Asian-American females	3.0
7	European-American females	2.9
8	African-American females	1.6

Source: National Vital Statistics Report, 49(11), October 12, 2001.

Why the Ethnic Differences in Suicide? The low suicide rate among Asian-Americans is probably because of high rates of Asian immigration. In every ethnic group, U.S. teenagers born in another nation use fewer guns, drink less alcohol, and kill themselves less often than do their U.S.-born peers of the same ancestry. The full explanation for Native Americans' high rates is not known, but both genetic and sociocultural factors are involved. Native American elders have much lower suicide rates than the elderly population as a whole, so something about the interface between culture and adolescence, rather than something innate, is probably to blame. When protective factors are in place for Native American youth, they are very powerful, particularly the ability to discuss problems with friends and family (Borowsky et al., 1999).

internalizing problems Emotional problems that are manifested inward, when troubled individuals inflict harm on themselves.

externalizing problems Emotional problems that are manifested outward, when people "act out," injuring others, destroying property, or defying authority.

Rebellion and Destructiveness

As you learned in Chapter 10, psychologists categorize emotional problems in two broad ways, as either internalizing or externalizing. **Internalizing problems** are manifested inward, when troubled individuals inflict harm on themselves. **Externalizing problems** are, at least superficially, the opposite: People "act out," injuring others, destroying property, or defying authority.

Internalizing disorders include the various manifestations of depression that we have just reviewed, as well as anorexia, bulimia, self-mutilation, and overuse of sedative drugs. Suicide is usually considered internalizing, since completed suicides are the ultimate example of self-harm. However, some individuals, especially adolescents, use suicide as a strategy to "get back at" someone—and this would make suicide externalizing, an attack on someone, especially in cases of what is called "suicide by cop," when a teenager deliberately provokes an armed police officer.

Both internalizing and externalizing problems suddenly increase at adolescence, with a marked gender difference: Externalizing problems are more common among boys. Is some degree of rebellion and defiance normal, particularly for adolescent boys? Most psychologists influenced by the psychoanalytic perspective answer "yes." A leading advocate of this view was Anna Freud, who believed that adolescent rebellion against parental authority was "welcome . . . beneficial . . . inevitable." Indeed, a lack of defiance was considered a psychological problem. She explained:

> We all know individual children who, as late as the ages of fourteen, fifteen or sixteen, show no such outer evidence of inner unrest. They remain, as they have been during the latency period, "good" children, wrapped up in their family relationships, considerate sons of their mothers, submissive to their fathers, in accord with the atmosphere, idea and ideal of their childhood background. Convenient as this may be, it signifies a delay of their normal development and is, as such, a sign to be taken seriously.
>
> [Freud, 1958/2000, p. 263]

Erikson, who was both a student and a patient of Anna Freud, described the identity crisis as inevitably difficult—and he thought that foreclosure was an inferior, insecure choice that short-circuited this normal developmental crisis. If the goal of adolescence is to achieve identity, to become one's true self, Erikson reasoned, then becoming independent and questioning adult authority are essential. Self-assertion and even aggression might be required.

If You Were His Father or Mother... Would you agree with Anna Freud that teenage rebellion is welcome and beneficial?

Many other perspectives on the adolescent years agree. For example, the cognitive perspective finds that adolescents are logical when they act contrary to adult wishes by taking risks: "An adolescent male may drive too fast to confirm his masculine identity" (O'Donoghue & Rabin, 2001, p. 36). Youths might choose to have unprotected sex, take illicit drugs, or drop out of school because of the "immediate benefits," including pleasure, friendship, "identity formation, or establishing autonomy" (O'Donoghue & Rabin, 2001, p. 46).

Each of the five major theories outlined in Chapter 2 has an explanation for adolescent rebellion. The sociocultural and epigenetic systems theories in particular explain why externalizing problems are more prevalent in Western nations today than they were 50 years ago: The global requirement for advanced schooling means that adolescents must be physically dependent on their parents for food and shelter for years after their bodies and hormones urge them to become independent. This compels them to assert psychological independence, often through defiance.

LELAND BOBBE / STONE / GETTY IMAGES

Self-assertion is what normal adolescents do, not only according to the five theories but in fact. Remember the research about the many domains of self-concept? One domain is behavioral competence, which fell even more than other competencies at puberty and then remained low (Cole et al., 2001). Behavioral competence was measured by how strongly children agreed that the following described them: "Act as supposed to . . . try to do the right thing . . . behave well . . . don't get into trouble . . . don't do things I shouldn't." The researchers found that teenagers, girls and boys, were not as "competent" in behavior as they had been as children. If competency is measured by good behavior, a dip is not surprising. Some externalizing behavior is normal and expected during adolescence.

Such acting out may signify genuine trouble in three ways:

- Externalizing actions may prove harmful—driving at high speed, for instance, could result in permanent paralysis or brain damage.
- Externalizing behavior often harms others. Even if the perpetrator enjoys and needs aggressive behavior, society cannot allow unchecked damage to people or social values.
- For a significant minority, externalizing disorders signal the need for intervention, not only because acting-out teenagers may harm themselves or others but because they are suffering from serious mental disturbance.

For all three of these reasons, distinguishing normal from abnormal externalizing actions, is a challenge to be met (Steinberg & Morris, 2001). Now we illustrate this challenge by examining another common yet dangerous externalizing behavior: delinquency.

Breaking the Law

Delinquency is one indication of the emotional stress that many adolescents feel. Worldwide, arrests are more likely in the second decade of life than at any other time; they rise rapidly at about age 12, peak at about age 16, and then decline slowly with every passing year (Rutter, 1998). In the United States, 44 percent of all arrests for serious crimes (crimes of violence, arson, or theft involving thousands of dollars) are of persons between the ages of 10 and 20 (Maguire & Pastore, 1998).

Incidence and Prevalence

The statistics in the preceding paragraph are arrest **incidence** data; they are obtained by determining how all official arrests are distributed among the various age groups of arrestees. They tell us that many arrestees are teenagers, but they cannot tell us **prevalence** of adolescent crime—that is, how widespread law-breaking is among adolescents.

Suppose that, as some contend, a small minority of repeat offenders commit almost all the crimes. In this case, even though the incidence might be high, the prevalence of adolescent lawbreaking would be low (Farrington, 1994). *If* this were true, and *if* adolescents on the path to a criminal career could be spotted early and then imprisoned, the *incidence* of adolescent crime would plummet, because those few offenders could no longer commit their many crimes. This supposition and strategy lead to attempts to "crack down on" and "put away" young criminals.

Developmentalists over the past decades have shown that this supposition is false: Juveniles are mostly experimenters; they have not yet settled on any career, not even crime. Most have no more than one serious brush with the law, and even chronic offenders typically have a mix of offenses—some minor, some

incidence How often a particular behavior or circumstance occurs.

prevalence However widespread within a population a particular behavior or circumstance is.

Do You Know This Boy? His name is Andy Williams. Is he a 15-year-old freshman lost in a large California high school and ignored by his parents? Or is he a crazed killer, who brought his father's revolver to school one day, murdered two schoolmates, and wounded 13 more? In fact, he is both, and that was the reason for this court hearing where the judge decided that Williams should be tried as an adult. Later, Williams pleaded guilty.

?Observational Quiz (see answer, page 516): Who are the adults with Andy?

Response for Parents of Teenagers (from page 513): Remember: Communicate, do not control. Say something—neutral, if possible—and let your child talk about the meaning of the hairstyle. Remind yourself that it is not your hair, and a hairstyle in itself is harmless. Don't say "What will people think?" or "Does this mean you are using drugs?" or express any other thought that might give a rebellious young adolescent a reason to break off the communication with you.

serious, and usually only one violent crime. In fact, of every 100 youths who are arrested at least once, only 1.3 have committed more than one violent offense. In other words, serious adolescent crimes are committed by many one-time offenders rather than by a few multiple offenders. The high incidence of adolescent crime is caused by its high prevalence, not by a few very active delinquents (Snyder, 1997).

The prevalence of adolescent crime is even greater than official records report, especially if all acts of "juvenile delinquency" (major or minor lawbreaking by youths under age 18) are considered (Rutter et al., 1998). Actual prevalence rates are higher than statistics indicate, because many teen crimes never come to the attention of the police and because many police officers do not arrest a young first-time offender. For example, in a confidential longitudinal study (Fergusson & Horwood, 2002), the average teenage boy admitted to three serious offenses and the average girl to one—although virtually none of the subjects had been arrested (see Figure 16.5).

Official U.S. statistics show that adolescent males are three times as likely to be arrested as females, that African-Americans are three times as likely to be arrested as European-Americans, and that European-Americans are three times as likely to be arrested as Asian-Americans (U.S. Department of Justice, 2001). But

FIGURE 16.5 Teenage Crime: How Prevalent?
Adolescent crime is more common than official statistics indicate. Over the 10 years from age 11 to age 20, boys in this longitudinal study admitted that they had committed an average of 3.7 crimes for which they might have been—but for the most part were not—arrested; for girls, the average was 1.4 offenses. The probability that an adolescent will commit some crime (major or minor) peaks at age 16–17 for both boys and girls.

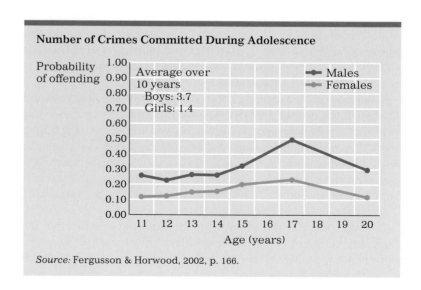

Source: Fergusson & Horwood, 2002, p. 166.

confidential studies find much smaller gender and ethnic differences than those reflected in official arrest data (Rutter et al., 1998). When all illegal acts—including such minor infractions as underage drinking, disorderly conduct, breaking a community curfew, playing hooky, sneaking into a movie or onto a bus without paying, and buying cigarettes or beer—are taken into account, virtually every adolescent is a repeat offender (Rutter, 1998).

The victims of adolescent crime also tend to be teenagers. The overall victimization rate of adolescents is two to three times that of adults, and the victimization rate for violent crimes (assault, rape, murder) shows an even greater ratio of teenagers compared to adults (Hashima & Finkelhor, 1997). (See Appendix A, Figures A-13 and A-14.)

Research in the United States, Britain, and Iceland finds that a major risk factor for becoming a violent criminal is being a victim of violence, and vice versa (Bjarnason et al., 1999). Perhaps as a consequence, teenagers who carry a weapon are likely to view doing so as defensive. Unfortunately, offense and defense usually go hand in hand, making homicide the leading nonaccidental cause of teenage death.

Crime Prevention

A useful distinction can be made between the many **adolescence-limited offenders,** whose criminal activity stops by age 21, and the few who are **life-course-persistent offenders,** who become career criminals (Moffitt, 1997a).

Life-course-persistent offenders are recognizable long before adulthood. They are the first of their cohort to have sex and use gateway drugs; they are among the least involved in school activities and most involved in "hanging out" with older, lawbreaking youths; and they are arrested many times for increasingly serious offenses throughout their teen years. They are antisocial in preschool and elementary school. Even earlier, they show signs of brain damage—perhaps being slow to express ideas in language, or being hyperactive, or having poor emotional control (Farrington, 1994; Rutter et al., 1998; Sampson et al., 1997).

Such youngsters are at high risk, and almost all career criminals have this ominous history. However, only about half of the children with these characteristics become serious criminals. Intervention measures—a particularly cohesive neighborhood, an especially effective school, a supportive peer group, a stable family, or a best friend who discourages crime—can halt the progression in early adolescence (Yoshikawa, 1994). If this fails, or if neighborhood, school, and peers fail to discourage serious crime, then intensive intervention that teaches life-course-persistent teenagers new ways of coping with their long-standing biological, cognitive, and psychosocial problems may help, especially if parents and teachers are taught as well (Rutter et al., 1998).

In general, a developmental perspective emphasizes primary prevention:

> Rather than waiting until violence has been learned and practiced, and then devoting increased resources to hiring policemen, building more prisons, and sentencing three-time offenders to life imprisonment, it would be more effective to redirect the resources to early violence prevention programs, particularly for young children and early adolescents.
>
> *[Slaby & Eron, 1994]*

Intensive, residential incarceration in a prison or reform school is needed for only a few. Even special programs can backfire if young lawbreakers become friends with other externalizing, deviant youth (Dishion et al., 1999; Mahoney et al., 2001). If a young adolescent offender is taken from family, school, and friends and placed in a context where toughness and defiance are required for survival, then temporary externalizing is likely to become habitual, a way of life. For

adolescence-limited offender A person whose criminal activity stops by age 21.

life-course-persistent offender A person whose criminal activity typically begins in early adolescence and continues throughout life; a career criminal.

! *Answer to Observational Quiz* (from page 514): They are not Andy's parents, who were not present at this hearing. Andy is flanked by his court-appointed defense attorneys.

Especially for Police Officers: You see some 15-year-olds drinking beer in a local park when they belong in school. What do you do?

younger children, externalizing behavior is learned at home; for adolescents, cultural context and peers are more important (McCabe et al., 2001).

Researchers began to look for early signs of risk for life-course-persistent delinquency several years ago. They stopped because labeling a particular young boy (maleness was one of the risk factors) "high risk" would stigmatize the innocent and would unfairly target minorities, children of single mothers, and the poor (other risk factors). Obviously, such sociological categories are unfair when used to predict the future behavior of any individual.

Nonetheless, some individuals (not groups) show neurological, genetic, and attachment signs of later violent crime. Children who have been abused or neglected, who have few friends, who are early substance users, or who are bullies are at higher risk (Rutter et al., 1998; Woodward & Fergusson, 1999). We can make fairly accurate risk assessments by age 10, or even younger. If early diagnosis leads to early punishment, it is wrong. If, instead, it leads to early intervention, it may prevent lives from being wasted.

Family and Friends

The changing seas of development are never sailed alone. At every turn, a voyager's family, friends, and community provide sustenance, provisions, directions, ballast for stability, and a safe harbor or at least an anchor when it is time to rest. Through example or insistence, societal forces also provide a reason to move ahead. In adolescence, when the winds of change blow particularly strong, parents and peers become powerful influences. The self-destruction of internalizing problems and the anger and social destruction of externalizing problems can be averted with the support of family and friends.

Parents

generation gap The distance between generations in values, behaviors, and knowledge, marked by a mutual lack of understanding.

Adolescence is often characterized as a time of waning adult influence, when the values and behaviors of young people are said to become increasingly distant and detached from those of their parents and other adults. According to all reports, however, the **generation gap,** as the distance between the younger generation and the older one has been called, is not necessarily wide. In fact, younger and older generations have very similar values and aspirations. This is especially true when adolescents are compared not with adults in general but with their

Not in My Kitchen Both parents and teenagers are invested in their relationship, but each generation has its own stake, or perspective, on their interactions. The generational stake may result in bickering, often over minor issues. This mother's folded arms show her determination to keep her son in line. The young man sits on the kitchen counter and wears his cap in the house to stress his independence.

own parents (Elder & Conger, 2000). (An exception occurs when the parents grew up in a very different place and time, as when parents lived in a rural region of a developing nation and their teenager is growing up in a big city in a developed nation [Harris, 1998].)

The fact that the generation gap is typically small by objective measures does not mean that all is harmonious at home. In fact, each generation has its own distinct **generational stake** (Bengtson, 1975). That is, each generation has a natural tendency to interpret parent–adolescent interactions from the viewpoint of its own position in the family. Parents have a stake in believing that all is well and that their children are basically loyal to the family despite a superficial show of rebellion. Adolescents have a stake in believing that their parents are limited, old-fashioned, and out of touch. This divergence occurs for good reason, since human evolution requires that adolescents break free from parental restraints to find their own mates and peers (Weisfeld, 1999). As we have seen, the search for autonomy inevitably seems to produce clashes.

Consider a conflict about a curfew. A parent may see it merely as a problem of management, the latest version of trying to get the child to bed on time, but a teenager may consider it evidence of the parents' outmoded values or lack of trust. On a deeper level, teenagers may see parental rules as an attempt to control and dominate; parents may see them as an attempt to love and protect. No wonder they disagree about some specifics.

Parent–Adolescent Conflict

As long as parents and adolescents live under the same roof, a certain amount of conflict occurs in most families when the young person's drive for independence clashes with the parents' tradition of control. The extent of the conflict depends on many factors, including the child's age and gender and the cultural context.

Parent–adolescent conflict typically emerges in early adolescence, particularly with daughters who mature early and with mothers more than fathers (Arnett, 1999a; Caspi et al., 1993). The reason younger adolescent girls and their mothers are conflict-prone is easy to understand, once you know what the typical issues are. **Bickering** (repeated, petty arguments, more like nagging than fighting) occurs about habits of daily life—hair, neatness, and clothing issues, for example—that traditionally fall under the mother's supervision. These issues are also ones that girls had been more pressured about, and more docile about, than boys, making a daughter's rebellion more surprising and more noticeable to the parents. In addition, most parents curb their daughters' sexual freedom more than their sons', thus evoking resistance. And it is the relatively young adolescent who feels compelled to make a statement—with green hair or blaring music—to establish in unmistakable terms that a new stage has arrived. Bickering follows.

Adolescents—both male and female—generally believe that they should be granted the privileges of adult status much earlier, and more extensively, than parents do (Holmbeck & O'Donnell, 1991). This dispute over status and age stems from the generational stake. Twelve-year-olds believe that controversies between themselves and their parents involve basic values such as personal privacy and freedom, which ought not to be interfered with by parents. Parents believe that the same issues (sleeping late on weekends, engaging in long telephone conversations, wearing tight or torn clothing, and leaving one's room in a mess) ought to be within their authority, since they have the child's well-being at heart.

Few parents can resist making a critical comment about the dirty socks on the floor, and few adolescents can calmly listen to "expressions of concern" without feeling they are being unfairly judged (Smetana & Asquith, 1994). In general, bickering peaks in early and midadolescence; family life becomes less conflicted as the parents grant more autonomy (Steinberg & Morris, 2001).

generational stake The need of each generation to view family interactions from its own perspective, because each has a different investment in the family scenario.

bickering Petty, peevish arguing, usually repeated and ongoing.

Response for Police Officers (from page 516): Avoid both extremes: Don't let them think this situation is either harmless or serious. You might bring them to the police station and call their parents in. However, these adolescents are not life-course-persistent offenders; jailing or grouping them with other lawbreakers might encourage more serious acts of rebellion.

An ethnic variation is found in the *timing* of parent–child conflict. For Chinese-, Korean-, and Mexican-American teens, stormy relations with parents may not surface until late in adolescence. It may be that because these cultures encourage dependency in children and emphasize family closeness, the typical teenager's quest for autonomy is delayed (Greenberger & Chen, 1996; Molina & Chassin, 1996).

The implication is that conflict is inevitable at some time. However, this may be a North American, middle-class perspective. Pakistani girls, Dutch boys and girls, and Filipino-American boys and girls seem to get along well with their parents and to be better students because of it (Salazar et al., 2001; Stewart et al., 2000; Van Wel et al., 2000).

Interesting as these variations are, we should stress that adolescents have *never* been found to benefit from families that are permissive to the point of laxness *or* strict to the point of abuse (Maccoby, 2000). The ethnic differences we are discussing occur within the range of normal authoritative and authoritarian parenting (see Chapter 10), not at the extremes. Families that are high in conflict, or parent–child relationships that are low in support, are almost always hard on the adolescent, no matter what the family structure or culture (Demo & Acock, 1996). If conflict reaches the point where the adolescent becomes a runaway or, more often, a throwaway—kicked out of the house—disaster is likely to follow in the form of suicide, indiscriminate sex, drug abuse, or violence (Yoder et al., 1998).

Single mothers who were teenagers when their children were born have a particularly hard time when the children become adolescents, because they tend to be too harsh or too lax, unable to find the proper balance in dealing with a young person who is as developed, and seems almost as mature, as the mothers themselves are (Borkowski et al., 2002; Loeber et al., 2000). In addition, the worse a neighborhood is, the stronger the pull of deviant peers and externalizing actions is and the more important parental guidelines, monitoring, and support are (Walker-Barnes & Mason, 2001).

Other Family Qualities

Conflict is only one of the dimensions of the parent–teenager relationship that have been studied. Other aspects include the following:

- Communication (Can they talk openly with one another?)
- Support (Do they rely on one another?)
- Connectiveness (How close are they?)
- Control (Do parents encourage or limit autonomy?)

These four elements vary a great deal from family to family. No researcher doubts that support and communication are beneficial, if not essential; hundreds of studies throughout the world confirm their importance. However, connection and control on the part of parents seem especially crucial to adolescents' development.

The degree to which a close family exercises control, restricting the adolescent's autonomy, is an especially tricky aspect of family functioning. On the one hand, some steps to limit freedom are beneficial. A powerful deterrent for delinquency, risky sex, and drug abuse is **parental monitoring,** that is, parental vigilance regarding where one's child is, what he or she is doing, and with whom (Fletcher et al., 1995; Rogers, 1999; Sampson & Laub, 1993). Monitoring helps limit access to alcohol, drugs, and guns by keeping the adolescent in places the parent considers acceptable.

Other sources of monitoring are people in the community: neighbors, store owners, and so on. Because many delinquent acts occur in late afternoon, between the closing school bell and the evening meal, after-school programs with adult supervision, particularly sports leagues or drama workshops that are attractive and available for boys as well as girls, can make a decided difference

parental monitoring Parents' awareness of what their children are doing, where, and with whom.

ELLEN SENISI / THE IMAGE WORKS

A Guiding Hand Organized extracurricular activities, with appropriate adult supervision, supplement parental monitoring as a way of helping adolescents stay out of trouble. Note, however, the front row is 70 percent female, and the cluster at the back is 80 percent male. Boys are particularly likely to rebel against organized, coed after-school programs.

(Levin, 1999). Community closeness, which allows neighbors to know which teenagers might be getting into trouble and who their parents are, significantly decreases delinquency (Sampson, 1997).

Conversely, too much parental interference and control are strong predictors of adolescent depression. A tactic called psychological control (threatening withdrawal of love and support) is particularly harmful (Barber, 2002; Pettit et al., 2001). Some freedom helps adolescents feel competent, trusted, and loved (Barber, 2002). Parents need to show involvement without interference, concern without restriction. Psychological intrusiveness, when parents not only know where the child is but also make the child feel guilty and anxious, may make the child unhappy and sometimes rebellious (Larson & Gillman, 1999). In fact, parental monitoring itself may be harmful when, instead of indicating a close relationship with the adolescent, it derives from harsh, suspicious parenting (Stattin & Kerr, 2000).

To summarize, most parent–teen relationships are supportive during adolescence, which is fortunate since family connection underlies psychological functioning. Some conflict is common, typically in early adolescence and centering on day-to-day details like musical taste, domestic neatness, and sleeping habits, not on world politics or moral issues (Barber, 1994). The ideal balance is not simple.

Peers

Friendships, already prominent in middle childhood, become even more influential during early adolescence (Erwin, 1998; Harris, 1998). From hanging out with a large group in the schoolyard or at the mall to having whispered phone conversations with a trusted confidant or with a romantic partner, relations with peers are vital to the transition from childhood to adulthood. Intimacy and trust are obviously very personal, not easily replaced. Most adolescent friendships are quite durable, with more stability from year to year than at younger ages (Degirmencioglu et al., 1998; Erwin, 1998).

Peer Pressure

The constructive role of peers is contrary to the notion of **peer pressure**, the idea that peers force adolescents to do things that they otherwise would not do. The idea of peer pressure is not completely false, but it is exaggerated in three ways:

- The pressure to conform to peers is strong only for a few years; it rises dramatically in early adolescence, until about age 14. Then it declines.

peer pressure Social pressure to conform with one's friends or contemporaries in behavior, dress, and attitude; usually considered a negative force, as when adolescent peers encourage each other to defy adult authority.

- Peer-group conformity can be constructive. It eases the transition for a young person who is trying to abandon childish modes of behavior, including dependence on parents, but who is not yet ready for full independence.
- Peer standards are not always negative. Generally, peer-group membership promotes higher grades and prosocial behavior and eases distress and antisocial behavior (Wentzel & Caldwell, 1997). Peers encourage each other to join sports teams, study for exams, avoid smoking, apply to colleges, and so on.

The reality of positive peer pressure does not negate another reality: Young people sometimes lead each other into trouble. When no adults are present, the excitement of being together and the desire to defy adult restrictions can result in risky, forbidden, and destructive behavior (Dishion et al., 1995; Lightfoot, 1997). Peer pressure is particularly likely to be negative in periods of uncertainty. For example, young people are more likely to admire aggressive boys when they themselves are new to a school, are experiencing the physical changes of puberty, and are uncomfortable with heterosexual attraction—as they might be in the first months of middle school (Bukowski et al., 2000).

Peers sometimes influence friends who are ambivalent about their values and activities but not those who are already set on a particular path (Vitaro et al., 1997). Indeed, peers choose each other; teenagers associate with other teenagers whose values and interests they share, particularly in regard to behavior such as drug use and involvement in academics (Hamm, 2000).

Collectively, peers sometimes become involved in escapades that none of them would engage in alone. The reason for such behavior is not peer pressure but peer solidarity. As one adolescent described it:

> The idea of peer pressure is a lot of bunk. What I heard about peer pressure all the way through school is that someone is going to walk up to me and say "Here, drink this and you'll be cool." It wasn't like that at all. You go somewhere and everyone else would be doing it and you'd think, "Hey, everyone else is doing it and they seem to be having a good time—now why wouldn't I do this?" In that sense, the preparation of the powers that be, the lessons that they tried to drill into me, they were completely off. They had no idea what we are up against.
>
> [quoted in Lightfoot, 1997]

Fortunately, most peer-inspired misbehavior is a short-lived experiment rather than a foreshadowing of long-term delinquency; that is, it is adolescence-

Homeless Teens Altanchimeg, a 17-year-old girl, was kicked out of her impoverished home at age 9. Now she is eight months pregnant and is one of 3,000 to 4,000 street children in Mongolia. She is shown sleeping beside her 15-year-old girlfriend, so she is not completely without peer support, but the baby's father is nowhere to be found.

? *Observational Quiz* (see answer, page 522): Are Altanchimeg and her friend in a homeless shelter?

PAULA BRONSTEIN /LIAISON / NEWSMAKERS / ONLINE USA / GETTY IMAGES

limited rather than life-course-persistent. The teenager who argues that he or she *must* engage in a particular activity, dress a certain way, or hang out in certain parts of town because "everyone else does it" is trying to lighten the burden of responsibility for some demeanor, style, or philosophy that he or she is trying out. Peers help with identity formation by allowing the adolescent to experiment with possible selves (Ungar, 2000). In a way, therefore, "peer pressure" acts as a buffer between the relatively dependent world of childhood and the relatively independent world of young adulthood.

The Peer Group for Immigrants

Conflict between peers and family may arise in ethnic groups that revere closeness to family, respect for elders, and self-sacrifice for the sake of kin (Harrison et al., 1990). This ideal clashes with the peer-group emphasis on adolescent freedom and self-determination.

This is potentially problematic for immigrants, because the adolescent's physical and cognitive drives hit full force several years before they would in traditional societies, where puberty occurs later and the age for marriage and adult work follows soon after. For many immigrant families, the normal strain between the generations is thus extended for several years longer than it would be in traditional cultures. Some minority adolescents (mostly girls) give in to parental control (perhaps docilely living at home until an early marriage), while others (mostly boys) rebel completely (perhaps leaving home in a fury).

Some immigrant boys join a delinquent group, typically consisting of other boys from the same ethnic group. In this case, peers provide an identity that comes complete with codes of behavior, standards of dress, and social bonding experiences. Such groups are common in immigrant communities living in multiethnic cities (Johnson-Powell & Yamamoto, 1997; Wong, 1999) and actually make psychological sense as a transition experience. A study of Latino gang members found that young people joined gangs by choice, to "satisfy their desire for self-identity," especially when their family was unwilling or unable to provide much affection or supervision (Arfaniarromo, 2001).

In the United States, virtually no adolescent is able to associate only with peers of the exact same background (even if he or she wanted to), because every individual has somewhat different roots. In the long term, most psychologists would consider this liberating. But in the immediate context, establishing ethnic identity is not easy. Minority individuals take years—even decades—to sort through the divergent historical roots, gender roles, peer loyalties, vocational aspirations, religious beliefs, and political values of cultures that surround them (Staples & Johnson, 1993; Suarez-Orozco & Suarez-Orozco, 2001).

Young Asian-Americans had not been the topic of significant research until recently. Now it is apparent that teenage descendants of Asian immigrants follow the same sequence as other groups over the years (Tse, 1999; Ying & Lee, 1999):

- Foreclosure on traditional ancestral values
- Rejection of tradition in favor of mainstream values (negative identity)
- Moratorium
- Identity achievement by connecting with other young Asian-Americans

Notice that the final step includes both rejection of parental traditions and solidarity with a peer group that shares some of the same traditional background. Research also finds that families in Asia, and first-generation Asian families in the United States, tend to be stricter and to have adolescents who are more successful academically and more respectful of their elders than European-American families (Chao, 2001). Thus, simply knowing ethnicity is not enough to understand an adolescent and his or her family; one must consider family cohesion, respect, and cultural assimilation as well (Fuligni, 1998).

!Answer to Observational Quiz (from page 520): No. They are sleeping near underground heating pipes in Ulaan Bataar, the capital of Mongolia and one of the coldest cities in Asia. One clue is the lighted candles, forbidden in most shelters.

Similar results come from a very different context: immigrants to Finland from Russia, Somalia, Turkey, and Vietnam. As in the United States, immigrant adolescents who were protected from discrimination and who identified with traditional family values were found to have the highest sense of well-being and achievement (Liebkind & Jasinskaja-Lahti, 2000).

Boys and Girls Together

During most of early and middle childhood, voluntary segregation of the sexes is common (Maccoby, 1998). Then, as puberty begins, boys and girls begin to notice one another in a new way. However, given the diversity of sex roles in today's world, developing a sexual identity and then expressing it with a partner are almost impossible to do without friends, as the following Thinking Like a Scientist feature explains in detail.

Thinking Like a Scientist

Finding a Partner: Step by Step

The progression of heterosexual involvement, first described 40 years ago (Dunphy, 1963), follows this general pattern:

- Groups of friends, exclusively one sex or the other
- A loose association of a girls' group and a boys' group, with all interactions very public
- A smaller, mixed-sex group, formed from the more advanced members of the larger association
- A final peeling off of heterosexual couples, with private intimacies

Cultural patterns affect the timing and manifestation of these stages, but the basic sequence seems biologically based and hence consistent across the centuries, cultures, and even species (Weisfeld, 1999). In modern developed nations, where puberty begins at about age 11 and marriage does not occur until a decade or two later, each of these stages typically lasts several years, with exclusive same-sex groups dominant in elementary school and heterosexual couples in later high school or college.

The overall sequence of sexual friendship patterns was documented in a study of students in a large, multiethnic public school outside Chicago (Richards et al., 1998). These students were beeped at random times of the day or evening and asked to record who was with them, how they felt at the moment, and what they were thinking. As they got older, these adolescents gradually spent more time with the other sex and enjoyed it more. Freshmen were happiest when they were with companions of their own sex or in mixed-sex groups, while juniors and seniors were happiest when with one member of the other sex.

JEFF GREENBERG / PHOTOEDIT

Young Lovers Young lovers spend as much time together as possible, gazing into each other's eyes, sharing food, and touching (if only at the elbows and knees). Progression into further physical displays of affection depends on the couple's peers, culture, and parents.

Peers and Other-Sex Friends

To get a sense of the time adolescents spend with peers, look at Figure 16.6. In the fifth and sixth grades, when they were on the edge of adolescence, children spent about 1 percent of their waking time (less than an hour a week) with the other sex. (Classroom time was not counted.) By the eleventh grade, however, boys were spending 5 hours a week with girls, and girls about 10 hours with boys. (The numbers are not equal

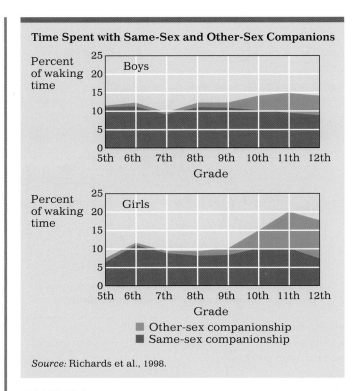

Time Spent with Same-Sex and Other-Sex Companions

Source: Richards et al., 1998.

FIGURE 16.6 We'll Still Be Friends Through adolescence, young people spend increasing amounts of time with peers of the other sex, while almost maintaining the amounts of time spent with same-sex friends. Note, though, that older girls spend much more of their time with opposite-sex friends than older boys do.

because most mixed-sex time was in groups that included more girls than boys; also, girls tended to be with older boys.) Related research found that adolescents spent about as much time thinking about the other sex as actually interacting (Richards et al., 1998). Obviously, heterosexual relationships are time-consuming and thought-provoking—something parents do not seem to understand and peers love to discuss.

The need to talk about the other sex is one reason adolescents continue to spend time with same-sex peers even after

romantic relationships develop. One reason such talk is essential is that same-sex friends are chosen for their loyalty, but heterosexual intimacy is fraught with problems, especially the likelihood of rejection (Fischer & Rose, 1996; Furman & Wehner, 1994). Typically, early romances are intense but soon over (Feiring, 1996). Having supportive friends to cushion the pain, offer reassurance and solace, and validate emotions and self-worth is essential when rejection does occur.

Usually, the first sign of heterosexual attraction is not an overt, positive interest but a seeming dislike (see Table 16.5). The pace of the change depends on several factors, which vary from culture to culture. One factor is the biology of puberty, with early maturers likely to be first to reach out to the other sex. This is one reason Asian-Americans are less likely to have sex or give birth during adolescence: They tend to mature more slowly. More powerful is the influence of culture and peers who may push a given teenager to date, dance, or whatever. Parents are another strong influence; the closeness of their supervision and the personal example they set have a substantial impact. The final factor is availability, which hinges on quite personal characteristics, such as appearance and boldness. For all these reasons, some teenagers are much more advanced romantically than their classmates—or even than some 20-year-olds.

Homosexual Youth

For those adolescents who are gay or lesbian, added complications usually slow down romantic attachments. To begin with, there is the hurdle of realizing that one is, in fact, homosexual. A confidential study of more than 3,000 ninth- to twelfth-grade teenagers found that only 0.5 percent identified themselves as gay or lesbian (Garofalo et al., 1999). Since estimates of the actual proportion of adult homosexuals range from 2 to 10 percent (depending on definitions), obviously many of the teenagers surveyed had not yet recognized their sexual orientation. Even including those who said they were bisexual (2 percent) and "not sure" (1.3 percent) did not bring the total to the probable 5 percent. Once a young person identifies as homosexual, other problems

TABLE 16.5 Typical Adolescent Responses to the Opposite Sex*

	From Girls	From Boys
Age 11	"Boys are a sort of disease."	"Girls are a pin prick in the side."
Age 13	"Boys are stupid although important to us."	"Girls are great enemies."
Age 15	"Boys are strange—they hate you if you're ugly and brainy but love you if you are pretty but dumb."	"Girls are the main objective."
Age 16	"Boys are a pleasant change from the girls."	"Girls have their good and bad points—fortunately, the good outnumber the bad."

*The quotations come from a study of adolescents in New Zealand.
Source: Kroger, 1989.

arise, including the difficulty of finding both romantic partners and loyal friends.

Especially in homophobic cultures, many young men with homosexual feelings deny these feelings altogether or try to change or conceal them by becoming heterosexually involved. Similarly, many young women who will later identify themselves as lesbian spend their teenage years relatively oblivious to, or in denial of, their sexual urges.

One difference between the sexes here is that lesbian adolescents find it easier to establish strong friendships with same-sex heterosexual peers than homosexual teenage boys do. The probable reason is that female friendships generally tend to be close and intimate, whereas males are often wary of close friendships with other males, especially those whose sexual orientation is in doubt. In many cases, a homosexual boy's best friend is a girl, who is more at ease with his sexuality than a same-sex peer might be (D'Augelli & Hershberger, 1993; Savin-Williams, 1995).

The rates of depression and suicide are much higher among homosexual than heterosexual youth. Ideally, teachers, parents, and peers should be more aware that—sexual orientation aside—every adolescent needs companionship and understanding.

"We slam danced 'til dawn, then we both got tattoos and had our noses pierced. It was so romantic."

Some Enchanted Evening In every generation, shared experiences bring couples closer together. The nature of those experiences varies from cohort to cohort and culture to culture.

Parents and Peers Together: Influencing Sexual Behavior

Parents and peers usually work together, rather than at cross-purposes, in helping adolescents develop values and maturity. To become healthy adults, teenagers need both; parents should neither abandon their teenager to the peer group nor forbid all contact with friends. It is true that peers sometimes lead in directions adults do not condone, but often such peers are older siblings or groups that the parents encourage the child to join (Dishion & Bullock, 2002; Windle, 2000).

To clarify these generalities about the relationship between parents and peers, let's consider a specific example: sexual behavior. As you will see, when a teenager engages in some damaging sexual activity, it often is because parents and peers failed to discourage it.

Embarrassing Mother

Sex-education programs, in schools as well as in churches and community groups, often encourage, and sometimes require, adolescents to talk to their parents about sex. The reason is that such conversations correlate "with less risky sexual behavior, less conformity to peer norms, and a greater belief that parents provide the most useful information about sex" (Blake et al., 2001). However, with or without mandated conversations, most parents hesitate to discuss sex and love in a manner that allows their children to express and evaluate their own opinions without feeling that their parents are ignorant or judgmental. Mothers are far more likely to talk about sex with their children than fathers are, although teenagers of both sexes would like to hear what their fathers think.

Few parents are adequate sex educators. For one thing, they start too late. Many parents do not begin discussing sexual issues until long after the children have been informed, or misinformed, by friends, intuition, television, or personal experience. Adolescents who learn about sex at home learn mainly from their older siblings and almost never from their parents (Ansuini et al., 1996).

For another, parents fool themselves. For example, one mother confidently explained, "If you spend a lot of time talking with your children . . . they know how we feel about it [premarital intercourse]. As a result, we don't have any major conflict at all." In truth, however, conflicts about sex in this particular family were avoided not by communication but by silence. Their daughter never told her parents she was sexually active, because "they simply do not want to know" (quoted in du Bois-Reymond, 1995).

In another study, mothers were asked whether their teens had had sex and then the teens were asked for the truth. The difference between the two sets of replies was astounding (see Figure 16.7). For instance, 35 percent of 14-year-olds were sexually active, but only 14 percent of mothers knew it.

In this study, mothers who were more religious and more disapproving of teen sex were less likely to know when their children were sexually active (Jaccard et al., 1998). Did these young people avoid the discussion because they already knew their parents' attitudes? No. Few teenagers accurately assessed their mothers' attitudes on a variety of sexual issues—particularly on the practical consequences of pregnancy (such as having to quit school or marry the wrong person).

Fully 72 percent of the mothers reported that they had talked with their teens at least once about sex, but only 45 percent of the teens agreed (Jaccard et al., 1998). Thus, 27 percent of mother–child pairs did not agree about whether or not they had talked about sex—a gap that remained when this study was replicated (Jaccard et al., 2000). This later research also explored why conversations were not more frequent. Both mothers and teens cited embarrassment as the most common reason. Mothers were also concerned that the teenagers would ask something the mothers did not know. There is some validity to this later concern, especially if the parents' own teenage years had occurred:

■ Before the AIDS epidemic began
■ Before the appearance of contraceptive implants and injections, which are now the most common method of medical birth control among teenagers; the pill and the diaphragm are considered old-fashioned
■ Before "good" girls were acknowledged to be interested in sex
■ Before "real" boys were expected to be careful in sexual situations
■ Before sexual activity was an acceptable topic of conversation for couples

The final item in the list may be the most important. Although many contemporary parents of 12-year-olds were sexually active before marriage, they experienced shame, secrecy, and embarrassment, especially when talking with their

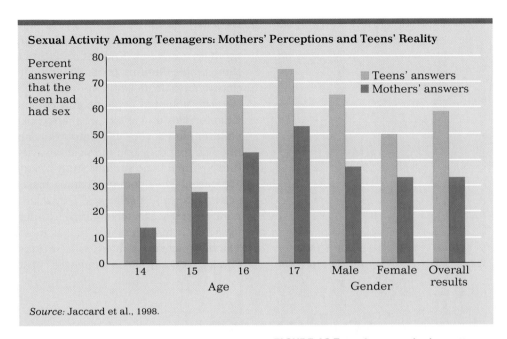

Sexual Activity Among Teenagers: Mothers' Perceptions and Teens' Reality

Percent answering that the teen had had sex

Teens' answers
Mothers' answers

Age

Gender

Overall results

Source: Jaccard et al., 1998.

FIGURE 16.7 **Mother Doesn't Always Know**
This graph shows the discrepancy between the answers mothers gave to "Is your child sexually active?" and the answers teenagers gave when asked for the truth. Notice which age group and gender had the largest gap—the younger boys!

own parents. One consequence is that most college students (95 percent) sometimes lie to their parents; girls from intact families are most likely to lie to their mothers about sex (Knox et al., 2001). Given that boys are more likely to do risky things, this finding probably indicates that those 5 percent who never lied (mostly boys from single-mother families) simply were never asked.

The potential negative consequences of not talking about sex (discussed in Chapter 14—unwanted pregnancy, disease, abortion, infertility, or chronically ill children) are severe. It is important not only that parents listen to their children but also that they communicate exactly what they think. According to Ad Health (the National Longitudinal Study of Adolescent Health first mentioned in Chapter 15), parent–child communication, trust, and closeness are predictors of less sexual activity as well as safer sex. However, if parents only stress ways to avoid pregnancy and disease, teenagers may infer that their parents approve of sexual activity. That "mixed message" makes intercourse (albeit with a condom) more likely. The best parental strategy is to include information about "the social, emotional, familial, and moral consequences" of sexual activity (Jaccard & Dittus, 2000).

In Person

Talk to the Children; Be Careful What You Say

When our daughter Bethany was newborn, toothless, and perfect, my husband worried about how we would pay for her teenage orthodonture. I knew he was being ridiculous (neither he nor I ever wore braces). I thought my own worry was more sensible, arising from my experience teaching high school students and from the mistakes my own parents made. My worry was that I would not be able to talk to my baby girl about sex when the time came.

My worry turned out to be fantasy as well. Armed with my ongoing understanding of developmental science, I answered the questions of all my children as soon as they asked, and I clarified mistaken ideas they had heard from their friends. For example, my daughter Rachel invited a classmate to her twelfth birthday party at a roller rink, but the child was forbidden to come because her parents thought she might catch AIDS in any place that was open to the public. I promptly explained how HIV is actually transmitted. Especially when puberty drew near, I tried to make sure that my children trusted me, that communication channels were open, that I met their friends, that I knew where they were going and how they were getting there, that they knew I cared. No need to rush into marriage or parenthood, I taught them.

When Bethany was about 16, she showed us a friendship ring her boyfriend had given her. We didn't even know she had a boyfriend, and we were worried, until we met him—a polite, shy kid. By the time we gave our approval, it was already too late: Bethany and he had broken up, partly because they didn't agree about their favorite music. That was the only time we felt any concern about our teenage daughters' boyfriends; all their relationships seemed quite innocent. The fears I had when Bethany was born—drugs, diseases, pregnancy—were unfounded, at least as far as I know. (One of my college students has called me naive about this.) My husband was actually wiser than I was: Bethany did wear braces on her teeth for two years.

My eldest two daughters are now older than I was when they were born, and neither is a wife or mother. Once Bethany met a wonderful man—brilliant, witty, interested in her. She said they had a lot of fun together, but "no sparks"! Another time I arranged a blind date for her. She telephoned me, laughing: "Mom, you are crazy. You're lucky you found Dad, because you have horrible judgment in men." I think she is wrong about that, but I do wonder whether some of my past parenting was a product of my context and cohort, not necessarily objectively correct.

I am reassured by statistics that show young adults in this current generation becoming parents later than my generation did, and I am very proud of the women my daughters are. But I have another fear. My own epigenetic clock makes me want grandchildren. My grandmother married before she was 20 and gave birth to 14 children; I would feel I had failed if any of my children did the same. However, I wonder whether the message of my generation—be careful about sex and become an independent woman—was incomplete, and whether my grandmother and even my mother knew something I forgot to communicate.

Peers and Sex

Remember that peers and parents complement each other. Parents hesitate to discuss sex, but peers readily provide information on the topic. In fact, peers are crucial, whether for good or ill. It is difficult for a teenager to abstain from sex if all his or her friends are sexually active—unless that one teenager is already unusually studious, closely chaperoned, or a loner. Certainly the early-maturing girls who date older boys are likely to become sexually active.

Current research finds that the particular peer group can make a decided difference: Some contemporary U.S. teenagers take a "virginity pledge," which usually means they do postpone having sexual intercourse until after high school—*if* the pledge is voluntary and *if* those who pledge feel they are a special group, resisting the dominant trends followed by other teenagers (Bearman & Bruckner, 2001). Culture and context obviously are very powerful.

No matter what their attitudes, promises, or behavior, all adolescents are interested in sex, spending hours looking, talking, fantasizing about sexual partners and feeling fear, guilt, and pleasure simultaneously. Many young adolescent girls swoon over movie or music stars, whose posters are on their bedroom walls; many young adolescent boys stare avidly at magazine photographs of semi-clad women. That fascination parents cannot stop, nor should they. In the normal course of growing up, private interaction with another real person comes much later, preceded by heterosexual groups, public exchange of glances, and long conversations with best friends about romantic possibilities.

When teens do pair off, they are increasingly inclined to make decisions about sex and contraception as a couple, not in isolation (Kvalem & Traeen, 2000; Manning et al., 2000). In terms of postponing sex and using contraception, it's best to have a romantic partner who is truly a peer, someone of the same age and background (Ford et al., 2001; Marin et al., 2000).

Unfortunately, many boys still mistakenly believe that they have no control over their sexual impulses (Eyre & Millstein, 1999), especially when they have been drinking and a girl seems available They believe it is more appropriate for a boy to have several sexual partners than for a girl (Feldman et al., 2000). In fact, cultural attitudes about young men and sex are considered the prime reason AIDS is spreading faster in Africa among heterosexual couples than any other group (Akindade, 2001).

Most girls depend on other girls to support a long and slow sequence of romantic involvement. Although boys may feel pushed to prove themselves to other boys, they also are more willing than boys in previous cohorts to talk about sex with their partners. Peers provide information on contraception, abortion, and disease (many teachers are not permitted to say, and many parents do not know). Adolescent peers, however, are not ideal sex educators:

■ They are reluctant to judge a friend's behavior.
■ Their analysis can be askew. For example, they exaggerate the risk of contracting HIV from one sexual encounter, but at the same time, they think that ten encounters are not much riskier than one (Linville et al., 1993).
■ The personal fable lets them deny responsibility. If they consider sex bad but have sex anyway, they blame their partner, their hormones, or even the devil (Schifter & Madrigal, 2000).
■ They underestimate the difficulties of raising a child, romanticize the joy and status a new baby brings, and overestimate the bonding of intimacy.

This last problem may be the most significant. For instance, in one study, those adolescent girls who thought that their boyfriends would be more committed to them and that they would still finish high school if they had a baby were later more likely to have a baby (Ungar, 2000). As we know from other research, doing so decreases their chances of marriage and further education.

Especially for an Adult Friend of a Teenager: If your 14-year-old friend asks you where to get "the pill," what do you say?

Conclusion

As you can see from this example, neither parents nor peers necessarily do a good job of helping adolescents through their teen years. Despite their best efforts, problems emerge regarding drugs, delinquency, suicide, and all the other topics we have discussed in these three chapters on adolescence. From a developmental perspective, parents and peers together can provide the support, encouragement, guidance, and knowledge that every teenager needs.

As this unit (Chapters 14–16) draws to a close, let us look again briefly at adolescence. Except perhaps for the very first months of life, no other developmental period is characterized by such multifaceted and compelling biological changes. Nor are developing persons at any other age likely to experience a more fascinating, unnerving, and potentially confusing sequence of intellectual and social transitions. The adolescent's developmental tasks—to reach adult size and sexuality, to adjust to changed educational expectations and intellectual patterns, to develop autonomy from parents and intimacy with friends, to achieve a sense of identity and purpose—are too complex to be accomplished without surprises. No wonder every young person, in every family and culture, experiences disruption of some sort (Arnett, 1999; Kroger, 2000; Schlegel & Barry, 1991).

As you have seen, most adolescents, most families, and most cultures survive this transition fairly well. Parents and children bicker and fight, but they still respect and love each other. Teenagers skip school, eat unwisely, drink too much, experiment with drugs, break laws, feel depressed, rush into sexual activity, conform to peer pressure, disregard their parents' wishes—but all these behaviors typically stay within limits. For most young people, the teenage years overall are happy ones, during which they escape potentially serious problems and discover the rewards of maturity.

While all adolescents have some minor difficulties, those with at least one serious problem often have several others as well (Galambos & Leadbeater, 2000). For instance, girls who become mothers by age 16 are also more likely to be from troubled families, to leave school, and to experiment with hard drugs. Boys who become chronic criminals also tend to be alienated from their families, to fail in school, to abuse drugs, and to have brain damage (Rutter et al., 1998). Suicidal adolescents typically have been heartbreakingly lonely and seriously depressed for years, with inadequate social support from family and friends (Davila & Daley, 2000).

In almost every case, these problems stem from earlier developmental events. They begin with genetic vulnerability and prenatal insults and continue with family disruptions and discord in early childhood and then with learning disabilities and aggressive or withdrawn behavior in elementary school—all within a community and culture that do not provide adequate intervention. With the inevitable stresses of puberty, problems become worse, more obvious, and more resistant to change.

An encouraging theme emerges, however: No developmental path is set in stone by previous events; adolescents are, by nature, innovators, idealists, and risk takers, open to new patterns, goals, and lifestyles. Some break free from destructive or ominous beginnings (Belsky et al., 2001). Plasticity means not only that people's lives are not determined by their genes but also that early experiences can be overcome. Research on effective schools, on teenage sex, on the positive role of friendship, and on identity achievement shows that every problem can be adolescence-limited. Young people can find a path that leads them away from the restrictions and burdens of their past, alive and ready for their future. Our task, now that we know more about development, is to do what we can to make that future bright.

Response for an Adult Friend of a Teenager (from page 527): Practical advice is important: Steer your friend to a reputable medical center that provides counseling for adolescents about various methods of avoiding pregnancy (including abstinence). You don't want your friend using ineffective or harmful contraception, or becoming sexually active before he or she is ready. Try to respond to the emotions behind the question, perhaps addressing the ethics and values involved in sexual activity. Remember that adolescents do not always do the things they talk about, nor are they always logical; but they can analyze alternatives and assess consequences if you lead them in that direction.

SUMMARY

The Self and Identity

1. Adolescence is a time for self-discovery, which begins as adolescents try out various roles and personalities. A period of multiple selves may include some selves that the person considers false—perhaps as a means of exploration, perhaps in reaction to parental criticism.

2. According to Erikson, as adolescents seek to resolve their identity crisis, they must overcome role confusion, particularly in four areas—vocation, politics, religion, and gender. None of these issues are easy to resolve: Many adolescents opt for a hasty foreclosure or for postponement via moratorium. Some may react against parental and social pressure by taking on a negative, or oppositional, identity.

3. During the identity crisis, which can last 10 years or more, almost every adolescent experiences a period of identity diffusion. Values and goals shift, and the teenager seems adrift, without direction.

4. Adolescents achieve a sexual, or gender, identity by figuring out whether they are male or female, heterosexual or homosexual. They accept the roles and behaviors that society assigns to that sexual identity.

5. Young people who are not members of the dominant cultural group are particularly concerned to establish their ethnic identity. Some foreclose the search by sticking to their traditional identity; some assimilate the majority's values; and some achieve their own identity by blending two or more cultural traditions.

6. Social conditions and historical contexts affect the complexity and length of the identity crisis. Some cultures provide a distinct rite of passage, a ceremony that signifies entry to adulthood, that makes it easier to achieve identity.

7. Surprisingly, major political and economic shifts, such as those experienced in many nations of Eastern Europe since 1990, have had little impact on the identity crises of adolescents in those nations. Worldwide, adolescents seem more affected by personal concerns than by public events.

Depression and Self-Destruction

8. Almost all adolescents lose some of the confidence and self-esteem they had when they were children. A sizable minority contemplate suicide at some time. According to psychoanalytic theory, emotional turbulence is normal during these years.

9. A few individuals become chronically sad and depressed, intensifying problems they have had since childhood. Parasuicide (suicide attempts) is not rare, especially among adolescent girls, although few adolescents actually kill themselves. Suicide rates are higher in adulthood than in adolescence, and higher among males than females.

10. Not only gender but also ethnic differences are apparent in completed suicide, with Native American males having the highest rates and Asian-American females the lowest. Even better predictors of the risk of suicide are individual factors, such as drug and alcohol use, gun availability, alienation from parents, and lifelong depression.

11. Suicide rates in some nations are lower, in others much higher, than in the United States. Among the reasons are variations in the prevalence of the four factors listed in item 10. In every case, friends and family members who are alert to the warning signs can intervene to stop potential suicide.

Rebellion and Destructiveness

12. Almost all adolescents become more independent and rebellious as part of growing up. Often this rebelliousness manifests itself in minor lawbreaking, especially by adolescent boys.

13. Adolescence-limited delinquents stop breaking the law when they reach adulthood. If they are arrested, they should not be punished in a way that teaches them to become worse criminals; instead, they should be redirected and prevented from hurting themselves or others in the process. Life-course-persistent offenders are more difficult to treat, because their problems typically start in early childhood and extend into adulthood.

Family and Friends

14. Parents continue to influence children during adolescence, despite bickering over minor issues. Ideally, communication and warmth remain high within the family as control by parents decreases and the adolescent is allowed to develop autonomy. Cultural differences are apparent in autonomy, independence, and parenting styles (authoritative versus authoritarian). Parental neglect or hostility is always destructive.

15. Friends help the developing adolescent cope with the conflicting demands of school, family, peers, and physical growth. Peer pressure can be either beneficial or harmful.

16. Peers can be crucial for immigrant adolescents, depending on when the family emigrated and how thoroughly they have adjusted to the new culture. Immigrant adolescents who have a strong commitment to family values tend to be successful in school and unlikely to rebel by using drugs or in other ways.

17. Peers are particularly likely to offer each other guidance in dealing with romance, including physical affection and contraception. One reason many adolescents turn to their peers is that parents do not talk with their children about the specifics of love and sex. Adolescents benefit from communication with, and cooperation among, all the adults who interact with them.

KEY TERMS

identity (p. 497)
possible selves (p. 497)
false self (p. 498)
identity versus role confusion
(p. 498)
identity achievement (p. 498)
foreclosure (p. 499)
negative identity (p. 499)

identity diffusion (p. 499)
identity moratorium (p. 499)
gender identity (p. 501)
rite of passage (p. 505)
suicidal ideation (p. 508)
parasuicide (p. 510)
cluster suicide (p. 511)
internalizing problems (p. 512)

externalizing problems
(p. 512)
incidence (p. 513)
prevalence (p. 513)
adolescence-limited offender
(p. 515)
life-course-persistent offender
(p. 515)

generation gap (p. 516)
generational stake (p. 517)
bickering (p. 517)
parental monitoring (p. 518)
peer pressure (p. 519)

KEY QUESTIONS

1. What is the difference between finding a false self and achieving identity?

2. What factors might make it particularly easy, or particularly difficult, for someone to establish his or her ethnic identity?

3. Give several examples of decisions a person must make in establishing gender identity.

4. What aspects of a high school graduation might help a young person achieve identity?

5. In what ways can adolescent suicide be considered common and in what ways uncommon?

6. How do personal and cultural factors increase the risk of adolescent suicide?

7. How are adolescence-limited and life-course-persistent delinquents similar, and how are they different?

8. Why and how do parents remain influential during their children's teen years?

9. How and when can peer pressure be helpful, and how can it be harmful?

10. What is the usual developmental pattern of relationships between boys and girls?

11. What are the common mistakes that parents make in regard to their adolescent children's sexuality?

12. How should society's treatment of adolescents be affected by the fact that many problems occur together?

BIOSOCIAL

Physical Growth Sometime between the ages of 8 and 14, puberty begins with increases in various hormones that trigger a host of changes. Within a year of the hormonal increases, the first perceptible physical changes appear—enlargement of the girl's breasts and the boy's testes. About a year later, a growth spurt begins, when boys and girls gain in height, weight, and musculature.

Sexual Maturation Toward the end of puberty, primary sexual development includes menarche in girls and ejaculation in boys. Secondary sexual characteristics also develop. Males become taller than females and develop deeper voices and characteristic patterns of facial and body hair. Females become wider at the hips; breast development continues for several years. Some teenagers become vulnerable to sexual abuse and/or unhealthy dieting. Others use drugs at an age or dose that is harmful to healthy growth. Both sexes risk diseases and premature parenthood unless they are cautious regarding biological impulse.

COGNITIVE

Adolescent Thinking Adolescent thought can deal with the possible as well as the actual, thanks to a newly emerging ability to think hypothetically, to reason deductively, and to explain theoretically. At the same time, adolescent egocentrism, along with feelings of uniqueness and invincibility, can make them extraordinarily self-absorbed, thinking intuitively rather than rationally.

Education The specific intellectual advancement of each teenager depends greatly on education. Each culture and each school emphasizes different subjects, values, and modes of thinking, a variation that makes some adolescents much more sophisticated in their thoughts and behavior than others. Lack of motivation, school violence, and high-stakes tests pose potential problems. For some adolescents, risk taking is more attractive than rational planning. This is apparent regarding vocational choices and sex education. Culture and cohort are powerful in an adolescent's every thought, emotion, and choice.

PSYCHOSOCIAL

Identity One goal of adolescence is self-understanding and identity achievement. Achieving identity can be affected by personal factors—including relationships with family and peers—the nature of the society, and the economic and political circumstances of the times. Identity achievement can be especially problematic for members of a minority group in a multi-ethnic society.

Peers and Parents The peer group becomes increasingly important in fostering independence and interaction, particularly with members of the other sex. Parents and young adolescents are often at odds over issues centering on the child's increased assertiveness or lack of self-discipline. Depression and thoughts about suicide are common in adolescence, especially among girls, although boys are more likely to actually complete a suicide. While most adolescents break the law in some way, the minority who commit serious crimes often come from a troubled family and a debilitating social context. More supportive communities can moderate these problems, as can constructive peer pressure and authoritative parenting.

Appendix A
Supplemental Charts, Graphs, and Tables

Often, examining specific data is useful, even fascinating, to developmental researchers. The particular numbers reveal trends and nuances not apparent from a more general view. For instance, many people mistakenly believe that the incidence of Down syndrome babies rises sharply for mothers over 35, or that even the tiniest newborns usually survive. Each chart, graph, or table in this appendix probably contains information not generally known.

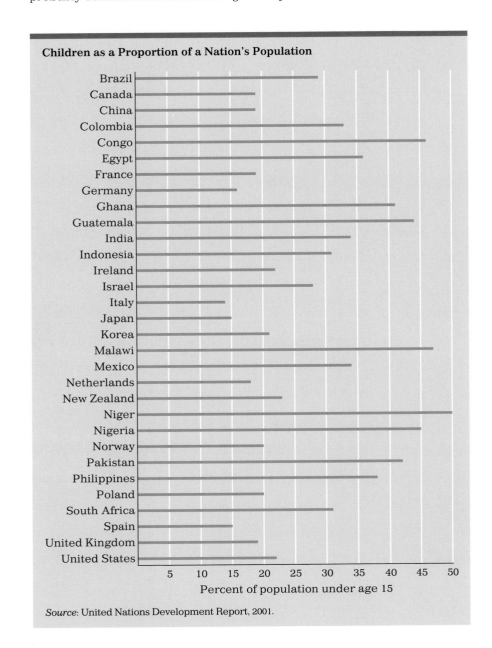

Children as a Proportion of a Nation's Population

Percent of population under age 15

Source: United Nations Development Report, 2001.

More Children, Worse Schools? (Chapter 1)

Nations that have high birth rates also have high death rates, short life spans, and more illiteracy. A systems approach suggests that these variables are connected: For example, the Montessori and Reggio-Emilio early-childhood education programs, said to be the best in the world, originated in Italy, and Italy has the lowest proportion of children under 15 of all the countries in this graph.

Ethnic Composition of the U.S. Population (Chapter 2)

Thinking about the ethnic makeup of the U.S. population can be an interesting exercise in social comparison. If you look only at the table, you will conclude that not much has changed over the past 30 years: Whites are still the majority, Native Americans are still a tiny minority, and African-Americans are still about 11 percent of the population. However, if you look at the chart, you can see why every group feels that much has changed. Because the proportions of Hispanic-Americans and Asian-Americans have increased dramatically, European-Americans see the current nonwhite population at almost one-third of the total, and African-Americans see that Hispanics now outnumber them.

?Observational Quiz (see answer, page A-4): Which ethnic group is growing most rapidly?

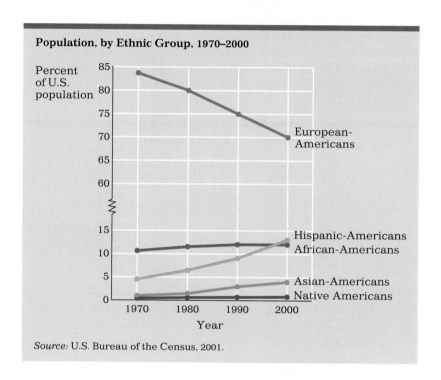

Source: U.S. Bureau of the Census, 2001.

	PERCENT OF U.S. POPULATION			
ETHNIC ORIGIN	1970	1980	1990	2000
European (white)	83.7	80	75	70
African (black)	10.6	11.5	12	12
Latino (Hispanic)	4.5	6.4	9	13
Asian	1.0	1.5	3	4
Native American	.4	.6	.7	.8

The Genetics of Blood Types (Chapter 3)

Blood types A and B are dominant traits, and type O is recessive. The percentages given in the first column of this chart represent the odds that a child born to the parents with the various combinations of genotypes will have the genotype given in the second column.

Genotypes of Parents*	Genotype of Offspring	Phenotype	Can Donate Blood To (Phenotype)	Can Receive Blood From (Phenotype)
AA + AA (100%) AA + AB (50%) AA + AO (50%) AB + AB (25%) AB + AO (25%) AO + AO (25%)	AA (inherits one A from each parent)	A	A or AB	A or O
AA + OO (100%) AB + OO (50%) AO + AO (50%) AO + OO (50%) AB + AO (25%) AB + BO (25%)	AO	A	A or AB	A or O
BB + BB (100%) AB + BB (50%) BB + BO (50%) AB + AB (25%) AB + BO (25%) BO + BO (25%)	BB	B	B or AB	B or O
BB + OO (100%) AB + OO (50%) BO + BO (50%) BO + OO (50%) AB + AO (25%) AB + BO (25%)	BO	B	B or AB	B or O
AA + BB (100%) AA + AB (50%) AA + BO (50%) AB + AB (50%) AB + BB (50%) AO + BB (50%) AB + BO (25%) AO + BO (25%)	AB	AB	AB only	A, B, AB, O ("universal recipient")
OO + OO (100%) AO + OO (50%) BO + OO (50%) AO + AO (25%) AO + BO (25%) BO + BO (25%)	OO	O	A, B, AB, O ("universal donor")	O only

*Blood type is not a sex-linked trait, so any of these pairs can be either mother-plus-father or father-plus-mother.
Source: Adapted from Hartl & Jones, 1999.

Odds of Down Syndrome by Maternal Age and Gestational Age (Chapter 4)

The odds of any given fetus, at the end of the first trimester, having three chromosomes at the 21st site (trisomy 21) and thus having Down syndrome is shown in the 10-weeks column. Every year of maternal age increases the incidence of trisomy 21. The number of Down syndrome infants born alive is only half the number who survived the first trimester. Although obviously the least risk is at age 20 (younger is even better), there is no year when the odds suddenly increase (age 35 is an arbitrary cut-off). Even at age 44, less than 4 percent of all newborns have Down syndrome. Other chromosomal abnormalities in fetuses also increase with mother's age, but the rate of spontaneous abortion is much higher, so births of babies with chromosomal defects is not the norm, even for women over age 45.

AGE (YRS)	GESTATION (WEEKS)		LIVE BIRTHS
	10	35	
20	1/804	1/1,464	1/1,527
21	1/793	1/1,445	1/1,507
22	1/780	1/1,421	1/1,482
23	1/762	1/1,389	1/1,448
24	1/740	1/1,348	1/1,406
25	1/712	1/1,297	1/1,352
26	1/677	1/1,233	1/1,286
27	1/635	1/1,157	1/1,206
28	1/586	1/1,068	1/1,113
29	1/531	1/967	1/1,008
30	1/471	1/858	1/895
31	1/409	1/745	1/776
32	1/347	1/632	1/659
33	1/288	1/525	1/547
34	1/235	1/427	1/446
35	1/187	1/342	1/356
36	1/148	1/269	1/280
37	1/115	1/209	1/218
38	1/88	1/160	1/167
39	1/67	1/122	1/128
40	1/51	1/93	1/97
41	1/38	1/70	1/73
42	1/29	1/52	1/55
43	1/21	1/39	1/41
44	1/16	1/29	1/30

Source: Snijders & Nicolaides, 1996.

Saving Young Lives: Childhood Immunizations (Chapter 5)

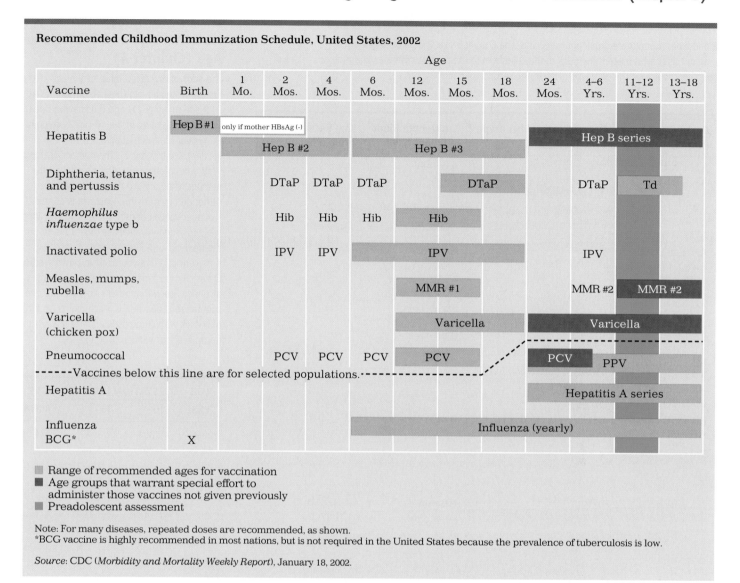

Recommended Childhood Immunization Schedule, United States, 2002

Vaccine	Birth	1 Mo.	2 Mos.	4 Mos.	6 Mos.	12 Mos.	15 Mos.	18 Mos.	24 Mos.	4–6 Yrs.	11–12 Yrs.	13–18 Yrs.
Hepatitis B	Hep B #1 only if mother HBsAg (-)		Hep B #2			Hep B #3				Hep B series		
Diphtheria, tetanus, and pertussis			DTaP	DTaP	DTaP		DTaP			DTaP	Td	
Haemophilus influenzae type b			Hib	Hib	Hib	Hib						
Inactivated polio			IPV	IPV		IPV				IPV		
Measles, mumps, rubella						MMR #1				MMR #2	MMR #2	
Varicella (chicken pox)						Varicella			Varicella			
Pneumococcal			PCV	PCV	PCV	PCV			PCV	PPV		
Hepatitis A									Hepatitis A series			
Influenza						Influenza (yearly)						
BCG*	X											

------Vaccines below this line are for selected populations.------

▨ Range of recommended ages for vaccination
■ Age groups that warrant special effort to administer those vaccines not given previously
▨ Preadolescent assessment

Note: For many diseases, repeated doses are recommended, as shown.
*BCG vaccine is highly recommended in most nations, but is not required in the United States because the prevalence of tuberculosis is low.

Source: CDC (*Morbidity and Mortality Weekly Report*), January 18, 2002.

First Sounds and First Words: Similarities Among Many Languages (Chapter 6)

	BABY'S WORD FOR:	
LANGUAGE	**Mother**	**Father**
English	mama, mommy	dada, daddy
Spanish	mama	papa
French	maman, mama	papa
Italian	mamma	babbo, papa
Latvian	mama	tēte
Syrian Arabic	mama	baba
Bantu	ba-mama	taata
Swahili	mama	baba
Sanskrit	nana	tata
Hebrew	ema	abba
Korean	oma	apa

!Answer to Observational Quiz (from page A-2): Asian-Americans, whose share of the U.S. population has quadrupled in the past 30 years.

Mothering: Knowledge Over Instinct (Chapter 7)

Differentiating excellent from destructive mothering is not easy, once basic needs for food and protection are met. However, as the Toni and Jacob examples in Chapter 7 make clear, psychosocial development depends on responsive parent–infant relationships. Breast-feeding is one sign of intimacy between mother and infant. Regions of the world differ dramatically in rates of breast-feeding, with the highest worldwide in Southeast Asia, where half of all 2-year-olds are still breast-fed.

In the United States, the South is lowest and the West is highest in rate of breast-feeding at one month. The overall rate increased from 39 percent in 1993 to 52 percent in 1999. In the United States, other factors that affect the likelihood of breast-feeding (not shown here) are ethnicity (Latinas are more likely, and African-Americans less likely, to breast-feed than European-Americans); maternal age (a positive correlation between age and breast-feeding); and newborn weight (low-birthweight babies are less likely to be breast-fed). The most marked influence of all is the mother's education.

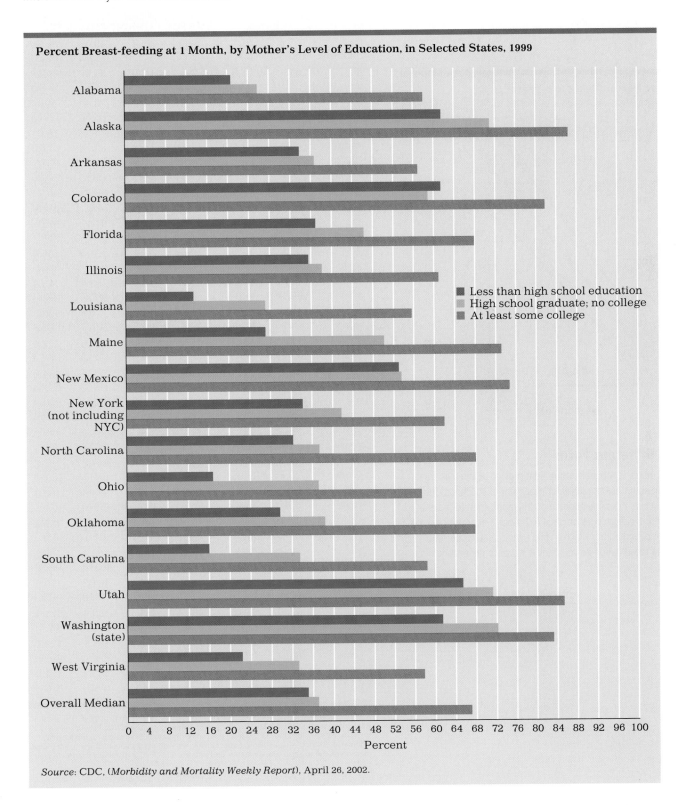

Percent Breast-feeding at 1 Month, by Mother's Level of Education, in Selected States, 1999

Legend:
- Less than high school education
- High school graduate; no college
- At least some college

States (top to bottom): Alabama, Alaska, Arkansas, Colorado, Florida, Illinois, Louisiana, Maine, New Mexico, New York (not including NYC), North Carolina, Ohio, Oklahoma, South Carolina, Utah, Washington (state), West Virginia, Overall Median

Percent (x-axis): 0 4 8 12 16 20 24 28 32 36 40 44 48 52 56 60 64 68 72 76 80 84 88 92 96 100

Source: CDC, (*Morbidity and Mortality Weekly Report*), April 26, 2002.

Height Gains from Birth to Age 18 (Chapter 8)

The range of height (on this page) and weight (see page A-7) of children in the United States. The columns labeled "50th" (the fiftieth percentile) show the average; the columns labeled "90th" (the ninetieth percentile) show the size of children taller and heavier than 90 percent of their contemporaries; and the columns labeled "10th" (the tenth percentile) show the size of children who are taller than only 10 percent of their peers. Note that girls are slightly shorter, on average, than boys.

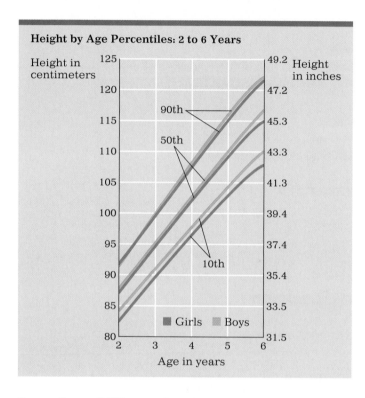

Height by Age Percentiles: 2 to 6 Years

Same Data, Different Form

The columns of numbers in the table at the right provide detailed and precise information about height ranges for every year of childhood. The illustration above shows the same information in graphic form for ages 2–6. The same is done for weight ranges on page A-7. Ages 2–6 are singled out because that is the period during which a child's eating habits are set. Which form of data presentation do you think is easier to understand?

Length in Centimeters (and Inches)

AGE	BOYS: PERCENTILES			GIRLS: PERCENTILES		
	10th	50th	90th	10th	50th	90th
Birth	47.5 (18¾)	50.5 (20)	53.5 (21)	46.5 (18¼)	49.9 (19¾)	52.0 (20½)
1 month	51.3 (20¼)	54.6 (21½)	57.7 (22¾)	50.2 (19¾)	53.5 (21)	56.1 (22)
3 months	57.7 (22¾)	61.1 (24)	64.5 (25½)	56.2 (22¼)	59.5 (23½)	62.7 (24¾)
6 months	64.4 (25¼)	67.8 (26¾)	71.3 (28)	62.6 (24¾)	65.9 (26)	69.4 (27¼)
9 months	69.1 (27¼)	72.3 (28½)	75.9 (30)	67.0 (26½)	70.4 (27¾)	74.0 (29¼)
12 months	72.8 (28¾)	76.1 (30)	79.8 (31½)	70.8 (27¾)	74.3 (29¼)	78.0 (30¾)
18 months	78.7 (31)	82.4 (32½)	86.6 (34)	77.2 (30½)	80.9 (31¾)	85.0 (33½)
24 months	83.5 (32¾)	87.6 (34½)	92.2 (36¼)	82.5 (32½)	86.5 (34)	90.8 (35¾)
3 years	90.3 (35½)	94.9 (37¼)	100.1 (39½)	89.3 (35¼)	94.1 (37)	99.0 (39)
4 years	97.3 (38¼)	102.9 (40½)	108.2 (42½)	96.4 (38)	101.6 (40)	106.6 (42)
5 years	103.7 (40¾)	109.9 (43¼)	115.4 (45½)	102.7 (40½)	108.4 (42¾)	113.8 (44¾)
6 years	109.6 (43¼)	116.1 (45¾)	121.9 (48)	108.4 (42¾)	114.6 (45)	120.8 (47½)
7 years	115.0 (45¼)	121.7 (48)	127.9 (50¼)	113.6 (44¾)	120.6 (47½)	127.6 (50¼)
8 years	120.2 (47¼)	127.0 (50)	133.6 (52½)	118.7 (46¾)	126.4 (49¾)	134.2 (52¾)
9 years	125.2 (49¼)	132.2 (52)	139.4 (55)	123.9 (48¾)	132.2 (52)	140.7 (55½)
10 years	130.1 (51¼)	137.5 (54¼)	145.5 (57¼)	129.5 (51)	138.3 (54½)	147.2 (58)
11 years	135.1 (53¼)	143.33 (56½)	152.1 (60)	135.6 (53½)	144.8 (57)	153.7 (60½)
12 years	140.3 (55¼)	149.7 (59)	159.4 (62¾)	142.3 (56)	151.5 (59¾)	160.0 (63)
13 years	145.8 (57½)	156.5 (61½)	167.0 (65¾)	148.0 (58¼)	157.1 (61¾)	165.3 (65)
14 years	151.8 (59¾)	63.1 (64¼)	173.8 (68½)	151.5 (59¾)	160.4 (63¼)	168.7 (66½)
15 years	158.2 (62¼)	169.0 (66½)	178.9 (70½)	153.2 (60¼)	161.8 (63¾)	170.5 (67¼)
16 years	163.9 (64½)	173.5 (68¼)	182.4 (71¾)	154.1 (60¾)	162.4 (64)	171.1 (67¼)
17 years	167.7 (66)	176.2 (69¼)	184.4 (72½)	155.1 (61)	163.1 (64¼)	171.2 (67½)
18 years	168.7 (66½)	176.8 (69½)	185.3 (73)	156.0 (61½)	163.7 (64½)	171.0 (67¼)

Source: These data are those of the National Center for Health Statistics (NCHS), Health Resources Administration, DHHS. They were based on studies of The Fels Research Institute, Yellow Springs, Ohio. These data were first made available with the help of William M. Moore, M.D., of Ross Laboratories, who supplied the conversion from metric measurements to approximate inches and pounds. This help is gratefully acknowledged.

Weight Gains from Birth to Age 18 (Chapter 8)

These height and weight charts present rough guidelines; a child might differ from these norms and be quite healthy and normal. However, if a particular child shows a discrepancy between height and weight (for instance, at the 90th percentile in height but only the 20th percentile in weight) or is much larger or smaller than most children the same age, a pediatrician should see if disease, malnutrition, or genetic abnormality is part of the reason.

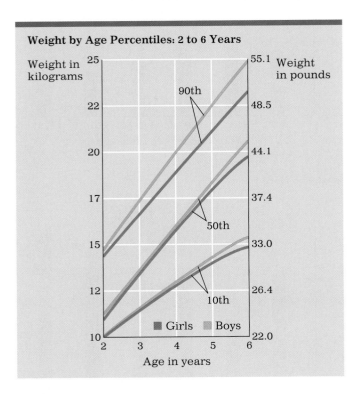

Weight by Age Percentiles: 2 to 6 Years

Comparisons

Notice that the height trajectories in the graph on page A-6 are much closer together than the weight trajectories shown in the graph above. By age 18, the height range amounts to only about 6 inches, but there is a difference of about 65 pounds between the 10th and the 90th percentiles.

?Critical Thinking Question (see answer, page A-8): How can this discrepancy between height and weight ranges be explained?

Weight in Kilograms (and Pounds)

AGE	BOYS: PERCENTILES			GIRLS: PERCENTILES		
	10th	50th	90th	10th	50th	90th
Birth	2.78 (6¼)	3.27 (7¼)	3.82 (8½)	2.58 (5¾)	3.23 (7)	3.64 (8)
1 month	3.43 (7½)	4.29 (9½)	5.14 (11¼)	3.22 (7)	3.98 (8¾)	4.65 (10¼)
3 months	4.78 (10½)	5.98 (13¼)	7.14 (15¾)	4.47 (9¾)	5.40 (12)	6.39 (14)
6 months	6.61 (14½)	7.85 (17¼)	9.10 (20)	6.12 (13½)	7.21 (16)	8.38 (18½)
9 months	7.95 (17½)	9.18 (20¼)	10.49 (23¼)	7.34 (16¼)	8.56 (18¾)	9.83 (21¾)
12 months	8.84 (19½)	10.15 (22½)	11.54 (25½)	8.19 (18)	9.53 (21)	10.87 (24)
18 months	9.92 (21¾)	11.47 (25¼)	13.05 (28¾)	9.30 (20½)	10.82 (23¾)	12.30 (27)
24 months	10.85 (24)	12.59 (27¾)	14.29 (31½)	10.26 (22½)	11.90 (26¼)	13.57 (30)
3 years	12.58 (27¾)	14.62 (32¼)	16.95 (37¼)	12.26 (27)	14.10 (31)	16.54 (36½)
4 years	14.24 (31½)	16.69 (36¾)	19.32 (42½)	13.84 (30½)	15.96 (35¼)	18.93 (41¾)
5 years	15.96 (35¼)	18.67 (41¼)	21.70 (47¾)	15.26 (33¾)	17.66 (39)	21.23 (46¾)
6 years	17.72 (39)	20.69 (45½)	24.31 (53½)	16.72 (36¾)	19.52 (43)	23.89 (52¾)
7 years	19.53 (43)	22.85 (50¼)	27.36 (60¼)	18.39 (40½)	21.84 (48¼)	27.39 (60½)
8 years	21.39 (47¼)	25.30 (55¾)	31.06 (68½)	20.45 (45)	24.84 (54¾)	32.04 (70¾)
9 years	23.33 (51½)	28.13 (62)	35.57 (78½)	22.92 (50½)	28.46 (62¾)	37.60 (83)
10 years	25.52 (56¼)	31.44 (69¼)	40.80 (90)	25.76 (56¾)	32.55 (71¾)	43.70 (96¼)
11 years	28.17 (62)	35.30 (77¾)	46.57 (102¾)	28.97 (63¾)	36.95 (81½)	49.96 (110¼)
12 years	31.46 (69¼)	39.78 (87¾)	52.73 (116¼)	32.53 (71¼)	41.53 (91½)	55.99 (123½)
13 years	35.60 (78½)	44.95 (99)	59.12 (130¼)	36.35 (80¼)	46.10 (101¾)	61.45 (135½)
14 years	40.64 (89½)	50.77 (112)	65.57 (144½)	40.11 (88½)	50.28 (110¾)	66.04 (145½)
15 years	46.06 (101½)	56.71 (125)	71.91 (158½)	43.38 (95¾)	53.68 (118¼)	69.64 (153¼)
16 years	51.16 (112¾)	62.10 (137)	77.97 (172)	45.78 (101)	55.89 (123¼)	71.68 (158)
17 years	55.28 (121¾)	66.31 (146¼)	83.58 (184¼)	47.04 (103¾)	56.69 (125)	72.38 (159½)
18 years	57.89 (127½)	68.88 (151¾)	88.41 (195)	47.47 (104¾)	56.62 (124¾)	72.25 (159¼)

Source: Data are those of the National Center for Health Statistics, Health Resources Administration, DHHS, collected in its Health Examination Surveys.

Day Care and Family Income (Chapter 9)

Note that, in both years, the wealthier families were less likely to have children exclusively in parental care and more likely to have children in center-based care.

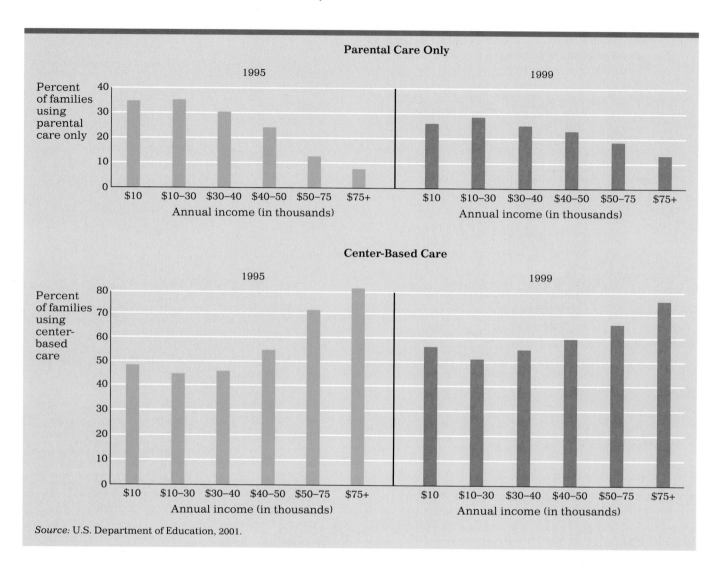

Parental Care Only

Center-Based Care

Source: U.S. Department of Education, 2001.

! Answer to Critical Thinking Question
(from page A-7): Nutrition is generally adequate in the United States, and that is why height differences are small. But as a result of the strong influence that family and culture have on eating habits, almost half of all North Americans are overweight or obese.

Rates of Poverty, by State and by Age Group

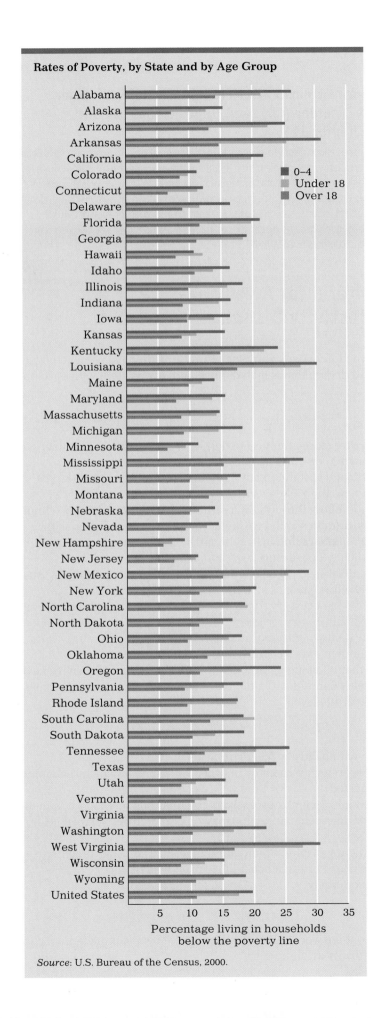

0–4
Under 18
Over 18

Percentage living in households
below the poverty line

Source: U.S. Bureau of the Census, 2000.

Babies Are the Poorest Americans
(Chapter 10)

Is poverty worse for adults than for children? Most developmentalists would say the opposite, and would wonder why every state has more poor children—especially young children—than poor adults.

? *Observational Quiz* (see answer, page A-10): Which state has the highest poverty rate for adults? For children under 18? For children from birth to age 4?

DSM-IV-R Criteria for Attention-Deficit/Hyperactivity Disorder (AD/HD), Conduct Disorder (CD), and Oppositional Defiant Disorder (ODD) (Chapter 11)

The specific symptoms for these various disorders overlap. Many other childhood disorders also have some of the same symptoms. Differentiating one problem from another is the main purpose of DSM-IV-R. That is no easy task, which is one reason the book is now in its fourth major revision and is now 943 pages long. Those pages include not only the type of diagnostic criteria shown here but also discussions of prevalence, age and gender statistics, cultural aspects, and prognosis for about 400 disorders or subtypes, 40 of which appear primarily in childhood. Thus, the diagnostic criteria reprinted here for three disorders represent less than 1 percent of the contents of DSM-IV-R.

Diagnostic Criteria for Attention-Deficit/Hyperactivity Disorder

A.   Either (1) or (2):

(1) Six (or more) of the following symptoms of **inattention** have persisted for at least 6 months to a degree that is maladaptive and inconsistent with developmental level:

Inattention

(a) often fails to give close attention to details or makes careless mistakes in schoolwork, work, or other activities
(b) often has difficulty sustaining attention in tasks or play activities
(c) often does not seem to listen when spoken to directly
(d) often does not follow through on instructions and fails to finish schoolwork, chores, or duties in the workplace (not due to oppositional behavior or failure to understand instructions)
(e) often has difficulty organizing tasks and activities
(f) often avoids, dislikes, or is reluctant to engage in tasks that require sustained mental effort (such as schoolwork or homework)
(g) often loses things necessary for tasks or activities (e.g., toys, school assignments, pencils, books, or tools)
(h) is often easily distracted by extraneous stimuli
(i) is often forgetful in daily activities

(2) Six (or more) of the following symptoms of **hyperactivity-impulsivity** have persisted for at least 6 months to a degree that is maladaptive and inconsistent with developmental level:

Hyperactivity

(a) often fidgets with hands or feet or squirms in seat
(b) often leaves seat in classroom or in other situations in which remaining seated is expected
(c) often runs about or climbs excessively in situations in which it is inappropriate (in adolescents or adults, may be limited to subjective feelings of restlessness)
(d) often has difficulty playing or engaging in leisure activities quietly
(e) is often "on the go" or often acts as if "driven by a motor"
(f) often talks excessively

Impulsivity

(g) often blurts out answers before questions have been completed
(h) often has difficulty awaiting turn

(i) often interrupts or intrudes on others (e.g., butts into conversations or games)
B. Some hyperactive-impulsive or inattentive symptoms that caused impairment were present before age 7 years.
C. Some impairment from the symptoms is present in two or more settings (e.g., at school [or work] and at home).
D. There must be clear evidence of clinically significant impairment in social, academic, or occupational functioning.

Diagnostic Criteria for Conduct Disorder

A. A repetitive and persistent pattern of behavior in which the basic rights of others or major age-appropriate societal norms or rules are violated, as manifested by the presence of three (or more) of the following criteria in the past 12 months, with at least one criterion present in the past 6 months:

Aggression to people and animals

(1) often bullies, threatens, or intimidates others
(2) often initiates physical fights
(3) has used a weapon that can cause serious physical harm to others (e.g., a bat, brick, broken bottle, knife, gun)
(4) has been physically cruel to people
(5) has been physically cruel to animals
(6) has stolen while confronting a victim (e.g., mugging, purse snatching, extortion, armed robbery)
(7) has forced someone into sexual activity

Destruction of property

(8) has deliberately engaged in fire setting with the intention of causing serious damage
(9) has deliberately destroyed others' property (other than by fire setting)

Deceitfulness or theft

(10) has broken into someone else's house, building, or car
(11) often lies to obtain goods or favors or to avoid obligations (i.e., "cons" others)
(12) has stolen items of nontrivial value without confronting a victim (e.g., shoplifting, but without breaking and entering; forgery)

Serious violations of rules

(13) often stays out at night despite parental prohibitions, beginning before age 13 years
(14) has run away from home overnight at least twice while living in parental or parental surrogate home (or once without returning for a lengthy period)
(15) is often truant from school, beginning before age 13 years
B. The disturbance in behavior causes clinically significant impairment in social, academic, or occupational functioning.

Diagnostic Criteria for Oppositional Defiant Disorder

A. A pattern of negativistic, hostile, and defiant behavior lasting at least 6 months, during which four (or more) of the following are present:

(1) often loses temper
(2) often argues with adults
(3) often actively defies or refuses to comply with adults' requests or rules
(4) often deliberately annoys people
(5) often blames others for his or her mistakes or misbehavior
(6) is often touchy or easily annoyed by others
(7) is often angry and resentful
(8) is often spiteful or vindictive

Note: Consider a criterion met only if the behavior occurs more frequently than is typically observed in individuals of comparable age and developmental level.

B. The disturbance in behavior causes clinically significant impairment in social, academic, or occupational functioning.

Source: American Psychiatric Association, 2000.

Changes in Ranking of 16 Nations on Science and Math Knowledge Between Fourth and Eighth Grades (Chapter 12)

Only high-scoring nations are included in these rankings. Many other countries, such as Portugal and Iran, rank much lower. Still others, including all the nations of Latin America and Africa, do not administer the tests on which these rankings are based. Identical rankings indicate ties between nations on overall scores. International comparisons are always difficult and often unfair, but two general conclusions have been confirmed: Children in East Asian countries tend to be high achievers in math and science, and children in the United States lose ground between the fourth and eighth grades.

Science Knowledge				Math Knowledge			
Nation	Rank in Fourth Grade	Rank in Eighth Grade	Change in Rank	Nation	Rank in Fourth Grade	Rank in Eighth Grade	Change in Rank
Korea	1	2	−1	Korea	1	3	−2
Japan	2	3	−1	Singapore	1	1	0
Netherlands	3	5	−2	Japan	3	2	+1
Australia	5	9	−4	Hong Kong	4	4	0
United States	5	11	−6	Netherlands	5	8	−3
Austria	5	6	−1	Czech Republic	6	5	+1
Czech Republic	7	4	+3	Austria	7	6	+1
Canada	8	10	−2	Hungary	8	6	+2
Singapore	8	1	+7	Australia	10	11	−1
England	10	6	+4	Ireland	10	9	+1
Hong Kong	11	11	0	United States	10	15	−5
Hungary	11	6	+5	Canada	12	9	+3
Ireland	13	11	+2	Israel	13	12	+1
Norway	14	11	+3	England	14	15	−1
New Zealand	14	11	+3	New Zealand	15	13	+2
Israel	16	16	0	Norway	16	13	+3

Source: Third International Mathematics and Science Study (TIMMS), 1998.

Changes in the Average Weekly Amount of Time Spent by 6- to 11-Year-Olds in Various Activities (Chapter 12)

Data can be presented graphically in many ways. The data given here were collected in the same way in 1981 and in 1997, so the changes are real (although the age cutoff in 1997 was 12, not 11). What do you think would be the best way to show this information? What is encouraging and what is problematic in the changes that you see? One possibility is shown below the table: The changes are presented as percentages in a bar graph.

| Activity | Average Amount of Time Spent in Activity, per Week | | Change in Time Spent |
	In 1981	In 1997	
School	25 hrs, 17 min.	33 hrs, 52 min.	+8 hrs, 35 min.
Organized sports	3 hrs, 5 min.	4 hrs, 56 min.	+1 hr, 51 min.
Studying	1 hr, 46 min.	2 hrs, 50 min.	+1 hr, 4 min.
Reading	57 min.	1 hr, 15 min.	+18 min.
Being outdoors	1 hr, 17 min.	39 min.	–38 min.
Playing	12 hrs, 52 min.	10 hrs, 5 min.	–2 hours, 47 min.
Watching TV	15 hrs, 34 min.	13 hrs, 7 min.	–2 hours, 27 min.

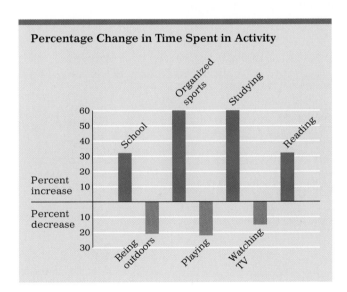

Percentage Change in Time Spent in Activity

Who Is Raising the Children? (Chapter 13)

Most children still live in households with a male/female couple, who may be the children's married or unmarried biological parents, grandparents, stepparents, foster parents, or adoptive parents. However, the proportion of households headed by single parents has risen—by 500 percent for single fathers and by almost 200 percent for single mothers. (In 2000, 52 percent of U.S. households had *no* children under age 18.)

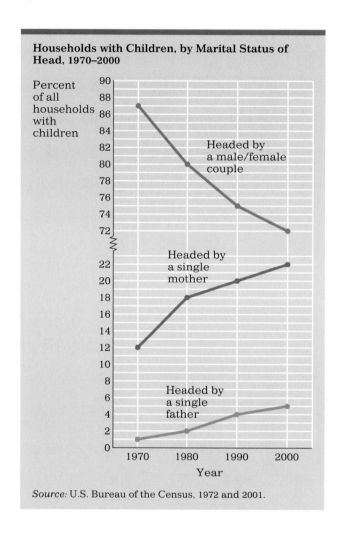

Households with Children, by Marital Status of Head, 1970–2000

Source: U.S. Bureau of the Census, 1972 and 2001.

Smoking Behavior Among U.S. High School Students, 1991–2001 (Chapter 14)

The data in these two tables reveal many trends. For example, do you see that African-American adolescents are much less likely to smoke than Hispanics or European-Americans, but that this racial advantage is decreasing? Do you see that white females smoked more than white males until 2001?

? *Observational Quiz:* (see answer, page A-16): If we compare the 2001 data with only the 1991 data, the news about teen smoking is bad: The percentages of current smokers increased overall and for almost every group. However, what evidence is provided by the data that might encourage public-health workers?

Percentage of High School Students Who Reported Smoking Cigarettes

Smoking behavior	1991	1993	1995	1997	1999	2001
Lifetime (ever smoked)	70.1	69.5	71.3	70.2	70.4	63.9
Current (smoked at least once in past 30 days)	27.5	30.5	34.8	36.4	34.8	28.5
Current frequent (smoked 20 or more times in past 30 days)	12.7	13.8	16.1	16.7	16.8	13.8

Percentage of High School Students Who Reported Current Smoking, by Sex, Race/Ethnicity, and Grade

Characteristic	1991	1993	1995	1997	1999	2001
Sex						
Female	27.3	31.2	34.3	34.7	34.9	27.7
Male	27.6	29.8	35.4	37.7	34.7	29.2
Race/ethnicity						
White, non-Hispanic	30.9	33.7	38.3	39.7	38.6	31.9
Female	*31.7*	*35.3*	*39.8*	*39.9*	*39.1*	*31.2*
Male	*30.2*	*32.2*	*37.0*	*39.6*	*38.2*	*32.7*
Black, non-Hispanic	12.6	15.4	19.2	22.7	19.7	14.7
Female	*11.3*	*14.4*	*12.2*	*17.4*	*17.7*	*13.3*
Male	*14.1*	*16.3*	*27.8*	*28.2*	*21.8*	*16.3*
Hispanic	25.3	28.7	34.0	34.0	32.7	26.6
Female	*22.9*	*27.3*	*32.9*	*32.3*	*31.5*	*26.0*
Male	*27.9*	*30.2*	*34.9*	*35.5*	*34.0*	*27.2*
Grade						
9th	23.2	27.8	31.2	33.4	27.6	23.9
10th	25.2	28.0	33.1	35.3	34.7	26.9
11th	31.6	31.1	35.9	36.6	36.0	29.8
12th	30.1	34.5	38.2	39.6	42.8	35.2

Source: CDC (*Morbidity and Mortality Weekly Report*), May 17, 2002, p. 411.

Sexual Behaviors of U.S. High School Students: State-by-State Variations (Chapter 15)

These percentages, as high as they are, are actually lower than they were in the early 1990s.
The data in this table reflect responses from students in the 9th to 12th grades. When only high school seniors are surveyed, the percentages are higher. In every state, more than half of all high school seniors have had sexual intercourse, and about 25 percent have had four or more sex partners.

State	Ever had sexual intercourse (%)			First sexual intercourse before age 13 (%)			Four or more sex partners during lifetime (%)			Currently sexually active* (%)			Currently abstinent (%)		
	Female	Male	Total	Female	Male	Total	Female	Male	Total	Female	Male	Total	Female	Male	Total
Alaska	43.8	42.2	43.3	5.0	8.6	7.0	14.6	13.2	14.1	29.3	24.0	26.9	33.2	42.8	37.8
Arkansas	56.6	55.3	55.9	7.6	15.0	11.4	18.8	24.0	21.5	41.3	39.0	40.1	27.2	29.2	28.1
Delaware	50.9	58.2	54.6	6.6	13.7	10.2	16.8	23.3	20.3	38.6	41.3	40.0	24.1	29.2	26.9
Hawaii	40.1	41.7	41.0	5.1	8.6	6.8	10.6	13.8	12.2	30.0	26.3	28.5	25.2	36.7	30.4
Massachusetts	41.8	46.4	44.1	3.0	9.0	6.0	9.7	14.7	12.2	32.0	31.7	32.0	24.0	32.0	28.1
Michigan	44.2	45.1	44.6	4.2	9.5	6.9	12.3	15.2	13.7	31.4	31.4	31.4	28.8	30.7	29.7
Mississippi	58.5	62.3	60.3	7.6	24.8	16.0	18.6	33.3	25.7	45.8	43.5	44.8	21.6	30.0	25.7
Missouri	56.1	57.4	56.8	5.0	14.0	9.5	15.3	23.4	19.5	42.9	40.2	41.6	23.3	30.0	26.6
Montana	41.0	43.7	42.5	3.4	7.0	5.3	10.9	13.0	12.1	29.4	29.1	29.2	28.4	33.6	31.3
Nevada	48.5	54.0	51.3	3.1	10.4	6.8	12.9	22.7	17.9	37.5	36.6	37.1	22.5	32.2	27.5
New York	39.0	45.8	42.4	2.6	9.7	6.1	8.2	15.8	12.0	29.4	30.1	29.7	24.5	34.7	29.9
North Dakota	NA	NA	NA	3.2	4.7	3.9	11.8	11.0	11.4	NA	NA	NA	NA	NA	NA
Ohio	45.2	48.7	46.9	2.3	8.5	5.4	15.1	16.4	15.7	32.9	34.2	33.6	27.1	30.0	28.5
South Carolina	56.2	60.2	58.1	7.4	21.3	14.1	16.8	28.0	22.2	39.4	39.9	39.7	29.7	33.6	31.7
South Dakota	44.0	44.0	44.0	3.5	5.7	4.6	12.5	12.7	12.6	33.5	30.4	32.0	23.5	30.8	27.2
Tennessee	52.3	52.3	52.4	4.6	12.9	8.9	16.7	21.8	19.3	41.7	37.9	39.7	20.0	27.0	23.7
Vermont	NA	NA	NA	3.9	9.6	6.9	11.1	15.7	13.5	31.4	30.6	31.1	NA	NA	NA
West Virginia	51.3	57.9	54.8	5.5	12.1	8.9	15.5	21.6	18.6	38.6	42.0	40.4	24.8	27.4	26.2
Wisconsin	41.7	41.1	41.5	3.7	4.8	4.3	9.7	10.7	10.3	31.9	28.8	30.5	23.5	29.5	26.4
Wyoming	47.8	47.8	47.9	3.4	8.9	6.2	15.2	16.8	16.1	36.0	32.7	34.5	24.7	31.5	28.0

NA = Not available.
*Active in 3 months prior to survey.
Source: CDC (*Morbidity and Mortality Weekly Report*), June 9, 2000, pp. 76–77.

!*Answer to Observational Quiz* (from page A-15): The main piece of evidence is that the 2001 numbers are much better than those for 1997 and 1999, so the recent trends offer hope. Since cigarette prices skyrocketed and public-service announcements against smoking increased during those years, teenagers may be thinking twice before lighting up. Notice that the percentage of high school students who have never smoked has also increased—another hopeful sign.

Education Affects Income (Chapter 15)

Although there is some debate about the cognitive benefits of college education, there is no doubt about the financial benefits. No matter what a person's ethnicity or gender, an associate's degree more than doubles his or her income compared to that of someone who has not completed high school.

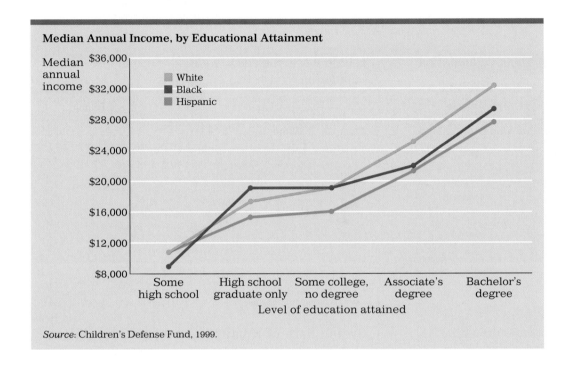

Median Annual Income, by Educational Attainment

Median annual income

White
Black
Hispanic

Level of education attained

Some high school / High school graduate only / Some college, no degree / Associate's degree / Bachelor's degree

Source: Children's Defense Fund, 1999.

United States Homicide Victim and Offender Rates, by Race and Gender, Ages 14–17 (Chapter 16)

Teenage boys are more often violent offenders than victims. The ratio of victimization to offense has varied for teenage girls over the years. The good news is that rates have decreased dramatically over the past ten years for every category of adolescents—male and female, black and white. (Similar declines are apparent for Asian- and Hispanic-Americans.) The bad news is that rates are still higher in the United States than in any other developed nation.

Homicide Victimization Rates per 100,000 Population for 14- to 17-Year-Olds

	Male		Female	
Year	White	Black	White	Black
1976	3.7	24.6	2.2	6.4
1981	4.4	23.6	2.4	6.2
1986	4.2	27.4	2.3	6.6
1991	8.7	73.6	2.6	9.6
1996	8.4	53.3	2.1	8.9
1999	5.0	31.0	1.7	6.0

Source: U. S. Bureau of Justice Statistics, 2001.
Tabulations based on FBI Supplementary Homicide Reports and U.S. Census Bureau, Current Population Reports.

Estimated Homicide Offending Rates per 100,000 Population for 14- to 17-Year-Olds

	Male		Female	
Year	White	Black	White	Black
1976	10.4	72.4	1.3	10.3
1981	10.9	73.1	1.3	8.6
1986	12.3	72.2	1.1	5.6
1991	21.9	199.1	1.3	12.1
1996	17.4	134.8	1.7	7.8
1999	10.2	67.3	1.2	5.3

Source: U. S. Bureau of Justice Statistics, 2001.
Tabulations based on FBI Supplementary Homicide Reports and U.S. Census Bureau, Current Population Reports. Rates include both known perpetrators and estimated share of unidentified perpetrators.

All the charts, graphs, and tables in this Appendix offer readers the opportunity to analyze raw data and draw their own conclusions. The same information may be presented in a variety of ways. On this page, you can create your own bar graph or line graph, depicting some noteworthy aspect of the data presented in the three tables. First, consider all the possibilities the tables offer by answering these six questions:
1. Are white male or female teenagers more likely to be victims of homicide?
2. These are annual rates. How many African-Americans in 1,000 were likely to commit homicide in 1999?
3. Which age group is *most* likely to commit homicide?
4. Which age group is *least* likely to be victims of homicide?
5. Which age group is *almost equally* likely to be either perpetrators or victims of homicide?
6. Of the four groups of adolescents, which has shown the greatest decline in rates of both victimization and perpetration of homicide over the past decade? Which has shown the least decline?
Answers: 1. Boys—at least twice as often. 2. Less than one (actually, only .36, if boys and girls are averaged together.) 3. 18–24. 4. 0–13. 5. 25–34. 6. Black males had the greatest decline, and white females had the least (but these two groups have always been highest and lowest, respectively, in every year).
Now—use the grid provided at right to make your own graph.

Overall Rate of Homicide by Age, 1999, United States (Chapter 16)

Late adolescence and early adulthood are the peak times for murders—both as victims and offenders. The question for developmentalists is whether something changes before age 18 to decrease the rates in young adulthood.

Age group	Victims (per 100,000 in age group)	Killers (per 100,000 in age group)
0–13	1.6	0.2
14–17	5.9	10.7
18–24	15.5	27.7
25–34	10.0	11.0
35–49	5.9	5.0
50+	2.6	1.5

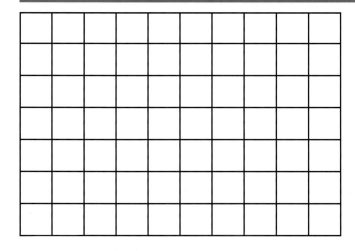

Appendix B
More About Research Methods

The first part of this appendix details some pointers on how to go about gathering more information about human development. The second part expands on Chapter 1's discussion of ways to ensure that research is valid.

Learning More

There are many ways to deepen your understanding of human development, including thinking about your own life and watching the children around you with careful attention to details of expression and behavior. Indeed, such thoughts may become second nature, as you realize how much there is to learn through reflection and observation. But more systematic research, and further book learning, bring insight and understanding that make development even more intriguing.

Library Research

To learn more about a particular topic, focus on readings that are current and scholarly. For instance, if something in a popular magazine or newspaper catches your attention, remember that the writer may have sensationalized, exaggerated, or biased the reporting. You might first check what this textbook says about the topic, and then look at the references cited.

This can begin effective library research. Start with recently published material and then find material from the bibliographies. In addition, there are two collections of abstracts that review current articles from a variety of developmental journals:

- *Psychscan: Developmental Psychology* is published four times a year by the American Psychological Association and includes abstracts of articles from almost 40 scholarly journals, from *Adolescence* to *Psychological Review*. Volume 22 covers the year 2002.
- *Child Development Abstracts and Bibliography* is published three times a year by the Society for Research in Child Development and is organized topically by author. Included are not only journal articles in biology, cognition, education, personality, and theory but also reviews of major books in the field. Volume 75 covers the year 2001. The online address is www.srcd.org.

"Handbooks," which summarize and evaluate research on various topics, are published every ten years or so. The most recent one in child development is in four volumes: *Handbook of Child Psychology* (1998), William Damon (Ed.), New York: Wiley.

To find the most current research, even before it appears in these abstracts and handbooks, look at the most recent issues of the many research journals. The three that cover all three domains (biosocial, cognitive, and psychosocial) are *Developmental Psychology,* published by the American Psychological Association (750 First St., NE, Washington, DC 20002); *Child Development,* published by Blackwell Publishers for the Society for Research in Child Development (Blackwell Publishers: 350 Main St., Malden, MA 02138; Society for Research in

Child Development: University of Michigan, 505 East Huron St., Suite 301, Ann Arbor, MI 48104-1522); and *Human Development,* published by Karger (P.O. Box CH-4009, Basel, Switzerland). These three journals differ somewhat in the types of articles and studies they publish; together they provide a good overview of development.

These suggestions are only a start. There are hundreds of other professional journals that focus on one aspect or another of human development; many are devoted to a particular age group or topic or to research from a particular nation. All of us who are professors hope you begin with one topic and soon lose track of time and subject, finding your interest drawn from one journal or book to another.

Using the Internet

The Internet is a boon for every student, from the novice just beginning to learn about a particular issue to the experienced researcher who wants today's data about an arcane topic. However, using the Internet carries certain risks. To maximize the benefits and reduce the costs of your Internet research, keep the following two advantages and two disadvantages in mind.

Advantages

It's All There

Virtually everything you might want to know is on the Internet, not only massive government statistics carefully collected and tallied but also very personal accounts of rare maladies. Every journal has a Web site, with tables of contents, usually abstracts of articles, and often full texts. Photos, charts, quizzes, ongoing experiments, newspapers from around the world, videos, and much more are available at the click of a mouse.

Quick and Easy

Just by sitting in front of a computer, any time of the day or night, you can research almost any topic. Every library (especially in colleges) has computers hooked up to the World Wide Web and librarians who can help you get started. Other students, co-workers, family members, and even strangers are experts in one aspect or another of Internet use, and usually they are flattered to be asked for specific suggestions. On your own, alone with your personal computer, you can access the Web and teach yourself everything you need to know, using online tutorials, help buttons, and exploration. This last route takes the most time, but some people learn best by teaching themselves—and do not get discouraged by the inevitable frustration when a particular tactic leads to a dead end.

Disadvantages

There's Too Much

You can spend hours sifting through information that turns out to be useless, trash, or tangential. *Directories* (which list general topics or areas and then move you step by step in the direction you choose) and *search engines* (which give you all the sites that use a particular word or words) sort information to help you find what you want. Each directory or search engine is different, and each provides somewhat different lists; none provides only the most comprehensive and accurate sites. You can take advantage of several search engines at once by using a metasearch engine (such as www://metacrawler.com or www://dogpile.com), but here, too, the selection process may not yield exactly what you want. With experience and help, you will get better at choosing the best sites for you, but resign yourself to sorting through some junk no matter what you do.

From Quality to Quackery

Anybody can put anything on the Web. There is no evaluation of bias, or even of evil; racist hate groups' Web sties and explicit child pornography abound on the Internet. You must evaluate and sift for yourself. Make sure you have several divergent sources for every "fact" you find; consider who put the information on the Internet, and for what reason. As the author of a very useful book on psychology on the Web explains: "There is no such thing as a truly free lunch, and there is no such thing as truly neutral information" (Varnhagen, 2002).

Imagine going to your local newsstand and buying a copy of every magazine and newspaper it carries. Then imagine blindly picking one—and reading it uncritically, as if it were the whole truth. You might be lucky and find a publication that was fairly objective, but more often you would find one that was designed for a particular audience that advocated a particular point of view—pro-gun, pro-environment, pro-sex, pro-Catholic, pro-Conservative, and so on. Or you might find one that assumed that sailing or traveling or crossword puzzles or whatever was the most important activity known to humankind. The Internet has the same problem, only much worse. Every controversial issue in child development has several sites that advocate radically opposite viewpoints; often they do not even suggest that there might be another side to the issue.

The Bottom Line

What these advantages and disadvantages come down to is that everyone will find the Internet useful for every topic, but anyone can waste time and be led astray. If you use the Web for research, also check print resources and more experienced researchers.

If you write a paper using Internet resources, bear in mind that massive plagiarism and prejudiced perspectives are common problems. Cite every source you use (so your reader can check your references) and evaluate objectivity, validity, and credibility even more carefully than you do for print resources. Expect your readers or your professors to be suspicious of Internet-based papers, and allay their fears by making your sources explicit and using published materials as well as electronic ones.

To help you get started, here are ten Internet addresses. They are all useful, but always remember to read with a critical eye.

- www.worthpublishers.com/berger   Includes links to Web sites, quizzes, PowerPoint slides, and activities keyed to every chapter of the textbook.
- http://www.psych.umn.edu/psylabs/mtfs/   Describes the findings and ongoing work of the Minnesota Twin Family Study, which seeks to identify the genetic and environmental influences on the development of psychological traits.
- http://embryo.soad.umich.edu/   The Multidimensional Human Embryo. Presents MRI images of a human embryo at various stages of development, accompanied by brief explanations.
- www.kidshealth.org   Web site on children's health, with a large number of articles by experts on various aspects of children's health. Sponsored by the Nemours Foundation.

- www.cdipage.com   A useful site, with links and articles on child development and information on common childhood psychological disorders.
- http://www.piaget.org/main.html   The Jean Piaget Society. Home page of an international, interdisciplinary organization devoted to "exploring the nature of the developmental construction of human knowledge." Some information about Piaget and his theories is provided, along with references and links to other sites.
- http://ericeece.org/eeceweb.html   ERIC Clearinghouse on Elementary and Early Childhood Education: World Wide Web Sites Sponsored or Maintained by ERIC/EECE. Provides links to many education-related sites and provides brief descriptions of each.
- http://education.indiana.edu/cas/adol/adol.html   Adolescence Directory online (ADOL) is an electronic guide to information on adolescent issues. It is a service of the Center for Adolescent Studies at Indiana University.
- http://www.psychREF.com   Contains an index of references in psychology. Not all of them are relevant to human development, but almost every topic in this text is referenced on this Web site.

Ways to Make Research More Valid

As emphasized throughout this text, the study of development is a science. All social scientists use many methods to make their research more objective and therefore more valid. Several basic techniques are described in Chapter 1, including observation and experiments, correlation and statistical significance, independent and dependent variables, and cross-sectional, longitudinal, and cross-sequential research designs. Six additional terms or techniques pertaining to the validity of research are described here. Understanding them will help you evaluate research read about on the Internet, from library reading, or in textbooks.

Population and Subjects

population The entire group of individuals who are of particular concern in a scientific study, such as all the children of the world or all newborns who weigh less than 3 pounds.

subjects The people who are studied in a research project.

The entire group of people about whom a scientist wants to learn is called the **population.** Generally, a research population is quite large—not usually the world's entire population of 6 billion, but perhaps all the 4 million babies born in the United States last year, or all the 500,000 Japanese currently over age 65, or even all the 70,000 low-income fifth-graders attending New York City public schools in 2003. The particular individuals who are studied in a specific research project are called the **subjects.** Typically, the subjects reflect the characteristics of the population. Indeed, every published study reports who the subjects were and how they did, or did not, reflect the population.

Sample Size

sample A group of individuals drawn from a specified population. A sample might be the low-birthweight babies born in four particular hospitals that are representative of all hospitals.

To make statements about people in general, scientists study particular subjects chosen from the larger population. Each group of research subjects, called a **sample,** must be large enough to ensure that if a few extreme cases happen to be included, they do not distort the statistical picture the sample gives of the population. Suppose, for instance, that researchers want to know the average age at which children begin to walk. Since they cannot include every infant in their study, they choose a sample of infants, determine the age of walking for each subject in the sample, and then calculate the sample average. If the sample is typical, the average walking age will be very close to the average for the entire infant population.

The importance of an adequate **sample size** can be seen if we assume, for the moment, that one of the infants in the sample had an undetected disability and did not walk until age 24 months. Assume also that all the other infants walked at 12 months, the current norm. If the sample size was less than 10 infants, then one late walker would add more than a month to the age at which the "average" child is said to walk. However, if the sample contained more than 500 children, the one abnormally late walker would not change the results by even one day.

sample size The number of individuals who are being studied in a single sample in a research project.

Representative Sample

Data collected from one group of subjects may not be valid (that is, applicable and accurate) for other people who are different in some significant way, such as gender or ethnic background. Thus, every sample should be a **representative sample**—that is, should consist of people who are typical of the population the researchers wish to learn about. In a study of the average age of walking, for example, the sample population should reflect—in terms of male/female ratio, socioeconomic and ethnic background, and other characteristics—the entire population of infants. Ideally, other factors might be taken into consideration as well. For instance, if there is some evidence that first-born children walk earlier than later-born children, the sample should also be representative of the population's birth order.

representative sample A group of research subjects who reflect the relevant characteristics of the larger population whose attributes are under study.

The importance of representative sampling is revealed by its absence in two classic studies of age of walking for infants in the United States (Gesell, 1926; Shirley, 1933). Both studies used a relatively small and unrepresentative sample (all the children were European-American and most were middle-class). Partly because the samples were not representative of the general population of infants, both studies arrived at an average walking age of 15 months. This is 3 months later than the current U.S. norm, which was obtained through research on a much larger, more representative sample that included some low-SES children and some children of African and Latino descent—groups known to have high proportions of early-walking children. Another reason the earlier studies found babies walking 3 months later is that infants 80 years ago received much less physical stimulation, so their motor skill development was slowed down. In other words, infants actually did start to walk somewhat later then, perhaps at 13 months, which the researchers would have found if their sample had been representative.

"Blind" Experimenters and Subjects

When experimenters have specific expectations about their research findings, those expectations can unintentionally affect the research results. As much as possible, therefore, the people who actually gather the data should be in a state of **"blindness"**—that is, they should be unaware of the purpose of the research.

blindness A situation in which data gatherers and their subjects are deliberately kept ignorant of the purpose of the research so that they cannot unintentionally bias the results.

Suppose we are testing the hypothesis that first-born infants walk sooner than later-borns. Ideally, the examiner who measures the subjects' walking ability should not know the hypothesis or the infants' age or birth order. The subjects of the research should also be kept blind to its purpose, especially when the subjects are older children or adults, who might be influenced by their own expectations.

Operational Definitions

When planning a study, researchers establish *operational definitions* of whatever phenomena they will be examining. That is, they define each variable in terms of specific, observable behavior that can be measured with precision. Even a simple variable, such as whether or not a toddler is walking, requires an operational definition. For example, does "walking" include steps taken while holding onto someone or something, or must the steps be taken without support? Is one unsteady step enough to meet the definition, or must the infant be able to move a certain distance without faltering? For a study on age of first walking to be meaningful, the researchers would need to resolve questions like these in a clear and thorough definition. In fact, the usual operational definition of walking is "takes at least three steps without holding on."

Understandably, operational definitions become much harder to establish when personality or intellectual variables are being studied. It is nonetheless essential that researchers who are investigating, say, "aggression" or "sharing" or "reading" define the trait in terms that are as precise and measurable as possible. Obviously, the more accurately operational definitions describe the variables to be examined, the more objective and valid the results of the study will be.

Experimental and Comparison Groups

To test a hypothesis adequately in an experiment, researchers gather data on two samples that are similar in every important way except one. They compare an **experimental group,** which receives some special experimental treatment, and a **comparison group,** or *control group,* which is matched to the experimental group in every respect but one: It does not receive the experimental treatment.

Suppose a research team hypothesizes that infants who are provided with regular exercise to strengthen their legs begin to walk earlier than babies who do not receive such exercise. In other words, they hypothesize that the independent variable of exercise affects the dependent variable of walking. To find out if this hypothesis is true, the researchers would first select two representative samples of children and examine both groups to make sure they are equivalent in motor skills, such as the ability to roll over and sit up. Then one sample (the experimental group) would receive daily "workouts" devoted to leg-strengthening between, say, their sixth and twelfth months; and the other sample (the control group) would get no special leg exercise. Results for the two groups would then be compared to test the hypothesis.

To put all this together with the techniques discussed in Chapter 1: A researcher might find 1,000 subjects *(sample size),* randomly chosen from all babies *(population)* born throughout the United States on a particular day *(representative sample)* and visit them at home once a month from age 8 months to 18 months *(longitudinal research),* seeing *(naturalistic observation)* which ones take three unaided steps *(operational definition)* at what age. Then, in follow-up research with a similar sample, two groups of subjects would be matched on every variable except one: The parents of half the babies *(experimental group)* would be shown how to exercise their infants' legs *(independent variable)* and be encouraged, perhaps even paid, to do this every day. These babies' age of walking *(dependent variable)* could be compared with that of the non-exercised babies *(comparison group)* by a researcher who doesn't know *(blind)* which babies are in which group. If differences between the groups emerge, they could be analyzed to see if they exceed random variability (that is, they could be tested for *statistical significance).*

experimental group Research subjects who experience the special condition or treatment that is the crux of the research.

comparison group Research subjects who are comparable to those in the experimental group in every relevant dimension except that they do not experience the special condition or treatment that is the key aspect of the experiment. Also called a *control group.*

Appendix C
Suggestions for Research Assignments

The best way to study child development is to do some investigation yourself, not only reading the textbook and expressing your ideas in speech and writing but also undertaking some research of your own. Writing a term paper is the usual mode in most college courses: You and your instructor already know the importance of setting a deadline for each stage (topic selection, outline, first draft, final draft), of asking several readers to evaluate your paper (perhaps including other students or a professor), and of having the final version typed with references correctly cited and listed. Some suggestions for effective use of journals and the Internet are given in Appendix B.

The subject of human development is also ideal for more personal study, so suggestions for conducting observations, case studies, surveys, and experiments are offered here.

Learning Through Observation

Much can be learned by becoming more systematic in your observations of the children around you. One way to begin is to collect observations of ten different children, in differing contexts, during the semester. Each profile should be approximately one page and should cover the following four items:

1. *Describe the physical and social context.* You will want to describe where you are, what day and time it is, and how many people you are observing. The weather and age and gender of those who are being observed might also be relevant. For example:

   Neighborhood playground on (street), at about 4 P.M. on (day, date), thirty children and ten adults present.

   OR

   Supermarket at (location) on Saturday morning (day, date), about 20 shoppers present.

2. *Describe the specific child who is the focus of your attention.* Estimate age, gender, and so on of the target child and anyone else who interacts with the child. Do not ask the age of the child until after the observation, if at all. Your goal is to conduct a naturalistic observation that is unobtrusive. For example:

   Boy, about 7 years old, playing with four other boys, who seem a year or two older. All are dressed warmly (it is a cold day) in similar clothes.

   OR

   Girl, about 18 months old, in supermarket cart pushed by woman, about 30 years old. The cart is half full of groceries.

3. *Write down everything that the child does or says in three minutes.* (Use a watch with a second hand.) Record gestures, facial expressions, movements, and words. Accurate reporting is the goal, and three minutes becomes a surprisingly long time if you write down everything. For example:

Child runs away about 20 feet, returns, and says, "Try to catch me." Two boys look at him, but they do not move. Boy frowns. He runs away and comes back in 10 seconds, stands about four feet away from the boys, and says, "Anyone want to play tag?" [And so on.]

OR

Child points to a package of Frosted Flakes cereal and makes a noise. (I could not hear if it was a word.) Mother says nothing and pushes the cart past the cereal. Child makes a whining noise, looks at the cereal, and kicks her left foot. Mother puts pacifier in child's mouth. [And so on.]

4. *Interpret what you just observed.* Is the child's behavior typical of children that age? Is the reaction of others helpful or not helpful? What values are being encouraged, and what skills are being mastered? What could have happened differently? This section is your opinion, but it must be based on the particulars you have just observed and on your knowledge of child development, ideally with specific reference to concepts (e.g., the first may be a rejected child; the second child's language development may not be encouraged).

Structuring a Case Study

A case study is more elaborate and detailed than an observation report. Select one child (ask your instructor if family members can be used), and secure written permission from the caregiver and, if the child is old enough, the child him- or herself. Explain that you are not going to report the name of the child, that the material is for your class, that the child or caregiver can stop the project at any time, and that they would be doing you a big favor in helping you learn about child development. Most people are quite happy to help in your education, if you explain this properly.

Gather Your Data

First, collect the information for your paper by using all the research methods you have learned. These methods include:

1. *Naturalistic observation.* Ask the caregiver when the child is likely to be awake and active, and observe the child for an hour during this time. Try to be as unobtrusive as possible; you are not there to play with, or care for, the child. If the child wants to play, explain that you must sit and write for now and that you will play later.

   Write down, minute by minute, everything the child does and that others do with the child. Try to be objective, focusing on behavior rather than interpretation. Thus, instead of writing "Jennifer was delighted when her father came home, and he dotes on her," you should write "5:33: Her father opened the door, Jennifer looked up, smiled, said 'dada,' and ran to him. He bent down, stretched out his arms, picked her up, and said, 'How's my little angel?' 5:34: He put her on his shoulders, and she said, 'Giddy up, horsey.'"

   After your observation, summarize the data in two ways: (a) Note the percentage of time spent in various activities. For instance, "Playing alone, 15 percent; playing with brother, 20 percent; crying, 3 percent." (b) Note the frequency of various behaviors: "Asked adult for something five times; adult granted request four times. Aggressive acts (punch, kick, etc.) directed at brother, 2; aggressive acts initiated by brother, 6." Making notations like these will help you evaluate and quantify your observations. Also, note any circumstances that might have made your observation atypical (e.g., "Jenny's mother said she hasn't been herself since she had the flu a week ago," or "Jenny kept trying to take my pen, so it was hard to write").

Note: Remember that a percentage can be found by dividing the total number of minutes spent on a specific activity by the total number of minutes you spent observing. For example, if, during your 45-minute observation, the child played by herself for periods of 2 minutes, 4 minutes, and 5 minutes, "playing alone" would total 11 minutes. Dividing 11 by 45 yields .244; thus the child spent 24 percent of the time playing alone.

2. *Informal interaction.* Interact with the child for at least half an hour. Your goal is to observe the child's personality and abilities in a relaxed setting. The particular activities you engage in will depend on the child's age and temperament. Most children enjoy playing games, reading books, drawing, and talking. Asking a younger child to show you his or her room and favorite toys is a good way to break the ice; asking an older child to show you the neighborhood can provide insights.

3. *Interview adults responsible for the child's care.* Keep these interviews loose and open-ended. Your goals are to learn (a) the child's history, especially any illnesses, stresses, or problems that might affect development; (b) the child's daily routine, including play patterns; (c) current problems that might affect the child; (d) a description of the child's temperament and personality, including special strengths and weaknesses.

    You are just as interested in adult values and attitudes as in the facts; therefore, you might concentrate on conversing during the interview, perhaps writing down a few words. Then write down all you remember as soon as the interview has been completed.

4. *Testing the child.* Assess the child's perceptual, motor, language, and intellectual abilities by using specific test items you have prepared in advance. The actual items you use will depend on the age of the child. For instance, you might test object permanence in a child between 6 and 24 months old; you would test conservation in a child between 3 and 9 years old. Likewise, testing language abilities might involve babbling with an infant, counting words per sentence with a preschooler, and asking a school-age child to make up a story.

Write Up Your Findings

Second, write the report, using the following steps:

1. Begin by reporting relevant background information, including the child's birth date and sex, age and sex of siblings, economic and ethnic background of the family, and the educational and marital status of the parents.

2. Describe the child's biosocial, cognitive, and psychosocial development, citing supporting data from your research to substantiate any conclusions you have reached. Do *not* simply transcribe your interview, test, or observation data, although you can attach your notes as an appendix, if you wish.

3. Predict the child's development in the next year, the next five years, and the next ten years. List the strengths in the child, the family, and the community that you think will foster optimal development. Also note whatever potential problems you see (either in the child's current behavior or in the family and community support system) that may lead to future difficulties for the child. Include discussion of the reasons, either methodological or theoretical, that your predictions may not be completely accurate.

Finally, show your report to a classmate (your instructor may assign you to a peer mentor) and ask if you have been clear in your description and predictions. Discuss the child with your classmate to see if you should add more details to your report. Your revised case study should be typed and given to your professor, who will evaluate it. If you wish, send me a copy (Professor Kathleen Berger, c/o Worth Publishers, 41 Madison Avenue, New York, NY 10010).

Experiments and Surveys

As you learned in Chapter 1, experiments and surveys are wonderful ways to learn more about development, but each study needs to be very carefully designed and undertaken to avoid bias and to ensure that all the ethical considerations are taken into account. Accordingly, I recommend that an experiment or survey be undertaken by a group of students, not by an individual. Listening carefully to other opinions, using more than one person to collect data, and checking with your professor before beginning the actual study are ways to make sure that your results have some validity.

If you do this, structure your work in such a way that everyone contributes and that contrary opinions are encouraged. (The normal human response is for everyone to agree with everyone else, but, as you learned in Chapter 15, seeking alternate, logical explanations can move an entire group forward to deeper, more analytic thought.) You might designate one person to be the critic, or your group might spend one day designing your study and another day finding problems with the design. (Some problems simply need to be recognized and acknowledged, but some of them can be fixed by changing the design.)

Specific topics for experiments or surveys depend on your group's interests and on your professor's requirements for the course. For ideas, check this book's Subject Index or Study Guide. Since development is multidisciplinary and multicontextual, almost any topic can be related to child development. Just remember to consider theory and practice, change and continuity, social interaction and cultural impact . . . and then try to limit your initial experiment or survey to one small part of this fascinating, ever-changing subject!

Glossary

accommodation The process of taking new information into the mind in such a way as to readjust, refine, or expand previous mental categories, or schemas. (p. 169)

achievement tests Measures of reading ability, math knowledge, science facts, writing skills, or any other subject matter that has actually been mastered. (p. 346)

activity level A measure of how active children are, taking into account both body movements while in one place and movement from one spot to another. (p. 244)

AD/HD (attention-deficit/hyperactivity disorder) A condition in which a child has great difficulty concentrating for more than a few moments at a time and, as a result, is inattentive, impulsive, and overactive. (p. 351)

adaptation The cognitive process by which new information is taken in and responded to. (p. 168)

additive gene A gene that, through interaction with other genes, affects a specific trait (such as skin color or height). (p. 79)

adolescence The period of biological, cognitive, and psychosocial transition from childhood to adulthood, usually lasting a decade or so. (p. 431)

adolescence-limited offender A person whose criminal activity stops by age 21. (p. 515)

adolescent egocentrism A characteristic of adolescent thinking that sometimes leads young people to focus on themselves to the exclusion of others and to believe, for example, that their thoughts, feelings, and experiences are unique. (p. 472)

adoption The process whereby legally designated, nonbiological parents are given custody and care of a child. (p. 258)

adoptive family A family that consists of one or more nonbiological children whom an adult individual or couple have voluntarily, legally, and permanently taken to raise as their own. (p. 410)

adrenal glands A pair of glands located above the kidneys that secrete the hormones epinephrine (adrenaline) and norepinephrine (noradrenaline), which help to arouse the body in time of stress. (p. 432)

affordance An opportunity for perception and interaction that is offered by people, places, and objects in the environment. (p. 177)

age of viability The age (about 22 weeks after conception) at which a fetus can survive outside the mother's uterus if specialized medical care is available. (p. 107)

aggression Hostile attitudes and hurtful or destructive actions that stem from anger or frustration. (p. 302)

aggressive-rejected Referring to children who are actively rejected by their peer group because of their aggressive, confrontational behavior. (p. 400)

allele One of the normal versions of a gene that has several possible sequences of base pairs. (p. 71)

anal stage Freud's term for the second stage of psychosexual development, in which the anus becomes the main source of gratification, particularly the sensual pleasure of bowel movements and, eventually, the psychological pleasure of controlling them. (p. 215)

androgyny A balance, within a person, of traditionally male and female psychological characteristics. (p. 320)

anorexia nervosa A serious eating disorder in which a person restricts eating to the point of emaciation and possible starvation. Most victims are high-achieving females in early puberty or early adulthood. (p. 452)

anoxia A lack of oxygen that, if prolonged, can cause brain damage or death. (p. 126)

antisocial Behaving in ways that are deliberately hurtful or destructive. (p. 302)

Apgar scale A means of quickly assessing a newborn's body functioning. The baby's color, heart rate, reflexes, muscle tone, and respiratory effort are scored (from 0 to 2) one minute and five minutes after birth and compared with a standard for healthy babies (a perfect 10). (p. 123)

apprentice in thinking Vygotsky's term for the young child whose intellectual growth is stimulated and directed by older and more skilled members of society, often parents or teachers, who act as tutors or mentors. (pp. 49, 266)

approach–withdrawal The term used in the NLYS for a trait whose measurement helps classify children as fearful, outgoing, or low-reactive. (p. 206)

aptitude The potential to learn, or master, a particular skill or body of knowledge. (p. 346)

Asperger syndrome A set of less severe symptoms of autism, in which the individual has fairly normal speech and intelligence but severely impaired social interaction. (p. 343)

assimilation The process of taking new information into the mind by incorporating it into previously developed mental categories, or schemas. (p. 168)

assisted reproductive technology (ART) A general term for the various techniques designed to help couples conceive. (p. 76)

asthma A chronic inflammatory disorder of the airways. (p. 335)

attachment According to Ainsworth (1973), "an affectional tie that one person or animal forms between himself and another specific one—a tie that binds them together in space and endures over time." (p. 218)

attention-deficit disorder (ADD) A condition in which a child has great difficulty concentrating (but, unlike a hyperactive child, is not impulsive and hyperactive); the child may be prone to anxiety and depression and may seem lost in thought, spaced out, or distracted. (p. 351)

authoritarian parenting Baumrind's term for a style of child rearing in which standards for proper behavior are high, misconduct is strictly punished, and parent–child communication is low. (p. 309)

authoritative parenting Baumrind's term for a style of child rearing in which the parents set limits and provide guidance for their child but are willing to listen to the child's ideas and to make compromises. (p. 309)

autism A pervasive developmental disorder marked by an inability to relate to other people in an ordinary way, by extreme self-absorption, and by an inability to learn normal speech. (p. 343)

automatization A process by which thoughts and actions are repeated in sequence so often that they become automatic, or routine, and no longer require much conscious thought. (p. 338)

autonomy versus shame and doubt Erikson's term for the second crisis of psychosocial development, in which toddlers either succeed or fail in gaining a sense of self-rule over their own actions and bodies. (p. 216)

axon A nerve fiber that extends from a neuron and transmits electrical impulses from that neuron to the dendrites of other neurons. (p. 141)

B

babbling The extended repetition of certain syllables, such as *ba-ba-ba,* that begins at about 6 or 7 months of age. (p. 187)

baby talk The high-pitched, simplified, and repetitive way adults speak to infants; also called *child-directed speech, motherese.* (p. 185)

behavioral genetics The study of the genetic origins of psychological characteristics, such as personality patterns, psychological disorders, and intellectual abilities. (p. 81)

behavioral teratogens Teratogens that tend to harm the prenatal brain, affecting the future child's intellectual and emotional functioning. (p. 111)

behaviorism A grand theory of human development that focuses on the sequences and processes by which behavior is learned. (Also called *learning theory.*) (p. 40)

bickering Petty, peevish arguing, usually repeated and ongoing. (p. 517)

Big Five A central group of personality traits that seem to be evident in all humans: extroversion, agreeableness, conscientiousness, neuroticism, and openness. (p. 206)

binocular vision The ability to focus the two eyes in a coordinated manner in order to see one image. (p. 148)

biosocial domain The part of human development that includes the brain and body, as well as changes in our biological selves and in the social influences that direct our physical growth. (p. 6)

blended family A family that consists of two adults, the biological children from a previous union of one or both adults, and any children the adults have together. (p. 410)

blindness A situation in which data gatherers and their subjects are deliberately kept ignorant of the purpose of the research so that they cannot unintentionally bias the results. (p. B-5)

body image A person's concept of how his or her body appears. This self-evaluation may be quite different from the opinions of others or from any objective measures. (p. 443)

body mass index (BMI) A measure of obesity, determined by dividing a person's weight in kilograms by height in meters squared. (p. 450)

breathing reflex An involuntary physical response, involving inhaling and exhaling, that ensures an adequate supply of oxygen and the discharge of carbon dioxide. (p. 149)

bulimia nervosa An eating disorder in which the person, usually a female, engages repeatedly in episodes of binge eating followed by purging through induced vomiting or use of laxatives. (p. 454)

bullying A child's repeated, systematic efforts to inflict harm on another, particular child through physical, verbal, or social attacks. (p. 402)

bullying aggression Aggressive behavior that takes the form of an unprovoked physical or verbal attack on another person. (p. 303)

butterfly effect The idea that a small action or event (such as the breeze created by the flap of a butterfly's wings) may set off a series of changes that culminate in a major event (such as a hurricane). (p. 2)

C

carrier A person who has a gene in his or her genotype that is not evident as part of the phenotype but that can be passed on to the person's offspring. (p. 78)

case study A research method in which one individual is studied intensively. (p. 125)

centration A characteristic of preoperational thought in which the young child focuses on one aspect of a situation to the exclusion of all others. (p. 263)

cerebral palsy A disorder that results from damage to the brain's motor centers, usually as a result of events during or before birth. People with cerebral palsy have difficulty with muscle control, which can affect speech or other body movements. (p. 126)

cesarean section A means of childbirth in which the fetus is taken from the mother surgically, through an incision that extends from the mother's abdomen through the uterus. (p. 125)

child abuse Deliberate action that is harmful to a child's physical, emotional, or sexual well-being. (p. 251)

child maltreatment All intentional harm to, or avoidable endangerment of, anyone under 18 years of age. (p. 251)

child neglect Failure to meet a child's basic physical, educational, or emotional needs. (p. 251)

child sexual abuse Any activity in which an adult uses a child for his or her own sexual stimulation or pleasure—even if the use does not involve physical contact. Child pornography, fondling, and lewd comments by strangers are all examples of child sexual abuse. (p. 448)

child with special needs A child who, because of a physical or mental disability, requires extra help in order to learn. (p. 340)

chromosome A carrier of genes; one of the 46 molecules of DNA (in 23 pairs) that each cell of the body contains and that, together, contain all human genes. (p. 69)

classical conditioning The process by which a neutral stimulus becomes associated with a meaningful stimulus so that the organism responds to the former stimulus as if it were the latter. (Also called *respondent conditioning.*) (p. 40)

classification The process of organizing things into groups (or categories or classes) according to some property they have in common. (p. 360)

cluster suicide A group of suicides that occur in the same community, school, or time period. (p. 511)

code of ethics A set of moral principles that is formally adopted by a group or organization. (p. 29)

code-switching The ability to change one's speech and tone from one form to another. (p. 371)

cognitive domain The part of human development that includes our thought processes, perceptual abilities, and language mastery, as well as the educational institutions that encourage our intellectual growth. (p. 6)

cognitive equilibrium In cognitive theory, the state of mental balance that enables a person to reconcile new experiences with existing understanding. People strive to attain cognitive equilibrium. (p. 45)

cognitive theory A grand theory of human development that focuses on the structure and development of thinking, which shapes people's attitudes, beliefs, and behaviors. (p. 44)

cohort A group of people whose shared birth year, or decade, means that they travel through life together experiencing the same major historical changes. (p. 8)

colic A condition in which indigestion causes an infant to engage in prolonged bouts of crying and to sleep less at night than other infants. (p. 208)

comorbidity The presence of more than one disorder in one person at the same time. (p. 351)

comparison group Research subjects who are comparable to those in the experimental group in every relevant dimension except that they do not experience the special condition or treatment that is the key aspect of the experiment. Also called a *control group*. (pp. 23, B-6)

concrete operational thought Piaget's term for the ability to reason logically about the things and events that one perceives. (p. 359)

conditioning According to behaviorism, any process in which a behavior is learned. See **classical conditioning** and **operant conditioning**. (p. 40)

conservation The principle that the amount of a substance is unaffected by changes in its appearance. (p. 264)

contact-maintaining behaviors Actions (such as clinging, resisting being put down, and using social referencing) that are evidence of attachment—specifically, the desire to remain physically close to the person to whom one is emotionally attached. (p. 219)

control processes The mechanism—selective attention, emotional regulation, and strategic thinking—that put memory, processing speed, and knowledge together in order to regulate the analysis and flow of information within the information-processing system. (p. 365)

conventional moral reasoning Kohlberg's second level of moral reasoning, in which emphasis is placed on social rules. (p. 373)

corpus callosum A long, narrow strip of nerve fibers that connects the left and right (hemispheres) of the brain. (p. 240)

correlation A number indicating the degree of relationship between two variables, expressed in terms of the likelihood that one variable will occur when the other variable does. A correlation is not an indication that one variable *causes* the other. (p. 22)

cortex The outer layer of the brain in humans and other mammals; it is the location of most thinking, feeling, and sensing. (p. 141)

criterion-referenced Of achievement-test scores, based on a certain standard of performance. (p. 346)

critical period In prenatal development, the time when a particular organ or other body part is most susceptible to teratogenic damage. A time when a certain type of development must occur or it will never happen. (pp. 112, 278)

cross-sectional research A research method in which groups of people who differ in age but share other important characteristics are compared. (p. 26)

cross-sequential research A hybrid research method in which researchers first study several groups of people of different ages (a cross-sectional approach) and then follow those groups over the years (a longitudinal approach). (Also called *cohort-sequential* or *time-sequential research*.) (p. 29)

culture The specific manifestations of a social group's design for living, developed over the years to provide a social structure for the group members' life together. (p. 10)

D

deductive reasoning Reasoning from a general statement or principle, through logical steps, to a specific conclusion. (p. 467)

deferred imitation A mental combination in which an infant perceives something that someone else does and then performs the same action a few hours or even days later. (p. 174)

Defining Issues Test (DIT) A questionnaire devised by James Rest that measures moral thinking by asking people to read various dilemmas and then to rank 12 statements as possible resolutions for each situation. (p. 375)

dendrite A nerve fiber that extends from a neuron and receives electrical impulses transmitted from other neurons via their axons. (p. 141)

dependent variable In an experiment, the variable that may change as a result of the introduction of or changes made in the independent variable. (p. 23)

developmental psychopathology A field in which knowledge about normal development is applied to the study and treatment of various disorders, and vice versa. (p. 342)

developmental theory A systematic statement of principles and generalizations that provides a coherent framework for studying and explaining development. (p. 35)

***Diagnostic and Statistical Manual of Mental Disorders* (DSM-IV-R)** The American Psychiatric Association's official guide to the diagnosis of mental disorders. The fifth edition will soon be published. (p. 343)

differential response A way of reacting to child-maltreatment reports that distinguishes between those that require immediate investigation (possibly leading to foster care and legal prosecution) and those that are less serious (possibly leading to supportive measures to encourage better care). (p. 253)

disorganized A category of attachment that is neither secure nor insecure but is marked by the child's and caregiver's inconsistent behavior toward each other. (p. 221)

dizygotic twins Twins who were formed when two separate ova were fertilized by two separate sperm at roughly the same time. Such twins share about half their genes, like any other siblings. (p. 76)

dominant gene The stronger of an interacting pair of genes. (p. 79)

drug abuse The ingestion of a drug to the extent that it impairs the user's biological or psychological well-being. (p. 456)

drug addiction A situation in which a person craves more of a drug in order to feel physically or psychologically at ease. (p. 456)

drug use The ingestion of a drug, regardless of the amount or effect. (p. 456)

dynamic perception Perception that is primed to focus on movement and change. (p. 179)

dynamic systems A process of continual change within a person or group, in which each change is connected systematically to every other development in each individual and every society. (p. 2)

dyscalculia Unusual difficulty with mathematics. (p. 349)

dyslexia Unusual difficulty with reading. (p. 349)

E

eclectic perspective The approach taken by most developmentalists, in which they apply aspects of each of the various theories of development rather than adhering exclusively to one theory. (p. 62)

egocentrism A type of centration in which the young child contemplates the world exclusively from his or her personal perspective. (p. 263)

Electra complex In the phallic stage of psychosexual development, the female version of the Oedipus complex: Girls have sexual feelings for their fathers and accompanying hostility toward their mothers. (p. 347)

embryonic period Approximately the third through the eighth week after conception, the period during which the rudimentary forms of all anatomical structures develop. (p. 103)

emergent theories Recently formulated theories that bring together information from many minitheories but that have not yet cohered into theories that are comprehensive and systematic. (p. 36)

emotional intelligence Goleman's term for the understanding of how to interpret and express emotions. (p. 300)

emotional regulation The ability, beginning in early childhood, to direct or modify one's feelings, particularly feelings of fear, frustration, and anger. (p. 295)

empathy A person's true understanding of the emotions of another, including the ability to figure out what would make that person feel better. (p. 302)

epigenetic systems theory An emergent theory of development that emphasizes the interaction of genes and the environment—that is, both the genetic origins of behavior (within each person and within each species) and the direct, systematic influence that environmental forces have, over time, on genes. (p. 51)

estrogen A sex hormone, secreted in greater amounts by females than by males. (p. 433)

ethnic group A collection of people who share certain attributes, almost always including ancestral heritage and often including national origin, religion, customs, and language. (p. 16)

ethology The study of patterns of animal behavior, particularly as that behavior relates to evolutionary origins and species survival. (p. 54)

experience-dependent Refers to brain functions that depend on particular, and variable, experiences in order to grow. (p. 143)

experience-expectant Refers to brain functions that require basic common experiences (which the infant can be expected to have) in order to grow. (p. 143)

experiment A research method in which the researcher tries to determine the cause-and-effect relationship between two variables by manipulating one variable (called the *independent variable*) and then observing and recording the resulting changes in the other variable (called the *dependent variable*). (p. 23)

experimental group Research subjects who experience the special condition or treatment that is the crux of the research. (pp. 23, B-6)

explicit memory Memory that is available for instant recall; often involves material that was deliberately studied and memorized. (p. 184)

extended family A family that consists of three or more generations of biologically related individuals. (p. 410)

externalizing problems Difficulties that arise from a person's tendency to externalize emotions, or to express them outwardly, lashing out in impulsive anger and attacking other people or destroying things. (pp. 295, 512)

F

failure to thrive A situation in which an infant or young child gains little or no weight, despite apparent, normal health. (p. 251)

false self A set of behaviors that is adopted by a person to combat rejection, to please others, or to try out as a possible self. (p. 498)

family function The ways in which a family operates to nurture the development of its children's potential: meeting their physical needs for food, clothing, and shelter; encouraging them to learn; developing their self-esteem; nurturing their friendships with peers; and providing harmony and stability at home. (p. 408)

family structure The legal and genetic relationships among the members of a particular family. (p. 408)

fast mapping The speedy and not very precise process of acquiring vocabulary by mentally "charting" new words. (p. 279)

fetal alcohol syndrome (FAS) A cluster of birth defects, including abnormal facial characteristics, slow physical growth, and retarded mental development, that is caused by the mother's drinking excessive quantities of alcohol when pregnant. (p. 115)

fetal period The ninth week after conception until birth, the period during which the organs grow in size and complexity. (p. 103)

fine motor skills Physical abilities involving small body movements, especially of the hands and fingers, such as drawing and picking up a coin. (p. 150)

fMRI Functional magnetic resonance imaging, a technique in which the brain's magnetic properties are measured to detect changes in activity levels anywhere in the brain. (p. 176)

focus on appearance A characteristic of preoperational thought in which the young child ignores all attributes except appearance. (p. 263)

foreclosure Erikson's term for premature identity formation, which occurs when an adolescent adopts parents' or society's roles and values wholesale, without questioning and analysis. (p. 499)

formal code Speech that is characterized by extensive vocabulary, complex syntax, and lengthy sentences. Also called *elaborated code.* (p. 371)

formal operational thought In Piaget's theory, the fourth and final stage of cognitive development; arises from a combination of maturation and experience. (p. 468)

foster care A legally sanctioned, publicly supported plan that transfers care of maltreated children from parents to someone else. (p. 257)

foster family A family in which one or more orphaned, neglected, or delinquent children are temporarily cared for by an adult individual or couple to whom they are not biologically related. (p. 410)

fragile-X syndrome A genetic disorder in which part of the X chromosome is attached to the rest of it by a very thin string of molecules; often produces mental deficiency in males who inherit it. (p. 92)

G

gamete A reproductive cell; that is, a cell that can reproduce a new individual if it combines with a gamete from the other sex. (p. 69)

gateway drugs Drugs—usually tobacco, alcohol, and marijuana—whose use increases the risk that a person will later use harder drugs, such as cocaine and heroin. (p. 456)

gender differences Culturally imposed differences in the roles and behavior of males and females. (p. 314)

gender identity A person's identification of the self as either male or female, with acceptance of all the roles and behaviors that society assigns to that sex. (p. 501)

gene The basic unit for the transmission of heredity instructions. (p. 69)

generation gap The distance between generations in values, behaviors, and knowledge, marked by a mutual lack of understanding. (p. 516)

generational forgetting The tendency of a particular cohort of young people to be ignorant of what the previous cohort learned about the consequences of the use of a drug because the younger group has not personally witnessed the effects of that drug. (p. 458)

generational stake The need of each generation to view family interactions from its own perspective, because each has a different investment in the family scenario. (p. 517)

genetic code The sequence in which pairs of chemical bases appear along each segment of the DNA molecule. (p. 70)

genetic counseling A process of consultation and testing that enables individuals to learn about their genetic heritage, including conditions that might harm any children they may have. (p. 96)

genetic imprinting The tendency of certain genes to be expressed differently when they are inherited from one parent rather than the other. (p. 80)

genotype A person's entire genetic inheritance, including genes that are not expressed in the person. (p. 78)

germinal period The first two weeks of development after conception; characterized by rapid cell division and the beginning of cell differentiation. (p. 103)

goal-directed behavior Purposeful action initiated by infants in anticipation of events that will fulfill their needs and wishes. (p. 171)

gonads The pair of sex glands in humans. In females, they are called the ovaries; in males, they are called testes or testicles. (p. 433)

goodness of fit A pattern of smooth interaction between the individual and the social milieu, including family, school, community. (p. 206)

grammar All the methods—word order, verb forms, and so on—that languages use to communicate meaning, apart from the words themselves. (p. 189)

grand theories Comprehensive theories that have traditionally inspired and directed thinking about development. Psychoanalytic theory, behaviorism, and cognitive theory are all grand theories. (p. 36)

grandparent family A family that consists of children living with their grandparents instead of with their parents. (p. 410)

graspability The perception of whether or not an object is of the proper shape, size, texture, and distance to afford grasping. (p. 178)

gross motor skills Physical abilities involving large body movements, such as waving the arms, walking, and jumping. (p. 150)

growth spurt The period of relatively sudden and rapid physical growth of every part of the body that occurs during puberty. (p. 436)

guided participation In sociocultural theory, the process by which a skilled person helps a novice learn by providing not only instruction but also a direct, shared involvement in the learning process through social experiences and exploration. (pp. 49, 266)

H

habituation The process of getting used to an object or event through repeated exposure to it. (p. 176)

head-sparing A phenomenon by which the brain continues to grow even though the body stops growing as a result of malnutrition. (p. 136)

hidden curriculum The unofficial, unstated, or implicit rules and priorities that influence the academic curriculum and every other aspect of school learning. (p. 386)

high risk Term used by educators to refer to a child whose chances of poor achievement are notably higher than average. More generally, high risk refers to someone with an increased likelihood of some negative experience, such as catching a disease or dropping out of school. (p. 288)

high-stakes tests Tests whose results have serious consequences for the children who take them—determining, for example, whether they will be promoted to the next grade or allowed to graduate from high school. (p. 484)

holophrase A single word that is used to express a complete, meaningful thought. (p. 188)

HPA axis The hypothalamus/pituitary/adrenal axis, a route followed by many kinds of hormones to trigger the changes of puberty and to regulate stress, growth, sleep, appetite, sexual excitement, and various other bodily changes. (p. 433)

Human Genome Project An international effort to map the complete human genetic code. (p. 70)

human immunodeficiency virus (HIV) A virus that gradually overwhelms the body's immune responses, leaving the individual defenseless against a host of pathologies that eventually manifest themselves as AIDS. (p. 114)

hypothalamus An area at the base of the brain that, in addition to regulating several maintenance activities (eating, drinking, and body temperature), directs the production of hormones via the pituitary gland. (p. 432)

hypothesis A specific prediction that is stated in such a way that it can be tested and either confirmed or refuted. (p. 20)

hypothetical thought Thought that includes propositions and possibilities that may or may not reflect reality. (p. 456)

I

identification A defense mechanism that lets a person symbolically take on the behaviors and attitudes of someone more powerful than him- or herself. (p. 316)

identity In Piaget's theory, the idea that certain characteristics of an object remain the same even if other characteristics change. (p. 361)

identity As used by Erikson, a consistent definition of one's self as a unique individual, in terms of roles, attitudes, beliefs, and aspirations. (p. 497)

identity achievement Erikson's term for the attainment of identity, or the point at which a person understands who he or she is as a unique individual, in accord with past experiences and future plans. (p. 498)

identity diffusion A situation in which an adolescent does not seem to know or care what his or her identity is. (p. 499)

identity moratorium Erikson's term for a pause in identity formation that allows young people to explore alternatives without making final identity choices. (p. 499)

identity versus role confusion Erikson's term for the fifth stage of development, in which the person tries to figure out "Who am I?" but is confused as to which of many roles to adopt. (p. 498)

imaginary audience A teenager's false belief, stemming from adolescent egocentrism, that others are intensely interested in his or her appearance and behavior. (p. 473)

imaginary companion A make-believe person or other creature that a young child talks to and plays with. (p. 277)

immunization A process that stimulates the body's immune system to defend against attack by a particular contagious disease. (p. 155)

implantation Beginning about a week after conception, the burrowing of the organism into the lining of the uterus, where it can be nourished and protected during growth. (p. 104)

implicit memory Memory of events, objects, and experiences that can be recognized when certain cues are present but cannot be recalled without reminders. (p. 184)

incidence How often a particular behavior or circumstance occurs. (p. 513)

inclusion A policy under which learning-disabled children are included in the regular class, as in mainstreaming, but are supervised by a specially trained teacher or paraprofessional for all or part of the day. (p. 354)

independent variable In an experiment, the variable that is introduced or changed to see what effect it has on the dependent variable. (p. 23)

inductive reasoning Reasoning from one or more specific experiences or facts to a general conclusion. (p. 467)

indulgent parenting An abusive style of child rearing in which the parents accommodate the child's every whim. (p. 310)

industry versus inferiority The fourth of Erikson's eight crises of psychosexual development, in which school-age children attempt to master many skills and develop a sense of themselves as either industrious and competent or incompetent and inferior. (p. 393)

infantile amnesia The inability, hypothesized by Freud, to remember anything that happened before the age of 2 or anything except very important events before the age of 5. (p. 182)

infertile Referring to a couple who are unable to produce a baby after at least a year of trying. (p. 76)

informal code Speech that is characterized by the use of relatively few words and simpler syntax and by reliance on gestures and intonation to convey meaning. Also called *restricted code*. (p. 372)

information-processing theory A perspective that compares human thinking processes, by analogy, to computer analysis of data, from sensory input through brain reactions, connections, and stored memories to output. (p. 176)

initiative versus guilt The third of Erikson's eight stages of psychosocial development, in which the young child eagerly begins new projects and activities and feels guilt when his or her efforts result in failure or criticism. (p. 300)

injury control/harm reduction The idea that accidents are not random but can be made less harmful with proper control. In practice, this means anticipating, controlling, and preventing dangerous activities. (p. 248)

insecure attachment A relationship that is unstable or unpredictable; in infancy such relationships are characterized by the child's fear, anxiety, anger, clinging, or seeming indifference toward the caregiver. (p. 219)

insecure-avoidant Referring to a pattern of attachment in which one person tries to avoid any connection with another, as an infant who is uninterested in the caregiver's presence or departure and ignores the caregiver on reunion. (p. 219)

insecure-resistant/ambivalent Referring to a pattern of attachment in which anxiety and uncertainty keeps one person clinging to another, as an infant who resists active exploration, is very upset at separation, and both resists and seeks contact on reunion. (p. 219)

instrumental aggression Aggressive behavior that is aimed at getting or keeping an object desired by another. (p. 303)

interaction effect The phenomenon in which a teratogen's potential for causing harm increases when it is combined with another teratogen or another risk factor. (p. 113)

internalizing problems Difficulties that arise from a person's tendency to internalize emotions, or to inhibit their expression, being fearful and withdrawn or inflicting harm on themselves. (pp. 295, 512)

invincibility fable A teenager's false belief, stemming from adolescent egocentrism, that he or she cannot be conquered or even harmed by anything that might vanquish a normal mortal, such as unprotected sex, drug abuse, or high-speed driving. (p. 472)

in vitro fertilization (IVF) A technique for helping couples conceive in which ova are surgically removed from a woman, mixed with sperm, and inserted into the woman's uterus once viable zygotes have formed. (p. 76)

IQ tests Aptitude tests designed to measure a person's intellectual aptitude, or ability to learn in school. This aptitude was originally defined as mental age divided by chronological age, times 100—hence, intelligence quotient, or IQ. An example:
Actual age of three children: 12, 12, 12
Mental ages of the three: 15, 12, 8
IQ of each of these three:
$15/12 = 1.25 \times 100 = 125$ (superior)
$12/12 = 1 \times 100 = 100$ (average)
$8/12 = .75 \times 100 = 75$ (slow learner)
(p. 346)

irreversibility A characteristic of preoperational thought in which the young child fails to recognize that reversing a process can restore whatever existed before the transformation occurred. (p. 265)

K

kinship care A form of foster care in which a relative of the maltreated child becomes the approved caregiver. (p. 257)

knowledge base A broad body of knowledge in a particular subject area that makes it easier to master new learning in that area. (p. 364)

kwashiorkor A disease of chronic malnutrition in which a deficiency of protein causes the child's face, legs, and abdomen to bloat, or swell with water, and makes the child more vulnerable to other diseases, such as measles, diarrhea, and influenza. (p. 161)

L

language acquisition device (LAD) Chomsky's term for a hypothesized brain structure responsible for the innate human ability to learn language, including the basic aspects of grammar. (p. 192)

latency Freud's term for middle childhood, during which children's emotional drives are quieter, their psychosexual needs are repressed, and their unconscious conflicts are submerged. (p. 393)

lateralization Literally, "sidedness," here referring to the differentiation of the two sides of the body or brain so that one side specializes in a certain function; brain lateralization means that the left side of the brain controls the right side of the body, and vice versa. (p. 240)

learning-disabled Having a marked delay in a particular area of learning that is not associated with any obvious physical handicap, overall mental retardation, or unusually stressful home environment. (p. 346)

least restrictive environment (LRE) A legally required school setting that offers children with special needs as much freedom as possible to benefit from the instruction available to other children; often, in practice, the general classroom. (p. 353)

life-course-persistent offender A person whose criminal activity typically begins in early adolescence and continues throughout life; a career criminal. (p. 515)

life-span perspective A view of human development that takes into account all phases of life, not just childhood or adulthood. (p. 5)

linear change A process in which change occurs in a gradual, regular, predictable sequence. (p. 2)

"little scientist" Piaget's term for the stage-five toddler (age 12 to 18 months), who actively experiments with objects to learn about their properties. (p. 174)

long-term memory The component of the information-processing system in which virtually limitless amounts of information can be stored indefinitely. (p. 364)

longitudinal research A research method in which the same individuals are studied over a long period of time. (p. 28)

low birthweight (LBW) A birthweight of less than $5\frac{1}{2}$ pounds (2,500 grams). (p. 119)

M

mainstreaming A policy (mandated by the Education of All Handicapped Children Act in 1975) under which children with special needs must be taught in "the least restrictive environment" available, which usually means that they are taught with other children in the general classroom. (p. 353)

marasmus A disease of severe protein–calorie malnutrition in which growth stops, body tissues waste away, and the infant eventually dies. (p. 161)

menarche A female's first menstrual period. (p. 434)

mental combinations Sequences of actions that the toddler in Piaget's stage six of sensorimotor intelligence (age 18 to 24 months) develops intellectually before actually performing them. (p. 174)

mentally retarded Having severe delays in all areas of mental development. (p. 346)

metacognition "Thinking about thinking," or the ability to evaluate a cognitive task to determine how best to accomplish it, and then to monitor and adjust one's performance on that task. (p. 366)

middle childhood The period from age 7 to 11. (p. 331)

minitheories Theories that focus on some specific area of development but are less general and comprehensive than the grand theories. (p. 36)

modeling In social learning theory, the process in which people observe and then copy the behavior of others. (p. 43)

molecular genetics The study of genetics at the molecular level, including the study of the chemical codes that constitute a particular molecule of DNA. (p. 83)

monozygotic twins Twins who have identical genes because they were formed from one zygote that split into two identical organisms very early in development. (p. 75)

morality of care In Gilligan's view, the tendency of females to be reluctant to judge right and wrong in absolute terms because they are socialized to be nurturant, compassionate, and nonjudgmental. (p. 375)

morality of justice In Gilligan's view, the tendency of males to emphasize justice over compassion, judging right and wrong in absolute terms. (p. 375)

multicontextual A characteristic of development, referring to the fact that each human life takes place within a number of contexts—historical, cultural, and socioeconomic. (p. 5)

multicultural A characteristic of development, referring to the fact that it takes place within many cultural settings worldwide and thus reflects a multitude of values, traditions, and tools for living. (p. 5)

multidirectional A characteristic of development, referring to its nonlinear progression—gains and losses, compensations and deficits, predictable and unexpected changes. (p. 5)

multidisciplinary A characteristic of development, referring to the fact that many academic fields contribute data and insight to the science of development. (p. 5)

multifactorial Referring to inherited traits that are influenced by many factors, including factors in the environment, rather than by genetic influences alone. (p. 78)

myelination The process by which axons become insulated with a coating of *myelin*, a fatty substance that speeds transmission of nerve impulses from neuron to neuron in the brain. (p. 239)

N

naming explosion A sudden increase in an infant's vocabulary, especially in the number of nouns, that begins at about 18 months of age. (p. 187)

nature A general term for the traits, capacities, and limitations that each individual inherits genetically from his or her parents at the moment of conception. Nature refers only to genes, not to other biological forces. (p. 60)

negative identity An identity that is taken on with rebellious defiance, simply because it is the opposite of whatever parents or society expects. (p. 499)

neglectful parenting An abusive style of child rearing in which the parents do not seem to care about their child at all. (p. 310)

neural tube A fold of outer embryonic cells that appears about three weeks after conception and later develops into the central nervous system. (p. 105)

neuron A nerve cell of the central nervous system. Most neurons are in the brain. (p. 141)

norm A standard, or average, that is derived or developed for a specific group or population. (p. 135)

norm-referenced Of achievement-test scores, based on a certain level of achievement that is usual, or normal (such as a certain grade level). (p. 346)

nuclear family A family that consists of a father, a mother, and the biological children they have together. (p. 410)

nurture A general term for all the environmental influences that affect development after an individual is conceived. Nurture includes the prenatal environment, as well as all the ecosystems described in Chapter 1. (p. 60)

O

obesity A body weight that is 20 percent or more above the weight that is considered ideal for the person's age and height. (p. 332)

object permanence The realization that objects (including people) still exist even when they cannot be seen, touched, or heard. (p. 171)

Oedipus complex In the phallic stage of psychosexual development, the sexual desire that boys have for their mothers and the related hostility that they have toward their fathers. (p. 316)

operant conditioning The process by which a response is gradually learned via reinforcement or punishment. (Also called *instrumental conditioning*.) (p. 41)

oral stage Freud's term for the first stage of psychosexual development, in which the infant obtains pleasure through sucking and biting. (p. 215)

overextension The application of a word beyond its true meaning, as when a child calls two or more people *Mama*. (p. 189)

overregularization The young child's tendency to apply the rules of grammar even when doing so is not necessary or appropriate. (p. 281)

overweight A body weight that is up to 20 percent above the weight that is considered ideal for the person's age and height. (p. 332)

P

parasuicide A deliberate act of self-destruction that does not end in death. Parasuicide may be a fleeting gesture, such as a small knife mark on the wrist, or potentially lethal, as when a person swallows an entire bottle of sleeping pills. (p. 510)

parental monitoring Parents' awareness of what their children are doing, where, and with whom. (p. 518)

parent–newborn bond The strong feelings of attachment that arise between parents and their newborn infants. (p. 128)

peer group An aggregate of individuals of roughly the same age and social status who play, work, or learn together. (p. 397)

peer pressure Social pressure to conform with one's friends or contemporaries in behavior, dress, and attitude; usually considered a negative force, as when adolescent peers encourage each other to defy adult authority. (p. 519)

peers People who are about the same age and status as oneself. (p. 301)

percentile Any point on a ranking scale of 1 to 99. For example, the 50th percentile is at the midpoint of such a scale, with half the subjects ranking higher and half ranking lower on a given value, such as height or weight. (p. 136)

perception The mental processing of sensory information. (p. 146)

permanency planning The search for a long-term solution to a problem. In the case of an abused child, such a plan may involve return to parents who have changed, long-term foster care, or adoption. (p. 257)

permissive parenting Baumrind's term for a style of child rearing in which the parents seldom punish, guide, or control the child but are nurturant and communicate well with the child. (p. 309)

perseveration The tendency to persevere, or stick to, one thought or action even when it has become useless or inappropriate. (p. 243)

personal fable A teenager's false belief, stemming from adolescent egocentrism, that he or she is destined to have a unique, heroic, or even legendary life. (p. 473)

person–environment fit The match between a person at a given stage of development and his or her setting, including society, family, and peer group. (p. 478)

pervasive developmental disorders Severe problems, such as autism, that affect many aspects of psychological growth of a child under age 3. (p. 343)

phallic stage Freud's term for the third stage of psychosexual development, which occurs in early childhood and in which the penis becomes the focus of psychological concern as well as physiological pleasure. (p. 316)

phenotype All the genetic traits, including physical characteristics and behavioral tendencies, that are expressed in a person. (p. 78)

phobia An irrational fear that is strong enough to make a person avoid the feared object or experience. (p. 297)

phonics approach The teaching of reading by requiring children to learn the sounds of each letter before they begin to decipher simple words. (p. 381)

pituitary gland A gland that, in response to a biochemical signal from the hypothalamus, produces hormones that regulate growth and control other glands, including the adrenal glands. (p. 432)

placenta The disk-shaped temporary organ that connects the wall of the uterus and the umbilical cord. The placenta allows oxygen and nourishment to flow to the fetus and permits carbon dioxide and wastes to flow away but maintains the separation of the mother's and fetus's circulatory systems. (p. 106)

plastic A characteristic of development, referring to the fact that individuals—including their personalities as well as their bodies and minds—change throughout the life span. (p. 5)

polygenic Referring to inherited traits that are influenced by many genes, rather than by a single gene. (p. 78)

population The entire group of individuals who are of particular concern in a scientific study, such as all the children of the world or all newborns who weigh less than 3 pounds. (p. B-4)

possible selves Various intellectual fantasies about what the future might bring if one or another course of action is chosen. (p. 497)

postconventional moral reasoning Kohlberg's third level of moral reasoning, in which emphasis is placed on moral principles. (p. 373)

postformal thought A type of reasoning that, many psychologists believe, develops after formal operational thought. Postformal thought is well suited to solving real-world problems because it is less abstract and absolute than formal thought, more adaptable to life's inconsistencies, and more dialectical—capable of combining contradictory elements into a comprehensive whole. (p. 469)

postpartum depression The profound feeling of sadness and inadequacy that is experienced by some new mothers, leading to an inability to eat, sleep, or care normally for their newborns. (p. 129)

post-traumatic stress disorder (PTSD) A syndrome in which a victim or witness of a trauma or shock has lingering symptoms, which may include hyperactivity and hypervigilance, displaced anger, sleeplessness, sudden terror or anxiety, and confusion between fantasy and reality. (p. 256)

poverty line The minimum annual income a family needs to pay for basic necessities, as determined by the federal government. A family whose income falls below that amount is considered poor. (p. 14)

preconventional moral reasoning Kohlberg's first level of moral reasoning, in which emphasis is placed on getting rewards and avoiding punishments. (p. 373)

prefrontal cortex The area at the front of the cortex of the brain that specializes in the "executive function," planning, selecting, and coordinating thoughts. (Also called the *frontal lobe* or *frontal cortex*.) (p. 242)

preoperational thought Piaget's term for cognitive development between the ages of about 2 and 6; characterized by centration (including egocentrism), focus on appearance, static reasoning, and irreversibility. (p. 263)

preterm birth Birth that occurs three weeks or more before the full term of pregnancy has elapsed, that is, at 35 or fewer weeks past conception rather than at the full term of about 38 weeks. (p. 120)

prevalence However widespread within a population a particular behavior or circumstance is. (p. 513)

primary circular reactions The first of three types of feedback loops, this one involving the infant's own body, in which the infant takes in experiences and tries to make sense of them. (p. 168)

primary prevention Actions that change overall background conditions to prevent some unwanted event or circumstance, such as injury, disease, or drug abuse. (p. 248)

primary sex characteristics The sex organs—those parts of the body that are directly involved in reproduction, including the vagina, uterus, ovaries, testicles, and penis. (p. 439)

private speech Vygotsky's term for the internal dialogue which occurs when people talk to themselves and through which new ideas are developed and reinforced. (p. 267)

prosocial Behaving in ways that help other people without obvious benefit to oneself. (p. 302)

protein–calorie malnutrition A condition in which a child does not consume sufficient food of any kind to thrive. (p. 160)

proximity-seeking behaviors Actions (such as approaching, following, and climbing into the lap) that are evidence of attachment—specifically, the desire to be physically close to someone to whom one is emotionally attached. (p. 219)

psychoanalytic theory A grand theory of human development that holds that irrational, unconscious drives and motives, many of which originate in childhood, underlie human behavior. (p. 36)

psychosocial domain The part of human development that includes emotions, personality, and interpersonal relationships with family, friends, and the wider community. (p. 6)

puberty A period of rapid growth and sexual change that occurs in early adolescence and produces a person of adult size, shape, and sexual potential. (p. 432)

R

race A social construction by which biological traits (such as hair or skin color, facial features, and body type) are used to differentiate people whose ancestors came from various regions of the world. (p. 16)

reaction time The length of time it takes a person to respond to a particular stimulus. (p. 336)

reactive aggression Aggressive behavior that is an angry retaliation for some intentional or accidental act by another person. (p. 303)

recessive gene The weaker of an interacting pair of genes. (p. 79)

reinforcement The process by which a behavior is followed by results that make it more likely that the behavior will be repeated. This occurs in operant conditioning. (p. 41)

relational aggression Aggressive behavior that takes the form of insults or social rejection. (p. 303)

REM sleep Rapid eye movement sleep, a stage of sleep characterized by flickering eyes behind closed lids, dreaming, and rapid brain waves. (p. 139)

reminder session A perceptual experience that makes a person recollect an idea or thing but that does not test one's actual memory for it. (p. 182)

replication The repetition of a scientific study, using the same procedures on another group of subjects, to verify or refute the original study's conclusions. (p. 20)

reported maltreatment Maltreatment about which the police, child welfare agency, or other authorities have been officially notified. (p. 251)

representative sample A group of research subjects who reflect the relevant characteristics of the larger population whose attributes are under study. (p. B-5)

resource room A room set aside in some schools for special-needs children to spend part of each day with a teacher who is trained and equipped to work with their disabilities. (p. 354)

reversibility The idea that sometimes a thing that has been changed can be returned to its original state by reversing the process by which it was changed. (p. 361)

risk analysis The process of weighing the potential outcomes of a particular event, substance, or experience to determine the likelihood of harm. In teratology, risk analysis involves an attempt to evaluate all the factors that increase or decrease the likelihood that a particular teratogen will cause harm. (p. 111)

rite of passage A dramatic ceremony that marks the transition from childhood to adulthood. (p. 505)

rooting reflex An involuntary physical response in which babies seek a nipple by turning their heads toward anything that brushes against their cheeks and trying to suck on it. (p. 150)

rough-and-tumble play Play that mimics aggression through wrestling, chasing, or hitting but that actually occurs purely in fun, with no intent to harm. (p. 304)

S

sample A group of individuals drawn from a specified population. A sample might be the low-birthweight babies born in four particular hospitals that are representative of all hospitals. (p. B-4)

sample size The number of individuals who are being studied in a single sample in a research project. (p. B-5)

scaffold A sensitive structuring of the young child's participation in learning encounters. (p. 267)

scientific method An approach to the systematic pursuit of knowledge that, when applied to the study of development, involves five basic steps: Formulate a research question, develop a hypothesis, test the hypothesis, draw conclusions, and make the findings available. (p. 20)

scientific observation A method of testing hypotheses by unobtrusively watching and recording subjects' behavior either in a laboratory or in a natural setting. (p. 21)

scientific study of human development The science that seeks to understand the ways in which people change and remain the same as they grow older. (p. 1)

script A mental road map of a familiar sequence of events. (p. 273)

secondary circular reactions The second of three types of feedback loops, this one involving people and objects, in which the infant takes in experiences and tries to make sense of them. (p. 170)

secondary prevention Actions that avert harm in the immediate situation, such as stopping a car before it hits a pedestrian. (p. 248)

secondary sex characteristics Body characteristics that are not directly involved in reproduction but that indicates sexual maturity, such as a man's beard or a woman's breasts. (p. 439)

secure attachment A relationship of trust and confidence; during infancy, a relationship that provides enough comfort and reassurance to enable independent exploration of the environment. (p. 219)

secure base for exploration The caregiver's role in a relationship of secure attachment, in which the child freely ventures forth and returns. (p. 219)

selective adaptation The idea that humans and other animals gradually adjust to their environment; specifically, the process by which the frequency of particular genetic traits in a population increases and others decrease over generations, depending on whether a given trait contributes to the survival of the species. (p. 52)

selective attention The ability to screen out distractions and to focus on the details that will help in later recall of information. (p. 366)

self-awareness A person's realization that he or she is a distinct individual whose body, mind, and actions are separate from those of other people. (p. 213)

self-concept People's understanding of who they are. (p. 298)

self-efficacy In social learning theory, the belief that one is effective; self-efficacy motivates people to change themselves and their contexts. (p. 44)

self-esteem People's pride in themselves. (p. 298)

self-handicapping A person's deliberate selection of choices that will impede his or her success. Adolescents who do not study, who hand in homework late, who rush through tests, and who skip sleep are handicapping their academic success. (p. 483)

sensation The response of a sensory system when it detects a stimulus. (p. 146)

sensitive period A time when a certain type of development occurs most rapidly. (p. 278)

sensorimotor intelligence Piaget's term for the intelligence of infants during the first (sensorimotor) period of cognitive development, when babies think by using their senses and motor skills. (p. 168)

sensory register The component of the information-processing system in which incoming stimulus information is stored for a split second to allow it to be processed. (p. 363)

separation anxiety Fear of abandonment, exhibited at the departure of a beloved caregiver; usually strongest at 9 to 14 months. (p. 203)

sex differences Biological differences between males and females. (p. 314)

sexual abuse The use of an unconsenting person for one's own sexual pleasure. Sexual activity is abusive whenever it is not mutual, whenever consent is not freely given, or whenever a person does not understand or feels obligated to agree to a sexual encounter. (p. 448)

sexually active Traditionally, a euphemism for sexual intercouse; still in use, even though today many adolescents engage in many behaviors other than penile–vaginal penetration. (p. 490)

sexually transmitted diseases (STDs) Disease spread by sexual contact. Such diseases include syphilis, gonorrhea, herpes, chlamydia, and AIDS. (p. 445)

shaken baby syndrome A serious condition caused by maltreatment involving shaking a crying infant back and forth, sharply and quickly. Severe brain damage results from internal hemorrhaging and broken neural connections. (p. 255)

single-parent family A family that consists of one parent and his or her biological children. (p. 410)

small for gestational age (SGA) A term applied to newborns who weigh substantially less than they should, given how much time has passed since conception. (Also called *small-for-dates*.) (p. 121)

social cognition A person's awareness and understanding of human personality, motives, emotions, intentions, and actions. (p. 396)

social cognitive theory A perspective that highlights how the school-age child advances in learning, cognition, and culture, building on maturation and experience to become more articulate, insightful, and competent. (p. 394)

social comparison The tendency to assess one's abilities, achievements, social status, and other attributes by measuring them against those of other people, especially one's peers. (p. 397)

social construction An idea that is built more on shared perceptions of social order than on objective reality. (p. 9)

social learning theory An application of behaviorism that emphasizes that many human behaviors are learned through observation and imitation of other people. (p. 43)

social mediation A function of speech by which a person's cognitive skills are refined and extended. (p. 268)

social referencing Seeking information about an unfamiliar or ambiguous object or event by observing someone else's expressions and reactions. That other person becomes a reference, consulted when the infant wants to know how to react. (p. 210)

society of children The social culture of children, consisting of the games, vocabulary, dress codes, and rules of behavior that characterize their interactions. (p. 398)

sociocultural theory An emergent theory that holds that human development results from the dynamic interaction between each person and the surrounding culture, including all the social forces, near and distant, that affect that person. (p. 48)

sociodramatic play Pretend play in which children act out various roles and themes in stories that they create themselves. (p. 305)

socioeconomic status (SES) An indicator of a person's social and economic standing, measured through a combination of family income, educational level, place of residence, occupation, and other variables. (p. 14)

source memory The ability to recall the person who said or did something or the place where something occurred. (p. 271)

spermarche A male's first ejaculation of live sperm, whether through masturbation, a dream, or sexual contact with another person. (p. 434)

spontaneous abortion The naturally occurring termination of a pregnancy before the fetus is fully developed. (Also called *miscarriage*.) (p. 89)

static reasoning A characteristic of preoperational thought in which the young child assumes that the world is unchanging. (p. 264)

still face technique A method of studying synchrony by assessing the infant's reaction when the caregiver stops engaging in synchronous behavior and merely stares at the baby for a minute or two. (p. 210)

Strange Situation A laboratory procedure developed by Mary Ainsworth to measure attachment by evoking an infant's reactions to stress, specifically episodes of a caregiver's or stranger's arrival at and departure from a playroom where the infants can play with many toys. (p. 220)

stranger wariness Fear of unfamiliar people, exhibited fleetingly at 6 months and at full force by 10 to 14 months. (p. 203)

stunting A condition in which a person's height is at the bottom 3 percent of the norm as a result of chronic malnutrition. (p. 139)

subjects The people who are studied in a research project. (p. B-4)

substantiated maltreatment Maltreatment that has been reported, investigated, and verified. (p. 251)

sucking reflex An involuntary physical response in which newborns suck anything that touches their lips. (p. 150)

sudden infant death syndrome (SIDS) A set of circumstances in which a seemingly healthy infant, at least 2 months of age, dies unexpectedly in his or her sleep. (p. 156)

suicidal ideation Thinking about suicide, usually with some serious emotional and intellectual or cognitive overtones. (p. 508)

superego In psychoanalytic theory, the part of the personality that is self-critical and judgmental and that internalizes the moral standards set by parents and society. (p. 316)

survey A research method in which information is collected from a large number of people by personal interview, by written questionnaire, or by some other means. (p. 25)

synapse The intersection between the axon of one neuron and the dendrites of other neurons. (p. 142)

synchrony A coordinated interaction between caregiver and infant, who respond to each other's faces, sounds, and movements very rapidly and smoothly. (p. 208)

T

temperament According to Rothbart and Bates (1998), "constitutionally based individual differences in emotion, motor, and attentional reactivity and self-regulation." (p. 204)

teratogens Agents and conditions, including viruses, drugs, chemicals, stressors, and malnutrition, that can impair prenatal development and lead to birth defects or even death. (p. 111)

tertiary circular reactions The third of three types of feedback loops, this one involving active exploration and experimentation, in which the infant takes in experiences and tries to make sense of them. (p. 174)

tertiary prevention Actions that are taken after an adverse event occurs, aimed at reducing the harm or preventing disability. Immediate and effective medical treatment of illness or injury is tertiary prevention. (p. 248)

testosterone A sex hormone, secreted in greater amounts by males than by females. (p. 433)

theory of mind An understanding of human mental processes. (p. 275)

theory-theory Gopnik's term for the idea that children attempt to construct a theory to explain everything they see and hear. (p. 265)

threshold effect The phenomenon in which a particular teratogen is relatively harmless in small doses but becomes harmful once exposure reaches a certain level (the threshold). (p. 113)

time-out A disciplinary technique in which the child is required to stop all activity and sit in a corner or stay indoors for a few minutes. (p. 312)

total immersion An approach to teaching a second language in which instruction occurs entirely in that language and the learner's native language is not used at all. (p. 384)

transient exuberance The great increase in the number of neurons, dendrites, and synapses that occurs in an infant's brain over the first 2 years of life. (p. 142)

trust versus mistrust Erikson's term for the first crisis of psychosocial development, in which the infant learns whether the world is essentially a secure place where basic needs are always met or an unpredictable arena where needs (for food, comfort, etc.) are sometimes unmet. (p. 215)

twenty-third pair The chromosome pair that, in humans, determines the zygote's (and hence the person's) sex, among other things. (p. 72)

U

underextension The too-narrow application of a word, as when a toddler uses *cat* to refer only to the family cat and no other feline. (p. 188)

undernutrition Inadequate nutrition that does not cause visible wasting or stunting but causes the person to be shorter than the norm for healthy, well-fed members of the same ethnic group. (p. 162)

V

variables The qualities that may differ, or vary, during a scientific investigation. (p. 20)

visual cliff An experimental apparatus designed to provide the illusion of a sudden dropoff between one horizontal surface and another. (p. 178)

volatile mismatch A lack of fit between a person and his or her environment, which can change rapidly as the person or the environment changes. (p. 479)

W

wasting A condition in which a person's body weight is at the bottom 3 percent of the norm as a result of acute malnutrition. (p. 139)

Wechsler Intelligence Scale for Children (WISC) An IQ test designed for school-age children; it is administered by a trained examiner to one child at a time, and the questions are varied to hold the child's interest and to assess many abilities, including vocabulary, general knowledge, memory, and spatial comprehension. (p. 347)

whole-language approach The teaching of reading by encouraging children to develop all their language skills—talking and listening, reading and writing—all with the goal of communication. (p. 381)

withdrawn-rejected Referring to children who are actively rejected by their peer group because of their withdrawn, anxious behavior. (p. 400)

working memory The component of the information-processing system in which current conscious mental activity occurs. Also called *short-term memory*. (p. 363)

working model In cognitive theory, a set of assumptions that are used to organize perceptions and experiences. (p. 217)

X

X-linked Referring to a gene that is on the X chromosome. (p. 79)

XX A twenty-third pair that consists of two X-shaped chromosomes, one from the mother and one from the father. (p. 72)

XY A twenty-third pair that consists of one X-shaped chromosome from the mother and a Y-shaped chromosome from the father. (p. 72)

Z

zone of proximal development (ZPD) In sociocultural theory, the range of skills that a learner can exercise and master with assistance but cannot yet perform independently. According to Vygotsky, learning can occur within this zone. (pp. 50, 267)

zygote The single cell formed from the fusing of a sperm and an ovum. (p. 69)

Aboud, Frances E., & Mendelson, Morton J. (1996). Determinants of friendship selection and quality: Developmental perspectives. In William M. Bukowski, Andrew F. Newcomb, & Willard W. Hartup (Eds.), *The company they keep: Friendship in childhood and adolescence.* Cambridge, England: Cambridge University Press.

Achenbach, Thomas M., Howell, Catherine T., Quay, Herbert C., & Conners, C. Keith. (1991). National survey of problems and competencies among four- to sixteen-year-olds. *Monographs of the Society for Research in Child Development, 56* (Serial No. 225), 3.

Ackerman, Brian P., Kogos, Jen, Youngstrom, Eric, Schoff, Kristen, & Izard, Carroll. (1999). Family instability and the problem behaviors of children from economically disadvantaged families. *Developmental Psychology, 35,* 258–268.

Adams, Gerald R., Gullotta, Thomas P., & Montemayor, Raymond (1992). *Advances in adolescent development: Adolescent identity formation.* New York: Russell Sage.

Adams, Marilyn Jager, & Bruck, M. (1995). Resolving the "great debate." *American Educator 19,* 10–20.

Adams, Marilyn Jager, Treiman, Rebecca, & Pressley, Michael. (1998). Reading, writing, and literacy. In William Damon (Series Ed.), Irving E. Sigel, & K. Ann Renninger (Vol. Eds.), *Handbook of child psychology:* Vol. 4. *Child psychology in practice* (5th ed., pp. 275–357). New York: Wiley.

Adler, Scott A., Wilk, Amy, & Rovee-Collier, Carolyn. (2000). Reinstatement versus reactivation effect on active memory in infants. *Journal of Experimental Child Psychology, 75,* 93–115.

Adolph, Karen E., Vereijken, Beatrix, & Denny, Mark A. (1998). Learning to crawl. *Child Development, 69,* 1299–1312.

Aguilar, Benjamin, Sroufe, L. Alan, Egeland, Byron, & Carlson, Elizabeth. (2000). Distinguishing the early-onset/persistent and adolescent-onset antisocial behavior types: From birth to 16 years. *Development and Psychopathology, 12,* 109–132.

Aguirre-Molina, Marilyn, Molina, Carlos W., & Zambrana, Ruth Enid (Eds.). (2001). *Health issues in the Latino community.* San Francisco: Jossey-Bass.

Ainsworth, Mary D. Salter. (1967). *Infancy in Uganda: Infant care and the growth of love.* Baltimore: Johns Hopkins Press.

Ainsworth, Mary D. Salter. (1973). The development of infant-mother attachment. In Bettye M. Caldwell & Henry N. Ricciuti (Eds.), *Review of child development research* (Vol. 3). Chicago: University of Chicago Press.

Ainsworth, Mary D. Salter. (1993). Attachment as related to mother-infant interaction. In C. Rovee-Collier & L.P. Lipsitt (Eds.), *Advances in infancy research* (Vol. 8). Norwood, NJ: Ablex.

Akhtar, Nameera, Jipson, Jennifer, & Callanan, Maureen A. (2001). Learning words through overhearing. *Child Development, 72,* 416–430.

Akindade, E. A. (2001). Risk-taking behavior and substance abuse vis-à-vis HIV transmission in African societies. *Journal of Instructional Psychology, 28,* 3–8.

Alarcon, Marciela, Pennington, Bruce, Filipek, Pauline A., & DeFreis, John C. (2000). Etiology of neuroanatomical correlates of reading disability. *Developmental Neuropsychology, 17,* 339–360.

Aldous, Joan, Mulligan, Gail M., & Bjarnason, Thoroddur. (1998). Fathering over time: What makes the difference? *Journal of Marriage and the Family, 60,* 809–820.

Aldwin, Carolyn M. (1994). *Stress, coping, and development.* New York: Guilford Press.

Alexander, Robin. (2000). *Culture and pedagogy: International comparisons in primary education.* Oxford, England: Blackwell.

Allison, Clara. (1985). Development direction of action programs: Repetitive action to correction loops. In Jane E. Clark & James H. Humphrey (Eds.), *Motor development: Current selected research.* Princeton, NJ: Princeton Book Company.

Allwood, Carl Martin, & Selart, Marcus (Eds.). (2001). *Decision making: Social and creative dimensions.* Dordrecht, Netherlands: Kluwer.

Als, Heidelise. (1995). The preterm infant: A model for the study of fetal brain expectation. In Jean-Pierre Lecanuet, William P. Fifer, Norman A. Krasnegor, & William A. Smkotherman (Eds.), *Fetal development: A psychobiological perspective.* Erlbaum: Hillsdale, NJ.

Altshuler, Sandra J., & Gleeson, James P. (1999). Completing the evaluation triangle for the next century: Measuring child "well-being" in family foster care. *Child Welfare, 78,* 125–147.

Alvarez, Jeannette M., Ruble, Diane N., & Bolger, Niall. (2001). Trait understanding or evaluative reasoning? An analysis of children's behavioral predictions. *Child Development, 72,* 1409–1425.

Aman, Christine J., Roberts, Ralph J., & Pennington, Bruce F. (1998). A neuropsychological examination of the underlying deficit in attention deficit hyperactivity disorder: Frontal lobe versus right parietal lobe theories. *Developmental Psychology, 34,* 956–969.

Aman, Michael G., & Langworthy, Kristen S. (2000). Pharmacotherapy for hyperactivity in children with autism and other pervasive developmental disorders. *Journal of Autism and Developmental Disorders, 30,* 451–459.

Amato, Paul R. (1993). Children's adjustment to divorce: Theories, hypotheses, empirical support. *Journal of Marriage and the Family, 55,* 23–38.

Amato, Paul R. (2000). The consequences of divorce for adults and children. *Journal of Marriage and the Family, 62,* 1269–1287.

Ambrosi-Randic, Neala. (2000). Perception of current and ideal body size in preschool age children. *Perceptual and Motor Skills, 90,* 885–889.

American Psychiatric Association. (1994). *Diagnostic and Statistical Manual of Mental Disorders—DSM-IV.* Washington, DC: American Psychiatric Press.

American Psychiatric Association. (2000). *Diagnostic and statistical manual of mental disorders (DSM-IV-R).* Washington, DC: American Psychiatric Press.

American Society for Reproductive Medicine. (2002). Assisted reproductive technology in the United States. *Fertility and Sterility, 77,* 18–31.

Ammerman, Robert T., Lynch, Kevin G., Dorovan, John E., & Martin, Christopher S. (2001). Constructive thinking in adolescents with substance use disorders. *Psychology of Addictive Behaviors, 15,* 89–96.

Anderson, Daniel R., Huston, Aletha C., Schmitt, Kelly L., Linebarger, Deborah L., & Wright, John C. (2001). Early childhood television viewing and adolescent behavior: The recontact study. *Monographs of the Society for Research in Child Development, 66*(Serial No. 264).

Angel, Ronald J., & Angel, Jacqueline L. (1994). *Painful inheritance: Health and the new generation of fatherless families.* Madison: University of Wisconsin Press.

Angold, Adrian, Erkanli, Alaattin, Egger, Helen L., & Costello, E. Jane. (2000). Stimulant treatment for children: A community perspective. *Journal of the American Academy of Child and Adolescent Psychiatry, 39,* 975–984.

Ansuini, Catherine G., Fiddler-Woite, Julianna, & Woite, Robert S. (1996). The source, accuracy, and impact of initial sexuality information on lifetime wellness. *Adolescence, 31,* 283–289.

Apgar, Virginia. (1953). A proposal for a new method of evaluation in the newborn infant. *Current Research in Anesthesia and Analgesia, 32,* 260.

Archer, Sally. (1994). *Interventions for adolescent identity development.* Thousand Oaks, CA: Sage.

Arendell, Terry. (1997). A social constructionist approach to parenting. In Terry Arendell (Ed.), *Contemporary parenting: Challenges and issues.* Thousand Oaks, CA: Sage.

Arfániarromo, Albert. (2001). Toward a psychosocial and sociocultural understanding of achievement motivation among Latino gang members in U.S. high schools. *Journal of Instructional Psychology, 28,* 123–136.

Aries, Philippe. (1962). *Centuries of childhood: A social history of family life.* New York: Knopf.

Armstrong, Neil, & Welsman, Joanne. (1997). *Young people and physical activity.* Oxford, England: Oxford University Press.

Arnett, Jeffrey Jensen. (1999a). Adolescent storm and stress, reconsidered. *American Psychologist, 54,* 317–326.

Arnett, Jeffrey Jensen. (1999b). Learning to stand alone: The contemporary American transition to adulthood in cultural and historical context. *Human Development, 41,* 295–315.

Aron, David C., Gordon, Howard S., Di Guiseppe, David L., Harper, Dwain L., & Rosenthal, Gary E. (2000). Variations in risk-adjusted Cesarean delivery rates according to race and health insurance. *Medical Care, 38,* 35–44.

Aronson, Elliot. (2000). *Nobody left to hate: Teaching compassion after Columbine.* New York: Freeman.

Ashby, F. Gregory, & Waldron, Elliott M. (2000). The neuropsychological bases of category learning. *Current Directions in Psychological Science, 9,* 1014.

Ashman, Sharon B., & Dawson, Geraldine. (2002). Maternal depression, infant psychobiological development, and risk for depression. In Sherryl H. Goodman & Ian H. Gotlib (Eds.), *Children of depressed parents: Mechanisms of risk and implications for treatments.* Washington, DC: American Psychological Association.

Aslin Richard N., & Hunt, Ruskin H. (2001). Development, plasticity, and learning in the auditory system. In Charles A. Nelson & Monica Luciana (Eds.), *Handbook of developmental neuroscience* (pp. 149–158). Cambridge, MA: MIT Press.

Aslin, Richard N., Jusczyk, Peter W., & Pisoni, David B. (1998). Speech and auditory processing during infancy: Constraints on and precursors to language. In William Damon (Series Ed.), Deanna Kuhn, & Robert S. Siegler (Vol. Eds.), *Handbook of child psychology: Vol. 2. Cognition, perception and language* (5th ed., pp. 147–198). New York: Wiley.

Astington, Janet Wilde, & Gopnik, Alison. (1988). Knowing you've changed your mind: Children's understanding of representational change. In J.W. Astington, P.L. Harris, & D.R. Olson (Eds.), *Developing theories of mind.* Cambridge, England: Cambridge University Press.

Aviezer, Ora, van IJzendoorn, Marinus H., Sagi, Abraham, & Shuengel, Carlo. (1994). "Children of the Dream" revisited: 70 years of collective childrearing in Israel kibbutzim. *Psychological Bulletin, 116,* 99–116.

Babb, L. Anne. (1999). *Ethics in American adoption.* Westport, CT: Bergin and Garvey.

Bachman, Jerald G., & Schulenberg, John. (1993). How part-time work intensity relates to drug use, problem behavior, time use, and satisfaction among high school seniors: Are these consequences or merely correlates? *Developmental Psychology, 29,* 220–235.

Bagley, Christopher & Thurston, Wilfreda E. (1996). *Understanding and preventing child sexual abuse.* Hants, England: Ashgate.

Baildam, E. M., Hillier, V. F., Menon, S., Bannister, R. P., Bamford, F. N., Moore, W. M. O., & Ward, B. S. (2000). Attention to infants in the first year. *Child: Care, Health & Development, 26,* 199–216.

Bailey, J. Michael, Kirk, K. M., Zhu, G. Dunne, M. P., & Martin, M. P. (2000). Do individual differences in sociosexuality represent genetic or environmentally-contingent strategies: Evidence from the Australian Twin Registry. *Journal of Personality & Social Psychology, 78,* 537–545.

Bailey, J. Michael, Pillard, Richard C., & Knight, Robert. (1993). At issue: Is sexual orientation biologically determined? *CQ Researcher, 3,* 209.

Baillargeon, Renee. (1987). Object permanence in 3.5- and 4.5-month-old infants. *Developmental Psychology, 23,* 655–664.

Baillargeon, Renee. (1999). Young infants' expectations about hidden objects: A reply to three challenges. *Developmental Science, 2,* 115–163.

Baker, Jeffrey P. (2000). Immunization and the American way: Childhood vaccines. *American Journal of Public Health, 90,* 199–207.

Baker, Susan P. (2000). Where have we been and where are we going with injury control? In Dinesh Mohan & Geetam Tiwari (Eds.), *Injury prevention and control* (pp. 19–26). London: Taylor & Francis.

Baldwin, Dare A. (1993). Infants' ability to consult the speaker for clues to word referencing. *Journal of Child Language, 20,* 395–418.

Baldwin, Dare A. (2000). Interpersonal understanding fuels knowledge acquisition. *Current Directions in Psychological Science, 9,* 40–45.

Baltes, Paul B., Lindenberger, Ulman, & Staudinger, Ursula M. (1998). Life span theory in developmental psychology. In William Damon (Series Ed.) & Richard M. Lerner (Vol. Ed.), *Handbook of child psychology*: Vol. 1. *Theoretical models of human development* (5th ed., pp. 1029–1144). New York: Wiley.

Baltes, Paul B., Smith, Jacqui, & Staudinger, Ursula. (1992). Wisdom and successful aging. In T. Sonderegger (Ed.), *Psychology and aging: Nebraska Symposium on Motivation* (Vol. 39). Lincoln: University of Nebraska Press.

Bamford, F.N., Bannister, R., Benjamin, C.M., Hillier, V.F., Ward, B.S., & Moore, W.M.O. (1990). Sleep in the first year of life. *Developmental and Child Neurology, 32,* 718–734.

Bandura, Albert. (1986). *Social foundations of thought and action: A social cognitive theory.* Englewood Cliffs, NJ: Prentice-Hall.

Bandura, Albert. (1997). The anatomy of stages of change. *American Journal of Health Promotion, 12,* 8–10.

Bandura, Albert. (2001). Social cognitive theory: An agentive perspective. *Annual Review of Psychology, 52,* 1–26.

Bandura, Albert, Barbaranelli, Claudio, Caprara, Gian Vittorio, & Pastorelli, Concetta. (1996). Multifaceted impact of self-efficacy beliefs on academic functioning. *Child Development, 67,* 1206–1222.

Bandura, Albert, Barbaranelli, Claudio, Caprara, Gian Vittorio, & Pastorelli, Concetta. (2001). Self-efficacy beliefs as shapers of children's aspirations and career trajectories. *Child Development, 72,* 187–206.

Banerjee, Robin, & Linstern, Vicki. (2000). Boys will be boys: The effect of social evaluation concerns on gender-typing. *Social Development, 9,* 397–408.

Banich, Marie T. (1998). Integration of information between the cerebral hemispheres. *Current Directions in Psychological Science, 7,* 32–37.

Banich, Marie T., & Heller, Christine. (1998). Evolving perspectives on lateralization of function. *Current Directions in Psychological Science, 7,* 1–2.

Barber, Bonnie L., Jacobson, Kristen C., Miller, Kristelle E., & Petersen, Anne C. (1998). Ups and downs: Daily cycles of adolescent moods. In Ann C. Crouter & Reed Larson (Eds.), *Temporal rhythms in adolescence: Clocks, calendars, and the coordination of daily life. New directions for child and adolescent development* (pp. 23–36). San Francisco: Jossey-Bass.

Barber, Brian K. (1994). Cultural, family, and personal contexts of parent-adolescent conflict. *Journal of Marriage and the Family, 56,* 375–386.

Barber, Brian K. (Ed.). (2002). *Intrusive parenting: How psychological control affects children and adolescents.* Washington, DC: American Psychological Association.

Barkow, Jerome H., Cosmides, Leda, & Tooby, John (Eds.). (1992). *The adapted mind: Evolutionary psychology and the generation of culture.* New York: Oxford University Press.

Barnard, Kathryn E., & Martell, Louise K. (1995). Mothering. In Marc H. Bornstein (Ed.), *Handbook of parenting: Status and social conditions of parenting.* Mahwah, NJ: Erlbaum.

Barnett, Mark A., Bartel, Jeffrey S., Burns, Susan R., Sanborn, Fred W., Christensen, N. E., & White, M. M. (2000). Perceptions of children who lie: Influence of lie motive and benefit. *Journal of Genetic Psychology, 161,* 381–383.

Barnett, S. Anthony. (1998). *The science of life.* St. Leonards, Australia: Allen & Unwin.

Barnhill, Gena, Hagiwara, Taku, Smith Myles, Brenda, & Simpson, Richard L. (2000). Asperger syndrome: A study of the cognitive profiles of 37 children and adolescents. *Focus on Autism and Other Developmental Disabilities, 15,* 146–153.

Baron-Cohen, Simon. (2000). Is Asperger syndrome/high-functioning autism necessarily a disability? *Development and Psychopathology, 12,* 489–500.

Barr, Rachel, & Hayne, Harlene. (1999). Developmental changes in imitation from television during infancy. *Child Development, 70,* 1067–1081.

Barrett, Martyn (Ed.). (1999). *The development of language.* Hove, England: Psychology Press.

Bassett, Mary Travis. (2002). Ensuring a public health impact of program to reduce HIV transmission from mothers to infants: The place of voluntary counseling and testing. *American Journal of Public Health, 92,* 347–351.

Bates, Elizabeth, Devescovi, Antonella, & Wulfeck, Beverly. (2001). Psycholinguistics: A cross-language perspective. *Annual Review of Psychology, 52,* 369–396.

Bates, John E., Pettit, Gregory S., Dodge, Kenneth A., & Ridge, B. (1998). Interaction of temperamental resistance to control and restrictive parenting in the development of externalizing behavior. *Developmental Psychology, 34,* 982–995.

Bates, John E., Viken, Richard J., Alexander, Douglas B., Beyers, Jennifer, & Stockton, Lesley. (2002). Sleep and adjustment in preschool children: Sleep diary reports by mothers relate to behavior reports by teachers. *Child Development, 73,* 62–74.

Bauer, Henry H. (1992). *Scientific literacy and the myth of the scientific method.* Urbana: University of Illinois Press.

Bauer, Patricia J., & Dow, Gina. (1994). Episodic memory in 16- and 20-month-old children. Specifics are generalized but not forgotten. *Developmental Psychology, 30,* 403–417.

Bauer, Patricia J., Liebl, Monica, & Stennes, Leif. (1998) PRETTY is to DRESS as BRAVE is to SUITCOAT: Gender-based property-to-property inferences by 4–10-year-old children. *Merrill-Palmer Quarterly, 44,* 355–377.

Bauer, Patricia J., & Mandler, Jean M. (1992). Putting the horse before the cart: The use of temporal order in recall of events by one-year-old children. *Developmental Psychology, 28,* 441–452.

Bauer, Ursula E., Johnson, Tammie M., Hopkins, Richard S., & Brooks, Robert G. (2000). Changes in youth cigarette use and intentions following implementation of a tobacco control program. *Journal of the American Medical Association, 284,* 723–728.

Baumrind, Diana. (1967). Child-care practices anteceding three patterns of preschool behavior. *Genetic Psychology Monographs, 75,* 43–88.

Baumrind, Diana. (1971). Current patterns of parental authority. *Developmental Psychology, 4* (Monograph 1), 1–103.

Baumslag, Naomi, & Michels, Dia L. (1995). *Milk, money, and madness: The culture and politics of breasteeding.* Westport, CT: Bergin & Garvey.

Baynes, R.D., & Bothwell, T.H. (1990). Iron deficiency. *Annual Review of Nutrition, 10,* (Palo Alto: Annual Reviews), 133.

Beal, Carole R. (1994). *Boys and girls: The development of gender roles.* New York: McGraw-Hill.

Beal, Susan Mitchell, & Porter, C. (1991). Sudden infant death syndrome related to climate. *Acta Paediatrica Scandinavica, 80,* 278–287.

Bearman, Peter S. & Bruckner, Hannah. (2001). Promising the future: Virginity pledges and first intercourse. *American Journal of Sociology, 106,* 859–912.

Beauvais, Fred. (2000). Indian adolescence: Opportunity and challenge. In Raymond Montemayor, Gerald R. Adams, & Thomas P. Gullotta (Eds.), *Adolescent diversity in ethnic, economic, and cultural contexts.* Thousand Oaks, CA: Sage.

Beck, Martha. (1999). *Expecting Adam.* New York: Times Books.

Beckwith, Leila, Cohen, Sarale E., & Hamilton, Claire E. (1999). Maternal sensitivity during infancy and subsequent life events relate to attachment representation at early adulthood. *Developmental Psychology, 35,* 693–700.

Bedi, Gail C. (2001). Experience dependent plasticity and the treatment of children with specific language impairment or dyslexia. In Charles A. Nelson & Monica Luciana (Eds.). *Handbook of Developmental Neuroscience* (pp. 309–318). Cambridge, MA: MIT Press.

Behrend, Douglas A., Scofield, Jason, & Kleinknecht, Erica E. (2001). Beyond fast mapping: Young children's extensions of novel words and novel facts. *Developmental Psychology, 37,* 698–705.

Behrman, Richard E. (1992). *Nelson textbook of pediatrics.* Philadelphia: W.B. Saunders.

Beidel, Deborah C., & Turner, Samuel M. (1998). *Shy children, phobic adults: Nature and treatment of social phobia.* Washington DC: American Psychological Association.

Beiser, Morton, Hou, Feng, Hyman, Ilene, & Tousignant, Michel. (2002). Poverty, family process, and the mental health of immigrant children in Canada. *American Journal of Public Health, 92,* 220–227.

Belamarich, Peter F., & Ayoob, Keith Thomas. (2001). Keeping teenage vegetarians healthy and in the know. *Contemporary Pediatrics, 18*(10), 89–90, 95–100, 103, 107–108.

Bell, Carl C., & Jenkins, Esther J. (1993). Community violence and children on Chicago's Southside. *Psychiatry, 56,* 46–54.

Bell, Martha A., & Fox, N. A. (1992). The relations between frontal brain electrical activity and cognitive development during infancy. *Child Development, 63,* 1142–1163.

Bellantoni, Michele F., & Blackman, Marc R. (1996). Menopause and its consequences. In Edward L. Schneider & John W. Rowe (Eds.), *Handbook of the biology of aging.* San Diego, CA: Academic Press.

Belle, Deborah. (1999). *The after-school lives of children: Alone and with others while parents work.* Mahwah, NJ: Erlbaum.

Belsky, Jay. (2001). Emanuel Miller Lecture: Developmental risks (still) associated with early child care. *Journal of Child Psychology and Psychiatry and Allied Disciplines, 42,* 845–859.

Belsky, Jay, Domitrovich, Celene, & Crnic, Keith A. (1997). Temperament and parenting antecedents of individual differences in 3-year-old boys' pride and shame reactions. *Child Development, 37,* 456–466.

Belsky, Jay, Jaffee, Sara, Hsieh, Kuang-Hua, & Silva, Phil A. (2001). Child-rearing antecedents of intergenerational relations in young adulthood: A prospective study. *Developmental Psychology, 37,* 801–813.

Belsky, Jay, Steinberg, Lawrence, & Draper, Patricia. (1991). Childhood experience, interpersonal development, and reproductive strategy: An evolutionary theory of socialization. *Child Development, 62,* 647–670.

Bem, Sandra L. (1989). Genital knowledge and gender constancy in preschool children. *Child Development, 60,* 649–662.

Benes, Francine M. (2001). The development of prefrontal cortex: The maturation of neurotransmitter systems and their interactions. In Charles A. Nelson & Monica Luciana (Eds.), *Handbook of developmental neuroscience* (pp. 79–92). Cambridge, MA: MIT Press.

Bengtson, Vern L. (1975). Generation and family effects in value socialization. *American Sociological Review, 40,* 358–371.

Bengtson, Vern L. (2001). Beyond the nuclear family: The increasing importance of multigenerational bonds. *Journal of Marriage and the Family, 63,* 1–16.

Benoit, Diane, & Parker, Kevin C. (1994). Stability and transmission of attachment across three generations. *Child Development, 65,* 1444–1456.

Benson, Peter L., Leffert, Nancy, Scales, Peter C., & Blyth, Dale A. (1998). Beyond the "village" rhetoric: Creating healthy communities for children and adolescents. *Applied Developmental Science, 2,* 138–159.

Bentley, Gillian R., & Mascie-Taylor, C. G. Nicholas. (2000). Preface. In Gillian R. Bentley & C. G. Nicholas Mascie-Taylor. (Eds.), *Infertility in the modern world.* Cambridge, England: Cambridge University Press.

Berkley, C. S., Gardner, J. D., Frazier, A. L. & Colditz, G. A. (2000). Relation of childhood diet and body size to menarche and adolescent growth in girls. *Epidemiology, 152,* 446–452.

Bernardes, J. (1996). Multidimensional developmental pathways: A proposal to facilitate the conceptualization of "family diversity." *The Sociological Review, 39,* 590–610.

Berrick, Jill Duerr. (1998). When children cannot remain home: Foster family care and kinship care. *The Future of Children: Protecting children from abuse and neglect, 8,* 4–22.

Bertenthal, Bennett I., & Clifton, Rachel K. (1998). Perception and action. In William Damon (Series Ed.), Deanna Kuhn, & Robert S. Siegler (Vol. Eds.), *Handbook of child psychology:* Vol. 2. *Cognition, perception and language* (5th ed, pp. 51–102). New York: Wiley.

Betts, J. (1995). Does school quality matter: Evidence from the National Longitudinal Survey of Youth. *Review of Economics and Statistics, 77,* 231–250.

Beunen, Gaston P., Malina, Robert M., Van't Hof, Martin A., Simons, Jan, Ostyn, Michel, Renson, Roland, & Van Gerven, Dirk. (1988). *Adolescent growth and motor performance: A longitudinal study of Belgian boys.* Champaign, IL: Human Kinetics Books.

Bialystok, Ellen. (2001). *Bilingualism in development: Language, literacy, and cognition.* Cambridge, England: Cambridge University Press.

Biener, Lois, & Heaton, Alan. (1995). Women dieters of normal weight: Their motives, goals, and risks. *American Journal of Public Health, 85,* 714–717.

Bigelow, Ann E. (1999). Infants' sensitivity to imperfect contingency in social interaction. In Philippe Rochat (Ed.), *Early social cognition: Understanding others in the first months of life* (pp. 137–154). Mahwah, NJ: Erlbaum.

Bijou, Sidney W., & Baer, Donald M. (1978). *Behavior analysis of child development*. Englewood Cliffs, NJ: Prentice-Hall.

Bingham, C. Raymond, Miller, Brent C., & Adams, Gerald R. (1990). Correlates of age at first sexual intercourse in a national sample of young women. *Journal of Adolescent Research, 5,* 7–17.

Biro, Frank M., McMahon, Robert P., Striegel-Moore, Ruth, Crawford, Patricia B., Obarzanek, Eva, Morrison, John A., et al. (2001). Impact of timing of pubertal maturation on growth in black and white female adolescents: The National Heart, Lung, and Blood Institute Growth and Health Study. *Journal of Pediatrics, 138,* 636–643.

Bishop, Virginia E. (1993). Peter and the watermelon seeds. In P.J. McWilliam & Donald B. Bailey, Jr. (Eds.), *Working together with children & families*. Baltimore: Brookes.

Bissex, Glenda L. (1980) *GNYS AT WRK: A child learns to write and read.* Cambridge, MA: Harvard University Press.

Bjarnason, Thoroddur, Sigurdardottir, Thordis J., & Thorlindsson, Thorolfur. (1999). Human agency, capable guardians, and structural constraints: A lifestyle approach to the study of violent victimization. *Journal of Youth & Adolescence, 28,* 105–119.

Bjorkqvist, Kaj, & Osterman, Karin. (1999). Finland. In Peter K. Smith, Yohji Morita, Josine Junger-Tas, Dan Olweus, Richard F. Catalano, & Phillip T. Slee (Eds.), *The nature of school bullying: A cross-national perspective*. London: Routledge.

Blake, Susan M., Simkin, Linda, Ledsky, Rebecca, Perkins, Cheryl, & Calabrese, Joseph M. (2001). Effects of a parent-child communications intervention on young adolescents' risk for early onset of sexual intercourse. *Family Planning Perspectives, 33,* 52–61.

Bledsoe, Caroline H., & Cohen, Barney. (Eds.). (1993). *Social dynamics of adolescent fertility in sub-Saharan Africa*. Washington, DC: National Academy Press.

Block, Lauren G., Morwitz, Vicki, Putsis, William P., & Sen, Subrata K. (2002). Assessing the impact of anti-drug advertising on adolescent drug consumption: Results from a behavioral economic model. *American Journal of Public Health, 92,* 1346–1351.

Bloom, Floyd, Nelson, Charles A., & Lazerson, Arlyne. (2001). *Brain, mind, and behavior* (3rd ed.). New York: Worth Publishers.

Bloom, Lois. (1993). *The transition from infancy to language: Acquiring the power of expression*. New York: Cambridge University Press.

Bloom, Lois. (1998). Language acquisition in its developmental context. In William Damon (Series Ed.), Deanna Kuhn, & Robert S. Siegler (Vol. Eds.), *Handbook of child psychology*: Vol. 2. *Cognition, perception and language* (5th ed., pp. 309–370). New York: Wiley.

Bloom, Lois. (2000). Commentary. In George J. Hollich, Kathy Hirsh-Pasek, and Roberta Michnick Golinkoff. Breaking the language barrier: An emergentist coalition model for the origins of word learning. *Monographs of the Society for Research in Child Development, 65*(3, Serial no. 262).

Bloom, Lois, & Tinker, Erin. (2001). The intentionality model and language acquisition: Engagement, effort, and the essential tension in development. *Monographs of the Society for Research in Child Development, 66,* (4 Serial no. 267).

Blum, Robert W., Beuhring, Trisha, Shew, Marcia L., Bearinger, Linda H., Sieving, Renee E., & Resnick, Michael D. (2000). The effect of race/ethncity, income, and family structure on adolescent risk behavior. *American Journal of Public Health, 90,* 1879–1884.

Bogin, Barry. (1995). Plasticity in the growth of Mayan refugee children living in the United States. In C.G.N. Mascie-Taylor & B. Bogin (Eds.), *Human variability and plasticity*. Cambridge, England: Cambridge University Press.

Bogin, Barry. (1996). Human growth and development from an evolutionary perspective. In C.J.K. Henry & S.J. Uliajaszel (Eds.), *Long-term consequences of early environment: Growth, development and the lifespan developmental perspective*. Cambridge, England: Cambridge University Press.

Bolger, Kerry E., Patterson, Charlotte J., & Kupersmidt, Janis B. (1998). Peer relationships and self-esteem among children who have been maltreated. *Child Development, 69,* 1171–1197.

Bonner, Barbara L., Crow, Sheila M., & Logue, Mary Beth. (1999). Fatal child neglect. In Howard Dubowitz (Ed.), *Neglected children: Research, practice, and policy* (pp. 156–173). Thousand Oaks, CA: Sage.

Boom, Jan, Brugman, Daniel, & van der Heijden, Peter G. M. (2001). Hierarchical structure of moral stages assessed by a sorting task. *Child Development, 72,* 535–548.

Boonstra, Heather. (2000). Promoting contraceptive use and choice: France's approach to teen pregnancy and abortion. *The Guttmacher Report on Public Policy, 3*(3), 3–4.

Booth, Alan, & Amato, Paul R. (2001). Parental predivorce relations and offspring postdivorce wellbeing. *Journal of Marriage and the Family, 63,* 197–212.

Booth, Tony, & Ainscow, Mel. (1998). *From them to us*. London: Routledge.

Borders, L. DiAnne, Penny, Judith M., & Portnoy, Francie. (2000). Adult adoptees and their friends: Current functioning and psychosocial well-being. *Family Relations, 49,* 407–418.

Borgaonkar, Digamber S. (1997). *Chromosomal variation in man: A catalog of chromosomal variants and anomalies* (8th ed.). New York: Wiley.

Borkowski, John G., Bisconti, Toni, Willard, Christine C., Keogh, Deborah A., Whitman, Thomas L, & Weed, Keri. (2002). The adolescent as parent: In John G. Borkowski, Sharon Landesman Ramey & Marie Bristol-Power (Eds.), *Parenting and the child's world: Influences on academic, intellectual, and social-emotional development*. Mahwah, NJ: Erlbaum.

Borland, Moira, Laybourn, Ann, Hill, Malcolm, & Brown, Jane. (1998). *Middle childhood: The perspectives of children and parents*. London: Jessica Kingsley Publishers.

Bornstein, Marc H. (Ed.). (1995a). *Handbook of parenting: Vol. 4. Applied and practical parenting*. Mahwah, NJ: Erlbaum.

Bornstein, Marc H. (1995b). Parenting infants. In Marc H. Bornstein (Ed.), *Handbook of parenting: Childhood and parenting*. Mahwah, NJ: Erlbaum.

Borowsky, Iris Wagman, Resnick, Michael, Ireland Marjorie, & Blum, Robert. (1999). Suicide attempts among American Indian and Alaska Native youth. *Archives of Pediatric and Adolescent Medicine, 153,* 573–580.

Bosworth, Kris, Espelage, Dorothy L., & Simon, Thomas R. (1999). Factors associated with bullying behavior in middle school students. *Journal of Early Adolescence, 19,* 341–362.

Bouchard, Thomas J. (1994). Genes, environment, and personality. *Science, 264,* 1700–1701.

Bouchard, Thomas J. (1997). Twin studies of behavior. In Alain Schmitt, Klaus Atzwanger, Karl Grammer, & Katrin Schafer (Eds.), *New aspects of human ethology*. New York: Plenum Press.

Boulton, Michael J. (1999). Concurrent and longitudinal relations between children's playground behavior and social preference, victimization, and bullying. *Child Development, 70,* 944–954.

Boulton, Michael J., & Smith, Peter K. (1989). Issues in the study of children's rough-and-tumble play. In Marianne N. Bloch & Anthony D. Pellegrini (Eds.), *The ecological context of children's play*. Norwood, NJ: Ablex.

Bourgeois, J.-P. (2001). Synaptogenesis in the neocortex of the newborn: The ultimate frontier for individuation? In Charles A. Nelson & Monica Luciana (Eds.), *Handbook of developmental neuroscience* (pp. 149–158). Cambridge, MA: MIT Press.

Bower, Bruce. (1999). Gene may alter Ritalin's effects in ADHD. *Science News, 156,* 359.

Bowerman, Melissa, & Choi, Soonja. (2001). Shaping meanings for language: Universal and language specific in the acquisition of spatial semantic categories. In Melissa Bowerman & Stephen C. Levinson (Eds.), *Language acquisition and conceptual development*. Cambridge, England: Cambridge University Press.

Bowerman, Melissa, & Levinson, Stephen C. (2001). Introduction. In Melissa Bowerman & Stephen C. Levinson (Eds.), *Language acquisition and conceptual development*. Cambridge, England: Cambridge University Press.

Bowlby, John. (1969). *Attachment and loss: Vol. 1. Attachment*. New York: Basic Books.

Bowlby, John. (1973). *Attachment and loss: Vol. 2. Separation anxiety and anger*. New York: Basic Books.

Bowlby, John. (1988). *A secure base: Clinical applications of attachment theory*. London: Routledge.

Boyland, Moira, Laybourn, Ann, Hill, Malcolm, & Brown, Jane. (1998). *Middle childhood*. London: Jessica Kingsley.

Boysson-Bardies, Benedicte de. (1999). *How language comes to children* (M. B. DeBevoise, Trans.). Cambridge, MA: MIT Press.

Boysson-Bardies, Benedicte, Halle, Pierre, Sagart, Laurent, & Durand, Catherine. (1989). A crosslinguistic investigation of vowel formants in babbling. *Journal of Child Language, 16,* 1–17.

Bradley, Robert H. (1995). Environment and parenting. In Marc H. Bronstein (Ed.), *Handbook of parenting: Vol. 2. Biology and ecology of parenting*. Mahwah, NJ: Erlbaum.

Bradley, Robert H., Corwyn, Robert F., Pipes McAdoo, Harriette, & Garcia Coll, Cynthia. (2001). The home environment of children in the United States. Part I: Variations by age, ethnicity, and poverty status. *Child Development, 72,* 1844–1867.

Brandtstädter, Jochen. (1998). Action perspectives on human development. In William Damon & Richard M. Lerner (Eds.), *Handbook of child psychology: Vol. 1. Theoretical models of human development* (5th ed., pp. 807–863). New York: Wiley.

Brannen, Julia, Heptinstall, Ellen, & Kalwant, Bhopal. (2000). *Connecting children: Care and family life in later childhood*. London: Routledge.

Bransford, John D., Brown, Ann L., & Cocking, Rodney R. (Eds.). (1999). *How people learn: Brain, mind, experience and school*. Washington, DC: National Academy Press.

Branson, Robert K. (1998). Teaching-centered schooling has reached its upper limit: It doesn't get any better than this. *Current Directions in Psychological Science, 7,* 126–135.

Braungart-Rieker, Julia M., Garwood, Molly M., Powers, Bruce P., & Wang, Xiaoyu. (2001). Parental sensitivity, infant affect, and affect regulation: Predictors of later attachment. *Child Development, 72,* 252–270.

Brazelton, T. Berry, & Cramer, Bertrand. (1991). *The earliest relationship*. London: Karnac.

Brendgen, Mara, Vitaro, Frank, Bukowski, William J., Doyle, Anna Beth, & Markiewicz, Dorothy. (2001). Developmental profiles of peer social preference over the course of elementary school: Associations with trajectories of externalizing and internalizing behavior. *Developmental Psychology, 37,* 308–320.

Brennan, Robert T., Kim, Jimmy, Wenz-Gross, Melodie, & Siperstein, Gary N. (2001). The relative equitability of high-stakes testing versus teacher-assigned grades: An analysis of the Massachusetts Comprehensive Assessment System (MCAS). *Harvard Educational Review, 71,* 173–216.

Brent, David A., Baugher, Marianne, Bridge, Jeffrey, Chen, Tuhao, & Chiappetta, Laurel. (1999). Age- and sex-related risk factors for adolescent suicide. *Journal of the American Academy of Child and Adolescent Psychiatry, 38,* 1497–1505.

Bressler, Steven L. (2002). Understanding cognition through large-scale cortical networks. *Current Directions in Psychological Science, 11,* 58–61.

Bretherton, Inge, & Munholland, Kristine A. (1999). Internal working models in attachment relationships: A construct revisited. In Jude Cassidy & P. R. Shaver (Eds.), *Handbook of attachment: Theory, research, and clinical applications*. New York: Guilford Press.

Briley, Mike, & Sulser, Fridolin (Eds.). (2001). *Molecular genetics of mental disorders*. London: Dunitz.

Bronfenbrenner, Urie. (1979). *The ecology of human development: Experiments by nature and design*. Cambridge, MA: Harvard University Press.

Bronfenbrenner, Urie, & Morris, Pamela A. (1998). The ecology of developmental processes. In William Damon (Series Ed.) & Richard M. Lerner (Vol. Ed.), *Handbook of child psychology: Vol. 1. Theoretical models of human development* (5th ed., pp. 993–1028). New York: Wiley.

Brook, Judith S., Richter, Linda, Whiteman, Martin, & Cohen, Patricia. (1999). Consequences of adolescent marijuana use: Incompatibility with the assumption of adult roles. *Genetic, Social, & General Psychology Monographs, 125,* 193–207.

Brooks-Gunn, Jeanne. (1991). Maturational timing variations in adolescent girls, antecedents of. In Richard M. Lerner, Ann C. Petersen, & Jeanne Brooks-Gunn (Eds.), *Encyclopedia of adolescence: Vol. 2.* New York: Garland.

Brooks-Gunn, Jeanne, Klebanov, Pam K., Liaw, Fong-ruey, & Spiker, Donna. (1993). Enhancing the development of low-birthweight, premature infants: Changes in cognition and behavior over the first three years. *Child Development, 64,* 736–753.

Brown, Bernard. (1999). Optimizing expression of the common human genome for child development. *Current Directions in Psychological Science, 8,* 37–41.

Brown, Larry K., Lourie, Kevin J., & Pao, Maryland. (2000). Children and adolescents living with HIV and AIDS: A review. *Journal of Child Psychology & Psychiatry & Allied Disciplines, 41,* 81–96.

Bruner, Jerome. (1996). *The culture of education.* Cambridge, MA: Harvard University Press.

Buckner, John C., Bassuk, Ellen L., Weinreb, Linda F., & Brooks, Margaret G. (1999). Homelessness and its relation to the mental health and behavior of low-income school-age children. *Developmental Psychology, 35,* 246–257.

Buhrmester, Duane. (1996). Need fulfillment, interpersonal competence, and the developmental contexts of early adolescent friendship. In William M. Bukowski, Andrew F. Newcomb, & Willard W. Hartup (Eds.), *The company they keep: Friendship in childhood and adolescence.* Cambridge, England: Cambridge University Press.

Bukowski, William M., & Sippola, Lorrie. (2001). Groups, individuals, and victimization: A view of the peer system. In Jaana Juvchen & Sandra Graham (Eds.), *Peer harassment in school: The plight of the vulnerable and victimized.* New York: Guilford Press.

Bukowski, William M., Sippola, Lorrie K., & Newcomb, Andrew F. (2000). Variations in patters of attraction to same- and other-sex peers during early adolescence. *Developmental Psychology, 36,* 147–154.

Burlingham, Dorothy, & Freud, Anna. (1942). *Young children in wartime.* London: Allen & Unwin.

Burton, Linda M. (1995). Intergenerational patterns of providing care in African-American families with teenage childbearers: Emergent patterns in an ethnographic study. In Vern L. Bengtson, K. Warner Schaie, & Linda M. Burton (Eds.), *Adult intergenerational relations: Effects of societal change.* New York: Springer.

Buschman, N. A., Foster, G., & Vickers, Pauline. (2001). Adolescent girls and their babies: Achieving optimal birthweight. *Child: Care, Health, and Development, 27,* 163–171.

Bushman, Brad J., & Anderson, Craig A. (2001). Media violence and the American public. *American Psychologist, 56,* 477–489.

Buss, David M. (1994). *The evolution of desire: Strategies of human mating.* New York: Basic Books.

Buss, David M., Haselton, Martie G., Shackelford, Todd K., Bleske, April L., & Wakefield, Jerome C. (1998). Adaptations, exaptations, and spandrels. *American Psychologist, 53,* 533–548.

Byram, Michael. (1998). Cultural identities in multilingual classrooms. In Jasone Cenoz & Fred Genesee (Eds.), *Beyond bilingualism: Multilingualism and multilingual education.* Clevedon, England: Multilingual Matters.

Byrd, Robert S., Neistadt, Allyson M., Howard, Cynthia R., Brownstein-Evans, Carol, & Weitzman, Michael. (1999). Why screen newborns for cocaine: Service patterns and social outcomes at age one year. *Child Abuse & Neglect, 23,* 523–530.

Byrnes, James P. (1998). *The nature and development of decision-making: A self-regulation model.* Mahwah, NJ: Erlbaum.

Cabrera, Natasha J., Tamis-LeMonda, Catherine S., Bradley, Robert H., Hofferth, Sandra, & Lamb, Michael E. (2000). Fatherhood in the twenty-first century. *Child Development, 71,* 127–136.

Cairns, Robert B., & Cairns, Beverly D. (1994). *Lifelines and risks: Pathways of youth in our time.* Cambridge, England: Cambridge University Press.

Cairns, Robert B., & Cairns, Beverly D. (2001). Aggression and attachment: The folly of separation. In Arthur C. Bohart & Deborah J. Stipek (Eds.), *Constructive and destructive behavior: Implications for family, school, and society* (pp. 21–47). Washington, DC: American Psychological Association.

Calam, Rachel, & Waller, Glenn. (1998). Are eating and psychological characteristics in early teenage years useful predictors of eating characteristics in early adulthood? A 7-year longitudinal study. *International Journal of Eating Disorders, 24,* 351–362.

Caldwell, J. C., & Caldwell, P. (2000). From STD epidemics to AIDS: A socio-demographic and epidemiological perspective on sub-Saharan Africa. In Gillian R. Bentley & C. G. Nicholas Mascie-Taylor (Eds.), *Infertility in the modern world.* Cambridge, England: Cambridge University Press.

Calkins, Susan D. (1994). Origins and outcomes of individual differences in emotional regulation. *Monographs of the Society for Research in Child Development, 59* (2–3, Serial No. 240), 53–72.

Calkins, Susan D., Fox, Nathan A., & Marshall, Timothy R. (1996). Behavioral and physiological antecedents of inhibited and uninhibited behavior. *Child Development, 67,* 523–540.

Cameron, Judy L. (2001). Effects of sex hormones on brain development. In Charles A. Nelson & Monica Luciana (Eds.), *Handbook of developmental neuroscience* (pp. 59–78). Cambridge, MA: MIT Press.

Campbell, Darren W., & Eaton, Warren O. (1999). Sex differences in the activity level of infants. *Infant and Child Development, 8,* 1–17.

Campbell, Frances A., Pungello, Elizabeth P., Miller-Johnson, Shari, Burchinal, Margaret, & Ramey, Craig T. (2001). The development of cognitive and academic abilities: Growth curves from an early childhood education experiment. *Developmental Psychology, 37,* 231–242.

Campbell, Susan B. (1995). Behavior problems in preschool children: A review of recent research. *Journal of Psychology & Psychiatry & Allied Disciplines, 36,* 113–149.

Campos, Joseph J., Hiatt, Susan, Ramsay, Douglas, Henderson, Charlotte, & Svejda, Marilyn. (1978). The emergence of fear on the visual cliff. In Michael Lewis & Leonard A. Rosenblum (Eds.), *The development of affect.* New York: Plenum.

Cannon, Tyrone D., Rosso, Isabelle M., Bearden, Carrie E., Sanchez, Laura E., & Hadley, Trevor. (1999). A prospective cohort study of neurodevelopmental processes in the genesis and epigenesis of schizophrenia. *Development and Psychopathology, 11,* 467–485.

Cappella, Elise, & Weinstein, Rhona S. (2001). Turning around reading achievement: Predictors of high school students' academic resilience. *Journal of Educational Psychology, 93,* 758–771.

Caprara, Gian Vittorio, Barbaranelli, Claudio, & Pastorelli, Concetta. (2001). Prosocial behavior and aggression in childhood and pre-adolescence. In Arthur C. Bohart & Deborah J. Stipek (Eds.), *Constructive and destructive behavior: Implications for family, school and society* (pp. 187–204). Washington, DC: American Psychological Society.

Cardon, Lon R., Smity, Shelley D., Fulker, David W., Kimberling, William J., Pennington, B.R., & DeFries, J.C. (1994). Quantitative trait locus for reading disability on chromosome 6. *Science, 266,* 276–279.

Caretta, Carla Mucignat, Caretta, Antonio, & Cavaggioni, Andrea. (1995). Pheromonally accelerated puberty is enhanced by previous experience of the same stimulus. *Physiology and Behavior, 57,* 901–903.

Carey, Susan. (1999). Sources of conceptual change. In Ellin K. Scholnick, Katherine Nelson, Susan A. Gelman, & Patricia H. Miller (Eds.), *Conceptual development: Piaget's legacy.* Mahwah, NJ: Erlbaum.

Carlson, Bruce M. (1994). *Human embryology and developmental biology.* St. Louis, MO: Mosby.

Carlson, Marcia J., & Corcoran, Mary E. (2001). Family structure and children's behavioral and cognitive outcomes. *Journal of Marriage and the Family, 63,* 779–792.

Carmichael, Catherine A., & Hayes, Brett K. (2001). Prior knowledge and exemplar encoding in children's concept acquisition. *Child Development, 72,* 1071–1090.

Carnegie Council on Adolescent Development. (1989). *Turning points: Preparing American youth for the 21st century.* New York: Carnegie Corporation.

Carpendale, Jeremy I. M. (2000). Kohlberg and Piaget on stages and moral reasoning. *Developmental Review, 20,* 181–205.

Carpenter, Siri. (1999). Modern hygiene's dirty tricks: The clean life may throw off a delicate balance in the immune system. *Science News, 156,* 108–110.

Carr, Janet. (1995). *Down's Syndrome: Children growing up: A longitudinal perspective.* Cambridge, England: Cambridge University Press.

Carraher, Terezinha Nunes, Carraher, David W., & Schliemann, Analúcia D. (1985). Mathematics in the streets and in schools. *British Journal of Developmental Psychology, 3,* 21–29.

Carraher, Terezinha Nunes, Schliemann, Analúcia D., & Carraher, David W. (1988). Mathematical concepts in everyday life. In G.B. Saxe & M. Gearhart (Eds.), *New directions for child development: Vol. 41. Children's mathematics.* San Francisco: Jossey-Bass.

Carruthers, Peter, & Smith, Peter. (1996). *Theories of theories of mind.* Cambridge: Cambridge University Press.

Carson, Ronald A. (1999). The fate of the responsible self in a genetic age. In Ronald A. Carson & Mark A. Rothstein (Eds.), *Behavioral genetics: The clash of culture and biology* (pp. 189–199). Baltimore: Johns Hopkins Press.

Carter, Jimmy. (2001). *An hour before daylight: Memories of a rural boyhood.* New York: Simon & Schuster.

Case, Robbie. (1998). The development of conceptual structures. In William Damon (Series Ed.), Deanna Kuhn, & Robert S. Siegler (Vol. Eds.), *Handbook of child psychology: Vol. 2. Cognition, perception, and language* (5th ed., pp. 745–800). New York: Wiley.

Case, Robbie, & Okamoto, Yukari. (1996). The role of central conceptual structures in the development of children's thought. *Monographs of the Society for Research in Child Development, 61*(1-2, Serial No. 246).

Casey, B. J. (2001). Disruption of inhibitory control in developmental disorders: A mechanistic model of implicated frontostriatal circuitry. In James L. McClelland & Robert S. Siegler (Eds.), *Mechanisms of cognitive development: Behavioral and neural perspectives* (pp. 327–352). Mahwah, NJ: Erlbaum.

Casey, B. J., Thomas, Kathleen M., & McCandliss, Bruce. (2001). Applications of magnetic resonance imaging to the study of development. In Charles A. Nelson & Monica Luciana (Eds.), *Handbook of developmental neuroscience* (pp. 59–78). Cambridge, MA: MIT Press.

Caspi, Avshalom, Lynam, Donald, Moffit, Terrie, & Silva, Phil A. (1993). Unraveling girls' delinquency: Biological, dispositional, and contextual contributions to adolescent misbehavior. *Developmental Psychology, 29,* 19–30.

Cassel, William S., Roebers, Claudia E.M., & Bjorklund, David F. (1996). Developmental patterns of eyewitness responses to repeated and increasingly suggestive questions. *Journal of Experimental Child Psychology, 61,* 116–133.

Cassidy, Jude, & Shaver, Philip R. (Eds.). (1999). *Handbook of attachment: Theory, research, and clinical applications.* New York: Guilford Press.

Casswell, Sally. (1996). Alcohol use: Growing up and learning about drinking—Children in Dunedin in the 1980s. In Phil A. Silva & Warren R. Stanton (Eds.), *From child to adult: The Dunedin multidisciplinary health and development study.* Auckland: Oxford University Press.

Ceballo, Rosario, Dahl, Trayci A., Aretakis, Maria T., & Ramirez, Cynthia. (2001). Inner-city children's exposure to community violence: How much do parents know? *Journal of Marriage and the Family, 63,* 927–940.

Ceci, Stephen J., & Bruck, Maggie. (1998). Children's testimony: Applied and basic issues. In William Damon (Series Ed.), Irving E. Sigel, & K. Ann Renninger (Vol. Eds.), *Handbook of child psychology: Vol. 4. Child psychology in practice* (5th ed, pp. 713–775). New York: Wiley.

Centers for Disease Control and Prevention (CDC). (1993). *1992 Annual Report.* Division of STD/HIV prevention. Atlanta: GA.

CDC. (1994, April 22). Programs for the prevention of suicide among adolescents and young adults. *Morbidity and Mortality Recommendations and Reports, 43,* 1–7.

CDC. (1994, April 22). Suicide contagion and the reporting of suicide. *Morbidity and Mortality Weekly Report, 43,* 13–18.

CDC. (1994, April 29). Zidovudine for the prevention of HIV transmission from mother to infant. *Morbidity and Mortality Weekly Report, 43,* 285–287.

CDC. (1994, August 19). Changes in the cigarette brand preferences of adolescent smokers—United States, 1989–1993. *Morbidity and Mortality Weekly Report, 43,* 577–581.

CDC. (1994, October 21). Reasons for tobacco use and symptoms of nicotine withdrawal among adolescent and young adult tobacco users—United States, 1993. *Morbidity and Mortality Weekly Report, 43,* 745–750.

CDC. (1995, March 24). Youth risk behavior surveillance—United States, 1993. *Morbidity and Mortality Weekly Report, 44*(No. SS–1), 1–56.

CDC. (1996, September 27). Youth risk behavior surveillance—United States, 1995. *Morbidity and Mortality Weekly Report, 45,* 20.

CDC. (1996, October 11). Sudden Infant Death Syndrome—1983–1994. *Morbidity and Mortality Weekly Report, 45,* 859–865.

CDC. (1997, February 28). Update: Trends in AIDS incidence, deaths, and prevalence—United States, 1996. *Morbidity and Mortality Weekly Report, 46,* 165–173.

CDC. (1997, April 25). Alcohol consumption among pregnant and childbearing-aged women—United States, 1991–1995. *Morbidity and Mortality Weekly Report, 46,* 346–350.

CDC. (1997, May 16). Varicella-related deaths among adults—United States, 1997.

Morbidity and Mortality Weekly Report, 46, 409–412.

CDC. (1998, April 3). Youth risk behavior surveillance—United States, 1997. Tobacco use among high school students. *Morbidity and Mortality Weekly Report, 47,* 229–233.

CDC. (1998, April 17). Measles—United States, 1997. *Morbidity and Mortality Weekly Report, 47,* 273–276.

CDC. (1998, August 14). Youth risk behavior surveillance—United States, 1997. *Morbidity and Mortality Weekly Report, 47.*

CDC. (1998, September 11). Characteristics of health education among secondary schools—School health education profiles, 1996. *Morbidity and Mortality Weekly Report, 47,* 1–31.

CDC. (1998, September 18). Trends in sexual risk behaviors among high school students—United States, 1991–1997. *Morbidity and Mortality Weekly Report, 47,* 1–31.

CDC. (1999, September 24). Prevalence of selected maternal and infant characteristics, pregnancy risk assessment monitoring system (PRAMS), 1997. *Morbidity and Mortality Weekly Report, 48,* 1–37.

CDC. (1999, December 31). Summary of notifiable diseases, United States, 1998. *Morbidity and Mortality Weekly Report, 47,* 1–93.

CDC. (2000, January 7). Notifiable Diseases/Deaths in Selected Cities Weekly Information. *Morbidity and Mortality Weekly Report, 48,* 1183–1190.

CDC. (2000, January 21). Immunization schedule. *Morbidity and Mortality Weekly Report, 48,* 1209–1213.

CDC. (2000, June 9). Youth risk behavior surveillance—United States 1999. *Morbidity and Mortality Weekly Report, 49,* 1–96.

CDC. (2000, August 18). Surveillance for characteristics of health education among secondary schools–School health education profiles, 1998. *Morbidity and Mortality Weekly Report, 49,* 1–41.

CDC. (2000, September 22). Surveillance for vaccination coverage among child and adults—United States. *Morbidity and Mortality Weekly Report, 49,* No. SS-9.

CDC. (2000, November 3). Progress toward interrupting indigenous measles transmission—region of the American, January 1999–September 2000. *Morbidity and Mortality Weekly Report, 49,* 986–990.

CDC. (2001, June 22). Vaccinia (smallpox) vaccine: Recommendations of the Advisory Committee on Immunization Practices (ACIP), 2001. *Morbidity and Mortality Weekly Report, 50,* No. RR-10.

CDC. (2002, January 4). Summary of provisional cases of selected notifiable diseases, United States, cumulative, week ending December 29, 2001 (52nd week). *Morbidity and Mortality Weekly Report, 50,* 1169.

CDC. (2002, January 18). Immunization schedule. *Morbidity and Mortality Weekly Report, 51.*

CDC. (2002, February 8). Progress toward elimination of perinatal HIV infection—Michigan, 1993–2000. *Morbidity and Mortality Weekly Report, 51,* 93–97.

CDC. (2002, April 5). Prevalence of selected maternal behavior and experiences, Pregnancy risk assessment monitoring system (PRAMS), 1999. *Morbidity and Mortality Weekly Report, 51,* SS-2.

CDC. (2002, April 26). Alcohol use among women of childbearing age—United States, 1991–1999. *Morbidity and Mortality Weekly Report, 51,* 273–276.

CDC. (2002, May 17). Trends in cigarette smoking among high school students—United States, 1991–2001. *Morbidity and Mortality Weekly Report, 51.*

CDC. (2002, June 28). Youth risk behavior, surveillance—United States, 2001. *Morbidity and Mortality Weekly Report, 51,* No. SS-4.

CDC. (2002, July 26). Cigarette smoking among adults—United States 2000. *Morbidity and Mortality Weekly Report, 51,* 542–645.

Cepeda, Nicholas J., Kramer, Arthur R., & Gonzalez de Sather, Jessica C. M. (2001). Changes in executive control across the life span: Examination of task-switching performance. *Developmental Psychology, 37,* 715–730.

Ceron-Mireles, Prudencia, Harlow, Sioban D., & Sanchez-Carrillo, Constanza I. (1996). The risk of prematurity and small-for-gestational-age birth in Mexico City: The effects of working conditions and antenatal leave. *American Journal of Public Health, 86,* 825–831.

Chao, Ruth. (2001). Extending research on the consequences of parenting style for Chinese Americans and European Americans. *Child Development, 72,* 1832–1843.

Chen, Shing-Jen. (1996). Positive childishness: Images of childhood in Japan. In

C. Philip Hwang, Michael E. Lamb, & Irving E. Sigell (Eds.), *Images of childhood.* Mahwah, NJ: Erlbaum.

Cherkes-Julkowski, Miriam. (1998). Learning disability, attention-deficit disorder, and language impairment as outcomes of prematurity: A longitudinal descriptive study. *Journal of Learning Disabilities, 31,* 294–306.

Cherlin, Andrew. (1992). *Marriage, divorce, remarriage.* Cambridge, MA: Harvard University Press.

Chess, Stella, Thomas, Alexander, & Birch, Herbert. (1965). *If your child is a person.* New York: Viking Press.

Chiang, W-C., & Wynn, Karen. (2000). Infants' representation and tracking of multiple objects. *Cognition, 77,* 169–195.

Chikkatur, Anita. (1997). A shortcut to independence. In Andrea Estepa & Philip Kay (Eds.), *Starting with I: Personal essays by teenagers.* New York: Persea Books.

Children's Defense Fund. (1999). *The state of America's children, yearbook 1999.* Washington, DC: Publications Department.

Chisholm, Kim. (1998). A three year follow-up of attachment and indiscriminate friendliness in children adopted from Romanian orphanages. *Child Development, 69,* 1092–1106.

Chomitz, Virginia Rall, Cheung, Lilian W.Y., & Lieberman, Ellice. (1995). The role of lifestyle in preventing low birth weight. *The Future of Children: Low Birth Weight, 5,* 121–138.

Chomsky, Noam. (1968). *Language and mind.* New York: Harcourt, Brace, World.

Chomsky, Noam. (1980). *Rules and representations.* New York: Columbia University Press.

Chorney, Michael J., Chorney, K., Seese, N., Owen, M.J., Daniels, J., McGuffin, P., et al. (1998). A quantitative trait locus associated with cognitive ability in children. *Psychological Science, 3,* 159–166.

Choudhury, Naseem, & Gorman, Kathleen. (2000). The relationship between attention and problem solving in 17–24 month old children. *Infant and Child Development, 9,* 127–146.

Chow, Gregory E., & Yancey, Michael K. (2001). Labor and delivery: Normal and abnormal. In Frank W. Ling & Patrick Duff (Eds.), *Obstetrics and gynecology: Principles for practice.* New York: McGraw Hill.

Christoffel, Tom, & Gallagher, Susan Scavo. (1999). *Injury prevention and public health.* Gaithersberg, MD: Aspen.

Cicchetti, Dante, & Sroufe, L. Alan. (2000). The past as prologue to the future: The times, they've been a changing. *Development and Psychopathology, 12,* 255–264.

Cicchetti, Dante, & Toth, Sheree L. (1998). Perspectives on research and practice in developmental psychopathology. In William Damon (Series Ed.), Irving E. Sigel, & K. Ann Renninger (Vol. Eds.), *Handbook of child psychology:* Vol. 4. *Child psychology in practice* (5th ed., pp. 479–483). New York: Wiley.

Cicchetti, Dante, & Walker, Elaine F. (2001). Stress and development: Biological and psychological consequences. *Development and Psychopathology, 13,* 413–418.

Clark, Eve V. (1995). Later lexical development and word formation. In P. Fletcher and B. MacWhinney (Eds.). *The handbook of child language* (pp. 393–412). Cambridge, MA: Blackwell.

Clark, Eve V. (2001). Emergent categories in first language acquisition. In Melissa Bowerman & Stephen C. Levinson (Eds.), *Language acquisition and conceptual development* (pp. 45–69). Cambridge, England: Cambridge University Press.

Clark, Tim, & Rees, John. (1996). *Practical management of asthma.* London: Martin Dunitz.

Clarke, Jeffrey M., McCann, Christina M., & Zaibel, Eren. (1998). The corpus callosum and language: Anatomical-behavioral relationships. In Mark Beeman & Christina Chiarello (Eds.), *Right hemisphere language comprehension: Perspectives from cognitive neuroscience.* Mahwah, NJ: Erlbaum.

Clayton, Richard R., Cattarello, Anna M., & Johnstone, Bryan M. (1996). The effectiveness of Drug Abuse Resistance Education (Project DARE): 5-year follow-up results. *Preventive Medicine, 25,* 307–318.

Cnattingius, Sven, & Haglund, Bengt. (1997). Decreasing smoking prevalence during pregnancy in Sweden: The effect on small-for-gestational-age births. *American Journal of Public Health, 87,* 410–413.

Cobb, Paul. (2000). Conducting classroom teaching experiments in collaboration with teachers. In A. Kelly & R. Lesh (Eds.), *Handbook of research design in mathematics and science education.* Mahwah, NJ: Erlbaum.

Cobb, Paul, Wood, Terry, & Yackel, Erna. (1993). Discourse, mathematical thinking and classroom practice. In Ellice A. Forman, Norris Minick, & C. Addison Stone (Eds.), *Contexts for learning.* New York: Oxford University Press.

Cochran, Susan D., & Mays, Vickie. (2000). Lifetime prevalence of suicide symptoms and affective disorders among men reporting same-sex sexual partners: Results from NHANES III. *American Journal of Public Health, 90,* 573–578.

Cohen, Deborah, Spear, Suzanne, Scribner, Richard, Kissinger, Patty, Mason, Karen, & Wilgen, John. (2000). "Broken windows" and the rash of gonhorrea. *American Journal of Public Health, 90,* 230–236.

Coie, John D., & Dodge, Kenneth A. (1998). Aggression and antisocial behavior. In William Damon & Nancy Eisenberg (Eds.), *Handbook of child psychology:* Vol. 3. *Social, emotional, and personality development* (5th ed., pp. 786–788). New York: Wiley.

Colby, Anne. (2000). The place of moral interpretation and habit in moral development. *Human Development, 43,* 161–164.

Colder, Craig, Mott, Joshua A., & Berman, Arielle S. (2002). The interactive effects of infant activity level and fear on growth trajectories of early childhood behavior problems. *Development and Psychopathology, 14,* 1–23.

Cole, David A., Maxwell, Scott E., Martin, Joan M., Peeke, Lachlan G., Seroczynski, Alesha D., Tram, Jane M., et al. (2001). The development of multiple domains of child and adolescent self-concept: A cohort sequential longitudinal design. *Child Development, 72,* 1723–1746.

Cole, Michael. (1996a). *Cultural psychology: A once and future discipline.* Cambridge, MA: Belknap Press.

Cole, Michael. (1996b). Interacting minds in a life-span perspective: A cultural/historical approach to culture and cognitive development. In Paul B. Baltes & Ursula M. Staudinger (Eds.), *Interactive minds: Life-span perspective on the social foundation of cognition* (pp. 57–89). New York: Cambridge University Press.

Coles, Robert. (1990). *The spiritual life of children.* Boston: Houghton Mifflin.

Coles, Robert. (1997). *How to raise a moral child: The moral intelligence of children.* New York: Random House.

Colin, Virginia L. (1996). *Human attachment.* Philadelphia: Temple University Press.

Coll, Cyntich T. Garcia, Meyer, Elaine C., & Brillon, Lisa. (1995). Ethnic and minority parenting. In Marc H. Bornstein (Ed.), *Handbook of parenting (Vol. 2): Biology and ecology of parenting.* Mahwah, NJ: Erlbaum.

Collinge, John, Sidle, Katie C., Meads, Julie, Ironside, James, & Hill, Andrew F. (1996). Molecular analysis of prion strain variation and the aetiology of "new variant" CJD. *Nature* (London) *383,* 685–690.

Collins, W. Andrew. (1990). Parent-child relationships in the transition to adolescence: Continuity and change in interaction, affect, and cognition. In R. Montemayor, G. Adams, & T. Gullotta (Eds.), *From childhood to adolescence: A transitional period? Advances in adolescent development: Vol. 2. The transition from childhood to adolescence.* Beverly Hills, CA: Sage.

Collins, W. Andrew, Maccoby, Eleanor E., Steinberg, Laurence, Hetherington, E. Mavis, & Bornstein, Marc H. (2000). Contemporary research on parenting: The case for nature and nurture. *American Psychologist, 55,* 218–232.

Comery, Thomas A., Harris, Jennifer B., Willems, Patrick J., Oostra, Ben A., Irwin, Scott A., Weiler, Ivan Jeanne, & Greenough, William T. (1997). Abnormal dendritic spines in Fragile-X knockout mice: Maturation and pruning deficits. *Proceedings of the National Academy of Sciences, 94,* 5401–5404.

Comstock, George, & Scharrer, Erica. (1999). *Television: What's on, who's watching, and what it means.* San Diego: Academic Press.

Conner, David B., Knight, Danica K., & Cross, David R. (1997). Mothers' and fathers' scaffolding of their two-year-olds during problem-solving and literacy interactions. *British Journal of Developmental Psychology, 15,* 323–338.

Conrad, Marilyn, & Hammen, Constance. (1993). Protective and resource factors in high- and low-risk children: A comparison of children with unipolar, bipolar, medically ill, and normal mothers. *Development and Psychopathology, 5,* 593–607.

Constable, Catherine. (1987). Talking with teachers. Increasing our relevance as language interventionists in the schools. *Seminars in Speech & Lanugage, 8,* 345–356.

Cookson, William O. C. M., & Moffatt, Miriam F. (1997). Asthma: An epidemic in the absence of infection? *Science, 275,* 41–42.

Coontz, Stephanie. (1992). *The way we never were: American families and the nostalgia trap.* New York: Basic Books.

Coontz, Stephanie (Ed.). (1998). *American families: A multicultural reader.* New York: Routledge.

Cooper-Hilbert, Beth. (1998). *Infertility and involuntary childlessness: Helping couples cope.* New York: Norton.

Cornwell, A. Christake, Feigenbaum, P., & Kim, A. (1998). SIDS, abnormal nighttime REM sleep and CNS immaturity. *Neuropediatrics, 29,* 72–79.

Corter, Carl M., & Fleming, Alison S. (1995). Psychobiology of maternal behavior in human beings. In Marc H. Bornstein (Ed.), *Handbook of parenting: Biology and ecology of parenting.* Mahwah, NJ: Erlbaum.

Costello, Anthony & Manandhar, Dharma. (2000). *Improving newborn infant health in developing countries.* London: Imperial College Press.

Cote, James E., & Levine, Charles G. (2001). Attitude versus aptitude: Is intelligence or motivation more important for positive higher education outcomes. *Journal of Adolescent Research, 15,* 58–80.

Covington, Martin V. (2000). Goal theory, motivation, and school achievement. *Annual Review of Psychology, 51,* 171–200.

Covington, Martin V., & Dray, Elizabeth. (2002). The developmental course of achievement motivation: A need-based approach. In Allan Wigfield & Jacquelynne S. Eccles (Eds.), *Development of achievement motivation.* San Diego, CA: Academic Press. 33–56.

Cowan, Nelson. (Ed.). (1997). *The development of memory in childhood.* Hove, East Sussex, England: Psychology Press.

Cowan, Philip A., & Cowan, Carolyn P. (2001). What an intervention design reveals about how parents affect their children's academic achievement and behavior problems. In John G. Borkowski, Sharon Landesman Ramey & Marie Bristol-Power (Eds.). *Parenting and the child's world: Influences on intellectual, academic, and social-emotional development.* Mahwah, NJ: Erlbaum. 75–97.

Cox, Martha J., & Brooks-Gunn, Jeanne. (Eds.). (1999). *Conflict and cohesion in families: Causes and consequences.* Mahwah, NJ: Erlbaum.

Cox, Maureen. (1993). *Children's drawings of the human figure.* Hove, England: Erlbaum.

Cox, Maureen. (1997). *Drawings of people by the under-5s.* London: Falmer Press.

Creasy, Robert K. (Ed.). (1997). *Management of labor and delivery.* Malden, MA: Blackwell Science.

Crick, Nicki R., Casas, Juan F. & Ku, Hyon-Chin. (1999). Relational and physical forms of peer victimization in preschool. *Child Development, 35,* 376–385.

Crittenden, Patricia McKinsey. (1999). Child neglect: Causes and contributors. In Howard Dubowitz (Ed.), *Neglected children: Research, practice, and policy* (pp. 47–68). Thousand Oaks, CA: Sage.

Crittenden, Patricia M., Claussen, Angelika H., & Sugarman, David B. (1994). Physical and psychological maltreatment in middle childhood and adolescence. *Development and Psychopathology, 6,* 145–164.

Crockenberg, Susan, & Litman, Cindy. (1990). Autonomy as competence in 2-year-olds: Maternal correlates of child defiance, compliance, and self-assertion. *Developmental Psychology, 26,* 961–971.

Cross, Susan E., & Madson, Laura. (1997). Models of the self: Self-construals and gender. *Psychological Bulletin, 122,* 5–37.

Csikszentmihalyi, Mihaly, Rathunde, Kevin, & Whalen, Samuel. (1993). *Talented teenagers: The roots of success and failure.* Cambridge: Cambridge University Press.

Csikszentmihalyi, Mihaly, & Schneider, Barbara. (2000). *Becoming adult: How teenagers prepare for the world of work.* New York: Basic Books.

Cummings, E. Mark, Goeke-Morey, Marcie C., & Graham, Marybeth A. (2002). Interparental relations as a dimension of parenting. In John G. Borkowski, Sharon Landesman Ramey, & Marie Bristol-Power (Eds.), *Parenting and the child's world: Influences on academic, intellectual and social-emotional development.* Mahwah, NJ: Erlbaum.

Curtis, Patrick A., Boyd, Jennifer D., Liepold, Mary, & Petit, Michael. (1995). *Child abuse and neglect: A look at the states: The CWLA stat book.* Washington, DC: Child Welfare League of America.

Curtis, Patrick A., Dale, Grady, Jr., Kendall, Joshua C. (Eds.). (1999). *The foster care crisis: Translating research into policy and practice.* Lincoln: University of Nebraska.

Czech, Christian, Teemp, Günter, & Pradier, Laurent. (2000). Presenilinst Alzheimer's disease: Biological functions and pathogenic mechanism. *Neurobiology, 60,* 363–384.

Dales, Loring, Hammer, Sandra Jo, & Smith, Natalie J. (2001). Time trends in autism and in MMR immunization coverage in California. *Journal of the American Medical Association, 285,* 1183–1185.

Daniluk, Judith C. (1998). *Women's sexuality across the lifespan: Challenging myths, creating meanings.* New York: Guilford.

Danis, Agnes, Bernard, Jean-Marc, & Leproux, Christine. (2000). Shared picture-book reading: A sequential analysis of adult-child verbal interaction. *British Journal of Developmental Psychology, 18,* 369–388.

Darling, Nancy E., & Steinberg, Lawrence. (1997). Community influences on adolescent achievement and deviance. In Jeanne Brooks-Gunn, George Duncan, & J. Lawrence Aber (Eds.) *Neighborhood poverty: Vol. 3. Policy implications in studying neighborhoods* (pp. 120–131). New York: Russell Sage.

Darling, Stephen, Della Sala, Sergio, Gray, Colin, & Trivelli, Cristina. (1998). Putative functions of the prefrontal cortex: Historical perspectives and new horizons. In Giuliana Mazzoni & Thomas O. Nelson (Eds.), *Metacognition and cognitive neuropsychology: Monitoring and control processes.* Mahwah, NJ: Erlbaum.

Darroch, Jacqueline E., Landry, David J., & Susheela, Singh. (2000). Changing emphases in sexuality education in U.S. public secondary schools, 1988–1999. *Family Planning Perspectives, 32,* 204–211, 265.

Datan, Nancy. (1986). Oedipal conflict, platonic love: Centrifugal forces in intergenerational relations. In Nancy Datan, Anita L. Greene, & Hayne W. Reese (Eds.), *Life-span developmental psychology: Intergenerational relations.* Mahwah, NJ: Erlbaum.

D'Augelli, Anthony R., & Hershberger, Scott L. (1993). Lesbian, gay and bisexual youth in community settings: Personal challenges and mental health problems. *American Journal of Community Psychology, 21,* 421–448.

David. (2002, January 15). Conversation between David Stassen and author.

Davidson, Philip W., Cain, Nancy N., Sloane-Reeves, Jean E., & Van Speybroech, Alec. (1994). Characteristics of community-based individuals with mental retardation and aggressive behavioral disorders. *American Journal of Mental Retardation, 98,* 704–716.

Davies, Lorraine, Avison, William R., & McAlpine, Donna D. (1997). Significant life experiences and depression among single and married mothers. *Journal of Marriage and the Family, 59,* 294–308.

Davila, Joanne, & Daley, Shannon E. (2000). Depression and suicide. In Thomas Joiner & M. David Rudd (Eds.). *Suicide science: Expanding the boundaries.* Dordrecht, Netherlands: Kluwer.

Davis, Jennifer Nerissa, & Daly, Martin. (1997). Evolutionary theory and the human family. *The Quarterly Review of Biology, 72,* 407–435.

Davis, Nanette J. (1999). *Youth crisis: Growing up in the high-risk society.* Westport, CT: Praeger.

Davis-Floyd, Robbie E. (1992). *Birth as an American rite of passage.* Berkeley: University of California Press.

Davis-Kean, Pamela E., & Sandler, Howard M. (2001). A meta-analysis of measures of self-esteem for young children: A framework for future measures. *Child Development, 72,* 887–906.

Dawson, Geraldine, & Ashman, Sharon B. (2000). On the origins of a vulnerability to depression: The influence of the early social environment on the development of psychobiological systems related to risk for affective disorder. In Charles A. Nelson (Ed.), *The Minnesota Symposia on Child Psychology: Vol. 31. The effects of early adversity on neurobehavioral development.* Mahwah, NJ: Erlbaum.

Dawson, Geraldine, Ashman, Sharon B., & Carver, Leslie. (2000). The role of early experience in shaping behavioral and brain development and its implications for social policy. *Development and Psychopathology, 12,* 695–712.

Dearing, Eric, McCartney, Kathleen, & Taylor, Beck A. (2001). Change in family income-to-needs matters more for children with less. *Child Development, 72,* 1779–1793.

De Bellis, Michael D. (2001). Developmental traumatology: The psychobiological development of maltreated children and its implications for research, treatment, and policy. *Development and Psychopathology, 13,* 539–564.

De Bellis, Michael D., Clark, D. B., Beers, S. R., Soloff, P. H., Boring, A. M., Hall, J., Kersh, H., & Keshavan, M. S. (2000). Hippocampal volume in adolescent-onset al-cohol use disorders. *American Journal of Psychiatry, 157,* 737–744.

Degirmencioglu, Serdar M., Urberg, Kathryn A., Tolson, Jerry M., & Richard, Protima. (1998). Adolescent friendship networks: Continuity and change over the school year. *Merrill-Palmer Quarterly, 44,* 313–337.

DeKeseredy, Walter S., & Schwartz, Martin D. (1998). *Women abuse on campus: Results from the Canadian National Survey.* Thousand Oaks, CA: Sage.

Delaney, Carol. (2000). Making babies in a Turkish village. In Judy DeLoache & Alma Gottlieb (Eds.), *A world of babies.* Cambridge, England: Cambridge University Press.

Del Mundo, Amor S., Pumariega, Andres J., & Vance, Hubert R. (1999). Psychopharmacology in school-based mental health services. *Psychology in the Schools, 36,* 437–450.

DeLoache, Judy, & Gottlieb, Alma (Eds.). (2000). *A world of babies.* Cambridge, England: Cambridge University Press.

Delpit, Lisa. (1995). *Other people's children: Cultural conflict in the classroom.* New York: New Press.

De May, Langha, Baartman, Herman E.M., Schulze, Hans-J. (1999). Ethnic variation and the development of moral judgment of youth in Dutch society. *Youth and Society, 31,* 54–75.

D'Emilio, Frances. (2002, May 25). Tiny baby spends first day at home. *Associated Press.*

Demo, David H., & Acock, Alan C. (1996). Family structure, family process, and adolescent well-being. *Journal of Research on Adolescence, 6,* 457–488.

Demo, David H., & Cox, Martha J. (2000). Families with young children: A review of the research in the 1990s. *Journal of Marriage and the Family, 62,* 876–895.

Dent-Read, Cathy, & Zukow-Goldring, Patricia. (1997). Introduction: Ecological realism, dynamic systems, and epigenetic systems approaches to development. In Cathy Dent-Read & Patricia Zukow-Goldring (Eds.), *Evolving explanations of development.* Washington, DC: American Psychological Association.

de Onis, Mercedes, Frongillo, Edward A., & Blössner, Monika. (2000). Is malnutrition declining? An analysis of changes in levels of child malnutrition since 1980. *Bulletin of the World Health Organization, 78,* 1222–1233.

Derochers, Stephen, Ricard, Marcelle, Dexarie, Therese Gouin, & Allard, Louise. (1994). Developmental syncronicity between social referencing and Piagetian sensorimotor causality. *Infant Behavior and Development, 17,* 303–309.

de Róiste, Áine & Bushnell, Ian W.R. (1996). Tactile stimulation: Short- and long-term benefits for pre-term infants. *British Journal of Developmental Psychology, 14,* 41–53.

Deveraux, Lara L. & Hammerman, Ann Jackoway. (1998). *Infertility and identity: New strategies for treatment.* San Francisco: Jossey-Bass Publishers.

de Villiers, Jill G., & de Villiers, Peter A. (2000). Linguistic determination and the understanding of false beliefs. In Peter Mitchell & Kevin J. Riggs (Eds.), *Children's reasoning and the mind* (pp. 191–228). Hove, England: Psychology Press.

Diamond, Adele. (2000). Close interrelation of motor development and cognitive development and of the cerebellum and prefrontal cortex. *Child Development, 71,* 44–56.

Diamond, Ronny, Kezur, David, Meyers, Mimi, Scharf, Constance N., & Weinshel, Margot. (1999). *Couple therapy for infertility.* New York: Guilford.

Diederich, P. B. (1973). *Research 1960–1970 on methods and materials in reading.* Princeton, NJ: Educational Testing Service.

Diekstra, Rene F. W. (1995). Depression and suicidal behaviors in adolescence: Sociocultural and time trends. The positive effects of schooling. In Michael Rutter (Ed.), *Psychosocial disturbances in young people: Challenges for prevention.* Cambridge, England: Cambridge University Press.

Diekstra, Rene F.W., Kienhorst, C.W.M., & de Wilde, E.J. (1995). Suicide and suicidal behavior among adolescents. In Michael Rutter & David J. Smith (Eds.), *Psychosocial disorders in young people: Time trends and their causes.* New York: Published for Academia Europaea by J. Wiley.

Diener, Marissa. (2000). Gift from the Gods: A Balinese guide to early child rearing. In Judy DeLoache and Alma Gottlieb (Eds.). *A world of babies.* Cambridge, England: Cambridge University Press.

Dietz, Tracy L. (1998). An examination of violence and gender role portrayals in video games: Implications for gender socialization and aggressive behavior. *Sex Roles, 38,* 425–442.

Dietz, William H. (1995). Childhood obesity. In Lilian W.Y. Cheung & Julius B. Richmond (Eds.), *Child health, nutrition, and physical activity.* Champaign, IL: Human Kinetics.

Dietz, William H. (1999). Barriers to the treatment of childhood obesity: A call to action. *Journal of Pediatrics, 134,* 535–536.

DiPietro, Janet A., Hodgson, Denice M., Costigan, Kathleen A., & Hilton, Sterling C. (1996). Fetal neurobehavioral development. *Child Development, 67,* 2553–2567.

Dishion, Thomas J., Andrews, David W., & Crosby, Lynn. (1995). Antisocial boys and their friends in early adolescence: Relationship characteristics, quality, and interactional processes. *Child Development, 66,* 139–151.

Dishion, Thomas J., & Bullock, Bernadette Marie. (2002). Parenting and adolescent problem behavior: An ecological analysis of the nurturance hypothesis. In John G. Borkowski, Sharon Landesman Ramey, & Marie Bristol-Power (Eds.), *Parenting and the child's world: Influences on academic, intellectual and social-emotional development.* Mahwah, NJ: Erlbaum.

Dishion, Thomas J., McCord, Joan, & Poulin, Francois. (1999). When interventions harm: Peer groups and problem behavior. *American Psychologist, 54,* 755–764.

Dishion, Thomas J., & McMahon, Robert J. (1998) Parental monitoring and the prevention of child and adolescent problem behavior: A conceptual and empirical formulation. *Clinical Child and Family Psychology Review, 1,* 61–75.

Dixon, Roger A., & Lerner, Richard M. (1999). History and systems in developmental psychology. In Marc H. Bornstein & Michael E. Lamb (Eds.), *Developmental psychology: An advanced textbook.* Mahwah, NJ: Erlbaum.

Dodge, Kenneth A. (2002). Mediation, moderation, and mechanisms in how parenting affects children's aggressive behavior. In John G. Borkowski, Sharon Landesman Ramey, & Marie Bristol-Power (Eds.), *Parenting and the child's world: Influences on academic, intellectual and social-emotional development.* Mahwah, NJ: Erlbaum.

Dodge, Kenneth A., Pettit, Gregory S., & Bates, John E. (1994). Effects of physical maltreatment on the development of peer relations. *Development and Psychopathology, 6,* 43–55.

D'Odorico, Laura, Carubbi, Stefania, Salerni, Nicoletta, & Calvo, Vincenzo. (2001). Vocabulary development in Italian children: A longitudinal evaluation of quantitative and qualitative aspects. *Journal of Child Language, 28,* 351–372.

Donovan, Patricia. (1997). Can statutory rape laws be effective in preventing adolescent pregnancy? *Family Planning Perspectives, 29,* 30–34, 40.

Dornbusch, Sanford M., Herman, Melissa R., & Morley, Jeanne A. (1996). Domains of adolescent achievement. In Gerald R. Adams, Raymond Montemayor, & Thomas P. Gullotta (Eds.), *Psychosocial development in adolescence* (pp. 181–231). Beverly Hills, CA: Sage.

Dornbusch, Sanford M., Lin I-Chun, Munroe, Paul T., & Bianchi, Alison J. (1999). Adolescent polydrug use and violence in the United States. *International Journal of Adolescent Health and Medicine, 11,* 197–219.

Douglas, Ann. (2002). *The mother of all pregnancy books.* Indianapolis, IN: Hungry Minds.

Dounchis, Jennifer Zoler, Hayden, Helen A., & Wilfley, Denise E. (2001). Obesity, body image, and eating disorders in ethnically diverse children and adolescents. In J. Kevin Thompson & Linda Smolak (Eds.), *Body image, eating disorders, and obesity in youth* (pp. 67–98). Washington, DC: American Psychological Association.

Downs, A. Chris. (1990). The social biological constraints of social competency. In Thomas P. Gullotta, Gerald R. Adams, & Raymond R. Montemayor (Eds.), *Developing social competency in adolescence.* Newbury Park, CA: Sage.

Downs, A. Chris, & Fuller, M. J. (1991). Recollections of spermarche: An exploratory investigation. *Current Psychology: Research and Review, 10,* 93–102.

Dozier, Mary, Stovall, K. Chase, Albus, Kathleen E., & Bates, Brady. (2001). Attachment for infants in foster care: The role of caregiver state of mind. *Child Development, 72,* 1467–1477.

Drake, Brett, & Zuravin, Susan. (1998). Bias in child maltreatment reporting: Revisiting the myth of classlessness. *American Journal of Orthopsychiatry, 68,* 295–304.

DSM-IV. See American Psychiatric Association.

du Bois-Reymond , Manuela. (1995). The role of parents in the transition period of young people. In Manuela du Bois-Reymond, Rene Diekstra, Klaus Hurrelmann, & Els Peters (Eds.), *Childhood and youth in Germany and the Netherlands: Transitions and coping strategies of adolescents.* Berlin: Mouton de Gruyter.

Dubowitz, Howard. (1999). Neglect of children's health care. In Howard Dubowitz (Ed.), *Neglected children: Research, practice, and policy* (pp. 109–130). Thousand Oaks, CA: Sage.

Duggal, Sunita, Carlson, Elizabeth A., Sroufe, L. Alan, & Egeland, Byron. (2001). Depressive symptomatology in childhood and adolescence. *Development and Psychopathology, 13,* 143–164.

Duggar, Celia E. (2001, April 22). Abortion in India is tipping scales sharply against girls. *The New York Times,* pp. A1, 10.

Duncan, Greg J., & Brooks-Gunn, Jeanne. (2000). Family poverty, welfare reform, and child development. *Child Development, 71,* 188–196.

Dunn, Judy, Bretherton, Inge, & Munn, Penny. (1987). Conversations about feeling states between mothers and their young children. *Developmental Psychology, 23,* 132–139.

Dunn, Judy, & Hughes, Claire. (2001). "I got some swords and you're dead": Violent fantasy, antisocial behavior, friendship, and moral sensibility in young children. *Child Development, 72,* 491–505.

Dunphy, Dexter C. (1963). The social structure of urban adolescent peer groups. *Sociometry, 26,* 230–246.

Durbrow, Eric H. (1999). Cultural processes in child competence: How rural Caribbean parents evaluate their children. In Ann S. Masten (Ed.), *The Minnesota Symposia on Child Psychology: Vol. 29. Cultural processes in child development.* Mahwah, NJ: Erlbaum.

Durlak, Joseph A. (1998). Common risk and protective factors in successful prevention programs. *American Journal of Orthopsychiatry, 68,* 512–520.

Durrant, Joan E. (1996). Public attitudes toward corporal punishment in Canada. In Detlev Frehsee, Wiebke Horn, & Kai-D. Bussmann (Eds.), *Family violence against children: A challenge for society.* Berlin: de Gruyter.

Duster, Troy. (1999). The social consequences of genetic disclosure. In Ronald A. Carson & Mark A. Rothstein (Eds.), *Behavioral genetics: The clash of culture and* biology (pp. 172–188). Baltimore: Johns Hopkins Press.

Dutton, Donald G. (2000). Witnessing parental violence as a traumatic experience shaping the abusive personality. In Robert A. Geffner, Peter G. Jaffe, & Marlies Sudermann (Eds.). *Children exposed to domestic violence*. Binghamton, NY: Haworth.

Duval, Thomas Shelley, & Silvia, Paul J. (2002). Self-awareness, probability of improvement and the self-serving bias. *Journal of Personality and Social Psychology, 82,* 49–61.

Dweck, Carol S. (1999). *Self-theories: Their role in motivation, personality, and development*. Philadelphia: Psychology Press.

Dybdahl, Ragnhild. (2001). Children and mothers in war: An outcome study of a psychosocial intervention program. *Child Development, 72,* 1214–1230.

Dykens, Elisabeth M., Hodapp, Robert M., & Leckman, James F. (1994). *Behavior and development in fragile X syndrome*. Thousand Oaks, CA: Sage.

Eaton, Warren O., & Yu, Alice Piklai. (1989). Are sex differences in child motor activity level a function of sex differences in maturational status? *Child Development, 60,* 10051011.

Eccles, Jacquelynne S., & Barber, Bonnie L. (1999). Student Council, volunteering, basketball or marching band: What kinds of extracurricular involvement matters? *Journal of Adolescent Research, 14,* 10–43.

Eccles, Jacquelynne S., Wigfield, Allan, & Schiefele, Ulrich. (1998). Motivation to succeed. In William Damon (Series Ed.) & Nancy Eisenberg (Vol. Ed.), *Handbook of child psychology:* Vol. 3. *Social, emotional, and personality development* (5th ed., pp. 1017–1098). New York: Wiley.

Edwards, John R. (1994). *Multilingualism*. London: Routledge.

Efron, Robert. (1990). *The decline and fall of hemispheric specialization*. Hillsdale, NJ: Erlbaum.

Eggebeen, David J., & Knoester, Chris. (2001). Does fatherhood matter for men? *Journal of Marriage and the Family, 63,* 381–393.

Ehrenberg, Ronald G., Brewer, Dominic J., Gamoran, Adam, & Willms, Douglas J. (2001). Class size and student achievement. *Psychological Science in the Public Interest, 1,* 1–30.

Eid, Michael, & Diener, Ed. (2001). Norms for experiencing emotions in different cultures: Inter- and intra-national differences. *Journal of Personality and Social Psychology, 81,* 869–885.

Eisenberg, Nancy. (1986). *Altruistic emotion, cognition, and behavior*. Mahwah, NJ: Erlbaum.

Eisenberg, Nancy. (2000). Emotion, regulation, and moral development. *Annual Review of Psychology, 51,* 665–697.

Eisenberg, Nancy, Cumberland, Amanda, Spinrad, Tracy L., Fabes, Richard A., Shepard, Stephanie A., Reiser, Mark, et al. (2001). The relations of regulation and emotionality to children's externalizing and internalizing problem behavior. *Child Development, 72,* 1112–1134.

Eisenberg, Nancy, Fabes, Richard A., & Murphy, Bridget C. (1996). Parents' reactions to children's negative emotions: Relations to children's social competence and comforting behavior. *Child Development, 67,* 2227–2247.

Eisenberg, Nancy, Fabes, Richard A., Shepard, Stephanie A., Murphy, Bridget C., Guthrie, Ivanna K., Jones, Sarah, et al. (1997). Contemporaneous and longitudinal prediction of children's social functioning from regulation and emotionality. *Child Development, 68,* 642–664.

Elbert, Thomas, Pantev, Christo, Wienbruch, Christian, Rockstroh, Brigitte, & Taub, Edward. (1995). Increased cortical representation of the fingers of the left hand in string players. *Science, 270,* 305–307.

Elder, Glen H., Jr. (1974). *Children of the great depression: Social change in life experience*. Chicago: University of Chicago Press.

Elder, Glen H., Jr. (1998). Life course theory and human development. *Sociological Analysis, 1*(2), 1–12.

Elder, Glen H., Jr., & Conger, Rand D. (2000). *Children of the land: Adversity and success in rural America*. Chicago: University of Chicago Press.

Elder, Glen H., Jr., Rudkin, Laura, & Conger, Rand D. (1995). Intergenerational continuity and change in rural America. In Vern L. Bengtson, K. Warner Schaie, & Linda M. Burton (Eds.), *Adult intergenerational relations: Effects of societal change*. New York: Springer.

Elkind, David. (1967). Egocentrism in adolescence. *Child Development, 38,* 1025–1034.

Elkind, David. (1981). *The hurried child*. Boston: Addison-Wesley.

Elkind, David. (1984). *All grown up and no place to go*. Reading, MA: Addison-Wesley.

Ellis, Bruce J., & Garber, Judy. (2000). Psychosocial antecedents of variation in girls' pubertal timing: Maternal depression, stepfather presence, and marital and family stress. *Child Development, 71,* 485–501.

Elmore, Richard F., & Rothman, Robert (Eds.). (1999). *Testing, teaching, and learning*. Washington, DC: National Academy Press.

Elo, Irma T., King, Rosalind Berkowitz, & Furstenberg, Frank F., Jr. (1999). Adolescent females: Their sexual partners and the fathers of their children. *Journal of Marriage and the Family, 61,* 74–84.

El-Sheikh, Mona, & Harger, JoAnn. (2001). Appraisals of marital conflict and children's adjustment, health, and physiological reactivity. *Developmental Psychology, 37,* 875–885.

Emler, Nicholas. (1998). Sociomoral understanding. In Anne Campbell & Steven Muncer (Eds.), *The social child*. East Sussex, England: Psychology Press.

Enkin, Murray, Keirse, Marc J.N.C., & Chalmers, Iain. (1989). *Effective care in pregnancy and childbirth*. Oxford, England: Oxford University Press.

Ennett, Susan T., Tobler, Nancy S., Ringwalt, Christopher L., & Flewelling, Robert L. (1994). How effective is drug abuse resistance education? A meta-analysis of Project DARE outcome evaluations. *American Journal of Public Health, 84,* 1394–1401.

Epstein, Seymour. (1994). Integration of the cognitive and psychodynamic unconscious. *American Psychologist, 49,* 709–724.

Erdley, Cynthia A., & Asher, Steven R. (1996). Children's social goals and self-efficacy perceptions as influences on their responses to ambiguous provocation. *Child Development, 67,* 1329–1344.

Erel, Osnat, Oberman, Yael, & Yirmiya, Nurit. (2000). Maternal versus nonmaternal care and seven domains of children's development. *Psychological Bulletin, 126,* 727–747.

Erikson, Erik H. (1963). *Childhood and society* (2nd ed.). New York: Norton.

Erikson, Erik H. (1968). *Identity, youth, and crisis.* New York: Norton.

Erwin, Phil. (1998). *Friendship in childhood and adolescence.* London: Routledge.

Esbensen, Bonnie M., Taylor, Marjorie, & Stoess, Caryn J. (1997). Children's behavioral understanding of knowledge acquisition. *Cognitive Development, 12,* 53–84.

Etaugh, Claire, & Liss, Marsha B. (1992). Home, school, and playroom: Training ground for adult gender roles. *Sex Roles, 26,* 129–147.

Ethics Committee of the American Society for Reproductive Medicine. (2001). Preconceptual gender selection for non-medical reasons. *Fertility and Sterility, 75,* 861–864.

Evans, David W., Leckman, James F., Carter, Alice, Reznick, J. Steven, Henshaw, Desiree, King, Robert A., & Pauls, David. (1997). Ritual, habit, and perfectionism: The prevalence and development of compulsive-like behavior in normal young children. *Child Development, 68,* 58–68.

Evans, Ian M., Galyer, Karma T., & Smith, Kyle J. (2001). Children's perceptions of unfair reward and punishment. *The Journal of Genetic Psychology, 162,* 212–227.

Eveleth, Phyllis B., & Tanner, James M. (1991). *Worldwide variation in human growth* (2nd ed.). Cambridge, England: Cambridge University Press.

Ewing, Charles Patrick. (1990). *Kids who kill.* Lexington, MA: Lexington Books.

Eyer, Diane E. (1992). *Maternal-infant bondings: A scientific fiction.* New Haven, CT: Yale University Press.

Eyre, Stephen L., & Millstein, Susan G. (1999). What leads to sex? Adolescents preferred partners and reasons for sex. *Journal of Research on Adolescence, 9,* 277–307.

Faberow, Norman L. (1994). Preparatory and prior suicidal behavior factors. In Edwin S. Shneidman, Norman L. Faberow, & Robert E. Litman (Eds.), *The psychology of suicide* (rev. ed.). Northwale, NJ: Aronson.

Fabes, Richard A. (1994). Physiological, emotional, and behavioral correlates of gender segregation. In C. Leaper (Ed.), *Childhood gender segregation: Causes and consequences.* San Francisco: Jossey-Bass.

Fabes, Richard A., Leonard, Stacie A., Kupanoff, Kristina, & Martin, Carol Lynn.

(2001). Parental coping with children's negative emotions: Relations with children's emotional and social responding. *Child Development, 72,* 907–920.

Fagot, Beverly I. (1995). Parenting boys and girls. In Marc H. Bornstein (Ed.), *Handbook of parenting: Vol. 1. Children and parenting.* Mahwah, NJ: Erlbaum.

Fagot, Beverly I., & Leinbach, Mary D. (1993). Gender-role development in young children: From discriminating to labeling. *Developmental Review, 13,* 205–224.

Fagot, Beverly I., Pears, Katherine C., Capaldi, Deborah M., Crosby, Lynn, & Leve, C. S. (1998). Becoming an adolescent father: Precursors and parenting. *Developmental Psychology, 34,* 1209–1219.

Fairburn, Christopher G., & Wilson, G. Terence. (Eds). (1993). *Binge eating: Nature, assessment and treatment.* New York: Guilford Press.

Falcon, Angelo, Aguirre-Molina, Marilyn, & Molina, Carlos W. (2001). Latino health policy: Beyond demographic determinism. In Marilyn Aguirre-Molina, Carlos W. Molina, & Enid Zambrana (Eds.), *Health issues in the Latino community* (pp. 3–22). San Francisco: Jossey-Bass.

Falk, Ruma, & Wilkening, Freidrich. (1998). Children's construction of fair chances: Adjusting probabilities. *Developmental Psychology, 23,* 1340–1357.

Farber, Susan L. (1981). *Identical twins reared apart: A reanalysis.* New York: Basic.

Farrington, David P. (1994). Interactions between individual and contextual factors in the development of offending. In Rainer K. Silbereisen & Eberhard Todt (Eds.), *Adolescence in context: The interplay of family, school, peers, and work in adjustment.* New York: Springer-Verlag.

Feiring, Candice. (1996). Concepts of romance in 15-year-old adolescents. *Journal of Research on Adolescence, 6,* 181–200.

Feldman, Ruth, Greenbaum, Charles W., Mayes, Linda C., & Erlich, Samuel H. (1997). Change in mother-infant interactive behavior: Relations to change in the mother, the infant, and the social context. *Infant Behavior & Development, 20,* 151–163.

Feldman, Ruth, Greenbaum, Charles W., & Yirmiya, Nurit. (1999). Mother-infant affect synchrony as an antecedent of the emergence of self-control. *Developmental Psychology, 35,* 3–19.

Feldman, S. Shirley, Cauffman, Elizabeth, Jensen, Lene Arnett, & Arnett, Jeffrey J. (2000). The (un)acceptability of betrayal: A study of college students' evaluation of sexual betrayal by a romantic partner and betrayal of a friend's confidence. *Journal of Youth and Adolescence, 29,* 499–523.

Fenson, Larry, Dale, Philip S., Resnick, J. Steven, Bates, Elizabeth, Thal, Donna J., & Petchick, Stephen J. (1994). Variability in early communicative development. *Monographs of the Society for Research in Child Development, 59* (Serial No. 242).

Ferguson, Mark W. J., & Joanen, Ted. (1982) Temperature of egg incubation determines sex in *Alligator mississippiensis. Nature, 296,* 850–853.

Ferguson, William G. L. (1997). Normal labor and delivery. In Robert K. Creasy (Ed.), *Management of labor and delivery.* Malden, MA: Blackwell Science.

Fergusson, David M., & Horwood, L. John. (2002). Male and female offending trajectories. *Development and Psychopathology, 14,* 159–178.

Fergusson, David M., Lynskey, Michael, & Horwood, L. John. (1995). The adolescent outcomes of adoption: A 16-year longitudinal study. *Journal of Child Psychology and Psychiatry and Allied Disciplines, 36,* 597–615.

Fergusson, David M., & Woodward, Lianne J. (1999). Maternal age and educational psychosocial outcomes in early adulthood. *Journal of Child Psychology & Psychiatry & Allied Disciplines, 40,* 479–489.

Ferrari, Michel, & Sternberg, Robert J. (1998). The development of mental abilities and styles. In William Damon (Series Ed.), Deanna Kuhn, & Robert S. Siegler (Vol. Eds.), *Handbook of child psychology:* Vol. 2. *Cognition, perception, and language* (5th ed., pp. 399–946). New York: Wiley.

Ferron, Christine. (1997). Body image in adolescence: Cross-cultural research. *Adolescence, 32,* 735–745.

Feynman, Richard P. (1985). *Surely you're joking, Mr. Feynman: Adventures of a curious character.* New York: Bantam Books.

Field, Tiffany. (1994). The effects of mother's physical and emotional unavailability on emotion regulation. In Nathan A. Fox (Ed.), *The development of emotion regulation: Biological and behavioral considerations. Monographs of the Society for Research in Child Development, 59* (2-3, Serial No. 240).

Field, Tiffany, Diego, Miguel, & Sanders, Christopher E. (2001). Exercise is positively related to adolescents' relationships and academics. *Adolescence, 36,* 105–110.

Fifer, William P., & Moon, Chris M. (1995). The effects of fetal experience with sound. In Jean-Pierre Lecanuet, William P. Fifer, Norman A. Krasnegor, & William P. Smotherman (Eds.), *Fetal development: A psychobiological perspective.* Mahwah, NJ: Erlbaum.

Finkelhor, David. (1994). Current information on the scope and nature of child sexual abuse. *The Future of Children, 4,* 31–53.

Finn, J. D., Gerber, S. B., Achilles, C. M., & Boyd-Zaharias, J. (2001). The enduring effects of small classes. *Teachers College Record, 103,* 145–183.

Fiscella, Kevin, Kitzman, Harriet J., Cole, Robert E., Sidora, Kimberly, Olds, David. (1998). Delayed first pregnancy among African-American adolescent smokers. *Journal of Adolescent Health, 23,* 232–237.

Fischer, Kurt W., Ayoub, Catherine, Sigh, Ilina, Noam, Gil, Maraganore, Andronicki, & Raya, Pamela. (1997). Psychopathology as adaptive development along distinctive pathways. *Development and Psychopathology, 9,* 749–779.

Fischer, Kurt W., & Bidell, Thomas R. (1998). Dynamic development of psychological structures in action and thought. In William Damon (Series Ed.) & Richard M. Lerner (Vol. Ed.), *Handbook of child psychology:* Vol. 1. *Theoretical models of human development* (5th ed., pp. 467–561). New York: Wiley.

Fischer, Kurt W., & Rose, Samuel P. (1996). Dynamic growth cycles of brain and cognitive development. In Robert Thatcher, G. Reid Lyon, J. Rumsey, & N. Krasnegor (Eds.), *Developmental neuroimaging: Mapping the development of brain and behavior* (pp. 263–279). New York: Academic Press.

Fishbein, M., Hall-Jamieson, K., Zimmer, E., von Haeften, I., & Nabi, R. (2002). Avoiding the boomerang: Testing the relative effectiveness of anti-drug public service announcements before a national campaign. *American Journal of Public Health, 92,* 238–245.

Fishel, Simon, Dowell, Ken, & Thornton, Simon. (2000). Reproductive possibilities for infertile couples: present and future. In Gillian R. Bentley & C. G. Nicholas Mascie-Taylor (Eds.), *Infertility in the modern world.* Cambridge, England: Cambridge University Press.

Fisher, Barbara C. (1997). *Attention deficit disorder misdiagnosis.* Boca Raton, FL: CRC Press.

Fisher, Celia B., Jackson, Jacqueline Faye, & Villarruel, Francisco A. (1998). The study of African American and Latin American children and youth. In William Damon (Series Ed.) & Richard M. Lerner (Vol. Ed.), *Handbook of child psychology:* Vol. 1. *Theoretical models of human development* (5th ed., pp. 1145–1207). New York: Wiley.

Fisher, Jennifer O., & Birch, Leann L. (2001). Early experience with food and eating: Implications for the development of eating disorders. In J. Kevin Thompson & Linda Smolak (Eds.), *Body image, eating disorders, and obesity in youth* (pp. 261–292). Washington, DC: American Psychological Association.

Fisher, Simon E., Marlow, Angela J., Lamb, Janine, Maestrini, Elena, Williams, Dianne F., Richardson, Alex J., Weeks, Daniel E., Stein, John F., & Monaco, Anthony P. (1999). A quantitative-trait locus on chromosome 6p includes different aspects of developmental dyslexia. *American Journal of Human Genetics, 64,* 146–156.

Flavell, John H., Miller, Patricia H., & Miller, Scott A. (2001). *Cognitive development* (4th ed.). Upper Saddle River, NJ: Prentice-Hall.

Fleming, Alison S., & Corter, Carl M. (1995). Psychobiology of maternal behavior in nonhuman mammals. In Marc H. Bornstein (Ed.), *Handbook of parenting: Biology and ecology of parenting.* Mahwah, NJ: Erlbaum.

Fletcher, Anne C., Darling, Nancy, & Steinberg, Laurence. (1995). Parental monitoring and peer influences on adolescent substance use. In Joan McCord (Ed.), *Coercion and punishment in long-term perspectives.* New York: Cambridge University Press.

Flieller, Andre. (1999). Comparison of the development of formal thought in adolescent cohorts aged 10 to 15 years (1967–1996 and 1972–1993). *Developmental Psychology, 35,* 1048–1058.

Flores, Glenn, & Zambrana, Ruth Enid. (2001). The early years: The health of children and youth. In Marilyn Aguirre-Molina, Carlos W. Molina, & Ruth Enid Zambrana (Eds.). *Health issues in the Latino community.* San Francisco: Jossey-Bass.

Fonagy, Peter, & Target, Mary. (2000). The place of psychodynamic theory in developmental psychopathology. *Development and Psychopathology, 12,* 407–425.

Fonzi, Ada, Genta, Maria Luisa, Menesini, Ersilia, Bacchini, Dario, Bonino, Silvia, & Costabile, Angela. (1999). Italy. In Peter K. Smith, Yohji Morita, Josine Junger-Tas, Dan Olweus, Richard F. Catalano, & Phillip T. Slee (Eds.), *The nature of school bullying: A cross-national perspective.* London: Routledge.

Ford, Kathleen, Sohn, Woosung, & Lepkowski, James. (2001). Characteristics of adolescents' sexual partners and their association with use of condoms and other contraceptive methods. *Family Planning Perspectives, 33,* 100–105, 132.

Fox, Nathan A., Henderson, Heather A., Rubin, Kenneth H., Calkins, Susan D., & Schmidt, Louis A. (2001). Continuity and discontinuity of behavioral inhibition and exuberance: Psychophysiological and behavioral influences across the first four years of life. *Child Development, 72,* 1–21.

Fox, Nathan A., Sobel, Ana, Calkins, Susan, & Cole, Pamela. (1996). Inhibited children talk about themselves: Self-reflection on personality development and change in 7-year-olds. In Michael Lewis & Margaret Wolan Sullivan (Eds.), *Emotional development in atypical children.* Mahwah, NJ: Erlbaum.

Frankenburg, William K., Frandel, A., Sciarillo, W., & Burgess, D. (1981). The newly abbreviated and revised Denver Developmental Screening Test. *Journal of Pediatrics, 99,* 995–999.

Franklin, Deborah. (1984). Rubella threatens unborn in vaccine gap. *Science News, 125,* 186.

Freda, B. (1997). *Personal communication.*

Fredricks, Jennifer A., & Eccles, Jacquelynne S. (2002). Children's competence and value beliefs from childhood through adolescence: Growth trajectories in two male-sex-typed domains. *Developmental Psychology, 38,* 519–533.

Freedman, David S., Dietz, William H., Srinivasan, Sathanur R., & Berenson, Gerald S. (1999). The relation of overweight to cardiovascular risk factors among children and adolescents. *Pediatrics, 103,* 1175–1182.

Freeman, Michael (Ed.). (2000). *Overcoming child abuse: A window on a world problem.* Aldershot, England: Dartmouth.

Freud, Anna. (1958/2000). Adolescence. In *The psychoanalytic study of the child* (Vol. 13, pp. 255–278). New York: International Universities Press.

Freud, Sigmund. (1918/1963). *Three case histories.* New York: Collier.

Freud, Sigmund. (1933/1965). *New introductory lectures on psychoanalysis.* (James Strachey, Ed. & Trans.). New York: Norton.

Freud, Sigmund. (1935). *A general introduction to psychoanalysis* (Joan Riviare, Trans.). New York: Modern Library.

Freud, Sigmund. (1938). *The basic writings of Sigmund Freud.* (A.A. Brill, Ed. & Trans.). New York: Modern Library.

Freud, Sigmund. (1940/1964). *An outline of psychoanalysis: Vol. 23. The standard edition of the complete psychological works of Sigmund Freud.* (James Strachey, Ed. & Trans.). London: Hogarth Press.

Friedman, Michael K., Powell, Kenneth E., Hutwagner, Lori, Graham, LeRoy M., & Teague, Gerald. (2001). Impact of changes in transportation and commuting behaviors during the 1996 Summer Olympics Games in Atlanta on air quality and childhood asthma. *Journal of the American Medical Association, 285,* 897–905.

Friedrich, William N. (1998). Behavioral manifestations of child sexual abuse. *Child Abuse and Neglect, 22,* 523–531.

Fuligni, Andrew J. (1998). Authority, autonomy, and parent-adolescent conflict and cohesion: A study of adolescents from Mexican, Chinese, Filipino and European backgrounds. *Developmental Psychology, 34,* 782–792.

Fuligni, Andrew J. (2001). A comparative longitudinal approach to acculturation among children from immigrant families. *Harvard Educational Review, 71,* 566–578.

Furman, Wyndol, & Wehner, Elizabeth A. (1994). Romantic views: Toward a theory of adolescent romantic relationships. In R. Montemayor, G.M. Adams, & C.T. Gullotta (Eds.), *Personal relationships during adolescence.* Thousand Oaks, CA: Sage.

Furstenberg, Frank F. (1998). Social capital and the role of fathers in the family. In Alan Booth and Nancy Crouter (Eds.), *Men in families: When do they get involved? What difference does it make?* (pp. 295–301). Mahwah, NJ: Erlbaum.

Furstenberg, Frank F., & Cherlin, Andrew J. (1991). *Divided families: What happens to children when parents part.* Cambridge, MA: Harvard University Press.

Furstenberg, Frank F., & Kiernan, Kathleen E. (2001). Delayed parental divorce: How much do children benefit? *Journal of Marriage and the Family, 63,* 446–457.

Furth, Hans G. (1996). *Desire for society: Children's knowledge as social imagination.* New York: Plenum Press.

Fuson, Karen C., & Kwon, Youngshim. (1992). Korean children's understanding of multidigit addition and subtraction. *Child Development, 63,* 491–506.

Gabrieli, John D. E. (1998). Cognitive neuroscience of human memory. *Annual Review of Psychology, 49,* 87–115.

Galambos, Nancy L., & Leadbeater, Bonnie J. (2000) Trend in adolescent research for the new millennium. *International Journal of Behavioral Development, 24.*

Galatzer-Levy, Robert J., & Kraus, Louis. (Eds.). (1999). *The scientific basis of child custody decisions.* New York: Wiley.

Gall, Stanley A. (1996). *Multiple pregnancy and delivery.* St. Louis, MO: Mosby.

Ganong, Lawrence H., & Coleman, Marilyn. (1994). *Remarried family relationships.* Thousand Oaks, CA: Sage.

Ganong, Lawrence H., & Coleman, Marilyn. (1999). *Changing families, changing responsibilities: Family obligations following divorce and remarriage.* Mahwah, NJ: Erlbaum.

Gantley, M., Davies, D.P., & Murcott, A. (1993). Sudden infant death syndrome: Links with infant care practices. *British Medical Journal, 306,* 16–20.

Garbarino, James, & Collins, Cyleste C. (1999). Child neglect: The family with a hole in the middle. In Howard Dubowitz (Ed.), *Neglected children: Research, practice and policy* (pp. 1–23). Thousand Oaks, CA: Sage.

Garbarino, James, Kostelny, Kathleen, & Barry, Frank. (1997). Value transmission in an ecological context: The high-risk neighborhood. In Joan E. Grusec & Leon Kuczynski (Eds.), *Parenting and children's internalization of values: A handbook of contemporary theory.* New York: Wiley.

Gardner, Howard. (1980). *Artful scribbles: The significance of children's drawings.* New York: Basic Books.

Gardner, Howard. (1983). *Frames of mind: The theory of multiple intelligences.* New York: Basic Books.

Gardner, Howard. (1993). *Multiple intelligences: The theory in practice.* New York: Basic Books.

Garmezy, Norman. (1985). Stress-resistant children: The search for protective factors. In J. E. Stevenson (Ed.), *Recent research in developmental psychopathology.* Oxford, England: Pergamon.

Garmezy, Norman. (1993). Vulnerability and resilience. In David C. Funder, Ross D. Parke, Carol Tomlinson-Keasy, & Keith Widaman (Eds.), *Studying lives through time.* Washington, DC: American Psychological Association.

Garner, Pamela W., & Spears, F. M. (2000). Emotion regulation in low income preschool children. *Social Development, 9,* 246–264.

Garofalo, Robert, Cameron, Wolf, Wissow, Lawrence S., Woods, Elizabeth R., & Goodman, Elizabeth. (1999). Sexual orientation and risk of suicide. *Archives of Pediatric & Adolescent Medicine, 513,* 487.

Garrity, Carla & Baris, Mitchell A. (1996). Bullies and victims. *Contemporary Pediatrics, 13,* 90–114.

Garrod, Andrew. (Ed.). (1993). *Approaches to moral development: New research and emerging themes.* New York: Teachers College Press.

Garvin, James P. (1994). *Learning how to kiss a frog: Advice for those who work with pre- and early adolescents.* Newburyport, MA: Garvin Consultant Association.

Gaulin, Steven J.C. (1993). How and why sex differences evolve, with spatial ability as a paradigm example. In Marc Haug, Richard Whalen, Claude Aron, & Kathie Olsen (Eds.), *The development of sex differences and similarities in behavior.* Boston: Kluwer.

Gauvain, Mary. (1998). Cognitive development in social and cultural context. *Current Directions in Psychological Science, 7,* 188–192.

Gdalevich, Michael, Mimouni, Daniel, & Mimouni, Marc. (2001). Breast-feeding and the risk of bronchial asthma in childhood: A systematic review with meta-analysis of prospective studies. *Journal of Pediatrics, 139,* 261–266.

Ge, Xiaogia, Conger, Rand D., & Elder, Glen H., Jr. (2001). Pubertal transition, stressful life events, and the emergence of gender differences in adolescent depressive symptoms. *Developmental Psychology, 37,* 404–417.

Geiger, Brenda. (1996). *Fathers as primary caregivers.* Westport, CT: Greenwood Press.

Gelles, Richard. (1999). Policy issues in child neglect. In Howard Dubowitz (Ed.), *Neglected children: Research, practice, and policy* (pp. 278–298). Thousand Oaks, CA: Sage.

Gelles, Richard. (2000). Controversies in family preservation programs. In Robert A. Geffner, Peter G. Jaffe, & Marlies Sudermann (Eds.), *Children exposed to domestic violence* (pp. 239–253). Binghamton, NY: Haworth Press.

Gelman, Rochel, & Williams, Earl M. (1998). Enabling constraints for cognitive development and learning: Domain specificity and epigenesis. In William Damon (Series Ed.), Deanna Kuhn, & Robert S. Siegler (Vol. Eds.), *Handbook of child psychology: Vol. 2. Cognition, perception, and language* (5th ed., pp. 575–630). New York: Wiley.

Genesee, Fred. (1998). A case study of multilingual education in Canada. In Jasone Cenoz & Fred Genesee (Eds.), *Beyond bilingualism: Multilingualism and multilingual education.* Clevedon, England: Multilingual Matters.

Gentner, Dedre, & Boroditsky, Lera. (2001). Individuation, relativity, and early word learning. In Melissa Bowerman & Stephen C. Levinson (Eds.), *Language acquisition and conceptual development.* Cambridge, England: Cambridge University Press.

Georgieff, Michael K., & Rao, Raghavendra. (2001). The role of nutrition in cognitive development. In Charles A. Nelson & Monica Luciana (Eds.), *Handbook of developmental neuroscience* (pp. 149–158). Cambridge, MA: MIT Press.

Gergely, Gyoergy, & Watson, John S. (1999). Early socio-emotional development: Contingency perception and the social-biofeedback model. In Philippe Rochat (Ed.), *Early social cognition: Understanding others in the first months of life* (pp. 101–136). Mahwah, NJ: Erlbaum.

Gerhardstein, Peter, Liu, Jane, & Rovee-Collier, Carolyn. (1998). Perceptual constraints on infant memory retrieval. *Journal of Experimental Child Psychology, 69,* 109–131.

Gesell, Arnold. (1926). *The mental growth of the pre-school child: A psychological outline of normal development from birth to the sixth year including a system of developmental diagnosis.* New York: Macmillan.

Gibbons, Ann. (1998). Which of our genes makes us human? *Science, 281,* 1432–1434.

Gibbs, J. C., Basinger, K. S., & Fuller, D. (1992). *Moral maturity: Measuring the development of sociomoral reflection.* Hillsdale, NJ: Erlbaum.

Gibson, Eleanor Jack. (1969). *Principles of perceptual learning and development.* New York: Appleton-Century-Crofts.

Gibson, Eleanor Jack. (1988). Levels of description and constraints on perceptual development. In Albert Yonas (Ed.), *Perceptual development in infancy.* Mahwah, NJ: Erlbaum.

Gibson, Eleanor Jack. (1997). An ecological psychologist's prolegomena for perceptual development: A functional approach. In Cathy Dent-Read & Patricia Zukow-Goldring (Eds.), *Evolving explanations of development: Ecological approaches to organism-environment systems.* Washington, DC: American Psychological Association.

Gibson, Eleanor Jack, & Walk, Richard D. (1960). The visual cliff. *Scientific American, 202,* 64–72.

Gibson, Eleanor Jack, & Walker, Arlene S. (1984). Development of knowledge of visual-tactile affordances of substance. *Child Development, 55,* 453–460.

Gibson, James J. (1979). *The ecological approach to visual perception.* Boston: Houghton Mifflin.

Gibson-Cline, Janice. (Ed.). (1996). *Adolescence: From crisis to coping.* London: Routledge.

Gibson-Cline, Janice. (Ed.). (2000). *Youth and coping in twelve nations.* London: Routledge.

Gillham, Jane E., Carter, Alice S., Volkmar, Fred R., & Sparrow, Sara. (2000). Toward a developmental operational definition of autism. *Journal of Autism and Developmental Disorders, 30,* 269–278.

Gilliam, Franklin D., & Bales, Susan Nall. (2001). Strategic frame analysis: Reframing America's youth. *Social Policy Report, 15*(3), 1–14.

Gilligan, Carol. (1982). *In a different voice: Psychological theory and women's development.* Cambridge, MA: Harvard University Press.

Gilligan, Carol, Murphy, John M., & Tappan, Mark B. (1990). Moral development beyond adolescence. In Charles N. Alexander & Ellen J. Langer (Eds.), *Higher stages of human development.* New York: Oxford University Press.

Ginsburg, Herbert P., Klein, Alice, & Starkey, Prentice. (1998). The development of children's mathematical thinking: Connecting research with practice. In William Damon (Series Ed.), Irving E. Sigel, & K. Ann Renninger (Vol. Eds.), *Handbook of child psychology:* Vol. 4. *Child psychology in practice* (5th ed., pp. 401–476). New York: Wiley.

Girouard, Pascale C., Baillargeon, Raymond H., Tremblay, Richard E., Glorieux, Jacqueline, Lefebvre, Fred, & Robaey, P. (1998). Developmental pathways lending to externalizing behaviors in 5 year olds born before 29 weeks of gestation. *Journal of Developmental & Behavioral Pediatrics, 19,* 244–253.

Glasgow, Kristin L., Dornbusch, Sanford M., Troyer, Lisa, Steinberg, Laurence, & Ritter, Philip L. (1997). Parenting styles, adolescents' attributions, and educational outcomes in nine heterogeneous high schools. *Child Development, 68,* 507–529.

Glauber, James H., Farber, Harold J., & Homer, Charles S. (2001). Asthma clinical pathways: Toward what end? *Pediatrics, 107,* 590–592.

Glick, Jennifer E., & Van Hook, Jennifer. (2002). Parents' coresidence with adult children: Can immigration explain racial and ethnic variation? *Journal of Marriage and the Family, 64,* 240–253.

Glidden, Laraine Masters. (2000). Adopting children with developmental disabilities: A long-term perspective. *Family Relations, 49,* 397–405.

Goetzel, Laura, & D'Alton, Mary. (2001). Prenatal diagnosis. In Frank W. Ling & Patrick Duff (Eds), *Obstetrics and gynecology: Principles for practice.* New York: McGraw Hill.

Gogate, Lakshmi J., Bahrick, Lorraine E., & Watson, Jilayne D. (2000). A study of multimodal motherese: The role of temporal synchrony between verbal labels and gestures. *Child Development, 71,* 878–894.

Gold, Rachel Benson, & Nash, Elizabeth. (2001). State-level policies on sexuality, STD education. *The Guttmacher Report on Public Policy, 4*(4), 4–7.

Goldberg, Melissa C., Maurer, Daphne, & Lewis, Terri L. (2001). Developmental changes in attention: The effects of endogenous cueing and of distracters. *Developmental Science, 4,* 209–219.

Goldberg, Susan, & Divitto, Barbara. (1995). Parenting children from preterm. In Marc H. Bornstein (Ed.), *Handbook of parenting: Children and parenting.* Mahwah, NJ: Erlbaum.

Goldberg, Susan, Muir, Roy, & Kerr, John. (Eds.). (1995). *Attachment theory: social, developmental, and clinical perspectives.* Hillsdale, NJ: Analytic Press.

Goldberg-Reitman, Jill. (1992). Young girls' conception of their mother's role: A neostructural analysis. In Robbie Case (Ed.), *The mind's staircase: Exploring the conceptual underpinning of children's thought and knowledge.* Mahwah, NJ: Erlbaum.

Golden, Michael H. N. (1996). The effect of early nutrition on later growth. In C.J.K. Henry & S.J. Uliajaszel (Eds.), *Long-term consequences of early environment: Growth, development and the lifespan developmental perspective.* Cambridge, England: Cambridge University Press.

Goldenberg, Robert L., Iams, Jay D., Mercer, Brian M., Meis, Paul J., Moawad, Atef H., Copper, Rachel L., et al. (1998). The preterm prediction study: The value of new vs. standard risk factors in predicting early and all spontaneous preterm births. *American Journal of Public Health, 88,* 233–238.

Goldfield, Eugene C. (1995). *Emergent forms: Origins and early development of human action and perception.* New York: Oxford University Press.

Goldman, Herbert I. (2001). Parental reports of 'MAMA' sounds in infants: An exploratory study. *Journal of Child Language, 28*(2), 497–506.

Goldsmith, H. Hill, Gottesman, Irving I., & Lemery, Kathryn S. (1997). Epigenetic approaches to developmental psychopathology. *Development and Psychopathology, 9,* 365–387.

Goleman, Daniel. (1998). *Building emotional intelligence.* APA Convention, San Francisco.

Golombok, Susan, MacCallum, Fiona, & Goodman, Emma. (2001). The "test-tube" generation: Parent-child relationships and the psychological well-being of in vitro fertilization children at adolescence. *Child Development, 72,* 599–624.

Golombok, Susan, & Tasker, Fiona. (1996). Do parents influence the sexual orientation of their children? Findings from a longitudinal study of lesbian families. *Developmental Psychology, 32,* 3–11.

Golub, Sharon. (1992). *Periods: From menarche to menopause.* Newbury Park, CA: Sage.

Goodman, Alan H. (2000). Why genes don't count (for racial differences in health). *American Journal of Public Health, 90,* 1699–1702.

Goodman, Gail S., Rudy, Leslie, Bottoms, Bette L., & Aman, Christine. (1990). Children's concerns and memory: Issues of ecological validity in the study of children's eyewitness testimony. In Robyn Fivush & Judith A. Hudson (Eds.), *Knowing and remembering in young children.* Cambridge, England: Cambridge University Press.

Goodman, Sherryl H., & Gotlib, Ian H. (1999). Risk for psychopathology in the children of depressed mothers: A developmental risk model for understanding mechanisms of transmission. *Psychological Review, 106,* 458–490.

Goodman, Sherryl H., & Gotlib, Ian H. (2002). Transmission of risk to children of depressed parent: Integration and conclusions. In Sherryl H. Goodman & Ian H. Gotlib (Eds.), *Children of depressed parents: Mechanisms of risk and implications for treatments.* Washington, DC: American Psychological Association.

Goodnow, Jacqueline J. (1997). Parenting and the transmission and internalization of values: From social-cultural perspectives to within-family analyses. In Joan E. Grusec & Leon Kuczynski (Eds.), *Parenting and children's internalization of values: A handbook of contemporary theory.* New York: Wiley.

Goodwin, Marjorie H. (1990). *He-said-she-said: Talk as social organization among black children.* Bloomington: Indiana University Press.

Gopnik, Alison. (2001). Theories, language, and culture: Whorf without wincing. In Melissa Bowerman & Stephen C. Levinson (Eds.), *Language acquisition and conceptual development* (pp. 19–44). Cambridge, England: Cambridge University Press.

Gordon, Debra Ellen. (1990). Formal operational thinking: The role of cognitive-developmental processes in adolescent decision-making about pregnancy and contraception. *American Journal of Orthopsychiatry, 60,* 346–356.

Gordon, Richard A. (2000). *Eating disorders: Anatomy of a social epidemic* (2nd ed.). Oxford, England: Blackwell.

Gorenstein, Ethan E., & Comer, Ronald J. (2002). *Case studies in abnormal psychology.* New York: Worth Publishers.

Gottlieb, Alma. (2000). Luring your child into this life: A Beng path for infant care. In Judy DeLoache & Alma Gottlieb (Eds.). *A world of babies.* Cambridge, England: Cambridge University Press.

Gottlieb, Gilbert, Wahlsten, Douglas, & Lickliter, Robert. (1998). The significance of biology for human development: A developmental psychobiological systems view. In William Damon (Series Ed.) & Richard M. Lerner (Vol. Ed.), *Handbook of child psychology*: Vol. 1. *Theoretical models of human development* (5th ed., pp. 233–274). New York: Wiley.

Gould, Stephen J. (1999). *Rocks of ages: Science and religion in the fullness of life* (Library of contemporary thought). New York: Ballantine Books.

Graber, Julia A., Brooks-Gunn, Jeanne, Paikoff, Roberta L., & Warren, Michelle P. (1994). Prediction of eating problems: An 8-year study of adolescent girls. *Developmental Psychology, 30,* 823–834.

Graham, Sandra, & Juvonen, Jaana. (1998). Self-blame and peer victimization in middle school: An attributional analysis. *Developmental Psychology, 34,* 587–599.

Grandin, Temple. (1996). *Thinking in pictures: And other reports from my life with autism.* New York: Vintage.

Grantham-McGregor, Sally, Powell, Christine, Walker, Susan, Chang, Susan, & Fletcher, Patricia. (1994). The long-term follow up of severely malnourished children who participated in an intervention program. *Child Development, 65,* 428–439.

Green, Jonathan, Gilchrist, Anne, Burton, Di, & Cox, Anthony. (2000). Social and psychiatric functioning in adolescents with Asperger syndrome compared with conduct disorders. *Journal of Autism and Developmental Disorders, 30,* 279–293.

Green, Michael F. (2001). Teratology. In Frank W. Ling & Patrick Duff (Eds.), *Obstetrics and gynecology: Principles for practice.* New York: McGraw Hill.

Greenberger, Ellen, & Chen, Chuansheng. (1996). Perceived family relationships and depressed mood in early and late adolescence: A comparison of European and Asian Americans. *Developmental Psychology, 32,* 707–716.

Greenberger, Ellen, & Steinberg, Laurence. (1986). *When teenagers work.* New York: Basic Books.

Greene, Sheila. (1997). Child development: Old themes and new directions. In Ray Fuller, Patricia Noonan Walsh, & Patrick McGinley (Eds.), *A century of psychology* (pp. 250–268). London: Routledge.

Greenfield, Thomas K., Midanik, Lorraine T., & Rogers, John D. (2000). A k10-year national trend study of alcohol consumption, 1984–1995: Is the period of declining drinking over. *American Journal of Public Health, 90,* 47–52.

Greenough, William T. (1993). Brain adaptation to experience: An update. In Mark H. Johnson (Ed.), *Brain development and cognition* (pp. 319–322). Oxford, England: Blackwell.

Greenough, William T., Black, James E., & Wallace, Christopher S. (1987). Experience and brain development. *Child Development, 58,* 539–559.

Greenough, William T., & Volkmar, Fred R. (1973). Pattern of dendritic branching in occipital cortex of rats reared in complex environments. *Experimental Neurology, 40,* 491–504.

Greydanus, Donald Everett. (1997a). Disorders of the skin. In Adele Dellenbaugh Hofmann & Donald Everett Greydanus (Eds.), *Adolescent medicine* (3rd ed.). Stamford, CT: Appleton and Lange.

Greydanus, Donald Everett. (1997b). Neurological disorders. In Adele Dellenbaugh Hofmann & Donald Everett Greydanus (Eds.), *Adolescent medicine* (3rd ed.). Stamford, CT: Appleton and Lange.

Griffin, Kenneth E., Scheier, Lawrence M., Botvin, Gilbert J., & Diaz, Tracy. (2001). Protective role of personal competence skill in adolescent substance use: Psychological well-being. *Psychology of Addictive Behaviors, 15,* 194–203.

Grifo, James A., Tang, Y.X., Munné, S., Alikani, M., Cohen, J., & Rosenwaks, Z. (1994). Healthy deliveries from biopsied human embryos. *Human Reproduction, 9,* 912–916.

Grilo, C.M., & Pogue-Geile, M. F. (1991). The nature of environmental influences on weight and obesity: A behavior genetic analysis. *Psychological Bulletin, 10,* 520–537.

Grolnick, Wendy S., Deci, Edward L., & Ryan, Richard M. (1997). Internalization within the family: The self-determination theory perspective. In Joan E. Grusec &

Leon Kuczynski (Eds.), *Parenting and children's internalization of values: A handbook of contemporary theory.* New York: Wiley.

Grossman, K., Thane, K., & Grossman, K.E. (1981). Maternal tactile contact of the newborn after various postpartum conditions of mother-infant contact. *Developmental Psychology, 17,* 159–169.

Grotevant, Harold D. (1998). Adolescent development in family contexts. In William Damon (Series Ed.) & Nancy Eisenberg (Vol. Ed.), *Handbook of child psychology:* Vol. 3. *Social, emotional, and personality development* (5th ed., pp. 1097–1149). New York: Wiley.

Grotevant, Harold D., & Kohler, Julie K. (1999). Adoptive families. In Michael E. Lamb (Ed.), *Parenting and child development in "nontraditional" families* (pp. 161–190). Mahwah, NJ: Erlbaum.

Groze, Victor, & Ileana, Daniela. (1996). A follow-up study of adopted children from Romania. *Child and Adolescent Social Work Journal, 13,* 541–565.

Gruber, Jonathan. (2001). Introduction. In Jonathan Gruber (Ed.), *Risky behavior among youth: An economic analysis* (pp. 1–42). Chicago: The University of Chicago Press.

Guberman, Steven R. (1996). The development of everyday mathematics in Brazilian children with limited formal education. *Child Development, 67,* 1609–1623.

Gullone, Eleonora, Moore, Susan, Moss, Simon, & Boyd, Candace. (2000). The adolescent risk-taking questionnaire. *Journal of Adolescent Research, 15,* 231–250.

Gunnar, Megan R. (2000). Early adversity and the development of stress reactivity and regulation. In Charles A. Nelson (Ed.), *The Minnesota symposia on child psychology: Vol. 31. The effects of early adversity on neurobehavioral development.* Mahwah, NJ: Erlbaum.

Gunnar, Megan R., Morison, Sara J., Chisholm, Kim, & Schuder, Michelle. (2001). Salivary cortisol levels in children adopted from Romanian orphanages. *Development and Psychopathology, 13,* 611–628.

Gunnar, Megan R., & Vasquez, Delia M. (2001). Low cortisol and a flattening of expected daytime rhythm: Potential indices of risk in human development. *Development and Psychopatholoy, 13,* 515–538.

Habermas, Tilmann, & Bluck, Susan. (2000). Getting a life: The emergence of the

life story in adolescence. *Psychological Bulletin, 126,* 748–769.

Hack, Maureen, Klein, Nancy, & Taylor, H. Gerry. (1995). Long-term developmental outcomes of low-birthweight infants. *The Future of Children: Low Birth Weight, 5,* 176–196.

Hacker, Karen A., Amare, Yared, Strunk, Nancy, & Horst, Leslie. (2000). Listening to youth: Teen perspectives on pregnancy prevention. *Journal of Adolescent Health, 26,* 279–288.

Haden, Catherine A., Ornstein, Peter A., Eckerman, Carol O., & Didow, Sharon M. (2001). Mother-child conversational interactions as events unfold: Linkages to subsequent remembering. *Child Development, 72,* 1016–1031.

Hagerman, Randi J. (1996). Biomedical advances in developmental psychology: The case of Fragile X syndrome. *Developmental Psychology, 32,* 416–424.

Haier, Richard J. (2001). PET studies of learning and individual differences. In James L. McClelland & Robert S. Siegler (Eds.), *Mechanisms of cognitive development: Behavioral and neural perspectives* (pp. 123–148). Mahwah, NJ: Erlbaum.

Haith, Marshall M., & Benson, Janette B. (1998). Infant cognition. In William Damon (Series Ed.), Deanna Kuhn, & Robert S. Siegler (Vol. Eds.), *Handbook of child psychology:* Vol. 2. *Cognition, perception, and language* (5th ed.). New York: Wiley.

Hala, Suzanne, & Chandler, Michael. (1996). The role of strategic planning in accessing false-belief understanding. *Child Development, 67,* 2948–2966.

Hall, G. Stanley. (1904). *Adolescence: Its psychology and its relation to physiology, anthropology, sociology, sex, crime, religion and education.* New York: Appleton.

Hallahan, Daniel P., & Keogh, Barbara K. (2001). Introduction. In Daniel P. Hallahan and Barbara K. Keogh (Eds.), *Research and global perspectives in learning disabilities* (pp. 1–24). Mahwah, NJ: Erlbaum.

Halliday, Michael A.K. (1979). One child's protolanguage. In Margaret Bullowa (Ed.), *Before speech: The beginning of interpersonal communication.* Cambridge, England: Cambridge University Press.

Halterman, Jill S., Aligne, C. Andrew, Auinger, Peggy, McBride, John T., & Szilagyi, Peter G. (2000). Inadequate therapy for asthma among children in the United States. *Pediatrics, 105,* 272–276.

Hamer, Dean H. (1999). Genetics and male sexual orientation. *Science, 285,* 803.

Hamer, Dean H., Hu, Stella, Magnuson, Victoria L., Hu, Nan, & Pattatucci, Angela M.L. (1993). A linkage between DNA markers on the X chromosome and male sexual orientation. *Science, 261,* 321–327.

Hamilton, Stephen A., & Wolfgang, Lempert. (1996). The impact of apprenticeship on youth: A prospective analysis. *Journal of Research on Adolescence, 6,* 427–455.

Hamm, Jill V. (2000). Do birds of a feather flock together? The variable bases for African American, Asian American, and European American adolescents' selection of similar friends. *Developmental Psychology, 36,* 209–219.

Hankin, Benjamin, & Abramson, Lyn Y. (2001). Development of gender differences in depression: An elaborated cognitive vulnerabilty-transactional stress theory. *Psychological Bulletin, 127,* 773–796.

Hansen, Karen Kirhofer. (1998). Folk remedies and child abuse: A review with emphasis on *caida de mullera* and its relationship to shaken baby syndrome. *Child Abuse & Neglect, 22,* 117–127.

Hanushek, E. A. (1999). The evidence on class size. In S. Mayer & P. Peterson (Eds.), *Earning and learning: How schools matter* (pp. 131–168). Washington, DC: Brookings.

Hardy, Janet B., Astone, Nan M., Brooks-Gunn, Jeanne, Shapiro, Sam, & Miller, Therese L. (1998). Like mother, like child: Intergenerational patterns of age at first birth and associations with childhood and adolescent characteristics and adult outcomes in the second generation. *Developmental Psychology, 34,* 1220–1232.

Hariri, Ahmed R., Mattay, Venkata S., Tessitore, Alessandro, Kolachana, Bhaskar, Fera, Francesco, Goldman, David, Egan, Michael F., & Weinberger, Daniel R. (2002). Serotonin transporter genetic variation and the response of the human amygdala. *Science, 297,* 400–403.

Harlow, Clara Mears (Ed.). (1986). *From learning to love: The selected papers of H.F. Harlow.* New York: Praeger.

Harlow, Harry F. (1958). The nature of love. *American Psychology, 13,* 673–685.

Harnack, Lisa, Stang, Jamie, & Story, Mary. (1999). Soft drink consumption among US children and adolescents: Nutritional consequences. *Journal of the American Dietetic Association, 99,* 436–441.

Harris, Judith Rich. (1998). *The nurture assumption: Why children turn out the way they do.* New York: Free Press.

Harris, Judith Rich. (2002). Beyond the nurture assumption: Testing hypotheses about the child's environment. In John G. Borkowski, Sharon Landesman Ramey, & Marie Bristol-Power (Eds.), *Parenting and the child's world: Influences on academic, intellectual and social-emotional development.* Mahwah, NJ: Erlbaum.

Harrison, Algea O., Wilson, Melvin N., Pine, Charles J., Chan, Samuel Q., & Buriel, Raymond. (1990). Family ecologies of ethnic minority children. *Child Development, 61,* 347–362.

Hart, Betty, & Risley, Todd R. (1995). *Meaningful differences in the everyday experiences of young American children.* Baltimore: Brookes.

Hart, Carole L., Smith, George Davey, Hole, David J., & Hawthorne, Victor M. (1999). Alcohol consumption and mortality from all causes, coronary heart disease, and stroke: Results from a prospective cohort study of Scottish men with 21 years of follow up. *British Medical Journal, 318,* 1725–1729.

Hart, Sybil, Field, Tiffany, & Nearing, Graciela. (1999). Depressed mothers' neonates improve following the MABI and a Brazelton demonstration. *Journal of Pediatric Psychology, 23,* 351–356.

Harter, Susan. (1996). Developmental changes in self-understanding. In Arnold J. Sameroff & Marshall M. Haith (Eds.), *The five to seven year shift: The age of reason and responsibility.* Chicago: The University of Chicago Press.

Harter, Susan. (1998). The development of self-representations. In William Damon (Ed.), *Handbook of child psychology: Vol. 3. Social, emotional and personality development* (5th ed., pp. 553–618). New York: Wiley.

Harter, Susan. (1999). *The construction of the self: A developmental perspective.* New York: Guilford Press.

Harter, Susan, Marold, Donna B., Whitesell, Nancy R., & Cobbs, Gabrielle.

(1996). A model of the effects of perceived parent and peer support on adolescent false self behavior. *Child Development, 67,* 360–374.

Harter, Susan, Waters, P., & Whitesell, Nancy R. (1997). Lack of voice as a manifestation of false self behavior: The school setting as a stage upon which the drama of authenticity is enacted. *Educational Psychologist, 32,* 153–173.

Hartl, Daniel L., & Jones, Elizabeth W. (1999). *Essential genetics* (2nd ed.). Sudbury, MA: Jones & Bartlett.

Hartman, Donald P., & George, Thomas P. (1999). Design, measurement, and analysis in developmental research. In Mark H. Bornstein & Michael E. Lamb (Eds.), *Developmental psychology: An advanced textbook* (4th ed.). Mahwah, NJ: Erlbaum.

Hartup, Willard W. (1996). The company they keep: Friendships and their developmental significance. *Child Development, 67,* 1–13.

Hartup, Willard W., & Stevens, Nan. (1999). Friendship and adaptation across the life span. *Current directions in psychological science, 8,* 76–79.

Haselager, Gerbert J. T., Cillessen, Antonius H. N., Van Lieshout, Cornelius F. M., Riksen-Walraven, J. Marianne A., & Hartup, Willard W. (2002). Heterogeneity among peer-rejected boys across middle childhood: Developmental pathways of social behavior. *Developmental Psychology, 38,* 446–456.

Hashima, Patricia, & Finkelhor, David. (1997). *Violent victimization of youth versus adults in the National Crime Victimization Survey.* Paper accepted for presentation at the Fifth International Family Violence Research Conference, Durham, NH.

Haskins, Ron. (1989). Beyond metaphor: The efficacy of early childhood education. *American Psychologist, 44,* 274–282.

Hassold, Terry J., & Patterson, David (1999). *Down syndrome: A promising future together.* New York: Wiley.

Haugaard, Jeffrey J. (2000). The challenge of defining child sexual abuse. *American Psychologist, 55,* 1036–1039.

Hawkins, J. D., Catalono, R. F., Kosternam, R., Abbott, R., & Hill, K. G. (1999). Preventing adolescent health-risk behaviors by strengthening protection during childhood. *Archives of Pediatrics and Adolescent Medicine, 153,* 226–234.

Hay, Dale F., Pawlby, Susan, Sharp, Deborah, Asten, Paul, Mills, Alice, & Kumar, R. (2001). Intellectual problems shown by 11-year-old children whose mothers had postnatal depression. *Journal of Child Psychology & Psychiatry & Related Disciplines, 42,* 871–889.

Heath, Andrew C., Bucholz, Kathleen K., Madden, Pamela A.F., Dinwiddie, Stephen H., Slutske, Wendy S., Bierut, Laura J., et al. (1997). Genetic and environmental contributions to alcohol dependence risk in a national twin sample: Consistency of findings in women and men. *Psychological Medicine, 27,* 1381–1396.

Heimann, Mikael, & Meltzoff, Andrew N. (1996). Deferred imitation in 9- and 14-month-old infants: A longitudinal study of a Swedish sample. *British Journal of Developmental Psychology, 14,* 55–64.

Held, Richard. (1995). Binocular vision. In P.D. Gluckman & M.A. Heymann (Eds.), *Developmental physiology: A pediatric perspective* (2nd ed.). London: Arnold.

Hellerstedt, Wendy L., Himes, John H., Story, Mary, Alton, Irene R., & Edwards, Laura E. (1997). The effects of cigarette smoking and gestational weight change on birth outcomes in obese and normal-weight women. *American Journal of Public Health, 87,* 591–596.

Helmuth, Laura. (2001). Where the brain tells a face from a place. *Science, 292,* 196–198.

Helwig, Charles C. (1995). Adolescents' and young adults' conceptions of civil liberties: Freedom of speech and religion. *Child Development, 66,* 152–166.

Helwig, Charles C., & Jasiobedzka, Urszua. (2001). The relation between law and morality: Children's reasoning about socially beneficial and unjust laws. *Child Development, 72,* 1382–1393.

Henry, Bill, Caspi, Avshalom, Moffitt, Terrie E., & Harrington, HonaLee. (1999). Staying in school protects boys with poor self-regulation in childhood from later crime: A longitudinal study. *International Journal of Behavioral Development, 23,* 1049–1073.

Henry, C. Jeya K. (1996). Early environmental and later nutritional needs. In C. Jeya K. Henry & S. J. Uliajaszel (Eds.), *Long-term consequences of early environment: Growth, development and the lifespan developmental perspective.* Cambridge, England: Cambridge University Press.

Herbert, Jane, & Hayne, Harlene. (2000). Memory retrieval by 18–30 month-olds: Age-related changes in representational flexibility. *Developmental Psychology, 36,* 473–484.

Herman-Giddens, Marcia E., Wang, Lily, & Koch, Gary. (2001). Secondary sexual characteristics in boys: Estimates from the national health and nutrition examination survey III, 1988–1994. *Archives of Pediatrics and Adolescent Medicine, 155,* 1022–1028.

Hernandez, Donald J., & Charney, Evan. (Eds.). (1998). *From generation to generation: The health and well-being of children in immigrant families.* Washington, DC: National Academy Press.

Hernandez, J. (1995). The concurrence of eating disorders with histories of child abuse among adolescents. *Journal of Child Sexual Abuse, 4,* 73–85.

Hetherington, E. Mavis, Bridges, Margaret, & Insabella, Glendessa M. (1998). What matters? What does not? Five perspectives on the association between marital transitions and children's adjustment. *American Psychologist, 53,* 167–184.

Hetherington, E. Mavis, & Kelly, John. (2002). *For better or for worse: Divorce reconsidered.* New York: Norton.

Hetherington, E. Mavis, & Stanley-Hagan, Margaret. (1999). Divorce and the adjustment of children: A risk and resiliency perspective. *The Journal of Child Psychology and Psychiatry, 40,* 129–140.

Heyman, Bob, & Henriksen, Mette. (2001). *Risk, age, and pregnancy.* New York: Palgrave.

Hill, Hope M., Soriano, Fernando I., Chen, S. Andrew, & LaFromboise, Teresa D. (1994). Sociocultural factors in the etiology and prevention of violence among ethnic minority youth. In Leonard D. Eron, Jacquelyn H. Gentry, & Peggy Schlegel (Eds.), *Reason to hope: A psychosocial perspective on violence and youth.* Washington, DC: American Psychological Association.

Hinde, Robert A. (Ed.). (1983). *Primate social relationships.* Oxford, England: Blackwell.

Hinde, Robert A. (1995). Foreward. In Marc H. Bornstein (Ed.), *Handbook of parenting: Vol. 4. Applied and practical parenting.* Mahwah, NJ: Erlbaum.

Hines, Marc. (1993). Hormonal and neural correlates of sex-typed behavioral development in human beings. In Marc Haug, Richard Whalen, Claude Aron, & Kathie Olsen (Eds.), *The development of sex differences and similarities in behavior.* Boston: Kluwer.

Hirsch, E. Donald, Jr. (2001, May 2). The latest dismal NAEP scores. *Education Week, 20*(33), 41, 60.

Hitchens, Christopher. (1998). Goodbye to all that: Why Americans are not taught history. *Harper's, 297* (1782), 37–47.

Hobson, R. Peter. (2000). The grounding of symbols: A social-developmental account. In Peter Mitchell & Kevin John Riggs (Eds.), *Children's reasoning and the mind* (pp. 11–35). Hove, England: The Psychology Press.

Hodder, Harbour Fraser. (1997). The new fertility: The promise—and perils—of human reproductive technologies. *Harvard Magazine,* 54–64, 97–99.

Hodges, Ernest V.E., Boivin, Michel, Vitaro, Frank, & Bukowski, William M. (1999). The power of friendship: Protection. *Developmental Psychology, 35,* 258–268.

Hofer, Myron A. (1995). Hidden regulators: Implications for a new understanding of attachment, separation and loss. In Susan Goldberg, Roy Muir, & John Kerr (Eds.), *Attachment theory: Social, developmental and clinical perspectives.* Hillsdale, NJ: The Analytic Press.

Hofer, Myron A., & Sullivan, Regina M. (2001). Toward a neurobiology of attachment. In Charles A. Nelson & Monica Luciana (Eds.), *Handbook of developmental neuroscience* (pp. 149–158). Cambridge, MA: MIT Press.

Hoffman, Martin L. (2001). Toward a comprehensive, empathy-based theory of prosocial moral development. In Arthur C. Bohart & Deborah J. Stipek (Eds.). *Constructive and destructive behavior: Implications for family, school and society* (pp. 61–86). Washington, DC: American Psychological Society.

Hofman, Adele Dellenbaugh. (1997). Adolescent growth and development. In Adele Dellenbaugh Hofmann & Donald Everett Greydanus (Eds.), *Adolescent medicine* (3rd ed.). Stamford, CT: Appleton & Lange.

Hogan, Dennis P., Sun, Rongjun, & Cornwell, Gretchen T. (2000). Sexual and fertility behaviors of American females age 15–19 years: 1985, 1990, and 1995. *American Journal of Public Health, 90,* 1421–1425.

Holden, Constance. (2000). Asia stays on top, U.S. in middle in new global rankings. *Science, 290,* 1866.

Hollich, George J., Hirsh-Pasek, Kathy & Golinkoff, Roberta Michnick. (2000). Breaking the language barrier: An emergentist coalition model for the origins of word learning. *Monographs of the Society for Research in Child Development, 65* (3, Serial No. 262).

Holloman, Holly A., & Scott, Keith G. (1998). Influence of birth weight on educational outcomes at age 9: The Miami site of the infant health and development program. *Journal of Developmental and Behavioral Pediatrics, 19,* 404–410.

Holmbeck, Grayson N., & O'Donnell, Kim. (1991). Discrepancies between perceptions of decision making and behavioral autonomy. In R.L. Paikoff (Ed.), *New directions for child development: No. 51. Shared views in the family during adolescence.* San Francisco: Jossey-Bass.

Hoover, J.H., Oliver, R., & Hazler, R. J. (1992). Bullying: Perceptions of adolescent victims in the midwestern USA. *School Psychology International, 13,* 5–16.

Horan, P. F., Phillips, J., & Hagen, N. E. (1998). The meaning of abstinence for college students. *Journal of HIV/AIDS Prevention and Education for Adolescence and Children, 2,* 51–66.

Horgan, John. (1999). *The undiscovered mind.* New York: Free Press.

Horney, Karen. (1967). *Feminine psychology.* (Harold Kelman, Ed.). New York: Norton.

Horowitz, Frances Degen. (1994). John B. Watson's legacy: Learning and environment. In Ross D. Parke, Peter A. Ornstein, John J. Rieser, & Carolyn Zahn-Waxler (Eds.), *A century of developmental psychology.* Washington, DC: American Psychological Association.

Horowitz, Frances, & Paden, L. (1973). The effectiveness of environmental intervention programs. In Bettye M. Caldwell & Henry Noel Ricciuti (Eds.). *Review of child development research,* (Vol. 3). Chicago: University of Chicago Press.

Howard, Robert W. (1996). Asking nature the right questions. *Genetic, Social & General Psychology Monographs, 122,* 161–178.

Howe, Christine J. (1998). *Conceptual structure in childhood and adolescence.* London: Routledge.

Howe, Mark L. (1997). Children's memory for traumatic experiences. *Learning and Individual Differences, 9,* 153–174.

Hsu, Hui-Chin, Fogal, Alan, & Cooper, Rebecca B. (2000). Infant vocal development during the first 6 months: Speech quality and melodic complexity. *Infant and Child Development, 9,* 1–16.

Hudson, Judith A. (1990). The emergence of autobiographical memory in mother-child conversation. In Robyn Fivush & Judith A. Hudson (Eds.), *Knowing and remembering in young children.* Cambridge, England: Cambridge University Press.

Huesmann, L. Rowell, & Reynolds, Meredith A. (2001). Cognitive processes and the development of aggression. In Arthur C. Bohart & Deborah J. Stipek (Eds.), *Constructive and destructive behavior: Implications for family, school & society* (pp. 249–270). Washington, DC: American Psychological Society.

Huffman, Lynne C., Bryan, Yvonne E., del Carmen, Rebecca, Pedersen, Frank A., Doussard-Roosevelt, Jane A., & Porges, Stephen W. (1998). Infant temperament and cardiac vagal tone: Assessments at twelve weeks of age. *Child Development, 69,* 624–635.

Hughes, Dana, & Simpson, Lisa. (1995). The role of social change in preventing low birth weight. *The Future of Children: Low Birth Weight, 5,* 87–102.

Hughes, Edward G., & Giacomi, Mita. (2001). Funding in vitro fertilization treatment for persistent subfertility: The pain and the politics. *Fertility and Sterility, 76,* 431–442.

Hughes, Jan N., Cavell, Timothy A., & Grossman, Pamela B. (1997). A positive view of self: Risk or protection for aggressive children? *Development and Psychopathology, 9,* 75–94.

Hulanicka, Barbara. (1999). Acceleration of menarcheal age of girls from dysfunctional families. *Journal of Reproductive and Infant Psychology, 17,* 119–132.

Hunt, Morton M. (1999). *The new know-nothings: The political foes of the scientific study of human nature.* New Brunswick, NJ: Transaction.

Hurst, Laurence D. (1997). Evolutionary theories of genomic imprinting. In Wolf Reik & Azim Surani (Eds.), *Genomic imprinting.* Oxford, England: IRL Press.

Huston, Aletha C., Wright, John C., Marquis, Janet, & Green, Samuel B. (1999). How two young children spend their time: Television and other activities. *Developmental Psychology, 35,* 912–925.

Huttenlocher, Janellen, Levine, Susan, & Vevea, Jack. (1998). Environmental input and cognitive growth: A study using time-period comparisons. *Child Development, 69,* 1012–1029.

Huttenlocher, Peter R., & Dabholkar, Arun S. (1997). Regional differences in synaptogenesis in human cerebral cortex. *The Journal of Comparative Neurology, 387,* 167–178.

Hwang, C. Philip, Lamb, Michael E., & Sigel, Irving E. (Eds.). (1996). *Images of childhood.* Mahwah, NJ: Erlbaum.

Hyde, Kenneth E. (1990). *Religion in childhood and adolescence: A comprehensive review of the research.* Birmingham, AL: Religious Education Press.

IFFS Surveillance 01. (2001). A survey of 39 nations. *Fertility and Sterility, 76,* Supplement 2, No. 5.

Ingersoll, Evan W., & Thoman, Evelyn B. (1999). Sleep/wake states of preterm infants: Stability, developmental change, diurnal variation, and relation with caregiving activity. *Child Development, 70,* 1–10.

Inhelder, Bärbel, & Piaget, Jean. (1958). *The growth of logical thinking from childhood to adolescence.* New York: Basic Books.

Inhelder, Bärbel, & Piaget, Jean. (1964). *The early growth of logic in the child.* New York: Harper and Row.

Isabella, Russell A., & Belsky, Jay. (1991). Interactional synchrony and the origins of infant-mother attachment: A replication study. *Child Development, 62,* 373–384.

Isolauri, Erika, Sutas, Yelda, Salo, Matti K., Isosomppi, Riitta, & Kaila, Minna. (1998). Elimination diet in cow's milk allergy: Risk for impaired growth in young children. *Journal of Pediatrics, 132,* 1004–1009.

Itoigawa, Naosuke, Minami, T., Kondo-Ikemura, K., Tachibana, H., et al. (1996). Parenting and family support in Japan for 6- to 8-year-old children weighing under 1000 grams at birth. *International Journal of Behavioral Development, 19,* 477–490.

Iverson, Jana M., Tender, Heather L., Lany, Jill, & Golden-Meadow, Susan. (2000). The relation between gesture and speech in congenitally blind and sighted children. *Journal of Nonverbal Behavior, 24,* 105–130.

Ivry, Richard, & Robertson, Lynn C. (1998). *The two sides of perception.* Cambridge, MA: MIT Press.

Jaccard, James & Dittus, Patricia J. (2000). Adolescent perceptions of maternal approval of birth control and sexual risk behavior. *American Journal of Public Health, 90,* 1426–1430.

Jaccard, James, Dittus, Patricia J., & Gordon, Vivian V. (1998). Parent-adolescent congruency in reports of adolescent sexual behavior and in communications about sexual behavior. *Child Development, 69,* 247–261.

Jaccard, James, Dittus, Patricia J., & Gordon, Vivian V. (2000). Parent teen communication about premarital sex. *Journal of Adolescent Research, 15,* 187–208.

Jackson, Yo, & Warren, Jared S. (2000). Appraisal, social support, and life events: Predicting outcome behavior in school-age children. *Child Development, 71,* 1441–1457.

Jacob's father. (1997). Jacob's story: A miracle of the heart. *Zero to Three, 17,* 59–64.

Jacobs, Edward A., Copperman, Stuart M., Joffe, Alain, Kulig, John, McDonald, Catherine A., Rogers, Peter D., & Shah, Rizwan Z. (2000). Fetal alcohol syndrome and alcohol related neurodevelopmental disorders. *Pediatrics, 106,* 358–361.

Jacobs, Janis E., Lanza, Stephanie, Osgood, D. Wayne, Eccles, Jacquelynne S., & Wigfield, Allan. (2002). Changes in children's self-competence and values: Gender and domain differences across grades one through twelve. *Child Development, 73,* 509–527.

Jacobson, Joseph L., & Jacobson, Sandra W. (1996). Methodological considerations in behavioral toxicology in infants and children. *Developmental Psychology, 32,* 390–403.

Jaffe, Joseph, Beebe, Beatrice, Feldstein, Stanley, Crown, Cynthia L., & Jasnow, Michael D. (2001). Rhythms of dialogue in infancy: Coordinated timing in development. *Monographs of the Society for Research in Child Development, 66*(2, Serial No. 265), vi-131.

Jaffee, Sara, Caspi, Avshalom, Moffitt, Terrie E., Belsky, Jay, & Silva, Phil. (2001). Why are children born to teen mothers at risk for adverse outcomes in young adulthood? Results from a 20-year longitudinal study. *Development and Psychopathology, 13,* 377–397.

Jahns, Lisa, Siega-Riz, Anna Maria, & Popkin, Barry M. (2001). The increasing prevalence of snacking among US children from 1977 to 1996. *Journal of Pediatrics, 138,* 493–498.

Jaswal, Vikram K., & Markman, Ellen M. (2001). Learning proper and common names in inferential versus ostensive contexts. *Child Development, 72,* 768–786.

Jenkins, Jennifer M., & Astington, Janet Wilde. (1996). Cognitive factors and family structure associated with theory of mind development in young children. *Developmental Psychology, 32,* 70–78.

Jensen, Peter S., & Hoagwood, Kimberly. (1997). The book of names: DSM-IV in context. *Development and Psychopathology, 9,* 231–249.

Jha, P., Nagelkerke, N. J. D., Ngugi, E. N., Rao, J. V. R. Prasada, Willbond, B., Moses, S., & Plummer, Frances A. (2001). Reducing HIV transmission in developing countries. *Science, 292,* 224–225.

Johnson, Byron R., Jan, Sung Joon, Li, Spencer De, & Larson, David. (2000). The "invisible institution" and Black youth crime: The church as an agency of local social control. *Journal of Youth and Adolescence, 29,* 479–498.

Johnson, C. Merle. (1991). Infant and toddler sleep: A telephone survey in one community. *Journal of Developmental and Behavioral Pediatrics, 12,* 108–114.

Johnson, Dana E. (2000). Medical and developmental sequelae of early childhood institutionalization in Eastern European adoptees. In Charles A. Nelson (Ed.), *The Minnesota symposia on child psychology: Vol. 31. The effects of early adversity on neurobehavioral development.* Mahwah, NJ: Erlbaum.

Johnson, David W., & Johnson, Roger T. (1994). *Learning together and alone: Cooperative, competitive, and individualistic learning* (4th ed.). Boston: Allyn & Bacon.

Johnson, Mark H. (1998). The neural basis of cognitive development. In William Damon (Series Ed.), Deanna Kuhn, & Robert S. Siegler (Vol. Eds.), *Handbook of child psychology: Vol. 2. Cognition, perception, and language* (5th ed., pp. 1–49). New York: Wiley.

Johnson, Mark H. (1999). Developmental neuroscience. In Marc H. Bornstein & Michael E. Lamb (Eds.), *Developmental psychology: An advanced textbook.* Mahwah, NJ: Erlbaum.

Johnson-Powell, Gloria, & Yamamoto, Joe. (1997). *Transcultural child development: Psychological assessment and treatment.* New York: Wiley.

Johnston, Lloyd D., O'Malley, Patrick M., & Bachman, Jerald G. (1998a). *Drug use by American young people begins to turn downward.* (University of Michigan News and Information Services Press Release, December, 1998). Ann Arbor: University of Michigan.

Johnston, Lloyd D., O'Malley, Patrick M., & Bachman, Jerald G. (1998b). *Monitoring the future study: Drug use among American teens shows some signs of leveling after a long rise.* (University of Michigan News and Information Services Press Release, December, 1998). Ann Arbor: University of Michigan.

Johnston, Lloyd D., O'Malley, Patrick M., & Bachman, Jerald G. (1998c). *Smoking among American teens declines some.* (University of Michigan News and Information Services Press Release, December, 1998). Ann Arbor: University of Michigan.

Johnston, Lloyd D., O'Malley, Patrick M., & Bachman, Jerald G. (2001). *Monitoring the future: National survey results on drug use, 1975–2000* (NIH Publication No. 01-4924). Bethesda, MD: National Institute of Drug Abuse.

Johnston, Lloyd D., O'Malley, Patrick M., & Bachman, Jerald G. (2002). *Monitoring the future: National survey results on drug use.* Bethesda, MD: National Institute of Drug Abuse.

Johnston, Timothy D., & Edwards, Laura. (2002). Genes, interactions, and the development of behavior. *Psychological Review, 109,* 26–34.

Joiner, Thomas E., Jr. (1999). The clustering and contagion of suicide. *Current Directions in Psychological Science, 8,* 89–92.

Jones, Elizabeth, & Reynolds, Gretchen. (1992). *The play's the thing: Teachers' roles in children's play.* New York: Teacher's College Press.

Jones, Howard W., & Schnorr, John A. (2001). Multiple pregnancies: A call for action. *Fertility and Sterility, 75,* 11–17.

Jones, Mary Cover. (1957). The later careers of boys who were early- or late-maturing. *Child Development, 28,* 113–128.

Jones, Mary Cover. (1965). Psychological correlates of somatic development. *Child Development, 36,* 899–911.

Jones, N. Burton. (1976). Rough-and-tumble play among nursery school children. In Jerome S. Bruner, Alison Jolly, & Kathy Sylva (Eds.), *Play.* New York: Basic Books.

Jones, Robin, Schlank, Anita, & Le Guin, Louis. (1999). Assessment of adolescent sex offenders. In Jon A. Shaw (Ed.) *Sexual aggression*. Washington, DC: America Psychiatric Press.

Joseph, Rhawn. (2000). Fetal brain behavior and cognitive development. *Developmental Review, 20*, 81–98.

Jusczyk, Peter W. (1997). *The discovery of spoken language*. Cambridge, MA.: MIT Press.

Kachur, S. Patrick, Potter, Lloyd B., James, Stephen P., & Powell, Kenneth E. (1995). *Suicide in the United States: 1980–1992* (Violence Surveillance Summary Series No. 1). Atlanta, GA: National Center for Injury Prevention and Control.

Kagan, Sharon Lynn, Moore, Evelyn, & Bredekamp, Sue. (1995). *Reconsidering children's early development and learning: Toward common views and vocabulary* (Report No. 95-03). Washington, DC: National Education Goals Panel.

Kagen, Jerome. (1994). *Galen's prophecy*. New York: Basic Books.

Kahana-Kalman, Ronit, & Walker-Andrews, Arlene S. (2001). The role of person familiarity in young infants' perception of emotional expressions. *Child Development, 72*, 352–369.

Kahn, Jeffrey P., Mastroianni, Anna C., & Sugarmen, Jeremy. (Eds.). (1998). *Beyond consent: Seeking justice in research*. New York: Oxford University Press.

Kandel, Denise B., & Davies, Mark. (1996). High school students who use crack and other drugs. *Archives of General Psychiatry, 53*, 71–80.

Kanner, Leo. (1943). Autistic disturbances of affective contact. *Nervous Child, 2*, 217–250.

Kaplan, Bonnie J., Crawford, Susan G., Dewey, Deborah M., & Fisher, Geoff C. (2000). The IQs of children with ADHD are normally distributed. *Journal of Learning Disabilities, 33*, 425–432.

Karatekin, Canan. (2001). Developmental disorders of attention. In Charles A. Nelson & Monica Luciana (Eds.), *Handbook of developmental neuroscience* (pp. 561–576). Cambridge, MA: MIT Press.

Karoly, Lynn A., Greenwood, Peter W., Everingham, Susan S., Houbé, Jill, Kilburn, M. Rebecca, Rydell, C. Peter, et al.

(1998). *Investing in our children: What we know and don't know about the costs and benefits of early childhood interventions*. Santa Monica, CA: RAND.

Karpov, Yuriy, & Haywood, H. Carl. (1998). Two ways to elaborate Vygotsky's concept of mediation: Implications for instruction. *American Psychologist, 53*, 27–36.

Kaufman, Alan S., & Lichtenberger, Elizabeth O. (2000). *Essentials of WISC-III and WPPSI-R Assessment*. New York: Wiley.

Kaufman, Joan, & Charney, Dennis. (2001). Effects of early stress on brain structure and function: Implications for understanding the relationship between child maltreatment and depression. *Development and Psychopathology, 13*, 431- 471.

Keil, Frank C., & Lockhart, Kristi L. (1999). Explanatory understanding in conceptual development. In Ellen Kofsky Scholnick, Katherin Nelson, Susan A. Gelman, & Patricia H. Miller (Eds.), *Conceptual development: Piaget's legacy* (pp. 103–130). Mahwah, NJ: Erlbaum.

Kelley, Sue A., Brownell, Celia A., & Campbell, Susan B. (2000) Mastery motivation and self-evaluative affect in toddlers: Longitudinal relations with maternal behavior. *Child Development, 71*, 1061–1071.

Kellogg, Rhoda. (1967). *The psychology of children's art*. New York: CRM Press/Random House.

Kelly, Karen. (1998). Working teenagers: Do after-school jobs hurt? *The Harvard Education Letter, 14*, 1–3.

Kempe, C. Henry, Silverman, Frederic N., Steele, Brandt F., Droege-Muller, P. W., & Silver, H. K. (1962). The battered-child syndrome. *Journal of the American Medical Association, 181*, 17–24.

Kerig, Patricia K., Fedorowicz, Anne E., Brown, Corina A., & Warren Michelle. (2002). Assessment and intervention for PTSD in children exposed to violence. In Robert A. Geffner, Peter G. Jaffe, and Marlies Sudermann (Eds.), *Children exposed to domestic violence: Current issues in research, intervention, prevention and policy development* (pp. 161–184). Binghamton, NY: Haworth.

Kerr, Margaret, Lambert, William W., & Bem, Daryl J. (1996). Life course sequelae of childhood shyness in Sweden: Comparison with the United States. *Developmental Psychology, 32*, 1100–1105.

Kessler, Seymour. (2000). *Psyche and helix: Psychological aspects of genetic counseling*. New York: Wiley.

Khaleque, Abdul, & Rohner, Ronald P. (2002). Perceived parental acceptance-rejection and psychological adjustment: A meta-analysis of cross cultural and intracultural studies. *Journal of Marriage and the Family, 64*, 54–64.

Kilbride, Howard, Castor, Cheri, Hoffman, Edward, & Fuger, Kathryn L. (2000). Thirty-six-month outcome of prenatal cocaine exposure for term or near-term infants: Impact of early case management. *Developmental and Behavioral Pediatrics, 21*, 19–26.

Killen, Melanie, & Stangor, Charles. (2001). Children's social reasoning about inclusion and exclusion in gender and race in race peer group contexts. *Child Development, 72*, 174–186.

Kim, Kenneth & Smith, Peter K. (1998). Retrospective survey of parental marital relations and child reproductive development. *International Journal of Behavioral Development, 22*, 729–751.

Kisilevsky, Barbara S., & Low, James A. (1998). Human fetal behavior: 100 years of study. *Developmental Review, 18*, 1–29.

Kitzinger, Sheila. (1989). *The complete book of pregnancy and childbirth*. New York: Knopf.

Klaczynski, Paul A. (2000). Motivated scientific reasoning biases, epistemological beliefs, and theory polarization: A two-process approach to adolescent cognition. *Child Development, 71*, 1347–1366.

Klaczynski, Paul A. (2001). Analytic and heuristic influences on adolescent reasoning and decision-making. *Child Development, 72*, 844–861.

Klaus, Marshall H., & Kennell, John H. (1976). *Maternal-infant bonding: The impact of early separation or loss on family development*. St. Louis, MO: Mosby.

Klein, Melanie. (1957). *Envy and gratitude*. New York: Basic Books.

Klepinger, Daniel H., Lundberg, Shelly, & Plotnick, Robert D. (1995). Adolescent fertility and the educational attainment of young women. *Family Practice Perspectives, 27*, 23–28.

Klesges, Robert. (1993). Effects of television on metabolic rate: Potential implications for childhood obesity. *Pediatrics, 91*, 281–286.

Klopfer, Peter. (1971). Mother love: What turns it on? *American Scientist, 49,* 404–407.

Kluckhohn, Clyde. (1949). *Mirror for man.* New York: McGraw-Hill.

Klug, William S., & Cummings, Michael R. (2000). *Genetics* (6th ed.). Upper Saddle River, NJ: Prentice Hall.

Knowles, Richard. (2001). *Solving problems in genetics.* New York: Springer.

Knox, David, Zusman, Marty E., McGinty, Kristen, & Gescheidler, Jennifer. (2001). Deception of parents during adolescence. *Adolescence, 36,* 611–614.

Kochanska, Grazyna. (1997). Multiple pathways to conscience for children with different temperaments: From toddlerhood to age 5. *Developmental Psychology, 33,* 228–240.

Kochanska, Grazyna. (2001). Emotional development in children with different attachment histories: The first three years. *Child Development, 72,* 474–490.

Kochanska, Grazyna, Coy, Katherine C., & Murray, Kathleen T. (2001). The development of self-regulation in the first four years of life. *Child Development, 72,* 1091–1111.

Kochanska, Grazyna, Murray, Kathleen, & Coy, Katherine C. (1997). Inhibitory control as a contributor to conscience in childhood: From toddler to early school age. *Child Development, 68,* 263–278.

Kochenderfer-Ladd, Becky, & Wardrop, James L. (2001). Chronicity and instability of children's peer victimization experiences as predictors of loneliness and social satisfaction trajectories. *Child Development, 72,* 134–151.

Koepke, Jean E., & Bigelow, Ann E. (1997). Observations of newborn suckling behavior. *Infant Behavior & Development, 20,* 93–98.

Kohlberg, Lawrence. (1963). Development of children's orientation towards a moral order (Part I). Sequencing in the development of moral thought. *Vita Humana, 6,* 11–36.

Kohlberg, Lawrence. (1981a). *Essays on moral development* (Vol. 1). New York: Harper & Row.

Kohlberg, Lawrence. (1981b). *The philosophy of moral development.* New York: Harper & Row.

Kohnstamm, Geldoph A., Halverson, Charles F., Havil, Valeri L., & Mervielde, Ivan. (1996). Parents' free descriptions of child characteristics: A cross cultural search for the developmental antecedents of the big five. In Sara Harkness & Charles M. Super (Eds.), *Parents' cultural belief systems: The origins, expressions, and consequences.* New York: Guilford Press.

Kools, Susan M. (1997). Adolescent identity development in foster care. *Family Relations, 46,* 263–271.

Koopman, Peter, Gubbay, John, Vivian, Nigel, Goodfellow, Peter, & Lovell-Badge, Robin. (1991). Male development of chromosomally female mice transgenic for Sry. *Nature, 351,* 117–122.

Korbin, Jill E., Coulton, Claudia J., Chard, Sarah, Platt-Houston, Candis, & Su, Marilyn. (1998). Impoverishment and child maltreatment in African American and European American neighborhoods. *Development and Psychopathology, 10,* 215–233.

Koren, Gideon, Nulman, Irena, Rovet, Joanne, Greenbaum, Rachel, Loebstein, Michal, & Einarson, Tom. (1998). Long-term neurodevelopmental risks in children exposed in utero to cocaine. The Toronto Adoption Study. *Annals of the New York Academy of Science, 846,* 306–313.

Kornhaber, Mindy, & Orfield, Gary. (2001). *Raising standards or raising barriers? Inequality and high-stakes testing in public education.* New York: Century Foundation Press.

Kovacs, Donna M., Parker, Jeffrey G., & Hoffman, Lois W. (1996). Behavioral affective, and social correlates of involvement in cross-sex friendship in elementary school. *Child Development, 67,* 2269–2286.

Kozol, Jonathan. (1991). *Savage inequalities.* New York: Crown.

Kraft, Joan Creech, & Willhite, Calvin C. (1997). Retinoids in abnormal and normal embryonic development. In Sam Kacew & George H. Lambert (Eds.), *Environmental toxicology and human development.* Washington DC: Taylor & Francis.

Kramer, Michael S., Goulet, Lise, Lydon, John, Séguin, Louise, McNamara, Helen, Dassa, Clément, et al. (2001). Socio-economic disparities in preterm birth: causal pathways and mechanisms. *Paediatric and Perinatal Epidemiology, 15* (supplement 2), 104–123.

Kroger, Jane. (1989). *Identity in adolescence: The balance between self and other.* London: Routledge.

Kroger, Jane. (2000). *Identity development: Adolescence through adulthood.* Thousand Oaks, CA: Sage.

Kromelow, Susan, Harding, Carol, & Touris, Margot. (1990). The role of the father in the development of stranger sociability during the second year. *American Journal of Orthopsychiatry, 6,* 521–530.

Kuhl, Patricia K. (1994). Speech perception. In F. Mimifie (Ed.), *Introduction to communication sciences and disorders* (pp. 77–148). San Diego, CA: Singular.

Kuhl, Patricia K., & Meltzoff, Andrew N. (1988). Speech as an intermodal object of perception. In A. Yonas (Ed.), *Minnesota symposia on child psychology: Vol. 20. Perceptual development in infancy.* Mahwah, NJ: Erlbaum.

Kuhn, Deanna. (2000). Theory of mind, metacognition, and reasoning: A life-span perspective. In Peter Mitchell & Kevin J. Riggs (Eds.), *Children's reasoning and the mind* (pp. 301–326). Hove, England: Psychology Press.

Kuller, Jeffrey A., Strauss, Robert A., & Cefalo, Robert C. (2001). Preconceptual and prenatal care. In Frank W. Ling & Patrick Duff (Eds.), *Obstetrics and gynecology: Principles for practice.* New York: McGraw Hill.

Kvalem, Ingela Lundin & Traeen, Benter. (2000). Self-efficacy scripts of love and intention to use condoms among Norwegian adolescents. *Journal of Youth and Adolescence, 29,* 337–352.

La Leche League International. (1997). *The womanly art of breastfeeding.* New York: Plume.

Ladd, Gary W. (1999). Peer relationships and social competence during early and middle childhood. *Annual Review of Psychology, 50,* 333–359.

Lagattuta, Kristin H., & Wellman, Henry M. (2001). Think about the past: Early knowledge about links between prior experiences, thinking and emotion. *Child Development, 72,* 82–102.

Lahey, Benjamin B., & Loeber, Rolf. (1994). Framework for a developmental model of oppositional defiant disorder and conduct disorder. In Donald K. Routh (Ed.), *Disruptive behavior disorders in childhood.* New York: Plenum Press.

Laible, Deborah J., & Thompson, Ross A. (1998). Attachment and emotional understanding in preschool children. *Developmental Psychology, 34,* 1038–1045.

Laird, Robert D., Jordan, Kristi Y., Dodge, Kenneth A., Pettit, Gregory S., & Bates,

John E. (2001). Peer rejection in childhood, involvement with antisocial peers in early adolescence, and the development of externalizing behavior problems. *Developmental and Psychopathology, 13,* 337–354.

Lamb, Michael E. (1982). Maternal employment and child development: A review. In Michael E. Lamb (Ed.), *Nontraditional families: Parenting and child development.* Mahwah, NJ: Erlbaum.

Lamb, Michael E. (1997). The development of father-infant relationships. In M.E. Lamb (Ed.), *The role of the father in child development.* New York: Wiley.

Lamb, Michael E. (1998). Nonparental care: Context, quality, correlates, and consequences. In William Damon (Series Ed.), Irving E. Sigel, & K. Ann Renninger (Vol. Eds.), *Handbook of child psychology:* Vol. 4. *Child psychology in practice* (5th ed., pp. 73–133). New York: Wiley.

Lamb, Michael E. (2000). Research on father involvement: An historical overview. In Elizabeth H. Peters, Gary W. Peterson, Suzanne K. Steinmetz, and Randal D. Day (Eds.), *Fatherhood: Research, interventions, and policies.* New York: Haworth.

Lamb, Michael E., Sternberg, Kathleen J., & Esplin, Phillip W. (2000). Effects of age and delay on the amount of information provided by alleged sex abuse victims in investigative interviews. *Child Development, 71,* 1586–1596.

Lambert, Wallace E., Genesee, Fred, Holobow, Naomi, & Chartrand, Louise. (1993). Bilingual education for majority English-speaking children. *European Journal of Psychology of Education, 8,* 3–22.

Landry, David J., Singh, Susheela, & Darroch, Jacqueline E. (2000). Sexuality education in fifth and sixth grades in U.S. public schools, 1999. *Family Planning Perspectives, 32,* 212–219.

Langer, Jonas M. (2001). The mosaic evolution of cognitive and linguistic ontogeny. In Melissa Bowerman & Stephen C. Levinson (Eds.), *Language acquisition and conceptual development* (pp. 19–44). Cambridge, England: Cambridge University Press.

Langer, Jonas M., Schlesinger, Matthew, Spinozzi, Giovanni, & Natale, Francesco. (1998). Developing classification in action: I. Human infants. *Human Evolution, 13,* 107–124.

Langkamp, Diane L., Kim, Young, & Pascoe, John M. (1998). Temperament of preterm infants at four months of age: Maternal ratings and perceptions. *Developmental and Behavioral Pediatrics, 19,* 391–396.

Lansford, Jennifer E., Cebello, Rosario, Abbey, Antonia, & Stewart, Abigail J. (2001). Does family structure matter? A comparison of adoptive, two-parent biological, single-mother, stepfather, and stepmother households. *Journal of Marriage and the Family, 63,* 840–851.

Lapsley, D. K. (1993). Toward an integrated theory of adolescent ego development: The "new look" at adolescent egocentrism. *American Journal of Orthopsychiatry, 63,* 562–571.

Largie, Shay, Field, Tiffany, Hernandez-Reif, Maria, Sanders, Christopher E., & Diego, Miguel. (2001). Employment during adolescence is associated with depression, inferior relationships, lower grades and smoking. *Adolescence, 36,* 395–401.

Larivee, Serge, Normandeau, Sylvie, & Parent, Sophie. (2000). The French connection: Some contributions of French-language research in the post-Piagetian era. *Child Development, 71,* 823–839.

Larner, Mary B., Stevenson, Carol S., & Behrman, Richard E. (1998). Protecting children from abuse and neglect: Analysis and recommendations. *Future Child, 8,* 4–22.

Larsen, William J. (1998). *Essentials of human embryology.* New York: Churchill-Livingstone.

Larson, David E. (Ed.). (1990). *Mayo Clinic family health book.* New York: Morrow.

Larson, Reed W. (2000). Toward a psychology of positive youth development. *American Psychologist, 55,* 170–183.

Larson, Reed W. (2001). Commentary. In Daniel R. Anderson, Aletha C. Huston, Kelly L. Schmitt, Deborah L. Linebarger, & John C. Wright (Eds.). Early childhood television viewing and adolescent behavior. *Monographs of the Society for Research in Child Development, 66*(Serial No. 264).

Larson, Reed W., & Gillman, Sally. (1999). Transmission of emotions in the daily interactions of single-mother families. *Journal of Marriage and the Family, 61,* 21–37.

Larson, Reed W., & Ham, Mark. (1993). Stress and "storm and stress" in early adolescence: The relationship of negative events with dysphoric affect. *Developmental Psychology, 29,* 130–140.

Law, James. (2000). Factors affecting language development in West African children: A pilot study using a qualitative methodology. *Child: Care, Health, and Development, 26,* 289–308.

Leach, Penelope. (1997). *Your baby & child: From birth to age 5.* New York: Knopf.

Leaper, C., & Anderson, K. J. (1997). Gender development and heterosexual romantic relationships during adolescence. In S. Shulman & William A. Collins (Eds.), *Romantic relationships during adolescence.* San Francisco: Jossey-Bass.

Leaper, Campbell, Anderson, Kristin J., & Sanders, Paul. (1998). Moderators of gender effects on parents' talk to their children: A meta-analysis. *Developmental Psychology, 34,* 3–27.

Lee, K. (2000). Crying patterns of Korean infants in institutions. *Child: Care, Health & Development, 26,* 217–228.

Leekam, Susan R., López, Beatriz, & Moore, Chris. (2000). Attention and joint attention in preschool children with autism. *Developmental Psychology, 36,* 261–273.

Leffert, Nancy, & Petersen, Anne C. (1995). Patterns of development during adolescence. In Michael Rutter & David J. Smith (Eds.), *Psychosocial disorders in young people: Time trends and their causes.* Chichester: Wiley.

Leifer, A.D., Leiderman, P.H., Barnett, C.R., & Williams, J.A. (1972). Effects of mother-infant separation on maternal attachment behavior. *Child Development, 43,* 1203–1218.

Lemery, Kathryn S., Goldsmith, H. Hill, Klinnert, Mary D., & Mrazel, David A. (1999). Developmental models of infant and childhood temperament. *Developmental Psychology, 35,* 189–204.

Lenneberg, Eric H. (1967). *Biological foundations of language.* New York: Wiley.

Leonard, Kenneth E. & Blane, Howard T. (Eds.). (1999). *Psychological theories of drinking and alcoholism* (2nd ed.). New York: Guilford Press.

Lerner, Harriet E. (1978). Adaptive and pathogenic aspects of sex-role stereotypes: Implications for parenting and psychotherapy. *American Journal of Psychiatry, 135,* 48–52.

Lerner, Janet. (2000). *Learning disabilities: Theories, diagnosis, and teaching strategies* (8th ed.). Boston: Houghton Mifflin.

Lerner, Richard M. (1998). Theories of human development: Contemporary perspectives. In William Damon (Series Ed.) & Richard M. Lerner (Vol. Ed.), *Handbook of child psychology:* Vol. 1. *Theoretical models of human development* (5th ed., pp. 1–24). New York: Wiley.

Levin, Jack. (1999, May 7). An effective response to teenage crime is possible and cities are showing the way. *The Chronicle of Higher Education, 35.*

LeVine, Robert A., Dixon, Suzanne, LeVine, Sarah, Richman, Amy, Leiderman, P. Herbert, Keeferk, Constance H. & Brazelton, Berry. (1994). *Child care and culture: Lessons from Africa.* New York: Cambridge University Press.

Levinson, David. (1989). Physical punishment of children and wife beating in cross-cultural perspective. *Child Abuse & Neglect, 5,* 193–195.

Lew, Adine R., Bremner, J. Gavin, & Lefkovitch, Leonard P. (2000). The development of relational landmark use in six- to twelve-month old infants in a spatial orientation task. *Child Development, 71,* 1179–1190.

Lewin, Tamar. (2002, March 18). In testing, one size may not fit all. *New York Times,* p. A-16.

Lewis, Lawrence B., Antone, Carol, & Johnson, Jacqueline S. (1999). Effects of prosodic stress and serial position on syllable omission in first words. *Developmental Psychology, 35,* 45–59.

Lewis, Marc D., & Granic, Isabela (Eds.). (2000). *Emotion, development and self-organization: Dynamic systems approaches and emotional development.* Cambridge, England: Cambridge University Press.

Lewis, Michael. (1997). *Altering fate.* New York: Guilford Press.

Lewis, Michael, & Brooks, J. (1978). Self-knowledge and emotional development. In Michael Lewis & L.A. Rosenblum (Eds.), *The development of affect.* New York: Plenum Press.

Lewis, Michael, Sullivan, Margaret W., Stanger, Catherine, & Weiss, Maya. (1989). Self development and self-conscious emotions. *Child Development, 60,* 146–156.

Lewit, Eugene M., & Kerrebrock, Nancy. (1998). Child indicators: Dental health. *The Future of Children: Protecting Children from Abuse and Neglect, 8,* 4–22.

Liebkind, Karmela, & Jasinskaja-Lahti, Inga. (2000). Acculturation and psychological well-being among immigrant adolescents in Finland: A comparative study of adolescents from different cultural backgrounds. *Journal of Adolescent Research, 15,* 446–469.

Lightfoot, Cynthia. (1997). *The culture of adolescent risk-taking.* New York: Guilford Press.

Lillard, Angeline. (1998). Ethno-psychologies: Cultural variations in theories of mind. *Psychological Bulletin, 123,* 3–32.

Lindsey, Elizabeth W. (2001). Foster family characteristics and behavioral and emotional problems of foster children: Practice implications for child welfare, family life education, and marriage and family therapy. *Family Relations, 50,* 19–22.

Linville, Patricia W., Fischer, Gregory W., & Fischoff, Baruch. (1993). AIDS risk perceptions and decision biases. In John B. Pryor & Glenn D. Reeder (Eds.). *The social psychology of HIV infection.,* Mahwah, NJ: Erlbaum.

Livson, Norman, & Peskin, Harvey. (1980). Perspectives on adolescence from longitudinal research. In Joseph Adelson (Ed.), *Handbook of adolescent psychology.* New York: Wiley.

Loeber, Rolf, & Farrington, David P. (2000). Young children who commit crimes: Epidemiology, developmental origins, risk factors, early interventions, and policy implications. *Development and Psychopathology, 12,* 737–762.

Loeber, Rolf, Drinkwater, Matthew, Yin, Yanming, Anderson, Stewart J., & Schmidt, L. C. (2000). Stability of family interaction from ages 6 to 18. *Journal of Abnormal Child Psychology, 28,* 353–369.

Loehlin, John C. (1992). *Genes and environment in personality development.* Newbury Park, CA: Sage.

Loovis, E. Michael, & Butterfield, Stephen A. (2000). Influence of age, sex, and balance in mature skipping by children in grades K-8. *Perceptual and Motor Skills, 90,* 974–978.

Lorenz, John M., Wooliever, Diane E., Jetton, James R., & Paneth, Nigel. (1998). A quantitative review of mortality and developmental disability in extremely premature newborns. *Archives of Pediatric & Adolescent Medicine, 152,* 425–435.

Lovett, Marsha. (2001). A collaborative convergence on studying reasoning processes: A case study in statistics. In Sharon M. Carver & David Klahr (Eds.), *Cognition and instruction: Twenty-five years of progress.* Mahwah, NJ: Erlbaum.

Lozoff, Betsy, Jimenez, Elias, Hagen, John, Mollen, Eileen, & Wolf, Abraham W. (2000). Poorer behavioral and developmental outcome more than 10 years after treatment for iron deficiency in infancy. *Pediatrics, 105,* E-5l.

Luria, Alexander R. (1976). *Cognitive development: Its cultural and social foundations.* Cambridge, MA: Harvard University Press.

Luthar, Suniya S., Cicchetti, Dante, & Becker, Bronwyn. (2000). The construct of resilience: A critical evaluation and guidelines for future work. *Child Development, 71,* 543–562.

Lutz, Donna J., & Sternberg, Robert J. (1999). Cognitive development. In Marc H. Bornstein & Micheal E. Lamb (Eds.), *Developmental psychology: An advanced textbook* (4th Ed.). Mahwah, NJ: Erlbaum.

Lyall, Sarah. (2002, March 24). For Europeans, love, yes; Marriage, maybe. *The New York Times,* pp. 1, 18.

Lynam, Donald R., Milich, Richard, Zimmerman, Rick, Novak, Scott P., Logan, Tamra Kinkner, Martin, Catherine, et al. (1999). Project DARE: No effects at 10-year follow up. *Journal of Consulting and Clinical Psychology, 67,* 590–593.

Lynch, Michael, & Cicchetti, Dante. (1998). An ecological-transactional analysis of children and contexts: The longitudinal interplay among child maltreatment, community violence, and children's symptomatology. *Development and Psychopathology, 10,* 235–258.

Lyons, Peter, & Rittner, Barbara. (1998). The construction of the crack babies phenomenon as a social problem. *American Journal of Orthopsychiatry, 68,* 313–320.

Lyons-Ruth, Karlen. (1996). Attachment relationships among children with aggressive behavior problems: The role of disorganized early attachment patterns. *Journal of Consulting and Clinical Psychology, 64,* 64–73.

Lyons-Ruth, Karlen, Bronfman, Elisa, & Parsons, Elizabeth. (1999). Maternal frightened, frightening, or atypical behaviors and disorganized infant attachment patterns. In Joan I. Vondra & Douglas Barnett (Eds.),

Atypical attachment in infancy and early childhood among children at developmental risk. *Monographs of the Society for Research in Child Development 64* (Serial No. 258), 25–44.

Maccoby, Eleanor E. (1998). *The two sexes: Growing up apart, coming together.* Cambridge, MA: Belknap Press of Harvard University Press.

Maccoby, Eleanor E. (2000). Parenting and its effects on children: On reading and misreading behavior genetics. *Annual Review of Psychology, 51,* 1–27.

Maccoby, Eleanor E. (2002). Parenting effects: Issues and controversies. In John G. Borkowski, Sharon Landesman Ramey & Marie Bristol-Power (Eds.). *Parenting and the child's world: Influences on academic, intellectual, and social-emotional development.* Mahwah, NJ: Erlbaum. 35–46.

Macfie, Jenny, Cicchetti, Dante, & Toth, Sheree L. (2001). The development of dissociation in maltreated preschool-aged children. *Development and Psychopathology, 13,* 233–254.

Macpherson, Alison, Roberts, Ian, & Pless, I. Barry. (1998). Children's exposure to traffic and pedestrian injuries. *American Journal of Public Health, 88,* 1840–1845.

Macrae, C. Neil, & Bodenhausen, Galen V. (2000). Social cognition: Thinking categorically about others. *Annual Review of Psychology, 51,* 93–120.

Maddox, John. (1993). Willful public misunderstanding of genetics. *Nature, 364,* 281.

Maehr, Martin L., & Yamaguchi, Ryoko. (2001). Cultural diversity, student motivation and achievement. In Faridah Salili, Chi-Yue Chiu, & Ying-Yi Hong (Eds.), *Student motivation.* New York: Kluwer.

Magnusson, David. (1996). *The life-span development of individuals: Behavioral, neurobiological, and psychosocial perspectives.* Cambridge, England: Cambridge University Press.

Magnusson, David. (2000). The individual as the organizing principle in psychological inquiry: A holistic approach. In Lars R. Bergman, Robert B. Cairns, Lars-Goran Nilsson, & Lars Nystdt (Eds.), *Developmental science and the holistic approach* (pp. 34–48). Mahwah, NJ: Erlbaum.

Maguire, Kathleen, & Pastore, Ann L. (Eds.). (1998). *Sourcebook of criminal justice statistics, 1997.* Washington, DC: U.S. Government Printing Office.

Mahady Wilton, Melissa M., Craig, Wendy M., & Pepler, Debra J. (2000). Emotional regulation and display in classroom victims of bullying: Characteristic expression of affect, coping styles and relevant contextual factors. *Social Development, 9,* 226–245.

Mahler, Margaret S., Pine, Fred, & Bergman, A. (1975). *The psychological birth of the human infant: Symbiosis and individuation.* New York: International Universities Press.

Mahoney, Joseph L., Stattin, Hakan, & Magnusson, David. (2001). Youth recreation centre participation and criminal offending: A 20-year longitudinal study of Swedish boys. *International Journal of Behavioral Development, 25,* 509–520.

Mahowald, Mary B., Verp, Marion S., & Anderson, R.R. (1998). Genetic counseling: Clinical and ethical challenges. *Annual Review of Genetics, 32,* 547–559.

Maier, Susan E., Chen, Wei-Jung A., & West, James R. (1996). The effects of timing and duration of alcohol exposure on development of the fetal brain. In Ernest L. Abel (Ed.), *Fetal alcohol syndrome: From mechanism to prevention.* Boca Raton, FL: CRC Press.

Main, Mary. (1995). Recent studies in attachment. In Susan Goldberg, Roy Muir, & John Kerr (Eds.), *Attachment theory: Social, developmental, and clinical perspectives.* Hillsdale, NJ: Analytic Press.

Males, Mike A. (1999). *Framing youth: Ten myths about the next generation.* Monroe, ME: Common Courage Press.

Malina, Robert M. (1990). Physical growth and performance during the transitional years (9–16). In Raymond Montemayor, Gerald R. Adams, & Thomas P. Gullotta (Eds.), *From childhood to adolescence: A transitional period?* Newbury Park, CA: Sage.

Malina, Robert M., & Bouchard, Claude. (1991). *Growth, maturation, and physical activity.* Champaign, IL: Human Kinetics Books.

Malina, Robert M., Bouchard, Claude, & Beunen, Gaston. (1988). Human growth: Selected aspects of current research on well-nourished children. *Annual Review of Anthropology, 17,* 187–219.

Mandler, Jean M., & McDonough, Laraine. (1998). On developing a knowledge base in infancy. *Developmental Psychology, 34,* 1274–1288.

Mange, Elaine Johnson, & Mange, Arthur P. (1999). *Basic human genetics.* Sunderland, MA: Sinauer Associates.

Manning, Wendy D., Longmore, Monica A., & Giordano, Peggy C. (2000). The relationship context of contraceptive use at first intercourse. *Family Planning Perspectives, 32,* 104–110.

Manning, Wendy D., & Smock, Pamela J. (2000). "Swapping" families: Serial parenting and economic support for children. *Journal of Marriage and the Family, 62,* 111–122.

Marcia, James E. (1966). Development and validation of ego identity status. *Journal of Personality and Social Psychology, 3,* 551–558.

Marcia, James E., Waterman, Alan S., Matteson, David R., Archer, Sally L., & Orlofsky, Jacob L. (Eds.). (1993). *Ego identity: A handbook for psychosocial research.* New York: Springer-Verlag.

Marcus, Gary F. (2000). *Pabiku* and *Ga Ti Ga:* Two mechanisms infants use to learn about the world. *Current Directions in Psychological Science, 9,* 145–147.

Marin, B.V. (2000). Older boyfriends and girlfriends increase risk of sexual initiation in young adolescents. *Journal of Adolescent Health, 27,* 409–418.

Markman, Ellen M. (1989). *Categorization and naming in children: Problems of induction.* Cambridge, MA: MIT Press.

Markus, Hazel R., Cross, Susan, & Wurf, Elissa. (1990). The role of the self-system in competence. In Robert J. Sternberg & John Kolligian, Jr. (Eds.) *Competence considered* (pp. 205–226). New Haven, CT: Yale.

Markus, Hazel R., & Kitayama, S. (1991). Culture and the self: Implications for cognition, emotion, and motivation. *Psychological Review, 98,* 224–253.

Markus, Hazel R., & Nurius, Paula. (1986). Possible selves. *American Psychologist, 41,* 954–969.

Marsh, Herbert E., Hau, Kit-Tai, & Kong, Chit-Kwong. (2000). Late immersion and language of instruction in Hong Kong high schools: Achievement growth in language and nonlanguage subjects. *Harvard Educational Review, 70,* 302–346.

Marsh, Herbert W. (1989). Age and sex effects in multiple dimensions of self-concept: Preadolescence to early adulthood. *Journal of Educational Psychology, 81,* 417–430.

Marshall, Paul. (2001). *Religious freedom in the world.* Nashville, TN: Broadman and Holman.

Marsiglio, William, Amato, Paul, Day, Randal D., & Lamb, Michael D. (2000). Scholarship on fatherhood in the 1990s and beyond. *Journal of Marriage and the Family, 62,* 1173–1191.

Martin, Carol Lynn, Eisenbud, Lisa, & Rose, Hilary. (1995). Children's gender-based reasoning about toys. *Child Development, 66,* 1453–1471.

Martin, Carol Lynn, & Fabes, Richard. (2001). The stability and consequences of young children's same-sex peer interactions. *Developmental Psychology, 37,* 431–446.

Martin, Joyce A., Hamilton, Brady E., Ventura, Stephanie J., Menacker, Fay, & Park, Melissa M. (2002, February 12). Births: Final data for 2000. *National Vital Statistics Report, 50*(5).

Martin, Karin A. (1996). *Puberty, sexuality, and the self: Boys and girls at adolescence.* New York: Routledge.

Martin, Sandra L., English, Kathleen T., Clark, Kathryn Andersen, Cilenti, Dorothy, & Kupper, Lawrence L. (1996). Violence and substance use among North Carolina pregnant women. *American Journal of Public Health, 86,* 991–998.

Martin, Sandra L., Kim, Haesook, Kupper, Lawrence I., Meyer, Robert E., & Hays, Melissa. (1997). Is incarceration during pregnancy associated with infant birthweight? *American Journal of Public Health, 87,* 1526–1531.

Marvin, Robert S. (1997). Ethological and general systems perspectives on child-parent attachment during the toddler and preschool years. In Nancy L. Segal, Glenn E. Weisfeld, & Carol C. Weisfeld (Eds.), *Uniting psychology and biology: Integrative perspectives on human development.* Washington, DC: American Psychological Association.

Masataka, Nobuo. (1992). Early ontogeny of vocal behavior of Japanese infants in response to maternal speech. *Child Development, 63,* 1177–1185.

Masoro, Edward J. (1999). *Challenges of biological aging.* New York: Springer.

Massimini, Fausto, & Delle Fave, Antonella. (2000). Individual development in a biocultural perspective. *American Psychologist, 55,* 24–33.

Masten, Ann S. (2001). Ordinary magic. *American Psychologist, 56,* 227–238.

Masten, Ann S., & Coatsworth, J. Douglas. (1998). The development of competence in favorable and unfavorable environments: Lessons from research on successful children. *American Psychologist, 53,* 205–220.

Masterpasqua, Frank. (1997). Toward a dynamic developmental understanding of disorder. In Frank Masterpasqua & Phyllis A. Perna (Eds.), *The psychological meaning of chaos: Translating theory into practice.* Washington, DC: American Psychological Association.

Masterpasqua, Frank, & Perna, Phyllis A. (1997). *The psychological meaning of chaos: Translating theory into practice.* Washington, DC: American Psychological Association.

Matsuda, Fumiko. (2001). Development of concepts of interrelationships among duration, distance, and speed. *International Journal of Behavioral Development, 25,* 466–480.

Mauro, Christine F., & Harris, Yvette R. (2000). The influence of maternal child-rearing attitudes and teaching behaviors on preschoolers' delay of gratification. *Journal of Genetic Psychology, 161,* 292–306.

Maxwell, Jan Carlisle. (2000). Changes in drug use in Australia and the United States: Results from the 1995 and 1998 national household surveys. *Drug and Alcohol Review, 20,* 37–48.

Mayberry, Rachel I., & Nicoladis, Elena. (2000). Gesture reflects language development. *Current Directions in Psychological Science, 9,* 192–195.

Mayes, Susan D., Calhoun, Susan L., & Crowell, Errin W. (2000). Learning disabilities and ADHD: Overlapping spectrum disorders. *Journal of Learning Disabilities, 33,* 417–424.

McCabe, Kristen M., Hough, Richard, Wood, Patricia A., & Yeh, Mary. (2001). Childhood and adolescent onset conduct disorder: A test of the developmental taxonomy. *Journal of Abnormal Child Psychology, 29,* 305–316.

McCarty, Michael E., & Ashmead, Daniel H. (1999). Visual control of reaching and grasping in infants. *Developmental Psychology, 35,* 620–631.

McCloskey, Laura Ann, & Stuewig, Jeffrey. (2001). The quality of peer relationships among children exposed to family violence. *Development and Psychopathology, 13,* 83–96.

McCrae, Robert R., Costa, Paul T. Jr., de Lima, Margarida Pedroso, Simões, António, Ostendorf, Fritz, Angleitner, Alois, et al. (1999). Age differences in personality across the adult life span: Parallels in five cultures. *Developmental Psychology, 35,* 466–477.

McDevitt, Thomas M. (1998). *World population profiles: 1998.* Washington, DC: U. S. Commerce Department.

McDonald, Katrina Bell, & Armstrong, Elizabeth M. (2001). De-romanticizing black intergenerational support: The questionable expectations of welfare reform. *Journal of Marriage and the Family, 63,* 213–223.

McDonough, Laraine, & Mandler, Jean M. (1994). Very long term recall in infants: Infantile amnesia reconsidered. In Robyn Fivush (Ed.), *Long-term retention of infant memories.* Hove, England: Erlbaum.

McGroder, Sharon M. (2000). Parenting among low-income, African-American single mothers with preschool-age children: Patterns, predictors, and developmental correlates. *Child Development, 71,* 752–771.

McGue, Matthew. (1995). Mediators and moderators of alcoholism inheritance. In J.R. Turner, L.R. Cardon, & J. K. Hewitt (Eds.), *Behavior genetic approaches to behavioral medicine.* New York: Plenum Press.

McGuffin, Peter, Riley, Brien, & Plomin, Robert. (2001). Toward behavioral genomics. *Science, 291,* 1232–1249.

McHale, Susan M., Crouter, Ann C., & Tucker, Corinna J. (2001). Free-time activities in middle childhood: Links with adjustment in early adolescence. *Child Development, 72,* 1764–1778.

McKenzie, Kwame, & Murray, Robin M. (1999). Risk factors for psychosis in the U.K. Afro-Caribbean population. In D. Bhugra & V. Bahl (Eds.), *Ethnicity: An agenda for mental health* (pp. 48–59). London: Gaskell.

McKusick, Victor A. (1994). *Mendelian inheritance in humans* (10th ed.). Baltimore: Johns Hopkins University Press.

McLanahan, Sara S., & Sandefur, Gary. (1994). *Growing up with a single parent: What hurts, what helps.* Cambridge, MA: Harvard University Press.

McLoyd, Vonnie C. (1998a). Children in poverty: Development, public policy, and practice. In William Damon (Series Ed.), Irving E. Sigel, & K. Ann Renninger (Vol. Eds.), *Handbook of child psychology*: Vol. 4.

Child psychology in practice (5th ed., pp. 135–210). New York: Wiley.

McLoyd, Vonnie C. (1998b). Socioeconomic disadvantage and child development. *American Psychologist, 2,* 185–204.

McLoyd, Vonnie C., & Smith, Julia. (2002). Physical discipline and behavior problems in African American, European American, and Hispanic children: Emotional support as a moderator. *Journal of Marriage and the Family, 64,* 40–53.

Meadows, Sara. (1993). *The child as thinker: The development and acquisition of cognition in childhood.* London: Routledge.

Medved, Michael. (1995, October). Hollywood's 3 big lies. *Reader's Digest, 147,* 155–158.

Meis, Paul J., Goldenberg, Brian, Mercer, Brian M., Moawad, Atef, Das, Anita, McNellis, et al. (1995). The preterm prediction study: Significance of vaginal infections. *American Journal of Obstetrics and Gynecology, 173,* 1231–1235.

Melhuish, Edward C. (2001). The quest for quality in early day care and preschool experience continues. *International Journal of Behavioral Development, 25,* 1–6.

Merrell, Kenneth W., & Gimpel, Gretchen A. (1998). *Social skills of children and adolescents: Conceptualization, assessment, treatment.* Mahwah, NJ: Erlbaum.

Merriman, William E. (1998). Competition, attention, and young children's lexical processing. In B. MacWhinney (Ed.), *The emergence of language.* Mahwah, NJ: Erlbaum.

Merzenich, Michael M. (2001). Cortical plasticity contributing to child development. In James L. McClelland & Robert S. Siegler (Eds.), *Mechanisms of cognitive development: Behavioral and neural perspectives* (pp. 67–96). Mahwah, NJ: Erlbaum.

Messinger, Daniel S., Fogel, Alan, & Dickson, K. Laurie. (1999). What's in a smile? *Developmental Psychology, 35,* 701–708.

Metallinos-Katsaras, Elizabeth & Gorman, Kathleen S. (1999). Effects of undernutrition on growth and development. In Daniel B. Kessler and Peter Dawson (Eds.). *Failure to thrive and pediatric undernutrition* (pp. 375–384). Baltimore: Brooks.

Midanik, Lorraine, & Greenfield, Thomas K. (2000). Trends in social consequences and dependence symptoms in the United States: The national alcohol surveys, 1984–1995. *American Journal of Public Health, 90,* 53–56.

Midgley, Carol, & Urdan, Tim. (2001). Academic self-handicapping and achievement goals: A further examination. *Contemporary Educational Psychology, 26,* 61–75.

Mihalic, Sharon Wofford, & Elliott, Delbert. (1997). Short- and long-term consequences of adolescent work. *Youth & Society, 28,* 464–498.

Miller, Alison L., & Olson, Sheryl L. (2000). Emotional expressiveness during peer conflicts: A predictor of social maladjustment among high-risk preschoolers. *Journal of Abnormal Child Psychology, 28,* 339–352.

Miller, Brent C., Fan, Xitao, Christensen, Mathew, Grotevant, Harold D., & van Dulmen, Manfred. (2000). Comparisons of adopted and non-adopted adolescents in a large, nationally representative sample. *Child Development, 71,* 1458–1473.

Miller, Jane E., & Davis, Diane. (1997). Poverty history, marital history, and quality of children's home environments. *Journal of Marriage and the Family, 59,* 996–1007.

Miller, M., Bowen, J. R., Gibson, F. L., Hand, P. J., & Ungerer, Judy A. (2001). Behavior problems in extremely low birthweight children at 5 and 8 years of age. *Child: Care, Health, and Development, 27,* 569–581.

Miller, Orlando J., & Therman, Eeva. (2001). *Human chromosomes* (4th ed.). New York: Springer.

Miller, Patricia H. (2002). *Theories of developmental psychology* (4th ed.). New York: Worth Publishers.

Miller, Patricia Y., & Simon, William. (1980). The development of sexuality in adolescence. In J. Adelson (Ed.). *Handbook of adolescent psychology* (pp. 383–407). New York: Wiley.

Mills, James L., McPartlin, Joseph M., Kirke, Peadar N., & Lee, Young J. (1995). Homocysteine metabolism in pregnancies complicated by neural-tube defects. *Lancet, 345,* 149–151.

Min, Pyong Gap. (2000). Korean Americans' language use. In Sandra Lee McKay & Sauling Cynthia Wong (Eds.), *New immigrants in the United States* (pp. 306–332). Cambridge, England: Cambridge University Press.

Mintz, Laurie B., & Kashubeck, Susan. (1999). Body image and disordered eating among Asian American and Caucasian college students. *Psychology of Women Quarterly, 23,* 781–796.

Mitchell, Katherine. (2001). Education for democratic citizenship: Transnationalism, multiculturalism, and the limits of liberalism. *Harvard Educational Review, 71,* 51–78.

Mitchell, Peter, & Kikuno, Haruo. (2000). Belief as construction: Inference and processing bias. In Peter Mitchell & Kevin J. Riggs (Eds.), *Children's reasoning and the mind* (pp. 281–300). Hove, England: Psychology Press.

Mitchell, Peter, & Riggs, Kevin J. (Eds.). (2000). *Children's reasoning and the mind.* Hove, England: Psychology Press.

Moats, Louisa C. (2001). Overcoming the language gap: Invest generously in teacher professional development. *American Educator, 25*(2), 4–9.

Moffitt, Terrie E. (1993a). Adolescence-limited and life-course persistent antisocial behavior: A developmental taxonomy. *Psychological Review, 100,* 674–701.

Moffitt, Terrie E. (1993b). The neuropsychology of conduct disorder. *Development and Psychopathology, 5,* 135–151.

Moffitt, Terrie E. (1997a). Adolescence—Limited and life-course-persistent offending: A complementary pair of developmental theories. In Terence P. Thornberry (Ed.), *Development theories of crime and delinquency.* New Brunswick, NJ: Transaction.

Moffitt, Terrie E. (1997b). Helping poor mothers and children. *Journal of the American Medical Association, 278,* 680–682.

Moffitt, Terrie E., & Caspi, Avshalom. (2001). Childhood predictors differentiate life-course persistent and adolescence-limited antisocial pathways among males and females. *Development and Psychopathology, 13,* 355–375.

Moffitt, Terrie E., Caspi, Avshalom, Belsky, Jay, & Silva, Paul A. (1992). Childhood experience and the onset of menarche. *Child Development, 63,* 47–58.

Moffitt, Terrie E., Caspi, Avshalom, Harrington, Hona Lee, & Milne, Barry J. (2002). Males on the life-source-persistent and adolescent-limited antisocial pathways: Follow-up at 26 years. *Developmental Psychopathology, 59.*

Mohan, Dinesh. (2000). Injury control and safety prevention: Ethics, science, and practice. In Dinesh Mohan & Geetam Tiwari (Eds.), *Injury prevention and control.* London: Taylor & Francis.

Molfese, Victoria J. , & Martin, Tina B. (2002). Intelligence and achievement: measurement and prediction of developmental variations. In Dennis L. Molfese & Virginia J. Molfese. (Eds.). *Developmental variation in learning.* Mahwah, NJ: Erlbaum. 275–308.

Molina, Brooke S.G., & Chassin, Laurie. (1996). The parent-adolescent relationship at puberty: Hispanic ethnicity and parent alcoholism as moderators. *Developmental Psychology, 32,* 675–686.

Montemayor, Raymond. (2000). The variety of adolescent experiences. In Raymond Montemayor, Gerald R. Adams, & Thomas P. Gullotta (Eds.), *Adolescent diversity in ethnic, economic, and cultural contexts* (pp. 258–271). Thousand Oaks, CA: Sage.

Moon, Christine, Cooper, Robin Panneton, & Fifer, William P. (1993). Two-day olds prefer their native language. *Infant Behavior & Development, 16,* 495–500.

Moore, Keith L., & Persaud, T. Vidhya N. (1998). *The developing human: Clinically oriented embryology.* Philadelphia: Saunders.

Morgenstern, Hal, Bingham, Trista, & Reza, Avid. (2000). Effects of pool-fencing ordinances and other factors on childhood drowning in Los Angeles County, 1990–1995. *American Journal of Public Health, 90,* 595–601.

Morita, Yohji, Soeda, Haruo, Soeda, Kumiko, & Taki, Mitsuru. (1999). Japan. In Peter K. Smith, Yohji Morita, Josine Junger-Tas, Dan Olweus, Richard F. Catalano, & Phillip T. Slee (Eds.*), The nature of school bullying: A cross-national perspective.* London: Routledge.

Morrison, Frederick J., Griffith, Elizabeth M., & Alberts, Denise M. (1997). Nature-nurture in the classroom: Entrance age, school readiness, and learning in children. *Developmental Psychology, 33,* 254–262.

Morrongiello, Barbara A., Fenwick, Kimberley D., & Chance, Graham. (1998). Crossmodal learning in newborn infants: Inferences about properties of auditory-visual events. *Infant Behavior & Development, 21,* 543–553.

Mortensen, Preben Bo, Pedersen, Carsten B., Westergaard, Tine, Wohlfahrt, Jan, Ewald, Henrik, Mors, Ole, et al. (1999). Effects of family history and season of birth on the risk of schizophrenia. *New England Journal of Medicine, 340,* 603–608.

Mortimer, Jeylan T., Finch, Michael D., Dennehy, Katherine, Lee, Chaimun, & Beebe, Timothy. (1994). Work experience in adolescence. *Journal of Vocational Education Research, 19,* 39–70.

Mortimer, Jeylan T., Finch, Michael D., Ryu, Seongryeol, Shanahan, Michael J., & Call, Kathleen T. (1996). The effects of work intensity on adolescent mental health, achievement, and behavioral adjustment: New evidence from a prospective study. *Child Development, 67,* 1243–1261.

Morton, J. Bruce, & Trehub, Sandra E. (2001). Children's understanding of emotion in speech. *Child Development, 72,* 834–843.

Moses, Louis J. (2001). Executive accounts of theory-of-mind development. *Child Development, 72,* 688–690.

Moshman, David. (1998). Cognitive development beyond childhood. In William Damon (Series Ed.), Deanna Kuhn & Robert S. Siegler (Eds.), *Handbook of child psychology: Vol. 2. Cognition, perception, and language* (5th ed., pp. 947–978). New York: Wiley.

Moshman, David. (1999). *Adolescent psychological development: Rationality, morality, and identity.* Mahwah, NJ: Erlbaum.

Moshman, David. (2000). Diversity in reasoning and rationality: Metacognitive and developmental considerations. *Brain and Behavioral Science, 23,* 689–690.

Moshman, David, & Geil, M. (1998). Collaborative reasoning: Evidence for collective rationality. *Thinking and Reasoning, 4,* 231–248.

Moster, Dag, Lie, Rolv T., Irgens, Lorentz M., Bjerkedal, Tor, & Markestad, Trond. (2001). The association of Apgar score with subsequent death and cerebral palsy: A population-based study in term infants. *Journal of Pediatrics, 138,* 798–803.

Mott, Frank L., Kowaleski-Jones, Lori, & Menaghan, Elizabeth G. (1997). Paternal absence and child behavior: Does a child's gender make a difference? *Journal of Marriage and the Family, 59,* 103–118.

Mpofu, Elias, & van de Vijver, Fons J. R. (2000). Taxonomic structure in early to middle childhood: A longitudinal study with Zimbabwean schoolchildren. *International Journal of Behavioral Development, 24,* 204–212.

Mulvey, Edward O., & Cauffman, Elizabeth. (2001). The inherent limits of predicting school violence. *American Psychologist, 56,* 797–802.

Murphy, J. Michael, Wehler, Cheryl A., Pagona, Maria E., Little, Michelle, Kleinman, Ronald E., & Jellinek, Michael S. (2001). Relation between hunger and psychosocial functioning. In Margaret E. Hertzig & Ellen A. Farber (Eds.). *Annual progress in child psychiatry and child development, 1999* (pp. 215–228). New York: Brunner/Routledge.

Murphy, Shane. (1999). *The cheers and the tears: A healthy alternative to the dark side of youth sports today.* San Francisco: Jossey-Bass.

Muuss, Rolf E. (1996). *Theories of adolescence.* New York: McGraw Hill.

Myers, B. J. (1987). Mother-infant bonding as a critical period. In M.H. Bornstein (Ed.), *Sensitive periods in development: Interdisciplinary perspectives.* Mahwah, NJ: Erlbaum.

Myers, David G. (2001). Do we fear the right things? *APS Observer, 14*(10), 3, 31.

Nagin, Daniel S., & Tremblay, Richard E. (1999). Trajectories of boys' physical aggression, opposition, and hyperactivity on the path to physically violent and nonviolent juvenile delinquency. *Child Development, 70,* 1181–1196.

Naito, Mika, & Miura, Hisayoshi. (2001). Japanese children's numerical competencies: Age- and school-related influences on the development of number concepts and addition skills. *Developmental Psychology, 37,* 217–230.

Nakamura, Suad, Wind, Marilyn & Danello, Mary Ann. (1999). Review of hazards associated with children placed in adult beds. *Archives of Pediatrics and Adolescent Medicine, 153,* 1019–1023.

Nantais, Kristin, & Schellenberg, E. Glenn. (1999). The Mozart effect: An artifact of preference. *Psychological Science, 10,* 370–373.

Nasser, Mervat. (1997). *Culture and weight consciousness.* London and New York: Routledge.

Nation, Kate, & Snowling, Margaret J. (1998). Individual differences in contextual facilitation: Evidence from dyslexia and poor reading comprehension. *Child Development,* *69,* 996–1011.

National Academy of Sciences. (1994). *Assessing genetic risks: Implications for health and social policy.* Washington DC: National Academy Press.

National Center for Education Statistics. (2001). *Digest of Education Statistics: 2000.* Washington, DC: U.S. Department of Education.

National Center for Health Statistics. (1999). *Health, United States, 1999: With health and aging chartbook.* Hyattsville, MD: National Center for Health Statistics.

National Center for Health Statistics. (2000). *Health, United States, 2000.* Hyattsville, MD: Centers for Disease Control and Prevention.

National Center on Child Abuse and Neglect. (2001). *Child maltreatment 2000: Reports from the States.* Washington, DC: NCCAN.

National Endowment Goals Panel. (1997). *National endowment goals panel monthly.* Washington DC: National Endowment Goals Panel.

National Research Council and Institute of Medicine. (2000). *From neurons to neighborhoods: The science of early childhood development.* Jack P. Shonkoff & Deborah A. Phillips (Eds.). Washington, DC: National Academy Press.

National Vital Statistics Report. (2001, September 25). Births to teenagers in the United States: 1940–2000. *Vital Statistics, 49,* (10), entire issue.

Nazzi, Thierry, Bertoncini, Josiane, & Mehler, Jacques. (1998). Language discrimination by newborns: Towards an understanding of the role of rhythm. *Journal of Experimental Psychology: Human Perception and Performance, 24,* 756–766.

Nelson, Adie. (2000). The pink dragon is female: Halloween costumes and gender markers. *Psychology of Women Quarterly, 24,* 137–144.

Nelson, Charles A. (1997). The neurobiological basis of early memory development. In Nelson Cowan & Charles Hulme (Eds.), *The development of memory in childhood: Studies in developmental psychology.* Hove, East Sussex, England: Psychology Press.

Nelson, Katherine. (1981). Individual differences in language development: Implications for development and language. *Developmental Psychology, 17,* 171–187.

Nelson, Katherine. (1996). *Language in cognitive development.* New York: Cambridge University Press.

New York Times (1998, November 2). Metropolitan diary, p. B-2.

NICHD Early Child Care Research Network. (1996). Characteristics of infant child care: Factors contributing to positive child caregiving. *Early Childhood Research Quarterly, 11,* 469–306.

NICHD Early Child Care Research Network. (1997). The effects of infant child care on infant-mother attachment security. Results of the NICHD study of early child care. *Child Development, 68,* 860–879.

NICHD Early Child Care Research Network. (1998). Early child care and self-control, compliance, and problem behavior at 24 and 36 months. *Child Development, 69,* 1145–1170.

NICHD Early Child Care Research Network. (1999). Child care and mother-infant interaction in the first three years of life. *Developmental Psychology, 35,* 1399–1413.

NICHD Early Child Care Research Network. (2000). The relation of child care to cognitive and language development. *Child Development, 71,* 960–980.

NICHD Early Child Care Research Network. (2001). Child care and children's peer interaction at 24 and 36 months: The NICHD study of early child care. *Child Development, 72,* 1478–1500.

NICHD Early Child Care Research Network. (2002). Parenting and family influences when children are in child care: Result from the NICHD study of early child care. In John G. Borkowski, Sharon Landesman Ramey, and Marie Bristol-Power (Eds.). *Parenting and the child's world: Influences on academic, intellectual, and social-emotional development.* Mahwah, NJ: Erlbaum.

Nichols, Francine, & Zwelling, Elaine. (1997) *Maternal newborn nursing.* Philadelphia: Saunders.

Nielsen Media Research. (2000). Nielsen Media Research.

Nieto, Sonia. (2000). *Affirming diversity* (3rd ed.). New York: Addison Wesley Longman.

Nixon, James. (2000). Injury prevention and human rights. In Dinesh Mohan & Geetam Tiwari (Eds.), *Injury prevention and control.* London: Taylor & Francis.

Noppe, Ilene C. (2000). Beyond broken bonds and broken hearts: The bonding of theories of attachment and grief. *Developmental Review, 20,* 514–538.

North, Adrian C., Hargreaves, David J., & O'Neill, Susan. (2000). The importance of music to adolescents. *British Journal of Educational Psychology, 70,* 255–272.

Nunan, David, & Lam, Agnes. (1998). Teacher education for multilingual contexts: Models and issues. In Jasone Cenoz & Fred Genesee (Eds.), *Beyond bilingualism: Multilingualism and multilingual education.* Clevedon, England: Multilingual Matters.

O'Connor, Thomas G. & Croft, Carla M. (2001). A twin study of attachment in pre-school children. *Child Development, 72,* 1501–1511.

O'Connor, Thomas G., Rutter, Michael, Beckett, Celia, Keaveney, Lisa, Kreppner, Jana M., & English and Romanian Adoptees Study Team. (2000). The effects of global severe privation on cognitive competence: Extension and longitudinal follow-up. *Child Development, 71,* 376–390.

O'Donnell, Mike, & Sharpe, Sue. (2000). *Uncertain masculinities: Youth, ethnicity, and class in contemporary Britain.* London: Routledge.

O'Donoghue, Ted, & Rabin, Matthew. (2001). Risky behavior among youths: Some issues from behavioral economics. In Jonathan Gruber, (Ed.), *Risky behavior among youth: An economic analysis* (pp. 29–67). Chicago: The University of Chicago Press.

Offenbacher, Steven, Katz, Vern, Fertik, Gregory, Collins, John, Boyd, Doryck, Maynor, Gayle, McKaig, Rosemary, & Beck, James. (1996). Periodontal infection as a possible risk factor for preterm low birth weight. *Journal of Periodontology, 67,* 1103–1113.

Ogbu, John U. (1993). Differences in cultural frames of reference. *International Journal of Behavioral Development, 16,* 483–506.

O'Hara, Michael W. (1997). The nature of postpartum depressive disorders. In Lynne Murray & Peter J. Cooper (Eds.), *Postpartum depression and child development.* New York: Guilford.

Ohsako, Toshio. (1999). The developing world. In Peter K. Smith, Yohji Morita,

Josine Junger-Tas, Dan Olweus, Richard F. Catalano & Phillip T. Slee (Eds.), *The nature of school bullying: A cross-national perspective.* London: Routledge.

Olausson, Petra Otterblad, Haglund, Bengt, Weitoft, Gunilla Ringbäck, & Cnattingius, Sven. (2001). Teenage childbearing and long-term socioeconomic consequences: A case study in Sweden. *Family Planning Perspectives, 33,* 70–74.

Oliver Ryalls, Brigette. (2000). Dimensional adjectives: Factors affecting children's ability to compare objects using novel words. *Journal of Experimental Child Psychology, 76,* 26–49.

Oliver Ryalls, Brigette, Gul, Robina, & Ryalls, Kenneth R. (2000). Infant imitation of adult and peer models: Evidence for a peer model advantage. *Merrill-Palmer Quarterly, 46,* 188–202.

Olweus, Dan. (1992). Bullying among schoolchildren: Intervention and prevention. In Ray D. Peters, Robert J. McMahon, & Vernon L. Quinsey (Eds.). *Aggression and violence throughout the life span.* Newbury Park, CA: Sage.

Olweus, Dan. (1993a). *Bullying at school: What we know and what we can do.* Oxford, England: Blackwell.

Olweus, Dan. (1993b). Victimization by peers: Antecedents and long-term outcomes. In K.H. Rubin & J.B. Asendorf (Eds.), *Social withdrawal, inhibition, and shyness in childhood.* Mahwah, NJ: Erlbaum.

Olweus, Dan. (1999). Norway. In Peter K. Smith, Yohji Morita, Josine Junger-Tas, Dan Olweus, Richard F. Catalano, & Phillip T. Slee (Eds.), *The nature of school bullying: A cross-national perspective.* London: Routledge.

Olweus, Dan. (2001). Peer harassment: A critical analysis and some important issues. In Jaana Juvonen and Sandra Graham (Eds.). *Peer harassment in school: The plight of the vulnerable and victimized* (pp. 3–20). New York: Guilford Press.

O'Neill, Daniela K., & Chong, Selena C. F. (2001) Preschool children's difficulty understanding the type of information obtained through the five senses. *Child Development, 72,* 803–815.

O'Neill, Molly. (1998, March 14). Feeding the next generation: Food industry caters to teenage eating habits. *The New York Times,* D1.

Ong, Elisa K., & Glantz, Stanton A. (2001). Constructing "sound science" and "good epidemiology": Tobacco, lawyers, and public relations firms. *American Journal of Public Health, 91,* 1749–1757.

Oosterlaan, Jaap, Logan, Gordon D., & Sergeant, Joseph A. (1998). Response inhibition in AD/HD, CD, comorbid AD/HD + CD, anxious, and control children: A meta-analysis of studies with the stop task. *Journal of Child Psychology & Psychiatry & Allied Disciplines, 39,* 411–425.

Opie, Iona. (1993). *The people in the playground.* Oxford, England: Oxford University Press.

Oppenheim, David. (1998). Perspectives on infant mental health from Israel: The case of changes in collective sleeping on the kibbutz. *Infant Mental Health Journal, 19,* 76–86.

Orford, Jim. (2001). *Excessive appetites* (2nd ed.). New York: Wiley.

Organization for Economic Cooperation and Development. (2000). *Education at a glance: OECD indicators, 2000.* Paris: OECD.

Orme, John G., & Buehler, Cheryl. (2001). Foster family characteristics and behavioral and emotional problems of foster children: A narrative review. *Family Relations, 50,* 3–15.

Oswald, Ramona Faith. (2002). Resilience within the family networks of lesbians and gay men: Intentionality and redefinition. *Journal of Marriage and the Family, 64,* 374–383.

Overton, Willis F. (1998). Developmental psychology: Philosophy, concepts, and methodology. In William Damon (Series Ed.) & Richard M. Lerner (Vol. Ed.), *Handbook of child psychology:* Vol. 1. *Theoretical models of human development* (5th ed., pp. 107–188). New York: Wiley.

Oyserman, Daphna, Coon, Heather, & Kemmelmeier, Markus. (2002). Rethinking individualism and collectivism: Evaluation of theoretical assumptions and meta-analyses. *Psychological Bulletin, 128,* 3–72.

Panchaud, Christine, Singh, Sushela, Feivelson, Dina, & Darroch, Jacqueline. (2000). Sexually transmitted diseases among adolescents in developed countries. *Family Planning Perspectives, 32,* 24–32.

Panksepp, Jaak. (1998). Attention deficit hyperactivity disorders, psychostimulants, and intolerance of childhood playfulness: A tragedy in the making? *Current Directions in Psychological Science, 7,* 91–98.

Parke, Ross D. (1995). Fathers and families. In Marc H. Bornstein (Ed.) *Handbook of parenting: Status and social conditions of parenting.* Mahwah, NJ: Erlbaum.

Parke, Ross D. (1996). *Fatherhood.* Cambridge, MA: Harvard University Press.

Parke, Ross D., & Buriel, Raymond. (1998). Socialization in the family: Ethnic and ecological perspectives. In William Damon & Nancy Eisenberg (Eds.), *Handbook of child psychology:* Vol. 3. *Social, emotional, and personality development* (5th ed., pp. 463–552). New York: Wiley.

Parke, Ross D., Ornstein, Peter A., Rieser, John J., & Zahn-Waxler, Carolyn. (1994). The past as prologue: An overview of a century of developmental psychology. In Ross D. Parke, Peter A. Ornstein, John J. Rieser, & Carolyn Zahn-Waxler (Eds.), *A century of developmental psychology.* Washington, DC: American Psychological Association.

Parker, Richard. (2002). The global HIV/AIDS pandemic, structural inequalities, and the politics of international health. *American Journal of Public Health, 92,* 347–351.

Parten, Mildred B. (1932). Social participation among preschool children. *Journal of Abnormal and Social Psychology, 27,* 243–269.

Pasupathi, Monisha, Staudinger, Ursula M., & Baltes, Paul B. (2001). Seeds of wisdom: Adolescents' knowledge and judgment about difficult life problems. *Developmental Psychology, 37,* 351–361.

Patel, Dilip R., & Luckstead, Eugene F. (2000). Sport participation, risk-taking and health risk behaviors. *Adolescent Medicine: State of the Art Reviews, 11,* 141.

Patrick, Helen, & Pintrich, Paul R. (2001). Conceptual change in teachers' intuitive conceptions of learning, motivation and instruction: The role of motivational and epistemological beliefs. In Bruce Torff & Robert J. Sternberg (Eds.), *Understanding and teaching the intuitive mind: Student and teacher learning* (pp. 117–144). Mahwah, NJ: Erlbaum.

Patterson, Charlotte J. (1995). Lesbian mothers, gay fathers, and their fathers. In Anthony R. D'Augelli & Charlotte J. Patterson (Eds.), *Lesbian, gay, and bisexual identities over the lifespan: Psychological perspectives.* New York: Oxford University Press.

Patterson, Charlotte J., & Redding, Richard E. (1996). Lesbian and gay families with children: Implications of social science research for policy. *Journal of Social Issues, 52*(3), 29–50.

Patterson, Gerald R. (1998). Continuities— A search for causal mechanisms: Comment on the special section. *Developmental Psychology, 34,* 1263–1268.

Patterson, Serena J., Sochting, Ingrid, & Marcia, James E. (1992). The inner space and beyond: Women and identity. In Gerald R. Adams, Thomas P. Gullotta, & Raymond Montemeyor (Eds.), *Adolescent identity formation* (pp. 9–24). Newbury Park, CA: Sage.

Pecheux, Marie Germaine, & Labrell, Florence. (1994). Parent-infant interactions and early cognitive development. In Andre Vyt, Henriette Bloch, & Marc H. Bornstein (Eds.), *Early child development in the French tradition:* Contributions from current research. Mahwah, NJ: Erlbaum.

Pellegrini, Anthony D., & Smith, Peter K. (1998). Physical activity play: The nature and function of a neglected aspect of play. *Child Development, 69,* 577–598.

Pellegrini, Anthony D., & Smith, Peter K. (2001). Physical activity play: The nature and function of a neglected aspect of play. In Margaret E. Hertizig & Ellen A. Farber (Eds.). *Annual progress in child psychiatry and child development, 1999* (pp. 1–36). New York: Brunner Routledge.

Pennington, Bruce F. (2001). Genetic methods. In Charles A. Nelson & Monica Luciana (Eds.), *Handbook of developmental neuroscience* (pp. 149–158). Cambridge, MA: MIT Press.

Pennisi, Elizabeth, & Roush, Wade. (1997). Developing a new view of evolution. *Science, 277,* 34–37.

Pepler, Debra, Craig, Wendy M., & O'Connell, Paul. (1999). Understanding bullying from a dynamic systems perspective. In Alan Slater & Darwin Muir (Eds.), *The Blackwell reader in developmental psychology.* Oxford, England: Blackwell.

Perner, Josef. (2000). About + belief + counterfactual. In Peter Mitchell & Kevin J. Riggs (Eds.), *Children's reasoning and the mind* (pp. 367–401). Hove, England: Psychology Press.

Perriello, Vita. (2001). Aiming for healthy weight in wrestlers and other athletes. *Contemporary Pediatrics, 18*(9), 55–74.

Peterson, Anne C., Compas, Bruce E., Brooks-Gunn, Jeanne, Stemmler, Mark, Ey, Sydney, & Grant, Kathryn E. (1993). Depression in adolescence. *American Psychologist, 48,* 155–168.

Peterson, Carole, & Rideout, Regina. (1998). Memory for medical emergencies experienced by one- and two-year-olds. *Developmental Psychology, 34,* 1059–1072.

Petitto, Anne, & Marentette, Paula F. (1991). Babbling in the manual mode: Evidence for the ontogeny of language. *Science, 251,* 1493–1496.

Pettit, Gregory S., Laird, Robert D., Dodge, Kenneth A., Bates, John E., & Criss, Michael M. (2001). Antecedents and behavior-problem outcomes of parental monitoring and psychological control in early adolescence. *Child Development, 72,* 583–598.

Pew Environmental Health Commission. (2000). Attack asthma: Why American needs a public health defense system to battle environmental threats. Baltimore, MD: Johns Hopkins School of Public Health.

Phelps, Richard P. (1998). The demand for standardized student testing. *Educational Measurement: Issues and Practice, 17,* 5–23.

Phinney, Jean S. (1990). Ethnic identity in adolescents and adults: Review of research. *Psychological Bulletin, 108,* 499–514.

Phipps, Maureen G., & Sowers, MaryFran. (2002). Defining early adolescent childbearing. *American Journal of Public Health, 92,* 125–128.

Piaget, Jean. (1952a). *The child's conception of number.* London: Routledge & Kegan Paul.

Piaget, Jean. (1952b). *The origins of intelligence in children* (Margaret Cook, Trans.). New York: International Universities Press.

Piaget, Jean. (1962). *Play, dreams, and imitation in childhood.* New York: Norton.

Piaget, Jean. (1970a). *The child's conception of movement and speed.* (G.E.T. Holloway & M.J. Mackenzie, Trans.). New York: Basic Books.

Piaget, Jean. (1970b). *The child's conception of time.* (A.J. Pomerans, Trans.). New York: Basic Books.

Pinderhughes, Ellen E., Nix, Robert, Foster, E. Michael, Jones, Damon, & The Conduct Problems Prevention Research Group. (2001). Parenting in context: Impact of neighborhood poverty, residential stability, public services, social networks, and danger on parental behaviors. *Journal of Marriage and the Family, 63,* 941–953.

Pinel, John P. J., Assanand, Sunaina, & Lehman, Darrin R. (2000). Hunger, eating, and ill health. *American Psychologist, 55,* 1105–1116.

Pinker, Steven. (1994). *The language instinct.* New York: Harper-Collins.

Pipe, Margaret-Ellen, Gee, Susan, Wilson, J. Clare, & Egerton, Janice M. (1999). *Developmental Psychology, 35,* 781–789.

Pipp-Siegel, Sandra, Siegel, Clifford J., & Dean, Janet. (1999). Neurological aspects of the disorganized/disoriented attachment classification system: Differentiating quality of the attachment relationship from neurological impairment. In Joan I. Vondra & Douglas Barnett (Eds.), Atypical attachment in infancy and early childhood among children at developmental risk. *Monographs of the Society for Research in Child Development, 64*(Serial No. 258), 25–44.

Pisecco, Stewart, Baker, David B., Silva, Phil A., & Brooke, Mark. (2001). Boys with reading disabilities and/or ADHD: Distinctions in early childhood. *Journal of Learning Disabilities, 34,* 98–106.

Plomin, Robert, DeFreis, John C., McClearn, Gerald E., & McGuffin, Peter. (2001). *Behavioral genetics* (4th ed.). New York: Worth Publishers.

Plunkett, Kim. (1997). Theories of early language acquisition. *Trends in Cognitive Sciences, 1,* 146–153.

Poehlmann, Julie, & Fiese, Barbara. (2001). The interaction of maternal and infant vulnerabilities on developing attachment relationships. *Development and Psychopathology, 13,* 1–11.

Pollack, Harold A., & Frohna, John G. (2001). A competing risk model of sudden infant death syndrome in two US birth cohorts. *Journal of Pediatrics, 138,* 661–667.

Pollak, Seth D., Cicchetti, Dante, Hornung, Katherine, & Reed, Alex. (2000). Recognizing emotion in faces: Developmental effects of child abuse and neglect. *Developmental Psychology, 36,* 679–688.

Pollitt, Ernesto, Golub, Mari, Gorman, Kathleen, Levitsky, David, Schurch, Beat, Strupp, Barbara, & Wachs, Theodora. (1996). A reconceptualization of the effects of undernutrition on children's biological, psychological and behavioral development. *Social Policy Report of the Society for Research in Child Development, 10,* (5), 1–32.

Ponsoby, Anne-Louise, Dwyer, Terence, Gibbins, Laura E., Cochrane, Jennifer A., & Wang, Yon-Gan. (1993). Factors potentiating the risk of sudden infant death syndrome associated with the prone position. *New England Journal of Medicine, 329,* 377–382.

Pool, Robert. (1993). Evidence for the homosexuality gene. *Science, 261,* 291–292.

Poplau, Ronald W. (2002). Student creativity. In Randi Stone (Ed.), *Best practices for high school classrooms.* Thousand Oaks, CA: Sage.

Popper, Karl R. (1965). *The logic of scientific discovery.* New York: Harper.

Porter, Richard, Varendi, H., Christensson, K., Porter, R. H. and Winberg, J. (1998). Soothing effect of amniotic fluid smell in newborn infants. *Early Human Development, 51,* 47–55.

Posada, German, Gao, Yuan, Wu, Fang, Posada, Roberto, Tascon, Margarita, Schöelmerich, Axel, et al. (1995). The secure-base phenomenon across cultures: Children's behavior, mothers' preferences, and experts' concepts. In Everett Waters, Brian E. Vaughn, German Posada, & Kiyomi Kondo-Ikemura (Eds.), *Caregivng, cultural and cognitive perspectives on secure-base behavior and working models: New growing points of attachment theory and research. Monographs of the Society for Research in Child Development, 60*(Serial No. 244), 27–48.

Posner, Michael I. & Rothbart, Mary K. (2000). Developing mechanisms of self-regulation. *Development and Psychopathology, 12,* 427–441.

Poulin, François, & Boivin, Michel. (2000). The role of proactive and reactive aggression in the formation and development of boys' friendships. *Developmental Psychology, 30,* 233–240.

Prinstein, Mitchell J., Boergers, Julie, Spirito, Anthony, Little, Todd D., & Grapentine, W. L. (2000). Peer functioning, family dysfunction, and psychological symptoms in a risk factor model for adolescent inpatients' suicidal ideation severity. *Journal of Clinical Child Psychiatry, 29,* 392–405.

Proos, L. A., Hofvander, Y., & Tuvemo, T. (1991). Menarcheal age and growth pattern of Indian girls adopted in Sweden. *Acta Paediatrica Scandinavica, 80,* 852–858.

Pufall, Peter B. (1997). Framing a developmental psychology of art. *Human Development, 40,* 169–180.

Puuronen, Vesa, Sinisalo, Pentti, Miljukova, Irina, & Shvets, Larissa (Eds.). (2000). *Youth in a changing Karelia.* Aldershot, England: Ashgate.

Pyke, Karen. (1999). The micropolitics of care in relationships between aging parents and adult chidlren: Individualism, collectivism, and power. *Journal of Marriage and the Family, 61,* 661–672.

Quinn, Paul C., Cummins, Maggie, Kase, Jennifer, Martin, Erin, & Weissman, Sheri. (1996). Development of categorical representations for above and below spatial relations in 3- to 7-month-old infants. *Developmental Psychology, 32,* 942–950.

Rall, Jaime, & Harris, Paul L. (2000). In Cinderella's slippers? Story comprehension from the protagonist's point of view. *Developmental Psychology, 36,* 202–208.

Ramey, Craig T., Bryant, Donna B., Wasik, Barbara H., Sparling, Joseph J., Fendt, K.H., & Levange, L.M. (1992). The Infant Health and Development Program for low birth weight, premature infants: Program elements, family participation, and child intelligence. *Pediatrics, 89,* 454–465.

Ramey, Craig T. & Ramey, Sharon L. (1998). Early intervention and early experience. *American Psychologist, 53,* 109–120.

Ramey, Craig T., Ramey, Sharon Landesman, Lanzi, Robin Gaines, & Cotton, Janice N. (2002). Early educational intervention for high-risk children: How center-based treatment can augment and improve parenting effectiveness. In John G. Borkowski, Sharon Landesman Ramey, and Marie Bristol-Power (Eds.). *Parenting and the child's world: Influences on academic, intellectual, and social-emotional development.* Mahwah, NJ: Erlbaum.

Ramey, Sharon Landesman, & Ramey, Craig T. (2000). Early childhood experiences and developmental competence. In Sheldon Danziger & Jane Waldfogel (Eds.), *Securing the future* (pp. 122–150). New York: Russell Sage Foundation.

Ramey, Sharon Landesman. (2002). The science and art of parenting. In John G. Borkowski, Sharon Landesman Ramey, & Marie Bristol-Power (Eds.), *Parenting and the child's world: Influences on academic, intellectual and social-emotional development.* Mahwah, NJ: Erlbaum.

Ranyard, Rob, Crozier, W. Ray, & Svenson, Ola. (Eds.). (1997). *Decision making: Cognitive model and explanations.* New York: Routledge.

Rao, Raghavendra, & Georgieff, Michael K. (2000). Early nutrition and brain development. In Charles A. Nelson (Ed.), *The Minnesota Symposia on Child Psychology: Vol. 31. The effects of early adversity on neurobehavioral development.* Mahwah, NJ: Erlbaum.

Raskin-White, Helene, Loeber, Rolf, Stouthamer-Loeber, Magda, & Farrington, David P. (1999). Developmental associations between substance use and violence. *Development and Psychopathology, 11,* 785–803.

Ratner, Hilary Horn, Foley, Mary Ann, & Gimpert, Nicole. (2000). Person perspective on children's memory and learning: What do source monitoring failures reveal? In Kim P. Roberts & Mark Blades (Eds.), *Children's source monitoring.* Mahwah, NJ: Erlbaum.

Rauscher, Frances H., & Shaw, Gordon L. (1998). Key components of the Mozart effect. *Perceptual and Motor Skills, 86,* 835–841.

Rauscher, Frances H., Shaw, Gordon L., & Ky, Katherine N. (1993). Music and spatial task performance. *Nature, 365,* 611.

Rayner, Keith, Foorman, Barbara R., Perfetti, Charles A., Pesetsky, David, & Seidenberg, Mark S. (2001). How psychological science informs the teaching of reading. *Psychological Science in the Public Interest, 2,* 31–74.

Reed, Edward S. (1993). The intention to use a specific affordance: A conceptual framework for psychology. In Robert H. Wozniak & Kurt W. Fischer (Eds.), *Development in context: Acting and thinking in specific environments.* Mahwah, NJ: Erlbaum.

Reese, Elaine, Haden, Catherine A., & Fivush, Robyn. (1993). Mother-child conversations about the past: Relationships of style and memory over time. *Cognitive Development, 8,* 403–430.

Reid, John B., Patterson, Gerald R., & Snyder, James J. (2002). *Antisocial behavior in children and adolescents.* Washington, DC: American Psychological Association.

Reiss, David. (1997). Mechanisms linking genetic and social influences in adolescent development: Beginning a collaborative search. *Current Directions in Psychological Science, 6,* 100–105.

Reiss, David, & Neiderhiser, Jenae M. (2000). The interplay of genetic influences and social processes in developmental theory: Specific mechanisms are coming into view. *Development and Psychopathology, 12,* 357–374.

Reiter, Edward O., & Lee, Peter A. (2001). Have the onset and tempo of puberty changed? *Archives of Pediatrics and Adolescent Medicine, 155,* 988–989.

Remez, Lisa. (2000). Oral sex among adolescents: Is it sex or is it abstinence? *Family Planning Perspectives, 32,* 298–303.

Renninger, K. Ann, & Amsel, Eric. (1997). Change and development: An introduction. In Eric Amsel & K. Ann Renninger (Eds.), *Change and development: Issues of theory, method, & application.* Mahwah, NJ: Erlbaum.

Rest, James R. (1983). Morality. In Paul H. Mussen (Ed.), *Handbook of child psychology: Vol. 3. Cognitive development.* New York: Wiley.

Rest, James R., Narvaez, Darcia, Bebeau, Muriel J., & Thoma, Stephen J. (1999a). A neo-Kohlbergian approach: The DIT and scheme theory. *Educational Psychology Review, 11,* 291–324.

Rest, James R., Narvaez, Darcia, Bebeau, Murel J., & Thoma, Stephen J. (1999b). *Postconventional moral thinking: A neo-Kohlbergian approach.* Mahwah, NJ: Erlbaum.

Reynolds, Arthur J. (2000). *Success in early intervention: The Chicago child-parent centers.* Lincoln: University of Nebraska.

Reznick, J. Steven, Chawarska, Katarzyna, & Betts, Stephanie. (2000). The development of visual expectation in the first year. *Child Development, 71,* 1191–1204.

Rice, Amy L., Sacco, Lisa, Hyder, Adnan, & Black, Robert E. (2000). Malnutrition as an underlying cause of childhood deaths associated with infectious diseases in developing countries. *Bulletin of the World Health Organization, 78,* 1207–1221.

Rice, George, Anderson, Carol, Risch, Neil, & Ebers, George. (1999). Male homosexuality: Absence of linkage to microsatellite markers at Xq28. *Science, 284,* 665–667.

Richards, Maryse, Crowe, Paul A., Larson, Reed, & Swarr, Amy. (1998). Developmental patterns and gender differences in the experience of peer companionship during adolescence. *Child Development, 69,* 154–163.

Richardson, Gale A. (1998). Prenatal cocaine exposure: A longitudinal study of development. *Annals of the New York Academy of Science, 846,* 144–152.

Ridley, Matt. (1999). *Genome.* London: Fourth Estate Limited.

Rigby, Ken, & Slee, Phillip T. (1999). Australia. In Peter K. Smith, Yohji Morita, Josine Junger-Tas, Dan Olweus, Richard F. Catalano, & Phillip T. Slee (Eds.), *The nature of school bullying: A cross-national perspective.* London: Routledge.

Riley, Lisa A., & Glass, Jennifer L. (2002). You can't always get what you want—infant care preferences and use among employed mothers. *Journal of Marriage and the Family, 64,* 2–15.

Rind, Bruce, Tromovitch, Philip, & Bauserman, Robert. (1998) A meta-analytical examination of assumed properties of child sexual abuse using college students. *Psychological Bulletin, 124,* 22–53.

Riordan, Jan, & Auerbach, Kathleen. (1998). *Breast feeding and human lactation* (2nd ed.). Boston: Jones and Bartlett.

Rios-Ellis, Britt, Bellamy, Laura, & Shoji, Junichi. (2000). An examination of specific types of Ijime within Japanese schools. *School Psychology International, 21,* 227–241.

Rivara, Fred P. (1994). Unintentional injuries. In Ivan Barry Pless (Ed.), *The epidemiology of childhood disorders.* New York: Oxford University Press.

Robert, Elizabeth. (1996). Treating depression in pregnancy, editorial. *New England Journal of Medicine, 335,* 1056–1058.

Roberts, Ken, Clark, S. C., Fagan, Colette, & Tholen, Jochen. (2000). *Surviving post-Communism.* Cheltenham, England: Elgar.

Roberts, Kenneth. (1988). Retrieval of a basic-level category in prelinguistic infants. *Developmental Psychology, 24,* 21–27.

Roberts, Kim P. (2000). An overview of theory and research on children's source monitoring. In Kim P. Roberts & Mark Blades (Eds.), *Children's source monitoring.* Mahwah, NJ: Erlbaum.

Robin, Daniel J., Berthier, Neil E., & Clifton, Rachel K. (1996). Infants' predictive reaching for moving objects in the dark. *Developmental Psychology, 32,* 824–835.

Robinson, Thomas N., & Killen, Joel D. (2001). Obesity prevention for children and adolescents. In J. Kevin Thompson & Linda Smolak (Eds.), *Body image, eating disorders, and obesity in youth* (pp. 261–292). Washington, DC: American Psychological Association.

Rochat, Philippe. (2001). *The infant's world.* Cambridge, MA: Harvard University Press.

Rodier, Patricia H. (2000). The early origins of autism. *Scientific American, 282* (2). 56–63.

Roehlkepartain, Eugene, Benson, Peter L., & Sharman, Anu. (1994). *Growing up adopted.* Minneapolis: Search Institute.

Rogers, Kathleen Boyce. (1999). Parenting processes related to sexual risk-taking behaviors of adolescent males and females. *Journal of Marriage and the Family, 61,* 99–109.

Rogoff, Barbara. (1990). *Apprenticeship in thinking: Cognitive development in social context.* New York: Oxford University Press.

Rogoff, Barbara. (1997). Evaluating development in the process of participation: Theory, methods, and practice building on each other. In Eric Amsel & K. Ann Renninger (Eds.), *Change and development: Issues of theory, method, & application.* Mahwah, NJ: Erlbaum.

Rogoff, Barbara. (1998). Cognition as a collaborative process. In William Damon (Series Ed.), Deanna Kuhn & Robert S. Siegler (Vol. Eds.), *Handbook of child psychology: Vol. 2. Cognition, perception, and language* (5th ed., pp. 679–744). New York: Wiley.

Rohlen, Thomas P., & LeTendre, Gerald K. (1996). *Teaching and learning in Japan.* Cambridge, England: Cambridge University Press.

Rolls, Edmund T. (2000). Memory systems in the brain. *Annual Review of Psychology, 51,* 599–630.

Romaine, Suzanne. (1999). Bilingual language development. In M. Barrett (Ed.), *The development of language* (pp. 251–275). Hove, England: Psychology Press.

Romo, Harriett D., & Falbo, Toni. (1996). *Latino high school graduation: Defying the odds.* Austin: University of Texas Press.

Roosa, Mark W., Reinholtz, Cindy, & Angelini, Patti Jo. (1999) The relation of child sexual abuse and depression in young women: Comparisons across four ethnic groups. *Journal of Abnormal Child Psychology, 27,* 65–76.

Rose, Amanda J., & Asher, Steven R. (1999). Children's goals and strategies in response to conflicts within a friendship. *Developmental Psychology, 35,* 69–79.

Rose, Susan A., & Feldman, Judith F. (2000). The relation of very low birth weight to basic cognitive skills in infancy. In Charles A. Nelson (Ed.), *The Minnesota Symposia on Child Psychology: Vol. 31. The effects of early adversity on neurobehavioral development.* Mahwah, NJ: Erlbaum.

Rose, Susan A., Feldman, Judith F., & Jankowski, Jeffrey J. (2001a). Attention and recognition memory in the first year of life: A longitudinal study of preterm and full-term infants. *Developmental Psychology, 37,* 135–151.

Rose, Susan A., Feldman, Judith F., & Jankowski, Jeffrey J. (2001b). Visual short-term memory in the first year of life: Capacity and recency effects. *Developmental Psychology, 37,* 539–549.

Rosenblith, Judy F. (1992). *In the beginning: Development from conception to age two* (2nd ed.). Newbury Park, CA: Sage.

Rosenblum, Gianine D., & Lewis, Michael. (1999). The relations among body image, physical attractiveness, and body mass in adolescence. *Child Development, 70,* 50–64.

Rosenthal, M. Sara. (1996). *The fertility sourcebook.* Lincolnwood, Illinois: Lowell House.

Rosser, Pearl L., & Randolph, Suzanne M. (1989). Black American infants: The Howard University normative study. In J. Kevin Nuegent, Barry M. Lester, & T. Berry Brazelton (Eds.), *The cultural context of infancy: Vol 1. Biology, culture, and infant development.* Norwood, NJ: Ablex.

Rothbart, Mary K., & Bates, John E. (1998). Temperament. In William Damon (Series Ed.), Nancy Eisenberg (Vol. Ed.), *Handbook of child psychology: Vol. 3. Social, emotional, and personality development* (5th ed., pp. 105–176). New York: Wiley.

Rothbaum, Fred, Pott, Martha, Azuma, Hiroshi, Miyake, Kazuo, & Weisz, John. (2000). The development of close relationships in Japan and the United States: Paths of symbolic harmony and generative tension. *Child Development, 71,* 1121–1142.

Rotheram-Borus, Mary Jane, & Wyche, Karen Fraser. (1994). Ethnic differences in identity development in the United States. In

Sally L. Archer (Ed.), *Interventions for adolescent identity development.* Thousand Oaks, CA: Sage.

Rovee-Collier, Carolyn K. (1987). Learning and memory in infancy. In J. Doniger Osofsky (Ed.), *Handbook of infant development* (2nd ed.). New York: Wiley.

Rovee-Collier, Carolyn K. (1990). The "memory system" of prelinguistic infants. In A. Diamond (Ed.), *The development and neural bases of higher cognitive functions.* New York: New York Academy of Sciences.

Rovee-Collier, Carolyn K. (2001). Information pick-up by infants: What is it, and how can we tell. *Journal of Experimental Child Psychology, 78,* 35–49.

Rovee-Collier, Carolyn K., & Gerhardstein, Peter. (1997). The development of infant memory. In Nelson Cowan & Charles Hulme (Eds.), *The development of memory in childhood: Studies in developmental psychology.* Hove, East Sussex, England: Psychology Press.

Rovee-Collier, Carolyn K., & Hayne, Harlene. (1987). Reactivation of infant memory: Implications for cognitive development. In H.W. Reese (Ed.), *Advances in child development and behavior* (Vol. 20). New York: Academic Press.

Rovee-Collier, Carolyn K., Hayne, Harlene, & Colombo, Michael. (2001). *The development of implicit and explicit memory.* Amsterdam: John Benjamins.

Rowan, Leonie, Knobel, Michele, Bigum, Chris, & Lankshear, Colin. (2002). *Boys, literacy, and schooling.* Buckingham, England: Open University.

Rowe, David C., & Jacobson, Kristen C. (1999). In the mainstream: Research in behavioral genetics. In Ronald A. Carson & Mark A. Rothstein (Eds.), *Behavioral genetics: The clash of culture and biology* (pp. 12–34). Baltimore: Johns Hopkins Press.

Rowland, David L., Zabin, Laurie S., & Emerson, Mark. (2000). Household risk and sexual abuse in a low income urban sample of women. *Adolescent and Family Health, 1,* 29–39.

Rubenstein, Adam J., Kalakanis, Lisa, & Langlois, Judith H. (1999). Infant preferences for attractive faces: A cognitive explanation. *Developmental Psychology, 35,* 848–855.

Rubin, Glenna B., Fagen, Jeffrey W., & Carroll, Marjorie H. (1998). Olfactory context and memory retrieval in 3-month-old

infants. *Infant Behavior & Development, 21,* 641–658.

Rubin, Kenneth H., Bukowski, William, & Parker, Jeffrey G. (1998). Peer interactions, relationships, and groups. In William Damon (Series Ed.) & Nancy Eisenberg (Vol. Ed.), *Handbook of child psychology: Vol. 3. Social, emotional, and personality development* (5th ed., pp. 619–700). New York: Wiley.

Ruble, Diane N., & Martin, Carol Lynn. (1998). Gender development. In William Damon & Nancy Eisenberg (Eds.), *Handbook of child psychology,* Vol. 3. *Social, emotional and personality development* (5th ed., pp. 933–1016). New York: Wiley.

Rumbert, Ruben, & Portes, Alejandro. (2001). *Ethnicities: Children of immigrants in America.* University of California Press/ Russell Sage Foundation.

Russell, Mark. (2002). Institute helps spread use of vaccines in Asia. *Science, 295,* 611–612.

Rust, John, Golombok, Susan, Hines, Melissa, Johnson, Katie, Golding, Jean, & ALSPAC Study Team. (2000). The role of brothers and sisters in the gender development of preschool children. *Journal of Experimental Child Psychology, 77,* 292–303.

Rutstein, Shea O. (2000). Factors associated with trends in infant and child morality in developing countries during the 1990s. *Bulletin of the World Health Organization, 78,* 1256–1270.

Rutter, Michael. (1998). Some research considerations on intergenerational continuities and discontinuities: Comment on the special section. *Developmental Psychology, 34,* 1269–1273.

Rutter, Michael. (2002). Nature, nurture, and development: From evangelism through science toward policy and practice. *Child Development, 73,* 1–12.

Rutter, Michael, Giller, Henry & Hagell, Anne. (1998). *Antisocial behavior by young people.* Cambridge, England: Cambridge University Press.

Rutter, Michael, & Rutter, Marjorie. (1993). *Developing minds: Challenge and continuity across the life span.* New York: Basic Books.

Rutter, Michael, & Sroufe, L. Alan. (2000). Developmental psychopathology: Concepts and challenges. *Development and Psychopathology, 12,* 265–296.

Rutter, Michael, Thorpe, K., & Golding, J. (2000). *Twins as a natural experiment to study the causes of language delay.* Report to the Mental Health Foundation, London.

Sabbagh, Mark A., & Baldwin, Dare A. (2001). Learning words from knowledgeable versus ignorant speakers: Links between preschoolers' theory of mind and semantic development. *Child Development, 72,* 1054–1070.

Sackett, Paul R., Schmitt, Neal, Ellingson, Jill E., & Kabin, Melissa B. (2001). High-stakes testing in employment, credentialing, and higher education: Prospects in a post-affirmative-action world. *American Psychologist, 56,* 302–318.

Sacks, Oliver. (1995). *An anthropologist on Mars: Paradoxical tales.* New York: Random House.

Sacks, Peter. (1999). *Standardized minds: The high price of America's testing culture and what we can do to change it.* Cambridge, MA: Perseus Books.

Sadeh, Avi, Raviv, Amiram, & Gruber, Reut. (2000). Sleep patterns and sleep disruptions in school-age children. *Developmental Psychology, 36,* 291–301.

Saffran, Jenny R., Aslin, Richard N., & Newport, Elissa L. (1996). Statistical learning by 8-month-old infants. *Science, 274,* 1926–1928.

Salazar, Lilia P., Schludermann, Shirin M., Schludermann, Eduard H., & Huynh, Cam-Loi. (2001). Filipino adolescents' parents' socialization for academic achievement in the United States. *Journal of Adolescent Research, 15,* 564–586.

Salzarulo, Piero, & Fagioli, Igino. (1999). Changes of sleep states and physiological activities across the first year of life. In A. F. Kalverboer, Maria Luisa Genta, & J. B. Hopkins (Eds.), *Current issues in developmental psychology.* Dordrecht, Netherlands: Kluwer.

Sampaio, Ricardo C., & Truwit, Charles L. (2001). Myelination in the developing human brain. In Charles A. Nelson & Monica Luciana (Eds.), *Handbook of developmental neuroscience* (pp. 35–44). Cambridge, MA: MIT Press.

Sampson, Paul D., Streissguth, Ann P., Bookstein, Fred L., Little, Ruth E., Clarren, Sterling K., Dehaene, Philippe, et al. (1997). Incidence of fetal alcohol syndrome and prevalence of alcohol-related neurodevelopmental disorder. *Teratology, 56,* 317–326.

Sampson, Robert J. (1997). Collective regulation of adolescent misbehavior. *Journal of Adolescence Research, 12,* 227–244.

Sampson, Robert J., & Laub, John. (1993). *Crime in the making: Pathways and turning points through life.* Cambridge, MA: Harvard University Press.

Sampson, Robert J., Raudenbush, Stephen W., & Earls, Felton. (1997). Neighborhoods and violent crime: A multilevel study of collective efficacy. *Science, 277,* 918–924.

Sanchez, Maria del Mar, Ladd, Charlotte O., & Plotsky, Paul M. (2001). Early adverse experience as a developmental risk factor for later psychopathology: Evidence from rodent and primate models. *Development and Psychopathology, 13,* 419–450.

Sandelowski, Margarete. (1993). *With child in mind: Studies of the personal encounter with infertility.* Philadelphia: University of Pennsylvania Press.

Sanders, S. A., & Reinisch, J. M. (1999). Would you say you had sex if...? *Journal of the American Medical Association, 281,* 275–277.

Santelli, John S., Lindberg, Laura Duberstein, Abma, Joyce, McNeely, Clea Sucoff, & Resnick, Michael. (2000). Adolescent sexual behavior: Estimates and trends from four nationally representative surveys. *Family Planning Perspectives, 32,* 156–165, 194.

Sapolsky, Robert M. (1997). The importance of a well-groomed child. *Science, 277,* 1620–1621.

Sapp, Felicity, Lee, Kang, & Muir, Darwin. (2000). Three-year-olds' difficulty with the appearance-reality distinction: Is it real or is it apparent? *Developmental Psychology, 36,* 547–560.

Sargent, James D., Stukel, Therese A., Dalton, Madeline A., Freeman, Jean L., & Brown, Mary Jean. (1996). Iron deficiency in Massachusetts communities: Socioeconomic and demographic risk factors among children. *American Journal of Public Health, 86,* 544–550.

Satcher, David. (2001). *The Surgeon General's call to action to promote sexual health and responsible sexual behavior.* Washington, DC: U.S. Government Printing Office.

Savin-Williams, Ritch C. (1995). An exploratory study of pubertal maturation timing and self-esteem among gay and bisexual male youths. *Developmental Psychology, 31,* 56–64.

Savin-Williams, Ritch C., & Diamond, Lisa M. (1997). Sexual orientation as a developmental context for lesbians, gays, and bisexuals: Biological perspectives. In Nancy L. Segal, Glenn E. Weisfeld, & Carol C. Weisfeld (Eds.), *Uniting psychology and biology: Integrative perspectives on human development.* Washington, DC: American Psychological Association.

Saxe, Geoffrey B. (1999). Sources of concepts: A cultural-developmental perspective. In Ellen Kofsky Scholnick, Katherine Nelson, Susan A. Gelman, & Patricia H. Miller (Eds.), *Conceptual development: Piaget's legacy* (pp. 253–268). Mahwah, NJ: Erlbaum.

Saxe, Geoffrey, Guberman, Steven R., & Gearhart, Maryl. (1987). Social processes in early number development. *Monographs of the Society for Research in Child Development, 52* (Serial No. 216).

Schacter, Daniel L., & Badgaiyan, Rajendra D. (2001). Neuroimaging of priming: New perspectives on implicit and explicit memory. *Current Directions in Psychological Science, 10,* 1–4.

Schaffer, Rudolph H. (2000). The early experience assumption: Past, present, and future. *International Journal of Behavioral Development, 24,* 5–14.

Schaffner, Kenneth F. (1999). Complexity and research strategies in behavioral genetics. In Ronald A. Carson & Mark A. Rothstein (Eds.), *Behavioral genetics: The clash of culture and biology* (pp. 61–88). Baltimore: Johns Hopkins Press.

Schaie, K. Warner. (1996). *Intellectual development in adulthood: The Seattle Longitudinal Study.* Cambridge, England: Cambridge University Press.

Scharf, Miri. (2001). A "natural experiment" in childrearing ecologies and adolescents' attachment and separation representation. *Child Development, 72,* 236–251.

Scheuffgen, Kristina, Happe, Francesca, Anderson, Mike, & Firth, Uta. (2000). High "intelligence," low "IQ"? Speed of processing and measured IQ in children with autism. *Development and Psychopathology, 12,* 83–90.

Schifter, Jacobo & Madrigal, Johnny. (2000). *The sexual construction of Latino youth.* New York: Haworth Hispanic/Latino Press.

Schirmer, Barbara R. (2000). *Language and literacy development in children who are deaf* (2nd ed.). Boston: Allyn and Bacon.

Schlegeal, Alice, & Barry, Herbert. (1991). *Adolescence: An anthropological inquiry.* New York: Free Press.

Schneider, Wolfgang. (1998). The development of procedural metamemory in childhood and adolescence. In Guiliana Mazzoni & Thomas O. Nelson (Eds.), *Monitoring and control processes in metacognition and cognitive neuropsychology* (pp. 1–21). Mahwah, NJ: Erlbaum.

Schneider, Wolfgang, & Bjorklund, David F. (1998). Memory. In William Damon (Series Ed.), Deanna Kuhn, & Robert S. Siegler (Vol. Eds.), *Handbook of child psychology: Vol. 2. Cognition, perception, and language* (5th ed., pp. 467–522). New York: Wiley.

Schneider, Wolfgang, Bjorklund, David F., & Maier-Bruckner, Wolfgang. (1996). The effects of expertise and IQ on children's memory: When knowledge is, and when it is not enough. *International Journal of Behavioral Development, 19,* 773–796.

Schneider, Wolfgang, & Pressley, Michael. (1997). *Memory development: Between two and twenty.* Mahwah, NJ: Erlbaum.

Schwab, Jacqueline, Kulin, Howard E., Susman, Elizabeth J., Finkelstein, Jordan W., Chinchilli, Vernon M., Kunselman, Susan J., Liben, Lynn S., D'Arcangelo, M. Rose, & Demers, Laurence M. (2001). The role of sex hormone replacement therapy on self-perceived competence in adolescents with delayed puberty. *Child Development, 72,* 1439–1450.

Schwartz, David, Chang, Lei, & Farver, JoAnn M. (2001). Correlates of victimization in Chinese children's peer groups. *Developmental Psychology, 37,* 520–532.

Schweder, Richard A., Goodnow, Jacqueline, Hatano, Giyooo, LeVine, Robert A., Markus, Hazel, & Miller, Peggy. (1998). The cultural psychology of development: One mind, many mentalities. In William Damon (Series Ed.) & Richard M. Lerner (Vol. Ed.), *Handbook of child psychology: Vol. 1. Theoretical models of human development* (5th ed., pp. 865–937). New York: Wiley.

Schweinhart, Lawrence J., & Weikart, David P. (1997). *Lasting differences: The High/Scope preschool curriculum comparison study through age 27.* Ypsilanti, MI: High/Scope Educational Research Foundation.

Scott, Fiona J., & Baron-Cohen, Simon. (1996) Logical, analogical, and psychological reasoning in autism: A test of the Cosmides theory. *Development and Psychopathology, 8,* 235–245.

Scott, Stephen, Spender, Quentin, Doolan, Moira, Jacobs, Brian, Aspland, Helen, & Webster-Stratton, Carolyn. (2001). Multicentre controlled trial of parenting groups for childhood antisocial behavior in clinical practice. *British Medical Journal, 323,* 194–197.

Scovel, Thomas. (1988). *A time to speak: A psycholinguistic inquiry into the critical period for human speech.* New York: Newbury.

Sedlak, Andrea J., & Broadhurst, Diane D. (1996). *Third national study of child abuse and neglect: Final report.* Washington DC: U.S. Department of Health and Human Services.

Sena, Rhonda, & Smith, Linda B. (1990). New evidence on the development of the word Big. *Child Development, 61,* 1034–1052.

Sénéchal, Monique, & LeFevre, Jo-Anne. (2002). Parental involvement in the development of children's reading skill: A five-year longitudinal study. *Child Development, 73,* 445–460.

Senghas, Ann, & Coppola, Marie. (2001). Children creating language: How Nicaraguan Sign Language acquired a spatial grammar. *Psychological Science, 12,* 323–328.

Shahin, Hashem, Walsh, Tom, Sobe, Tama, Lynch, Eric, King, Marie-Claire, Avraham, Karen B., & Kanaan, Moien. (2002). Genetics of congenital deafness in the Palestine population. *Human Genetics, 110,* 284–289.

Shanahan, Michael J., Elder, Glen H., Jr., Burchinal, Margaret, & Conger, Rand D. (1996). Adolescent paid labor and relationships with parents: Early work-family linkages. *Child Development, 67,* 2183–2200.

Shanahan, Michael J., & Flaherty, Brian P. (2001). Dynamic patterns of time use in adolescence. *Child Development, 72,* 385–401.

Shatz, Marilyn. (1994). *A toddler's life.* New York: Oxford University Press.

Shaw, Daniel S., Vondra, Joan I., Hommerding, Katherine Dowdell, Keenan, Kate, & Dunn, Marija. (1994). Chronic family adversity and early child behavior problems. A longitudinal study of low income families. *Journal of Child Psychology and Psychiatry, 35,* 1109–1122.

Shedler, Jonathan, & Block, Jack. (1990). Adolescent drug use and psychological health: A longitudinal inquiry. *American Psychologist, 45,* 612–630.

Sheinberg, Marcia, & Fraenkel, Peter. (2001). *The relational trauma of incest.* New York: Guilford Press.

Sherman, Stephanie L. & Waldman, Irwin D. (1999). Identifying the molecular genetic basis of behavioral traits. In Ronald A. Carson & Mark A. Rothstein (Eds.), *Behavioral genetics: The clash of culture and biology* (pp. 35–60). Baltimore: Johns Hopkins Press.

Shi, Rushen, Werker, Janet F., & Morgan, James L. (1999). Newborn infants' sensitivity to perceptual cues to lexical and grammatical words. *Cognition, 72,* B-11—B-21.

Shiono, Patricia H., Rauh, Virginia A., Park, Mikyung, Lederman, Sally A., & Zuskar, Deborah. (1997). Ethnic differences in birthweight: The role of lifestyle and other factors. *American Journal of Public Health, 87,* 787–793.

Shirley, Mary M. (1933). *The first two years: A study of twenty-five babies.* (Institute of Child Welfare Monograph No. 8.) Minneapolis: University of Minnesota Press.

Shneidman, Edwin S. (2001). *Contemplating suicide: Landmarks in 20th century psychology.* Washington DC: American Psychological Association.

Shneidman, Edwin S., & Mandelkorn, Philip. (1994). Some facts and fables of suicide. In Edwin S. Shneidman, Norman L. Faberow, & Robert E. Litman (Eds.), *The psychology of suicide* (Rev. ed.). Northwale, NJ: Aronson.

Shonkoff, Jack P. (2000). Science, policy, and practice: Three cultures in search of a shared mission. *Child Development, 71,* 181–187.

Shore, R. Jerald, & Hayslip, Bert, Jr. (1994). Custodial grandparenting: Implications for children's development. In Adele Eskeles Gottfried & Allen W. Gottfried (Eds.), *Redefining families: Implications for children's development.* New York: Plenum Press.

Shrebman, Laura. (2000). Intensive behavioral/psychoeducational treatment for autism: Research needs and future directions. *Journal of Autism and Pervasive Developmental Disorders, 30,* 373–378.

Shute, Nancy, Locy, Toni, & Pasternak, Douglas. (2000, March 6). The perils of pills. *U.S. News and World Report,* 45–49.

Sickmund, Melissa, Snyder, Howard N., & Poe-Yamagata, Eileen. (1997). *Juvenile offenders and victims: 1997 update on violence.* Washington, DC: Office of Juvenile Justice and Delinquency Prevention.

Siegler, Robert S., & Jenkins, E. A. (1989). *How children discover new strategies.* Hillsdale, NJ: Erlbaum.

Silbereisen, Rainer K., & von Eye, Alexander. (1999). *Growing up in times of social change.* Berlin: Walter de Gruyter.

Silk, Jennifer S., Nath, Sanjay R., Siegel, Lori R., & Kendall, Philip C. (2000). Conceptualizing mental disorders in children: Where have we been and where are we going? *Development and Psychopathology, 12,* 713–735.

Silva, Phil A. (1996). Health and development in the early years. In Phil A. Silva & Warren R. Stanton (Eds.), *From child to adult: The Dunedin multidisciplinary health and development study.* New Zealand: Oxford University Press.

Silver, Rawley. (2001). *Art as language.* Philadelphia: Psychology Press.

Simmons, Roberta G., & Blyth, Dale A. (1987). *Moving into adolescence: The impact of pubertal change and school context.* New York: de Gruyter.

Simon, Herbert A. (2001). Learning to research about learning. In Sharon M. Carver & David Klahr (Eds.), *Cognition and instruction* (pp. 205–226). Mahwah, NJ: Erlbaum.

Simons, Ronald L. (1996). *Understanding differences between divorced and intact families.* Thousand Oaks, CA: Sage.

Simpson, Joe Leigh, Grito, Jamie A., Handyside, Alan, & Verlinsky, Yury. (1999). Preimplantation genetic diagnosis: The new frontier. *Contemporary Ob/Gyn, 44,* 55–78.

Singh, Susheela, Wulf, Deirdre, Samara, Renee, & Cuca, Yvette P. (2000). Gender differences in the timing of first intercourse: Data from 14 countries. *International Family Planning Perspectives, 26,* 21–28, 43.

Siperstein, Gary N., Leffert, James S., & Wenz-Gross, Melodie. (1997). The quality of friendships between children with and without learning problems. *American Journal on Mental Retardation, 102,* 111–125.

Siqueira, Lorena, Rolnitsky, Linda A., & Rickart, Vaughn. (2001). Smoking cessation in adolescents. *Archives of Pediatrics and Adolescent Medicine, 155,* 489–495.

Skinner, Burrhus Frederic. (1953). *Science and human behavior.* New York: Macmillan.

Skinner, Burrhus Frederic. (1957). *Verbal behavior.* New York: Appleton-Century-Crofts.

Slaby, Ronald J., & Eron, Leonard D. (1994). Afterword. In Leonard D. Eron, Jacquelyn H. Gentry, & Peggy Schlegel (Eds.), *Reason to hope: A psychosocial perspective on violence and youth.* Washington, DC: American Psychological Association.

Slobin, Dan I. (2001). Form-function relations: How do children find out what they are? In Melissa Bowerman & Stephen C. Levinson (Eds.), *Language acquisition and conceptual development* (pp. 406–449). Cambridge, England: Cambridge University Press.

Smetana, Judith G., & Asquith, Pamela. (1994). Adolescents' and parents' conceptions of parental authority and adolescent autonomy. *Child Development, 65,* 1147–1162.

Smetana, Judith G., Killen, Melanie, & Turiel, Elliot. (1991). Children's reasoning about interpersonal and moral conflicts. *Child Development, 62,* 629–644.

Smith, George Davey. (2000). Learning to live with complexity: Ethnicity, socio-economic position, and health in Britain and the United States. *American Journal of Public Health, 90,* 1694–1698.

Smith, Jacqui, & Baltes, Paul B. (1999). Trends and profiles of psychological functioning in very old age. In P. B. Baltes & K. U. Mayer (Eds*.), The Berlin aging study: Aging from 70 to 100.* New York: Cambridge University Press.

Smith, Linda. (1995). Self-organizing processes in learning to learn words. In C.A. Nelson (Ed.), *Basic and applied perspectives on learning, cognition, and development* (Minnesota Symposium on Child Psychology, Vol. 28). Mahwah, NJ: Erlbaum.

Smith, Peter K., Morita, Yohji, Junger-Tas, Josine, Olweus, Dan, Catalano Richard, & Slee, Phillip. (1999). *The nature of school bullying: A cross-national perspective.* London: Routledge.

Smith, Peter K., Shu, Shu, & Madsen, Kirsten. (2001). Characteristics of victims of school bullying: Developmental changes in coping strategies and skills. In Jaana Juvonen and Sandra Graham (Eds.). Peer harassment in school: The plight of the vulnerable and victimized (pp. 332–351). New York: Guilford Press.

Snarey, John R. (1993). *How fathers care for the next generation: A four-decade study.* Cambridge, MA: Harvard University Press.

Sniezek, Janet A. (1999). Issues in self-control theory and research: Confidence, doubt, expectancy bias, and opposing forces. In Robert S. Wyer (Ed.), *Perspectives on behavioral self-regulation* (pp. 217–229). Mahwah, NJ: Erlbaum.

Snijders, R.J.M., & Nicolaides, K.H. (1996). *Ultrasound markers for fetal chromosomal defects.* New York: Parthenon.

Snow, Catherine E. (1984). Parent-child interaction and the development of communicative ability. In Richard L. Schiefelbusch & Joanne Pickar (Eds.), *The acquisition of communicative competence.* Baltimore: University Park Press.

Snyder, Howard N. (1997). *Serious, violent, and chronic juvenile offenders: An assessment of the extent of and trends in officially-recognized serious criminal behavior in a delinquent population.* Pittsburgh, PA: National Center for Juvenile Justice.

Society for Research in Child Development (SRCD). (1996). Ethical standards for research with children. *SCRD Directory of Members, 337–339.*

Soken, Nelson H., & Pick, Anne D. (1999). Infants' perception of dynamic affective expressions: Do infants distinguish specific expressions? *Child Development, 70,* 1275–1282.

Sonnenschein, S., Brody, G., & Munsterman, K. (1996). The influence of family beliefs and practices on children's early reading development. In L. Baker & P. Afflerbach (Eds.), *Developing engaged readers in school and home communities* (pp. 3–20). Mahwah, NJ: Erlbaum.

Soussignan, Robert, & Tremblay, Richard. (1996). Other disorders of conduct. In Seija Sandberg (Ed.). *Hyperactivity disorders of childhood* (pp. 195–245). Cambridge, England: Cambridge University Press.

Spelke, Elizabeth S. (1993). Physical knowledge in infancy: reflections on Piaget's theory. In Susan Carey & Rochel Gelman (Eds.), *The epigenesis of mind: essay on biology and cognition.* Hillsdale, NJ: Erlbaum.

Spelke, Elizabeth S., & Tsivkin, Sanna. (2001). Initial knowledge and conceptual change: space and number. In Melissa Bowerman & Stephen C. Levinson (Eds.), *Language acquisition and conceptual development* (pp. 70–97). Cambridge, England: Cambridge University Press.

Spieker, Susan J., Larson, Nancy C., Lewis, Steven M., Keller, Thomas E., & Gilchrist, Lewayne. (1999). Developmental trajectories of disruptive behavior problems in preschool children of adolescent mothers. *Child Development, 70,* 443–458.

Spock, Benjamin. (1976). *Baby and child care.* New York: Pocket Books.

Springer, Sally P., & Deutsch, Georg. (1997). *Left brain, right brain: Perspectives from cognitive neuroscience* (5th ed.). New York: Freeman.

Sridher, Dheepa, & Vaughn, Sharon. (2001). Social functioning of students with learning disabilities. In Daniel P. Hallahan and Barbara K. Keogh (Eds.), *Research and global perspectives in learning disabilities* (pp. 65–91). Mahwah, NJ: Erlbaum.

Sroufe, L. Alan. (1996). *Emotional development: The organization of emotional lie in the early years.* Cambridge, England: Cambridge University Press.

Sroufe, L. Alan. (2002). From infant attachment to promotion of adolescent autonomy: Prospective, longitudinal data on the role of parents in development. In John G. Borkowski, Sharon Landesman Ramey, and Marie Bristol-Power (Eds.). *Parenting and the child's world: Influences on academic, intellectual, and social-emotional development.* Mahwah, NJ: Erlbaum. 187–202.

Stanovich, Keith E. (1999). *Who is rational? Studies of individual differences in reasoning.* Mahwah, NJ: Erlbaum.

Stanovich, Keith E. (2000). Progress in understanding reading: Scientific foundations and new frontiers. New York: Guilford.

Staples, Robert, & Johnson, Leanor B. (1993). *Black families at the crossroads.* San Francisco: Jossey-Bass.

Stassen, David. (2002, January 15). Conversation between David Stassen and the author.

Stattin, Hakan, & Kerr, Margaret. (2000). Parental monitoring: A reinterpretation. *Child Development, 71,* 1072–1085.

Stecher, B. M., & Bohrnstedt, G. W. (2000). *Class size reductions in California: The 1998–99 evaluation findings.* Sacramento, CA: California Department of Education.

Steele, Kenneth M., Bass, Karen E., & Crook, Melissa D. (1999). The Mozart effect: An artifact of preference. *Psychological Science, 10,* 370–373.

Steinberg, Adria. (1993). Adolescents and schools: Improving the fit. *The Harvard Education Letter.*

Steinberg, Lawrence. (1996). *Beyond the classroom: Why school reform has failed and what parents need to do.* New York: Simon & Schuster.

Steinberg, Lawrence, & Dornbusch, Sanford M. (1991). Negative correlates of part-time employment during adolescence: Replication and elaboration. *Developmental Psychology, 27,* 304–313.

Steinberg, Laurence, & Morris, Amanda Sheffield. (2001). Adolescent development. *Annual Review of Psychology, 52,* 83–110.

Stern, Daniel N. (1985). *The interpersonal world of the infant.* New York: Basic Books.

Stern, David. (1997). What difference does it make if school and work are connected? Evidence on cooperative education in the United States. *Economics of Education Review, 16,* 213–229.

Sternberg, Robert J. (1996). *Successful intelligence.* New York: Simon & Schuster.

Sternberg, Robert J. (2002). Everything you need to know to understand the current controversies you learned from psychological research. *American Psychologist, 57,* 193–197.

Sternberg, Robert J., Grigorenko, Elena Y., & Bundy, Donald A. (2001). The predictive value of IQ. *Merrill-Palmer Quarterly, 47,* 1–41.

Stevenson, Jim. (1999). The treatment of the long-term sequelae of child abuse. *Journal of Child Psychology & Psychiatry & Allied Disciplines, 40,* 89–111.

Stewart, Deborah A. (1997). Adolescent sexual abuse, sexual assault, and rape. In Adele Dellenbaugh Hofmann & Donald Everett Greydanus (Eds.), *Adolescent medicine* (3rd ed.). Stanford, CT: Appleton & Lange.

Stewart, Sunita Mahtani, Bond, Michael H., Ho, L. M., Zaman, Riffat Moazan, Dar, Rabiya, & Anwar, Muhammad. (2000). Perceptions of parents and adolescent outcomes in Pakistan. *British Journal of Developmental Psychology, 18,* 335–352.

Stigler, James W., & Hiebert, James. (1999). *The teaching gap.* New York: The Free Press.

Stiles, Deborah A., Gibbons, Judith L., Sebben, Daniel J., & Wiley, Deane C. (1999). Why adolescent boys dream of becoming professional athletes. *Psychological Reports, 84,* 1075.

Stiles, Joan. (1998). The effects of early focal brain injury on lateralization of cognitive function. *Current Directions in Psychological Science, 7,* 21–26.

Stipek, Deborah. (2001). Pathways to constructive lives: The importance of early school success. In Arthur C. Bohart & Deborah J. Stipek (Eds.), *Constructive and destructive behavior: Implications for family, school & society* (pp. 291–316). Washington, DC: American Psychological Society.

Stipek, Deborah J., Feiler, Rachell, Daniels, Denise, & Milburn, Sharon. (1995). Effects of different instructional approaches on young children's achievement and motivation. *Child Development, 66,* 209–223.

Stormshak, Elizabeth, Bierman, Karen, & The Conduct Problems Prevention Research Group. (1998). The implications of different developmental patterns of disruptive behavior problems for school adjustment. *Development and Psychopathology, 10,* 451–468.

St. Pierre, Robert G., Layzer, Jean I., Goodson, Barbara D., & Bernstein, Lawrence S. (1997). *The effectiveness of comprehensive, case management interventions: Findings from the national evaluation of the comprehensive child development program.* Cambridge, MA: Abt Associates.

Strassberg, Zvi, Dodge, Kenneth A., Pettit, Gregory S., & Bates, John E. (1994). Spanking in the home and children's subsequent aggression toward kindergarten peers. *Development and Psychopathology, 6,* 445–462.

Straus, Murray A. (1994). *Beating the devil out of them: Corporal punishment in American families.* Lexington, MA: Lexington Books.

Strauss, David, & Eyman, Richard K. (1996). Mortality of people with mental retardation in California with and without Down syndrome, 1986–1991. *American Journal on Mental Retardation, 100,* 643–653.

Streissguth, Ann P., & Connor, Paul D. (2001). Fetal alcohol effects and other effects of prenatal alcohol: Developmental cognitive neuroscience implications. In Charles A. Nelson & Monica Luciana (Eds.), *Handbook of developmental neuroscience*. Cambridge, MA: MIT Press.

Streitmatter, Janice L. (1988). Ethnicity as a mediating variable of early adolescent identity development. *Journal of Adolescence, 11*, 335–346.

Suarez-Orozco, Carola, & Suarez-Orozco, Marcelo M. (2001). *Children of immigration*. Cambridge, MA: Harvard University Press.

Suizzo, Marie-Anne. (2000). The social-emotional and cultural contexts of cognitive development: Neo-Piagetian perspectives. *Child Development, 71*, 846–849.

Suls, Jerry, Lemos, Katherine, & Stewart, H. Lockett. (2002). Self-esteem, construal, and comparison with the self, friends, and peers. *Journal of Personality and Social Psychology, 82*, 252–261.

Sun, Yongmin, & Li, Yu. (2001). Marital disruption, parental investment and children's academic achievement: A prospective analysis. *Journal of Family Issues, 22*, 27–62.

Suomi, Stephen. (2002). Parents, peers, and the process of socialization in primates. In John G. Borkowski, Sharon Landesman Ramey, & Marie Bristol-Power (Eds.), *Parenting and the child's world: Influences on academic, intellectual, and social-emotional development*. Mahwah, NJ: Erlbaum.

Susman, Elizabeth J. (1997). Modeling development complexity in adolescence: Hormones and behavior in context. *Journal of Research on Adolescence, 7*, 283–306.

Susman, Elizabeth J., Schmeelk, Karen H., Ponirakis, Angelo, & Gariepy, Jean Louis. (2001). Maternal prenatal, postpartum, and concurrent stressors and temperament in 3-year-olds: A person and variable analysis. *Development and Psychopathology, 13*, 629–652.

Sutton-Smith, Brian. (1997). *The ambiguity of play*. Cambridge, MA: Harvard University Press.

Swain, Merrill, & Johnson, Robert K. (1997). Introduction. In Robert K. Johnson & Merrill Swain (Eds.), *Immersion Education: International Perspectives*. Cambridge, England: Cambridge University.

Swanson, H. Lee. (1999). *Interventions for students with learning disabilities: A meta-analysis of treatment outcomes*. New York: Guilford.

Swenson, Nora C. (2000). Comparing traditional and collaborative settings for language intervention. *Communication Disorders Quarterly, 22*, 12–18.

Szatmari, Peter. (2001, Spring). Thinking about autism, Asperger disorder, and PDD-NOS. *Newsletter of the Centre for Studies of Children at Risk*, 4.

Szkrybalo, Joel, & Ruble, Diane N. (1999). "God made me a girl": Sex-category constancy judgments and explanations revisited. *Developmental Psychology, 35*, 392–402.

Takahashi, T., Nowakowski, Richard S., & Caviness, Verne S., Jr. (2001). Neocortical neurogenesis: Regulation, control points, and a strategy of structural variation. In Charles A. Nelson & Monica Luciana (Eds.), *Handbook of developmental neuroscience*. Cambridge, MA: MIT Press.

Talukder, M. Q.-K. (2000). The importance of breastfeeding and strategies to sustain high breastfeeding rates. In Anthony Costello & Dharma Manandhar (Eds.), *Improving newborn infant health in developing countries*. London: Imperial College Press.

Tamis-LeMonda, Catherine S., Bornstein, Marc H., & Baumwell, Lisa. (2001). Maternal responsiveness and children's achievement of language milestones. *Child Development, 72*, 748–767.

Tangney, June Price. (2001). Constructive and destructive aspects of shame and guilt. In Arthur C. Bohart & Deborah J. Stipek (Eds.). *Constructive and destructive behavior: Implications for family, school and society* (pp. 249–270). Washington, DC: American Psychological Society.

Tanner, James M. (1978). Fetus into Man: Physical growth from conception to maturity. Cambridge, MA: Harvard University Press.

Tanner, James M. (1991a). Growth spurt, adolescent. In Richard M. Lerner, Ann C. Petersen, & Jeanne Brooks-Gunn (Eds.), *Encyclopedia of adolescence* (Vol. 1). New York: Garland.

Tanner, James M. (1991b). Menarche, secular trend in age of. In Richard M. Lerner, Ann C. Petersen, & Jeanne Brooks-Gunn (Eds.), *Encyclopedia of adolescence* (Vol. 2). New York: Garland.

Tarter, Ralph, Vanyukov, Michael, Giancola, Peter, Dawes, Michael,

Blackson, Timothy, Mezzich, Ada, & Clark, Duncan B. (1999). Etiology of early age onset substance use disorder: A maturational perspective. *Development and Psychopathology, 11*, 657–683.

Tatar, Moshe. (1998). Teachers as significant others: Gender differences to secondary school pupils' perceptions. *British Journal of Educational Psychology, 68*, 217–227.

Tatz, Colin. (2001). *Aboriginal suicide is different*. Canberra: Aboriginal Studies Press.

Taylor, H. Gerry, Klein, Nancy, & Hack, Maureen. (2000). School-age consequences of birth weight less than 750 grams: A review and an update. *Developmental Neuropsychology, 17*, 289–321.

Taylor, H. Gerry, Klein, Nancy, Schatschneider, Christopher, & Hack, Maureen. (1998). Predictors of early school age outcomes in very low birth weight children. *Journal of Developmental and Behavioral Pediatrics, 19*, 235–243.

Taylor, Marjorie. (1999). *Imaginary companions and the children who create them*. Oxford, England: Oxford University Press.

Teicher, Martin H. (2002). Scars that won't heal: The neurobiology of child abuse. *Scientific American, 286,* (3), 68–75.

Teitelbaum, Philip, Teitelbaum, Osnat, Nye, Jennifer, Fryman, Joshua, & Maurer, Ralph G. (1998). Movement analysis in infancy may be useful for early diagnosis of autism. *Proceedings of the National Academy of Sciences, 23*, 13982–13987.

Terrell, J., & Modell, J. (1994). Anthropology and adoption. *American Anthropologist, 96*, 155–161.

Terwogt, Mark Meerum, & Stegge, Hedy. (1998). Children's perspective on the emotional process. In Anne Campbell & Steven Muncer (Eds.), *The social child*. East Sussex, England: Psychology Press.

Thapar, Anita, Holmes, J., Poulton, K., & Harrington, R. (1999). Genetic basis of attention deficit and hyperactivity. *British Journal of Psychiatry, 174*, 105–111.

Theimer, Christine E., Killen, Melanie, & Stangor, Charles. (2001). Young children's evaluation of exclusion in gender-stereotypic peer contexts. *Developmental Psychology, 37*, 18–27.

Thelen, Esther, Corbetta, Daniela, Kamm, Kathi, Spencer, John P., Schneider, K., & Zernicke, R.F. (1993). The transition to reaching: Mapping intention and intrinsic dynamics. *Child Development, 64,* 1058–1098.

Thomas, Alexander, & Chess, Stella. (1977). *Temperament and development.* New York: Brunner/Mazel.

Thomas, Alexander, Chess, Stella, & Birch, Herbert G. (1963). *Behavioral individuality in early childhood.* New York: New York University Press.

Thomas, Jeanne L., Sperry, Len, & Yarbrough, M. Sue. (2000). Grandparents as parents: Research findings and policy recommendations. *Child Psychiatry and Human Development, 31,* 3–22.

Thompson, Frances E., & Dennison, Barbara. (1994). Dietary sources of fats and cholesterol in U.S. children aged 2 through 5 years. *American Journal of Public Health, 84,* 799–806.

Thompson, Richard F. (2000). *The Brain* (3rd ed.). New York: Worth.

Thompson, Ron A., & Sherman, Roberta. (1993). *Helping athletes with eating disorders.* Bloomington, IN: Human Kinetics Books.

Thompson, Ross A. (1992). Developmental changes in research risk and benefit: A changing calculus of concerns. In B. Stanley & J.E. Sieber (Eds.), *Social research on children and adolescents: Ethical issues.* Newbury Park, CA: Sage.

Thompson, Ross A. (1998). Early sociopersonality development. In William Damon & Nancy Eisenberg (Eds.), *Handbook of child psychology*: Vol. 3. *Social, emotional, and personality development* (5th ed., pp. 25–65). New York: Wiley.

Thompson, Ross A. (2000). The legacy of early attachments. *Child Development, 71,* 145–152.

Thompson, Ross A. (2001). Panel discussion of *From neurons to neighborhoods.* Biennial meeting of Society for Research in Child Development, Minneapolis, Minnesota.

Thompson, Ross A., & Nelson, Charles A. (2001). Developmental science and the media: Early brain development. *American Psychologist, 56,* 5–15.

Tobin, Allan J. (1999). Amazing grace: Sources of phenotypic variation in genetic boosterism. In Ronald A. Carson & Mark A. Rothstein (Eds.), *Behavioral genetics: The clash of culture and biology.* (pp. 1–11). Baltimore: Johns Hopkins Press.

Tomasello, Michael. (2000). Culture and cognitive development. *Current Directions in Psychological Science, 2,* 37–45.

Tomasello, Michael. (2001). Perceiving intentions and learning words in the second year of life. In Melissa Bowerman & Stephen C. Levinson (Eds.), *Language acquisition and conceptual development* (pp. 132–158). Cambridge, England: Cambridge University Press.

Torff, Bruce, & Gardner, Howard. (1999). The vertical mind: The case for multiple intelligences. In M. Anderson (Ed.), *The development of intelligence.* London: University College Press.

Torff, Bruce, & Sternberg, Robert J. (Eds.). (2001). *Understanding and teaching the intuitive mind: Student and teacher learning.* Mahwah, NJ: Erlbaum.

Tremblay, Richard E. (2000). Quoted in Constance Holden. The violence of the lambs. *Science, 298,* 580–581.

Triandis, H. C. (1989). The self and social behavior in differing cultural contexts. *Psychological Review, 96,* 506–520.

Tronick, Edward S. (1989). Emotions and emotional communication. *American Psychologist, 44,* 112–119.

Tronick, Edward S., Als, Heidelise, Adamson, Lauren, Wise, S., & Brazelton, T. Berry. (1978). The infant response to entrapment between contradictory messages in face-to-face interaction. *Journal of the American Academy of Child Psychiatry, 17,* 1–13.

True, Mary McMahan, Pisani, Lelia, & Oumar, Fadimata. (2001). Infant-mother attachment among the Dogon of Mali. *Child Development, 72,* 1451–1466.

Tse, Lucy. (1999). Finding a place to be: Ethnic identity exploration of Asian Americans. *Adolescence, 34,* 121–138.

Tsui, Amy O., Waserheit, Judith N., & Haaga, John G. (Eds.; Panel on Reproductive Health, National Research Council). (1997). *Reproductive health in developing countries: Expanding dimensions, building solutions.* Washington, D.C.: National cademy Press.

Tucker, G. Richard. (1998). A global perspective on multilingualism and multilingual education. In Jasone Cenoz & Fred Genesee (Eds.), *Beyond bilingualism: Multilingualism and multilingual education.* Clevedon, England: Multilingual Matters.

Turiel, Elliot, Smetana, Judith G., & Killen, Melanie. (1991). Social context in social cognitive development. In William M. Kurtines & Jacob L. Gewirtz (Eds.), *Handbook of moral behavior and development: Vol. 2. Research.* Mahwah, NJ: Erlbaum.

Uhlenberg, Peter. (1996). Mutual attraction: Demography and life-course analysis. *Gerontologist, 36,* 226–229.

Umilta, Carlo, & Stablum, Franca. (1998). Control processes explored by the study of closed head injury patients. In Giuliana Mazzoni & Thomas O. Nelson (Eds.), *Metacognition and cognitive neuropsychology*: *Monitoring and control processes.* Mahwah, NJ: Erlbaum.

Ungar, Michael T. (2000). The myth of peer pressure. *Adolescence, 35,* 167–180.

United Nations Development Program. (2001). *Human Development Report.* New York: Oxford University Press.

Updegraff, Kimberly A., Madden-Derdich, Debra A., Estrada, Ana Ulloa, Sales, Lara J., & Leonard, Stacie A. (2002). Young adolescents' experiences with parents and friends: Exploring the connections. *Family relations, 51,* 72–80.

U. S. Bureau of the Census. (1972). *Statistical abstract of the United States, 1972* (92nd ed.). Washington, DC: U.S. Department of Commerce.

U. S. Bureau of the Census. (1986). *Statistical abstract of the United States.* Washington, DC: U. S. Department of Commerce.

U. S. Bureau of the Census. (1999). *Statistical abstract of the United States, 1999* (119th ed.). Washington, DC: U.S. Department of Commerce.

U. S. Bureau of the Census. (2000). *Statistical abstract of the United States, 2000* (120th ed.). Washington, DC: U.S. Department of Commerce.

U. S. Bureau of the Census. (2001). *Statistical abstract of the United States, 2001* (121th ed.). Washington, DC: U.S. Department of Commerce.

U. S. Congress. (2000, July 26). Joint statement on the impact of entertainment violence on children, presented at the Public Health Summit, Washington, DC.

U. S. Department of Education. (2001). *Digest of education statistics, 2000* (NCES

2001-034). Washington, DC: Office of Educational Research and Improvement, U.S. Department of Education.

U. S. Department of Health and Human Services. (2000). *Trends in the well-being of America's children and youth.* Washington, DC: U.S. Government Printing Office.

U. S. Department of Health and Human Services. (2001). *Child maltreatment 1999: Reports from the States.* Washington, DC: U. S. Government Printing Office.

U. S. Department of Health and Human Services. (2002, February 14). Annual update of HHS poverty guidelines. *Federal Register, 67,* 6931–6933.

U. S. Department of Justice. (2002). *Source book of Criminal Justice Statistics.* Washington DC.

Uttal, William R. (2000). *The war between mentalism and behaviorism.* Mahwah, NJ: Erlbaum.

Valois, Robert F., Oeltmann, John E., Waller, Jennifer, & Hussey, James R. (1999). Relationship between number of sexual intercourse partners and selected health risk behavior among public high school adolescents. *Journal of Adolescent Health, 25,* 328–335.

Valsiner, Jaan. (1997). Constructing the personal through the cultural redundant organization of psychological development. In Eric Amsel & K. Ann Renninger (Eds.), *Change and development: Issues of theory, method, & application.* Mahwah, NJ: Erlbaum.

van Hoorn, Judith Lieberman, Komlosi, Akos, Suchar, Elzbieta, & Samelson, Doreen A. (2000). *Adolescent development and rapid social change.* Albany, NY: SUNY Press.

van IJzendoorn, Marinus H., & Hubbard, Frans O. A. (2000). Are infant crying and maternal responsiveness during the first year related to infant-mother attachment at 15 months? *Attachment and Human Development, 2,* 371–391.

van IJzendoorn, Marinus H., & Kroonenberg, P. (1988). Cross-cultural patterns of attachment: A meta-analysis of the Strange Situation. *Child Development, 59,* 3–9.

van IJzendoorn, Marinus H., Moran, Greg, Belsky, Jay, & Pederson, David. (2000). The similarity of siblings' attachments to their mother. *Child Development, 71,* 1086–1098.

Van Tuijl, Cathy, Leseman, Paul P. M., & Rispens, Jan. (2001). Efficacy of an intensive home-based educational intervention programme for 4–6 year-old ethnic minority children in the Netherlands. *International Journal of Behavioral Development, 25,* 148–159.

Van Wel, Frits, Linsson, Hub, & Abma, Ruud. (2000). The parental bond and the well-being of adolescents and young adults. *Journal of Youth and Adolescence, 29,* 307–318.

Vandell, Deborah L., Hyde, Janet S., Plant, E. Ashby, & Essex, Marilyn J. (1997). Fathers and "others" as infant care providers: Predictors of parents' emotional well-being and marital satisfaction. *Merrill-Palmer Quarterly, 43,* 361–385.

Varendi, Heili, Christensson, Kyllike, Porter, Richard H., & Winberg, Jan. (1998). Soothing effect of amniotic fluid smell in newborn infants. *Early Human Development, 51,* 47–55.

Varnhagen, Connie. (2002). *Making sense of psychology on the Web.* New York: Worth.

Vartanian, Lesa Rae. (2001). Adolescent reactions to hypothetical peer group conversations: Evidence for an imaginary audience? *Adolescence, 36,* 347–393.

Veldhuis, Johannes, Yoshida, Kohji, & Iranmanesh, Ali. (1997). The effects of mental and metabolic stress on the female reproductive system and female reproductive hormones. In John R. Hubbard & Edward A. Workman (Eds.). *Handbook of stress medicine: An organ system approach.* Boca Raton, FL: CRC Press.

Ventura, Stephanie J., Matthews, T. J., & Hamilton, Brady E. (2001, September 25). Births to teenagers in the United States, 1940–2000. *National Vital Statistics Reports, 49,* 1–24.

Verschueren, Karine, Buyck, Petra, & Marcoen, Alfons. (2001). Self-representations and socioemotional competence in young children: A 3-year longitudinal study. *Developmental Psychology, 37,* 126–134.

Vickers, James C., Dickson, Tracey C., Adlard, Paul A., Saunders, Helen L., King, Carolyn E., & McCormack, Graeme. (2000). The causes of neural degeneration in Alzheimer's disease. *Neurobiology, 60,* 139–165.

Victora, Cesar; Bryce, Jennifer; Fontaine, Liver, & Monasch, Roeland. (2000). Reducing deaths from diarrhea through oral rehydration therapy. *Bulletin of the World Health Organization, 78,* 1246–1255.

Vincent, Maureen A., & McCabe, Marita P. (2000). Gender differences among adolescents in family and peer influences on body dissatisfaction, weight loss, and binge-eating behaviors. *Journal of Youth and Adolescence, 29,* 205–222.

Vinden, Penelope. (1996). Junin Quechua Children's understanding of the mind. *Child Development, 67,* 1707–1716.

Vitaro, Frank, Tremblay, Richard E., Kerr, Margaret, Pagani, Linda, & Bukowski, William M. (1997). Disruptiveness, friends' characteristics, and delinquency in early adolescence: A test of two competing models of development. *Child Development, 68,* 676–689.

Vizmanos, B., & Marti-Henneberg, C. (2000). Puberty begins with a characteristic subcutaneous body fat mass in each sex. *European Journal of Clinical Nutrition, 54,* 203–206.

Volker, Susanne, Keller, Heidi, Lohaus, Arnold, & Cappenberg, Martina. (1999). Maternal interactive behaviour in early infancy and later attachment. *International Journal of Behavioral Development, 23,* 921–936.

Vondra, Joan I., & Barnett, Douglas (Eds.) (1999). *Atypical attachment in infancy and early childhood among children at developmental risk. Monographs of the Society for Research in Child Development, 64*(Serial No. 258), 145–171.

Vygotsky, Lev S. (1925/1994). Principles of social education for deaf and dumb children in Russia. In Rene van der Veer & Jaan Valsiner (Eds., 1994), *The Vygotsky Reader.* Oxford, U.K.: Blackwell.

Vygotsky, Lev S. (1934/1986). *Thought and language.* Cambridge, MA: MIT Press.

Vygotsky, Lev S. (1934/1994). The development of academic concepts in school aged children. In Rene van der Veer & Jaan Valsiner (Eds.), *The Vygotsky Reader,* Blackwell.

Vygotsky, Lev S. (1978). *Mind in society: The development of higher psychological processes.* Cambridge, MA: Harvard University Press.

Vygotsky, Lev S. (1987). *Thinking and speech* (N. Minick, Trans.). New York: Plenum Press.

Wachs, Theodore D. (1999). Celebrating complexity: Conceptualization and assessment of the environment. In S. Freidman & T.D. Wachs (Eds.), *Measuring environment across the lifespan: Emerging methods and concepts*. Washington, DC: American Psychological Association.

Wachs, Theodore D. (2000). *Necessary but not sufficient*. Washington, DC: American Psychological Association.

Wainryb, Cecilia, Shaw, Leigh A., Laupa, Marta, & Smith, Ken R. (2001). Children's, adolescents' and young adult thinking about different types of disagreements. *Developmental Psychology, 37,* 373–386.

Wainryb, Cecilia, & Turiel, Elliot. (1995). Diversity in social development: Between or within cultures? In Melanie Killen & Daniel Hart (Eds.), *Morality in everyday life: Developmental perspectives*. Cambridge, England: Cambridge University Press.

Waldfogel, Jane. (1998). Rethinking the paradigm for child protection. *The Future of Children: Protecting Children from Abuse and Neglect, 8,* 4–22.

Waldron, Nancy L. & McLeskey, James. (1998). The effects of an inclusive school program on students with mild and severe learning disabilities. *Exceptional Children, 64,* 395–405.

Walker, Lawrence J. (1988). The development of moral reasoning. *Annals of Child Development, 55,* 677–691.

Walker, Lawrence J., Gustafson, Paul, & Hennig, Karl H. (2001). The consolidation/transition model in moral reasoning development. *Developmental Psychology, 37,* 187–197.

Walker, Lawrence J., Hennig, Karl H., & Krettenauer, Tobias. (2000). Parent and peer contexts for children's moral reasoning development. *Child Development, 71,* 1033–1048.

Walker, Lawrence J., Pitts, Russell C., Hennig, Karl H., & Matsuba, M. Kyle. (1995). Reasoning about morality and real-life moral problems. In Melanie Killen & Daniel Hart (Eds.), *Morality in everyday life: Developmental perspectives*. Cambridge, England: Cambridge University Press.

Walker-Barnes, Chanequa J., & Mason, Craig A. (2001). Ethnic differences in the effect of parenting on gang involvement and gang delinquency: A longitudinal, hierarchical linear modeling perspective. *Child Development, 72,* 1814–1831.

Walsh, Froma. (2002). A family resilience framework: Innovative practice applications. *Family Relations, 51,* 130–137.

Walton, Irene, & Hamilton, Mary. (1998). *Midwives and changing childbirth*. Cheshire, England: Books for Midwives Press.

Warash, Bobbie Gibson, & Markstrom-Adams, Carol. (1995). Preschool experiences of advantaged children. *Psychological Reports, 77,* 89–90.

Warshofsky, Fred. (1999). *Stealing time: The new science of aging*. New York: TV Books.

Wartella, Ellen A., & Jennings, Nancy. (2000). Children and computers: New technology—old concerns. *The Future of Children, 10,* (2), 31–43.

Waters, Mary C. (2000). *Black identities: West Indian immigrant dreams and American realities*. Cambridge, MA: Harvard University Press.

Watson, John B. (1924). *Behaviorism*. Chicago: University of Chicago Press.

Watson, John B. (1928). *Psychological care of the infant and child*. New York: Norton.

Watson, John B. (1998). *Behaviorism*. New Brunswick, NJ: Transaction.

Wegar, Katarina. (2000). Adoption, family ideology and social stigma: Bias in community attitudes, adoption research, and practice. *Family Relations, 49,* 363–370.

Weinberg, M. Katherine, Tronick, Edward Z., Cohn, Jeffrey F., & Olson, Karen L. (1999). Gender differences in emotional expressivity and self-regulation during early infancy. *Developmental Psychology, 35,* 175–188.

Weisfeld, Glenn. (1999). *Evolutionary principles of human adolescence*. New York: Basic Books.

Weissbluth, Marc. (1999). *Healthy sleep habits, happy child* (Rev. ed.). New York: Fawcett.

Weizman, Zehave Oz, & Snow, Catherine E. (2001). Lexical input as related to children's vocabulary acquisition: Effects of sophisticated exposure and support for meaning. *Developmental Psychology, 37,* 265–279.

Wellman, Henry M., Cross, David, & Watson, Julanne. (2001), Meta-analysis of theory-of-mind development: The truth about false belief. *Child Development, 72,* 655–684.

Wendland-Carro, Jaqueline, Piccinini, Cesar A., & Millar, W. Stuart. (1999). The role of an early intervention on enhancing the quality of mother-infant interaction. *Child Development, 70,* 713–721.

Wentworth, Naomi, Benson, Janette B., & Haith, Marshall M. (2000). The development of infants' reaches for stationary and moving targets. *Child Development, 71,* 576–601.

Wentzel, Kathryn R. (2002). Are effective teachers like good parents? Teaching styles and student adjustment in early adolescence. *Child Development, 73,* 287–301.

Wentzel, Kathryn R., & Caldwell, Kathryn. (1997). Friendships, peer acceptance, and group membership: Relations to academic achievement in middle school. *Child Development, 68,* 1198–1209.

Werner, Emmy E. (1994). Overcoming the odds. *Journal of Developmental and Behavioral Pediatrics, 2,* 131–136.

Werner, Emmy E., & Smith, Ruth S. (1992). *Overcoming the odds: High risk children from birth to adulthood*. Ithaca, NY: Cornell University Press.

Wertsch, James V. (1985). *Vygotsky and the social formation of mind*. Cambridge, MA: Harvard University Press.

Wertsch, James V., & Tulviste, Peeter. (1992). L.S. Vygotsky and contemporary developmental psychology. *Developmental Psychology, 28,* 548–557.

Whitaker, Daniel J., Miller, Kim S., & Clark, Leslie F. (2000). Reconceptualizing adolescent sexual behavior: Beyond did they or didn't they? *Family Planning Perspectives, 32,* 111–117.

Whitaker, Robert C., Wright, Jeffrey A., Pepe, Margaret S., Seidel, Kristy D., & Dietz, William H. (1997). Predicting obesity in young adulthood from childhood and parental obesity. *New England Journal of Medicine, 337,* 869–873.

Whitam, Frederick L., Diamond, Milton, & Martin, James. (1993). Homosexual orientation in twins: A report on 61 pairs and three triplet sets. *Archives of Sexual Behavior, 22,* 187–206.

White, Barbara Prudhomme, Gunnar, Megan R., Larson, Mary C., Donzella, Bonny, & Barr, Ronald G. (2000). Behavioral and physiological responsivity, sleep, and patterns of daily cortisol production in infants with and without colic. *Child Development, 71,* 862–877.

White, Lynn, & Rogers, Stacy J. (2000). Economic circumstances and family outcomes: A review of the 1990s. *Journal of Marriage and the Family, 62,* 1035–1051.

Whiting, Beatrice Blyth, & Edwards, Carolyn Pope. (1988). *Children of different worlds: The formation of social behavior.* Cambridge, MA: Harvard University Press.

Wierson, Michelle, Long, Patricia J., & Forehand, Rex L. (1993). Toward a new understanding of early menarche: The role of environmental stress in pubertal timing. *Adolescence, 28,* 913–924.

Wigfield, Allan, & Eccles, Jacquelynne S. (2002). The development of competence beliefs, expectancies for success, and achievement values from childhood through adolescence. In Allan Wigfield & Jacquelynne S. Eccles (Eds.), *Development of achievement motivation.* San Diego, CA: Academic Press. 91–120.

Wigfield, Allan, Eccles, Jacquelynne, Yoon, Kwang Suk, Harold, Rena D., Arbreton, Amy, Freedman-Doan, Carol, & Blumenfeld, Phyllis. (1997). Changes in children's competency beliefs and subjective tasks values across the elementary school years: A 3-year study. *Journal of Educational Psychology, 89,* 451–469.

Willatts, Peter. (1999). Development of means-end behavior in young infants: Pulling a support to retrieve a distant object. *Developmental Psychology, 35,* 651–667.

Williams, Benjamin R., Ponesse, Jonathan S., Schachar, Russell J., Logan, Gordon D., & Tannock, Rosemary. (1999). Development of inhibitory control across the life span. *Developmental Psychology, 35,* 205–213.

Williams, Joanne M., & Currie, Candace. (2000). Self-esteem and physical development in early adolescence: Pubertal timing and body image. *Journal of Early Adolescence, 20,* 129–149.

Wills, Thomas Ashby, Dandy, James M., & Yaeger, Alison. (2001). Time perspective and early-onset substance use: A model based on stress-coping theory. *Psychology of Addictive Behaviors, 15,* 118–125.

Wills, Thomas Ashby, McNamara, G., Vaccaro, D., & Hirky, A. E. (1996). Escalated substance use: A longitudinal groups analysis from early to middle adolescence. *Journal of Abnormal Psychology, 105,* 166–180.

Windle, Michael. (2000). Parental, sibling, and peer influences on adolescent substance use and alcohol problems. *Applied Developmental Science, 4,* 98–110.

Winer, Gerald A., Cottrell, Jane E., Gregg, Virginia, Fournier, Jody S., & Bica, Lori A. (2002). Fundamentally misunderstanding visual perception: Adults' belief in visual emissions. *American Psychologist, 57,* 417–424.

Wingerson, Lois. (1998). *Unnatural selection: The promise and the power of human gene research.* New York: Bantam Doubleday Dell.

Winsler, Adam, Carlton, Martha, & Barry, Maryann J. (2000). Age-related change in preschool children's systematic use of private speech in a natural setting. *Journal of Child Language, 27,* 665–687.

Winsler, Adam, Díaz, Rafael M., Espinosa, Linda, & Rodríguez, James L. (1999). When learning a second language does not mean losing the first: Bilingual language development in low-income, Spanish-speaking children attending bilingual preschool. *Child Development, 70,* 349–362.

Wishart, Jennifer G. (1999). Learning and development in children with Down's syndrome. In Alan Slater and Darwin Muir (Eds.) *The Blackwell reader in developmental psychology.* Oxford, England: Blackwell.

Wolfe, David A., Wekerle, Christine, Reitzel-Jaffe, Degborah, & Lefebvre, Lorrie. (1998). Factors associated with abusive relationships among maltreated and nonmaltreated youth. *Development and Psychopathology, 10,* 61–85.

Wolfson, Amy R., & Carskadon, Mary A. (1998). Sleep schedules and daytime functioning in adolescents. *Child Development, 69,* 875–887.

Wollons, Roberta Lynn. (2000). *Kindergartens and cultures: The global diffusion of an idea.* New Haven, CT: Yale University Press.

Wolraich, Mark L., Hannah, Jane N., Baumgaertel, Anna, & Feurer, Irene D. (1998). Examination of DSM-IV criteria for attention deficit hyperactivity disorder in a county-side sample. *Journal of Developmental & Behavioral Pediatrics, 19,* 162–168.

Wong, Sau-ling C., & Lopez, Miguel G. (2000). English language learners of Chinese background: A portrait of diversity. In Sandra Lee McKay & Sau-ling Cynthia Wong (Eds.), *New immigrants in the United States* (pp. 263–305). Cambridge, England: Cambridge University Press.

Wong, Siu Kwong. (1999). Acculturation, peer relations, and delinquent behavior of Chinese-Canadian youth. *Adolescence, 34,* 108–119.

Woodward, Amanda L., & Markman, Ellen M. (1998). Early word learning. In William Damon (Series Ed.), Deanna Kuhn, & Robert S. Siegler (Vol. Eds.), *Handbook of child psychology: Vol. 2. Cognition, perception and language* (5th ed., pp. 371–420). New York: Wiley.

Woodward, Lianne J., & Fergusson, David M. (1999). Childhood peer relationship problems and psychosocial adjustment in late adolescence. *Journal of Abnormal Child Psychology, 27,* 87–104.

Woolley, Jacqueline D., Phelps, Katrina E., Davis, Debra L., & Mandell, Dorothy J. (1999). Where theories of mind meet magic: The development of children's beliefs about wishing. *Child Development, 70,* 571–587.

World Health Organization (WHO). (1990). *The Innocenti declaration on the protection, promotion, and support of breastfeeding.* Adopted by the WHO and UNICEF. Florence, Italy, August 1.

World Health Organization. (1998). *Obesity: Preventing and managing the global epidemic: Report of a WHO consultation on obesity.* Geneva: World Health Organization.

Wright, Charlotte M., & Talbot, E. (1996). Screening for failure to thrive: What are we looking for? *Child: Care, Health & Development, 22,* 223–234.

Wright, William. (1998). *Born that way.* New York: Knopf.

Wyman, Peter A., Cowen, Emory L., Work, William C., Hoyt-Meyers, Lynne, Magnus, Keith B., & Fagen, Douglas B. (1999). Caregiving and developmental factors differentiating young at-risk urban children showing resilient versus stress-affected outcome: A replication and extension. *Child Development, 70,* 645–659.

Wysong, Earl, Aniskiewicz, Richard, & Wright, David. (1994). Truth and DARE: Tracking drug education to graduation and as symbolic politics. *Social Problems, 41,* 448–472.

Xu, Fujie, Schillinger, Julia A., Markowitz, Lauri E., Sternberg, Maya R., Aubin, Mark R., & St. Louis, Michael E. (2000). Repeat *chlamydia trachomatis* infection in women: Analysis through a surveillance case registry in Washington State, 1993–1998. *American Journal of Epidemiology, 152,* 1164–1170.

Ying, Yu-Wen, & Lee, Peter A. (1999). The development of ethnic identity in Asian-American adolescents: Status and outcome. *American Journal of Orthopsychiatry, 69,* 182–193.

Yoder, Kevin A., Hoyt, Dan R., & Whitbeck, Les B. (1998). Suicidal behavior among homeless and runaway adolescents. *Journal of Youth & Adolescence, 27,* 753–771.

Yoos, H. Lorrie, Kitzman, Harriet, & Cole, Robert. (1999). Family routines and the feeding process. In Daniel B. Kessler & Peter Dawson (Eds.), *Failure to thrive and pediatric undernutrition* (pp. 375–384). Baltimore: Brooks.

Yoshikawa, Hirokazu. (1994). Prevention as cumulative protection: Effects of early family support and education on chronic delinquency and its risks. *Psychological Bulletin, 115,* 28–54.

Yoshikawa, Hirokazu, & Hsueh, JoAnn. (2001). Child development and public policy: Toward a dynamic systems perspective. *Child Development, 72,* 1887–1903.

Yowell, Constance M. (2000). Possible selves and future orientation: Exploring hopes and fears of Latino boys and girls. *Journal of Early Adolescence, 20,* 245–280.

Zahn-Waxler, Carolyn, Schmitz, Stephanie, Fulker, David, Robinson, Joann, & Emde, Robert. (1996). Behavior problems in 5-year-old monozygotic and dyzygotic twins: Genetic and environmental influences, patterns of regulation, and internalization of control. *Development and Psychopathology, 8,* 103–122.

Zarbatany, Lynne, Hartmann, Donald P., & Rankin, D. Bruce. (1990). The psychological functions of preadolescent peer activities. *Child Development, 61,* 1067–1080.

Zeifman, Debra, Delaney, Sarah, & Blass, Elliott. (1996). Sweet taste, looking, and calm in two- and four-week-old infants: The eyes have it. *Developmental Psychology, 32,* 1090–1099.

Zeskind, Philip Sanford, & Barr, Ronald G. (1997). Acoustic characteristics of naturally occurring cries of infants with "colic." *Child Development, 68,* 394–403.

Ziatas, Kathryn, Durkin, Kevin, & Pratt, Chris. (1998). Belief term development in children with autism, Asperger syndrome, specific language impairment, and normal development: Links to theory of mind development. *Journal of Child Psychology & Psychiatry & Allied Disciplines, 39,* 755–763.

Zigler, Edward. (1998). School should begin at age 3 years for American children. *Journal of Developmental and Behavioral Pediatrics, 19,* 37–38.

Zigler, Edward, & Muenchow, Susan. (1992). *Head Start: The inside story of America's most successful educational experiment.* New York: Basic Books.

Zigler, Edward, & Styfco, Sally J. (Eds.). (1993). *Head Start and beyond: A national plan for extended childhood intervention.* New Haven, CT: Yale University Press.

Zigler, Edward, & Styfco, Sally J. (2001). Can early chidhood intervention prevent deliquency? A real possibility. In Arthur C. Bohar & Deborah J. Stipek (Eds.). *Constructive and destructive behavior: Implications for family, school and society* (pp. 231–248). Washington, DC: American Psychological Association.